lonely planet

Germany

Andrea Schulte-Peevers
Jeremy Gray
Anthony Haywood
Steve Fallon
Nick Selby

LONELY PLANET PUBLICATIONS
Melbourne • Oakland • London • Paris

GERMANY

BERLIN
Visit world-class museums by day and bustling bars, pubs and clubs by night

NORTH FRISIAN ISLANDS
Experience the ruggedly beautiful landscapes of Sylt, Amrum and Föhr

HARZ MOUNTAINS
Hike, bike or ski your way around this year-round sporting paradise

COLOGNE
Visit the magnificent Cologne cathedral which dominates the city skyline

100 km
50
0

BALTIC SEA

NORTH SEA

SWEDEN
Trelleborg

DENMARK

POLAND

NETHERLANDS

SCHLESWIG-HOLSTEIN

MECKLENBURG-WESTERN POMERANIA

BRANDENBURG

SAXONY-ANHALT

LOWER SAXONY

NORTH RHINE-WESTPHALIA

BERLIN
POTSDAM

HAMBURG

BREMEN

HANOVER

MAGDEBURG

SCHWERIN

KIEL

Kage
Næstved
Odense
Kolding
Esbjerg

Flensburg
Husum
Westerland
North Frisian Islands
Norddeich
Emden
Groningen
Emmerich
Duisburg

Rügen Island
Sassnitz
Binz
Stralsund
Barth
Greifswald
Rostock
Warnemünde
Wismar
Poel Island
Puttgarden
Neubrandenburg
Pasewalk
Szczecin (Stettin)
Frankfurt an der Oder
Lübben
Cottbus
Lutherstadt-Wittenberg
Dessau
Rheinsberg
Neustrelitz
Müritz
Lübeck
Neumünster
Lüneburg
Celle
Wolfsburg
Stendal
Salzwedel
Quedlinburg
Bad Harzburg
Harz Mountains
Goslar
Braunschweig
Hildesheim
Paderborn
Göttingen
Bielefeld
Osnabrück
Münster
Hamm
Rheine
Bad Bentheim
Recklinghausen
Oberhausen
Gelsenkirchen
Bochum
Dortmund
Vechta
Oldenburg
Wilhelmshaven
Bremerhaven
Cuxhaven
East Frisian Islands

Elbe River
Hunte River
Weser River
Oder River

SWEDEN
Trelleborg

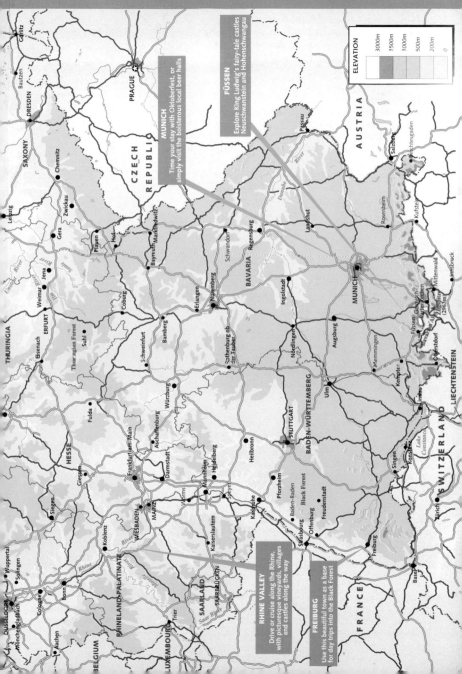

GERMANY

MUNICH
Time your stay with Oktoberfest, or simply visit the boisterous local beer halls

FÜSSEN
Explore King Ludwig's fairy-tale castles Neuschwanstein and Hohenschwangau

RHINE VALLEY
Drive or cruise along the Rhine, with picturesque vineyards, villages and castles along the way

FREIBURG
Use this beautiful town as a base for day trips into the Black Forest

ELEVATION

3000m
1500m
1000m
500m
200m
0

Germany
2nd edition – March 2000
First published – March 1998

Published by
Lonely Planet Publications Pty Ltd A.C.N. 005 607 983
192 Burwood Rd, Hawthorn, Victoria 3122, Australia

Lonely Planet Offices
Australia PO Box 617, Hawthorn, Victoria 3122
USA 150 Linden St, Oakland, CA 94607
UK 10a Spring Place, London NW5 3BH
France 1 rue du Dahomey, 75011 Paris

Photographs
Many of the images in this guide are available for licensing from
Lonely Planet Images.
email: lpi@lonelyplanet.com.au

Front cover photograph
Gargoyles welcome visitors to the medieval Wartburg Castle, Eisenach.
(David Peevers)

ISBN 0 86442 788 3

text & maps © Lonely Planet 2000
photos © photographers as indicated 2000

Printed by The Bookmaker Pty Ltd
Printed in China

Contents – Text

BAVARIA

BADEN-WÜRTTEMBERG

RHINELAND-PALATINATE

4 Contents – Text

Contents – Maps

RHINELAND-PALATINATE

SAARLAND

HESSE

NORTH RHINE-WESTPHALIA

BREMEN

LOWER SAXONY

HAMBURG

SCHLESWIG-HOLSTEIN

MAPS

Germany's Changing Borders p34
German Railways p151
German Autobahns p157
Travel Distance Chart p158

BALTIC SEA

NORTH SEA

POLAND

Schleswig-Holstein p860

Hamburg p831

Mecklenburg-Western Pomerania p384

NETHERLANDS

Bremen p759

Lower Saxony p771

Brandenburg p232

Greater Berlin p168

Berlin colour maps pp177-84

Saxony-Anhalt p333

Harz Mountains p361

North Rhine-Westphalia p699

Saxony p255

Thuringia p297

Hesse p668

BELGIUM

Rhineland-Palatinate p619

LUXEMBOURG

CZECH REPUBLIC

Saarland p660

Bavaria pp420-1

Baden-Württemberg p537

FRANCE

LIECHTENSTEIN

AUSTRIA

0   50   100 km

SWITZERLAND

ITALY

SLOVENIA

The Authors

Andrea Schulte-Peevers

Andrea is a Los Angeles-based writer, editor and translator who owes her love of languages and travel to her mother, who began lugging her off to foreign lands when she was just a toddler. She got her high-school education in Germany, then left for London and stints as an au-pair, market researcher and foreign language correspondent. In the mid-80s, Andrea swapped England for Southern California and the hallowed halls of UCLA. She hit the job market armed with a degree in English literature and chartered a course in travel journalism. Assignments have taken her to all continents except Antarctica, and she's *still* dreaming about seeing the Himalayas.

Andrea has previously contributed to *California & Nevada* and the first edition of *Germany*, and is also the author of Lonely Planet's city guides *Berlin* and *Los Angeles*.

Jeremy Gray

A Louisiana native, Jeremy studied German literature in the wilds of Texas before moving to Mainz, Germany on a scholarship in 1984. He stayed on to teach English, translate and (with his usual single-mindedness) file plumbing orders for the US Air Force. Later he took a master's degree in international relations at Canterbury and became a journalist in bustling Woking, Surrey.

Much of the 1990s were spent in scenic Frankfurt, alternating stints at wire services, newspapers and television. He upped stakes in 1998 to freelance for the *Financial Times* in the Netherlands and, as a reminder of the better things in life, for Lonely Planet.

Jeremy lives in Amsterdam with Petra, his graphic-designer wife. *Germany* is his first book for Lonely Planet.

Anthony Haywood

Anthony was born in Fremantle, Australia, in 1959. He first pulled anchor at 18 to spend two years travelling through Europe and the USA. He studied literature and Russian language at university, and worked for various companies in Melbourne as a technical writer and trainer. He moved to Germany in 1992, where he lives with his wife Sylvia and works as an author for LP, journalist and translator.

Anthony has also contributed to *Russia, Ukraine & Belarus*, *Western Europe* and the first edition of *Germany*.

From the Authors

Andrea Schulte-Peevers My portion of *Germany* is dedicated to my husband David Peevers whose love, patience and unfailing support reached almost superhuman levels throughout this project. Thanks for the hugs, words of encouragement and smiles!

Heaps of thanks go to Walter and Ursula Schulte who so generously gave me a home away from home (not to mention superb food and wine) and to these wonderful friends who shared their living space, ideas and knowledge: Kerstin & Marco Göllrich, Jörg Thelen, Bettina and Torsten Piltz, Georg Letsch, Joachim Brust and Christina Rasch.

Tourist office representatives who went beyond the call of duty were Wolfgang Thieme of Rheinland-Pfalz-Information, Mandy Müller of Thüringer Tourismus GmbH and Jörg Hoenicke and Martina Schneider of Hamburg Tourism. Deserving special mention are Klaus Busch and Frau Schlösser (Worms), Jürgen Schmidt (Mainz), Julia Bickmann (Kaiserslautern), Albert Becker (Trier), Petra Bechler (Saalfeld), Bernd Buhmann (Berlin) and Gunter Winkler (DZT).

Thanks also go to the following people who let me in on their cities' scenes and secrets: Martina Schumacher of Hamburg; Ralf Kuhlmann of Cologne's Station Backpacker Hostel; Hans Peter Ahr of Erfurt; Jürgen Nitzsche of Weimar; and, in Berlin, Francis, Chris and Mickey of Insider Tours, Peter and Sven of the Odyssee Hostel, and Nick and Serena of Berlin Walks.

Finally, a heartfelt danke schön to all the folks at the LP office in Melbourne who worked so hard to make this book great, including Liz Filleul, Chris Wyness and Mark Griffiths.

Jeremy Gray Large, neatly-packed parcels of gratitude go out to Gunter Winkler at the German National Tourist Office, who connected me to other well-connected people in the local tourist offices. Local heroes include Vera Golücke (Munich), who should get a putty medal for her tireless efforts; Astrid Werner and Ute Meesmann (Potsdam), for hospitality beyond the call; Sabine Müller (Bamberg), for those niggling details; Annett Morche (Leipzig), for her unadulterated sense of fun; Sabine Teisinger (Regensburg), for showing me her secret pubs; Christine Lambrecht (Dessau) for her literary inspiration; and Christof Heller (Freiburg) for his grasp of historical detail. Fellow Lonely Planet authors Andrea Schulte-Peevers, Ryan ver Berkmoes and Steve Fallon also deserve special mention for helping keep me afloat on this maiden voyage. Finally, the biggest thanks of all goes to my wife, Petra Riemer, for putting up with my prolonged absences, late-night phone calls and generally obsessive behaviour during this project.

Anthony Haywood I would like to thank the staff at various tourist offices throughout Germany. Special thanks go to Herr Holzberg in Celle, Frau Neumann in Braunschweig and Frau Knoblauch in Osnabrück for their kind assistance. Also worthy of special mention are the German Wine Institute and the Deutsche Brauwirtschaft e.V., which provided information and illustrative material for this new edition. Thanks also to the readers who sent us information and suggestions. Very warm thanks to friends and family who have shared their knowledge about Germany or assisted on a personal level. And last but not least, thanks to Liz Filleul and Jane Fitzpatrick at LP in Melbourne and the cartographers and editors who worked so hard to bring this second edition to life.

This Book

The first edition of *Germany* was researched and written by Steve Fallon, Anthony Haywood, Andrea Schulte-Peevers and Nick Selby.

For this second edition, Andrea updated the Facts for the Visitor chapter, as well as Berlin, Thuringia, Rhineland-Palatinate, North Rhine-Westphalia and Hamburg. She was also coordinating author of the book.

Jeremy Gray updated the chapters of Baden-Württemberg, Bavaria, Brandenburg, Mecklenburg-Western Pomerania, Saxony and Saxony-Anhalt, as well as Getting There & Away and Getting Around. He also taste-tested for the German Beer & Wine special section.

Anthony updated the Facts about Germany chapter, as well as chapters on the Harz Mountains, Hesse, Bremen, Lower Saxony and Schleswig-Holstein. He also wrote the new German Beer & Wine special section.

From the Publisher

The second edition of Germany was produced in the Melbourne office. The editing was jointly coordinated by Susie Ashworth and Rebecca Turner, the design was coordinated by Paul Dawson, and Jacqui Saunders was responsible for the mapping.

Editing and proofing assistance was given by Russ Kerr, Sarah Mathers, Anne Mulvaney, Kalya Ryan and Jane Thompson. Joelene Kowalski, Birgit Jordan and Mark Griffiths also lent a helping hand with the maps.

Thanks to Jamieson Gross for the cover, Quentin Frayne for the language section, Darren Elder for his work on the index, Mick Weldon for the cartoons, Matt King for his help with the illustrations, Leonie Mugavin for extra travel information and Tim Uden for his Quark expertise. Thanks to Lonely Planet Images for their assistance, especially Valerie Tellini.

Our thanks also go to the Berlin transport office (BVG), the Munich Transport Authority (MVV) and the German Brewers' Association for permission to use their material.

And finally, thanks to our authors for their patience, good humour and hard work throughout the production of the book.

THANKS
Many thanks to the travellers who used the last edition and wrote to us with helpful hints, advice and interesting anecdotes. Your names appear in the back of this book.

Foreword

ABOUT LONELY PLANET GUIDEBOOKS

The story begins with a classic travel adventure: Tony and Maureen Wheeler's 1972 journey across Europe and Asia to Australia. Useful information about the overland trail did not exist at that time, so Tony and Maureen published the first Lonely Planet guidebook to meet a growing need.

From a kitchen table, then from a tiny office in Melbourne (Australia), Lonely Planet has become the largest independent travel publisher in the world, an international company with offices in Melbourne, Oakland (USA), London (UK) and Paris (France).

Today Lonely Planet guidebooks cover the globe. There is an ever-growing list of books and there's information in a variety of forms and media. Some things haven't changed. The main aim is still to help make it possible for adventurous travellers to get out there – to explore and better understand the world.

At Lonely Planet we believe travellers can make a positive contribution to the countries they visit – if they respect their host communities and spend their money wisely. Since 1986 a percentage of the income from each book has been donated to aid projects and human rights campaigns.

Updates Lonely Planet thoroughly updates each guidebook as often as possible. This usually means there are around two years between editions, although for more unusual or more stable destinations the gap can be longer. Check the imprint page (following the colour map at the beginning of the book) for publication dates.

Between editions up-to-date information is available in two free newsletters – the paper *Planet Talk* and email *Comet* (to subscribe, contact any Lonely Planet office) – and on our Web site at www.lonelyplanet.com. The *Upgrades* section of the Web site covers a number of important and volatile destinations and is regularly updated by Lonely Planet authors. *Scoop* covers news and current affairs relevant to travellers. And, lastly, the *Thorn Tree* bulletin board and *Postcards* section of the site carry unverified, but fascinating, reports from travellers.

Correspondence The process of creating new editions begins with the letters, postcards and emails received from travellers. This correspondence often includes suggestions, criticisms and comments about the current editions. Interesting excerpts are immediately passed on via newsletters and the Web site, and everything goes to our authors to be verified when they're researching on the road. We're keen to get more feedback from organisations or individuals who represent communities visited by travellers.

Lonely Planet gathers information for everyone who's curious about the planet – and especially for those who explore it first-hand. Through guidebooks, phrasebooks, activity guides, maps, literature, newsletters, image library, TV series and Web site we act as an information exchange for a worldwide community of travellers.

Research Authors aim to gather sufficient practical information to enable travellers to make informed choices and to make the mechanics of a journey run smoothly. They also research historical and cultural background to help enrich the travel experience and allow travellers to understand and respond appropriately to cultural and environmental issues.

Authors don't stay in every hotel because that would mean spending a couple of months in each medium-sized city and, no, they don't eat at every restaurant because that would mean stretching belts beyond capacity. They do visit hotels and restaurants to check standards and prices, but feedback based on readers' direct experiences can be very helpful.

Many of our authors work undercover, others aren't so secretive. None of them accept freebies in exchange for positive write-ups. And none of our guidebooks contain any advertising.

Production Authors submit their raw manuscripts and maps to offices in Australia, USA, UK or France. Editors and cartographers – all experienced travellers themselves – then begin the process of assembling the pieces. When the book finally hits the shops, some things are already out of date, we start getting feedback from readers and the process begins again …

WARNING & REQUEST

Things change – prices go up, schedules change, good places go bad and bad places go bankrupt – nothing stays the same. So, if you find things better or worse, recently opened or long since closed, please tell us and help make the next edition even more accurate and useful. We genuinely value all the feedback we receive. Julie Young coordinates a well travelled team that reads and acknowledges every letter, postcard and email and ensures that every morsel of information finds its way to the appropriate authors, editors and cartographers for verification.

Everyone who writes to us will find their name in the next edition of the appropriate guidebook. They will also receive the latest issue of *Planet Talk*, our quarterly printed newsletter, or *Comet*, our monthly email newsletter. Subscriptions to both newsletters are free. The very best contributions will be rewarded with a free guidebook.

Excerpts from your correspondence may appear in new editions of Lonely Planet guidebooks, the Lonely Planet Web site, *Planet Talk* or *Comet*, so please let us know if you *don't* want your letter published or your name acknowledged.

Send all correspondence to the Lonely Planet office closest to you:

Australia: PO Box 617, Hawthorn, Victoria 3122
USA: 150 Linden St, Oakland, CA 94607
UK: 10A Spring Place, London NW5 3BH
France: 1 rue du Dahomey, 75011 Paris

Or email us at: talk2us@lonelyplanet.com.au

For news, views and updates see our Web site: www.lonelyplanet.com

HOW TO USE A LONELY PLANET GUIDEBOOK

The best way to use a Lonely Planet guidebook is any way you choose. At Lonely Planet we believe the most memorable travel experiences are often those that are unexpected, and the finest discoveries are those you make yourself. Guidebooks are not intended to be used as if they provide a detailed set of infallible instructions!

Contents All Lonely Planet guidebooks follow roughly the same format. The Facts about the Destination chapters or sections give background information ranging from history to weather. Facts for the Visitor gives practical information on issues like visas and health. Getting There & Away gives a brief starting point for researching travel to and from the destination. Getting Around gives an overview of the transport options when you arrive.

The peculiar demands of each destination determine how subsequent chapters are broken up, but some things remain constant. We always start with background, then proceed to sights, places to stay, places to eat, entertainment, getting there and away, and getting around information – in that order.

Heading Hierarchy Lonely Planet headings are used in a strict hierarchical structure that can be visualised as a set of Russian dolls. Each heading (and its following text) is encompassed by any preceding heading that is higher on the hierarchical ladder.

Entry Points We do not assume guidebooks will be read from beginning to end, but that people will dip into them. The traditional entry points are the list of contents and the index. In addition, however, some books have a complete list of maps and an index map illustrating map coverage.

There may also be a colour map that shows highlights. These highlights are dealt with in greater detail in the Facts for the Visitor chapter, along with planning questions and suggested itineraries. Each chapter covering a geographical region usually begins with a locator map and another list of highlights. Once you find something of interest in a list of highlights, turn to the index.

Maps Maps play a crucial role in Lonely Planet guidebooks and include a huge amount of information. A legend is printed on the back page. We seek to have complete consistency between maps and text, and to have every important place in the text captured on a map. Map key numbers usually start in the top left corner.

> Although inclusion in a guidebook usually implies a recommendation we cannot list every good place. Exclusion does not necessarily imply criticism. In fact there are a number of reasons why we might exclude a place – sometimes it is simply inappropriate to encourage an influx of travellers.

Introduction

Germany (Deutschland), deep in the heart of Europe, has had a greater impact on the Continent's history than any other country. From Charlemagne and the Holy Roman Empire to Otto von Bismarck's German Reich, Nazi Germany and the rise and fall of the Berlin Wall, no other nation has moulded Europe the way Germany has – for better or for worse.

It is the home of Bach and Beethoven, of Goethe and Schiller, of Einstein and Marx, of the fairy tales of our childhood. Until the late 19th century the English-speaking world looked not to Italy and France for its cultural cues but to Germany, with German the most popular foreign language learned in schools. But then, in the last century especially, emerged another Germany: a Germany of war, the land-grabbing search for *Lebensraum* and genocide committed in the name of the *Reich* and *Führer*. This dichotomy

is one the world and indeed the Germans are still struggling to understand.

Germany's reunification in 1990 was the beginning of yet another chapter. Though it's been one country for over a decade, the cultural, social and economic divide formed during 40 years of separation will take many more years to bridge. Nevertheless, the integration of the two former Germanys is proceeding apace, so much so that first-time visitors may not notice big differences between them at all.

Much of Germany's history and culture is easily explored by travellers. No matter where you go – whether major metropolis or tiny town – fascinating sights and attractions abound. There are museums on every subject, glorious architecture from 2000 years and a heavy emphasis on cultural activity. Its infrastructure is extremely developed, there is plenty of accommodation and the beer, food and wine are excellent.

But Germany is not just a mecca for history buffs and culture vultures. Outdoor activity is part of the German way of life, with endless opportunities for cycling, skiing, hiking and mountaineering, horse riding or just relaxing in a thermal spa. It is also a land of staggering physical beauty, from the Bavarian Alps and the majestic, castle-lined Rhine River to the windswept North Sea islands, the enchanting Black Forest, and the 'museum' towns of half-timbered houses and soaring Gothic cathedrals.

Large parts are indeed still steeped in tradition and live up to this romantic image.

What often surprises many visitors, though, is that it's also a thoroughly modern nation where you're more likely to listen to techno than to oompah and where the Turkish doner kebab vies with *Bratwurst* for most popular snack. The cities especially are vibrant, progressive centres of multiculturalism and the creative avant-garde, with the constantly evolving Berlin the most happening place in Europe.

No matter where your journey through Germany takes you, you'll be sure to find a country of constant surprises and eye-opening discoveries.

Willkommen und Gute Reise!

Facts about Germany

HISTORY

The origins of German history can be found in the Teutonic tribes that once inhabited northern Europe. But a 'German' history only dates from about the 9th century, when the Frankish Reich, or empire, was first divided up and regions east of the Rhine began to develop their own cultural identity. Compared with Britain and France, Germany was slow to shake off the yoke of regional dynastic rule and become a centralised state. The subsequent development of its principalities into the Federal Republic of Germany is a history of feudalism, unification, fascism, occupation, division and reunification.

Today, Germany is the main player in the push for a united Europe. The German nation is finding a new voice as a mediator between established capitalist countries to the west and former communist countries to the east.

Early History

The first inhabitants of Germany were Celts, who were gradually displaced by Germanic tribes from the north. Although the exact origins of the tribes are uncertain, Bronze Age populations are believed to have inhabited a region extending southwards from Sweden and Denmark to the North German plains and Harz Mountains. By about 100 AD, six broad settlement groups had formed, scattered roughly between what is today Denmark in the north, Kaliningrad in the north-east, the Danube in the south-east and the Rhine region in the west.

Romans

Clashes between Germanic tribes and conquering Romans occurred as early as the 1st century BC. Although the Romans suffered defeats, the tribes had difficulty holding onto newly won land and were usually pushed back eastwards across the Rhine. In 71 BC regions west of the Rhine were taken by Atovius, a powerful tribal military leader hailing from the north, before reoccupation

under Julius Caesar in 58 BC led to alliances that temporarily kept the peace. After the defeat of Roman legions at the hands of Arminius in the Teutoburger Wald in 9 AD, the Romans abandoned plans to extend control to the Elbe River. They consolidated southern fortifications in about 90 AD and began Romanising conquered populations. Arminius was a talented tribal leader who had enjoyed Roman citizenship and fought with the legions before staging his own revolt.

Trade contacts ensured that something of the Romans rubbed off on the tribes. Many signs of the occupation can be found today, especially in Trier, one of the most important administrative centres in the Western Empire. Others were Cologne, Mainz, Koblenz, Augsburg and Regensburg.

A lot of what we know about the early Germans comes from the Roman scholar Tacitus and his work *Germania*, published in 98 AD. According to Tacitus, who often idealised the tribes, they cultivated crops, produced most of their goods within the household, traded in slaves with the Romans and lived on a diet largely consisting of milk, cheese and meat. He was probably the first scholar to draw attention to their proclivity for beer and a bet.

In the 4th century, Hun horsemen galloped in from Central Asia and triggered the Great Migration throughout Europe. This caused the displacement of Germanic tribes, who packed their bags in the 5th century and overran southern Europe. The threat ended when Attila, the leader of the Huns, died in 453.

Then, in 486, with the collapse of the Western Empire, the tables turned and the Romans sought protection among resettled Germanic tribes. By that time the Germanic population had adopted large chunks of Roman administrative, financial and political structures. The later use of the title *Kaiser* (from 'Caesar') was a direct legacy of Roman times.

The Frankish Reich

Based in lands on the western bank of the Rhine, the Frankish Reich was the most important European political power in the early Middle Ages. In its heyday it included present-day France, Germany, the Low Countries and half the Italian peninsula. One reason for its success was that Clovis (482-511), its first Merovingian king, and his successors were able to unite diverse population groups. After converting to Christianity, missionaries such as the English St Boniface were sent across the Rhine to convert the pagan tribes. But when fighting broke out among the aristocratic clans in the 7th century, the Merovingians were replaced by the Carolingians.

The Carolingians introduced hierarchical Church structures into duchies east of the Rhine to control the local populations. Charlemagne (768-814), the Reich's most important king, conquered Lombardy, won territory in Bavaria, successfully waged a 30-year war against the Saxons in the north and was crowned Kaiser by the pope in 800, ruling from his residence in Aachen. By licking the Lombards on the battlefield, he affirmed the Franks' role in protecting the newly created papal state in Italy, which was granted to the popes by his father.

The cards were reshuffled in the 9th century, though, when attacks by Danes, Saracens and Magyars threw the eastern portion of Charlemagne's empire into turmoil. Around this time four main tribal duchies emerged. They were Bavaria, Franconia, Swabia and Saxony.

On Charlemagne's death, a bun fight ensued between his sons, resulting in the Treaty of Verdun (843) and a gradual carve-up of the Reich. When Louis the Child, a grandson of Charlemagne, died in 911 without leaving an heir, the East Frankish (ie German) dukes elected a king from their own ranks, creating the first 'German' monarch.

Birth of the Holy Roman Empire

Louis the German, as his name suggests, promoted a distinctly German cultural identity. This identity was reinforced when the dukes decided to elect Konrad I (911-18) as king. When Konrad died, the crown passed to Heinrich I (919-36), a Saxon dandy whose pastimes included bird-catching and placating popes. It's said that Heinrich (also known as Henry the Fowler) was out trapping finches in Quedlinburg when he was told he had been elected king. The ranks of the nobility began to swell during Heinrich's reign, with many clerics scaling the

What was the Holy Roman Empire?

An idea, mostly, and not a very good one, it grew out of the Frankish Reich, which was seen as the legitimate successor state to the defunct Roman Empire. When Charlemagne's father, Pippin, helped a beleaguered pope (Charlemagne would later do the same), he received the title *Patricius Romanorum*, or Protector of Rome, virtually making him Caesar's successor. Soon afterwards, he gave the pope a state of his own – the Vatican. This reconstituted 'Roman Empire' then passed into German hands.

The empire was known by various names throughout its lifetime. It formally began (for historians, at least) in 962 with the crowning of Otto I as Kaiser, and finally collapsed in 1806, when Kaiser Franz II abdicated. Sometimes it included Italy as far south as Rome. Sometimes it didn't – the pope usually had a say in that. It variously encompassed present-day Holland, Belgium, Switzerland, Lorraine and Burgundy (in France), Sicily, Austria and an eastern swathe of land which lies in the Czech Republic, Poland and Hungary.

This was the so-called 'First Reich'. The Second Reich was created by Otto von Bismarck in 1871, while the notorious Third Reich was Adolf Hitler's attempt to cash in on this dubious glory.

social ladder. But his greatest achievement was a series of military campaigns in 925 that established hegemony over French-speaking Lorraine.

Heinrich's son, Otto I (936-73), continued Charlemagne's policy of assimilating Church figures into civil administration and revitalised the Reich's power over Italy as far south as Rome. He also consolidated *Markgrafschaften* (marches) on the eastern border, administrative buffer regions that gradually turned into duchies.

In 962 Otto answered a call for help from the pope, renewing Charlemagne's promise to protect the papacy. The pope responded by pledging his loyalty to the Kaiser, breathing life back into a complicated mutual dependence (without the pope, a king could not be crowned Kaiser) that caused numerous power struggles over the centuries. This marked the founding of a nebulous state known as the Holy Roman Empire, which survived under various names until 1806 (see the boxed text 'What was the Holy Roman Empire?').

Otto III (983-1002), grandson of Otto I, was three years old when elected to the throne, and for 11 years the Reich was successively ruled by two women, Theophano, his mother, and Adelheid, his grandmother. Otto then tried to make Rome the capital of the Holy Roman Empire and resurrect its former classical glory. He failed and most of the land won under Otto I was forfeited. In 1024 power fell to the Salians, an established Franconian noble house.

Investiture Conflict

In the 11th century, the papacy tried to stamp out the practice of symony (selling religious office), which led to a major power struggle, the Investiture Conflict, with Heinrich IV (1056-1106). At stake was the right to appoint bishops. In 1076 Heinrich was excommunicated – the first of two times – but absolved a short time later through a sensational act of penance, when he stood barefoot in the snow for three days in front of the castle at Canossa, in northern Italy, begging the pope's forgiveness. This divided his enemies, resulting in a 20-year civil war to control bishoprics and, of course, their wealth. By this time, however, the days of the Salian dynasty were numbered. Its downfall was delayed when Heinrich V (1106-25) took power, but he failed to deliver the dynasty an heir.

The issue of symony was eventually resolved by the Treaty of Worms (1122), which gave local bishops their independence from the Reich.

Hohenstaufen Rule

Kings had always had to submit to some form of election in Germany, but relatives usually held the best cards. But importantly, by 1125 this principle had been abandoned. Rather than dust down an obscure nephew of Heinrich V's, the *Kurfürsten* (prince electors) chose one of their own number in Lothar III (1125-37), a Saxon noble who had scaled the dynastic ladder by marriage. A good marriage between his daughter and a member of the powerful Welf family allied Bavarian and Saxon rulers against the rival Swabian family of the Hohenstaufens. When Lothar died, however, the electors opted for Konrad III (1138-52), beginning a period of Hohenstaufen rule.

Under Friedrich I Barbarossa (1152-89) the fortunes of the Reich improved, but Friedrich – as German rulers were inclined to do – soon fell foul of the pope, who saw a series of Italian campaigns begun by Friedrich as a threat to his power. In the meantime, Heinrich der Löwe (Henry the Lion), a Welf whose interests lay in Saxony and part of Bavaria, had been extending influence eastwards in campaigns to Germanise and convert the Slavs. But when he in turn fell out with Friedrich I, he went into exile and Saxon interests were carved up and given to the Reich. Bavaria ended up in the hands of the powerful Wittelsbach family. While the Reich divided up the spoils, Heinrich der Löwe made a dramatic, if untimely, exit, dying in 1189 on the 3rd crusade, at the threshold to the Holy Land.

Things ended badly for Heinrich der Löwe, but for the Reich, now ruled by

Heinrich VI (1190-97), the champagne goblets seemed set to clink everywhere. It married into Sicily around this time (causing another papal nerve attack), but Heinrich VI's sudden death caught the Reich unawares, producing a fight for the crown between Welfs and Hohenstaufens. This led to the election of a king and (pope-backed) anti-king in Phillip von Schwaben and Heinrich der Löwe's son, Otto IV.

The idea of electing rulers often turned monarchs into lackeys of the Kurfürsten, who pursued their own dynastic interests and prevented the creation of a unified Reich. By 1250, authority had fallen into the hands of squabbling local rulers. Friedrich II (1212-50), a papal-nominated replacement for the unfortunate Phillip von Schwaben (who was murdered in sticky circumstances during an Italian sojourn), left government administration to the princes, which accelerated fragmentation.

When Friedrich II tried to flex muscle in Italy, he was nullified by Pope Innocent IV, leading to the Great Interregnum, or 'Terrible Time' (1254-73). The Reich, suddenly flush with kings, lost virtually all central authority. Richard of Cornwall, an obscurely related English nominee, managed four visits to his realm, making sure he never strayed far from the Rhine, while his anti-king, Alfonso X of Spain, did not manage to pay his subjects even a flying visit.

Settlement in the East

Chaos and dynastic rivalry in the German Reich did not, however, inhibit expansion eastwards, which had always been the prerogative of individual princes. By the mid-12th century many German peasants and city-dwellers had settled east of the Oder River in Silesia and Moravia. Settlement only got under way in the early 13th century with the Teutonic Knights. Originally part of a charity organisation formed in the Holy Land to care for fallen crusaders, the knights took on a military character and, with the crusades behind them, returned to Europe. After answering a call from the king of Poland to fight the Prussians, they

pushed eastwards under their grand master, Hermann of Salza, establishing fortresses which later grew into towns, such as Königsberg (present-day Kaliningrad). Granted protection rights over their conquests, the knights subsequently built a unified state that, at its peak, stretched from the Oder to Estonia.

By the mid-14th century, plague and trouble with Poland and the gentry had brought decline, and by 1525 a reduced area controlled by the knights became the Duchy of Prussia, a vassal state of Poland until the rise of Brandenburg-Prussia around the 17th century.

Cities & the Hanseatic League

From about the mid-11th century, a swelling population, land pressure and greater mobility had encouraged the growth of cities. Some were imperial (controlled by the Reich before being granted autonomy by crown charter), others were free cities (those that had shaken off their clerical rulers). The main difference was that imperial cities retained military and financial obligations to the Reich. Laws in cities were more liberal than in the countryside, which was often under the thumb of oppressive feudal lords. Any peasant who managed to flee to a city and stay there for one year and one day could become a resident. This gave rise to the expression *Stadtluft macht frei* (City air liberates).

Leagues were established to protect common interests, the most important of which was the Hanseatic League, whose origins lay in guilds and associations formed by out-of-town merchants. By 1358 these had formally joined to create the Hanseatic League, dominated by Lübeck, which controlled a large slice of European shipping trade. At its zenith, the league had over 150 member cities. It earned a say in the choice of Danish kings after the Danes inspired wrath by sinking a flotilla of the league's ships off Gotland in 1361. The resulting Treaty of Stralsund turned the league into northern Europe's most powerful economic and political entity.

As well as Lübeck, the league included such cities as Riga and Danzig (now Gdansk) on the Baltic Sea, Hamburg and Bremen on the North Sea, and inland cities like Cologne, Dortmund and Hildesheim. By the 15th century, however, competition from Dutch and English shipping companies, internal disputes and a shift in the centre of world trade from the North and Baltic seas to the Atlantic had caused decline. Hamburg, Bremen and Lübeck are still known as Hanse cities, with Hamburg and Bremen remaining separate German states in their own right.

Plague

The Terrible Time lived up to its name, but the plague, which wiped out about 25% of Europe's population in the mid-14th century, was worse. It hit Germany from 1348 to 1350 and produced panic lynchings, pogroms against Jews, labour shortages and a rush to the cities, where tensions rose between old and new city-dwellers. Large tracts of marginal farmland were abandoned. The bright side of the plague was that anyone who survived enjoyed slightly better conditions by being able to demand more for labour.

Guilds

The higher price of labour corresponded to an increase in the power of craft guilds (precursors to trade unions). In the 13th and 14th centuries, guilds became important institutions that challenged merchant dominance and often city authorities as well. They formed alliances with powerful families and some even held their own church services. Those excluded from the guilds, such as journeymen (day labourers), usually had a hard time in the cities.

The Habsburgs

But the plague, full course of settlement in the east and the Hanseatic League's development into a real power were still to come when the Habsburg dynasty, in the person of Rudolf (1273-91), took the throne, thus ending the Terrible Time. This dynasty would dominate much of European affairs into the 20th century.

Under the Habsburgs, the focus of the Reich was shifted to the south-east and Austria, the family's traditional stamping ground. By Rudolf's time, the power to elect kings had fallen to seven Kurfürsten – three secular and four clerical – who shaped the politics of the Reich. But in the decades after Rudolf's death the crown passed between powerful dynasties that continued to promote their own interests at the expense of the Reich's. Rudolf had merely been a flicker of light in what was still a pretty bad time, and something had to change.

The first change came in 1338 with the Declaration of Rense, which dispensed with the pope's confirmation of elected kings. Election to king now automatically bestowed the title of Kaiser, ending centuries of built-in conflict. The second change was introduced under Karl IV (1347-78) with the signing of the Golden Bull (1356), Germany's most important early constitutional document. This laid down written rules for the election of Kaisers and regulated the relationship between the Kaiser and the princes. But the Kaiser still had to dance to the tune of the princes, setting the tone for a weak central authority up to the 19th century.

The reign of Karl IV (a Luxemburg) saw the establishment of Prague University (he was also king of Bohemia). In the next half-century other universities followed: Heidelberg, Cologne and Erfurt. The Reich (as opposed to local rulers) soon asserted itself in European affairs after the Great Schism (1378-1417) brought forth two popes (one French, the other Italian), weakening the Church's influence in German matters.

By the time of Maximilian I (1493-1519), the Reich was Habsburgian again and would remain so until its collapse in 1806. Maximilian was an impressive fellow who was often referred to as 'the last knight', which said as much about his predilection for medieval tournaments as the fact that the days of knights were numbered. But the Reformation would soon drive the Reich to the brink of collapse.

Reformation

The Great Schism was a low point for the Church. By squandering Church money on self-aggrandisement, competing popes alienated the common folk. They increasingly sold 'indulgences', whereby the wealthy could buy freedom from punishment for sin. Jan Hus, a cleric at Prague University, had raised a storm about this in about 1400, inflaming Czech nationalist sentiments, which ended with the departure of German professors. The Church burnt him at the stake in 1415.

On 31 October 1517, plagued by the questions of faith and salvation, Martin Luther, a theology professor at Wittenberg University, made public his '95 Theses', in which he questioned the selling of indulgences. Though in Latin and intended only for theologians, the theses quickly spread by word of mouth across Germany and found popular support.

The following year Luther was given a hearing by anxious Church authorities in Augsburg. Having refused to repudiate the theses, he broke from the Catholic (ie 'Universal') Church and expanded on his beliefs in reformist writings in 1520.

That year the pope threatened Luther with excommunication. Luther burnt the letter. With the thumbscrews tightening, he was invited to a *Reichstag* (one of the many meetings to discuss issues of the day) by Karl V (1519-56), where he again refused to repudiate his theses. He was banned by the Reich, only to be hidden in Wartburg (south of Eisenach in Thuringia), where he translated the New Testament into German.

Spurred on by Luther's teachings, townsfolk in Wittenberg began destroying their church. Luther returned to restore order, with Latin mass later being replaced by the Protestant service, which relied heavily on German hymns.

Also inspired by Luther and growing weary of their feral nobility, peasants elsewhere demanded better conditions from lords and the free election of priests. Insurrections occurred. Luther, to the dismay of

Martin Luther's controversial ideas triggered the Reformation.

many, sided with the lords, who repressed the violence. The *Bauernkriege* (Peasants' War) of 1524-25 ensued, immediately following a failed uprising by the knights, who wanted to save the last of their power by carving up principalities.

Karl V was too busy puzzling over his own dynastic crises to understand what was actually happening around him. He tried to force the Lutherans back into the Catholic Church, but eventually he succumbed to the princes' demands in the Peace of Augsburg (1555). This gave each prince the right to decide the religion of their principality and put the Catholic and Lutheran churches on an equal footing.

Except for small areas, the more secular northern principalities adopted Luther's teachings, while the clerical lords in the south, south-west and Austria adhered to the Catholic Church. This compromise is reflected in the religious make-up of Germany today. When Rudolf II took the throne in 1576, a Counter-Reformation movement gained momentum.

Thirty Years' War

The religious issue would not die. What began as a conflict between newly formed Protestant and Catholic leagues degenerated into one of Europe's most bloody dynastic wars. The Thirty Years' War (actually several wars) began in 1618 in Bohemia. In 1625 it was picked up by an alliance of Protestant Danes and Saxons who felt threatened by attempts to re-Catholicise the north. In 1630 Sweden jumped in, joined in 1635 by France, which saw a chance to weaken the Habsburgs by taking the Protestant side.

By the time calm was restored with the Peace of Westphalia (1648), the Reich was ravaged. It had over 300 states and about 1000 smaller territories. Switzerland and the Netherlands gained independence, France won chunks of Alsace and Lorraine, and Sweden helped itself to the mouths of the Elbe, Oder and Weser rivers. The Reich had turned into a nominal, impotent state, its population depleted by the war.

Absolutism & Enlightenment

Much can happen in a century, but Germany took that long to recover from the war. From the middle of the 17th century, the Reich's fortunes were in the hands of a rabble of competing autocratic princes. Some developed the nasty habit of selling their subjects as cannon fodder for foreign wars, notably to the British in the War of American Independence. They built grand baroque residences such as those in Würzburg, Karlsruhe, Mannheim and Ludwigsburg. Although the Enlightenment was slow to gain momentum in Germany, it produced composers like Johann Sebastian Bach and Georg Friedrich Händel, and a wave of *Hochkultur* (high culture). This, of course, excluded the masses, who remained largely illiterate and at the mercy of absolutist rulers. In 1714 the English crown fell into the hands of the House of Hanover, beginning a union between Hanover and Britain that ended with the death of William IV in 1837.

Areas formerly controlled by the Teutonic Knights had been united under Brandenburg-Prussia. Largely through the efforts of kings Friedrich Wilhelm I (the Soldier King) and his son, Friedrich II (Frederick the Great), the Hohenzollerns rose to challenge the power of the Habsburgs. This marked the rise of Brandenburg-Prussia.

The Habsburgs had extended imperial power across south-east Europe to Hungary and the Balkans, having repelled an army of 200,000 Turks near Vienna in 1683. This created the foundation for an Austro-Hungarian empire. Nevertheless, with Austria distracted by the Turks, France had gradually helped itself to the rest of Alsace, including Strasbourg and the Palatinate in the 1680s.

Brandenburg-Prussia annexed Silesia after the Seven Years' War (1756-63) with Austria, and subsequently sliced up Poland in a series of partitions. When peace returned, both Prussia and the Habsburgs set about revamping their administrations and armies.

Towards the end of the 18th century, the Age of Enlightenment was in full swing and the scales had tipped in favour of a centralised state. Rulers were quick to recognise the expediency of the Enlightenment for the survival of their own government. At the same time, a self-made class of public servants, academics, theologians and merchants questioned the right of the nobility to rule and stressed individual achievement.

A newly established imperial deputation secularised and reconstituted German territory between 1801 and 1803, much of this at the behest of Napoleon, who was to do more for German unity than any German had ever done. In 1806 the Rhine Confederation was formed, which supported Napoleon's ambitions by eradicating about 100 principalities. Sniffing the end of the Holy Roman Empire, Kaiser Franz II (1792-1806) packed his bags for Austria, renamed himself Franz I of Austria and abdicated in 1806. Thus, it was not a frightened pope or an ambitious prince who had sounded the death knell of the anachronistic Holy Roman Empire, but a Frenchman.

Its fragmentation meant that Germany was no serious match for Napoleon. In 1806 Brandenburg-Prussia fell to the French armies, which occupied Berlin. But Napoleon abandoned earlier plans to completely abolish this new power. The humiliation of defeat prompted Brandenburg-Prussia to reform, bringing it closer to civil statehood. Importantly, the Jews were granted equality, but it also nipped the guilds in the bud, and by abolishing bonded labour it laid the foundations for industrialisation.

In 1813, with French troops driven back by the Russians, Leipzig was the scene of one of Napoleon's most significant defeats. At the Congress of Vienna (1815), held to hammer out a post-Napoleon Europe, Germany was reorganised into a confederation of 35 states, an unsatisfactory solution that only minimally improved on the Holy Roman Empire. Under the auspices of the charismatic Austrian diplomat Klemens von Metternich, an ineffective Reichstag was established in Frankfurt. It poorly represented the most populous states, however, and failed to rein in Austro-Prussian rivalry.

Industrial Age

The first half of the 19th century was a crucial time in the development of Germany and Europe as a whole. The decay of feudal structures, an accumulation of great wealth in new hands and industrial innovation changed the economic and social ground rules, feeding into nationalist calls for a centralised state.

In 1837 construction of the first substantial railway line in Germany was begun between Dresden and Leipzig. This was expanded on in later years to become an efficient transportation system, coinciding with new customs unions that abolished feudal tariffs. Also significant was the growth of an industrial, urban proletariat. Workers' movements were banned, which is why the Trier-born Karl Marx and his collaborator, Friedrich Engels, would publish their influential works in exile.

With the scrapping of monarchical birthright in France in 1830, calls by liberals for reform in Germany grew louder. Fearing revolution, many states belatedly introduced the constitutions promised to the people at the Congress of Vienna. The 'Young Germany' movement of satirists formed, and lampooned the powerful of the day. In Prussia, Friedrich Wilhelm IV had taken the throne, but he disappointed everyone who wanted substantial change.

The French revolution of 1848 soon found a counterpart in Germany. Metternich was promptly dispensed with. Berlin erupted in riots. German leaders responded by quelling demands for more radical reforms by setting up a provisional parliament in the Paulskirche in Frankfurt. However, delays in agreeing on a constitution slowly sapped its prestige. One reason for this tardiness was the so-called *Grossdeutsch-Kleindeutsch* (greater or lesser Germany) question – mainly whether Austria would belong to a reconstituted Germany.

Austria wrote its own constitution, broke away and then relapsed into monarchism. Friedrich Wilhelm IV drafted his own constitution in 1850 (it remained in force until 1918), but failed when he tried to form a North German Confederation.

Although revolution fizzled, it did turn Prussia into a constitutional state, albeit with limited franchise. The confederation was revived in Frankfurt under Austrian presidency, and the clock turned back on reforms in the German parliament, the *Bundestag*. One member of the Bundestag was a certain Otto von Bismarck.

Unification

When a new era of reform began in Prussia in the 1850s, Bismarck went into 'cold storage on the Neva' in Russia, returning to become Prussian prime minister only after a constitutional crisis had changed the political atmosphere. Bismarck's grand ambition was to create a unified Germany, preferably with Prussia at the helm. An old-guard militarist, he successfully waged war against Denmark (with Austria his ally) over Schleswig-Holstein in 1864. In 1866 he unified northern Germany after the Seven Weeks' War against Austria, creating his own North German Confederation the following year.

MICK WELDON

The 'Iron Chancellor' Otto von Bismarck created a united Germany in 1871.

With northern Germany under his belt, Bismarck turned his attention to the south. Through skilful diplomacy, he isolated France and manoeuvred it into declaring war on Prussia in 1870. The pretence he used was a dispute with France over nominating a successor to the Spanish throne. Prussia backed down on the nomination issue, renouncing all future claims to the Spanish throne, but some tricky editing of a telegram to this effect (the *Emser Depesche*) by Bismarck offended the French. Bismarck then surprised Napoleon III by winning the backing of most southern German states. War with France resulted in Bismarck's annexation of Alsace-Lorraine.

By 1871, having won over the south German princes, he had created a unified Germany with Berlin as its capital. The Reich extended roughly from Memel (Klaipeda in present-day Lithuania) to the present-day Dutch border, including Alsace-Lorraine in the south-west and Silesia in the south-east. It was a masterful achievement and Western Europe's largest state. On 18 January 1871 the king of Prussia was crowned Kaiser of the Reich at Versailles (the ultimate humil-iation for the French), with Bismarck its 'Iron Chancellor'.

The new Reich was a bicameral, constitutional monarchy dominated by Prussia. Suffrage was limited to men, and real policy decisions were often made outside the elected Reichstag. The national colours were black, white and red, those of the old North German Confederation. Bismarck's power was based on the support of merchants and *Junker*, a noble class of landowners (without knighthood) that had formed in the Middle Ages.

He quickly embarked on a campaign called *Kulturkampf* to curb Catholic power. With the Catholic Zentrum (Centre) party the second-largest in the Reichstag, Bismarck feared a possible alliance of party interests with France and Austria-Hungary. Laws designed to nip the Catholic Church in the bud only increased support for Zentrum, however, and the policy was eventually abandoned.

The achievements of the Bismarck era were largely based on a dubious 'honest Otto' policy, whereby he acted as a broker between European powers, encouraging colonial vanities to divert attention from his own deeds. He built up a web of alliances to cover his back against Russia, Austria-Hungary, France, Italy and Britain, and even enjoyed good press in Britain. Germany began to catch up to Britain industrially and the number of Germans emigrating tailed off substantially from the peak levels of the 1840s and 1850s. Bismarck belatedly graced the Reich of Kaiser Wilhelm I with a few African jewels after 1880, acquiring colonies in central, south-west and east Africa as well as numerous Pacific paradises, such as Tonga, where a weary Prussian prince might one day lay down his steel helmet and crack coconuts.

The mid-19th century also saw the rise of democratic socialist parties, including predecessors of the present-day German Social Democratic Party (Sozialdemokratische Partei Deutschlands, or SPD). It was founded in 1875 as the Socialist Workers'

Party and got its present name in 1890. One leading social democrat, August Bebel, antagonised Bismarck with repeated calls for universal suffrage and economic equality. The chancellor's chief opponent, he was sentenced to two years' prison in 1872 for high treason and offence to the monarchy. In 1886, after a crackdown on socialists, he was convicted of belonging to a 'secret society'.

By the late 19th century, Germany was a wealthy, unified country. Bismarck had painted himself in liberal colours to buy inches and stop socialist demands for miles, providing health and accident benefits and invalid pensions. But the reform issue was to be his downfall. When Wilhelm II became Kaiser in 1888 (Friedrich, son of Wilhelm I, was sickly and ruled for only 99 days), divisions arose between the Kaiser, who wanted to extend the social security system, and Bismarck, who enacted his stricter antisocialist laws.

Europe badly missed Bismarck's diplomacy after the Kaiser's scalpel finally excised him from the political scene in March 1890. The period up to the outbreak of World War I in 1914, called the 'new direction', was an aimless one under the personal rule of Wilhelm II, who brought his weak chancellors to heel. Although industrially advanced (especially in chemical and electrical industries) and having produced some of the best social-revolutionary minds, Germany paddled towards the new century with incompetent leaders at its helm.

The legacy of Bismarck's diplomacy slowly unravelled. Wilhelm II had already given up Zanzibar for the return of Helgoland from Britain in 1890, frightening Russia, which fled into amorous French arms and a treaty in 1894. England came out of isolation and signed up with Japan against Russian hegemony in East Asia, later with France and then with Russia in 1907. Austria-Hungary teetered on the brink of collapse and dreamed of pan-Germanism. Meanwhile, the decline of the Ottoman Empire had thrown the Balkans into disarray and local wars.

The Great War

No war can be great, but technological advances and the hardening of Europe into large colonial power blocs made WWI probably the worst since the Thirty Years' War. It began with the assassination of the heir to the Austro-Hungarian throne, Archduke Franz-Ferdinand, in 1914 in Sarajevo. Austria-Hungary wrongly believed that Serbia was behind the assassination, leading to war between Serbia and Austria-Hungary. Russia mobilised, ready to jump in on the side of Serbia. With the Russian rejection of a German ultimatum to demobilise, Germany declared war on Russia, followed two days later by a declaration of war on France, based on the Schlieffen Plan.

This dictated that in the event of a two-front war (ie against Russia in the east and France in the west) Germany would attack France where it was most vulnerable, via Belgium, then fight the Russians afterwards. By doing so, however, Germany drew Britain, Belgium's ally, into the war. The lights of Europe, as the British foreign minister noted, had gone out. It soon escalated into a European and Middle Eastern war. Britain, France, Italy and Russia fought against Germany, Austria-Hungary and Turkey.

The horror of the Great War was to change the psychological landscape of Europe forever. It began well enough for Germany, but when one of its submarines sank the British passenger liner *Lusitania* in 1915, killing 120 US citizens, the Americans began to reconsider noninterventionism. Fearful of arousing American hostility, Germany abandoned its submarine attacks. By 1917, however, these had been unwisely renewed and America entered the war.

In the meantime, hunger had produced widespread pessimism in Germany. In Russia, communist revolution had deposed the tsarist government. Russia won peace with Germany in March 1918 through the humiliating treaty of Brest-Litovsk, which saw Russia renounce vast territories. With an allied counter-offensive and Germany's collapse on the western front following many bloody battles, Germany was prepared to negotiate a cease-fire and the acceptance of US president Woodrow Wilson's 14-point peace plan.

Peace & Abdication

To facilitate negotiations, Prince Max von Baden, a liberal, took over leadership of the government and the constitution was changed to make the chancellor responsible to parliament: Germany's first truly parliamentary party system. Though a good idea on paper, it successfully shifted any blame for peace negotiations onto the parties, creating a potent link between the stigma of defeat and democracy. This, a revolution from above that excused the military for defeat, would heavily burden Germany's first democratic experience, the Weimar Republic.

The bells finally tolled for Kaiser Wilhelm II in September 1918, when sailors mutinied in Kiel. This escalated into a workers' revolt, culminating in a revolution in Berlin and the abdication of the Kaiser, ending monarchical rule in Germany. Two days later, on 11 November 1918, the armistice was signed.

Weimar Republic

Peace meant the end of war, but it did not create stability in Germany. The period after the armistice hailed a struggle between socialist and democratic socialist parties, including the radical Spartacus League. Founded by Rosa Luxemburg and Karl Liebknecht, the Spartacus League wanted to create a republic based on Marx's theories of proletarian revolution. In practice, this meant transferring power to a soldiers' and workers' council (a council was established, but only briefly). Opposed by moderate socialists, the Spartacus League in 1919 came together with other groups to form the German Communist Party (Kommunistische Partie Deutschlands, or KPD). Following the bloody quashing of an uprising in Berlin, both Luxemburg and Liebknecht were arrested and murdered by *Freikorps* soldiers (war volunteers) and their bodies dumped in Berlin's Landwehrkanal. In the meantime, a new democratic republic had been proclaimed.

MICK WELDON

Co-founder of the German Communist Party, Rosa Luxemburg came to a gruesome end.

Germany paid dearly for the war. The Treaty of Versailles forced it to relinquish its colonies, to cede Alsace-Lorraine and territory in western Poland and to pay high reparations. Article 231 of the treaty made Germany responsible for all losses incurred by its enemies. The treaty was passed by a newly elected national assembly in 1919.

The federalist constitution of the new republic was adopted in July 1919 in the city of Weimar, where the constituent assembly had sought refuge from the chaos of Berlin. It gave women the vote and established basic human rights, but it was also unwieldy and gave too much power to the president, who could rule by decree in times of emergency – a clause that would later be abused by Paul von Hindenburg, Germany's second president.

A broad coalition government was formed by left and centre parties, led by president Friedrich Ebert of the SPD, the largest party until 1932. Too many forces in Germany rejected the republic, however, and it satisfied neither communists nor monarchists.

More trouble occurred in 1920 when a right-wing military circle staged the 'Kapp Putsch', occupying the government quarter of Berlin. Called on by the government to act (it had fled to Dresden), workers and trade unions went on strike, and the *Putsch* (revolt) collapsed.

By August 1923, economic difficulties had alienated the middle classes, whose savings were ravaged by hyperinflation. A new currency, the *Rentenmark*, was introduced but for many it was already too late.

In 1923 another attempt, the Munich Putsch, was made to topple the republic, led by a young Austrian called Adolf Hitler. Born in 1889 in Braunau am Inn, Austria, Hitler quit school after the death of his father in 1903 and dedicated himself to painting and a self-conceived mystical philosophy based on anti-Semitism, knights and Germanic folklore. In 1913 he moved to Munich and enlisted as a volunteer in the German army during WWI, rising to the rank of corporal and returning to civilian life after a gas attack left him temporarily blind.

A bad watercolour painter who was twice rejected by the Vienna Institute of Art as talentless, Hitler exploited anti-Berlin (red Berlin) sentiments and a Bavarian state of emergency. He tried to persuade the Bavarian government to march on the capital, imitating Mussolini's march on Rome a year earlier. He and other members of his National Socialist German Workers' Party (NSDAP) set off through the Munich streets and were promptly arrested. The party was banned and Hitler wound up in jail, where he wrote his turgid, nationalist and anti-Semitic work, *Mein Kampf*. After his early release in 1925, he set about rebuilding the party, having sworn to authorities that he would thereafter only pursue legal means of change.

Reparations had bitten deeply into the German economy, breeding widespread dissatisfaction. The French, increasingly distrustful of Germany meeting their demands, had occupied the Ruhr region in 1923, leading to passive resistance by workers, the creation of a French-backed Ruhr separatist movement, and a German backdown to save the already ailing economy. Although the French ultimately let the separatist issue slide, the conflict spelt out a need to solve the reparations problem.

This was done by the Dawes Plan, which provided for cheap loans. (Payments would later again be readjusted under the Young Plan in 1930.) The Locarno Pact (1925), largely the work of Gustav Stresemann as foreign minister, saw Germany accept its western borders with France and Belgium, which incited the wrath of nationalists but eased Franco-German tensions.

The most ambitious project in international relations, however, was the establishment of the League of Nations, originally part of Wilson's 14-point plan and the Treaty of Versailles. It was an early, commendable attempt to create international order (Germany joined in 1926, the USSR in 1934), but its power was undermined because the USA never joined.

After 1923 the economic situation began to stabilise and the Weimar years brought forth a cultural explosion. *Die wilden Zwanziger* (the wild twenties) saw film and radio gain importance and *Kabarett* (cabaret) capture the public imagination. Germany witnessed the literary flowering of the likes of Thomas Mann and Bertolt Brecht and the creative outpourings of the Bauhaus and Dada art movements.

Following the death of Ebert in 1925, Field Marshal Paul von Hindenburg became president. The election of the 78-year-old Hindenburg, a gritty monarchist, would prove disastrous to the republic.

Karl Marx had long met his maker when the New York Stock Market crashed on 24 October 1929. The ensuing Great Depression undermined an already fragile German democracy and bred support for extremist parties. Hindenburg, who had his own views on the crisis, used his emergency powers to circumvent parliament and appoint the Catholic Centre Party's Heinrich Brüning as chancellor. Brüning deflated the economy, forced down wages and destroyed whatever savings – and faith – the middle classes might have built up after the last economic debacle. It earned him the epitaph 'the Hunger Chancellor'.

The Hitler Era

In 1930 Hitler's NSDAP made astounding gains, winning 18% of the vote. Hitler set his sights on the presidency in 1932, running against Hindenburg; he received 37% of the second-round vote. In the same year, Brüning was replaced by Franz von Papen as chancellor. Papen was a hard-core monarchist associated with the *Deutscher Herrenklub*, a right-wing club for industrialists and the gentry in Berlin. He called two Reichstag elections, hoping to build a parliamentary base, but Hindenburg soon replaced him with Kurt von Schleicher, a military old boy.

Schleicher's attempt to pump prime the economy with public money – a policy begun by Papen – failed when it alienated industrialists and landowners. Finally in January 1933, won over by the right and advised by both Papen and Schleicher to nominate Hitler, Hindenburg continued his tradition of ignoring parliament. He dismissed Schleicher and appointed Hitler as chancellor, with a coalition cabinet of National Socialists and Papen's Nationalists. The National Socialists (Nazis) were by far the largest single party but still short of a majority.

The Nationalists – conservatives, old aristocrats and powerful industrialists who controlled Hindenburg – thought they could do the same with Hitler, but they were gravely mistaken. Hitler consolidated power by creating new ministries, which he filled with his own henchmen. In March 1933, without a clear majority, he called Germany's last halfway-free prewar elections. With the help of his intimidating party militia, the *Sturmabteilung* (SA), and the dubious Reichstag fire, which gave him an excuse to use emergency laws to arrest communist and liberal opponents, he won 43% of the vote – still not a majority.

The turning point was reached with the Enabling Law, which gave Hitler the power to decree laws and change the constitution without consulting parliament. A state of emergency remained until 1945.

By June 1933 the SPD had been banned and other parties disbanded. Hitler's NSDAP governed alone. So began the Third Reich.

In the early 1930s laws limited the independence of the states and banned unions, whose members were reorganised into the *Deutsche Arbeitsfront*, a crony association designed to eliminate worker opposition (the workers had voted against Hitler in 1933). SA and SS *(Schutzstaffel)* troops stepped up their terror campaigns. Meanwhile, Joseph Goebbels, head of the well-oiled Ministry for Propaganda, had begun to crack down on intellectuals and artists. This resulted in the burning of 'un-German' books on 10 May 1933 by students in Berlin and university towns across the country. Many intellectuals and artists packed their bags for America and elsewhere. The respected author Ricarda Huch boldly resigned her post as head of the Prussian Academy of the Arts in protest at the expulsion of Jews. Membership of the *Hitlerjugend* (Hitler Youth) became compulsory for young women and men aged between 10 and 18, while other youth organisations were disbanded except those of the Catholic Church.

Hitler, aware of the problems caused by unhappy popes in German history, signed an agreement that protected the Catholic Church (it was, after all, keen to sign up against 'godless Bolshevism') but excluded it from party political activities. In these early days, Hitler also enjoyed the support of the Protestant Church.

Röhm Putsch

Originally formed to guard public meetings, the SA had by 1934 become a powerful force that pushed to accelerate change. With rumours of revolt circulating, on 30 June elite SS troops (originally Hitler's bodyguards) rounded up and executed high-ranking SA officers, including their leader, Ernst Röhm. This gave the SS unchallenged power, but its leader, Hermann Göring, and his lieutenants also exploited the occasion to settle old (sometimes homophobic) scores with Hitler's opponents. Hindenburg's death that year allowed Hitler to merge the positions of president and chancellor.

The Plight of Jews

Although anti-Semitism was not unique to German society, its level of institutionalisation and brutality was. A boycott of Jewish businesses, including medical and legal practices, was organised by Goebbels in April 1933. Soon after, Jews were expelled from the public service and non-Aryans were banned from engaging in many professions, trades and industries. An 'Aryan' is anyone who speaks an Indo-European or Indo-Iranian language, but Hitler misused the term and 'non-Aryan' usually meant *Roma* or *Sinti* (Gypsies), non-whites and Jews. With the Nuremberg Laws of 1935, non-Aryans (mostly Jews, but also Roma and other groups) were deprived of German citizenship and forbidden from marrying or having sexual relations with Aryans. The death penalty was usually imposed on Germans and 'non-Germans' who broke race laws. In a bizarre twist, those sentenced to death were made to pay for their trial and execution costs.

On 9 November 1938 the horror escalated with the *Reichspogromnacht* (often called *Kristallnacht* or 'the night of broken glass'). In retaliation for the assassination of a German consular official by a Polish Jew in Paris, synagogues and Jewish cemeteries, property and businesses across Germany were desecrated, burnt or demolished. About 90 Jews died that night and the following day, while another 30,000 were arrested and incarcerated. Jewish businesses were expropriated and transferred to non-Jews through forced sale at below-market prices.

The Road to War

Economic success was one reason for Hitler's phenomenal popularity among the middle and lower-middle classes. He achieved this by pumping large sums into employment programs, such as *Autobahn* construction, and by encouraging employers to adopt military principles ('the employer is the *Führer*, the employee takes the orders').

Hitler reintroduced conscription and built up the air force. His first major lick of the Versailles wounds came in March 1936 with Germany's occupation of the Rhineland, which had been demilitarised under the treaty. He would later describe the 48 hours when he awaited international reaction as the most exciting of his life. It was a thrill the world could do without. Mild international protest was registered. A nonaggression pact with Poland, a friendship agreement with Mussolini and a naval agreement with Britain already under his belt, Hitler introduced a four-year plan in 1936 to rearm Germany and develop heavy industry. The SS established its own industries, initially relying on a compulsory 'volunteer workforce' of all women and men aged 18 to 25 (women worked in the fields or farmhouses). The Volkswagen factory opened in Wolfsburg in 1938.

That year Hitler's troops marched into Austria, greeted by enthusiastic crowds. The *Anschluss* (annexation) created the greater Germany that had been deliberated on in the previous century. It boosted Hitler's popularity at home. Meanwhile, foreign powers, hopelessly unprepared both militarily and psychologically for another war, pursued an increasingly untenable policy of appeasement.

With the Munich Agreement of September 1938 – signed by Hitler, Mussolini, Britain's Neville Chamberlain and France's Édouard Deladier – the largely ethnic German Sudetenland of Czechoslovakia was relinquished to Hitler, who assured everyone that German expansionism would stop at this. The British and French compromise, intended to buy time and save the remainder of Czechoslovakia, left the Czechs defenceless. Chamberlain returned home and declared there would be 'peace in our time', but began to rearm. By March 1939, Moravia and Bohemia had fallen into German hands.

When Hitler signed a nonaggression pact with Stalin's USSR in August 1939, the Tokyo-Berlin-Rome axis (Hitler had earlier signed agreements with Italy and Japan) was expanded to include Moscow, paving the way for an invasion of Poland. Hitler bought Soviet neutrality by signing a secret Soviet-German protocol that divided up Eastern Europe into spheres of interest.

In late August an SS-staged attack on a German radio station in Gleiwitz (Gliwice) gave Hitler the excuse he needed to march into Poland. Three days later, on 3 September 1939, France and Britain declared war on Germany.

WWII

Early Victories Although it resisted strongly, Poland was no match for Hitler's army and the persecution and murder of intellectuals left it without effective leadership. Jews were driven into ghettos and forced to wear the yellow Star of David. Meanwhile, ethnic Germans were resettled (about 900,000 up to 1944) in west Poland from areas occupied by the USSR under the terms of the secret protocol. The thumbscrews of the SS under Heinrich Himmler were tightened a notch. The SS ran concentration camps, the Gestapo (secret police) and provided the war machine with elite troops. At home there were food shortages and greater political oppression.

Belgium and the Netherlands fell quickly to Germany, as did France, where a collaborationist government was installed under Marshal Pétain. Hitler signed the French armistice in the same railway carriage used for the signing of the humiliating 1918 armistice. By the summer of 1940, the British had evacuated mainland Europe at Dunkirk but withstood the Battle of Britain and the bombing of major cities *(Blitzkrieg)*, including Coventry, which was almost completely destroyed.

In June 1941 Hitler attacked the USSR in Operation Barbarossa. This broke the nonaggression pact with Stalin and opened up a new front. But delays in staging the operation – caused by problems in the Mediterranean – would be his downfall. Although Barbarossa was successful at first, lines became over-stretched. Hitler's troops, bogged down and ill-prepared for the bitter winter of 1941-42, were forced into retreat. With the defeat of the German 6th army at Stalingrad (Volgograd) the following winter, morale flagged both at home and on the fronts.

The Final Solution The treatment of Jews further deteriorated after the outbreak of war. Himmler's SS troops systematically terrorised or executed local populations in occupied areas, while war with the USSR was portrayed as a fight against 'subhuman' Jews and Bolsheviks. The Nazis, abandoning vague plans to resettle European Jewry on the African island of Madagascar, began deportation to east Germany and Eastern Europe.

At Hitler's behest, Göring commissioned his functionaries to find an *Endlösung* (final solution) to the Jewish question. A conference in January 1942 on Berlin's Wannsee resulted in a protocol clothed in ugly bureaucratic jargon that laid the basis for the murder of millions of Jews. The Holocaust would be an efficient, systematic, bureaucratic and meticulously documented genocidal act carried out by about 100,000 Germans, but with the tacit agreement of a far greater number.

Concentration Camps Although not a Nazi invention, concentration camps reached a new level of efficiency under Nazism. Among the main groups incarcerated were Jews, Roma, political opponents, priests (especially Jesuits), homosexuals, resistance fighters and habitual criminals. The network of camps was expanded throughout the war, reaching a total of 22 (mostly in Eastern Europe). There were another 165 work camps, with many (eg Auschwitz-Birkenau) providing a labour force for big industry, such as IG Farbenindustrie AG, producer of Zyklon B, a cyanide gas. Initially tested on Soviet prisoners, the gas was later used in gas chambers to murder over three million Jews. About seven million people were sent to concentration camps. Only 500,000 survived to be liberated by Soviet and Allied soldiers.

Resistance Resistance to Hitler from socialist, social democratic and workers' groups had been effectively quashed during the 1930s, with members either sent to camps or forced to go underground or abroad. Following the outbreak of war with the USSR in 1941, the Gestapo smashed the Rote Kapelle Soviet spy ring that had penetrated Nazi ministries. The efficiency of the SS meant that, with notable exceptions, resistance tended to be small-scale.

In 1942 a group of Munich students formed the Weisse Rose (White Rose) group, which exploited the pessimism after Stalingrad by distributing anti-Nazi leaflets. See the boxed text 'The White Rose' in the Bavaria chapter.

When the war seemed lost, Claus Graf Schenk von Stauffenberg and other high-ranking army officers planned to assassinate Hitler and seize power from the SS on 20 July 1944. The attempt failed and when sensitive documents fell into Nazi hands over 200 people from the underground were immediately arrested and executed. Over 7000 people would be arrested, and several thousand of them executed.

Total War With the Normandy invasion of June 1944, the Allies returned to the European mainland, supported by systematic air raids on German cities. The brunt of the bombings was suffered by the civilian population. Over a year earlier, Goebbels had delivered his speech on total war to a gathering of the high and mighty in Berlin, rejecting Allied demands for unconditional surrender. Children and the elderly were called to join the newly formed *Volkssturm* (People's Army).

The Soviet advance from the east continued, often with brutal retributions, especially against women (rape was common, as was a particularly nasty strain of venereal disease, the so-called 'Russian syphilis'). The British bombed Dresden on 13 February 1945, killing 35,000 people, many of them refugees.

Hitler, broken and paranoid, ordered the destruction of all German industry and infrastructure, a decree that was largely ignored. He committed suicide, along with his wife, Eva Braun (they married the previous day), and Goebbels, on 30 April, with Soviet troops just outside Berlin. The capital fell two days later.

On 7 May, after a delay that allowed refugees to reach Allied areas, Germany capitulated and peace was signed at the US headquarters in Rheims. It was signed again, at Stalin's request, the next day at Soviet headquarters in Berlin.

Surrender & Occupation

With the declaration of unconditional surrender on 8 May 1945, Germany lay in ruins. In line with agreements reached at the Yalta Conference (1944), it was divided into four zones of occupation. Similarly, Berlin was carved up into 12 administrative areas under British, French and US control and another eight under Soviet control. At the Potsdam Conference in July-August 1945, regions east of the Oder and Neisse rivers were transferred to Poland as compensation for earlier territorial losses to the USSR.

Soviet demands for high reparations, a bone of contention between the Allies and Soviets that soon led to a breakdown in cooperation, were ultimately met from its own zone of occupation. In practice, this meant factory production was requisitioned, and able-bodied men and POWs were put to work in forced-labour camps on Soviet reconstruction.

Resettlement & Persecution

The westward advance of the Red Army had caused the displacement of millions of ethnic Germans in the east. At Potsdam a 'humane expulsion' of remaining ethnic German populations in Poland, Czechoslovakia and Hungary was agreed upon. This was accompanied, however, by retribution from the local populace. About 6.5 million ethnic Germans migrated or were expelled in a matter of months. The *Aussiedler* (foreign German settlers) and their descendants formed their own support groups to help locate missing family members, but these soon developed right-wing overtones. Many of these groups, often a source of friction with eastern neighbours today, remain an arch-conservative force in German politics.

Political & Economic Developments

In the Soviet zone, the KPD and SPD were forcibly united into the Socialist Unity Party (Sozialistische Einhartspartei Deutschlands, or SED) and given preferred status. Meanwhile, having removed a ban on political parties, the Allies set up regional and state administrative bodies – institutional forerunners of West German federalism. The SPD was joined by the Christian Democratic Union (CDU) and its Bavarian offshoot, the Christian Social Union (CSU).

The first free elections since 1933 were held in the Allied zones in 1946-47, resulting in the formation of elected state parliaments.

The Marshall Plan

War devastated the German economy. Inflation strained the currency and critical food shortages meant many city-dwellers went hungry. About 50 to 70% of houses in Cologne, Hamburg, Dortmund and Kiel had been destroyed in air raids, a problem aggravated by the need to house German refugees from Eastern Europe.

The Allies, keenly aware of the role an unhealthy German economy had played in the Nazi rise to power, founded economic councils, took control of some of Germany's nonmilitary industries and, in 1948, implemented the Marshall Plan, an economic aid package. The plan provided for the delivery of goods, food parcels, credit and raw materials. Money paid for aid was deposited in European bank accounts, creating a pool of funds to inflate the economy. The Marshall Plan provided the basis for West Germany's *Wirtschaftswunder* (economic miracle). But it widened the rift between Soviet and Allied zones.

Berlin Blockade

Currency reform in Allied zones in June 1948 prompted the USSR to issue its own. Angry at the lack of consultation, it began an economic blockade of West Berlin that would last almost a year and see almost 300,000 flights supply the west of the city. The air lift was a remarkable achievement. At its height

American, Canadian, British and several Australian air crews flew in the equivalent of 22 freight trains of 50 carriages daily, at intervals of 90 seconds. These flights earned the name *Rosinenbomber* (raisin bombers) because they carried so much dried fruit.

In this climate of frosty east-west relations, the Allies began setting up their own government institutions. In September 1948, representatives of West German states met in Bonn to discuss a draft constitution for the Federal Republic of Germany (FRG, or BRD by its German initials), which received the nod of approval by the Allies. The first elections were held in 1949 and Konrad Adenauer, 73, a mayor of Cologne during the Weimar years, became West Germany's first chancellor. Bonn was chosen as the provisional capital.

Reaction in the East

With the foundation of a West German state, the idea of creating a unified Germany faded. Tension in Korea led to greater east-west polarisation, while Marshal Tito's independent policy course in Yugoslavia complicated the situation and created a Soviet need to consolidate power in East Germany. At the same time, the idea of an independent, uniquely German socialism was dropped in favour of Stalinism.

East Germany adopted its own constitution for the German Democratic Republic (GDR, or DDR by its German initials) in 1949. The constitution was based largely on the Weimar model and, on paper at least, guaranteed press and religious freedom and the right to strike. Berlin became the East German capital. A bicameral system was set up (one chamber was later abolished), Wilhelm Pieck was voted the country's first president and Otto Grotewohl became its premier and cabinet head.

Although on paper East Germany was a parliamentary democracy, the dominance of the SED was such that party boss Walter Ulbricht called the shots. The early years saw a party takeover of economic, judicial and security functions, including the establishment of the notorious Ministry for State Security, or Stasi, which set about neutralising

GERMANY'S CHANGING BORDERS

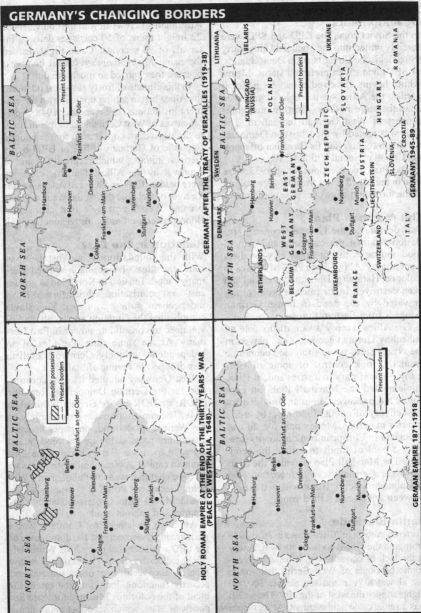

GERMANY AFTER THE TREATY OF VERSAILLES (1919-38)

GERMANY 1945-89

HOLY ROMAN EMPIRE AT THE END OF THE THIRTY YEARS' WAR
(PEACE OF WESTPHALIA, 1648)

GERMAN EMPIRE 1871-1918

opposition to the SED. In keeping with centralist policies, the states of Mecklenburg-Western Pomerania, Saxony, Saxony-Anhalt and Thuringia were reorganised into 14 regional administrations, which also removed a source of possible opposition.

De-Nazification

The task of weeding out Nazis had begun early in all zones, especially in Soviet zones in the areas of justice, education and the public service. Whereas justice in the areas under Soviet control tended to be swift and harsh, the Allies went ahead with war-crimes trials in Nuremberg, creating a precedent in international justice. In 1946 12 prominent Nazis, including Göring, were sentenced. Trials continued up to 1948, when Cold War politics and adverse public reaction led to their abandonment.

The Nuremberg sentences were never recognised by the West German government. Adenauer, a lawyer by profession, disputed their validity and later used the judgments as a Cold War bargaining chip against a US government keen to draw West Germany into the western fold. The stance adopted by Adenauer ensured that convictions were never entered onto criminal records.

Economic Transformation

In the early 1950s both East and West Germany concentrated on economic reconstruction. In East Germany, this was largely achieved by collectivising farms and tightening state control. Two and five-year plans were introduced in 1948 and 1950 respectively, with the declared aim of creating a broad production base in major industrial sectors and to ensure independence from the west. The social effect of these policies was an increased economic dependence by workers on the state, which delivered the SED another lever of control.

Economic Miracle

Under Konrad Adenauer's coalition of Christian and Free Democrats, the FRG built up its ties to the west and embarked on a policy of welfare-state capitalism, which coincided with an economic boom throughout the 1950s and most of the 1960s. Its architect, Ludwig Erhard, known as 'the father of the Wirtschaftswunder', oversaw policies that encouraged investment and sparked economic activity, aided by the Marshall Plan and a trend towards European economic integration. *Gastarbeiter* (guest workers) were called in from southern Europe (mainly Turkey, Yugoslavia and Italy) to solve a labour shortage. (See Population & People later in this chapter.)

In line with Adenauer's integrationist policies and deep-seated fear of the USSR, West Germany became a founding member of the European Coal and Steel Community, which regulated coal and steel production in France, Italy, West Germany and the Benelux countries. This was a first important step towards a European free trade zone. With the signing of the Treaty of Rome in 1958, West Germany took its place in the newly formed European Economic Community, now the expanded European Union.

Soviet Offers

In 1950 the East German premier, Otto Grotewohl, suggested a council be established to prepare the ground for a unified provisional government. This was taken up two years later by Stalin, who, faced with a west-oriented, thriving FRG, reiterated the offer, spiced with free elections held under the observation of the occupying powers. This was intended as the precursor to a peace treaty and the establishment of a unified, neutral Germany with its own defence policy. Adenauer rejected the offer, fearing a reversion to the bad old days of four-power occupation and continued his policy of integration with the west. These policies were subsequently endorsed by voters in 1953 and again in 1957, when the coalition of the CDU/CSU and FDP (the free-market Free Democrats) won elections resoundingly. Germany remained divided.

Uprising

By 1953 the first signs of discontent appeared in the East. The causes were mostly economic – production was stifled by bottlenecks, heavy industrial goods were given priority over consumer goods and industrial workers resented higher productivity demands forced upon them by party honchos. But there was another cause: the death of Stalin had raised hopes of reform but brought little real change. Under pressure from Moscow, the government backed down on a decision to raise prices, but refused to budge on tougher production goals. Strikes and calls for reform turned to unrest in the urban and industrial centres, culminating in demonstrations and riots on 17 June 1953 that involved about 10% of the country's workers. The government proved incapable of containing the situation. Soviet troops stationed in East Germany quashed the uprising, with scores of deaths and the arrest of about 1200 people. This did nothing to raise the morale of East Germans, who began voting with their feet.

Defence Alliances

In May 1955 the FRG joined the North Atlantic Treaty Organisation (NATO), which completed its military integration into the west. West Germany also changed its constitution to allow German-based armed forces, and a year later it introduced conscription. East Germany's response was to join the Warsaw Pact defence alliance and the Eastern bloc trade organisation Comecon.

As early as 1957 there were calls to arm West Germany with nuclear weapons, a policy supported strongly by both the USA and leading West German political figures, including Adenauer. Despite public protests, a parliamentary resolution to this effect was passed one year later, though never acted upon. In the same year, a proposal by Poland (the Rapacki Plan) to ban all nuclear weapons on German, Polish and Czechoslovakian soil failed miserably. The reason for its lack of success – that Warsaw Pact troops clearly outnumbered NATO's – would subsequently dominate talks on disarmament right into the 1970s.

The Wall

The flow of refugees seeking better fortunes in the west increased after the crackdown. In 1953 about 330,000 East Germans fled to the west. Most of them were young, well-educated and employed. This placed a strain on the already troubled economy. The exodus reached such a level that it threatened East Germany's Comecon commitments. On the night of 12 August 1961, with the approval of Warsaw Pact countries, East Germany built the wall between East and West Berlin, creating one of the Cold War's most potent symbols. At the same time, the FRG-GDR border was fenced off and mined.

Building walls to keep people out may be one thing, but building one to keep your own citizens in amounted to an admission of failure by the SED. In a period of economic stabilisation in the 1960s, the East German government tried to make the system more flexible and attractive. Its New Economic Policy was extremely successful: the standard of living rose to the highest in the Eastern bloc and East Germany became its second largest industrial power (behind the USSR). Party head Walter Ulbricht, who had been slow to pick up on changes in Moscow under Khrushchev, was considered too inflexible. In 1971 he was replaced by Erich Honecker, opening the way for rapprochement with the west and greater international acceptance.

Ministry for State Security (Stasi)

Based on the Soviet KGB, the Stasi was founded in 1950. The 'shield and sword' of the SED, it soon developed into a state within the state. By 1989 it had a spy network of about 90,000 full-time employees and 180,000 *inoffizielle Mitarbeiter* (unofficial co-workers). The Stasi accumulated about six million files in its lifetime and in January 1990 its Berlin headquarters was stormed by angry protesters demanding to see them. With the fall of the SED, the Stasi was disbanded and a public office, the Gauck Behörde, was established to assess records, which continue to be a source of controversy.

Stasi Best Friends

The Stasi knew few limits when it came to tracking down dissidents. One unusual collection of files found in its Berlin archive kept a record of dissidents' body odour. Some dissidents who had been hauled in for interrogation were made to deliver an odour sample, usually taken with a cotton wool pad from the unfortunate victim's crotch. The sample was then stored in an hermetic glass jar for later use if a dissident suddenly disappeared. To track down a missing dissident by odour, Stasi sniffer dogs were employed. These specially trained groin-sniffing curs were euphemistically known as 'smell differentiation dogs'. What happened to these dogs after the Stasi was disbanded is unclear. They were probably put to service on matters more mundane, like sniffing drugs.

MICK WELDON

Developments in the West

By the end of 1956 Warsaw Pact troops had crushed Hungarian reformists, the last German internee was released by the USSR, and the KPD had been banned in West Germany for its rather rash call for the violent overthrow of the 'Adenauer regime'. Undeterred, Adenauer pushed ahead with his 'love your friends, don't recognise your enemies' policy by signing a friendship treaty with France in 1963 and maintaining the Hallstein Doctrine, which rejected recognition of East Germany. His 'I'm OK, you're OK' meeting with French president Charles de Gaulle was to be his last triumph. Later that year Adenauer was replaced by Ludwig Erhard, who still rested on his laurels as the 'father of the Wirtschaftswunder' but now faced a troubled economy. In 1966 the CDU/CSU and SPD formed a broad coalition, a period of government most Germans found dispiriting because there was no effective opposition.

The absence of parliamentary opposition in the late 1960s served to fuel radical demands by the student movement. Students sought reform of West Germany's antiquated university system and teaching programs (many of Germany's textbooks either ignored Nazism or took a soft line), an open discussion of the Hitler years, and a more flexible policy towards the Eastern bloc. New emergency acts passed to protect the FRG's political system evoked public outrage. In 1969, the SPD, having dispensed with revolutionary elements of its platform, formed a government (with the FDP) under Willy Brandt.

Whereas Adenauer had spent the Hitler years quietly tending his rose garden in Cologne, Brandt (a pen name – his real name was Herbert Ernst Karl Frahm) had worked as a journalist in exile in Scandinavia, where he was stripped of German citizenship for anti-Nazi writings. He was also later the mayor of Berlin (1957-66). Brandt took the broom to the Hallstein Doctrine and instigated an *Ostpolitik* of coexistence to normalise East-West relations.

In December 1972 the two Germanys signed the Basic Treaty. This guaranteed sovereignty in international and domestic affairs, but fudged formal recognition, which was precluded by the West German constitution. This paved the way for both countries to join the United Nations.

Brandt signed separate treaties with Poland, recognising the Oder-Neisse border, and Czechoslovakia. In Poland he paid his respects to Jews killed in the Warsaw ghetto uprising, provoking outrage among hardliners at home and approving nods abroad. On top of this came the Four-Power Agreement, which eased conditions in Berlin. Somewhat of a legend in his own time, Brandt dragged more retrograde elements of German society kicking and screaming into a new era.

He was replaced by Helmut Schmidt in 1974 after a scandal (one of Brandt's close advisers turned out to be a Stasi spy). In the period of government that followed, anti-nuclear and green issues moved onto the agenda, opposed by Schmidt and ultimately leading to the election of Greens party representatives to the Bonn parliament in 1979.

The 1970s also brought a sharp rise in terrorism in West Germany, with the abduction and assassination of prominent business and political figures by the notorious Red Army Faction. This group was anti-capitalist, but many of its acts were attempts to free prisoners, or simple revenge. By 1976, however, its leading members, Ulrike Meinhof and Andreas Baader, had committed suicide (both in prison) and remaining members found themselves either in prison, in hiding, or taking refuge across the border in East Germany, where political change would one day expose them to West German attempts to bring them to justice.

In 1982 the SPD lost power to a conservative coalition government under Helmut Kohl, who set about grooming relations between east and west, while dismantling parts of the welfare state at home. Kohl would fulfil Erich Honecker's dream by receiving him with full state honours on a visit to Bonn in 1987. It might have been Erich's kiss of death.

Reunification

The Honecker era saw changes to the East German constitution. Ominously, reunification clauses were struck out in 1974 and replaced by one declaring East Germany's irrevocable alliance to the USSR. Nevertheless, the Basic Treaty of 1972 had created some semblance of order in the East German household. Honecker fell in line with Soviet policies, rode out world recession and an oil crisis in the early 1970s, and

oversaw a period of housing construction, pension rises and help for working mothers.

In the mid-1980s, however, prices for consumer goods rose sharply and, with East Germany struggling to keep pace with technological innovations elsewhere in the world, the country began to stagnate. Reforms in Poland and Hungary, and especially Mikhail Gorbachev's new course in the USSR, put pressure on an increasingly recalcitrant SED leadership to introduce reforms.

The end began in May 1989, when Hungary announced it would suspend its Travel Agreement, which prevented East Germans from entering the west via Hungary. It began to dismantle installations along its Austrian border, suddenly making it possible for East Germans to cross safely – they did so in numbers. The SED responded to the exodus by tightening travel restrictions. East German discontent peaked, with heavy-handed police actions against demonstrators and the falsification of regional election results. Adding insult to injury, the party doggedly prepared East Germany's 40th anniversary celebrations.

Replying to a question about reforms in the USSR, SED party ideologist Kurt Hager was quoted as saying you didn't need to wallpaper your flat just to keep up with your neighbours. However, it was Gorbachev's decision not to intervene in German affairs that ultimately brought change.

In East Germany the churches had become a focal point of opposition, and more and more East Germans filled West German consulates and embassies in East Berlin, Warsaw, Prague and Budapest, seeking to emigrate. The turning point was reached on 10 September 1989, when Hungary's foreign minister, Gyula Horn, opened the Hungarian border to Austria, allowing refugees to cross legally to the west. Two weeks later the SED arranged transport to the west for several thousand of those who had taken refuge in diplomatic buildings. This triggered another wave of refugees seeking asylum.

In Leipzig the number of demonstrators attending traditional Monday church services swelled throughout October to more

The Rise & Fall of Erich Honecker

A miner's son, Erich Honecker was born in Neunkirchen, Saarland, on 25 August 1912. He worked as a roof tiler, joined the central committee of the communist youth organisation in the 1920s and led the group's underground activities in southern Germany after Hitler took power. He was imprisoned for 10 years from 1935. On release he became president of the Freie deutsche Jugend (Free German Youth) organisation.

In 1958 he was appointed Politburo member and secretary of the central committee, handling state security. A diligent if unspectacular functionary, in 1971 he succeeded Walter Ulricht as state secretary and by 1976 he rose to party general secretary and head of East Germany.

Honecker continued the policy of limiting relations with West Germany and made himself unpopular in the west by raising the minimum sum of money West Germans had to exchange when visiting the GDR. Like West German chancellor Helmut Schmidt, he tried to prevent international tensions from flowing over into friction between the two German states.

Honecker's period of leadership was one of lethargy and disillusionment. He stepped down as SED leader in October 1989 and was stripped of all party and political functions soon after. In December he was investigated for treason, corruption and abuse of public office and put under house arrest. He was put in jail in 1990, released shortly afterwards due to bad health and moved to a Soviet military hospital.

With an arrest order hanging over him, Honecker fled to the USSR in March 1991. By November he had sought refuge in the Chilean embassy. When the Russians applied pressure on Chile, he was returned to Germany and placed on trial for manslaughter (for his role in giving the order to shoot fleeing East Germans), but his ill health led to the case being abandoned. In 1993 Honecker went to Chile, and died of liver cancer the following year.

than 250,000. A wave of opposition groups, notably *Neues Forum* (New Forum), formed, leading calls for human rights and an end to the SED political monopoly, supported by church figures. This brought about a SED leadership crisis and the replacement of Honecker by Egon Krenz. About 500,000 demonstrators turned up at Berlin's Alexanderplatz on 4 November and whistled as Markus Wolf, the Stasi head, tried to lodge a defence of Stasi activities. By this time, East Germany was losing its citizens at a rate of about 10,000 per day.

The Monday demonstrations sealed the fate of the GDR. These were the largest demonstrations that had been held since the unsuccessful workers' uprising in 1953. To his credit, Erich Honecker had signed an order instructing police and troops not to provoke the demonstrators and forbidding the use of weapons or violence against them.

On 9 November, the floodgates opened when the GDR *Politbüro* approved direct travel to the west, announced in a televised press conference by SED boss Günter Schabowsky. Asked by one reporter *when* this would come into effect, Schabowsky searched his notes uncomfortably and, at a loss, then mistakenly announced, 'right away'. Tens of thousands passed through border points in Berlin, watched by perplexed guards, who, though they knew little or nothing about this new regulation, did not intervene. Amid scenes of wild partying, the Wall had fallen.

Under pressure from opposition groups, so-called 'round table talks' were established between government representatives and opposition groups to hammer out a course. In March 1990 free elections were held in East Germany, the first since 1949, in which an alliance headed by Lothar de Maizière of the CDU won convincingly. The

SPD, which took an equivocal view of re-unification, was punished by voters accordingly. The old SED administrative regions were abolished and the *Länder* (states) revived. Common currency and economic union came into force in July 1990.

In late 1990 the two Germanys, the USSR and Allied powers signed the Two-Plus-Four Treaty, ending post-war occupation zones. Shortly afterwards the East German state was dissolved and Germany's first unified post-WWII elections were held.

Recent Trends

The era of reunification is synonymous with the era of Helmut Kohl. Kohl set up the *Treuhandanstalt* (trust agency; see Economy later in this chapter) to privatise industry, while in foreign policy, he strove to placate worried neighbours by signing friendship treaties. Soviet troops had withdrawn by August 1994. Shortly afterwards the Allied powers withdrew from Berlin. Attempts were made to bring former East German functionaries to justice, notably Erich Honecker. This contradictory policy – bearing in mind that West Germany did not formally recognise the Nuremberg convictions – has only been partly successful.

If not for the surprising events in East Germany, the Kohl era might have gone down on record as one of Germany's least remarkable. Instead, it was one of Germany's most dramatic. After 16 years, however, the Kohl era came to an end when a coalition of Social Democrats and Greens took office in 1998, the first time the Greens party has co-governed at a federal level.

Known as the 'Tony Blair of German politics', Chancellor Gerhard Schröder, an economic pragmatist belonging to the SPD, is leading Germany into a new era, known as the 'Berlin Republic' because Berlin is again the seat of government. The decision to move the parliament back to Berlin, taken by Helmut Kohl and his CDU/CSU coalition in 1991, was originally resisted by the opposition parties of the day and many ordinary Germans. Nevertheless, most people now support the move, signalling their confidence in Germany as a modern, democratic country that has come to terms with the tumultuous and tragic events of its past.

Germany, restored to its position as 'the land in the middle', now juggles its inward looking reunification process with an outward looking commitment to European integration, while gaining new confidence on the international stage.

GEOGRAPHY

Germany covers 356,866 sq km and shares borders with Poland and the Czech Republic in the east; Austria and Switzerland in the south; France, Belgium, the Netherlands and Luxembourg in the west; and Denmark in the north. Its landscape tends to be flat in the north and north-east, gradually building up in height further to the south. Its highest mountain, Zugspitze, rises to 2962m and is near the Austrian border.

Most of Germany's rivers run to the north or north-west, following the lie of the land, and drain into the North or Baltic seas. The Danube, an exception, flows eastwards. Of all its natural features, Germany's most potent national symbol is the Rhine River. It begins in the Swiss Alps and winds 1320km to the Netherlands' North Sea coast. The Rhine has long been an important natural border between Germany and France. The middle Rhine between Bingen and Bonn is the most beautiful stretch.

The North Sea coast is mostly flat, partly consisting of drained land and dikes. Islands extend from East Friesland near the Netherlands up to Schleswig-Holstein. The shallow North Sea along this coast is known as the Wattenmeer and is subject to extreme tides that make it possible to walk to some of the islands across the tidal flats at low tide. Storm tides sometimes submerge a group of smaller islands, known as the Halligen, leaving only diked houses visible above the sea.

In Schleswig-Holstein, the Baltic Sea coast is slightly hillier and has numerous bays and fjords. These give way to sandy inlets, spits and occasional cliffs in eastern Germany. Rügen, Germany's largest Baltic Sea island, is famous for its chalk cliffs. In cold winters the Baltic Sea freezes, as does the North Sea in the Wattenmeer.

The north of Germany is characterised by the Northern Lowlands, a broad expanse of low-lying land that sweeps across about one-third of the country. This is part of a larger European plain extending from the Netherlands to the Urals. Some parts consist of marshland and heath, such as around the lower Elbe, and others of glacial lakes, mainly in Mecklenburg-Western Pomerania. The Spreewald, a favourite holiday area south-east of Berlin, is a picturesque wetland with narrow, navigable waterways.

The Central Uplands region is a complicated patchwork of mountain ranges, rifts and valleys. In German it is called the *Mittelgebirge*, which refers to the region itself and a type of medium-altitude mountain range, mostly less than 500m high. The Central Uplands roughly includes the area between the Black Forest, the Sauerland (near Cologne), the Elbsandsteingebirge (south-west of Dresden), and the Bavarian Forest, which runs along the Czech border. The Danube marks its southern boundary. Although physically a Mittelgebirge area, the Harz Mountains lie north of the main body of ranges.

The Central Uplands are especially picturesque in the west around the Rhine massifs and the Moselle River, where the slopes of warm valleys provide Germany's best wine-growing conditions and some good hiking. The Eifel Upland north of the Moselle River is volcanic and famous for its *Maare*, or crater lakes.

The Alpine Foothills, a wedge between the Danube and the Alps, are typified by moorland in eastern regions near the Danube, low rolling hills and subalpine plateaus. Also here are several large glacial lakes such as the Chiemsee and Ammersee, and hundreds of smaller ones.

The German portion of the Alps lies entirely within Bavaria and runs from Lake Constance (Bodensee), Germany's largest lake, to Berchtesgaden in the east. Though lower than their brethren to their south, many peaks are well above 2000m, rising spectacularly from the Alpine Foothills.

CLIMATE

Germany has a much milder climate than its eastern neighbours, but a collision of Atlantic westerly winds and continental air masses from the north-east can sometimes cause changeability. Conditions also fluctuate greatly from year to year, which makes it difficult for the visitor to know what to expect.

In a harsh winter, temperatures plunge well below 0°C and can remain there for several weeks, with much of the country blanketed by snow. The next year might be mild and damp, however; in that case you can count on daytime temperatures of about 0°C. The temperature is between about 14°C and 20°C in July, and -4°C and 3°C in January, depending on the region.

Annual rainfall distribution is fairly even, although regional summer droughts sometimes occur. November can often be drizzly, with overcast conditions adding to the climatic misery of the locals. Most of Germany gets between 600mm and 800mm annually, but the north-east averages less. Areas in the Alpine Foothills, the Alps, the western Harz Mountains and the Black Forest receive over 1200mm. The western slopes of mountain ranges are generally wetter than eastern slopes and afternoon thunderstorms are fairly common in summer.

Spring is especially beautiful but it can be slow to arrive. In a good year, however, jackets can be stripped off in early April, and summer temperatures reach the high 20°Cs or low 30°Cs. An Indian summer might set in around October and the winter will remain crisp and dry. Cross your fingers, though: all too often spring can be a cold washout, run into a cool, wet summer with temperatures that only occasionally rise above 20°C in some regions, and turn into dark, equally wet November weather that lingers until the following spring.

Areas in the east and south-east are subject to a more continental climate and greater temperature extremes, with colder, drier winters. It is not uncommon for bays, lakes and rivers to freeze over in winter.

The western third of Germany is milder. The wind can make the lowlands a couple of

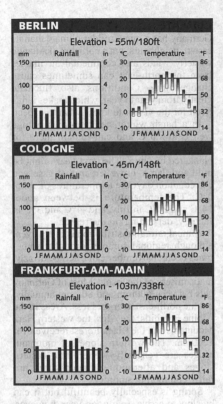

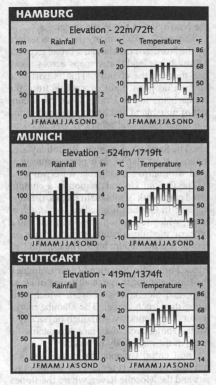

degrees cooler, while the breezy North Sea coast is often cooler again. Germans say the North Sea coast has a *Reizklima*, a healthy, bracing climate. Windmills dot the landscape in Schleswig-Holstein and East Friesland. Bathers rent *Strandkörbe*, large wicker shelters, as protection from the wind.

The warmer latitude enjoyed by the south is generally offset in winter by its higher altitude. The south-west corner, around Freiburg, has a reputation for receiving more sunshine than any other part of Germany. The valleys of the Central Uplands often enjoy slightly higher summer daytime temperatures than elsewhere.

Germans have a few indigenous expressions for their weather patterns. A brief cool period that occurs regularly in May is called

die drei Eisheiligen (the three ice saints). *Schafskälte* (loosely a 'sheep's cold spell') corresponds with shearing time in June. *Altweibersommer* (old maid's summer) is an Indian summer, while frequently warmer weather between Christmas and New Year is called *Weihnachtstauwetter* (Christmas thaw weather).

One interesting phenomenon is the *Föhn*, an autumn wind that occurs in the German Alps and Alpine Foothills. It is caused by the rapid descent and warming of cool air as it passes over the Alps. The Föhn can bring clear skies and temperatures of over 20°C in autumn while the rest of Germany has rain. If it doesn't give you a headache (locals blame it for all sorts of ailments), it may be worth seeking out during a wet spell. Winds can intensify unexpectedly, however, so you need to be careful if boating on one of the lakes during *Föhnig* weather.

ECOLOGY & ENVIRONMENT

Germany's population density and long history of settlement have placed enormous pressure on the environment, with few areas escaping human impact. Industrialisation, urban encroachment and an extensive road system have dramatically reduced the amount of natural open space, especially in urban conglomerations such as the Ruhr region.

Many watercourses have been altered to facilitate internal shipping. Levels of air and water pollution are relatively high, which is complicated by some pollution coming from neighbouring countries, meaning only coordinated Europe-wide agreements can bring about significant improvement.

Nevertheless, the situation has improved substantially in the past few years. A vehicle tax system strongly encourages the use of advanced catalysers, but the car is worshipped as a symbol of freedom in Germany and technically, there is no speed limit on autobahns, though there are segments with limits ranging from 100 to 130km/hr (see the boxed text 'Pedal to the Metal' in the Baden-Württemberg chapter). Smog alerts are commonplace during the summer months, which is unlikely to change until Germans wean themselves off their cars.

Germans have become fiercely protective of their natural environment and participate enthusiastically in waste-recycling programs. There is a refund system for many types of bottles and jars, and nonrefundable glass is disposed of according to colour (green, clear and brown) in special containers placed throughout towns and cities.

Greenpeace is extremely active in Germany. In 1995 it successfully opposed controversial plans by Shell to sink the Brent Spar oil platform in the North Sea. The organisation also played a crucial role in stopping the transportation of reprocessed nuclear waste to an underground facility near the northern town of Gorleben. The issue resulted in demonstrations, clashes and the sabotage of railway links, with a massive police presence required to protect trains transporting the waste. Transportation was suspended in 1998 when it was discovered the containers 'weeped' radioactive substances. In the long term, the current government intends to close down the country's nuclear power stations, but, if plans are realised, it is likely to take two decades before the last plant goes offline.

The Bergwald Projekt group is an interesting option for anyone wishing to become actively involved in environmental field work. Based in Switzerland, the group organises land-care programs to improve and safeguard forests in Germany, Austria and Switzerland. Also see Volunteer Work in the Facts for the Visitor chapter.

Environment in Eastern Germany

Environmental conditions in East Germany were little short of disastrous. Industrial sites were contaminated, sewerage facilities were inadequate and air pollution in some areas posed a serious health danger. Particularly insidious were uranium slag heaps in parts of Saxony and Thuringia. One environmental aim of the Unification Treaty of 1990 was to iron out the differences between eastern and western Germany by 2000. On the whole, the policy was successful, although the uranium tailings and use of brown coal in several power stations remain problems.

Despite the environmental destruction, large areas of eastern Germany have survived intact. Areas along the Oder River and some estuaries on the Baltic coast are a haven for species, mainly birds, now rare or extinct elsewhere in Germany.

Forest Destruction

Deforestation reached a peak in the late 18th century, when early industries such as glass-making created a high demand for wood. Cleared areas were replanted with fast-growing conifers, turning what were once mixed deciduous forests into a monoculture. The lower Harz Mountains, originally beech and oak, are one such example. This practice has been abandoned and attempts are being made to re-create original forest conditions using species mixtures.

About 73% of forest stands in eastern Germany are affected to some degree by acid rain, compared with a national figure of about 60%. The rate among mature trees in the Erzgebirge, the Bavarian Alps and the Rhön and Harz mountains is as high as 90%! Damage initially occurs in the crown, which means it is often barely noticeable.

Measures have been taken to reduce the effects of acid rain, such as applying lime to reduce unnaturally high acidity levels in the soil, but the only real solution is to reduce air pollution levels in the long term.

Rivers & Seas

Environmental disasters in the 1970s and 1980s have led to increased awareness of pollution in Germany's rivers and seas. In 1988 about 18,000 seals were washed up dead along the Atlantic coast, 8300 in the Wattenmeer in Germany alone. Scientists discovered that pollutants, mainly heavy metals, had weakened the seals' immune systems, making them susceptible to viruses. High nitrogen and phosphate levels have also produced algal blooms in the Baltic Sea. Better sewage disposal systems in eastern Germany are helping to reduce the problem, but both seas are in a sorry state. The Wattenmeer is showing particular signs of stress, which poses a threat to the feeding and breeding grounds of migratory birds. Coastal shipping is also a serious hazard: in 1998 a timber transport ship caught fire and spilt 600 tonnes of oil in the Wattenmeer off the coast of Amrum, an island in Schleswig-Holstein, killing about 20,000 birds.

The Rhine River was dead in 1970, with contamination so bad near Cologne that authorities declared a 250km stretch through the Ruhr region a hazard to human health. If that wasn't enough, a chemical spill from a Swiss factory in 1986 temporarily turned it green. A couple of years later, Germany's environment minister of the day donned a wetsuit and swam a few laps to reassure the populace. The aquatic minister may have placated some, but salmon and sea trout decided to wait until 1997 before venturing into the upper Rhine – for the first time in 50 years.

FLORA

Despite environmental pressures, German forests remain beautiful places to relax and get away from the crowd – especially in summer, when most Germans prefer to soak up sun in various states of undress in open parks and meadows. Most cities and towns have their own forest (Stadtwald), which can be easily reached by public transport or on foot. The prettiest ones are planted with varieties of beech, oak, birch, chestnut (mostly horse chestnut with nonedible fruit), lime, maple or ash.

Many forest regions have mixed deciduous forest at lower altitudes, changing to coniferous species as you ascend, so with a little planning it's possible to find the type of forest you want. River valleys are usually the best place to find deciduous forest.

Waldfrüchte (berries) are particularly colourful and, for the most part, poisonous in Germany, so avoid the taste test unless you know exactly what you are about to eat. The same applies to mushrooms, which are essential for the development of healthy root systems in trees, especially in deciduous forests. It is always a good idea to limit your pick. Pfifferlinge, or chanterelle mushrooms, are just one of the seasonal culinary delights.

Alpine regions have a wide range of wildflowers – orchids, cyclamen, gentians, pulsatilla, alpine roses, edelweiss and buttercups, just to mention a few. Meadow species are particularly colourful in spring and summer, and great care is taken these days not to cut pastures until plants have seeded. Visitors can help by keeping to paths, especially in alpine areas and coastal dunes where ecosystems are especially fragile.

One popular attraction is the heather blossom on the Lüneburg Heath north-east of Hanover in late August. It draws visitors each year from all over Germany, and a couple of towns in the region compete to elect their own *Heideköniginnen*, or Heather Queens, who lead parades through the streets.

FAUNA

Germany remains home to a wide variety of animals, although many have found their way onto the endangered species list. But gone are the days when declining numbers only caused concern if there was too little game for the hunter to bag. That said, the most common large mammals you are likely to see in forests will be game species like deer and wild boar, or those that have adapted well to human activities, such as squirrels and foxes.

One common non-native among the mammals is the raccoon, which was introduced from America and is especially prevalent in eastern Germany. The alpine marmot inhabits the Alps up to the tree line, although it tends to avoid the northern slopes. This sociable rodent lives in colonies and lets out a shrill whistle-like sound when disturbed. If you're lucky, you'll meet one that's used to being fed by hikers.

Wild goats were almost wiped out by hunters in the 19th century; those now found in the Alps (above the tree line) were reintroduced from northern Italy. Chamois are widespread in the Alps and Alpine Foothills, with small introduced populations in the Black Forest, the Swabian Alps and Elb-sandsteingebirge (south of Dresden).

Beavers were endangered as early as the Middle Ages, faced extinction in the 19th century and are now more common. Originally found throughout Germany, populations cluster around the Oder and Elbe rivers in eastern Germany. Attempts are being made to reintroduce them into other wetland areas.

The hare is on the list of endangered species but can be seen frequently in fields in less-populated regions, whereas the snow hare, whose fur is white in winter, is fairly common in the Alps. Visitors may also come across martens, badgers, hamsters and otters.

Lynx died out in Germany in the 19th century. Reintroduced populations were then illegally hunted to extinction in the 1980s. Since the removal of fences along

the Czech border, about 25 to 30 brave souls have tried their luck again in the national park of the Bavarian Forest, which unfortunately means that your chances of seeing one in the wild are virtually zero. Others have been sighted in upland regions of eastern Germany. The wild cat, another indigenous feline, has returned to forest regions after being almost hunted to extinction in the 1930s. The Harz Mountains have the largest population. Wild cats often breed with domestic cats, making it hard to distinguish between the two.

Wolves regularly cross the Oder River from Poland into eastern Germany. European moose, which also torment guards with their border activities, are occasionally sighted in mixed forests and on moors in eastern Germany.

It is common to see seals on the North Sea and Baltic Sea coasts, especially on sandbanks in northern Germany's Wattenmeer. The Wattenmeer is also excellent for observing migratory birdlife, especially from March to May and August to October, when many different species make a stopover to feed on the region's rich marine life. You can recognise sandpipers in summer by their rust-brown back and dark stripes on a white breast, while colourful shelduck have a green head, a broad white stripe around the neck and a red beak. Marsh geese and eider are also frequent visitors.

Sea eagles, almost extinct in western Germany, are now fairly plentiful in eastern Germany. If you are very lucky, you might see a golden eagle in the Alps. More common are falcons, white storks and cranes, especially in eastern Germany. In the Alpine Foothills you'll often see jays (look for the flashes of blue on their wings), which imitate the calls of other species and spend most of their time flying about. Forests everywhere in Germany provide a habitat for a wide variety of songbirds as well as woodpeckers.

Endangered Species

As you would expect in a highly industrialised, densely populated country like

Germany, many species of flora and fauna are endangered or already extinct. Conditions have not improved much in recent years. About 120 hectares of natural landscape – the equivalent of 143 soccer fields – has been sacrificed to housing and road construction *daily* over the past 10 years. What's more, the richness of flora and fauna in eastern Germany distorts the severity of the problem in western Germany.

The situation for a lot of reptile and beetle species is grim and a larger number of ant and butterfly species are also threatened with extinction. About one-third of the 100 mammals studied for the 'Red List', a list of endangered or extinct species, are in danger of dying out, including shrews and field hamsters. Permanent populations of large mammals such as wolves and European moose have virtually ceased to exist. The news is not all bad, though: sea eagles, osprey, cormorants, cranes and white storks are no longer endangered, and bats and beavers are also back in numbers.

Urban encroachment has also done little to help the 3000 species of ferns and flowering plants. Around one-third are endangered and 47 species are already extinct. Germany is trying to reverse this trend by creating a linked network of vegetation habitats that hopefully will one day span the country. In the long run, this will also benefit the native fauna.

NATIONAL PARKS

Germany has 12 national parks. The following is an overview of what you can expect to find. For information on facilities and accommodation refer to the relevant section in the regional chapter.

Bavarian Forest National Park

Near the Czech border, the Bayerischer Wald National Park covers an area of 131 sq km and consists of mountain forest (mostly beech, fir and spruce) with upland moors. Parts of the forest have been severely damaged by acid rain. Nevertheless, it has some fine walking tracks.

Berchtesgaden National Park

This park covers 210 sq km and is near the Austrian border, rising in altitude from about 60m to 2700m. The landscape is a contrast of lakes, limestone and dolomite cliffs, meadows, mixed forests and sub-alpine spruce stands. Arguably Germany's most beautiful park, this is where you can best view alpine plants and wildlife.

Saxon Switzerland

The main attraction of the Sächsische Schweiz, a 93 sq km national park south of Dresden, is its spectacular sandstone and basalt rock formations, especially in the Bastei region on the Elbe. Its proximity to Dresden means the park can get a bit crowded in summer, but things quieten down on the walking tracks farther away from the river.

Wattenmeer National Parks

The three national parks of the Wattenmeer, in Schleswig-Holstein, Lower Saxony and around the mouth of the Elbe River near Hamburg, have a combined area of 5367 sq km. The largest is in Schleswig-Holstein. The tidal flats are rich in sealife and host an extraordinary variety of birds. The islands are also very attractive, especially the sand dunes and beaches on Amrum and Sylt. The best time to observe birds is in spring and autumn. Summer, late spring and early autumn are the best times to walk the Wattenmeer, but it is highly advisable to have a guide.

Boddenlandschaft

Covering an area of 805 sq km, this park takes in the Baltic Sea coast from Rostock to Stralsund, several islands and peninsulas, as well as Rügen's west coast. Its main feature is the coastal landscape, with dunes, pine forests, meadows and heath.

Jasmund

On the island of Rügen and covering only 30 sq km, this small national park protects the chalk cliffs along the Jasmund Peninsula. Forest, creeks and moors can be found inland. It can get extremely crowded in mid-summer.

The Case of the Vanishing National Park

For a country the size of Germany, 12 national parks is a modest tally, especially when you consider that three of these – the national parks of the Wattenmeer – would be one if they weren't in three different states. But wait, in 1998, a 13th national park was declared near the Elbe River. The number 13 proved to be a bad omen, for a local resident contested its status, a local court slammed down its mallet in his favour and the park vanished into thin air. The reason? It failed to meet the criteria for a national park.

The ex-Elbtalaue National Park near Lüneburg in Lower Saxony is by no means an isolated incident. Several of Germany's other parks are open to challenge. To satisfy the requirements of a national park, three-quarters of the declared area must be 'undisturbed' by human beings. In practice, most German national parks fail to fulfil this criterion.

In the Nationalpark Harz, locals are already launching a challenge because the park is crisscrossed by roads. And fishing is permitted in virtually all of Schleswig-Holstein's national park in the Wattenmeer. Only 13% of Mecklenburg-Western Pomerania's Boddenlandschaft National Park is undisturbed. The situation in the Odertal, though not quite as severe, is similar. Brandenburg, which passed a state law to protect the park, graciously interprets the label 'national park' for the Odertal to mean an area designated for protection. The idea is that it will one day meet the criteria.

And that's the dilemma. If the parks don't meet the strict criteria, they risk being relegated to humble nature reserves by local courts. But without protecting and regenerating damaged habitats (and also misusing the designation 'national park') Germany will have to wait a long time before it gets its 13th park.

Unteres Odertal

An example of European cooperation, this 329-sq-km German-Polish park (105 sq km in Poland) is a unique wetland with an enormous range of flora and fauna, especially waterfowl. Meadows, marshland and deciduous forest make up a big proportion. Many of Germany's rarer species are found here, including migratory species.

Müritz

The designated national park area covers about 318 sq km. This includes the Mecklenburg Lakes between the eastern shore of Lake Müritz and Neustrelitz. The park consists largely of moorland, with about 60 lakes, some comprising important breeding grounds for sea eagles and cranes.

Harz & Hochharz

Near the former East German border, these parks are made up of mostly spruce forest, with occasional meadows, moorland and deciduous forests. There are also caves and several spectacular rock formations in the area. The western portion (Harz) covers 158 sq km and is more developed than the Hochharz (about 58 sq km) to the east. Weekends can turn the more popular walking tracks (especially those leading to Brocken, northern Germany's highest peak) into crowded ant trails.

GOVERNMENT & POLITICS

Germany is a constitutional democracy with a president and a bicameral system based on the Bundestag (lower house) and the *Bundesrat* (upper house). The lower house is a popularly elected people's chamber, with the upper house made up of delegates representing the 16 states.

With reunification, eastern Germany's original (pre-1952) states of Brandenburg, Mecklenburg-Western Pomerania, Saxony, Saxony-Anhalt and Thuringia were re-established. These are often referred to as *neue Bundesländer* (new states). Berlin became a separate city-state. The *alte Bundesländer* (old states) are Baden-Württemberg, Bavaria Bremen, Hamburg, Hesse, Lower Saxony, North Rhine-Westphalia, Rhineland-Palatinate, Saarland and Schleswig-Holstein.

Presidents are elected by an unwieldy body consisting of parliamentary representatives, state parliament delegates and respected public figures. Their term is five years and they can only be re-elected once. The position is largely ceremonial, with a few built-in safety mechanisms for troubled times. Presidential powers to dismiss a government, as existed in the Weimar constitution, were abolished to prevent a repeat of the chaotic circumstances that culminated in Hitler becoming chancellor in 1933. In 1999 Johannes Rau was elected president, replacing Roman Herzog.

The Bundestag elects the chancellor and initiates most legislation, often relying on closed door parliamentary commissions which consult experts to hammer out compromises. A simple majority is required for ordinary laws, a two-third majority in both houses for constitutional changes. Elections are held every four years and the chancellor can only be unseated by a so-called 'constructive vote of no confidence', which means a new chancellor must already have been assured a majority before the old one can be dispensed with. The only time such a motion has been successful was when Kohl replaced Schmidt in 1982.

About half the Bundestag is made up of direct candidates, those elected from constituencies. The other half are listed candidates, who are party delegates and do not have electorates. The idea behind this is to prevent parochial issues from dominating the political agenda. A party has to gain 5% of the national vote to be represented in the Bundestag. This has often prevented small radical parties and splinter groups from getting a seat in parliament. Bundesrat members are appointees of the state parliaments.

The next tier of government is the state parliament, or *Landtag*. Each Landtag has its own prime minister – a lord mayor in city-states – and cabinet. States also have their own constitutions. A federal law overrides state law on any single issue. In practice, co-operation means there is a high degree of uniformity between state and federal laws. Below state level are several tiers of local government, including city administrations.

Voting is not compulsory. Women have voted in Germany since 1918 and make up 26% of the Bundestag. The federal election turnout by German voters is consistently high, usually around 80%.

Germany's longest serving chancellors are Adenauer (14 years) and Kohl (16 years). Kohl, who earned the epitaph of the 'unification chancellor', was voted out of office in 1998, when his coalition of Christian Democrat and Liberals (CDU/CSU and FDP) was replaced by a coalition of the SPD-Greens party/Bündnis 90 coalition. Despite this success, the Greens party has consistently failed to woo the young voters vital for its future survival, and the future of the coalition is rather uncertain.

One controversial policy favoured by the Greens is to close the country's nuclear power stations. Amendments enacted to Germany's laws on citizenship (see Population & People later in this chapter) also proved divisive. When the coalition lost its majority in the upper house after a state election in Hesse, it was forced to water down some policies to get the agreement of opposition parties. Dissent, in-fighting and power struggles have marked the early period in office, which saw Schröder, a moderate, consolidate his position at the helm of government.

The interests of eastern Germany are still largely represented by the former communist party of East Germany, now called the Party of Democratic Socialists (PDS), which received over 5% of the vote in the 1998 election, winning seats in the Bundestag for the first time. This surprised many political pundits, who had written off the PDS long ago as an insignificant force at national level.

In 1999 the German parliament moved from Bonn to Berlin and now convenes in the restored and enlarged Reichstag building. Most departments, including the foreign ministry, are now in Berlin, but some, such as defence, health and agriculture, will probably remain in Bonn permanently. The move, which may cost as much as DM20 billion, has produced a flurry of logistical activity in Berlin – new houses being built for parliamentarians, buildings being restored to accommodate ministries, even finding a new playing field for the parliamentary soccer team.

ECONOMY

Germany is the world's third largest economic power (behind the USA and Japan), a committed member of the EU and a member of the expanded G8 group of industrial nations since 1974.

Although Germany was already a leading industrial power in the late 19th century, its real economic success was achieved in the post-war years with West Germany's Wirtschaftswunder. From 1951 to 1961, the economy averaged an annual growth rate of about 8%. This was helped to a large extent by the multiple effects of the Marshall Plan (see History earlier in this chapter), a labour supply swelled by returned soldiers, refugees and foreign workers, and a system known as the social market economy *(Sozialmarktwirtschaft)*.

Although the Sozialmarktwirtschaft is taking somewhat of a hammering, it still ensures a broad safety net of benefits for employees and unemployed that is anchored in the constitution. This is coupled with a free market guaranteeing private ownership and competition.

Of particular importance to German economic success has been the centralised wage-bargaining system and the creation of 'super unions', industry-based unions that often act in economic partnership with employer groups to fix wage levels and conditions. It means that all employees of one industrial sector, regardless of their specific job, belong to a single union. Until recently, this system has helped keep industrial disputes to a minimum.

Employees are represented on works committees and often have a say in decisions made by management – the *Mitbestimmungsrecht* (right of co-determination). Much of the social security system is run by private insurance institutions.

The traditional mainstay of the German economy is the manufacturing sector, which employs about 33% of the total workforce. It mainly consists of medium-sized companies of less than 100 employees and excels in automotive, chemical, electronic and machine-building industries. Industrial giants like Siemens, Volkswagen, Daimler-Benz and BASF manufacture abroad. Siemens employs over 370,000 people worldwide.

Other important industrial sectors are environmental technology, in which Germany has cornered 18% of the world market, and food processing, clothing and steel. Almost a million Germans work in fields directly or indirectly related to environmental protection (as many as in the automotive industry), many of these in waste management. Germany's service industries grew rapidly in the 1990s and employ 38% of the workforce.

The economy is heavily focused on exports, with about one-fifth of workers employed in export industries. About half of Germany's trade is with other EU countries and another 13% with the Asia-Pacific region. Its major trading partners (in descending order of combined import-export volume) are France, the Netherlands, Italy, the USA and Great Britain. But one-quarter of its trade is with non-EU European countries like Poland, the Czech Republic and Russia.

The German economy is under strong pressure from foreign competition, so many companies have moved production abroad, especially to Eastern Europe, where wages and social security overheads are lower (Germany's are the highest in the world). Political figures have tried to reverse the trend by appealing to business leaders' loyalty, but the decisions are financial, not sentimental, and change is unlikely in the near future.

The shift of government to Berlin has not drawn many corporations in its wake: of the

500 largest corporations active in Germany, only 11 are based in the capital, whereas 50 are based in Hamburg and 30 in Munich.

In 1999 Germany joined the European Monetary Union, although many Germans, mindful of the hyperinflation of the Weimar period, remain uncomfortable with the decision to abandon the solid D-Mark. That year, the German unemployment rate was running at 9% in western Germany and 18% in eastern Germany, with an inflation rate of less than 1%. One positive sign of economic integration is that wages in eastern Germany are around 90% of those in western Germany.

Economic Integration

East Germany's post-war recovery was even more remarkable given the wartime destruction, looting by the USSR, loss of skilled labour and isolation from western markets. By 1989, however, stagnation had set in. A secret paper prepared for the government revealed that deficits could not be reversed without a 20 to 25% cut in living standards. Such a cut would have made the country ungovernable, although it became ungovernable anyway.

About 80% of the East German workforce was engaged in state industries before reunification, mostly in the manufacturing sector, an old West German stronghold. After initial optimism, the problems became clear: its industries were overstaffed, massively subsidised, and too heavily focused on Eastern European markets, which dried up with the collapse of the Comecon trading bloc. Its capital stock was badly rundown and productivity lagged behind West German levels.

The introduction of a 1:1 exchange rate for the *Ostmark* (East German Mark) was a big setback for economic development. Overnight, this gave East Germans the means to buy Western consumer goods, but robbed East Germany of its greatest advantage – low wage costs. Nevertheless, wage levels in eastern Germany are currently about 90% of the level in western Germany, but its level of productivity is only 57% of western Germany's.

In 1990 the *Treuhandanstalt* (Trust Agency) was set up to privatise East German assets. Its brief ranged from selling off the large industrial combines through to flogging Honecker's holiday home and the SED party organ *Neues Deutschland* (New Germany). But West German companies were reluctant to invest. Many East German companies were returned to former owners, others scaled down, broken up or bought out in management takeovers. The Treuhandanstalt tallied up enormous debts in its lifetime, draining rather than contributing to the cash-strapped German economy. In fact, financing unification has transformed Germany, once a big lender, into a big spender hooked on foreign capital.

POPULATION & PEOPLE

Germany has a population of about 82 million people, with about 15.5 million living in eastern Germany. This makes it one of Europe's most densely populated countries (third behind the Netherlands and Belgium). Most Germans live in villages and small towns, and even Germany's largest cities tend to be modest by world standards. Its decentralisation is a direct legacy of a history of political fragmentation.

The most densely populated areas are Greater Berlin, the Ruhr region, the area around Frankfurt-am-Main, Wiesbaden and Mainz, and another region taking in Mannheim and Ludwigshafen. The east is much less densely populated, with roughly 20% of the nation's people living on about 33% of the land area. The population of eastern Germany has fallen below the 1906 level. The most sparsely populated state is Mecklenburg-Western Pomerania.

Oddly, a post-unification population boom in Berlin has been offset recently by the exodus of young families from the capital into the surrounding countryside. Early predictions of Berlin becoming a metropolis of over eight million inhabitants have been revised and the capital may even shrink, not grow, in the near future.

Modern Germany has become an *Einwanderungsland* (country of immigrants) and

Top 10 German Towns

Germany has 19 cities with over 300,000 inhabitants. Only two are in eastern Germany. The greatest proportion of the population (49.3 million) lives in small cities of between 2000 and 100,000 inhabitants. About 26 million people (nearly one-third) live in the 84 cities with over 100,000 inhabitants.

The 10 biggest cities in Germany (and their populations) are:

1.	Berlin	3,400,000
2.	Hamburg	1,708,000
3.	Munich	1,236,000
4.	Cologne	966,000
5.	Frankfurt-am-Main	650,000
6.	Essen	615,000
7.	Dortmund	599,000
8.	Stuttgart	586,000
9.	Düsseldorf	571,000
10.	Bremen	549,000

almost as culturally diverse as New World countries and former colonial powers such as France and Britain. Historically, it has always had many immigrants, whether they were French Huguenots escaping religious persecution (about 30% of Berlin's population in 1700 were Huguenots), Polish miners who settled in the Ruhr region in the 19th century, post-war Gastarbeiter, or asylum seekers in the 1990s. About 9% of the population are foreigners. Around half of these have lived in Germany for 10 years or more.

In 1999 a law was passed that revamped Germany's archaic citizenship laws. The old laws, which date back to 1913, defined nationality according to blood, not birthplace or residency, producing an absurd situation whereby generations of 'foreigners' born in Germany were not automatically entitled to citizenship. Most affected by this were the children of former Gastarbeiter.

Although the new law stops short of allowing people falling into this group from possessing dual citizenship, it does dispense with the principle of blood. Anyone born to non-German parents is now entitled to a 'provisional' citizenship. By the age of 23, they must decide whether to retain the nationality of their parents, thus renouncing rights to German citizenship, or whether to relinquish their foreign passport.

Germany has an ageing population and a low birthrate, making immigration necessary if the standard of living is to be maintained. About 200,000 immigrants annually would be required to hold the population (and keep pension funds afloat) at 74 million in 2040.

Ethnic Minorities

The Sorbs, a Slavonic minority, live in the south-east in Saxony and Brandenburg. They developed their own written language around the time of the Reformation and enjoyed a nationalist revival in the 19th century. Hitler tried to eradicate them, while in GDR times the SED attempted to politically integrate them into its power monopoly by offering generous cultural support. They have their own Institute for Sorb Studies at Leipzig University, as well as schools, press and 'national' literature.

There is also a Danish minority based around Flensburg with its own schools and cultural life.

Gastarbeiter

Rather than develop an immigration program to solve a labour shortage in the 1950s, Germany signed treaties with several countries (mostly Mediterranean) to import foreign workers. The first treaty was signed with Italy in 1955, followed by others with Greece, the former Yugoslavia, Portugal, Spain, Morocco, Tunisia and Turkey. About 1.6 million Gastarbeiter worked in Germany throughout the 1960s, rising to a peak of 2.3 million in 1973, when the oil crisis and economic recession ended the program. Instead of returning home, as was envisaged, many stayed on. They were joined by families, or established families of their own, and form an important component of German society.

The Turkish ethnic community is the largest (about two million), followed by

Italian (563,000) and Greek (351,000) communities. A smaller community of Vietnamese lived in East Germany before reunification – about 200,000 workers arrived from 'fraternal socialist countries', most living in housing ghettos for foreigners. Plans by the German government to repatriate them are proving difficult, and many live a marginalised existence selling cigarettes (illegally) on the streets.

Spätaussiedler

Though German by legal definition (ie having German blood), *Spätaussiedler* (literally 'German settlers from abroad') form another important ethnic group. Since 1987 over two million immigrants with distant German connections have settled in Germany, most hailing from Eastern Europe, and Kazakhstan. These days the government is applying strict language tests, while pumping aid into German villages in Kazakhstan to encourage people to stay. Just over 100,000 Spätaussiedler migrate to Germany annually.

Asylum Seekers

One indirect effect of the Nazi years was the creation of liberal asylum laws for the politically persecuted. In 1992 almost 80% of all asylum seekers accepted by EU countries were living in Germany. This amounted to about 438,000 people, mainly due to war in the former Yugoslavia. Since then, the German constitution has been changed to tighten up regulations. These days just under 100,000 asylum seekers arrive in Germany annually. Only about 4% are allowed to stay.

EDUCATION

Germany has a highly educated population and one of the world's most thorough education systems, providing the country with a skilled workforce and a strong research industry. Education is compulsory for 12 years and financed by the state. There are many private and religious schools, but the overwhelming majority of students attend government schools. Because of reunification, and education being a state government responsibility, there are quite a few regional differences.

The first port of call for many is kindergarten (indeed, a German word). Children then attend a *Grundschule* (basic school), usually at age six. In most states, this lasts for four years. They then spend two years in an orientation phase, after which they are divided into streams and allocated a school type. Here is where the whole system becomes more complicated.

Excluding schools for the disabled, there are five different types of school. The first three are the *Hauptschule* (main school), *Realschule* (practical school) and a combined *Hauptschule-Realschule*. Students who have been to one of these schools then enter the workforce and/or attend a *Berufsschule* (vocational college) after the ninth or 10th year. In addition to vocational colleges, there are several types of specialist colleges – some trades oriented, others focusing on a specific field of business or industry. These colleges are integrated into the school system and attendance in one form or another is compulsory until the full 12 years have been completed.

A certificate known as the *Mittlere Reife* is given to students who successfully complete the 10th year at the Realschule.

Gesamtschule (comprehensive school) combines all types of schools. The *Gymnasium* (senior secondary school) is usually where students do the *Abitur* – the university entrance qualification. Most students do the exam when they are 19. It is extremely rigorous, sometimes lasting six hours for one subject. All students, regardless of their school type, have to study at least one foreign language.

Germany has some of Europe's most respected universities, with Heidelberg, its first, founded in 1386. This followed the foundation of Prague University in 1348, which was at that time part of the German Reich. Based on the ideas of Wilhelm von Humboldt, who founded the University of Berlin, universities were originally devoted to pure learning, but this has changed recently. There are about 290 universities or equivalent institutions in Germany, mostly under the wing of the individual states and funded in part by the federal government.

The high demand for university places these days means that it is almost impossible for students to pick and choose the town in which they want to study. Most places are allocated by a central board. Often students then swap places among themselves.

Students study for a *Diplom* (diploma) or *Staatsexamen* (state examination), *Magister* (master of arts), or *Doktortitel* (doctorate). The minimum study period is eight or nine semesters, about 4½ years, but the usual length of stay at a German university is seven years. Together with the late entry age and military service for men, this means many people are 28 before they leave the education system. This may change in future if plans to introduce a shorter bachelor degree are realised. Women comprise 46% of university students.

Parents are legally obliged to support their children's education, and those who cannot afford it receive income-tested assistance.

The third pillar of the education system is vocational training. Germans are very proud of their 'dual training system', which combines on-the-job training with formal classes. Formal qualifications are highly regarded in Germany, untrained experience less so.

Influenced by the USSR, East Germany dispensed with the streamed-school system and most of its students attended the *Einheitsschule*, something like West Germany's Gesamtschule. There were also schools offering courses in specialised areas such as music, sport, languages and certain sciences.

Officially, the tenet of this system was to create a 'harmoniously developed socialist personality'. Despite this wild claim, the system did function, and the strong involvement of parents in school matters ensured that there was much more to it than the official line suggests. However, the number of students able to study at university was much lower than in West Germany. With reunification, English replaced Russian as the first foreign language (making some teachers redundant), Marxist-Leninist programs were axed and many universities had trouble gaining formal recognition. The proportion of women attending university in East Germany was 5% higher than in West Germany.

SCIENCE & PHILOSOPHY

Germany, with its rigorous education system based on the ideas of the philologist and statesman Wilhelm von Humboldt (1767-1835), has made enormous contributions to the disciplines of philosophy and the natural sciences. The importance of Germans in the social sciences and physics in particular is inestimable. By 1939, 10 out of 45 Nobel Prizes in physics had gone to Germans.

Immanuel Kant (1724-1804), who was born in Königsberg (now Kaliningrad), provided Germany with a philosophy for the Enlightenment in his *Critique of Pure Reason* (1781) and, as a founder of German idealism, he paved the way for Georg Wilhelm Friedrich Hegel (1770-1831).

In *The Phenomenology of the Spirit* (1807), Hegel developed a theory of dialectics, or opposites that culminated idealistically in pure consciousness. His influence extended to Arthur Schopenhauer (1788-1860), an idealist with pessimist predilections, who was associated with Goethe and Schiller in Weimar.

If Schopenhauer drove German idealism to its subjective limits, the Trier-born Karl Marx (1818-83) injected it with an historical basis and reinterpreted Hegel's pure consciousness as proletarian revolution. Marx's *Das Kapital*, written in the reading room of London's British Museum, is arguably the most influential work of the past two centuries.

As an economist, Marx occupies a place alongside his British predecessor, David Ricardo (1772-1823). As a social theorist, his brilliance was in describing the change from feudalism to modern capitalism. As a revolutionary, he laid the groundwork for 20th-century political developments.

Friedrich Nietzsche (1844-1900) shared Schopenhauer's idealism but saw subjectivity as a positive condition. Much of his work focuses on power and the human will. His ideas on an *Übermensch* (superman), however, were distorted by Hitler and used to justify racial abuses.

Gottlob Frege (1848-1925), a logician and founder of so-called analytical philosophy, greatly influenced the English philosopher Bertrand Russell. Another important German philosopher is Max Weber (1864-1920), who was born in Erfurt and is considered the founder of modern sociology. The ideas of Martin Heidegger (1889-1976), who was influenced by the Dane Søren Kierkegaard, formed the basis of existentialism.

Germany's achievements in the natural sciences are no less impressive. Geographer and naturalist Alexander von Humboldt (1769-1859), the younger brother of Wilhelm, stands out as an important figure for his extensive study of flora and species geography, physical geography and meteorology. His data taken from expeditions to Cuba and Central and South America contributed greatly to the knowledge of our environment.

Physics, however, is the field in which Germany has particularly excelled. Three distinguished Germans stand out among the many Nobel laureates. Albert Einstein (1879-1955) was born in Ulm and at 15 emigrated to Switzerland, where he worked in the patents office in Bern. His theories on the atomic structure of matter were followed by his theory of relativity. In 1933 Einstein moved to the USA and became an American citizen in 1940. Max Planck (1858-1947) is considered the founder of quantum physics. Werner Heisenberg (1901-76) achieved recognition with his research into hydrogen.

The German tradition of excellence in the social and natural sciences continues to this day, supported by a network of elite Max Planck Institutes and the financial backing of private research by large German international corporations.

ARTS
Music
Early Music The Church was the focal point of much early German music. The term *Lied* (song) describes a variety of popular styles sung as marching tunes or to celebrate victory or work. These later divided into *Volkslieder* (folk songs) and *Kunstlieder* (artistic songs). Among the latter were religious songs, such as the *Marienlied*, which had a mixture of German and Latin lyrics.

From 1100 to 1300, the *Hof* (court) was the focus of music. *Minnesang*, as the new style was called, had Moorish origins and was imported from southern France. These love ballads praised the woman of the court and were often performed by knights. The most famous minstrel was Walther von der Vogelweide (about 1170-1230), whose work has been rerecorded by modern artists.

Meistergesang Around the 15th century the troubadour tradition was adopted by a class of burghers who earned a living from music and were often tradesmen on the side. They established schools and guilds, and created strict musical forms *(Meistergesang)*. Their model was the tradesmen's guild, with *Altmeister* and *Jungmeister* (old and young masters). To become a *Meistersinger*, a performer had to pass a test and bring something new to melody and lyric. One famous Meistersinger, Hans Sachs (1494-1576), was the subject of a Richard Wagner opera, *Die Meistersinger von Nürnberg*, in the 19th century.

Renaissance The Lied remained an important secular form in the 15th and 16th centuries, with Ludwig Senfl (1486-1546) one of the most important composers.

The most significant development took place in the Church, when Luther created the tradition of Protestant hymns. He collaborated with Johann Walther (1496-1570) to publish the first book of hymns sung in German. Also a translator of Latin hymns and an amateur musician, Luther wrote a dozen of his own, some set to the melodies of Volkslieder.

Baroque Dietrich Buxtehude (1637-1707) was one famous organist who influenced Johann Sebastian Bach (1685-1750). The latter is said to have walked several hundred kilometres to Lübeck to hear Buxtehude play. Bach's legacy includes his *Brandenburg Concertos*, passions, cantata and oratorios. Bach and Georg Friedrich Händel (1685-1759) are synonymous with the baroque period.

Händel's music was greatly influenced by his Italian travels. He wrote operas, instrumental works, and oratorios such as his *Messiah*. From 1714 he lived and worked almost exclusively in London. Halle and Göttingen both celebrate his works with annual festivals.

Wiener Klassik The late 18th century saw a shift in musical focus to Vienna, although none of the three great names associated with the movement came from there. Both Joseph Haydn (1732-1809) and Wolfgang Amadeus Mozart (1756-91) were Austrian, but not Viennese, and therefore not really German in today's sense. Nevertheless, their influence on German music is immeasurable. Ludwig

Johann Sebastian Bach is synonymous with baroque music.

MICK WELDON

van Beethoven (1770-1827) was born in Bonn and went to Vienna, where he was taught by Haydn and Antonio Salieri. His work reflects the Enlightenment and he intended to dedicate his third symphony, *Eroica*, to Napoleon until he saw a betrayal of democratic ideals in Napoleon accepting the imperial crown. Beethoven's compositions became more abstract with the onset of deafness. By 1819 he had lost all hearing. Four years later, inspired by a Schiller ode, he composed his monumental ninth symphony, which included a choral finale.

One of Europe's best orchestras was at the Residenz in Mannheim. Bach's son Carl Philipp Emanuel Bach (1714-88) became a significant composer in his own right. Christoph Willibald Gluck (1714-87) was an early composer who began with Italian opera styles and moved on to a simpler, classical style.

Romantic Romantic composers of the 19th century continued the tradition of musical independence (ie living from their work) established in Beethoven's time. This fit in well with the ideology of the free, if sometimes hungry, artist. Felix Mendelssohn-Bartholdy (1809-47) from Hamburg gave his first concert recital at nine years old and at 17 composed his first overture, based on Shakespeare's *A Midsummer Night's Dream*. He later dug up works by JS Bach and gave the latter the fame he enjoys today.

Carl Maria von Weber (1786-1826) set the Romantic tone early with idealisations of Germanic myths. But the most influential composer of the 19th century was Richard Wagner (1813-83), who balanced all the components of operatic form to produce the *Gesamtkunstwerk* (complete work of art). He was strongly influenced by Weber, Beethoven and Mozart. He once described *Die Meistersinger von Nürnberg* as his most perfect work. *Der Fliegende Holländer* (The Flying Dutchman) is another of Wagner's famous operas popular today. His choice of mythological themes also made him popular with Nazis, but Nietzsche, another Nazi favourite, fell out with him metaphysically and condemned his works. Wagner's innovations in opera made him controversial even in his own time, and no future composer could ignore him.

Johannes Brahms' (1833-97) fine symphonies, chamber and piano works, and Lieder were important landmarks. Robert Schumann (1810-56) began his career as a pianist, turning to composition after suffering paralysis of the fingers. In 1840 he married Clara Wieck (1819-96), a gifted pianist in her own right who had begun concert tours at 13. In 1843 Schumann opened a music school at Leipzig with Mendelssohn-Bartholdy.

The Hungarian-born Franz Liszt (1811-86) was at the centre of a group of composers in Weimar from 1844 to 1860. Richard Strauss (1864-1949) worked in the late Romantic tradition of Wagner, only to delve into a style reminiscent of Mozart at the end of his career.

20th Century Arnold Schönberg (1874-1951) was born in Vienna and died in Los Angeles. He lived in Berlin in the 1920s and exerted an enormous influence on Germany's classical music. He is arguably the inventor of a new tonal relationship.

Hanns Eisler (1898-1962) was a pupil of Schönberg's who went into exile in 1933 and returned to teach in East Berlin in 1950. Eisler wrote classical music, pop songs, film music, scores for Brecht and the East German national anthem, his most notorious work. Paul Dessau (1894-1979) also collaborated with Brecht and composed in a broad range of styles. Paul Hindemith (1895-1963) emerged as a talented composer before WWII. Banned by the Nazis, he emigrated to the USA in 1938 and only returned for tours and brief visits after the war. His early works had baroque leanings; his late orchestral compositions, mostly completed in America, confirm his status as one of Germany's best modern composers.

The German classical tradition continues to thrive: the Dresden Opera and Leipzig Orchestra are known worldwide, and musical performances are hosted almost daily in every major theatre in the country.

The Studio for Electronic Music, which is located in Cologne, is a centre for cutting-edge developments.

Contemporary Germany also has a strong jazz tradition, which had a flavour of protest in the 1950s. One of the world's best exponents of free jazz is trumpeter Albert Mangelsdorff. Passport, headed by Klaus Doldinger, is one of the most interesting German bands playing jazz-rock fusion.

German rock began to roll in 1969, when Amon Düul released its first album – a psychedelic work with long instrumental breaks. Can, a Cologne-based experimental group, earned a name with its *Monster Movie* album. Better known internationally is Tangerine Dream, which gained recognition with its 1974 *Phaedra* album.

Old hands will remember Kraftwerk's *Autobahn* album, which hit the turntables worldwide in the early 1970s. This band, one of the first to recognise the potential of computer-assisted music, is hailed as the 'mother of techno'.

Rolf Kaiser was an important producer in the 1970s who did much to promote German music, but British and American bands usually thrived at the expense of local talent. The advent of punk initially left the industry gaping at its guitars. A local movement – *neue deutsche Welle* (German new wave) – soon took shape with German lyrics.

Nena's extremely tame *99 Luftballons* (released in Britain and Australia as *99 Red Balloons*) was a No 1 in the UK; in the USA, where the original German version was released, it was No 2. Spliff, Ideal and Palais Schaumberg were other bands that built up strong reputations.

Nina Hagen, born in East Berlin, was the foster child of writer Wolf Biermann. After Biermann was stripped of East German citizenship, she followed him to West Germany and soon became a symbol of German punk. She worked with the British all-girl group The Slits and as The Nina Hagen Band struck gold with her first album. Her laconic Berlin style blended well enough with English-American punk for *New Musical*

Express to describe her as an epileptic Edith Piaf and a cross between Johnny Rotten, Maria Callas and Bette Midler.

Neue deutsche Welle grew weary and lost momentum around the early 1980s, with few new bands to emerge. Nevertheless, Udo Lindenberg, who was involved in early bands, went solo with political engagement, and anarchists still have a soft spot beneath their leather for the old rocker. Rock became more conservative, a lot of it indistinguishable from *Schlager* (see later in this section).

Herbert Grönemeyer (dubbed 'the German Springsteen') achieved success in 1984 with his *Bochum* album, which stayed in the charts for 79 weeks. His single *Männer* was another big hit. Grönemeyer's strained vocal style is not everyone's cup of tea, but his lyrics often had a nice irony. BAP is a renowned Cologne-based band which sings in the local *kölsch* dialect, which means most Germans can't understand the words either. Cologne has a lively rock scene and BAP is worth seeing if rock archaeology is your interest.

Marius Müller-Westernhagen is a friend of Boris Becker, which makes him doubly famous. His *Freiheit* single became the unofficial reunification anthem after the Berlin Wall fell (sung by the audience, cigarette lighters held aloft, fingers getting sizzled).

Fury in the Slaughterhouse is currently one of Germany's most important mainstream rock bands. Die Toten Hosen (literally 'the dead trousers', but based on an expression to say nothing much is going on) continues to serve up orthodox punk, much of it in English, while heavy metal group The Scorpions still chooses to groom an international image at the expense of its German roots.

The rap group Die Fantastischen Vier, which lent German rap popular tones in the early 1990s, has proved to be a survivor. Other well known rap bands and performers to follow in their wake are Fischmob, Rödelheim Hartreim Project, Fettes Brot, 5-Sterne Deluxe, Eins/Zwo, Die Absoluten Beginner and Sabrina Setlur.

Techno fans might like to return to the womb of creation by dropping in on the Love Parade, held in Berlin each summer. It has turned into Germany's most important music event, with over one million fans thronging the capital annually, many in special 'love trains'.

Schlager & Chanson Schlager is what Germans call your traditional nondescript pop song. Some have a country and western or folk flavour, others are influenced by French and Italian pop. You can hear it all over Germany, but especially in mountaintop restaurants. Schlager is one of those musical forms which, high-brow critics will point out, defies any attempt to raise its standard. Even some of the most shameless parodies have turned into unashamed, thigh-slapping Schlager successes.

Those in the know try to distinguish between Schlager and the more respectable *Chanson* or Lied. The Lied can be traced back to medieval times (see Early Music earlier in this section) and is an integral part of *Kabarett* (German cabaret). One of Germany's more fascinating Schlager singers is Heino, something like a tranquillised albino 'Ken' doll who sports dark glasses and is fast achieving the status of a national treasure. Guildo Horn, nicknamed 'Der Meister' (The Master), is also someone who has dragged German Schlager to new and dubious heights in recent years.

Kabarett Originally imported as cabaret from Paris' Montmartre district in the late-19th century, Kabarett (the German form of cabaret) has a strong political flavour and relies heavily on satire and the Lied.

In Berlin in 1922 there were over 38 venues to help Germans forget about the troubled Weimar Republic. A few of these, such as Schall and Rauch (Noise and Smoke), were political snakepits.

Many well known creative figures of the era worked in Kabarett – including Brecht, Erich Kästner and Kurt Tucholsky. Tucholsky wrote lyrics for the famous Gussy Holl (nicknamed 'the silver-blonde elegant witch'). Annemarie Hase, Trude Hesterberg and Rosa Valletti were three other Kabarett stars of the 1920s.

It is said that when Brecht read his *Legende vom toten Soldaten* (Legend of the Dead Soldier) before a full house in the late 1920s, its antimilitarism was so provocative that brawling broke out among the divided public. Hesterberg, who was Jewish, tormented Nazis in the audience by hanging swastikas and Star of David symbols on the curtain during one of her numbers, *Die Dressur* (The Taming).

In 1933 the stakes were raised by Hitler's power takeover. Almost all political Kabarett was closed down, with performers and writers forced into exile. Others died in concentration camps.

Nevertheless, the tradition is still alive and kicking in Germany. If you think your German is up to the humour, keep an eye on listings in major cities. Dieter Hildebrandt is an old hand, Jutta Wübbe's stage persona, the awkward, drab housewife Marlene Jaschke, is quite witty, as is Rüdiger Hoffmann, who has a strong rural Westphalian element.

Literature

Early Literature The earliest form of German literature was an oral tradition among the tribes. It was usually polytheistic and based on an epic deed. During Charlemagne's reign (circa 800) educated clerical figures diligently recorded what remained of the oral tradition, giving us the *Hildebrandslied*, a father-son epic with shades of the Oedipus myth. Christian and Teutonic traditions were sometimes combined, as in *Ludwigslied*, which celebrated victory over the Normans, or *Heliand*, a story about Christ in which Jesus is recast as a tribal leader.

Clerical dominance continued under the Ottonian dynasty. Hrotsita von Gandersheim (circa 960) was a nun who wrote religious moral dramas. In the 12th century *Hofliteratur* (literature of the royal court) brought a shift away from the Church. It was French-inspired, epic and performed by the author, who was often a knight. The *Nibelungenlied*, an anonymous work, draws heavily on Germanic mythology.

Wolfram von Eschenbach's (circa 1170) epic, *Parzival*, took the themes of mortal

beings, God and compassion, and was later turned into a libretto by Wagner. Less conventional is Gottfried von Strassburg's (circa 1200) *Tristan und Isolde*. It tells of a rarefied illicit love that clashes with social custom, belief and the heroes' duty. *Minnesang*, a musical cousin of Hofliteratur, was directed at the women of the court. Walther von der Vogelweide (circa 1170-1220), the best lyricist, went beyond love themes to produce works with a political and philosophical edge.

Meister Eckhard (1260-1327), Heinrich Seuse (1295-1365) and Johannes Tauler (1300-61) wrote works with strong mystical tones, an important element of the 13th and 14th centuries.

Luther revolutionised literary language in the 16th century with his translation of the Bible into common German. As he once wrote: '... look at their gobs to find out how they speak, then translate so they understand and see you're speaking to them in German.' Luther's translation was printed using a revolutionary technique invented by Johannes Gutenberg (1397-1468). Reusable lead printing blocks replaced wooden ones, providing the technological basis for mass circulation.

Baroque Much of baroque literature reflects the Thirty Years' War and conflict surrounding the Reformation. The 17th century saw a conscious attempt to groom the German language. Language societies were established to formalise grammar and oversee usage, and with this came a dose of literary absolutism.

Martin Opitz (1597-1639) created the basis for a new German poetry with his influential and theoretical work *Buch der deutschen Poeterey* (Book of German Poetry). Andreas Gryphius (1616-54) was a poet and playwright who played on baroque ideas of earthly transience and the grandiose meaninglessness of life. In his *Katharina von Georgien* (Katharine of Georgia) the heroine dies a Christian martyr rather than marry the Shah of Persia. His sonnet *Tränen des Vaterlandes* (Tears of the Fatherland) explored the horrors of the Thirty Years'

War. HJC von Grimmelshausen's (1622-76) classic *Simplicissimus* (Adventures of a Simpleton) is a picaresque tale about a peasant youth who, having become caught up in the war, returns home as a hermit. It is an important predecessor of the German novel, and influenced Günter Grass.

Enlightenment Led by French philosopher Descartes and his German counterpart, Gottfried Wilhelm von Leibniz (1646-1716), the Enlightenment dispensed with superstition and baroque folly and turned to human reason.

Johann Christian Gottsched (1700-66) left his native Königsberg allegedly because Friedrich Wilhelm I liked his size and wanted to conscript him. In Leipzig he remodelled German theatre along French lines. His theoretical work *Versuch einer critischen Dichtkunst* (Essay on Critical Poetics) was a milestone of the era.

Also significant was Christoph Martin Wieland (1733-1813), whose *Geschichte des Agathon* (Agathon) is considered Germany's first *Bildungsroman* (a novel showing the development of the hero). At the centre of the novel is an ambitious attempt to find a harmony of emotion and reason.

Gotthold Ephraim Lessing (1729-81) wrote critical works, fables and tragedies, throwing his hat into the ring with Gottsched, whose French inclinations he rejected in favour of Shakespearian dramatic forms. Lessing dug up the old Greek idea that tragedy employed empathy and fear to evoke the audience's passion (Brecht later threw his hat in too).

Lessing's *Miss Sara Samson*, *Emilia Galotti* and *Nathan der Weise* (Nathan the Wise) are his best known dramatic works. One recurring theme in his plays is of the daughter who is 'created' by the father but later becomes his sacrifice.

Sturm und Drang This era (literally 'Storm and Stress'), from 1767 to 1785, marks the beginning of a golden age dominated by the two heavyweights Goethe (1749-1832) and Schiller (1759-1805).

Goethe, unlike his contemporaries, came from the upper class and lived to a ripe old age. He earned fame with his early work *Götz von Berlichingen*, following up with the movement's first novel, *Die Leiden des jungen Werthers* (The Sorrows of Young Werther). During this period Schiller wrote *Die Räuber* (The Robbers) and *Kabale und Liebe* (Cabal and Love). Their importance is immeasurable, and their arrival signalled the start of a modern national literature.

Neoclassicism Storm and Stress was merely a short stopover in a greater literary flight plan. Neoclassicists looked to ancient Greece and Rome for inspiration and ideals, tightened up formal aspects and cultivated the idea of the 'beautiful soul'. This artistic ideal aimed at human improvement often meant authors hailed their own, alleged, genius.

Goethe's *Italienische Reise* (Italian Journey) was a new turn in his development. The years 1794-1805 saw a fruitful collaboration with Schiller in Weimar and Jena, during which the Bildungsroman *Wilhelm Meisters Lehrjahre* (Wilhelm Meister's Apprenticeship) was published. Goethe's finest

MICK WELDON

Johann Wolfgang von Goethe was the heavyweight of German *Hochkultur*.

work is considered his two-part *Faust*, which he worked on for most of his life. Based on a pact with the devil, *Faust* explores the human struggle for ultimate power and knowledge. Among Schiller's important works are his Wallenstein trilogy and *Maria Stuart*, *Die Jungfrau von Orleans* (The Maid from Orleans) and *Wilhelm Tell*.

Romanticism Early Romanticism began as a complement to neoclassicism, keeping and developing the Greek and Roman elements but taking the individual deep into fancy and imagination. Friedrich Hölderlin (1770-1843) was an important figure who, like Goethe, spanned several periods. Germany's best Romantic poet, he strove for perfect balance and rhythm in his work – much of which is in classical meter or free verse. His career was cut short, however, by the onset of madness in his 30s.

John-Paul (1763-1825) wrote novels which often have a whimsical, sentimental edge. Novalis (1772-1801) created the symbol of Romantic yearning, the blue flower, in one of his early novels. His best work, the poems *Hymnen an die Nacht* (Hymns to the Night), deals with death and grief.

Ernst Theodor Amadeus Hoffmann (1776-1822) is best known for his bizarre tales. His *Mademoiselle de Scudérie* is considered the forerunner of the mystery genre. Annette von Droste-Hülshoff (1797-1848) was a Catholic socialist whose *Die Judenbuche* (The Beech Tree of the Jews), like most of her work, has a tranquil mood and is set in a village.

The brothers Jakob (1785-1863) and Wilhelm (1786-1859) Grimm are famous worldwide for their collections of fairy tales and myths. As scholars, however, they created a basis for the serious study of German language and literature.

Heinrich Heine & Junges Deutschland
The Junges Deutschland (Young Germany) movement grew up around the 1830s as a reaction to nonpolitical romanticism. Literature was subject to harsh censorship, causing many writers to resort to satire. Heinrich Heine's (1797-1856) *Deutschland: Ein*

Wintermärchen (Germany: A Winter's Tale) is a politically scathing work based on a trip from Aachen to Hamburg. His early *Buch der Lieder* (Book of Songs) is ranked as one of Germany's best collection of love poems. Heine's work was banned in 1835 – and it had nothing to do with the love poems. In Georg Büchner's (1813-37) *Woyzeck*, one of the best plays of the era, a simple hero gets caught up in hostile social forces. Büchner lent his characters a complex psychology and employed plot structures that anticipated the Theatre of the Absurd.

Realism The realist movement, which broke in Germany around 1840, saw the novel become the dominant literary form. Many took on a regional flavour. Theodor Storm (1817-88) wrote poetry, short stories and novels set in his native Schleswig-Holstein, often creating a raw North Sea atmosphere. Wilhelm Raabe (1831-1910) is hailed for his social descriptions. His *Else von der Tanne* is about a woman killed by fellow villagers made distrustful by war. Better known is Wilhelm Busch (1832-1908), whose illustrated *Max und Moritz* delights adults and children today. Busch's skill was in the simplicity of his tales and cartoons, full of wit and irony.

With the crossover to naturalism, things became grimier and more descriptive. Arno Holz's (1863-1929) *Buch der Zeit* (Book of the Times) was a landmark in big-city poetry. Gerhart Hauptmann's (1862-1946) *Bahnwärter Thiel* (Thiel the Crossing Keeper) is a bleak novella with madness, murder, sexual dependence and a railway theme – just the thing for a long train journey.

20th Century The 20th century kicked off in fine style with the poetry of Rainer Maria Rilke (1875-1926), who was born in Prague. One of Germany's best lyric poets, Rilke wrote *Das Stunden Buch* (The Book of Hours), a search for spiritual wellbeing in an industrial age.

Thomas Mann (1875-1955) has a place of honour approaching Goethe's. He won the Nobel prize for literature in 1929. Born in Lübeck, he moved to Munich around

1900 and later travelled to Italy. His greatest novels focus on the society of his day. In *Buddenbrooks* he describes declining bourgeois values. *Der Zauberberg* (The Magic Mountain) links personal and social illness around the time of the Great War, while in *Doktor Faustus* the central character makes a pact with the devil, exchanging health and love for creative fulfilment. Its tone is set by the menace of Nazism. A good Mann starter is his magnificently crafted *Tod in Venedig* (Death in Venice).

Hermann Hesse (1864-1947), like Mann, was a Nobel Prize winner. His *Steppenwolf* took the theme of the outsider. A 'new Romantic', he was profoundly influenced by a journey to India in 1911 and imbued his work with spirituality.

Ricarda Huch (1864-1947) was described by Thomas Mann as 'Germany's first lady'. She stands out in her own right as a courageous opponent of Nazism, having resigned in protest from the Prussian Academy of the Arts. Her work includes poetry, novels and biographies, including one on the Russian anarchist Mikhail Bakunin.

Heinrich Mann (1871-1950) took a stronger political stance than his younger brother, Thomas. His *Professor Unrat* was the raw material for the film *Der blaue Engel*, with Marlene Dietrich (see the boxed text 'Marlene Dietrich' in this chapter). Alfred Döblin's (1878-1957) *Berlin Alexanderplatz*, another important novel of the era, provides a dose of big city lights and the underworld during the Weimar Republic.

The Prague-born Franz Kafka (1883-1924) only fleetingly graced Germany, but his influence on its literature is enormous. Guilt and the human condition underscore most of his works. In *Die Verwandlung* (Metamorphosis), the hero inexplicably wakes up as a dung beetle. The hero of *Der Prozess* (The Trial) is condemned by an imaginary court on charges he never learns.

Erich Maria Remarque (1898-1970) achieved worldwide success with his anti-war novel from 1929, *Im Westen nichts Neues* (All Quiet on the Western Front), one of the most widely read German books. It

was banned in 1933 and Remarque emigrated to America in 1939.

Bertolt Brecht The 'epic theatre' of Brecht (1898-1956) was loosely Marxist, rejecting Lessing's Greek leanings for political, didactic forms. His *Leben des Galilei* (Life of Galileo) and *Die Dreigroschenoper* (The Threepenny Opera) are two of his most popular dramatic works, which overshadow his fine poetry.

Brecht went into exile during the Nazi years, then surfaced in Hollywood as a scriptwriter and was called in to explain himself during the McCarthy communist witch hunts. He ended up in East Berlin after the war – where he could count on a sympathetic audience. Empathy, Brecht claimed, numbed the faculties of the theatre audience: his epic theatre relied on alienation techniques designed to allow the audience to reason. For more on Brecht, see the boxed text in the Berlin chapter.

Kurt Tucholsky (1890-1935) and Erich Kästner (1899-1974), two political satirists, are also recommended for anyone interested in the period between the wars.

Post-1945 The post-war period saw the return of many writers-in-exile and the emergence of Heinrich Böll (1917-85) and Günter Grass (1927-) as key figures in West Germany. Both were members of the political Gruppe 47 circle of writers, which focused on post-war social questions and the German psyche, and both won Nobel prizes for literature, Grass in 1999. In Böll's *Ansichten eines Clowns* (The Clown), the central character, a washed-up pantomime artist, takes a sceptical look at family, society, Church and state. Grass' tour-de-force, *Die Blechtrommel* (The Tin Drum), humorously traces recent German history through the eyes of Oskar, a child who refuses to grow up. This first novel turned Grass into a household name. He followed it up with an impressive body of novels, plays and poetry.

Christa Wolf (1929-) grew up in East Germany and is one of its best, if controversial, writers. *Der geteilte Himmel* (Divided

Heaven) has an industrial backdrop and tells the story of a woman's love for a man who fled to West Germany. Sarah Kirsch (1935-), who emigrated from East Germany, has earned a reputation as a highly respected poet. Stefan Heym (1913-), like Brecht, went into exile and returned after the war to settle in East Germany. He has been politically active with the PDS (the former East German SED) and his *Auf Sand gebaut* (Built on Sand), a collection of stories, looks at the situation of East Germans around 1990.

Heiner Müller (1929-95) had the honour of being unpalatable in both Germanys. It is said that Müller worked for the Stasi, but that his messages were so ambiguous as to be worthless. His acerbic wit produced gems such as 'five Germans are more stupid than one'. His *Der Lohndrücker* (The Man who Kept Down Wages) is a good place to start.

A leading literary figure over the past two decades has been Botho Strauss, whose work has a strong mystical edge. Patrick Süskind has been one of Germany's more popular young writers in recent years. Süskind's *Das Parfum* (Perfume) is the extraordinary tale of a psychotic 18th century perfume-maker with an obsessive genius.

Architecture

Visitors to Germany are often surprised by the number of fine buildings that survived the ravages of wartime bombing. Many damaged buildings were restored, others so painstakingly reconstructed from rubble as to defy the believability of pictures of ruins. This section explains the many styles you'll find.

Carolingian The grand buildings around the 9th century were loosely based on styles and techniques used in Italy. The finest remaining example is the Pfalzkapelle of Charlemagne's palace in Aachen, which dates from about 800. It was probably inspired by San Vitale in Ravenna and its classical columns were brought from Italy.

Romanesque The main influences of the Romanesque era (circa 1000) were Carolin-

gian, Christian (Roman) and Byzantine. Bishop Bernward, Otto III's tutor, returned from Rome wanting to turn Hildesheim into the cultural centre of the empire. Michaelskirche in Hildesheim and the elegant Stiftskirche in Gernrode are fine examples of the style, which aimed for a proportional interior and integrated columns. The cathedrals of Worms, Speyer, Mainz and Bamberg are considered Germany's most significant examples of Romanesque.

Gothic The Gothic movement, which began in northern France around 1150, was slow to reach Germany. The Magdeburger Dom (begun in 1209), one of Germany's first Gothic cathedrals, was based on a French design but kept many Romanesque elements. Gothic interiors usually have ribbed vaults, pointed arches and flying buttresses – allowing height and larger windows. The Elizabethkirche in Marburg an der Lahn and Liebfraukirche in Trier (both about 1240) are good examples.

Germany's most famous Gothic building is the massive Dom in Cologne (a UNESCO World Heritage building), which was begun in 1248 and not completed until 1880. The Ulm Münster is a good example of how high Gothic can go in Germany (161m, in this case), as are Freiburg's Münster and the Marienkirche in Lübeck. Late Gothic (from about the 15th century) buildings tended to have more elaborately patterned vaults, and hall churches (where the nave is the same height as the aisles) became more common. Munich's Frauenkirche and Michaelkirche are good examples of late Gothic. The *Rathaus* (town hall) buildings in Bremen and Lübeck are both in secular Gothic styles.

Renaissance The Renaissance had a slow birth in Germany, gaining importance only around the mid-16th century, overlapping with late Gothic. Its main centre was in southern Germany and around the trade routes of the Rhine, where there was a great deal of contact with Italy. Herms (usually stone heads of Hermes) placed on structural features, leafwork and sculptured human figures used as columns and pillars became popular. The Ottheinrichsbau (1556), the part of Heidelberg Castle built by Count Ottheinrich, is an example of German Renaissance architecture matching Italian standards. The Haus zum Ritter, also in Heidelberg, is another.

The 16th century brought colour and decorative facades to half-timbered houses, many with elaborately carved surfaces.

Weser Renaissance is a northern German secular style found in regions near the Weser River. Typical is a balanced multiple-wing castle with winding staircases ascending a tower. The finest example is the picturesque castle and grounds in Celle. Early styles often incorporated Gothic decoration on facades.

Baroque Loosely describing a period in German architecture from the early 17th century to the mid-18th century, baroque is linked to the period of absolutism after the Thirty Years' War, when feudal rulers asserted their importance through grand residences. Many took their inspiration from the palace of Versailles. Structures tended to dominate their surroundings, with grand portals, wide staircases and wings that created enclosed courtyards. Ornate and excessive, baroque buildings also incorporated sculpture and painting into their design. During this period many Italian architects, such as Barelli (who created Schloss Nymphenburg in Munich) and Zuccalli, worked in Germany.

Karlsruhe was founded in the baroque period, with the castle its focal point. Dresden's Zwinger, the Residenz in Würzburg and portions of Dom St Stephan in Passau are also fine examples.

The north was predominantly Protestant, Dutch-influenced and geometric; in the Catholic south, however, baroque tended to be freer and more ornamental. Schloss Sanssouci, in Potsdam, was begun during the late baroque, or rococo, period.

Neoclassicism In the late 18th century, baroque folly and exuberance were replaced by the strict geometry of neoclassicism, typified by Berlin's Brandenburg Gate, based on a Greek design. Friedrich Wilhelm II tried to turn Berlin into a European centre of culture by linking Prussian nationalism with the greatness of ancient Greece. Columns, pediments and domes were the dominant architectural forms. A leading architect of the style was Karl Friedrich Schinkel. His Altes Museum, Neue Wache and Schauspielhaus, all in Berlin, are pure forms of neoclassicism.

In Munich, Leo von Klenze, another leading figure, chiselled his way through virtually every ancient civilisation, with eclectic creations such as the Glyptothek and Propyläen on Munich's Königsplatz.

Revivalism The late 19th century brought a wave of derivative architecture based on old styles, leading to the completion of Cologne's Dom after original plans were discovered in 1814 and 1816. Georg von Nauberisser's Munich Rathaus (Marienplatz) is secular neogothic.

A German peculiarity was the so-called 'rainbow style', blending Byzantine and Roman features. The Heilandskirche in Potsdam typifies the style. Georg Adolph Demmler's Schloss in Schwerin is an example of Renaissance revivalism.

A prominent example of neobaroque, often called 'Wilhelmian style', is Paul Wallots' Reichstag building (begun 1884) in Berlin. Damaged in the fire of 1933, it was repaired without the original cupola and, now restored with a glass cupola, again houses the German parliament.

Neuschwanstein, Ludwig II's grandiose, fairy-tale concoction, was built in a neo-Romanesque style.

Art Nouveau The use of steel in the late 19th century allowed greater spans and large glass surfaces (exemplified by your average Hauptbahnhof), which was taken up by the Art Nouveau movement in the early 20th century. German impetus for the movement came from a group called Der Deutsche Werkbund, founded in 1907. It consisted of architects, designers, tradespeople and industrialists, and aimed to raise the quality of German industrial products. One of the many Art Nouveau factories is the AEG Turbinenhalle in Berlin. Alfred Messel's Wertheim department store in Berlin is another good example.

Between 1910 and 1925, an expressionist style arose that employed more fantasy, typified by the stalactite interior of the Grosses Schauspielhaus in Berlin or Erich Mendelsohn's Einsteinturm (1920) in Potsdam.

Bauhaus The Bauhaus movement took the industrial forms of Art Nouveau and drove them to functional limits. It began in 1919 with Walter Gropius' founding of the Staatliches Bauhaus, a modern art and design institute in Weimar. The institute later moved to Dessau, then to Berlin, before being closed by the Nazis in 1933. Gropius' aim, set out in his Bauhaus Manifest, was to bring together architects, painters, furniture designers and sculptors to create a unity of the arts. Detractors claim that it was often functional and impersonal, relying too heavily on cubist and constructivist forms. The institute's building in Dessau is typical of the style, but you can find the influence of Bauhaus everywhere in modern design. Painters Wassily Kandinsky and Paul Klee taught at the institute before going into exile.

Post-1945 Nazi architecture, like Nazism itself, revelled in pomposity. Hitler's architect and political crony, Albert Speer, received the order to create works that would befit the Thousand Year Reich. Unfortunately for Speer, classicism had two 'neo' prefixes by the time he got his hands on it, which perhaps explains why Nazi monumentality often seemed absurd. Werner March's lavishly embellished Olympisches Stadion and grounds in Berlin is one of the better examples to survive.

After Hitler, it took German architects a few years to plug back into the world scene. Post-war reconstruction demanded cheap buildings that could be erected quickly. Hubert Petschnigg's Thyssenhaus in Düsseldorf

is considered one of the best works of the 1960s. The interior of Hans Scharoun's Philharmonie (1963) in Berlin hints at a terraced vineyard. Günther Behnisch and Frei Otto's tent-like Olympisches Stadion, built for the 1972 Munich games, is one of Germany's best post-war constructions. Otto had earlier achieved fame with his German pavilion at the 1967 Montreal World Expo.

The 361.5m-high Fernsehturm in the former East Berlin, built in 1969, is to the memory of GDR architecture what Donna Summer is to disco. A tradition of monumentalism continued in the East (Berlin's Frankfurterallee is a sugar-cake version) until political disappointment among East Germans made this untenable in the 1960s. East Germany also inadvertently created one of the world's most potent architectural symbols in the Berlin Wall.

More recently, Richard Meier integrated an old villa into a design with ramps, blocks and ship motifs for his Museum für Kunsthandwerk (1984) in Frankfurt-am-Main.

Architectural activity in Berlin continues at a frenzied pace, with what is referred to as the 'project of the century' at Potsdamer Platz. More inventive is the new Jüdisches Museum in the Kreuzberg district, a zig-zag construction designed by American Daniel Libeskind. These, and other ambitious post-reunification projects, are creating a new face for the capital.

Film
Silent Film Germany's first public film screening was in Berlin in 1895. Early films were shown in booths at annual town fairs or in refurbished shops. In 1917 Ufa (Universum Film AG) was established by the government to raise production standards and improve the image of Germany abroad.

Silent films in Germany often took up morbid, pathological themes and used images and clever cutting to create character psychology. The influence of Sigmund Freud is clear in Stellan Rye's 1913 classic *Der Student von Prag* (The Student from Prague), which tells of a student who sells his mirror image to a stranger and ends up fleeing his own self. *Das Kabinett des Dr Caligari* (The Cabinet of Dr Caligari; 1919) by Robert Wiene, about a hypnotist who makes his patients commit murder, has expressionist influences and deals with tyranny. Another *Gruselfilm* (horror or Gothic film) is FW Murnau's *Nosferatu* (1921), a seminal Dracula work in which the plague is brought to a north German town. It hints at collective fear in the early days of the Weimar Republic.

The 1920s was a period of intense creativity, with quality films such as GW Pabst's *Die freudlose Gasse* (The Joyless Street; 1925) and Joe May's *Asphalt* (1929). Pabst, who worked in New York theatre before WWI, dominated the film scene in the 1920s and 1930s, using montage intelligently to elucidate character and create visual sequence. In *Die freudlose Gasse*, he takes two women – one a society lady, the other a prostitute – to illustrate a perceived loss of values.

Fritz Lang's *Metropolis* (1926) stands out as an ambitious cinema classic. It depicts the revolt of a proletarian class that lives underground. Walther Ruttmann's *Berlin – Die Sinfonie einer Grossstadt* (Berlin – Symphony of a Big City; 1927), set over 24 hours, provides excellent early documentation of Berlin.

Sound Films of the 1930s

In 1927 Ufa passed from the Deutsche Bank into the hands of the Hugenberg group, which was sympathetic to right-wing movements. The new film era resulted in the Marlene Dietrich classic *Der blaue Engel* (The Blue Angel; 1930), directed by Joseph von Sternberg and loosely based on Heinrich Mann's novella *Professor Unrat*. It tells of a pedantic professor who is hopelessly infatuated with a sexy Kabarett singer (Dietrich). Our learned man is destroyed at the end, but the film created the vamp image Marlene enjoyed all her life.

Pabst's *Dreigroschenoper* (Threepenny Opera; 1931), based on Brecht's play (music by Kurt Weill), is set in the gangster milieu around Mackie Messer (Mack the Knife). Apparently, Brecht was unhappy with changes, and tried to prevent its screening. A year earlier, Pabst had made *Westfront – 1918* (The Western Front – 1918), a pacifist

film that depersonalised characters to depict them caught up in the machinery of war.

Leontine Sagan's *Mädchen in Uniform* (Girls in Uniform; 1931) is set in a girls' boarding school, where pupils are taught obedience and prepared for a future as good mothers and soldiers' wives. *Das Testament des Dr Mabuse* (The Testament of Dr Mabuse; 1932) was Lang's first talkie. It is about a psychiatric patient who devises plans to take over the world. If that somehow rings a bell, it is worth remembering that the Nazis prevented the German premiere, forcing Lang to shift it to Austria.

Nazi Period Hitler's power takeover ruptured German cultural life, and film was no exception. Financial trouble at Ufa between 1933 and 1937 allowed the Nazis to anonymously buy out Hugenberg and step up control over the industry (the government owned 99.25% of the shares). All films had to get the nod of approval from Goebbels' Reichskulturkammer (chamber of culture). Censorship laws and bans drove over 500 actors and directors into exile. Many were murdered, while others, including many Jews, went to Hollywood and played parts as stereotypical German Nazis. Some directors and actors were successful, but the majority struck a language barrier and sank into oblivion.

László Loewenstein, an ethnic-German Hungarian better known as Peter Lorre, had already played a pathological child-killer in Lang's *M* (1931) before cropping up as the edgy, hunted Ugarte in *Casablanca*. Lorre later returned to Germany to act and direct.

Carl Froelich's *Traumulus* squeezed past the censors in 1935. It is a period film, set in the provinces, about an idealistic school director who loses touch with reality. Austrian Emil Jannings played the lead in a masterful performance.

Post-1945 Films shot directly after the war are known as *Trummerfilme* (literally 'rubble films') and usually deal with Nazism or war. DEFA (Der Deutsche Film AG), a new East German film corporation, was established in the Soviet zone (the USSR was

Marlene Dietrich

Marlene Dietrich, whose real name was Marie Magdalena von Losch, was born in Berlin into a good middle-class family on 27 December 1901. After attending acting school, she worked in the fledgling German silent film industry in the 1920s, stereotyped as a hard living, libertine flapper. In the 1927 film *Wenn ein Weib den Weg verliert* (When a Girl Loses the Way) she played a well-mannered young woman who falls into the clutches of a gigolo. She soon carved a niche in the film fantasies of lower middle-class men as the dangerously seductive *femme fatale*, best typified by her 1930 talkie *Der blaue Engel* (The Blue Angel), which also made her a Hollywood star.

There's a story that Dietrich landed the role only through the insistence of director Josef von Sternberg, who had watched her perform in a theatre review. Nevertheless, he still had to convince Heinrich Mann. Mann had written the novel and wanted to give the part to his lover, Trude Hesterberg, a cabaret artist. Meanwhile, the film's scriptwriter was doing his best to get his lover into the role. Dietrich won the part and Mann lost his lover.

Working closely with Sternberg, Dietrich built on her image of erotic opulence – dominant, severe, always with a touch of self-irony. When she put on men's suits for *Marocco* in 1930, she lent her 'sexuality is power' attitude bisexual tones, winning a new audience overnight.

Marlene stayed in Hollywood after the Nazi rise to power, though Hitler, no less immune to her charms, reportedly promised perks and the red carpet treatment if she moved back to Germany. She responded with an empty offer to return if she could bring Sternberg – a Jew and no Nazi favourite.

When Allied GIs rolled into Paris in 1944, Marlene was there, too. Asked once whether there was any truth to the rumour that she had slept with General Eisenhower, she apparently replied, 'How could I have? He was never at the front'.

After the war, Dietrich made only occasional appearances in films, choosing instead to cut records and perform live. Discrete, uncompromising and, contrary to the film image, always the well-bred woman from Berlin, Dietrich retreated from the public eye as age and illness slowly caught up with her.

She died in 1992, aged 90. The Deutsche Bahn has named one of its Berlin ICE trains after her.

MICK WELDON

its chief shareholder), producing Germany's first post-war film, *Die Mörder sind unter uns* (The Murderers Are Among Us; 1946) by Wolfgang Staudte. Set at Christmas 1945, it tells of a guilt-ridden army doctor who encounters a commanding officer responsible for the execution of women and children in Russia. He threatens the officer with a pistol as the latter is celebrating with his wife and children.

Bernhard Wicki's *Die Brücke* (The Bridge; 1959) is an exceptional and highly recommended film about a group of boys who faithfully try to defend an insignificant bridge against advancing Americans in the last days of the war.

Strassenbekanntschaft (Street Acquaintance; 1948), a Soviet-zone educational film about the dangers of venereal disease, is an interesting document for its conservative portrayal of women's roles in peacetime. The East German *Sterne* (Stars; 1958) is about a prisoner and guard who fall in love in a concentration camp in Bulgaria. Konrad Wolf earned a name as East Germany's best director and the film won an award at Cannes.

Since the 1960s The new decade brought the Oberhausener Gruppe, a group of directors who rejected old cinema norms with the declaration 'Papa's cinema is dead' in its 1962 manifesto. A highlight was Vesely's *Das Brot der frühen Jahre* (The Bread of Early Years; 1962), an adaptation of a Böll work about an electrical mechanic who surrenders his humdrum existence after encountering an old friend and falling in love. Vesely's film paved the way for a new wave of directors.

Volker Schlöndorff emerged as a key figure in a movement known as Der junge deutsche Film, a German form of the French new wave. His *Der Junge Törless* (Törless; 1965) is set in a boys' boarding school and deals with hierarchy and power, culminating in the maltreatment of a Jewish boy. *Abschied von Gestern* (Goodbye to Yesterday; 1966) by Alexandra Kluge, and Edgar Reitz's *Mahlzeiten* (Meals; 1967) are two other fine films.

Der geteilte Himmel (Divided Heaven; 1964) is an adaptation by Konrad Wolf of a novel by Christa Wolf. *Nackt unter Wölfen* (Naked Among Wolves; 1963), directed by Frank Beyer, tells of a child smuggled into Buchenwald concentration camp and the moral dilemmas it presents for other inmates by endangering a resistance movement.

Werner Herzog, Rainer Werner Fassbinder, Margarethe von Trotta, Wim Wenders and Doris Dörrie all emerged to join Schlöndorff as significant directors in the 1970s and 1980s. Terrorism became a popular theme. Schlöndorff's *Die verlorene Ehre*

der Katharina Blum (The Lost Honour of Katharina Blum; 1975) was an adaptation of a Böll story on the subject. Von Trotta worked with Schlöndorff on the film and later dealt with the theme again in *Das zweite Erwachen der Christa Klages* (The Second Awakening of Christa Klages; 1978) and *Die Bleierne Zeit* (Leaden Time; 1981).

Herzog's *Kaspar Hauser – Jeder für sich und Gott gegen alle* (Kaspar Hauser – Every Man for Himself and God Against All; 1974) is based on the true story of a foundling in 1829 who, having grown up isolated from civilisation, is exploited as an object of research. As in so many 1970s German films, Herzog portrayed society as a threat to self-identity. His *Fitzcarraldo* (1982), which took four years to complete and received mixed reviews from critics, is about a dreamer who defies social norms and self-limits to drag a boat inland across Peru.

Fassbinder's films are more eclectic, at times more grotesque, in their exploration of society, sexuality and the human psyche. He has won nine awards in Germany alone, and his trilogy – *Die Ehe der Maria Braun* (The Marriage of Maria Braun; 1979), *Lola* (1981) and *Die Sehnsucht der Veronika Voss* (The Longing of Veronika Voss; 1982) – is highly acclaimed.

Wenders won a Golden Palm at Cannes for *Paris, Texas* (1984). He pushed the *Erzählkino* (literally 'narrative cinema') style to its limit, as, for example, in *Der Himmel über Berlin* (Wings of Desire, 1987), based on two angels who move through divided Berlin.

With the collapse of the Wall, the GDR's Babelsberg film lot was sold to a French corporation. It has been upgraded to a tourist attraction while continuing to produce films and provide production services and studios.

The 1990s brought a shift to relationship themes. Sönke Wortmann's 1992 *Kleine Haie* (a pun on 'little sharks' and the title of a book of elocution exercises for actors) is a gentle comedy about male friendship. In *Keiner liebt mich* (Nobody Loves Me; 1994), Doris Dörrie created an offbeat film with black humour about the single woman in the 1990s. Dörrie built on her success with the release of *Bin ich schön?* (Am I Beautiful?; 1997).

Detlev Buck's 1993 *Wir können auch anders* (titled 'No More Mr Nice Guy' in English) is arguably the best film to emerge since reunification. It is a comic road movie about two innocent brothers from the backwoods of Schleswig-Holstein who set off for the wilds of eastern Germany to claim an inheritance. Buck's next film, *Männerpension* (Men's Pension; 1995), starred Til Schweiger, the current German heart-throb.

Film buffs should drop into the Deutsches Filmmuseum on the 'Museum Bank' in Frankfurt-am-Main. It has a book and video library, and screenings of German and international films. To learn more about the early days of German cinema – the UFA era – visit the Filmmuseum in Potsdam.

Painting & Sculpture

Early Works The two dominant art forms during the Carolingian period (around 800) were frescoes and manuscript illumination. Few frescoes have survived, but one example is in the crypt of St Maximin in Trier, excavated in the 1930s. Reichenau, an island in Lake Constance, was an early centre of Christian culture and manuscript illumination. Other schools sprang up in Trier, Cologne, Fulda and Hildesheim. The Stiftskirche St Georg on Reichenau has frescoes from the late 10th century depicting miracles, which are among Germany's most important early works. Stained glass, such as in the cathedral at Augsburg (about 1100), was common during the Salian dynasty. The cycle in Augsburg cathedral is the earliest in Central Europe and depicts Jonas, Daniel, Hosea, Moses and David. Augsburg's stone Bischofsthron (Bishop's Throne), set on two lions, dates from the same period. The ceiling painting of the Michaelskirche in Hildesheim, dating from around 1200, depicts biblical scenes.

Gothic Building techniques enabling large windows meant that stained glass played an important role between the 12th and 15th centuries. However, the price paid by Gothic art was the loss of space for frescoes. Good examples of glass painting can be found in Cologne in St Kunibert and in the choir of the Dom. An excellent early Gothic work is in the cathedral in Limburg an der Lahn. Manuscript illumination gained a density of colour with solemn shades of gold, dark green and purple. Iconography became common on church panels.

The Cologne school dropped the usual gold background and began painting rudimentary landscapes. The best example of an early realistic landscape depiction is *Die Meerfahrt der Heiligen* (Sea Voyage of Mary Magdalena), probably painted by Lukas Moser in 1432. It's in the Pfarrkirche in Tiefenbronn near Pforzheim. The background showing ships is remarkably evocative and realistic, creating a great sense of movement. Another famous work is Meister Bertram's religious panel *Erschaffung der Tiere* (Creation of the Animals; circa 1340), with its fine depiction of animals. Originally in the Petrikirche in Hamburg, it is now in that city's Kunsthalle.

Renaissance This era saw human elements gain importance in painting: religious figures were often depicted surrounded by mortals. In Germany, the Renaissance is synonymous with one great figure, Albrecht Dürer (1471-1528), who was born in Nuremberg. His influence was so great that the period is often referred to as the Dürerzeit (Age of Dürer). Dürer began as an apprentice goldsmith and travelled widely throughout Germany before spending time in Venice and Bologna. He was the first German to grapple seriously with the theory and practice of Italian Renaissance art. Closely tied to a Gothic tradition in early years, his woodcuts often had apocalyptic elements. His drawings of nature and animals were exact in their detail, and he left a surviving legacy of about 70 paintings, 350 woodcuts and 900 drawings. Some of his work is displayed in the Alte Pinakothek in Munich.

Dürer had an important influence on Lucas Cranach the Elder (1472-1553) and Hans Holbein (1497-1543). Cranach's landscape paintings contain many Gothic elements, as in his *Apollo und Diana in waldiger Landschaft* (Apollo and Diana in a Forest Landscape; 1530), in Berlin's New Picture Gallery. It depicts both figures naked in primal forest, Diana seated upon an acquiescent stag. Cranach was at the centre of a south German school of Mannerism, a movement that idealised beauty and dropped some of the Renaissance naturalist elements. Portraits often depicted stylised figures detached from their environment.

Of the Renaissance sculptors, Tilman Riemenschneider (1460-1531) was the best known. He fell foul of authorities by supporting the peasants in the *Bauernkriege* of 1525, lost his job as mayor and was tossed in jail and tortured. His greatest skill was in giving his stone sculpture qualities resembling wood. Like his life, his woodcuts show a strong play of light and shadow.

Baroque & Rococo The period around the 17th and 18th centuries brought an elaborate integration of painting, sculpture and architecture to form a *Gesamtkunstwerk* (total artwork). Sculpture was integrated into architectural design and gardens. Andreas Schlüter (1660-1714) was both a sculptor and architect whose *Reiterdenkmal des Grossen Kurfürsten* (Horseman's Monument of the Great Prince Elector), one of his most famous works, now stands before Berlin's Schloss Charlottenburg. He was called to St Petersburg by Peter the Great in 1713.

The fresco re-emerged as an important form, employed in the palaces to create the illusion of extended space. But baroque German painters were thin on the ground, with the two most important figures, Adam Elsheimer (1578-1610) and Johann Liss (1597-1630), both working in Italy. Many of Germany's palace frescoes of the time were done by Italians. Johann Baptist Zimmermann (1680-1758) was an important southern German fresco painter who worked in pastels typical of the rococo style. In northern Germany, Friedrich I employed the Frenchman Antoine Pesne (1683-1757) to satisfy his taste for the French rococo style.

Neoclassicism From about the mid-18th century neoclassicism brought a formal shift to line and body, with an emphasis on Roman and Greek mythology. The human figure also came back into fashion. In Germany the movement was influenced by the theorist Johann Winckelmann (1717-68), who, before being murdered in Italy, published works on classical painting and sculpture, including a history of classical art. His influence extended to Anton Mengs (1728-79), who became a painter of the royal court in Dresden. Johann Heinrich Tischbein (1751-1829) painted still lifes, animals and Goethe. He belonged to Goethe's circle of friends during the latter's Italian journey, and his *Goethe in der Campagna* (1787) shows Germany's most famous writer reclining in a suitably classical landscape surrounded by an assortment of antique objects. The painting is in the Frankfurt-am-Main Städel Art Institute.

Johann Gottfried Schadow (1764-1850) was the most important sculptor of the time. His most prominent work is the four-horse chariot with Victoria on Berlin's Brandenburg Gate. Napoleon liked it so much he took it with him in 1806. Returned in 1816, it was damaged during WWII and restored in 1956.

Romanticism The 19th century saw a shift back to more conventional religious themes. Great emphasis was placed on inner spirituality. Caspar David Friedrich's (1774-1840) paintings had a religious symbolic element. His *Das Kreuz im Gebirge* (Cross in the Mountains) depicts Christ's crucifixion among fir trees on a hill top, light filtering supernaturally through a mackerel sky. Philipp Otto Runge (1777-1810) belonged to the Dresden school and also imbued his paintings with mysticism. He was a founder of the German Romantic movement, wrote several theoretical works and his work is well represented in Hamburg's Kunsthalle. Raphael's influence can be seen in the paintings of a group of artists known as Nazarener (Nazareths), a derogatory term for intensely religious painters such as Johann Overbeck (1789-1869) and Franz Pforr (1788-1812).

Realism & Naturalism Romanticism had stagnated by the mid-19th century. The industrial age saw painters set up their easels outdoors and strive to recreate detail, whether natural or urban. Cologne-born Wilhelm Leibl (1844-1900) studied in Munich and specialised in painting Bavarian folk. His style gradually became more impressionistic. Some of his paintings are in Hamburg's Kunsthalle.

Hans Thoma (1838-1924) belonged to Leibl's circle and produced still lifes, portraits and lithographs. Adolph Menzel (1815-1905), ranked alongside Leibl as one of the best realist painters, was largely self-taught and went unnoticed until he began doing works based on the life of Friedrich I. His 1852 *Das Flötenkonzert* (The Flute Concert), at Berlin's New Picture Gallery, accurately re-creates costume and a room interior with a realist brush.

Impressionism A truly impressionist school of painting emerged in Germany in the 1880s and 1890s with Max Liebermann (1847-1935) and Fritz von Uhde (1848-1911). Liebermann's paintings were often dismissed as 'ugly' and 'socialist'. The movement was long considered un-German, which perhaps reflects the lingering social influence of romanticism. Liebermann began by painting gloomy naturalist works of the proletariat before adopting brighter impressionistic tones. Lovis Corinth's (1858-1925) late work *Die Kindheit des Zeus* (Childhood of Zeus; 1905) is a richly coloured frolic in nature with intoxicated, grotesque elements, and is now housed in the Bremen Kunsthalle with others of its ilk.

Expressionism In the same year that Corinth painted *Die Kindheit*, a group calling itself Die Brücke (The Bridge) emerged from the Dresden art scene. The movement worked with bright, dynamic surfaces, striving for a direct and true representation of creative force. Its members admired the work of Paul Gauguin and often employed primitivist and cubist elements. Its founding members were Ernst Kirchner (1880-1936), Erich Heckel (1883-1971) and Karl Schmidt-Rottluff (1884-1976). Members often lived in artists' communes, turning their studios into exhibition space.

Emil Nolde (1867-1956), arguably Germany's best expressionist painter, was an artistic lone wolf who only fleetingly belonged to Die Brücke. Nolde was forbidden from working by the Nazis in 1941.

A second group of expressionists, Der Blaue Reiter (Blue Rider), was based in Munich around the key figures of Wassily

'Degenerate' Art

Abstract expressionism, surrealism and Dadaism were definitely not Hitler's favourite movements. The Nazis created a popular offensive against such so-called 'Jewish subversion' and 'artistic bolshevism'. This peaked around 1937, when the German term *Entartung* (degeneracy) was borrowed from biology to describe virtually all modern movements. That was the year in which paintings by Klee, Beckmann, Dix and others, works supposedly spawned by the madness of 'degenerates', were exhibited in Munich defaced with signatures in protest.

Around 20,000 people visited the exhibition daily, most to frown upon the works. If that wasn't enough, a year later a law allowed for the forced removal of degenerate works from private collections. Many art collectors, however, managed to keep their prized works out of Nazi hands. A local citizen in Quedlinburg saved numerous works by the German-American dadaist Lionel Feininger which are exhibited in a gallery there. But the fate of many other artists' works was less fortunate: although a lot of works were sold abroad to rake in foreign currency, in 1939 about 4000 paintings were burned publicly in Berlin and lost forever.

Kandinsky (1866-1944), Gabrielle Münter (1877-1962), Paul Klee (1879-1940) and Franz Marc (1880-1916). Like Die Brücke, the movement tried to find a purer, freer spirit through colour and movement. Kandinsky's 1909 *Eisenbahn bei Murnau* (Railway at Murnau) shows a train passing through an evocatively colourful landscape. It is in Munich's Städtische Gallerie im Lenbachhaus, where many of the movement's works are housed. The Russian-born Kandinsky wrote much about expressionist theory, comparing the creation of form to the creation of life. Oskar Kokoschka (1886-1980) was an Austrian who exerted great influence on the expressionist scene both as an artist and professor in Dresden.

Neue Sachlichkeit 'New Objectivity' describes a loose movement in the early 20th century that reached its zenith with Bauhaus. Architecture formed the basis of Bauhaus, but ideas spilled over into painting with the publication of the movement's ninth book by Kandinsky, who had moved on from expressionism.

Kandinsky's *Punkt und Linie zu Fläche: Beitrag zur Analyse der Malerischen Elemente* (Point and Line to Surface: Contribution to the Analysis of Elements of Painting) was a landmark in Bauhaus art theory. As well as Kandinsky and Klee, the movement included sculptor Gerhard Marcks (1889-1981).

Otto Dix's (1891-1969) work crossed from expressionism into Dadaism, a movement mocking the bourgeoisie that developed briefly in Germany around 1916, whereas Max Ernst (1891-1976), a painter, sculptor and graphic artist, moved in later years from Dadaism to grotesque surrealism.

George Grosz (1893-1959), co-founder of German Dadaism and later the Rote Gruppe (Red Group), took the pencil and brush to society in the 1920s with witty, skilful caricatures. He escaped execution by the skin of his teeth after a military court sentenced him to death in 1918, and was received by Lenin on a 1922 trip to Russia. None of this made him the favourite artist of Hitler, who

stripped him of German citizenship and classified him as *entartet* (degenerate). Many of Grosz's works in private hands were confiscated or destroyed. He went into exile in New York, returning only in 1957.

John Heartfield (1891-1968) was another member of the futurist-Dadaist club who kicked around Berlin in the 1920s and 1930s. He worked closely with Grosz on satirical magazines. His *Die Saat des Todes* (The Seed of Death; 1937) depicts a skeleton in a wasteland sprinkled with swastikas. Käthe Kollwitz (1867-1945) was a 'Renaissance woman' who worked her way through naturalist and expressionist movements to arrive at agitprop and socialist realism. Some of her works are housed in the Käthe Kollwitz museums in both Berlin and Cologne.

With war approaching, art became increasingly bleak, often taking the themes of silence and death. Many artists suffered the fate of being classified 'degenerate' like Grosz or were forced to resign their positions and go into exile. Others were murdered or went into 'internal exile'.

Nazi Art Hitler was no great fan of 20th century painting unless he had done it himself. Few people place much value on Nazi art. It lay stacked in a basement for 50 years before being rolled out for a didactic exhibition in the mid-1990s. A 1999 exhibition in Weimar juxtaposed Nazi art with works produced in the GDR. On a more bizarre note, some of Hitler's art surfaced recently in Iran.

Post-1945 After the war, respected figures such as Nolde, Schmidt-Rottluff and Kandinsky returned to pull Germany's devastated cultural scene back onto its feet. Willi Baumeister and Ernst Nay are considered two of Germany's best post-war abstract expressionists. Nay tried to capture rhythm in his work, often using erotic motifs and mythology.

The Düsseldorf-based Gruppe Zero (Group Zero) plugged into the Bauhaus legacy. Key members Otto Piene (1928-) and Heinz Mack (1931-) used light and space cleverly in endeavours to create a harmonious whole. Mack's sculpture is mostly metal, while Piene has used projection techniques to create his so-called 'light ballets'. More recently, Anselm Kiefer (1945-) has gone for size in his 32-tonne work *Zweistromland* (Mesopotamia), 200 lead books arranged on shelves.

The Neue Wilde (New Wild Ones) movement of the late 1970s and early 1980s brought together new-wave music and the visual arts, with Cologne, Berlin and Hamburg its main centres. Markus Lüpertz (1941-) is one survivor from the scene active today.

In the GDR, the Leipzig Kunsthochschule was an important centre of socialist realism. Wolfgang Matheuer emerged as a respected painter and sculptor who relied on mythological personae (Icarus, Sisyphus). He produced a large body of work that includes self-portraits and landscapes.

For a good overview of German painting and sculpture visit: Hamburg's Kunsthalle, the Alte and Neue Pinakothek in Munich, Dresden's New Masters Gallery, Berlin's New Picture Gallery, the Städel Art Institute in Frankfurt-am-Main, Braunschweig's Herzog Anton Ulrich Museum and Stuttgart's Staatsgallerie. Schwerin's Staatliches Museum has an excellent collection of Dutch 17th century masters.

SOCIETY & CONDUCT

It's difficult to get around the fact that Germany has an image problem. Think of Italy, and good food, wine and classical monuments spring to mind. France has fashion, more good food and wine, and the language of love and diplomacy. Think of Germany, and *Sauerkraut*, two world wars, a Cold War, Hitler, the Holocaust and a bevy of pessimistic philosophers waltz before your eyes.

Take, for instance, a 1996 survey of British schoolchildren conducted for the Goethe Institut. It revealed that for 68% of those asked, Adolf Hitler was still the most well-known German. Next came Jürgen Klinsmann, Boris Becker and Steffi Graf. About 16% mentioned Ludwig van Beethoven. It gets worse: in a recent survey,

children were shown photographs of various people and asked to rate each on a 'sympathy' scale. When the children were told a particular person was from Germany, ratings plummeted!

But what are the Germans really like?

National Identity

Contrary to popular belief, Germans on the whole are not particularly nationalistic. Germany achieved nationhood very late and this was closely associated with social unrest, war and authoritarianism, all of which lend the very idea of 'the German nation' negative connotations. Germans still cannot celebrate their country as innocently as, say, Americans or French can theirs – the stigma is too great.

Grass, Germany's most famous modern writer, is quoted as saying his people didn't deserve a country of their own after Auschwitz. Waving a flag or singing the national anthem in the FRG after 1945 was generally avoided. Meanwhile, good East Germans were taking their government's advice and busily turning 'swords into ploughshares'. This mood is gradually changing since reunification. Now you can even hear the German football team struggling through the approved third verse of *Das Deutschland Lied* – which doesn't stop reporters asking them *why* they sing.

But national identity for most Germans remains a delicate tightrope walk between the many positive aspects of German culture and the horror of the country's history. Volkhard Knigge, responsible for the upkeep of the Buchenwald concentration camp memorial outside Weimar, probably best summed up the situation in an interview with *Der Spiegel* magazine: 'When you talk about Goethe, you can't hold your tongue on Buchenwald'.

Wall in the Head

It is still too early to see Germany as one single country. Although the Wall no longer exists physically, 40 years of living apart have left behind a wall in the head.

In East Germany, national identity was thrown into one bag with class struggle and socialism. Although this potpourri had taken on a bitter flavour by the 1980s, many East Germans developed a sense of nation. Stripped of socialist clothing, many still cling nakedly to a now defunct national identity. Some feel done out of their country and most eastern Germans will tell you that it was not all a nightmare. Their identity may be expressed in *Ostalgie* (a pun on 'east' and 'nostalgia') or a predilection for Rotkäppchen sparkling wine ('Little Red Riding Hood', as if she were always a paid-up party member) and other eastern products.

Paradoxically, however, East Germans were more predisposed to reunification than West Germans, using it to express discontent with the SED. But isolation bred unrealistic expectations: the grass was always greener on the other side of the wall.

Daniela Dahn, an ex-GDR journalist who wrote what has come to be seen as a survival handbook for eastern Germans, believes one of the biggest culture shocks occurred in the workplace. Eastern Germans, she says, were unused to the level of competition between employees in western Germany. Many East Germans identified with their workplace and co-workers, even if that meant less work was done. 'It was ineffective,' she explained in an interview with the *Frankfurter Rundschau*, 'but effectiveness knows no human measure'. Dahn has become something of a high priestess of *Ost-Trotz* (eastern defiance) and likens reunification to 'banishment to Paradise'.

Few people in eastern Germany seriously wish to re-create the conditions. Surveys show they value their newly won freedom of movement and choice, cleaner environment and better leisure facilities (Thuringia is rumoured to be the 'swimming pool capital' of Germany). But many miss the security they once enjoyed and don't feel they have much more political influence than they had under single-party rule.

Changes for Women in the GDR

Almost 90% of all women in the GDR were employed or in training programs. By June

The National Anthem

Germans have had an ambiguous relationship with their national anthem. Although a lot of young West Germans were familiar with the words, those who sang it before reunification were generally dismissed as either fools or hard-core nationalists. These days Germans feel less inhibited about singing along.

Based on an obscure Croatian folk song, the music for the German national anthem was composed by Joseph Haydn in 1797 and set to words penned by Hoffmann von Fallersleben in 1841 (including the original words 'God preserve Franz the Kaiser' – an Austrian, in fact). It didn't become the formal anthem until 1922. During the Nazi period it was usually sung in conjunction with *Die Fahne Hoch* (Raise the Flag), an uninspiring ditty composed in 1927.

The national anthem was retained after 1945 largely due to the efforts of Konrad Adenauer – minus the first two verses, which either listed a set of borders that now lie in neighbouring countries or sounded like a drinking song. A 1990 court decision ruled that only the third verse was protected as a national symbol.

The East German national anthem, *Auferstanden aus Ruinen* (Resurrected from Ruins) joined the long list of unsung communist golden oldies once the socialist fatherland was abolished. Proclaimed in 1949, its pro-unification lyrics fell out of favour among party honchos after the construction of the Berlin Wall in 1961, when only the tune was permissible. In November 1989, it was sung in protest by demonstrators. This received the blessing of the Ministry of Culture a couple of weeks later, and the anthem was played accordingly on radio and television before being finally abolished in 1990.

1992, 63% of women in eastern Germany found themselves out of work. Reunification also brought the closure of childcare centres, an end to free contraception and cuts in health programs. It pushed some women back into more traditional roles. Although a disproportionate number of women remain out of work, career attitudes of younger generations are beginning to resemble those in western Germany. Polls suggest that in eastern Germany around 13% of employed women place more importance on their careers than on having a family, compared to around 14% in western Germany. One large difference, however, is the lower priority women in eastern Germany give to 'self-development' – they do it for the money and a better standard of living.

Unemployment has had a big impact on middle-aged women's use of leisure time. In the former GDR, leisure was organised strongly around the workplace. So for a lot of women, unemployment has meant isolation and a less satisfying social life.

Abortion

Abortion was one of the trickiest issues to resolve after unification. In the GDR, it was legal within three months of conception. Due to strong opposition from women's groups to the adoption of less liberal West German abortion laws, the issue was fudged in the Unification Treaty. Abortion, according to old West German law, was illegal, but certain preconditions made it unpunishable (eg a 'social indication' meant termination within 12 weeks was often possible after counselling). Each state enforced this law as it saw fit, resulting in abortion tourism, whereby women sought abortions in states with a pro-choice approach.

It took five years to resolve the issue, with abortion made illegal (except when medical or criminal indications exist) but unpunishable if carried out within 12 weeks of conception and after compulsory counselling.

Right-Wing Violence

A disturbing social phenomenon to emerge after unification was attacks on foreigners.

Often attributed to youth unemployment and readjustment problems in eastern Germany, the problem was not confined to this area. Government leaders in both regions were blamed for failing to unequivocally condemn early attacks. Police were also criticised for focusing too heavily on the substantial *Autonomen* (left-wing anarchist) scene and too little on the skinhead problem.

Right-wing extremists had been an active but insignificant group at Monday demonstrations in Leipzig in 1989, but by 1991 the level of right-wing violence had increased fivefold. That year, encouraged by many locals who obstructed the police, skinheads attacked a refugee hostel in Hoyerswerda, south of Cottbus. Instead of clamping down on the skinheads, authorities relocated the refugees in a nearby town, further encouraging extreme right-wing elements. Rostock erupted a year later with similar scenes. The attacks spread: a house in Solingen (near Düsseldorf) occupied by Turks was burnt to the ground, killing five people; arsonists set fire to the Lübeck synagogue; and a group of Africans was brutally beaten in Magdeburg.

By and large, the situation has improved in most regions in the past decade. Brandenburg and Saxony, however, continue to have disgraceful records. Sadly, though, recent figures suggest that attacks are on the rise again elsewhere. Black and Asian travellers should be a bit more cautious in these states.

Dos & Don'ts

You'll find travelling in Germany a rewarding experience if you try to approach the country on its own terms. Forget the clichés about the cool, efficient Prussian, or of Bavarians in *Lederhosen* (leather trousers) descending from the hills twice a year to dance and slap together hands or various other body parts. Images like these usually induce bewilderment and frustrated groans among young Germans.

Nevertheless, tradition does remain dear to the German heart. Hunters still wear green, master chimney sweeps get around in pitch-black suits and top hats, some

Bavarian women don the *Dirndl* (skirt and blouse), while Bavarian menfolk occasionally sport Lederhosen, a *Loden* (short jacket) and felt hat. In contrast, most young Germans these days graduate from nappies to jeans and jogging shoes, completely sidestepping the leather phase.

It *is* OK to mention the war, if done with tact and relevance. After all, a lot of people you will meet have grown up demanding explanations. What causes offence is a 'victor' mentality, which is perceived as righteous and gloating, or the concept that fascist ideas are intrinsically German.

You might find yourself tripping up occasionally (you'll notice the blank stare) on German historical or cultural taboos. What may be an innocuously 'liberal' view at home can sometimes go down in Germany as political dynamite. No discussion of euthanasia can ignore abuses under the Nazi regime. Similarly, abortion has almost always been illegal (see earlier in this chapter), but under the Nazi regime criminals and non-Aryans – notably Jews and Gypsies – were encouraged and often forced to have abortions as a means of population control.

When Naked Vegetarians Pump Iron

The idea of the strapping young German frolicking unselfconsciously naked in the healthy outdoors is nothing new. A German *Körperkultur* (physical culture) first took shape in the late 19th century, closely connected with vegetarian and strong-man movements. The idea behind the movement was to remedy the so-called 'physical degeneration' caused by industrial society. Germany's modern *Freikörper* (naturist) movement grew out of this era.

There was much more to naturism then than just hopping about on a beach in your birthday suit. The early movement was something of a right-wing, anti-Semitic animal, whose puritanical members were scorned by some outsiders as 'the lemonade bourgeoisie'.

Achieving total beauty was the name of the game. Anathema to the movement, for example, was someone with a lascivious 'big-city lifestyle' that included smoking, fornicating, eating meat, drinking, wearing clothes made of synthetic fibres, or anyone with predilections for artificial light.

It was around this time that Germany's first vegetarian *Reform* restaurants and shops sprang up; a reminder of these is the present-day chain of Reformhaus shops found throughout the country.

The most interesting characters to develop out of this odd era were bodybuilders. A lot of early German bodybuilders were vegetarians and most were also naturists; but they were also internationalist in spirit. Some of these Germans achieved fame abroad under pseudonyms. Others were immortalised in Germany by sculptors, who employed them as models for their works.

Famous pioneers of the movement in Germany were the Kaliningrad-born Eugene Sandow, 'Professor' Attila (from Baden), Hans Ungar, who became famous under the pseudonym Lionel Strongfort, and Theodor Siebert, who hailed from Alsleben, near Halle in eastern Germany.

MICK WELDON

Push firmly but politely in dealings with German bureaucracy. Shouting will invariably bring down the shutters. In fact, Germans often lower their voice, not raise it, in mildly heated moments. Insist on talking to the boss. Ask for it in writing *(eine schriftliche Begründung)*. German work hierarchies are still rock solid and obstinacy crops up occasionally as a form of passing the buck. In that case, unfortunately, the boss will quite possibly be a higher and more unpleasant manifestation of your lowly buck-passer.

Give your name at the start of any phone call, especially when booking a room by telephone. Germans consider it impolite or simply get annoyed when no name is given.

If you don't want to (eg when dealing with bureaucracy), make one up.

Germans usually face each other squarely in conversation, with a lot of eye contact used to signal interest and attention. If John Wayne had been German, he would have intently analysed the pupils of his interlocutor during those big moments, not gazed meaningfully at the horizon. This stance can seem overbearing and unnerving or refreshingly direct. Shaking hands is common both among men and women, as is a hug or a kiss on the cheek among young people.

Much importance is still attached to academic titles (Herr or Frau Doktor). Addressing someone by the surname is a must

Jews in Germany

The first Jews arrived in present-day Germany with the conquering Romans, settling in important Roman cities on or near the Rhine, such as Cologne, Trier, Mainz, Speyer and Worms. As non-Christians, Jews had a separate political status. Highly valued for their trade connections, Jews were formally invited to settle in Speyer in 1084, granted trading privileges and the right to build a wall around their quarter. A charter of rights granted to the Jews of Worms in 1090 by Henry IV allowed local Jews to be judged according to their own set of laws.

The First Crusade (1095-99) resulted in a wave of pogroms in 1096, usually against the will of local rulers and townspeople. Many Jews resisted before committing suicide once their situation became hopeless. This, the *Kiddush ha-shem* (martyr's death), established a precedent of martyrdom that became a tenet of European Judaism in the Middle Ages. But the attacks also set the tone for persecution by mobs during troubled times. Jews fared better in the Second Crusade (1147-49), taking refuge in castles until the danger had passed.

In the 13th century Jews were declared crown property by Frederick II, an act that afforded protection but exposed them to royal whim. The Church also prescribed distinctive clothing for Jews, which later meant that in some towns Jews had to wear badges.

Things deteriorated with the arrival of the plague in the mid-14th century, when Jews were accused of having poisoned Christians' drinking wells. Persecution, including trials and burnings, was now sanctioned by the state. Political fragmentation meant Jews were financially exploited by both the Kaiser and local rulers, and libellous notions circulated throughout the Christian population. The 'blood libel' accused Jews of using the blood of Christians in rituals. The even more bizarre 'host-desecration libel' accused Jews of desecrating or torturing Christ by, among other dastardly deeds, sticking pins into communion wafers, which then wept tears or bled.

Moneylending continued to be the main source of income for Jews in the 15th century, but many moved back into local trade, including the wine trade in southern Germany. Expulsions remained commonplace, with large numbers emigrating to Poland, where Yiddish developed. The Reformation marked another low point, with Martin Luther calling at various times for the confiscation of Jewish religious texts, expulsion of Jews, serfdom and the

unless you are on informal '*du*' terms. If you have a title, you might like to move mountains with it (it's legally part of your name and you can insist on its use). If Herr Professor Doktor Vollschnauze nods or bows his head slightly when he shakes your hand, he's signalling respect for you as an equal. It's not that he feels humbled by your presence (always good to know). In that case, a subtle nod in response is the usual grace. If he insists on being addressed with both 'Dr' titles, you might like to think seriously about the kind of people you attract.

Great importance is also placed on the formal '*Sie*' form, which is used more often than most non-Germans expect. It is worth

trying to get it right, as correct use will make things a lot easier.

In the workplace, only employees who are also good friends say 'du'. It is quite common to use 'Sie' even after 20 years of close contact. This, of course, can turn your average German Christmas office party into a minefield once the drink and 'du' start flowing. One psychologist, interviewed on TV about inadvertently becoming 'familiar under the influence', suggested that fellow workers innocently revert to 'Sie' and pretend they were too drunk to remember. This might be worth a try in other predicaments too. Germans often celebrate the change to the familiar. Young people and eastern Germans are much

Jews in Germany

destruction of Jewish homes. Deeper fragmentation after the Thirty Years' War again exposed Jews to the whims of competing territorial and central authorities, but by the 17th century they were valued again for their economic contacts.

Napoleon granted Germany's Jews equal rights, but reforms were repealed by the 1815 Congress of Vienna. Anti-Jewish feelings in the early 19th century coincided with German nationalism and a more vigorous Christianity. Pressure was applied on Jews to assimilate. Famous assimilated Jews, such as Heinrich Heine, often exerted a liberal influence on society.

With unification in 1871, Jews enjoyed almost equal status in Germany, but they were still barred from government and could not become army officers. In the late 19th century Germany became a world centre of Jewish cultural and historical studies. There was a shift to large cities such as Leipzig, Cologne, Breslau (now Wroclaw in Poland), Hamburg, Frankfurt-am-Main, and to the capital, Berlin, where one-third of German Jews lived.

The Weimar Republic meant emancipation for the 500,000-strong Jewish community. Many assumed a direct political role in democratic and socialist parties (Hugo Preuss drafted Germany's first democratic constitution). But economic disasters in the 1920s soon brought a backlash. Despite over 100,000 Jews serving Germany in the armed forces during WWI, they became scapegoats for Germany's defeat, the humiliating peace and ensuing economic woes.

Many unassimilated Eastern European Jews immigrated to Germany in the 1920s. Meanwhile, German Jews continued to assimilate. Germany also became an important centre for Hebrew literature after Russian writers and academics fled the revolution of 1917.

After Hitler came to power, the fate of German Jewry was sealed by new race laws. Increasing persecution led many to emigrate, and by 1939 less than half the 1933 population figure remained in Germany. By 1943 Germany was declared *Judenrein*, or clean of Jews. This ignored the hundreds of thousands of Eastern European Jews incarcerated on 'German' soil. Around six million Jews died in Europe as a direct result of Nazism and its barbarity.

Germany's current Jewish community numbers around 61,000, a figure boosted by the influx of Jews from the former Soviet Union.

more relaxed about 'Sie' and 'du' (in bars, where a lot of young people gather, 'du' is often used), but don't even consider saying 'du' to a shop assistant unless you want to incite wrath and bad service.

On the whole, Germans are not prudish. Nude bathing and mixed saunas are commonplace (many women, however, prefer single-sex saunas). Nude bathing areas are marked FKK, or form spontaneously in certain areas on beaches or the shores of lakes.

RELIGION

The constitution guarantees religious freedom in Germany. The two main religions are Catholicism and Protestantism, each with about the same number of adherents. This situation dates back to the Peace of Augsburg (1555), when, as a result of the Peasants' War (see the earlier History section), the Catholic and Protestant churches were granted equal status. Each ruler was free to choose the denomination of their principality, which left the south predominantly Catholic and the north Protestant. Nevertheless, several Catholic diasporas continue to exist in the north, while there are both Catholic and Protestant Sorbs. A large influx of Huguenots (French Protestants) arrived in the late 17th century, making up a substantial chunk of Berlin's population (about 30%) by 1700. There are also about 1.7 million Muslims, 61,000 Jews and many smaller denominations.

About 530,000 Jews lived in Germany in 1933, before the community was devastated by emigration and the Holocaust. Some surviving Jews chose to remain, and the Jewish community has grown recently due to immigration from the former Soviet Union. The largest groups are in Berlin, Frankfurt-am-Main and Munich.

Germans who belong to a recognised denomination have to pay a Church tax (about 9% of income). Many leave the Church for financial reasons. A survey conducted in 1996 for *Der Spiegel* magazine found that only 51% of Germans believed in God. In eastern Germany, the figure was 20%.

In the former GDR, Protestants overwhelmingly outnumbered Catholics. Church membership was officially frowned upon by the party, and no party member could belong to the Church. Religious lessons were conducted solely outside the school system. Church and state existed side by side with formal agreements regulating Church activities. For example, a 1957 agreement allowed Protestant pastors to visit military barracks, but the state paid for this, also organising and controlling all visits. The Protestant Church played a major role in the overthrow of the SED by providing a forum for antigovernment protesters.

The Church in former East Germany took a distrustful view of the armed forces and supported conscientious objectors. In West Germany there was a more conservative approach to the issue of pacifism. This fact, and the much closer relationship between Church and state in unified Germany, means many eastern Germans view the role of the Church with scepticism.

LANGUAGE

German belongs to the Indo-European language group and is spoken by over 100 million people in countries throughout the world, including Austria and part of Switzerland. There are also ethnic-German communities in neighbouring Eastern European countries such as Poland and the Czech Republic, although expulsion after 1945 reduced their number dramatically.

See the Language chapter at the back of this book for pronunciation details and useful phrases. The glossary, also at the back, contains some common German words.

Facts for the Visitor

HIGHLIGHTS
Cities
Germany's major cities offer a wide range of sightseeing, museums, nightlife, entertainment, shopping and other, often unique, experiences. Bustling Berlin, the capital, is perhaps the best place to put your finger on the Zeitgeist, but other vibrant and fascinating destinations include Hamburg, Cologne, Frankfurt and Munich.

Castles
With castles of all periods and styles, Germany is a great place to indulge in fairy-tale fantasies. If you're into castles, make sure you visit Heidelberg, Neuschwanstein, Burg Rheinfels on the Rhine River, Burg Eltz on the Moselle, Wartburg Castle in Eisenach, Renaissance Wittenberg Castle, baroque Schloss Moritzburg near Dresden and romantic Wernigerode Castle.

Museums & Galleries
Germany is a museum-lover's dream. Munich has the huge Deutsches Museum, and Frankfurt's Museumsufer (Museum Embankment) has enough museums for any addict. Berlin has major collections of international stature, as does Hamburg, with its Kunsthalle and numerous other museums. On the Rhine, Cologne and Düsseldorf also have major art collections, while Dresden has the New Masters Gallery.

Theme Roads
Germany has several scenic theme routes, which are generally best explored by car or motorbike. For maps and route highlights, contact the route's tourist office or any of the local tourist offices along the way. Theme roads covered in this book include the Romantic Road in Bavaria, the Fairy-Tale Road from Hanau to Bremen, the German Wine Road in the Rhineland-Palatinate, the Black Forest Highway in Baden-Württemberg and the Vineyard Road in Saxony-Anhalt.

Historic Towns
Time stands still in many parts of Germany, and some of the best towns in which to relive the 'days of yore' include Rothenburg ob der Tauber, Goslar and Regensburg. Meissen and Quedlinburg have a fairy-tale atmosphere, Weimar holds a special place in German culture, and Bamberg and Lübeck are two of Europe's true gems. The old district *(Altstadt)* remains the heart and highlight of many large cities.

SUGGESTED ITINERARIES
Depending on your interests and the length of your stay, you may want to take in the following destinations:

One week
    Berlin/Potsdam, Munich and an alpine resort like Berchtesgaden
Two weeks
    As for one week, plus Trier, Cologne, Heidelberg, the Rhine Valley, Freiburg, Weimar and Dresden
One month
    As for two weeks, plus Aachen, Hamburg, Lübeck, Rügen Island and Erfurt
Two months
    As for one month, plus the Romantic Road, Harz Mountains, Münster, Ahr Valley, Mainz, Worms, Speyer, German Wine Road, Bamberg, Moselle Valley, Thuringian Forest, the southern Black Forest and one or two of the North Frisian Islands

PLANNING
When to Go
Any time can be the best time to visit Germany, depending on what you want to do. However, the climate can vary quite a bit according to the location, season and even the year, so it's best to be prepared for all types of weather at all times. The most reliable weather lasts from May to October, coinciding, of course, with the standard tourist season (except for skiing). The shoulder seasons can bring fewer tourists and surprisingly pleasant weather. In April and

May, for instance, flowers and fruit trees are in bloom, and the weather is often mild and sunny. Indian summers that stretch well into the autumn are not uncommon.

Eastern Germany lies in a transition zone between the temperate Atlantic climate of Western Europe and the harsher Continental climate of Eastern Europe, and the two air masses meet here. The mean annual temperature in Berlin is 11°C, the average range of temperatures varying from -1°C in January to 18°C in July. The average annual precipitation for all of Germany is 690mm and there is no special rainy season. The camping season generally runs from May to September, though some sites open as early as Easter and close in late/October or even November; a few remain open year round.

If you're keen on winter sports, ski resorts, slopes and cross-country trails in the Alps, Harz Mountains and Black Forest begin operating in November (usually late) and move into full swing after the New Year, closing down again when the snow begins to melt in March.

The Climate section and the Climate Charts in the preceding Facts about the Country chapter explain what to expect and when to expect it.

Maps

Locally produced maps of Germany are among the best in the world. Most tourist offices distribute free (but often very basic) city maps. Two auto associations, Allgemeiner Deutscher Automobil Club (ADAC) and Automobilclub von Deutschland (AvD), produce excellent road maps. More detailed maps can be obtained at most bookshops. Some of the best city maps are made by Falkplan, with a patented folding system, though some people prefer the one-sheet maps published by Hallwag or RV Verlag's EuroCity maps. If you are going to stay for a considerable length of time in any one city, you might invest in a street atlas such as the *Städteatlas* series, published by RV Verlag and available in bookshops and tourist offices everywhere in Germany.

What to Bring

Take along as little as possible; if you forget to bring it, you can buy it in Germany.

In general, standard dress in Germany is very casual, but fairly conservative outside the largest cities. Jeans are generally accepted throughout the country, though denim and trainers (sneakers) are banned at certain upmarket discos. Men needn't bother bringing a necktie; it will seldom – if ever – be used, except maybe at casinos. Layers of clothing are best, as weather can change drastically from region to region and from day to night.

If you plan to stay at hostels, pack or buy a towel and a plastic soap container when you arrive. Bedclothes are almost always provided (often at a fee), though you might want to take along your own sheet bag. You'll sleep easier with a padlock on one of the storage lockers usually provided at hostels.

Other items you might need include a torch (flashlight), an adaptor plug for electrical appliances (such as a cup or coil immersion heater to make your own tea or instant coffee), a universal bath/sink plug (a plastic film canister sometimes works), sunglasses, a few clothes pegs and premoistened towelettes or a large cotton handkerchief that you can soak in fountains and use to cool off while touring cities and towns in the warmer months.

TOURIST OFFICES

Tourism in Germany runs like the train system – very efficiently. Small and large tourist offices are incredibly helpful and well informed. Don't hesitate to make use of their services.

Local Tourist Offices

Germany's national tourist office (Deutsche Zentrale für Tourismus, or DZT) has its headquarters at Beethovenstrasse 69, 60325 Frankfurt-am-Main (☎ 069-97 46 40, fax 75 19 03). Its Web page is at www.german-tourism.de.

For local information, the office to head for in cities and towns throughout Germany is Tourist Information, sometimes also called *Verkehrsamt* or, in spa or resort towns, *Kurverwaltung* (resort administration). These are listed in the Information section of each town.

Tourist Offices Abroad

DZT branch and representative offices abroad include:

Australia
(☎ 02-9267 8148, fax 9267 9035)
PO Box A980, Sydney South, NSW 1235

Austria
(☎ 01-513 27 92, fax 513 27 92 22,
email 106167.3214@compuserve.com)
Schubertring 12, 1010 Vienna

Canada
(☎ 416-968 1570, fax 968 1986,
email germanto@idirect.com)
175 Bloor St East, North Tower, Suite 604,
Toronto, Ont M4W 3R8

France
(☎ 01 40 20 01 88, fax 01 40 20 17 00,
email gnto_par@compuserve.com)
9 Blvd de la Madeleine, 75001 Paris

Japan
(☎ 03-3586 5046, fax 3586 5079,
email dzt_tokyo@compuserve.com)
7-5-56 Akasaka, Minato-ku, Tokyo 107-0052

Netherlands
(☎ 020-697 8066, fax 691 2972,
email duitsland@compuserve.com)
Hoogoorddreef 76, 1101 BG Amsterdam ZO

Russia
(☎ 095-975 3001, fax 975 2383)
c/o Lufthansa German Airlines, Hotel Olympic Penta, Olimpiski prospekt 18/1, 129 110 Moscow

South Africa
(☎ 011-643 1615, fax 484 2750)
c/o Lufthansa German Airlines, 22 Girton Rd, Parktown, PO Box 10883, Johannesburg 2000

Switzerland
(☎ 01-213 22 00, fax 212 01 75,
email gnto_zrh@compuserve.com)
Talstrasse 62, 8001 Zürich

UK
(☎ 020-7317 0908, fax 7495 6129,
email 106167.3216@compuserve.com)
PO Box 2695, London W1A 3TN

USA
(☎ 212-661 7200, fax 661 7174)
Chanin Bldg, 122 East 42nd St, 52nd Floor,
New York, NY 10168-0072
(☎ 312-644 0723, fax 644 0724)
401 North Michigan Ave, Suite 2525,
Chicago, IL 60611

Additional offices are in Brussels, Budapest, Copenhagen, Helsinki, Hong Kong, Madrid, Mexico City, Milan, Oslo, Prague, São Paulo, Seoul, Stockholm, Tel Aviv and Warsaw.

VISAS & DOCUMENTS
Passport

Your most important travel document is your passport, which should remain valid until well after your trip. If it's just about to expire, renew it before you go. This may not be easy to do overseas, and some countries insist your passport remains valid for a specified minimum period (usually three months) after your visit.

Applying for or renewing a passport can be an involved process taking from a few days to several months, so don't leave it till the last minute. Bureaucracy usually grinds faster if you do everything in person rather than relying on the mail or agents. First, check what is required: passport photos, birth certificate, population register extract, signed statements, exact payment in cash etc.

Australian citizens can apply at post offices, or the passport office in their state capital; Canadians can apply at regional passport offices; New Zealanders can apply at any district office of the Department of Internal Affairs; and US citizens must apply in person (but may usually renew by mail) at a US Passport Agency office or some courthouses and post offices.

Visas

Citizens of Australia, Canada, Israel, Japan, New Zealand, Singapore and the USA require only a valid passport (no visa) to enter Germany for stays up to three months. European Union (EU) nationals and those from certain other European countries, including Switzerland and Poland, can enter on either a passport or their official identity card.

Nationals from most other countries need a so-called Schengen Visa, named after the Schengen Agreement that abolished passport controls between Austria, the Netherlands, Belgium, Luxembourg, Germany, France, Spain, Portugal, Italy and Greece. A visa for any of these countries should, in theory, be valid throughout the area, but it pays to double-check with the embassy or consulate of each country you intend to visit (the French in particular may be difficult). Residency status in any of the Schengen countries negates the need for a visa, regardless of your nationality.

Three-month tourist visas are issued by German embassies or consulates. They can take a while to be processed, so leave enough time before departure to apply. You'll need a valid passport and sufficient funds to finance your stay. Fees vary depending on the country.

Travel Insurance

No matter which way you're travelling to Germany, be sure to take out travel insurance. Depending on the scope of your coverage, this will protect you against sudden medical or legal expenses, luggage theft or loss, personal liability, and cancellation or delays. Before you take out any insurance, be certain that you understand all the ramifications and what to do in case you need to file a claim. Also check your medical policy at home, as some already provide coverage worldwide, in which case you only need to protect yourself against other problems (also see Health later in this chapter).

Buy travel insurance as early as possible. If you buy it the week before you leave, for example, you may find that you are not covered for delays to your trip caused by strikes or industrial action. Some policies also cover ticket loss, so be sure to keep a photocopy of your ticket in a separate place. It's also a good idea to make a copy of your policy, in case the original is lost.

Paying for your airline ticket with a credit card often provides limited travel accident insurance, and you may be able to reclaim the payment if the operator doesn't deliver. Ask your credit card company what it's prepared to cover.

Driving Licence

If you don't hold a European driving licence and plan to drive in Germany, obtain an International Driving Permit (IDP) from your local automobile association before you leave – you'll need a passport photo and a valid licence. They are usually inexpensive and valid for one year only. You're not required by law to carry an IDP when driving in Germany, but having one helps Germans make sense of your unfamiliar local licence (make sure you take that with you, too) and can make life much simpler, especially when hiring cars and motorcycles.

Camping Card International

Your local automobile association can also issue the Camping Card International, which is basically a camping ground ID. Cards are also available from your local camping federation, and sometimes on the spot at camping grounds. They incorporate third-party insurance for damage you may cause, and some camping grounds offer a small discount if you sign in with one.

Hostel Cards

You must be a member of a Hostelling International-affiliated organisation in order to stay at hostels run by the Deutsches Jugendherbergswerk (DJH). Non-Germans who don't have a HI card may obtain a so-called International Guest Card (IGC) at any hostel. It costs DM30 and is valid for one year. If you don't want it, DM6 per night will be added to your regular hostel rate; you'll be given a pass that is stamped once for each night and after six nights you automatically get the IGC. If you're German or have residency status in Germany, you can buy the DJH/HI cards at the hostel (DM21/DM34 for juniors/seniors) when checking in.

Independent hostels, usually called 'non-DJH hostel' in this guide, don't require a card, but in some cases you will be charged less if you have one.

Student & Youth Cards

The most useful of these is the International Student Identity Card (ISIC), a plastic ID-style card with your photograph, which provides discounts on many forms of transport (including airlines and local public transport), cheap or free admission to museums and sights, and cheap meals in some student restaurants.

If you're aged under 26 but you're not a student, you can apply for a GO25 card issued by the Federation of International Youth Travel Organisations (FIYTO) or the Euro<26 card, which go under different names in various countries. Both give much the same discounts and benefits as an ISIC.

All these cards are issued by student unions, hostelling organisations or youth-oriented travel agencies. They do not automatically entitle you to discounts, and some companies and institutions refuse to recognise them altogether, but you won't find out until you flash the card.

Photocopies

The hassles caused by losing your passport can be considerably reduced if you have a photocopy of the relevant data pages. Other documents to photocopy might include your airline ticket and credit cards. Also record the serial numbers of your travellers cheques (cross them off as you cash them).

Keep this emergency material separate from the original documents, along with a small amount of emergency cash. Leave extra copies with someone reliable at home. If your passport is stolen or lost, notify the police immediately, get a statement and contact your nearest embassy or consulate.

EMBASSIES & CONSULATES
Your Own Embassy

As a tourist, it's important to realise what your own embassy – the embassy of the country of which you are a citizen – can and can't do.

Generally speaking, it won't be much help in emergencies if the trouble you're in is remotely your own fault. Remember that you are bound by the laws of the country you're visiting. Your embassy will not be sympathetic if you end up in jail after committing a crime locally, even if such actions are legal in your own country.

In genuine emergencies you might get some assistance, but only if other channels

have been exhausted. For example, if you need to get home urgently, a free ticket home is exceedingly unlikely – the embassy would expect you to have insurance. If you have all your money and documents stolen, it might assist in getting a new passport, but a loan for onward travel is out of the question.

Embassies used to keep letters for travellers or have a small reading room with home newspapers, but these days the mail holding service has been stopped and even newspapers tend to be out of date.

German Embassies Abroad

German embassies around the world include the following:

Australia
  (☎ 02-6270 1911)
  119 Empire Circuit, Yarralumla, ACT 2600
Austria
  (☎ 0222-711 54)
  Metternichgasse 3, Vienna 3
Canada
  (☎ 613-232 1101)
  1 Waverley St, Ottawa, Ont K2P 0T8
France
  (☎ 01 53 83 45 00)
  13-15 Ave Franklin Roosevelt, 75008 Paris
Ireland
  (☎ 01-269 3011)
  31 Trimleston Ave, Booterstown, Dublin 4
Japan
  (☎ 03-3473 0151)
  4-5-10 Minami-Azabu, Minato-ku, Tokyo 106
Netherlands
  (☎ 070-342 0600)
  Groot Hertoginnelaan 18-20, 2517 EG The Hague
New Zealand
  (☎ 04-473 6063)
  90-92 Hobson St, Wellington
Russia
  (☎ 095-956 1080)
  Ul Mosfilmovskaya 56, 119285 Moscow
South Africa
  (☎ 012-427 8900)
  180 Blackwood St, Arcadia, Pretoria 0083
Switzerland
  (☎ 031-359 4111)
  Willadingweg 83, 3006 Bern
UK
  (☎ 020-7824 1300)
  23 Belgrave Square, London SW1X 8PZ

USA
  (☎ 202-298 4000)
  4645 Reservoir Rd NW, Washington, DC
  20007-1998

Embassies & Consulates in Germany

With the transfer of the German government from Bonn to Berlin in 1999, numerous diplomatic missions have followed suit and moved their embassies to the capital. For the moment, several countries are maintaining a diplomatic presence in Bonn, though some offices may have already closed by the time you read this. Consulates are also based in other major German cities like Hamburg, Düsseldorf and Munich.

Australia
  Embassy:
  (☎ 030-880 08 80)
  Uhlandstrasse 181-183, Berlin
  Embassy:
  (☎ 0228-810 30)
  Godesberger Allee 105-107, Bonn
Austria
  Embassy:
  (☎ 030-229 05 65)
  Friedrichstrasse 60, Berlin
  Embassy:
  (☎ 0228-53 00 60)
  Johanniterstrasse 2, Bonn
  Consulate:
  (☎ 089-99 81 50)
  Ismaninger Strasse 136, Munich
Belgium
  Embassy:
  (☎ 030-20 35 20)
  Friedrichstrasse 95, Berlin
  Consulate:
  (☎ 286 60 90)
  Brienner Strasse 14, Munich
Canada
  Embassy:
  (☎ 030-20 31 20)
  Friedrichstrasse 95, Berlin
  Embassy:
  (☎ 0228-96 80)
  Friedrich-Wilhelm-Strasse 18, Bonn
  Consulate:
  (☎ 089-219 95 70)
  Tal 29, Munich
Czech Republic
  Embassy:
  (☎ 030-22 63 80)
  Wilhelmstrasse 44, Berlin
  Embassy:
  (☎ 0228-919 70)
  Ferdinandstrasse 27, Bonn
  Consulate:
  (☎ 089-95 01 24/25/26)
  Siedlerstrasse 2, Unterföhring, Munich
Denmark
  Embassy:
  (☎ 030-25 00 10, visa
  information ☎ 030-229 28 83)
  Wichmannstrasse 5, Berlin
  Embassy:
  (☎ 0228-72 99 10)
  Pfälzer Strasse 14, Bonn
France
  Embassy:
  (☎ 030-204 39 90)
  Französische Strasse 23, Berlin
  Consulate:
  (☎ 030-88 59 02 43)
  Kurfürstendamm 211, Berlin
  Embassy:
  (☎ 0228-36 20 31 36)
  An der Marienkapelle 3, Bonn
  Consulate:
  (☎ 089-419 41 10)
  Möhlstrasse 5, Munich
Ireland
  Embassy:
  (☎ 030-34 80 08 22)
  Ernst-Reuter-Platz 10, Berlin
  Embassy:
  (☎ 0228-95 92 90)
  Godesberger Allee 119, Bonn
  Honorary Consulate:
  (☎ 089-98 57 23)
  Mauerkircherstrasse 1a, Munich
Japan
  Embassy:
  (☎ 030-819 12 57)
  Kleiststrasse 23, Berlin
  Embassy:
  (☎ 0228-819 10)
  Godesberger Allee 102-104, Bonn
  Consulate:
  (☎ 089-417 60 40)
  Prinzregentenplatz 10, Munich
Netherlands
  Embassy:
  (☎ 030-201 20 23)
  Friedrichstrasse 95, Berlin
  Embassy:
  (☎ 0228-530 50)
  Strässchensweg 10, Bonn
  Consulate:
  (☎ 089-545 96 70)
  Nymphenburger Strasse 1, Munich

New Zealand
  Embassy:
  (☎ 0228-22 80 70)
  Bundeskanzlerplatz 2-10, Bonn
Poland
  Embassy:
  (☎ 030-220 25 51)
  Unter den Linden 72-74, Berlin
  Consulate:
  (☎ 089-418 60 80)
  Ismaninger Strasse 62a, Munich
Russia
  Embassy:
  (☎ 030-229 11 10)
  Unter den Linden 63-65, Berlin
  Consulate:
  (☎ 030-229 12 07)
  Behrenstrasse 66, Berlin
  Consulate:
  (☎ 0228-31 20 74)
  Waldstrasse 42, Bonn
  Consulate:
  (☎ 089-59 25 28)
  Seidlstrasse 28, Munich
Slovakia
  Embassy:
  (☎ 030-204 45 38)
  Leipziger Strasse 36, Berlin
  Embassy:
  (☎ 0228 91 45 50)
  August-Bier-Strasse 31, Bonn
  Consulate:
  (☎ 089-910 20 60)
  Vollmannstrasse 25d, Munich
South Africa
  Embassy:
  (☎ 030-394 40 21)
  Douglasstrasse 9, Berlin
  Embassy:
  (☎ 0228-820 10)
  Auf der Hostert 3, Bonn
Switzerland
  Embassy:
  (☎ 030-394 41 21)
  Kirchstrasse 13, Berlin
  Embassy:
  (☎ 0228-81 00 80)
  Gotenstrasse 156, Bonn
  Consulate:
  (☎ 089-286 62 00)
  Brienner Strasse 14, Munich
UK
  Embassy:
  (☎ 030-20 18 40)
  Unter den Linden 32-34, Berlin
  Consulate:
  (☎ 089-21 10 90; also for Australian nationals

during Oktoberfest)
  Bürkleinstrasse 10, Munich
USA
  Embassy:
  (☎ 030-238 51 74)
  Neustädtische Kirchstrasse 4-5, Berlin
  Consulate:
  (☎ 030-832 92 33)
  Clayallee 170, Berlin
  Consulate:
  (☎ 089-288 80, ☎ 089-288 87 22 for US
  citizen services and passport issues)
  Königinstrasse 5, Munich
  Visa Information Service
  (☎ 0190-91 50 00, DM2.42/minute)

CUSTOMS

Articles that you take to Germany for your personal use may be imported free of duty and tax with some conditions. The usual allowances apply to *duty-free goods* purchased at the airport or on ferries:

Tobacco
  200 cigarettes or 100 cigarillos or 50 cigars or 250g of loose tobacco
Alcohol
  1L of strong liquor or 2L of less than 22% alcohol by volume *and* 2L of wine
Coffee & Tea
  500g or 200g of extracts *and* 100g of tea or 40g tea extracts
Perfume
  50g of perfume or scent *and* 0.25L of eau de toilette
Additional products up to a value of DM350

Tobacco products and alcohol may only be brought in by people aged 17 and over; the importation of duty-free coffee, oddly, is barred to those under 15. There are no currency import restrictions.

Do not confuse these with *duty-paid* items (including alcohol and tobacco) bought at normal shops and supermarkets in another EU country and brought into Germany, where certain goods might be more expensive. Then the allowances are more than generous: 800 cigarettes, 200 cigars, or 1kg of loose tobacco; 10L of spirits (more than 22% alcohol by volume), 20L of fortified wine or aperitif, 90L of wine or 110L of beer; and petrol reserves of up to 10L.

Note that duty-free shopping within the EU was abolished in mid-1999. This means that you can still enter a EU country, like Germany with duty-free items, from another country like the United States or Australia, but you can't buy duty-free goods in, say, France and go to the United Kingdom.

MONEY
Currency

The German Mark, or Deutschmark (DM), usually just called the Mark or D-Mark (pronounced 'day-mark'), consists of 100 Pfennig. Coins include one, two, five, 10 and 50 Pfennigs, as well as DM1, DM2 and DM5. There are banknotes of DM5, DM10, DM20, DM50, DM100, DM200, DM500 and DM1000.

Exchange Rates

country	unit		Deutschmark
Australia	A$1	=	DM1.23
Austria	AS1	=	DM0.14
Belgium	fl	=	DM0.05
Canada	C$1	=	DM1.29
Czech Republic	1Kč	=	DM0.05
Denmark	1Dkr	=	DM0.26
euro	€1	=	DM1.96
France	1FF	=	DM0.30
Japan	¥100	=	DM1.81
Netherlands	fl	=	DM0.89
New Zealand	NZ$1	=	DM0.99
Poland	1zł	=	DM0.45
South Africa	R1	=	DM0.31
Switzerland	Sfr	=	DM1.22
UK	UK£1	=	DM3.04
USA	US$1	=	DM1.89

Introducing the euro

On 1 January 1999 a new currency, the euro, was introduced in Europe. It's all part of the harmonisation of the European Union (EU) countries. Along with national border controls, the currencies of various EU members are being phased out. Not all EU members have agreed to adopt the euro, however: Denmark, Greece, Sweden and the UK rejected or postponed participation. The 11 countries which have participated from the beginning of the process are Austria, Belgium, Finland, France, Germany, Ireland, Italy, Luxembourg, the Netherlands, Portugal and Spain.

The timetable for the introduction of the euro runs as follows:

- On 1 January 1999 the exchange rates of the participating countries were irrevocably fixed to the euro. The euro came into force for 'paper' accounting and prices could be displayed in local currency and in euros.
- On 1 January 2002 euro banknotes and coins will be introduced. This ushers in a period of dual use of euros and existing local notes and coins (which will, in effect, simply be temporary denominations of the euro).
- By July 2002 local currencies in the 11 countries will be withdrawn. Only euro notes and coins will remain in circulation and prices will be displayed in euros only.

The €5 note in France is the same €5 note you will use in Italy and Portugal. There will be seven euro notes. In different colours and sizes, they come in denominations of 500, 200, 100, 50, 20, 10 and five euros. There are eight euro coins, in denominations of two and one euros, then 50, 20, 10, five, two and one cents. On the reverse side of the coins each participating state will be able to decorate the coins with their own designs, but all euro coins can be used anywhere that accepts euros.

So, what does all this mean for the traveller? It is somewhat uncertain exactly what practices will be adopted between 1999 and 2002, and travellers will probably find differences in 'euro-readiness' between different countries, between different towns in the same country,

Exchanging Money

The easiest places to change money are banks or foreign-exchange counters at the airport and train stations. Post offices often have money-changing facilities as well, and rates for cash – though not for travellers cheques – tend to be better than at banks. Commissions here are DM2 for cash transactions if the exchanged amount is under DM200, and no fee if it's higher. Travellers cheques cost a flat DM6 each.

At banks and exchange offices, the charge is usually between DM5 and DM10 per transaction. Some banks have currency exchange machines outside the main entrance but they don't give very good rates.

Cash Nothing beats cash for convenience ... or risk. If you lose it, it's gone forever and very few travel insurers will come to your rescue. Those that will, limit the amount to about US$300.

It's still a good idea, though, to bring some local currency in cash, if only to tide you over until you get to an exchange facility or find an automatic teller machine (ATM). The equivalent of, say, US$50 should usually be enough. Remember that banks and exchange offices always accept paper money but very rarely coins in foreign currencies.

Travellers Cheques The main idea of carrying travellers cheques rather than cash is the protection they offer from theft, though their popularity is waning as more travellers – including those on tight budgets – deposit their money in their bank at

Introducing the euro

or between different establishments in the same town. It is certain, however, that euro cheque accounts and travellers cheques will be available. Credit card companies can bill in euros, and shops, hotels and restaurants might list prices in both local currency and euros. Travellers should check bills carefully to make sure that any conversion from local currency to euros has been calculated correctly. The most confusing period will probably be between January 2002 and July 2002, when there will be two sets of notes and coins.

Luckily for travellers, the euro should make everything easier. One of the main benefits will be that prices in the 11 countries will be immediately comparable, avoiding all those tedious calculations.

Also, once euro notes and coins are issued in 2002, you won't need to change money at all when travelling to other single-currency members. Banks may still charge a handling fee (yet to be decided) for travellers cheques, but they won't be able to profit by buying the currency from you at one rate and selling it back to you at another, as they do at the moment. However, even EU countries not participating may price goods in euros and accept euros over shop counters.

There are many Web sites dealing with the introduction of the euro but most are devoted to the legal implications and the processes by which businesses may adapt to the single currency, and are not particularly interesting or informative for the traveller. The Lonely Planet Web site, www.lonelyplanet.com, has a link to a currency converter and up-to-date news on the integration process.

Australia	A$1	=	€0.62	Japan	¥100	=	€0.92
Canada	C$1	=	€0.65	New Zealand	NZ$1	=	€0.50
France	1FF	=	€0.15	UK	UK£1	=	€1.55
Germany	DM1	=	€0.51	USA	US$1	=	€0.96

euro currency converter DM1 = €0.51

home and withdraw it as they go along through ATMs.

Travellers cheques are *not* commonly used to pay for store-bought goods, at restaurants or hotels, especially if they are not issued in Deutschmarks. Cheques issued in any other currency must be exchanged into local currency at a bank, exchange office or post office (bring your passport). Most commonly recognised are American Express and Thomas Cook cheques, and neither company charges commission for exchanges at their own offices. Both also have efficient replacement policies.

Eurocheques Using guaranteed personal cheques is another way of carrying money or obtaining cash. Eurocheques cover a maximum of DM400. Until recently, they have been widely accepted in Germany, but their popularity is decreasing because of the high commission (DM4 to DM6 per cheque) charged by banks.

ATMs Automatic teller machines are ubiquitous in Germany, though occasionally you may have to swipe your card through an entry slot to gain entry to a secure area. Most machines take Visa and MasterCard, and if your bank at home is part of the Cirrus, Plus or Maestro systems, you'll be able to use your ATM card to withdraw money right out of your home bank account. Check the fees and availability of services with your bank before you leave. Always keep the number handy for reporting lost or stolen cards.

Credit Cards All the major international cards – eg MasterCard, Visa and American Express – are recognised but still not widely accepted, except at major hotels, petrol stations and large shops and department stores. Don't assume that you'll be able to pay for your meal, room or purchase with a card. Some shops may require a minimum purchase, while others may refuse to accept a credit card even if the credit card companies' logos are displayed in the window. Nevertheless, it can't hurt to take your card along, if only for emergencies or for renting a car.

Check with your credit card issuer about fees and interest rates for cash withdrawals through ATMs.

International Transfers Money sent by wire transfer from your bank to a bank in Germany should reach you within a week. Note that some banks charge an exorbitant amount just for receiving the money (fees of up to DM50 are common), unless you have an account with them. Opening an account, however, may well be impractical or even impossible to do.

For emergencies, Western Union or MoneyGram offer ready and fast international cash transfers through agent banks such as Postbank or Reisebank. Cash sent becomes available as soon as the order has been entered into the computer system, ie instantly. Commissions are paid by the person making the transfer; the amount varies from country to country. Count on about US$40 for amounts up to US$300 and US$70 for amounts over US$500 but under US$1000.

Costs

Naturally, it's easy to spend lots of money in Germany and a bit harder to spend little. The secret to spending less is to cut costs where you can, such as with accommodation and food. Hostels, private rooms and simple pensions all cost well under DM50 per person.

Buying passes keeps public transport costs way down (see the Getting Around chapter). Students with valid ID (see Student & Youth Cards earlier in this chapter), seniors and children are usually eligible for discounted prices. Unless otherwise stated, prices for tickets and admissions in this book reflect this adult/concession distinction.

If you're very economical, you can expect to survive on DM60 to DM90 per day. If you can afford to spend twice that, you can start living quite comfortably. Accommodation costs tend to be higher in the eastern states, though this is usually compensated by lower food and entertainment costs. Preparing your own meal or getting food from an *Imbiss* (snack bar) can save you a bundle, and many cafes and restaurants have small, inexpensive dishes that are tasty and filling. Avoid having lots of drinks, since even nonalcoholic beverages tend to be quite expensive.

Tipping & Bargaining

At restaurants, the service charge (Bedienung) is always included in bills and tipping is not compulsory. If you're satisfied with the service, simply round up the amount by 5 to 10%. (Also see the boxed text 'Eating Out' later in this chapter.) Taxi drivers, too, expect a small tip. In general, a tip of 10% is considered generous.

Bargaining almost never occurs in Germany, certainly not in shops or restaurants. At hotels, you can sometimes ask for a lower rate which you may get if business is slow. Haggling is commonplace, however, at flea markets and you should be able to get at least 10 to 25% off the asking price as long as you appear confident. Prices at produce markets are usually not negotiable, though vendors may throw in an extra tomato or two towards the end of the day.

Taxes & Refunds

Most German goods and services include a value-added tax (VAT) called Mehrwertsteuer (or MwSt) of 16%. Non-EU residents leaving the EU can have this tax (minus processing fee) refunded for goods (not services) bought, which is definitely worth it for large purchases.

Check that the shop where you're buying has the necessary Tax-Free Shopping Cheque forms. The shop will issue you a cheque for the VAT amount to be refunded, which you can cash in at VAT Cash Refund offices when leaving the country. Before you can get your money, the Tax-Free Shopping Cheque, together with the invoices/receipts, must be stamped by German customs as you're leaving the country. You're not allowed to use the items purchased until you're outside of Germany.

If you want to avoid the lines at the VAT Cash Refund office, you can mail the stamped forms and receipts to them after you return home and ask that the refund be issued to your credit card or mailed as a cheque.

If you are unable to obtain the necessary seal or stamp before leaving Germany, you may obtain it at a German embassy or consulate in your home country. The items purchased must be shown to a mission official and sales slips, tax forms and passport must be presented.

Some 17,000 shops, including Germany's biggest department stores, are affiliated with the Tax-Free Shopping Cheque service; they can be identified by a special label on their window reading 'Tax-Free for Tourists'. Printed information is available at affiliated shops, some tourist offices, major hotels, airports and harbours.

POST & COMMUNICATIONS

Main post offices in larger cities are usually open from 8 am to 6 pm on weekdays and till noon on Saturday. Occasionally, there will be a late counter offering limited services up to 8 pm, and to 2 pm on Saturday. In major cities, the main post office may also open for an hour or so on Sunday morning. Branch offices in the suburbs, or those in small towns and villages, close during lunchtime and at 5 or 5.30 pm. You'll often find main post offices located at or near the main train station.

Stamps are sold at post offices only, though there may be stamp machines outside the main entrance. Occasionally, souvenir and postcard shops in tourist resorts also carry stamps.

Letters sent within Germany usually take only one day for delivery; those addressed to destinations within Europe or to North America take four to six days, and to Australasia five to seven days. Most post offices also exchange currency and travellers cheques, and are a good place to fall back on when the banks are closed (see the Exchanging Money section earlier in this chapter).

Postal Rates

Within Germany and the EU, normal-sized postcards cost DM1, a 20g letter is DM1.10 and a 50g letter is DM2.20. Postcards to North America and Australasia cost DM2, a 20g airmail letter is DM3 and a 50g airmail letter is DM4. If the postcard or letter is oversized, there is a significant surcharge, sometimes up to triple the base rate. German postal workers can be very finicky about this and are bound to measure any letter that looks even remotely nonstandard. A parcel up to 2kg within Germany costs DM6.90. Surface-mail parcels up to 2kg within Europe are DM12 and to destinations elsewhere DM15. Fees for airmail parcels depend on weight and destination. For instance, a 2kg parcel sent to somewhere within Europe is DM38, to the US it costs DM71 and to Australia DM91.

Sending & Receiving Mail

Mail can be sent poste restante to any post office (select one, then inquire about the exact address). German post offices will hold mail for only two weeks, so plan your drops carefully. Ask those sending you mail to clearly mark the letter or package *Postlagernd* and to write your name, followed by the address of the post office. Remember to bring your passport or other photo ID when picking up mail. There is no fee for this service.

You can also have mail sent to American Express offices in large cities, a free service if you have an American Express card or travellers cheques (otherwise it's DM2 per item). Make sure you include the words 'Client's Mail' somewhere on the envelope. American Express holds mail for 30 days but won't accept registered mail or parcels.

Note that the German equivalent of PO Box is *Postfach*.

Telephone

Making phone calls in Germany is simple. You can make international phone calls from just about any post office, but it's cheaper and more convenient to go to a pay phone and use phonecards that allow you to make calls of any length to anywhere in the world. If you're calling abroad, look for a pay phone marked 'International'.

Most public phones in Germany accept only phonecards nowadays, which saves you carrying around a pocketful of change. To cover contingencies, though, it's a good idea to carry both a card and a few coins.

Cards are sold at post offices and occasionally at tourist offices, news kiosks and public transport offices.

German phonecards are available for DM12 and for DM50. When using coins or the DM12 card, call units cost DM0.20; with the DM50 card it's DM0.19 per unit. If you can, refrain from calling from your hotel room, since you'll often be charged DM0.60 or even DM0.80 per unit. You can save considerably if the person you want to contact is willing to call you back. Just place a short call to relay your hotel and room number and tell whoever is calling you back to dial their international access code plus 4930 and that number. You can do the same thing from pay phones that also receive calls by passing on the number next to the notation '*Standort*' (location) somewhere in the box/booth.

Also note that calls made *to* cellular phones cost a lot more than those to a stationary number, though how much more depends on the service used by the cellular-phone owner. Numbers starting with 0130 are toll-free.

There's a wide range of local and international phonecards. Lonely Planet's eKno Communication Card (see the insert at the back of this book) is aimed specifically at travellers and provides cheap international calls, a range of messaging services and free email – for local calls, you're usually better off with a local card. You can join online at www.ekno.lonelyplanet.com, or by phone from Germany by dialling ☎ 0800 000 7138. Once you have joined, to use eKno from Germany, dial ☎ 0800 000 7139.

For directory assistance within Germany, dial ☎ 11833; for numbers abroad it's ☎ 11834.

Telephone Rates Since the monopoly status enjoyed by Deutsche Telecom (DT) was lifted on 1 January 1998, a bewildering number of other long-distance providers have entered the market, driving prices down. (DT retains its grip on local calls.) In most cases, getting the low rates means dialling a five digit access number before the number you're trying to reach. This only works from private lines and *not* from pay phones, which are all owned by DT (so far).

Faced with competition, DT has also lowered rates, though these still do not apply to calls made from pay phones! This means that, for now, travellers will continue to depend on DT and their incredibly confusing rate plan divided into zones and time periods.

How long you can talk per phone unit depends on where and when you are calling. Assuming a DM0.20 per unit pay-phone rate, a three minute call from, say, Berlin to Munich made at 3 pm on a weekday costs DM3; the same call after 9 pm costs DM1.60. If you're in Cologne and calling Düsseldorf, you pay DM1.20 at 3 pm and DM0.80 after 9 pm for three minutes.

International calls are also subject to zones and time periods. Reduced rates are available after 6 pm and before 8 am to EU countries, and between 3 am and 2 pm to the USA and Canada. Calls to Australia and New Zealand cost the same all day. The length of time you can talk per unit is:

country	standard rates	reduced rates
Australia/NZ	3 seconds	3 seconds
EU countries	7.2 seconds	9 seconds
USA/Canada	5 seconds	5.46 seconds

In other words, a three minute call to the USA will cost you DM7.20 (DM6.60 reduced), to an EU country DM5 (DM4 reduced) and to Australia DM12 (any time).

To ring abroad from Germany, dial ☎ 00 followed by the country and local area codes and number. The country code for Germany is 49.

A reverse-charge call (or *R-Gespräch*) from Germany is only possible to a limited number of countries. For calls through the German operator, dial ☎ 0010. To reach the operator direct in the USA and Canada, dial ☎ 0130 followed by ☎ 0010 (AT&T), ☎ 0012 (MCI), ☎ 0013 (Sprint) or ☎ 0014 (Canada). To Australia, dial ☎ 0130 80 06 61 for the Optus operator and ☎ 0130 80 00 61 for Telstra.

Fax & Telegraph

If you're staying at upmarket hotels, fax transmissions are generally not a problem. There's usually no fee for receiving faxes, though sending them can cost you a bundle, so it pays to check in advance. Most copy shops will also let you send faxes, as will some Internet cafes.

If you carry a laptop with a fax modem, you only pay for the cost of the telephone call (keep in mind that hotel phone rates are exorbitant). Cheaper, in most cases, is the use of public fax phones now in place at larger post offices. These operate with a phonecard from which the regular cost of the call, plus a DM2 service charge, is deducted if the connection succeeds. Occasionally you can also find public fax phones in train stations.

If you need to send a telegram, you can do so at post offices, from many hotels, or by calling ☎ 01805 12 12 10/11 (for telegrams sent within Germany) or ☎ 0800 330 11 33 (outside Germany). Within Germany, up to 10 words costs DM29, while up to 30 words is DM35. Up to 20 words within Europe costs DM40, and outside Europe it's DM50.

Email & Internet Access

In order to maintain your Internet connectivity while in Germany, you can buy online time at an Internet cafe usually for around DM5 to DM7 per half hour. These are listed under various cities throughout this book.

Alternatively, you can bring along your laptop PC and modem and dial your home country service provider (or even take out a local account).

Getting your modem to work with German phone lines can be quite frustrating. German phone plugs are rather unique and you're quite likely to need an adaptor to get online. It's best to pick one up in your home country, though they're also sold at electronics stores in Germany. There are usually no problems getting connected from a line in a private home. At some hotels, however, you'll find that the phone cable is wired right into the wall and/or the phone itself. Larger hotels sometimes have digital

(ISDN) lines or complex internal phone systems that require you to make changes to your modem string in order to get an outside line. Finding competent help is almost impossible. It's best to contact your service provider before leaving home to see if it can offer any specific advice about Germany.

INTERNET RESOURCES

There's a bewildering amount of information on all aspects of Germany (culture, travel, education, institutions etc) on the Internet. Most towns have their own Web site, the most useful of which are also listed in this book. You can look for them via the usual search engines. Most of the sites listed here also provide useful cross links.

Please note that Web site addresses, though correct at press time, are particularly prone to change.

www.germany-info.org
Run by the German Information Center in New York and the German Embassy in Washington, this site is packed with useful general information and links to just about everything, be it language or exchange programs, German media, the postal-code directory, political foundations, business, law and, of course, travel (in English).

www.germany-tourism.de
Information on travel in Germany from the German National Tourist Office (in English and German)

www.ltu.com
Comprehensive travel guide with sections on arts, entertainment and shopping (in English)

www.tii.de
Operated by Tourismus Internet Info, this site offers general travel information, background reports on regions and cities. It's constantly updated (in English and German).

www.hotelstravel.com
Primarily a hotel directory, this site also provides general travel information, maps and links (in English).

www.dwelle.de/english
English news from Deutsche Welle (in English)

www.goethe.de
Site of the nonprofit Goethe Institut language and cultural centres, with info on German-language courses in Germany and around the world (in English)

BOOKS

Most books are published in different editions by different publishers in different countries. As a result, a book might be a hardcover rarity in one country while it's readily available in paperback in another. Fortunately, bookshops and libraries can search by title or author, so your local bookshop or library is the best place to find out about the availability of the following recommendations.

Lonely Planet

Lonely Planet's *Central Europe*, *Western Europe* and *Europe on a shoestring* all include a big Germany chapter for those on a grand 'shoestring' tour, in which case the *Central Europe phrasebook* might also come in handy. Lonely Planet also publishes a *German phrasebook*. For those spending more time in Germany, LP's city guides *Berlin* and *Munich* should be useful.

Guidebooks

Those able to read German will find a seemingly endless choice of guidebooks, many of which focus on just one region or city. Cultural guidebooks are very popular, and any German speaker with a special interest in architecture and the arts should pick up a copy of *Knaurs Kulturführer*.

The Falk Verlag, best known for its excellent maps, also publishes a series of magazine-sized guidebooks that are most useful for getting a pictorial overview of a particular area (DM14.80). In the same vein are the *Bildatlas* published by HB Verlag (DM14.80).

The DCC *Campingführer, Europa* series is one of the best annual camping guides on the market, with special entries on environmentally friendly camping grounds and those set in particularly attractive surroundings.

Travel

A Tramp Abroad by Mark Twain includes chapters on Germany during one of the author's two visits in the 1880s. In his postscript 'The Awful German Language', he wittily vents his spleen on the language.

The Temple by Stephen Spender is an autobiographical novel by one of Britain's most celebrated 20th century poets. It was reworked from a 1929 draft based on time the author spent in Germany during the Weimar Republic. *European Witness*, by the same author, picks up the threads in 1945, when Spender travelled the Rhine region and the British zone of occupation.

From the same school of writing comes *Mr Norris Changes Trains* and *Goodbye to Berlin* by Christopher Isherwood, which are ideal for those interested in literary or semi-autobiographical accounts of life in Berlin during the Weimar Republic.

In a German Pension by Katherine Mansfield is a collection of short stories by this New Zealand-born author, whose great skill in extracting meaning out of vignettes makes it a worthwhile read.

History & Politics

General *The Origins of Modern Germany* by Geoffrey Barraclough is an excellent introduction to the complex history of this country. *A History of Modern Germany* by Hajo Holborn is a three volume work that begins with the 15th century and traces developments up to the division in 1945. *The German Empire 1871-1918* by Hans-Ulrich Wehler is a translation of an authoritative German work on the period from Bismarck to the Weimar Republic. Another highly readable translation is *The History of Germany since 1789* by Golo Mann. *Germany 1866-1945* by Gordon Craig is also worthwhile as a general overview.

Bismarck, the Man and the Statesman by the same author is a revealing study of the Iron Chancellor placed in historical context. *The Wars of Frederick the Great* by Dennis Showalter focuses on 18th century Prussia.

Of the books dealing with Martin Luther, *Here I Stand* by Roland Bainton is one of the best. *Young Man Luther* by Eric Erikson focuses on Luther's early development from a psychoanalytical perspective.

The Great War, 1914-18 by Marc Ferro is considered one of the best books on WWI. *The Struggle for Europe* by Chester Wilmot

is an interesting account of WWI by a British journalist who was in the thick of things. *German Liberalism and the Dissolution of the Weimar Party System* by Larry E Jones is recommended for those interested in the politics of the 1920s.

Third Reich Naturally there's a plethora of English-language books about Nazi Germany, a subject that continues to inspire enormous fascination. *The Rise and Fall of the Third Reich* by William Shirer remains one of the most powerful works of reportage ever written. His portrait of the Berlin of those times – a city which he loved, grew to fear and eventually fled – is the literary equivalent of the brutal north face of the Eiger.

Inside the Third Reich by Albert Speer, Hitler's architect and confidant, is one of the best books about the day-to-day operations of the Führer's inner clique.

The Fall of Berlin by Anthony Read & David Fisher is considered one of the standards on the subject of the apocalyptic last days of the war and the Wagnerian death of Adolf Hitler. Still, the defining work on the subject is *The Last Days of Hitler* by Hugh Trevor-Roper, in which much idle speculation about Hitler's ultimate fate is firmly laid to rest. The writing style is atrocious but forgivable: it was written by a young intelligence officer in 1947. *The Road to Berlin* by John Erickson is an exhaustive military chronicle of the Soviet persecution of the war against the Nazis.

Another worthwhile book is the classic *Hitler: A Study in Tyranny* by Allan Bullock. *Hitler and Stalin: Parallel Lives* is a related work by this highly respected historian.

The Origins of the Second World War by AJP Taylor is another good work by the well known British historian, and *The Longest Day* by Cornelius Ryan is an account of the D-Day landings.

The Holocaust by Martin Gilbert is one of the best general histories on the subject, whereas *A Train of Powder* by Rebecca West is one of the most informative books on the Nuremberg trials. *Hitler's Willing*

euro currency converter DM1 = €0.51

Executioners by Daniel Goldhagen provides a controversial analysis of who was responsible for the Holocaust.

GDR & Cold War Books providing glimpses into the life and times of the GDR include *Man Without a Face: The Memoirs of a Spymaster* by Markus Wolf & Anne McElvoy. It is the autobiography of Wolf, who was the enormously successful chief of East Germany's intelligence services, the hated Stasi, and sort of an admirable monster. For a more withering look at Wolf, read *Spymaster: The Real Life Karla* by Leslie Colitt.

Berlin and the Wall by Ann Tusa is a saga about the events, trials and triumphs of the Cold War, the building of the Wall and its effects on the people and the city of Berlin. *Anatomy of a Dictatorship* by Mary Fulbrook focuses on East Germany from 1949 to its collapse in 1989. *The Adenauer Era* by Richard Hiscocks examines the period under Germany's postwar political architect.

Reunification *After the Wall* by Marc Fisher is an interesting book on German society, with great emphasis on life after the *Wende* (fall of communism). Fisher was bureau chief for the *Washington Post* in Bonn and gives us some perceptive social insights. It is both a professional and personal account.

Germany and the Germans by John Ardagh has been revised since reunification and is highly recommended for anyone interested in finding out how the country and its people tick. *The Rush to German Unity* by Konrad H Jarausch is more academic, mostly focusing on the 1989-90 period.

Society *The Germans* by Gordon A Craig is one of the most intelligent books available on German life and an excellent introduction to the country's politics, religion, the Jews, women, academic life and literature, dealt with from a historical perspective. It concludes with a chapter on the German language, playing on Mark Twain's ironic contribution.

Special Interest

Art *Artists and Revolution: Dada and the Bauhaus, 1917-25* by Allan C Greenberg is an informative look at the Bauhaus movement and art in the Weimar Republic.

New German Cinema: A History by Thomas Elsaesser covers the area of German films from 1950 to 1980.

Art as History: Episodes in the Culture and Politics of Nineteenth Century Germany by Peter Paret is for more serious art buffs, as is *The Classical Centre: Goethe and Weimar, 1775-1832* by TJ Reed.

Brecht: A Choice of Evils by Martin Esslin is highly recommended for anyone interested in Brecht and Germany's cultural scene in the 1920s. *Bertolt Brecht: Chaos According to Plan* by John Fuegi focuses on Brecht's methods.

FILMS

For a detailed discussion of films by local film-makers, see the Arts section in the Facts about Germany chapter.

NEWSPAPERS & MAGAZINES

German Germany has only a few national daily newspapers, none of them very good. The most widely read are the sensationalist *Bild* (actual headline: 'Sex Waves From Space!') and the conservative *Die Welt. Die Zeit* is an excellent weekly newspaper with in-depth reporting on everything from politics to fashion.

Regional daily papers with national appeal include the *Süddeutsche Zeitung* of Munich and Berlin's *Die Tageszeitung*, both fine, centrist and respected. Also widely read is the *Frankfurter Allgemeine Zeitung*.

Der Spiegel and *Focus*, both popular weekly magazines, offer hard-hitting investigative journalism, a certain degree of government criticism, and other deep thoughts between covers often featuring scantily clad models. *Stern* used to be similar but has become more lightweight and trivial in its coverage.

English You'll almost always find English-language newspapers and magazines in the newsstands at major city train stations, and increasingly in smaller towns as well. They are almost exclusively from the UK and USA, though in very big cities you'll find papers from all over the world.

The *International Herald Tribune*, edited in Paris with wire stories from the *New York Times* and *Washington Post*, is the most commonly available English-language daily paper and sells for DM3.50.

The biggies on offer from the UK include the *Guardian* (DM3.80), the *Financial Times* (DM4.30), the *London Times* (DM5), as well as tabloids like the *Daily Mail* and the *Sun*. From the USA, *USA Today* (DM3.50) has made huge inroads, and the *Wall Street Journal* (DM4.20) is also available.

The *Economist* (DM8) is a magazine that's on sale widely, as are the international editions of *Time* (DM6.80) and *Newsweek* (DM6.90). In addition, practically the whole gamut of women's, car, lifestyle and speciality magazines is available. *Spotlight* (DM9) is a monthly English-language magazine for Germans who want to learn English, with good feature articles and travel pieces.

RADIO

German radio is much like that of many other western countries. Pop, rock, adult contemporary and oldies dominate, with classical and opera offerings at the lower end of the dial. The inevitable Morning Zoo format is in great vogue here, so during commuting time you're bound to hear jovial German DJs giggling, honking horns and making fart noises.

The BBC World Service (on varying AM and FM wavelengths depending on which part of the country you happen to be in) and National Public Radio (NPR; available via cable channel 22) have radio programs in English. NPR is also available on AM radio in and around Frankfurt and Berlin. It features the excellent international news program *Morning Edition* daily from noon to 3 pm.

The American Armed Forces Radio & Television Service (AAFRTS) is available

in parts of southern Germany on the AM dial; it offers news broadcasts read by US service people. In North Rhine-Westphalia and other western states, the British BFBS offers much the same.

TV

Several English-language channels can now be received in Germany. The quality of the reception, though, depends on the location, on whether the TV is hooked up to cable or to a satellite dish and on the quality of the TV set. In theory, you can get BBC World, CNN, the Sky Channel and CNBC.

Germany has two national (public) channels, the ARD (Erstes Deutsches Fernsehen) and ZDF (Zweites Deutsches Fernsehen). In addition, there are the 'Dritten Programme', regional stations like the Cologne-based WDR (Westdeutscher Rundfunk) and the Munich-based BR (Bayrischer Rundfunk).

Generally, programming is quite highbrow, with lots of political coverage, discussion forums and foreign films. Advertising is limited to the two hours between 6 and 8 pm when it is shown in eight to 10-minute blocks roughly every half an hour.

These channels can usually be easily received with a TV antenna; no cable connection or satellite dish is necessary.

Private TV stations have proliferated in Germany in recent years. They offer the familiar array of sitcoms and soap operas (including many dubbed US shows), chat and game shows and, of course, feature films of all kinds. DSF and EuroSport are dedicated sports channels, and MTV and its German equivalent VIVA can also be received. Commercial breaks are frequent on these stations.

Overall, the content of private TV is very liberal. One recent ad for margarine featured a completely nude young couple enthusiastically engaged in the act of coupling. There are frequent 'documentaries' about bizarre sexual behaviour that come within a hair of being all-out XXX. One very popular show is hosted by an elegant transvestite. And you have to wonder what

Mum and Dad might think when watching a 13-year-old girl advising her peers on successful orgasm techniques.

A recent development are several Turkish-language channels that cater for Germany's large population with roots in Turkey. Don't expect religious programming, though! Scantily clad women and explicit subjects are just as commonplace here as they are on German-language TV.

In order to receive most of these private channels, a cable connection or satellite dish is required. These are ubiquitous and you'll rarely find a hotel or private home without access to at least 15 different channels.

Those living near another European country are usually able to receive programming from there as well. You'll see Polish TV in Saxony and Brandenburg, Danish TV in Schleswig-Holstein, Dutch TV in North Rhine-Westphalia and Italian TV in Bavaria. Of these, the most interesting to English speakers is Dutch TV, which usually shows American or British movies, soaps and sitcoms in the original language with Dutch subtitles.

VIDEO SYSTEMS

German video and TV operates on the PAL (Phase Alternative Line) system, predominant in most of Europe and Australia. It is not compatible with the American and Japanese NTSC or French SECAM standards, so prerecorded videotapes bought in countries using those standards won't play in Germany and vice versa. Dual standard VCRs, which play back NTSC and PAL (but only record in PAL), are available in better electronics and duty-free shops; you should expect to pay somewhere around DM500 for a decent one. A standard VHS tape costs about DM6 to DM10, depending on the brand.

PHOTOGRAPHY & VIDEO

Germany is a photographer's dream, with the Bavarian Alps in the south, the stark North Sea and Baltic Sea coasts in the north, and countless castles and picturesque old towns.

Film & Equipment

German photographic equipment is among the best in the world, and all makes and types are readily available, as are those manufactured in other countries. Print film is sold at supermarkets and chemists, but for B&W and slide film you'll have to go to a photographic store. The latter two are sometimes hard to find (or sold at inflated prices) outside major cities.

In general, buy film for the purpose you intend to use it. For general-purpose shooting – for either prints or slides – 100 ASA film is just about the most useful and versatile, as it gives you good colour and enough speed to capture most situations on film. If you plan to shoot in dark areas or in brightly lit night scenes without a tripod, switch to 400 ASA.

The best and most widely available films are made by Fuji, Kodak and Agfa. Fuji Velvia and Kodak Elite are easy to process and provide good slide images. Stay away from Kodachrome: it's difficult to process quickly and can give you lots of headaches if not handled properly. For print film you can't beat Kodak Gold, though Fuji and Agfa have just about perfected their films for print as well.

Film of any type is rather inexpensive in Germany, so there's no need to stock up at home. For a roll of 36-exposure standard print film, expect to pay around DM6. The cost for good slide film should be around DM10 to DM13. The cost per roll goes down significantly if you buy in packages of five or 10 rolls, so shop around. Occasionally, processing is included with the purchase of the film, which is a great deal if you have the time to wait. With slide film, unless you specify that you want the images framed *(gerahmt)*, you will get them back unframed.

It's worth carrying a spare battery for your camera to avoid disappointment when your camera dies in the middle of nowhere. If you're buying a new camera for your trip, do so several weeks before you leave and practise using it.

Chemists and supermarkets are cheap places to get your film processed, provided

Half-timbered houses in Thuringia's capital, Erfurt

Ulm's claim to fame? The world's highest steeple!

You'll enjoy a heavenly brew at Kloster Andechs.

The distinctive Berliner Dom rises from the Spree.

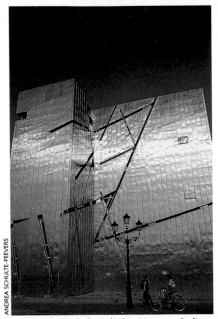

Libeskind's symbolic Jüdisches Museum, Berlin

Befreiungshalle, outside Kelheim

Brassica napus or rape seed: cultivated for fodder, soap oil and photographic opportunities

you don't need professional quality developing. Standard developing for print film is about DM4, plus DM0.40 for each 10 by 15cm print (allow about four days), and about DM0.60 per print for overnight service. Processing slide film costs about DM3.50 in these shops; if you want it mounted, your total comes to about DM7. All prices quoted are for rolls of 36.

Technical Tips

When the sun is high in the sky, photographs tend to emphasise shadows and wash out highlights. It's best to take photos during the early morning or the late afternoon when light is softer. This is especially true of landscape photography.

A polarising filter is a most useful piece of gear, as it deepens the blue of the sky and water, can eliminate many reflections and makes clouds appear quite dramatic. It's best used to photograph scenes in nature. But using one at high altitudes where the sky is already deep blue can result in pictures with a nearly black and unrealistic sky. The effect of a polariser is strongest when you point your camera 90° away from the sun.

In forests you'll find that light levels are surprisingly low, and fast film or using your camera's fill-flash function may be helpful. A monopod or lightweight tripod is an invaluable piece of gear for 'steadying up' your camera for slow exposure times or when using a telephoto lens.

Film can be damaged by excessive heat. Don't leave your camera and film in the car on a hot day, and avoid placing your camera on the dash while you are driving.

Frame-filling expanses of snow come out a bit grey unless you deliberately *overexpose* about a half to one stop. Extreme cold can play tricks with exposure, so 'bracket' your best pictures with additional shots about one stop under and overexposed.

Photographing People

Germans tend to be deferential around photographers and will make a point of not walking in front of your camera, even if you want them to. No one seems to mind being photographed in the context of an overall scene, but if you want a close-up shot, you should ask first. Then the problem is to have the subject look natural.

Video

American-bought video recorders can record with German-bought tapes and then play back with no problems. The size of the tapes are the same, only the method of recording and playback differs between PAL and NTSC standards.

Airport Security

All aircraft passengers have to pass their luggage through X-ray machines. In general, airport X-ray technology isn't supposed to jeopardise lower-speed film (under 1600 ASA). Recently, however, new high-powered machines designed to inspect *checked* luggage have been installed at major airports around the world. These machines are capable of conducting high-energy scans that may destroy unprocessed film. Make sure that you carry film and loaded cameras in your hand-luggage and ask airport security people to inspect them manually. Pack all your film into a clear plastic bag that you can quickly whip out of your luggage. This not only saves time at the inspection points but also helps minimise confrontations with security staff. In this age of terrorism, their job is tough but they can also add to your pre-flight hell, big time.

TIME

Throughout Germany, clocks are set to Central European Time (GMT/UTC plus one hour), the same time zone as Madrid and Warsaw. Daylight-saving time comes into effect at 2 am on the last Sunday in March, when clocks are turned one hour forward. On the last Sunday in October they're turned back an hour. Without taking daylight-saving times into account, when it's noon in Berlin, it's 11 am in London, 6 am in New York, 3 am in San Francisco, 8 pm in Tokyo, 9 pm in Sydney and 11 pm in Auckland. Official times (eg shop hours, train schedules, film screenings etc) are usually indicated by the 24 hour clock, eg 6.30 pm is 18.30.

ELECTRICITY

Electricity is 220V, 50 Hz AC. Plugs are the European type with two round pins. Your 220V appliances may be plugged into a German outlet with an adaptor, though their 110V cousins (eg from the USA) require a transformer. Some electric devices like laptops or shavers work on both 110V and 220V.

WEIGHTS & MEASURES

Germany uses the metric system – there's a conversion table at the back of this book. Like other Continental Europeans, Germans indicate decimals with commas and thousands with points (ie 10,000.00 is 10.000,00).

Clothing sizes – especially those for women's clothing – are quite different from those in the USA and in Great Britain. Women's size 8 in the USA (size 10 in the UK) equals size 36 in Germany. Sizes then increase in increments of two, making German size 38 a US 10 and a UK 12 and so on. Look for the sign '*Anprobe*' to find the fitting room.

Shoes are another matter altogether. A US 5 (UK 3) is size 36 in Germany. It continues in increments of one, so that US 6 (UK 4) equals size 37. To make things more complicated, men's sizes are a bit different again. A men's 41 equates to a US 8 and a UK 7. A men's 42 would be a US 9 and a UK 8, etc.

LAUNDRY

You'll find coin-operated laundrettes *(Münzwäscherei)* in most cities and smaller towns. Normal opening hours are from 6 am to 9 or 10 pm. A load of washing costs DM6 to DM7, including soap powder; the dryer is DM1 per 10 minutes. In most laundrettes you select your machine and deposit the coin(s) in a central machine with numbers corresponding to the washers and dryers. The panel also distributes the soap powder, so have one of the plastic cups strewn around the laundrette at the ready.

The dryers in German laundrettes are cooler than those in the USA or Australia, which means a sopping wet load can take up to an hour to dry. To save time and money, use the extractor. It's the bomb-shaped aluminium device that costs DM0.50. Spread your clothes inside it (making sure to balance the load), close it up and start it. It takes about five minutes to spin vigorously, removing much of the excess water from the clothes and cutting drying time by at least half.

Some camping grounds and a few hostels have washers and dryers for guests' use. If you're staying in a private room, your host might take care of your washing for a fee. Major hotels provide laundering services for fairly steep fees.

TOILETS

Finding a public lavatory when you need one is not usually a problem in Germany, but you may have to pay anything from DM0.20 to DM1.50 for the convenience. Ducking into a bar or restaurant is an easy alternative, though it's best to pick a busy place to avoid glaring stares from the staff. Perhaps better are the public facilities in department stores. If there's an attendant, it's nice to tip DM0.50, at least if the toilet was clean. All train stations have toilets, and at some main stations you can even shower for between DM2 and DM10. The standard of hygiene is usually very high, although occasionally toilets can be surprisingly grotty – especially in some pubs and nightclubs.

Public toilets also exist in larger parks, pedestrian malls and inner-city shopping areas, where ultra-modern self-cleaning pay toilet pods (with wide automatic doorways for easy wheelchair access) are increasingly being installed (DM0.50). Instructions come in English, French and German.

HEALTH

Generally speaking, Germany is a healthy place to visit. There are no prevalent diseases or risks associated with travelling here, and the country is well served by hospitals. In a serious emergency, call ☎ 112 for an ambulance to take you to the nearest hospital emergency room.

Predeparture planning

No vaccinations are required to visit Germany, except if you're coming from an infected area – a jab against yellow fever is the most likely requirement. If you're going to Germany with stopovers in Asia, Africa or Latin America, check with your travel agent or with the German embassy or consulate nearest you.

If you require a particular medication, take an adequate supply, as it may not be available locally. Take the part of the packaging showing the generic name rather than the brand, which will make replacements easier to obtain. It's a good idea to have a legible prescription or letter from your doctor to show that you legally use the medication.

Health Insurance Health care is excellent in Germany, but it's also expensive unless you're a citizen from an EU country, in which case first aid and emergency health care are free with an E111 form. For anyone else, without insurance, even minor health concerns can easily bust your entire travel budget. Unless your health plan at home provides worldwide coverage, definitely take out travel health insurance.

Wide varieties of policies are available and your travel agent should have recommendations. International student travel policies handled by STA Travel and other organisations are usually good value. Some policies specifically exclude 'dangerous activities' like scuba diving, motorcycling and even trekking. If these activities are on your agenda, search for policies that include them.

Be sure to keep all receipts and documentation. Some policies ask you to call back (reverse charges) to a centre in your home country for an immediate assessment of your problem. Also check whether the policy covers ambulance fees or an emergency flight home. Also see Travel Insurance under Visas & Documents earlier in this chapter.

Medical Problems & Treatment

In case of an accident or other emergency, call ☎ 112. In any other circumstance, ask for a referral to a doctor at your hotel or check the phone book under *Ärzte*. Occasionally, you'll also find referral service numbers listed under Information in the various destination sections in this book, which may prove useful.

Except for emergencies, it is not customary to go to a hospital for treatment; instead you'd go to a doctor in private practice.

The only place to obtain over-the-counter *(rezeptfrei)* medications for minor health concerns, like flu or a stomach upset, is a pharmacy *(Apotheke)*. For more serious conditions, you will need to bring a prescription *(Rezept)* from a licensed physician. The names and addresses of pharmacies open after hours (it rotates) are posted in any pharmacy window.

Environmental Hazards

Diarrhoea A change of water, food or climate can all cause a mild bout of diarrhoea, but a few rushed toilet trips with no other symptoms is not indicative of a major problem. In any case, diarrhoea is not likely to occur in Germany.

If it does, watch out for dehydration, the main danger with diarrhoea, particularly in children or the elderly. Fluid replacement (at least equal to the volume being lost) is the most important thing to remember. Weak black tea with a little sugar, soda water, or flat soft drinks diluted 50% with clean water are all good. With severe diarrhoea a rehydrating solution is preferable to replace minerals and salts.

Commercially available oral rehydration salts (ORS) are very useful; add them to boiled or bottled water. In an emergency you can make up a solution of six teaspoons of sugar and a half teaspoon of salt to a litre of boiled or bottled water. Keep drinking small amounts often. Urine is the best guide to the adequacy of replacement – if you have small amounts of concentrated urine, you need to drink more. Stick to a bland diet as you recover.

Heat Exhaustion Dehydration or salt deficiency can cause heat exhaustion. Take time to acclimatise and drink sufficient liquids. Salt deficiency is characterised by fatigue, lethargy, headaches, giddiness and muscle cramps; salt tablets may help, but adding extra salt to your food is better.

Hypothermia If you are planning on hiking, mountaineering or cross-country skiing while in Germany, you should be prepared for sudden weather changes, especially outside the summer months. Hypothermia occurs when the body loses heat faster than it can produce it and the core temperature of the body falls. It is surprisingly easy to progress from very cold to dangerously cold due to a combination of wind, wet clothing, fatigue and hunger, even if the air temperature is above freezing.

Dress in layers; silk, wool and some of the new artificial fibres are all good insulating materials. A hat is important, as a lot of heat is lost through the head. A strong, waterproof outer layer (and a 'space' blanket for emergencies) is essential. Carry basic supplies, including food containing simple sugars to generate heat quickly, and fluids to drink.

Symptoms of hypothermia are exhaustion, numb skin (particularly toes and fingers), shivering, slurred speech, irrational or violent behaviour, lethargy, stumbling, dizzy spells, muscle cramps and violent bursts of energy. Irrationality may take the form of sufferers claiming they are warm and trying to take off their clothes.

Get hypothermia victims out of the wind or rain and make sure they're in warm and dry clothing. Give them hot liquids – not alcohol – and some high-calorie, easily digestible food. Do not rub victims: instead, allow them to slowly warm themselves. This should be enough to treat the early stages of hypothermia.

Severe hypothermia is a critical condition.

Infectious Diseases

HIV & AIDS Infection with the human immunodeficiency virus (HIV) may lead to acquired immune deficiency syndrome (AIDS), which is a fatal disease. Any exposure to blood, blood products or body fluids may put the individual at risk. The disease is often transmitted through unprotected sex or dirty needles, including those used for vaccinations, acupuncture, tattooing and body piercing. Fear of HIV infection should never preclude treatment for serious medical conditions.

Sexually Transmitted Diseases Gonorrhoea, herpes and syphilis are among these diseases; sores, blisters or rashes around the genitals and discharges or pain when urinating are common symptoms. In some STDs, such as wart virus or chlamydia, symptoms may be less marked or not observed at all, especially in women. Syphilis symptoms eventually disappear completely but the disease continues and can cause severe problems in later years. While sexual abstinence is the only 100% effective prevention, using condoms is also effective. The treatment of gonorrhoea and syphilis is with antibiotics. Different sexually transmitted diseases require specific antibiotics. There is no cure for herpes or AIDS, though only AIDS will ultimately lead to death.

Bites & Stings

Insect Bites & Stings Bee and wasp stings are usually painful rather than dangerous. However, in people who are allergic to them, severe breathing difficulties may occur and require urgent medical care.

Calamine lotion or Stingose spray will give relief, and ice packs will reduce the pain and swelling.

Ticks You should always check all over your body if you have been walking through a potentially tick-infested area, as ticks can cause skin infections and other more serious diseases. The forest tick, which burrows under the skin, can cause inflammation, even encephalitis. You might consider a vaccination against tick-borne encephalitis if you plan to do some extensive hiking and camping in Germany.

Lyme disease is another serious tick-transmitted infection which may be picked up in forested areas of Germany. The illness usually begins with a spreading rash at the site of the tick bite and is accompanied by fever, headache, extreme fatigue, aching joints and muscles and mild neck stiffness. If untreated, these symptoms usually dissipate over several weeks, but over subsequent weeks or months disorders of the nervous system, heart and joints may develop.

Treatment works best early in the illness. Medical help should be sought. If a tick is found attached, press down around its head with tweezers, grab the head and gently pull upwards. Avoid pulling the rear of the body, as this may squeeze the tick's gut contents through the attached mouth parts into the skin, increasing the risk of infection and disease. Smearing chemicals on the tick will not make it let go and is not recommended.

WOMEN TRAVELLERS

Women should not encounter particular difficulties or forms of harassment in Germany, though naturally it pays to use common sense.

Attitudes Towards Women

Younger German women especially are quite outspoken and emancipated, but self-confidence hasn't yet translated into equality in the workplace, where they are often still kept out of senior and management positions. Sexual harassment in the workplace is more commonplace and tolerated here than in countries like the USA and Australia. Many women juggle jobs and children, but there's an extensive network of public, church-run and private kindergartens to fall back on.

In larger cities, German women are just as likely to initiate contact with the opposite sex as men are. Getting hassled in the streets happens infrequently and is most likely to be encountered when walking past a bunch of construction men on a break. Wolf whistles and hollering are best ignored, as any form of response will be interpreted as encouragement.

Safety Precautions

Women often face different situations when travelling than men do. If you are a woman traveller, especially a solo traveller, it's not a bad idea to develop a little extra awareness of your surroundings.

In general, you must exercise more vigilance in large cities than in rural areas. Try to avoid the 'bad' or unsafe neighbourhoods or districts; if you must go into or through these areas, it's best to go in a private vehicle (car or taxi). It's more dangerous at night, but in the worst areas crime can even occur in the daytime. If you are unsure which areas are considered unsafe, ask at your hotel or telephone the tourist office for advice. Tourist maps can sometimes be deceiving, compressing areas that are not tourist attractions and making the distances look shorter than they are.

While there is less to watch out for in rural areas, women may occasionally be harassed by men unaccustomed to seeing women travelling alone. Try to avoid hiking or camping alone, especially in unfamiliar places. Hikers all over the world use the 'buddy system,' not only for protection from other people, but also for aid in case of unexpected falls or other injuries.

Women must recognise the extra threat of rape, which is a problem not only in urban but also in rural areas, though to a lesser degree. Avoiding vulnerable situations and using common sense will help you to avoid most problems. You're more vulnerable if you've been drinking or using drugs.

If you are assaulted, call the police immediately (☎ 110). Major cities have rape crisis centres and women's shelters that provide help and support (some are listed throughout this book).

In cities, going into a bar alone is quite doable. If you don't want company, most men will respect a firm but polite 'no thank you'. If someone continues to harass you, protesting loudly will often make the offender slink away with embarrassment – or will at least draw attention to your predicament.

Don't hitchhike alone, and don't pick up hitchhikers when you're driving alone. Be extra careful at night on public transport, and remember to check the times of the last bus or train before you go out at night.

To deal with potential dangers, many women protect themselves with a whistle, some karate training, mace or cayenne pepper spray. The latter two are widely available in Germany; small canisters may be purchased without a permit for around DM15.

Organisations

Most larger cities have women-only cafes, ride and accommodation-sharing services, or cultural organisations just for women. These include the Frauenkulturhaus (☎ 089-470 52 12) at Richard-Strauss-Strasse 21 in Munich, the Frankfurt Frauenkulturhaus (☎ 069-70 10 17), at Industriehof 7-9, and the Fraueninfothek (☎ 030-282 39 80) at Dircksenstrasse 47 in Berlin.

Crisis centres for victims of harassment or violence are also ubiquitous, even in smaller towns. Places to turn to include the Frauenhaus München (☎ 089-354 83 11, 24-hour service ☎ 089-354 83 0) in Munich, the Frauenberatungsstelle (☎ 040-652 77 11) in Hamburg, and LARA – Krisen und Beratungszentrum für vergewaltigte Frauen (Crisis and Counselling Centre for Raped Women; ☎ 030-216 88 88) in Berlin.

GAY & LESBIAN TRAVELLERS

Gays are known as *Schwule* (formerly a pejorative term equivalent to 'queer' but now a moniker worn with pride and dignity), and lesbians are *Lesben*. Germans are generally fairly tolerant of homosexuality, but gays and lesbians still don't enjoy quite the same social acceptance as in certain other northern European countries. Most progressive are the largest cities, especially Berlin, Hamburg, Cologne and Frankfurt, where the sight of homosexual couples holding hands is not uncommon, and kissing in public is becoming more practised and accepted. In general, homosexuals are more likely to encounter discrimination and possibly even violence in certain eastern German areas (eg, Magdeburg, Frankfurt an der Oder and parts of eastern Berlin).

Organisations

Larger cities have many gay and lesbian bars, as well as other meeting places for homosexuals, such as Berlin's Mann-O-Meter (☎ 030-216 80 08) in Schöneberg and Schwulenzentrum (SchwuZ; ☎ 030-693 70 25 or ☎ 694 75 27) in Kreuzberg; the Lesbisch-Schwules Kulturhaus (☎ 069-297 72 96) in Frankfurt; and in Hamburg, there's Hein & Fiete (☎ 040-24 03 33) in St Georg.

Deutsche AIDS-Hilfe (German AIDS Help, ☎ 030-690 08 70) is a political interest group fighting for the rights of the HIV-positive. Its offices are at Dieffenbachstrasse 33 in Berlin-Kreuzberg.

DISABLED TRAVELLERS

Overall, Germany caters well for the needs of the disabled *(Behinderte)*, especially the wheelchair-bound. You'll find access ramps and/or lifts in many public buildings, including toilets, train stations, museums, theatres and cinemas. However, other disabilities (like blindness or deafness) are less catered for, and German organisations for disabled people continue to lobby for improvements.

All InterCity Express (ICE), InterCity/EuroCity (IC/EC), InterRegio (IR) trains, suburban (S-Bahn) and underground (U-Bahn) trains and ferry services have wheelchair access, but stepped entrances to trams and buses remain obstacles.

Organisations

There are a number of organisations and tour providers that specialise in the needs of disabled travellers.

Access-Able Travel Source
(☎ 303-232 2979, fax 303-239 8486)
PO Box 1796, Wheat Ridge, CO 80034
(has an excellent Web site with many links at www.access-able.com)
Mobility International
(☎ 541-343 1284, fax 541-343 6812, email info@miusa.org)
PO Box 10767, Eugene, OR 97440;
(☎ 020-7403 5688)
228 Borough High St, London SE1 1JX
(advises disabled travellers on mobility issues and runs an educational exchange program)

Society for the Advancement of Travel for the
  Handicapped (SATH)
  (☎ 212-447 7284, email sathtravel@aol.com)
  347 Fifth Ave, Suite 610, New York,
  NY 10016
Royal Association for Disability and Rehabilita-
  tion (RADAR)
  (☎ 020-7250 3222)
  12 City Forum, 250 City Rd, London,
  EC1V 8AF
  (publishes the helpful *Holidays & Travel
  Abroad: A Guide for Disabled People*)
Twin Peaks Press
  (☎ 360-694 2462, 800-637 2256)
  PO Box 129, Vancouver, WA 98666
  (publishes a quarterly newsletter, as well as
  directories and access guides)

SENIOR TRAVELLERS

Senior citizens are entitled to discounts in
Germany on things like public transport and
museum admission fees. In some cases they
might need a special pass.

Occasionally, discounts will not be
posted, so simply ask '*Gibt es Ermässi-
gungen für Senioren?*'. If you're on quite a
tight budget, keep in mind that there's no
age limit for stays at DJH hostels (except in
Bavaria) and most independent hostels, and
that the student cafeterias at the university
are open to anyone. European residents
aged over 60 are eligible for the Rail Europe Senior Card.

TRAVEL WITH CHILDREN

Successful travel with young children requires planning and effort. Don't try to
overdo things; even for adults, packing too
much into the time available can cause
problems. And make sure the activities include the kids as well – balance that day at
the Museumsufer in Frankfurt with a visit
to the city's wonderful zoo. Include the
kids in the trip planning; if they've helped
to work out where you are going, they will
be much more interested when they get
there. *Travel with Children* by Lonely
Planet co-founder Maureen Wheeler is a
good source of information.

Children's discounts are widely available
for everything from museum admissions to
bus fares and hotel stays. The definition of a
child varies – some places consider anyone

under 18 eligible for children's discounts,
while others only include children under six.

Most car-rental firms in Germany have
children's safety seats for hire at a nominal
cost, but it is essential that you book them in
advance. The same goes for highchairs and
cots (cribs); they're standard in most restaurants and hotels, but numbers are limited. The
choice of baby food, infant formulas, soy and
cow's milk, disposable nappies (diapers) and
the like is great in German supermarkets, but
the opening hours may be restricted. Run out
of nappies on Saturday afternoon and you're
facing a very long and messy weekend.

It's perfectly acceptable to bring your
kids, even toddlers, along to casual restaurants (though you would raise eyebrows at
upmarket ones, especially at dinnertime),
cafes and daytime events.

DANGERS & ANNOYANCES

Theft and other crimes against travellers are
relatively rare. In the event of problems, the
police are helpful and efficient.

Be careful in crowded train stations,
where pickpockets are often active. Don't
allow anyone to help you put your luggage
into a coin locker. Once they've closed the
locker, they might switch keys and later
come back to pick up your things. Begging
for small change is becoming prevalent in
big city centres.

Africans, Asians and southern Europeans
may encounter racial prejudice, especially
in eastern Germany where they have been
singled out as convenient scapegoats for
economic hardship. However, you'll probably find that the animosity is directed
against immigrants, not tourists. People in
eastern Germany are becoming used to foreigners, though a few may still feel a bit
awkward in your presence. See Dangers &
Annoyances in the individual cities and
towns for more specific warnings.

In the event of a real emergency, the following are the most important telephone
numbers to remember:

Police	☎ 110
Fire/Ambulance	☎ 112

LEGAL MATTERS

German police are well trained, fairly 'enlightened' and usually treat tourists with respect. Most can speak some English, though you may encounter communication problems in rural areas or in eastern Germany. By German law, you must carry some form of picture identification like your passport, national identity card or driving licence.

Reporting theft to the police is usually a simple, if occasionally time-consuming, matter. Remember that the first thing to do is show some form of identification.

If driving in Germany, you should carry your driving licence and obey road rules carefully (see Road Rules under Car & Motorcycle in the Getting Around chapter). Penalties for drinking and driving are stiff. The highest permissible blood-alcohol level is 0.05% nationwide. If you are caught exceeding this limit, your licence will be confiscated immediately and a court then decides within three days whether or not you get it back. The same applies if you are involved in an accident and you have a blood-alcohol level exceeding 0.03%, regardless of whether or not the accident was your fault.

In some cities, the police take a dim view of cyclists' misdemeanours, and you will receive an on-the-spot fine if caught. Offences may include riding through a pedestrian zone or on a footpath, or crossing an intersection against the red traffic signal. It is also illegal to use a bicycle path on the left-hand side of a road (ie against the flow of traffic). Cyclists are not required to wear helmets. As a pedestrian, you are expected to keep off bike paths.

Penalties for the possession of drugs are generally harsh. Travellers coming from Amsterdam should be aware that German authorities are less liberal in this regard than their Dutch cousins. Despite the abolition of border formalities, customs officers still spot-check passengers on trains and also on roads on both sides of the border. Though treated as a minor offence, the possession of even small quantities of cannabis for personal consumption remains illegal; if you are caught it may involve a court appearance.

BUSINESS HOURS

Official shop trading hours in Germany were liberalised a few years ago and are now weekdays from 7 am to 8 pm, and to 4 pm on Saturday, plus a maximum of three hours on Sunday. Consumer interest in this development has been mixed. Except in major cities like Berlin, Hamburg or Munich, you'll find that most shops do not take advantage of the extended hours. After experimenting with longer hours for a year or two, retail stores in smaller towns now usually close at 6 or 6.30 pm, while those in mid-size cities may stay open until 7 pm. Exceptions are department stores and supermarkets. Outside tourist resorts, shops almost never open on Sunday, bakeries excepted. Train stations in larger cities usually have a supermarket or general goods store that doesn't close until 9 or 10 pm. Petrol stations are also convenient – if expensive – places to stock up on basic food and drink when everything else is closed.

Banking hours are generally weekdays from 8.30 am to 1 pm and from 2.30 to 4 pm (many stay open till 5.30 pm on Thursday). Travel agencies and other offices are usually open weekdays from 9 am to 6 pm and on Saturday till noon. Government offices, on the other hand, close for the weekend as early as 1 pm on Friday. Museums are almost universally closed on Monday; opening hours vary greatly, although many art museums are open late one evening per week.

Restaurants tend to open from 10 am to midnight, with varying closing days *(Ruhetag)*. All shops and banks are closed on public holidays.

PUBLIC HOLIDAYS & SPECIAL EVENTS
Public Holidays

National public holidays include: New Year's Day; Good Friday, Easter Sunday & Easter Monday; Labour Day (1 May); Ascension Day (40 days after Easter); Whit/Pentecost Sunday & Monday (May or June); Corpus Christi (10 days after Pentecost); Day of German Unity (3 October), and Christmas and Boxing/St Stephen's Day. Epiphany (6 January), Assumption Day (15 August),

Reformation Day (31 October), All Saints' Day (1 November) and Repentance Day (14 November) are also holidays in some states.

Special Events

There are many festivals, fairs and cultural events throughout the year in Germany. Highlights include the following:

January & February
The Carnival *(Fasching)* season before Lent features many colourful events in large cities, notably in Cologne, Munich, Düsseldorf and Mainz. Another highlight is the International Film Festival in Berlin.

March
Events include the Frankfurt Music Fair, Thuringian Bach Festival, Frühlingsdom in Hamburg, Dresden Opera Festival and many spring fairs throughout Germany.

April
This month's highlights include the Stuttgart Jazz Festival, Munich Ballet Days, Mannheim May Fair, Walpurgisnacht Festivals (May Day's Eve in the Harz Mountains) and Berlin Music Festival.

May
May is the month for the Red Wine Festival in Rüdesheim, Brahms Festival in Lübeck, Dresden International Dixieland Jazz Festival, Dresden Music Festival, Rock am Ring at Nürburgring race track, Bonn Summer Festival (through to September), Africa Festival in Würzburg, Karl May Festival near Dresden, Rheingau Gourmet Weeks, men's Tennis Championships in Hamburg and women's German Open in Berlin.

June
Events include the Rheingau Music Festival, Händel Festival in Halle, Kieler Woche sailing regatta, Munich Film Festival, International Music Festival in Freiburg, Lüneburg Bach Festival, Mozart Festival in Würzburg, Tollwood Festival in Munich, Christopher Street Day (especially in Berlin) and Thuringian Organ Summer (through to August).

July
Folk festivals throughout Germany are highlights this month, as well as the Munich Opera Festival, Richard Wagner Festival in Bayreuth, Love Parade in Berlin, Domstufenfestspiele in Erfurt, Trier Antiquity Festival, Schleswig-Holstein Music Festival (through to August) and marksmen festivals throughout Germany, including Hanover, Dresden, Düsseldorf and Wolfenbüttel.

August
The Heidelberg Castle Festival is a feature, as well as wine festivals throughout the Rhineland area, Nuremberg Autumn Folk Festival and Hanse Sail Rostock.

September
It's time for Munich's Oktoberfest and the Canstatt Folk Festival in Stuttgart (both through to October), Frankfurt Book Fair, Gewandhaus Festival in Leipzig, Beethoven Marathon in Bonn and Backfischfest in Worms.

October
Highlights are the Leipzig Jazz Festival, Hamburg Bach Festival (through to November), Onion Fair in Weimar, Bremer Freimarkt and Frankfurt Marathon.

November
The St Martin's Festival throughout Rhineland and Bavaria kicks off, as well as Six-Day Cycle Racing in Munich.

December
Christmas fairs are run throughout Germany, including those in Munich, Nuremberg, Berlin, Lübeck, Münster, Stuttgart and Heidelberg.

ACTIVITIES

The Germans are outdoors people, which means there are plenty of facilities for visitors in search of active pursuits.

Cycling

Cycling is popular both in cities and the countryside, with over 170 long-distance cycling tracks totalling some 35,000km. Many routes are marked, and eastern Germany has much to offer cyclists in the way of lightly travelled back roads and a well-developed hostel network, especially in the flat, less populated north.

Offshore islands, especially the North Frisian group, are tailor-made for keen pedal-pushers. The eastern Harz is also excellent. If you want to do some rural cycling in one region, simply pick up a local topographic map and look for the *Forstwege* (forestry tracks), which are often part of the network of hiking tracks. With a compass and a good map, you can completely avoid traffic.

Bicycles can be hired in most towns; see the Getting Around sections of the individual cities and towns. See also the detailed general discussion under Bicycle in the Getting Around chapter. Always have a good lock for your bike.

Skiing

The German Alps have the most extensive downhill and cross-country skiing in the country, and Garmisch-Partenkirchen is the most popular alpine resort. Those who want to avoid the glitz, glamour and high prices there may want to try the Black Forest or the Harz Mountains, both excellent for cross-country skiing and ski hikes. The compact upper Harz (Hochharz), with its national parks and well-developed tourist facilities, is a good region for anyone wishing to undertake a ski hike of several days or more. Full clothing and safety precautions should be taken, and a good topographic map is indispensable for anything more than a local loop.

The skiing season generally runs from late November/early December to March. In the shoulder season, discounted ski package weeks are advertised by Weisse Woche (White Week) signs in tourist offices, hotels and ski resorts. Daily ski-lift passes start at around DM30.

All winter resorts have equipment-rental facilities. The lowest daily rate for downhill gear is about DM20, less if you rent gear for longer periods. Cross-country equipment costs slightly less.

Hiking & Mountaineering

The German countryside is crisscrossed by more than 100,000km of marked trails. Popular areas for hiking are the Black Forest, the Harz Mountains, the Bavarian Forest, the Saxon Switzerland area, the Thuringian Forest and the Sauerland. The German Alps offer the most inspiring scenery, however, and are the centre of mountaineering in Germany, with some 50 mountain huts available to climbers and walkers.

The Verband Deutscher Gebirgs- und Wandervereine (Federation of German Mountain and Hiking Clubs; ☎ 0681-390 46 50), Reichsstrasse 4, 66111 Saarbrücken, is the umbrella organisation of all local and regional hiking clubs, like the Harzklub, Rennsteigverein, Sauerländischer Gebirgsverein and Schwarzwaldverein.

The Deutscher Alpenverein (German Alpine Club; ☎ 089-14 00 30), Von-Kahr-Strasse 2-4, 80997 Munich, is a good resource of information on walking and mountaineering in Germany. The Web site (in German only) is at www.alpenverein.de.

Hikers should always seek information on weather conditions and make sure their footwear, clothing and provisions are adequate for the hike. Always carry water and high-energy food. Although conditions are not extreme in the Central Uplands, you should still be prepared for sudden changes, especially outside the summer months. Weather conditions are particularly changeable in the Alps. It is always advisable to let someone know where you intend to hike.

Also see the Health section earlier in this chapter for potential problems and how to deal with them.

Thermal Spas & Saunas

Germans love to sweat it out in the sauna, and most public baths (Stadtbäder) have sauna facilities, usually with fixed hours for men and women as well as mixed sessions. Prices start from around DM12. Booking in for a regimen of sauna, bath, massage and exercise in a spa resort (Kurort) is also popular. Treatments vary according to the qualities of the region. The local spa centre (Kurzentrum) or spa administration (Kurverwaltung) will have price lists for services. Expect to pay upwards of DM40 for a full massage. Sauna/massage combinations are popular. Services can usually be booked at short notice, and most spa towns have regular activity programs such as short guided hikes or music and theatre performances.

Horse Riding

Anyone with a passion for horse riding will have no trouble finding well-equipped Reiterhöfe (riding stables) in Germany. Most towns have one, and many riding centres also rent out rooms or holiday flats. Options range from individual lessons for beginners through to dressage, jumping and riding excursions *(Ausritt)*, often in the forest. Prices vary considerably, but adults can expect to pay DM15 to DM35 per hour for excursions. The best place to pick up addresses is from local tourist offices.

Steam Trains

Railway enthusiasts will be excited by the wide range of special excursions on old steam trains organised by Deutsche Bahn (DB). For more information, ask for the free booklet *Nostalgiezüge* at any large train station in Germany. The eastern Harz has a spectacular network of narrow-gauge lines, popular with enthusiasts and general visitors alike. A permanent steam-train service runs to the Brocken (1142m) and regular steam services operate on other lines. There are also special excursions available. For information on timetables and excursions, see the boxed text 'Narrow-Gauge Railways' in the Harz chapter.

Another narrow-gauge train, the Molli Schmalspurbahn, operates in Bad Doberan in Mecklenburg-Western Pomerania (see that chapter for details). Historic trains are also the subject of the Eisenbahnmuseum in Bochum in North Rhine-Westphalia (see that chapter), which also operates excursions through the Ruhr Valley in summer.

COURSES

You need pretty good German-language skills for most courses, but you may get by with English on more practical courses such as pottery, sculpture or skiing. If in doubt, contact the course leader; most Germans speak a little English and, where practicable, may be prepared to help you out with rudimentary translations.

The best sources of information are the local or regional tourist offices, particularly in popular resort areas like the Black Forest or the German Alps. Local newspapers are another good place to look.

Foreigners who want to study at a German university do not have to pay more than the standard guild fees and administration fees paid by Germans. However, you will have to take a language-proficiency test, known as the DHS. The only exemptions are if you can show certain Goethe Institut certificates or have qualified for university entrance at a German school. Information can be obtained from the Deutscher Akademischer Austauschdienst (DAAD; ☎ 0228-88 20, fax 88 24 44), Kennedyallee 50 in Bonn (Postfach 20 04 04, 53134 Bonn if inquiring by post).

Universities also offer a wide range of summer courses, a few of which are held in English or aimed at foreigners wishing to improve their German. Most courses include accommodation in student hostels. The DAAD publishes a multilingual *Sommerkurse in Deutschland* booklet with useful course descriptions, locations and prices.

Language

A *Sprachaustausch* (language exchange), whereby you help someone out with English or another language in exchange for German lessons, is an informal way to learn the language and make German friends. University language faculties are the best places to start looking.

Goethe Institut The Goethe Institut is a nonprofit, government-subsidised cultural and language organisation that promotes German language and culture abroad. Besides offering a comprehensive course program, it's also engaged in staging some 10,000 cultural events year round, including theatre performances, symposia, lectures, film and music festivals.

Goethe Institut language courses cater to all age groups and stages of proficiency – from absolute beginner to professional level. The program is divided into three general levels – *Grundstufe* (basic), *Mittelstufe* (intermediate) and *Oberstufe* (advanced) – and each is further divided into sublevels.

The Goethe Institut has centres in Berlin, Bonn, Bremen, Dresden, Düsseldorf, Frankfurt-am-Main, Freiburg im Breisgau, Göttingen, Iserlohn, Mannheim, Munich, Murnau, Prien, Rothenburg ob der Tauber, Schwäbisch Hall and Staufen, as well as summer schools in Konstanz and Rosenheim.

Intensive courses cost DM2940 to DM3140 (eight weeks), DM1690 (four weeks) and DM1360 (two weeks), excluding accommodation and meals. The institute also runs three-week summer programs for children and youths aged 10 to 20 years from DM3250.

Get course information from branches of the Goethe Institut or its central registration office (☎ 089-15 92 12 00, fax 15 92 14 44), Helene-Weber-Allee 1, 80637 Munich. You can also find information on the Internet at www.goethe.de.

Volkshochschulen Courses offered at *Volkshochschulen* (VHS; adult education centres) are good value and open to everyone. Most reasonably sized towns have their own VHS, which might offer anything from Japanese origami to language courses. The length of courses varies from several hours to several months. Language courses, which usually last three or four months and include an examination and certificate, cost around DM30 per teaching hour. One popular option is to combine au pair work with a German course.

WORK

Finding work in Germany is much tougher than it used to be. Most people can't even remember the days of the 'economic miracle' when workers could pick and choose jobs in a climate of full employment. Today you have to be well qualified and able to back up your skills with an impressive array of certificates. Germans place great importance on formal qualifications, and the country has a highly trained workforce. On the whole, local qualifications are more highly valued than those gained abroad.

All non-EU citizens who wish to work in Germany require both a work permit *(Arbeitserlaubnis)* and a residency permit *(Aufenthaltserlaubnis)*. Special conditions exist for citizens of so-called 'recognised third countries', including the USA, Canada, Australia, New Zealand, Japan, Israel and

Switzerland. Citizens of these countries who have a firm job offer may apply for the necessary permits, providing the job cannot be filled by a German or EU citizen.

You can begin your job search either before leaving home or on arrival in Germany. Once you receive a firm offer, the local employment office *(Arbeitsamt)* checks that the position cannot otherwise be filled, then issues a specific work permit for that position. You will also need to apply for the residency permit from the *Ausländerbehörde* (foreigners' office).

EU citizens don't need a work permit, and basically enjoy the same rights as Germans. However, they do need an EU residency permit *(EU-Aufenthaltserlaubnis)* from the local authority.

The same conditions apply for seasonal work such as fruit picking, but Germany has agreements (mostly with its neighbours to the east) allowing citizens of some countries to engage in seasonal jobs for a maximum of three months.

The best places to look for work are Arbeitsamt offices, which have an electronic data bank on vacant positions throughout the country. National newspapers are also a good option, especially the *Frankfurter Allgemeine Zeitung* and *Süddeutsche Zeitung*.

It is also possible to find work teaching English at language schools in the large cities, but you will still need work and residency permits, as well as valid health insurance at all times.

You won't get rich teaching English privately to adults or school children, but it might help keep your head above water or prolong a trip. The hourly rate varies dramatically – from a low of DM20 per hour to DM70 for qualified professionals in large cities. Local papers are the best way to advertise, but other good places to start are noticeboards at universities, photocopy shops or even local supermarkets.

In these days of record postwar unemployment, authorities are cracking down on illegal workers, especially on building sites, where raids are fairly common. You are unlikely to make friends among your German colleagues either, who will see you as a threat to their wage and work conditions.

Busking is often equated with begging.

Work as an au pair is easy to find. *The Au Pair and Nanny's Guide to Working Abroad* by Susan Griffith & Sharon Legg will help. *Work Your Way Around the World*, also by Susan Griffith, is another suggestion. There are numerous approved au pair agencies in Germany.

Volunteer Work

Voluntary environmental field work is a good way to meet people and do something for the environment. The Switzerland-based Bergwald Projekt, supported by Greenpeace and the World Wildlife Fund (Switzerland), has been active in reforestation programs in Germany, Switzerland and Austria since 1987. Accommodation is usually in forest huts or tents. Food and accident insurance are provided, but you must pay your own travel costs. Projects generally last one week and run almost weekly from spring to autumn (Sunday to Saturday). They are very popular, so register several months in advance. The address for information and registration is Bergwald Projekt (☎ 081-252 41 45, fax 252 41 47), Rigastrasse 14, 7000 Chur, Switzerland; or you can check the detailed Web page at www.bergwaldprojekt.ch.

ACCOMMODATION

Accommodation in Germany is generally well organised. Since reunification eastern Germany has been a little short on budget beds, though there are usually plenty of inexpensive private rooms available.

Accommodation normally includes breakfast, which takes the form of an all-you-can-eat buffet in most hotels. Sometimes breakfast is brought to your room.

A nightly *Kurtaxe* (resort tax) is charged in certain resorts and spas. This may be a nominal DM0.50 or a hefty DM6 and is usually not included in the quoted room rate. Paying the tax is compulsory and usually gets you a *Kurkarte* (spa card), which entitles you to small discounts to museums

or concerts and other events. In some places – like Sylt Island – you'll need the card just to get onto the beach.

The DZT associate, ADZ Room Reservation Service (☎ 069-74 07 67, fax 75 10 56), Corneliusstrasse 34, 60325 Frankfurt-am-Main, is a national booking agency. Reservations can also be made through tourist offices – some will require written confirmation – or by calling hotels directly. If making a reservation by telephone, remember to give your name at the start. Always tell the owner what time they can expect you and stick to it or ring again. Many well-meaning visitors have lost rooms by turning up late.

Camping

With over 2000 organised sites, camping makes an excellent budget alternative. If camping is to be your main form of accommodation, however, you will probably need your own mode of transport, since sites tend to be far from city centres and are usually not well served by public transport.

Most camping grounds are open from May to September, but several hundred stay open all year. The range of facilities varies greatly, from the primitive to the overequipped and serviced. Some camping grounds, especially in eastern Germany, rent out small bungalows. For camping on private property, permission from the landowner is required. Nightly costs in camping grounds vary according to the standard, but DM5 to DM10 is common for tent sites. Many then charge around DM7 per person and DM3 for cars. The best source of information is the Deutsche Camping Club (☎ 089-380 14 20, fax 33 47 37, email info@camping-club.de), Mandlstrasse 28, 80802 Munich. Its Web site is at www.camping-club.de.

Hostels

The Deutsches Jugendherbergswerk (DJH; ☎ 05231-740 10, fax 74 01 49, or write to DJH Hauptverband, Postfach 14 55, 32704 Detmold) coordinates all affiliated Hostelling International (HI) hostels in Germany. You'll find the Web site at www.djh.de.

For advance hostel reservations anywhere in Germany, write to Deutsches Jugendherbergswerk (☎ 264 95 20, fax 262 04 37), Tempelhofer Ufer 32, 10963 Berlin.

With more than 600 hostels throughout the country, Germany's hostel network is arguably the best and most extensive in the world – which is to be expected of the country that pioneered the concept. Almost all hostels in Germany are open all year. Guests must be members of a Hostelling International-affiliated organisation. If you're not a member, don't despair but read the text under Hostel Cards in the Visas & Documents section earlier in this chapter.

The charge for a dorm bed in a DJH hostel varies from about DM18 to DM30. Camping at a hostel (where permitted) is usually half that price. If you don't have a hostel-approved sheet bag, it usually costs from DM5 to DM7 to hire one (some hostels insist you hire one anyway). Breakfast is always included in the price. Lunch or an evening meal costs between DM5 and DM9.

Theoretically, visitors aged under 27 get preference, but in practice prior booking or arrival time determines who gets the room – not age. In Bavaria, though, the strict maximum age for anyone except group leaders or parents accompanying a child is 26.

Check-in hours vary, but you must usually be out by 9 am. You don't need to do chores at the hostels and there are few rules. Most have a curfew (as early as 10 pm, but often midnight or even 2 am in metropolises) and require you to leave hostel premises in the daytime. In April/May and September/October, many are filled with rambunctious German school groups.

Most DJH hostels have recently been modernised and many have been turned into *Jugendgästehäuser* (youth guesthouses). These offer considerably greater comfort and can be downright luxurious, with amenities like indoor pool or breakfast buffet. Rooms usually sleep just two or four and each has a private shower and WC. However, all this splendour does have a price: usually around DM37.50 per person. This makes stays here potentially more expensive than those in private rooms or some pensions.

Germany also has plenty of independent (non-DJH) hostels, especially in large cities. Usually slightly more expensive than member youth hostels, they tend not to have curfews and are often staffed by hip young people in the know about their city.

Pensions

Pensions offer the basics of hotel comfort without charging hotel prices. Many of these are private homes somewhat out of the centre of town with several rooms to rent. Most charge around DM40 to DM60 for singles and DM60 to DM80 for doubles; pensions are usually more common in major cities and less in villages.

Hotels

Budget hotel rooms can be a bit hard to come by in Germany during summer, although there is usually not much seasonal variation in price. The cheapest hotels only have rooms with shared toilets and showers in the corridor. Prices here don't differ much from those of private rooms. It's increasingly rare to find single rooms with facilities for less than DM45, and most are in the DM50 to DM70 bracket. Doubles work out substantially cheaper – you will find good quality ones in many cities for DM120 or less. Prices are higher in major cities like Berlin, Frankfurt, Hamburg and Munich.

Expensive hotels in Germany offer few advantages for their upmarket prices. The best time to splurge on them is on weekends or during a lull in trade-fair and conference activity, when you can sometimes take advantage of a package deal or special discounts. Top-end hotels really only come into their own if they have sauna and gym facilities – and if you have the time and inclination to use them. Otherwise, you would be better off sticking to quality medium-priced hotels.

The sky is the limit for big-city splurges in Germany. Spa towns are a good place to go the whole hog, as you can also splash out on massages.

Private Rooms

If you are after a private (or even a hotel) room, head straight for the tourist office and use their room-finding service *(Zimmervermittlung)*. The cost of this service varies from DM3 to DM5, or it may be 'free', in which case the tourist office often takes a commission from the owner. This means that in some cases you can rent rooms slightly cheaper by dealing directly with owners. Tourist office staff will usually go out of their way to find something in your price range, although telephone bookings are not always accepted.

Many owners will often inquire about the length of your stay before giving room prices. Generally, the longer you stay, the cheaper the daily room price. If you intend to stay for more than one night, it is always a good idea to say so at the start. In some resort towns, owners are reluctant to let rooms for just one night. It is generally a little more difficult to find singles than doubles, and for use of a double room as a single room *(Einzelbelegung)* you might end up paying 75% of the double-room rate.

In eastern Germany the quality and price of accommodation is less predictable. Tourist offices often weed out the absolute hovels, but occasionally you stumble upon unlisted rooms let at exorbitant prices by owners with unrealistic expectations. This can be Dickensian and highly amusing at first when, for example, the owner throws open the door to a crumbling dump and proudly announces, 'The Quedlinburg Room', but the amusement soon wears off.

In the absence of a tourist office, look for signs saying *'Zimmer frei'* (rooms available) or *'Fremdenzimmer'* (tourist rooms) in house or shop windows.

Farm Stays

Tourist offices can help with rooms or holiday flats on farms. This may be a basic room on a fully-fledged farm where 'Junior', waving from the tractor, makes hay while the sun shines, or one holiday flat among many, nominally on a farm, where tourists are the main crop. Bavaria is a popular place for farm stays, but you will also find them elsewhere in Germany. In parts of eastern Germany and Lower Saxony these are sometimes called *Heu* (hay) hotels.

Germany also has lots of riding stables *(Reiterhöfe)*, where horsey types can find accommodation, mostly holiday flats. In the wine-growing regions, it is possible to stay at wine estates. Facilities range from the rustic and simple through to modern hotels where visitors arrive by the coachload.

Rental Accommodation

Renting an apartment for a few days or more is a popular form of holiday accommodation in Germany. Tourist offices have lists of *Ferienwohnungen* or *Ferien-Appartements* (holiday flats or apartments). Most have cooking facilities (which means breakfast isn't included) and can be rented in cities and the country for a minimum period, usually three days.

Some guesthouses and hotels also have a couple of apartments, and occasionally owners are willing to rent holiday flats for one night for a surcharge. This can be truly budget accommodation for groups of two to four people. Another place to look for holiday flats is in newspaper classifieds.

Mitwohnzentralen (or accommodation-finding services) are a good bet for long-term accommodation in cities. These match up visitors to apartments, houses or vacant rooms in shared houses.

Rates vary by agency and type of accommodation but are always less than what you'd pay in hotels. In general, the longer you rent, the less expensive it gets.

Even if you're not staying, say for an entire month, it may still work out cheaper to pay the monthly rent and leave early. Added to the rate will be the agency's commission, which comes to around 25% of the rent, plus 16% VAT.

Verband der Mitwohnzentralen (☎ 089-194 45, fax 271 20 19), Georgenstrasse 45, 80799 Munich, is an umbrella association of over 40 such services throughout Germany that can help with long-term needs in major cities.

FOOD

Germans are hearty eaters. But while this is truly meat-and-potatoes country, vegetarian and health-conscious restaurants are beginning to sprout up. Restaurants always display their menus outside with prices, but watch for daily specials listed on blackboards. Beware of early closing hours and of the dreaded *Ruhetag* (rest day, usually Tuesday) at some establishments.

At home Germans might eat their heaviest meal at lunchtime and then have lighter evening fare (*Abendbrot* or *Abendessen*, consisting of cheeses, sliced meats and bread). That's not to say that dinner isn't important. Especially in business situations, it's a full meal, and restaurants in large cities on Friday and Saturday night can get crowded, so it's best to book a table.

German Cuisine

Sausages Sausage *(Wurst)*, in its hundreds of incarnations, is the single most popular dish in Germany. It's traditionally served

Continued on page 129

Eating Out

Restaurants

German restaurants are often formal places, with uniformed waiters, full menus, tablecloths, good service and high prices. Many town halls have an atmospheric restaurant, or *Ratskeller*, in the basement, serving traditional German dishes, but we found that these are usually the most expensive in town, with the worst food. If you're fine with paying for atmosphere, great, but if you like your food, check carefully.

Gaststätte

A *Gaststätte* is less formal than a restaurant, though it will have a large menu, daily specials and perhaps a beer garden attached out the front or back.

Wine & Beer Cellars

A *Weinkeller* or *Bierkeller* is, literally, a cellar serving wine or beer. But many small bistros call themselves this as well, and generally they're nice places to have a glass of either wine or beer and a light meal.

Cafes & Bars

Much of German social life revolves around these institutions, which are often hard to separate, as both coffee and alcohol are usually served. They're great places to meet local people without spending too much money – you can sit for hours mulling over your cup of coffee or beer. Note that almost every cafe is shrouded in cigarette smoke.

A wonderful German invention is the quick-and-cheap *Stehcafé*, a stand-up cafe where you indulge in that sinful German habit of coffee and cakes – without spending too much time and money doing so.

Paying & Tipping

Everywhere except in Stehcafés and at snack bars, bills are paid directly at the table. A service charge is always included in the bill and German waiters tend to be paid fairly well anyway. Nevertheless, unless the service was truly abhorrent, most people leave a small tip, usually just rounding up the amount of the bill. Rather than leaving the money on the table, tip as you're handing over the money by telling the waiter the amount you want to pay. For example, say *'Sechzig, bitte'* if your bill comes to DM57 and you want to give a DM3 tip. If you have the exact amount, just say *'Stimmt so'* (roughly 'that's fine').

GERMAN BEER
& WINE

Hövels: Don't let the name fool you!

The beginning of a good German vintage

The physics of beer drinking: when ein stein is not enough

BEER

Few countries in the world can match Germany for the quality and variety of its beer. Whether you like your brew bottom or top-fermented, out of a 0.2L glass or served in a traditional Stein, accompanied by Wurst under chestnut trees in the Bavarian Alps or with pickled herring in a northern coastal resort; dark, light, heavily malted or *hoppy*, Germany offers it all.

As you would expect in a country that takes such pride in its beer, Germany also has lots of interesting microbreweries where you can eat regional dishes, drink the local product and listen to music till late. The Ruhr region has much to offer, as do cities such as Cologne and Düsseldorf. But you'll find microbreweries serving quality beer in many towns across Germany. Most serve just two or three types, and if you really like the product, you can usually buy bottles to take home or drink in your hotel.

Title Page: Rhineland's Cistercian Monastery, Eberbach (photograph by David Peevers)

Right: Microbrewery, Kaltenberg

Inset photograph by David Peevers

DAVID PEEVERS

Favourite Beer Halls
Augustiner Gaststätte, Löwenbräukeller, Hofbräuhaus (Munich)
Brauhaus Sion, Früh am Dom, Päffgen, Brauerei zur Malzmühle
  (Cologne)
Zum Uerige & Zum Schlüssel (Düsseldorf)
Hövels Hausbrauerei (Dortmund)
Pinkus Müller (Münster)

Recommended Brewery Tours
Beck's Brewery (Bremen)
Friesisches Brauhaus zu Jever (in the town of Jever)
Maisel's Brauerei- und Büttnerei-Museum (Bayreuth)

Recommended Microbreweries
Hausbrauerei Rampendahl (Osnabrück)
Zum Uerige (Düsseldorf)
Altes Brauhaus (Wolfsburg/Fallersleben)
Zum Löwen (Braunschweig)
Hansens Brauerei (Flensburg)
Brauerei Schleswig (Schleswig)
Klosterbrauerei (Kiel)
Alte Klosterbrauerei (Vierzehnheiligen, Bavaria)

Authors' Favourite Local Beers
Köstritzer (from Bad Köstritz, Thuringia)
Drei Kronen Weizen (Memmelsdorf, Bavaria)
Rechenberger (Rechenberg, Saxony)
Schlenkerla (Bamberg)
Ruppaner Schimmele Pils (Constance)
Uerige Alt (Düsseldorf)
Päffgen Kölsch (Cologne)

Widely distributed favourites
Flensburg
Jever
Warsteiner

Apparently, good beer
equals good living.

The Beer Facts

- Germany has over 1270 breweries and about 5000 different labels of beer.
- 80% of all breweries in Europe are located in Germany.
- It produces 10% of the world's beer output.
- Germans are the second-largest consumers of beer in the world (130L per head). The largest, the Czech Republic (160L per head), pipped Germany after its separation from Slovakia.
- In 1835 Germany's first railway line was opened between Nuremberg and Fürth. It carried a full cargo of beer.

The importance of Germany's favourite drink is reflected everywhere.

MARTIN MOOS

GERMAN BEER & WINE

Nectar of the Gods

Long before the Roman conquest, the Germanic tribes brewed beer, incorporating it into their sacrificial rituals. The Roman scholar Tacitus mentioned the Germans' proclivity for beer and gambling in his work *Germania*, which was published in 98 AD.

Originally, all sorts of herbs and spices were used in beer production. Around 1000 AD, however, beer started flowing in German monasteries, where the monks used hops, improving the quality enormously. Because beer is a drink rather than a foodstuff, monks were allowed to drink it as a source of nourishment during fasting periods. It was also customary to ply pilgrims and wayfarers generously with the monastic brew.

Brewing eventually turned into a lucrative sideline for the monasteries. Because they were exempt from taxes imposed by local rulers on the private breweries, rulers – Kaiser Sigismund (1410-37) was the first culprit – decided to shore up revenue by forbidding the monks from selling their wares.

Meanwhile, brewing and exporting beer gradually developed into a useful source of income for many secular city governments as well. By the 19th century, brewing by monks or nuns had virtually ceased. Today only 11 monasteries still brew their own beer; the most famous is Kloster Andechs, near Munich.

For details on Munich's famous Oktoberfest, see the boxed text 'Oktoberfest' in the Bavaria chapter.

German Beer Purity Law

The German *Reinheitsgebot* (purity law) for beer is said to be the world's oldest food and beverage law. It was introduced by Duke Wilhelm IV in Bavaria in 1516 and soon spread throughout Germany. There were, however, several earlier laws regulating beer production. Brewing 'bad' beer, for instance, was a punishable offence in Augsburg in around 1165, and in Munich itself a similar law was passed in 1487. According to the German Beer Purity Law, only four ingredients may be used: malt, yeast, hops and water.

GERMAN BREWERS' ASSOCIATION

With age-old recipes and purity laws, Germans have always taken their brewing very seriously.

Bad Luck (hic!)

Ye olde barrel-making, a tough business indeed, could still be witnessed in Germany's local breweries (particularly in the south) as
late as the mid-1960s. Craftsmen were typically he-men and bore
names such as Böttcher or Schäffler (cooper). And they could fling
around those vats – weighing up to 150kg bone dry – with con-
summate ease.

The coopers also spread *Pech*, a gooey cocktail of tar and
resin, around the insides to seal them against natural toxins that
could spoil the beer (such as the tannic acid oozed by oak wood).
This method, which dates back to the 15th century, didn't guar-
antee lasting results and the pitch usually peeled off after a few
years, leaving unseemly
black scales in some poor
pub-goer's glass of beer.
'You've got pitch!' was the
customary cry among
drinking buddies.

The defect was referred
to the coopers, who usually
smeared the offending vat
with the same sticky mass.
Today, modern brewers
prefer to store the suds in
flake-free stainless steel, but
the centuries-old German
idiom for bad luck – *'Pech
gehabt!'* – has stuck.

Beer Glossary

German beer is divided into four different classes. Low Alcohol Beer
(Bier mit niedrigem Stammwürzegehalt) has an alcohol content of up
to 2.8%; *Schankbier* or draught beer contains around 2.8 to 4.6%
alcohol; *Vollbier* (literally 'full beer') has an alcohol content of 4.6 to
5.6%; and the potent *Starkbier* (strong beer) has over 5.5% alcohol.

Obergäriges Bier (top-fermented beer) is brewed at a higher temperature than *untergäriges Bier* (bottom-fermented beer). They differ
in the type of yeast used and whether the yeast rises to the top – where
it is removed – or sinks to the bottom of the vat.

Alkoholfreies Bier (Nonalcoholic Beer) Most breweries produce
their own 'nonalcoholic' beer, but it generally contains 0.5% alcohol. Virtually every type is available: Kölsch, Weizenbier, Pilsener, you name it.

GERMAN BEER & WINE

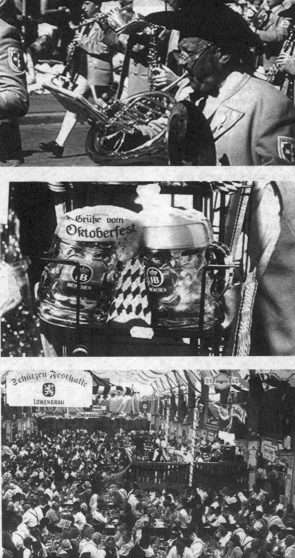

MARTIN MOOS

MARTIN MOOS

MARTIN MOOS

Germany is home to the largest beer festival in the world, Oktoberfest.

Alt (Old) A top-fermented full beer, it's prevalent in the lower Rhine region around Düsseldorf, where it's usually drunk out of 0.2L glasses or mugs. Altbierbowle is an Altbier with punch added.

Berliner Weisse With around 2.8% alcohol, draught or Schankbier is mostly brewed in and around Berlin. It contains lactic acid, giving it a slightly sour taste, and a blend of malted wheat and barley. Top-fermented, it's often drunk *mit Grün* (with green), which is with woodruff syrup, or *mit Schuss*, with raspberry syrup.

Bockbier/Doppelbock These two strong beers have around 7% alcohol, but Doppelbock is slightly stronger. Though usually bottom-fermented, Weizenbock and Weizendoppelbock are two top-fermented wheat beers produced in the south. There's a 'Bock' for almost every occasion: Maibock (usually drunk in May/spring), Weihnachtsbock (brewed for Christmas) etc. All Bock beers originate from Einbeck, near Hanover. Eisbock (ice bock) is dark and more aromatic.

Dampfbier (Steam Beer) Originating from Bayreuth in Bavaria, it's top-fermented and has a fruity flavour.

Dunkles Lagerbier (Dark Lager) *Dunkel* (dark) is brewed throughout Germany, but especially in Bavaria. With a light use of hops, it's full-bodied, with a strong malt aroma. Malt is dried at a high temperature, lending it a dark colour, and it's bottom-fermented.

Export Traditionally with higher alcohol to help it survive a long journey, this beer is closely associated today with Dortmund, and is often dry to slightly sweet.

Helles Lagerbier (Pale Lager) *Helles* (pale or light) refers to the colour, not alcohol content, which is still around 4.6 to 5%. Brewing strongholds are in Bavaria, Baden-Württemberg and in the Ruhr region. Bottom-fermented, it has strong malt aromas and is slightly sweet.

Hofbräu This is a brewery belonging to a royal court or *Hof* – for some time in Bavaria only a few nobles enjoyed the right to brew wheat beer.

All the makings of a quality brew: wheat, fermenting beer and hops

DAVID PEEVERS

Klosterbräu This type of brewery belongs to a monastery.

Kölsch By law, this top-fermented beer can only be brewed in or around Cologne. It has about 4.8% alcohol, a solid hop flavour and pale colour, and is served in glasses (0.2L) called Stangen.

Leichtbier (Light Beer) These low-alcohol beers have about 2 to 3.2% alcohol.

Malzbier (Malt Beer) A sweet, aromatic, full-bodied beer, it is brewed mainly in Bavaria and Baden-Württemberg.

Märzen (March) Full-bodied with strong malt aromas, it's traditionally brewed in March. Today, it's associated with the Oktoberfest.

Pils (Pilsener) This bottom-fermented full beer with pronounced hop flavour and a creamy head has an alcohol content of around 4.8% and is served throughout Germany.

Radler This shandy is also known as Alster or Alsterwasser in Hamburg.

Rauchbier (Smoke Beer) This dark beer has a fresh, spicy or 'smokey' flavour.

Schwarzbier (Black Beer) Slightly stronger, this dark, full beer has an alcohol content of about 4.8 to 5%. Full-bodied, it's bottom-fermented using roasted malt.

Weizenbier/Weissbier (Wheat Beer) Predominating in the south, especially in Bavaria, it has around 5.4% alcohol. A Hefeweizen has a stronger shot of yeast, whereas Kristallweizen is clearer with more fizz. Fruity and spicy, it's sometimes served with a slice of lemon, which ruins the head and, beer purists say, also the flavour.

Zwickelbier This type of beer is unfiltered.

Contacts

If you'd like to find out more about German beer, contact the Deutscher Brauer-Verband (☎ 0228-95 90 60, fax 959 06 17), Annaberger Strasse 28, 53175 Bonn, or check out the German-only Web site at www.brauer-bund.de. Another useful Internet address on German beer is www.bier.de. The site is constantly being expanded, is particularly strong on beers and bars in the Ruhr region, and is gradually developing pages in English.

WINE

A trip to Germany would not be complete without trying at least a few of the country's many good wines.

Wine and wine-making techniques were brought to Germany by the Romans, who conquered southern regions in about 100 BC. Monasteries began producing their own wine, but when Napoleon carved up the church vineyards in the early 19th century, they were sold to private buyers. Most vineyards are located in the south-west on southern facing slopes, usually around one of the major rivers like the Rhine or Moselle.

Local wines are classified by the ripeness of the grapes at harvest. Because of the cool climate, grapes ripen slowly, which means they develop an intense aroma and flavour. At their worst, they can be extremely acidic; good German wine, though, is very lively and has a fruity acidity. The basic wine categories are *trocken* (dry), *halb-trocken* (medium-dry) or *lieblich* (sweet), but this doesn't always appear on the label.

Right: Taking the taste test in a German wine museum.

Inset photograph by David Peevers

DAVID PEEVERS

Recommended Cellars for Wine Tasting

Weingut Georg Breuer (Rüdesheim, Rheingau, Rhineland-Palatinate)

Kloster Eberbach (near Rüdesheim, Rheingau, Rhineland-Palatinate)

Landesweingut Kloster Pforta (Schulpforte, Saale-Unstrut region, Saxony Anhalt)

Juliusspital (Würzburg, Franken region, Bavaria)

Haus des Frankenweins (near Friedensbrücke, Franken region, Bavaria)

Bürgerspital (Würzburg, Franken region, Bavaria)

Vinothek (Bernkastel-Kues, Mosel-Saar-Ruwer region, Rhineland-Palatinate)

Burg Metternich (Beilstein, Mosel-Saar-Ruwer region, Rhineland-Palatinate)

Wine Glossary

Auslese A 'selected harvest', it is usually intense and sweet.

Beerenauslese (BA) Grapes are picked overripe, and it's usually a dessert wine.

Deutscher Landwein (Country Wine) Landwein is usually dry or semi-dry. Some can be surprisingly pleasant and good value if bought from local wine shops or the vineyard.

Deutscher Tafelwein (Table Wine) This is the lowest category of wine and mostly poor quality. If the label doesn't say Deutscher, it's imported.

DAVID PEEVERS

A German wine seller advertises its wares.

Eiswein The grapes are picked and pressed while frozen (very sweet).

Kabinett This is the lightest QmP wine (see Qualitätswein).

Qualitätswein Qualitätswein comes from one of the 13 defined wine-growing regions and has to pass a tasting test. QbA (Qualitätswein bestimmter Anbaugebiete) is the lowest category of quality wine; QmP (Qualitätswein mit Prädikat) is top quality. QbA just means 'Quality Wine of a Specific Region'; QmP means 'Quality Wine of Distinction'.

What distinguishes a QmP wine is the ripeness (ie sweetness) of the grapes.

Sekt Sparkling wine in Germany is called Sekt. Most are made from Riesling grapes.

Spätauslese Literally 'selected late-harvest', this type of wine has concentrated flavours, but is not necessarily sweet.

Trockenbeerenauslese (TBA) The grapes are so overripe they are shrivelled (intensely sweet) and resemble raisins.

Popular Grape Varieties
White
Gewürztraminer Very spicy, it also has an intense bouquet.

Kernier This is a popular new white variety which is a cross between the red Trollinger variety and Riesling (it's very similar to a Riesling).

Rhine river cruises go round the bend.

DAVID PEEVERS

GERMAN BEER & WINE

DAVID PEEVERS

The low mountains surrounding Baden-Baden are ideal for grape-growing.

The Wine Facts

- There are about 100,000 hectares of vineyards in Germany. Only 19% of this area is planted with red wine grape varieties; the rest is planted with white wine varieties.
- When 85% or more of a wine consists of a single grape variety, the bottle may be labelled with this variety.

Müller-Thurgau The most widely planted variety in Germany ripens early and has a slight muscat flavour. Lively and less acidic than Riesling, it is best when young. This grape is now also called Rivaner.

Riesling Top of the range, this grape variety ripens late, and can be drunk young or old. It's racy and fragrant with a fruity bouquet. If you buy only one bottle of wine on your trip, make it a Rheingau or Moselle-Saar-Ruwer Riesling.

Ruländer (Grauburgunder) Robust, soft and full-bodied, it's known as Pinot gris or Pinot grigio to the rest of the world. Only about 2% of vineyards are planted with this variety.

Silvaner With a fairly neutral nose and mild acidity, this full-bodied wine should be drunk young.

Red

German reds tend to be light, with fruity acidity.

Portugieser Originally from Austria, not Portugal, Portugieser is a very light, mild red wine.

Spätburgunder This red, also known as pinot noir, can be velvety and full-bodied. The best have an almond taste.

Trollinger Hearty, fruity and quite acidic, this wine is grown only in Württemberg and ripens late. It has a fragrant nose.

Major Wine-Growing Regions

There are 13 major wine regions in Germany. Regions are divided up into various sub-regions called *Bereiche*, which usually take their name from the largest town in the area. A sub-region may have lots of vineyards huddled together, in which case they form a *Grosslage*; or it may consist of scattered vineyards, called *Einzellagen*.

Ahr One of Germany's smallest wine-growing regions, it extends along the Ahr River, which flows north-east into the Rhine about midway between Koblenz and Bonn. The region mainly produces red wines. About half of its area is given over to Spätburgunder, but Portugieser and Dornfelder red varieties are becoming more popular. Typically, the wines are mellow to fiery, and quite spicy. It's rarely sold outside the region.

Mittelrhein The name of the grape here is Riesling. There's even a variety – Rhine sailors beware – called the Loreley Riesling, a medium dry wine that was first released in 1990. Though Mittelrhein wine is good, the highlight of the region, which extends about 100km south along the Rhine River from Bonn, is the scenery. The locals drink most of what they produce, and in bad years they sell the rest to Sekt producers, who value the high acidity. Wines tend to be fresh and fragrant, often pithy or austere. Boppard, Bacharach and Oberwesel are the major towns.

Mosel-Saar-Ruwer Some of Germany's best wines are produced along these three rivers, the backbone of which is formed by the spectacular Moselle River. The Moselle has some of the world's steepest slopes under vine, which means much of the picking is done by hand. The slate soil gives the wines a flinty taste. A good Moselle wine is fragrant, fruity and light, and Riesling predominates. Müller-Thurgau is also widely planted, and there's an ancient Roman variety called the Elbing, which is cultivated in chalky soils.

Rheingau The Rheingau region falls roughly between Hochheim, on the River Main, and Lorch, near the Rhine River. It boasts some of Germany's most established wine-growing families. The Rheingau was one of the first regions to recognise the advantages of the grape fungus, noble rot (botrytis). Although fragrant and lively Riesling is the mainstay, excellent Spätburgunder (especially around Assmannshausen) is also produced.

Nahe The Nahe region, east of the Moselle River, produces some fragrant, fruity and full-flavoured wines using Müller-Thurgau, Riesling and Silvaner grapes.

Pfalz More wine is produced in the Pfalz (Palatinate), near the French border, than in any other German region. The best vineyards are in the northern Pfalz. Müller-Thurgau, Kerner, Silvaner and Morio-Muscat, as well as Riesling grape varieties, produce mild, well-rounded and full-bodied whites.

Rheinhessen The Rheinhessen is a broad valley bordered by the Nahe River in the west and the Rhine in the north and east. It's most famous as the birthplace of the ubiquitous Liebfraumilch wine (today the grapes come from several regions).

A wide variety of wines are produced here, due to its many different soil types. Riesling wines from the Rhine town of Nierstein rate among Germany's finest.

Franken Würzburg forms the centre of the Franken region, which produces dry and earthy wines. Wine is usually sold in a small green flagon known as a *Bocksbeutel*.

Hessische Bergstrasse Extending from Darmstadt to just north of Heidelberg, the Hessische Bergstrasse is a small region. Its wine is consumed locally and the festivals are usually better than the wines – try Heppenheim in late June.

Württemberg Nearly half of the wines produced in Württemberg are reds, making it Germany's largest red-wine producing region. The major city in the region is Stuttgart. White wines tend to be vigorous and the reds quite fruity.

DAVID PEEVERS

Harvesting grapes
in Baden-Baden

GERMAN BEER & WINE

Baden The Baden wine region, running south from Heidelberg to the northern shore of Lake Constance, takes in the Black Forest and the volcanic soils of the famous Kaiserstuhl area. It produces some fine whites from Müller-Thurgau, Ruländer (pinot gris), Gutedel and the spicy Gewürztraminner. Its Spätburgunder wines from Kaiserstuhl are full-bodied and racy. The Spätburgunder Weissherbst, a rose wine, is popular.

Saale/Unstrut Being Germany's northernmost wine region, the Saale/Unstrut region produces medium-bodied whites. Its young QbA and Kabinett wines are good. Freyburg is the main centre. Try Rotkäppchen (Little Red Riding Hood) Sekt, a favourite among ex-GDR citizens.

Sachsen Dresden and Meissen are the two major cities in the Sachsen region. The speciality is an Elbtaal (Elbe Valley) Sekt.

Other Wines
'Apple wine' *(Ebbelwei or Ebbelwoi)* is a popular drink in southern Hesse, especially in Frankfurt. You can drink it pure, *sauer gespritzt* (with a shot of mineral water) or *süss gespritzt* (with lemonade), which is like cider.

Glühwein, a hot, mulled wine drink, is served throughout the country in the weeks leading up to Christmas. Take it slowly, though – it sneaks up on you and leaves you with a hangover!

Wine Tastings & Tours
Tourist offices in all wine-producing regions can give you loads of information on local wine tastings, winery routes and organised tours. A good central source of information is the Deutsches Weininstitut (German Wine Institute; ☎ 06131-282 90, fax 28 29 50) Gutenberg-platz 3-5, 55116 Mainz (Postfach 1660, 55006 by post). It distributes excellent free booklets called *Vintners to Visit* and holds courses on German wine and wine regions.

Your choice of courses will be much greater if you can speak German. Most last just one day and are priced from DM100. Every autumn, the bilingual German Wine Academy takes place during a week-long river cruise from Düsseldorf to the Swiss border (operated by KD Lines), and includes a tight schedule of seminars held both aboard and at wine estates. Trust us: you'll learn a lot, though your memory of it may be a bit foggy! For details, contact the German Wine Institute or check the Web site at www.deutscheweine.de.

The majority of Germany's wine regions are in the south-west, around the Rhine and its tributaries. Boat cruises, trains and well marked roads and hiking paths link the vineyards, which offer tours, tastings and accommodation.

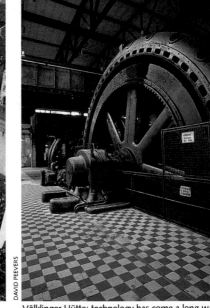

DAVID PEEVERS

A Romantic Road highlight, Rothenburg

DAVID PEEVERS

Völklinger Hütte: technology has come a long way

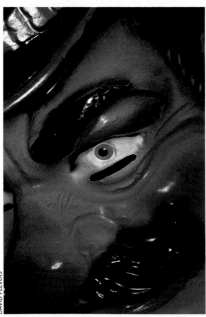

DAVID PEEVERS

A carnival mask at Bad Waldsee, near Ulm

DAVID PEEVERS

Cologne's biggest attraction is its imposing Dom.

Continued from page 112

with sweet *(süss)* or spicy *(scharf)* mustard *(Senf)*, with either sauerkraut or potato salad, and a piece of bread or a roll. Favourites, now usually found throughout the country but originating in particular regions, include:

Bratwurst – generic spiced sausage, found throughout Germany

Weisswurst – veal sausage, found mainly in southern Germany

Bregenwurst – yes, brain sausage, found mainly in Lower Saxony and western Saxony-Anhalt

Blutwurst – blood sausage

Frankfurter – hot-dog type of sausage

Thüringer – long, thin, spiced sausage

Krakauer – thick, paprika-spiced sausage of Polish origin

Side Dishes Main courses are almost invariably accompanied by a salad and either *Sauerkraut* (shredded cabbage in white wine vinegar and cooked slowly, sometimes with apple, sometimes in wine), *Blaukraut* or *Rotkohl* (the same, but made with red cabbage), or any number of potato dishes.

Potatoes are prepared in umpteen ways: fried *(Bratkartoffeln)*, mashed *(Kartoffelpüree)*, grated and then fried (the Swiss *Rösti*, known in the USA as hash browns), or as chips/French fries *(Pommes frites)*. A Thuringian speciality is *Klösse*, a ball of mashed potato cooked to produce something like a dumpling. This is similar to the Bavarian *Kartoffelknödel*. There are even restaurants throughout the country called Kartoffelhaus (or some variation), which base their entire menu around a vegetable most of the world considers only a side dish. In Baden-Württemberg, potatoes are often replaced with *Spätzle*, a noodle type.

Other Specialities See the introductions and Places to Eat sections of each chapter for suggestions on local specialities. Some of the more renowned dishes include:

Schnitzel – Pork, veal or chicken breast pounded flat, coated in egg, dipped in breadcrumbs and pan-fried. This is a standard German menu item, and unless otherwise stated, it's pork.

Eisbein – pickled pork knuckles

Rippenspeer – spare ribs

Rotwurst – black pudding

Rostbrätl – grilled meat

Sauerbraten – marinated and roasted beef served with a sour cream sauce

Rosthähnchen – roast chicken

Putenbrust – turkey breast

Menu Items A German menu *(Speisekarte)* and daily specials (on the *Tageskarte*) are usually broken up by category – meat, fish and vegetable. Menu vocabulary includes:

Fleisch – Meat

Rindfleisch – Beef

Schweinefleisch – Pork

Lammfleisch – Lamb

Kalbfleisch – Veal

Hackfleisch – Chopped or minced meat

Hähnchen or *Huhn* – Chicken

Schinken – Ham

Fisch – Fish

Forelle – Trout

Dorsch – Cod

Karpfen – Carp

Lachs – Salmon

Wild – Game

Wildschwein – Wild boar

Hirsch – Male deer

Reh – Venison

Kaninchen – Rabbit

Truthahn – Turkey

Geräuchert – Smoked

Gebacken – Baked

Frittiert – Deep-fried

Paniert – Breaded

Gegrillt – Grilled

Gebraten – Pan-fried

Gefüllt – Stuffed

Gekocht – Boiled

Desserts

Dessert *(Nachspeise* or *Nachtisch)* is not usually considered an important part of a German meal and usually consists of something relatively light. Popular desserts include custards, sometimes served with fruit; *Rote Grütze*, a delicious tart fruit compote, served with warm vanilla sauce; and ice cream, again served with fruit or whipped cream.

Cakes are not usually eaten as dessert but figure prominently during another German tradition: *Kaffee und Kuchen* – the afternoon coffee break.

Fruit

Except, perhaps, for bananas, Germans are moderate fruit eaters. Grocery stores and markets generally have a broad, if expensive, selection of fruits, which are often air-freighted from as far away as California, Israel, South Africa and New Zealand.

The most expensive way to buy fruit is at specialised neighbourhood fruit shops, which have the very finest of everything. They may also stock excellent wines and high-end pasta and other delicacies. Prices are usually twice that of the supermarkets.

Fast Food

You can get a quick feed at any stand-up food stall *(Schnellimbiss* or simply *Imbiss)*

throughout the country. There are almost always Imbisse in train stations and around the centre of town selling quite reasonable and filling fare.

Germany's sizeable Turkish population has significantly enlarged the country's snack repertory. In every city or village you'll find kiosks and takeaway restaurants selling doner kebab – a sandwich made from slices of roasted beef, chicken or lamb on pitta bread with onions, tomato, tahini and spices – for between DM5 and DM6.

Almost all places that do doner will also accommodate vegetarians by making a vegie version, and almost all sell salads, which cost from DM3.50 to DM7. Salads and some sandwiches are covered with tzatziki, a tasty Greek-style garlic, cucumber and yoghurt sauce (the Turkish version is called *cacik*).

What Germans Eat, and When

Breakfast

A traditional German breakfast *(Frühstück)* usually includes bread rolls, butter, jam, cheese, salami and other sliced meats, a boiled egg and coffee or tea. Most hotels and hostels and even some camp sites include a buffet breakfast as part of the cost of a night's stay. The better hotels and restaurants also include yoghurt, quark, and fresh or canned (or both) fruit salads and cereals in their buffets.

If your hotel doesn't serve breakfast or you arrive in the morning, your best bets are bakeries with Stehcafés and designer restaurants that feature breakfast buffets.

Lunch

Lunch *(Mittagessen)* is traditionally the main meal of the day. Getting a main meal in the evening is never a problem, but you may find that the dish or menu of the day only applies to lunch.

In larger cities, many restaurants offer set lunch specials, usually a main course, salad or soup or an appetiser and sometimes a drink as well, for a fixed price. These are especially prevalent in Chinese eateries and in many restaurants in business centres like Frankfurt. In many places, these are offered by top-end restaurants trying to increase their lunchtime turnover, with the same offered at dinnertime at a third or half off the price.

Dinner

There are no surprises here. Restaurants serve dinner *(Abendessen)* from about 4 pm to about 11 pm. Restaurant prices are highest at dinnertime. Most restaurants figure on only one or two seatings per evening, so you don't have to feel rushed after you've finished your meal. If you like, you may well stay on for another hour or so just nursing a drink, chatting and enjoying the atmosphere. The bill will only be presented to you when you request it.

Another delicious and filling non-meat alternative is Turkish pizza *(lahmacun)*. This tasty snack is made by putting lots of salad vegetables onto a pancake-shaped bread that's been topped with a spicy red sauce, drizzling it all with tzatziki and rolling it up like a burrito.

Other street offerings include small slices of pizza (DM2 to DM5), sausage (DM2 to DM3.50) and simple sandwiches (a ham sandwich in Germany is likely to contain bread and ham, *maybe* butter but usually nothing else; from DM2 to DM5). In the north, you'll also find herring and other marinated fish.

Nordsee, a fast-food chain with branches throughout the country, serves inexpensive and sometimes even creative seafood, along with beer and wine. Some are Stehcafés, some are sit-down restaurants and some are kiosks.

Imbiss stalls and some vans sell excellent roasted chicken (DM4.50 per half).

You'll find that American-style fast-food restaurants are taking over Germany at a jaunty clip. Offerings include McDonald's, Burger King and Pizza Hut. The price of burgers at the first two establishments is far higher in Germany than elsewhere, and the quality is generally not as good. Additionally, you have to pay for tomato sauce (ketchup) and mayonnaise (up to DM0.50 per serving). Burger King and McDonald's have meat-free vegie burgers at all their German outlets.

Vegetarian

Vegetarians should look for *Vegetarische Gerichte* on the menu. Note that Germans sometimes won't consider vegetables that are cooked with meat to contain meat, and sometimes they will offer chicken as an alternative to meat – this whole vegie thing is new here. Vegans have a serious problem, as most salads come with cheese and/or a mayonnaise-based salad dressing. Some 'vegetarian' pizzas contain eggs *(Eier)*. Always ask, and say (for men) '*Ich bin ein Vegetarier*' or (for women) '*Ich bin eine Vegetarierin*'.

Self-Catering

It's very easy and relatively cheap to put together a picnic. Head for the local market or supermarket and stock up on breads, sandwich meats, cheeses, wine and beer. Chains such as PennyMarkt, Aldi and Norma are inexpensive and good places to start, though they may lack a wide range.

Produce markets are great sources of some of the best, freshest and either cheapest or dearest ingredients. In much of the country they're held daily or several times a week, usually in the centre of the city, almost always at the Marktplatz.

Bakeries Bakeries are some of Germany's best features, offering a mind-boggling array of breads, rolls, sweets and snacks, usually very cheaply and always freshly prepared. Some are also Stehcafés, serving coffee, chocolate and cappuccino in addition to their bakery goods.

Bread & Bread Rolls German bread is arguably the best in the world; there are almost 100 varieties of it, everything from light and crusty French-style baguettes to corkboard-like *Vollkornbrot* that's heavy enough to kill someone with. *Bauernlaib* is a dark, sour brown bread, and *Sonnenblumenbrot* is another sour brown bread covered with sunflower seeds.

Bread rolls (*Semmeln* in southern Germany, *Brötchen* in the north) also come in dozens of varieties, including those covered in melted cheese *(Käsesemmel)*, nuts and grains (several types), made from whole grain *(Vollkornsemmel)*, covered in sesame seeds *(Sesamsemmel)* or rye rolls covered in caraway seeds *(Kümmelsemmel)*. All are made fresh daily or more often. *Brez'n*, the delicious traditional pretzels covered in rock salt, are available at bakeries throughout the country.

Biscuits & Cakes If you have a sweet tooth, welcome to heaven. Every German bakery offers dozens of types of cakes and biscuits/cookies, presliced and chopped into snack-size pieces that sell for between DM1

euro currency converter DM1 = €0.51

and DM3. Mouthwatering quark and cream-filled treats topped with fruit and laced with chocolate abound.

DRINKS

Drinks can be expensive in Germany. Be very careful at restaurants and, if you like lots of liquids, make a point of buying your drinks (alcoholic or not) in supermarkets or, even better, in drink shops that specialise in beer and soft drinks.

Almost all bottles in Germany are subject to a deposit *(Pfand)*, which varies according to the manufacturer. You get your deposit back when you bring the bottle back to a shop, even if it's not the one you bought it from.

Nonalcoholic Drinks

Water & Soft Drinks Soft drinks, which come in cans *(Dosen)* and bottles from 33cL to 2L, are widely available throughout the country, although the diet versions are often not. If familiar brands like Pepsi or Coca-Cola taste slightly different from what you're used to, it's because they've been reformulated to meet German tastes.

German tap water is fine to drink but most Germans prefer bottled mineral water *(Mineralwasser)*. Each region produces its own brand, which comes with lots of bubbles *(mit Kohlensäure)* or with little *(wenig Kohlensäure)*. Truly still water, like Evian, is rare and more expensive.

Asking for a glass of tap water at a restaurant will raise brows at best and may be refused altogether because they want to sell you an expensive bottle of mineral water. If you're really thirsty and on a seriously tight budget, remember that water from the sink in the WC is free.

Coffee & Tea Coffee is king in Germany and is usually served fresh and strong. It comes in cups *(Tasse)* or pots *(Kännchen)* and you should remember to specify what you want when ordering. Normally, condensed milk and sugar will be served alongside. In trendy cafes, you'll often see people nursing a huge bowl of coffee; this is

Milchkaffee (milk coffee) and contains a large amount of hot milk.

One warning: the bottomless cup is *not* a concept here, and a single cup can cost as much as DM5. If you just want a quick cuppa, grab it at a Stehcafé or the counters of the Eduscho or Tschibo coffee stores where it'll cost around DM2.50.

A very annoying custom, especially prevalent in tourist resorts, is the refusal to serve you just a cup of coffee if you are sitting on the outdoor terrace of a cafe or restaurant. There's nothing less endearing than the sound of a waitress snarling a '*Draussen nur Kännchen*' (Pots only outside) at you.

With tea, if you don't want a pot, ask for *ein Glass Tee* (a glass of tea); it'll usually be served in the form of a tea bag with sugar and maybe a slice of lemon. If you want milk, ask for *Tee mit Milch*.

Beer Nonalcoholic beer *(alkoholfreies Bier)* is very good and has become quite popular. Clausthaler is a popular brand, and Löwenbräu is also a tasty nonalcoholic beer that is frequently served on tap.

Alcoholic Drinks

With over 5000 different labels of beer and a wide selection of local wines, Germany is a tippler's delight. For an insight on the history of German beer and wine, the choices available and where to sample them, see our special section 'German Beer & Wine'.

Schnapps Schnaps is the German word for spirits or hard liquor – and it's drunk more as an aperitif or digestive than as a method of getting blotto. Most German schnapps are made from either apples *(Apfelschnaps)*, pears *(Birnenschnaps)*, plums *(Pflaumenschnaps)* or, in Bavaria, *(Zwetschgengeist)* or wheat *(Kornschnaps)*. But there are others made from different fruits such as *Himbeergeist*, from raspberries. Schnapps is best served at room temperature, tipped back in shots.

German digestive liqueurs *(Magenbitter)*, like Jägermeister, are often served free of charge in restaurants after an evening meal.

ENTERTAINMENT

The German heritage is associated with high culture, and the standard of theatre performances, concerts and operas is among the highest in Europe. Berlin is unrivalled when it comes to concerts and theatre, Dresden is famed for its opera, and Hamburg is now synonymous with the musical *Cats*.

Tickets to all cultural performances – classical music, dance, theatre, cabaret, pretty much anything except films – are almost always available through the local tourist office and at the box office of the venue itself. Except for travelling shows, there's rarely the need to reserve far in advance. Student discounts usually apply to all performances.

Cinemas

Films are widely attended in Germany, but foreign films are usually dubbed into German. If the film is shown in the original language with German subtitles, it will say 'OmU' on the advertisement, which means *Original mit Untertiteln* (original with subtitles). If the film is screened in the original language, it will say 'OF' *(Originalfassung)* or 'OV' *(Originalversion)*. These types of screenings are mostly limited to large cities like Berlin, Munich, Cologne, Hanover, Hamburg and Frankfurt.

Alternative cinemas – usually called *Kommunales Kino* or *Programmkino* – are wonderful places to see movies from around the world in their original language, sometimes with German subtitles.

German cinemas often lag a few months behind a film's first release, especially for US productions.

Tickets tend to be quite expensive (up to DM17 for a Saturday night screening of a first release), though steep discounts (usually about 50%) are offered on one day of the week *(Kinotag)*; the day varies from one cinema to the next.

Discos & Clubs

Germany is infamous as the home of techno music, and discos are hugely popular in larger towns and cities. In many smaller towns, the blaring thud, thud, thud is overpowered by more traditional German meeting places such as cafes and pubs.

Germans are very good at freeing up unorthodox spaces for discos – old city airports, bomb shelters, bank vaults and abandoned coal mines, you name it. As in many other countries in the world, old places become boring and new places become popular very quickly.

Discos in business hotels are usually overflowing with suits in complicated eyewear and pastel ties bopping the night away and doing thumbs-up-sign waves on the dance floor.

Generally, admission to clubs is between DM5 and DM10, though it can be as much as DM20. Check if there's a minimum drink purchase in addition to the admission, or whether the price already includes a drink or two. In some cities, like Leipzig and Berlin, there aren't any mandatory closing times, but in most places discos close between 1 and 3 am.

Opera & Classical Music

Most cities in Germany have active musical calendars, featuring either their own or visiting philharmonics and opera companies. There are also many opportunities to hear classical and choral works in churches – particularly in the home towns of some of the country's most famous sons.

Ballet and opera are usually held in the same venues as classical music performances, though in larger cities like Munich, Frankfurt, Berlin, Leipzig and Dresden, they have their own venue.

Theatre

Traditional German theatre is a treat even if you're not following the language, as productions are usually lavish and the acting, well, let's just say it can get very over the top. In larger cities you can enjoy *Kabarett*, which is political and satirical entertainment featuring clever monologues and short skits. Also in larger cities, road shows of West End and Broadway musicals – *Rocky Horror Picture Show*, *Evita*, *Cats* etc – pass through regularly.

Cultural Centres

Cultural centres have proliferated in Germany over the last decade or so. These mixed-use venues are usually housed in abandoned warehouses, department stores, breweries and other large buildings. The space is divided into several rooms dedicated to various forms of entertainment. Some may contain all or a mix of the following: cinema, dance and concert halls, theatre, bars, cafes, restaurants, gallery space, a circus and workshops. Depending on the centre, events are mainstream to cutting-edge, with a good dose of multiculturalism thrown in.

Rock

Local bands are best heard in bars, beer halls, beer gardens and small arenas. There are frequent big-name rock concerts throughout the country, and there's an energy to German local bands that's absolutely unique. Venues are unpredictable and in many instances as creative as those used for discos – the Olympic Stadium in Munich, the Volkswagen employee car park in Wolfsburg, etc. Check each city's Entertainment section for a listing of what's-on magazines.

Jazz

Jazz is big in Germany and most larger cities have dedicated jazz clubs. Check each city's Entertainment section for more information. Some city tourist offices publish jazz calendars (usually free), showing upcoming performances.

Folk & Traditional Music

Much of the folk and traditional music you're likely to encounter during a trip to Germany is found at Irish pubs. Most people think of oompah band music as typically German, but it's actually typically Bavarian; you'll find it at beer gardens throughout the state. In fact, German folk music is played mostly in drinking venues throughout the country, though sometimes there are special performances at theatres and small concert halls. It is not popular among young Germans, especially those living outside rural areas.

Pubs & Bars

Pubs and bars are less common in Germany than are beer gardens and cafes, where most casual drinking is done. Beer gardens are outdoor areas, sometimes in parks or outside castles, sometimes just attached to a restaurant. Here, you sit at long wooden tables while drinking huge glasses of beer and eating. In many Bavarian beer gardens, you're permitted to bring your own food (though there's also food for sale), but not in other states. Beer garden food is usually of the simple, hearty variety: roast chicken, Wurst, huge pretzels and other quick snacks. Usually you'll be required to pay a deposit on the glass.

In all German cities and towns there are *Kneipen* (pubs), which range from absolute dives packed with drunks slugging down rotgut to stylish affairs with good food and drink. You'll usually be able to tell rather quickly which one you're in. There are also standard American-style stand-up bars in most larger cities. While beers are relatively inexpensive, mixed cocktails are outrageously priced – sometimes as high as DM15 or DM20. Wine is also rather expensive.

Beer Halls

Beer halls are like large pubs, rustic and plain in their decor and dedicated drinking places. They are usually affiliated with a particular brewery and only serve its product. Beer halls are especially prevalent in Munich (who doesn't know the Hofbräuhaus?), but you'll also find them in places like Cologne and Düsseldorf. Bavarian beer halls will often have live entertainment, usually in the form of oompah bands, which creates a jolly, sometimes raucous atmosphere. Food is served in these places, though that's not the main reason people come here.

SPECTATOR SPORTS

Germans are mad about sport, and on the whole they play it well. At the heart of German sporting success are the *Sportvereine*, small, well-organised sports associations that are as much social clubs as sports clubs. The idea of the Sportverein dates back to the 19th century, when many were founded to remedy 'unhealthy' industrialisation. Today, around 26 million people, or about one in three Germans, belongs to some sort of sports club.

The GDR usually outshone West Germany in the Olympic Games, and the rigorous East German system of early talent identification and special training centres paid dividends in national prestige.

Doping, informally sanctioned by some sports clubs, tarnished the image of GDR sport and when East Germany won 12 out of 13 Olympic gold medals in women's swimming events in Montreal in 1976, even good GDR citizens began to have their suspicions. After Germany's reunification, many top competitors received suspensions. But even without the doping, a strong sporting tradition had taken hold, and a new generation of eastern Germans excels in international competition, especially swimmers.

Football

Football (Fussball), or soccer, is by far the most popular sport. One of Germany's most important football figures was Sepp Herberger; the centenary of his birth was celebrated in 1997. Herberger's great achievement was to coach the West German team to victory against Hungary in the 1954 World Cup in Switzerland, a triumph referred to as 'the miracle of Bern'. The victory, which restored pride to a defeated Germany, was greeted in West Germany by spontaneous public celebrations – no simple matter after WWII.

West Germany had to wait 20 years to repeat the triumph, this time with a new generation of players under the leadership of Franz Beckenbauer, one of the most technically proficient players the world has seen. Also important for national prestige was the success of the unified German side (this time coached by Franz 'the Kaiser' Beckenbauer) in the 1990 World Cup in Italy.

East Germany was less successful than its larger neighbour, although it seemed to be geared up for a rosy future when it picked up the European Championship for juniors in 1986. One member of this team, Matthias Sammer, became the first eastern German to play in the unified German team. He went on to win both the German Footballer of the Year award and the German Championship twice with his team, Borussia Dortmund.

Among other renowned players, the recently retired Jürgen Klinsmann, who comes from Stuttgart, won accolades in Britain with Tottenham Hotspur, one of his stopovers after Monte Carlo and Italy. As national captain, he led Germany to victory in the 1996 European Championship. He retired in 1999.

Some of the best matches are the local derbies, such as those between Bayern-München and 1860 Munich, usually held at Munich's Olympic Stadium, or VFL Bochum and Borussia Dortmund. First-division teams to watch out for are VfB Stuttgart, 1 FC Kaiserslautern, Hertha BSC, Bayer Leverkusen, Hamburger SV, Karlsruher SC, Borussia-Mönchengladbach and 1 FC Köln.

National League (Bundesliga) games are usually played from Friday to Sunday. The DFB Cup, based on a knockout system and often more exciting, is usually played during the week, as are European Cup play-offs.

The season runs from September to June, with a winter break from Christmas to mid-February. Tickets, which can be bought at the grounds or in advance from designated ticket offices locally, cost DM10 to DM20 for Stehplätze (standing-room places) and around DM30 for cheap seats.

Tennis

Tennis was a minor sport in Germany until a somewhat awkward carrot-top by the name of Boris Becker won Wimbledon in 1985 at 17 years of age and became the youngest player, first unseeded player and first German ever to do so. He won again in 1986 and 1989, picked up the US Open in

1989, and the Australian Open in 1991 and 1996. Becker officially retired from the game in 1998, then came back to play Wimbledon in 1999 where he once again announced his retirement. In recent years, Becker has assumed a mentoring and coaching role with younger German talent, like Thomas Haas and Nicolas Kiefer.

Michael Stich, despite his extraordinary skill, was condemned to the role of the eternal No 2 of German tennis. Not even a win over Becker in the 1991 Wimbledon final could make him Germany's No 1 in the public's eyes. His best year was 1993, when he was ranked second in the world and won the Davis Cup for Germany, but Stich announced his retirement in 1997, aged 28.

Steffi Graf has been the most consistently brilliant of all German tennis players, perhaps of all players anywhere. She ranked No 1 for longer than any other player in history, man or woman. Graf also holds a special place in history as the only player to achieve the Golden Slam – all four Grand Slam titles and the Olympic gold medal, in 1988.

Less dramatic on court than Becker, Graf's ability to roll over opponents exposed her to unfair accusations of having made tennis dull. The same cannot be said of Steffi's off-court activities. Her father, Peter Graf, was imprisoned for tax evasion in 1997, and Graf narrowly escaped charges herself. Perfectionism has taken its toll on Graf physically and psychologically. After injuries kept her off the courts for much of 1998, Steffi returned triumphantly to Paris to become the 1999 French Open champion and to Wimbledon where only Lindsay Davenport could stop her from winning her eighth Wimbledon title. Steffi's dramatic comeback was sadly shortlived, as she announced her retirement in August 1999.

Thanks largely to the success of Becker and Graf, Germany has become the biggest tennis market in the world, hosting plenty of top tennis tournaments. The men's outdoor season gets under way in Munich in late April, followed by the German Open in Hamburg in early May. The World Team Cup is held in mid-May in Düsseldorf. A grass tournament is then played in Halle in mid-June in preparation for Wimbledon. Then it's back on clay in Stuttgart in mid-July, and indoors for the Grand Slam Cup in Munich in late September. The men's professional tour culminates with the ATP World Championship in early November in Hanover.

Women's tournaments are held in Hanover in mid-February, Hamburg in late April, Berlin in mid-May, Leipzig in late September/early October, and Stuttgart in early October.

The address of the Deutscher Tennis Bund (☎ 040-41 17 80, fax 41 17 82 22) is Postfach 13 02 71, 20102 Hamburg.

Athletics

Germany has many quality athletics meetings. Locations vary from year to year. The most important indoor event is the Leichtathletik-Hallenmeisterschaft, held in February each year, which is the German qualification for international indoor events that usually follow in May.

Other good events are held annually in February and March in Chemnitz, Karlsruhe, Stuttgart and nearby Sindelfingen.

The outdoor athletics season runs roughly from May to early September. Its high point, the Deutsche Leichtathletik Meisterschaft, is reached each year at the end of June, when top athletes gather and compete to represent Germany in the next international championship.

There are also numerous commercial gatherings, usually 'parade events' after the completion of important international championships (usually by late August), two of which are the Internationales Stadion-Fest in Berlin's Olympic Stadium and the ASV Sportfest in Cologne. Both are Grand Prix events.

For more information on track and field events, contact the Deutscher Leichtathletik-Verband (☎ 06151-770 80, fax 77 08 11), Postfach 11 04 63, 64219 Darmstadt.

Other Spectator Sports

For information on swimming events, contact the Deutscher Schwimmverband (☎ 0561-94 08 30, fax 940 83 15), Korbacher Strasse 93, 34132 Kassel.

Top ski-jumping events are held in Oberstdorf in late December and in Garmisch-Partenkirchen on 1 January. The dates and locations of alpine events vary; tourist offices in ski areas are the best sources of information.

Information on equestrian events can be obtained from the Deutsche Reiterliche Vereinigung (☎ 02581-636 20, fax 621 44) Postfach 11 02 65, 48204 Warendorf.

Fans of Michael Schumacher might like to watch the FIA Formula 1 World Championship, normally held in the last week of July at the Hockenheim-Ring near Heidelberg. A motorcycle grand prix is usually held in late May or early June.

A calendar of events is published each year by Hockenheim-Ring (☎ 06205-95 00, fax 95 02 99). The address of the Deutscher-Motorsport-Verband (☎ 069-695 00 20, fax 69 50 02 20) is Otto-Fleck-Schneise 12, 60528 Frankfurt-am-Main.

SHOPPING

Products made in Germany are high quality but rarely cheap.

Munich is a good place to buy Bavarian traditional dress. Much of it is aimed at the children's market, but you will also find a large range of adult wear. Expect to spend at least DM400 for a quality adult leather jacket or a *Dirndl* (women's dress). Bavaria is also the place to buy hunting gear, especially if you have a penchant for traditional hunting hats.

Germany excels in optical goods such as binoculars and lenses, and its Leica and Zeiss brands have an excellent reputation worldwide. Beer steins are best bought from breweries or beer halls.

In the Harz Mountains there's a roaring trade in puppets, marionettes, carved wooden figures and embroidered cloth, much of this on the theme of witches. A good wooden marionette witch costs around DM200. Glassware is another speciality in the Harz Mountains.

Anyone seeking quality toys should visit Nuremberg, where a tradition of toy manufacture dates back to the 16th century. The city was famous for its wooden dolls with movable limbs, and later for toys made out of tin. It remains a centre for toys, traditional as well as modern plastic, many of which can be found at its Christmas market.

The Bavarian Forest is famous for its crystal glassware, and Meissen should be a port of call for anyone interested in modern or antique porcelain. The symbol of Meissen porcelain is the crossed swords, and a much imitated local form is the so-called *Einschnitt*, which has distinctive curved rims and rich decorative patterns. Quality antique porcelain designed by Graf Marcolini in the late 18th century has a small star beneath the crossed swords. Porcelain is also produced in the Thuringian Forest, while a good place for ceramics is Kannenbäckerstrasse in the Westerwald in Rhineland-Palatinate.

Germany produces some fine regional white wines which, due to the cool climate, have a distinctive refreshing acidity. The most famous vineyards are along the Rhine and Moselle rivers, but throughout most of southern Germany you will find places selling vintages from the cellar door (see the 'German Beer & Wine' special section).

Other typical shopping items include colourful heraldic emblems, cuckoo clocks from the Black Forest and ships in bottles from coastal towns. Therapeutic footwear, such as the sandals and shoes made by Birkenstock and orthopaedic inlays by Scholl, is a niche market where Germany excels.

Art reproductions, books and posters are sold in some museums and speciality shops. Also of high quality are illustrated calendars and coffee-table books.

The annual Christmas markets (*Christkindlmarkt* in Nuremberg and Munich, *Weihnachtsmärkte* elsewhere) are good places to pick up presents. Wax candles and ceramic goods are always well represented. Wooden toys and wooden boards (used by Germans for breakfast and the evening meal, or *Abendbrot*) are other options.

Collectors of antiquarian books will find a large selection in *Antiquariat* bookshops in the major centres or university towns. English-language books, except for those used in schools, tend to be overpriced; if you need to stock up on reading material, go to larger second-hand bookshops or shop around before you buy.

It is difficult to find real bargains at flea markets where 1970s junk dominates. But collectors of kitsch will be in their element; records and cassettes can usually be picked up for a couple of Deutschmarks and second-hand souvenirs for even less.

Window shoppers will enjoy Germany's many *Passagen* (arcades), and Berlin's Kaufhaus des Westens (KaDeWe) and Wertheim department stores are well worth a visit for their sheer range of goods.

Getting There & Away

If you live outside Europe, flying is pretty much the only way to get to Germany. Even if you're already in Europe, a flight may still be the fastest and cheapest option, especially from faraway places like Greece, Spain or southern Italy.

Otherwise, train travel is the most efficient and comfortable option, though buses are a viable, and usually cheaper, alternative from some capital cities. Keep in mind that seats fill up quickly and prices often increase considerably during the summer school holidays.

AIR
Airports & Airlines
The main gateways are Frankfurt-am-Main, Munich and Düsseldorf. Most of the cheaper tickets will get you as far as Frankfurt – the busiest airport in Europe after London's Heathrow – where you can catch connecting flights to other German cities.

Lufthansa Airlines is Germany's premier airline, with services within Germany, Europe and overseas. The Web site is at www.lufthansa.com and its international partners are SAS, United Airlines, Air Canada and Thai Airways; its subsidiary Condor has charter flights mainly to holiday destinations in southern Europe.

LTU International Airways is an independent charter airline with flights to cities around the world. Eurowings is a regional airline that offers primarily short hops from major European cities to regional and international airports in Germany. It's also a feeder airline for KLM-Royal Dutch Airlines, Northwest Airlines and Air France.

One major domestic competitor for Lufthansa is Deutsche BA, a subsidiary of British Airways.

Buying Tickets
If you're flying to Germany from outside Europe, the plane ticket will probably be the single most expensive item in your bud-

get, and buying it can be an intimidating business. There is likely to be a multitude of airlines and travel agents hoping to separate you from your money, and it is always worth putting aside a few hours to research the current state of the market. Start early: some of the cheapest tickets have to be bought months in advance, and some popular flights sell out early. Ask other travellers for recommendations, look at ads in newspapers and magazines (including those catering specifically for the German community in your country), consult reference books and watch for special offers. Then phone several agents for bargains. Find out the fare, the route, how long the ticket is valid and any restrictions on the ticket.

Cheap tickets are available in two distinct categories: official and unofficial. Official ones have a variety of names, including advance purchase tickets, advance purchase excursion (Apex) fares, super-Apex and simply budget fares. Unofficial discount tickets are released by the airlines through selected travel agents, and it is worth shopping around to find them. If you call the airlines directly, they may not quote you the cheapest fares available, except perhaps if there's an air-fare war on between competing airlines. In most cases, return tickets are cheaper than two one-way tickets.

If you are flying to Germany from the UK, USA or South-East Asia, you may find that the cheapest flights are being advertised by obscure agencies whose names haven't yet reached the telephone directory. Many such firms are honest and solvent, but there are a few rogues who will take your money and disappear, to reopen elsewhere a month or two later under a new name. If you feel suspicious about a firm, don't give them all the money at once – leave a deposit of 20% or so and pay the balance when you get the ticket. If they insist on cash in advance, go somewhere else or be prepared to take a big risk. And once you have the ticket, ring the

Air Travel Glossary

Baggage Allowance This will be written on your ticket and usually includes one 20kg item to go in the hold, plus one item of hand luggage.

Bucket Shops These are unbonded travel agencies specialising in discounted airline tickets.

Bumped Just because you have a confirmed seat doesn't mean you're going to get on the plane (see Overbooking).

Cancellation Penalties If you have to cancel or change a discounted ticket, there are often heavy penalties involved; insurance can sometimes be taken out against these penalties. Some airlines impose penalties on regular tickets as well, particularly against 'no-show' passengers.

Check-In Airlines ask you to check in a certain time ahead of the flight departure (usually one to two hours on international flights). If you fail to check in on time and the flight is overbooked, the airline can cancel your booking and give your seat to somebody else.

Confirmation Having a ticket written out with the flight and date you want doesn't mean you have a seat until the agent has checked with the airline that your status is 'OK' or confirmed. Meanwhile you could just be 'on request'.

Courier Fares Businesses often need to send urgent documents or freight securely and quickly. Courier companies hire people to accompany the package through customs and, in return, offer a discount ticket which is sometimes a phenomenal bargain. In effect, what the companies do is ship their freight as your luggage on regular commercial flights. This is a legitimate operation, but there are two shortcomings – the short turnaround time of the ticket (usually not longer than a month) and the limitation on your luggage allowance. You may have to surrender all your allowance and take only carry-on luggage.

Full Fares Airlines traditionally offer 1st class (coded F), business class (coded J) and economy class (coded Y) tickets. These days there are so many promotional and discounted fares available that few passengers pay full economy fare.

ITX An ITX, or 'independent inclusive tour excursion', is often available on tickets to popular holiday destinations. Officially it's a package deal combined with hotel accommodation, but many agents will sell you one of these for the flight only and give you phoney hotel vouchers in the unlikely event that you're challenged at the airport.

Lost Tickets If you lose your airline ticket, an airline will usually treat it like a travellers cheque and, after inquiries, issue you with another one. Legally, however, an airline is entitled to treat it like cash and if you lose it, then it's gone forever. Take good care of your tickets.

MCO An MCO, or 'miscellaneous charge order', is a voucher that looks like an airline ticket but carries no destination or date. It can be exchanged through any International Association of Travel Agents (IATA) airline for a ticket on a specific flight. It's a useful alternative to an onward ticket in those countries that demand one, and is more flexible than an ordinary ticket if you're unsure of your route.

No-Shows No-shows are passengers who fail to show up for their flight. Full-fare passengers who fail to turn up are sometimes entitled to travel on a later flight. The rest are penalised (see Cancellation Penalties).

Air Travel Glossary

On Request This is an unconfirmed booking for a flight.

Onward Tickets An entry requirement for many countries is that you have a ticket out of the country. If you're unsure of your next move, the easiest solution is to buy the cheapest onward ticket to a neighbouring country or a ticket from a reliable airline which can later be refunded if you do not use it.

Open Jaw Tickets These are return tickets where you fly out to one place but return from another. If available, this can save you backtracking to your arrival point.

Overbooking Airlines hate to fly empty seats and since every flight has some passengers who fail to show up, airlines often book more passengers than they have seats. Usually, excess passengers make up for the no-shows, but occasionally somebody gets 'bumped' onto the next available flight. Guess who it is most likely to be? The passengers who check in late.

Point-to-Point Tickets These are discount tickets that can be bought on some routes in return for passengers waiving their rights to a stopover.

Promotional Fares These are officially discounted fares, available from travel agencies or direct from the airline.

Reconfirmation If you don't reconfirm your flight at least 72 hours prior to departure, the airline may delete your name from the passenger list. Ring to find out if your airline requires reconfirmation.

Restrictions Discounted tickets often have various restrictions on them – such as needing to be paid for in advance and incurring a penalty to be altered. Others are restrictions on the minimum and maximum period you must be away, such as a minimum of 14 days or a maximum of one year.

Round-the-World Tickets RTW tickets give you a limited period (usually a year) in which to circumnavigate the globe. You can go anywhere the carrying airlines go, as long as you don't backtrack. The number of stopovers or total number of separate flights is decided before you set off and they usually cost a bit more than a basic return flight.

Stand-by This is a discounted ticket where you only fly if there is a seat free at the last moment. Stand-by fares are usually available only on domestic routes.

Transferred Tickets Airline tickets cannot be transferred from one person to another. Travellers sometimes try to sell the return half of their ticket, but officials can ask you to prove that you are the person named on the ticket. This is less likely to happen on domestic flights, but on an international flight tickets are compared with passports.

Travel Agencies Travel agencies vary widely and you should choose one that suits your needs. Some simply handle tours, while full-service agencies handle everything from tours and tickets to car rental and hotel bookings. If all you want is a ticket at the lowest possible price, then go to an agency specialising in discounted fares.

Travel Periods Ticket prices vary with the time of year. There is a low (off-peak) season and a high (peak) season, and often a low-shoulder season and a high-shoulder season as well. Usually the fare depends on your outward flight – if you depart in the high season and return in the low season, you pay the high-season fare.

airline to confirm that you are actually booked onto the flight.

You may decide to pay more than the rock-bottom fare in favour of the safety of a better-known travel agent. Reliable firms such as STA Travel (www.statravel.com) and Council Travel (www.counciltravel.com) with offices worldwide, Travel CUTS (www.travelcuts.com) in Canada, and Flight Centre (www.flightcentre.com) in Australia are not going to disappear overnight, leaving customers clutching a receipt for a non-existent ticket.

Once you have your ticket, make a photocopy or at least write down its number, the flight number and other relevant details, and keep the information somewhere separate. If the ticket is lost or stolen, this will help you get a replacement.

Round-the-world (RTW) tickets are often real bargains, and can work out to be no more expensive – or even cheaper – than an ordinary return ticket. Official airline RTW tickets are usually put together by a combination of two or more airlines and permit you to fly anywhere you want on their route systems as long as you do not backtrack. Other restrictions are that you (usually) must book the first sector in advance (cancellation penalties then apply). There may be restrictions on how many stops (or miles/km) you are permitted. Usually, the tickets are valid for 90 days up to a year from the date of the first outbound flight. Prices start at about UK£800/US$1300/A$1700, depending on the season and length of validity. An alternative type of RTW ticket is one put together by a travel agent using a combination of discounted tickets. These can be much cheaper than the official ones but usually carry a lot of restrictions.

Travellers with Special Needs

If you have special needs of any sort – you're vegetarian or require a special diet, you're travelling in a wheelchair, taking the baby, terrified of flying, whatever – let the airline know as soon as possible so that they can make the necessary arrangements. Remind them when you reconfirm your booking (at least 72 hours before departure) and again when you check in at the airport. It may also be worth ringing around the airlines before you make your booking to find out how they can handle your particular needs.

Airports and airlines can be surprisingly helpful, but they do need advance warning. Most international airports will provide escorts from check-in desk to plane where needed, and there should be ramps, lifts, accessible toilets and reachable phones. Aircraft toilets, on the other hand, are likely to present a problem; travellers should discuss this with the airline at an early stage and, if necessary, with their doctor.

Guide dogs for the blind will often have to travel in a specially pressurised baggage compartment with other animals, away from their owner, though smaller guide dogs may be admitted to the cabin. All guide dogs will be subject to the same quarantine laws (six months in isolation etc) as any other animal.

Deaf travellers can ask for airport and inflight announcements to be written down for them.

Children aged under two travel for 10% of the full fare (or free on some airlines) as long as they don't occupy a seat. They don't get a baggage allowance in this case. 'Skycots', baby food and nappies (diapers) should be provided by the airline if requested in advance. Prams and strollers can often be taken as hand luggage. Children aged between two and 12 can usually occupy a seat for half to two-thirds of the full fare. They do get a standard baggage allowance.

Departure Tax

A departure tax of DM6 to DM8 per person and airport security fees are included in the price of an airline ticket purchased in Germany. You shouldn't have to pay any more fees at the airport.

The USA

Flights to Germany from major cities in the USA abound and bargains are often available. Several airlines fly directly to Germany, most landing in Frankfurt, where you can catch a connecting flight to other cities in the country. Lufthansa connects Frankfurt with Chicago, New York, Los Angeles and other major US cities. American carriers serving Frankfurt include American Airlines, Delta Air Lines and United Airlines. There are also direct flights to other German cities, including LTU's flights to Düsseldorf from Los Angeles, Phoenix and Daytona. Generally, though, flights to Frankfurt are the cheapest. One-way budget fares to Frankfurt in summer cost from about US$250 from New York, US$350 from Los Angeles and US$380 from Chicago (although you could easily do better than this).

The *New York Times*, *Los Angeles Times*, *Chicago Tribune*, *San Francisco Examiner* and many other major Sunday newspapers produce weekly travel sections with lots of travel agents' advertisements.

Standard fares on commercial airlines are expensive and best avoided, especially since various types of discounts on scheduled flights are usually available. Besides advertised discount fares, options include charter flights, stand-by fares and courier flights. The US-based *Travel Unlimited* newsletter (PO Box 1058, Allston, Massachusetts 02134) publishes details of the cheapest airfares and courier possibilities, and is a treasure trove of information. A single monthly issue costs US$5 and a year's subscription is US$25 (US$35 abroad).

Charter Flights These are often cheaper than scheduled flights. Reliable travel agents specialising in charter flights, as well as budget travel for students, include STA Travel and Council Travel, both of which have offices in major US cities.

STA Travel
(☎ 212-865 2700) 2871 Broadway Ave, Columbia University, New York, NY 10025;
(☎ 310-824 1574) 920 Westwood Blvd, Los Angeles, CA 90024;
(☎ 415-391 8407) 51 Grant Ave, San Francisco, CA 94108;
(☎ 312-786 9050) 429 S Dearborn St, Chicago, IL 60605

Council Travel
(☎ 212-254 2525) 148 West 4th St, New York, NY 10012;
(☎ 212-822 2700) 205 East 42nd St, New York, NY 10017;
(☎ 310-208 3551) 10904 Lindbrook Dr, Los Angeles, CA 90024;
(☎ 415-421 3473) 530 Bush St, Ground Floor, San Francisco, CA 94108;
(☎ 312-951 0585) 1153 N Dearborn St, 2nd Floor, Chicago, IL 60610

Stand-by Fares These tickets are often sold at 60% of the standard price for one-way tickets. You will need to give a general idea of where and when you want to go; a few days before departure, you will be presented with a choice of two or three flights.

Airhitch specialises in stand-by tickets. Fares are incredibly cheap, but at the same time service can be iffy and the flight selection limited (eg just two airlines between Continental Europe and the US West Coast). Its main European office is at 5 Rue de Crussol, 75011 Paris (☎ 01 47 00 16 30), and it also has three US offices: New York City (☎ 212-864 2000 or toll-free ☎ 800 326 2009), Los Angeles (☎ 310-726 5000 or ☎ 800 397 1098) and San Francisco (☎ 415-834 9192 or ☎ 800 834 9192). You'll find the Airhitch Web site at www.airhitch.org.

Air-Tech in New York (☎ 212-219 7000) is a smaller but more professional outfit, providing stand-bys from New York to Frankfurt and Düsseldorf from as little as $169. Flights offered may not get you exactly where you want to go, but the savings are so huge that you might opt for an onward train or bus. Check out the Web site at www.airtech.com.

If you're feeling particularly enterprising, Priceline in Connecticut (toll-free ☎ 800 774 235 463) offers an auction-based booking system for flights. The catch is, bookings are nonrefundable and you may end up flying at weird times on weird airlines. The Web site is at www.priceline.com.

Courier Flights Travelling as a courier means that you accompany freight to its destination, usually only on the outgoing flight. You don't have to handle any shipment personally, either at departure or arrival, and most likely will not even get to see it. All you need to do is carry an envelope with the freight papers with you on board and hand it to someone at your destination. The freight takes the place of your check-in luggage, so you will be restricted to what you are allowed to carry on the plane. You may have to be a US resident and present yourself in person before the company will take you on. Also keep in mind that only a relatively small number of these tickets are available, so it's best to call two or three months in advance and be somewhat flexible with the departure dates.

Most courier flights depart from New York, and a New York-Frankfurt return may cost as little as US$100 in the low season. Generally, you are required to return within a specified period (sometimes within one or two weeks, but often up to one month). Good sources of information on courier flights are the International Association of Air Travel Couriers (☎ 561-582 8320, fax 582 1581) and the Worldwide Courier Association (☎ 718-252 0555 or toll-free ☎ 800 780 4359), 1789 Flatbush, Brooklyn NY 11210. Check out their Web sites at www.courier.org and www.wallstech.com respectively.

Canada

Air Canada and Lufthansa offer flights to Frankfurt from Toronto, Vancouver and Montreal. Travel CUTS (☎ 888-838 2877) specialises in discount fares for students and has offices in major cities. Also check the travel sections of the Toronto-based *Globe & Mail* and *Toronto Star*, and the *Vancouver Sun* for travel agents' ads. The magazine *Great Expeditions* (PO Box 8000-411, Abbotsford, BC V2S 6H1) is a useful source as well.

Australia

Qantas flies from Melbourne and Sydney to Frankfurt via Singapore or Bangkok. STA Travel and Flight Centre are major dealers in cheap airfares, though your local travel agent may also offer some heavily discounted fares. Check the Saturday travel sections of the *Sydney Morning Herald* and Melbourne's *Age* for ads offering cheap fares to Europe, but don't be surprised if they happen to be 'sold out' when you contact the agents (who then offer you a more expensive fare) or if they turn out to be low-season fares on obscure airlines with lots of conditions attached.

Discounted return airfares on major airlines through reputable agents can be surprisingly cheap, with low-season fares around A$1399 and high-season fares up to A$2500. Useful contacts include:

STA Travel
  (☎ 03-9663 7365) Level 4, Union Bldg, RMIT, Melbourne, Vic 3000;
  (☎ 02-9411 6888) Shop 17, 3-9 Spring St, Chatswood, Sydney, NSW 2067;
  (☎ 08-9380 2302) 1st Floor, New Guild Bldg, University of Western Australia, Crawley, Perth, WA 6009
Flight Centre
  (☎ 03-9650 2899) Bourke Street Flight Centre, 19 Bourke St, Melbourne, Vic 3000;
  (☎ 02-9235 0166) Martin Place Flight Centre, Shop 5, State Bank Centre, 52 Martin Place, Sydney, NSW 2000;
  (☎ 08-9325 9222) City Flight Centre, Shop 25, Cinema City Arcade, Perth, WA 6000

New Zealand

STA Travel and Flight Centre are popular travel agents in New Zealand. The cheapest fares to Europe are routed through the USA, and a round-the-world ticket may be cheaper than a simple return. Air New Zealand has flights from Auckland to Frankfurt, either with a stop-over in Asia or in Los Angeles. Otherwise, you can fly to Melbourne or Sydney to pick up a connecting flight there. Useful addresses include:

STA Travel
  (☎ 09-307 0555) 2nd Floor, Student Union Bldg, Princes St, Auckland University, Auckland
Flight Centre
  (☎ 09-309 6171) Auckland Flight Centre, Shop 3A, National Bank Towers, 205-225 Queen St, Auckland

The UK

London is the discount-flight capital of Europe, and finding a cheap airfare to Germany should not be a problem. The main airlines are British Airways and Lufthansa, with flights several times a day to Frankfurt, Düsseldorf, Munich, Hamburg, Berlin and other cities. CityFlyer Express offers flights out of London-Gatwick, and Air UK flies from London-Stansted to Düsseldorf. New airline, buzz offers low-cost flights from London-Stansted to Berlin, Düsseldorf and Frankfurt. Return tickets from Heathrow or Gatwick to Frankfurt in high season cost between UK£78 (with British Midland) and UK£137 (with British Airways/Lufthansa). Fares to other German cities are not significantly more expensive.

Bucket shops abound in London. They generally offer the cheapest tickets, though usually with restricted validity. However, many may not be registered with the ABTA (Association of British Travel Agents), which guarantees a refund or an alternative if you have paid for your flight and the agent then goes out of business.

Time Out magazine, the weekend papers and the *Evening Standard* carry ads for cheap fares. Also look for the free magazines and papers widely available in London, especially *TNT* – you can often pick them up outside main train and tube stations.

Trailfinders head office is a good place to go for budget airfares; it also has a travel library, bookshop, visa service and immunisation centre. STA Travel also has branches in the UK. Useful addresses include:

STA Travel
   (☎ 020-7361 6161 for Europe, ☎ 020-7361 6262 for long-haul) 86 Old Brompton Rd, London SW7
Trailfinders
   (☎ 020-7937 5400) 194 Kensington High St, London W8 7RG
Council Travel
   (☎ 020-7437 7767) 28a Poland St, London W1
Usit Campus
   (☎ 020-7730 7285) 52 Grosvenor Gardens, London SW1W OAG

Continental Europe

Discount flights to various airports in Germany are available from many major cities in Continental Europe. Sometimes it may actually be cheaper – and faster – to catch a plane than to use ground transportation, especially on longer journeys. Smaller regional airlines, like Eurowings, are a good alternative to national carriers, specialising in inexpensive short hops. Full-time students and those under 26 occasionally qualify for special discount rates.

Asia

Flights to Frankfurt are available from Hong Kong, Kuala Lumpur and Tokyo. Lauda Air offers one-way/return flights from Hong Kong and Kuala Lumpur via Vienna for A$559/949 in the low season and A$759/1249 in the high season. KLM has one-way/return flights from Hong Kong, Kuala Lumpur and Tokyo to Frankfurt via Amsterdam for A$570/950 in the low season, rising to A$660/1095 in the high season.

LAND
Train

The train is another good way to get to Germany if you're already in Europe, and it's more comfortable than the bus. It's not worth spending the extra money on a 1st class ticket, since travelling 2nd class on German trains is perfectly comfortable.

Long-distance trains from major German cities to other countries are called EC (EuroCity) trains. The city of Cologne has direct connections to Amsterdam, Basel, Brussels, Copenhagen, Paris, Rome and London (on Eurostar trains, via the Channel Tunnel). There are direct links from Hamburg to Copenhagen and there's also an overnight service to Budapest. From Munich, trains travel to Rome, Milan, Florence, Verona, Prague, Paris, Strasbourg, Salzburg and Zürich.

Overnight international trains are increasingly made up of mostly sleeper carriages, and there may be only one or two carriages with seats. A berth in a four-

Security

In recent years, the number of crimes committed on trains – especially at night – has increased. There have been horror stories of passengers robbed after being drugged or made unconscious with gas blown in through the ventilation ducts. While this should not stop you from using the train, it pays to be aware and to take a few precautions. Never leave your baggage out of sight, especially the bag holding your personal documents, tickets and money. Lock your suitcases, backpacks or bags; better yet, buy a lock and fasten them to the luggage rack. In general, travel in the daytime is safer, though it's easier to catch some sleep (and save accommodation costs) on night trains. If you travel at night, at least try to lock the compartment, if possible. If you're travelling in a sleeping compartment (as opposed to a couchette), it will be lockable and only the attendant (guard) will have a key.

person compartment will cost you a supplement of DM31 to DM49; in a six person compartment it's DM24 to DM38. Supplements for single-bed sleepers are DM140 to DM221, while doubles are an extra DM70 to DM110 per person.

If you have a sleeper or sleeping berth on international train trips, the train conductor will usually collect your ticket before you go to sleep and hand it back to you in the morning. If you're in a regular seat, however, expect to be woken up by conductors coming aboard in each country to check your ticket.

Be sure to make a seat reservation on EC trains, especially during the peak summer season and around major holidays. Trains can get extremely crowded, and you may find yourself stuck in a narrow corridor for hours. Reservations cost DM5 and can be made as late as a few minutes before departure. Examples of standard one-way 2nd-class fares from Germany are

Frankfurt-Paris DM154, Hamburg-London DM288 and Berlin-Amsterdam DM202. For the various train passes on offer – both international and German – see the Getting Around chapter.

Bus

In some cases, bus travel is a good alternative to the train if you're already in Europe and on your way to Germany. Especially for shorter distances, it's usually, though not always, cheaper than taking the train. The downside is, of course, that it's slower. Some of the coaches are quite comfortable, with toilet, air-conditioning and snack bar. Advance reservations may be necessary at peak travel times. In general, return fares are markedly cheaper than two one-way fares.

Eurolines is the umbrella organisation of numerous European bus companies, with service between major cities across Europe. You'll find the Web site at www.eurolines.com. Its offices in Europe include those listed below, although information and tickets are also available from most travel agents.

France
(☎ 01 49 72 51 51) Gare Routière Internationale, 28 Ave du Général de Gaulle, 75020 Paris
Germany
(☎ 069-790 32 88) Am Römerhof 17, 60486 Frankfurt-am-Main
Netherlands
(☎ 020-560 87 87) Amstel Busstation, Julianaplein 5, 1097 DN Amsterdam
UK
(☎ 01582-404 511) 52 Grosvenor Gardens, Victoria, London SW1 OAU

Buses connect major German cities like Düsseldorf, Cologne, Frankfurt, Hamburg, Munich and Aachen with London, Brussels and Amsterdam daily, with Paris up to six times a week, and with Prague three times a week. Examples of one-way/return fares are London-Frankfurt DM137/209, Paris-Hamburg DM115/169 and Amsterdam-Bremen DM70/104. If you're under age 26 or a student, you get a 10% discount. For frequent travellers, there's the Eurolines Pass, offering unlimited travel between 18 cities for either 30 or 60 days, but you can only buy it from the Eurolines representative office in the Frankfurt Hauptbahnhof. If you're under 26, it costs DM429/529 for 30/60 days in low season and DM559/699 in high season. If you're over 26, you pay DM529/629 for 30/60 days in low season and DM649/769 in high season.

BerlinLinienBus (☎ 0130-83 11 44) runs daily buses between German destinations (especially Berlin) and a number of European cities. Sample single fares (regular and for those under 26/over 60) include Amsterdam-Berlin (DM100/90, nine hours), Paris-Berlin via Brussels (DM139/109, 13½ hours), Brussels-Hanover (DM79/69, 9½ hours) and Vienna-Dresden (DM69/59, eight hours). Check out the Web site at www.bex.de.

Gullivers Reisen (☎ 030-311 02 11) covers several international destinations to/from Berlin. They include Amsterdam (DM100/90, nine hours) and London-Victoria (DM185/165, 16½ hours via Amsterdam). See www.gullivers.de on the Web.

Busabout (☎ 020-7950 1661, fax 7950 1662) is a UK-based budget alternative to Eurolines. Though aimed at younger travellers, it has no upper age limit. It runs coaches along five interlocking European circuits. The Busabout Pass costs around UK£250 (UK£199 for youth and student card holders) for 15 days travel on as many of the five circuits as you like. Routes include Amsterdam-Berlin (10 hours), Heidelberg-Frankfurt (1½ hours), Berlin-Prague (eight hours), Cologne-Amsterdam (4½ hours) and Lucerne-Munich (six hours). For more information, check the Web site at www.busabout.com.

Car & Motorcycle

Driving in Germany can be a lot of fun, since the overall quality of the roads is very high and having your own vehicle provides you with the most flexibility to get off the beaten track. The disadvantage is that traffic in urban areas can be horrendous, and parking in the cities is usually restricted to expensive car parks. See the Getting Around chapter for more detailed coverage (roads, road rules, motoring organisations etc) of driving in Germany.

If you're taking your own vehicle, you should always carry proof of ownership. Driving licences from most countries are valid in Germany for one year. You must also have third-party insurance to enter the country. It is compulsory to carry a warning (hazard) triangle and first-aid kit in your car at all times.

If you're coming from the UK, the quickest option (apart from the Channel Tunnel) is to take the car ferry or Hovercraft from Dover, Folkestone or Ramsgate to Calais in France; you can be in Germany in three hours from there. The main gateways to southern Germany are Munich, Freiburg and Passau. Heading for Poland and to the Czech Republic, you may encounter long border delays.

For information about car rental and purchase while in Germany, see the Getting Around chapter.

Bicycle

Cycling is a cheap, convenient, healthy, environmentally sound and above all fun way of travelling. If you are bringing your bicycle to Germany, check for wear and tear before you leave and fill your repair kit with every imaginable spare. As with cars and motorcycles, you won't necessarily be able to buy that crucial gizmo for your machine when it breaks down somewhere in the back of beyond.

Bicycles can travel by air, which can be surprisingly inexpensive, especially with some charter airlines. The independent charter airline LTU, for instance, charges only DM30 to transport a bicycle. You *can* take them to pieces and put them in a bike bag or box, but it's much easier simply to wheel your bike to the check-in desk, where it will (or should) be treated as a piece of baggage. You may have to remove the pedals and turn the handlebars sideways so that your bike will take up less space in the aircraft's hold; check all of this with the airline well in advance, preferably before you pay for your ticket. For information about transporting your bicycle by train in Germany, see the Bicycle section in the Getting Around chapter.

Hitching & Ride Services

Lonely Planet does not recommend hitching (see the Hitching section of the Getting Around chapter). However, travellers who do decide to hitch should not have too many problems getting to and from Germany via the main autobahns and highways.

Aside from hitching, the cheapest way to get to Germany is as a paying passenger in a private car. If you're leaving Germany or travelling within the country, such rides are arranged by *Mitfahrzentralen*, ride-share agencies that can be found in all major cities and many smaller ones as well. For local listings of Mitfahrzentralen see the Getting There & Away section in the individual cities and towns. There's also a Web site at www.mitfahrzentrale-carnet.com which has fares posted.

Most agencies belong to umbrella Mitfahrzentrale networks like Arbeitsgemeinschaft Deutscher Mitfahrzentralen (ADM; ☎ 194 40 in most cities) or Citynetz Mitfahr-Zentrale (☎ 194 44).

The fare you pay comprises a commission to the agency and a per-kilometre charge to the driver. Expect to pay about DM33 for a one-way Hamburg-Berlin trip, DM55 for Hamburg-Frankfurt and DM78 for Hamburg-Munich. From Berlin to Paris will cost about DM90, and to Budapest DM95.

The people answering the phone at Mitfahrzentrale offices usually speak good English. If you arrange a ride a few days in advance, it's best to call the driver the night before and again on the morning of departure just to make sure they are still going.

SEA

Germany's main ferry ports are Kiel and Travemünde in Schleswig-Holstein, and Rostock and Sassnitz (Rügen Island) in Mecklenburg-Western Pomerania. All have services to Scandinavia. Ferries to the UK leave from Hamburg. Return tickets are often cheaper than two one-way tickets. Keep in mind that prices fluctuate dramatically according to the season, the day and time of departure and, for overnight ferries, cabin amenities. All prices quoted are for one-way fares. For more details see Getting There & Away in the individual port towns.

The UK

Hamburg-Harwich The car ferry run by Scandinavian Seaways (☎ 040-389 03 71 in Hamburg) operates year round at least twice weekly and takes 20 hours. One-way fares range from DM97 for a berth in an inner four-bed cabin in low season to DM495 for a single-bed outer suite with private bath in high season. Cars up to 6m long cost an additional DM80/110 in low/high season.

Hamburg-Newcastle Scandinavian Seaways also operates the ferry between Hamburg and Newcastle. It sails every four days from May to August. The crossing takes 24 hours and costs DM138 to DM515.

Sweden

Sassnitz-Trelleborg Scandlines Hansa-Ferry (☎ 0180-534 34 43 or ☎ 038392-614 20 in Sassnitz) operates a quick ferry to Sweden, popular with day-trippers. There are five departures daily. The trip takes four hours and costs DM30/20 in summer/winter. Cars cost DM155 to DM195, including all passengers.

Travemünde-Trelleborg Up to four TT-Line ferries (☎ 040-360 14 42 in Hamburg) make the 7½ hour trip daily, which costs a flat DM50. Cars, including driver, are DM180 to DM300. Students pay half price.

Kiel-Gothenburg The daily overnight ferry run by Stena Line (☎ 0180-533 36 00 or ☎ 0431-9099 in Kiel) takes 14 hours and costs DM132/100 in high/shoulder season. From November to April, tickets are DM70. Passengers under 26 pay DM48 throughout the year. Single sleeping berths in four-bunk cabins start at DM39.

Denmark

Sassnitz-Rønne Three ferries operated by Scandlines HansaFerry (☎ 0180-534 34 43) make the journey daily to this town on Bornholm Island. The trip takes four hours and costs DM38 in summer, DM18 in winter one-way. If you return the same day, you travel back for free.

Rostock-Gedser Scandlines (☎ 0381-673 12 17) in Rostock runs its Vogelfluglinie ferries at least nine times daily to Gedser, about 100km south of Copenhagen. The trip (one to two hours) costs DM85 (DM115 in high season) for cars up to 6m in length, DM40 for motorbikes, and DM5 per adult.

Norway

Kiel-Oslo Color Line (☎ 0431-730 00 in Kiel) makes this 19½ hour journey almost daily. The fare, including a berth in the most basic two bed cabin, is DM150 and about 30% more in summer. Students pay half price in the off-season.

Finland

Travemünde-Helsinki Finnjet-Silja Line (☎ 0381-350 43 50 in Rostock) makes several trips weekly, which take 25 hours and cost from DM250 in four-bunk cabins in summer and DM180 during low season. Students get a 20% discount (50% if booked a week or less before departure).

Poseidon Passagierdienst (☎ 0451-150 74 43 in Lübeck) also makes the run to Helsinki year round at least once a week. The price per person in a three bed cabin is DM320 in low season and DM450 in peak season. It also goes to Turku (34½ hours).

LAKE
Switzerland

The Friedrichshafen-Romanshorn ferry provides the fastest way across Lake Constance from Germany to Switzerland. It's operated by Bodensee-Schiffsbetriebe (☎ 07541-201 38 9 in Friedrichshafen) year round (hourly in daylight), takes 45 minutes and costs DM9.40 (students DM5.80). Cars, including two passengers, are DM28 to DM36 depending on the size.

RIVER

The Köln-Düsseldorfer fleet operates on Germany's larger rivers, offering day trips and cruises on the Rhine, Moselle, Elbe and Danube to Amsterdam, Budapest, Vienna, Basel and other cities. However, you'll need lots of time and cash: the Amsterdam-Cologne trip takes two days, and a two bed berth costs DM350 per person (meals are included). You can reserve ahead at KD Deutsche Flusskreuzfahrten (☎ 0221-208 82 88, fax 208 82 31), Frankenwerft 1, 50667 Cologne, or try one of its many foreign agencies. Also check out the Web site, www.koeln-duesseldorf.de.

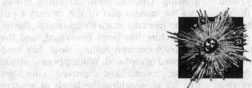

Getting Around

The Germans are whizzes at moving people around, and the nation's transportation network is among the best in Europe. Though it's not cheap, it's usually good value.

The two best ways of getting around are car and train – probably in that order. While air connections are very good, they're aimed at the business market and priced accordingly; in any case, Germany is compact enough to make surface travel a better way to go. Buses tend to be far less convenient than trains, though regional bus service is crucial in the rare places not yet adequately served by the rail network.

AIR

There are lots of flights within Germany, but costs can be prohibitive compared with the train. Lufthansa Airlines, together with its Team Lufthansa partners (Augsburg Airways, Cimber Air and Contact Air), is by far the most popular airline in the country, flying an average of nearly 12,000 flights a week in and outside Germany. For reservations, call Lufthansa (☎ 0180-380 38 03 or ☎ 0561-99 33 44). Team Lufthansa members are franchise partners that fly under their own livery under contract to Lufthansa. Foreign airlines also offer services between major cities, and two major competitors for Lufthansa are now Deutsche BA, a subsidiary of British Airways, and Eurowings, a regional airline that connects major European cities with regional and international airports in Germany.

Several small airlines offer service between regional cities, as well as to and from the North Frisian Islands.

There is only 'tourist' (economy) and business class on Lufthansa domestic flights. While discount tickets are available through travel agents, Lufthansa City Centre offices and even direct from Lufthansa itself, the cheapest scheduled prices for economy travel (with a seven or 14-day advance purchase excursion ticket) between any two points in the country ranges from DM240 to DM270. This fare would apply, for example, to a ticket from Munich to Hamburg, Berlin to Stuttgart or Frankfurt to Dresden. But you can do much better than these 'officially discounted' fares.

Infants generally travel on an adult passenger's lap for a 90% discount of the applicable fare. Children aged two to 11 travel at a 33% to 50% discount of the applicable fare. Unaccompanied children (over five years old only) can travel at the same 33% to 50% discount off the applicable fare, plus a handling fee of DM50.

Full-fare tickets are valid for one year from the start of travel. You do not have to reconfirm domestic flights.

Check-in for domestic flights is generally at least 30 minutes before departure, though in Frankfurt-am-Main and Berlin, passengers without baggage may check in as late as 20 minutes before departure time.

TRAIN

Operated almost entirely by the recently privatised Deutsche Bahn (DB), the German train system is arguably the most efficient in Europe. A wide range of services and ticket options are available, making travelling by rail the most attractive way to get around the country, sometimes even better than car.

There's rail service to almost every place you could think of going in Germany. With 41,000km of track, the network is Europe's most extensive, and over 7000 cities and towns are served. Service is usually excellent.

The future of rail in the former GDR is glowing. DB has been shovelling money into the eastern part of the country's rail system like coal into a steam engine; the infrastructure has been renovated, and the country's decrepit rolling stock has been upgraded or replaced. While prices continue to rise, services have improved to the point that it's approaching the levels of western

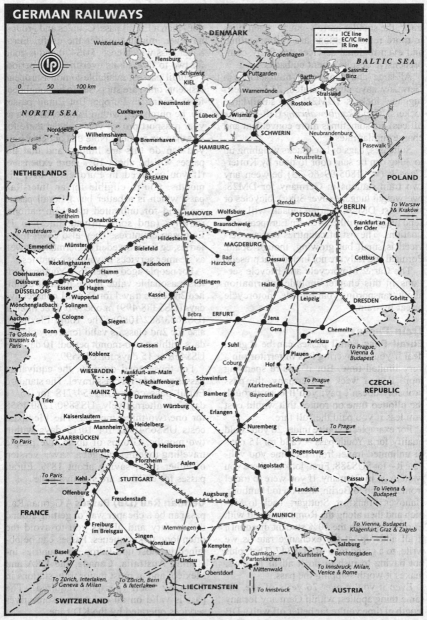

GERMAN RAILWAYS

- ···· ICE line
- — EC/IC line
- – – IR line

DENMARK

BALTIC SEA

NORTH SEA

Westerland
Flensburg
To Copenhagen
Schleswig
KIEL
Puttgarden
Sassnitz
Binz
Barth
Neumünster
Warnemünde
Stralsund
Cuxhaven
Lübeck
Wismar
Rostock
Norddeich
Wilhelmshaven
Bremerhaven
SCHWERIN
Neubrandenburg
Emden
HAMBURG
Pasewalk

NETHERLANDS

Oldenburg
BREMEN
Neustrelitz
POLAND
Bad Bentheim
Osnabrück
HANOVER
Wolfsburg
Stendal
POTSDAM
BERLIN
To Warsaw & Kraków
To Amsterdam
Rheine
Braunschweig
Frankfurt an der Oder
Emmerich
Münster
Bielefeld
Hildesheim
MAGDEBURG
Recklinghausen
Paderborn
Bad Harzburg
Dessau
Cottbus
Oberhausen
Hamm
Dortmund
Göttingen
Halle
Duisburg
Hagen
Kassel
Leipzig
DRESDEN
Görlitz
DÜSSELDORF
Essen
Wuppertal
Bebra
ERFURT
Mönchengladbach
Solingen
Aachen
Cologne
Siegen
Jena
Chemnitz
To Ostend, Brussels & Paris
Bonn
Giessen
Gera
Zwickau
To Prague, Vienna & Budapest
Koblenz
Fulda
Suhl
Plauen
Hof
WIESBADEN
Frankfurt-am-Main
Coburg
To Prague
MAINZ
Aschaffenburg
Schweinfurt
Marktredwitz
CZECH REPUBLIC
Trier
Darmstadt
Bamberg
Bayreuth
Würzburg
Erlangen
To Prague
Kaiserslautern
Heidelberg
SAARBRÜCKEN
Mannheim
Nuremberg
To Paris
Karlsruhe
Heilbronn
Schwandorf
Pforzheim
Regensburg
To Paris
Aalen
Ingolstadt
Kehl
STUTTGART
Landshut
Passau
Offenburg
Freudenstadt
Ulm
Augsburg
To Vienna & Budapest
FRANCE
MUNICH
To Vienna, Budapest Klagenfurt, Graz & Zagreb
Freiburg im Breisgau
Memmingen
Basel
Singen
Kempten
Salzburg
Berchtesgaden
Konstanz
Garmisch-Partenkirchen
Kurfstein
Lindau
To Zürich, Interlaken, Geneva & Milan
To Zürich, Bern & Interlaken
Oberstdorf
Mittenwald
To Innsbruck, Milan, Venice & Rome
LIECHTENSTEIN
To Innsbruck
SWITZERLAND
AUSTRIA

0   50   100 km

euro currency converter DM1 = €0.51

Germany. Apart from new rolling stock and track, the smaller narrow-gauge steam lines in more remote regions are still operating, and even regional services are fairly comprehensive despite recent cutbacks.

All large (and many small) train stations in Germany have coin-operated, 24-hour left-luggage lockers (DM2/4 for small/large lockers). *Gepäckaufbewahrung* (left-luggage offices) are sometimes more convenient and charge similar rates.

Suitcases, bags or backpacks weighing up to 30kg can be sent door to door by Kurier-Gepäck (☎ 01805-99 66 33) between any two train stations in Germany for DM28; overweight luggage (over 30kg), bicycles or skis cost DM46. KurierGepäck will also send luggage to other Western European destinations. The list of countries that are serviced is small but growing, though Spain, Portugal and Italy are not included at present.

The Car & Motorcycle and Bicycle sections in this chapter include information about transporting your bicycle, motorcycle or car by train.

Train Passes

Eurail Pass Eurail passes can be a great deal if you're covering lots of territory in a very limited time. But if you're spending more than a week in Germany, the pass probably doesn't pay: you'll burn through the allotted time on routes that would cost you less if you paid the full fare.

For example, if you're under 26 you could qualify for a Youth pass – valid for 15 days of unlimited travel from the time you validate it – for $US388. First, look at where you want to go in Germany. If you were to travel from Munich to Berlin, then on to Hamburg, Hanover, Frankfurt, Stuttgart, back to Munich and then along the Romantic Road with Europabus (with the 10% student discount), it all adds up, at the exchange rate as we write, to a grand total of $US347. That, plus not having to rush to do it all in 15 days, makes it worth skipping the pass.

Even if you're over 26 years of age, the same thing applies; within Germany for any length of time you're far better off with a DB

BahnCard (see BahnCard later in this section) than a Eurail pass. Couples and groups, however, might consider the useful Euro-Saver pass which costs $US470 and is good for two to five adults over the same period.

Eurail passes, available to non-European residents only, are supposed to be bought before arriving in Europe. But Eurail passes *can* be purchased within Europe, as long as your passport proves you've been there for less than six months. Note that outlets where you can do this are limited and that the passes will be about 10% more expensive. (If you've lived in Europe for over six months, you're eligible for an Inter-Rail pass, which is a better buy.) Eurail passes are valid for unlimited travel on national railways (and some private lines) in 19 European countries. They also cover many ferries, eg from Sweden to Germany, as well as steamer services in various countries.

For people aged under 26, a Youthpass offers reasonable value in the form of unlimited 2nd class travel for 15 or 21 consecutive days (US$388/499) or one/two/three months (US$623/882/1089). The Youth Flexipass, also for 2nd class, is valid for freely chosen days within a two-month period: 10 days for US$458 or 15 days for US$599.

For those aged over 26, the equivalent passes provide 1st class travel. The standard Eurail pass costs US$554/718 for 15/21 days, or alternatively, US$890/1260/1558 for one/two/three months. The Flexipass costs US$654/862 for 10/15 days within two months. Groups of up to five people travelling together can get a 'saver' version of either pass, saving about 18%. Eurail passes for children are also available.

German Rail (DB) Passes A German Rail pass can be a cheaper way of getting around the country and allows you to avoid the often long ticket queues. Passes can be obtained in most non-European countries including Australia, Canada, the USA and Mexico, and at most major train stations in Germany itself (passport required). The pass is valid on all trains, and some river services operated by the KD Line.

The standard German Rail pass is available to any non-German citizen not resident in Germany and entitles you to unlimited 1st or 2nd class travel for four/seven/10 days within a one-month period. The 2nd class German Rail pass costs US$174/240/306.

You must validate your rail pass before using it. If you haven't done so by the time you arrive in Germany, do so at any DB train station in the country.

Similar to the German Rail pass is the German Rail Youth pass, limited to 2nd class travel for those aged between 12 and 25. It costs US$138/174/239 for four/seven/10 days of travel. Two adults travelling together should check out the German Rail Twin pass which costs US$261/360/459 for four/seven/10-day passes in 2nd class.

If you're going to the Czech Republic, consider buying the Prague Excursion Pass sold by DB. It covers round-trip travel (and all supplements) to Prague from the Czech border and back within seven days. The 2nd class pass costs DM60 (DM45 if you're under 26) from Deutsche Bahn offices or EurAide in Munich or Berlin.

BahnCard If you plan to travel within Germany for more than a month, the BahnCard may be a cheaper option than just buying tickets at the counter. Once you pay what amounts to a sign-up fee, you're allowed to buy train tickets (including InterCity and InterCity Express, but *not* S-Bahn or U-Bahn ones) and many regional bus tickets for half-price. A 2nd class BahnCard costs DM260 (DM120 for those between 17 and 22 years of age, students under 27, anyone over 60 and card holders' spouses) and is valid for one year. People aged 17 or under pay only DM60 for the BahnCard.

Discount Tickets

There are youth, student and senior discounts available on certain DB fares to those with proper ID. Those with physical disability can get a certificate entitling them to discounted or free DB services. Contact DB for a copy of its excellent free access guide *Information für behinderte Reisende* (German only).

There are also various permanent and temporary reduced-rate ticket offers available.

Sparpreis The Sparpreis, a return ticket between any two stations in Germany, costs DM249, and accompanying passengers pay only DM125. It is valid for 30 days but the return trip cannot be completed within a single Monday-to-Friday period. The Sparpreis is not valid on InterCity Express (ICE) trains.

Guten-Abend-Ticket If arriving very late is not a problem, the Good-Evening-Ticket is good value. It's valid for unlimited train travel from 7 pm until 2 am (from 2 pm Saturdays) and costs DM59 in 2nd class (DM69 in 2nd class on an ICE train). There are blacked-out periods around Easter and Christmas – check with DB for detailed information. A flat DM15 surcharge is levied at the weekend.

Schönes-Wochenende-Ticket Without much fanfare, DB has instituted one of the finest train deals in Europe – the so-called Nice-Weekend-Ticket. This allows you and up to four accompanying passengers to travel anywhere in Germany from midnight Saturday until 2 am Monday for just DM35. The catch is that you have to use local trains and *not* InterCity Express (ICE), InterCity (IC), ICN (InterCity Night) or InterRegio (IR) trains. That's not so bad, though – you can get clear across the country on the slower trains (and no German train is *that* slow).

Train Services

The most straightforward way of finding out a train's schedule and price is at the station, where large yellow posters show all trains departing each hour (but not fares). Once you know the time you want to go, write down the information and ask at the ticket window. If you can't speak German, write down the train number, time, destination, class desired and slide it through the window.

Single tickets of over 100km are valid for up to four days, and there's normally no problem breaking your journey (though you should advise the conductor). Return tickets cost exactly double, but if the combined distance is more than 100km they're valid for one month (two months for international return tickets). Long-distance train tickets and passes are also valid on the S-Bahns.

Tickets can usually be bought from the conductor for a surcharge of DM5 (or DM10 on ICE trains), but an increasing number of services (generally slower, regional ones) operate without a conductor. For these trains passengers are required to buy a ticket *before* boarding, so ask if you are in doubt. Anyone caught without a valid ticket is liable for a fine of DM60.

At many train stations passengers must buy tickets from vending machines for distances under 100km – it's generally more convenient anyway. If you're travelling further than anywhere indicated on the machine, press button 'X' for the maximum fare and contact the conductor on board. Holders of the BahnCard (see Train Passes) should press the '-1/2' or 'Kind' (child) button for a half-price ticket.

There are travel centres *(Reisezentrum)* in most larger train stations where staff will help you plan an itinerary, though English is sometimes a problem.

For ticket and timetable info (in English) by telephone you can ring ☎ 01805-99 66 33 from anywhere in Germany for DM0.24 per minute. Timetable and/or fare information is available from several sites on the Internet, including DB at www.bahn.de.

Reservations On holidays and in the busy summer season, reservations are recommended for longer journeys or sleeping compartments. The fee is a flat DM5, regardless of the number of seats booked. Most night trains are equipped with 1st class (two-berth) and 2nd class (four or six-berth) sleeping compartments, which must be booked at least one day in advance; otherwise turn up on the platform and ask the conductor.

For all EuroCity (EC) and IC trains a supplementary reservation charge applies (DM7, or DM9 if bought from the conductor), though holders of Eurail, Inter-Rail and German Rail passes do not pay supplements

on ICE or IC trains. On many IR and Regional Express (RE) trains as well as on the few remaining D trains you pay an extra DM3 to DM5 for trips of up to 50km.

Costs The average per-kilometre price of 2nd class train travel is currently DM0.27; for 1st class the average is DM0.41 per kilometre. In this book we round train fares to the nearest DM0.50 and list only 2nd class fares. Children three and younger travel free, children from four to 11 pay half-price.

Though train travel in Germany does offer good value, without a rail pass or a ticket bought through a special offer, it can be expensive: it costs about DM120 for a Munich-Frankfurt ticket on non-ICE service and DM147 on an ICE train. Read the Train Passes and Discount Tickets sections for more information, and shop around.

InterCity Express Deutsche Bahn's InterCity Express (ICE) trains offer travellers ultra-rapid service aboard space-age bullet trains, and special fares apply. Travelling at speeds of up to 280km/h, ICE trains now dominate some long-distance routes between large cities, such as Frankfurt-Berlin (DM200, four hours) and Hamburg-Munich (DM268, six hours).

A symbol of Germany's technical prowess, ICEs were regarded as very safe trains until a horrendous train accident at the town of Eschede killed over 100 people in 1998. The authorities checked rolling stock for safety and, after an exhaustive probe, determined that material fatigue (on an inferior part long out of service on all other major rail services!) had been at fault, and fired a few higher-ups as scapegoats.

Services aboard ICE trains are challenging those of domestic air travel. There are restaurants and bistros, telephones, computer data ports, huge picture windows and generally great service. All ICE trains – and some toilets and compartments – are wheelchair accessible. Smoking is permitted only in the first 1st class and last 2nd class carriages of the trains, and prohibited in restaurant and buffet cars.

ICE service continues to expand all the time, but representative services include Hamburg-Frankfurt (DM191, three hours), Frankfurt-Basel (DM120, 2¾ hours) and Berlin-Hanover (DM101, three hours). As this book went to press, a direct Cologne-Frankfurt line was being laid which promised to shave almost an hour off the scheduled service through the Rhine valley via Mainz (DM68, 2¼ hours).

InterCity & EuroCity These are less rapid intercity trains than the ICEs. All run between 6 am and 10 pm; InterCity (IC) trains go between German cities and EuroCity (EC) trains between German cities and cities throughout Europe. They're still comfortable and relatively fast, but ICE trains they ain't.

InterRegio & Regional Express InterRegio (IR) trains cover regional and a growing number of cross-country routes at two-hour intervals. They're often a cheaper (and slower) alternative to ICs and ICEs; for trips longer than two hours, you can usually get there faster by transferring from an IR to a high-speed train. Regional Express (RE) trains are local trains that make limited stops and link the rural areas to the national and commuter networks.

Local Services Deutsche Bahn runs local services that rate just above, and sometimes complement, metropolitan public transport networks. One good example of this are the SchnellBahn (S-Bahn) services, essentially suburban-metropolitan shuttle lines. These originate in a Hauptbahnhof and reach far-flung suburbs; in the case of Munich, Frankfurt and Stuttgart, the S-Bahn also serves as the main city-to-airport train link.

The StadtExpress (SE) is an extended commuter link in metropolitan areas, calling at all stations outside the S-Bahn network (if there is one) and at a few stops in town. The RegionalBahn (RB) is the slowest DB train, not missing a single cow town or junction of roads – so sit back and enjoy.

Narrow-Gauge & Cog-Wheel Trains

There are several narrow-gauge steam trains still in operation in Germany, mainly in the east. Notable services include the Molli, running between Bad Doberan and the towns of Heiligendamm and Kühlungsborn, and the Rasender Roland between Putbus and Göhren (see the Mecklenburg-Western Pomerania chapter). Other popular steam-powered services are the *Harzquerbahn* from Wernigerode in the Harz Mountains (see that chapter) and the *Bimmelbahn* from Zittau into the Zittau Mountains (see the Saxony chapter).

Zahnradbahnen are privately-run cogwheel railways, with trains that grind their way up some of Germany's steepest mountains, mainly in the Bavarian Alps. They're a wonderful trip back in time, and if you get a chance to ride one, jump aboard! You can usually take a Zahnradbahn up the mountain and a cable car down.

Sleepers

Standard sleeper services are available on longer routes in Germany and have one to three-bed compartments or four to six-bed couchettes. Sleeping on a train is a great way to save on accommodation – though the cost of the bed is not included in the fare, and supplements are charged for sheets and towels. There are no showers, and you may feel a little uncomfortable about sleeping in a room with strangers. But it's a comfortable method of overnight travel and, with a few common-sense precautions, pretty safe (see boxed text 'Security' in the Getting There & Away chapter). The surcharge for the simplest 2nd class sleeping bunk is DM24 with sheets and other services; more expensive sleeping-car fares are available for three or two-bed compartments, and also one-bed compartments in 1st class.

A relatively new arrival, InterCity Night (ICN) trains, on limited services between major German cities, have one and two-person compartments complete with showers and toilets in 'comfort class', and aeroplane-style reclining şeats in 'tourist class'. There's also a new type of couchette available on ICN trains called *Kajütliegwagen*. Prices (eg Berlin-Munich DM203) include breakfast. This could be worth it if you have a BahnCard (see Train Passes), which would bring the 2nd class fare down to DM147.

BUS

The bus network in Germany is excellent and comprehensive but not a popular mode of transport. For trips of any distance the train is faster and generally just as cheap. Buses are better geared towards regional travel in areas where the terrain makes train travel more difficult or impossible, and in this book we only list bus services if they're a viable and sensible option.

Each city in Germany has a central bus station (*Busbahnhof* or *Zentraler Omnibus Bahnhof/ZOB*), from where almost all bus service originates. It is generally very close or adjacent to the central train station (*Hauptbahnhof*). Tickets can be bought directly from the bus companies, which often have offices or kiosks at the bus station, or from the driver on board. Since the privatisation of most regional bus services run by the German national railway, Deutsche Bahn (DB), a slew of companies have sprung up to provide regional service.

Europabus, the bus network of Europe's railways, still operates within Germany as Deutsche Touring, a subsidiary of DB. Europabus services include the Romantic and Castle roads in southern Germany, as well as organised bus tours of Germany lasting a week or more. See the Frankfurt and Romantic Road sections for details, contact the Deutsche Touring main booking office (☎ 069-790 30), Römerhof 17, 60486 Frankfurt-am-Main, or visit the (German-only) Web site at www.deutsche-touring.com.

CAR & MOTORCYCLE

Most German roads are excellent, and as a result, motoring can be a great way to tour the country. *Autobahnen* (motorways) run throughout Germany. Road signs (and most motoring maps) indicate national autobahn

routes in blue with an 'A' preceding the number while international routes have green signs with an 'E' and a number. Though very efficient, the autobahns are often busy, and literally life in the fast lane. While border signs proudly indicate that there's no speed limit, there are actually many restricted segments (not that many German drivers take much notice). Tourists often have trouble coping with the very high speeds and the dangers involved in overtaking – don't overestimate the time it takes for a car in the rear-view mirror to close in at 180km/h.

Traffic Jams

The severity of German traffic jams *(Staus)* seems to be somewhat of a national obsession. Traffic jams are a subject of intense interest to motorists in Germany and are the focus of typical German thoroughness: you can actually get an annual Traffic Jam Calendar from the ADAC (see Motoring Organisations).

Some breakfast television stations also show the worst-afflicted sections every day, and German radio stations broadcast a special tone that interrupts cassette and CD players during traffic reports. Ask the rental agent to disable it unless you want all your music peppered with poetic phrases like, *'Die Autobahn von Frankfurt nach Stuttgart ist gebumper-zu-bumper ...*

Normal Staus, however, are nothing when compared with the astounding *Stau aus dem Nichts* – the 'Traffic Jam from Nowhere'. You can be sailing along at 180km/h and suddenly find yourself screeching to a halt and taking the next eight, 10 ... even 30km at a crawl. Most frustrating is that in the vast majority of cases, you'll end up speeding back up again and never seeing what caused the back-up in the first place. These 'Traffic Jams from Nowhere' are so prevalent that the government actually funded a study of the phenomenon!

GERMAN AUTOBAHNS

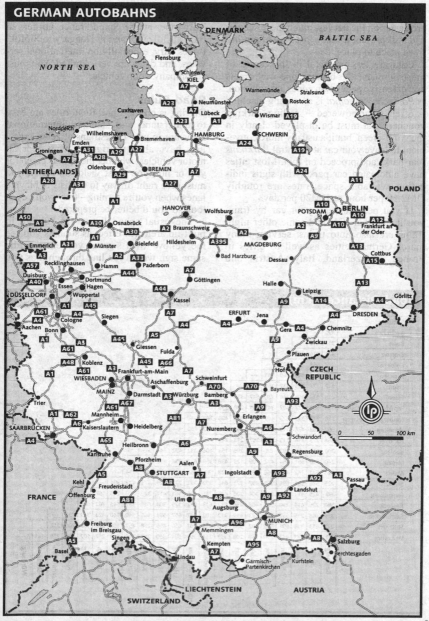

euro currency converter DM1 = €0.51

Secondary roads, dubbed 'B' highways, are easier on the nerves, much more scenic, and still present a fairly fast way of getting from place to place.

Cars are less practical in the centre of most German cities because one-way streets and extensive pedestrian zones are common. A *Parkscheinautomat* is a vending machine – often solar-powered – selling parking vouchers that must be displayed clearly in the windscreen, but it's usually more convenient to leave your car at a central *Parkhaus* (car park) and proceed on foot. Most cities have automated car parks with signs indicating available space; rates are roughly DM2.50 per hour or DM20 per day.

If you need to send your car by train, you'll find that ICN and some other night trains are also auto trains, serving many major German cities as well as cities in France, Switzerland, Italy, Austria and Hungary. Service to France is limited to Narbonne, at the Spain/France border; to Italy at Bolzano; and in Hungary to Siófok. Prices vary, especially on international services, and dates are very limited. You must accompany your vehicle.

Road Rules

Driving is on the right. Road rules are easy to understand and standard international signs are in use. Pedestrians at zebra crossings have absolute right of way over all motor vehicles; whether the light is green for you or not, you must yield. Similarly, you must give right of way to cyclists in bicycle lanes when you're turning – they won't even look so you'd better be prepared.

The usual speed limits are 50km/h in built-up areas (in effect as soon as you see the yellow town sign as you enter to the same sign with a red line through it as you

Road Distances (km)

	Bamberg	Berlin	Bonn	Bremen	Cologne	Dresden	Erfurt	Essen	Frankfurt-am-Main	Freiburg im Breisgau	Hamburg	Hanover	Koblenz	Leipzig	Mainz	Munich	Nuremberg	Rostock	Saarbrücken	Stuttgart	Würzburg
Bamberg	---																				
Berlin	395	---																			
Bonn	353	596	---																		
Bremen	471	376	335	---																	
Cologne	377	558	28	307	---																
Dresden	275	187	549	460	565	---															
Erfurt	147	277	335	332	351	216	---														
Essen	416	514	105	246	69	547	336	---													
Frankfurt-am-Main	196	507	177	407	347	451	238	396	---												
Freiburg im Breisgau	388	778	393	673	419	662	509	488	269	---											
Hamburg	502	282	476	115	413	453	354	356	482	750	---										
Hanover	354	273	314	115	288	357	213	243	327	593	150	---									
Koblenz	300	564	61	392	88	508	295	153	106	332	492	344	---								
Leipzig	240	160	591	354	472	109	123	438	359	627	354	250	415	---							
Mainz	226	542	142	437	166	487	273	228	39	261	512	357	80	394	---						
Munich	225	576	561	696	569	457	371	646	392	332	777	629	473	422	394	---					
Nuremberg	60	425	412	531	397	304	206	446	216	355	561	417	320	270	246	157	---				
Rostock	580	226	614	290	587	408	430	532	613	882	175	300	641	357	645	762	609	---			
Saarbrücken	359	688	215	552	243	633	419	312	182	267	657	503	165	540	146	423	349	792	---		
Stuttgart	222	613	318	591	345	492	350	410	183	167	650	495	258	180	228	182	180	780	212	---	
Würzburg	82	475	271	463	294	358	208	339	114	305	504	350	217	320	143	257	102	656	276	141	---

The Finger & Other Banned Gestures

German drivers are known for their aggressive road behaviour. It comes, says Oliver Bengl, a professional driver and commentator on things roadworthy, from the average German's belief that (a) they are excellent drivers while everyone else on the road is an execrable one, and that (b) the average German's highly conservative daytime role creates a 'King of the Road' mentality after leaving the workplace.

Road rage in Germany became so serious that German authorities stepped in and made any sort of offensive gesture illegal. If you give another driver 'the finger' (both British and American styles apply), tap your temple with your index finger, wave an inward-turned open palm up and down in front of your eyes, raise a fist or even give an Italian-style under-the-chin finger flick, the person at whom the gesture is directed can write down your registration number and report you to the police. You can be fined up to DM1500.

leave) and 100km/h on non-autobahn highways. Technically, there is no speed limit on autobahns but, in an effort to increase safety and curb noise pollution, many segments have limits ranging from 100 to 130km/h.

The highest permissible blood-alcohol level for drivers is 0.05%. Obey the road rules carefully: the German police are very efficient and issue stiff on-the-spot fines; speed and red-light cameras are in widespread use, and notices are sent to the car's registration address wherever that may be.

Note that in eastern Germany (and a few places in the west), a fixed green arrow on a traffic signal means that even when the signal is red, you are still permitted to make a right turn – after you have come to a full stop.

There are emergency phones every kilometre or so along most autobahns, even in the east, to be used in the event of breakdown. Lift the metal flap, follow the (pictorial) instructions and help will arrive.

Motoring Organisations

Germany's main motoring organisation, the Allgemeiner Deutscher Automobil Club (ADAC; ☎ 089-767 60, fax 089-76 76 28 01), Am Westpark 8, 81373 Munich, has offices in all major cities and many smaller ones, including a highly reassuring presence in eastern Germany. In this book we list ADAC offices under Information in many city sections.

The ADAC provides some of the best on and off-road services of any motoring club in the world. Members (DM74 annually domestic, DM139 worldwide) can get help planning trips, free road maps, discounts on auto insurance and even international health insurance from any ADAC office in the country, as well as roadside breakdown assistance *(Pannenhilfe)* 24 hours a day.

ADAC's services, including their roadside assistance program, are available to members of participating motoring organisations around the world – including American or Australian AAA, Canadian CAA and British AA. Call the ADAC road patrol (☎ 0180-222 22 22) if your car breaks down. Technicians probably won't speak English, but gestures work very well – impersonate the sound your heap was making before it died, and the mechanic will probably figure it out directly. ADAC mechanics also carry a multilingual auto-part dictionary, so they can tell you if it's your brake lining or fuel pump.

Petrol

Fuel prices in Germany are quite stiff, even by European standards, costing a little more than in the UK and a bit less than in Scandinavia. Depending on the time of year, prices vary from DM1.55 to DM1.74 for unleaded regular, DM1.65 to DM1.80 for unleaded super, and DM1.25 to DM1.45 for

euro currency converter DM1 = €0.51

diesel (by the way, taxes account for 80% of the bill). Autobahn filling stations are slightly more expensive than main-street ones and can be found every 40km or so throughout the country. Most stations in Germany are open late; the major players – Aral, BP, Elf and Agip – usually run 24-hour operations complete with mini-markets selling soggy, overpriced sandwiches, Shaun Cassidy cassettes and porno magazines.

Rental

In general, to rent a car in Germany you'll need to be at least 21 years old and hold a valid driving licence (an international licence is not necessary) and a major credit card. Amex, Diners Club, Visa and Euro Card/MasterCard are almost always accepted; JCB (Japan Credit Bank) is good only sometimes at airports, and they'll almost never take a Discover Card unless you've prepaid in the USA. There may be a supplement for additional driver(s). Safety seats for children under four are not required by law but are highly recommended. Bring one from home or be prepared to shell out at least DM10 per day for one from the car-rental firm. Ski and luggage racks are available from rental companies for about DM50 per rental.

Generally speaking, you're allowed to drive cars rented in Germany pretty much anywhere in Western Europe, and pretty much nowhere in Eastern Europe (except eastern Germany). Countries specifically forbidden include: Albania, Belarus, Bosnia, Bulgaria, Croatia, Czech Republic, Estonia, Hungary, Latvia, Lithuania, Macedonia, Poland, Romania, Russia, Slovakia, Slovenia, Turkey and Yugoslavia.

If you enter these places with a rental car, your insurance is revoked, the rental agreement rendered void and the rental company could even report the car as stolen. However, Auto Europe lets you go into Poland and the Czech Republic if you tell them in advance and pay an extra charge.

Rental Companies Germany's main rental companies are Avis (☎ 040-50 71 09 40), Eu-

ropcar (☎ 069-942 15 70), Hertz (☎ 01805-33 35 35) and Sixt (☎ 01805-525 25 25), but there are a number of smaller local ones too. Alamo (☎ 069-69 07 23 60) has recently been expanding its operations in Germany and generally has lower prices than the others.

The outfits listed have offices in so many German cities that printing them here is folly. Suffice to say that wherever you are – from Aachen to Zwickau – there's a rental office nearby, usually at the airport and often in the city or town centre.

Rental rates are usually rather high if you simply walk up to the counter, even taking into account special weekend rates and discounts. It's generally more economical to make reservations ahead of time with the central reservation office in your country. If you haven't done that in advance, make sure you shop around. Check out the smaller agencies in particular, though the larger firms, feeling the crunch, often have some exceptional deals on offer. For example, a three-day weekend rental of a budget car – an Opel Corsa or a Ford Fiesta, sometimes with a free upgrade to a spiffier model – can cost as little as DM89.

One rental agency offering some of the best deals around is Auto Europe, a US company with offices around the world that you can simply call up on their toll-free numbers. If you're already in Germany, dial ☎ 0130-82 21 98. In the US, it's ☎ 800-223 5555; in Australia ☎ 1-800-126 409; in New Zealand ☎ 0800-440 722; in France ☎ 0590 1770; and in the UK ☎ 0800-899 893. The smallest car available costs around US$80 for three days (the minimum rental period), including unlimited kilometres, value-added tax (or VAT equivalent) *and* third-party insurance.

Fly-drive deals can be excellent value for money; Lufthansa offers deals from around US$25 per day if you book for longer than three weeks. You may also get a better deal by calling the rental company's reservations number in the USA or the UK – even from within Germany – and asking the price for a rental in your home country. It often results in better deals. Otherwise, shop around upon arrival.

The new Reichstag inside the old

Cruising along Berlin's canals

DAVID PEEVERS

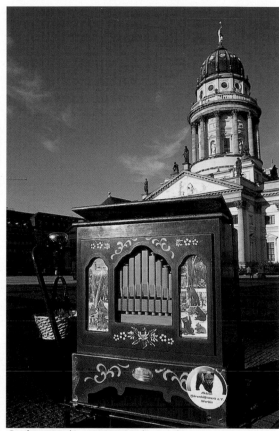

Gendarmenmarkt: a quiet spot, at least on the organ grinder's day off

DAVID PEEVERS

New Synagogue

DAVID PEEVERS

Wars of Liberation monument

DAVID PEEVERS

East Side Gallery

DAVID PEEVERS

The goddess of victory atop the Brandenburger Tor

Now a symbol of unity, the Brandenburg Gate

View of Kaiser-Wilhelm-Gedächtniskirche

Berliner Dom overshadows an equine monument

Insurance You could seriously screw yourself by driving uninsured or even underinsured. Germans are very pernickety about their cars, and even nudging another car at a red light could lead to months of harassing phone calls until you pay for an entire new rear bumper if you're uninsured.

Liability insurance covers you for legal action filed against you when you crash your car against anyone or their property. This is generally not included in the rental price but available for an extra charge.

Collision damage waiver (CDW) is protection for the car. It reduces the amount you'll have to reimburse the rental company (if their car is stolen or you bash it to bits) to DM300 if you're over 24 years old and DM1000 if under. It is available for an extra DM20 to DM50 per day.

American Express and some Visa and EuroCard/MasterCard holders are automatically covered for CDW on renting a car if they decline the policy on offer from the rental company. Check with your company to see what coverage they offer in Germany before assuming it will cover you, and note that CDW is *not* liability coverage.

Personal accident insurance (PAI) covers you and your passenger(s) for medical costs incurred as the result of an accident. If your health insurance from home does this as well, save yourself the DM10 to DM20 per day the rental firm will charge you.

Purchase

Unless you're going to stay put in Germany for a while, buying a car here tends to be an unwise decision due to the costs and paperwork involved. If you are an EU national, you must register the car with the Ordnungs- und Strassenverkehrsamt (Public Order & Traffic Office) which can be found in most larger towns. You will need proof of ownership, proof of insurance and a passport or ID. You're also subject to a motor vehicle tax. The vehicle also has to pass a safety inspection by the Technical Supervision Agency (TÜV) every two years in order to be kept legally on the road.

If you're not an EU national, it's generally not possible to buy and register a car in Germany, since you have to be a resident to do so. The only way to get around that requirement is to have a friend or relative buy the car for you, though they may not feel comfortable about jeopardising their driving record and insurance rates.

If you still want to buy a car, be warned: experienced car dealers from Eastern Europe get to the real bargains first, so it's a lot easier purchasing (and reselling) a vehicle in other Western European countries, especially Holland and Belgium.

Berlin and Munich are the best places in Germany to shop around for used cars if you know what to look for. And don't buy any vehicle without checking first that it has its *current* TÜV certificate of roadworthiness. The Berlin newspaper *Zweite Hand* has a separate car edition with thousands of listings each week.

BICYCLE

Bicycle touring *(Radwandern)* is very popular in Germany. In urban areas the pavement is often divided into separate sections for pedestrians and cyclists. Even outside towns and cities there are often separate cycling routes so you don't have to use the roads and highways; cycling is strictly *verboten* on the autobahns.

In Germany, the northern flatlands are especially suitable for long bike explorations, but you need to be in excellent shape to tackle the central highlands and certainly the mountainous areas of the south. Favoured routes include those along the Rhine, Moselle and Danube rivers and in the Lake Constance area.

Hostel-to-hostel biking is an easy way to go, and route guides are often sold at DJH hostels. There are well equipped cycling shops in almost every town, and a fairly active market for used touring bikes.

You can take a bicycle with you on most trains in Germany though you'll have to buy a separate ticket for it. For information, check the DB Radfahrer-Hotline (☎ 0180-319 41 94). On IC, IR, RB and SE trains the charge is DM12 with the special bike compartment; advance bookings are necessary. The cost on regional trains for less than 100km is DM6. The railway also sells a useful but bulky booklet, *Bahn&Bike Radtouren* (DM9.80) with tours, map insets and bargain hotel tips for most regions.

Germany's main cyclist organisation is the Allgemeiner Deutscher Fahrrad Club (ADFC, ☎ 089-55 35 75, fax 55 24 58), Landwehrstrasse 16, 80336 Munich. There's another office at Postfach 107747, 28077 Bremen (☎ 0421-34 62 90, fax 0431-346 29 50). See also Activities in the Facts for the Visitor chapter.

Rental & Purchase

Simple three-gear bicycles can be hired from train stations for around DM12/56 a day/week, and more robust mountain bikes from DM15/90; holders of train passes or valid train tickets sometimes get a small discount. See DB's *Fahrrad am Bahnhof* brochures for lists of stations offering this service. If you plan to spend longer than several weeks in the saddle, buying a second-hand bike works out cheaper than renting a bike or bringing your own; good reconditioned models go for DM300 to DM400.

HITCHING

Hitching is never entirely safe in any country in the world, and we don't recommend it. Travellers who decide to hitch should understand that they are taking a small but potentially serious risk. People who do choose to hitch will be safer if they travel in pairs and let someone know where they are planning to go. The advice that follows should help to make the journey as fast and safe as possible.

Hitching *(Trampen)* is considered an acceptable way of getting around in Germany and average waits are short. Don't waste time hitching in urban areas: take public transport to the main exit routes. It's illegal to hitchhike on autobahns or their entry/exit ramps, but service stations can be very good places to pick up a ride. Prepare a sign clearly showing your intended destination in German (eg 'München', not 'Munich'

though 'Hanover' will probably get you to 'Hannover'). You can save yourself a lot of trouble by arranging a lift through a *Mitfahrzentrale* (see Hitching & Ride Services in the Getting There & Away chapter).

BOAT

Boats are mostly used for basic transport when travelling to or between the Frisian Islands, though cruises along the Rhine and Moselle rivers are also popular.

In summer, there are frequent services on Lake Constance, but apart from the Constance-Meersburg and Friedrichshafen-Romanshorn car ferries, these boats are really more for sightseeing than actual transport. From April to October, excursion boats ply the lakes and rivers of eastern Germany and are an excellent, inexpensive way of seeing the country. Paddle-wheel steamers operating out of Dresden are a fine way to tour the Elbe River. Cruises are also popular between Berlin and Potsdam.

LOCAL TRANSPORT

Local transport includes buses, trams, S-Bahn and/or U-Bahn (underground train system). Most public transport systems integrate buses, trams and trains; fares are determined by the zones or the time travelled, or sometimes both. Multi-ticket strips or day passes are generally available and offer far better value than single-ride tickets. See town and city Getting Around sections for details.

Bus & Tram

Cities and towns operate their own local bus, trolleybus and/or tram services. In most places you must have a ticket before boarding, and validate it aboard (or risk paying a fine of around DM60). Tickets are sold mainly from vending machines at train stations and tram or bus stops. Bus drivers usually sell single-trip tickets as a service to forgetful passengers, but these are more expensive than tickets bought in advance.

Train

Most large cities have a system of suburban train lines called the S-Bahn. Trains on these lines cover a wider area than buses or trams, but tend to be less frequent. S-Bahn lines are often linked to the national rail network, and sometimes interconnect urban centres. Train passes and conventional train tickets between cities are generally valid on these services.

The larger cities, such as Berlin, Munich, Hanover and Frankfurt, have a fast and efficient underground/subway system known as the U-Bahn.

Taxi

Taxis are expensive in Germany and, given the excellent public transport systems, not recommended unless you're in a real hurry. (They can actually be slower if you're going to/from the airport.) Look up *Taxi Ruf* in the phone directory to find the nearest taxi rank. Taxis are metered and cost up to DM4.50 at flag fall and DM2.50 per kilometre; in some places higher night tariffs apply.

DB has put together an exceptional deal for travellers heading from major city train stations between 5 and 1 am: BahnTaxi is a flat-rate taxi service from the station to most city destinations.

The main cities served and costs per person are: Frankfurt-am-Main DM12, Nuremberg DM12, Berlin DM21, Munich DM15, Mannheim DM15 and Leipzig DM15.

You can order a BahnTaxi at all Reisezentrum offices in the station, or in advance from the train staff (who will usually announce the BahnTaxi shortly before arrival at the station). See the Getting Around sections in the appropriate city chapters for more information on taxis.

ORGANISED TOURS

Local tourist offices offer tour options, from city sightseeing trips lasting an hour or two to adventure, spa-bath and wine-tasting packages over several days.

There are many other international and national tour operators with specific options, many with European tours integrating German destinations. It's also worth contacting the German National Tourist Office in your home country (see the Facts for the Visitor chapter under Tourist Offices for a list of offices outside Germany).

Of the options available, DER Travel Service in the UK (☎ 020-7290 11 11, fax 7629 74 42), 18 Conduit Street, London W1R 9TD or the USA (☎ 310-479 4140 or toll free 800 937 1235, fax 847-692 4141), 11933 Wilshire Blvd, Los Angeles, CA 90025, has a huge selection including self-catering, guesthouse, independent package holidays and river cruises. The Web site (in German) is at www.der.de.

Two good city tour operators (both based in the UK) are Moswin Tours Ltd (☎ 0116-271-9922), 21 Church Street, Oadby, Leicester LE2 5DB, and the German Travel Centre (☎ 020-8429 2900), 403-409 Rayner's Lane, Pinner, Middlesex HA5 5ER.

Cyclists should contact Euro-Bike Tours in the USA (☎ 815-758 8851 or toll-free 800-321 6060), PO Box 990, De Kalb IL 60115, which offers a range of two-wheel tours, including the spectacular Rhine River Valley. Uniquely Europe (☎ 425-455 4445, fax 425 2111), 116th Avenue NE, Bellevue, WA 98804, is a worthy rival.

The German railways (DB) offer some excellent tours including transport and very nice room and board (often from just DM100 per couple per night) from towns within Germany. There are some unusual regional options as well, such as steam-train or river-boat outings. Foreign offices include:

Australia
  (☎ 02-9248 6129, fax 9248 6217)
  321 Kent Street, Sydney, NSW 2000
UK
  (☎ 044181-390 3840, fax 044181-399 4700)
  Suite 4, The Sanctuary, 23 Oakhill Grove,
  Surbiton, Surrey KT6 6DU
USA
  (☎ 310-479 4140 or toll-free 800-937 1235,
  fax 479 2239)
  11933 Wilshire Blvd, Los Angeles, CA 90025

Berlin

☎ 030 • pop 3.45 million

Berlin, the largest city in Germany, has more to offer visitors than any other in the country. Like New York, Berlin is a city that never sleeps. Bustling pubs and raucous nightclubs teem with restless energy. The wealth and quality of Berlin's cultural life is peerless, with world-class museums, opera and theatre, music – from classical to countercultural – and a lively art and gallery scene. Despite the ravages of war and the sad neglect of the eastern parts of the city, surviving palaces, monuments and historic structures spur the imagination and lift the spirit. A vast green belt of forests, parks and lakes surrounding the city makes escape from the urban grit and pace a simple matter of a quick ride on the U-Bahn.

No other city has ever undergone the kind of peacetime trauma that has been visited on Berlin. Nowhere else has a city been sliced in half by a brutal and impenetrable wall, its people forcibly and ideologically separated for 40 years (see the boxed text 'The Berlin Wall'). Once at the very epicentre of the Cold War, Berlin has become the bridge between east and west. Its physical scars are healing and the progress made – in a scant few years – to bring the infrastructure of east and west on a par has been quite astonishing.

But while the city may be reunited, its people have not easily rejoined. The 'wall' that lingers in the minds and hearts of *Berliners* has proven as difficult to bring down as the one that they looked across with such longing for four decades (see also Society & Conduct in the Facts about Germany chapter). But Berlin demands that its people get on with their lives and Berliners have responded to this challenge as they have to all others; they're nothing if not resilient.

Berliners pride themselves on their directness in their speech and tolerance of different views. This open-mindedness is reflected in the facts that one in eight residents are not

HIGHLIGHTS

Berlin Luminaries: Marlene Dietrich, Frederick the Great, Walter Gropius, George Grosz, Alexander von Humboldt, Max Liebermann, Leni Riefenstahl, Margarete von Trotta, Kurt Tucholsky, Katarina Witt

- Partying at Berlin's bizarre nightclubs
- Bar hopping in the districts of Mitte, Prenzlauer Berg and Friedrichshain
- Exploring Berlin on foot with Berlin Walks or the Insider Tour
- Discovering the Potsdamer Platz area, Berlin's new 'city within a city'
- Visiting Pergamon Museum
- Strolling along Unter den Linden from the Brandenburg Gate to Alexanderplatz
- Enjoying the sounds and sights at the Turkish Market or Winterfeldtmarket
- Seeing Berlin for DM3.90 with Bus 100

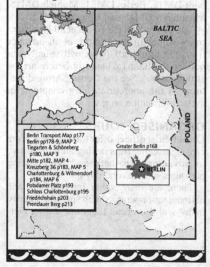

BALTIC SEA

POLAND

Berlin Transport Map p177
Berlin pp178-9, MAP 2
Tiergarten & Schöneberg p180, MAP 3
Mitte p182, MAP 4
Kreuzberg 36 p183, MAP 5
Charlottenburg & Wilmersdorf p184, MAP 6
Potsdamer Platz p193
Schloss Charlottenburg p195
Friedrichshain p203
Prenzlauer Berg p213

Greater Berlin p168

BERLIN

ethnic Germans and that Europe's largest gay and lesbian scene flourishes here.

All this makes Berlin a most 'un-German' city. The structure of social hierarchy so prevalent in much of German society is less rigid here. Where you come from doesn't matter as much as what you can do. Nowhere else in the country is it easier for entrepreneurs to realise their ambitions or for people to participate culturally or politically.

The world has always looked to this most dramatic city – sometimes in fascination, sometimes in horror and sometimes even in deep sympathy. At the same time repellent and seductive, light-hearted and brooding, Berlin continues to be a city of extremes in both its accomplishments and its problems.

HISTORY

Berlin's 'modern' history began in the 13th century with the founding of the trading posts of Cölln and Berlin by itinerant merchants in today's Nikolaiviertel in the Mitte district. Thanks to their strategic location at the crossroads of medieval trading routes,

the two settlements soon developed into *Handelsstädte* (trade centres). In 1307, they merged into the double city of Berlin-Cölln.

A self-confident merchant class managed to keep the city – also a member of the Hanseatic League in the 14th and 15th centuries – largely independent. Eventually, though, even they could not prevent it from being absorbed into the sphere of power of the Hohenzollern dynasty.

In the 1440s, under Elector Friedrich II, Berlin and Cölln gradually lost their independence as the ruler dissolved their administrative council. He laid the foundation for a city palace, the future Berliner Schloss, which stood until the GDR demolished the war-damaged ruin in 1950. By the time the elector's nephew Johann inherited the title in 1486, Berlin-Cölln had become a residential city and the capital of the March of Brandenburg.

Under the electors, Berlin continued to blossom economically and grew into a powerful and civilised city. It would take the Thirty Years' War (1618-48) to – at least

This copy of an original engraving appeared in an 1851 edition of *The Iconographic Encyclopaedia of Science, Literature and Art*. Just 20 years on, the city's population had tripled and change was afoot.

temporarily – put an end to this expansion. At the end, the entire Holy Roman Empire, including Berlin, had been ravaged, its population reduced to a mere 6000.

Replenishing the population was foremost on the mind of Elector Friedrich Wilhelm (called the 'Great Elector'; ruled 1640-88). He shrewdly accomplished this by inviting foreigners to settle in Berlin. In 1671, he asked 50 wealthy Jewish families who had been kicked out of Vienna to come to the city with the proviso that they bring their enormous fortunes with them.

The bulk of new settlers, though, were Huguenot refugees from France. Some 6000 arrived after King Louis XIV, in 1685, revoked the Edict of Nantes, which had granted the Protestants religious freedom. Berlin's population swelled by 25% and the French language superseded German in some districts. By 1700, one in five inhabitants was of French descent.

Elector Friedrich III, the Great Elector's son, was a man with great ambition and a penchant for the arts and sciences. Joined by his beloved wife, Sophie Charlotte, he presided over a lively and intellectual court, founding the Academy of Arts (1696) and the Academy of Sciences (1700). One year later, Friedrich promoted himself to King Friedrich I of Prussia, making Berlin a royal residence and capital of the new state of Brandenburg-Prussia.

His son, Friedrich Wilhelm I (ruled 1713-40), was quite antithetical to him. Frugal and militarily minded, he was obsessed with building an army of 80,000 (he's known as the *Soldatenkönig*, or Soldier King), which he partially achieved by building a city wall to prevent the desertion of Berlin males. (Little did he know that some 230 years later a different government would steal his idea to keep its people from leaving.)

Everyone breathed a sigh of relief when his son Friedrich II – better known to English-speakers as Frederick the Great (ruled 1740-86) and to his subjects as '*der alte Fritz*' (Old Freddy) – came to the throne. He sought greatness through building and was known for his political and

military savvy. Berlin flourished as a great cultural centre and became known as *Spree-Athen*, 'Athens on the Spree'.

The Enlightenment arrived with some authority – playwright Gotthold Ephraim Lessing, thinker and publisher Friedrich Nikolai and philosopher Moses Mendelssohn, grandfather of composer Felix Mendelssohn-Bartholdy helped make Berlin a truly international city.

Prussia went into a downwards spiral after the death of Friedrich II, culminating with the defeat of its army by Napoleon's forces at Jena, east of Weimar, in 1806. The French occupied Berlin for the next seven years. In 1848 a bourgeois democratic revolution was suppressed, stifling the political development that had been set in motion by the Enlightenment and had swept across Europe. From 1850 to 1870 the population more than tripled to just under 500,000 as the Industrial Revolution, spurred on by such companies as Siemens and Borsig, took hold. In 1871 Chancellor Otto von Bismarck united Germany under Kaiser Wilhelm I, marking the start of the *Gründerzeit* (literally 'Foundation Time'). The population of Berlin was almost two million in 1900.

Before WWI Berlin had become an industrial giant, but the war and its aftermath led to revolt throughout Germany. On 8-9 November 1918, following the abdication of Wilhelm II, the Social Democratic Party (SPD) proclaimed the German Republic from a balcony of the Reichstag (German Parliament) with their leader, Friedrich Ebert, at the head. Hours later Karl Liebknecht, the founder of the German Communist Party (KPD; then known as the Spartacus League) proclaimed a free socialist republic from Berliner Schloss balcony. In January 1919 Liebknecht and fellow Spartacist Rosa Luxemburg were murdered by the *Freikorps*, remnants of the old imperial army (allied with Ebert), which brought the socialist revolution to a bloody end. Ebert was elected president later that month; the Weimar Republic was born.

Berlin gained the reputation as a tolerant and indulgent centre in the 1920s. Outsiders

– including the English writers WH Auden and Christopher Isherwood – flocked to this city of cabaret, dada and jazz. In 1920 eight towns and dozens of small communities were amalgamated to form *Gross Berlin* (Greater Berlin).

But not all was right in Berlin. As elsewhere in Germany, in Berlin crippling war reparations, strikes and the worst hyperinflation ever known brought poverty and discontent. The year before the Nazi takeover in 1933, the Communist Party under Ernst Thälmann was the strongest single party in 'Red Berlin', polling 31% of votes in the 1932 elections.

Berlin was heavily bombed by the Allies in WWII. The final Battle of Berlin began on 16 April 1945. More than 1.5 million Soviet soldiers approached the capital from the east, reaching Berlin on 21 April and encircling it on 25 April. Two days later, they were in the city centre. Hitler committed suicide on 30 April, the capital fell two days later and on 7 May 1945 Germany capitulated. By the end of the war, some 125,000 Berliners had lost their lives and only 7000 of its 160,000 Jews had survived.

In August 1945, the Potsdam Conference sealed the postwar fate of Berlin by agreeing that each of the victorious powers – the USA, Britain, France and the Soviet Union – would occupy a separate zone. In June 1948 the city was split in two when the three western Allies introduced a western German currency and established a separate administration in their sectors. The Soviets then blockaded West Berlin, but the Allies kept it in the western camp through an amazing operation called the Berlin Airlift. In October 1949 East Berlin became the capital of the German Democratic Republic.

The construction of the Berlin Wall in August 1961 prevented the drain of skilled labour (between 1945 and 1961 three million East Germans were lured westwards by higher wages). So great was the animosity and mistrust on both sides of the Wall that even as late as 1987, when Berlin marked its 750th anniversary, separate celebrations were held in the East and West.

The *Wende* (change) began in May 1989, when Hungary announced it would suspend its Travel Agreement, which had prevented East Germans from entering the west via Hungary. The GDR government responded by tightening up travel restrictions. Meanwhile, more and more East Germans filled West German consulates and embassies in East Berlin, Warsaw, Prague and Budapest, seeking to emigrate. The breakthrough came on 10 September 1989, when Hungary's foreign minister, Gyula Horn, opened the Hungarian border to Austria, allowing refugees to cross legally to the west.

The collapse of the communist regimes in Eastern Europe, including the GDR, was now unstoppable. On 9 November 1989 the Wall opened. Currency and economic union became a reality in July 1990. With reunification, Berlin once again became the German capital in 1990, as had been agreed by the two German governments. In 1991, a small majority (338 versus 320) of members of the *Bundestag* (German Parliament) voted in favour of moving the federal government to Berlin. This move began in May 1999 and should be finished by the end of 2000.

ORIENTATION

Berlin is surrounded by the *Bundesland* (federal state) of Brandenburg. The city-state of Berlin measures some 892 sq km while the municipal boundaries encompass 234 sq km. Roughly one-third of the municipal area is made up of parks, forests, lakes and rivers; in spite of WWII bombing, there are more trees here than in Paris and more bridges than in Venice. Much of the natural beauty of rolling hills and quiet shorelines is in the city's south-east and south-west.

The improvement and maintenance of these natural features was imperative in giving people recreational areas after the erection of the Berlin Wall, when West Berlin became an 'island' in the GDR 'sea'. As Berliners used to say, 'No matter whether you go north, south, east or west from Berlin, you're still going East'.

The Spree River wends its way across the city for over 30km, from the Grosser

BERLIN

GREATER BERLIN

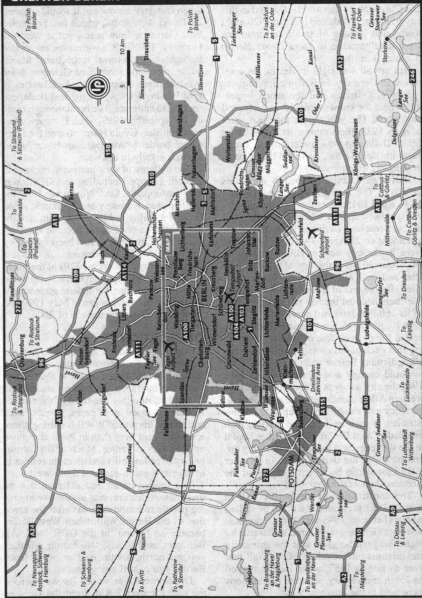

Müggelsee, the city's largest lake, in the east, to Spandau in the west. North and south of Spandau, the Havel River widens into a series of lakes, from Tegel to below Potsdam. A network of canals links the waterways to each other and to the Oder River in the east on the Polish border.

Berlin has 23 independent administrative districts *(Bezirke)*, although most travellers will visit only the eight 'core' ones: (clockwise from the west) Charlottenburg, Tiergarten, Mitte, Prenzlauer Berg (locals say Prenz'lberg), Friedrichshain, Kreuzberg, Schöneberg and Wilmersdorf. Kreuzberg, quite different in its eastern and western sections, is split in this book into Kreuzberg 36 and Kreuzberg 61 for clarity, according to its old postal codes.

For now, Berlin has two commercial centres reflecting its 40-year division: the western around Zoo station and Kurfürstendamm (Map 6), and the eastern in Mitte along Unter den Linden and Alexanderplatz.

Unter den Linden (Map 4), the fashionable avenue of aristocratic old Berlin, and its continuation, Karl-Liebknecht-Strasse, extend east from the Brandenburger Tor (Brandenburg Gate) to Alexanderplatz, once the heart of socialist East Germany. Some of Berlin's finest museums are on Museumsinsel in the Spree (though most are closed for renovation). The major entertainment district has sprung up around the Hackesche Höfe and along Oranienburger Strasse.

South of the Brandenburger Tor, in areas once occupied by the Wall, Berlin's newest quarter is emerging around Potsdamer Platz, as well as Leipziger Platz. But Berlin's macabre erstwhile landmark hasn't been forgotten altogether; sections remain for public viewing around the city (see the boxed text 'The Berlin Wall').

Back in former West Berlin, the ruin of the shattered Kaiser-Wilhelm-Gedächtniskirche (Kaiser Wilhelm Memorial Church; Map 6), on Breitscheidplatz in Charlottenburg, a block away from the Zoologischer Garten (usually referred to as just 'Zoo' and pronounced 'Zoe') train station, is the most visible landmark. The main tourist office

branch and hundreds of shops are in the Europa-Center on the east side of the square. The Kurfürstendamm, the main thoroughfare here (known as the 'Kudamm'), runs 3.5km west from Breitscheidplatz to Halensee.

To the north-east, between Breitscheidplatz and the Brandenburg Gate, is Tiergarten, a district named after the city park that was once a royal hunting domain. The area north of the park, along the bend in the Spree (the Spreebogen) and between Lehrter Stadtbahnhof and Bellevue S-Bahn stations, is being transformed into the government and diplomatic district. The Lehrter Stadtbahnhof now operates as an S-Bahn station, but will become the capital's main station for long-distance and suburban train travel.

Street numbers usually run sequentially up one side of the street and down the other (important exceptions are Unter den Linden and, in Schöneberg, Martin-Luther-Strasse and Lietzenburger Strasse). Number guides appear on most corner street signs. Also be aware that a continuous street may change names several times, and that on some streets (eg Kurfürstendamm, Kantstrasse and Knesebeckstrasse) numbering sequences continue after interruptions caused by squares. The names of some streets and other landmarks have been changed for political reasons and more will follow; recently renamed are Dimitroffstrasse (now Danziger Strasse) in Prenzlauer Berg and central Marx-Engels-Platz on Museumsinsel, which has once again become Schlossplatz.

Maps

For a detailed map of the city, there's Lonely Planet's Berlin city map. It has three scales (Berlin & Vicinity 1:60,000; Central Berlin 1:34,500; and Zoo, Tiergarten, Mitte 1:20,000), an index to all streets and sights, and costs AUS $7.95 (UK £3.99).

Other good choices are from Falkplan (either the standard sheet map or the Falk Megaplan with a patented folding system), ADAC's 1:25,000 map or the RV Verlag Euro City 1:27,500 version. Maps cost from DM7 to DM15.

The Berlin Wall

This Cold War symbol has sparked much debate, especially since the *Wende*. It wasn't the Soviets who built what was known around the world as *Die Mauer* (the Wall) on 13 August 1961 – the East Germans did. But it was only made possible by Nikita Khrushchev's decision to give responsibility for security in Berlin's Soviet sector to GDR leader Walter Ulbricht and his Socialist Unity Party (SED) earlier that year.

Until then, many East Berliners worked in the west and attended concerts, films etc, returning at night. But the allure of the more prosperous west was too great, so by the summer of 1961 up to 20,000 East Germans a month were leaving the GDR via West Berlin. The GDR built its so-called 'Anti-Fascist Protection Barrier' to keep workers in and the GDR economy from haemorrhaging. It took only hours before concrete and barbed wire kept tens of thousands of people separated from jobs, friends and family members.

The Wall stood for more than 28 years, some 165km of ugly prefab slabs that you could reach out and touch (or paint) on the western side but which was protected by a no-man's-land of barbed wire, land mines, attack dogs and watchtowers in the east. The first victim, who tried to jump into the west from the window of his house, died only a few days after the Wall went up. On 24 August 1961, the first shooting and killing of a runaway by GDR border police occurred. The full extent of the system's cruelty became blatantly apparent on 17 August 1962 when 18-year-old Peter Fechtner was shot during his attempt to flee, then left to bleed to death with the East German police looking on.

At first, the GDR tried to completely seal itself off from the west, but over time restrictions for travel *into* East Berlin were loosened. In December 1963, the first West Berliners were allowed to visit friends and family in the east. Nine months later, senior citizens got permission to cross the border into the city's western section. Within a year, the GDR began levying an 'admission fee' – mandatory minimum exchange of German marks into 'Ostmark', its currency. In 1980, this was raised to DM25 per day. But in the end nothing could prevent the collapse of the Wall: on 9 November 1989, thousands of East Berliners streamed into the west – the euphoria was endless.

If you plan to explore the city thoroughly or stay longer than a week, invest in a street atlas. RV Verlag's atlas (DM24.80) has more than 150 detailed maps (1:20,000) of the city, suburbs and Potsdam; an index with new street names; public transport routes; and descriptive info and listings (in German).

Newsagents and most bookshops stock a decent supply of maps to the city and surrounding area.

INFORMATION
Tourist Offices

The main office of Berlin Tourismus Marketing (BTM; Map 6) is in the Europa-Center at Budapester Strasse 45 near Zoo station. It is open Monday to Saturday from 8.30 am to 8.30 pm and Sunday from 10 am to 6.30 pm. A second branch (Map 3) is in the south wing of the Brandenburg Gate and is open daily from 9.30 am to 6 pm. Both offices handle in-person hotel (but not private room) reservations at no charge.

Smaller tourist offices with fewer services, called Info Points, are in the Reisecenter on the ground floor of the KaDeWe department store (Map 6) at Tauentzienstrasse 21 (open weekdays from 9.30 am to 8 pm, and Saturday from 9 am to 4 pm) and in the main hall of Tegel airport at the left-luggage office opposite Gate O (open daily from 5 am to 10.30 pm).

The Berlin Wall

Almost immediately, thousands of people began chiselling off chips of the Wall. Soon after most of it was taken down and, in some cases, sold off to museums and private collectors. However, some stretches still stand, silent symbols not just of an era of division but also of the triumph of freedom and individuality over an oppressive and unjust political system:

East Side Gallery
A 1300m-long section along Mühlenstrasse painted by more than 100 international artists during post-reunification euphoria (U/S-Bahn Warschauer Strasse).

Niederkirchnerstrasse
This 160m section runs along Niederkirchnerstrasse from Martin-Gropius-Bau to Wilhelmstrasse near the former Preussischer Landtag (Prussian State Parliament; U/S-Bahn Potsdamer Platz).

Invalidenfriedhof
This cemetery, just north of the Hamburger Bahnhof Museum of Contemporary Art, has two sections measuring about 150m in total (U6 to Zinnowitzer Strasse).

Gedenkstätte Berliner Mauer
The new Berlin Wall Memorial, a lengthy section of the Wall plus border installations, is on the corner of Bernauer Strasse and Gartenstrasse (S-Bahn Nordbahnhof).

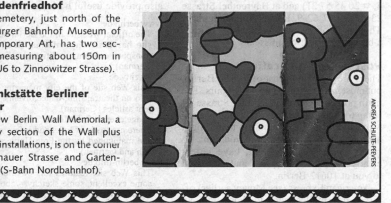

ANDREA SCHULTE-PEEVERS

For telephone information or reservations, you must now call the new BTM Hotline at ☎ 0190 75 40 40. Calls from within Germany cost an exorbitant DM2.42 per minute. The BTM Hotline number for calls from outside Germany is ☎ (49) 1805 75 40 40. A considerably cheaper alternative is the BTM's Web site at www.btm.de.

All tourist offices sell maps, books and the heavily touted Berlin WelcomeCard (DM29). It entitles one adult and up to three children under 14 years of age to 72 hours of public transport within the Berlin-Potsdam area and minor discounts on admissions to museums, shows, attractions, sightseeing tours and boat cruises. The WelcomeCard is also available at hotels and public-transport ticket offices.

The ADAC car club (☎ 868 60) has offices at Bundesallee 29-30 in Wilmersdorf and at Alexanderplatz 5 (Map 4).

Information for disabled people is available from the Berliner Behindertenverband (☎ 547 51 05), which is open weekdays from 8 am to 6 pm; SERIS (☎ 892 66 02); Movado (☎ 471 51 45); Service-Ring-Berlin (☎ 859 40 10), open weekdays from 10 am to 6 pm; and the Verband Geburts- und anderer Behinderter (Disabled Persons' Association; ☎ 341 17 97). The last two also have a wheelchair hire service, the latter for free.

Money

Among the most central exchange offices *(Wechselstuben)* is the Reisebank (Map 6, ☎ 881 71 17), Hardenbergplatz 1, outside the Zoo station and open daily from 7.30 am to 10 pm. Another branch at Ostbahnhof (☎ 296 43 93) has slightly shorter weekend hours. Euro-Change (Map 6, ☎ 261 14 84) inside the Europa-Center is open from 9 am to 6 pm, and Saturday to 4 pm.

American Express cashes its travellers cheques at no commission but sometimes gives a very ordinary rate. Branches are opposite the Galeries Lafayette department store at Friedrichstrasse 172 in Mitte (Map 4, ☎ 20 45 57 21) and at Bayreuther Strasse 23 (☎ 21 47 62 92) near Wittenbergplatz. Thomas Cook (Map 4, ☎ 20 16 59 16) has a branch at Friedrichstrasse 56.

Post & Communications

There are dozens of post offices in Berlin, but most have restricted opening hours. The main post office is at Budapester Strasse 42 (Map 6), near the tourist office, and is open Monday to Saturday from 8 am to midnight and on Sunday from 10 am to midnight. To receive poste restante mail, have letters clearly marked '*Postlagernd*' and addressed to you at 10612 Berlin.

American Express (see Money earlier) offers a free mail service to those with an American Express card or travellers cheques (DM2 fee otherwise). The sender should make sure that the words 'Client's Mail' appear somewhere on the envelope. The office will hold mail for 30 days but won't accept registered post or parcels.

Email & Internet Access Expect to pay from DM5 to DM7 for 30 minutes at an Internet cafe. Café Website (Map 6, ☎ 88 67 96 30), Joachimsthaler Strasse 41, near Zoo station has 40 PCs and stays open until 2 am. Across the street, on the top floor of the Karstadt Sporthaus, is Cyberb@r (Map 6, ☎ 88 02 40), open during regular shop hours; there's a second branch at KaDeWe (Map 6). Six-month email accounts cost DM15.

The Alpha Café (☎ 447 90 67), Dunckerstrasse 72 in Prenzlauer Berg (S8 or S10 to Prenzlauer Allee), is a fun place with 10 computers, aol, netscape, printers, scanners and other office equipment. It's open daily from 3 pm to midnight.

Internet Café Hai Täck (Map 3, ☎ 85 96 14 13), Brünnhildestrasse 8, in Schöneberg (U9 and S4/45/46 to Bundesplatz) has aol and compuserve, a fax service and good food. It's open from 11 am to 1 am.

Internet Resources

You'll find lots on Berlin's culture, institutions etc on the Internet. Most sites listed also provide useful hotlinks.

www.berlin.de
The official Web site of the Berlin Senate, this site has basic city information on culture, transport, economy, politics etc (English and German).

www.zitty.de
This Web site of the city magazine *Zitty* has info on theatre, film, dance, events, plus current articles (German).

userpage.chemie.fu-berlin.de
There are loads of links and info on this Web site maintained by the Free University (English and German).

www.berlin-info.de
This Web site features lots of information – some excellent, some sketchy – about hotels, sightseeing and Berlin generally (English and German).

Travel Agencies

Travel agencies offering cheap flights advertise in the *Reisen* classified section *(Kleinanzeigen)* of the popular city magazines *Zitty* and *Tip* (see the Entertainment section later in this chapter). One of the better discount operators is Alternativ Tours (Map 6, ☎ 881 20 89), Wilmersdorfer Strasse 94, in Wilmersdorf (U7 to Adenauerplatz) which specialises in unpublished, discounted fares to anywhere.

Another good option is Rainbow Tours (Map 6, ☎ 318 63 00), Kantstrasse 116, which operates incredibly cheap bus trips to Prague, London, Munich and Paris.

Kilroy Travel (☎ 310 00 40) has especially good deals on air tickets, bus travel and car hire. There's a branch at Hardenbergstrasse 9 in Charlottenburg (Map 6). Others are at Georgenstrasse 3 in Mitte (Map 4) and at Takustrasse 47, on the corner of Königin-Luise-Strasse in Dahlem (U1 to Dahlem-Dorf). Kilroy also sells the GO25 card issued by the Federation of International Youth Travel Organisations (FIYTO) and ISIC student cards (DM15; one photo and ID required).

STA Travel also caters largely for young people and issues ISIC cards. There are branches at Goethestrasse 73 (Map 6, ☎ 311 09 50) and at Dorotheenstrasse 30 (☎ 20 16 50 63; U/S-Bahn to Friedrichstrasse).

Flugbörse is a good place for discounted air tickets, including student and youth fares. There are 11 branches throughout Berlin. Check the Yellow Pages for details.

Agencies specialising in Eastern Europe are on Budapester Strasse, south of Zoo station. LOT Polish Airlines (Map 6, ☎ 261 15 05) is at No 18 and Malév Hungarian Airlines (Map 6, ☎ 264 95 45) at No 10. Information on travel to the Czech Republic is available from Čedok (Map 4, ☎ 204 46 44), Leipziger Strasse 60. The Aeroflot office (Map 4, ☎ 226 98 10), Unter den Linden 51, near the corner of Friedrichstrasse has information about Russia.

Bookshops

Cosmopolitan Berlin has many bookstores that specialise in English-language material. The friendly British Bookshop (Map 4, ☎ 238 46 80), Mauerstrasse 83-84, in Mitte has books on the history of Berlin and of Germany in general, an excellent selection of the latest British and US novels, and reference works on subjects like German cuisine, the arts and travel, including Lonely Planet books.

Books in Berlin (Map 6, ☎ 313 12 33), Goethestrasse 69, in Charlottenburg has new and used English-language books. For used books there's also Fair Exchange (Map 5, ☎ 694 46 75) at Dieffenbachstrasse 58 in Kreuzberg 61 (U7 to Südstern).

The excellent Hugendubel (Map 6, ☎ 21 40 60), Tauentzienstrasse 13, seems to have

just about every German book in print, plus a decent selection of English novels and Lonely Planet books. Browsing is encouraged and a cafe and comfortable sofas invite reading. A smaller branch is in the Potsdamer Platz Arkaden mall.

Kiepert has a similar selection and an old-fashioned layout; its branches are at Hardenbergstrasse 4-5 in Charlottenburg (Map 6, ☎ 311 00 90) and at Friedrichstrasse 63 (Map 4, ☎ 208 25 11) in Mitte.

Libraries

Berlin has a comprehensive network of about 350 public libraries crammed with about four million tomes. You can browse the stacks at any of them for free, but to check out books you'll need a library card, only available to Berlin residents. Major libraries include:

Amerika-Gedenkbibliothek (AGB)
   The America Memorial Library (Map 3, ☎ 69 08 40) is the largest circulating library in Germany (850,000 items). It is at Blücherplatz 1 (U6 or U7 to Mehringdamm) and open Monday from 3 to 7 pm (Tuesday to Saturday from 11 am).
Zentrum für Berlin-Studien
   The Centre for Berlin Studies (Map 4, ☎ 20 28 61 49) at Breite Strasse 35-36 stocks 350,000 books on anything you ever wanted to know about Berlin. It's open weekdays from 10 am to 7 pm and Saturday from 1 to 6 pm.
Staatsbibliothek
   The State Library (Map 4, ☎ 201 50) at Unter den Linden 8 in Mitte is open weekdays from 9 am to 9 pm and Saturday to 5 pm. There's a free tour in German at 10.30 am every first Saturday of the month. A second branch (Map 3, ☎ 26 61) is across from the Kulturforum at Potsdamer Strasse 33. It's open weekdays from 10 am to 7 pm (Saturday to 1 pm). Free guided tours here are offered on the third Saturday of every month at 10.30 am. The Staatsbibliothek is not part of the public library system. To understand how to read or borrow books, pick up the leaflet 'Notes for First-Time Users' as you enter (bring your passport).

Universities

Berlin has Germany's third-largest student body (after Munich and Cologne) with a total of 165,000 students, including 17% foreigners. These three major universities are Humboldt Universität Berlin (Map 4, ☎ 209 30) at Unter den Linden 6 in Mitte; the Freie Universität Berlin (☎ 83 81) at Kaiserwertherstrasse 16-18 in Zehlendorf; and Technische Universität (Map 6, ☎ 31 41) at Hardenbergstrasse and Strasse des 17 Juni in Mitte. In addition, there are four arts academies and nine polytechnics *(Fachhochschulen)*.

International Centres

Amerika Haus (Map 6, ☎ 31 10 73), Hardenbergstrasse 22-24, in Charlottenburg is open Wednesday to Friday from 1 to 5 pm. The British Council (Map 6, ☎ 31 10 99 10) is next door at Hardenbergstrasse 20. There's an Institut Français (Map 6, ☎ 885 90 20) at Kurfürstendamm 211.

Laundry

The Schnell und Sauber chain has outlets across Berlin: at Uhlandstrasse 53 (Map 6, U1 to Hohenzollernplatz); at Wiener Strasse 15 near the corner of Lausitzer Strasse in Kreuzberg 36 (Map 5, U15 to Görlitzer Bahnhof); and on Mehringdamm at the corner of Gneisenaustrasse, right opposite the Mehringdamm U-Bahn station exit, in Kreuzberg 61.

The other major chain is called Wasch-center, with a branch at Bergmannstrasse 109 in Kreuzberg 61 (U6 and U7 to Mehringdamm). Independent laundrettes include Öko-Express, Rosenthaler Strasse 71 near the corner of Torstrasse (Map 4, U8 to Rosenthaler Platz) in Mitte; and Waschcafé at Revaler Strasse 15 and Aqua-Wasch at Lenbachstrasse 22, both in Friedrichshain.

Left Luggage

At Zoo station, coin lockers cost DM2 or DM4, and the left-luggage office (open from 5 am to 11 pm) charges DM4 per item per day. The left-luggage office at Zentraler Omnibus Busbahnhof is open daily from 5.30 am to 9.30 pm.

Medical Services

Berlin has about 6000 doctors and 2600 dentists, so you're quite likely to find one nearby by simply checking under *Ärzte* in the phonebook. For a referral to a doctor in your neighbourhood, or in emergencies, call ☎ 31 00 31 (24 hours).

Emergency referrals to dentists *(Zahn-arzt)* are at ☎ 89 00 43 33. The Zahnklinik Medeco has some English-speaking doctors. They're at Königin-Louise-Platz 1 (☎ 841 91 00) in Dahlem and at Klosterstrasse 17 (☎ 351 94 10) in Spandau and are open daily from 7 am to midnight. Most major hotels also have either doctors available or can refer you to one.

Hospitals affiliated with the universities with large, 24-hour emergency rooms include: Charité Hospital (Map 4, ☎ 280 20, emergencies ☎ 28 02 47 66), Schumann-strasse 20-21 (U6 to Oranienburger Tor); the Virchow Klinikum (☎ 450 50, emergencies ☎ 45 05 20 00), Augustenburger Platz 1, in Wedding; and Uniklinikum Benjamin Franklin (☎ 844 50, emergencies ☎ 84 45 30 15/25), Hindenburgdamm 30, in Steglitz.

Emergency

If you're in an emergency that requires police attention, call ☎ 110. Otherwise, there are police stations all over the city, including the City-Wache at Joachimstaler Strasse 14-19 just south of Zoo station (Map 6). For mishaps on trains, see the *Bahnpolizei* at major stations.

Police headquarters (Map 3, ☎ 69 95) and the municipal lost and found office (Map 3, ☎ 69 93 64 44) are at Platz der Luftbrücke 6 beside Tempelhof airport. The latter is open Monday and Tuesday from 7.30 am to 2 pm, Wednesday from noon to 6.30 pm and Friday from 7.30 am till noon.

If you've lost something on public transport, contact the BVG (☎ 25 62 30 40), Fraunhofer Strasse 33-36 (9th floor, room No 119); it's open Monday to Thursday, from 9 am to 6 pm (Friday to 2 pm). The Deutsche Bahn lost and found office (☎ 29 72 96) is at Mittelstrasse 20 in Schönefeld S-Bahn station.

If your car breaks down, contact the ADAC car club at ☎ 01802-22 22 22.

Dangers & Annoyances

By all accounts, Berlin is a rather safe and tolerant city. Walking alone at night is not usually dangerous, although of course there's always safety in numbers in any urban environment.

As everywhere, train stations often attract drunks, druggies and other, mostly harmless, unsavouries. Non-whites and openly gay people might encounter problems in certain eastern districts like Marzahn, Niederschönhausen and Lichtenberg. If you see any 'white skins' (skinheads wearing jackboots with white boot laces), run the other way – and fast.

Berlin has an estimated 5000 prostitutes who are harmless but annoying with their solicitations ('You datin' tonight, honey?' – or words to that effect). Their stomping grounds are the Ku'damm, Oranienburgerstrasse, Kurfürstenstrasse, Lietzenburgerstrasse, Strasse des 17 Juni and Stuttgarter Platz. Often these areas aren't the safest because they also attract pimps and junkies, so be careful. Drugs should be avoided for obvious reasons but in particular because a lot of the stuff going around is distributed by mafia-like organisations and is often dangerously impure.

Most U/S-Bahn stations are equipped with electronic information and emergency devices labelled 'SOS/Notruf/Information' and illustrated with a large red bell. If you require emergency assistance simply push the 'SOS' button. The Information button allows you to speak directly with one of the station masters. The fierce-looking private guards accompanied by even fiercer-looking muzzled dogs occasionally ride on U-Bahns and are a convincing deterrent. If you're riding S-Bahns to the outer – especially eastern – districts late at night, stay in the compartment right behind the driver which is usually the safest.

ALEXANDERPLATZ AREA (MAP 4)

Former East Berlin's main hub, **Alexanderplatz** – 'known as Alex for short' – was named after Tsar Alexander I who visited

Berlin in 1805. Today, it's a mere shadow of the low-life district described so evocatively by Alfred Döblin in his novel *Berlin Alexanderplatz* (1929). It was bombed in WWII and completely reconstructed in the 1960s. On 4 November 1989, some 700,000 people gathered here to rally against the GDR regime. They were vociferous but peaceful and they were heard: five days later, the Wall collapsed.

The first impression of Alexanderplatz is overwhelming. Nothing seems to be built on a human – or humane – scale. A jumble of concrete and glass high-rises combines with a treeless asphalt desert to form one of the most hideous and disorienting squares. This is a good place for a quick overview of the soulless architectural styles en vogue in the GDR.

Alexanderplatz has few sights, a minor being the **World Time Clock** (1969) with enamel and aluminium panelling (don't use the subterranean men's loo nearby unless you want to be stared down by 101 homosexuals on permanent prowl). The other attraction is the 365m-tall spiky monstrosity called the **Fernsehturm** (TV Tower; ☎ 242 33 33). If it's a clear day and the queue isn't too long, it's worth paying the DM8/3 for adults/children to go up the tower, open daily from 9 am to 1 am (10 am to midnight, November to March). At the 207m level is the **Telecafé**, which makes a complete revolution twice an hour.

Marienkirche

The Marienkirche just west of Alex on Karl-Liebknecht-Strasse is a 700-year-old Gothic three-nave church and one of Berlin's few surviving medieval buildings. The main attraction is the badly faded 23m-long *Totentanz* (Dance of Death) fresco portraying a shrouded Death in 14 guises leading people from all walks of life to their graves. The church is open Monday to Thursday from 10 am to noon and 1 to 5 pm, Saturday from noon to 5 pm and Sunday from 1 to 4 pm (free).

Nearby is the opulent **Neptunbrunnen** (Neptune Fountain; 1891) by Reinhold

The Secrets of SMB Museums

Berlin has 170 museums but many of the major ones are being consolidated and reorganised, meaning they are temporarily closed.

Berlin's most internationally important museums are run by the Staatliche Museen Berlin (State Museums Berlin; denoted in this book with 'SMB'). Information about any of them is available via a hotline at ☎ 20 99 55 55. Admission to most is DM4/2 per entry, or DM8/4 for a day card valid at all SMB museums. You must buy a day card to get into the Pergamon Museum, Hamburger Bahnhof, New National Gallery, New Picture Gallery, Egyptian Museum and Berggruen Collection. The Drei-Tages-Touristenkarte for DM15 gives unlimited access for three consecutive days to all SMB museums. Admission to all SMB museums is free on the first Sunday of the month.

Display captions are frequently in German only, but some museums have English-language pamphlets available at ticket counters or information desks which you may borrow for free or take with you. Increasingly popular are taped, self-guided audio-tours in several languages (free to DM8). Unless noted otherwise, museums detailed in this chapter are closed on Monday.

Begas. The female figures symbolise the rivers Rhine, Elbe, Oder and Weichsel.

The tall building just south is the **Rotes Rathaus** (Red Town Hall; 1860), home of Berlin's governing mayor and the Berlin Senate. It gets its name from the colour of the brick used in its construction (not from the political leanings of its occupants).

MUSEUMSINSEL (MAP 4)

This little island in the Spree is commonly known as Museumsinsel because of its cluster of world-class museums. On its eastern end looms the great neo-Renaissance **Berliner Dom** (Berlin Cathedral; 1905), the former court church of the Hohenzollern family (members of which are also buried here). It's open daily from 9 am to 8 pm and admission is DM8/5 for the church, crypt and viewing gallery (DM5/3 for church and crypt). There are free daily organ recitals at 3 pm.

Some of the island's museum buildings are undergoing badly needed face-lifts, with only two of the five museums open.

The SMB **Alte Nationalgalerie** (Old National Gallery) is scheduled to reopen in 2001, its permanent exhibit of 18th and 19th century masterpieces having been fused with the Gallery of the Romantics collection at Charlottenburg Palace.

Meanwhile, highlights from the Alte Nationalgalerie are on view on the upper floor of the SMB **Altes Museum** (Old Museum), an imposing neoclassical edifice by Karl Friedrich Schinkel at Bodestrasse 1-3. It was one of the first purpose-built museums in Europe and has a famed rotunda featuring Roman statues of the Greek gods. Look for works by Renoir, Monet, Manet and the Max trio: Beckmann, Liebermann and Slevogt. On the ground floor is a collection of antiquities. Museum hours are 10 am to 6 pm (DM8/4).

Immediately behind it is the SMB **Neues Museum**, which is being rebuilt to house the Egyptian Museum. Its reopening is scheduled for 2005. Closed until at least 2004 is the neobaroque SMB **Bodemuseum**, on the island's northern tip.

Pergamon Museum (SMB)

The huge Pergamon Museum is a feast of classical Greek, Babylonian, Roman, Islamic and Middle Eastern art and architecture. It will wear you out if you're not careful. The three sections (Collection of Classical Antiquities, Museum of Near Eastern Antiquities and Museum of Islamic Art) are all worth seeing, but the following are musts.

Continued on page 185

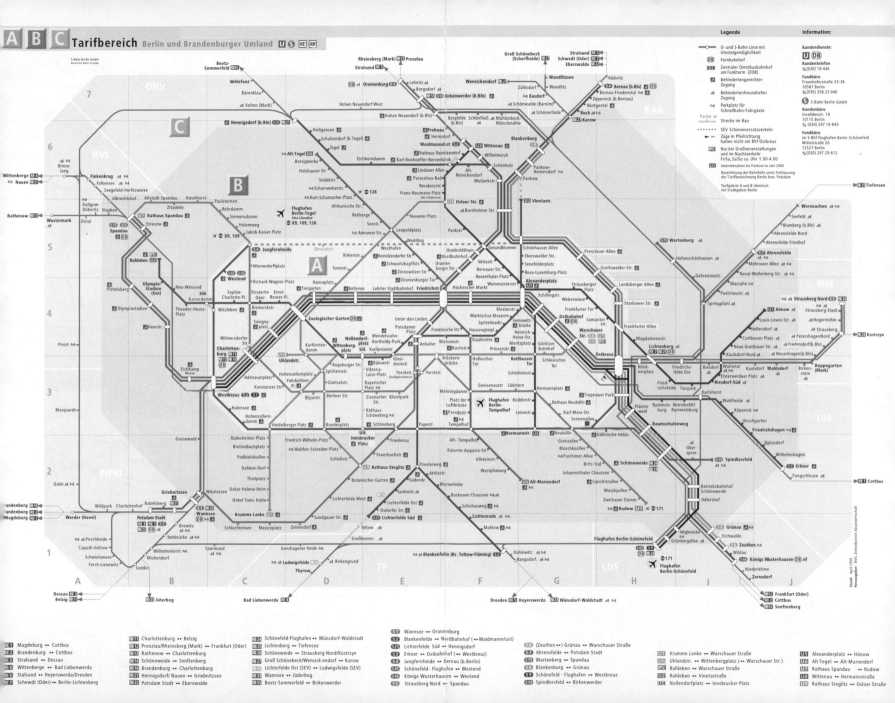

Map 1 BERLIN

LP

0   0.5   1 km

Berlin-Tegel Airport

WEDDING

Rehberge

Nauener Platz

Seestrasse

Leopold-Platz

Volkspark Rehberge

111

Saatwinkler Damm

Amrumer Strasse

Wedding

Reinickendorfer Strasse

Westhafen

Volkspark Jungfernheide

Falkenseer Chaussee

Seegfelder Strasse

Klosterbusch Weg

Havel River

Gatow Felder Strasse

Paulsternstr.

Altstadt Spandau

Zitadelle

Am Juliusturm

Haselhorst

Nonnendammallee

Paulsternstrasse

Rohrdamm

Siemens-damm

Halemweg

Jak-Kaiser-Platz

Goerdeller Damm

Birkenstrasse

Seiler Str.

Rathaus Spandau

Siemens Damm

Stadtring

Jungfernheide

100

SPANDAU

Brunsbütteler Damm

Ruhlebener Strasse

Charlottenburger

Ruhleben

See Schloss Charlottenburg Map

Schlossgarten Charlottenburg

Mierendorff Platz

Map 3

Turmstrasse

Turmstrasse

Fritz-Schloss-Park

Sexlitzstrasse

Heerstrasse

Wilhelm Strasse

Pichelsdorferstrasse

Spandauer Damm

Fürstenbrunner Weg

Kaiserin Augusta Allee

Alt Moabit

Alt Meabit

CHARLOTTENBURG

Waldbühne

Olympia-Stadion (Ost)

Neu-Westend

Reichsstrasse

Königin Elisabeth Str.

Stadtring

Richard-Wagner-Platz

Otto-Suhr-Allee

Helmholtzstr.

Hansa-Platz

TIERGARTEN

Des 17 Juni Strasse

Heerstrasse

Olympic Stadium

Olympische Strasse

Preussenallee

Sophie-Charlotte-Platz

Bismarck-strasse

Bismarckstr.

Deutsche Oper

E-Reuter-Platz

Tiergarten

Kaiser Damm

Theodor-Heuss-Platz

Kaiser-damm

Kantstrasse

Kaiser-Friedrich-Str.

Zoologischer Garten

Zoologischer Garten

Budapester Str.

Schöneberge

Havelchaussee

Havel River

Messe Damm

Kantstrasse

Wilmersdorfer Strasse

Kantstrasse

Uhland-strasse

Kurfürstendamm

Kurfürsten-damm

Wittenberg-platz

Kurfürsten-strasse

Lützow Ufer

Am Postfenn

Teufelssee Chaussee

Adenauer-platz

Kurfürstendamm

Lietzenburger Str.

Augsburger Strasse

Luise-Platz

Nollendorf-platz

Kleistr.

Bülow-strasse

Gleise

Spichernstrasse

Nachodstr.

Hohenstaufen Str.

Pallas Str.

Goeben Str.

Map 6

Hohenzollern Platz

Konstanzer Strasse

Fehrbelliner Platz

Güntzel-strasse

Kleistpark

Yorckstr.

Westfälischestrasse

Hohenzollern Damm

Berliner Str.

Berliner Str.

Eisenacher Strasse

Brandenburgische

Bayerischer Platz

WILMERSDORF

Berlinerstrasse

Blissestrasse

Uhlandstr.

Badensche Str.

Volkspark

Rathaus Schöneberg

Dominicus Strasse

SCHÖNEBERG

Gatower Heide

Heidelberger Platz

Bundes-platz

Innsbrucker Platz

Sachsendam

Kronprinzenweg

Stadt Ring

Hubertus

100

Hagenstrasse

SCHMARGENDORF

Hundekehlestr.

Mecklenburgische

Rüdesheimer Platz

Wies Badener Str.

Breitenbachplatz

Friedrich-Wilhelm-Platz

Saarstrasse

Glasgaram.

103

Avus

GRUNEWALD

Koenigsallee

Clay Allee

Hutten Weg

Podbielskiallee

Laubacher Str.

W-Schreiber-Platz

Kustower Damm

Potsdamer Chaussee

Berliner Grunewald

Teplitzer

Schildhorns

ZEHLENDORF

To Wannsee

115

To Dahlem Museum Complex

Podbielski-allee

Berlin Transport Map
(see overleaf)

Map 3 TIERGARTEN, SCHÖNEBERG & KREUZBERG 61

Map 3 TIERGARTEN, SCHÖNEBERG & KREUZBERG 61

Classical art and architecture feature in Berlin's Pergamon Museum.

DAVID PEEVERS

Map 4 MITTE

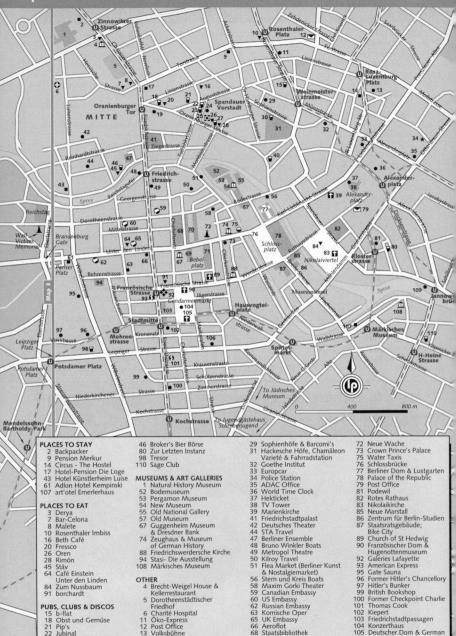

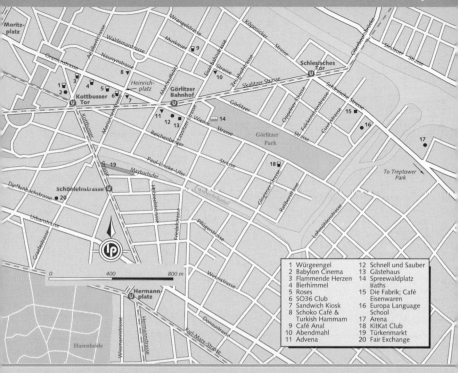

1 Würgeengel	12 Schnell und Sauber
2 Babylon Cinema	13 Gästehaus
3 Flammende Herzen	14 Spreewaldplatz
4 Bierhimmel	Baths
5 Roses	15 Die Fabrik; Café
6 SO36 Club	Eisenwaren
7 Sandwich Kiosk	16 Europa Language
8 Schoko Café &	School
Turkish Hammam	17 Arena
9 Café Anal	18 KitKat Club
10 Abendmahl	19 Türkenmarkt
11 Advena	20 Fair Exchange

The German parliament has returned to Berlin and a new state-of-the-art Reichstag.

Map 6 CHARLOTTENBURG & WILMERSDORF

PLACES TO STAY
11 Hecker's Hotel
43 Pension Peters
44 Hotel Crystal
48 Hotel-Pension Majesty
51 Pension Alexandra
64 Pension Fischer; Hotel-Pension Nürnberger Eck
70 Hotel Garni Augusta
76 Hotel Bleibtreu
78 Olivaer Apart Hotel
79 Hotel Agon
80 Hotel-Pension Margrit
81 Hotel Savigny
82 Hotel-Pension Curtis
Jugendgästehaus Central

PLACES TO EAT
5 Café Hardenberg
6 Technische Universität Mensa
9 Satyam
10 Samadhi
16 Good Friend
17 Ashoka Bar
37 Marché
41 Arche Noah
42 Schwarzes Café
53 Ali Baba
54 Einhorn
56 Aschinger
65 Salomon Bagels
69 Soup Kultur
71 Café Wintergarten
75 Piccola Taormina

OTHER
1 Kiepert
2 Concert & Theaterkasse City
3 Renaissance Theatre
4 Kilroy Travel
7 College of Arts Concert Hall
8 Post Office
12 STA Travel
13 Books in Berlin
14 Sack + Pack
15 Aldi Supermarket
18 Dicke Wirtin
19 British Council
20 Amerika Haus
21 Theater des Westens; Quasimodo; Delphi Film Palast
22 Erotik Museum
23 Aldi Supermarket
24 Reisebank
25 BVG Information Kiosk
26 Filmzentrum Zoo-Palast; Hekticket
27 Humana 2nd Hand Clothing
28 Berlin Zoo & Aquarium
29 Hertz; Avis
30 Sixt Budget; LOT Polish Airlines
31 Malév Hungarian Airlines
32 Main Post Office
33 Main Tourist Office
34 Europa-Center
36 Kaiser-Wilhelm-Gedächtniskirche
38 Café Website
39 Olympia Cinema
40 Karstadt Sporthaus & Cyberb@r
45 Hegel
46 A-Trane
47 Abraxas
48 Rainbow Tours
50 Alternativ Tours
52 Kaiser's Supermarket
55 Australian Embassy
57 Tour Bus Stop (Café Kranzler)
58 Wertheim Department Store
59 Hugendubel
60 Apollo Sauna
61 Kaiser's Supermarket; Einhorn Buffet
62 American Express
63 KaDeWe Department Store, Info Point & Cyberb@r
66 Synagogue
67 City-Wache (Police Station)
68 Theaterkasse Centrum
72 Käthe-Kollwitz-Museum
73 Lufthansa City Centre
74 Institut Français; French Consulate
83 Aldi Supermarket
84 Schnell und Sauber
86 Flöz

Continued from page 176

In Room 2 of the Collection of Classical Antiquities is the reconstructed **Pergamon Altar** from Asia Minor (165 BC), a gargantuan raised-marble altar with a 120m frieze of the gods doing battle with the giants. In Room 6 is the Roman **Gate of Miletus**, built under Emperor Hadrian in the early 2nd century AD. The **Orpheus Mosaic** in the same room is from a villa in Miletus.

You pass through the gate to enter the Museum of Near Eastern Antiquities and another culture and century: Babylon during the reign of Nebuchadnezzar II (604-562 BC). Here is the museum's *pièce de résistance*: the world-renowned **Ishtar Gate**, fronted by a 30m-long 'Processional Way' made of the same blue and ochre glazed bricks with reliefs of lions, horses, dragons and unicorns. It's so awesome you can almost hear the fanfare.

On the upper floor, in the Museum of Islamic Art, the first highlight awaits in rooms 9 and 10 in the form of the exterior wall of the **Caliph's palace in Mshatta**, probably built during the reign of Caliph al-Walid II (743-744 AD). Not to be missed either is the 17th century **Aleppo Room** (room 17) from the house of a Christian merchant in today's Syria. Each square centimetre of wall space is overlaid with colourful wooden panelling painted with dizzying detail.

The Pergamon is open from 10 am to 6 pm (DM8/4). 'Listening wands' with four hours of taped commentary in English may be hired for DM8.

SCHLOSSPLATZ (MAP 4)
Nothing of sterile Schlossplatz, just south of the Berliner Dom, serves as a reminder that on the spot occupied by the **Palace of the Republic** a real imperial palace, the Berliner Schloss, once stood. The war-damaged building was torn down in 1950 and replaced with a glitzy pile of concrete and golden mirrors that, until 1990, was the home of the GDR parliament, the Volkskammer (People's Chamber). The complex was used by the public during congresses, balls and concerts.

After the Wende it was discovered that asbestos had been used in its construction, so it was closed immediately. For years demolition looked inevitable but, amid discussions about its fate, it's just been left to crumble, an eyesore in a blossoming Berlin. In 1993-94, one step ahead of Christo and his wrapped Reichstag, a French artist clad the structure with plastic sheets designed to look like the old City Palace, sparking some interest in rebuilding the original structure.

The only surviving section from the original palace is the triumphal-arch portal, now incorporated into the **Staatsratsgebäude** (State Council Building) on the southern side of Schlossplatz. Immediately east of the Staatsrat is the turn-of-the-century **Neue Marstall** (New Royal Stables), housing the City Archives.

NIKOLAIVIERTEL (MAP 4)
Across the Spree to the east between Rathausstrasse and Mühlendamm is the rather twee and old-world Nikolaiviertel (Nicholas Quarter). Some of the city's oldest houses stood here until flattened by bombs in 1944. What you see today is the not entirely unsuccessful attempt by socialist architects to re-create a medieval town to celebrate Berlin's 750th anniversary in 1988.

The result is a maze of narrow alleys lined by diminutive houses, lorded over by the spindly twin spires of the **Nikolaikirche** (Church of St Nicholas), a three-nave hall church that is Berlin's oldest (1230). One of the few buildings which were restored rather than newly built, it has a moderately interesting exhibit on the city's history until 1648. It's open from 10 am to 6 pm (DM5/2.50).

UNTER DEN LINDEN (MAP 4)
A stroll west of Museumsinsel along fashionable Unter den Linden (Under the Linden Trees) takes in the greatest surviving monuments of the former Prussian capital. After crossing the lovely **Schlossbrücke** (Palace Bridge), with its eight clusters of marble statues tracing the training and development of a Greek warrior, the very first building on the right at Unter den Linden 2 is the **Deutsches**

Historisches Museum (Museum of German History; ☎ 20 30 40). In the former Zeughaus (Armoury, 1706, by Andreas Schlüter), it normally houses an extensive and fascinating collection of objects, paintings, maps and photos tracing German history from 900 AD, as well as excellent changing exhibits. Closed until at least late 2001, it will reopen with a modern extension designed by Chinese-American architect IM Pei who is also crowning the original baroque building with a new glass roof. Meanwhile, part of the exhibit has been moved across the street to the beautiful, colonnaded **Kronprinzen-Palais** (Crown Prince's Palace; 1732). It's open Thursday to Tuesday from 10 am to 6 pm (closed Wednesday). Entry is free.

To the west of the Zeughaus is Schinkel's restored **Neue Wache** (New Guardhouse; 1818), Germany's central memorial to the victims of fascism and militarism. It harbours the tombs of an unknown soldier, resistance fighter and concentration camp victim, as well as Käthe Kollwitz's sculpture *Mother and her Dead Son*. It's open daily from 10 am to 6 pm (free).

Humboldt Universität (1753), the next building to the west, was originally a palace of Prince Heinrich, brother of King Friedrich II of Prussia. It was converted to a university building in 1810. At No 8 is the massive **Staatsbibliothek** (State Library; 1914). An equestrian **statue of Friedrich II** usually stands in the middle of the avenue in front of the university but was removed in October 1997 and still under renovation at the time of writing.

Across from the university is **Bebelplatz**, where the Nazis held their first official book-burning on 10 May 1933, destroying works of numerous writers, including Bertolt Brecht, Heinrich Mann and Alfred Döblin. A poignant below-ground memorial of empty bookshelves marks the spot.

Bebelplatz is framed by several historical buildings. To the east is the baroque **Alte Königliche Bibliothek** (Old Royal Library; 1780), now part of the legal faculty of the university. Opposite is Wenzeslaus von Knobelsdorff's **Staatsoper Unter den Lin-**

den (1743). On the south-eastern corner sits the domed **Church of St Hedwig** (1783), partly modelled on Rome's Pantheon. It was Berlin's only Catholic church until 1854.

A short distance east along Französische Strasse and then Werderstrasse is the **Friedrichswerdersche Kirche** (☎ 208 13 23), with a permanent exhibit on the architecture and sculptures of Karl Friedrich Schinkel. It's open Tuesday to Sunday from 10 am to 6 pm (DM4/2).

South-west of Bebelplatz is **Gendarmenmarkt**, a lovely, quiet square framed by a trio of magnificent buildings. The **Deutscher Dom** (German Cathedral; ☎ 22 73 21 41), at the southern end of the square, was originally constructed in 1708 and rebuilt in 1785, 1882 and 1995. It houses an excellent exhibition on German history from 1800. It's open daily from 10 am to 6 pm, and to 7 pm in June, July and August (free).

At the square's northern end, the **Französischer Dom** (French Cathedral) – so called because it was once the seat of French Huguenots – contains the **Hugenottenmuseum** (Huguenot Museum; ☎ 229 17 60), which covers the 18th century French Protestants' contributions to Berlin life. For a great view, climb the tower. The museum is open Tuesday to Saturday from noon to 5 pm, and Sunday from 1 pm (DM3/2). Between the two cathedrals is the opulent **Konzerthaus** (Concert Hall), designed by Schinkel in 1819.

Back on Unter den Linden, on the south-east corner with Charlottenstrasse, is the **Guggenheim Museum** (☎ 202 09 30), which opened in late 1997. It is the fifth permanent exhibition space set up by the Guggenheim family, which incidentally is of German descent. The stark galleries with high ceilings host three to four high-calibre shows of modern and contemporary art annually. It's open daily from 11 am to 8 pm (DM8/5, free on Monday).

Brandenburg Gate

The landmark Brandenburger Tor – the only surviving city gate – marks the western terminus of Unter den Linden. Once the

JON DAVISON

Once a symbol of division, the Brandenburg Gate now represents German unity.

boundary between East and West Berlin, it is now the symbol of reunification.

The gate is crowned by the **Quadriga**, a two-wheeled chariot drawn by four horses and driven by the winged goddess of victory. The gate's northern wing contains the **Raum der Stille** (Room of Silence), where the weary and frenzied can sit and contemplate peace.

The gate opens up to **Pariser Platz**, which is being restored to its prewar grandeur, when it was called the 'emperor's reception hall'. By the time it's finished, it will have statuesque buildings on three sides. The **embassies** of the United States, UK and France will be supplemented by banks, offices and the exhibition space of the **Academy of Arts**.

Hotel Adlon, the grande dame of Berlin caravansaries, has already been re-created in its original spot. Its first incarnation stems from 1907, when it counted Charlie Chaplin, Greta Garbo and Thomas Mann among its guests. Famous names or deep pockets are once again a requirement for spending the night with front-row seats on the Brandenburg Gate (see Places to Stay).

ORANIENBURGER TOR AREA (MAP 4)

A short walk north-west of Oranienburger Tor U-Bahn station (U6) is the **Brecht-Weigel Gedenkstätte** (Brecht-Weigel House; ☎ 283 05 70 44) at Chausseestrasse 125. Here the Marxist playwright Bertolt Brecht and his actress wife, Helene Weigel, lived from 1948

until their deaths. Brecht's living quarters are on the 1st floor, and Weigel's are on the ground floor. They can be seen on guided tours offered half-hourly Tuesday to Friday from 10 am to noon (Thursday also from 5 to 7 pm), Saturday from 9.30 am to noon and 12.30 to 2 pm, and Sunday (hourly) from 11 am to 6 pm (DM6/3). Reservations won't hurt. The entrance is upstairs to the right from the rear courtyard.

Behind the house is the **Dorotheenstädtischer Friedhof** (Dorotheenstadt Cemetery), with the tombs of architect Schinkel, the philosopher Georg Friedrich Hegel, the writer Heinrich Mann as well as Brecht and Weigel. There's a complete list of names and a map with grave locations at the end of the walkway leading to the cemetery. It's open roughly from 8 am to sunset, though make sure you check the sign by the entrance for details, since you'll be in for one hell of a climbing adventure if the gates are locked.

Nearby at Invalidenstrasse 43, Humboldt University's **Museum für Naturkunde** (Natural History Museum, 1810; ☎ 20 93 85 91), has a good collection of dinosaurs (including the world's largest on show: it's 23m long and 12m tall!) and prehistoric birds as well as minerals and meteorites. It is open 9.30 am to 5 pm (DM5/2.50).

About a 10 minute walk west is Berlin's premier contemporary art museum, the SMB **Hamburger Bahnhof** (Map 3, ☎ 397 83 40) at Invalidenstrasse 50-51. It picks up where the New National Gallery at the Kulturforum leaves off, with big names like Joseph Beuys, Andy Warhol and Robert Rauschenberg forming the core collection.

At least as interesting as the art is the architecture of the building. From the outside, the gleaming white, three-winged former train station exudes a palatial aura, though the clock in the right tower points to its more humble origin. Inside is a huge vaulted hall with the loftiness of a three-nave cathedral; it's painted white and carried by an exposed skeleton of steel beams. Museum hours are 10 am to 6 pm (Thursday to 8 pm), weekends from 11 am (DM8/4).

Bertolt Brecht

Bertolt Brecht (1898-1956), the controversial poet and play-wright, spent the last seven years of his life in East Berlin. He wrote his first play, *Baal*, while studying medicine in Munich in 1918. His first play to reach the stage, *Trommeln in der Nacht* (Drums in the Night; 1922), won the coveted Kleist Prize, and two years later he moved to the Deutsches Theater in Berlin to work with the Austrian director Max Reinhardt. Over the next decade, in plays like *Die Dreigroschenoper* (The Threepenny Opera; 1928), he developed his theory of 'epic theatre', which, unlike 'dramatic theatre', forces its audience to detach themselves emotionally from the play and its characters and to reason intellectually.

With the rise of Hitler in 1933, Brecht – a dedicated Marxist – went into exile with his wife, the actress Helene Weigel. He first went to Switzerland, then to Denmark, Finland and then the USA. He wrote most of his best plays during this time: *Mutter Courage und ihre Kinder* (Mother Courage and her Children; 1941), *Leben des Galilei* (The Life of Galileo; 1943), *Der gute Mensch von Sezuan* (The Good Woman of Sezuan; 1943) and *Der kaukasische Kreidekreis* (The Caucasian Chalk Circle; 1948).

MICK WELDON

After having to testify before the House of Un-American Activities Committee in 1947, Brecht left for Europe, arriving in East Berlin in 1949. There he founded the Berliner Ensemble at the Theater am Schiffbauerdamm with Weigel, who directed it until her death in 1971.

During his lifetime Brecht was both under suspicion in the East for his unorthodox aesthetic theories and scorned (and often boycotted) in much of the West for his communist principles. A staple of left-wing directors throughout the 1960s and 70s, Brecht's plays are now under reassessment, though his influence in freeing the theatre from the constraints of a 'well made play in three acts' is undeniable. The superiority of Brecht's poetry, so little known in English, remains undisputed.

SPANDAUER VORSTADT (MAP 4)

The quarter south-east of U-Bahn station Oranienburger Tor – on both sides of Oranienburger Strasse – is called the Spandauer Vorstadt. Today it is often mistakenly referred to as the Scheunenviertel (Barn Quarter), which is actually only the small section of the Spandauer Vorstadt around Rosa-Luxemburg-Platz.

For centuries, the area was a centre of Berlin's Jewish community and it is becoming so again. It is also one of the city's premier entertainment districts with an edgy mix of pubs (artistic to grungy), avant-garde bars, ethnic restaurants and culture centres, especially along Oranienburger Strasse, Auguststrasse and Tucholskystrasse.

Hackesche Höfe & Sophienhöfe

These two beautifully restored series of courtyards are mixed-use complexes, combining living quarters with restaurants, theatres and shops in an artistic fashion.

The main entrance to the Hackesche Höfe is off Rosenthaler Strasse which immediately puts you into the nicest courtyard, Hof No 1, whose facades are smothered in colourful, intricately patterned Art Nouveau tiles. Also here is the Chamäleon Varieté (see Entertainment); the other seven courtyards contain a cinema, a nightclub, galleries and shops.

At its eastern end, the Hackesche Höfe spill out onto Sophienstrasse. Turn left, walk for about 50m and on your right will be the **Sophienhöfe** (the entrance looks like a normal house entrance). This is a much smaller development, with only three courtyards containing galleries and a cafe, and has a dignified, quiet atmosphere. The connecting walkways are lined with primary colour neon lights.

Neue Synagoge

At Oranienburger Strasse 29 is the lovingly restored Neue Synagoge (New Synagogue). Built in the Moorish-Byzantine style, it opened in 1866 as the nation's largest synagogue (3200 seats). During the *Reichspogromnacht* on 9/10 November 1938, SA thugs tried to set fire to it, as they had to almost all other 13 synagogues in Berlin, but were prevented by a district police chief. A plaque on the facade commemorates this act of courage. The synagogue was nonetheless desecrated by the Nazis, though it wasn't destroyed until hit by bombs in 1943.

Today it is not a functioning synagogue but a memorial museum called **Centrum Judaicum** (☎ 28 40 12 50) with a permanent exhibition called 'Open the Gates: The New Synagogue 1866-1995'. On display are original furnishings and liturgical objects – including a dented eternal lamp found in the concrete flooring, a rusted doorknob, a shard of broken glass – retrieved from the wreckage.

The Centrum Judaicum is open Sunday to Thursday from 10 am to 6 pm, Friday to 4 pm (DM5/3). Guided tours in German cost an extra DM3/1.50 and are held Wednesday at 4 pm and Sunday at 2 and 4 pm. Beside the synagogue, at Oranienburger Strasse 31, is the **Jewish Art Gallery** (☎ 282 86 23).

TIERGARTEN (MAPS 3 & 4)

Just north of the Brandenburg Gate, the **Reichstag** (1894) is another Berlin landmark. In May 1999, it once again became the seat of the Bundestag, the German parliament. British architect Sir Norman Foster has created a state-of-the-art parliamentary facility, only preserving the building's historical shell. Its most striking feature is a glistening glass dome above the plenary hall. You can take an elevator to a rooftop viewing terrace, then walk inside the mirror-clad 'beehive' via a spiralling ramp. There's also a cafe. Elevators to the terrace operate till midnight, last admission at 10 pm (free).

The Reichstag has been at the centre of momentous times in German history. After WWI, Philipp Scheidemann proclaimed the German republic from one of its windows. The Reichstag fire on the night of 27-28 February 1933 destroyed large sections and allowed Hitler and the NSDAP to blame the communists. A dozen years later, bombs and the victorious Soviets nearly finished the job. Restoration – *sans* dome – wasn't finished until 1972. At midnight on 2 October 1990 the reunification of Germany was enacted here. In summer 1995, the artist Christo and his wife, Jeanne-Claude, wrapped the edifice in fabric for two weeks.

Tours of the Reichstag itself are free but must be reserved by writing to: Deutscher Bundestag, Besucherdienst, 11011 Berlin.

West of the Reichstag, the **Federal Chancellory**, the **Chancellor's Garden** and other government office buildings are being built.

Just south of the Reichstag, near the start of Scheidemannstrasse, is the **Wall Victims Memorial** to some of the 191 people who died trying to cross the Wall – one only nine months before it came tumbling down.

If you head westwards on Scheidemannstrasse and its continuation John-Foster-Dulles-Allee, you'll pass the 68-bell **Carillon** of black marble and bronze, the largest in Europe, with regular chime concerts. Just beyond is the **Haus der Kulturen der Welt** (House of World Cultures, 1957; ☎ 39 78 71 75), nicknamed the 'pregnant oyster' for its odd shape. The photo and art exhibits inside,

BERLIN

usually from Africa, Asia or Latin America, are worth a look. It's open Tuesday to Sunday from 10 am to 7 pm (admission varies).

The huge city park, **Tiergarten**, stretches westwards from the Brandenburg Gate to Zoo station in Charlottenburg. It became a park in the 18th century and in the mid-19th century was landscaped with lakes and streams. During the frigid winter of 1946-47 impoverished local residents chopped down virtually all the trees for firewood.

Strasse des 17 Juni, named by the West Berlin government in honour of the 1953 workers' uprising in East Berlin, leads westwards from the Brandenburg Gate through the park. Hitler's showy entrance to Berlin, it was known as the East-West Axis during the Nazi era. On the northern side, just west of the gate, is a **Soviet War Memorial** flanked by the first two Russian tanks (Nos 200 and 300) to enter the city in 1945. The brown marble is said to have come from Hitler's chancellory, which once stood on Wilhelmstrasse. (More of this recycled marble was used in building the Soviet Memorial in Treptower Park.)

Farther west along Strasse des 17 Juni, on the Grosser Stern (Big Star) roundabout, is the 69m-tall **Siegessäule** (Victory Column, 1873). It commemorates 19th century Prussian military adventures and was moved here by the Nazis in 1938 from Königsplatz in front of the Reichstag. Crowned by a gilded statue of Victoria, it has a spiral staircase (285 steps) leading to the top, with a worthwhile view. It's open daily from 9 am to 6 pm, but is closed Monday morning (DM2/1).

Just north-east is **Schloss Bellevue** (1785), built for Prince Ferdinand, the youngest brother of King Friedrich II, and now the German president's official residence. Kaiser Wilhelm II disliked the building and used it as a school for his children. The Nazis turned it into a Museum of German Ethnology.

KULTURFORUM (MAP 3)

In the 1950s, one of the premier architects of the time, Hans Scharoun, was asked to create a design concept for what would become known as Kulturforum, a cluster of museums and concert halls on the south-eastern edge of Tiergarten. The first building was the **Berliner Philharmonie** (1961) at Herbert-von-Karajan-Strasse 1; the golden-coloured aluminium facade was only added in 1981.

Scharoun also designed the adjacent, smaller **Kammermusiksaal** (Chamber Music Hall, 1987) and the SMB **Musikinstrumenten-Museum** (Musical Instruments Museum; ☎ 25 48 10), in an annexe on the north-eastern side of the Philharmonie. Harpsichords from the 17th century, medieval trumpets and shepherds' bagpipes may not be everyone's cup of tea, but the museum displays them in a unique and wonderful way. Historical paintings and porcelain figurines portray people playing instruments, while earphones sprinkled throughout the museum let you hear what they sound(ed) like.

Pride of place goes to the **Gray Organ** (1820) from Bathwick, Somerset, but our favourite is the **'mighty Wurlitzer' organ** (1929) with more buttons and keys than a Beefeater guard. Guided tours (DM3) at 11 am on Saturday culminate with a noon recital on this white and gold confection (you don't have to go on the tour to hear this). Chamber music concerts are held at the museum most Sundays at 11 am. Museum hours are from 9 am to 5 pm on weekdays and weekends from 10 am (DM4/2).

The red-brick **St Matthäus Kirche** (1846), south of the Philharmonie, is one of the few

ANDREA SCHULTE-PEEVERS

Marble from Hitler's chancellory was used to create the Soviet War Memorial.

places with **English-language services**, held on Sunday at 12.30 pm in winter and 9 am in summer. A well kept secret is the bird's-eye view from atop the bell tower (DM1) The church is open Wednesday to Sunday from noon to 6 pm.

Neue Gemäldegalerie (SMB)

If you only see one museum at the Kulturforum, make it the Neue Gemäldegalerie (New Picture Gallery), which opened in June 1998 in a gloriously designed building. Focused on European painting from the 13th to the 18th century, it merges collections from the Bodemuseum (in the former East) and the Gemäldegalerie in Dahlem (in the former West). More than 1100 major paintings are on view in this vast museum. Highlights come from Flemish/Dutch masters like Rembrandt and Rubens; Germans such as Cranach, Dürer and Holbein; Italians like Botticelli, Raffael and Titian; Frenchmen like Watteau and de la Tour; Brits like Gainsborough and Reynolds; and Spaniards like Goya and Velázquez. The galleries are accessed from the football-field-sized, pillared Great Hall, lit via circular skylights.

Its hours are 10 am to 6 pm, and weekends from 11 am (DM8/4). Admission includes free audio guides (German or English) with commentary on selected paintings.

Other Kunstforum Museum

The never-ending SMB **Kunstgewerbemuseum** (Museum of Decorative Arts; ☎ 266 29 02) shows arts and crafts ranging from 16th century chalices of gilded silver to Art Deco ceramics and 20th century appliances. Don't miss Carlo Bugatti's crazy suite of furniture (1885) upstairs, with elements of Islamic, Japanese and Native American design all in one. It's open from 10 am to 6 pm, and weekends from 11 am (DM4/2).

Across the plaza is the SMB **Kupferstichkabinett** (Copperplate Etchings Gallery; ☎ 266 20 23) – you can safely miss this one – and, to the south-east at Potsdamer Strasse 50, the SMB **Neue Nationalgalerie** (New National Gallery, 1968; ☎ 266 26 62), with a collection of 19th and 20th century paintings

and sculptures including works by Klee, Munch, Miró, Max Ernst, Juan Gris and Henry Moore. But the main emphasis is on German expressionism; you can't miss the works of Otto Dix (eg *Old Couple*, 1923), Beckmann's triptychs and the wonderful 'egghead' figures of George Grosz. The sculpture garden in the back is a great place to put your feet up and catch a few rays if the sun is shining. The **State Library** branch (1976) across the street contains reading, periodical and exhibition rooms.

Bauhaus Archiv/Museum für Gestaltung

About 1km to the west along the Landwehr Canal is the Bauhaus Archives/Museum of Design (☎ 254 00 20), Klingelhöferstrasse 14. It is devoted to the artists of the Bauhaus School (1919-33), who laid the basis for much contemporary architecture. (See the boxed text 'The Bauhaus' in the Saxony-Anhalt chapter.) The collection includes

ANDREA SCHULTE-PEEVERS

Bauhaus School founder, Walter Gropius designed the distinctive Bauhaus Museum.

works by Klee, Wassily Kandinsky and Oskar Schlemmer. It is in a building with distinctive glass-panelled gables designed by school founder, Walter Gropius (1883-1969), nephew of the architect Martin Gropius. The museum is open from 10 am to 5 pm, but is closed Tuesday (DM5/2.50).

POTSDAMER PLATZ AREA

Just east of the Kulturforum, in an area once occupied by the Wall, a slow and difficult birth is being given to Berlin's largest-scale new development (shown on the B&W Potsdamer Platz map). Since construction began in 1993, Potsdamer Platz has been ranked as one of Berlin's top tourist attractions, which is no surprise. The mammoth effort to rebuild the centre of an entire living, breathing city in one fell stroke is unprecedented. It's a challenge, and an opportunity, to reflect the Zeitgeist at the dawn of a new millennium.

For an overview of the work, visit the Info-Box (☎ 226 62 40), a nail-polish red, three-storey container on stilts above U-Bahn station Potsdamer Platz (U2). Inside is a free multimedia exhibit called 'See the City of Tomorrow Today' which explains all elements of the gigantic project with scale models, historical footage, computer simulations, posters and more. It will be open at least until December 2000, daily from 9 am to 7 pm (Thursday to 9 pm). For a bird's-eye view of the new district, head to the Info-Box's rooftop terrace (DM2).

A work in progress for many more years to come, Potsdamer Platz is slowly taking shape. By the time you read this, Helmut Jahn's glass and steel Sony Center should have opened, while the DaimlerChrysler section was inaugurated in October 1998. More than DM4 billion has been invested in this 23,000 sq metres mixed-use area. Its design is based on a masterplan by Renzo Piano (best known as the creator of the Centre Pompidou in Paris) and Christoph Kohlbecker. They were joined by an illustrious cast of architects including Arata Isozaki, the creator of a waffle-patterned, coffee-coloured bank building; Rafael Moneo, who conceived the sleek, minimalist Grand Hyatt Hotel; and Richard Rogers, who planned office buildings and an integrated shopping mall. Piano designed six of the 19 structures, including the entertainment ensemble of music theatre, IMAX and

The Reincarnation of Potsdamer Platz

The dawn of Potsdamer Platz came with the construction of the first railway line to Potsdam in 1838. From the late 19th century to the Weimar era, the square evolved into the heart of metropolitan life and entertainment in Berlin, becoming the European equivalent of New York's Times Square. Thousands of people came daily, stopping for a tea at Café Josty, a beer at Pschörr brewery or gathering in the lobby of the elegant Hotel Esplanade. Potsdamer Platz had become such an important traffic nexus that Europe's first (hand-operated) traffic light was installed in 1924 to control the daily flow of more than 100,000 people, 20,000 cars and 30 tram lines.

War sucked all life out of Potsdamer Platz, which was 80% destroyed. It soon plunged into a coma before being bisected by the Wall in 1961. On the GDR side was the infamous 'death strip', while in the west sprawled an abandoned and desolate wasteland. Nearly all the remaining historical buildings were demolished at that time, except the ruined Hotel Esplanade, the erstwhile belle of Bellevuestrasse. (Its cafe was moved, with the help of some wizardly technology, when the hotel was torn down in 1996. It has been incorporated into the new Sony Center.)

With the fall of the Wall – and communism – capitalism took over instantly. It didn't take long to realise the enormous commercial potential of this huge slice of prime real estate, which was soon gobbled up by powerful investors like Daimler-Benz (now DaimlerChrysler).

POTSDAMER PLATZ

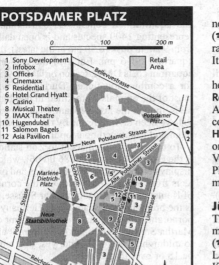

1 Sony Development	
2 Infobox	
3 Offices	
4 Cinemaxx	
5 Residential	
6 Hotel Grand Hyatt	
7 Casino	
8 Musical Theater	
9 IMAX Theatre	
10 Hugendubel	
11 Salomon Bagels	
12 Asia Pavilion	

casino, all orbiting the central Marlene-Dietrich-Platz. Also his work is the adjacent Debis Building with its dramatic cathedral-like atrium.

CHECKPOINT CHARLIE AREA (MAP 4)

About 1km east of the Potsdamer Platz development is the site of the former Checkpoint Charlie, the only gateway for foreigners between the two Berlins during the Cold War. Almost nothing remains of the famous spot, but if you want to see where the barrier actually stood, go to the intersection of Friedrichstrasse and Zimmerstrasse. You'll see the famous sign 'You are now leaving the American sector'. The little guard cabin that used to house the western military police is now at the Allied Museum in Zehlendorf (see Other Museums later in this chapter).

The history of the Wall is commemorated nearby in the **Haus am Checkpoint Charlie** (☎ 253 72 50), a private museum of memorabilia and photos at Friedrichstrasse 43-44. It's open daily from 9 am to 10 pm (DM8/4).

North-west of here, on the corner of Wilhelmstrasse and Vosstrasse, stood the **Neue Reichskanzlei**, Hitler's chancellory built by Albert Speer in 1938. Today, an apartment complex and kindergarten occupy the site. **Hitler's bunker**, where the madman suicided on 30 April 1945, was farther west along Vosstrasse, just north-east of Potsdamer Platz. A sandy mound overgrown with weeds marks the spot.

Jüdisches Museum

The most provocative addition to Berlin's museum landscape is the Jewish Museum (☎ 25 99 33) by Daniel Libeskind. It's at Lindenstrasse 9-14, a short walk east of Kochstrasse U-Bahn station.

The daring structure by the Polish-born architect is a rare example of crisp modernism in New Berlin. Zinc-clad walls rise skywards in a sharply angled zigzag ground plan. The general outline is echoed in the windows – triangular, trapezoidal and irregular gashes in the building's gleaming skin. The interior seeks to reflect the history of the Jewish people in its design. The building is accessible only from the adjacent 18th century former Berlin Museum – they're connected by an underground level.

Exhibits won't be on view until at least October 2000. At the time of writing, fascinating architectural tours of the museum were conducted in German and English several times weekly (DM8/5). Reservations (☎ 28 39 74 44) were required.

TREPTOWER PARK (MAP 2)

Treptower Park, along with the Plänterwald, forms a recreational area of 230 hectares in the south-east of central Berlin. At its heart is the city's largest **Sowjetisches Ehrenmal** (Soviet Memorial, 1949), a gargantuan complex attesting both to the immensity of WWII's losses and to the overblown self-importance of the Soviet state under Stalin.

The monument is always open. From the S-Bahn station Treptower Park, head southwards for about 750m on Puschkinallee, then enter the park through the bombastic stone gate.

As you approach the memorial, you'll first pass a statue of Mother Russia, grieving for her dead children. Next are two mighty walls made from marble retrieved from Hitler's New Chancellory and fronted by kneeling soldiers.

From here opens up a wide plaza, lined on either side by eight sarcophagi representing the then 16 Soviet republics. Each block is covered with reliefs of war scenes and quotes from Stalin (in Russian and German). The large field in the centre is the burial site of the 5000 soldiers that fell in the Battle of Berlin. It culminates in a mound topped with a 13m-high statue of a Russian soldier clutching a child, his great sword resting on a shattered swastika. In the plinth is a socialist-realism mosaic of grateful Soviet citizens, including workers and peasants.

KURFÜRSTENDAMM AREA (MAP 6)

Breitscheidplatz, at the start of the broad Kurfürstendamm, is the heart and formal centre of western Berlin. Here stand the stark ruins of the **Kaiser-Wilhelm-Gedächtniskirche** (Kaiser Wilhelm Memorial Church; 1895), engulfed in roaring commercialism and flashiness. The Allied bombing of 22 November 1943 left only the broken western tower of the church still standing. The **Gedenkhalle** (Memorial Hall) below the ruined tower contains original ceiling mosaics, marble reliefs, liturgical objects and photos from before and after the bombing; it's open Monday to Saturday from 10 am to 4 or 5 pm. The octagonal modern **church** (1961), with its bluer-than-blue stained glass, is open to visitors daily from 9 am to 7.30 pm, except during services.

On the eastern side of Breitscheidplatz looms the **Europa-Center** (1965), a shopping and restaurant complex. North-east of here, on Budapester Strasse, is the Elephant Gate (complete with a chinoiserie-style roof) to

Germany's oldest **zoo** (1844; ☎ 25 40 10) and **aquarium**. It contains 13,000 animals representing 1400 species and is open daily from 9 am to dusk (6.30 pm at the latest), the aquarium till 6 pm. Entry to the zoo and aquarium costs DM12/6 each or DM19/9.50 for a combination ticket. During the war most of the animals were killed in bombing raids, though the last elephant, Siam, is said to have been driven insane by the pandemonium and trumpeted nonstop in terror.

To the west, and adjacent to Zoo station is the **Erotik Museum** (☎ 886 06 66), which displays erotic sculptures, drawings and objects from around the world. On the corner of Kantstrasse and Joachimstaler Strasse, it is the brainchild of Beate Uhse, Germany's porno and sex toy marketing equivalent of Martha Stewart, and open daily from 9 am to midnight (DM10/8). And, yes, you must be 18 or over to get in.

SCHLOSS CHARLOTTENBURG

Schloss Charlottenburg is an exquisite baroque palace and one of the few remaining sites in Berlin that reflects the former splendour and grandeur of the royal Hohenzollern clan. Built at the end of the 17th century by Elector Friedrich III (later King Friedrich I) as a summer residence for Queen Sophie-Charlotte (1668-1705), it is on Spandauer Damm, 3km north-west of Zoo station. Along with several important buildings in the **Palace Garden** (Schlossgarten; free), there are five fine museums inside and in the area. To get here, take U2 to Sophie-Charlotte-Platz and then bus 110 for three stops (or walk north about 1km from the station along Schlossstrasse to the entrance).

Each of the palace buildings charges separate admission (see later in this section), but if you decide to see most of them you should get the Day Card (DM15/10). Note that this does not give you entry to the museums in and around the palace.

Nering-Eosander Building

In the palace's central Nering-Eosander Building are the former royal living quarters, which must be visited on a boring, 50 minute guided tour in German (a detailed room by room description in English may be borrowed for free at the ticket office). The tour takes in 21 rooms which each seem to be trying to outdo one another in brocade, gilt and overall opulence. Among the highlights are the **Hall of Mirrors** (Room 118); the lovely **Oval Hall** (Room 116), with views of the French gardens and distant Belvedere; the wind gauge in **Friedrich I's bedchamber** (Room 96); the fabulous **Porcelain Chamber** (Room 95), covered from floor to ceiling in Chinese blueware and figures; and the **Eosander Chapel** (Room 94) with its *trompe l'oeil* arches.

After the tour you are free to explore the upper floor, with more paintings, silverware, vases, tapestries, weapons, Meissen porcelain and other items essential to a royal lifestyle. Tours take place Tuesday to Friday from 9 am to 5 pm, weekends from 10 am (DM8/4). On weekends and during summer holidays, the demand for tickets may exceed capacity, so show up as early as possible.

Knobelsdorff Wing

The reign of King Friedrich II saw the addition of the elongated eastern Knobelsdorff Wing (1746). You'll find some of the palace's most beautiful rooms, including the confection-like **White Hall**, the former dining hall, with its elaborate concave ceiling; the **Golden Gallery**, a rococo extravaganza of mirrors and gilding; and the **Concert Hall**. To the right of the staircase are the comparatively austere **Winterkammern** (Winter Chambers) of Friedrich Wilhelm II. Its hours are the same as the Nering-Eosander Building (DM5/3).

Galerie der Romantik On the ground floor of the Knobelsdorff Wing is the superb SMB Gallery of the Romantics (☎ 32 09 11) with works by Caspar David Friedrich *(Abbey in the Oak Wood)*, the Gothic fantasies of Karl Friedrich Schinkel and Carl Blechen, and some fine examples of neoclassical and Biedermeier art. It's open Tuesday to Friday from 10 am to 6 pm (closed Monday), and weekends from 11am to 6pm (DM4/2).

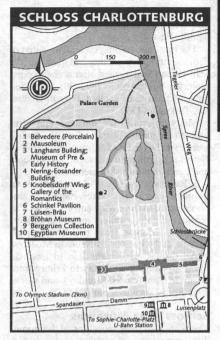

SCHLOSS CHARLOTTENBURG

0   150   300 m

Palace Garden

1 Belvedere (Porcelain)
2 Mausoleum
3 Langhans Building;
   Museum of Pre &
   Early History
4 Nering-Eosander
   Building
5 Knobelsdorff Wing;
   Gallery of the
   Romantics
6 Schinkel Pavilion
7 Luisen-Bräu
8 Bröhan Museum
9 Berggruen Collection
10 Egyptian Museum

Schlossbrücke

To Olympic Stadium (2km)
Spandauer   Damm
                            9   8   Luisenplatz
                          10
To Sophie-Charlotte-Platz
U-Bahn Station

Palace Garden Buildings

Buildings within the Palace Garden include the 1824 **Schinkel Pavilion** with Schinkel art and bric-a-brac. It's open Tuesday to Sunday from 10 am to 5 pm, with shorter hours between late October and late March (DM3/2). The rococo **Belvedere** folly (same hours and admission), built in 1788, contains an impressive collection of porcelain from the royal manufacturer, KPM. The neoclassical **Mausoleum** contains the tombs of Queen Luise (1776-1810) and her husband, Friedrich Wilhelm III (1770-1840), among others. It's open late March to October from Tuesday to Sunday from 10 am to 5 pm (DM2/1).

Museum of Pre & Early History

Occupying the palace's west wing (or Langhans Building) is the SMB Museum für Vor- und Frühgeschichte. It contains archaeological artefacts from Stone, Bronze and Iron Age cultures in Europe and the Middle East.

The most outstanding collection is that of Trojan antiquities on the 2nd floor in the **Schliemann Saal**, named after archaeologist Heinrich Schliemann (1822-90), who discovered the site of ancient Troy in Hissarlik, Turkey, in 1871.

Many objects in the museum and elsewhere (2.5 million works of art, it is said) were looted by the Red Army after the fall of Berlin and brought to museums in Moscow and Leningrad (now St Petersburg).

What's left in Berlin is nonetheless an impressive array of bronzes, huge clay amphorae used to store wine and oil, as well as replicas of gold jewellery and other objects from the 'Priamos Treasure', whose originals are at the Pushkin Museum in Moscow.

All display panels are also in English. Museum hours are Tuesday to Friday from 10 am to 6 pm (closed Monday), and weekends from 11 am to 6 pm (DM4/2).

Schloss Area Museums

There are also three museums in the immediate area well worth visiting. Unless noted, hours are Tuesday to Friday from 10 am to 6 pm, and weekends from 11 am.

Egyptian Museum (SMB) The undisputed highlight of the Ägyptisches Museum (☎ 32 09 11), south of the palace at Schlossstrasse 69b, is the **bust of Queen Nefertiti**, she of the long graceful neck and stunning looks (even after all these years – about 3300, give or take a century or two). The bust, in a darkened room, was never finished (the right eye, for example, is not inlaid) as this was just a model for other portraits of the queen, the wife of the Pharaoh Ikhnaton (ruled 1379-62 BC). His bust is in one of the niches in the main exhibition room.

All objects were found at Amarna, an ancient city on the Nile, halfway between Thebes and the Mediterranean Sea. On your way to the main exhibition room, you'll pass through the **Kalabsha Gate**, a sandstone arch from the 20th century BC, given

to Germany as a gift for its help in saving archaeological treasures during the construction of the Aswan Dam (1960-70).

The main exhibition room is divided into darkened niches, each devoted to a particular person or subject such as 'Ikhnaton's family', 'courtier and soldiers', or 'women and music'. All objects, including more busts, statues, reliefs and totemic animal figurines, are intimately spot-lit. The exhibit continues upstairs. Admission is DM8/4.

Berggruen Collection In the West Stüler Building, opposite the Egyptian Museum, is the SMB Sammlung Berggruen (☎ 326 95 80). Entitled 'Picasso and His Time' and on loan for a decade from Dr Heinz Berggruen, art connoisseur and FOP (Friend of Picasso), the collection only opened in 1996. There are some 75 paintings, drawings and sculptures by Picasso and about as many works by Cézanne, Van Gogh, Gauguin and Braque. On the 2nd floor are 31 smaller pieces by Klee from 1917 to 1940 as well as three Giacometti sculptures. Admission is DM8/4.

Bröhan Museum This lovely museum (☎ 321 40 29), just south of the Berggruen Collection at Schlossstrasse 1a, focuses on decorative arts and design from 1889 to 1939; it was donated to the city by Karl Bröhan in 1982. On the ground floor are the outstanding fully furnished and decorated **Art Nouveau and Art Deco rooms** (some by Hector Guimard and Émile Ruhlmann). The collection of silverwork, glass, porcelain and enamelware seems endless but astonishes at every turn. On the top floor are changing exhibitions and a **Henry van de Velde** (1863-1957) room, with furniture, tableware and other objects by this multitalented artist. Admission is DM6/4.

OLYMPIA STADION

The Olympic Stadium, built by Hitler for the 1936 Olympic Games in which the African-American athlete Jesse Owens won four gold medals and put paid to the Nazi theory that Aryans were the all-powerful *Übermenschen*, lies south-west of Schloss

Charlottenburg. The 85,000-seat stadium, one of the best examples of Nazi-era neoclassical architecture, is still used for soccer, athletics and other sporting events. It is open to visitors on nonevent days from 9 am to sunset (DM1/0.50). To reach it take U2 to Olympia-Stadion Ost, then follow the signs (a 15 minute walk).

A short distance to the west is the 77m **Glockenturm** (Clock Tower), which offers superb views over the stadium, the city and the Havel. Check out the Nazi bell – it weighs 2.5 tonnes and is inscribed: *'Ich rufe die Jugend der Welt'* (I call upon the youth of the world). The tower is open May to October daily from 10 am to 5.30 pm (DM3/1.50).

DAHLEM MUSEUMS

The biggest draw in the leafy south-western district of Zehlendorf used to be the Dahlem Museum complex (U1 to Dahlem-Dorf), with seven museums all under the one roof. But this complex has been affected like no other by the sweeping reorganisation of Berlin's collections.

The entire Gemäldegalerie (Picture Gallery) has moved into its new home at the Kulturforum (see earlier in this chapter). The collection of the **Museum of Islamic Art** has been integrated with that at the Pergamon museum. The **Museum of Indian Art** and the **Museum of East Asian Art** closed in May 1998 and won't reopen until at least 2001 while the collections are being reorganised and expanded. The former **Museum für Volkskunde** (Folklore Museum) was being converted into the **Museum für Europäische Kulturen** (Museum of European Cultures) and reopened in the summer of 1999. Hours are Tuesday to Friday from 10 am to 6 pm, and weekends from 11 am (DM4/2).

Museum of Ethnology

The only museum in the complex that is partly open is the SMB Museum für Völkerkunde (☎ 830 14 38), Lansstrasse 8. It takes you on a journey back in time and around the world to the early Americas, the South Seas (ie Australasia), Africa and South and East Asia. The museum's collections on Europe, the Islamic Orient and Native Americans are only shown during special exhibitions.

Some highlights of the **pre-Columbian collection** are the stone sculptures from Guatemala, and Mayan figurines, sculptures and weapons. Pre-Columbian gold jewellery and helmets deserve a closer look. Cult objects from New Guinea, Tonga, Melanesia and other islands, some of which used to belong to Captain James Cook, form part of the South Seas section. Especially impressive are the enormous outriggers in the boat hall. Upstairs, such treats as a royal Hawaiian feather coat await. In the **East Asian section** is a 19th century carved teak wall from a house in central Java. In the basement are the two hands-on rooms: the **Junior Museum** for children and the **Blinden Museum** for the blind.

Note that sections of the museum may be temporarily closed, so if you're interested in anything in particular, call ahead. It's open Tuesday to Friday from 10 am to 6 pm (closed Monday), and weekends from 11 am (DM4/2).

Allied Museum

A couple of U-Bahn stops south of Dahlem-Dorf (get off at Oskar-Helene-Heim) is the Allierten Museum (☎ 818 19 90), an excellent multimedia exhibition that documents the history of the western Allies in post-WWII Berlin. It's housed in the former Outpost cinema for US soldiers at Clayallee 135. In the yard is the guard cabin from Checkpoint Charlie, a piece of the Wall and guard tower and other objects. It's open from 10 am to 6 pm (closed Monday; free). This fascinating museum is, sadly, undervisited, probably because it's perceived to be hard to get to. This is not really the case: the trip from Wittenbergplatz station on the U1 takes about 20 minutes, followed by a five to 10 minute walk north on Clayallee. It's worth the effort.

OTHER MUSEUMS

We don't have the space to describe all of Berlin's 170 museums, but here's a selection of a few more worthwhile ones.

Akademie der Künste

The Academy of Arts (Map 3, ☎ 39 07 60) at Hanseatenweg 10 (U9 to Hansaplatz) hosts exceptionally fine revolving exhibits, often in conjunction with other museums. It's open daily from 10 am to 7 pm (Monday from 1 pm; DM8/4, Wednesday free).

Museum Berlin-Karlshorst

This fascinating exhibition (☎ 509 86 09) on the German-Soviet Union relationship from 1917 to the Wende is in the villa where the unconditional surrender of the German army was signed, ending WWII in Europe. Documents, objects, uniforms and photographs explore every stage in the relations with a particular focus on WWII. It's at Zwieseler Strasse 4 (corner of Rheinsteinstrasse), Karlshorst (S3 to Karlshorst, north on Treskowallee, then right on Rheinsteinstrasse for a 10 minutes). It's open from 10 am to 6 pm (closed Monday; free). Ask for the free English-language pamphlet.

Brücke Museum

This small museum (☎ 831 20 29), Bussardsteig 9, in Zehlendorf exhibits works by the expressionist painters of Die Brücke (The Bridge), a group founded in Dresden in 1910 by Karl Schmidt-Rottluff, Erich Heckel and Ernst Ludwig Kirchner. It's open from 11 am to 5 pm (closed Tuesday; DM6/3).

Deutsches Technikmuseum

The German Museum of Technology (Map 3, ☎ 25 48 40), Trebbiner Strasse 9, in Kreuzberg 61 (U15 to Möckernbrücke or Gleisdreieck) examines technology through the ages – from printing and transport to information technology. The new Spectrum annexe displays more than 200 operating historical machines. It's open Tuesday to Friday from 9 am to 5.30 pm, and weekends from 10 am to 6 pm (closed Monday; DM5/3).

Käthe-Kollwitz-Museum

This private museum (Map 6, ☎ 882 52 10), Fasanenstrasse 24, is dedicated to one of the greatest woman artists of the 20th century. An extensive collection of graphics, lithographs, woodcuts, sculptures and drawings show the socialist artist's work in all its versatility and complexity. It's open from 11 am to 6 pm (closed Tuesday; DM8/4). Audio guides (in English too) are DM3.50.

Märkisches Museum

The Mark of Brandenburg Museum (Map 4, ☎ 30 86 60), a red-brick, cathedral-like pile at Am Köllnischen Park 5, focuses on Berlin history, art and culture. Thematic highlights include theatre, music and literature, glass and art and crafts. Best of all are the *Automato-*

phone, 18th century mechanical musical instruments that are wound up and made to go through their noisy paces every Wednesday and Sunday at 3 pm. The museum is open from 10 am to 6 pm (closed Monday; DM8/4).

Museum für Post und Kommunikation

This museum, another merger of East and West Berlin collections, was scheduled to reopen at Leipziger Strasse 16 in late 1999. Presumably it will once again trace the history of the German-Prussian postal system from the late Middle Ages to the present; there's also a telecommunications section. Call ☎ 75 01 68 01 for opening hours and admission.

Schwules Museum

The Gay Museum (Map 3, ☎ 693 11 72), Mehringdamm 61, has hit-or-miss special exhibitions, and collections of photographs, posters and newspapers. It's open Wednesday to Sunday from 2 to 6 pm, with a guided tour at 5 pm on Saturday (DM7/4).

Stasi Museum – Lichtenberg

In the one-time Stasi headquarters at Ruschestrasse 103 (House 1), the Forschungs- und Gedenkstätte Normannenstrasse (☎ 553 68 54) is a memorial and research site where you can see cunning surveillance devices, Communist paraphernalia and blood-chilling documents about GDR internment camps. It's open Tuesday to Friday from 11 am to 6 pm (weekends from 2 pm; DM5/3). Take the U5 to Magdalenenstrasse.

Stasi – Die Ausstellung

This engaging exhibition (Map 4, ☎ 22 41 74 70), Mauerstrasse 34-38, in Mitte sheds light on the all-pervasive power of the GDR secret police, including methods of infiltration, the recruitment of IM (inoffizielle Mitarbeiter, ie 'unofficial co-workers' ie 'spies') and the invasion of privacy of normal citizens. It helps if you read German. It's open Monday to Saturday from 10 am to 6 pm (free).

BERLIN FOR FREE

It's easy to spend a fortune in Berlin but some of the most fascinating and enjoyable things cost nothing. The following free activities and sights are described in detail in this chapter.

- Stroll along Unter den Linden and admire the historical buildings
- Attend a show at the A-Trane, Quasimodo or other jazz clubs on a Tuesday or Wednesday night

- Walk or picnic in the gardens of Charlottenburg Palace, Tiergarten or any other city park
- Take in the aromas and sights of the Turkish Market in Kreuzberg
- Catch up with construction plans for Berlin at the Info-Box
- Hear a carillon (glockenspiel) recital at the House of World Cultures
- Catch a free organ recital at a church
- Hunt for the tombs of famous people at the Dorotheenstadt Cemetery
- Tour the historical State Library, either at Unter den Linden or near the Kulturforum
- Get a different perspective on Berlin from the Reichstag dome or take a tour of the revamped building
- Visit the Allied Museum, Museum of German History at Kronprinzenpalais, Deutscher Dom historical exhibition, Museum Berlin-Karlshorst, Stasi museums in Lichtenberg and Mitte, all state museums (SMB) on the first Sunday of the month, Guggenheim Museum (Monday only) and Academy of Arts (Wednesday only)

LANGUAGE COURSES

The Goethe Institut (Map 4, ☎ 25 90 63, fax 25 90 64 00), Neue Schönhauser Strasse 20, has many courses at all levels. (See Courses in the Facts for the Visitor chapter.)

A private school teaching German to foreigners that seems to get high marks is the Europa Sprachenschule (Europa Language School; Map 5, ☎ 618 88 63, fax 618 95 57) at Taborstrasse 17 in Kreuzberg 36 (U15 to Schlesisches Tor). It offers weekly intensive courses at beginner and advanced levels from DM66 (groups of up to 15) to DM180 (groups of five). Other options are available too. For more information, contact the school.

ORGANISED TOURS
Bus Tours

Most city sightseeing tours operate on the get-on, get-off as often as you wish principle and there's very little difference between operators. Most take in 12 main sights – including Kurfürstendamm, Brandenburg Gate, Schloss Charlottenburg, Berliner Dom and Alexanderplatz – on loops that take about two hours without getting off. Taped commentary comes in, count 'em, eight languages. Buses leave roughly every half-hour, with the first tour usually around 10 am somewhere near the Gedächtniskirche; buses stop running around 6 pm (earlier in winter). The cost is DM30.

The buses of Severin + Kühn (☎ 880 41 90) leave from Kurfürstendamm 216; BBS (☎ 35 19 52 70) from Kurfürstendamm, on the corner of Rankestrasse; and BVB (☎ 885 98 80) departs from Kurfürstendamm 229 opposite Café Kranzler.

These operators also have a Super Berlin Tour, a more conventional, narrated nonstop 3½ hour tour which costs DM39 and is offered in the morning and in the afternoon. A 50% discount applies to children under 13.

Between Easter and October, there's also Top-Tour-Berlin (☎ 25 62 47 40), operated by BVG, which has departures every 30 minutes from outside Café Kranzler at Kurfürstendamm 18. It makes 20 stops and costs DM35 (DM29 for children ages six to 14). Tickets bought after 3 pm are valid until the end of the following day.

Guide Friday/Tempelhofer Reisen (☎ 752 40 57) does two different routes: the 'red loop' takes in mostly western Berlin, while the 'green loop' covers the eastern section. Each costs DM25 and buses leave every 45 minutes. There's live commentary in German and English.

Walking Tours

Berlin has three companies that do English-language tours which are excellent, informative and entertaining.

Certainly among the best walking tours we've ever been on are those operated by The Original Berlin Walks (☎ 301 91 94). Its Discover Berlin tour covers the heart of the city, giving interesting and unbiased historical background and architectural information. It leaves daily at 10 am and 2.30 pm from late March to the end of October and at 10 am only the rest of the year.

Other options are the fascinating Infamous Third Reich Sites and Jewish Life in Berlin tours. Tours last between two and three hours and cost DM15/10, free for children under 14. They leave from outside the main entrance of Zoo station (Map 6) at the top of the taxi rank. Just show up armed with a BVG *Langstrecke* ticket (DM3.90; see Public Transport in the Getting Around section). Rail-pass holders don't need one for the Discover Berlin and Jewish Life tours as the S-Bahn is used. There are no tours from January to mid-March.

Berlin Walks' main competitor, The Insider Tour by the Yellow Walking Tour Company (☎ 692 31 49), is also great fun. It's run by a team of young, hip Australians who pepper their informative commentary with anecdotes and interesting trivia. Their tour covers all main sights in both western and eastern Berlin – from Zoo station to Alex – all on foot! Wear sturdy shoes and be prepared for a three to four hour walk. Tours cost DM15 and leave daily at 10 am and 2.30 pm (10 am only from November to March) from outside McDonald's and the Zoo station main entrance. The price includes a nifty brochure packed with useful information about Berlin.

The last in the trio of English-language walking tour operators is Terry's Top Hat Tour, which enjoys a good reputation as well. It leaves twice daily from the New Synagogue and the Circus and Backpacker hostels in Mitte (see Places to Stay), costs DM10 and lasts about four hours.

Cruises
In the warmer months, tourist boats cruise Berlin's waterways, calling at main historical sights in the centre as well as picturesque villages, parks and castles. Food and drink are sold on board, but are quite expensive, so take along something.

Stern und Kreis Schiffahrt (Map 4, ☎ 536 36 00) operates various cruises from April to December. A 3½ hour cruise (DM15/25.50 one way/return) from Jannowitzbrücke near the Märkisches Museum past the northern boundary of Tiergarten park to Schlossbrücke near Charlottenburg Palace is offered up to six times a day. A one hour spin around Museumsinsel from the Nikolaiviertel (DM14) operates up to 16 times daily. Night tours (DM21.50) are offered Friday and Saturday at 7.30 pm (2½ hours).

Children under six travel for free, those under 14 get a 50% discount. Students and seniors get 15% off, though not on weekends and holidays. A Kombi-Tageskarte, giving you unlimited rides aboard regular Stern und Kreis cruises as well as U/S-Bahn, buses and trams in Berlin and Potsdam, costs DM26.

Reederei Bruno Winkler (☎ 349 95 95) has sightseeing cruises on the Spree River or the Landwehr Canal from March to September. The main landing stage is at Schlossbrücke, just east of the Charlottenburg Palace. Three-hour tours leave twice daily at 10.20 am and 2.20 pm (DM22). You can also hop aboard at the Friedrichstrasse landing at the Reichstagsufer which cuts the return-trip cost to DM18. Seniors and students get DM2 off. English-language audiotapes with commentary are available.

Berliner Wassertaxi Service (Map 4, ☎ 65 88 02 03), a water-taxi service just north of the Schlossbrücke, has one-hour spins (DM12/9) along the Spree between Spree Canal and Bahnhof Friedrichstrasse, leaving every half-hour between 10 am and 4.30 pm.

SPECIAL EVENTS
Berlin's calendar is loaded with annual fairs, festivals, concerts and parties; the following is just a small sampling.

International Film Festival
  The Internationale Filmfestspiele, the world's second-largest film festival (after Cannes), is held over 12 days in February.
Festtage at the Staatsoper
  This annual series of gala concerts and operas under the auspices of the Staatsoper Unter den Linden, brings renowned conductors, soloists and orchestras to Berlin for 10 days in late March/early April.
Karnival der Kulturen
  This lively street carnival features a parade of wacky, costumed people dancing and playing music on floats, in May.
Christopher Street Day
  The biggest annual gay event in the city takes place in late June with a parade from Savignyplatz in Charlottenburg to the eastern end of Unter den Linden.
Love Parade
  Berlin's top annual techno event held in mid-July attracts 1.5 million people. The parade is

followed by nonstop partying in clubs and the streets.

Berlin Festival Weeks
This month-long celebration in September features concerts, exhibits, plays and other cultural events related to a particular subject (eg the Berlin Airlift in 1998, Gustav Mahler in 1999).

JazzFest Berlin
This four-day jazz festival at various venues around the city takes place in early November.

Christmas Markets
Christmas markets are held from late November to 21 December at several locations around Berlin, including Breitscheidplatz (Map 6), open daily from 10 am to 9 or 10 pm; Alexanderplatz (Map 4), open daily from 1 to 10 pm; and the Marktplatz in Spandau, open daily from 9 am to 7 pm.

PLACES TO STAY

Berlin attracts tourists throughout the year, with the peak months being from May to September. If you'll be travelling to Berlin then, make reservations at least several weeks ahead of time. If you're driving, remember that most hotels don't have their own garages. Street parking may be hard to find and you may end up having to put your vehicle in an expensive parking garage (about DM25 a day) that may also be quite a distance from the hotel. The top-end hotels may have their own lots or offer to park your car for you in a public garage, though in either case this will add at least DM25 to your hotel bill.

PLACES TO STAY – BUDGET
Camping

Camping facilities in Berlin are neither plentiful nor particularly good. All of them are far from the city centre and complicated to reach unless you're motorised. They fill up quickly, with a lot of space taken up by caravans, so we highly recommend that you call ahead to inquire about space availability. Offices at all grounds are open daily from 7 am to 1 pm and 3 to 9 pm. Charges are DM9.70 per person plus from DM7.20 for a small tent site to DM12.70 for a larger tent with car space; showers are DM1. For specifics, contact the Deutscher Campingclub (☎ 218 60 71) at Geisbergstrasse 11 in Schöneberg.

Camping grounds convenient to public transport include *Campingplatz Kohlhasenbrück* (☎/fax 805 17 37, Neue Kreis Strasse 36), open early March to late October. It's in a peaceful location overlooking the Griebnitzsee in Zehlendorf, about 15km southwest of the centre. Take the S7 to the Griebnitzsee station from where it's a 10 minute walk. Alternatively, get off at the previous stop, Wannsee, and take bus No 118, which runs directly to the camping ground.

If Kohlhasenbrück is full, 2km to the east along the Teltow Canal at Albrechts-Teerofen is the *Campingplatz Dreilinden* (☎ 805 12 01), open early March to late October. It's 30 minutes on foot from the Griebnitzsee S-Bahn; bus No 118 from Wannsee station also stops here.

Berlin's other camping grounds are more complicated to reach if you're not motorised. *Campingplatz Kladow* (☎ 365 27 97, fax 365 12 45, Krampnitzer Weg 111-117), open all year, is in Spandau, 18km west of the city centre. If you must use public transport, take the U7 to Rathaus Spandau, then bus No 134 to the Alt-Kladow stop where you change to bus No 234. An alternative is nearby *Campingplatz Gatow* (☎ 36 54 340, fax 36 80 84 92, Kladower Damm 213-217), also served by bus No 134.

Campingplatz Am Krossinsee (☎ 675 86 87, fax 675 91 50, Wernsdorfer Strasse 45) is in Köpenick, 35km south-east of the city centre, and open all year. You'd have to take the S8 to Grünau, then tram No 68 to Schmückwitz and then bus No 755 to Königs Wusterhausen.

DJH Hostels

Berlin's three official DJH hostels fill up quickly on weekends and throughout summer. Until early July, they are often booked out by noisy school groups. None offers cooking facilities, but breakfast is included in the rates, with lunch and dinner usually available. The hostels are open all day year-round, but have curfews.

To secure a bunk, write several weeks in advance to Deutsches Jugendherbergswerk, Zentralreservierung, Kluckstrasse 3, 10785

Berlin. State precisely which nights you'll be in Berlin and enclose an international postal reply coupon so they can send back confirmation to you. You can also send a fax to 262 95 29. They do not take phone reservations but if you just want to inquire about space availability, you can simply call ☎ 262 30 24 weekdays from 8 am to 3 pm (Friday to 2 pm).

The only DJH hostel in the city centre is the impersonal 364-bed *Jugendgästehaus Berlin (Map 3, ☎ 261 10 97, fax 262 95 29, Kluckstrasse 3)*, which charges DM34/42 for juniors/seniors in multibed rooms. It's in Schöneberg near the Landwehr Canal (U15 to Kurfürstenstrasse). Curfew is at 3 am.

Jugendgästehaus am Wannsee (☎ 803 20 34, fax 262 95 29, Badeweg 1), on the corner of Kronprinzessinnenweg, has 264 beds and the most pleasant location of the three hostels. It's on Grosser Wannsee, the lake southwest of the city and at most an eight minute walk from the Nikolassee S-Bahn station (S1 and S7). From the station, walk westwards over the footbridge, turn left at Kronprinzessinnenweg and the hostel will be in sight on the right. The entire trip from the city centre takes about 45 minutes. The cost is DM34/42 for juniors/seniors in four-bed rooms, with a key deposit (DM20). Curfew is at a raging 1 am.

Jugendherberge Ernst Reuter (☎ 404 16 10, fax 404 59 72, Hermsdorfer Damm 48-50) is in the far north-west of Berlin. Take the U6 to Alt-Tegel, then bus No 125 right to the door. An overnight stay at this 110-bed facility costs DM28/35 for juniors/seniors. Curfew is at 1 am.

Non-DJH Hostels & Guesthouses

DJH cards are not needed for any of the hostels. None has a curfew and several are run by ex-backpackers who have travelled extensively, know what people want and need, and are extremely friendly and well informed about Berlin.

Charlottenburg & Wilmersdorf *Jugendhotel Berlin (☎ 322 10 11, fax 322 10 12, Kaiserdamm 3)* asks DM46/49/55 per person

in triples/doubles/singles, including breakfast but not the DM7 fee per sheet sleeping bag for stays under three nights. This facility caters primarily to those under 27, but will accept older people on a space-available basis at higher rates (DM183/143/92). All rooms have bath and WC (toilet).

Enormous, 450-bed *Jugendgästehaus Central (Map 6, ☎ 873 01 88, fax 861 34 85, Nikolsburger Strasse 2-4)* offers B&B for DM37 per person in double and multibed rooms; the DM7 sheet charge applies to stays under three nights (U1 to Hohenzollernplatz or U9 to Güntzelstrasse).

Studentenhotel Hubertusallee (☎ 891 97 18, fax 892 86 98, Delbrückstrasse 24), near the Hubertussee lake, charges DM80/110/126 for singles/doubles/triples with shower and WC. Students with a recognised card pay only DM45/70/90. Prices include breakfast. From Ku'damm, you can either catch bus No 119 going west and get off at the Hasensprung stop or take No 129 to the Delbrückstrasse stop. It's open from March to October.

Jugendhotel Vier Jahreszeiten (☎ 873 20 14/17, fax 873 82 23, Bundesallee 31a) in Wilmersdorf (U9 to Güntzelstrasse) charges DM39 for B&B in one to five-bed rooms. From November to February, the owners knock up to DM8 off the rates.

Jugendgästehaus St-Michaelis-Heim (☎ 89 68 80, fax 89 68 81 85, Bismarckallee 23) is a new arrival and has 35 modern and friendly rooms with shared showers for DM30 to DM33 per person without breakfast. At the attached hotel, singles/doubles start at DM70/150, also with shared facilities.

Friedrichshain This up-and-coming area has sprouted a couple of convivial hostels with staff that can make you feel 'plugged into' Berlin within a day or two.

Odyssee Globetrotter Hostel (☎ 29 00 00 81, Grünberger Strasse 23), in the 2nd backyard and on the 1st floor, is run by four young guys who grew up in pre-Wende East Berlin (and can tell a tale or two about those days). It offers 82 beds in new, clean dorms with lockers, as well as private rooms.

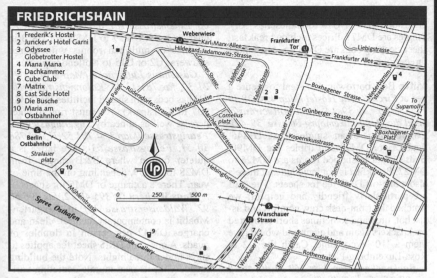

FRIEDRICHSHAIN

1 Frederik's Hostel
2 Juncker's Hotel Garni
3 Odyssee
  Globetrotter Hostel
4 Mana Mana
5 Dachkammer
6 Cube Club
7 Matrix
8 East Side Hotel
9 Die Busche
10 Maria am
   Ostbahnhof

Weberwiese
Karl-Marx-Allee
Hildegard-Jadamowitz-Strasse
Frankfurter Tor
Liebigstrasse
Frankfurter Allee
Strasse der Pariser Kommune
Rüdersdorfer Strasse
Gubener Strasse
Jasdelner Strasse
Kadiner Strasse
Wedekindstrasse
Marchwitzastrasse
Cornelius platz
Boxhagener Strasse
Grünberger Strasse
Warschauer Strasse
Niederbarnim strasse
To Supamolly
Berlin Ostbahnhof
Stralauer platz
Helsingforser Strasse
Kopernikusstrasse
Libauer Strasse
Simon-Dach-Strasse
Boxhagener Platz
Gabriel-Max-Strasse
Wühlischstrasse
Gärtnerstrasse
Mühlenstrasse
Revaler Strasse
Simplonstrasse
Modersohnstrasse
Spree Osthafen
Warschauer Strasse
Eastside Gallery
Warschauer Platz
Niederbergstrasse
Ehrenbergstrasse
Rudolfstrasse
Rotherstrasse

0   250   500 m

Check-out is at a civilised 1 pm and the breakfast buffet costs just DM5. The reception area doubles as a happening bar-lounge (both open 24 hours) with pool table and cheap beers (yes, the parties are legendary). Dorm bunks are DM24 to DM32, singles/doubles DM50/72, sheets included. From Ostbahnhof, take bus No 240 or 147; from U/S-Bahn Warschauer Strasse it's a five minute walk north.

Frederik's Hostel (☎ 29 66 94 50, fax 29 66 94 52, email hostel@frederiks.de, Strasse der Pariser Kommune 35) is another winner. Thirty large, quiet rooms are spread out in a historic building that was once a Jewish girls school. There's a large garden, 24-hour reception, Internet access, bike rental and an overall congenial atmosphere. A bed in a large dorm costs DM22 to DM25, while singles/doubles/triples are DM49/32/29 per person and sheets are DM4. To get there, take the U5 to Weberwiese.

Kreuzberg *Hotel Transit (Map 3, ☎ 789 04 70, fax 78 90 47 77, Hagelberger Strasse 53-54)* has multi-bed rooms with shower for

DM33 per person, big breakfast included. Singles/doubles go for DM90/105. The Transit tends to fill up with school groups from March to May and in September/October; it's also popular with backpackers.

Die Fabrik (Map 5, ☎ 611 71 16, fax 618 29 74, Schlesische Strasse 18) is in a converted factory (take the U15 to Schlesisches Tor) and has beds in a huge dorm on the ground floor for DM30 per person. Singles/doubles/triples/quads are spread out over five floors (no lift) and available for DM66/94/120/144; breakfast is an extra DM10 and served at the downstairs cafe called Eisenwaren.

Gästehaus (Map 5, ☎ 618 20 08, mobile ☎ 0177 618 20 08, fax 618 20 06, Wiener Strasse 14), operated by Wohnagentur Freiraum, is located in a renovated historic building near the cafes and nightlife in Kreuzberg 36 (U1/12/15 to Görlitzer Bahnhof). Singles/doubles/triples/quads are DM40/70/100/110.

The *Jugendgästehaus Schreberjugend (☎ 615 10 07, fax 61 40 11 50, Franz-Künstler-Strasse 4-10)* has 124 rooms and charges DM38.50 per night in two or three-bed rooms (U6 or U15 to Hallesches Tor). Singles are DM77. Prices include breakfast; sheet sleeping bags are DM6 for stays under three nights.

Mitte Beg, borrow and/or steal to secure a bed at *Circus – The Hostel (Map 4, ☎ 28 39 14 33, fax 28 39 14 84, email circus@ mind.de, Rosa-Luxemburg-Strasse 39-41)*. Comfortable, clean singles cost DM45, doubles are DM70 and triples are DM90. Beds in four to six-bed rooms are DM25 to DM27. Breakfast is not included and there's also a one-off DM3 fee for sheets. The staff are particularly friendly and helpful; we watched the front-desk crew comfort and assist hot, tired and sometimes short-tempered backpackers again and again and would give them a '10' every time. Catch the U2 to Rosa-Luxemburg-Platz.

Backpacker (Map 4, ☎ 262 51 40, ☎ 28 39 09 65, fax 28 39 09 35, email backpacker@snafu.de, Chausseestrasse 102) is a short walk from the nightlife areas. It offers simple digs for DM25 to DM28 in four to six-person dorms, DM30 in triples and DM38 in doubles (all per person); sheets are DM5. There are cooking facilities and services including bike rental (U6 to Zinnowitzer Strasse – north exit).

Prenzlauer Berg *Lette 'm Sleep (☎ 44 73 36 23, fax 44 73 36 25, email info@backpackers.de, Lettestrasse 7)* is a welcome addition to the hostel scene and right in the heart of some of Berlin's hottest nightlife. It's received ringing endorsements from readers who have called it 'spotlessly clean' and 'the most friendly'. Per person charges are DM25 to DM35 in three to six-bed dorms or DM45 in doubles (with kitchenette). It's a five-minute walk from U-Bahn station Eberswalder Strasse (U2).

Schöneberg & Tiergarten *Studentenhotel (Map 3, ☎ 784 67 20, fax 788 15 23, Meininger Strasse 10)* offers B&B for DM43 per person in a double room, DM39 in a quad (U4 to Rathaus Schöneberg).

CVJM (Map 3, ☎ 264 91 00, fax 261 43 08, Einemstrasse 10), the German YMCA, charges a flat DM39 to DM42 for B&B in doubles or multibed rooms with shared showers (U2 or U15 to Nollendorfplatz).

Gästehaus Luftbrücke (Map 3, ☎ 78 70 21 30, fax 781 13 47, Kolonnenstrasse 10-11) has beds with shared facilities for DM45 (U7 to Kleistpark). You must ring to enter here as well as at nearby *Jugendgästehaus Feurigstrasse (Map 3, ☎ 781 52 11, fax 788 30 51, Feurigstrasse 63)*. The latter is a quieter option where B&B ranges from DM28 to DM39, depending on the time of year. There's a charge of DM5 for sheets.

Haus Wichern (☎ 395 40 72, fax 396 50 92, Waldenserstrasse 31) in Tiergarten-Moabit is contemporary, central, clean and charges DM42 per person in doubles or quads. A one-time DM5 sheet fee applies to stays under three nights. Note the building facade with its neat murals depicting various crafts and trades.

Tegel If you're on a really tight budget and don't mind 'roughing it', head for the big tent at *Internationales Jugendcamp Fliesstal (☎ 433 86 40, fax 434 50 63, Ziekowstrasse 161)*, open in July and August. There's room for 260 people with spaces in communal tents costing DM10 per person (including blankets, foam mattresses and showers). Check-in is after 5 pm. No reservations are taken and officially this place is only for those aged 14 to 27, but usually no one gets turned away. The official maximum stay is three nights. Wake-up is 8 am and the place is closed until 5 pm. Inexpensive food and self-catering facilities are available.

The tents are right behind *Jugendgästehaus Tegel (☎ 433 30 46, fax 434 50 63)*, a stately, red-brick building with 220 beds. A night in three to eight-bed rooms is DM37.50 per person, including sheets and breakfast. There's no curfew. To get to either, take the U6 to Alt-Tegel, then bus No 222 to Titusweg.

Wedding The *Jugendgästehaus Nordufer (☎ 45 19 91 12, fax 452 41 00, Nordufer 28)* is operated by the same nonprofit Berliner Jugendclub (Berlin Youth Club) that also runs the Jugendgästehaus Tegel. Nordufer has 130 beds in 38 rooms and also charges DM37.50. Take the U9 to Westhafen, then walk left across the bridge and left again into Nordufer. It too is officially only for those under 27.

The *Bund Deutscher Pfadfinderinnen (Association of German Girl Scouts; ☎ 493 10 70, fax 494 10 63, Osloer Strasse 12)* charge DM30 per night, with sheets an extra DM8. There's a kitchen, but the staff also serve breakfast for DM4 or DM6. Hot and cold dinners are available also. You must phone ahead for reservations (U9 to Osloer Strasse).

Other Districts The *Karl-Renner-Haus (☎ 833 50 29/30, fax 833 91 57, Ringstrasse 76)* is in Steglitz and has beds in two to six-bed rooms for DM35 (breakfast included) or DM38 in rooms with shower. There's a DM5.50 charge for sheets the first night only. Take the S1 to Lichterfelde West.

Also in Steglitz is *Jugendgästehaus Lichterfelde (☎ 71 39 17 34, fax 71 39 17 51, Osdorfer Strasse 121)*, which caters exclusively to guests between 16 and 26 and charges DM40/55 for singles/doubles. Breakfast is included. Take the S25 to Osdorfer Strasse.

Jugendhotel am Flussbad (☎ 65 88 00 94, fax 65 88 00 93, Gartenstrasse 50) is a long way out in Köpenick. It has seven dorms with showers and WC on the floor and charges DM25 to DM35 per person, plus DM5 for linen. Take the S3 to Köpenick, then the S10 to Spindlerfeld.

Private Rooms & Long-Term Rentals

The BTM no longer books private rooms, but you can try the private agency Agentur Last Minute (☎ 30 82 08 85), which has rooms in a shared flat from DM35 per night per person (no commission). Monthly rentals start at DM350, though most rooms cost around DM450, plus a commission of 28% payable to the agency. Another good option is Berlin Projekte – Berliner Zimmer (☎ 312 50 03) which has singles for DM60 and doubles for DM95.

If you're planning to stay in Berlin for a month or longer, you might consider renting a room or an apartment through a *Mitwohnzentrale* (flat-sharing agency), which matches people willing to let their digs to those needing a temporary home. Accommodation can be anything from rooms in shared student flats to furnished apartments. Agencies to try include *Erste Mitwohnzentrale (☎ 324 30 31, Sybelstrasse 53)* in Charlottenburg; *Mitwohnagentur Kreuzberg (☎ 786 20 03, Mehringdamm 72)*; and *HomeCompany (☎ 194 45, Joachimsthaler Strasse 14)* in Charlottenburg.

Hotels

Unless noted, all the following hotel prices include breakfast.

Charlottenburg & Wilmersdorf There are a few reasonably priced places near Zoo station and north of the Ku'damm. *Pension München (☎ 85 79 120, fax 85 79 12 22, Güntzelstrasse 62, 3rd floor)* comes highly recommended. It has just eight rooms with shared facilities for DM66/90 a single/double. Breakfast costs an extra DM9 and is served in a nice room with tiled floor.

Pension Fischer (Map 6, ☎ 218 68 08, fax 213 42 25, Nürnberger Strasse 24a) charges DM50/70 (or DM70/130 with facilities). Breakfast costs DM8 to DM10. *Hotel-Pension Margrit (Map 6, ☎ 883 77 17, fax 882 32 28, Brandenburgische Strasse 24)* has clean but low-frills rooms at acceptable prices. Singles with shower but shared WC are DM60, doubles DM115. If you want full private facilities, you'll pay DM95/150.

Hotel Bogota (Map 6, ☎ 881 50 01, fax 883 58 87, Schlüterstrasse 45) is a reader recommendation, and we agree. It's in an early 20th century building on the corner of Ku'damm. Rates for the 125 rooms range from DM78/120 for those without facilities, to DM150/190 for those with private shower and WC.

Mitte *Hotel-Pension Die Loge (Map 4, ☎/fax 280 75 13, Friedrichstrasse 115)* has rooms from DM60/100 to DM90/130. There may be discounts for long-term stays. The pension is run by an affable young couple who serve up some mighty fine – wait for it – candlelight breakfasts for DM10 per person.

Equally artistic is *Hotel Künstlerheim Luise (Map 4, ☎ 280 69 41, fax 280 69 42, Luisenstrasse 19)*, which has received a full make-over and features 33 artist-designed rooms. Those without facilities start at DM50/70, those with are DM120/200. One of our readers stayed here and loved it.

Schöneberg & Tiergarten Budget options in Schöneberg include the large but dumpy *Hotel Sachsenhof (Map 3, ☎ 216 20 74, fax 215 82 20, Motzstrasse 7)*, which has depressing rooms but a good breakfast buffet (DM10 extra). Rooms start at an affordable DM57/99 (DM120/186 with facilities). The friendly *Hotel Gunia (Map 3, ☎ 218 59 40, fax 218 59 44, Eisenacher Strasse 10)* charges DM80/110 for rooms with shared bath and DM100/150 for those with private facilities. Both are in the heart of the area's gay quarter.

Those who like their accommodation with a personal touch should try the family-run *Hotel Les Nations (☎ 392 20 26, fax 392 50 10, Zinzendorfstrasse 6)*, in a quiet side street. It's popular among younger travellers for its comfortable rooms with shared facilities costing DM60/100. Those with shower and WC are DM135/195. A bonus for night-owls: breakfast is served around the clock.

PLACES TO STAY – MID-RANGE

Mid-priced pensions and hotels garnis (places without restaurants) are plentiful in Berlin, but most are small, plain and un-commercial, so don't expect luxury. Many are upstairs from shop fronts or located in apartment blocks, and some are quite difficult to find; often you must ring to enter. There are a few big places, but most have 20 beds or less.

Charlottenburg & Wilmersdorf

Pension Peters (Map 6, ☎ 312 22 78, fax 312 35 19, Kantstrasse 146) is quite nicely furnished with warm lighting in just eight rooms starting at DM75/95 (or DM110/130 with shower). *Hotel-Pension Majesty (Map 6, ☎ 323 20 61, fax 323 20 63, Mommsenstrasse 55)* is another good bet; it has 11 rooms without private bath or WC and charges DM80/100 without any private facilities or DM110/165 with a shower.

The *Hotel Crystal (Map 6, ☎ 312 90 47, fax 312 64 65, Kantstrasse 144)* is much larger and also more reasonably priced, charging from DM70/90 without facilities or DM120/150 with.

Hotel Garni Augusta (Map 6, ☎ 883 50 28, fax 882 47 79, Fasanenstrasse 22) is a frilly establishment with rooms without shower for DM110/150; for rooms with shower and WC, it costs DM145/195.

The attractive *Pension Alexandra (Map 6, ☎ 885 77 80, fax 88 57 78 18, Wielandstrasse 32)* offers nice simple rooms for DM110/135, or DM155/185 with full facilities; prices include a generous breakfast buffet. It's a few steps north of Ku'damm.

Hotel-Pension Nürnberger Eck (Map 6, ☎ 235 17 80, fax 23 51 78 99, Nürnberger Strasse 24a) has lots of original art and rooms decked out in the style of the 1920s and 30s for DM80/130 (DM100/160 with shower).

Friendly, small *Hotel-Pension Curtis (Map 6, ☎ 883 49 31, fax 885 04 38, Pariser Strasse 39-40)* has comfortable rooms with shower for DM75/120. Some larger rooms cost DM10 or DM20 more. Discounts for longer stays are available. In case they're booked, there are three other pensions in the same building – Austriana, Rügen and Marco Polo – that offer similar room rates.

Hotel Savigny (Map 6, ☎ 881 30 01, fax 882 55 19, Brandenburgische Strasse 21) is a good, well priced establishment in a historic Berlin building with high ceilings and a lift dating back to 1912. The large rooms have all amenities. Singles range from

DM90 to DM130 and doubles cost between DM130 and DM190.

Olivaer Apart Hotel (Map 6, ☎ 88 58 60, fax 88 58 62 22, Konstanzer Strasse 1) is a contemporary place that would make business types feel right at home. It's also near Ku'damm and has stylish, minimalist rooms costing DM140/180.

It may not win awards for style, yet *Hotel Agon (Map 6, ☎ 885 99 30, fax 885 99 31 23, Xantener Strasse 4)* scores points for its personable feel. Rooms are large and comfortable, offer all amenities and start at DM117/147, including breakfast buffet.

Friedrichshain

East Side Hotel (☎ 29 38 33, fax 29 38 35 55, Mühlenstrasse 60) has a great location opposite the East Side Gallery, the largest remaining stretch of the Wall. Rooms with full facilities in this pleasantly renovated 19th century hotel are friendly, well lit and cost DM140 to DM188 for singles and DM166 to DM235 for doubles.

Juncker's Hotel Garni (☎ 293 35 50, fax 29 33 55 55, Grünberger Strasse 21) offers pretty good value for money. Its 30 beds cost from DM90/110 to DM140/170, depending on location and size; all have private shower and WC. Breakfast is an extra DM10 per person.

Kreuzberg

Rooms at *Hotel am Anhalter Bahnhof (Map 3, ☎ 251 03 42, fax 251 48 97, Stresemannstrasse 36)* are spread across three floors; those facing away from the street cost from DM140/180 with private bath. Singles without facilities cost DM80, doubles DM110, triples DM150 and quads DM160. Prices include a buffet breakfast.

Mitte

The family operated *Pension Merkur (Map 4, ☎ 282 82 97, fax 282 77 65, Torstrasse 156)* charges from DM65/95 for a simple single/double to DM150/168 for those with private shower and WC. It's a little overpriced for what you get, but it has a few moderate family rooms.

Hotel Kastanienhof (☎ 44 30 50, fax 44 30 51 11, Kastanienallee 65), between Prenzlauer Berg and Mitte, has rooms with private shower and WC for DM130/160, though bigger, quieter rooms are also available at DM190/265.

PLACES TO STAY – TOP END

Splurge options in Charlottenburg include *Hotel Bleibtreu (Map 6, ☎ 88 47 40, fax 88 47 44 44, Bleibtreustrasse 31)*, which has a unique flair and creative rooms. Rates range from DM249/289 to DM349/389, not including the DM26 breakfast buffet.

Another good bet in this area is the stylish *Hecker's Hotel (Map 6, ☎ 889 00, fax 889 02 60, Grolmannstrasse 35)*, which has an imposing glass-fronted lobby and rooms with designer furniture costing from DM200/250.

A new crop of stylish top hotels has sprouted in Mitte. The reborn *Adlon Hotel Kempinski (Map 4, ☎ 226 10, fax 22 61 22 22, Unter den Linden 77)* is the *de rigueur* establishment with 337 rooms. Rooms start at DM390/460 (not including the DM39 breakfast buffet).

Staying at *art'otel Ermelerhaus (Map 4, ☎ 24 06 20, fax 24 06 22 22, Wallstrasse 70-73)* feels a bit like camping out at a museum. Public areas and rooms at this classy establishment abound, and original art works by Georg Basclitz are featured. Rates start at DM235/275, but it's almost worth the splurge.

Sorat Hotel Spree-Bogen (Map 3, ☎ 39 92 00, fax 39 92 09 99, Alt Moabit 99) offers another take on artsy environments. It's a state-of-the art affair that sits right on the river banks in Tiergarten-Moabit and has rooms from DM230/300, including the sumptuous breakfast buffet.

Over in Kreuzberg, the intimate 25-room *Hotel Riehmers Hofgarten (Map 3, ☎ 78 10 11, fax 786 60 59, Yorckstrasse 83)* is another upmarket hotel deserving special attention. Rooms cost DM170/200 or DM210/240, including a big breakfast buffet. It's housed in an elegant edifice (1892) that will delight romantics.

PLACES TO EAT

There are restaurants offering every cuisine under the sun in Berlin. In fact, there are so many *Spezialitäten* that you will soon regard German fare as unusual. Surprisingly, along with all the variety, good food is generally available at (by local standards) reasonable prices. A full lunch or dinner at an unpretentious restaurant can easily cost less than DM20.

If you want a wider selection of restaurants and other eateries than we can provide, consult the annual *Essen, Trinken, Tanzen in Berlin* (Eating, Drinking, Dancing in Berlin), published by the hip *Zitty* magazine and available at newsagents for DM8.50.

Berlin specialties to watch out for include *Bouletten* (meatballs), *Eisbein mit Sauerkraut/Erbsenpüree* (pork knuckle with sauerkraut/mushy peas), *Currywurst* (curried sausage), *Schusterjungen* (literally 'cobbler's kids'; or bread rolls made with rye flour) and *Soljanka*, a Ukrainian sour bean soup that has arrived via the GDR. Wash it down with any of these three beers: Berliner Kindl, Schultheiss or Berliner Weisse (a light, fizzy lager with fruit syrup added).

Restaurants

German A winner in Charlottenburg is *Aschinger (Map 6, ☎ 882 55 58, Kurfürstendamm 26)*, a cellar that serves 15 hearty dishes at DM9.80, an all-you-can-eat salad bar for DM4.80 and breakfasts for DM5 (coffee is extra). You must order at the self-service counter. A small glass of its dark home brew is DM2.80.

Luisen-Bräu (☎ 341 93 88, Luisenplatz 1) is a microbrewery where you can relax over a beer and a pretzel after a day of museum-hopping around Charlottenburg Palace. Filling fare includes a daily dish for DM9.80.

If you thought a schnitzel was a schnitzel was a schnitzel, go to *Gasthaus Dietrich Herz (☎ 693 11 73, Marheinekeplatz)* in Kreuzberg to find a dozen varieties starting from DM12.95. Hearty snacks under DM10 are also served in this old-time restaurant.

Stäv (Map 4, ☎ 282 39 65, Schiffbauerdamm 8), just east of the Reichstag, has a menu that reflects a distinct Rhine-Berlin connection. The name stands for *Ständige Vertretung*, the term used for the West German embassy in the former GDR.

The wood-panelled walls of *Zum Nussbaum (Map 4, ☎ 242 30 95, Am Nussbaum 3)* in the Nikolaiviertel have hosted the hungry and thirsty since 1571, making it Berlin's oldest restaurant. Tourists love the place, which has remained friendly and affordable.

At the *Kellerrestaurant (Map 4, ☎ 282 38 43, Chausseestrasse 125)* in the Brecht-Weigel House, you can eat rustic dishes (from DM20) based on the recipes of Brecht's wife, Helene Weigel.

You'll need slightly deeper pockets to dine at *Offenbachstuben (☎ 445 85 02, Stubbenkammerstrasse 8)*, a GDR relic with a menu that seems to feature the entire animal world, including deer and rabbit. Mains cost from DM20 to DM35.

Alte Meierei (Map 3, ☎ 39 07 97 21, Alt Moabit 99) in Tiergarten is a stylish gem tucked away in the stables of a former dairy. It serves updated versions of classic Berlin dishes to a monied clientele daily. Dinner mains start at DM28. If you're a gourmet on a budget, go at lunchtime.

Indian & Middle Eastern *Ashoka Bar (Map 6, ☎ 313 20 66, Grolmannstrasse 51)* in Charlottenburg is a tiny but hugely popular eatery, open daily from 10 am to 2 am. Most curries and meat-based dishes cost less than DM10 and just fly over the counter from the steamy open kitchen. Equally delicious food (vegetarian only) is found at *Satyam (Map 6, ☎ 312 90 79, Goethestrasse 5)*, which is open the same hours.

Chandra Kumari (Map 3, ☎ 694 12 03, Gneisenaustrasse 4) in Kreuzberg 61 has dishes blending Sri Lankan and Indian influences, starting at DM7.50 for a vegetarian lentil dish and topping at DM95 for the 'wedding banquet' for two.

Delicious budget fare is available on Goltzstrasse in Schöneberg. Try Indian food from *Rani (Map 3, ☎ 215 26 73)* at No 32 and Persian from *Shayan (Map 3, ☎ 215 15 47)* at No 23. Sandwiches at the latter go for

DM5, rice dishes are DM7 to DM9 and ke-babs cost DM5 to DM18.

Oren (Map 4, ☎ 282 82 28, Oranienburger Strasse 28) in Mitte is pricier and more up-market. Patrons dine on delicious Israeli and Middle Eastern food, including a few fish dishes. Popular is the Orient-Express (DM19) platter sporting many mezze (appetisers). The menu is in Hebrew, English and German, and you can read Hebrew newspapers.

International *Deininger (Map 3, ☎ 694 19 93, Friesenstrasse 23)* in Kreuzberg 61 has an eclectic menu and different all-you-can-eat dishes for DM12 every Monday and Tuesday night. The themed Sunday brunch (10 am to 3 pm) is DM12 also. Reservations are advised.

borchardt (Map 4, ☎ 20 39 71 17, Französische Strasse 47) near Gendarmen-markt in Mitte is a stylish and trendy haunt of the famous and fabulous. The ceilings are as tall as the waiter's aprons are long; the food's Franco-German and pricey. Call for reservations.

Storch (Map 3, ☎ 784 20 59, Wart-burgstrasse 54) in Schöneberg is another upmarket yet cosy place with tuxedo-clad waiters serving delicious dishes with Alsa-tian touches. Expect to pay about DM30 for main courses, though *Flammekuchen* go for DM14 to DM17.

Kiezküche (Waldenserstrasse 2-4) is a hot tip for gourmets on a budget (enter the large yard, then it's on the 1st floor behind the steel door in the first building on your left). The place is run by a nonprofit organ-isation that trains disadvantaged youth as certified chefs and restaurant managers. And they get to practise on you! Refined recipes such as poached salmon in chantilly sauce for a miraculous DM7 are typical. Seating is cafeteria style. It's open week-days from 11.30 am to 2 pm.

Italian *Piccola Taormina (Map 6, ☎ 881 47 10, Uhlandstrasse 29)* in Charlottenburg is a noisy, blue-walled labyrinth serving fast, good-value pizzas and pastas. It's possible to escape for DM10 (including coffee). *Ali*

Baba (Map 6, ☎ 881 13 50, Bleibtreustrasse 45), open daily till 3 am, serves superb pizza and fills as quickly as a 'free samples day' at a treasury. With prices topping DM13, you don't need to be rich to eat here.

Gargano (Map 3, ☎ 215 83 08, Goltz-strasse 52) in Schöneberg is a comfortable Italian eatery with specials like homemade vegetarian ravioli with tomato and basil (DM13) and saltimboca romana (DM18). In the same neighbourhood is the family run *Trattoria á Muntagnola (Map 3, ☎ 211 66 42, Fuggerstrasse 27)*, an authentic slice of southern Italy. Garlic strings and heavy chandeliers dangle above red-and-white chequered tablecloths where diners eat fresh pasta dishes (around DM20).

In Mitte, we recommend *Fressco (Map 4, ☎ 282 96 47, Oranienburger Strasse 48-49)*, a non-smoking gourmet Imbiss with tiled walls and huge daily specials for about DM11. The outrageous fruit cake sells for DM6 per piece.

Kosher Several restaurants claim to have strictly kosher food, but people in the know have told us it ain't so. These are reliable candidates, though.

Beth Café (Map 4, ☎ 281 31 35, Tu-cholskystrasse 10) in Mitte is a good-value kosher cafe-bistro with a pretty inner court-yard. It's affiliated with the Jewish congre-gation of Adass Jisroel and open daily except Saturday from 1 to 10 pm (Monday to 8 pm).

Arche Noah (Map 6, ☎ 882 61 38, Fasa-nenstrasse 79), inside the Jewish Commu-nity House in Charlottenburg, has a huge selection of Jewish and Israeli foods. You can eat a la carte or indulge in daily multi-course dinners for DM21, DM24 or DM26. The Tuesday hot and cold buffet with 30 items (DM35) starts at 6.30 pm.

Mexican & Spanish Mexican restaurants are only a recent arrival in Germany and have proliferated in Berlin. Unfortunately, they're often trendy places serving not ter-ribly authentic, overpriced fare. The fol-lowing are the better ones.

Tres Kilos (Map 3, ☎ 693 60 44, Marheinekeplatz 3) is a chic cantina in Kreuzberg 61 with tasteful decor and warm furnishings and lighting. It's open daily from 5 pm to 1 am. The food's pricey (mains around DM20) but really quite tasty. *Locus (Map 3, ☎ 691 56 37)*, next door at No 4, is equally popular, if less fancy and cheaper. *Lone Star Taqueria (Map 3, ☎ 692 71 82, Bergmannstrasse 11)* is another contender nearby.

Frida Kahlo (☎ 445 70 16, Lychener Strasse 37) in Prenzlauer Berg is a lively restaurant-bar with reasonably priced food, from breakfast to dinner.

Bar-Celona (Map 4, ☎ 282 91 53, Hannoversche Strasse 2), a friendly restaurant-bar near the Brecht-Weigel House, serves delicious paella for DM20 to DM26 (two person minimum) and tapas from DM3.50 to DM6.

A fashionable crowd munches on tapas, tortillas and bocadillos starting at DM3 at the atmospheric *Pasodoble (Map 3, ☎ 784 52 44, Crellestrasse 39)* in Schöneberg. Main dishes, like paella, cost around DM20.

South-East Asian & Chinese *Fisch & Vegetables (Map 3, ☎ 821 68 16, Goltzstrasse 32)* is a stellar Imbiss and takeaway in Schöneberg with cheap, good Thai dishes which you watch being made in the open kitchen. The stand-up tables are always full (sharing is okay) and everything is under DM10.

Stepping into *Tuk-Tuk (Map 3, ☎ 781 15 88, Grossgörschenstrasse 2)* in Schöneberg feels like walking into an intimate bamboo den in Jakarta. Meat-based and vegie Indonesian dishes start at DM18 and are served amid soothing gamelan music.

Angkor Wat (Map 3, ☎ 393 39 22, Paulstrasse 22) in Tiergarten-Moabit is a dark, cavernous place that serves Cambodian fondue, involving cooking your meat and vegies in a cauldron right at your table (DM60 for two). Other, usually coconut milk-based, dishes go for around DM20.

For authentic Chinese head for the bustling *Good Friend (Map 6, ☎ 313 26 59,* *Kantstrasse 30)*, a place that's short on decor but long on delicious food. It's hugely popular with both Chinese and non-Chinese clientele. Most meals cost less than DM20.

Turkish Despite the many Turks who call Berlin home, there are relatively few Turkish restaurants, though there are countless doner kebab places. *Malete (Map 4, ☎ 280 77 59, Chausseestrasse 131)* in Mitte is a friendly restaurant with interesting salads costing around DM10, vegetarian dishes from DM10 to DM18.50 and meat dishes from DM20. *Derya (Map 4, ☎ 281 75 36)*, up the street at No 116, is similar and also has a nice beer garden surrounding a fountain.

Vegetarian Not exclusively vegetarian but a central option for a cheap vegie meal is *Marché (Map 6, ☎ 882 75 78, Kurfürstendamm 14-15)*, with good salads from DM4 and pastas from DM9. Children under 1.2m eat for free.

Those hankering after an Asian fix should head for *Samadhi (Map 6, ☎ 313 10 67, Goethestrasse 6)*, also located in Charlottenburg. It has dishes seldom seen outside Thailand, with starters/main courses from DM8/16. The daily lunch menu is DM11.50.

For unadorned vegetarian fare, try *Einhorn (Map 6, ☎ 881 42 41, Mommsenstrasse 2)*, a buffet with salads from DM2.60 per 100g and main dishes from DM6.

The most upmarket vegetarian restaurant is *Abendmahl (Map 5, ☎ 612 51 79, Muskauer Strasse 9)* in Kreuzberg 36. It has an inventive menu, including fish dishes, with starters from DM8, main courses from DM25. It's a stylish place, watched over by a statue of Jesus.

Not far is *Advena (Map 5, ☎ 618 81 09, Wiener Strasse 11)*, a quiet oasis with excellent vegetarian specials (DM8.50 to DM12), salads (DM6) and soups (DM5.50) served in a relaxing, candlelight atmosphere. On Sunday the breakfast buffet is out till 4 pm.

Naturkost Vegetarisches Buffet (Map 3, ☎ 694 29 82, Mehringdamm 48) in Kreuzberg 61 (U6 or U7 to Mehringdamm) has good takeaway or sit-down choices. Blackboard specials are under DM10.

Cafes

Many Berlin cafes change identity, chameleon-like, over the course of a day, starting as a breakfast place, then offering a small lunch menu, featuring cakes in the afternoon and becoming a restaurant-bar or just a bar at night. Many of the places mentioned here would easily fit into the earlier Restaurant section or the Pubs & Bars section of Entertainment.

Café Einstein (Map 3, ☎ 261 50 96, Kurfürstenstrasse 58), is a Viennese-style coffee house and Berlin's most elegant and stylish cafe. Academics with credit cards will feel most comfortable, but it's fun to watch the crowd even if you can only afford a coffee. There's also a full menu, with starters from DM6.50 and main courses for about DM28. The staff tend to be a bit precious. *Café Einstein Unter den Linden (Map 4, Unter den Linden 42)* is a second branch.

Café Wintergarten (Map 6, ☎ 882 54 14, Fasanenstrasse 23) in Charlottenburg is a cosy place for deep conversation over a coffee or delicious international fare. In summer, the garden tables are the most coveted.

Schwarzes Café (Map 6, ☎ 313 80 38, Kantstrasse 148) near Zoo station is a perennial favourite of students and young travellers. It's open around the clock and a good place to visit if you roll into Berlin in the middle of the night. Breakfast from DM8.50 is served any time, while many simple dishes (around DM14), some a tad overpriced, are available also.

Students from the Technische Universität across the street treat *Café Hardenberg (Map 6, ☎ 312 26 44, Hardenbergstrasse 10)* as an extension of the student cafeteria. It's usually full which can have a deleterious effect on the service, so pack some patience.

Barcomi's (☎ 694 81 38, Bergmannstrasse 21) is a little deli whose freshly roasted coffee and American baked goods – like muffins and bagels – are the main attractions. A second, more upmarket, branch *(Map 4, ☎ 28 59 83 63)* is in the Sophienhöfe in Mitte.

Café am Neuen See (Map 3, ☎ 254 49 30, Lichtensteinallee 1), in Tiergarten park, is ideal on balmy summer nights. The beer garden service is pretty slow but that just gives you more time for people-watching and looking out over the lake.

Good cafes belong to trendy Schöneberg like froth on a cappuccino. *Café M (Map 3, ☎ 216 70 92, Goltzstrasse 33)* is a mainstay, despite decor with all the grungy charm of a train station waiting room. It's overpriced and overrated but the Schöneberg trendoids keep coming, so it's still good for taking in the scene.

Café Lux (Map 3, ☎ 215 96 74) next door, at No 35, is more low-key but also popular. It features kaleidoscopic canvases and a pool table.

Montevideo (Map 3, ☎ 213 10 20, Victoria-Louise-Platz 6) looks a bit like an American diner and makes killer breakfasts from around the world – Japanese, American, Canadian, Dutch, Italian, Finnish etc – from DM9.50 to DM19.

Student Cafeterias

These are called *Mensa* at German universities, which comes from the Latin for 'table' and has nothing to do with elite intellectual society. Anyone, student or not, may eat at the *Technische Universität Mensa (Map 6, Hardenbergstrasse 34)* in Charlottenburg, three blocks from Zoo station (entry is across from Steinplatz). Nonstudents pay slightly more, but you can still fill your tray with a three-course lunch for under DM10. It's open weekdays from 11.15 am to 2.30 pm. The *cafe* on the ground floor is open from 8 am to 7.45 pm and has drinks, snacks and basic mains for DM4 or DM5. On the 2nd floor is a smaller restaurant which is slightly more expensive (three courses for about DM12).

Humboldt Universität Mensa (Map 4) has the same hours (enter through the main portal at Unter den Linden 6, then take the first door on the left, turn right at the end of the corridor and follow your nose). You must show student ID (from any university) or pay nonstudent prices. *Freie Universität*

BERLIN

(Kiebitzweg 6) in Zehlendorf (U1 to Thielplatz) also has a Mensa (same hours).

Kantinen

On weekdays, you can enjoy a hot subsidised meal (DM5 to DM10) in a government cafeteria where you clear your own table. The *Kantine* in the *Rathaus Charlottenburg (Otto-Suhr-Allee 100)*, close to Schloss Charlottenburg, is in the basement. What's available is usually written on a blackboard at the far end of the counter. The cafeteria on the 10th floor of *Rathaus Kreuzberg (Map 3, Yorckstrasse 4-11)* is open weekdays from 7.30 am to 3 pm and offers great views. Everyone is welcome. Almost any *Arbeitsamt* (employment office) will have a cheap Kantine. A good one is in Arbeitsamt IV *(Charlottenstrasse 90)*; it's open weekdays from 9 am to 2 pm. Just walk straight in and take the lift on the left up to the 5th floor.

Snacks & Fast Food

Berlin is paradise for snackers on the go, with Turkish, Greek, Middle Eastern, Italian and Chinese specialities available at Imbiss stands and stalls throughout the city.

Restaurants offering takeaway or standup eating include *Habibi (Map 3, Winterfeldtplatz 24)* in Schöneberg, which has some of the city's best felafel and shwarma and stays open till 3 am (weekends to 5 am). Other branches are nearby at Akazienstrasse 9 and at Oranienstrasse 30 in Kreuzberg.

Rimón (Map 4, ☎ 28 38 40 32), on the corner of Oranienburger Strasse and Krausnickstrasse, rates even better with some people. The moderately priced restaurant makes all kinds of Jewish-Middle Eastern food (latkes, bagels, couscous), but at its takeaway (on Krausnickstrasse) you can get mouthwatering felafel for just DM3.50.

For the same price you can also get what's possibly the best doner kebab this side of Istanbul at the *Rosenthaler Imbiss (Map 4)*, a short distance away on Rosenthaler Platz, right outside the north-western U-Bahn exit. (Do not confuse this one with the other Imbiss immediately to the left).

Bagels are making inroads into German food consciousness, partly thanks to a new chain called *Salomon Bagels*, a friendly establishment that serves delicious sandwiches for around DM6; bagels are DM1.50 each. There's a branch at Joachimsthaler Strasse 13 *(Map 6, ☎ 881 81 96)* and another inside the Potsdamer Platz Arkaden mall *(☎ 25 29 76 26)*. Also in the mall is the *Asia Pavillion* where huge plates of steaming hot fried noodles are DM4.50, with most everything else less than DM10.

Soup Kultur (Map 6, ☎ 74 30 82 95, Kurfürstendamm 224) is a pint-sized standup place operated by a young team serving soups from around the world, from hearty potato to refreshing gazpacho to exotic South African *sousboontje*. Prices range from DM4.90 to DM8.50.

Taco Rico (Map 3, ☎ 23 62 13 43, Martin-Luther-Strasse 21) in Schöneberg is a good place for those hankering for decent Mexican food, but unwilling to pay the inflated prices of regular restaurants. You can fill up on enchiladas and burritos for well under DM10.

For sumptuous Spanish-style toasted sandwiches, spilling over with things like mozzarella or gorgonzola, tomato and salami (DM3 to DM5), head to the *Sandwich Kiosk (Map 5)* on Heinrichplatz (Oranienstrasse) in Kreuzberg 36.

Self-Catering

Try the discount Aldi, Lidl or Penny Markt supermarket chains, which have outlets throughout Berlin; Tip is less common. You may have to wait in long checkout queues but will pay considerably less for basic food items. Handy travelling food such as powdered fruit drinks and soups, dried and fresh fruit, bread, cheese, packaged salads, sandwich meats and chocolate bars are among the worthwhile items. These are also the cheapest places to buy beer and table wines. More upmarket chains include Kaiser's, Reichelt, Spar and Bolle. Plus is another discounter, with more outlets and a slightly larger range of goods.

Aldi is on Joachimstaler Strasse *(Map 6)*, on the 1st floor opposite Zoo station, at

Uhlandstrasse 42 *(Map 6)* and at Leibniz-strasse 72 *(Map 6)* near Kantstrasse in Charlottenburg. *Tip* and *Penny Markt* are side by side near the corner of Hohen-staufenstrasse and Martin-Luther-Strasse. *Kaiser*'s locations include the outlet on Nol-lendorfplatz *(Map 3)*, Wittenbergplatz *(Map 6)* and at Bleibtreustrasse 19 *(Map 6)*. Spar outlets are everywhere as well.

Markets There are some 100 neighbour-hood produce markets in Berlin, but listed here are two of the best. Fruit and vegies, bread loaves, olives, fetta and meats are just part of a mouthwatering culinary bonanza you'll find at the bazaar-like *Türkenmarkt (Map 5)* in Kreuzberg 36. Best of all, this Turkish Market's really cheap! The market is on Maybachufer along Landwehr Canal on Tuesday and Friday from noon to 6.30 pm. Take U1, U15 or U8 to Kottbusser Tor, then walk south for about 250m.

Another legendary market is the *Winter-feldtmarkt (Map 3)* on Winterfeldtplatz in Schöneberg where the produce is some of the freshest, though prices tend to be quite high. It's on Wednesday and Saturday from 8 am to 2 pm. Take the U1, U2, U4 or U15 to Nollendorfplatz, then walk five minutes south on Maassenstrasse.

ENTERTAINMENT

Berliners take their culture – and fun – ser-iously. All in all, there are 36 theatres, 49 off-theatres, 22 children's theatres, 14 cabarets, 95 cinemas, 170 museums and 300 galleries. Berlin's nightlife is spread over seven main areas. For fairly upmarket venues, go to Savignyplatz and side streets like Bleibtreustrasse and Grolmannstrasse in Charlottenburg (Map 6). The western theatre district is centred on and around Ku'damm (Map 6). The area around Mehringdamm, Gneisenaustrasse and Bergmannstrasse in Kreuzberg 61 (Map 3) is alternative but with trendy touches, while Kreuzberg 36 (Map 5) along Oranienstrasse and Wiener Strasse has preserved a grungy, slightly edgy feel. Around Winterfeldtplatz in Schöneberg (Map 3), you'll find few tourists and lots of

30-somethings tip-toeing between their fad-dish alternative lifestyles and the demands of their careers and parenthood.

In the eastern districts, the nightlife is by far more earthy, experimental and less sedentary. The energy is electric with new bars and restaurants opening in profusion and previously dull streets erupting into life, seemingly overnight.

The most dynamic scene is in the Prenz-lauer Berg (locals say Prenzl'berg) district, especially around Käthe-Kollwitz-Platz and its side streets but also on Knaackstrasse and the streets north of Danziger Strasse. More established are the clubs and cafes in Mitte along Oranienburger Strasse, August-strasse, Hackescher Markt and adjacent streets (Map 4). The eastern theatre district is nearby along Friedrichstrasse (Map 4, U/S-Bahn station Friedrichstrasse). The new frontier is Friedrichshain, which has

PRENZLAUER BERG

1 Schall und Rauch	9 Offenbachstuben
2 Café Amsterdam	10 X-Bar
3 Alpha Café	11 Kulturbrauerei
4 Lette 'm Sleep	12 Uluru Resort
5 Frida Kahlo	13 Kommandatur
6 Weinstein	14 Hotel Kastanienhof
7 Bibo Bar	15 Pfefferberg Cultural
8 La Bodeguita del Medio	Centre

lots of interesting new bars and restaurants along Simon-Dach-Strasse and around Boxhagener Platz.

Listings

The best sources for comprehensive what's-on listings are the bi-weekly *Zitty* (DM4) and *Tip* (DM4.50). Both are full of insider tips and colourful articles that capture the constantly evolving Berlin Zeitgeist. Read the free rag *030* for one-off parties, the coolest new clubs and other trendoid essentials. The monthly *Prinz* (DM4.50) and *Berlin Programm* (DM3) are not nearly as up-to-date and happening. All magazines are in German, but you should be able to understand listings even with a minimal command of the language.

Tickets

Outlets selling tickets to cultural and sports events are scattered all over the city. A commission charge of 15% of the ticket price is customary. Most agencies accept phone reservations with credit cards. If time permits, tickets will be mailed to you; if there isn't sufficient time, they'll be waiting for you at the box office.

Ticket offices are everywhere in the Ku'damm, including Theaterkasse Centrum (Map 6, ☎ 882 76 11) at Meineckestrasse 25 and Concert & Theaterkasse City (Map 6, ☎ 313 88 58) at Knesebeckstrasse 10. In Schöneberg, you'll find Box Office Theaterkasse (Map 3, ☎ 215 54 63) at Nollendorfplatz 7. The Showtime ticket counter (Map 6, ☎ 217 77 54) is in the KaDeWe department store at Tauentzienstrasse 21.

Cinemas

Films are quite expensive in Berlin; tickets on Saturday night can cost as much as DM17. In general, admission is cheaper on *Kinotag* (film day; usually Tuesday or Wednesday) and before 5 pm. Student discounts are rare.

There are numerous movie houses along Kurfürstendamm, most of them showing international first releases dubbed into German. One of the grandest is the historic *Zoo-Palast* (Map 6, ☎ 25 41 47 77, Hardenbergstrasse 29a), a multiplex with nine cinemas and prices through the roof. *Delphi Film Palast* (Map 6, Kantstrasse 12a), adjacent to the Theater des Westens, is another historical venue.

Cinemas which show films in the original language with subtitles (denoted OmU) include: *The Arsenal* (☎ 218 68 48, Welserstrasse 25) in Schöneberg (U4 to Victoria-Louise-Platz); *The Babylon* (Map 5, ☎ 61 60 91 93, Dresdner Strasse 126) in Kreuzberg 36; *The Odeon* (Map 3, ☎ 78 70 40 19, Hauptstrasse 116) in Schöneberg; and *The Olympia* (Map 6, ☎ 881 19 78, Kantstrasse 162) near Zoo station.

Discos & Clubs

Berlin has a reputation for unbridled and very late nightlife – nothing happens until midnight. As in every major city, it's hard to keep up with the ever-changing club scene. Before stepping out, call ahead to make sure the club's still there or, better yet, consult any of the what's-on rags (see Listings earlier in this section).

Cover charges range from DM5 to DM20 and usually don't include a drink. There are a lot of illegal 'squat' clubs too but for details on those you'll have to rely on the kindness (and knowledge) of strangers. Many clubs have perfected the fine art of the rave, and techno music has become quintessentially Berlin (see the boxed text 'Techno Town').

If you put a pin for every club on a map of Berlin, the biggest cluster would be in the eastern districts of Mitte, Friedrichshain and Prenzlauer Berg, which just shows how the scene has shifted since the Wende.

Tresor (Map 4, ☎ 609 37 02, Leipziger Strasse 128a) in Mitte has been a techno classic since 1991. It's inside the money vault of a former department store and open Wednesday and Friday to Sunday after 11 pm. Cover is DM5 to DM20.

Sophienklub (Map 4, ☎ 282 45 52, Sophienstrasse 6), a left-over from GDR days, changes the music style nightly – jazz, brasil, house, soul, funk, reggae, but *no*

Techno Town

House. Rave. Gabber. Jungle. Trance. Techno has come a long way since the Düsseldorf band Kraftwerk first gave vent to these mechanical beats some 20 years ago. Since then, techno's evolution has seen it morph into the mainstream to the point where you even hear it blaring from speakers in German supermarkets. A sound, a mantra and a way of life that Berlin has somehow made its own.

DAVID PEEVERS

DAVID PEEVERS

Thanks to the annual Berlin Love Parade (1.5 million people grooved here in the streets in 1999), techno has even gained recognition as a legitimate political expression: the Berlin Senate voted not only to allow the parade but also to pay for the huge post-event clean-up because the organisers had registered the event as a 'political demonstration'. Perhaps it's difficult to see a political connection in this movement whose unofficial motto is, after all, 'Friede, Freude, Eierkuchen' (Peace, Happiness, Pancakes), though it certainly qualifies as a culture.

techno. It has a low-key atmosphere and charges DM10 for cover, less during the week (U8 to Weinmeisterstrasse).

Sage Club (Map 4, Brückenstrasse 1), inside the Heine-Heine-Strasse U-Bahn station (U8), is a winner with sophisticated twenty-somethings. Funk, soul, house is on the turntables, water-spewing gargoyles are part of the decor.

Kurvenstar (Map 4, ☎ 28 59 97 10, Kleine Präsidentenstrasse 4) is a recent entry that merges music, dancing and food from around the world. It's open daily after 9 pm.

To wallow in GDR nostalgia, head to the **Cube Club** (☎ 292 87 56, Wühlischstrasse 29) in Friedrichshain. Upstairs is a cafe-bar; the intimate basement club opens Thursday to Saturday after 11 pm. Cover can be free or up to DM5.

Maria am Ostbahnhof (☎ 29 00 61 98, Strasse der Pariser Kommune 8-10) and **Matrix** (☎ 29 49 10 47, Warschauer Platz 18) are also in Friedrichshain. Both are major techno outposts in unique settings: Maria am Ostbahnhof holds court at an abandoned postal distribution centre, while Matrix rocks beneath the Warschauer Strasse U-Bahn arches.

In Prenzlauer Berg, head to the **Bibo Bar** (☎ 443 97 98, Lychener Strasse 12), a cocktail bar-cum-dance club that draws a wild, wacky and communicative crowd.

Back in the 'old west', check out **SO36** (Map 5, ☎ 61 40 13 06, Oranienstrasse 190) in Kreuzberg 36, a perennial favourite. It has theme nights: hip hop to house, ballroom (!) to drum and bass. Wednesday is gay-lesbian night.

euro currency converter DM1 = €0.51

90° Grad (Map 3, ☎ 262 89 84, Denne-witzstrasse 37) is still trendy after all these years (take U15 to Kurfürstenstrasse). DJs spin their tunes perched in a giant chancel in the middle of the dance floor. It's open Wednesday to Sunday from 11 pm; cover ranges from DM10 to DM15. Thursday is gay night.

Abraxas (Map 6, ☎ 312 94 93, Kant-strasse 134) in Charlottenburg is unpretentious, timeless and does jazz and Latin rhythms nightly except Monday. Cover is DM5 to DM10.

Live Music

Many pubs and bars offer live music. A cover charge of up to DM20 may be levied, but usually only on Friday and Saturday nights.

Junction Bar (Map 3, ☎ 772 76 77, Gneisenaustrasse 18) in Kreuzberg 61 is a basement venue with a musical menu that includes funk, soul, rock and jazz. It's open from 6 pm.

In Friedrichshain is *Mana Mana (Niederbarnimstrasse 23)*, a low-key hang-out popular with punks (only 'friendly' ones, we're assured). The decor is wild and creative, and so are the bands. Cocktails here are 'dirt-cheap' (DM6 to DM10), as far as cocktails go. *Supamolly (Jessner Strasse)* survived a period as a squatter haunt and is now a pub and live venue. Usually it's music, though theatre and film screenings pad the program. Cover is cheap, often under DM5.

Other area clubs with occasional live music are *Dachkammer (☎ 296 16 73, Simon-Dach-Strasse 39)*, which is otherwise a pleasant pub and cocktail bar and *Maria am Ostbahnhof* (see Discos & Clubs).

Zosch (Map 4, ☎ 280 76 64, Tucholsky-strasse) in Mitte is a scene dinosaur, popular with student-age patrons. It has friendly service and occasional bands in the basement (often free).

Major venues include the *Arena (Map 5, ☎ 533 20 30, Eichenstrasse 4)*, in an old bus depot in Treptow, which is a big party place and often has concerts with international headliners. *Waldbühne (☎ 23 08 82 30,*

Glockenturmstrasse) in Charlottenburg is Berlin's largest outdoor venue for rock and pop concerts, seating 22,000 people (U2 to Olympiastadion Ost, then walk or take the free shuttle).

Jazz

A-Trane (Map 6, ☎ 312 80 76, Bleibtreu-strasse 1) in Charlottenburg is still *the* place for nightly jazz of all main styles. Benches and coffeehouse-type tables and chairs wrap around the small stage in such a clever way that there's not a bad seat in the house. Cover is DM10 to DM20 but some nights, usually Tuesday and Wednesday, are free.

Quasimodo (Map 6, ☎ 312 80 86, Kantstrasse 12a), next to the Delphi Film Palast, has nightly live jazz, blues or rock acts in the basement and a stylish cafe on the ground floor. Cover ranges from DM15 to DM25, though Tuesday and Wednesday are free.

b-flat (Map 4, ☎ 283 31 23, Rosenthaler Strasse 13) in Mitte has concerts almost nightly at 9 pm and draws people of all ages and walks of life; otherwise it's a modern cafe-bar. *Flöz (Map 6, ☎ 861 10 00, Nas-sauische Strasse 37)* in Wilmersdorf (U7 or U9 to Berliner Strasse), has mostly modern jazz and boogie and a slightly more mature clientele. The pub section opens at 8 pm; the concert space in the basement at 9 pm.

Pubs & Bars

Hegel (Map 6, ☎ 312 19 48, Savignyplatz 2) in upmarket Charlottenburg serves drinks like Zarenblut (Tsar's blood) and Hegel's Todestrunk (Hegel's death drink). Things get downright nostalgic when someone takes a turn on the piano.

Flammende Herzen (Flaming Hearts; Map 5, ☎ 615 71 02, Oranienstrasse 170) and *Bierhimmel (Map 5, ☎ 615 31 22)* at No 181 are longtime favourites in Kreuzberg. Both are good places to read a newspaper or have a chat, and are also popular with gays and lesbians.

Nearby is *Würgeengel (Map 5, ☎ 615 55 60, Dresdner Strasse 122)*. With its dramatic blood-red velvet walls, matching big plump sofas and unique tile and stucco ceiling it may look like a Belle Epoque brothel, but the cocktails have a killer reputation.

Still in Kreuzberg is the open-air *Golgatha (Map 3, ☎ 785 24 53, Dudenstrasse 48-64)*, in the Viktoriapark. It's been around for as long as we can remember and is still a comfortable, low-key place. You can dance in your Birkenstocks here, ya rascal.

Moving east to Mitte, *Broker's Bier Börse (Map 4, ☎ 282 39 65, Schiffbauerdamm 8)* is a unique beer hall where, after 5 pm, demand determines the drinks' prices, just like in a mini stock exchange. Sure, tourists love it, but it's fun nonetheless. *Café Silberstein (Map 4, ☎ 281 28 01, Oranienburger Strasse 27)* is an avantgarde bar with an artistic assortment of oversized metal chairs and crazy sculptures. The music is at talking level and there's sushi on the menu.

Obst und Gemüse (Map 4, ☎ 282 96 47), on the same street at No 48/49, gets its name from the fruit and vegetable shop that used to occupy the spot. It's packed to the rafters most nights and is self-service.

Lychener Strasse in Prenzlauer Berg is a happening street. At No 6 is *La Bodeguita del Medio (☎ 441 74 12)*, a clamorous Cuban-style watering hole with a multicultural crowd and an assortment of rum and tequila, plus tapas from DM6. *Weinstein (☎ 441 18 42)* across the street at No 33 is a snug wine bar with a more 'civilised' atmosphere. You can sample wines (from DM4.50) from around Germany.

Kommandatur (☎ 442 77 25, Knaackstrasse 20) is still trashy, crowded, smoky and loud. And they just keep coming back.

For something not quite so Germanically dark, try the Australian-themed *Uluru Resort (☎ 44 04 95 22, Rykestrasse 17)*, which often has live music and a boisterous, friendly atmosphere.

Cocktail Bars The popularity of cocktail bars has exploded in Berlin in recent years, despite comparatively high prices. In Mitte is *Pip's (Map 4, Auguststrasse 84)*, for a trip back to the 70s. It's friendly, comfortable and not overly pretentious. Cocktails start at DM11 (or DM8 before 9 pm Sunday to Thursday). *Jubinal (Map 4, ☎ 28 38 73 77)*, nearby on the corner of Auguststrasse and Tucholskystrasse, is a similarly happening spot with minimalist decor that's a bit off the tourist track. There's occasional jazz, and cocktails cost from DM13.

In Friedrichshain is the rather subdued *Dachkammer* (see Live Music), a good place to come for a chat and a good glass of wine in the upstairs bar.

Prenzlauer Berg has *X-Bar (☎ 443 49 04, Raumerstrasse 17)*, where you'd need wads of money and lots of stamina to drink yourself through the cocktail menu. There's a sushi bar in the back.

Places in the western districts are considerably more grown-up with prices to match. *Bar am Lützowplatz (Map 3, ☎ 262 68 09, Lützowplatz 7)* was named 'Best Bar in Germany' in 1994 and it's still pouring it on, so to speak. Not to be outdone in the accolade department, *Harry's New York Bar (Map 3, ☎ 254 78 21, Lützowufer 15)*, inside the Hotel Esplanade, was voted 'Bar of 1996' by *Playboy* magazine. Both places are rather snooty and pricey (cocktails from DM16 to DM25).

Still chic, but without the suit and tie clientele, are these trendy bars in Schöneberg: *Mister Hu (Map 3, ☎ 217 21 11, Goltzstrasse 39)*, the *Zoulou Bar (Map 3, ☎ 784 68 94, Hauptstrasse 4)* and *N.N. (Map 3, ☎ 787 50 33, Hauptstrasse 159)*.

Berliner Kneipen Traditional Berlin pubs have their own style of hospitality – rustic, simple food, beer, humour and Schlagfertigkeit (quick-wittedness). As Berlin becomes more cosmopolitan, these places become a dying breed, but a few still survive. In Charlottenburg is *Dicke Wirtin (Map 6, ☎ 312 49 52, Carmerstrasse 9)*, an earthy pub with four daily stews for under DM6 and six varieties of beer on draft from DM4.50. It's popular with locals and students.

Stories abound about historic *Zur letzten Instanz (The Final Authority; Map 4, ☎ 242 55 28, Waisenstrasse 14)* in Mitte. It got its name 150 years ago, we are told, when a newly divorced couple came in from the nearby courthouse. By the time they were well oiled and ready to leave, they'd decided to remarry – at which one of those present exclaimed, 'This is the court of final authority!' (There's no final word on the couple's fate.) Another historic place is *Zum Nussbaum* (see Places to Eat).

E&M Leydicke (☎ 216 29 73, *Manstein-strasse 4*) in Schöneberg is another ancient Berlin pub (founded in 1877) which bottles its own flavoured schnapps and fruit wines on the premises.

Classical Music

The *Berliner Philharmonie (Map 3, ☎ 25 48 81 32, Herbert-Von-Karajan-Strasse 1)* is justly famous and has supreme acoustics; try to hear a concert here. Tickets cost from DM24 to DM78 and all seats are excellent, so just take the cheapest. Another treat is a concert at the lavish *Konzerthaus (Map 4, ☎ 203 09 21 01)*, on Gendarmenmarkt in Mitte, home to the renowned Berlin Symphony Orchestra. Tickets range from DM10 (standing) to DM75. The concert hall at the *Hochschule der Künste (College of Arts; Map 6, ☎ 31 85 23 74, Hardenbergstrasse 33)* is also busy in season.

Organ and other concerts are held in many of the city's churches, museums and other venues, including the *Marienkirche (Map 4)* on Karl-Liebknecht-Strasse in Mitte; *St Matthäus Kirche (Map 3)* at the Kulturforum in Tiergarten; the *Berliner Dom (Map 4)* on Museumsinsel; and the *Eosander Chapel* of Charlottenburg Palace.

Opera

The *Staatsoper Unter den Linden (Map 4, ☎ 208 28 61, Unter den Linden 5-7)* in Mitte hosts lavish productions with international talent under the stewardship of renowned Daniel Barenboim, who places much emphasis on Wagner and pre-Mozart operas. In Charlottenburg, you'll find the *Deutsche Oper (☎ 341 02 49, Bismarck-strasse 35)*, a glass and steel behemoth (1961). Classical works of predominantly

Italian and French composers (Verdi, Puccini, Bizet, Massenet, to name a few) feature largely in program schedules, as do contemporary composers. Productions at both are sung in the original language.

Back in Mitte is the *Komische Oper (Map 4, ☎ 20 26 03 60, Behrenstrasse 55-57)*, with classic opera and operetta. The box office is at Unter den Linden 41. The company popularises the opera, making it accessible through lively productions of light-hearted works performed in a theatrical way. All productions are sung in German.

Theatre

Berlin has more than 100 theatres, so there should be something for everybody. In the former eastern section, they cluster around Friedrichstrasse; in the western part of the city they are concentrated around Ku'damm. Many theatres are closed on Monday and from mid-July to late August.

Good seats are usually available on the evening of a performance, as unclaimed tickets are sold an hour before curtain time, sometimes at steep discounts.

Half-price theatre tickets are also available from Hekticket on the day of performance. Branches are on the ground floor in the Zoo Palast cinema at Hardenbergstrasse 29a (Map 6) and at Liebknechtstrasse 12 (Map 4), near Alexanderplatz (both ☎ 24 31 24 31 or ☎ 230 99 30). Choices are obviously limited to what's left unsold that day. Sales commence at 2 pm daily; tickets must be bought and paid for in person at the office but will actually be waiting for you at the venue.

We've listed here a cross-section of mainstream and off-theatre venues. Also check the listings in city magazines and newspapers for other (mostly smaller, experimental) theatres. Berlin's not stuffy, so you can attend theatre and cultural events dressed as you please.

Theater des Westens (Map 6, ☎ 882 28 88, Kantstrasse 12) in Charlottenburg has a varied program of theatre and musicals. Though this beautiful old theatre (1896) has style and often features excellent musicals, it's hard to see much from the cheapest seats.

Productions at nearby *Renaissance-Theater Berlin (Map 6, ☎ 312 42 02, Hardenbergstrasse 6)* have included obscure Brecht fragments but also light drama. It's usually interesting, no matter what's on.

In former East Berlin is the *Deutsches Theater (Map 4, ☎ 28 44 12 25, Schumannstrasse 13a)*, the centre of Berlin theatre life before World War II. Productions are usually top quality and range from classical to avant-garde. Nearby, the *Berliner Ensemble (Map 4, ☎ 282 31 60, Bertolt-Brecht-Platz 1)* is Brecht's original theatre and worth visiting for its architecture and the musical interludes alone. Not everything playing here is by Brecht.

The *Maxim Gorki Theater (Map 4, ☎ 20 22 11 15)* on Festungsgraben offers an interesting array of productions, from works by 20th century Russian and Eastern European playwrights to Harold Pinter and Tennessee Williams.

Nonconformist and radical, cutting-edge and provocative are the maximes of the *Volksbühne (Map 4, ☎ 24 06 56 61)* on Rosa-Luxemburg-Platz. Performances are not for tender souls.

If you don't speak German, you might enjoy a show by the misleadingly named *Friends of Italian Opera (Map 3, ☎ 693 56 92, Fidicinstrasse 40)* in Kreuzberg, which is Berlin's only English-language ensemble.

Cabaret & Varieté

Many venues are trying to revive the lively and lavish variety shows of the golden 1920s in Berlin. Programs include dancers and singers, jugglers, acrobats and other entertainers who each perform a short number. These 'cabarets' should not be confused with another form of entertainment called '*Kabarett*', which are political and satirical shows featuring a team of *Kabarettisten* in a series of monologues or short skits (see Music in the Facts about Germany chapter). They can be hilarious, though you should have passable skills in German to truly appreciate them. But the visual and sound extravaganzas listed here are understandable to anyone:

In Mitte, *Friedrichstadtpalast (Map 4, ☎ 23 26 24 74, Friedrichstrasse 107)* offers musical revues on a ritzy scale with an evening and a night show.

Variety shows at the intimate *Chamäleon Varieté (Map 4, ☎ 282 71 18, Hackesche Höfe)* include the usual comedy, juggling acts and singing but it's all put together in an unconventional and entertaining way. On Friday and Saturday there's a midnight show as well as one at 8.30 pm (closed Monday).

Tickets are hot at cool *Wintergarten-Das Varieté (Map 3, ☎ 261 60 60, ☎ 23 08 82 30, Potsdamer Strasse 96)*, which has a 1920s-style cabaret-variety show updated for the new millennium. Programs change every few months and vary in quality, but are worth checking out.

Bar jeder Vernunft (☎ 883 15 82, Schaperstrasse 24), in Wilmersdorf behind the car park, is a smallish venue, a tent in fact, bathed in red and mirrors where you sit at small tables or in *separeés* (niches). On weekdays, it becomes a piano bar after the show. Programs often have an experimental and/or bizarre character.

Cultural Centres

Podewil (Map 4, ☎ 24 74 96, Klosterstrasse 68-70) in Mitte offers a mixed bag of film, theatre and live music as well as a cafe, in a 1704 building. In fine weather, the beer garden is open to 9.30 pm.

An adventure playground for adults is *Tacheles (Map 4, ☎ 282 61 85, Oranienburger Strasse 54-56)*, in a dilapidated, graffiti-covered building. Before the war it was a Jewish-owned department store and was later left to crumble by the East Berlin authorities. Its post-atomic look belies its active cultural program that includes dance, jazz concerts, the Café Camera, cabaret, readings, workshops, artist studios and galleries and a theatre. Its Gartenhaus club and beer garden is great in summer.

Another multimedia culture club, though a bit tamer, is the *UFA-Fabrik (☎ 75 50 30, Viktoriastrasse 10-18)*, in the former UFA film studios in Tempelhof (U6 to Ullsteinstrasse). The hot spot in Prenzlauer Berg is

Life is a Cabaret

No other form of entertainment is so strongly associated with Berlin as cabaret – and not just since the Liza Minelli movie of that name. Cabaret catapulted to its heyday in the 'Golden Twenties', and at one point there were as many as 167 such theatres in Berlin. Night after night, each offered their own unique blend of singers, show girls, jugglers, magicians and other artists, many of whom had broken away from the circus.

MICK WELDON

The political and social circumstances of the 1920s proved to be rich nourishment for cabaret. Official censorship had only been lifted at the end of WWI and artists were quick to capitalise on their new freedoms. They could flaunt opinions that previously would have been treated as seditious, or worse. Satirising the politics of the day became popular, especially since politicians provided fodder through corruption scandals and other misdeeds.

The extreme inflation that had shaken Germany until late 1923 had made people rather fatalistic and drove them to party as though there were no tomorrow. The arrival of new music – especially jazz (or *yatz*, as it was called here) – further loosened libidos and earned Berlin a reputation for casual sex and 'perversion' on a grand scale.

Since the *Wende*, Berlin cabaret has had a renaissance. But those expecting encounters with Christopher Isherwood's world of lurid delights and amoral dalliances will be largely disappointed. Berlin's contemporary cabaret offerings reflect little of the raw sexuality that raged in those times. In many venues, you're more likely to encounter the *Pirates of Penzance* than an opium-besotted androgyne. Even the drag queen spectacles have become as respectable as church deacons. And in places such as the Wintergarten you'll find carefully choreographed, top-Deutschmark spectacles for the tourist market.

A walk along Kurfürstendamm may yet put you in mind of Berlin's gloriously tawdry past. At the former Wild Stage club in the basement of the Theater des Westens a still unknown Bertolt Brecht was forced off the stage while reciting one of his provocative poems. And it was also here where the scandalous Josephine Baker delighted audiences with her Banana Dance, wearing only ... guess what? A young future film director named Billy Wilder made a living by dancing with rich unescorted women. And Marlene Dietrich draped herself across a piano, looking out from behind heavily lidded eyes with a sexual challenge that the rest of the world wasn't yet ready for.

the **Kulturbrauerei** (☎ 441 92 69, Knaackstrasse 97), which was being developed into a mega-complex at the time of writing.

Nearby is the more alternative **Pfefferberg** (☎ 449 65 34, Schönhauser Allee 176), whose particular strength lies in promoting cross-cultural projects with events featuring ska and reggae; there's a gorgeous beer garden as well.

Gay Berlin

If you're reading this, you probably don't need to be told that Berlin is about the gayest city in Europe. Christopher Isherwood wrote in his autobiography *Christopher and his Kind* (covering 1929 to 1939) that Berlin meant boys and, for some of us, it still does – but nowadays it's spelt 'boyz'. It's estimated that up to 500,000 gays and lesbians call Berlin home; the numbers were augmented mostly by Ossies after the Wende, since East Berlin was the only place in the GDR where you could have any semblance of a lifestyle.

Anything goes in today's gay Berlin – and we mean *anything* – so please take the usual precautions. Discos and clubs are everywhere but don't really get going till about midnight. Before clubbing you can eat at a gay-owned and/or operated restaurant and nurse a drink at one of the dozens of gay cafes and bars. For listings check the gay and lesbian freebie *Siegessäule* or the strictly gay *Sergej Szene Berlin. Zitty* and *O30* also have listings. If you require even more information and listings than we or they are able to provide, get a copy of the bilingual *Berlin von Hinten* (Berlin from Behind; Bruno Gmünder Versand) for DM19.80. You can also seek advice and information from Mann-O-Meter (☎ 216 80 08) at Motzstrasse 5 in Schöneberg.

The main gay areas in Berlin are: around Nollendorfplatz in Schöneberg (Map 3); Oranienstrasse in Kreuzberg 36 (Map 5; U15 to Görlitzer Bahnhof); and Prenzlauer Berg, particularly around Gleimstrasse (U2 to Schönhauser Allee).

Around Nollendorfplatz Isherwood lived right in the thick of things at Nollendorf-

strasse 17, so who are we to question tradition? **Hafen** (Map 3, ☎ 214 11 18, Motzstrasse 19) is full of guppies fortifying themselves before they move on to (some say sneak into) **Tom's Bar** (Map 3, ☎ 213 45 70) next door, with its cavernous and very dark and active cellar. Hafen opens at 8 pm, Tom's at 10 pm (but if you're OFB – out for business – don't get to the latter before midnight). **Connection** (Map 3, ☎ 218 14 32, Fuggerstrasse 33) is arguably the best gay disco in town (DM10, first drink free) and has a huge darkroom. **Andreas Kneipe** (Map 3, ☎ 218 32 57, Ansbacher Strasse 29) is a good place to start the evening; it's a convivial pub with lots of locals and lots of cruising.

Kreuzberg 36 *Roses* (Map 5, ☎ 615 75 70, Oranienstrasse 187) has an over-the-top baroque, queeny decor. **Cafe Anal** (Map 5, ☎ 618 17 64, Muskauer Strasse 15), a gay and lesbian Berlin fixture, is an artsy-fartsy cafe and very low-key. Thursday nights are gay nights at the **KitKat Club** (Map 5, ☎ 611 38 33, Glogauer Strasse 2). **SO36** has a gay-lesbian party every Wednesday (also see Discos & Clubs earlier). Across the Oberbaum Bridge is **Die Busche** (☎ 589 15 85, Mühlenstrasse 11-12), the biggest gay place in eastern Berlin and a meat market popular, they say, with hairdressers.

Prenzlauer Berg *Schall und Rauch* (☎ 448 07 70, Gleimstrasse 23) has designer prices and attracts a 'young and beautiful' crowd. We came and we went. It's open daily to 3 am. **Café Amsterdam** (☎ 448 07 92), at No 24, is much more down-to-earth (we stayed) and is open to 6 am on the weekend. The ever-changing DJs here play great music.

Saunas Berlin has about a half-dozen gay saunas but one of the biggest, cleanest and most active is **Gate Sauna** (Map 4, ☎ 229 94 30, Wilhelmstrasse 81) in Mitte. It's open weekdays from 11 am to 7 am and nonstop over the weekends. Also popular is the **Apollo Sauna** (Map 6, ☎ 213 24 24, Kurfürstenstrasse 101), a traditional gay sauna with steam rooms, cruising hallways and cabins. It's famous for its Slivovitz sauna infusions and open daily from 1 pm to 7 am. Lockers at either cost from DM19 to DM27 (cabins an extra DM8 or DM10).

Lesbian Berlin

The Lesbenberatung (Lesbian Advice Centre; ☎ 215 20 00) is at Kulmer Strasse 20a in Schöneberg and holds discussions on issues like discrimination and safe sex. It's open from Monday to Thursday from 4 to 8 pm. Women's centres include EWA (☎ 442 55 42), Prenzlauer Allee 6, in Prenzlauer Berg and Frieda (☎ 442 42 76), Proskauer Strasse 7, in Friedrichshain.

The oldest lesbian bar-club (1973) in the city is the timelessly plush *Pour Elle (Map 3, ☎ 218 75 33, Kalckreuthstrasse 10)* in Schöneberg. Open daily from 9 to 5 am, it's popular with well-off lesbians over 35.

Begine (Map 3, ☎ 215 43 25, Potsdamer Strasse 139) is a warm cafe and culture centre for women, primarily lesbians. The program includes concerts, readings, films and songs.

Schoko Café (Map 5, ☎ 615 15 61, Mariannenstrasse 6) in Kreuzberg 36 (above the Turkish hammam) is a convivial meeting point with a good cake selection. *SO36* (see Discos & Clubs) goes gay-lesbian every Wednesday and the Jane Bond evening for women, lesbians and drag queens gets down on the 3rd Friday of the month.

SPECTATOR SPORTS

Berlin's football (soccer) club Hertha BSC plays in the Bundesliga and has had its ups and downs (though more ups lately). Seats at home games at the Olympic Stadium usually cost from DM12 to DM56. Call ☎ 300 92 80 for tickets.

Berlin's basketball team, ALBA, is a European-class team which won the German championship in the 1996/97 season. It plays in the Max-Schmeling-Halle (☎ 44 30 44 30 for tickets).

Berlin has three racecourses: Galopprennbahn Hoppegarten (☎ 03342-389 30) is at Goetheallee 1 in Dahlwitz-Hoppegarten, north-east of the city; Trabrennbann Karls-

horst (☎ 50 01 70) in Lichtenberg; and Trabrennbahn Mariendorf (☎ 740 10) at Mariendorfer Damm 222, Tempelhof.

The German Open is a women's ATP (Association of Tennis Professionals) tournament held every May at the Rot-Weiss Berlin tennis club in the Grunewald forest near the Hundekehlesee lake. It usually attracts high-ranking players and has been won by Steffi Graf umpteen times. Tickets cost from DM46 to DM115 (bookings ☎ 89 57 55 20, ☎ 89 57 55 21)

The Berlin Marathon is held in late September, the same month as the ISTAF, an international track & field meet.

SHOPPING

Berlin's decentralised character is also reflected in its lack of a clearly defined shopping artery like London's Oxford Street or New York's Fifth Avenue. Rather, you'll find numerous shopping areas in the various neighbourhoods, many of which have a localised feel. The closest Berlin gets to having an international shopping flair is in the area along Kurfürstendamm and its extension, Tauentzienstrasse, though Friedrichstrasse in Mitte is up and coming.

A good source of hip stores is *The Art of Shopping*, an annual booklet available in bookshops and some stores.

Department Stores & Malls

A couple of Berlin's most famous department stores hold forth on Ku'damm and Tauentzienstrasse. The famous KaDeWe (Kaufhaus des Westens; Map 6, ☎ 212 10), Tauentzienstrasse 21, is an amazing, seven-floor department store selling just about everything. Not far behind in terms of assortment, but with lower prices, is Wertheim (Map 6, ☎ 88 20 61), Kurfürstendamm 231.

The French chain Galeries Lafayette (Map 4, ☎ 20 94 80) has opened an outlet on Friedrichstrasse (U6 to Französische Strasse). It's part of the Friedrichstadt-Passagen, a chic indoor shopping complex that's more interesting for its architecture than for its expensive designer stores.

An excellent new place is Potsdamer Platz Arkaden, a stylish indoor mall with lots of neat boutiques, bookshops, supermarkets and fast-food restaurants. It has mostly mid-priced stuff.

Galleries

Berlin has about 300 private galleries holding forth in courtyards, stately patrician villas, old warehouses or factories or in spacious, elegant collections of rooms on major boulevards. They used to be concentrated along Ku'damm and Fasanenstrasse, but the more cutting-edge studios and galleries are in now in Mitte (Map 4), especially along Auguststrasse and in and around the Hackesche Höfe and Sophienhöfe.

For a complete and up-to-date overview, pick up a copy of *Berlin Artery – Der Kunstführer* (DM3.50) available at newsstands, bookstores and some museums.

Camping & Outdoors

For outdoor, expedition and camping gear, have a look at the range of Der Aussteiger (☎ 441 04 14), Schliemannstrasse 46, in Prenzlauer Berg and compare it with Bannat (☎ 882 76 01), Lietzenburger 65 (corner of Fasanenstrasse), in Wilmersdorf.

One of the best-known and largest stores is Globetrotter Ausrüstungen (☎ 850 89 20) at Bundesallee 88 in Friedenau (U9 to Walter-Schreiber-Strasse). Camp 4 (☎ 242 66 34), Dircksenstrasse 78, in Mitte has shoes, sleeping bags, tents, backpacks and more (U8 or S-Bahn to Jannowitzbrücke).

Second-Hand Clothing

You'll find several stores with funky preworn attire along Maassenstrasse and Goltzstrasse in Schöneberg, including Razzo (☎ 252 23 95), Goltzstrasse 32, and Megadress Berlin at No 13. A few blocks north, at Ahornstrasse 2, is Garage (Map 3, ☎ 211 27 60), where you buy by weight, with 1kg costing DM25. Much of it is tattered or soiled, though. Also in Schöneberg is Made in Berlin (Map 3, ☎ 262 24 31) at Potsdamer Strasse 106, which is a little more upmarket.

In Kreuzberg 61 are the crammed Checkpoint (Map 3, ☎ 694 43 44), Mehringdamm 57, and the big Colours (Map 3, ☎ 694 33 48) in the backyard at Bergmannstrasse 102 (on the 1st floor).

Humana is a chain of thrift shops with branches throughout town, including a big central one at Joachimsthaler Strasse across from Zoo station (Map 6) and a four-storey one at Frankfurter Tor (☎ 422 20 18; U5 to Petersburger Strasse), on the corner of Karl-Marx-Allee, east of Alexanderplatz.

For superb gowns and cocktail dresses from the 1950s to the 1980s, visit Sterling Gold, with branches at Paul-Lincke-Ufer 44 in Kreuzberg 36 (☎ 611 32 17) and inside the Heckmann-Höfe (Map 4), off Oranienburger Strasse 32, in Mitte (☎ 28 09 65 00). It's not cheap, but there is classy, well preserved stuff.

Flea & Antique Markets

Berlin's many flea markets are treasure troves of unique memorabilia, typical Berlin curiosities, bric-a-brac, antiques, eccentric clothing and simply cheap used stuff. Bargaining is definitely encouraged and, depending on your skills, you should be able to get between 10 and 50% off the asking price. As a general rule, offer half, then settle somewhere in between. Following is a list of regular markets:

Grosser Berliner Trödel- und Kunstmarkt (Big Berlin Junk & Art Market; Map 3) On Strasse des 17 Juni just west of the S-Bahn stop Tiergarten, this market is popular with tourists and expensive but fun to browse; it's open weekends from 8 am to 5 pm.

Berliner Kunst- und Nostalgiemarkt (Berlin's Art and Nostalgia Market, Map 4) On Am Kupfergraben at the north-eastern tip of Museumsinsel, this flea market has collectibles, books, ethnic crafts and GDR memorabilia (not always authentic); It's open weekends from 8 am to 5 pm (take bus No 100 to Lustgarten, then a few minutes' walk north; or U/S-Bahn station Friedrichstrasse, then a 10 minute walk east along Georgenstrasse).

Flohmarkt am Arkonaplatz This flea market is in Mitte on Arkonaplatz (U8 to Bernauer Strasse) and has 1950s collectibles and more; it's open Sunday from 10 am to 4 pm.

BERLIN

Flohmarkt Spandau
On Askanierring between Flankenschanze and Falkenseer Chaussee, this flea market has lots of private vendors, meaning prices are fairly low; it's open weekends from 8 am to 4 pm (U7 to Rathaus Spandau).

GETTING THERE & AWAY
Air
Berlin has three airports with Tegel (TXL; ☎ 410 11), about 8km north-west of Zoo station, primarily serving destinations within Germany, Europe and to North America. There's a luggage-storage office (open from 5.30 am to 10 pm), a BTM tourist information counter, a post office and a bank in the main hall.

Schönefeld (SXF; ☎ 60 91 51 12), some 22km from Zoo station, primarily operates international flights to/from Europe, Asia, Africa and Central America.

Berlin-Tempelhof (THF; ☎ 695 11), 6km south of the centre, is the main hub for domestic departures and flights within Central Europe.

The Lufthansa City Centre (Map 6, ☎ 88 75 38 00) is located at Kurfürstendamm 220. The 24-hour central reservation number is ☎ 0180-380 38 03. The Lufthansa number at Tegel airport is ☎ 88 75 61 27. Contact numbers for other airlines serving Berlin airports include:

Aeroflot
 ☎ 226 98 10
Air Canada
 ☎ 882 58 79
Air France
 ☎ 01805-36 03 70
British Airways/Deutsche BA
 ☎ 41 01 26 47
Delta Air Lines
 ☎ 0180-333 78 80
El Al Israel Airlines
 ☎ 201 77 90
KLM-Royal Dutch Airlines
 ☎ 01805-21 42 01, ☎ 41 01 38 44
LOT Polish Airlines
 ☎ 261 15 05
MALEV-Hungarian Airlines
 ☎ 264 95 45
Swissair
 ☎ 01805-25 85 75

Train
With the completion date for the futuristic Lehrter Bahnhof pushed back well into this decade, the bulk of train travel will continue to be borne by a few major stations, notably Bahnhof Zoo in the west and Ostbahnhof in the east. Many long-distance trains stop at both. Depending on your final destination, you may find that services arriving at one station link with services leaving from another. To connect, take the U-Bahn or S-Bahn (DM2.50 or DM3.90, depending on the distance), but allow ample time.

Conventional train tickets to/from Berlin are valid for all train stations on the city S-Bahn, which means that on arrival you can use the S-Bahn network (but not the U-Bahn) to connect or get to your destination. Conversely, you can use the S-Bahn to go to the station from where your train leaves for another city, if you have a booked ticket. Rail passes are also valid on the S-Bahn.

Bahnhof Zoologischer Garten More commonly known as Bahnhof Zoo, or Zoo station, this is the main station in the west for long-distance trains to cities including Hanover, Frankfurt and Cologne, as well as Paris, Amsterdam and Brussels. There are also frequent services to Hamburg and Munich and a direct train to Leipzig. The station has been renovated and has many shops and restaurants with extended hours.

The big Deutsche Bahn (DB) Reisezentrum (reservation and information office) is open from 5.15 am to 11 pm and offers quick service. Outside the main entrance on Hardenbergplatz is the BVG local transport information kiosk (Map 6), where you can get maps, information and tickets. Downstairs near the lockers is a spic-and-span place called McClean where a shower costs DM10.

Practically next door to McClean is the EurAide Office, a one-stop service for English-speaking travellers. Staff can help with buying the right train ticket, making a seat reservation or finding a place to stay. EurAide is open daily from 8 am to noon and 1 to 4.30 pm.

Other Train Stations After renovation, the Hauptbahnhof in eastern Berlin was renamed Ostbahnhof. Most long-distance trains (ICE, IC and IR) from the western parts of Germany (Hamburg, Cologne, Munich) that stop at Zoo station also stop here. It also handles regional services around Brandenburg, Saxony and, less so, around Mecklenburg-Western Pomerania.

Berlin's other main station is Bahnhof Lichtenberg on Weitlingstrasse in Lichtenberg, which is the hub for trains to Stralsund, Rostock and other cities in Mecklenburg-Pomerania, as well as Cottbus, Dresden, Erfurt, Halle, Magdeburg, Vienna, Moscow, Prague and Budapest.

Bus

The Zentraler Omnibus Busbahnhof (ZOB; Central Bus Station), Masurenallee 4-6, in Charlottenburg is opposite the spindly Funkturm radio tower (U2 to Kaiserdamm or S-Bahn No 45 to Witzleben). It is open from 5.30 am to 10 pm. The Reisebüro ZOB (☎ 301 80 28 for information, ☎ 302 52 94 for reservations) is open daily from 9 am to 6 pm (though tickets are available from many travel agencies and also Mitfahrzentralen in Berlin).

Several bus lines operate at ZOB, with services within Germany and abroad. The main lines are BerlinLinienBus and Gulliver's.

BerlinLinienBus (outside of Berlin, call toll-free ☎ 0800 666 69 99 or within Berlin ☎ 86 09 60) runs daily buses between Berlin and Munich (nine hours) via Leipzig, Bayreuth, Nuremberg and Ingolstadt. One way/return SuperSpar tickets, for passengers under 26 or over 60, cost DM76/139, while full-fare tickets are DM129/149. The Web page is at www.berlinlinienbus.de.

Gulliver's (☎ 311 02 11), which has SleeperSeats (practically full beds) on some of its routes for DM10 to DM40 extra, offers discounts to students, under 26s and over 60s and will transport a bike for DM50/80 one way/return.

Car & Motorcycle

The A10 ring road around the city links Berlin with other German and foreign cities, including the A11 to Szczecin (Stettin) in Poland; the A12 to Frankfurt an der Oder; the A13 to Dresden; the A9 to Leipzig, Nuremberg and Munich; the A2 to Hanover and the Ruhrgebiet cities; and the A24 to Hamburg.

Ride Services Berlin has several *Mitfahrzentrale* agencies, which charge a fixed amount payable to the driver plus commission, ranging from DM7 for short distances to DM20 for longer trips. Generally, a ride to Leipzig costs DM20, Frankfurt-am-Main is DM51, Munich DM56, Cologne DM50, Budapest DM95 and Paris DM89 (including commission).

One central agency is ADM Mitfahrzentrale (☎ 194 40) in Bahnhof Zoo on the Vinetastrasse platform of the U2. It is open weekdays from 9 am to 8 pm and weekends from 10 am to 6 pm. There's a second branch (☎ 241 58 20) in U-Bahn station Alexanderplatz, as you cross from U2 to U8, that's open weekdays from 10 am to 6 pm (Thursday to 8 pm) and weekends from 11 am to 4 pm.

The CityNetz Mitfahr-Zentralen have an office in the Kurfürstendamm U-Bahn station (☎ 882 76 04) and at Bergmannstrasse 57 near Südstern U-Bahn station (☎ 693 60 95). There's also a central number, ☎ 194 44, which can be called daily from 8 am to 8 pm.

Other agencies include the Mitfahrzentrale Prenzlauer Berg (☎ 448 42 75) at Oderberger Strasse 45 and the Mitfahrzentrale Berlin für Lesben und Schwule (☎ 216 40 20), at Yorckstrasse 52, which caters primarily for gays and lesbians.

The people answering the phone in these offices usually speak English well. If you arrange a ride a few days in advance, be sure to call the driver the night before and again on departure morning to make sure they're still going.

Hitching

Lonely Planet does not encourage hitchhiking for all the obvious reasons. In Germany, it has also gone somewhat out of fashion;

BERLIN

there are fewer people trying and fewer willing to pick them up.

If you're headed for Leipzig, Nuremberg, Munich and beyond, head to the Dreilinden service area on the A115. Take either the U1 to Krumme Lanke, then bus No 211 to Quantzstrasse, then walk down to the rest area. Alternatively, take the S1 or S7 to Wannsee, then bus Nos 113 or 211 to the Isoldestrasse stop. Bring a sign showing your destination in German, and consider waiting until you find someone going to your exact destination. If you're going to Hamburg or Rostock, go to the former border checkpoint Stolpe by catching the U6 to Alt-Tegel and then catching bus No 224 to Stolpe.

GETTING AROUND
To/From the Airport
Berlin's three airports can all be reached by train and/or bus. For general information, call ☎ 0180-500 01 86.

Tegel (☎ 410 11) is connected by bus No 109 to Zoo station, via Kurfürstendamm and Luisenplatz. Express bus X9 goes to Lützowplatz at Kurfürstenstrasse via Budapester Strasse and Zoo station. The trip between the airport and the western city centre takes about 30 minutes. If you want to connect to a U-Bahn, take either line to Jakob-Kaiser-Platz to switch to the U7, or bus No 128 to Kurt-Schumacher-Platz to connect to the U6. The first-class express bus, TXL Bus, travels between Tegel and Potsdamer Platz/Unter den Linden in about 30 minutes. Fees are a steep DM9.90 but this gets you air-conditioning, free newspapers and a display screen with flight departure information. A taxi to/from Tegel costs about DM35.

Schönefeld airport (☎ 60 91 51 12) is served by the Airport Express train from Zoo station every half-hour from 4.30 am to 11 pm. The slower alternative is the S9, which runs from Zoo station via Alexanderplatz every 20 minutes between 4 am and midnight. The less frequent S45 links Schönefeld and Tempelhof airports. The S-Bahn station (also a main train station) is about 300m away from the terminal; they're connected by a free shuttle bus. Bus

No 171 links the terminal directly with the U-Bahn station Rudow (U7) with connections to central Berlin. A taxi between Schönefeld and Zoo station costs between DM50 and DM70.

Tempelhof airport (☎ 695 11) is served by the U6 (get off at Platz der Luftbrücke) and by bus No 119 from Kurfürstendamm via Kreuzberg. A taxi to/from Zoo station costs about DM30.

Public Transport
Berlin's public transport system is composed of services provided by Berliner Verkehrsbetriebe (BVG; ☎ 194 49, daily from 6 am to 11 pm) and Deutsche Bahn (DB; ☎ 194 19). The BVG operates the U-Bahn, buses, trams and ferries, while DB is in charge of suburban and regional trains like the S-Bahn, Regionalbahn (RB) and Regionalexpress (RE). One type of ticket is valid on all transport (with the few exceptions noted later). The system is fairly efficient but, given the extensive construction around town, delays and schedule changes may occur. For 24-hour up-to-date BVG route information call ☎ 25 62 25 62. For DB's service, dial ☎ 29 71 29 71.

The BVG kiosk on Hardenbergplatz in front of Zoo station (Map 6) has free route network maps and general information on buses, U-Bahns, trams and ferries. It's open daily from 8 am to 10 pm and also sell tickets and passes. For information on S-Bahn, RE and RB connections, visit the Reisezentrum office inside the station.

Tickets & Passes Berlin's metropolitan area is divided into three tariff zones – A, B and C. Tickets are valid in at least two zones, AB or BC, or in all three zones, ABC. Unless you're venturing to Potsdam or the very outer suburbs, you'll only need the AB ticket. Taking a bike in marked carriages of the S-Bahn or U-Bahn costs DM2.50. On U-Bahn carriages, bikes are allowed between 9 am and 2 pm and from 5.30 pm to closing time on weekdays (any time on weekends). Dogs and one piece of luggage are free. The most common types of tickets are:

Kurzstrecke (Short Trip)
This ticket (DM2.50) allows three stops on U-Bahn or S-Bahn, or six stops on bus or tram; one change is allowed, but only between trains (not bus to train or bus to bus).

Langstrecke (Long Trip)
For DM3.90 you get unlimited travel for two hours within two of the three zones (AB or BC) in any direction.

Ganzstrecke (Entire Route System)
You have unlimited travel for two hours in zones ABC (DM4.20).

Tageskarte (Day Pass)
This pass provides unlimited travel for one day (DM7.80 for zones AB or BC, or DM8.50 for zones ABC).

7-Tage Karte (Seven-Day Pass)
This transferable pass allows unlimited travel for a week after validation (DM40 for zones AB, DM42 for zones BC and DM48 for zones ABC).

Buying & Using Tickets Bus drivers sell single and day tickets, but tickets for U/S-Bahn trains and other multiple, weekly or monthly tickets must be purchased in advance. Most are available from the orange vending machines (with instructions in English) in U/S-Bahn stations, as well as from the ticket window at station entrances and the BVG information kiosk.

Tickets must be stamped (validated) in a red machine *Entwerter* at the platform entrances to S-Bahn and U-Bahn stations or at bus stops before boarding. If you're using a timed ticket like the Langstrecke, validate it just as your train arrives to ensure full value. If you're caught by an inspector without a ticket (or even an unvalidated one), there's a DM60 fine.

Buses & Trams These are rather slow, although they offer a mighty fine – and inexpensive – way of sightseeing while comfortably ensconced on the upper level of a double-decker. Bus No 199 is a popular route – from Grunewald to Platz der Luftbrücke via the Ku'damm and Kreuzberg. An even better option is bus No 100 (see

Seeing Berlin From Bus No 100

Perhaps the best – and certainly the cheapest – way to get to know Berlin on the quick is a tour on the double-decker city bus No 100. Shuttling between Zoo station and Prenzlauer Berg, it passes by nearly every major sight in the city. And all you need is a DM3.90 bus ticket, which even allows you to get off and on as often as you like within the two hours of its validity. Since there's no commentary, it's a good idea to pick up a map and information leaflet from the BVG information kiosk outside Zoo station. This is also the ideal place to board, especially if you want to garner a coveted front window seat with panoramic views.

The first sight you see after the bus leaves Zoo station is the landmark Gedächtniskirche (Memorial Church) and the beginning of the Ku'damm before reaching the famous Zoological Garden. From here, the bus hooks north into the Tiergarten where you'll pass by the triumphant golden figure atop the Victory Column. Look quickly right as the bus crosses the Strasse des 17 Juni and you'll spot the Brandenburg Gate down the broad boulevard. Your next stop is Schloss Bellevue, the Berlin residence of Germany's president. The bus then follows streets paralleling the Spree river before passing the Reichstag. Soon after, it'll drive right through Brandenburg Gate, a privilege given only to taxis and city buses.

Now you're in former East Berlin and heading down Unter den Linden, passing the Berliner Dom and Humboldt University. Then you'll reach Alexanderplatz with its monster TV tower and, a few minutes later, you'll arrive at the bus' eastern terminus near Europe's largest Jewish cemetery. If you don't interrupt your trip, the one-way journey takes about 45 minutes (more during heavy traffic), which should give you enough sightseeing ideas to last at least a week.

the boxed text 'Seeing Berlin From Bus No 100').

Bus stops are marked with a large 'H' (for *Haltestelle*) and the name of the stop. Drivers sell tickets and can give change. The next stop is usually announced via a loudspeaker or displayed on a digital board. Push the button on the handrails if you want to get off.

Nightbus lines take over from the U/S-Bahn between 1 and 4 am, running roughly at 30-minute intervals. Buses leave from the major nightlife areas like Zoo station, Hackescher Markt in Mitte and Nollendorfplatz in Schöneberg and cover the entire Berlin area. Normal fares apply.

Trams only operate in the eastern districts.

U-Bahn/S-Bahn The most efficient way to travel around Berlin is by U-Bahn or S-Bahn. There are 10 U-Bahn and 13 S-Bahn lines which operate from 4 am until just after midnight. Exceptions are the U1 and the U9 which operate all night on a limited service (about two trains an hour). Most S-Bahns operate hourly on Saturday and Sunday between midnight and 4 am. Rail pass holders can use the S-Bahn for free.

The next station (including an *Übergang*, or transfer point) is announced on most U-Bahn (but not S-Bahn) trains and is also displayed at the end of carriages on some newer trains. It's best, though, to know the name of the station before you get to the one you need. To help you do this, large route maps are plastered on the ceilings above the doors in most U-Bahn cars. Large versions of the same maps are on station platforms.

Regional Trains The S-Bahn network is supplemented by the RB and RE, whose routes are also marked on the BVG network map. Only BVG Ganzstrecke and DB rail tickets (including rail passes) are valid on these routes.

Ferries The BVG operates several ferry services but you're only likely to need the F10 which shuttles between Kladow and Wannsee. The trip in itself is quite scenic and, since regular BVG tickets apply, makes for an inexpensive excursion. Ferries operate hourly all year, weather permitting.

Car & Motorcycle

Berlin is probably easier to drive around than many other big cities in Europe, but you will still run into roadworks in the eastern parts for some time yet. The A10 ring road gets you easily around the urban perimeter.

Parking in garages is expensive (about DM2 to DM3 per hour), but it'll often be your only choice if you want to be near the main shopping areas or attractions. Parking meters are rare but the 'pay and display' system is quite widespread. Free street parking, while impossible to find in these central areas, is usually available in residential streets, especially in the eastern districts. Watch out for signs indicating parking restrictions or you risk a ticket or even being towed.

Car Rental All the major international car-rental chains are represented in Berlin. Their lowest standard rates begin at around DM99 daily and between DM400 and DM500 weekly, including VAT and unlimited kilometres. The best deals are special weekend tariffs, in effect from Friday at noon to Monday 9 am, from DM120. Some arrangements also include collision insurance, which can save you up to DM40 a day. You must be at least 21 to rent from most agencies.

International agencies on and around Budapester Strasse near Zoo station are Hertz (☎ 261 10 53) at No 39, Avis (☎ 23 09 37 0) next door, SixtBudget (☎ 261 13 57) at No 18, and EuropCar (☎ 235 06 40) at Kurfürstenstrasse 101-104. For other branches and agencies, check the Yellow Pages under *Autovermietung*. A cheaper local agency is Robben und Wientjes with several branches, including one in Kreuzberg at Prinzenstrasse 90/91 (☎ 61 67 70).

We found that, with few exceptions, the best rates are usually available through a US-based company called AutoEurope. They have negotiated low rates and excellent conditions with all the major agencies. Reservations are made 24 hours via a toll-free number with an English-speaking operator. Cars are available in all sizes and categories, and there's no surcharge for one-way rentals or airport drop-offs. There's also no charge for cancellations or changes, and the minimum rental age is 19. They even let you travel into Poland and the Czech Republic if you tell them at the time of booking, though there is an extra charge. There is, however, a three-day minimum rental (but no penalty for turning it in early).

If you need a car and you're already in Germany, dial ☎ 0130-82 21 98. From North America, it's ☎ 800-223-5555; from Australia ☎ 1-800-12 64 09; from New Zealand ☎ 0800-44 07 22; from France it's ☎ 0800-90 17 70; and from Britain you can call ☎ 0800-89 98 93.

A small economy car will cost you around US$70 for the three-day minimum and US$110 for the weekly rental, which includes unlimited kilometres, VAT and third-party insurance but not collision insurance. If this is not covered by your credit card, you have to add up to US$15 per day to your rate. Even then, you'll probably spend less than when renting directly from a local agency.

Motorcycle Rental American Bike Rent (☎ 03301-701 55 5) is located at Magnus-Hirschfeld-Strasse 26, north of Berlin in Lehnitz (S1 to Lehnitz). Twenty-four hour/weekend rates for Harley-Davidsons range from DM139/163 to DM168/176 and the first 90km are free. The seven-day rates, including the first 720km, are DM815 to DM985. There is a deposit of DM1500 on cash rentals. It's open April to October on weekdays from 2 to 7 pm.

Another possibility is G Passeckel (☎ 781 18 73), Eisenacher Strasse 79, in Schöneberg (U7 to Eisenacher Strasse) which has smaller bikes for DM60 to DM80 a day (DM400 deposit) and bigger ones for DM100 and DM120 a day (DM800 deposit). It's only open from March to October, weekdays from 9 am to 6.30 pm and Saturday when the weather is fine.

Taxi

Taxi stands with 'call columns', *Rufsäule*, are beside all main train stations and throughout the city. Flag fall is DM4.20, then it's DM2.20 per kilometre for the first 6km and DM2 thereafter. Night (11 pm to 6 am) and weekend charges are higher by DM0.20 per kilometre, and a fifth passenger costs DM2.50 extra. If you order a taxi by phone (☎ 194 10, ☎ 21 01 01, ☎ 21 02 02), flag fall goes up to DM6. Sample fares: Nollendorfplatz to Schlesisches Tor is DM21.50; Hermannplatz to Schlesisches Tor is DM11.50.

If you need to travel quickly over a short distance, you can use the DM5 flat rate which entitles you to ride for five minutes or 2km, whichever comes first. This only applies if you flag down a moving taxi and ask for the DM5 rate before getting in.

Fairly new to Berlin are Velotaxis (☎ 44 35 89 90), pedicabs that seat two people (DM2 per person per kilometre).

Bicycle

Berlin is fairly user-friendly for cyclists, although you need to keep your wits about you in heavy traffic, especially where there are bike lanes. Outfits renting bicycles in Berlin include:

Bike City (☎ 39 73 91 45) has bikes for DM10 (students DM5). There's no deposit but you must bring ID. In the warmer months, rental stations (open daily from 10 am to 6 pm) are usually on the Schlossplatz by the Staatsrat building (Map 4); at U-Bahn station Hansaplatz (Lessingstrasse exit); and at Pohlstrasse 89, on the corner of Kluckstrasse (U15 to Kurfürstenstrasse). To confirm locations, call the office or the hotline at ☎ 0177-210 66 61.

Fahrradstation (reservations ☎ 28 38 48 48) is the largest bike rental agency and has branches all over the city, including one in courtyard No VII of the Hackesche Höfe in Mitte (Map 4). Other branches are at nearby Auguststrasse 29, Bergmannstrasse 9 in Kreuzberg and at Bahnhof Friedrichstrasse. City cruisers cost DM15/39/59 per day/three-day weekend/week rental. Mountain bikes are DM20/49/69. There's a deposit of DM200.

Brandenburg

With Berlin at its centre, the state of Brandenburg seems to have a hard act to follow, but it has more than its share of attractions. It is a region of lakes, marshes, rivers and canals connecting the Oder and Elbe rivers (utilising the Havel and Spree rivers, which meet at Spandau, west of Berlin). Brandenburg, with a land mass the size of Belgium and just as flat, is prime boating, fishing, hiking and cycling territory. The Spreewald, a wetlands area near Lübben and Lübbenau, has become the capital's playground since the *Wende* (fall of communism) and is still the centre of Germany's Sorbian minority, a Slavic people who have lived here since at least the 6th century.

Brandenburg's biggest draw is Potsdam, the 'Versailles of Germany', but visitors should not ignore places like Brandenburg, a lovely baroque city and once the capital of the Mark (March) of Brandenburg; Rheinsberg, with its graceful lakeside palace and summer concerts; the fine Gothic Cistercian monastery at Chorin; the impressive ship's lift at Niederfinow; or the hilly Märkische Schweiz region, where the playwright Bertolt Brecht spent his summers.

Brandenburg was originally settled by the Wends – the ancestors of the Sorbs – but they were overpowered in 1157 by Albrecht der Bär (Albert the Bear), who became the *Markgraf* (margrave) of Brandenburg. The Hohenzollern Friedrich I arrived in the early 15th century and by 1618, the electors of Brandenburg had acquired the eastern Baltic duchy of Prussia, merging the two states into a powerful union called the Kingdom of Prussia. This kingdom eventually brought all of Germany under its control, leading to the establishment of the German Empire in 1871.

Many Berliners will warn you about the 'Wild East', advising you not to stray too far afield in what they consider to be a backward and sometimes violent region. But Brandenburgers, ever *korrekt* in the Prussian style, sniff and ask what can you expect from a

HIGHLIGHTS

Brandenburg Luminaries: Theodor Fontane, Heinrich von Kleist, Karl Friedrich Schinkel, Friedrich August Wolf

- Wandering around the Chinese Teahouse in Potsdam's Sanssouci Park
- Exploring Rheinsberg and its magnificent Schloss
- Visiting the Sachsenhausen Concentration Camp Memorial & Museum at Oranienburg
- Viewing the ship's lift in Niederfinow from the upper platform
- Hiking through the Spreewald Biosphere Reserve to the Freilandmuseum of Sorbian architecture
- Taking a day trip to Brandenburg an der Havel, with its baroque churches and half-timbered houses

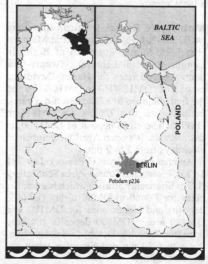

bunch of brash upstarts like the Berliners. In May 1996, Brandenburg held a referendum on whether to merge with Berlin; the result was an overwhelming *Nein*.

Potsdam & Havelland

The prime attraction of Brandenburg state and the most popular day trip from Berlin is Potsdam, a mere 24km south-west of Berlin's city centre and easily accessible by S-Bahn. But if time allows, try to make it to Brandenburg, the centre of the watery Havelland region another 36km west and the state's namesake. An attractive, untouristed city, it offers an interesting introduction to life in the new eastern Germany beyond the razzle-dazzle of Berlin.

POTSDAM
☎ 0331 • pop 142,000
Potsdam, on the Havel River just beyond the south-western tip of Greater Berlin, is the capital of Brandenburg state. In the 17th century, Elector Friedrich Wilhelm of Brandenburg (ruled 1640-88) made it his second residence. With the creation of the Kingdom of Prussia, Potsdam became a royal seat and garrison town; in the mid-18th century, Friedrich II (Frederick the Great, ruled 1740-86) built many of the marvellous palaces in Sanssouci Park to which visitors flock today.

In April 1945, RAF bombers devastated the historic centre of Potsdam, including the City Palace on Alter Markt, but fortunately most of the palaces escaped undamaged. To emphasise their victory over the German military machine, the Allies chose Schloss Cecilienhof for the Potsdam Conference of August 1945, which set the stage for the division of Berlin and Germany into occupation zones.

Orientation
Potsdam Stadt train station is just south-east of the town centre across the Havel River. The next two stops are Potsdam Charlot-

Frederick the Great's legacy is the impressive collection of palaces in Sanssouci Park.

tenhof and Potsdam Wildpark, which are closer to Sanssouci Park and all the palaces. However, they are served only by Regional-Bahn (RB) trains, not the Regional Express (RE) or S-Bahn Nos 3 and 7, which is how most people get here from Berlin. You can walk from Schloss Cecilienhof to Glienicker Brücke (and bus No 116 to Wannsee) in about 10 minutes. From Potsdam Stadt station to Charlottenhof is about 2km on foot. Do not confuse these stops with the Hauptbahnhof, an underutilised station serving destinations to the south.

Information
The tourist office (☎ 27 55 80, fax 275 58 99, email ptm@potsdam.de) is beside the Alter Markt at Friedrich-Ebert-Strasse 5. It sells a good variety of maps and brochures but can get very crowded. From April to October, hours are weekdays from 9 am to 8 pm, Saturday to 6 pm and Sunday to 4 pm. From November to March, weekday hours are

BRANDENBURG

ANDREA SCHULTE-PEEVERS

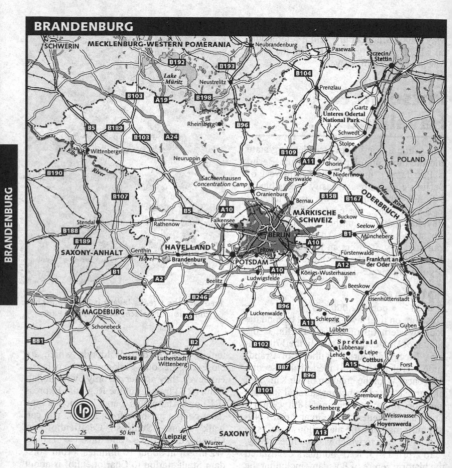

BRANDENBURG

from 10 am to 6 pm and weekends till 2 pm. A smaller branch (same telephone number) at Brandenburger Strasse 18 has similar hours but mainly sells tickets.

Both places sell the joint Berlin-Potsdam WelcomeCard (see the Information section of the Berlin chapter), which entitles you to unlimited transport and free or discounted admission to many attractions in both cities for 72 hours (DM29). The Sanssouci tourist office (☎ 969 42 00), with information on the park palaces, is near the old windmill opposite Schloss Sanssouci. It's open from April to October daily from 8.30 am to 5 pm, and 9 am to 4 pm the rest of the year.

Potsdam hosts the *Bundesgartenschau* (National Garden Show) in the summer of 2001, held at parks and gardens in and around town.

There's a Dresdner Bank at Yorkstrasse 28 and a Commerzbank in a beautiful neo-classical building on the corner of Charlottenstrasse and Lindenstrasse.

The post office is on Am Kanal north of the Alter Markt. The Internetcafé Staudenhof (☎ 280 05 55), at Alter Markt 10 across

Brandenburg on My Mind

Like the US state of Georgia, the German state of Brandenburg has strong musical associations, though they're a bit more highbrow in content than 'midnight trains' and 'rainy nights'. Even philistines have at least heard of the *Brandenburg Concertos*. They are the six *concerti grossi* composed by Johann Sebastian Bach in 1721 for Margrave Christian Ludwig of Brandenburg, the youngest son of Elector Friedrich Wilhelm I, based at Köthen in Saxony-Anhalt.

In 1747 Friedrich II (Frederick the Great) managed to lure Bach to Potsdam, where the great composer wrote *The Musical Offering* on a theme proposed by the king himself.

And how many people know *The Wedding March* was first performed here? No, not the catchy 'Here Comes the Bride' number; that's from Wagner's opera *Lohengrin* and is played when the bride walks *down* the aisle. We mean the one played for the exit of the married couple. It's the sixth number of Felix Mendelssohn's incidental music to *A Midsummer Night's Dream* (1842). The vogue for the piece started in 1858 when Queen Victoria's daughter, the Princess Royal (affectionately known as Vicky), had it played at her wedding at Windsor to Crown Prince Frederick of Prussia (later Kaiser Frederick III of Germany). So the next time you watch a couple of newlyweds make their way up the aisle and hear Mendelssohn's rather stirring tune, you should have Brandenburg on your mind.

from the tourist office, charges DM3 for half an hour of surfing.

Potsdam's comprehensive Web site is at www.potsdam.de (in German only).

Das Internationale Buch on Friedrich-Ebert-Strasse stocks maps and English-language publications.

If you've got laundry, the Waschsalon at Auf dem Kiewitt 14 charges DM5 per load

and another DM5 for drying. It's open all day but you have to use a magnetic card – sold only on Wednesday and Thursday from 6 to 8 pm. Take tram 91 or 94 to Potsdam West.

Sanssouci Park

This large park west of the city centre is open from dawn till dusk (free); the palaces and outbuildings all have different hours and admission prices. A day ticket, which includes all palaces and other sights in the park, costs DM20/15 for adults/children and a family card is DM25. But you have to work pretty fast to make it pay off. There's a 50% student discount on all separate admissions.

Sanssouci Park is a sprawling beast; take along the free map provided by the tourist office or you'll find yourself up the wrong path at almost every turn. The palaces are spaced fairly far apart – for example, it's 2km between the Neues Palais (New Palace) and the Schloss Sanssouci, and about 15km to complete the entire circuit. Sadly, cycling in the park is strictly *verboten*.

Schloss Sanssouci & Around Begin your park tour with Georg Wenzeslaus von Knobelsdorff's Schloss Sanssouci (1747), the celebrated rococo palace with glorious interiors. You have to take the guided tour, so arrive early and avoid weekends and holidays, or you may not get a ticket (DM10/5). Only 2000 visitors a day are allowed entry (a rule laid down by UNESCO for this World Heritage site), so tickets are usually sold out by 2.30 pm – even in the shoulder seasons. However, the tour run by the tourist office (see Organised Tours later in this section) guarantees entry.

Our favourite rooms include the frilly rococo **Konzertsaal** (Concert Hall) and the bed chambers of the **Damenflügel** (Ladies' Wing), including a 'Voltaire slept here' one. From the northern terrace of the palace you can see **Ruineberg**, a group of classical 'ruins' that actually make up a folly built by Frederick the Great in 1754. Schloss Sanssouci is open April to mid-October, Tuesday to Sunday from 9 am to 5 pm, and to 4 pm from November to April, with a half-hour break at 12.30 pm.

Just opposite is the **Historische Mühle** (Historic Windmill) designed, like the Queen's Hamlet at Versailles, to give the palace grounds a rustic, rural air. It's open from May to October, Saturday to Thursday from 10 am to 6 pm (DM3/2). The palace is flanked by the twin **Neue Kammern** (New Chambers), which served as a guesthouse and orangery. It includes the large Ovidsaal, with its gilded reliefs and green and white marble floor, and the Meissen porcelain figurines in the last room to the west. It's open from Saturday to Thursday from 10 am to 5 pm (DM4/2).

Next door, the **Bildergalerie** (Picture Gallery) was completed in 1764 as Germany's first purpose-built art museum. It contains a rich collection of 17th century paintings by Rubens, Van Dyck, Caravaggio and others. From mid-May to mid-October, it's open Tuesday to Sunday from 10 am to 5 pm, with a half-hour break at 12.30 pm (DM4/2).

Just west of the Neue Kammern is the **Sicilian Garden** (Sizilianischer Garten) of subtropical plants, which is laid out in the mid-19th century.

Orangerieschloss & Around The Renaissance-style Orangery Palace, built in 1864 as a guesthouse for foreign royalty, is the largest of the Sanssouci palaces but hardly the most interesting. The six sumptuous rooms on display include the Raphaelsaal, with copies of the Italian Renaissance painter's work done by 19th century German painters and a tower that can be climbed (DM2) for great views over the Neues Palais and the park.

Part of the Orangery's west wing is still used to keep some of the more sensitive plants alive in the cold north German winter. Hours are Tuesday to Sunday from 10 am to 5 pm, with a half-hour break at 12.30 pm (DM5/3).

Two interesting buildings west of the Orangery and within easy walking distance are the pagoda-like **Drachenhaus** (Dragon House, 1770), housing a cafe-restaurant (closed Monday) and the rococo **Belvedere**, the only building in the park to suffer serious damage during WWII but fully restored in 1999.

Neues Palais The late-baroque New Palace (1769), summer residence of the royal family, is one of the most imposing buildings in the park and the one to see if your time is limited. The tour (DM6/4) takes in about a dozen of the palace's 200 rooms, including the **Grottensaal** (Grotto Hall), a rococo delight of shells, fossils and baubles set into the walls and ceilings; the **Marmorsaal**, a large banquet hall of white Carrara marble with a wonderful ceiling fresco; the **Jagdkammer** (Hunting Chamber) with lots of dead furry things and fine gold tracery on the walls; and several chambers fitted out from floor to ceiling in rich red damask. Note the *Fahrstuhl*, an electric 'stair lift' from 1899 that transported ageing royals from the ground to the 1st floor. The **Schlosstheater** in the south wing has classical music concerts on the weekend; see the Entertainment section. Opposite the New Palace is the **Communs**, which originally housed the palace servants and kitchens but is now part of Potsdam University.

The palace opens from mid-May to mid-October, Tuesday to Sunday from 10 am to 5 pm; from April to mid-May, it's the same hours but on weekends and holidays only.

Schloss Charlottenhof & Around Karl Friedrich Schinkel's main contribution (1826) to the park must be visited on a 30 minute German-language tour (DM6/3), but don't wait around too long if the queues are long. In truth, the exterior (modelled after a Roman villa) is more interesting than the interior, especially the Doric portico and the bronze fountain to the east. Charlottenhof is open from April to October, Tuesday to Sunday from 10 am to noon and 12.30 to 5 pm.

A short distance to the north-east on the edge of the little Maschinenteich (Machine Pond) are the **Römische Bäder** (Roman Baths), built in 1836 by a pupil of Schinkel and never used. The floor mosaics and caryatids inspired by the baths at Herculaneum are impressive, but we also liked the flounder spitting into a clamshell near the entrance. The Roman Baths are open from mid-May to mid-October, Tuesday to Sunday from 10 am to 5 pm with a half-hour break at noon (DM3/2).

Follow the path north along the west bank of the Schafgraben to Ökonomieweg, then head east, and you'll come to what many consider to be the pearl of the park: the **Chinesisches Teehaus** (Chinese Teahouse, 1757), a circular pavilion of gilded columns, palm trees and figures of Chinese musicians and animals (one of the monkeys is said to have the features of Voltaire). It keeps the same hours as the Roman Baths, and costs DM2.

Altstadt

The baroque **Brandenburger Tor** (Brandenburg Gate), on Luisenplatz at the western end of the old town, pales in comparison with its namesake in Berlin but is actually older (1770). From this square, pedestrian Brandenburger Strasse runs due east to the **Sts Peter und Paul Kirche** (Church of Sts Peter & Paul, 1868). The **Französische Kirche** (French Church), to the south-east on Charlottenstrasse and once the seat of the town's Huguenots, was built in 1753.

North-west of here, on Friedrich-Ebert-Strasse, is the **Nauener Tor** (Nauen Gate, 1755), another monumental arch. The **Holländisches Viertel** (Dutch Quarter) to the south-east and bounded by Friedrich-Ebert-Strasse, Hebbelstrasse, Kurfürstenstrasse and Gutenbergstrasse, has some 134 gabled red-brick houses built for Dutch workers who came to Potsdam in the 1730s at the invitation of Friedrich Wilhelm I. (They didn't stay long.)

South-east of central Platz der Einheit is the great neoclassical dome of Schinkel's **Nikolaikirche** (1850) on Alter Markt. On the eastern side of the square is Potsdam's old **Rathaus** (1753), which now contains several art galleries upstairs. It's open from Tuesday to Sunday (free).

West of the Alter Markt on Breite Strasse and housed in the **Marstall**, the former royal stables designed by Knobelsdorff in 1746, is the smallish **Filmmuseum**. It contains exhibits on the history of the UFA and DEFA studios in Babelsberg, Marlene Dietrich costumes, and footage of Nazi-era and GDR films. It's open from Tuesday to Sunday from 10 am to 6 pm (DM5/3).

Across Breite Strasse and farther to the west on Henning-von-Tresckow-Strasse is the former **Kaserne** (military barracks, now the Finanzamt) where, according to local lore, the plot by Colonel Claus von Stauffenberg and other officers to assassinate Adolf Hitler in July 1944 was hatched. A short distance beyond the 'bay' of the Havel where Breite Strasse meets Zeppelinstrasse is the wonderful **Moschee** (mosque), a Moorish-style structure built in 1842 to house the palace waterworks. It can be visited from May to October on Saturday and Sunday from 10 am to 12.30 pm, and 1 to 5 pm (DM4/2).

Due north of this Moorish pump house on the south-eastern edge of Sanssouci Park is the **Friedenskirche** (Church of Peace), a neo-Romanesque pile completed in 1854 and containing the mausoleum of Friedrich Wilhelm IV (ruled 1840-61).

BRANDENBURG

ANDREA SCHULTE-PEEVERS

Older than Berlin's Brandenburg Gate, but less dramatic is Potsdam's Brandenburger Tor.

euro currency converter DM1 = €0.51

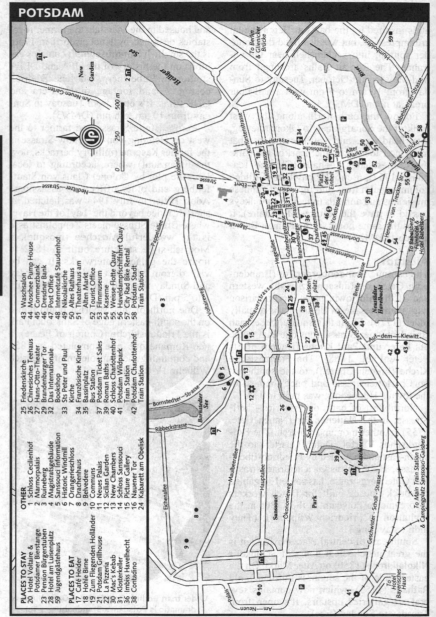

BRANDENBURG

POTSDAM

PLACES TO STAY
20 Hotel Voltaire &
     Potsdamer Bierstange
23 Pension Bürgerstuben
28 Hotel am Luisenplatz
59 Jugendgästehaus

PLACES TO EAT
17 Café Heider
18 Hohle Birne
19 Zum Fliegenden Holländer
21 Potsdam Grillhouse
22 La Pizzeria
30 Mac's Kebab
31 Klosterkeller
36 Imbiss Havelhecht
38 Contadino

OTHER
1   Schloss Cecilienhof
2   Marmorpalais
3   Ruineberg
5   Magistratsgebäude
6   Sanssouci Information
7   Historic Windmill
8   Orangerieschloss
9   Drachenhaus
10 Belvedere
11 Neues Palais
12 Sicilian Garden
13 New Chambers
14 Schloss Sanssouci
15 Picture Gallery
16 Nauener Tor
24 Kabarett am Obelisk

25 Friedenskirche
26 Chinesisches Teehaus
27 Hans-Otto-Theater
32 Brandenburger Tor
33 Das Internationale
     Bookshop
33 Sts Peter und Paul
     Kirche
34 Französische Kirche
35 Bassinplatz
37 Bus Station
37 Potsdam Ticket Sales
39 Roman Baths
40 Schloss Charlottenhof
41 Potsdam Wildpark
     Train Station
42 Potsdam Charlottenhof
     Train Station

43 Waschsalon
44 Moschee Pump House
45 Commerzbank
47 Dresdner Bank
48 Post Office
49 Intercafé Staudenhof
49 Nikolaikirche
50 Alte Rathaus
51 Theaterhaus am
     Alten Markt
52 Tourist Office
53 Filmmuseum
54 Kaserne
55 Weisse Flotte Quay
56 Haveldampfschiffahrt Quay
57 City Rad Bike Rental
58 Potsdam Stadt
     Train Station

New Garden

This winding lakeside park on the west bank of the Heiliger See and north-east of the city centre is a fine place to relax after all the baroque-rococo and high art of Sanssouci Park. The **Marmorpalais** (Marble Palace, 1792) by Carl Gotthard Langhans, right on the lake, has just been carefully restored. Note the gilded angels dancing around the cupola. From April to October it's open Tuesday to Sunday, from 10 am to noon and 12.30 pm to 5 pm; the rest of the year it's open to 4 pm (DM4/3).

Farther north is **Schloss Cecilienhof**, an English-style country manor which contrasts with the rococo palaces and pavilions in Sanssouci Park. Cecilienhof is remembered as the site of the 1945 Potsdam Conference, and large photos of the participants – Stalin, Truman and Churchill – are displayed inside. Note the star of red roses in the courtyard, planted especially for the gathering. The conference room can be visited on a guided tour daily (except Monday) from 9 am to noon and 12.30 to 5 pm (DM8/4). It closes an hour earlier in winter. Prices that include the rooms of the crown prince and princess are DM10/6.

Babelsberg

The **UFA film studios** (☎ 721 27 55), Germany's one-time response to Hollywood, are east of the city centre on August-Bebel-Strasse (enter from Grossbeerenstrasse). Shooting began in 1912 but the studio had its heyday in the 1920s when such silent-movie epics as Fritz Lang's *Metropolis* were made, along with some early Greta Garbo films.

Today the place resembles a mini-Universal Studios theme park, with haunted house, live shows with audience participation, an impressive stunt show and a few poky rides. During the studio tour, staff whisk you around the backlot for a peek at the film sets and production, as well as into the props and costumes room.

Opening hours are from March to October daily from 10 am to 6 pm (DM28/25, family ticket DM75). It's closed to visitors in winter.

It costs a mere DM3/2 to visit Schinkel's neo-Gothic **Schloss Babelsberg** near the lakes. It's open from April to October, Tuesday to Friday from 10 am to 12.30 pm and 1 to 5 pm, and weekends only during the rest of the year, from 10 am to 4 pm. You can also stroll in the pleasant park past Schinkel's **Flatowturm**, which is open from mid-May to mid-October on Saturday and Sunday only, from 10 am to 12.30 and 1 to 5 pm (DM3/2). A DM5 combination ticket will get you into both the palace and the tower.

Cruises

Weisse Flotte (☎ 275 92 20) operates boats on the Havel and the lakes around Potsdam, departing from the dock below the Hotel Mercure near Lange Brücke regularly from April to early October, between 9 am and 3.45 pm. There are frequent boats to Wannsee (DM15.50 return). Other popular trips are to Werder (DM16.50) and Spandau (DM22). Haveldampschiffahrt (☎ 270 62 29) has steamboat tours (DM18/10) of the same areas, leaving from the southern end of Lange Brücke (*opposite* the Weisse Flotte quay) daily except Monday and Friday from mid-April to late September.

Organised Tours

City tours (DM15) run by the tourist office leave from various points daily (except Monday) at 11 am and 2.30 pm from April to October, and at 11.30 am from Thursday to Sunday the rest of the year. There's also a combined Sanssouci Park/Schloss tour for DM49.

Special Events

Potsdam's biggest annual events include the Tulip Festival in the Dutch quarter in mid-April; the Musikfestspiele Potsdam Sanssouci (☎ 29 38 59 for tickets) during the second and third weeks of June; and the Filmfestival Potsdam in mid-June.

Places to Stay

Campingplatz Sanssouci-Gaisberg (☎/fax 03327-556 80, *An der Pirschheide 41*), about 3km south-west of the centre, is the closest camping ground. Take bus No 631 (direction: Werder) from Luisenplatz to Bahnhof Pirschheide – the grounds are to the south on the Templiner See lakeshore. Camping costs DM2.50/9.90 for a small/large tent site and DM9.50/3.90 per adult/child.

Jugendgästehaus Siebenschläfer (☎/fax 74 11 25, Lotte-Pulewka-Strasse 43) is great value for money in Potsdam, charging DM25 for juniors and DM31 for seniors in two and four-bed rooms. Bus No 695 from Potsdam Stadt train station stops almost in front of the door.

The tourist office can arrange *private rooms* from DM25 per person (☎ 289 15 87 for bookings). TourBu (☎ 888 10 12, fax 888 10 14), Saarmunder Strasse 60, is a private room-booking service with singles/doubles for around DM40/50.

Hotel Babelsberg (☎ 74 90 10, fax 70 76 68, Stahnsdorfer Strasse 68) is a five minute walk from the film studios, and charges from DM65/90 for singles/doubles, including breakfast.

Filmhotel Lili Marleen (☎ 74 32 00, fax 743 20 18, Grossbeerenstrasse 75), also near Babelsberg, has rooms with private bath for DM95/125.

Pension Bürgerstuben (☎ 280 11 09, fax 280 48 54, Jägerstrasse 10) is in the centre of Potsdam. Rooms with facilities go for DM90/150, including breakfast.

Hotel Bayerisches Haus (☎ 96 37 90, fax 97 23 29, Im Wildpark 1), in a lovely spot where Erich Honecker once slept, offers rooms from DM115/DM130.

Hotel am Luisenplatz (☎ 971 90 00, fax 971 90 19, email info@luisenplatz.de, Luisenplatz 5), run by a friendly Dutchman, offers a good upper-middle standard from DM139/218.

Arkona Hotel Voltaire (☎ 231 70, fax 231 71 00, Friedrich-Ebert-Strasse 88) has a posh address and is nicely renovated, central and expensive: rooms range between DM195/234 and DM265/304.

Places to Eat

Der Klosterkeller (☎ 29 12 18, Friedrich-Ebert-Strasse 94), near the corner of Guten-bergstrasse, has a restaurant, wine bar, beer garden and cocktail bar. The restaurant serves traditional regional dishes from about DM20.

Zum Fliegenden Holländer (☎ 27 50 30, Benkertstrasse 5) is located on a side street between Mittelstrasse and Gutenbergstrasse. It's an airy pub-restaurant on three levels, newly done up with lots of copper. Two-course lunch specials cost DM16.

Hohle Birne (☎ 280 07 15, Mittelstrasse 19) serves earthy but tasty German cuisine (eg mixed grill with mushroom sauce, cro-quettes and salad, DM19.50) and vegie dishes from DM9. There's a huge beer and wine menu, too.

Contadino (☎ 951 09 23, Luisenplatz 8) is a quality Italian place with soups for DM5.50, pizzas from DM8.50 and good mains (eg salmon pastry pockets with shrimp and lobster sauce) under DM20.

The two-floor *Potsdamer Bierstange (☎ 231 70, Friedrich-Ebert-Strasse 88)*, in the swanky Hotel Voltaire, has a lovely gar-den terrace, a 1920s feel inside and light dishes from DM10 to DM15.

Café Heider (☎ 275 42 11, Friedrich-Ebert-Strasse 29) was a prime meeting spot for GDR-era intellectuals, right by the Nauen Gate. Its daily specials cost DM10 to DM13.

La Pizzeria (☎ 280 04 29, Guten-bergstrasse 90) is popular with locals for its well priced pizzas and pastas.

Two places on pedestrian Brandenburger Strasse for a quick bite are *Imbiss Havel-hecht* at No 25 and *Mac's Kebab* on the corner of Lindenstrasse. The *Potsdam Grillhouse (Friedrich-Ebert-Strasse 92)* has doners and felafel from DM3.50, and stays open till midnight.

Entertainment

The box office (☎ 27 57 10) at *Theater-haus am Alten Markt (Alter Markt)* has tickets for performances there and at the *Hans-Otto-Theater (Zimmerstrasse 10)*. It also sells tickets for concerts held at the *Schlosstheater* in the Neues Palais (usu-ally Friday at 5.30 pm, Saturday at 4.30 pm and Sunday at 7 pm). Box office hours are

Monday to Thursday from 10 am to 6 pm, and Friday and Saturday to 1 pm.

From May to late October, there are organ concerts at various churches in Potsdam, including the *Friedenskirche* and *Nikolaikirche*. You can check with the tourist office for dates. *Kabarett am Obelisk (☎ 29 01 69, Schopenhauerstrasse 27)* presents satirical programs with contemporary themes from Tuesday to Sunday. The box office is open Tuesday to Friday from 4 to 8.30 pm, Saturday from 6 to 8.30 pm and Sunday from 5 to 7.30 pm. Tickets cost DM10 to DM25.

Getting There & Away
Train S-Bahn train Nos 3 and 7 link central Berlin with Potsdam Stadt Train Station near the centre of town about every 10 minutes. Some regional (RB) trains from Berlin-Zoo stop at all three train stations in Potsdam. There is no direct service to Berlin-Schönefeld airport, but you can take S-Bahn No 3 or 7 from Potsdam Stadt to Westkreuz in western Berlin and change to S-Bahn No 45 (or take bus No 602). Berlin transit passes must cover Zones A, B and C (DM4.20) to be valid for the trip to Potsdam by either S-Bahn or BVG bus.

Many trains between Hanover and Berlin Zoo also stop at Potsdam Stadt. Train connections from Potsdam Stadt south to Leipzig are poor, and most require a change in Magdeburg. Going to Dresden means changing trains at Berlin-Lichtenberg.

To reach Babelsberg from Berlin, take S-Bahn No 3 or 7 to Babelsberg station (one stop before Potsdam Stadt) and then bus No 692 to the Ahornstrasse stop. You can also get off the S-Bahn at Griebnitzsee station and take bus No 696 to the Drewitz stop.

Bus Potsdam's bus station, on Bassinplatz, is accessible from the Rathaus Spandau in Berlin on bus No 638 (hourly from 5 am to 9 pm) and from Schönefeld on bus No 602. If you're headed for Schloss Cecilienhof, take bus No 116 from Wannsee to Glienicker Brücke in Potsdam and walk from there.

Getting Around
Potsdam is part of Berlin's S-Bahn network but has its own local trams and buses; these converge on Lange Brücke near Potsdam Stadt train station. A short ride (up to six stops) costs DM1.90, regular tickets DM2.50, and a day pass DM7.80.

For a taxi, ring ☎ 29 29 29 or ☎ 70 70 70. Flag fall is DM4 and each additional kilometre costs DM1.90.

City Rad (☎ 61 90 52) rents out bikes from Bahnhofsplatz on the north side of Potsdam Stadt train station. In winter, ring ☎ 280 05 95. The rental fees (plus up to DM150 deposit) are DM15/20 per day for touring/trekking bikes (students get a 30% discount). It also offers a four-hour guided bike tour (called Tour Alter Fritz after Frederick the Great) on Saturday at 10 am for an additional DM20 per person.

BRANDENBURG AN DER HAVEL
☎ 03381 • pop 82,600
Brandenburg is the oldest town in the March of Brandenburg, with a history going back to at least the 6th century, when Slavs settled near today's cathedral. It was an important bishopric from the early Middle Ages and the seat of the Brandenburg *Markgrafen* until they moved to Berlin in the 15th century. Although badly damaged in WWII, the town is being restored and with its baroque churches and many half-timbered houses, makes an obvious day trip from Berlin.

Orientation & Information
Brandenburg is split into three sections by the Havel River, the Beetzsee and their canals: the Neustadt, on an island in the centre; Dominsel (Cathedral Island), to the north; and the Altstadt, to the west. There are worthwhile sights in all three areas, which are connected by six bridges. The train station is on Am Hauptbahnhof, 1.5km south of Neustädtischer Markt.

The tourist office (☎ 194 33, fax 22 37 43), at Hauptstrasse 51, is open weekdays from 10 am to 6 pm and to 2 pm on Saturday. There's a Dresdner Bank branch

BRANDENBURG

with an ATM at Neustädtischer Markt 10. The post office is due west at St Annan Strasse 30-36.

You can find the town's Web site at www.brandenburg.de; it has both German and English versions.

Walking Tour

Begin a stroll through Brandenburg at the Romanesque **Dom St Peter und Paul** (Cathedral of Sts Peter & Paul) on the northern edge of Dominsel.

Begun in 1165 by Premonstratensian monks and completed in 1240, it contains the wonderfully decorated Bunte Kapelle (Coloured Chapel), with a vaulted and painted ceiling; the carved 14th century Böhmischer Altar (Bohemian Altar) in the south transept (which may still be under renovation); a fantastic baroque organ (1723) restored in 1999; and the **Dommuseum** of liturgical treasures upstairs, which charges DM3/2 for adults/children.

Much of the cathedral is being rebuilt, so some items may have been moved around – or disappeared altogether. It's open from Monday to Saturday from 10 am to 4 pm (only to noon on Wednesday) and from 11 am on Sunday. The museum has identical hours, except that it opens at noon on Sunday.

From the cathedral, walk south on St Petri to Mühlendamm. Just before you cross the Havel to the Neustadt, look left and you'll see the **Hauptpegel**, the 'city water gauge' erected to measure the river's height. On the other side is the **Mühlentorturm**, the Mill Gate Tower that once marked the border between the separate towns of Dominsel and Neustadt.

Molkenmarkt, the continuation of Mühlendamm, runs parallel to Neustädtischer Markt and leads to the **Pfarrkirche St Katharinen** (Parish Church of St Catherine), a Gothic hall church which dates back to the early 1400s. It was under renovation at the time of writing. South-west of the church at the end of Steinstrasse is the **Steintorturm**, the second of four city towers still standing.

To reach the Altstadt, walk back up Steinstrasse to pedestrianised Hauptstrasse and then west over the Havel to the **Museum im Freyhaus** at Ritterstrasse 96. It's a local history museum with much emphasis on the EP Lehmann factory, which produced cute mechanical toys and pottery. The museum is open Tuesday to Friday from 9 am to 5 pm and Saturday and Sunday from 10 am to 5 pm (DM4/2).

Just a short distance north-east is the red-brick Gothic **Altstädtische Rathaus**, with a signature **statue of Roland** (1474) in front symbolising the town's judicial independence.

Cruises

Several boat companies offer cruises along the Havel from Am Salzhof in the Altstadt, including Weisse Flotte (☎ 22 39 59) and Bollman Flotte (☎ 66 35 90); the latter's program includes full-day trips to Spandau. You can also take one to two-hour tours (DM10 to DM15) on a historic steamer from Nordstern (☎ 45 50 19).

Special Events

Brandenburg's two big-ticket events are the Havelfest Brandenburg, a folk festival held throughout the Altstadt in mid-June, and the Musiktage der Havelstadt Brandenburg (Music Days of the Havel City of Brandenburg), with an emphasis on 20th century works, in the first half of September. Tickets can be purchased from the Brandenburger Theaterkasse (☎ 22 25 90) at Steinstrasse 42.

Places to Stay

The closest camp sites are on Breitlingsee, a large lake about 5km to the west. They include *Campingplatz Malge* (☎ 66 31 34) and *Campingplatz Insel Kiehnwerder* (mobile ☎ 0161 630 54 64), which are both open from April to October.

The DJH *Jugendherberge Brandenburg* (☎/fax 52 10 40, Hevellerstrasse 7), which backs onto the lake almost opposite the cathedral, charges juniors/seniors DM18/23 for B&B. Reception is open from 7 to 9 am and from 5 to 7 pm. It also rents out bikes, and there's no curfew.

The tourist office can arrange *private rooms* from about DM35 per person.

Pension Blaudruck (☎ 22 57 34, *Steinstrasse 21*) has basic singles/doubles for DM40/80. *Am Beetzseeufer* (☎ 30 33 13, *Beetzseeufer 6*) is a guesthouse north of Dominsel with nice rooms starting at DM85/140, including all facilities.

Hotel Am St Gotthard (☎ 529 00, *fax 52 90 30, Mühlentorstrasse 56*) is very central and charges from DM90/130. *Sorat Hotel Brandenburg* (☎ 59 70, *fax 59 74 44, Altstädtischer Markt 1*) is one of the nicer places, with clean rooms in a plain but modern building. Rooms with full facilities start at DM155/195.

Places to Eat

Dom Café (☎ 52 43 27, *Burghof 11*), just west of the cathedral, has salad platters from DM5.50 and main courses from DM15. It's open from April to September between 11 am and 6 pm.

Kartoffelkäfer (☎ 22 41 18, *Steinstrasse 56*) has potatoes in just about any form imaginable (soups from DM5.25, main courses from DM7.60 to DM25).

Blaudruck Café (☎ 0177 243 27 40, *Steinstrasse 21*) is a wild-looking pub with lots of game and a great wine list. Daily specials start at DM8, and at night it opens its snazzy wine cellar.

Cheap bites include *Pizzeria No 31* (*Steinstrasse 31*); *Orient Grill* (*Steinstrasse 43*), with doners from DM4; and an *Asia-Snack* (*Steinstrasse 65*).

Getting There & Around

Frequent regional trains link Brandenburg with Berlin-Zoo station (DM16.20, 40 minutes) and Potsdam (DM9.80, 20 minutes).

Tram Nos 6 and 9 run from Brandenburg Hauptbahnhof to Hauptstrasse via Steinstrasse and Neustädtischer Markt. A single ride is DM1.90 and four tickets cost DM7.60. There's a Fahrradstation (☎ 28 93 98) at the Hauptbahnhof renting bicycles for DM13 a day.

Spreewald

The Spreewald, the watery 'Spree Forest' (287 sq km) of rivers, canals and streams 80km south-east of Berlin, is the closest thing the capital has to a playground. Daytrippers and weekend warriors come here in droves to punt on more than 400km of waterways, hike the countless nature trails and fish in this region declared a 'Biosphere Reserve' by UNESCO in 1990. The focal points of most of this activity are the twin towns of Lübben and Lübbenau. The Spreewald is also home to most of Germany's Sorbian minority (see the boxed text 'The Sorbs'), who call the region the Blota. Its unofficial capital is Cottbus, 30km farther to the south-east.

LÜBBEN & LÜBBENAU

☎ 03546 • pop 15,000 (Lübben)
☎ 03542 • pop 23,800 (Lübbenau)

There's an ongoing debate among Berliners over Lübben (Lubin in Sorbian) and Lübbenau (Lubnjow), which lie 13km apart. Which is the more historical, touristy and picturesque 'Spreewald capital'? Lübben, a tidy and attractive town and the centre of the drier Unterspreewald (Lower Spreewald), has a history going back at least two centuries further than Lübbenau, boasts more interesting architecture and feels like a 'real' town. Lübbenau, in the Oberspreewald (Upper Spreewald), is equally picturesque but positively crammed year round with tourists trying to get out onto the canals on *Kähne* (punt boats), once the only way to get around in these parts. You'll find that a visit to both towns has its merits.

Orientation & Information

Lübben train station is south-west of the central Markt on Bahnhofstrasse. To reach the centre of town walk north-east along Friedensstrasse and then through the Hain, a large park. The train station and bus stations in Lübbenau are on Poststrasse, about 600m south of the tourist office.

BRANDENBURG

The Sorbs

The ancestors of the Sorbs, Germany's only indigenous minority (pop 60,000), were the Slavic Wends, who settled between the Elbe and Oder rivers in the 5th century in an area called Lusatia (Luzia in Sorbian, from *luz* or 'meadow').

Lusatia was conquered by the Germans in the 10th century, subjected to brutal Germanisation throughout the Middle Ages and partitioned in 1815. Lower Sorbia, centred around the Spreewald and Cottbus (Chosebuz), went to Prussia while Upper Sorbia around Bautzen (Budysin in Sorbian), 53km north-east of Dresden, went to Saxony. Upper Sorbian, closely related to Czech, enjoyed a certain prestige in Saxony, while the Kingdom of Prussia tried to suppress Lower Sorbian, which is similar to Polish. The Nazis tried to eradicate both.

The Sorbs were protected under the GDR, but their proud folk traditions and costumes didn't suit the bland 'proletarian' regime. Since German unification, interest in the culture has been revived through radio and TV broadcasts and theatre in the language. The more colourful Sorbian festivals include the Vogelhochzeit or Birds' Wedding on January 25, a horseback procession at Easter and a symbolic 'witch-burning' on April 30, a local variant of the Walpurgisnacht.

For further details, contact the Sorbian Institute (☎ 03591-497 20), Bahnhofstrasse 6, 02625 Bautzen; or the Institute of Sorbian Studies (☎ 0341-973 76 50), Augustusplatz 9, 04109 Leipzig.

Lübben's tourist office (☎ 30 90, fax 25 43) is in the Schloss Lübben at Ernst-von-Houwald-Damm 15, and opens weekdays from 10 am to 6 pm, Saturday to 4 pm and Sunday to 3 pm (shorter hours in winter).

The tourist office in Lübbenau (☎ 36 68, fax 467 70) is at Ehm-Welk-Strasse 15. From March to October, it's open weekdays from 9 am to 6 pm and weekends to 4 pm. During the rest of the year it's open only on weekdays from 9 am to 4 pm.

If you want to learn more about the Spreewald Biosphere Reserve, go to Haus für Mensch und Natur (☎ 89 21 30, fax 89 21 40) at Schulstrasse 9. Hours are 10 am to 5 pm weekdays and, between April and October, also on Saturday and Sunday.

Banks with ATMs on Hauptstrasse in Lübben include a Sparkasse at No 9-10 and a Dresdner Bank at No 13. Both banks also have branches, each with an ATM, in Lübbenau, facing one another on the Topfmarkt. The Dresdner Bank is at No 5 and the Sparkasse at No 8.

Hiking

The Spreewald has hiking and walking trails to suit everyone. The tourist offices sell the 1:25 000 *Oberspreewald* (No 4) and *Unterspreewald* (No 1) maps in the Landesvermessungsamt Brandenburg series for DM9.80 each. These maps are a must if you take your hiking seriously.

From Lübben an easy trail follows the Spree south to Lübbenau (13.2km) and north to Schlepzig (12.3km). From Lübbenau you can follow a nature trail (30 minutes) west to Lehde, the 'Venice of the Spreewald', with its wonderful **Freilandmuseum** of traditional Sorbian thatched houses and farm buildings, which charges DM6/4 for adults/children. The Leipscher Weg, which starts near the Grosser Hafen on Dammstrasse in Lübbenau, is part of the E10 European Walking Trail from the Baltic to the Adriatic and leads south-west to Leipe, accessible by boat only since 1936 (you can also take a punt back). Another popular walk is the 3km one from the Topfmarkt north-east to the Wotschofska restaurant, crossing 14 small bridges.

Boating

The Kahnfährhafen in Lübben, where you can board punts (DM5 to DM6 per person per hour), is along the Spree south-west of the tourist office. Bootsverleih Gebauer (☎ 71 94) rents out one/two-person kayaks for DM7/8 for the first hour and DM4/5 for each additional hour. Day rates are DM30/35 during the week and DM35/42 on the weekend. Canoes cost DM10/7 for the first hour/subsequent hour and DM49/56 per day during the week/weekend.

In Lübbenau there are two 'harbours': the Kleiner Hafen on Spreestrasse, about 100m north-east of the tourist office; and the Grosser Hafen, 300m south-east on Dammstrasse. From the former you can go on a two hour tour of the canals for DM10, or paddle as far as Lehde (DM15, three hours) and Leipe (DM35, seven hours, recommended over two days). The large Grosser Hafen has any number of punt and boat companies vying for business throughout the year.

Special Events

The highlight of the Spreewald Summer festival of cultural events is the Tage der Sorbischen Kultur/Dny serbskeje kultury (Days of Sorbian Culture), held in the Markt in Lübben during the first week in June. The Spreewaldfest, with its colourful *Kahnkorso* (punt competition), is held in Lübben in late September.

Places to Stay

Spreewald-Camping (☎ 70 53 *or* ☎ 33 35, *Am Burglehn)*, across the Spree from the tourist office in Lübben, charges DM5 per tent, DM3 per car and DM7/3 for each adult/child. It also rents out caravans accommodating two/three/four people for DM25/30/40. *Campingplatz Am Schlosspark* (☎/fax 35 33, *Schlosspark)* is a short distance east of Lübbenau palace.

The DJH *Jugendherberge Lübben* (☎/fax 30 46, *Zum Wendenfürsten 8)*, about 2.5km south of Lübben's centre, charges juniors/seniors DM21/26 for B&B. The DJH *Jugendherberge Burg* (☎/fax 035603-225, *Jugendherbergsweg 220)* in Burg, south-east of Lübbenau, charges the same rates.

Lübben and Lübbenau have plenty of *private rooms* from DM25 per person; the tourist offices can organise one for you for a DM5 booking fee. Prices listed are for mid-April to mid-October (many are about 20 to 30% lower in winter).

In Lübben, the central *Pension Am Markt* (☎ 45 76, fax 32 72, Hauptstrasse 5) has singles/doubles from DM65/90. The lovely *Hotel Spreeufer* (☎ 272 60, fax 80 69, Hinter der Mauer 4), near the bridge just south of Hauptstrasse, has rooms from DM80/100.

In Lübbenau, *Pension Am Haag* (☎ 21 40, Am Haag 3) has a quiet, central location on the water. Rooms cost DM60/80. The *Ebusch* (☎/fax 36 70, Topfmarkt 4), a dumpy pension with a restaurant, charges from DM75/100.

Pension Höhn (☎ 457 22, fax 468 88, Dammstrasse 38) is a fairly basic place with singles/doubles for DM65/85. For a real splurge, check in at the *Hotel Schloss Lübbenau* (☎ 87 30, fax 87 36 66, Schlossbezirk 6), east of the centre. Prices start at DM150/200.

Places to Eat

Goldener Löwe (☎ 73 09, Hauptstrasse 15) in Lübben is a somewhat touristy but decent place, with a lovely beer garden and freshwater fish dishes for DM12 to DM20. *Café Ambiente* (☎ 18 33 07), on the corner of Renatestrasse and Gerichtsstrasse, offers breakfast and light meals under DM10, and is open from 8 am to 6 pm. There are several cheap *Imbiss* (snack) stands just opposite the NKD Citykauf department store at the start of Hauptstrasse.

The cosy *Lübbenauer Hof* (☎ 831 62, Ehm-Welk-Strasse 20) is one of the nicest places for a meal in Lübbenau, with main courses from DM17. *Pension Spreewald-Idyll* (☎ 22 51, Spreestrasse 13) also has a good restaurant, with salads from DM5.50 and main courses from DM14. If you want to try eel, pike or perch *(Aal, Hecht, Zander)* pulled from the Spree, try *Strubel's* (☎ 27 98, Dammstrasse 3), where mains are about DM20.

The *butcher shop (Ehm-Welk-Strasse 3)* is open weekdays from 8 am to 6 pm and Saturday until noon, and has the usual ready-to-eat *Wurst* (DM2) and half-chickens.

BRANDENBURG

Getting There & Around

Daily regional trains serve Lübben and Lübbenau every one to two hours from Berlin-Lichtenberg and Berlin-Ostbahnhof (DM24.40, one hour) en route to Cottbus (DM7.60, 25 minutes).

The tourist office in Lübben rents out bicycles for DM10 a day, as does K-Heinz Oswald (☎ 40 63), An der Spreewaldbahn 6, north-west of the centre. In Lübbenau, try Kretschmann (☎ 34 33) at Poststrasse 16.

COTTBUS
☎ 0355 • pop 115,000

Cottbus (Chosebuz in Sorbian) is a pretty town with some wonderful architecture and a decent number of cultural offerings.

The tourist office (☎ 242 54, fax 79 19 31), Berliner Strasse 1, is open weekdays from 9 am to 6 pm and Saturday to 1 pm (2 pm in summer). Its friendly staff will find accommodation from about DM25, plus a DM5 booking fee.

The Sorbische Kulturinformation Lodka (☎ 79 11 10), in the Wendisch Haus at August-Bebel-Strasse 82, provides visitors with information about the Sorbs – and serves excellent (and authentic) Sorbian specialities at its cafe. It's open daily from 1.30 pm to midnight.

Those who are interested in Sorbian culture should check out the **Wendisches Museum/Serbski muzej** at Mühlenstrasse 12, which thoroughly examines this Slavic people's history, language and culture. It's open weekdays from 8.30 am to 5 pm and Saturday and Sunday from 2 to 6 pm (DM4/2 for adults/children).

Other places worth a visit in Cottbus include the 15th century **Oberkirche** on Oberkirchplatz, west of the central Altmarkt; the Jugendstil **Staatstheater** on Schillerplatz to the south-west; and **Branitzer Park** to the south-east, with its lovely 18th century baroque Schloss and the Seepyramide, a curious grass-covered pyramid 'floating' in a little lake.

Regional trains link Cottbus to Berlin-Lichtenberg (DM33, 1½ hours) about every hour. You can also reach Cottbus from the Spreewald twin towns (DM7.60, 25 minutes) and Frankfurt an der Oder (DM28.50, 1¼ hours).

Märkische Schweiz & Oderbruch

For a region where the highest 'peak' reaches a mere 129m (Krugberg, north of Buckow), 'Switzerland of the March of Brandenburg' is a rather grandiose label. But it is a lung for Berlin – a land of clear streams, lakes and beautiful, low-lying hills. The lovely town of Buckow, the 'pearl of the Märkische Schweiz', has long been a popular place for rest and recreation for Berliners. The Oderbruch region to the south couldn't be more different: it is flat, marshy, prone to flooding and has as its centre the dull city of Frankfurt an der Oder.

BUCKOW
☎ 033433 • pop 1800

In 1854 Friedrich Wilhelm IV's physician advised His Majesty to visit this village, where 'the lungs go as on velvet', and Fontane praised its 'friendly landscape' in *Das Oderland* (1863), the second book in his four volume travelogue. But Buckow really only made it on the map in the early 1950s, when Bertolt Brecht and Helene Weigel spent their summers here, away from the hot and humid capital of the new GDR.

Orientation & Information

Buckow, in the centre of the 205 sq km Märkische Schweiz Nature Park, is surrounded by five lakes; the largest is Schermützelsee (146 hectares in area, 45m deep). Wriezener Strasse, the main street where you'll find the tourist office (☎ 659 82, fax 659 20) at No 1a, runs parallel to the lake before becoming Hauptstrasse. From April to October, the tourist office is open weekdays from 9 am to noon and 1 to 5 pm, weekends from 10 am to 5 pm. From November to March, Saturday hours are 10 am to 2 pm, and it's shut on Sunday.

There's a Sparkasse with an ATM just west of the tourist office at Wriezener Strasse 2. The post office is at Hauptstrasse 84.

Things to See

Brecht-Weigel-Haus, where the GDR's first couple of the arts spent their summers from 1952 to 1955, is at Bertolt-Brecht-Strasse 29. The easiest way to reach it is to walk due west on Werderstrasse, but you'll probably find it's much more fun strolling along Ringstrasse and Bertolt-Brecht-Strasse admiring the posh villas and mansions of the prewar period. Brecht's house is a relatively simple affair with an overhanging roof, geometric patterns outside and a relief of Europa riding a bull over the front door.

Among the photographs, documents and original furnishings inside is Mother Courage's covered wagon; outside in the fine gardens are copper tablets engraved with Brecht's words. Brecht-Weigel-Haus (☎ 467) is open from April to October, Wednesday to Friday from 1 to 5 pm, and weekends to 6 pm. During the rest of the year it's open Wednesday to Friday from 10 am to noon and 1 to 4 pm, and on Sunday from 11 am to 4 pm. Admission is DM3/1.50.

The **Eisenbahnmuseum** (Railroad Museum) at the train station is open from May to October on Saturday and Sunday from 10 am to 4 pm (DM2/1). The Buchower Kleinbahn is the little forest train that has been running for 100 years between here and Müncheberg to the south.

The **Ehemaliges Rechenzentrum der Nationalen Volksarmee** (Former Computer Centre of the GDR National People's Army) is in a huge 70 room bunker some 15m underground at Gladowshöher Strasse 3 in Garzau, 12km south-west of Buckow. It can be visited on a two hour tour (DM15/5). Ring ☎ 033435-742 01 to make a booking. Unfortunately, Garzau is not served by public transport from Buckow. Don't forget to bring some warm clothes – it's a chilly 12°C down there in summer and 8°C in winter.

Activities

Buckow is paradise for hikers and walkers. You can follow the Panoramaweg from north of Buckow clear around the Schermützelsee (7.5km), the Drachenkehle north to Krugberg (5km), the Poetensteig to the north-east above the Kleiner Tornowsee, the Grosser Tornowsee to Pritzhagener Mühle (9km), or the Alter Schulsteig to Dreieichen (10km). The tourist office sells two useful maps with marked walks: *Märkische Schweiz Reisegebietskarte* (DM6.50) and the 1:25,000 *Märkische Schweiz Topographische Karte* (DM9.75). The Kneipp- und Heimatverein Märkische Schweiz (☎ 575 00), in the same building as the tourist office, organises walking tours in the area on some Saturday morning from April to October.

There's a *Strandbad* (beach) with a raft and diving board on the north-east tip of Schermützelsee. Entry is DM3. At the dock just south you can rent rowing boats or go on a cruise with Seetours (☎ 232). In season, the large MS *Scherri* sails hourly from Tuesday to Sunday between 10 am and 5 pm, while the little MS *Seeadler* sails Saturday and Sunday only from 10.30 am to 5.30 pm.

A trip to the Pension Buchenfried and Fischerkehle restaurant at the south-western end of the lake and back is DM7/3.50, or you can go just one way for DM5/2.50 (taking a bike along costs DM2). If you want to do some angling, visit Fred Schüler (☎ 571 28) at Wriezener Strasse 54. Four-hour/day-long fishing trips cost DM10/15. A permit is DM6 a day.

The Kurbahn, a mini-coach made up to look like a train that you wouldn't be caught dead on at home for fear of embarrassment, twirls around the nature park and leaves from the front of the Strandbad on Saturday and Sunday between noon and 6 pm (DM7/5).

Special Events

In July and August the open-air theatre in the Schlosspark behind the tourist office stages plays for children. Contact the Schlosspark Sommer Theater (☎ 562 97) at Neue Promenade 30-31 for details.

euro currency converter DM1 = €0.51

Places to Stay

The DJH *Jugendherberge Buckow (☎/fax 286, Berliner Strasse 36)*, south-west of the tourist office, charges DM21/26 for juniors/seniors. Walk north on Hauptstrasse and turn left (west) onto Berliner Strasse.

The tourist office can organise *private rooms* from DM30 per person, plus a DM2 booking fee.

The *Pension Grahl (☎ 572 83, Hauptstrasse 9)* has the narrowest driveway in the civilised world but has great singles/doubles with breakfast for DM40/55, with a nice lake view. *Rosemarie Krüger (☎ 296, Königstrasse 55)* is central on the corner of Wallstrasse, with rooms for DM30/50.

Zur Märkische Schweiz (☎/fax 464, Hauptstrasse 73), near the post office, has rooms from DM50/80. *Pension Buchenfried (☎ 575 63, fax 575 62, Am Fischerberg 9)* enjoys an enviable position on the south-western shore of Schermützelsee, but it's a bit far away from whatever action there is in Buckow. It costs DM76/110.

Pension Strandcafé (☎ 279, fax 68 06, Wriezener Strasse 28) is closer to town but still near the water, and charges DM65/110. *Bergschlösschen (☎ 573 12, fax 574 12, Königstrasse 38-41)*, though a bit down-at-heel, remains a swanky address, with rooms for DM110/160 with full facilities.

Stobbermühle (☎ 668 33, fax 668 44, Wriezener Strasse 2) is a very chi-chi 'apartment hotel' (suites from DM148, breakfast DM12 extra).

Places to Eat

The *Stobbermühle* restaurant is superb, with inventive starters/main courses from DM7/18 – it's worthy of a hotel in a world-class city, not poky (but pretty) little Buckow. Try the fabulous duck dishes (from DM20) or the lobster (DM36).

Fischerkehle (☎ 374, Am Fischerberg 7) is a popular, 85-year-old place on the south-west shore of the lake.

Buckow also boasts a Vietnamese restaurant called the *Minh Hoa (☎ 574 72, Königstrasse 33)*, and a stylish Chinese place called *Chao'sche (☎ 560 02, Bertolt-Brecht-Strasse 9)* in a lovely old villa. It's open daily from 11.30 am to 11.30 pm.

Café Am Markt (☎ 566 95, Markt 4) has cheap pizza from DM6 and attracts a boisterous crowd. It's open from Tuesday to Sunday.

The *Mini Grill* on Wriezener Strasse, almost opposite the tourist office, sells kebabs, pork steaks, sausages and more from 11 am to 8 pm.

Getting There & Around

There are frequent regional trains from Berlin-Lichtenberg to Buckow via Lindenberg (DM25, 1¾ hours). A slower but cheaper alternative is to take the S-Bahn No 5 to Strausberg and board the bus there (11 departures on weekdays, three on Saturday and Sunday) to Buckow via Hohenstein and Bollersdorf.

The Haus Wilhelmshöhe (☎ 246), a hotel at Lindenstrasse 10-11, has bicycles for rent.

FRANKFURT AN DER ODER

☎ 0335 • pop 84,000

Frankfurt, which lies 90km east of Berlin, has had its share of troubles despite an early successful start. At a strategic crossing on the Oder, it prospered as a centre of trade from the early 13th century, and within 150 years had become a member of the Hanseatic League. For centuries the town was known for its three annual fairs.

During WWII the city, with some 750 medieval houses, was evacuated. In the last few days before Germany's surrender in May 1945, a holdout group of Nazi guerrillas engaged in hand-to-hand combat with Polish soldiers. Frankfurt was burned to the ground in the process, with only five of the old houses left standing. In the summer of 1997, Frankfurt and the surrounding area was struck by the 'flood of the century', causing millions of Deutschmarks worth of damage.

Frankfurt is an easy gateway to Poland and points beyond. Slubice, just five minutes over the Oder and the town's one-time eastern suburb, seems to exist only to supply Frankfurters with cut-rate tobacco and booze.

Orientation & Information

Frankfurt's tourist office (☎ 32 52 16, fax 225 65) is at Karl-Marx-Strasse 8a, a stone's throw from the 23 storey, shoebox-like Oderturm (Oder Tower, 1976). It opens on weekdays from 10 am to 6 pm (with a half-hour break at noon) and from 10 am to 12.30 pm on Saturday. You can pick up a free copy of the town *Spaziergang* map with a marked route round the few sights.

There's a Sparkasse ATM on Schmalz-gasse off Karl-Marx-Strasse, and a Commerzbank with an ATM on the corner of Karl-Marx-Strasse and Logenstrasse. Just opposite, in the splendid Haus der Künste (1902), is the post office.

Things to See & Do

You might have a look inside the odd **St Gertraudkirche**, at Gertraudenplatz 6 (to the south, off Lindenstrasse). Its treasures were all brought here from the ruined **Marienklrche** (St Mary's Church) under-going renovation on Grosse Scharrnstrasse.

The 14th century **Rathaus**, on Markt just north of Bischofsstrasse, has a golden her-ring (Frankfurt had the trading monopoly on this salt-laden commodity) hanging from its lovely south gable. Inside is the **Galerie Junge Kunst** of GDR art, open daily except Monday from 11 am to 5 pm (DM3/2.10 for adults/children).

East of the tourist office, near the river in an 18th century military school building, is the **Kleist-Museum** (☎ 32 11 53), Faber-strasse 7, with displays on the life and works of Heinrich von Kleist, the German dramatist born in Frankfurt. It's also open daily (except Monday) from 11 am to 5 pm (DM4/3).

The **Konzerthalle CPE Bach** is an old Gothic church converted into the town's main concert hall. It houses an exhibit on the life of quirky composer Carl Philipp Emmanuel Bach, the son of JS Bach, which opens daily from 11 am to 5 pm (DM2).

Places to Stay & Eat

The tourist office can organise *private rooms* from DM35 per person plus a DM5 booking fee.

Pension Am Kleistpark (☎ 238 90, fax 53 39 88, Humboldtstrasse 14), near the city bridge, is perfectly located for an early morning getaway, with doubles for DM100.

Hotel Gallus (☎ 561 50, fax 561 53 33, Fürstenwalderstrasse 47) is reasonably central, with rates from DM59/78 for simple singles/doubles and DM79/108 with private shower/WC.

The *Broilereck* (☎ 42 22 86, Tunnel-strasse 48) serves chicken and salad (of sorts) for well under DM10. There are a few *Imbisse* next to the Kaiser's supermar-ket on Heilbronner Strasse.

Closer to town there's a *Mensa* (student cafeteria), on Kellenspring near the river, which is open from 8.30 am to 3.30 pm. *Pizzeria Roma* (Lindenstrasse 5) in the Haus der Künste has pizzas and pasta from DM8. *Kartoffel Haus* (☎ 53 07 86, Holz-markt 7), just north of the Kleist-Museum, has potato-based specialities from DM6.

Getting There & Around

Frankfurt is served hourly by regional trains from Berlin-Ostbahnhof (DM22, one hour) and Cottbus (DM22, 1¼ hours). There are also good connections to Ebers-walde via Niederfinow.

To reach the centre of town from the train station, walk north on Bahnhofstrasse and east on Heilbronner Strasse, or jump on tram No 1 or 3 (or bus A, B, D or G) and get off at Schmalzgasse. Short/regular tram tickets cost DM1.50/2.20.

The Fahrradstation (☎ 564 24 33) at the train station rents out bicycles for DM13 a day.

Northern Brandenburg

SACHSENHAUSEN CONCENTRATION CAMP

In 1936 the Nazis opened a 'model' *Konzen-trationslager* (concentration camp) for men in a disused brewery in Sachsenhausen, near the town of Oranienburg (pop 26,000),

BRANDENBURG

about 35km north of Berlin. Inmates (political undesirables, gays, Jews, gypsies – the usual Nazi targets) were forced to make bricks, hand grenades and weapons, counterfeit dollar and pound banknotes (to flood Allied countries and wreak economic havoc) and even to test out boot leather for days on end on a special track. By 1945 about 220,000 men from 22 countries had passed through the gates of Sachsenhausen KZ – labelled, as at Auschwitz in south-western Poland, *Arbeit Macht Frei* (Work Sets You Free). About 100,000 were murdered here, their mortal remains consumed by the fires of the horrible ovens.

After the war, the Soviets and the communist leaders of the new GDR set up *Speziallager No 7* (Special Camp No 7) for political prisoners, rightists, ex-Nazis, monarchists or whoever didn't happen to fit into *their* mould. An estimated 60,000 people were interned at the camp between 1945 and 1950, and up to 12,000 are believed to have died here. There's a mass grave of victims at the camp and another one 1.5km to the north.

The Sachsenhausen Memorial and Museum are open from April to September, Tuesday to Sunday from 8.30 am to 6 pm, and to 4.30 pm the rest of the year (free).

Orientation & Information

The walled camp (31 hectares) is about 2km north-east of Oranienburg train station, but it's an easy, signposted 20 minute walk. Follow Stralsunder Strasse north and turn east (right) onto Bernauer Strasse. After about 600m turn left at Strasse der Einheit and then right on Strasse der Nationen, which leads to the main entrance. You can also catch bus No 804 or 805 as far as the corner of Bernauer Strasse and Strasse der Einheit.

The Oranienburg tourist office (☎ 03301-70 48 33, fax 70 48 34) is in the Henrietta-Center on Breite Strasse (next to the old fire station). To get there, walk north from the train station, turn west (left) on Bernauer Strasse and go straight over the Schlossbrücke – it's 100m straight ahead. Hours are weekdays only from 8 am to 4 pm.

There's an information office (☎ 03301-80 37 15, fax 80 37 18) in the camp itself, selling maps, brochures and books.

Gedenkstätte und Museum Sachsenhausen

The Sachsenhausen Memorial and Museum consists of several parts. As you approach the entrance, along a quiet tree-lined lane, you'll see a **memorial** to the 6000 prisoners who died on the *Todesmarsch* (Death March) of April 1945, after the Nazis emptied the camp of its 33,000 prisoners and tried to drive them to the Baltic in advance of the Red Army.

Farther on is a mass grave of 300 prisoners who died in the infirmary after liberation on 22-23 April 1945, the camp commandant's house and the so-called Green Monster (where SS troops were trained in the finer arts of concentration-camp maintenance). At the end of the road is the **Neues Museum** (New Museum), with excellent exhibits, including a history of anti-Semitism and audiovisual material.

East of the New Museum are **Barracks 38 & 39**, reconstructions of two typical huts housing most of the 6000 Jewish prisoners brought to Sachsenhausen after Kristallnacht (9-10 November 1938). Number 38 has been rebuilt after being burnt to the ground by neo-Nazis in September 1992 just days after a visit by the late Israeli Prime Minister Yitzhak Rabin.

Just north of Barracks 38 & 39 is the **prison**, where particularly brutal punishment was meted out, and prisoners were confined in stifling blackened cells. Nearby is a **memorial**, bearing the pink triangle, to the homosexuals who died here, one of the few monuments you'll see anywhere to these 'forgotten victims' (there's another one at the Nollendorfplatz U-Bahn station in Berlin).

To get to the **Lagermuseum** (Camp Museum), with moth-eaten and dusty exhibits that focus on both the Nazi concentration camp and Special Camp No 7, walk north along the parade ground, where endless roll calls took place, past the site of the gallows.

The museum is housed in the building on the right, once the camp kitchen. In the former laundry room opposite, a particularly gruesome film of the camp after liberation is shown throughout the day. Steel yourself before entering.

Left of the tall, ugly monument – erected by the GDR in 1961 in memory of political prisoners interned here – is the **crematorium** and **Station Z extermination site**, a pit for shooting prisoners in the neck and a wooden 'catch' where bullets could be retrieved and reused. A memorial hall on the site of the **gas chamber** is a fitting visual metaphor for the 'glorious' Third Reich and the 'workers' paradise' of the GDR: subsidence has caused it to sink, its paving stones are cracked and the roof is toppling over an area containing, we're told, 'considerable remains from corpses incinerated in the crematorium'.

To the north-east, beyond the wall, are **stone barracks** built in 1941 to house Allied POWs. From 1945 German officers and others sentenced by the Soviet military tribunal were imprisoned here. To the north is a mass grave from the latter period.

Places to Eat

Food will probably be the last thing on your mind when you leave Sachsenhausen, but if you need a cup of coffee or a fortifying schnapps, seek out the cafe **Lena** (☎ *34 98, Bernauer Strasse 60)*. Opposite the tourist office is **Kro-El No 1** *(Stralsunder Strasse 3)* and an adjoining **Imbiss**, with pizzas, pastas and salads from DM4 to DM6. Between 5 and 7 pm all drinks here are half price.

Getting There & Away

The easiest way to get to Sachsenhausen from Berlin is to take the S-Bahn No 1 to Oranienburg (DM4.20, 50 minutes), which runs every 20 minutes. There are also Inter-Regio trains from Berlin-Lichtenberg (DM12, 30 minutes).

RHEINSBERG
☎ 033931 • pop 5300

Rheinsberg, which lies about 50km north-west of Berlin, has much to offer visitors: a charming Renaissance palace, walks in the lovely Schlosspark, boating on the lake and Rhin River and some top-notch restaurants.

Orientation & Information

Rheinsberg hugs the south-eastern shore of Grienericksee, a large lake. The central Markt lies about 1km north-west of the train station, with the friendly tourist office (☎/fax 20 59) in its Kavalierhaus. It's

BRANDENBURG

Brandenburg's Fontane of Knowledge

In 1859, Theodor Fontane (pronounced 'foon-**tah**-neh'), a Huguenot writer from Neuruppin in north-west Brandenburg, set out on a series of walking tours of the March. To the eternal gratitude of the state tourism association, Fontane wrote all about these experiences in his four volume *Wanderungen durch die Mark Brandenburg* (Travels through the March of Brandenburg), published between 1862 and 1882. His name is everywhere nowadays – in travel brochures, on 'Fontane Slept Here' plaques and in bookshop display windows. Wherever you find yourself, Fontane was there first.

Moving around the state, you might get the impression that Fontane (1819-98) was just an old travel hack who 'did' Brandenburg, and not the greatest master of the social novel German literature has known. But he did say a lot of nice things about the March – from Rheinsberg and Chorin to Buckow and the Spreewald.

Fontane is buried in the Französischer Friedhof (French Cemetery) in Berlin's Mitte district. But prepare for company; he still enjoys a wide following, and there are always pilgrims milling about his modest tombstone.

open Monday to Saturday from 9.30 am to 5 pm and Sunday from 10 am to 2 pm. Buses stop on Mühlenstrasse just south of Schlossstrasse.

Sparkasse has a branch at Berliner Strasse 16, and there's an ATM booth in Kirchplatz in front of the 13th century Kirche St Laurentius (Church of St Lawrence). The post office is on the corner of Schlossstrasse and Poststrasse.

The town's simple Web site (in German only) is at www.rheinsberg.de.

Schloss Rheinsberg

A moated castle stood on the shores of the Grienericksee from the early Middle Ages to protect the March of Brandenburg's northern border from the marauders of Mecklenburg. But Schloss Rheinsberg as we see it today only began to take shape in 1566, when its owner, Achim von Bredow, had it rebuilt in the Renaissance style.

Friedrich Wilhelm I purchased the castle in 1734 for his 22-year-old son, Crown Prince Friedrich (the future Frederick the Great), expanded the palace and cleaned up the town – paving roads, plastering house façades and tiling roofs. Prince Friedrich, who spent four years here studying and preparing for the throne, later said this period was the happiest of his life. He oversaw much of the remodelling of the palace by Johann Gottfried Kemmeter and Knobelsdorff; some say this was his 'test', on a minor scale, of the much grander Schloss Sanssouci (1747) in Potsdam.

During WWII, art treasures from Potsdam were stored at Schloss Rheinsberg. Alas, the palace was looted in 1945 and used as a sanatorium by the communists from 1953. Today, the place is a mere shadow of its former self, but it is being renovated at a furious pace.

A tour of the palace takes in about two dozen, mostly empty, rooms on the 1st floor, including the oldest ones: the **Hall of Mirrors**, where young Friedrich held flute contests; the **Tower Chamber**, where the future king studied and which he recreated in the Berlin Schloss in 1745; and the **Bacchus Room**, with a ceiling painting of a worn-looking Ganymede. Among our favourites, though, are the **Lacquer Room**, with its chinoiserie; **Prince Heinrich's bedchamber**, with an exquisite *trompe l'oeil* ceiling; and the rococo **Shell Room**.

The ground floor of the north wing contains the **Kurt Tucholsky Gedenkstätte**, a small memorial museum dedicated to the life and work of writer Kurt Tucholsky (1890-1935). He wrote a popular novel called *Rheinsberg – ein Tagebuch für Verliebte* (Rheinsberg – A Lovers' Diary), in which the young swain Wolfgang traipses through the Schloss with his beloved Claire in tow, putting the palace and the town of Rheinsberg firmly on the literary map.

The palace and museum are open from April to October, Tuesday to Sunday from 9.30 am to 5 pm, with a half-hour break at 12.30 pm. During the rest of the year it opens at 10 am and closes at 4 or 5 pm. Admission to the palace is DM6/4 for adults/children (family card DM15), and DM2/1 to the museum.

Activities

Reederei Halbeck (☎ 386 19), next to the tourist office at Markt 11, offers a number of lake and river cruises – from two hours for DM15 to 12 hours for DM35. The Untermühle guesthouse (☎ 20 42), at Untermühle 2, rents out canoes and two-person kayaks for DM50/200 a day/week. It also offers canoe and kayak day-tours of the Rhin River for DM80.

Ponyhof Fatima (☎ 27 97), at Schlossstrasse 35, offers pony rides and short treks for DM5/9 per half-hour/hour daily at 3 pm.

Special Events

The Rheinsberger Musiktage (Rheinsberg Music Days) is a three day festival of music round the clock – from jazz and chamber music to children's cabaret. It takes place around Whitsun/Pentecost in May/June. Ring ☎ 20 57 for information. The Musikakademie Rheinsberg (☎ 20 57), in the Kavalierhaus, performs opera and classical music in the Hall of Mirrors, the palace courtyard and Kirche St Laurentius from late June to mid-August. Tickets (DM15 to DM55) are available from the tourist office or, in Berlin, from the TAKS ticket agency (☎ 030-341 02 03).

Places to Stay

The closest hostel and camp sites are at Zechlinerhütte, about 6km north of Rheinsberg. *Campingplatz Berner Land (☎ 033921-702 83, Am Bikowsee 4)* is open all year; there's a twice-daily bus link to Rheinsberg on weekdays (6 am and 1.55 pm). The DJH *Jugendherberge Prebelow/ Zechlinerhütte (☎ 033921-222, Prebelow 2)* charges juniors/seniors DM18/23 for B&B; lunch/dinner is also available for DM6/5.50.

Private rooms (from DM20 per person) are plentiful in Rheinsberg. Just walk along Lange Strasse (eg at Nos 9, 11, 43 and 45), Paulshorster Strasse (Nos 9 and 31) and Menzerstrasse (No 2), which is the continuation of Schlossstrasse, looking for 'Zimmer Frei' signs.

The *Pension Butschak (☎/fax 2753, Menzerstrasse 6)* has spick-and-span singles/ doubles in a quiet garden for DM60/80. *Zum Jungen Fritz (☎ 40 90, fax 409 34, Schlossstrasse 8)*, near the Kirke St Laurentius, is a sweet little guesthouse with rooms from DM80/115.

Pension Am Rheinsberger Schlosspark (☎ 392 71, fax 392 70, Fontaneplatz 2), south of the palace in the park, charges just DM90/120.

Deutsches Haus Atrium Hotel (☎ 390 59, fax 390 63, email schlosshotel@t-online.de, Seestrasse 13) is the place to splurge, with rooms from DM120/200.

Places to Eat

Zum Alten Fritz (☎ 20 86, Schlossstrasse 11) is an excellent place for north German specialities like *Schlesischer Krustenbraten* (ham with beans and parsley potatoes, DM18) or *Märkische Rinderrouladen* (beef olives a la March, DM19).

Al Castello (☎ 380 84, Rhin Passage), on Rhinstrasse, has pizzas and pastas for DM7

and DM8.50 respectively. *Garden (☎ 378 11, Rhin Passage)* is a Chinese restaurant with starters/main courses from DM4.50/15 and cheap weekday lunches from DM13.

Seehof (☎ 383 03, Seestrasse 19c) is a 1st class restaurant with a lovely back courtyard. *Schloss Rheinsberg (☎ 27 77)*, inside the Deutsches Haus Atrium Hotel, is the town's silver-service restaurant, with prices to match.

Entertainment

When was the last time you watched a movie at a *drive-in*? There's one (☎ 033923-704 26) at Zempow, about 15km north-west of Rheinsberg, charging DM1 per car and DM7 per person. Obviously you'll need a car.

Shopping

Rheinsberg is a traditional centre of faïence and ceramics; you can visit the Rheinsbergische Keramik Manufaktur (RKM) in the Rhin Passage seven days a week from 10 am (9 am on Saturday) to 6 pm. Not surprisingly, there's a large outlet with RKM wares for sale.

Getting There & Around

Rheinsberg is serviced by direct regional trains every two hours from Berlin-Lichtenberg (DM24/40, 1½ hours) and Oranienburg (DM14.80, 1¼ hours). Links from Neubrandenburg involve a change at Löwenberg (DM34, 2½ hours). From Berlin, you could also take the S1 from Friedrichstrasse to Oranienburg and change to a DB train (or a bus) to Rheinsberg.

Two buses a day make the trip between Oranienburg train station and Rheinsberg, stopping at Mühlenstrasse south-east of the Markt.

The Fahrradhaus Thäns (☎ 26 22), also called Sporthaus, at Schlossstrasse 16, rents out bicycles from DM10/63 a day/week.

UNTERES ODERTAL NATIONAL PARK

North-eastern Brandenburg is home to one of the last relatively unspoiled delta regions in Europe, the Unteres Odertal (Lower Oder

BRANDENBURG

Valley). Established in 1995, the 105 sq km cross-border reserve (of which 60 sq km lie in Poland) has an enormous range of flora and fauna, and acts as a breeding ground for over 120 kinds of birds, including sea eagles, black storks and other endangered species. Meadows, marshland and deciduous forest make up a large part of the grounds, which is 60km long but just 2 to 3km wide in most spots. One-tenth has been designated a 'total reserve' (ie no human interference); by 2008, this percentage will rise to 50%. In October, the sky darkens when up to 13,000 migratory cranes stop off in the park on their way south – a spectacular sight.

Orientation & Information

Gartz is the northernmost town on the German side of the Oder, just across from the Polish city of Stettin (Szczecin). Stolpe is the largest settlement to the south, situated just off a globlet of park delta. Halfway in between lies Schwedt, gateway into the region and a suitable point to launch your cycling, canoeing or hiking tour.

The Nationalparkverwaltung (National Park Authority) Unteres Odertal, Bootsweg 1 in Schwedt (☎ 03332-254 70, fax 25 47 33) and the Schwedt tourist office (☎ 255 90, fax 25 59 59) at Lindenallee 36 organise three-hour **free guided tours** of sections of the park most Saturdays during summer. Departure is from the Schwedt tourist office and other points (either on foot or by bicycle). The latter also sells hiking and bicycle maps for the dozen-odd paths on the Brandenburg side between Stettin and Hohensaaten.

Campingplatz Mescherin (☎ 03332-807 07, Dorfstrasse 6) is the only camp site in the park, in Mescherin near its northern end.

Getting There & Away

Either RE or RB trains go to Schwedt from Eberswalde (DM12, one hour), Chorin (DM9.80, 50 minutes) and Berlin (DM28, 1¾ hours). There's also a slow regional service to Schwedt from Neubrandenburg (DM38, 2¼ hours). Trains from Rheinsberg take nearly five hours, go via Berlin-

Lichtenberg or Friedrichstrasse (DM50 to DM55) and require at least two changes.

For drivers, the park is 30 to 50km due east of the north-south Berlin-Stettin autobahn A11. Schwedt is at the junction of the B2, which runs north-south along the German border, and the B166, which leads east from the A11 to Choina (Königsberg) in Poland.

Getting Around

You can borrow bicycles from DM10 per day from shops including Fahrradhaus (☎ 03332-230 97), Virradenstrasse 31a in Schwedt; Hotel Stolper Turm (☎ 033338-333) in Stolpe; and Förderverein Gartz (☎ 033332-834), Stettiner Strasse 37c in Gartz. A number of places along the river rent out canoes and kayaks from DM5/30 per hour/day.

CHORIN
☎ 033366 • pop 522

Kloster Chorin (Chorin Monastery), in this little town 60km north-east of Berlin, is considered to be one of the finest red-brick Gothic structures in northern Germany, and the classical music festival (the Choriner Musiksommer) held here in summer is world-class. There's no tourist office, but the reception desk at the Hotel Haus Chorin (☎ 447) acts as a sort of de facto information centre.

Chorin was founded by Cistercian monks in 1273, and 500 of them laboured over six decades to erect their monastery and church of red brick on a granite base (a practice copied by the Franciscans at the Nikolaikirche and Marienkirche in Berlin). The monastery was secularised in 1542 following Elector Joachim II's conversion to Protestantism and, after the Thirty Years' War, it fell into disrepair. Renovation of the structure (instigated by Schinkel) has gone on in a somewhat haphazard fashion since the early 19th century.

The entrance to the monastery is through the bright red and ornate western facade and leads to the central cloister and ambulatory, where the summer concerts are held. To the north is the early-Gothic **Klosterkirche**, with its wonderful carved portals and long lancet windows in the apse. Have a look along the walls at floor level to see the layer of granite supporting the porous handmade bricks. The monastery is open daily from April to October between 9 am and 6 pm, and to 4 pm the rest of the year (DM4/2 for adults/children and DM5 for parking).

The celebrated Choriner Musiksommer takes place in the monastery cloister from June to August on most Saturdays and Sundays at 3 pm; expect to hear some top talent. For information, contact the organisers at ☎ 03334-65 73 10, Schickelstrasse 5, in Eberswalde Finow. Tickets are available through ticket agencies in Berlin. There are chamber music concerts in the church, said to have near perfect acoustics, on certain Sundays at 4 pm from late May to August.

Getting There & Away

Chorin is served by regional trains from Berlin-Ostbahnhof (DM16.20, 50 minutes) about every two hours. The train station in Chorin town is about 3km north-west of the monastery, but you can reach it via a marked trail in less than half an hour.

Buses link Chorin with Eberswalde Hauptbahnhof, which is served from Berlin as well as from Frankfurt an der Oder (1¾ hours). They stop close to the monastery entrance along the B2.

NIEDERFINOW
☎ 033362 • pop 700

The Schiffshebewerk (ship's lift) at Niederfinow, south-east of Chorin, is one of the most remarkable feats of engineering from the early 20th century. It's also fun, especially for kids. A mechanical hoist (1934) allows barges to clear the difference of 36m in height between the Oder River and the Oder-Havel Canal. This being Germany, technical data about the structure is posted everywhere ('60m high, 27m wide, 94m long' etc), but it's still an amazing sight watching 1200-tonne Polish barges laden with coal being hoisted in a watery cradle up from the Oder and deposited in the canal.

The lift can be viewed from Hebewerk-strasse for free, but it's much more fun to pay the DM2/1 and climb the steps to the upper platform to view the 10 minute operation from above. It's open daily from May to September between 9 am and 6 pm, and to 4 pm the rest of the year.

A tourist information point (☎ 701 95) is in the car park on Hebewerkstrasse next to the lift. It's open weekdays from 10 am to 6 pm and Saturday from 10 am to 2 pm. You can also contact the Eberswalde tourist office (☎ 03334-231 68) in the Pavillion am Markt.

Oder-Havel Schiffahrt (mobile ☎ 0171 551 80 85) has 1½ hour boat trips (DM10/8) along the Oder-Havel Canal and down onto the Oder via the Schiffshebewerk a couple of times a day between April and October. The embarkation point is along the canal about 3km west of the lift.

Niederfinow is reachable by regional train from Berlin-Lichtenberg (DM16.20, one hour), with a change at Eberswalde. The Schiffshebewerk is about 2km to the north of the station, and the way is signposted.

Saxony

Saxony (Sachsen) is the most densely populated and industrialised region in eastern Germany. Saxon tribes originally occupied large parts of north-western Germany, but in the 10th century they expanded southeast into the territory of the pagan Slavs.

The medieval history of the various Saxon duchies and dynasties is complex, but in the 13th century the Duke of Saxony at Wittenberg obtained the right to participate in the election of Holy Roman emperors. Involvement in Poland weakened Saxony in the 18th century, and ill-fated alliances, first with Napoleon and then with Austria, led to the ascendancy of Prussia over Saxony in the 19th century.

In the south, Saxony is separated from Bohemia in the Czech Republic by the Erzgebirge, eastern Germany's highest mountain range. The Elbe River cuts northwest from the Czech border through a picturesque area known as 'Saxon Switzerland' towards the capital, Dresden. Leipzig, a great educational and commercial centre on the Weisse Elster River, rivals Dresden in historic importance, and upstages it in accessibility and fun. Quaint little towns like Weesenstein, Görlitz and Meissen punctuate this colourful, accessible corner of Germany.

Accommodation

Note that you can book accommodation in all regions, at no extra charge, through the Information and Booking Office of the Saxony Tourism Association (☎ 0351-49 17 00, fax 496 93 06), Friedrichstrasse 24, 01067 Dresden.

Central Saxony

DRESDEN
☎ 0351 • pop 485,000
In the 18th century the Saxon capital, Dresden, was famous throughout Europe as 'the Florence of the north'. During the 69-year

HIGHLIGHTS

Saxony Luminaries: JC Bach, Hanns Eisler, GW Leibniz, Karl Liebknecht, Friedrich Wilhelm Nietzsche, Robert Schumann, Richard Wagner, Clara Wieck-Schumann

• Visiting the Stasi Museum and all-night cafes and bars in Leipzig

• Wandering through Dresden's Zwinger, Semperoper and museums

• Touring Meissen's porcelain factory

• Enjoying the wilds of Saxon Switzerland and the Bastei's stunning views

• Catching the steam train into the Zittau Mountains

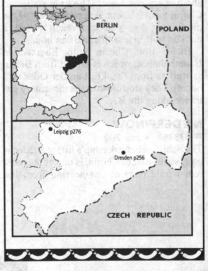

reign of Augustus the Strong and his son Augustus III, Italian artists, musicians, actors and master craftsmen, particularly from Venice, flocked to the court at Dresden.

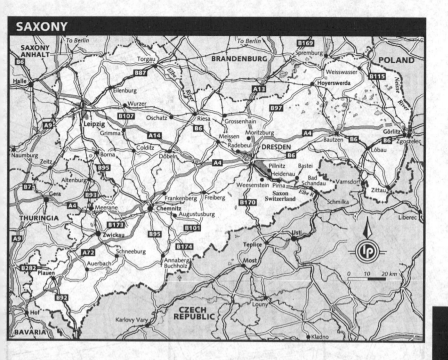

SAXONY

The Italian painter Canaletto depicted the era's rich architecture in many paintings, which now hang in Dresden's Old Masters Gallery alongside countless masterpieces purchased for Augustus III with income from the silver mines of Saxony.

Much of Dresden was devastated by Anglo-American fire-bombing raids in February 1945. At least 35,000 people died in the attack, which happened at a time when the city was jammed with refugees and the war was almost over. There's great debate about the bombing of Dresden, which was inspired more by vengeance than strategic necessity.

Quite a number of Dresden's great baroque buildings have been restored – although many of them still exude the carbonised elegance of the prewar and GDR periods. The city's former architectural masterpiece, the Frauenkirche, is in the early stages of a laborious reconstruction.

The Elbe River cuts a ribbon between the low, rolling hills, and despite its ugly outlying districts, this sprawling city invariably wins the affection of visitors. With its fine museums and baroque palaces, a stay of three nights is the minimum required to appreciate Dresden.

Orientation

The Elbe River cuts through town in a rough V-shape that splits the northern Neustadt, the bohemian pub district, from the Altstadt to the south.

Most of Dresden's priceless art treasures are south of the Elbe in two large buildings, the Albertinum and the Zwinger, which are at opposite sides of the Altstadt. From the Hauptbahnhof, the hideous, pedestrianised Prager Strasse leads north into the old centre. Major redevelopment is under way for the area around the Hauptbahnhof and

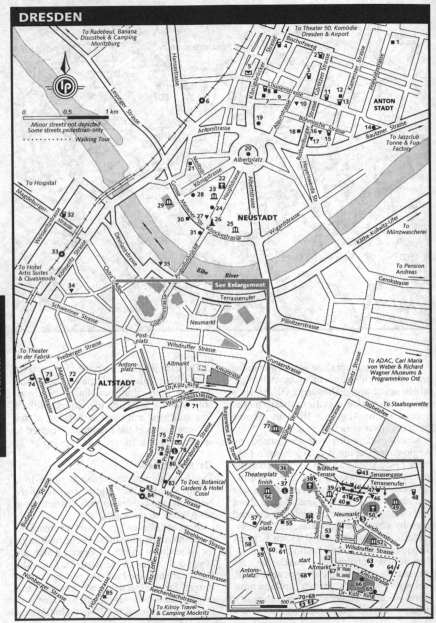

DRESDEN

PLACES TO STAY		68	Zum Goldenen Ring	36	Semperoper
1	Pension Edith	80	Schlemmerland	37	Tourist Office Schinkelwache
7	Hostel Mondpalast			38	Hofkirche
9	Jugendhotel Die Boofe	**PUBS & CLUBS**		39	Museum of Transport
12	Hotel Stadt Rendsburg	2	Café 100	43	Dock for Paddle-wheel
18	Rothenburger Hof	3	El Perro Borracho		Steamers
21	Hotel Martha Hospiz	4	Café Europa	44	Kasamatten
30	Westin Bellevue	8	Planwirtschaft	47	Kunstakademie
40	Dresden Hilton	11	Blumenau	49	Albertinum
55	Hotel Kempinski Taschenberg	13	Mona Lisa	50	Frauenkirche
	Palais & Sophienkeller	15	Lloyds Kaffeehaus	51	Dresdner Bank
64	Radisson SAS Hotel	32	Yenidze Disco	52	City Historical Museum
72	DJH Jugendgästehaus	41	Café Antik Kunst	53	Kulturpalast
	Dresden	48	Bärenzwinger	54	Schloss
75	Hotel Lilienstein			56	Zwinger
79	Hotel Königstein	**OTHER**		57	Staatsschauspiel
81	Hotel Bastei	5	Main Post Office	60	Haus Des Buches
82	Mercure Newa Dresden	6	Dresden-Neustadt Train	61	Lufthansa City Centre
85	Rudi Arndt Hostel		Station	63	Flugtheke Travel Agency
		14	Pfunds Molkerei	65	Neues Rathaus
PLACES TO EAT		19	Öko-Express Laundry	66	Das Internationale Buch
10	Scheunecafé	20	Fountains	67	Kreuzkirche
16	Raskolnikoff	22	Dreikönigskirche	69	Commerzbank
17	Marrakech	23	Museum of Early Dresden	70	Dresdner Bank
27	Andrea Doria		Romanticism & Kügelgenhaus	71	Karstadt, Cyberb@r &
34	brennNessel	24	Podium Theatre		Karstadt's Reisebüro
35	Four Restaurants	25	Museum of Saxon Folk Art	73	World Trade Centre
42	Crêpes Galerie	26	Goldener Reiter	74	Hostel Tram Stop
45	Dampf Schiff	28	ADM-Mitfahrzentrale	76	Post Office
46	Klepper Eck	29	Japanisch Palais &	77	Hygiene Museum
58	Pavillon		Ethnological Museum	78	Tourist Office
59	Sächsischer Feinbäcker	31	Blockhaus	83	Bus Station
62	McDonald's	33	Dresden-Mitte Train Station	84	Main Train Station

Prager Strasse, including a dozen new high-rise buildings, as well as pedestrian and traffic underpasses.

In Neustadt, the main attractions for visitors are the Albertplatz and Anton Stadt quarters. The charming Hauptstrasse is pedestrianised and connects Albertplatz with Augustusbrücke.

Train & Boat Stations Dresden has two important train stations: the Hauptbahnhof, on the southern side of town, and the nicer Dresden-Neustadt north of the river. Most trains stop at both, but the Hauptbahnhof is more convenient unless you're staying in Neustadt. Tram Nos 3 and 11, S-Bahns and many other trains make the 10 minute run between the two stations.

The forlorn Dresden-Mitte is a third station between the two main ones.

Paddle-wheel steamers run by Sächsische Dampfschiffahrt (☎ 86 60 90) are an important form of transport in the region; they leave from docks at Terrassenufer (see Organised Tours later in this section and Elbe River Excursions in the Around Dresden section).

Information
Tourist Offices The tourist information office (☎ 49 19 20, fax 49 19 21 16, email info@dresdentourist.de) is at Prager Strasse 21, on the eastern side of the pedestrian street leading away from the Hauptbahnhof. It's open weekdays from 9 am to 7 pm and Saturday from 9 am to 4 pm (closed Sunday). A

euro currency converter DM1 = €0.51

SAXONY

second office is in Schinkelwache, Theaterplatz 2 in the shadow of the Semperoper. It's open weekdays from 10 am to 6 pm and weekends to 4 pm. It's also open on some holidays when the others are closed.

Ask at all these offices about the 48 hour Dresden-Card (DM27), which gives free admission to 11 museums, discounts on city tours and river boats, as well as free use of public transport. As we went to press, the city was mulling over a sweeping revamp of its timetables – including bus and tram line numbers cited later in this chapter.

The German Auto Association, ADAC (☎ 44 78 80) is at Schandauer Strasse 46 and has a rental office (☎ 470 70 78) at the Hauptbahnhof.

Money The Reisebank has several branches with EC/Plus and Visa ATMs in the Hauptbahnhof. There are branches of the Commerzbank and Dresdner Bank at the northern end of Prager Strasse in the island between Waisenhausstrasse and Dr-Külz-Ring. There's another Dresdner Bank on Neumarkt near the Frauenkirche.

Post & Communications The main post office is in the Neustadt at Königsbrücker Strasse 21, north of Antonstrasse. There's a more central one at Prager Strasse 72 next to the tourist office. To surf the Web, the Cyberb@r on the top floor of the huge Karstadt department store, Prager Strasse 12, charges DM5 per half hour.

Internet Resources Dresden's multilingual Web site, with an events calendar and online hotel booking function, is at www.dresden.de.

Travel Agencies Karstadt's Reisebüro (☎ 861 25 10), Prager Strasse 12, is a leading city travel agent. There's an office of Kilroy Travel (☎ 472 08 64) at Zellescher Weg 21; and Flugtheke (☎ 496 02 48), Kreuzstrasse 3, is a discounter with some good deals. There's also a Lufthansa office (☎ 49 98 80) at Wilsdruffer 25-29.

Bookshops There's slim pickings at all three malodorous Hauptbahnhof bookshops, which have English newspapers and magazines on sale.

The best book selection (with lots of Lonely Planet titles) is in the Haus Des Buches (☎ 495 21 35), Wilsdruffer 29 at Postplatz. Das Internationale Buch (☎ 495 41 90) on Kreuzstrasse also has an excellent collection of English books, with some of the lowest prices in Germany.

Laundry The tiny Öko-Express, on the corner of Albertplatz and Königsbrückenstrasse, charges just DM3.50 per load, and DM1 for 10 minutes drying. There's also a Münzwascherei (☎ 442 22 00) on the south side of the Elbe at Pfeifferhannstrasse 13-15.

Medical Services Northwest of the Altstadt in the Friedrichstadt part of town is Krankenhaus Dresden-Friedrichstadt (☎ 48 00), a hospital and clinic. A Red Cross clinic is in the Hauptbahnhof for emergencies.

Dangers & Annoyances The train stations are all less than fabulous places after dark, attracting more than the usual number of layabouts, skinheads and other reprobates. Be especially cautious at night in the area around Dresden-Mitte station.

Historic Centre Walking Tour
Our 3.5km circuit begins at Altmarkt and makes an arc north-west along the Elbe, taking in the main churches, the Albertinum, the Semperoper and the Zwinger palace. It's a 1½ hour stroll, but stops at several places could easily stretch the tour to a day.

The Altmarkt area is the historic centre of Dresden. Today it looks and feels just like Warsaw did a few years ago. They seem to have used the same decorator, resulting in lots of granite, socialist-realist statues and an impractically wide area that's sometimes filled with a market. Many restaurants have set up street-side cafes, and when the markets aren't operating it's nice to sit outside and gaze across the square.

From its centre, proceed east to the rebuilt **Kreuzkirche** (1792). Originally the Nikolaikirche, the church was renamed for a cross *(Kreuz)* found floating in the Elbe River by fishermen. The church is famous for its 400-strong boys' choir, the Kreuzchor, which performs every Saturday at 6 pm (free, donations requested).

Behind the Kreuzkirche stands the neo-Renaissance **Neues Rathaus** (1905-10), topped by a shining golden statue of Hercules. Today it's the offices of the city administration, and while you can enter and gawk at the lobby, there are no scheduled tours of the building.

From Altmarkt to Albertinum Cross the wide Wilsdruffer Strasse to the **City Historical Museum** in a building erected in 1775. It contains exhibits on the city's history up to 1989. It's open Tuesday to Sunday from 10 am to 6 pm (DM4/2). Due west of here, oppsite the Altmarkt and the rather princely McDonald's, is a centre of the city's cultural life, the obnoxiously squat **Kulturpalast**, home to a huge range of concerts and performances year round. When they replace the air-conditioning system it should sound (and feel) great.

Pass through Galeriestrasse to the right of the Kulturpalast and you'll reach the grassy **Neumarkt** – no longer a market these days – with the **Frauenkirche** (Church of Our Lady) wrapped in scaffolding at its eastern end.

The Frauenkirche was built under the direction of baroque architect George Bähr from 1726 to 1738. Until the end of WWII it was Germany's greatest Protestant church, its enormous dome known as the 'stone bell'. The bombing raids of 13 February 1945 flattened it, and the communists decided to leave the rubble as a war memorial. After reunification, the grass-roots movement to rebuild the church prompted reconstruction and a huge archaeological dig to begin in 1992. Today you can see most of the building's 10,000 pieces in open shelters on Neumarkt. Reassembly of this huge puzzle is expected to take at least until 2006 (Dresden's 800th anniversary). You can take a one hour guided tour (several daily, German only) of the Frauenkirche site. It's free, but donations are greatly encouraged, especially so from British and American visitors, who are made to feel more than a little guilty for blowing it up in the first place.

From the Frauenkirche, turn east up Rampstrasse and veer north-east through the path which leads to the Brühlscher Garten, the lovely green park east of the main terrace.

In front stands the **Albertinum** (☎ 491 47 30) which houses many of Dresden's art treasures (and underneath, a brand-new parking garage). Inside you'll find the **New Masters Gallery**, with renowned 19th and 20th century paintings from leading French and German Impressionists, among others.

Here, too, is the **Grünes Gewölbe** (Green Vault), one of the world's finest collections of jewel-studded precious objects. Its treasures include the world's biggest green diamond – even size-conscious Texans would appreciate its 41 carats – and a stunning group of 137 gem-studded figures entitled *Court of Delhi on the Birthday of the Great Moghul*, fashioned by Johann Melchior Dinglinger, court jeweller of Augustus the Strong. Also in the Albertinum is the **Skulpturensammlung**, which includes classical and Egyptian works.

All museums are open from 10 am to 6 pm (closed Thursday) and cost DM7/4 for adults/children on a combined ticket. Eventually, the Grünes Gewölbe will be relocated to its original site in the Schloss, which is still under reconstruction.

From Brühlsche Terrasse to Zwinger From the Albertinum, do an about-face and go west, passing the gilded **Kunstakademie** (Academy of Arts) on your way to the **Brühlsche Terrasse**, a spectacular promenade. This has been called the balcony of Europe, with a pavement nearly 15m above the southern embankment of the Elbe. In summer it's a must for strolling, with expansive views of the river, the paddle-steamers and, across the river, the **Japanisch Palais** (Japanese Palace) and the baroque **Blockhaus**, a guardhouse designed by French architect Zacharias Longuelune.

Beneath the promenade is the Renaissance brick bastion commonly known as the **Kasamatten**. The museum inside is open daily (DM6/4). For an extra DM2 you can get a tape player and a cassette in English (or six other languages).

Take the double-sided staircase down to Brühler Gasse, which leads back to the Neumarkt. From here, turn right onto the fabulous Augustusstrasse, with its 102m-long *Procession of Princes* mural depicted on the outer wall of the former **Royal Stables**. The scene, a long row of horses, was first painted in 1876 by Wullhelm Walther and then transferred to some 24,000 Meissen porcelain tiles, which make up the mural. Join the crowds standing across the street and squinting.

Here you'll also find the **Verkehrsmuseum** (Transport Museum; ☎ 495 30 02), with its fascinating collection including penny-farthings, trams, dirigibles and carriages. Included in the admission is a great 40 minute film, *Dresden of the 1930s*, with original black-and-white footage and German commentary. It's shown daily at 10.45 am and 1.15, 2.30 and 3.45 pm. Museum hours are Tuesday to Sunday from 10 am to 5 pm (DM4/2).

Schlossplatz Augustusstrasse leads directly to Schlossplatz and the baroque Catholic **Hofkirche** (1755), with its crypt containing

The Procession of Princes Mural stretches for 102m and is made up of 24,000 porcelain tiles.

the heart of Augustus the Strong. Just south of the church is the neo-Renaissance **Schloss**, which is being reconstructed as a museum. Restoration of the palace is scheduled, a bit optimistically, to finish in 2006, although the Hausmannsturm (tower) and an exhibit on the reconstruction are now open to the public daily, except Monday (DM3/1.50).

Theaterplatz On the western side of the Hofkirche is Theaterplatz, with Dresden's picture-postcard **Semperoper**. The first opera house on the site opened in 1841 but burned down less than three decades later. Rebuilt in 1878, it was pummelled in WWII and re-opened only in 1985, after the communists invested millions in restoring this neo-Renaissance jewel. The Dresden opera has a tradition going back 350 years, and many works by Richard Strauss, Carl Maria von Weber and Richard Wagner premiered here.

Zwinger From the opera house, proceed south a few metres to reach the sprawling baroque Zwinger (1728), which occupies the southern side of Theaterplatz. Its lovely, fountain-studded courtyard is framed by an open-air gallery and several charming portals (one is reachable via a long footbridge over a moat). The Zwinger was badly damaged during the war but has been mostly rebuilt, although work is ongoing – you can watch the masons chiselling away in the rooftop workshop. Conceived by star architect Mattaeus Pöppelmann for royal tournaments and festivals, the exterior has some fine examples of baroque sculpture (which are endlessly photographed). Atop the western pavilion stands a tense-looking **Atlas** with the world on his shoulders. At the opposite end of the courtyard is a cutesy carillon of 40 Meissen porcelain bells, which chime on the hour.

The Zwinger houses five museums. The most important are the **Old Masters Gallery** (DM7/4), which features masterpieces including Raphael's *Sistine Madonna*; and the **Historical Museum** (DM3/1.50), with its superb collection of ceremonial weapons. Both are open Tuesday to Sunday from 10 am to 6 pm.

Other museums include the **Mathematics and Physics Salon** with old instruments, globes and timepieces. It's open 9.30 am to 5 pm, closed Thursday (DM3/2). The **Museum für Tierkunde** (Zoological Museum) has natural history exhibits and is open from 9 am to 4 pm, closed Tuesday (DM2/1). The dazzling **Porcelain Collection** is open from 10 am to 6 pm, closed Thursday (DM3/2). All are housed in opposite corners of the complex with separate entrances.

This walking tour ends with an ice-cream from one of the courtyard vendors (DM1 a scoop).

Yenidze

As your train rolls into Dresden-Mitte station, you can't miss a large building looking very much like a gaudy mosque, bearing the word *Yenidze* on its stained-glass onion dome. In 1907, the place opened as a to-bacco factory, manufacturing a cigarette named Salaam Alakhem. It was modelled after a mosque to inspire interest in its foreign intrigue and allegedly Turkish tobacco. (It didn't work.) The place has been in financial turmoil since an expensive post-unification facelift, but its nifty basement disco thuds on.

Neustadt

Neustadt is an old part of Dresden largely untouched by the wartime bombings. After unification, Neustadt became the centre of the city's alternative scene, but as entire street blocks are renovated it's gradually losing its bohemian feel. Königstrasse, which runs parallel and to the west of Hauptstrasse, is developing into a swish shopping district.

The **Goldener Reiter** statue (1736) of Augustus the Strong stands at the northern end of the Augustusbrücke. This leads to the pleasant pedestrian mall of Hauptstrasse. Here is the **Museum of Early Dresden Romanticism** (☎ 804 47 60) in the Kügelgenhaus, an impressive baroque structure at No 13. It's open Wednesday to Sunday from 10 am to 6 pm (DM3/1.50).

Moving north you'll come to the newly renovated **Dreikönigskirche**, the parish church designed by Pöppelmann. It houses some lovely Renaissance artworks, including the *Dance of Death* frieze which once hung in the Schloss.

On **Albertplatz** at its northern end there's an evocative marble **Schiller monument**, a pretty artesian well in front of the GDR-era Nudelturm tower, and two lovely **fountains** flanking the walkway down the centre.

Museums in the vicinity include the **Museum für Sächsische Volkskunst** (Museum of Saxon Folk Art; ☎ 491 46 19) at Köpckestrasse 1, which is open Tuesday to Sunday from 10 am to 6 pm (DM3/2); and the Japanisch Palais (1737) on Palaisplatz, which has Dresden's famous **Ethnological Museum** (☎ 814 48 51). The latter is open from 10 am to 5 pm daily, except Friday (DM3/1.50).

Pfunds Molkerei

It's billed as 'the world's most beautiful dairy shop', and for good reason: from top to bottom, the interior of Pfunds Molkerei is a riot of hand-painted tiles and enamelled sculpture. Founded by the Pfund brothers in 1880, the dairy claims to have invented condensed milk. The place was nationalised by the GDR in 1972 and fell into disrepair before restoration in 1995 (the tiles are all Villeroy & Boch and worth a fortune, so don't break anything). Located at Bautzner Strasse 79, the shop (☎ 816 20) sells lovely wines, cheeses and milk (DM2 a glass), and there's a cafe-restaurant upstairs with a strong milk-products theme.

Great Garden

South-east of the Altstadt is the Great Garden (Grosser Garten), enchanting in summer and home to the excellent **zoo** (☎ 47 80 60). With 2600 animals representing more than 400 species, it's open daily from 8.30 am to 6.30 pm, and to 4.30 pm from November to March (DM10/6). Last entry is 45 minutes before closing time. At the garden's north-western corner are the **Botanical Gardens** (free). The hothouse is especially lovely during a freezing Dresden winter.

SAXONY

Other Museums

In a park west of the Great Garden is the unique **Hygiene Museum** (☎ 484 60), Lingnerplatz 1, just off Blüher Strasse, established by Odol-mouthwash mogul Karl August Lingner. It'll appeal to anyone with a healthy interest in the human body, and contains cutaway models, the transparent man and other health related exhibits, including a good one on STDs and AIDS. It's open daily, except Monday (DM5/3).

On the south-eastern outskirts of town, on the way to Pillnitz, is the interesting **Carl Maria von Weber Museum** (☎ 261 82 34), Dresdner Strasse 44, the summer home of the composer and conductor who lived and worked here for several years before his death in England in 1826 at age 39. Staff are very keen, and there are regular concerts here as well. The museum is open Wednesday to Sunday from 1 to 6 pm (DM3/1.50). Take bus No 85 to Van-Gogh-Strasse in Pillnitz.

Also impressive is the **Richard Wagner Museum** (☎ 482 29), in a positively serene setting at Richard-Wagner-Strasse 6 in Graupa (bus No 83). Dedicated staff talk you through each detail of the stormy composer's life in GDR-style mind-numbing thoroughness. (The maestro's favourite breakfast food? We won't give it away.) But there are some very nice exhibits, and again, the grounds are lovely. It's open daily, except Monday, from 10 am to 5 pm (DM5/3.50).

Organised Tours

The tourist office on Prager Strasse books tours with a number of organisations.

You can get off the beaten track with thematic tours from Igeltour (☎ 804 45 57), starting at DM6. River tours are run by Sächsische Dampfschiffahrt (☎ 86 60 90) on rebuilt steam ships that lower their smokestacks to clear bridges. It prides itself on having the world's oldest fleet of paddle-wheel steamers. The 90-minute tours run daily at 11 am and 1, 3 and 5 pm (DM18/9). See also Elbe River Excursions in the Around Dresden section later in this chapter.

The Hamburger Hummelbahn (☎ 498 95 19) runs double-decker buses, 'choo-choo' trains and other touristy vehicles around the city, stopping at all the major sights (at clearly marked 'Hummelbahn' stops). Tours (also available in English) leave from Postplatz from April to October daily at the same hours as the boats (DM20/16, 1½ hours).

Special Events

Dresden's annual events calendar includes the **Parade of the Sächsische Dampfschiffahrt fleet** on May 1, a unique, smoke-puffing sight; the **International Dixieland Festival** in early May, with around 250 concerts at 60 venues; the **Dresden Music Festival** in May/June, with classical concerts in the palaces, theatres and churches; and the **Dresden City Festival** in late August, with something for everyone.

Places to Stay – Budget

Accommodation in Dresden can be horrendously expensive, with hotel rates among the highest in Germany. Luckily, several new budget places have emerged in or near the centre.

There are two camping grounds near Dresden. The closest is *Camping Mockritz* (☎/fax 471 52 50), open from March to December, 5km south of the city (take the frequent No 76 Mockritz bus from behind the Dresden Hauptbahnhof). Often full in summer, it also has bungalows available.

A more appealing, if distant, choice is the spacious *Camping Moritzburg* (☎ 035207-814 23), open from April to mid-October. It's a 10 minute walk from Schloss Moritzburg (see Around Dresden).

DJH Jugendgästehaus Dresden (☎ 49 26 20, fax 492 62 99, Maternistrasse 22) is a fantastic place in an old Communist Party training centre. Beds cost DM33/38 for juniors/seniors in basic twin or triple rooms; add DM5 for ones with private shower and WC (toilet). Singles cost an extra DM15. From the Hauptbahnhof, take tram No 7, 9, 10 or 26 to the corner of Ammonstrasse and Freiberger Strasse (look for the World Trade Centre building) and walk about one block east.

Hostel Mondpalast (☎/fax 804 60 61, Katharinenstrasse 11-13) is a leading Neustadt budget option, with bedrooms decorated by theme (Australia, Greece, space travel etc). The friendly owners charge from DM25 for beds in dorm rooms, and DM37/62 for simple singles/doubles. There's a nice kitchen and lounge with TV/stereo, a bright breakfast gallery and a great pub next door.

Jugendhotel Die Boofe (☎ 801 33 61, fax 801 33 62, Louisenstrasse 20) offers near-hotel standards at DM49.50/79 for singles/doubles. But it can get a bit noisy – there's a pub downstairs and a fire station next door.

The non-DJH *Rudi Arndt Hostel (☎ 471 06 67, fax 472 89 59, Hübnerstrasse 11)* is a 10 minute walk south of the Hauptbahnhof and offers dorm beds for DM24/29 for juniors/seniors.

The tourist office at Prager Strasse 21 finds *private rooms* from around DM35 per person (plus a fee of DM5 per person).

Deutscher Zentraler Zimmernachweis (☎ 830 90 61, fax 830 90 79), in the northern side of the Hauptbahnhof, is a private accommodation agency that is worth checking out. It books rooms in private flats from DM30, pensions from DM35, hotels outside the centre for DM70/110 for singles/doubles, or inside the centre from DM99/110.

Hotel Stadt Rendsburg (☎ 804 15 51, fax 802 25 86, Kamenzer Strasse 1), built in 1884, offers basic rooms with shared bath for DM65/95, including breakfast.

The *Pension Edith (☎ 802 83 42, fax 80 28 34 23 42, Priesnitzstrasse 63)* is in a quiet spot and has rooms with a private shower for DM78/103; it only has a few, so book well ahead.

Artis Service Wohnen (☎/fax 864 50, Berliner Strasse 25), 1km west of the centre, offers basic rooms from DM60/90 (without breakfast).

Hotel Cosel (☎ 471 94 95, fax 471 01 71, August-Bebel-Strasse 46) is about 2km south-east of the Altstadt and charges from DM65/100.

Places to Stay – Mid-Range

Pension Andreas (☎ 31 57 70, fax 315 77 55, Mendelssohnallee 40-42), in the eastern quarter of Blasewitz, has singles/doubles with all the private facilities for DM90/120.

Hotel Bastei (☎ 485 66 61, fax 495 40 76), *Hotel Königstein (☎ 485 66 66, fax 495 40 54)* and *Hotel Lilienstein (☎ 485 66 63, fax 495 25 06)* are three almost identical 1960s-style Ibis hotels along Prager Strasse. Staff are about as interchangeable as the rates, with rooms from DM110/130.

Rothenburger Hof (☎ 812 60, fax 812 62 22, Rothenburger Strasse 15-17) has rooms with shared bath for DM105/165. *Hotel Martha Hospiz (☎ 817 60, fax 817 62 22, Nieritzstrasse 11)*, near Neustadt train station, offers very cheerful, simple single rooms for DM95, but most have private WC and shower and cost DM140/190.

Mercure Newa Dresden (☎ 481 41 09, fax 495 51 37, St Petersburger Strasse 34) is perfectly located at the southern end of Prager Strasse, a minute's walk from the Hauptbahnhof. Clean, perfectly fine rooms cost from DM158/168.

The *Westin Bellevue (☎ 80 50, fax 805 16 09, email hotelinfo@westin-bellevue.de, Grosse Meissner Strasse 15)*, just south of the Japanisch Palais, has unparalleled views across to the Brühlsche Terrasse, the ferry terminal, Neues Rathaus and the Kreuzkirche. Rooms cost from DM160/180.

Places to Stay – Top End

The *Dresden Hilton (☎ 864 20, fax 864 27 25, email Dresden-Hilton@t-online.de, An der Frauenkirche 5)* manages to charge from DM295 for very mod (but very 60s) rooms.

The *Radisson SAS Gewandhaushotel (☎ 494 90, fax 494 94 90, email info@ drszh.vd.sas.com, Ringstrasse 1)*, just south of Wilsdruffer Strasse, has top-notch rooms from DM270, plus a very Scandinavian DM29 for breakfast.

The *Hotel Kempinski Taschenberg Palais (☎ 491 20, fax 491 28 12, email reservation@kempinski-dresden.de, Taschenberg 3)* drips luxury. In a restored 18th century mansion opposite the Zwinger, it has a swimming pool, health club, business centre, sauna and solarium. Rooms cost a heart-stopping DM390/450, but in July and August there are special rates of DM295 per room (including all the extras).

Places to Eat

Restaurants – Altstadt Interesting restaurants are scattered pretty thinly south of the Elbe. Beneath the Brühlsche Terrasse, Terrassengasse is a great place in summer, with cafes and cheap options for sitting and watching the world go by.

Crêpes Galerie (☎ *864 29 46, Terrassengasse)* has crepes from DM8 to DM12 and drinks from DM3. *Dampf Schiff* (☎ *864 28 26)* and *Klepper Eck* (☎ *864 24 39)*, both on the corner of Münzgasse, are street-side locales with good beer, decent food and great views of people walking up to the Brühlsche Terrasse.

Zum Goldenen Ring (☎ *495 23 20, Seestrasse 6)*, opposite the Kreuzkirche, is reasonable, with main courses for around DM13. The *brennNessel* (☎ *494 33 19, Schützengasse 18)* is a good vegetarian restaurant with meals like wholemeal noodles and sheep's cheese in bell pepper sauce (DM13.60) and leek, potato and sunflower seed casserole (DM14.50).

The *Sophienkeller* (☎ *49 72 60)*, under the Hotel Kempinski Taschenberg Palais, is a very interesting place, with good local specialities and wines and excellent service, even if staff do have a tendency to burst into song (they sing good German and folk songs, they don't beg for tips, and you can tell them to leave you alone). Full dinners are DM25 to DM40, while main courses are DM16 to DM28.

The *Four Restaurants/Opernrestaurant* (☎ *491 15 21, Theaterplatz 2)* is opposite the Semperoper and offers stylish surroundings and varied food, from Italian to German specialities, at equally stylish prices. It's also a nice spot for drinks after a performance.

Restaurants – Neustadt The *Andrea Doria* (☎ *803 29 49, Hauptstrasse 1a)* has

super service and nice street-side dining. Lunch main courses range from DM14 to DM20, and it's open from 11 to 2 am.

The hotel, *Rothenburger Hof* has alternating evening menus for around DM13 (closed Monday).

For something special, dine at the *Kügelgenhaus* (☎ *527 91, Hauptstrasse 13)*, below the Museum of Early Dresden Romanticism in Neustadt. It has a good range of local Saxon dishes, and there's a beer cellar below the restaurant.

The *Scheunecafé* (☎ *803 66 19, Alaunstrasse 36)* is good value, with a delicious five course Indian menu for just DM35 for two people.

Raskolnikoff (☎ *804 57 06, Böhmische Strasse 34)* is very bohemian, with cheap Russian dishes like *borscht* (beetroot soup) and *wareniki* (dough baked with potatoes and mushrooms). It's located underneath the Galerie Erhardt sign.

Despite its name, *Marrakech* (☎ *804 55 66, Rothenburger Strasse 16)* offers mainly Uzbeki and Russian dishes such as *blinktschik* (a spicy hamburger-and-onion pancake) for DM12, or borscht with beef, fish or *pelmeni* (stuffed pastry pockets) from DM8. The bearded chef looks a bit like Rasputin. It's only open in the evenings.

Snacks & Fast Food The three markets in the Hauptbahnhof are good for stocking up before a trip. The *Asia Markt* is the best of the lot, but there's also a *Markt im Hauptbahnhof* and the more expensive *Reise Point Markt*.

Schlemmerland on Prager Strasse is a collection of fast-food joints, selling doner kebabs, pizzas, fish, pastries and Asian dishes – much of it for DM6 or less. Along here there's also a *Burger King* and on Altmarkt, the inevitable *McDonald's*.

Around Postplatz there are several fast-food options, though the clientele at some is, shall we say, scruffy. The *Pavillon* is the nicest of these, with good doner (DM4), *Grillhaxe* (grilled pork leg) with sauerkraut (DM8.50) and half chickens (DM4.50). Across the road there's a good

Sächsischer Feinbäcker with pastry, cheese bread and the like.

Entertainment

The finest all-round listings guide to Dresden is *SAX* (DM2.50), available at newsstands around the city. It has listings for clubs, restaurants, schools, cafes, travel agencies, cheap tickets and a whole lot more. Freebies include *Blitz*, *Dresdner* and the *Kneipensurfer*, a useful map listing of Neustadt's better pubs.

Pubs & Cafes The best area to head to for a drink is the Neustadt, which has droves of cafe-pubs.

Bärenzwinger (☎ 495 14 09, Brühlscher Garten) is a cheap students' bar in an old cellar in the back of the Albertinum. It features pantomime, cabaret or live music most nights.

Café Antik Kunst (☎ 498 98 36, Terrassengasse), behind the Hilton, is an antique shop and cafe where you sit on really expensive furniture and sip good coffee (DM3 to DM9).

Neustadt's choice of late-night restaurant-bars includes the *Planwirtschaft (☎ 801 31 87, Louisenstrasse 20)*, a beer cellar through the courtyard. *Café 100 (☎ 801 77 29, Alaunstrasse 100)* is another enticing, candle-lit cellar pub.

Café Europa (☎ 38 99 23, Königsbrücker Strasse 68) is a relaxed place, with plenty of newspapers lying around and intimate lighting. *El Perro Borracho (☎ 803 67 23, Alaunstrasse 70)*, perhaps Dresden's best Hispanic pub, was being remodelled as we went to press.

Mona Lisa (☎ 803 31 51, Louisenstrasse 77) is a quasi-Caribbean cocktail bar, while the *Blumenau (☎ 802 65 02, Louisenstrasse 67)* nearby is a trendy pub, perfect for seeing and being seen. Both get pretty packed on warm summer evenings.

Lloyds Kaffeehaus (☎ 803 67 90, Martin-Luther-Strasse 17) is an intellectual but cosy place, with bookcases, homemade cakes and a plentiful range of coffees. There's live music every night.

Discos & Clubs The *Yenidze (☎ 494 00 94, Weisseritzstrasse 3)*, near Dresden-Mitte station, is a hip place in the basement of this weird former tobacco company. It attracts a mixed, table-dancing crowd who wear as little as possible. On Friday night women get in free and get a DM10 coupon for drinks.

Fun Factory (☎ 502 24 51, Bautzner Strasse 118) is a very popular spot with hip hop, acid jazz and some techno, but the bouncers can be very choosy.

Mega Drome (☎ 837 12 21, Meissner Landstrasse 507) is a techno temple in Radebeul. Older crowds find solace at *Banana Diskothek (☎ 84 20 40, Lommatzscher Strasse 82)* in the Elbepark/Stadthaus.

Theatre There's an active theatre scene in Dresden, with many small companies playing throughout the city; the best bet is to check in *SAX*. Dresden's two great theatres are the *Staatsschauspiel (☎ 49 13 50, Theaterstrasse 2)*, near the Zwinger, and the *Staatsoperette (Pirnaer Landstrasse 131)* in Leuben in the far east of the city.

Landesbühnen Sachsen (☎ 895 42 14, Meissner Strasse 152), in Radebeul, has a good range of drama, music and cabaret, along with some ballet and opera. *Podium (☎ 804 32 66, Hauptstrasse 11)* is a very cool alternative theatre. A couple more alternative places are *Theater in der Fabrik (☎ 421 45 05, Tharandter Strasse 33)* and, near the Jugendgästehaus Dresden, *theater 50 (☎ 859 09 95, Fechnerstrasse 2A)*, in the former GDR business centre near the World Trade Centre. Inside the latter is *Komödie Dresden)*, which is geared to comic plays.

Classical Music Dresden is synonymous with opera, and performances at the spectacular *Semperoper*, opposite the Zwinger, are brilliant. Performances by the renowned Philharmonic also take place in the Semperoper but mainly in the *Kulturpalast (☎ 486 63 06)*.

Tickets Theatre tickets can be bought at the Schinkelwache tourist office at Theaterplatz 2, the tourist office at Prager Strasse 21, or the theatre box office an hour before

SAXONY

performance. Tickets for the Semperoper cost from DM30, but they're usually booked out well in advance. In fact, the Schinkelwache office suggests that for major performances – *The Magic Flute*, *Der Freischütz*, *Fidelio* etc – you should reserve as far as a *year* in advance by writing to them at Besucherdienst Theaterkasse, Theaterplatz 2, Postfach 120712, 01067 Dresden.

Many theatres close for holidays from mid-July to the end of August.

Rock, Jazz & Other Music A huge variety of concerts are held in the *Kulturpalast* (☎ 486 63 06), which changes its programs daily.

The *Jazzclub Tonne* (☎ 802 60 17, Am Brauhaus 3) has live jazz five nights a week (entry DM10 to DM30). Take bus No 11 to Waldschlösschenstrasse – it's in the complex behind the old brewery.

There's a fun jazz and Dixieland cruise on paddle-steamers every Friday and Saturday from 7 to 10 pm, with music, food and drinks during a swing up the Elbe. It's organised by Sächsische Dampfschiffahrt (☎ 86 60 90, Hertha-Lindner-Strasse 10) and costs DM24/12 for adults/children.

The *Lloyds Kaffeehaus* (☎ 803 67 90, Martin-Luther-Strasse 17) has an eclectic evening program of live music, including jazz, classical, flamenco and Yiddish. Entry is free.

Cinema Undubbed English films are shown at *Programmkino Ost* (☎ 310 37 82, Schandauer Strasse 73) and less frequently at *Quasimodo* (☎ 866 02 11, Adlergasse 14).

Getting There & Away
Dresden-Klotzsche airport, 9km north of the city centre, is served by Lufthansa, KLM and other major airlines.

Dresden is just over two hours south of Berlin-Lichtenberg (DM59) by fast train. The Leipzig-Riesa-Dresden service (DM40, 1¼ hours) operates hourly. The double-deck S-Bahn trains run half hourly to Meissen (DM7.70, 30 minutes). There are direct trains to Frankfurt (DM143, 5¼ hours), Munich

(DM155, seven hours), Vienna (DM152, six hours) and Prague (DM82, 2¾ hours).

Dresden's bus station is next to the Hauptbahnhof; regional buses depart for more remote Saxon destinations.

To/from Leipzig, take the A14/A4. From Berlin, take the A113 to the A13 south. To the Czech Republic, take the B170 south. From Munich, take the A9 to the A72 and on to the A4.

There's an ADM-Mitfahrzentrale (☎ 194 40) at Königstrasse 10. Some destinations and prices (including fees) are Berlin (DM25), Hamburg (DM53), Prague (DM27) and Munich (DM50).

Getting Around
The Airport City Liner runs between Dresden-Klotzsche airport, Dresden-Neustadt station (DM6) and the Hauptbahnhof (DM8). It runs weekdays from 7.30 am to 8.45 pm, Saturday from 8.30 am to 1 pm and 2.30 to 9 pm, and Sunday from 10 am to 1 pm and 2.30 to 9 pm. It's anticipated that a new S-Bahn train link will begin operating between the airport and the city centre from 2001.

Dresden's transport network charges DM2.70 for a one-zone single ticket and DM10 for four-ride strip tickets. Day/weekly tickets cost DM8/24. The family day ticket, for two adults and up to four kids, is a good deal at DM12. Bicycles cost an extra DM1.90.

All major car-rental firms have offices at the airport. Driving in town is a cinch: signs are good and parking is easy. Note that there are parking ticket machines in the centre.

Flag fall for taxis is DM4.20. Taxis line up at the Hauptbahnhof and Dresdner-Neustadt station; you can also ring ☎ 21 12 11. The fare from the Hauptbahnhof to the airport costs about DM20.

The luggage counters at both the Hauptbahnhof and Dresden-Neustadt station rent out spanking new bicycles, all with baskets and some with child seats, for DM10 per day. The Hilton hotel rents out bikes for DM20 per day, or DM15 for five hours.

AROUND DRESDEN
Weesenstein

In Weesenstein, a charming, untouched town just 16km south-east of Dresden, **Schloss Weesenstein** is one of the most under-visited and untouched extant medieval castles in Germany. Built by the margraves of Dohna, who owned land stretching into Bohemia, the castle was begun in the 13th century as a fortification along busy trade routes.

In 1385, a feud began when a son of the margraves' family danced too closely to the wife of Jeschka, a knight from Colbitz. Over the next 20 years the feud escalated into full-scale battle between the families, and the margrave of Meissen was called in to be an impartial judge in the conflict. He awarded the castle to himself and gave it to his cronies in the Bühnau family, who lived here for the next 360 years. The castle was later the home of King Johann who, from

1860 on, ran the Saxon court from here rather than from Pillnitz.

Today, the castle is a mixture of Gothic, Renaissance and baroque architectural styles. Exhibits are designed to let you really see how royalty and servants lived here – right down to the toilets. The **Bier Keller**, where they have brewed Weesenstein beer since the 16th century, is open to visitors, as is the lovely **chapel**, which hosts regular concerts. Manuscripts of music by the Bühnau family's court composers have just been rediscovered in state archives, and a CD of recordings of the music is available (DM33) at the cashier.

Behind the castle are the story-book baroque **gardens**, open to the public and bisected by a stream, which is in turn fed by a waterfall.

The castle is open Tuesday to Sunday from 9 am to 6 pm (DM6/4, and an extra

---

Old Shatterhand

If you glimpse a teepee in the Saxon hinterlands, it's not a late claim to the white man's territory. More likely, it's a tribute to Germany's greatest adventure writer, Karl May (1842-1912), who ranks as one of the country's most widely-read authors. May's tales (set in the American west and the Orient) are still popular today, with more than 100 million copies sold in German and 33 other languages. The careful detail of his work – all 99 volumes of it – is all the more astounding given the prodigious Saxon hardly ever left Germany.

Born and raised in Hohenstein-Ernstthal near Chemnitz, May worked briefly as a teacher but soon landed in jail for petty deceits and kleptomania (he even stole dresses and ladies' furs). May spent seven years behind bars and, in prison libraries, read hungrily of frontier adventures such as the Californian Gold Rush and battles with the American Indians. In 1879, by then an editor in Dresden, May published *In the Far West* and began to create iconoclast heroes, such as Indian chief Winnetou and Old Shatterhand, the rifle-toting American settler.

May's tales made him a celebrity in the 1880s, posing for photos in cowboy duds and signing autographs as Old Shatterhand. Rich from royalties, the eccentric author built 'Villa Shatterhand' on the outskirts of Dresden in 1895 and filled it with exotic weapons, hunting trophies and other incongruous items from the Near East and America. In 1908, an ageing May finally visited the United States but, despite his lust for the Wild West, never ventured beyond Niagara Falls.

Villa Shatterhand is now the Karl-May-Museum (☎ 0351-83 73 30), Karl-May-Strasse 5, Radebeul. It's open Tuesday to Sunday from 9 am to 6 pm, and from 10 am to 4 pm in winter (DM8.50/5.50). In May the town hosts a huge **Karl May Festival**, a mecca for hard-drinking Germans in feather headdresses and chaps. From Dresden, it's about a 20 minute ride on the S1 north to Radebeul-Ost or on tram No 4 to Schildenstrasse.

SAXONY

DM5 to take photos). There are Sunday services in the chapel at 8.30 am.

Special Events In mid-May during the Pfingsten (Pentecost or Whitsun holiday), the town holds its **Mittelalter Fest** (Middle Ages Festival), which features jousting, medieval crafts, local speciality foods and freshly brewed beer (DM10/5 for adults/children). If the weather's fine, it's some of the most fun you can have in Germany and not at all on the tourist track.

Places to Eat *Schloss Café*, on a balcony overlooking the formal gardens, serves coffee (DM2 to DM4), beer (DM3 to DM4.50) and ice cream (DM6.50). It also has a lovely view.

Dresdeners drive to *Königliche Schlossküche (☎ 035027-53 78, Am Schlossberg 1)* for nice dinners out, and so should you. It has excellent Saxon specialities and very nice touches like flower petals in the *Lauch* (leek) soup. Superb game and beef dishes with local mushrooms and other vegies cost DM20 to DM35 for main courses, and DM9.50 to DM12.50 for starters.

Getting There & Away There are five trains a day (DM7.40, 20 minutes) from Dresden's Hauptbahnhof to Weesenstein's train station, about 500m south of the castle – follow the road up the hill and you can't miss it. By road, a lovely way to go is to head east out of Dresden along the B172 to Prohlis, turn right at the Bahr Baumarket (direction: Borthen), turn right again in Röhrsdorf (direction: Dohna), head through Dohna and follow the signs.

Pillnitz Palace

From 1765 to 1918, this exotic palace on the Elbe, about 10km south-east of Dresden, was the summer residence of the kings and queens of Saxony. The most romantic way to get there is on one of Dresden's old steamers. The cost for return passage (six departures a day from the Sächsische Dampfschiffahrt dock in Dresden) is DM22 and the journey takes 1¾ hours.

Otherwise, take tram No 14 from Wilsdruffer Strasse, or tram No 9 from in front of the Dresden Hauptbahnhof, east to the end of the line, then walk a few blocks down to the riverside and cross the Elbe on the small ferry, which operates year round. The museum (☎ 263 12 60) is open from May to mid-October daily (except Monday) from 9.30 am to 5.30 pm. However, the gardens stay open till 8 pm and the palace exterior, with its Oriental motifs, is far more interesting than anything inside – so don't worry if you arrive too late to get in.

Schloss Moritzburg

This palace rises impressively from its lake 14km north-west of Dresden. Erected as a hunting lodge for the Duke of Saxony in 1546, Moritzburg was completely remodelled in baroque style in 1730, and it has an impressive interior. It's open daily from 9 am to 5.30 pm, closed Monday in winter (DM7/5 for adults/children). Guided tours in German (DM3) are conducted hourly. The palace (☎ 035207-87 30) also has lovely parkland ideal for strolling. There are buses to Moritzburg from behind Dresden's Neustadt train station, as well as five trains a day (DM7.50, 40 minutes).

Elbe River Excursions

From May to November, Sächsische Dampfschiffahrt (☎ 0351-86 60 90, see Organised Tours under Dresden) has frequent services upriver from Dresden via Pirna (DM26) and Bad Schandau (DM28) to Schmilka (DM28). Here the Elbe River has cut a deep valley through the sandstone, producing abrupt pinnacles and other striking rock formations. Local trains return to Dresden from Schmilka-Hirschmühle (opposite Schmilka) about every half an hour until late in the evening (DM11.50, 54 minutes), with stops all along the river. Boats also run downriver as far as Meissen (DM26).

SAXON SWITZERLAND

Sächsische Schweiz (Saxon Switzerland) is a national park 50km south of Dresden near the Czech border. Its wonderfully wild, craggy country is dotted with castles and tiny towns along the mighty Elbe. The landscape varies unexpectedly and radically: its forests can look deceptively tropical, while the worn cliffs and plateau recall the parched expanses of New Mexico or central Spain (without the searing heat).

The region (not huge at 275 sq km) is a favourite with hikers and climbers, and here you'll see the archetypal German nature lovers in their element, complete with walking sticks, day packs and knee stockings. Highlights include the Bastei lookout and the border resort of Bad Schandau.

You can get information on hiking in the Sächsische Schweiz National Park from Dresden-Information (☎ 49 19 20, fax 49 19 21 16) at Prager Strasse 21.

Bastei

One of the most breathtaking spots in all of Germany is the Bastei, some 28km south-west of Dresden on the Elbe. Located on dramatic stone outcrops 305m above the river, the Bastei commands unparalleled views of the surrounding forests and mountains – it's so high that the Elbe looks like a stream and its barges and steamships like toys. The crags are linked by a series of footbridges that encompass the **Neue Felsenburg**, the 13th-century remains of a Saxon outpost.

The centre of the **Basteibrücke** was the site of a medieval catapult; during a siege, the bridge collapsed and the Bohemian attackers plummeted to their deaths. A replica stone-thrower and artefacts from the period are displayed in the terrain a few steps further on. It's open daily from 9 am to 6 pm (DM2/1), though you can pay into a can after 6 pm and still gain access. The bridge floors are pretty transparent, so it's definitely *not* for those afraid of heights.

There's a marked path leading down to the riverside resort of Rathen (25 minutes), which hosts open-air theatre in summer. Tickets cost DM6 to DM32; call ☎ 035024-77 70 for program details.

Places to Stay & Eat The most obvious option is the GDR-era *Berghotel Bastei*

(☎ 035024-704 06, fax 704 81), which has very comfy rooms and a decent restaurant despite the tourist kitsch outside. Singles/doubles cost DM100/150 from March to October, and are 15% cheaper at other times. Otherwise, you can find rooms from about DM25 per person (including breakfast) in Lohmen, a couple of kilometres due north-east. The Lohmen tourist office (☎ 03501-58 10 24, fax 58 10 25) is at Basteistrasse 79, in the building marked 'Gemeindeverwaltung'.

Getting There & Away If driving from Pirna, (12km south-west of Dresden), follow the many brown signs marked 'Bastei' to the turn-off. Parking costs DM10/5 for cars/motorcycles. By bus, take the frequent No 236/23T from Pirna train station (DM6, 35 minutes). There's also an open-topped double-decker bus from the Elbe parking lot in Bad Schandau (DM8/12 one-way/return, 45 minutes). In summer there's a shuttle service between the inner and outer Bastei parking lots – otherwise, it's a half hour walk from the main road.

Bad Schandau
☎ 035022 • pop 3200
Bad Schandau, a poky little spa town on the Elbe just 5km north of the Czech border, is a superb base for hikes in the region. The tourist office (☎ 900 31, fax 900 34, email info@bad-schandau.de), Markt 12, is open weekdays from 9 am to 6.30 pm, and Saturday (in summer only) from 9 am to 4 pm. Here's a good place to buy the excellent Seeger map of the Sächsische Schweiz National Park (DM9.80).

At the southern end of town you'll find the **Personenaufzug** (passenger lift), which will whisk you up a 50m-high tower for a commanding view. It's open daily from 9 am to 6 pm (DM4/2). The structure is linked to a pretty forest path at the back, via a 35m-long bridge through thin air.

Even more fun is the **Kirnitzschtalbahn**, a museum-piece tram which runs 7km north-east along the Kirnitzsch river to the **Lichtenhainer Wasserfall**, a good spot to

SAXONY

begin a hike along the sandstone cliffs so typical of the region. The tram runs at least hourly in summer (DM6/DM8 one-way/return) and departs from the train station.

A favourite day trip for locals is to the tiny community of **Hinterhermsdorf**, in a remote cul-de-sac about 14km west of Bad Schandau. Here you can rent flat-bottom boats (DM5 per hour) on the Kirnitzsch river, which is lined on either side by steep rock faces – you can't feel much more secluded than this. The regular bus No 241 goes from Bad Schandau (DM5.50, 45 minutes).

Places to Stay & Eat The camp site *Ostrauer Mühle (☎ 427 42)*, on the Kirnitzsch river east of Bad Schandau, charges from DM5/4 per site/adult. The *Jugendherberge Bad Schandau (☎ 424 08, fax 424 09, Dorfstrasse 14)* is in the village of Ostrau nearby, which is reachable by ferry. It charges DM24/29 for juniors/seniors.

Helpful staff at the tourist office will book *private rooms* from DM25 per person and from about DM45 in local hotels. *Hotel Zum Roten Haus (☎ 423 43, Marktstrasse 10)* is a reliable option, charging from DM70/100 for singles/doubles. Its restaurant also has a good menu, with Saxon dishes ranging from DM13 to DM25.

Getting There & Away There are trains to Dresden (DM8.40, 45 minutes) and Prague (DM45, two hours). The north-south B172 runs right through town. Sächsische Dampfschiffahrt boats run twice daily between Dresden and Bad Schandau (DM28, 6½ hours).

MEISSEN
☎ 03521 • pop 31,700

Some 27km north-west of Dresden, Meissen is a perfectly preserved old town and the centre of a rich wine-growing region. Its medieval fortress, the Albrechtsburg, crowns a ridge high above the Elbe River and contains the former ducal palace and Meissen Cathedral, a magnificent Gothic structure. Augustus the Strong of Saxony created Europe's first porcelain factory here in 1710.

Orientation

Meissen straddles the Elbe, with the old town on the western bank and the train station on the eastern. The train/pedestrian bridge behind the station is the quickest way across and presents you with a picture-postcard view of the river and the Altstadt.

From the bridge, continue up Obergasse, then bear right through Hahnemannsplatz and Rossplatz to the Markt, the town's central square. A new road bridge a kilometre downriver replaced the vehicle-choked Elbbrücke in late 1999.

Sächsische Dampfschiffahrt boats arrive and depart from the landing on the west side of the Elbe, about 300m east of the Markt. Helpful pointer signs throughout the city make it hard to get lost.

Information

The helpful Meissen-Information (☎ 45 44 70, fax 45 82 40, email tourist.meissen@t-online.de) is at Markt 3. From April to October, the office is open weekdays from 10 am to 6 pm and weekends to 3 pm. Winter opening hours are weekdays only from 9 am to 5 pm. It also sells maps of the wonderful Elbe bicycle trail, which runs from Lutherstadt-Wittenberg to the Czech border.

Change money at the Commerzbank in the Hauptbahnhof or at the Sparkasse, corner of Dresdner Strasse and Bahnhofstrasse.

Things to See & Do

On the Markt are the **Rathaus** (1472) and the 15th century **Frauenkirche** (open from May to October daily from 10 am to noon and 1 to 4 pm). The church's tower (1549) has a porcelain carillon, which chimes every quarter-hour. This, along with the church's traditional bells, makes an interesting acoustic contrast: *bink* ... BONG ... *pi-bink* BONG. Climb the tower (DM2) for fine views of Meissen's Altstadt; pick up the key in the church or from the adjacent Pfarrbüro (parish office).

Steep stepped lanes lead up to the **Albrechtsburg**, with its towering medieval cathedral (open daily; DM3.50/2.50) containing an altarpiece by Lucas Cranach the

Elder. Beside the cathedral is the remarkable 15th century **palace**, constructed with an ingenious system of internal arches. It's open daily, but closed in January (DM6/3).

There are two lovely carved-stone **drinking fountains**. The one in the Markt is new (1995); the other, at the northern end of Burgstrasse in Platz am Café Zieger, dates from 1884.

Meissen has long been renowned for its chinaware, with its trademark insignia of blue crossed swords. The Albrechtsburg palace was originally the manufacturing site, but the **Porzellan Manufaktur** (Porcelain Factory; ☎ 46 87 00) is now at Talstrasse 9, 1km south-west of town. There are often long queues for the workshop demonstrations (DM9/7), but you can view the porcelain collection upstairs at your leisure (another DM5). A highlight here is the 3.6m-high 'table-top temple' on the 2nd floor, built for Prince Elector Augustus II in 1749.

Saxon Speak

The Saxons speak a dialect as incomprehensible to non-Saxons as Bavarian is to outsiders. Many visitors may find themselves saying 'Huh?' more often than usual. It's as if the Saxons learned German from the Scots, with their very soft pronunciation of consonants. For example, when a Saxon says **'lah-lptsch'**, he means Leipzig. And the 'ü' sound is pronounced like an English short 'i' – **'bit-nershtrazze'** for Büttnerstrasse.

But Saxon-speak is far from an odd offshoot of German; on the contrary, it was from Saxony that the German language developed (as many a Saxon will proudly tell you). Martin Luther's translation of the Bible into the Saxon language laid the foundation for a standard German language.

Saxons might also hark back to a 1717 Dutch reference to the Saxon dialect as 'the purest, most comprehensible, charming and delightful to the ear of all German dialects'.

Both sections are open from 9 am to 6 pm. The factory's porcelain shop is downstairs but don't expect any real bargains, even on B-class wares.

Organised Tours

From April to October there are 1½ hour guided tours of the town in German daily at 1 pm (meet at the tourist office) for DM6/3.

Places to Stay

Budget accommodation is fairly scarce, but Meissen-Information can often find *private rooms* from around DM30 per person (plus a service fee of DM4 per person).

Camping Rehbocktal (☎/fax 45 26 80) is in a beautiful forest at Scharfenberg on the banks of the Elbe, 3km south-east of Meissen. Charges are DM3/5 per car/tent plus DM6.50 per person. The four-person bungalows are good value at DM17.50 per person for the first night, DM12.50 thereafter; take bus No 404 from the station.

The non-DJH *Jugendgästehaus (☎/fax 45 30 65, Wilsdrufferstrasse 28)*, about a 20 minute walk south of the Markt, offers beds in small dorms for DM20. Call first – if the place is full they say so on their answering machine.

Pension Burkhardt (☎ 45 81 98, fax 45 81 97, Neugasse 29) has attractive rooms, all with WC, shower, phone and TV, from DM70/110 a single/double. The *Pension Schweizerhaus (☎/fax 45 71 62, Rauhentalstrasse 1)* has six double rooms with private shower and WC from DM90. The friendly *Pension Goldgrund (☎ 40 12 03, fax 40 02 30, Goldgrund 15)*, on the southern edge of town, has rooms for DM70/100.

The *Hotel Am Markt 6 (☎ 410 70, fax 41 07 20)* has very smart rooms. All come with satellite TV and bathroom, and cost from DM95/165.

Places to Eat

For good pastry and pizzas, *Sächsisches Bäckerhaus Meissen* has several locations around town, including one opposite the Hauptbahnhof. *Kebaphaus (☎ 40 32 66, Neugasse 26)* has doners for DM4, tasty

Eibauer Dunkel beer for DM2.50 as well as schnitzels, salads and chicken.

Gaststätte Winkelkrug (☎ 45 37 11, Schlossberg 13) is near the Albrechtsburg in a quaint old building with a nice garden section, and you can eat from as little as DM8. It's closed on Monday and Tuesday. *Domkeller (☎ 45 76 76, Domplatz 9)* has breathtaking terrace views over town and good local dishes from about DM13.

Weinschänke Vincenz Richter (☎ 45 32 85, An der Frauenkirche 12) is an expensive place with oodles of atmosphere (check out the torture chamber). It's closed on Sunday and Monday. You can sample Meissen's fine wines in the *Probierstube (☎ 73 26 76, Bennoweg 9)*, a 10 minute walk north-east of the train station. It's run by the local wine-growers' cooperative and dishes up hearty food, too.

A fine place to sit on summer days is in the courtyard of *Café Antik (☎ 45 13 88, Burgstrasse 6)*, with drinks from DM2 to DM5 and most meals from DM11 to DM16.

Pizzeria Gallo Nero (☎ 45 27 35, Elbstrasse 10) comes highly recommended, with pizzas and pastas averaging DM7 to DM12.

Getting There & Around

Half-hourly S-Bahn trains run from Dresden's Hauptbahnhof and Neustadt train stations (DM7.70, 30 minutes), but a more interesting way to get here is by steamer (between May and September). Boats leave from the Sächsische Dampfschiffahrt dock in Dresden at 9.30 am for the two hour journey, which costs DM28 return. Boats head back to Dresden at 3.15 pm.

Meissen is compact and easily seen on foot. You can also rent two-wheelers at Fahrrad Rühle (☎ 45 23 28), Burgstrasse 9, for DM10 per day.

Western Saxony

CHEMNITZ
☎ 0371 • pop 263,000

Chemnitz (pronounced '**kem**-nits') is used to being called names. Its smokestack

industries prompted the nickname of 'Saxon Manchester' in the 19th century, and the GDR dubbed it 'Karl-Marx-Stadt' in 1952, although the great communist theorist had little in common with the place. The city, which lies in the northern Erzgebirge some 80km south-west of Dresden, still bears the heavy stamp of Stalinist planning, although more recent projects and a few Renaissance gems lend it human dimensions.

Orientation & Information

The River Chemnitz flows south to north along the western side of the Altstadt. The Markt and the Rathaus lie 1km south-west of the train station along Strasse der Nationen, while the bus station is just off the western side.

The tourist office (☎ 69 06 80, fax 690 68 20) is at Bahnhofstrasse 6, right opposite the Hauptbahnhof. It's open Monday to Friday from 9 am to 6 pm, and Saturday to 1 pm. There's a Reisebank in the Hauptbahnhof, and branches of BfG Bank and Dresdner Bank on the Markt.

The post office is on the corner of Posthof and Strasse der Nationen, the city's main drag. The Internet Café at Hainstrasse 106 (north-east of the centre) charges DM5 for half an hour of surfing. The town's Web site, www.chemnitz.de (in German only) includes sights and hotel listings.

Museums

Heading west out of the train station, go straight ahead to Strasse der Nationen, take a left and you'll reach the hulking König-Albert-Bau at Theaterplatz 1, containing the **Museum für Naturkunde** (Natural History Museum; ☎ 488 45 51) and the **Versteinerter Wald** (Petrified Forest) display outside its east wing. Some of the stony trunks are 250 million years old. It's open Tuesday to Friday from 9 am to noon and 2 to 5 pm (Wednesday to 7.30 pm), and weekends from 11 am to 5 pm (DM4/2 for adults/children).

The same building houses the **Kunstsammlungen** (Chemnitz Art Gallery; ☎ 488 44 24), including graphic arts and works by local artist Karl Schmidt-Rottluff, a noted expressionist painter and founding member of the Die Brücke group of artists. Hours are Tuesday to Friday from 11 am to 5 pm (Wednesday to 7.30 pm), and weekends from 11 am to 5 pm (DM4/2).

Karl-Marx-Denkmal

Moving south on Strasse der Nationen, turn right onto Brückenstrasse (formerly Karl-Marx-Strasse) and you'll see the bronze Karl Marx statue (1971) by Soviet artist Lew Kerbel. Behind it there's a plaque with the stirring appeal 'Workers of all countries, unite!' from Marx's *Communist Manifesto*.

Across the road is the ghastly GDR-era Stadthalle/Hotel Mercure complex. Behind and to its left stands the handsome 12th century **Roter Turm**, one of the city's oldest defence towers. Time it right and you can climb the tower. It's open Thursday from 2 to 6 pm, and Saturday from 9 am to noon (free).

Markt

The bustling Markt lies in the shadow of the **Altes Rathaus**, an imposing white 15th century building with a Renaissance portal showing the figures of Judith and Lucretia. Next door is the **Hoher Turm** and the **Neues Rathaus**, with some lovely Art Deco features in the foyer. Enter the east side and you'll see a marble **fountain**, turn around and look up at the painted **gallery**, with its vaults of ochre and grey leaves. The adjacent **Jakobikirche** is a Gothic church topped by a neat roof turret and updated with an Art Deco facade.

Schloss Area

Just north-east of the Altstadt is the Schlossteich, a large park-ringed pond with an artificial island. Concerts are held at the music pavilion in summer. Towering over it is the **Schlosskirche**, a 12th century Benedictine monastery later recast into a weighty Gothic hall church. Its treasures include Hans Witten's intriguing painting *Christ at the Column* (1515). Just south of the church stands the reconstructed **Schloss** itself, which houses the **Museum für Stadtgeschichte**

(City Historical Museum). The vaulted interior is actually better than the displays. It's open Tuesday to Friday from 11 am to 5 pm, and weekends from 10 am to 6 pm (DM4/2).

Places to Stay

Jugendherberge Chemnitz (☎ 713 31, fax 733 31, Augustusburger Strasse 369) charges DM18/24 for juniors/seniors, but is a good 40 minutes outside of town by public transport (including a 20 minute walk). The hostel in nearby Augustusburg is a better bet (see later this chapter).

The tourist office books accommodation for a DM3 fee. All hotels have cheaper weekend rates – just ask.

Pension Art Nouveau (☎ 402 50 71, fax 402 50 73, Hainstrasse 130), 1km northeast of the train station, has clean, simple singles/doubles for DM65/90; those with private shower/WC are DM95/150.

Pension am Zöllnerplatz (☎/fax 42 59 86, Mühlenstrasse 108), in a nice central location, charges DM70/110 for rooms with their own facilities.

Gunnewig Hotel Europa (☎ 68 11 28, fax 67 06 06, Strasse der Nationen 56) charges DM109/139 for convenient, if generic, rooms with private shower/WC.

Places to Eat

On Rathausstrasse just south-east of the Markt, there's a *Best Döner Kebap* selling tasty felafel for DM4.50; and *Fleischerei-Bäckerei Emil Riemann* has cheap sandwiches, soups, pastas and more.

Diebels Fasskeller (☎ 694 69 94, An der Markthalle 3) is a cosy pub in a modern complex on the river. It has a good vegie menu (eg potato and leek casserole, DM6.90) and lots of pasta and meat dishes under DM15.

Metropolitan (☎ 676 28 58, An der Alten Post 1-2) borders on kitsch but still has a splendid Art Deco interior, some decent regional dishes for around DM16 and a very, very long bar menu.

Ausspanne (☎ 330 02 25, Schlossberg 4) is away from it all in a lovely half-timbered house by the castle, and has a good fish menu and fine Saxon dishes for DM17 to DM25.

SAXONY

Getting There & Away

Chemnitz is on the fast Nuremberg-Dresden line. There are frequent trains to Dresden (DM20, 1¾ hours), Leipzig (DM33, 1½ hours), Prague (DM88, 4¾ hours via Dresden), Nuremberg (DM85, 4¼ hours) and Berlin (DM93, 2¾ hours). The autobahn A4 (Bad Hersfeld-Dresden) runs north of town, where the A72 (Munich) originates.

Getting Around

On public transport, short/regular journey tickets cost DM2.20/1.70, and a 24-hour bus and tram ticket costs just DM6. The regular City Bus (No 77) circles the city from the Hauptbahnhof, stopping at the Rathaus and several other main sights.

The tourist office lends out bicycles for *free*: hand over a DM20 deposit, and you'll get a KeyCard to access bicycles at special blue stands throughout the city.

AUGUSTUSBURG

☎ 037291 • pop 2300

The best antidote for Stalinist industrial blues is an afternoon – make it a few days – cooling your heels at Augustusburg, just 13km east of Chemnitz. Its medieval palace, on a steep mountain overlooking forests and rape seed meadows, is one of those relatively undiscovered gems you've read about, with friendly locals to boot.

Orientation & Information

All the sights and the old town are on the mountain or the surrounding hills. The funicular station is located just south-west of the Schloss.

The excellent tourist office (☎ 65 51, fax 65 52), at Marienberger Strasse 29b, is open Monday to Friday from 9 am to 5 pm from April to October (10 am to 4 pm at other times of the year). Saturday hours are from 9 am to 1 pm.

The tourist office also sells the useful *Wanderwege* (hiking) map of routes – easy and strenuous – in Augustusburg and environs (DM3.50). Slip into your walking gear and enjoy a look around this stunning unspoiled area.

Things to See & Do

The oversized **Schloss** is really the only show in town, encompassing the hostel, restaurants, three museums and a pleasant green area. The summer residence of the Elector August (1526-86), the great-great-great grandfather of Saxon ruler Augustus the Strong, this sprawling complex was built in just four years by Leipzig mayor and architect Hieronymus Lotter. With any luck you'll run into one of the 200 couples who get married here every year.

You'll also find the **Motorradmuseum** here, which houses Germany's largest collection of motorcycles, 170 in all, including classic Horch, NSU and BMW roadsters and some very rare models. In the outer courtyard is the **Kutschenmuseum**, with some of the snootiest horse-drawn coaches you'll ever see in the former castle stables. In the upper floors of the Schloss you'll find the **Hasenhaus**, with displays of hunting and game shown in dioramas and antler-filled rooms.

Outside the north entrance is the **Adler-und Falkenhof** (falconry) with buzzards, eagles, owls and other trained hunting birds. There are 45-minute demonstrations at 11 am and 3 pm (DM10/8), but a look at the feathered beauties on their perches from the moat bridge might be enough.

You really can't beat the *Sparkarte*, which gives you entrance to the museums and a castle tour for just DM10/6. Museum hours are from April to October daily from 9 am to 6 pm (or 10 am to 5 pm at other times of year).

Places to Stay & Eat

Jugendherberge Augustusburg (☎ 202 56, fax 63 41, Schloss Augustusburg) is a delight, with beds in newly renovated dorms once slept in by knights. It charges DM21/26 for juniors/seniors. Breakfast is terrible, but the atmosphere is so superb that it shouldn't bother you.

Hotel Waldhaus (☎ 203 17, fax 64 25, Am Kurplatz 7) charges from DM85/120 for simple singles/doubles. Facilities include billiards and table tennis.

Hotel Waldfrieden (☎ *203 79, fax 600 25)* offers reasonable rooms for DM77/110. Just uphill from the cable-car, the hotel restaurant (closed Monday) has an unexpectedly good shark steak (DM16.80) and a nice creamed goulash (DM14.80).

Gasthof Landsknecht (☎ *63 28, Markt 1)* is a rustic vaulted place that stresses its game dishes (eg venison goulash, DM18) and *Rauchemad,* a weird dessert made of potatoes, sugar, cinnamon and apple sauce. It's closed on Monday.

Augustuskeller (☎ *207 40),* in the Schloss courtyard, is *the* medieval lunch option, with lots of tasty game and traditional Saxon fare for DM15 to DM30. It's open only from 11 am to 6 pm (closed Monday). Also here is the *Schlossrestaurant* (☎ *63 75),* which is a cosy alternative (closed Tuesday).

Getting There & Away

Trains run from Chemnitz to Erdmannsdorf (DM8.40, 20 minutes), where you take the funicular railway to Augustusburg (DM4/6 one-way/return, 20 minutes). Motorists should take the B180, which arches round the east side of Chemnitz right past the castle.

LEIPZIG

☎ 0341 • pop 500,000

In Goethe's *Faust* a character named Frosch calls Leipzig 'a little Paris'. He was wrong – Leipzig is more fun.

Leipzig became the 'Stadt der Helden', or City of Heroes, for its leading role in the 1989 democratic revolution. Its residents organised protests against the communist regime in May of that year; by October, they were taking to the streets by the hundreds of thousands, placing candles on the steps of Stasi headquarters and attending peace services at St Nicholas Church.

By the time the secret police got round to pulping their files, Leipzigers were partying in the streets, and they still haven't stopped – from late winter, streetside cafes begin pouring out, and trendy and underground music clubs thud throughout the night.

But it's not *just* a party town. Leipzig has some of the finest classical music and opera in the country, and its art and literary scenes are flourishing. It was home to Bach, Wagner and Mendelssohn, and to Goethe, who set a key scene of *Faust* in the cellar of his favourite watering hole. And Leipzig's university attracts students from all over the world.

Leipzig has hosted trade fairs since medieval times, and during the communist era these provided a key east-west interface. After reunification, the city spent huge sums on an ultra-modern fairground with the aim of re-establishing its position as one of Europe's great fair cities.

Since the discovery of rich silver mines in the nearby Erzgebirge (Ore Mountains) in the 16th century, Leipzig (pronounced 'lah-iptsh' in the local Saxon dialect) has enjoyed almost continual prosperity. Today, it's an important business and transport centre, and arguably the most dynamic city in eastern Germany.

Orientation

Leipzig's centre lies within a ring road that outlines the town's medieval fortifications. To reach the city centre from the Hauptbahnhof, take the underpass below Willy-Brandt-Platz and continue south along Nikolaistrasse for five minutes; the central Markt is just a couple of blocks south-west.

The impressive, 26-platform Leipzig train station (1915) isn't just the largest passenger terminus in Europe. It houses a fabulous three storey shopping mall with more than 150 shops, and is probably the sole train station on the planet where it's genuinely fun to shop (many stores are open on Sunday too). Outside the southern entrance is the central tram stop.

The vast Augustusplatz, three blocks east of the Markt, is ex-socialist Leipzig, dominated by the boxy designs of the university, Neues Gewandhaus concert hall and opera house. The main post office is also here.

Leipzig's dazzling trade fairgrounds (Neue Messe) are 5km north of the Hauptbahnhof (take tram No 16).

SAXONY

LEIPZIG

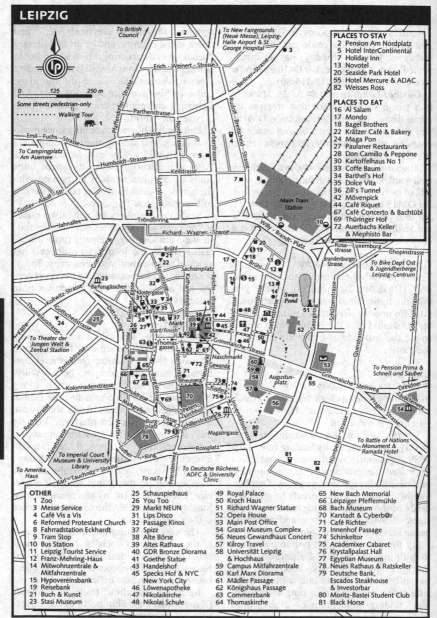

Information

Tourist Offices The excellent Leipzig Tourist Service (☎ 710 42 60/65, fax 710 42 71, email lipsia@aol.com) is at Richard-Wagner-Strasse 1, between the Hauptbahnhof and the Altes Rathaus. It's open Monday to Friday from 9 am to 7 pm, Saturday to 4 pm and Sunday to 2 pm. Useful pamphlets include the *Visitor Guide* and the superb *Museums In Saxony's Major Cities*.

The tourist office and some hotels sell the one or three-day Leipzig Card (DM9.90/21), allowing free or discounted admission to the city's museums and zoo, and free travel on trams and buses.

ADAC has an office (☎ 211 05 51) at Augustusplatz 5-6, next to the Hotel Mercure.

Money There's a Reisebank in the Hauptbahnhof on the first underground level in the south hall. For other major banks in the city centre, see the Banks entry in the Historic Centre Walking Tour section – they're as much sights as exchange offices.

Post & Communications The main post office is at Augustusplatz 1, with another branch inside the Hauptbahnhof. A good local Internet cafe is the Cyberb@r (☎ 126 24 18) on the top floor of the Karstadt, Neumarkt 38, which charges DM2.50 for every 15 minutes of surfing, and is open weekdays from 9.30 am to 8 pm, and 9 am to 4 pm on Saturday. You can send emails for free at the Investorbar (☎ 120 4473) below the Deutsche Bank at Martin-Luther-Ring 2. The staff are helpful, but surfing isn't allowed.

Internet Resources Leipzig's Web site, with a full English version and an online booking facility for accommodation, is at www.leipzig.de.

Travel Agencies Atlas Reisen (☎ 251 89 59) has a branch on the bottom floor of the Hauptbahnhof. Good bucket shops include Kilroy Travel (☎ 30 30 90) at Augustusplatz 10, and Messe Service (☎ 564 05 82) at Berliner Strasse 34.

Bookshops & Libraries Buch & Kunst (☎ 960 42 42) at Am Brühl 8 and Franz-Mehring-Haus (☎ 71 18 40) at Goethestrasse 3-5 have English-language novels and a good all-round selection.

The Deutsche Bücherei (☎ 227 10), Deutscher Platz 1, and its sister library in Frankfurt are the largest German-language libraries in the world. It houses almost every title published in German since 1913, and runs a book and printing museum (free entry). The university library (☎ 973 05 77) at Beethovenstrasse 6 has periodicals and foreign-language books.

University Universität Leipzig (☎ 971 08, email info@leipzig.de), formerly Karl Marx University, has 21,000 students studying languages, medicine, law and economics. The main campus is south of the Hauptbahnhof, with satellites throughout the city.

Cultural Centres Bastions of international cooperation include Amerika Haus (☎ 21 33 84 20) at Wilhelm-Seyfferth-Strasse 4 and the British Council (☎ 564 67 12) at Lumumbustrasse 11-13.

Laundry Wash your dirties at Maga Pon (☎ 960 79 22), a combination laundry and hip cafe at Gottschedstrasse 13. A load costs DM6 and drying is DM2. There's a more traditional Schnell und Sauber laundrette just south-east of the city centre at Dresdner Strasse 19.

Medical Services St George Hospital (St Georg Krankenhaus; ☎ 909 00), Delitzscher Strasse 141, is the largest in the area. To get there, take tram No 16 in the direction of Neue Messe. The University Clinic (Universitätsklinik; ☎ 971 08), at Liebigstrasse 21 in the centre, is both a hospital and a clinic for everyday ailments.

In an emergency, call ☎ 192 92 from 7 pm to 7 am for a doctor, or the Löwenapotheke (☎ 960 50 27/28), Grimmaische Strasse 19.

Dangers & Annoyances The area around the Hauptbahnhof is sleazy; be cautious at night. Don't leave valuables in your car, as there is plenty of smash-and-grab theft.

Historic Centre Walking Tour

This 4km circuit starts at the Markt and moves clockwise to Augustusplatz before exploring the attractive south of the old quarter. It's a 1½ hour walk, but will take the best part of a day with all the stops.

On the Markt, the Renaissance **Altes Rathaus** (1556), one of Germany's most stunning town halls, houses the **City History Museum**. It's open on Tuesday from 2 to 8 pm, Wednesday to Sunday from 10 am to 6 pm, and closed Monday (DM5/2.50 for adults/children).

At the southern end of the square is a wonderful **GDR bronze diorama** depicting the march of history, from medieval workers slaving away with pickaxes (at the left), through other historical milestones to the apex of civilisation (at the far right): socialist man and woman. Their muscles, taut and toned from lifting wheat and swinging sickles, ripple in the pleasure of building world communism.

Königshaus/Mädler Passages

Move south across the street and you'll enter the orange baroque **Apelshaus** (1606-07) with the lovely bay windows. It's now a shopping mall and is popularly known as the Königshaus Passage, but in its heyday its impressive list of overnight guests included Peter the Great and Napoleon. Walk in and open the steel door 10m ahead on the left, and you'll see a fabulous stone spiral staircase.

The Königshaus Passage leads directly into the Mädler Passage, which must be one of the world's most beautiful shopping centres. A mix of neo-Renaissance and Art Nouveau, it opened as a trade hall in 1914 and was renovated at great expense in the early 1990s. Today it's home to a group of chi-chi shops, restaurants, cafes and most notably, **Auerbachs Keller** (see Places to Eat). There are also Faust-related statues (students, Mephistopheles and Faust) at the eastern exit, where stairs lead down to the restaurant.

Naschmarkt Turn north out of the Mädler Passage and you'll reach the Naschmarkt – so named for the edible goodies once peddled here – which is dominated by the **Alte Börse** (1687), the ornate former trading house. In front is a **statue of Goethe** (1903), who studied law at Leipzig University. Today the Alte Börse is a cultural centre, with concerts, plays and readings throughout the year, and the courtyard is a wonderful place for a drink on sunny afternoons. On your right is the **Handelshof**, the old trade hall, which temporarily houses the **Museum of Fine Arts** (see Museums later in this section).

From the Naschmarkt, continue east along Grimmaische Strasse and turn left into another delightfully renovated passage called **Specks Hof**, which contains a great New York diner (see Places to Eat) and a beautiful series of tile and stained-glass reliefs by Halle artist Moritz Götze.

Nikolaikirche At the eastern portal of Specks Hof you'll see the Nikolaikirche (St Nicholas Church; 1165). Begun in Romanesque style, it was enlarged and converted to late Gothic, with an amazing classical interior. More recently, the church was the chief meeting point for peaceful demonstrators from May 1989, shortly before the GDR imploded. A pamphlet tells the story of 600 loyal party members being sent into the church to break up the services, but in the end listening to the sermon and joining the protesters. The church still runs its 'Swords to Ploughshares' services on Monday at 5 pm.

Augustusplatz Carry on east through the Theaterpassage to reach Augustusplatz, Leipzig's cultural nerve centre. The square is strewn with glass structures that glow at night, lending the concrete slabs some much-needed warmth. Pivot left and you'll see the neoclassical **Royal Palace**, now a university building.

To the north is the functional **Opernhaus** (opera house, 1956-60), with a **statue of Richard Wagner** out the back. The mini-shadow on your left is cast by the 11 storey **Kroch Haus**, Leipzig's first 'skyscraper', which is topped by a clock and a muscular bronze sentry who bashes the bell hourly. At the southern end of the square is the GDR-era **Universitäts Hochhaus** (1970), a genuine skyscraper vaguely shaped like an open book; and the unforgivably boxy **Neues Gewandhaus** (1981), which is home to the city's classical-music and jazz concerts.

Stop a moment to admire, on the west side of the square at the Leipzig University entrance, another revolting bronze diorama depicting Karl Marx with – we would swear to it – Lenin's forehead.

Moving south past the Gewandhaus fountain you'll arrive at the **Moritz-Bastei**, the stone fortress cellar that is surely Europe's largest student club (see Entertainment for more details). Half-hidden on the western side of the university building, up Universitätsstrasse, is the **Schinkeltor**, a mid-19th century gate that was one of the few bits of the original university to survive WWII and the GDR.

Innenhof Passage Just west of the Schinkeltor is the Innenhof Passage, in the spectacularly renovated Städtisches Kaufhaus. Pass the Kaiser Maximilian restaurant and you'll come upon a courtyard, formerly a cloth exchange (Gewandhaus) and site of the city's first concert house – which is why the city's concert hall is called Neues Gewandhaus. Composer Felix Mendelssohn once led a music school here; there are free concerts in summer.

Emerge from the Innenhof Passage and stroll east down Preussergasse to reach Petersstrasse, one of the city's main shopping boulevards. At No 43, don't miss **Café Richter** (☎ 960 52 35), which despite its name is the oldest coffee retailer in town (since 1879). This fabulous eclectic building, with its golden iron spiral staircase, is worth a gander, and the luscious beans (around DM8 for 500g) are wonderful too.

Banks From the Café Richter, you can wander south to the end of Petersstrasse for a glimpse of monetary history. In 1991, when the German government offered a 1:1 exchange rate for Ostmarks, tonnes of cash was shipped to the east. Leipzig held a lot of it in its safes, particularly in the **Deutsche Bank** on the corner of Schillerstrasse and Petersstrasse. Looking at its Italian Renaissance headquarters today, you might suspect they held back a little: gilt ceiling mouldings, marble pillars, etched glass and a skylight so large it illuminates the entire teller area.

Elsewhere in town, the **Commerzbank**, on the corner of Thomas Kirchhof and Klostergasse, has a facade that drips so much gold that the bank itself complained to the building's owner. Also not too shabby is the **Hypovereinsbank** on Nikolaistrasse just south of Brühl, with its aquamarine Art Nouveau tiles and copper-plated doors.

Neues Rathaus A few steps on from Deutsche Bank, after passing through Markgrafenstrasse to Burgplatz, you'll confront the baroque New Town Hall, with its impressive 108m-high tower. Although the building's origins date back to the 16th century, its current manifestation was completed in 1905. Recently renovated, the interior makes it one of the finest municipal buildings in Germany, with a grand staircase straight out of a Donald Trump dream. In the lobby are rotating art exhibitions, mostly on historical themes. It's open weekdays from 6.45 am to either 4.30 or 6.30 pm (free).

Thomaskirche From Burgplatz, turn north and walk up Burgstrasse to Thomaskirche (St Thomas Church; 1212), with the tomb of composer Johann Sebastian Bach in front of the altar. The church was extended and converted to the Gothic style in 1496, and was the site of the baptisms of Richard Wagner, Karl Liebknecht and all of Bach's offspring.

Bach worked here as a cantor from 1723 until his death in 1750. Outside the church is the **New Bach Memorial** (1908) showing the composer standing against an organ, with his left-hand jacket pocket turned inside-out (he always claimed to be broke, with 20 children from two marriages).

The St Thomas Choir, once led by Bach, is still going strong and now includes 80 boys aged eight to 18. See the Entertainment section for more information. Church services are held at 9.30 am on Sunday.

The walking tour ends here.

Museums

Bach Museum Opposite St Thomas Church, in a baroque house at Thomaskirchhof 16, is the Bach Museum, which focuses on the composer's life in Leipzig – where he wrote, among many other works, the *Matthäus Passion, Johannes Passion, Weihnachts Oratorium* and the *h-Moll Messe*. There are portraits, manuscripts and other Bach memorabilia. Guided tours in German are given at 11 am and 3 pm. It's open daily from 10 am to 5 pm (DM4/2.50).

Museum of Fine Arts The Museum der Bildenden Künste, with an excellent collection of works by the old masters, is housed temporarily in the Handelshof, Grimmaische Strasse 1-7 (☎ 21 69 90). Its new home will be on Sachsenplatz; the date of completion was uncertain at the time of writing. The museum is open Tuesday and Thursday to Sunday from 10 am to 6 pm, and Wednesday from 1 to 9.30 pm (DM5/2.50).

Stasi Museum At No 24 Dittrichring, where it intersects with Goerdelerring, is the former headquarters of the East German Ministerium für Staatssicherheit (or Stasi), the secret police. It's in the building known as the Runde Ecke (Round Corner) and is now a museum (☎ 961 24 43).

At the front are photographs of demonstrations in October and November 1989, and of Lieutenant General Manfred Hummitsch, the former head of the Stasi in Leipzig. Inside

Russia, Prussia and Austria combined forces to defeat Napoleon in Leipzig in the early 19th century.

are exhibits on propaganda, preposterous Stasi disguises, surveillance photographs and, in the back, mounds of papier-mache the Stasi created when they shredded and soaked secret documents before the fall of the GDR. Take a chunk home; it's free and plentiful.

The museum is open Wednesday to Sunday from 2 to 6 pm (free).

Egyptian Museum This museum at Leipzig University (☎ 973 70 10), Schillerstrasse 6, has a 9000-piece collection of Egyptian antiquities, making it one of the most important collections of its type in Europe. Displays include stone vessels from the first half of the third millennium BC, Nubian decorative arts and sarcophagi. It's open Tuesday to Saturday from 1 to 5 pm, and Sunday from 10 am to 1 pm (DM3/1.50).

Grassi Museum Complex There are three museums in the Grassi complex at Universität Leipzig, Täubchenweg 2 and 2c, all charging admission and closed Monday. The **Museum für Völkerkunde** (Ethnological Museum; ☎ 214 20) has a huge collection of cultural exhibits from around the world, and is open Tuesday to Friday from 10 am to 5.30 pm, and weekends to 5 pm. The **Musikinstrumenten-Museum** (☎ 214 21 20) boasts a collection of almost 1000 musical instruments and free guided tours on Sundays at 10.30 am. It's open Tuesday to Saturday from 10 am to 5 pm, and Sunday to 1 pm. The **Museum für Kunsthandwerk** (☎ 214 21 75) displays local arts and crafts, and is open Tuesday to Sunday from 10 am to 6 pm (to 8 pm on Wednesday). Entry is DM5/2 for each museum.

Zoo
Leipzig's zoo, north-west of the Hauptbahnhof, is renowned for its breeding of lions and tigers. It's open from May to September daily from 9 am to 7 pm, and 9 am to 5 pm from October to February (DM9/6).

Battle of Nations Monument
South-east of the centre is Leipzig's monolithic Völkerschlachtdenkmal from 1913, a 91m-high monument commemorating the decisive victory here by the combined Prussian, Austrian and Russian forces over Napoleon's army 100 years earlier. Climb the tower for a good view of the city and surrounding area. It's open from May to October daily from 10 am to 5 pm (DM5/2.50).

Organised Tours
Leipzig Tourist Service runs a two hour guided walk from Monday to Saturday at 4 pm, starting from its office (DM10). From April to December, there are also daily bus tours at 10.30 am and 1.30 pm, lasting two and 2½ hours and costing DM20/16 and DM28/20.

Special Events
Leipzig's annual events calendar includes the **Book Fair** in late March, which includes lots of readings and book-related events, and is the second biggest in the country after Frankfurt; and the **Pub Festival** in late May and early November, which is the largest of its kind in Europe, with a shuttle bus between drinking holes. Held in late July, the **Bach Festival** celebrates the 250th anniversary of Bach's death in 2000 with a crushing array of concerts; and **euro scene leipzig** in early November is one of Europe's top contemporary theatre and dance festivals.

Places to Stay – Budget
Campingplatz Am Auensee (☎ 465 16 00, Gustav-Esche-Strasse 5) is in a pleasant wooded spot on the city's north-western outskirts (take tram No 10 or 28 to the terminus at Wahren, then walk for about eight minutes). Camping is DM8 per person plus DM5 for a car/tent site. A-frame cabins/bungalows are also available for singles/doubles at DM50/90 per night.

The *Jugendherberge Leipzig-Centrum (☎ 245 70 11, fax 245 70 12, Volksgartenstrasse 24)* is in the eastern suburb of Schönefeld, in an office-type block. It charges DM24/29 for juniors/seniors. To get there, take tram No 17, 27, 37 or 57 towards Schönefeld and alight at Löbauer Strasse (seven stops).

euro currency converter DM1 = €0.51

Leipzig Tourist Service runs a free room-finding service (☎ 710 42 55), with singles/doubles from around DM45/80. You can make a reservation by faxing or mailing your order and a credit card number to Leipzig Tourist Service, Richard-Wagner-Strasse 1, 04109 Leipzig (fax 710 42 51).

The Mitwohnzentrale (☎ 194 30) at Goethestrasse 7-10 can arrange flat rental (from DM35 to DM50 per person per day). The office is open daily from 9 am to 8 pm.

Pension Prima (☎ 688 34 81, *Dresdner Strasse 82*) has a great deal on simple rooms for DM55/80, including breakfast. It's 2km east of the old town.

Elster Pension (☎ 479 80 39, fax 400 10 44, *Giesserstrasse 15*), near idle GDR-era factories in the south-western suburb of Plagwitz (tram No 2), charges DM65/90 for rooms with a shared shower.

Another option is the renovated *Weisses Ross* (☎ 960 59 51, *Rossstrasse 20*), which offers rooms for DM70/110 with shower or DM60/95 without.

Pension am Nordplatz (☎ 960 31 43, *Nordstrasse 58*) has basic rooms with shared bath for DM80/100 (or with private bath for DM130/140).

Places to Stay – Mid-Range

Hotel Mercure Leipzig (☎ 214 60, fax 960 49 16, *Augustusplatz 5-6)* offers a great location from DM99/139 for singles/doubles. Despite its joyless facade, inside it's quite comfy and breakfast is good.

The *Ramada Hotel Leipzig* (☎ 129 30, fax 129 34 44, *Gutenbergplatz 1-5)*, 500m east of the ring, has most of the west's creature comforts and good prices, from DM135.

The *Novotel* (☎ 995 80, fax 995 82 00, *Goethestrasse 11)*, opposite the train station, is one of the city's few air-conditioned hotels and charges from DM165 for both singles/doubles.

Places to Stay – Top End

The *Holiday Inn Garden Court* (☎ 125 10, fax 125 11 00, *Rudolf-Breitscheid-Strasse 3)* is a plush option, with singles/doubles from DM160/200.

Hotel InterContinental Leipzig (☎ 98 80, fax 988 12 29, *Gerberstrasse 15)* has rooms from DM195.

Seaside Park Hotel (☎ 985 20, fax 98 57 50, email seaside-hotels@regionett.de, *Richard-Wagner-Strasse 7)* occupies a nice Art Deco house in the town centre, with rooms from DM195/233; it also has a commendable restaurant.

Places to Eat

Restaurants – Traditional The *Thüringer Hof* (☎ 994 49 99, *Burgstrasse 19)*, Luther's favourite pub, was completely destroyed in WWII and what you see today is entirely new. There's a traditional vaulted-ceiling restaurant in front and an atrium in the back. It has great food and decent prices: vegie dishes from DM13 to DM17, and fish and meat mains from DM17 to DM26.

Zill's Tunnel (☎ 960 20 78, *Barfussgässchen 9)* offers wonderful Saxon specialties – the roast venison in red wine (DM22.70) is particularly good.

At the *Ratskeller* (☎ 123 62 02, *Neues Rathaus)*, the cream goulash with red cabbage and dumplings is good and costs DM12.90.

Barthel's Hof (☎ 141 31 13, *Hainstrasse 1)* is a sprawling, historic place with a fantastic lunch buffet (DM14.40) and some quirky Saxon dishes (eg *Heubraten*, marinated lamb roasted on hay, for DM24). Most mains cost between DM20 and DM35.

The two *Paulaner* restaurants (☎ 211 31 15, *Klostergasse 3 and 5)* are typically 'Munich' and offer great student deals such as spare ribs, Leberkäse or Nürnberger sausage with sauerkraut, bread and salad for just DM7.80.

Founded in 1525, the *Auerbachs Keller* (☎ 21 61 00, *Mädler Passage)* is one of Germany's classic restaurants. Goethe's *Faust – Part I* includes a scene here, in which Mephistopheles and Faust carouse with students before they ride off on a barrel. Ask to join a tour of the historic section of the restaurant, including the Goethe room (where the writer constantly drank – excuse us, gleaned inspiration), the

Weinfass and, beneath that, the genuinely spooky Hexenküche. Note the carved tree-trunk hanging in the Weinfass, featuring witches, Faust astride the barrel and a hoofed Mephisto in hot pursuit. The tour includes a Verjüngungstrunk (rejuvenation drink), buffet or fixed-menu dinner and costs DM100 per person.

Restaurants – International *Mövenpick* (☎ 211 77 22, Am Naschmarkt 1-3) is in the Handelshof and offers outstanding value, with a nightly buffet where you can help yourself to imaginative salads, casseroles and desserts for DM19.50 per person.

Kartoffelhaus No 1 (☎ 960 46 03, Barfussgässchen 12), in Mr Drinks Beerhouse, serves great potato dishes in absurd Bavarian decor. Main courses range from DM15 to DM22.

NYC New York City (☎ 211 07 07, Specks Hof Passage) is a diner that serves excellent-looking omelettes, vegie dishes, burgers and steaks, all for DM15 or less.

Escados Steakhouse & Bar (☎ 960 71 27, Nikolaistrasse 9), in the vault section of Deutsche Bank, is pricey but the atmosphere is so suave and the food so good that it's worth a shot. The place is tropical-meets-classical, with palm trees and rattan amid the columns. The food is mainly Argentinian beef and steaks, and prices are from DM22 to DM38.

Cafes The laundry-cafe, *Maga Pon (☎ 960 79 22, Gottschedstrasse 13)* is probably better as the latter than the former, with great atmosphere, friendly staff, high ceilings and healthy foods. A meal of soup and the special of the day is DM10, daily soups are DM6, and there's a great wine selection. It's open daily from 9 am and to 3 am most nights.

Barfussgässchen, one block west of the Markt, is a wonderful street that's chock-a-block with outdoor tables when the weather warms up. Along here you'll find two excellent pizzerias, *Dolce Vita (☎ 479 15 27)* and the upmarket *Don Camillo & Peppone (☎ 960 39 10)*.

Leipzig's oldest coffee bar, *Zum Arabischen Coffe Baum (☎ 965 13 21, Kleine Fleischergasse 4)* has a restaurant and cafe on floors one to three and a coffee museum on the top floor (free). Composer Robert Schumann met friends here, and you can sit at his regular table.

The cosy Italian cafe, *Mondo (☎ 961 68 38, Am Brühl 52)* has great coffee (DM3.50), sandwiches (DM4.50 to DM6) and a jaw-dropping wood carving on the wall.

Café Riquet (☎ 961 00 00), an upmarket cafe in a superb Art Nouveau building (identifiable by the bronze elephant heads above the entrance), stands on the corner of Reichsstrasse and Schuhmachergässchen. Other cafes worth a visit are the *Bachstübl (☎ 960 23 82)* and *Café Concerto (☎ 960 47 79)* on Thomaskirchhof next door to the Bach Museum.

Snacks & Fast Food The Hauptbahnhof is virtually a fast-food heaven, with Asian, burger, ice cream and pizza places spread over three levels. Petersstrasse also offers the usual French fries, Wurst and pizza.

The *Bagel Brothers (☎ 980 33 30)*, on the corner of Brühl and Nikolaistrasse, has really good filled bagels with a drink from just DM4.90. *Kratzer* is a cheap bakery and stand-up cafe at Hainstrasse 28.

The best Middle Eastern food we've had in ages was at *Al Salam (☎ 980 28 77, Nikolaistrasse 33)*. Enormous felafel and doners are on offer for DM4, as well as bursting-fresh salads and excellent hot dishes; everything is under DM10. The vegetarian platter is DM7.50, and there's a huge range of sweets.

Entertainment

Kreuzer is the best magazine for what's on in Leipzig, with great listings, the best events calendar and a good travel section. It's DM2.50 at newsstands and restaurants.

Leipzig Im is a monthly pamphlet available from the Leipzig Tourist Service. The two leading free listings magazines are *Fritz* and its thicker but inferior cousin *Blitz*, with listings and what's-on guides.

SAXONY

Check also the *Leipzig Jazz Kalender*, printed monthly and available at Leipzig Tourist Service.

Pubs & Clubs The bar at the *Mövenpick* (see Places to Eat) is great – grab peanuts from the huge barrel by the bar, shell 'em, eat 'em and throw the shells on the floor. There's free food from 5 to 7 pm daily.

The *Mephisto Bar* (☎ 216 10 22, *Mädler Passage)*, above Auerbachs Keller, continues the Faust theme with a mirror that laughs devilishly and, if the barman's in the mood, shows Satan himself.

The two most popular discos in town are at the *Moritz-Bastei* and *Spizz* (see Rock & Jazz), but two others are *You Too* (☎ 960 59 62, Grosse Fleischergasse 12)*, right near the Thomaskirche (with a room for Top 20 and a second section for African and world beat); and the popular *Lips Disco* (☎ 960 48 18, Barfussgässchen 12)*, which you enter from Kleine Fleischergasse.

Gay & Lesbian *Café Vis a Vis*, just north of the Hauptbahnhof at Rudolf-Breitscheid-Strasse 33, draws a largely gay clientele and is open 24 hours. Other popular gay bars include the *Black Horse* (☎ 284 01 6, Rossstrasse 12)*, a gay-friendly Irish pub, and *Markt NEUN* on Barfussgässchen.

Rock & Jazz Venues for large rock concerts include *Neue Messe Leipzig* (☎ 67 80)*, tram No 16; and *Zentral Stadion* (no phone), 10 minutes from the city centre near Jahnallee.

One of the best student clubs in Germany is *Moritz-Bastei* (☎ 70 25 90, Universitätsstrasse 9)*. Located in a spacious cellar below the old city walls, it has live bands or disco on most nights and runs films outside in summer.

Spizz (☎ 960 80 43, Markt 9)* is a very slick place and one of the coolest bars in town, with excellent live jazz and disco downstairs. It has three levels, slow service and a good range of wines and beers.

Moritz-Bastei is great for jazz, as is *naTo* (☎ 391 55 39, Karl-Liebknecht-Strasse 46)*, a cultural house, meeting spot and general

cool hang-out. There's also jazz at the *Neues Gewandhaus* and at the *Opernhaus*.

Ballet & Opera The Leipzig Ballet performs at the Opernhaus, featuring classics, the modern and just about everything in between. Ticket prices range from DM12 to DM35.

Composer Udo Zimmermann, the director of the Opernhaus, favours operas from Wagner and Albert Lortzing for their Leipzig connections. But he also likes modern opera, especially by Stockhausen, as well as electronic music and Jörg Herchet. Tickets range from DM12 to DM65.

Theatre & Cabaret The largest theatre is the *Schauspielhaus* (☎ 126 80, Bosestrasse 1)*, a few blocks west of the Markt, with classics typically infused with modern elements. Modern performances are also held at the Schauspielhaus' *Neue Szene* (*Gottschedstrasse 16)*; catch tram No 1 or 2 to Gottschedstrasse.

Theater der Jungen Welt (☎ 477 29 90, Lindenauer Markt 21)* specialises in plays with themes that appeal to younger audiences (late teens to early 20s), but also has puppet shows. The finest variety shows are done by *Krystallpalast* (☎ 14 06 60, Magazingasse 4)*, with snake women, Flamenco, trapeze acts and more.

The best known cabaret theatres are *Leipziger Pfeffermühle* (☎ 960 32 53, Thomaskirchhof 16)*; *Academixer* (☎ 960 48 48, Kupfergasse 3-5)*, where tickets start at just DM10; and *Sanftwut* (☎ 961 23 46, Mädler Passage)*. All three hold satirical performances poking fun at German life, especially east-west relations.

Classical Music The *Neues Gewandhaus* concert hall, located on Augustusplatz, has Europe's longest-established orchestra, with a tradition dating back to 1743 – Mendelssohn was one of its conductors. Today it covers the entire spectrum of classical music, with guest appearances by soloists, conductors and orchestras from around the world. Tickets range from

DM20 to DM60, and are available at the tourist office (☎ 710 42 60/65).

In July and August, there are free concerts every Monday at 6 pm in front of the Bach statue near the Thomaskirche. The St Thomas concerts include ones by its Boys' Choir. On Sunday there are concerts in the courtyard of the Bach Museum at 3 pm (DM10 to DM15). Free organ concerts take place in the St Thomas and St Nicholas churches every Saturday in July and August; at St Thomas they're at 6 pm and at St Nicholas at 5 pm.

Cinema *Kino Im Grassi* (☎ 960 48 38, *Täubchenweg 2d)* in the Grassi Museum Complex screens films in the original language, with German subtitles, as does the *Passage Kinos* (☎ 217 38 60, *Hainstrasse 19a).*

Getting There & Away

Air The enormous Leipzig-Halle airport, practically equidistant from both cities, is served by several airlines, including Lufthansa Airlines (☎ 224 16 00), Delta Airlines (☎ 0180-333 78 80) and Eurowings (☎ 224 18 59). It takes mainly domestic flights, but will be equipped for big international aircraft from June 2000. Most airlines have their offices in Terminal B at the airport.

Train Leipzig is an important link between eastern and western Germany, with connections to all major cities in the country. There are regular and frequent services between Leipzig and Frankfurt (DM111, 3¾ hours), Munich (DM133, seven hours), Dresden (DM33, 1½ hours), Berlin twice an hour (DM54, two to three hours), Hanover (DM75, 3¾ hours) and Hamburg (DM123, 4½ hours).

Car & Motorcycle Leipzig lies just south of the A14 Halle-Dresden autobahn and 15km east of the A9, which links Berlin to Nuremberg. Best leave your vehicle in one of the well marked parking lots that ring the Altstadt, as parking in the centre is, shall we say, a challenge.

Ride Services There are two local Mitfahrzentralen. One, combined with the Mitwohnzentrale (see Places to Stay), is at Goethestrasse 7-10 (☎ 194 40). The other, Campus Mitfahrzentrale (☎ 980 50 00), is at Reichsstrasse 2, in the Uni-Innenhof. Sample fares with booking fee include Berlin (DM22), Munich (DM44) and Frankfurt (DM41).

Getting Around

To/From the Airport Zubringerbusse Leipzig shuttles the 20km between Leipzig-Halle airport and the Hauptbahnhof (DM10 adults, DM5 for children aged six to 14), running from the airport every half an hour from 7 am to 10.45 pm, and from the Hauptbahnhof every half an hour from 5.30 am to about 10 pm.

Public Transport Trams are the main option, with the most important lines running via Willy-Brandt-Platz in front of the Hauptbahnhof. The S-Bahn circles the city's outer suburbs. Fares are zone *and* time-based – heaven knows why – with DM1.70 (15-minute) and DM3.40 (60-minute) adult tickets. Strip-tickets for five journeys cost DM8/16 for 15-minute/60-minute rides. There's also the off-peak '10 o'clock' ticket, valid from 10 am to 4 pm (DM6).

Taxi Taxi rates in Leipzig are DM3.50 flag fall and DM2 per kilometre. You can order one through Funktaxi (☎ 48 84) or Löwen Taxi (☎ 98 22 22). From 10 pm to 7 am, any bus or tram driver will arrange for a taxi to meet you at the bus or tram stop – the reservation is free, the taxi is not. The BahnTaxi costs DM15 per person and leaves from the west exit of the Hauptbahnhof.

Bicycle The ADFC (☎ 306 51 82) is at Bernhard-Göring-Strasse 52. For bicycle rental, try Fahrradstation Eckhardt (☎ 512 40), outside on the western side of the Hauptbahnhof, for DM15/90 per day/week, plus DM150 deposit. Bike Department Ost (☎ 689 33 34), Rosa-Luxemburg-Strasse 45, charges from DM10 per day.

euro currency converter DM1 = €0.51

AROUND LEIPZIG
Colditz Escape Museum

In the secluded Zwickauer Mulde valley, some 46km south of Leipzig, lies the sleepy town of Colditz and its impressive (though run-down) fortress. The Renaissance structure was used by Augustus the Strong as a hunting lodge in the 17th century, and after the dawn of German psychiatry in the 1800s, it became a mental hospital. Built on a crag high above town, it seemed the ideal site for a high-security prison in WWII, and the Nazis dubbed the place Oflag IVc (Officer's Camp IVc).

Its inmates, mostly cunning Allied officers who had already escaped elsewhere, proved this was a mistake. Between 1939 and 1945 there were over 300 escape attempts, which earned Colditz the reputation of a 'bad boys' camp. Some 31 men managed to flee, aided by ingenious self-made gadgetry, including a glider made of wood and bedsheets, and a home-made sewing machine for making German uniforms. Most astounding, perhaps, is a 44m-long tunnel (under the chapel) that French officers dug in 1941-42 before the Germans caught them.

A number of prisoners turned writer after the war, and their tales have spawned more than 70 Colditz books, several films and at least one BBC TV series. However, all this Allied glory embarrassed the GDR, which suppressed the story in the east after WWII.

Today the fortress houses an **Escape Museum**, which isn't big but is worthwhile, not least because it hasn't been fully commercialised. The place can be viewed only on daily guided tours (except Sunday) at 11 am and 1 and 3 pm (DM5), organised by the Städtisches Museum in the faded yellow house at Tiergartenstrasse 1. For further details, ring the Colditz Castle Society Office (☎ 034381-437 77) at Schlossgasse 1.

Getting There & Away Trains to Colditz from Leipzig, with a change at Grossbothen, take 1¼ hours (DM12). Colditz is at the junction of the B107 and B176 roads between Leipzig and Chemnitz.

ZWICKAU
☎ 0375 • pop 105,000

Once a major centre of GDR industry, Zwickau, one hour south of Leipzig, is perhaps best known as the place from where the mighty Trabants rolled ... slowly ... very slowly ... off their assembly lines.

First mentioned in 1118, Zwickau began life as a trading and silver-mining town, but it's been a seat of the German auto industry since 1904, when the Horch factory churned out roadsters. Horch was nationalised by the GDR, and when it had been sufficiently devolved, Trabant production began.

These days, the Trabi grounds have been completely renovated and taken over by the company that Trabant always tried to emulate, Volkswagen.

Zwickau was also the birthplace of the composer Robert Alexander Schumann (1810-56), and his house is now open as a museum. This, plus a lovely city centre and an impressive cathedral, make Zwickau worth a stop.

Orientation & Information

The Altstadt is surrounded by the circular Dr-Friedrichs-Ring. The Hauptbahnhof is west of the Altstadt, and is connected to it by Bahnhofstrasse and Schumannstrasse. Leipzigerstrasse is the main road jutting north from Dr-Friedrichs-Ring; it becomes the B175/B93, which splits off north of the city. There's a serious lack of street signs throughout the city.

Just south of the Markt and Rathaus, there's a spanking new terminus equipped to take Intercity trains running on the Dresden-Nuremberg line. They now roll right into the Altstadt, on rails parallel to the city trams. The Hauptbahnhof remains 1km west of the centre.

The tourist information office (☎ 83 52 70, fax 29 37 15, email info@zwickau-info.de) is at Hauptstrasse 6, right in the centre of the city. The staff are very friendly, have a huge range of pamphlets, books and magazines, and sell theatre tickets. It's open Monday to Friday from 9 am to 6.30 pm, and Saturday from 10 am to 4 pm.

Dresdner Bank and Deutsche Bank have branches at the intersection of Innere Plauensche Strasse and Dr-Friedrichs-Ring.

The central post office is opposite the Hauptbahnhof. Zwickau's rather simple Web site is www.zwickau-info.de.

There's also a Schnell und Sauber coin-operated laundrette at Leipzigstrasse 27.

City Centre

At Hauptmarkt, the southern end of Hauptstrasse, sits the **Rathaus**, looking for all the world like a theatre; and next door is the city **theatre**, looking like a city administration building. Here too is the prominent **Schumann monument** (1901), which was shuffled around town several times before returning to its original site in 1993.

Behind the theatre is the **Kleine Bühne Puppet Theatre** and **Theater in der Mühle** (see Entertainment).

Behind Hauptmarkt (though the address is actually Hauptmarkt 5) is the **Schumann Haus** (☎ 21 52 69), with exhibits on the composer and his wife, Clara, herself a noted pianist. Opening hours are Tuesday to Saturday from 10 am to 5 pm (DM5/3, children DM1.50).

The city's **Marienkirche** (1219), where Schumann was baptised, is justifiably a place of pride. It was converted to the late-Gothic style from 1453 to 1565, and the steeple was added in the late 17th century. Inside, the church has an impressive stone font (1538), and a wonderful high altar shrine. Next to the photo boards showing the Dom restoration,

The Inevitable Trabi Joke

The Trabant (1949-90) was intended to be the GDR's answer to Volkswagen – an economical, convenient car for the masses – but matched VW only in its ubiquity. Despite production times from hell (the *average* owner waited nine years to get this lemon), the 'Trabi', as it was affectionately called, is still one of the most common cars on the road in eastern Germany.

Each Trabi took so long to build because its plastic parts (that is, most of the vehicle aside from the frame, bonnet and other supporting sections) were made by workers running hand-operated moulding systems. Powered by a two-stroke engine – similar to that of a large lawnmower – this rolling environmental disaster pumped out five times the amount of fumes as the average western vehicle.

A plastic car with a lawnmower engine that you had to wait years to own? That reminds us of a little joke.

A Texas oil man heard that there were cars in East Germany so popular that buyers had to wait years for delivery. He immediately sent a cheque to the Trabi factory.

The directors sensed a propaganda coup in the making and arranged to send him the very next car off the line.

Two weeks later the oil man was in a bar, speaking with some friends.

'I ordered me one o' them Trabis that folks over there wait 12 years to get,' he drawled, 'and you know, them East Germans are so efficient. Why, just last week they sent me over a little plastic model so I can know what to expect.'

MICK WELDON

SAXONY

there's a particularly gruesome rendition of Christ – wearing a real wig up on the cross.

Just south of Marienkirche is the Korn-markt, which had a monopoly on Zwickau grain sales until 1832. On one side stands the eccentric **Schiffchen**, a 15th century house built in the form of a ship's prow. The place was originally owned by a family of ropemakers.

On Dr-Friedrichs-Ring, on the corner of Schillerstrasse and just in front of the West-sächsische Hochschule, is the **Solar Anlage**, an enormous solar-powered sculpture that shows the date, time and temperature.

Car Museum

The best thing about Zwickau's Automobil-museum (☎ 332 38 54), Walter-Rathenau-Strasse 51, isn't the excellent exhibit on auto production (from Horch through Audi and all makes of Trabant), but rather the gift shop, where for DM5 you can buy plastic wind-up toy Trabants, advertising posters and other Trabi trinkets.

The car displays are fantastic, with lots of different Trabant models and prototypes – you're really cruisin' in a three-cylinder IFA-F9 Trabant Cabrio (1949-53). Upstairs, there are classic Horch and Audi-Sachsen Ring cars, sleek limousines, fire engines and other great vehicles, plus a cutaway Trabant and samples of Trabi manufacturing equipment. Stay tuned: sponsor VW is coughing up DM12 million to expand the car selection.

The museum is open Tuesday to Thursday from 9 am to noon and 2 to 5 pm, and weekends from 10 am to 5 pm (DM5/3.50). Tours in German are DM5, and you'll have to pay DM1 to take photographs, and DM3 for video.

Johannesbad

North of the Altstadt is a beautiful old Art Deco swimming pool complex on the river, Zwickauer Mulde. It was being renovated when we visited, but work should be completed in May 2000. Even if you don't want to swim, the interior is terribly ornate and worth a look. From the centre, walk five minutes up Max-Pechstein-Strasse and take a right at Osterweihstrasse.

Places to Stay

There's no hostel or camping ground in Zwickau yet. The tourist office books *private rooms* and hotels for free.

Jugendhotel Bildungswerk Westsachsen (☎ 54 32 38, *Werdauer Strasse 160*), some 4km west of town at the forest's edge, charges DM30 for beds in clean dorm rooms. Take bus No 18 towards Königwalde and alight at Windberg.

The clean *AMON Hotel-Sachsenring* (☎ 21 62 51, fax 21 62 55, *Leipzigerstrasse 160*) has simple but comfortable singles/doubles from DM60/80 (DM85/120 with shower and WC).

The *Achat Hotel* (☎ 87 20, fax 87 29 99, *Leipzigerstrasse 180*), north of the Altstadt, is an absolutely spotless, totally modern place with large, comfortable rooms priced from DM99/190 (including breakfast) on weekdays; all rooms are DM88 from Friday to Sunday.

Hotel Park Eckersbach (☎ 47 55 72, fax 47 58 01, *Trillerplatz 1*), in an attractive old villa, charges from DM95/115.

Best Western Airport Hotel (☎ 560 20, fax 560 21 51, *Olzmannstrasse 57*), about 2km west of the centre, offers business-style comfort from DM136/168.

Places to Eat

Fleischerei Hopfe (*Marienstrasse 30*) is a great butcher's for a quick bite, with a Röster (sausage) and roll just DM2.10 and noodle dishes from DM4. *Athen* (☎ 52 73 52, *Schillerstrasse 8*) has gyros for DM4.50 at the takeaway window and good sit-down dishes in the back. If you must, there's a *Burger King* on Hauptmarkt.

Grünheimer Kapelle (☎ 536 16 33, *Peter-Breuer-Strasse 3*) is in an old chapel with fabulous carved furniture, uneven art exhibits and friendly service. Mains average DM18; we enjoyed the pheasant in red wine sauce (DM21.40).

The *Bistro Basilicum* at the Achat Hotel (see Places to Stay) is a nice, modern place with delicious desserts and friendly, if slow, service.

The *Trattoria Cinecittá* (☎ 230 96 01, *Katherinenstrasse 27)* has lots of movie knick-knacks inside and a wonderful quiet courtyard in the back. Its pizzas and pastas average DM12 to DM17, but the all-you-can-eat lunch menu costs just DM8.

The *Drei Schwäne* (☎ 204 76 50, *Heinrich-Heine-Strasse 69)* in Nordvorstadt is the place to splurge with tip-top French and Alsatian cuisine and fish dishes (closed Monday). Mains average DM36 to DM44. Take bus No 183 or tram No 7 to the Neue Welt stop.

Entertainment

The *Kommunales Kino* at *Kleine Bühne* (☎ 21 58 75) behind Hauptmarkt shows English-language films. There's lots of theatre, dance, concerts and puppet shows at the *Theater Zwickau* (☎ 83 46 47), *Kleine Bühne Puppentheater* (☎ 21 58 75) and *Theater in der Mühle* (☎ 21 60 09), all just behind or on Hauptmarkt.

Roter Oktober (☎ 29 44 93, *Kolpingstrasse 54)*, on the corner of Leipzigstrasse, is a scream: a tiny bar dedicated to all things GDR, with posters of communist luminaries, propaganda, flags and drink specials like Intershop Weissbier and Castro Libre.

The *1470* (☎ 28 27 28, *Mareinstrasse 50)* is a wonderful wooded pub over two floors that also serves decent food (open evenings only). *Ars Vivendi* (☎ 230 95 95, *Peter-Breuer-Strasse 10)* is a chic modern cocktail bar in a lovely old Art Nouveau building.

The *Pflaume* (☎ 29 15 86, *Hauptmarkt 24)*, a lively pub near the theatre, was undergoing a face-lift but should be open by the time you read this. The *Irish Harp Pub* (☎ 28 25 85, *Hauptmarkt 26)* is another very popular option, with cheap food and drinks specials on Friday evenings.

Getting There & Around

There are direct trains to Zwickau every two hours, or an hourly service with one change, from Leipzig's Hauptbahnhof (DM22, 1½ hours). By car, it's about a 1½ hour drive from Leipzig on the B93.

Trams and buses (DM2 per ride) service outlying areas, but it's generally easiest to walk in the Altstadt.

Eastern Saxony

BAUTZEN
☎ 03591 • pop 42,800

In the gentle hills of Upper Lusatia, Bautzen (Budysin in Sorbian) rises suddenly from steep granite cliffs above the River Spree in a flourish of medieval towers. The town is the cultural capital of the Sorbs, Germany's sole indigenous minority, whose Slav forebears settled in the present-day Saxony and Brandenburg in the 7th century (see the boxed text 'The Sorbs' in the Brandenburg chapter). A number of Sorb institutions are based here, and many visitors are surprised to find bilingual signs for streets and public buildings (although you'll be lucky to hear the language spoken).

Though badly damaged many times over its 1000-year history, the layout of the Altstadt has hardly changed for centuries and a large number of historic buildings remain. Many have been spruced up (and many haven't), and the old quarter is slowly evolving into a tourist centre, with the first smart pubs and hotels beginning to spring up. Its chief oddity is the joint Catholic-Protestant cathedral, which holds services for each denomination a couple of hours apart.

Orientation & Information

Bautzen's egg-shaped old quarter half-lies in a gentle arch of the River Spree and is centred around the Hauptmarkt, site of the towering Rathaus and the tourist information office. The Dom is a few metres to the north, on the adjacent Fleischmarkt, while the medieval Ortenburg complex lies at the eastern end. The Hauptbahnhof is a 15 minute walk south-east of the Altstadt, which is reached via Bahnhofstrasse and Karl-Marx-Strasse.

SAXONY

The tourist office (☎ 420 16, fax 53 43 09, email bautzen@imedia.de) is at Hauptmarkt 1. It's open Monday to Friday from 9 am to 6 pm and weekends from 10 am to noon (closed Sunday in winter). There's a Hypovereinsbank at Kornstrasse 2, just north of Markt. The post office is at Postplatz south-east of the centre.

The tiny SB-Waschsalon, on the corner of An der Friedensbrücke and Innere Lauenstrasse, charges DM5 per load (bring your own powder) and DM1 for 20 minutes' drying.

Reichenturm

As you come from the Hauptbahnhof you're likely to pass by the Reichenturm, looking a bit naked with its blanched medieval base and baroque cupola (the gate below was torn down in 1837). Also called the Leaning Tower, the 55m-high Reichenturm deviates 1.4m from the centre. Although it's no Pisa, this makes it one of the steepest leaning towers north of the Alps. You'll scarcely feel this from the viewing platform (DM1/0.50 for adults/children).

Hauptmarkt

The Reichenstrasse – Street of the Rich – leads west from the tower past some wealthy-looking baroque houses to the Hauptmarkt, site of thrice-weekly markets. The square is dominated by the impressive **Rathaus**, with an 18th century baroque exterior that masks a Gothic facade. The intriguing **sundial** on the yellow tower not only measures time but also the lengths of the days and nights for the respective date.

Opposite is the **Gewandhaus**, site of the first bazaar in Upper Lusatia, which today houses the Ratskeller, an Italian restaurant and a tatty GDR-style Imbiss (to be avoided at all costs).

Dom St Petri

Just north of the Rathaus is Fleischmarkt, the old meat market. Here you'll find St Peter's Cathedral, with an 85m-high tower that contains an apartment halfway up that's still occupied. You notice something odd as you enter the sanctuary: this is a so-called *Simultankirche* serving both Catholics and Protestants. When the Reformation reached Bautzen in 1524, both congregations agreed to share the church, with the Protestants taking the nave and the Catholics the choir. There's a waist-high iron grating separating the two (although a 4m-high barrier was deemed necessary until 1952). Both sections are equipped very differently, with a bombastic high altar in the Catholic area and a simple flat one for the Protestants.

Behind the Dom is the **Domstift** (Cathedral Chapter), housed in a courtyard palace with a richly decorated portal (1755). Inside is the ecclesiastical treasury, which can be viewed Monday to Friday from 10 am to noon and 1 to 4 pm (free, donations encouraged). In the courtyard you'll see a chimney on the west wing with the stone head of a man peeking out; this peculiarity dates from 1619, when a Catholic-Protestant feud led to a storming of the cathedral deanery. Legend has it that the dean crawled up the chimney to signal Ortenburg castle for help.

Schloss Ortenburg

On the western edge of town stands the Ortenburg, probably erected in 958 by Otto I to keep the *Milzener* (forebears of the Sorbs) at bay. The cliff-top location made strategic good sense but didn't stop it from burning down several times. The place came under Hungarian rule in the 15th century, and then-king Matthias Corvinus took a great interest in the creation of his own likeness. An ornate version took its place at the **Matthiasturm** above the main gate of the fortress.

The Ortenburg courtyard is home to the **Sorbian Museum**, which displays folk art, musical instruments, costumes and other items in the old salt storage. It's open from April to October daily from 10 am to 5 pm, and to 4 pm in winter (DM3/2).

Alte Wasserkunst

A few paces south, along the old town wall, you come to the Old Waterworks, which for centuries was Bautzen's most important building. Because of the town's site on granite, water supply was a tricky problem. A solution emerged in the late 15th century, when Spree waters were diverted into the tower and pumped up to city level. The wooden tower was replaced with a sturdy stone one (1558) that was operational until 1965. You can visit the **technical museum** (☎ 415 88) with pumpworks daily from 10 am to 5 pm (DM2/1.50); there's a nice view of the **Michaeliskirche**, with its distinctive square tower, from the viewing platform.

Places to Stay

Jugendherberge Bautzen (☎ 403 47, fax 403 48, Am Zwinger 1) is staffed by friendly folk and is in the old fortifications next to the Nicolaikirche. It charges DM18/23 for juniors/seniors in triple-bed rooms.

The tourist office can book *private rooms* from about DM30 per person. All listings below include breakfast.

Pension Stephan's (☎/fax 448 48, Schlossstrasse 1) has a classy location and offers one single room for DM60 and three doubles for DM100, all with private shower and WC.

Pension Dom-Eck (☎ 50 13 30, fax 50 13 34, Breitengasse 2), right by the Dom, has surprisingly modern rooms for DM60/120.

Hotel Alte Gerberei (☎ 30 10 11, fax 30 10 04, Uferweg 1) is on the banks of the Spree with a cosy courtyard, and charges from DM70/120 for rooms with amenities.

Schloss-Schänke (☎ 30 49 90, fax 49 01 98, Burgplatz 5) is in a nicely renovated, old Franciscan residence and charges DM90/120 for rooms with mod cons.

Places to Eat

The *Asia-Döner-Schnell-Imbiss Tram Lam (☎ 400 53, Wendische Strasse 6)* serves up doners as big as its name from DM4.50 (closed Saturday evening and Sunday).

Wjelbik (☎ 420 60, Kornstrasse 7) serves Sorb specialties such as the Sorbian Wedding (braised beef with horseradish sauce, DM16) under wonderful vaulted ceilings.

Apotheke (☎ 48 00 35, Schlossstrasse 21) is the closest Bautzen gets to a vegetarian restaurant, with great salads (eg with sorrel,

nettle or dandelion), pasta and wholemeal dishes (DM12.50 to DM18). Meat-eaters don't come up short, either.

Mönchshof (☎ 49 01 41, Burglehn 1) goes a bit overboard on the medieval knights theme, but the roast boar in red wine and thyme sauce is admittedly good (DM19.50).

Schloss-Schänke is the place to splurge, with seriously romantic dining halls, swish tableware and hushed service. A three-course meal and drinks will set you back DM50 or more.

Zum Haseneck (☎ 479 13, Kurt-Pchalek-Strasse 1), east of the Reichenturm, is a rabbit-eater's heaven with mains averaging around DM17.

Getting There & Away

IR trains service Bautzen to Görlitz (DM20, 1½ to two hours), Dresden (DM15, one hour) and Bad Schandau (DM16, two hours). There's also a bus to Hoyerswerda (DM15, one hour). The A4 Dresden-Görlitz autobahn runs just south of town.

GÖRLITZ
☎ 03581 • pop 66,000

Some 100km east of Dresden on the Neisse River, Görlitz emerged from WWII with its beautiful old town virtually unscathed, though the town was split in two under the Potsdam Treaty, which used the Neisse as the boundary between Germany and Poland.

A major trading city and cultural bridge between east and west and north and south, Görlitz's wealth is obvious from its buildings, which have survived wars but not, unfortunately, three great fires over the years. Sections destroyed in successive fires were rebuilt in the style of the day, and today the city's Renaissance, Gothic and baroque architecture is better preserved than that of any city its size in Saxony. Görlitz is receiving special federal funding to restore its entire Altstadt and many of its 3500 historic buildings.

Görlitz is a surprisingly cosmopolitan place, and it makes a very nice side trip from Dresden, or an overnight stopover between Germany and Poland.

Orientation & Information

The Altstadt spreads to the north of the Hauptbahnhof; Berliner Strasse and Jacobstrasse connect the two. There are several market squares. At the northern end of Jacobstrasse is Postplatz, containing the main post office. North of here is Demianiplatz/Marienplatz, home to the Karstadt department store and the town's main bus stop and tram stop. North of here is Elisabethstrasse, where a lively market takes place on Saturday, and still north of that is Obermarkt, for all intents and purposes, the main town square.

East of Obermarkt is Untermarkt, which leads to Neissestrasse and finally to the Neisse River. The Polish town of Zgorzelec (zgo-**zhe**-lets), part of Görlitz before 1945, is on the east side of the river.

West of the city towers is the Landeskrone, a dormant volcano topped with a viewing tower reachable by one of Saxony's sweetest narrow-gauge railways.

The tourist office (☎ 475 70, fax 47 57 27, email goerlitzinformation@t-online.de), is at Obermarkt 29. It's open Monday to Friday from 10 am to 6.30 pm, Saturday to 4 pm and Sunday (except in January and February) to 1 pm.

The city sits on 15° longitude, the dividing line for Central and Eastern European time. Cross over into Poland and you lose an hour.

There's a Deutsche Bank on Demianiplatz and a Dresdner Bank at Postplatz.

The main post office is at Postplatz 1. Surf the Web in the Cyberb@r, on the top floor of Karstadt, for DM3 per 15 minutes and DM5 for half an hour.

The town's Web site (mostly in German) has an accommodation listing and is at www.goerlitz.de.

Obermarkt & Southern Altstadt

The tourist office is not only interesting for its brochures but also for the fact that Napoleon stayed here in 1813 and addressed his troops from the balcony above the entrance. At the eastern end of Obermarkt is the 16th century **Dreifaltigkeitskirche**, a former cloister and guardhouse.

At the western end of Obermarkt are the remains of town fortifications, two structures now open as museums. The seven floors of the **Reichenbacherturm** were used until 1904 by 'tower families' entrusted to keep a watchful eye out for fires in the town. The **Kaisertrutz** (1490) is now home to temporary art exhibitions. Both are open Tuesday to Sunday from 10 am to 5 pm (DM3/2 each for adults/children).

Behind the Kaisertrutz is the city **theatre** and the **Blumenuhr**, a flower clock handy as a meeting point.

South of Postplatz is the newly restored **Strassburg Passage**, connecting Berliner Strasse and Jacobstrasse. It's at least as impressive as the Art Nouveau **Karstadt** department store at Demianiplatz/Marienplatz, once a hotel. Walk into its centre, look up and gawk at its amazing skylight.

At the northern end of Demianiplatz/Marienplatz is the **Dicke Turm**, also known as the Frauenturm and Steinturm, and almost 6m thick in some places.

Untermarkt

Perhaps the most beautiful section of town, Untermarkt is built around a fountain of Neptune and contains the **Rathaus**, begun in 1537 and built in three sections and three styles. The oldest is at the south-western corner of the square, and its tower features a spectacular astrological clock and goldplated lion (which roars for guided tours). Heading east on Neissestrasse brings you past the **Barockhaus/Library** at No 30, a museum (DM3/2) in the town's only purely baroque house; the **Biblisches Haus** next door, with a facade adorned with reliefs of Old and New Testament scenes; and finally to the river and the **Technical Museum** (free) beneath the easternmost restaurant in the country (see Places to Eat).

North from Untermarkt, walk along Peterstrasse to the Gothic **Peterskirche** (1497), containing a fascinating 'sun organ' built by Silesian-Italian Eugenio Casparini and his son, with pipes shooting off like rays. Free performances are every Thursday and Sunday at noon.

Organised Tours

Walking tours (DM5) leave from in front of the tourist office on Wednesday, Friday and Saturday at 2 pm, and Sunday and holidays at 11 am.

Places to Stay

The *DJH hostel* (☎/fax 40 65 10, Goethestrasse 17) charges DM21/26 for juniors/seniors. Exit the Hauptbahnhof via the Südlicher Ausgang, turn left and walk 15 minutes (or take tram No 1 to Goethestrasse). It's sober but well equipped.

The tourist office books rooms for free. Expect to pay DM25 to DM50 per person for a *private room*.

Familie Launer (☎ 40 53 83, Augustrastrasse 34) offers a fantastic B&B for DM35/70 for singles/doubles. The rooms are homy, breakfast is huge and Frau Launer utterly charming.

The next best bet in town is the charming *Gasthaus Zum Flyns* (☎ 40 06 97, Langenstrasse 1), with lovely restored rooms from DM50/70, friendly staff and a good restaurant downstairs (See Places to Eat).

The central *Gästehaus Lisakowski* (☎ 40 05 39, Landeskronstrasse 23) offers simple rooms from DM60/80.

Silesia (☎ 481 00, fax 48 10 10, Biesnitzer Strasse 11), in a quiet part of town, has old-style bohemian charm from DM95/130.

The most central hotel in town is the *Sorat Hotel Görlitz* (☎ 406 65 77, fax 40 65 79, Struvestrasse 1) on Marienplatz, with modern rooms from DM145/184.

Hotel Tuchmacher (☎ 473 10, fax 47 31 79, Peterstrasse 8), just by the Peterskirche, is the town's most tasteful option from DM175/230.

Places to Eat

For a quick bite, hit Berliner Strasse, which feeds from the train station to the heart of town. Here you'll find a *City Kebap* at No 20, a big *Sternenbäck* bakery at No 52 and a *Schlemmerimbiss* at No 50, with burgers, schnitzels, pastas and more. *Pizza Pasta* (☎ 41 26 23, Strassburg Passage) makes really fine pizzas.

Kartoffelhaus (☎ 41 27 02, Steinstrasse 10), near the Karstadt, is a tuber temple full of neat memorabilia, with baked potatoes from DM4.50 and Silesian dishes such as *bigosh* (potato-sauerkraut stew) for DM14.50.

Destille (☎ 40 53 02, Nicolaistrasse 6) is a top-notch but affordable place, with Silesian Heaven (pork fillet and smoked ham with baked fruit and breaded dumplings) for DM20. You can view the Jewish bath in the cellar for DM2 (or DM4.50 with a glass of Israeli wine).

As well as a lovely interior with vaulted ceilings, the restaurant in the *Gasthaus Zum Flyns* (see Places to Stay) has nice wines and local specialities like Flyns Steak (pork cutlet with baked banana, curry sauce and croquettes) for DM15.

The easternmost restaurant in Germany is the *Vierradenmühle* (☎ 40 66 61) at the site of one of the bridges that spanned the Neisse before WWII. Today there's a main filtration station here, with a technical museum of its workings beneath the restaurant. The food is excellent, with main courses for lunch from DM5 to DM8 and dinner mains from DM12 to DM22.

Zum Nachtschmied (☎ 41 16 57, Obermarkt 18) is an earthy inn with an open hearth and baroque dining hall.

Getting There & Away

More than a dozen daily trains run between Görlitz and Dresden (1½ to two hours, DM29). There are also about the same number of connections between Görlitz and Berlin (DM58, three to 3½ hours).

Görlitz is an important border crossing. Daily Frankfurt-Warsaw and Berlin-Kraków trains make a stop here before heading into Poland via the historic Neisseviadukt bridge (1847), a 475m-long, 35m-high span with 35 arches.

Trains run from Görlitz to Wroclaw at 12.30 and 8.04 am, and 8.24 pm (DM18, 2½ hours). The latter train continues to Warsaw (DM56, eight to nine hours).

NVG buses run frequently between Zittau and Görlitz (DM10, one hour).

SAXONY

Görlitz is just south of the A4 autobahn from Dresden – turn off just after the Königshainer Berge tunnel (Germany's longest). The national B6, B99 and B115 converge just north of town.

ZITTAU
☎ 03583 • pop 29,000
Saxony's most intriguing outpost is Zittau, 35km south of Görlitz. Situated on a knoblet of Germany with Poland and the Czech Republic on either side, the place has an unexpected Italian feel, with its town hall *palazzo*, warm hues and fountain-studded squares. Trade in textiles and machinery made it wealthy in the 17th and 18th centuries, aided by its proximity to passes through the Zittauer Gebirge (Zittau Mountains).

Orientation & Information
The Altstadt is a 10 minute walk south of the Hauptbahnhof via Bahnhofstrasse and Bautzener Strasse. The tourist office (☎ 75 21 38, fax 75 21 61, email stadt@zittau.de), at Markt 1 in the Rathaus, is open Monday to Friday from 8 am to 6 pm, and Saturday from 9 am to 1 pm. From May to October, it's also open on Sunday from 10 am to 1 pm. Staff will sell you the good LVA Sachsen hiking map (DM9.80) and find rooms in Zittau and environs for free. The office also runs two-hour guided city tours every Saturday at 11 am (DM5/3 for adults/children).

The post office is at Haberkornplatz 1 just north of the old town ring, and there's a Sparkasse (with an ATM) on the corner of Neustadt and Frauenstrasse. Zittau's Web site (in German), with descriptions of sights, is www.zittau.de.

Local youths with precious little to do loiter on the main squares. They're mostly harmless, but can be a little bit intimidating at times.

Things to See & Do
The Markt is lined with lovely patrician houses and the turreted **Rathaus** (1845), designed in Italian Renaissance style by architect Karl Friedrich Schinkel. Meet at the tourist office for a tour of the Rathaus on Wednesday at 3 pm (DM3/2). Behind it is the spacious Neustadt square, with several fountains and at one end, the weighty **Marstall** (stables) with a shiny red mansard roof. Originally a 16th century salt store, it now houses offices.

Just to the north of the Markt stands the **Johanneskirche**, a neoclassical church rebuilt in 1837 with unusual bits inside, including wooden Greek columns and an absolutely enormous rendition of Christ in the shallow nave. For a view of the mountains, climb the 60m tower weekdays from noon to 4.30 pm and weekends from 1 to 4 pm (DM3/2).

Exit the north portal to come to the **Kreuzkirche**, a fancy red church in the Bohemian Gothic style. Its most arresting features inside are its two **Fastentücher** (Lenten embroideries); the bigger one, from the late 15th century, shows a complete illustrated Bible with 90-odd scenes.

Just down Klosterstrasse is the **Klosterhof**, a former Franciscan monastery that houses the **Stadtmuseum** (City Museum; ☎ 51 02 70), with a cellar display of torture instruments and a working well. Hours are Tuesday to Sunday from 10 am to noon and 1 to 5 pm (DM3/2).

Zittau Mountains
The most romantic way into the Zittau Mountains is by the narrow-gauge *Bimmelbahn*, which puffs its way to the sleepy resort villages of Oybin and Jonsdorf near the Czech border. Originally laid for browncoal mining, the line snakes up into the mountains through thick forests and past tree-topped crags, splitting at Bernsdorf. The service to Oybin (four per day, DM15, 45 minutes) stops at the **Teufelsmühle** (Devil's Mill), built for silver miners in the 17th century; here you can glimpse the peak **Töpfer** (582m) to the east.

Alternatively, you can hike to Oybin from Zittau's Rathaus. The trail is clearly marked, taking you south along the Neisse River before veering off into the hills (11km, or about 3½ hours). Oybin and Jonsdorf both make good bases for extended hikes, though Oybin is a more picturesque place in its own right.

Berg Oybin, a former fortress and monastery on a hill just north of the town, was built by Bohemian king Charles IV. The dramatic ruins are an ideal setting for summer concerts, or for poking around on your own. It's open from May to August daily from 9 am to 6 pm, and to 4 pm at other times of year (DM4/3).

Places to Stay

The closest hostel is the lovely *Jugendherberge Jonsdorf* (☎ *035844-721 30, fax 721 31, Hainstrasse 14*), 8km south-west of Zittau and a five minute walk from the train station. It charges around DM21/26 for juniors/seniors.

Pension Dany (☎ *51 21 43, fax 51 21 44, Heydenreichstrasse 12*) has a pretty terrace near the Altstadt and singles/doubles for DM45/90, with private shower and WC.

Hotel Bergschlösschen (☎/*fax 51 07 17, Kummersberg 8*), on the edge of town, charges DM65/95 for nice rooms with private facilities.

The *Hotel Dreiländereck* (☎ *55 50, fax 55 52 22, Bautzener Strasse 9*), in the centre, offers very comfy rooms from DM105/130, and has a parking garage.

Places to Eat

The *Max & Moritz Schlemmereck*, on the corner of Bautzner Strasse and the Markt, sells burgers, schnitzels, doners, salads and more for under DM10.

Savi (☎ *70 82 97, Bautznerstrasse 10)* is a pleasant cafe-bar with a decent menu, including pastas and local dishes for DM10 to DM15 and tasty half-litres of Münch-Eibel beer for DM3.50.

Dornspachhaus (☎ *79 58 83, Bautzener Strasse 2*), in a 16th century house next to the Johanneskirche, has vaulted ceilings, dried flowers and a lovely courtyard. Most mains cost under DM20.

Getting There & Away

There are frequent trains to Bautzen (DM20, 1½ to two hours), Görlitz (DM9.80, one hour), Dresden (DM29, two hours) and Prague (DM86, four to 11½ hours).

The B96 (to Bautzen), B178 (to Löbau) and B99 (to Görlitz) all converge in the town centre. NVG buses run frequently between Zittau and Görlitz (DM10, one hour).

SAXONY

Thuringia

The 'green heart' – as Thuringia (Thüringen) is widely known – is an integral part of German tourism these days. Much of Thuringia's appeal lies in its landscape: large, lush forests and sprawling valleys offer limitless opportunities for outdoor activity.

But it is the state's cultural heritage that draws most visitors to Thuringia. It was here that Johann Wolfgang von Goethe and Friedrich Schiller penned most of their best-known works. Johann Sebastian Bach was born in Thuringia, and the Hungarian composer Franz Liszt founded a music school here. The Bauhaus architectural movement originated in this state, whose countryside inspired painters like the American Lyonel Feininger. The reformer Martin Luther preached here and took refuge in Wartburg castle. His nemesis, the revolutionary Thomas Müntzer, led the Peasants' War on Thuringian soil, and the 19th century saw the founding of the German workers' movement. In a grotesque irony, Weimar – the centre of the German Enlightenment, where nearly every house bears a plaque in a testament to the luminary who lived or worked within – exists scant kilometres from the horrors of the Buchenwald concentration camp.

With 16,250 sq km, Thuringia is the smallest of the five new German states. With 2.6 million people it is rather densely populated, although there are no big cities. Even the capital, Erfurt, has only 215,000 people.

Compared with other states of the former GDR, Thuringia's touristic infrastructure is fairly well developed because, along with the coastal resorts along the eastern Baltic, it was one of the top holiday areas for East Germans before the Wall came down.

Travelling within Thuringia is relatively easy, certainly by eastern German standards. Trains connect most towns, and one of the most scenic rides is from Erfurt to Meiningen through the Thuringian Forest. There's also a bus system, though it is usually slow, infrequent and often restricted to

HIGHLIGHTS

Thuringia Luminaries: Ernst Abbe, Johann Sebastian Bach, Karl Philipp Emanuel Bach, Max Weber, Carl Zeiss

- Exploring *Gesamtkunstwerk* Weimar, with its inspiring history, architecture, museums and parks
- Taking in the Kyffhäuser Monument and Panorama Museum in Bad Frankenhausen
- Hiking the Goethe Trail or at least parts of the Rennsteig, Germany's oldest and most famous trail
- Spending time in Wartburg Castle, Martin Luther's hideout, in Eisenach
- Wandering through Erfurt's romantic Old Town
- Visiting Gotha's Schloss Friedenstein, with its top-rated museums

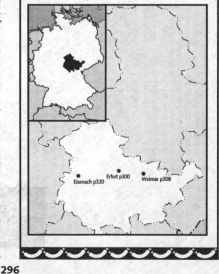

Eisenach p320   Erfurt p300   Weimar p308

THURINGIA

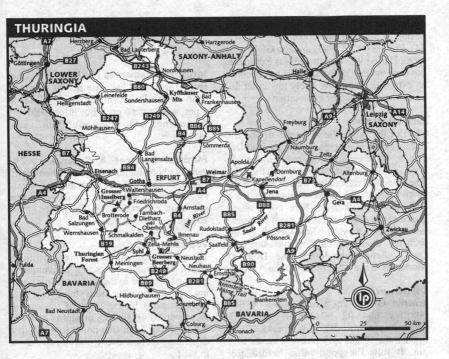

THURINGIA

weekdays. Despite the relatively short distances, if you're travelling by car or motorcycle be prepared for long hours on winding – though usually scenic – country roads.

State-of-the-art hotels have mushroomed since unification, though they tend to charge top Deutschmark. Budget options, on the other hand, are depressingly scarce. Besides hostels and camping grounds, your best bets are private rooms, though standards vary widely.

Central Thuringia

ERFURT
☎ 0361 • pop 215,000

Erfurt, the capital of Thuringia, was founded by St Boniface as a bishopric in 742. In the Middle Ages the city catapulted to prominence and prosperity for being on

an important trade route and for producing a precious blue pigment from the woad plant. The Altstadt's many well preserved buildings attest to that period's wealth. None, however, are from before the 15th century, on account of a major fire that raged through the city in 1472.

Erfurt's university was founded in 1392, not by the clergy but by rich merchants, which allowed students to study common law, not just church law. It became a stronghold of progressive thinking and humanist ideas that questioned traditional church dogma. Not surprisingly, the later Protestant reformer, Martin Luther, studied here. The university was refounded after the *Wende*, and the original main building is being restored.

Erfurt was also known as the 'Thuringian Rome' because some 90 churches stood within its walls; 20 of them still exist. Later

THURINGIA

on, it was governed successively by the bishop of Mainz, Napoleonic troops (1807-14), Prussia (1815-1945) and the GDR until 1990. During WWII, damage was extensive, but over the past decade, Erfurt has become an extremely attractive, lively town that deserves a day or two of exploration.

Orientation

Most of the car traffic is routed around the Altstadt via two ring roads, making it a pleasure to walk between the main sights (do watch out for the fast-moving trams, though). The train and bus stations are just beyond the south-eastern edge of the town centre. It's a five minute walk from here north along Bahnhofstrasse to Anger, the main shopping and business artery. The little Gera River bisects the Altstadt, spilling off into numerous creeks. Erfurt's landmark, the Dom St Marien, is at the western end of the Altstadt.

Information

Tourist Office The tourist office (☎ 664 00, fax 664 02 90, email service@ erfurt-tourist-info.de), Fischmarkt 27, is open from 10 am to 7 pm, weekends to 4 pm. It sells the good-value ErfurtCard, which buys admission to most museums, unlimited public transport, a guided city tour and minor entertainment discounts for a flat DM12 (24 hour validity) or DM25 (72 hours). The Erfurt Family Card (DM59) is good for two adults and for *all* of their own kids (no limit) for 72 hours, and includes additional benefits. For useful information on sights, hotels and events, pick up a copy of the free *Erfurt magazin*.

Money Banks cluster at the intersection of Bahnhofstrasse and Juri-Gagarin-Ring near the Hauptbahnhof. The Reisebank inside the station is open Tuesday to Friday to 7 pm, and Saturday and Monday to 4 pm. If it's closed, there's an ATM here as well.

Post & Communications The main post office on Anger is open weekdays to 7 pm, Saturday to 1 pm and is closed on Sunday. It has a public fax-phone and a copy machine.

Poste-restante mail is delivered here; letters should be clearly marked as *Postlagernd* and addressed to 99084 Erfurt.

Internet Resources For Internet access, try the Internet City cafe across from the train station at Lessingstrasse 8 (closes at 7 pm, weekends 6 pm). For information on the Internet, go to www.erfurt-tourist-info .de/online.

Medical Services & Emergency The general phone number for medical emergencies is ☎ 115. There's an emergency clinic (☎ 262 64) at Espachstrasse 2. For dental problems, call ☎ 516 18. The police (☎ 66 20) are at Andreasstrasse 38.

Walking Tour

Though a state capital, Erfurt is surprisingly small, and most sights are conveniently grouped together in the Altstadt. This walking tour begins at the train station and ends at Fischmarkt in the heart of the city. It takes you to all the major sights and will last anything from two hours to a full day, depending on how many places you choose to visit.

From the Hauptbahnhof head north on Bahnhofstrasse. Just after crossing Juri-Gagarin-Ring, you'll come upon the 14th century **Reglerkirche** on the eastern side of the street. The portal and the southern tower of the former monastery church are Romanesque, and the large carved altar dates back to 1460.

Bahnhofstrasse intersects with Anger, which is lined by houses from seemingly different historical periods, but most of them are only 100 years old. The quince-yellow, richly stuccoed **Angermuseum** (☎ 562 33 11) immediately to your left, however, is original baroque (1712). The rooms that once housed a packing and weighing station now harbour extensive and precious collections of medieval art and crafts, 19th and 20th century landscape paintings and 18th century Thuringian faïences (glazed earthenware). It's open from 10 am to 6 pm, but closed Monday (DM3/1.50).

As you head west on Anger, pay attention to the opulent facades at No 23 and No 37-38. You'll also pass the **Bartholomäusturm**, a tower with a 60 bell *Glockenspiel* (live concert Saturday at 11 am; automatic melodies several times daily).

When you get to the **Angerbrunnen**, where the street splits into a V, keep to the right – Regierungsstrasse – past **Wigbertikirche** to the part-Renaissance, part-baroque **Statthalterpalais**, once home to city governors and now the office of Thuringia's governor. Turn north on Meister-Eckehart-Strasse, then right on Barfüsserstrasse, where the haunting ruins of the **Barfüsserkirche** (☎ 562 33 11) await. A medieval gem, left as a memorial after WWII bombing, its restored choir now houses a small museum of medieval art. It's open from Easter to October, and closed between 1 and 2 pm (DM2).

Backtrack to Meister-Eckehart-Strasse and turn right to get to the 13th century **Predigerkirche**, a basilica with a reconstructed baroque organ. From the church head west on Paulstrasse and Kettenstrasse to the giant Domplatz, presided over by the stunning **Severikirche** and the imposing cathedral itself, joined by a flight of 70 stone steps.

Dom St Marien

St Mary's Cathedral had its origins as a simple chapel from 752 but wasn't completed until the 14th century. In order to build the choir, the hillside occupied by the earlier church had to be artificially raised, creating the enormous substructure on which the cathedral now perches. This also required construction of the stone staircase, which you must climb to enter the church via the richly ornamented triangular portal.

Highlights inside include the superb **stained-glass windows** (1370-1420), with Biblical scenes; the **Wolfram** (1160), a bronze candelabrum in the shape of a man; the **Gloriosa bell** (1497); a Romanesque stucco Madonna; and the 14th century **choir stalls**. Tours are available but you can guide yourself with the help of a free pamphlet, available as you enter.

Around the Dom

Adjacent to the cathedral is the **Severikirche** (1280), a five-aisled hall church boasting a stone Madonna (1345) and a 15m-high baptismal font (1467), as well as the sarcophagus of St Severus, whose remains were brought to Erfurt in 836.

North of the Dom complex, on a little hill, is the **Petersberg**, the site of a former citadel which can be entered through a baroque portal. The remains of the Romanesque **Peterskirche** grace the plateau, with especially fine views of the Altstadt. The main tourist office offers tours of the Petersberg at 2 pm on Saturday.

Back on the Domplatz, take a look at the ornate facades of the houses on its eastern side, then duck into the tiny Mettengasse. Immediately to your right is the **Waidspeicher**, now a puppet theatre and cabaret but formerly a storage house for *Waid* (woad), the plant that produced blue dye. A few metres farther is the **Haus zum Sonneborn** (1536), with its richly ornamented portal, now the city's wedding office.

Andreas Quarter

At the end of Mettengasse, turn north into Grosse Arche, cross Marktstrasse and head north-east on Allerheiligenstrasse. You're now in the former university quarter, which is still being restored. At Allerheiligenstrasse 20, you'll find the **Haus zur Engelsburg**, where a group of humanists met between 1510 and 1515 to compose at least two of the contentious *Dunkelmännerbriefe* (Obscurantists' Letters), a series of satirical letters mocking contemporary theology, science and teaching practices. It is now a student club.

Farther along lies the Gothic **Michaeliskirche**, where Martin Luther preached in 1522. Across the street diagonally opposite is the **Collegium Majus**, the site of the main building of Erfurt's venerable university. A WWII ruin until 1998, it was being reconstructed at the time of writing. The arched portal is the only section from the original structure. The university itself – founded in 1392, closed in 1816 and refounded after

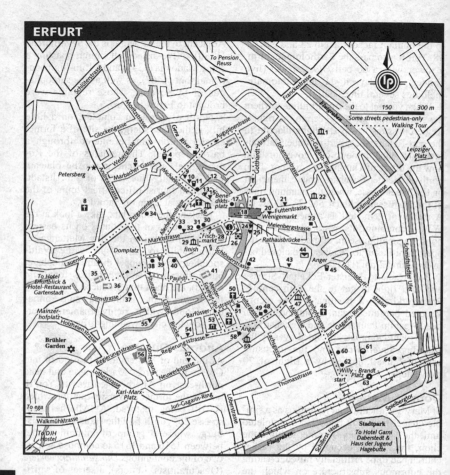

ERFURT

Some streets pedestrian-only

Walking Tour

0   150   300 m

To Pension Reuss

Leipziger Platz

Petersberg

To Hotel Erfurtblick & Hotel-Restaurant Gartenstadt

Mainzerhofplatz

Brühler Garten

To ega

Walkmühlstrasse

To DJH Hostel

Domplatz

Fisch-markt

Wenigemarkt

Futterstrasse

Meienbergstrasse

Rathausbrücke

Anger

Willy - Brandt - Platz
start

Stadtpark

To Hotel Garni Daberstedt & Haus der Jugend Hagebutte

the Wende – was once so prominent that Luther himself called it 'my mother to which I owe everything'.

Turning right onto Augustinerstrasse you'll see the **Augustinerkloster** (☎ 576 60 10), where Luther was a monk from 1505 to 1511 and also read his first mass after being ordained as a priest. The church has ethereal stained-glass windows, and the cloister exudes an otherworldly serenity.

Also on view are an exhibit on the Reformation and Luther's cell. Tours take place between April and October on the hour from 10 am to 4 pm daily except Monday, and at 10 am, noon and 2 pm the rest of the year (DM5.50/4). The grounds and church may be seen free of charge throughout the day. Enter either via Kirchgasse or Comthurgasse. An order of female Protestant nuns – the Communität Casteller Ring, formed in 1950 – has been in residence at the monastery since 1996. Their prayer services are held four times daily, and are open to the public.

THURINGIA

ERFURT

PLACES TO STAY
3   Hotel & Gasthof Nikolai
4   Pension & Pizzeria Don
    Camillo
19 Sorat Hotel & Zum Alten
    Schwan
23 Dorint Hotel
49 Hotel Zumnorde
51 Hotel Ibis

PLACES TO EAT
6   Double B
9   Zum Augustiner
10 Moses
12 Maximilian
15 Wirtshaus Christoffel
20 Drogerie Bistro; Ponte
    Vecchio
21 Louisiana
24 Eiscafé Riva
25 Silberschale
32 Güldenes Rad
39 Barock-Café
43 Anger Maier
54 Suppengrün
55 Altstadt Café
57 Dubliner Irish Pub

OTHER
1   Thüringer Volkskundemuseum
    & Museumskeller
2   Augustinerkloster & Café am
    Augustinerkloster
5   Hemingway
7   Police Station
8   Peterskirche
11 Whisky-Kneipe
13 Collegium Majus
14 Michaeliskirche
16 Galerie Waidspeicher &
    Kulturhof Krönbacken
17 Fayence & Porzellan
    Manufaktur Reindel
18 Krämerbrücke
22 Haus zum Stockfisch;
    Stadtmuseum
26 Begegnungsstätte Kleine
    Synagoge
27 Tourist Office
28 Rathaus
29 Haus zum Roten Ochsen &
    Galerie am Fischmarkt
30 Gildehaus & Jazzkeller
31 Haus zum Breiten
    Herd

33 Haus zur Engelsburg &
    Studentenclub Engelsburg
34 P33
35 Severikirche
36 Dom St Marien
37 Spar Supermarket
38 Theater Waidspeicher & Die
    Arche Cabaret
40 Haus zum Sonneborn
41 Predigerkirche
42 Eurospa & Breuninger
44 Main Post Office
45 Centrum
46 Reglerkirche
47 Angermuseum
48 Bartholomäusturm
50 Barfüsserkirche
52 Wigbertikirche
53 Statthalterpalais
56 Schauspielhaus
58 Angerbrunnen
59 Galerie Haus Dacheröden
60 Rewe Supermarket
61 Central Bus Station
62 Internet City Café
63 Main Train Station
64 Rewe Supermarket

From the monastery, Gotthardtstrasse leads south to the best view of the medieval **Krämerbrücke** (merchant bridge), an 18m-wide, 120m-long curiosity lined by two rows of houses and buttressed by six arches spanning the Gera River.

On the bridge's western end is **Fayence & Porzellan Manufaktur Reindel** (☎ 642 17 74), which sells lovely ceramics, made in the back of the store.

From the west end of Krämerbrücke, a short detour takes you to An der Stadtmünze 4/5 and the **Begegnungsstätte Kleine Synagoge** (☎ 646 46 71), a cultural and educational facility with an emphasis on Jewish tradition and history. It occupies a classicist building that was Erfurt's synagogue from 1840 until it outgrew the space in 1884. In the basement is an exhibit on Jews in Erfurt, as well as a small Mikve (a pool used for ritual purification). It's open Tuesday to Sunday from 11 am to 6 pm; admission and most events are free.

Fischmarkt
Head back to the western end of Krämerbrücke and walk down Marktstrasse to **Fischmarkt**, the medieval market square with a gilded statue of a Roman warrior at its centre. It is flanked by several noteworthy buildings, including the **Haus zum Breiten Herd** (1584), festooned with a rich Renaissance facade. The frieze depicting the five human senses continues with the four virtues on the adjacent **Gildehaus** (1892). Also note the **Haus zum Roten Ochsen** (1562), another Renaissance gem (and now a gallery) opposite the neo-Gothic **Rathaus** (1870-75), where a series of murals along the stairwell depicts scenes from the *Tannhäuser* and *Faust* legends. On the 3rd floor is an extravagant festival hall.

Museums
Unless noted otherwise, all museums mentioned here are open Tuesday to Sunday from 10 am to 6 pm (DM3/1.50).

THURINGIA

The medieval Krämerbrücke, with its two rows of houses, actually spans the Gera River.

At Johannesstrasse 169, at the eastern end of the Altstadt, is the late-Renaissance **Haus zum Stockfisch** with its intricately carved and painted facade. Once the home of a woad merchant, it is now occupied by the **Stadtmuseum** (☎ 562 58 88). Highlights here include a medieval bone carver's workshop and an exhibit on Erfurt in the 20th century, including the GDR era. For insight into the history of Thuringian folk art, visit the **Thüringer Volkskundemuseum** (☎ 642 17 65), at Juri-Gagarin-Ring 140a, where you can see the reassembled workshops of a glass blower, toy carver, mask maker and other craftspeople as well as their products, including pottery, carvings, painted furniture and traditional garments.

West of the city centre is the **ega** (☎ 22 32 20) – which stands for Erfurter Gartenausstellung – a huge garden show centred around **Cyriaksburg** castle (tram No 2 from Anger). It is open daily from 9 am to 6 pm (DM5).

Galleries

Erfurt has many galleries that are treasure troves of contemporary regional, national and international art and sculpture. Those interested should find the following rewarding: **Galerie Waidspeicher** in the Kulturhof Krönbacken (☎ 561 20 80), Michaelisstrasse 10; **Galerie Haus Dacheröden** (☎ 562 41 82), Anger 37/38; and **Galerie am Fischmarkt** (☎ 642 21 88), Fischmarkt 7. Opening hours vary, so call ahead.

Organised Tours

The tourist office offers a two hour walking tour of the historical Altstadt at 1 pm daily from April to December (weekends also at 11 am), and on weekends only the rest of the year (DM6/3). A night tour runs from May to September, Wednesday to Saturday at 7 pm (DM8/4).

Places to Stay

For DM5, the tourist office (☎ 194 33) will book you into a hotel or find you a private room from DM30 per person. Options are also listed in the free *Erfurt magazin*.

Places to Stay – Budget

The sprawling *Ferienpark Hohenfelden* (☎ 036450-420 81, fax 420 82), by a lake in the scenic Ilmtal, about 15km south of Erfurt, is one of Thuringia's largest and most modern camping facilities and is open all year. Take bus No 155 from the central bus station to Hohenfelden Stausee (DM5). It costs DM7.50/3.50/4 per person/tent/car. Another option is *Camping Drei Gleichen* (☎ 036256-227 15, fax 804 41), some 12km west of Erfurt, which charges DM6/5/2.

Erfurt's newly renovated *DJH hostel* (☎ 562 67 05, Hochheimer Strasse 12) is about 2km south of the city centre (tram No 5 from the train station to Steigerstrasse, then a five minute walk). B&B is DM24/28 for juniors/seniors; sheets are DM7. A pleasant alternative is the independent *Haus der Jugend Hagebutte* (☎/fax 655 15 32, Hagebuttenweg 47a). The nightly rate in twin rooms with private facilities is DM15 for those under age 27, DM30 for those older, plus DM5 for sheets. Optional breakfast is DM6. Take tram No 6 to Färberwaidweg.

Pension Reuss (mobile ☎ 0172 740 63 55, Spittelgartenstrasse 15), north of the city centre, is a great bargain, with singles/doubles for DM45/85. A budget option just south-east of the Altstadt is *Hotel Garni Daberstedt (☎/fax 373 15 16, Buddestrasse 2)* with singles from DM50, doubles from DM70, both topping out at DM90. All prices quoted are for rooms with shower and WC (toilet).

Places to Stay – Mid-Range

West of the Altstadt is the family-run *Hotel Erfurtblick (☎ 22 06 60, fax 220 66 22, Nibelungenweg 20)*, with singles/doubles for DM90/130; and the cute *Hotel-Restaurant Gartenstadt (☎ 210 45 12, fax 210 45 13, Binderslebener Landstrasse 212)*, which charges from DM95/125.

Another bargain is *Pension Don Camillo (☎ 642 29 23, Michaelisstrasse 29)*, where spacious, modern rooms with kitchenette cost DM100/120. The pizzeria downstairs is great, too (see Places to Eat). Opposite the Barfüsserkirche is a branch of the *Ibis (☎ 664 10, fax 664 11 11, Barfüsserstrasse 9)* chain. These are good, basic business hotels charging a flat DM120 per room, plus DM15 per person for breakfast. On slow weekends, rates may drop as low as DM79.

Fairly new but very popular is *Hotel & Gasthof Nikolai (☎ 59 81 70, fax 59 81 71 20, Augustinerstrasse 30)*, a rustic country inn with charming, individually furnished rooms costing from DM100/130.

Places to Stay – Top End

One of Erfurt's finest hotels, filled with character and amenities, is *Hotel Zumnorde (☎ 568 00, fax 568 04 00, Anger 50-51; enter from Weitergasse)*. It has classy atmosphere and large rooms from DM165/220. Another winner is the central *Dorint Hotel (☎ 594 90, fax 594 91 00, Meienbergstrasse 26-28)*, which has all the comforts of a state-of-the-art business hotel. Ask for a room in the historical wing (from DM190/210).

Housed in what's been a hotel since the Middle Ages, the *Sorat Hotel (☎ 674 00, fax 674 04 44, Gotthardtstrasse 27)* offers contemporary designer flair with pleasant rooms. It's in a dream location right by a willow-fringed arm of the Gera and the romantic Krämerbrücke. Prices of DM180/220 include a killer champagne buffet breakfast.

Places to Eat

German Restaurants Erfurt brims with traditional restaurants serving Thuringian and general German cuisine, though the quality varies widely. The tunnel-like *Anger Maier (☎ 566 10 58, Schlösserstrasse 8)* is an Erfurt institution. It's always crowded – no wonder, with snack prices (eg bagels) starting at DM3 and daily specials under DM10.

Other good candidates include the rustic *Wirtshaus Christoffel (Michaelisstrasse 41)* and the more sedate *Maximilian* next door, with its panoramic windows. Also good is the atmospheric *Güldenes Rad (☎ 561 35 06, Marktstrasse 50)*, which has a large beer garden where delicious Köstrizer is the beverage of choice.

A classier alternative is *Zum Alten Schwan (☎ 674 00)*, inside the Sorat Hotel (see Places to Stay), which has formal table settings, top-notch service and superior regional food with French touches.

Prices in the previous four restaurants are similar, with mains ranging from DM15 to DM35, though smaller dishes, like salads for around DM12, are also available.

Lighter German fare is on the menu at *Silberschale (☎ 21 09 10, Kürschnergasse 3)*, a friendly restaurant-pub that's an absolute local favourite, and one of ours, too. Seating is spread over three levels, including a winter garden and a terrace above the Gera river. Patrons of all ages, walks of life and wallet sizes will feel comfortable here.

Moses (Michaelisstrasse 35), serving stick-to-the-ribs fare, is popular with students; the all-you-can-eat special of pork and beer for DM25 is typical. Non-carnivores might want to stick with the budget-priced salads and casseroles.

THURINGIA

Other Restaurants For a change from German food, try the *Pizzeria Don Camillo* (☎ 260 11 45, Michaelisstrasse 29), where Aldo from Turin serves tasty pizza and pasta. More upmarket, but worth the splurge, is the charming *Drogerie Bistro* (☎ 642 28 50, Wenigemarkt 8). It's especially nice in summer when candle-lit tables spill out onto the small square at the foot of the Krämerbrücke. Delicious but more economical pizza and pasta dishes are available at *Ponte Vecchio*, the adjacent pizzeria that's in the hands of the same family.

A good place to meet people over a pint of Guinness and hearty fare from the Emerald Isle is the *Dubliner Irish Pub* (☎ 644 20 72, Neuwerkstrasse 47a). It often has live music.

Homesick Americans might want to try *Louisiana* (☎ 568 82 09, Futterstrasse 14), a modern eatery in an ancient, vaulted setting. The menu runs the gamut from steak (from DM16.50) to salad and nachos. It's open weekdays for dinner, and all day weekends.

Vegetarians will like *Suppengrün* (☎ 540 11 38, Regierungsstrasse 70), a clean, cafeteria-style place with a limited menu of organic-produce soups and salads under DM10 (open until 6 pm).

Cafes In summer, try to grab a terrace table above the little canal of the *Altstadt Café* (☎ 562 64 73, Fischersand 6), just west of Lange Brücke. A stylish place for traditional coffee and cake is the *Barock-Café* (☎ 644 22 20, Grosse Arche 16). The *Café am Augustinerkloster*, run by the resident nuns, offers a nice, quiet place to sit, as well as homemade cake, coffee and tea at prices that are practically at cost (closed Tuesday).

In warm weather, lines at the *Eiscafé Riva* (☎ 561 32 17, Lange Brücke 64) may be long – but with prices of 70 Pfennig for a 'small' portion of delicious ice cream in a cone, it still feels like a steal.

Self-Catering There are *Rewe* supermarket branches in the InterCity Hotel by the train station and on Bahnhofstrasse, about two minutes walk north of the station. A large *Eurospar* is in the basement of the Breuninger department store on Schlösserstrasse, on the corner of Junkerstand.

Entertainment
Besides *Erfurt magazin*, for listings there's also *takt*, available for free at pubs and restaurants around town.

Pubs & Bars Erfurt's former university quarter, the Andreasviertel, is a hub of nightlife, pubs, bars etc. The main drag here is Michaelisstrasse, where you'll find places like *Hemingway* (☎ 211 56 78) at No 26, with a faint Caribbean ambience; and the *Whisky-Kneipe*. Around the corner is *Double B* (☎ 642 16 71, Marbacher Gasse 10), a student pub that also serves some two dozen varieties of cooked breakfasts all day (and night).

Live Music & Disco The *Studentenzentrum Engelsburg (also called Eburg;* ☎ 562 90 36, 24 47 70, Allerheiligenstrasse 20-21), a student haunt in historic digs, has bands, disco and performances most nights after 9 pm. The *Museumskeller* (☎ 562 49 94, Juri-Gagarin-Ring 140a), in the vaulted cellars of the Thüringer Volkskundemuseum, has concerts on Friday and Saturday nights at 10.30 pm.

Thuringia's largest disco is the meat-market *MAD* (☎ 525 69 14, Am Nordstrand 4), outside of town. MAD stands for Music-Action-Dance: singles parties, fashion shows, plus four dance floors – you get the idea.

More sophisticated, but also a little bit outside the centre, is *Kantine* (☎ 562 81 11, Schlachthofstrasse 83), which does techno, 80s electronic and other machine-age music on Friday and Saturday nights. Back in town, *Centrum* (☎ 566 25 63, Anger 7) has an eclectic program of movies, disco and bands most nights. Enter through the alleyway across from the post office main entrance.

Jazz Quality jazz is performed at the *Jazzkeller* (☎ 561 25 35) in the Gildehaus at Fischmarkt 12/13, with concerts most Thursday nights at 8.30 pm. Enter through the alley next to the Meissen porcelain store. In summer, you might also catch a jazz concert in the *Kulturhof Krönbacken*, a courtyard anchored by an ancient chestnut tree and surrounded by an ensemble of former woad warehouses. It's at Michaelisstrasse 10.

Theatre & Classical Music The town's *Schauspielhaus (☎ 223 30, Klostergang)*, south of the Domplatz, has two stages and presents classical theatre, musical theatre and ballet. The ticket office (☎ 223 31 55) is at Dalbergsweg 2. The *Theater Waidspeicher (☎ 598 29 12, Domplatz 18)*, on the ground floor of a woad warehouse (in a courtyard reached via Mettengasse east off Domplatz), is a puppet theatre popular with all ages. Upstairs is the home of the satirical cabaret *Die Arche (☎ 598 29 24)*.

P33 (☎ 210 87 14, Pergamentergasse 33) is a warehouse-sized pub-theatre with beamed ceilings that presents a mixed bag of variété, cabaret and music Friday and Saturday nights and during Sunday brunch.

From the end of May throughout summer, classical concerts take place beneath linden trees in the romantic courtyard of the Michaeliskirche (Friday). Organ concerts are at the Predigerkirche (Wednesday) and at the Dom (Saturday).

Getting There & Away
Train Erfurt's Hauptbahnhof (☎ 194 19 or ☎ 562 48 22/23 for information) has direct IR or IC links every two hours to Berlin-Zoo (DM81, 3½ hours), Leipzig (DM39, two hours), Dresden (DM71, three hours) and Frankfurt-am-Main (DM72, three hours). There are also services to Meiningen (DM24.40, two hours) and Schmalkalden (change in Zella-Mehlis; DM22.20, 1½ hours), as well as to Mühlhausen (DM16.20, one hour). Trains to Weimar (DM7.60, 15 minutes) and Eisenach (DM14.80, 50 minutes) run several times hourly.

Bus Because it's so well connected by rail, bus service to/from Erfurt is fairly limited. There's one bus weekdays to Schmalkalden (No 618) and several to Rudolstadt (No 13). Buy your tickets from the driver.

Car & Motorcycle Erfurt is just north of the A4 (exit at Erfurt-West or Erfurt-Ost) and crossed by the B4 (Hamburg to Bamberg) and the B7 (Kassel to Gera). Most major car rental agencies have offices at the airport. Avis can be reached at ☎ 656 24 25, Hertz at ☎ 656 24 69 and Europcar at ☎ 656 24 44.

Getting Around
Bus No 891 runs four times daily from the Hauptbahnhof to the airport. You can also take tram No 1 to Hauptfriedhof, then change to bus No 91/92 to Flughafen. The trip takes about 30 minutes and costs DM2. A taxi should cost around DM20.

Erfurt's tram and bus system is divided into three zones, but you're likely to travel only within the city centre (yellow zone). Tickets are DM2.20, or DM8 for a five ticket block and DM5.50 for a day pass. For information, call ☎ 194 49. To order a taxi, ring ☎ 511 11 or ☎ 66 66 66.

GOTHA
☎ 03621 • pop 54,000

Gotha, a pleasant provincial town first mentioned in 775 in a document signed by Charlemagne, rose to prominence when Duke Ernst I made it his residence and built the enormous yet gracious Schloss Friedenstein. The descendants of this founder of the House of Saxe-Coburg-Gotha now occupy the British royal throne, having changed their name to Windsor after WWI. In the 18th century, an extended stay by the French philosopher Voltaire turned the court into a centre of the Enlightenment in Germany. Even today, the Schloss, which contains several top-rated museums and a resplendent baroque theatre, remains Gotha's cultural centre and its star attraction. Gotha is also a gateway to the Thuringian Forest and the terminus of the Thüringerwaldbahn, a historic tram that shuttles through the forest several times daily (also see the Friedrichroda section later in this chapter).

Orientation & Information
Schloss Friedenstein, sitting on a mound called Schlossberg, and its gardens take up

THURINGIA

about half of Gotha's city centre, with the Altstadt ensuing to the north. It's a brisk, 15 minute walk from the train station to the central square, the Hauptmarkt. The central bus station is on Mühlgrabenweg on the north-eastern edge of the city centre.

· The tourist office (☎ 85 40 36 or ☎ 22 21 38, fax 22 21 34) is a short walk east of the Hauptmarkt in a GDR-era building project at Blumenbachstrasse 1-3. It's open weekdays from 9 am to 5 pm and Saturday to noon, and makes free room reservations. Guided tours (in German) take place Wednesday at 11 am and Saturday at 2 pm from the Rathaus on Hauptmarkt (DM5/2.50).

For information on the Thuringian Forest, there's also the Tourismusverband Thüringer Wald (☎ 36 31 11, fax 36 11 13) in Margarethenstrasse 2-4, open one hour longer than the tourist office.

The GothaCard (DM15 for one adult and one child up to age 12) is good for 72 hours of unlimited public transport and admission to most museums. The Touristenticket (DM8, children DM5) entitles you to free transport (including the Thüringerwald-bahn) for one day and reduced admissions for a one month period.

The main post office on Ekhofplatz 1 has a public fax-phone and also exchanges currency, as do banks throughout the town.

Schloss Friedenstein

Built between 1643 and 1654, this horse-shoe-shaped palace was never destroyed, so its early baroque exterior remains largely unchanged. Note the two characteristic towers, one round, the other square. Among the museums it contains, the **Schlossmuseum** (☎ 823 40) deserves top billing. In fact, it's worth visiting Gotha only to tour its lavish baroque and neoclassical royal apartments and the eclectic collections they hold. Expect to spend at least two hours to see it all.

A main attraction of the medieval collection is the ethereal painting *Gothaer Liebespaar* (1484). This depiction of two lovers is considered the first double portrait in German painting. Also noteworthy are several artworks by Lucas Cranach the Elder,

including the haunting *Verdammnis und Erlösung* (Damnation and Deliverance, 1529).

On the 2nd floor, you'll find the **Festsaal**, an exuberant hall of stuccoed ceilings, walls and doors. The less flashy neoclassical wing contains a collection of sculptures, of which the Renaissance work by Conrad Meit called *Adam und Eve* deserves special mention. The **Kunstkammer** is jammed with miniature curiosities and treasures, including exotica like engraved ostrich eggs and a cherry pit sporting a carved portrait of Ernst the Pious. Highly unusual too are the cork models of ancient buildings, a craft in vogue in 18th century Italy. Finally, the palace also houses one of Europe's oldest Egyptian collections, including several mummies.

In the west tower is the **Museum für Regionalgeschichte und Volkskunde**, one of the most important museums of regional history in Thuringia. A real gem, though, is the refurbished **Ekhof-Theater**, one of the oldest baroque theatres in Europe. The stage tradition at Schloss Friedenstein goes back to 1683 and a still-functional mechanised set-changing device survives from that period. In 1775 Conrad Ekhof, the 'father of German theatre', founded the court theatre with a permanent ensemble. Performances take place during the summer festival in July and August, and there's also an exhibit on the history of this theatre.

The **Schlosskirche** occupies the north-eastern corner, while the east wing contains a **research library** with more than half a million books from 12 centuries.

Behind the Rose Garden to the south, along Parkallee, is the **Museum der Natur** (☎ 823 00), with stuffed animals grouped in dioramas and a popular dinosaur exhibit.

All Schloss museums are open daily from 9 am to 5 pm. Admission to the Schlossmuseum and the Museum für Regionalgeschichte is DM8/4 each. The Nature Museum is DM4/2. A combination ticket for all museums costs DM10/5.

Hauptmarkt

The **Rathaus**, with its gorgeously restored Renaissance facade and 40m-tall tower, commands the large rectangular Hauptmarkt, the focal point of the Altstadt. Built as a department store in 1567, the structure was later inhabited by Duke Ernst I until Schloss Friedenstein was completed and finally turned into the town hall in 1665. The market slopes up towards the palace, at the foot of which is the **Wasserkunst**, a cascading fountain. Noteworthy houses flanking the square include the one at No 42 where Martin Luther stayed in 1537 and the one at No 17, which is the birthplace of Lucas Cranach's wife. Of modest importance is the **Augustinerkirche**, one block west, where Luther preached four times and which has an unusual pulpit balancing on a slender wood pillar.

Places to Stay
The nearest camping ground is *Am Schwimmbad Georgenthal* (☎ 036253-413 14), about 15km south-west of Gotha at Am Flössgraben 3 (take bus No 864 from the central bus station). It's open from April to October and costs DM6.50/5/2.50 per person/tent/car.

Gotha's *DJH hostel* (☎ 854 08, Mozart-strasse 1) is in a historical building five minutes walk north of the train station. B&B costs DM20/25 for juniors/seniors.

The tourist office makes free room reservations, including private ones for DM25 to DM40 per person, though central budget options exist as well. At the foot of the palace is the quiet *Am Schloss* (☎/fax 85 32 06, Bergallee 3) where singles/doubles with shared bath cost DM40/70. Near the train station, you'll find the tiny *Café Suzette* (☎/fax 85 67 55, Bebelstrasse 8), which has adequate singles with private bath for DM63 and doubles for DM108.

Those who can afford to spend a bit more should try *St Gambrin* (☎ 309 00, fax 30 90 40, Schwabhäuser Strasse 47), which also has a fish restaurant and charges DM80/130 for rooms with full facilities. All prices include breakfast.

Places to Eat
Old-world coffee-house culture reigns in Gotha's Altstadt. *Cassignoel* (☎ 85 27 58,

Querstrasse 5) and the *Hof-Café Harmonie (Hauptmarkt 8)*, upstairs in a little arcade, are especially fine. Be aware that cafes usually close at 6 pm, as does the *Gockelgrill* (☎ 85 32 54, Hauptmarkt 26), which has decent grilled half chickens for DM4.50.

For more variation, head for the whimsical *Firlefanz* (☎ 85 67 45, Klosterstrasse 5), a restaurant-pub where you can spend as little as DM4 for a snack or up to DM20 for a full meal. For dining with a historical ambience, try *Weinschänke* (☎ 30 10 09, Gartenstrasse 28) or *Goldene Schelle* (☎ 89 19 50, Hauptmarkt 40). Mains at both places cost about DM15 to DM20.

Getting There & Away
Gotha is easily reached by train from Eisenach (DM7.60, 25 minutes), Erfurt (DM7.60, 20 minutes) and Weimar (DM12, 45 minutes). It's also an IR train stop (every two hours) to Berlin-Zoo (DM90, four hours) and Frankfurt (DM64, 2½ hours). Gotha is just north of the A4 (exit Gotha) and is crossed by the B247 and B7.

For easy access to the Thuringian Forest, take the Thüringerwaldbahn (tram No 4), which makes the trip to Friedrichroda and Tabarz several times hourly (DM4.50, one hour).

WEIMAR
☎ 03643 • pop 61,000
Neither a monumental town nor a medieval one, Weimar appeals to cultural and intellectual tastes and is something of a pilgrimage site for Germans. Its position as the epicentre of this country's Enlightenment, and the birthplace of much that is considered great in German thought and deed, is unrivalled. But these traditions are not always apparent to visitors in a hurry. The parks and small museums need to be savoured, not downed in one gulp.

The pantheon of intellectual and creative giants who lived and worked here amounts to a virtual Germanic hall of fame: Lucas Cranach the Elder, Johann Sebastian Bach, Christoph Martin Wieland, Friedrich Schiller, Johann Gottfried Herder, Johann

THURINGIA

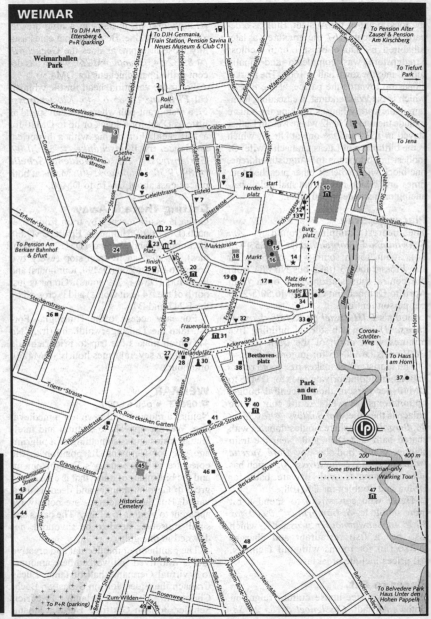

WEIMAR

PLACES TO STAY		32	Zum Weissen Schwan	21	Wittumspalais
11	rollover	39	Mensa	22	Bauhaus Museum
17	Hotel Elephant	44	Felsenkeller	23	Goethe & Schiller Statue
26	Hotel Alt Weimar			24	German National Theatre
28	Hotel Amalienhof	**OTHER**		25	Studentenclub Schütze
38	Dorint Hotel	1	Planbar	29	Rewe supermarket
42	DJH Am Poseckschen Garten	3	Main Post Office	30	Wieland Statue
46	Villa Hentzel	4	Studentenclub Kasseturm	31	Goethe Haus; Goethe
48	Wolff's Art Hotel	5	Mon Ami		Nationalmuseum
49	DJH Maxim Gorki	9	Stadtkirche St Peter &	33	Haus der Frau von Stein
			Paul/Herderkirche	34	Fürstenhaus & Music Academy
PLACES TO EAT		10	Stadtschloss &	35	Carl August Statue
2	Brasserie Central		Kunstsammlungen zu Weimar	36	Anna Amalia Library
6	Anno 1900	14	Police Station	37	Goethe's Gartenhaus
7	Scharfe Ecke	15	Tourist Office & Stadthaus	40	Liszt Haus
8	Zum Zwiebel	16	Cranachhaus	41	Bauhaus Universität
12	ACC	18	Rathaus	43	Nietzsche Archiv
13	Residenz-Café	19	Stiftung Weimarer Klassik	45	Goethe & Schiller Crypt
27	Sommer's Weinstuben	20	Schiller Haus	47	Römisches Haus

Wolfgang von Goethe, Franz Liszt, Friedrich Nietzsche, Walter Gropius, Lyonel Feininger, Vasili Kandinsky, Paul Klee, the list goes on. The latter four are associated with the Bauhaus School, the cornerstone of modern architecture, which was founded here in 1919.

Abroad, the town is best known as the place where Germany's first republican constitution was drafted after WWI (hence, the 1919-33 Weimar Republic; also see the boxed text), though there are few reminders of this historical moment here. The ghostly ruins of the Buchenwald concentration camp, on the other hand, still provide haunting evidence of the terrors of the Nazi regime that was so fervently embraced in this area.

Because of its historical significance, Weimar has received particularly large handouts for the restoration of its many fine buildings. In 1999 it was the European Capital of Culture.

Although Weimar does on occasion feel like a giant museum teeming with tourists, it is one of Germany's most fascinating places and belongs on any itinerary.

Orientation & Information

The town centre is a 20 minute walk south of the train station. Bus Nos 1, 5 and 8 all serve Goetheplatz on the north-western edge of the Altstadt.

The tourist office (☎ 240 00, fax 24 00 40, email tourist-info@weimar.de) is at Markt 10. From May to October, it's open weekdays from 10 am to 7 pm (in winter to 6 pm) and weekends to 5 pm (in winter to 3 pm). There's also a smaller information office (☎ 24 00 45) in the train station. Both offices sell the WeimarCard, which includes free or reduced entry to museums and travel on city buses, plus other benefits. Prices and benefits vary annually.

Most of Weimar's museums and many of its cultural activities are managed by a trust foundation, the Stiftung Weimarer Klassik (☎ 54 51 02). Its visitor information office, just off the Markt at Frauentorstrasse 4 (open from 8.30 am to 4.45 pm), sells a wide range of relevant literature, though most of it is in German.

You can change money at the Sparkasse at Graben 4 or at most other banks in town. The main post office (☎ 23 10) is at Goetheplatz 7-8, and has a public fax-phone and a photocopy machine. There's a police station (☎ 85 07 29) at Markt 15.

Opening Hours Museums and sights administered by the Stiftung Weimarer Klassik

THURINGIA

How the Weimar Republic Got Its Name

Despite its name, the Weimar Republic (1919-33), Germany's first dalliance with democracy, was never actually governed from Weimar. The town on the Ilm was merely the place where, in 1919, the National Assembly drafted and passed the country's first constitution.

Assembly delegates felt that the volatile and explosive political climate rocking post-WWI Berlin, the capital, would threaten the democratic process were it to take place there, and looked for an alternative location. Weimar had several factors in its favour: a central location, a suitable venue (the Deutsches National Theater), and the humanist tradition so antithetical to the militaristic Prussian spirit that had led to war, and from which the delegates sought to distance themselves.

Weimar's spot in the democratic limelight lasted only briefly: the government returned to Berlin just one week after passing the constitution on 31 July.

all have the following opening hours: mid-May to late August from 9 am to 7 pm, late October to mid-March to 4 pm, otherwise to 6 pm. These hours apply to the Goethe Haus, Goethe Nationalmuseum, Schiller Haus, Historischer Friedhof crypt, Wittumspalais, Liszt Haus, Goethe's Gartenhaus, Römisches Haus, Nietzsche Archiv, Schloss & Park Tiefurt and the Anna Amalia Library. Some are closed one day a week (see individual entries). For general information, contact ☎ 54 51 02.

Walking Tour

Our tour begins on Herderplatz, dominated by the **Stadtkirche St Peter und Paul** (1500). It is popularly known as Herderkirche after Johann Gottfried Herder, who Goethe brought to Weimar as court preacher in 1776. His statue stands on the church square and he's buried inside. The church itself has a famous altarpiece (1555), begun by Lucas Cranach the Elder and completed by his son. In the left aisle is an interesting triptych showing Martin Luther as a knight, professor and monk. The church is closed at lunchtime and after 3 or 4 pm.

Walk east on Mostgasse to Burgplatz, anchored by the Stadtschloss, the former residence of the ducal family of Saxe-Weimar. Inside are the **Kunstsammlungen zu Weimar**, with sculptures, paintings and arts and craft objects. Highlights include the Cranach Gallery, several portraits by Albrecht Dürer, and collections of Dutch masters and German romanticists. From April to October, it's open daily from 10 am to 6 pm (closed Monday), and to 4.30 pm the rest of the year (DM6/3).

South of here, on Platz der Demokratie, is the Fürstenhaus, a former palace that is now home of a renowned **music academy** founded by Franz Liszt in 1872. The statue in front represents Duke Carl August. On the eastern side of the square is the **Anna Amalia Library**, a rococo gem that was once managed by Goethe and harbours 900,000 books. It's only open from 11 am to 12.30 pm (closed November to March); tickets are sold at the Goethe Nationalmuseum (DM4/3).

The pink building behind the Fürstenhaus is the **Haus der Frau von Stein**. She was a married woman who was Goethe's long-time muse and – presumably only platonic – love. It is now home to the Goethe Institut, a language school and culture centre.

Head west on Ackerwand to Wielandplatz, with the **Wieland statue**, then turn north onto Frauenplan, where you'll find the **Goethe Haus** and **Goethe Nationalmuseum** (see their separate entries).

A short walk further north leads to the Markt with the neo-Gothic Rathaus (1841) to the left (west), opposite two Renaissance jewels: the **Cranachhaus**, in which the artist lived the final two years before his death in

1553, and the **Stadthaus**, which now houses the tourist office.

Backtrack a few steps, then turn right onto the pedestrianised Schillerstrasse which leads past the **Schiller Haus** to Theaterplatz. Here, the famous **statue of Goethe and Schiller** (1857) fronts the **German National Theatre**, best known as the place where the national assembly drafted the constitution of the Weimar Republic in 1919. The theatre has several artistic claims to fame: Goethe was director here from 1791 to 1817, and Liszt and Strauss were its music directors in the late 19th century.

Across from here is the **Bauhaus Museum**, adjacent to the baroque **Wittumspalais**, once a residence of Duchess Anna Amalia, the premier patron of the arts in late 18th century Weimar. Today it houses the **Wieland-museum**. It was Wieland (1733-1813) who first translated Shakespeare's works into German (closed Monday, DM6/4).

Goethe Haus

No other individual is as closely associated with Weimar as Johann Wolfgang von Goethe, who lived here from 1775 until his death in 1832. In 1792 his sponsor and employer, Duke Carl August, gave him a house on Frauenplan as a gift, and it was here that he worked, studied, read, researched and wrote such immortal works as *Faust*.

Goethe's original 1st-floor living quarters are reached via an expansive Italian Renaissance staircase decorated with sculpture and paintings brought back from his travels to Italy. Each of the rooms is painted in a different shade, according to Goethe's own theories about the correlation of mood and colour. You'll see his dining room, study and the bedroom with his deathbed.

Because demand often exceeds capacity, you will be given a time slot during which you're allowed to enter. Once inside, you may stay as long as you want. The house is closed Monday (DM8/5).

Goethe Nationalmuseum

Those who come here expecting to learn all about the great man of letters will probably be disappointed. Rather than focusing on Goethe himself, the exhibit offers a survey of the late 17th, early 18th century period, referred to as German Classicism. Goethe's fellow thinkers – like Wieland, Herder and Schiller – are given as much exposure as his ducal patrons (Anna Amalia and Carl August), his muses (Charlotte von Stein) and various bit-players, like Germaine de Staël and Karl Ludwig von Knebel.

Paintings, books, manuscripts, sculptures, letters and *objet d'art* are presented in a non-chronological, loose fashion on two main floors, connected by both a cascading staircase wrapped in warm wood paneling and a dramatically spiralling one.

Be sure to take a look inside the museum cafe, with its controversial mural which, aside from depicting Weimar's glorious Who's Who, also includes Adolf Hitler. The museum is open daily (DM8/5).

Schiller Haus

The dramatist Friedrich von Schiller lived in Weimar from 1799 until his early death in 1805 but, unlike Goethe, he had to buy his house at Schillerstrasse 12 with his own money. The little study at the end of the 2nd floor contains the desk where he penned *Wilhelm Tell* and other works, as well as his deathbed. His wife's quarters are on the 1st floor and the servants lived on the ground floor. Entry is via Neugasse. It is closed Tuesday (DM5/3).

Both Goethe and Schiller are interred on the **Historischer Friedhof** (Historic Cemetery) in a neoclassical crypt (see boxed text) along with Duke Carl August. It is closed Tuesday and from 1 to 2 pm (DM4/3).

Park an der Ilm

The sprawling Ilm Park, the eastern flank of the Altstadt, is an inspiring and romantic spot named after the little river that runs through it. Its most famous feature is **Goethe's Gartenhaus**. This simple cottage was an early present (1776) from Duke Carl August and was intended to induce Goethe to stay in Weimar. It worked. He lived in this building until 1782 and also helped

Goethe – May He Rest in Peace

This is a story with all the ingredients for a Gothic techno-thriller – sort of Robert Ludlum meets Anne Rice. Set at the height of the Cold War, it features a celebrity corpse, a crypt, a controversial scientific procedure, and a multi-level conspiracy.

On a November night in 1970, seven men huddle around a humble sarcophagus in Weimar's Historical Cemetery. They've come to check on the foul odours that have been emanating from the heavy oak casket, which is now carefully, slowly pried open. The group recoils at the sight before them: Johann Wolfgang von Goethe – German genius, cultural icon, sacred cow – devoured by flesh-eating fungi! Slamming the lid back down, the stunned and horrified men decide that something has to be done. Goethe's mouldy remains must be clutched from the voracious micro-organisms. And quickly!

'If anybody had found out about this, people would have said that the GDR allowed Goethe's corpse to go to waste,' explained Professor Franz Bolck, 80, the only surviving member of the expedition team of pathologists, archaeologists and restoration experts, in an interview with the German magazine, *Stern*. 'This was a political situation of the highest order,' he added.

Apparently, Goethe's corpse was originally embalmed, but his coffin had since been illegally opened, allowing humidity to creep inside, which caused the decomposition. To cover up the mess, Operation Maceration Goethe (tastefully named after the process of removing skin and soft tissue to preserve a skeleton) kicked off a few nights later. The group clandestinely returned to the crypt, leaving with the ailing corpse in tow.

What happened in the following two weeks is the subject of a meticulous report that resurfaced in early 1999, causing a minor scandal and a major stir in the press and among the general public. What had happened to the untouchable German demi-god?

According to the report, the cadaver was measured (determining a body height of 1.69m at the time of death), the bones counted (five were missing) and scrubbed with mild laundry detergent. The dusty brain mass was removed and the skull refilled with sand to measure the volume (1.55L). On 21 November, the bug-free relics were reinterred to – hopefully – forever rest in peace. The seven conspirators swore an oath of secrecy about the incident and the file was sealed.

It remained that way until the respected *Frankfurter Allgemeine Zeitung* got its hands on it and published the report in its entirety in March 1999. The body, they opined with a serious dose of indignation, had been treated with 'brutality' and 'roughness'. Not so, says Bolck with the clinical rationale of the pathologist. 'It was obvious: no conservation without maceration.'

---

landscape the park. Admission is limited and it's closed on Tuesday (DM4/3). In 1999, an exact replica of the house was built in the park to protect the original from the tourist invasions.

Within view of the Gartenhaus is the **Römisches Haus**, Carl August's summer retreat, built between 1792-97 under Goethe's supervision; the first neoclassical house in Weimar, it perches atop an artificial bluff. It

reopened in June 1999 with restored period rooms and an exhibit on the Ilm Park. It is closed Monday (DM4/3).

On the western edge of the park, at Marienstrasse 17, stands the **Liszt Haus**. The composer and pianist Franz Liszt resided in Weimar in 1848 and again from 1869 to 1886, a time during which he wrote *Hungarian Rhapsody* and *Faust Symphony*. It's closed Monday and from 1 to 2 pm (DM4/3).

Art Nouveau in Weimar

Architecture fans will want to make a trip out to **Haus Unter den Hohen Pappeln** (House Beneath the Tall Poplars; ☎ 85 38 08), at Belvederer Allee 58, the former private home of Belgian Art Nouveau architect, designer and painter Henry van de Velde. Van de Velde came to Weimar in 1902 at the instigation of Harry Graf Kessler and founded the Arts & Crafts School in 1908. Together they tried to blow the cobwebs out of what had become a provincial nest by creating a new artistic style, borrowing organic shapes from nature and creating a dynamic and decorative interplay of line and surface. Although they ultimately failed, van de Velde's legacy survives in numerous ways around town.

His own home, which looks a bit like a ship on its side, features natural stone, stylised chimneys, loggias and oversized windows. It's open from 10 am to 6 pm, and is closed on Monday (DM3/2). Take bus No 1 or 12 to the Papiergraben stop.

Van de Velde designed the entrance of the **Nietzsche Archiv**, Humboldtstrasse 36, where the philosopher spent his final years. The Archiv is open from 1 pm, closed Monday (DM4/3). He also designed the building now housing the **Bauhaus Universität** on Geschwister-Scholl-Strasse.

More splendidly restored Art Nouveau buildings cluster on Cranachstrasse, Gutenbergstrasse and Humboldtstrasse, just west of the Historischer Friedhof. Especially note the one at Cranachstrasse 15, once the home of Kessler, and the magnificent one at No 47.

Bauhaus in Weimar

The Bauhaus School and movement was founded in Weimar in 1919 by Walter Gropius, who managed to draw top artists including Kandinsky, Klee, Feininger and Schlemmer as teachers. In 1925 the Bauhaus moved to Dessau and from there to Berlin, in 1932, where it was dissolved by the Nazis. The **Bauhaus Museum**, on Theaterplatz, chronicles the evolution of the group, explains their innovations in design and architecture and spotlights the main players. From April to October, hours are 10 am to 6 pm (closed Monday), and to 4.30 pm the rest of the year (DM5/3).

Despite its later influence on modern architecture, only one Bauhaus building was ever constructed in Weimar. Called the **Haus am Horn**, Am Horn 61, it opened to the public in 1999 and can be entered on Wednesday and on weekends from 10 am to 6 pm (DM3).

For more on the Bauhaus, see the Berlin chapter, as well as Dessau and the boxed text 'The Bauhaus' in the Saxony-Anhalt chapter.

Neues Museum

A recent addition to Weimar's museum scene is this museum (☎ 54 60) with top-drawer contemporary art – Warhol, Baselitz, Rauschenberg etc – amassed by Paul Maenz, a gallery owner and collector from Cologne. It's open from 10 am to 6 pm (November to March to 4.30 pm), but is closed on Monday (DM5/3).

Belvedere & Tiefurt Parks

The lovely Belvedere Park outside of Weimar harbours Carl August's former hunting palace, with the **Rokokomuseum** displaying glass, porcelain, faïences and weapons from the late 17th and 18th centuries. The museum is open from 10 am to 6 pm (DM5/3). Also here is the **Collection of Historical Coaches**, on view from 10 am to 1 pm and 2 to 6 pm (DM1/0.50). Both museums are closed Monday and from November to March. Bus No 12 runs hourly from Goetheplatz to Belvedere.

A few kilometres east of the train station, Tiefurt Park is an English-style garden enveloping Anna Amalia's summer palace, her own 'temple of the muses': it was here where she held her round-table gatherings that often included Goethe. The palace is furnished and may be visited; it's closed Monday (DM6/4). Bus No 3 goes out to Tiefurt from Goetheplatz.

Places to Stay

Although Weimar's hotel capacity has increased enormously in recent years, demand may on occasion exceed supply. The tourist office also arranges private rooms (from DM25 to DM35 per person). Unless noted, all prices below include breakfast and are for rooms with shower and WC.

Places to Stay – Budget

The closest camping ground is *Campingplatz Ilmtal* (☎ 036453-802 64) at Oettern, 7km south-east of Weimar, but it's pretty basic. Open from mid-April to November, it charges DM4 to DM6 per person, DM2 per vehicle, plus DM5 per tent. A much better option, but about 25km south of town, is *Ferienpark Hohenfelden* (see Places to Stay in the Erfurt section).

At last count Weimar had four DJH hostels. The *Jugendherberge Germania* (☎ 85 04 90, fax 85 04 91, Carl-August-Allee 13), near the train station, is a modern facility charging juniors/seniors DM24/29. Most central is the recently refurbished *Am Poseckschen Garten* (☎ 85 07 92, fax 85 07 93, Humboldtstrasse 17) near the Historischer Friedhof, where beds cost DM24/29. *Jugendgästehaus Maxim Gorki* (☎ 85 07 50, fax 85 07 49, Zum Wilden Graben 12) is on the hilly southern side of town (take bus No 8 from the station to Rainer-Maria-Rilke-Strasse), while the *Jugendgästehaus Am Ettersberg* (☎ 42 11 11, fax 42 11 12, Ettersbergsiedlung) is in a nature preserve north of town (bus No 6 from the station to Obelisk). The latter two charge DM25/30; make reservations for both at the Maxim Gorki.

On a quiet side street near the train station, *Pension Savina II* (☎ 866 90, fax 86 69 11, Meyerstrasse 60) offers excellent value, with singles/doubles with kitchenette from DM60/100. *Pension Alter Zausel* (☎/fax 50 16 63, Carl-Von-Ossietzky-Strasse 13) asks from DM75/100.

A little bit west of the Altstadt is *Pension Am Berkaer Bahnhof* (☎ 20 20 10, Peter-Cornelius-Strasse 7), where rooms go for DM65/130. *Hotel-Pension Am Kirschberg* (☎ 87 19 10, fax 871 91 16, Am Kirschberg 27) near the Ilm Park charges from DM75/100.

Places to Stay – Mid-Range

Across from the Schloss is *rollover* (☎ 51 88 43, fax 51 88 44, Burgplatz 2), which asks DM80/140 for clean and functional rooms. Good value for money is offered by the church-affiliated *Hotel Amalienhof* (☎ 54 90, fax 54 91 10, Amalienstrasse 2), in a neo-classical villa with matching interior, right by the Goethe Haus. Rooms cost from DM130/180. Another excellent bet is the contemporary and friendly *Villa Hentzel* (☎ 865 80, fax 86 58 19, Bauhausstrasse 12), where 13 large, individually designed rooms range from DM90 to DM130 for singles and DM140 to DM190 for doubles. Those who like minimalist decor should try *Hotel Alt Weimar* (☎ 861 90, fax 86 19 10, Prellerstrasse 2), which charges DM140/190.

Places to Stay – Top End

Prices leap through the roof at Weimar's classic hostelry *Kempinski Hotel Elephant* (☎ 80 20, fax 80 26 10, Markt 19), where you must drop from DM300/365 for the privilege. Other top end choices with similar prices are the brand-new *Dorint Hotel* (☎ 87 20, 87 21 00, Beethovenplatz 1/2) and *Wolff's Art Hotel* (☎ 540 60, fax 54 06 99, Freiherr-vom-Stein-Allee 3a/b).

Places to Eat

The cheapest eats are at the university *Mensa*, entered at Marienstrasse 15, which has a huge selection and prices around DM5 for students and double that for nonstudents.

For an immersion in Thuringian cuisine, head to *Scharfe Ecke* (☎ 20 24 30, Eisfeld 2) or the slightly more expensive *Zum Zwiebel* (☎ 50 23 75, Teichgasse 6). *Anno 1900* (☎ 90 35 71, Geleitstrasse 12a), in an Art Nouveau-style winter garden, serves international favourites, including almost a dozen vegetarian dishes, topping out at DM18.

One of Weimar's most popular haunts is *Residenz-Café* (☎ 594 08, Grüner Markt 4), with its soft decor and lighting, cafe tables and plump sofas attracting tourists and locals alike. The moderately priced food is delicious and comes in super-sized portions. In business for 160 years, it's known as 'Resi' by the cognoscenti.

Around the corner, *ACC* (☎ *85 11 61, Burgplatz 1)*, which stands for 'autonomous culture centre', is a restaurant-cum-gallery heavily visited by students. The food is simple but healthily prepared; vegetarians won't feel left out here.

Sommer's Weinstuben (☎ *40 06 91, Humboldtstrasse 2)*, with its intimate, wood-panelled rooms, is where you can go for a beer and a chat or a full meal (dishes from DM12). North of the Altstadt is *Brasserie Central* (☎ *85 27 74, Rollplatz 8a)*, with a casual pub atmosphere and mains with a French influence for DM16 to DM20.

A Weimar institution, though often invaded by coach tourists, is *Felsenkeller* (☎ *85 03 66, Humboldtstrasse 37)* with delicious house brew and good food.

For gourmet cuisine, served in the same hallowed rooms once frequented by Goethe, Schiller and Liszt, it's off to the historical *Zum Weissen Schwan* (☎ *20 25 21, Frauentorstrasse 23)*, next to the Goethe Haus. Money better not matter.

There's a *Rewe* supermarket near the Goethe Haus on the corner of Steubenstrasse and Frauenplan.

Entertainment

The *Deutsches NationalTheater* (German National Theatre; ☎ *75 53 34)*, Theaterplatz, offers a grab-bag of performances: classic and contemporary plays, plus ballet, opera and classical concerts.

A Weimar classic of a different sort, the *Studentenclub Kasseturm* (☎ *85 16 70, Goetheplatz 1)* is in a historic round tower with three floors of live music, disco or cabaret most nights (open after 8 pm). A few steps away, at No 11, is *Mon Ami*, a cultural centre with cinema, bistro-cafe and dance club.

The *Studentenclub Schütze* (☎ *90 43 23, Schützengasse 2)*, just off Theaterplatz, is similar to Kasseturm. Young people also gather at the trendy *Planbar* (*Jacobsgasse 6)*, while 30-somethings may be comfortable at *Club C1* (*Carl-August-Allee 1)*,

where it's cocktails and live music around the grand piano several nights a week.

Getting There & Away

Train Weimar is an IC train stop on the route from Frankfurt to Leipzig (DM31.40, one hour) and Dresden (DM65, 2½ hours), and an IR stop en route to Berlin-Zoo (DM75, three hours). All leave at two-hour intervals. Erfurt (DM7.60, 15 minutes) and Eisenach (DM19.40, one hour) are served several times hourly. Berkaer Bahnhof is a second station west of the city centre, but only local trains depart from there.

Bus There's a bus service to Jena Westbahnhof several times daily (DM7.20, 1¼ hours), but the train connection is much more convenient.

Getting Around

Walking is the only way of getting around central Weimar. For trips outside the centre, there's a bus system with single tickets costing DM2.50 (day pass DM8).

Unless staying in an Altstadt hotel, drivers must leave their car in one of the parking lots outside the city centre. Look for the signs saying 'P+R'. Parking is free, and there are shuttle buses (DM2.50 one way) into town. Otherwise, it's a 15 to 20 minute walk.

Bicycles may be rented at Grüne Liga (☎ 531 30) on Rollplatz. For a taxi, call ☎ 90 36 00.

BUCHENWALD

The Buchenwald concentration camp museum and memorial are on Ettersberg Hill, 10km north of Weimar. You first pass the memorial erected atop the mass graves of some of the 56,500 victims from 18 nations, including German antifascists, Jews, and Soviet and Polish prisoners of war. The concentration camp and museum are 1km beyond the memorial. Many prominent German Communists and Social Democrats, Ernst Thälmann and Rudolf Breitscheid among them, were murdered here. After 1943, prisoners were exploited in the production of weapons. Many died during

THURINGIA

medical experimentation. Shortly before the end of the war, some 28,000 prisoners were sent on death marches. Between 1937 and 1945, more than one fifth of the 250,000 incarcerated here died. On 11 April 1945, as US troops approached and the SS guards fled, the prisoners rebelled (at 3.15 pm – and the clock tower above the entrance still shows that time), overwhelmed the remaining guards and liberated themselves.

After the war, the Soviet victors turned the tables by establishing Special Camp No 2, in which another 7000 so-called anticommunists and ex-Nazis were literally worked to death. Their bodies were found, after the Wende, in mass graves north of the camp and near the train station.

From May to September, free admission to the grounds – and to two separate exhibits on both eras – is from 9.45 am to 6 pm (last admission 5.15 pm); the rest of the year it's 8.45 am to 5 pm (last admission 4.15 pm). Pamphlets and books in English are sold at the bookshop. Bus No 6 travels here hourly via Goetheplatz and the train station.

Northern Thuringia

MÜHLHAUSEN
☎ 03601 • pop 42,000
About 30km north of Eisenach, in the picturesque Unstrut River valley, lies Mühlhausen, which experienced its greatest glory as a 'free imperial city' in the Middle Ages. Its historical core, criss-crossed by cobbled alleyways, reflects 800 years of architectural styles. There's a good collection of half-timbered houses with gorgeous carved and painted doors.

Information
The tourist office (☎ 45 23 35, fax 45 23 16, email info@mühlhausen.de) is at Ratsstrasse 20, and is open weekdays from 9 am to 5 pm. From May to October, it's also open weekends from 10 am to noon.

Banks on Untermarkt include a Deutsche Bank branch at No 27. The post office is at Bahnhofsplatz 1. There's a police station

(☎ 500) at Karl-Marx-Strasse 4. For an ambulance and in medical emergencies, call ☎ 33 23.

Things to See
Mühlhausen's historical core is encircled by its 12th century town wall, just under 3km long, with two of the gates and three towers still standing. It's partly accessible between Frauentor and Rabenturm (DM2/1).

Mühlhausen's skyline is characterised by the steeples and spires of 13 churches, of which the Marienkirche at Am Obermarkt, with its neo-Gothic steeple, is the most noticeable and notable. The five nave construction makes it the second largest church in Thuringia after the Dom in Erfurt. In 1525, Thomas Müntzer preached here to the rebels before the Peasants' War on the Schlachtberg (see boxed text 'Thomas Müntzer & the Peasants' War'). It now houses a memorial to the reformer (DM2/1).

A museum dedicated to the history of the Peasants' War is nearby in the Kornmarktkirche (DM2/1).

At the Divi-Blasii Kirche, just south of the Altstadt on Felchtaer Strasse, Johann Sebastian Bach – followed by his cousin and then by his fourth son – worked as organist, inaugurating a new organ in 1709. Also worth a look is the Rathaus (DM1/0.50), a sprawling cluster of buildings from several centuries built around a Gothic core.

Places to Stay & Eat
The DJH hostel (☎ 81 33 20, fax 81 33 18, Auf dem Tonberg 1) is about 2km from the city centre (bus No 5 or 6 from the train station to Blobach, then a 500m walk). B&B costs DM20/25 for juniors/seniors; sheets are DM7.

For budget place in town, try Pension an der Harwand (☎ 42 09 61, Hinter der Harwand 3), where rooms with private bath are DM40/80. Gästehaus Am Schwanenteich (☎ 44 00 52, Wanfrieder Landstraáe 16a) charges the same. More upmarket is the traditional Hotel Stadt Mühlhausen (☎ 45 50, fax 45 57 09, Untermarkt 18), with rooms for DM85/120.

Thomas Müntzer & the Peasants' War

In 1524-25, central and southern Germany were rocked by a series of peasant uprisings that culminated in May 1525 with the final bloody battle on the Schlachtberg in Bad Frankenhausen.

Motivated by extreme poverty and a dearth of rights, more than 8000 rebels banded together in their fight for freedom and justice. They were joined by the priest and radical reformer Thomas Müntzer, who served as their spiritual leader. In the war he preached, 'The lord of hosts will overthrow the tyrants and place the power in the hands of the faithful.'

The rebels' chance of winning against the superior forces of the princes' army was nil, however, and few survived the slaughter. Müntzer himself was captured, tortured and killed 12 days later outside the gates of Mühlhausen.

The government of the GDR saw an opportunity for its own legitimisation in this historical insurrection. Its interpretation of history regarded the Peasants' War as a precursor to the proletarian revolution that finally came to fruition 450 years later in the founding of the 'Workers' and Peasants' State'. Müntzer was given national-hero status.

Healthy portions of local food for between DM12 and DM20 are served at the **Postkeller** *(Steinweg 6)*. In the building behind (walk to the end of the tiled walkway) is the **Postkeller Club**, a pub with occasional live music. Thuringian fare is on the menu at **Zum Luftbad** *(Goetheweg 90)*, next to a park.

Getting There & Away

There are hourly trains from Erfurt (DM16.20, one hour), but coming from Eisenach (DM16.20, one hour) requires a change in Gotha. Mühlhausen is at the crossroads of the B249 from Sondershausen and the B247 from Gotha.

THE KYFFHÄUSER

The Kyffhäuser is a low forested mountain range wedged between the Harz Mountains to the north and the Thuringian Forest to the south. Besides being good hiking and cycling territory, it also harbours several unique and intriguing sights. A good base from which to explore the area is Bad Frankenhausen, a quiet spa town at the forest's southern edge; the central information office, the Kyffhäuser Information (☎ 034671-717 16/17, fax 717 19), Anger 14, is also here.

Kyffhäuser Monument

Above the dense forests and steep ravines of the 457m-high Kyffhäuser mountain looms this bombastic memorial (1896) to Emperor Wilhelm I. A statue showing him on horseback stands below a 60m-high tower and above the stone throne of Emperor Friedrich I (1125-90) – better known as Barbarossa – whom he considered his spiritual predecessor.

He found justification for this belief in a bizarre legend connected with the Kyffhäuser mountains. It goes like this ... after Barbarossa failed to return from the crusades, his subjects refused to believe that the popular emperor was dead. Instead, they thought that a spell had been cast which would confine him to live in the depth of a mountain – the Kyffhäuser – until he would one day return to earth to unite all the German people.

For centuries, Barbarossa whiled away the time in his mountain prison. Every hundred years, however, he woke up and sent a boy outside to check whether the ravens (a symbol of calamity) were still flying around the mountain. If the answer was yes, the emperor fell back asleep for another century. If the ravens were gone, however, the moment had come to return. So when the German

euro currency converter DM1 = €0.51

THURINGIA

people were united in 1871 under Emperor Wilhelm I, he considered himself – a tad immodestly – as the reincarnation of the beloved Barbarossa. And, incidentally, there are no more ravens on the Kyffhäuser ...

The monument stands on the foundations of the Oberburg (Upper Castle) of the medieval Burg Kyffhausen, Germany's largest castle complex (608m long, 60m wide) before its destruction in 1118. Today, only the ruins of the Unterburg (Lower Castle), as well as a gate and a 172m-deep well, remain.

The remote monument is best reached by car, but there's also sporadic bus service from Bad Frankenhausen. It's open from October to April daily from 9 am to 5 pm, and to 7 pm the rest of the year (DM6/3).

Panorama Museum

On the Schlachtberg north of Bad Frankenhausen's centre, where the final battle in the Peasants' War took place, stands a giant concrete cylinder that harbours a painting of truly epic proportions and content. Called *Frühbürgerliche Revolution in Deutschland* (Early Civil Revolution in Germany), the oil painting measures 14m by 123m (!) and was created in a style called 'fantastical realism' reminiscent of such classical artists as Bruegel and Hieronymus Bosch. More than 3000 figures, assembled in numerous scenes, metaphorically depict the tumultuous transition from the Middle Ages to the modern era in 15th and 16th century Europe.

It took artist Werner Tübke and his five assistants five years to complete this complex and allegorical *theatrum mundi* (theatre of the world), which opened in 1989 as one of the last official acts of the GDR government. The work's artistic merit and political context have been questioned, but its sheer size and ambitious themes do not fail to impress.

The museum is open from April to September daily, except Monday, from 10 am to 6 pm, and October to March to 5 pm. In July and August, it is also open on Monday from 1 to 6 pm (DM10/7, children DM2). Guided tours (in German) run hourly on the hour. English-language brochures are available.

Places to Stay

The nearest camping ground is *Stausee Kelbra* (☎ 034651-63 10, Lange Strasse 150), on a large reservoir in Kelbra, about 17km north of Bad Frankenhausen. There's a *hostel* (☎/fax 620 18, Bahnhofstrasse 6), only a five minute walk from the Bad Frankenhausen train station, which charges DM20/30.

Pension Krieg (☎ 034671-774 69, fax 644 02, Kyffhäuserstrasse 36) has single/double rooms with shower and WC from DM50/76 up to DM60/120. More upmarket is the central *Hotel Grabenmühle* (☎ 034671-798 82, fax 798 83, Am Wallgraben 1), which charges DM60/120.

Getting There & Around

Getting to Bad Frankenhausen by train usually requires a change in Bretleben. From Erfurt, the trip takes 1¼ hours and costs DM14.80. By car or motorcycle, take the B4, B86 and then the B85.

To reach the outlying sights, it's best to be under your own steam. For bike rental, try Fahrradhaus Gerhard Ritter (☎ 27 18) at Kräme 30.

Thuringian Forest

The Thuringian Forest, a mountainous area roughly bordered by the Werra River in the west and the Saale River in the east, sprawls out south of the A4. The tallest peaks are just under 1000m and provide good opportunities for winter sports. The Rennsteig, one of Germany's most popular trails, runs along the mountain ridges for 168km.

Not all of the forest is pristine; many of the trees are suffering the effects of acid rain from decades of air pollution, and several beautifully situated towns, like Suhl, have been ravaged by industry or blighted by high-rise apartment blocks typical of GDR architecture. Despite these drawbacks, its climate, dense woods, unhurried lifestyle and relative lack of commercialism still make the Thuringian Forest a wonderful place to explore.

EISENACH
☎ 03691 • pop 45,300

The birthplace of Johann Sebastian Bach, Eisenach is a small town on the edge of the Thuringian Forest with a long tradition as a car-manufacturing centre. Its main attraction is Wartburg castle. Richard Wagner based his opera *Tannhäuser* on a minstrel's contest that took place at the castle in 1206-07. It was the residence of the much revered Elisabeth, the wife of the landgrave of Thuringia. She was canonised shortly after her death in 1235 for trading a pompous lifestyle at court in favour of helping the poor and disadvantaged. In 1521-22 the reformer Martin Luther went into hiding in the Wartburg under the assumed name of Junker Jörg after being excommunicated and put under papal ban.

Eisenach itself is not without appeal, and many of the scars left by decades of neglect during the GDR regime have already been smoothed over.

Orientation & Information

The Markt is a 15 minute walk from the Hauptbahnhof. Except for the Wartburg, which is 2km south-west of town, most sights are close to the Markt. Eisenach has two bus stations: local buses stop right outside the train station; overland buses on Müllerstrasse one block west.

The Eisenach tourist office (☎ 792 30 or 194 33, fax 79 23 20, email tourist-info@ eisenach-tourist.de) is at Markt 2 and is open Monday from 10 am to 6 pm, Tuesday to Friday from 9 am, and Saturday from 10 am to 2 pm. There's a Volksbank at Schillerstrasse 16 to change money. The main post office is at the south-western corner of the Markt at No 6. The police (☎ 26 10) are at August-Bebel-Strasse 6.

Wartburg

This superb medieval castle, perched high above the town on a wooded hill, is said to go back to Count Ludwig der Springer, who in 1067, upon seeing the craggy hillside, exclaimed *'Wart, Berg, du sollst mir eine Burg werden'* (literally 'Wait, mountain, you shall be a castle for me'). Martin Luther

translated the New Testament from Greek into German while in hiding here, contributing enormously to the development of the written German language. His modest, wood-panelled study is part of the guided tour (in German, ask for a free English translation sheet), which is the only way to see the interior. The tour also takes in the museum and the amazing **Romanesque Great Hall**.

Tours of the castle, museum and Luther study run frequently between 8.30 am and 5 pm (9 am to 3.30 pm in winter) and cost DM11/6 (museum and Luther study only are DM6/5). Between Easter and October, crowds can be horrendous. To ensure admission, arrive before 11 am. For information, call ☎ 25 00.

To get to the Wartburg from the Markt, walk one block west to Wydenbrugkstrasse, then head up Schlossberg through the forest via Eselstation (40 minutes). A more scenic return route is via the Haintal (50 minutes).

From May to October, bus Nos 10 and 13 run to Eselstation just below the castle roughly every 1½ hours (DM2.50 return) from outside the train station.

City Centre

Museums mentioned here are closed Monday, unless noted. Guided tours run daily at 2 pm from the tourist office (DM5).

The Markt is dominated by the galleried **Georgenkirche**, where members of the Bach family, including Johann Sebastian himself, served as organists between 1665 and 1797. Its collection of ancient tombstones includes that of Wartburg founder, Ludwig der Springer. A few steps south, at Lutherplatz 8, is the half-timbered **Lutherhaus** (☎ 298 30), where Martin Luther lived as a schoolboy between 1498 and 1501. The exhibit traces important stages and accomplishments in the reformer's life through paintings, manuscripts and illustrated works, as well as through a series of interactive multimedia terminals (in German and English). It's open daily from 9 am to 5.45 pm (Monday from noon); in winter it closes at 4.45 pm (DM5/4).

THURINGIA

euro currency converter DM1 = €0.51

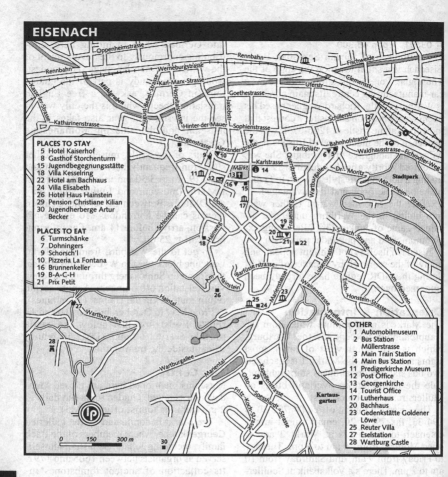

EISENACH

PLACES TO STAY
5 Hotel Kaiserhof
8 Gasthof Storchenturm
15 Jugendbegegnungsstätte
18 Villa Kesselring
22 Hotel am Bachhaus
24 Villa Elisabeth
26 Hotel Haus Hainstein
29 Pension Christiane Kilian
30 Jugendherberge Artur Becker

PLACES TO EAT
6 Turmschänke
7 Dohningers
9 Schorsch'l
10 Pizzeria La Fontana
16 Brunnenkeller
19 B-A-C-H
21 Prix Petit

OTHER
1 Automobilmuseum
2 Bus Station Müllerstrasse
3 Main Train Station
4 Main Bus Station
11 Predigerkirche Museum
12 Post Office
13 Georgenkirche
14 Tourist Office
17 Lutherhaus
20 Bachhaus
23 Gedenkstätte Goldener Löwe
25 Reuter Villa
27 Eselstation
28 Wartburg Castle

South of here, at Frauenplan 21, stands the **Bachhaus** (☎ 793 40), containing a memorial exhibit on the composer, who was born in 1685 in a now demolished house nearby. Each tour (in German) concludes with a little concert played on antique instruments. Hours are daily from 9 am to 5.45 pm, and in winter to 4.45 pm; it's also closed on Monday morning (DM5/4).

Fans of another composer, Richard Wagner, should check out the collection on his life and works presented at the **Reuter Villa**

(☎ 74 32 94), Reuterweg 2. It's open from 10 am to 5 pm (DM4/2).

The first nationwide proletarian movement, the Social Democratic Workers Party, was founded in Eisenach by August Bebel and Wilhelm Liebknecht in 1869. The **Gedenkstätte 'Goldener Löwe'** (literally 'Golden Lion Memorial Site'; ☎ 754 34), at Marienstrasse 57, has an interesting exhibit on the 19th century workers' movement in Germany. It's open weekdays from 9 am to 4 pm.

THURINGIA

Stone-faced Potsdam locals

MARK AVELLINO

A musical motif at Sanssouci Park

ANDREA SCHULTE-PEEVERS

One of the distinctive rococo ornaments found in Potsdam's Sanssouci Park

ANDREA SCHULTE-PEEVERS

Once likened to Rome, Erfurt is a city of churches, with 20 of its original 90 still standing today.

One of Leipzig's lively building facades

In the **Predigerkirche** (☎ 78 46 78) on Predigerplatz you'll find an exhibit on medieval art in Thuringia. It's open daily from 9 am to 5 pm (DM5/3). Eisenach's car-manufacturing tradition is the subject of the **Automobilmuseum** (☎ 772 12) at Rennbahn 8 where you can admire such GDR relics as the Dixi and the Wartburg 1.3. Hours are from 10 am to 5 pm (DM4/2).

Places to Stay

The nearest camping ground is the lakeside *Campingplatz Altenberger See* (☎/fax 21 56 37), 7km south of town in Wilhelmsthal (take the bus, direction: Bad Liebenstein, from the Müllerstrasse station). Charges are DM5 per tent, plus DM7 per person and DM2 per car/day.

Eisenach's DJH hostel, *Jugendherberge Artur Becker* (☎ 20 36 13, Mariental 24) is closed for renovation until at least July 2000. Contact the tourist office about the exact reopening and new rates. Meanwhile, a more central alternative is *Jugendbegegnungsstätte Hessen/Thüringen* (☎/fax 21 41 33, Auf der Esplanade) next to the Markt, which charges DM35 to DM45 for singles and DM40 to DM60 doubles (no breakfast but there is kitchen access), plus a one-off laundry fee for sheets and towels of DM8.

The tourist office has a free room-finding service. *Private rooms* start at DM30/50 a single/double. All prices quoted for private rooms and hotels include breakfast and a private bath.

For cheap stays in the centre of Eisenach, try the hostel-like *Gasthof Storchenturm* (☎ 21 52 50, fax 21 40 82, Georgenstrasse 43), which has rooms of monastic simplicity for DM52.50/85. For more comfort, try the new *Hotel am Bachhaus* (☎ 204 70, fax 204 71 33, Marienstrasse 7), which charges DM80/130.

Several lovely hotels are located among the cluster of handsome Art Nouveau villas in Eisenach's hilly south. The charming *Pension Christine Kilian* (☎/fax 21 11 22, Kapellenstrasse 8) has rooms from DM60/80. *Villa Kesselring* (☎/fax 73 20 49, Hainweg 32), a 10 minute walk up from the

Bachhaus in a small yellow home, offers nice rooms for DM60/96; it's very popular and often full.

Farther up the hill is the sprawling *Hotel Haus Hainstein* (☎ 24 20, fax 24 21 09, Am Hainstein 16) with great views of the Wartburg and quiet, stylish rooms from DM75/130. Nonsmokers might like *Villa Elisabeth* (☎ 770 52, fax 74 36 52, Reuterweg 1), in a mini-castle with crenellated turrets and rooms from DM70/120.

Places to Eat

For hearty Thuringian dishes, the *Brunnenkeller* (☎ 714 29) in an old monastery wine cellar on the south side of the Georgenkirche is a good destination, with meals costing from DM12 to DM25. For similar food in a cheerful, contemporary ambience, head to *B-A-C-II* (☎ 21 55 22, Frauenplan 8), opposite the Bachhaus. On the other side of the square is the small cafe *Prix Petit* (☎ 73 34 85, Frauenplan 13). The name means 'small price' and that's just what you get: snacks from DM4, big salads for DM8.50.

For pizza, pasta and salad all under DM10, you can't go wrong at *Pizzeria La Fontana* (☎ 74 35 39, Georgenstrasse 22). Across the street is *Schorsch'l* (☎ 21 30 49, Georgenstrasse 19), a happening bistro-pub with live music and simple meals. Trendy types (as far as that goes in Eisenach) hang out at *Dohningers* (Henkelsgasse 2), which serves pints of Fosters and hot snacks.

For an upmarket dining experience, your best bet is the *Turmschänke* (☎ 21 35 33, Wartburgallee 2), an atmospheric and classy wine restaurant in Eisenach's only surviving town gate. Four-course menus cost DM70, and mains range from DM21 to DM43.

Getting There & Away

Frequent direct trains run to Erfurt (DM14.80, 50 minutes), Gotha (DM7.60, 25 minutes) and Weimar (DM19.40, one hour). For Mühlhausen, change in Gotha (DM16.20, one hour). IR trains to Frankfurt-am-Main (DM57, 2¼ hours) and to Berlin-Zoo (DM98, four hours) also stop here. Bus

THURINGIA

service is sporadic at best, although useful connections include bus No 280b to Friedrichroda and bus No 30 to Mühlhausen.

If you're driving, Eisenach is right on the A4 (exits Eisenach Ost or Eisenach West) and crossed by the B7, B19 and B84.

RENNSTEIG

Eisenach is the western gateway to the Rennsteig, one of Germany's most popular long-distance walks. From the suburb of Hörschel, the trail wends 168km south-east along mountain ridges through largely uninterrupted forest to Blankenstein on the Saale River, offering beautiful views of dreamy valleys, snug villages and medieval hill-top castles. It's well maintained and signposted with markers bearing the letter 'R'. The best hiking time is May/June and September/October, though summers are tolerable too because most of the walking is done at elevations above 700m. You should be moderately fit, but no serious hiking experience or special equipment is required.

Hiking the entire distance can be done in five days, though day hikes – especially between Hörschel and Oberhof – are a pleasant way to sample the region. Although there's little in the way of accommodation directly on the trail, there are plenty of pensions and hotels in the villages below.

Before setting out, pick up maps (Kompass Wanderkarte's 1:50,000 map *Der Rennsteig* – No 118 is a good one) and information at the Rennsteigwanderhaus Hörschel (☎ 036928-91 19 94), Rennsteigstrasse 9 in Hörschel. Year-round hours are weekdays from 7.30 am to noon and 1 to 4 pm. From May to October, it's also open on weekends from 7.30 to 10.30 am and 3 to 5 pm.

· According to local tradition, you must dip your walking stick into the Werra and pick up a pebble from its waters before starting out. Upon leaving the Rennsteig, the pebble must be given back to the forest.

To get to the trailhead, take bus No 93 (direction: Oberellen) from the Müllerstrasse bus station in Eisenach. If you hike the entire distance to Blankenstein, you can then catch a train to Saalfeld, Jena and beyond.

FRIEDRICHRODA
☎ 03623 • pop 6000

Friedrichroda is scenically located on the northern edge of the Thuringian Forest about 20km south of Gotha. During GDR days, it was the country's second-busiest resort, with more than one million overnight stays a year. Numbers dropped dramatically after the Wende, but Friedrichroda is once again gaining in popularity, especially after improvements to infrastructure and a reorientation towards health and spa tourism. In 1998 a state-of-the-art therapeutic bath centre opened, where a variety of treatments are being offered. Another addition is a traditional Chinese medicine centre.

Orientation & Information

Friedrichroda has two train stations: Bahnhof Friedrichroda in the east of town, and Bahnhof Reinhardsbrunn north of the centre, which is the stop for the Thüringerwaldbahn tram to/from Gotha.

The tourist office (☎ 332 00, fax 33 20 29) is at Marktstrasse 13-15 (enter from Kirchgasse) and is open Monday to Thursday from 9 am to 5 pm, Friday to 6 pm and Saturday to noon.

Things to See & Do

Among Friedrichroda's prime attractions is the **Marienglashöhle** (☎ 30 49 53), a large gypsum cave featuring an underwater lake and a crystal grotto. You enter the latter in the dark, then – just to give you that otherworldly feel – a variation on the theme of the film *Close Encounters of the Third Kind* plays in the background as the light gradually brightens, unveiling a sparkling universe. Most of the crystallised gypsum here has been harvested and used to decorate statues of the Virgin Mary and altars in the region and beyond. Guided tours take place daily from 9 am to 5 pm in summer, and to 4 pm in winter (DM7/4). The cave is about a 20 minute walk from the city centre and is also a stop on the **Thüringerwaldbahn** (see Getting There & Away).

In the northern part of town, in the midst of a lavish English park with ancient trees, stands the neo-Gothic **Schloss Reinhardsbrunn** (1828), built on the foundations of a medieval Benedictine monastery founded by Wartburg builder Ludwig the Springer. Queen Victoria of England first met her cousin, Duke Albert of Saxe-Coburg-Gotha, here; they got married in 1840. The palace, which is being restored, can only be viewed from the outside, except for the parts housing a hotel.

For an easy day excursion into the forest surrounding Friedrichroda, you can take the **Thüringer Wald-Express** (DM7/5, return DM12/8) to the Heuberghaus on the mountain ridge, then hike along the ridge for about 90 minutes to the Inselsberg peak, then take the Inselsberg Express (DM3/2) down to Tabarz and catch the Thüringerwaldbahn back to Friedrichroda.

Places to Stay

The nearest camping ground is *Campingplatz Paulfeld* (☎ 036253-251 71, fax 251 65) in Catterfeld, a few kilometres southwest of Friedrichroda. The modernised *DJH hostel* (☎ 30 44 10, fax 30 50 03, Herzogsweg 25) is on the outskirts of town, a five minute walk from the Friedrichroda stop on the Thüringerwaldbahn and 20 minutes from Reinhardsbrunn train station. Beds here cost DM19/24 for juniors/seniors; sheets are DM7.

Near the hostel is the reasonably priced *Haus am Wald* (☎ 20 02 22, Waldstrasse 18), which charges from DM40/70 for singles/doubles, has bike rentals and a pleasant wine cellar. Perhaps the best bet, though, is the nearby *Pension Tannenrausch* (☎/fax 30 49 56, Waldstrasse 24), where spacious rooms with all modern amenities, shower and WC cost just DM70/80.

In town is the rustic but comfortable *Hotel Phönix* (☎ 20 08 80, fax 20 08 81, Tabarzer Strasse 3), with cosy rooms for DM70/110 and a restaurant serving vegetarian dishes.

Getting There & Away

There's regular local train service between Gotha and Bahnhof Reinhardsbrunn. The Thüringerwaldbahn (tram No 4), a historic, colourful tram, makes the trip between Gotha and Tabarz several times hourly (DM4.50, one hour). The most scenic stretch begins right after Friedrichroda through the forest to Tabarz. If you're driving, take the Waltershausen/Friedrichroda exit off the A4. The town is also on the B88 to Ilmenau.

ILMENAU

☎ 03677 • pop 28,000

Ilmenau is a sleepy little town enlivened by several handsome historical buildings and a small student population. In the Middle Ages, it derived its wealth from silver and copper mining, but when that was exhausted, it plunged into deep depression. It fell upon Johann Wolfgang von Goethe, in his capacity as minister to the court of Saxe-Weimar, to revive the mining industry, but even he had little success.

Goethe is still the main reason people make the pilgrimage to Ilmenau, which is the gateway to the famous Goethe Hiking Trail (see the boxed text).

The tourist office (☎ 20 23 58 or ☎ 194 33, fax 20 25 02, email stadtinfo@ilmenau.de), Lindenstrasse 12, is open weekdays 9 am to 6 pm and Saturday to noon. Web information is at www.ilmenau.de.

There's a camping ground in Manebach, a few kilometres west of Ilmenau. The modernised *DJH hostel* (☎ 88 46 81, fax 88 46 82, Am Stollen 49) charges juniors/seniors DM20/25 for bunks in four-bed dorms. For DM2, the tourist office makes reservations for hotels and private rooms (from DM25 per person). An excellent Ilmenau 'base camp' is *Hotel Tanne* (☎ 65 90, fax 659503, Lindenstrasse 38), which pampers guests with modern amenities, friendly service and features like a spa and bike rental station, at a reasonable DM95/135.

Direct trains to Erfurt leave about once an hour (DM14.80, one hour), but to Eisenach you have to change in Neudietendorf (DM22.20, two hours). Ilmenau is easily reached via the B88 from Ilmenach, the B4 from Erfurt and the B87 from Weimar.

THURINGIA

Goethe Trail

This lovely, at times challenging, 18.5km day hike follows in the footsteps of Johann Wolfgang von Goethe, who spent much time around Ilmenau in the employ of Carl August, Duke of Saxe-Weimar. The hike encompasses level forest terrain, steep climbs and everything in between; it's marked with the letter 'G' in Goethe's own handwriting. An excellent 1:30,000 hiking map by Grünes Herz is available at the tourist office (DM7.95).

The starting point is the Amtshaus, a subdued baroque structure on the Markt that was Goethe's Ilmenau home. Here, five rooms have been turned into a **memorial exhibit** (☎ 20 26 67), open daily to 4.30 pm (in winter to 4 pm), but closed at lunchtime (DM2/1).

From here the trail heads west to the village of Manebach, where the steep climb up the **Kickelhahn** (861m) begins. Near the top, you'll pass the replica of the little forest cabin where Goethe wrote the famous poem *Wayfarer's Night Song*. At the top is a restaurant and **lookout tower**, with views that make the Thuringian forest look like a giant green velvet blanket.

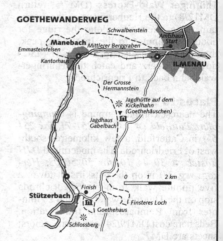

GOETHEWANDERWEG

The trail descends to **Jagdhaus Gabelbach** (☎ 20 26 26), a hunting lodge and former guesthouse of Duke Carl August who also liked to throw lavish parties here, often with Goethe in attendance. Today it contains an exhibit on the latter's scientific research. From here, the trail meanders south to the village of Stützerbach, where the **Goethehaus** (☎ 036784-502 77) features the originally furnished rooms where Goethe used to stay and work, plus an exhibit on the local glass industry. Opening hours of Gabelbach and the Goethehaus are Wednesday to Sunday from 9 am to 5 pm, and in winter to 4 pm (DM4/3). Check with the tourist office about bus service back to Ilmenau.

If you don't have much time or simply want to do a shorter hike, you can walk directly to the Kickelhahn from Ilmenau, bypassing Manebach, in about 1½ hours. Or you can drive up Waldstrasse to the parking lot at Herzogröder Wiesen, where it's a 25 minute uphill walk – past Jagdhaus Gabelbach – to the Kickelhahn peak.

SCHMALKALDEN
☎ 03683 • pop 18,000

Hugging the south-western slopes of the Thuringian Forest, Schmalkalden is about 17km south of Friedrichroda. Historically, the little town will forever be tied to the Reformation because it was here, in 1530, that the Protestant princes formed the Schmal-

kaldic League to counter the central powers of Catholic Emperor Charles V. The league met eight times until 1545; in 1537 Martin Luther presented the Schmalkaldic Articles of Faith, sealing the separation of the Catholic and Protestant churches in Germany. Charles V retaliated and beat the league in the Schmalkaldic Wars that same year, but he couldn't keep the Reformation movement down for long; with the Peace of Augsburg in 1546, each German state was allowed to choose its own religion.

Schmalkalden today offers few reminders of those tumultuous and eventful times, but it is a beautiful town that has preserved its medieval feel. Narrow streets are lined by carefully restored half-timbered houses, and there's a handsome hill-top castle, Schloss Wilhelmsburg, thrown in for good measure. In 1999 the town celebrated its 1125th anniversary.

Orientation & Information
It's about a 10 minute walk from the train and central bus stations to Altmarkt, the town's central square, and another seven minutes to Schloss Wilhelmsburg.

The tourist office (☎ 40 31 82, fax 60 40 14, email info@schmalkalden.de) is at Mohrengasse 1a and is open 9 am to 6 pm weekdays and 10 am to 3 pm on Saturday (to 1 pm in winter). There's a Sparkasse bank on Weidebrunner Gasse. The post office is at the southern end of Altmarkt. The police station is on Weidebrunner Gasse (☎ 68 10).

Things to See & Do
Towering above the city centre to the west is the well preserved late Renaissance-style **Schloss Wilhelmsburg** (☎ 40 31 86). It was built between 1585 and 1590 by Landgrave Wilhelm IV of Hessen as a hunting lodge and summer residence. Lavish murals and stucco decorate most rooms, of which the **Riesensaal**, with its coffered and painted ceiling is the most impressive. Notable, too, is the playful **Schlosskirche**, the palace chapel, whose ornate white and gilded decorations tend to reflect secular rather than religious themes. The rare wood organ still works.

Other highlights include an exhibit on the Reformation and Renaissance, and a copy of a 13th century mural depicting scenes from the *Iwein legend*, a variation on the King Arthur myth by German 12th century poet Hartmann von Aue. The original in the Hessenhof in the town centre is not accessible to the public.

The Schloss is open from 9 am to 5 pm (in winter to 4 pm) daily except Sunday (DM6/4).

The **Rathaus** (1419) on Altmarkt functioned as the meeting place of the Schmalkaldic League. The two incongruous towers of the late-Gothic **St Georgenkirche**, where Luther once preached, also look out over the square. The renovated **Lutherhaus**, where the reformer stayed, is a stately half-timbered building at the northern end of Steingasse on Lutherplatz. The emblem with the swan fastened to the facade is a symbol of Luther. Schmalkalden is also the western terminus of the **Martin-Luther-Weg**, a 17km easy to moderate hiking trail that ends at Tambach-Dietharz, from where there's bus service back to town (though not yet on weekends; check times with the tourist office).

Places to Stay & Eat
Gasthaus Zum Schmelztiegel (☎/fax 40 31 58, Stiller Tor 19) is in a lovely half-timbered house and charges DM50/100 for singles/doubles. Also recommended is the *Grünes Tor (☎ 66 30, fax 66 31 00, Weidebrunner Gasse 12)*. Each room in this galleried converted barn is furnished with much imagination and taste, and costs just DM80/120. Similarly priced and another good choice is *Hotel Teichhotel (☎/fax 40 26 61, Teichstrasse 21)*. All hotels have restaurants serving healthy portions of regional food; rooms all have private facilities. For cocktails and international dishes under DM12.50, younger people gather at *Maykel's (☎ 60 89 70, Lutherplatz 1)*.

Getting There & Away
Trains to Erfurt require changing in Zella-Mehlis (DM22.20, 1½ hours). Schmalkalden is about 5km east of the B19, which connects Eisenach and Meiningen.

MEININGEN
☎ 03693 • pop 23,000
Meiningen lies about 30km south of Schmalkalden, tucked between the Thuringian Forest and the Rhön mountain range. This idyllic town on the Werra River was once the residence of the dukes of Saxe-Meiningen and

THURINGIA

owes its continuing reputation as a regional cultural centre to the vision of Duke Georg II (1826-1914). In 1866 the duke founded a resident theatre troupe, which toured its lavish productions as far as Moscow and London. All in all, they gave 2591 performances in 38 cities. Georg also catapulted the court orchestra – the Meininger Hofkapelle – to international fame by appointing the pianist-conductor Hans von Bülow as musical director. He later passed the baton to Richard Strauss and Max Reger. The annual theatre festival in spring enjoys a fine reputation throughout German-speaking countries.

Orientation & Information

Two large parks, the Schlosspark to the west and the English Garden to the north, fringe Meiningen's town centre. The train and bus stations are on the eastern side of the English Garden, which also contains the Meiningen Theater. It's about a 10 minute walk to the Markt from here.

The friendly tourist office (☎ 446 50, fax 44 65 44, email info@meiningen.de) is at Bernhardstrasse 6, almost opposite the theatre, and is open weekdays from 9 am to 6 pm, and Saturday from 10 am to 3 pm. The main post office is at Eleonorenstrasse 1-3. The police station (☎ 591) is at Friedenssiedlung 9.

Schloss Elisabethenburg

The handsome baroque Schloss Elisabethenburg at the north-western edge of the town centre was built immediately after the founding of the duchy of Saxe-Meiningen in 1680 and served as ducal residence until 1918. It now contains several permanent exhibits highlighting the town's accomplishments in theatre and music. Among the prized items of the **Theater Museum** are 275 original stage backdrops from the early days of the Meininger Theater, some of which are on permanent display. There are also accomplished sketches of set designs and costumes drawn by Georg II himself, and historic photographs of well known actors.

Another wing holds the **Music Museum**, a series of rooms dedicated to the musical

directors of the Meininger Hofkapelle. A medieval and Renaissance **art collection** rounds out the exhibits.

The palace museums (☎ 50 36 41/43) open daily except Monday from 10 am to 6 pm, and 9 am to 5 pm from October to April (DM6/4).

Places to Stay & Eat

The tourist office makes free reservations for hotels and *private rooms*. One of the cheaper options is the small *Pension Pelzer* (☎ 442 10, fax 44 21 25, Georgstrasse 8), where singles/doubles with private facilities cost DM60/100. *Gasthaus Eleonore* (☎ 812 90, fax 81 29 10, Eleonorenstrasse 4) is similarly priced and near the Markt. Downstairs is a cafe with dancing from Thursday to Saturday.

The historic *Gasthof Schlundhaus* (☎ 81 38 38, fax 81 38 39, Schlundgasse 4) has charming rooms for DM105/180 and an atmospheric restaurant popular with locals. This is supposed to be the place where Thuringian potato dumplings, a regional speciality, were invented. *Henneberger Haus* (☎ 411 16, Georgstrasse 2) is a charming restaurant-bistro in a beautiful historic building. The baroque *Turmcafé* (☎ 50 36 41) in Schloss Elisabethenburg is a great place for afternoon coffee and cake.

Getting There & Away

Direct trains travel to Erfurt every two hours (DM24.40, two hours). Buses link Meiningen with Suhl, Zella-Mehlis and other towns in the Thuringian Forest. Meiningen is on the B19 from Eisenach to Schweinfurt in Bavaria, and is also on the B89 to Sonneberg in southern Thuringia.

The Saale Valley

JENA
☎ 03641 • pop 100,000
About 23km east of Weimar, the university town of Jena has also hosted a galaxy of German luminaries, though it lacks its

neighbour's charm and museum-like character. Industrialisation and architectural sins committed in GDR times have clearly left their mark, but recent restoration efforts are bearing pleasant results.

Science buffs will know about Jena in connection with the development of optical precision technology and names like Carl Zeiss, Ernst Abbe and Otto Schott. It's a tradition that continues to this day, given that the city's economic landscape is dotted with corporations like Carl Zeiss Jena, Jenaer Glaswerk, JENOPTIK and Jenapharm.

Surprisingly, one of Jena's greatest assets is found in nature. Flanked by 400m-high limestone hills, the city is blessed with a Mediterranean microclimate conducive to the growth of vines and 27 varieties of wild orchids. May and June are the best months to explore this unusual phenomenon.

Orientation & Information

Jena's main attractions are all within walking distance of each other. There are three train stations: Saalbahnhof in the north (take bus No 15 to get to the centre); Westbahnhof in the south-west; and Paradiesbahnhof, next to the Saale right in the centre.

The tourist information centre (☎ 586 30, fax 58 63 22, email tourist-info@jena.de) is at Johannisstrasse 23 and is open weekdays from 9 am to 6 pm and to 2 pm on Saturday.

Dresdner Bank at Am Holzmarkt 9 stays open from Monday to Thursday to 7 pm and Friday to 4 pm. The main post office is at Engelplatz 8. For information via the Web, go to www.jena.de.

A laundrette is at Lutherstrasse 63a (bus No 14 to Riedstrasse). For an ambulance, call ☎ 112 or ☎ 44 44 44. The police headquarters is at Käthe-Kollwitz-Strasse 1 (☎ 810).

Around the Markt

The Markt is one of the few places in Jena that still reflects some of the city's medieval heritage. At its southern end stands the Rathaus (1380), with an astronomical clock in its baroque tower. On the hour every hour, a little door opens and a devil/fool

called Schnapphans appears, trying to catch a golden ball – representing the human soul – dangling in front of him. The Schnapphans is one of the 'Seven Wonders of Jena', things designated as curiosities by the town's students.

The square is anchored by a **statue** of Prince-Elector Johann Friedrich I, founder of Jena's university and popularly known as 'Hanfried'. The handsome building with the half-timbered upper section at the western end contains the **Stadtmuseum Göhre** (☎ 44 32 45/75), which has an interesting regional history collection on themes as diverse as wine-making, the Reformation and student fraternities. This is occasionally supplemented by high-ranking special exhibits. It's open daily from 10 am to 5 pm, and Wednesday to 6 pm (DM5/3).

A walkway beneath the museum leads to the Gothic **Stadtkirche St Michael**, which contains the original engraved tombstone of Martin Luther. Another one of Jena's 'Seven Wonders' is the passageway right under the altar, which cannot be noticed from inside.

Universität Jena

Jena's university was founded as Collegium Jenense in 1558 in a former monastery in Kollegiengasse. Still part of the campus today, it features a nice courtyard festooned with the coat of arms of Johann Friedrich I. North of here, in an excellent example of urban re-engineering, is the former **Zeiss optics factory**, now part of the university. Several buildings wrap around Ernst Abbe Platz, dotted with abstract sculptures by Frank Stella. The copies of antique sculptures in the lobby of the main uni building here, though, prove a tad more aesthetic. The campus borders the **Goethe Galerie**, an American-style shopping mall with an interesting glass roof.

By contrast, the 120m-tall **Universitätshochhaus** (jokingly called *phallus Jenensis*) is a crime in city planning. In the early 1970s, the medieval Eichplatz was razed to make room for this concrete behemoth, built as a Zeiss research facility. When it turned out to be unsuitable for that purpose, it was

THURINGIA

A high-tech telescope shelters under the glass roof of the Goethe Galerie.

given to the university. It has since moved out as well, and the tower's fate is pending.

University **headquarters** are in a century-old complex on the north-eastern edge of the Altstadt at Fürstengraben 1. Inside are a Minerva bust by Rodin and a wall-sized painting showing Jena students going off to fight against Napoleon.

Goethe & Schiller

As minister for the elector of Saxe-Weimar, Goethe spent five years in Jena. When not busy regulating the flow of the Saale, building streets, designing the botanical garden or cataloguing the university library, he crafted his *Faust* and *Wilhelm Meister*. He also discovered an obscure jaw bone in the **Anatomieturm**, a former fortification tower on the corner of Teichgraben and Leutragraben. Most of the time he lived at Fürstengraben 26, which is now a **Goethe Gedenkstätte** (☎ 94 90 09) focused on his accomplishments as a natural scientist, poet

and politician. It's open Wednesday to Sunday from 11 am to 3 pm, closed from November to March (free). Goethe himself planted the ginkgo tree just east of here, which is part of the **Botanical Garden** (☎ 94 92 74); entry is DM2/1.

Goethe is also credited with bringing Schiller to Jena University. Schiller gave his inaugural lecture at the building that now houses the university headquarters (see the earlier Universität Jena entry). He liked Jena and stayed for 10 years – more than anywhere else – mostly in the **Gartenhaus** (☎ 93 11 88), a cottage at Schillergässchen 2. Schiller wrote *Wallenstein* in the little wooden shack in the garden, where he also liked to wax philosophical with Goethe. The house is open from 11 am to 3 pm, closed Monday; between November and March it's also closed Sunday (DM2/1).

Carl Zeiss & Ernst Abbe

These scientists are two more notables responsible for putting Jena on the map. Zeiss opened his first mechanical workshop here in 1846 and began building primitive microscopes. After enlisting Abbe's help in 1866, they developed the first scientific microscope. In cooperation with Otto Schott, the founder of Jenaer Glasswerke, they pioneered the production of optical precision instruments that propelled Jena to global prominence in the early 20th century.

Their life stories and the evolution of optical technology are the themes of the **Optisches Museum** (☎ 44 31 65), Carl-Zeiss-Platz 12. As well as microscopes, cameras, binoculars and other instruments, there's a collection of spectacles through the ages, plus an interactive room with various simplified eye tests. Ask to borrow an English-language pamphlet describing the exhibits. Tours of the reconstructed Zeiss workshop (1866) in the adjacent Volkshaus run Sunday at 10 am. The museum is open Tuesday to Friday from 10 am to 5 pm, Saturday from 1 to 4.30 pm and Sunday from 9.30 am to 1 pm (DM8/5).

The octagonal pavilion outside the museum, designed by Belgian Art Nouveau artist Henry van de Velde, dates from 1911 and contains a marble bust of Abbe. The **Zeiss Planetarium** (☎ 88 54 88), Am Planetarium 5 in the northern city centre, was the world's first public planetarium (1926). Today it boasts a huge state-of-the-art telescope. There are shows several times daily except Monday (DM8/6). A combination ticket for the Optical Museum and the planetarium is DM13/9.

Places to Stay

The camping ground closest to Jena is **Campingplatz Ilmtal** (see the Weimar section for details).

The **IB Jugendgästehaus** (☎ 68 72 30 or ☎ 68 70, fax 68 72 02, Am Herrenberge 9) is in a rather ugly GDR-era building outside of the centre. From Saalbahnhof, take bus No 1 to Holzmarkt, then bus No 10, 11, 33 or 40 to Mühlenstrasse; from there it's a 10 minute walk uphill. Singles are DM40, doubles DM60, triples DM75, including breakfast. There's a DM7 surcharge for one night stays.

The tourist office makes free reservations for hotels and **private rooms** (from DM35 per person). All prices here are for rooms with private bath and include breakfast. The cheapest options in the centre, asking about DM65/95 for singles/doubles, are **Pension H+R Stadtmitte** (☎ 44 20 83, fax 61 55 33, Neugasse 1) and **Gästehaus Lara** (☎ 463 90, fax 46 39 40, Lutherstrasse 47). At **Gasthof Zur Schweiz** (☎ 44 93 55, fax 44 93 54, Quergasse 15) you can expect to pay DM85/120. Not as central but in a historic house (with a brewery attached) is **Hotel Papiermühle** (☎ 459 80, fax 45 98 45, Erfurter Strasse 102), which charges DM81/126.

Top of the line is **Hotel Esplanade** (☎ 80 00, fax 80 01 50, Carl-Zeiss-Platz 4), central but quiet and with a dramatic atrium design. Rooms with full facilities start at DM140/170 but top out at DM225/255.

Places to Eat

One of the cheapest places is the **Mensa**, the university cafeteria on the ground floor of the main building on Abbe Platz. **Zur Rosen** (☎ 93 06 50, Johannisstrasse 13) is a student pub with tasty food costing around DM5 for students, double otherwise. For fishy snacks from DM3, there's **Nordsee** (☎ 48 91 94, Markt 23).

For a more grown-up atmosphere, and some of the best German food in town, head to **Zur Noll** (☎ 44 15 66, Oberlauengasse 19), a historical restaurant-pub decorated with original artwork. Good Thuringian food hits the plates at the old-fashioned **Roter Hirsch** (☎ 44 32 21, Holzmarkt 10), where daily specials cost DM10 to DM18 (try to get a table upstairs).

There are several fast-food options in the Goethe Galerie mall, where there's also the casually stylish **Rotonda** (☎ 80 00), which has international dishes around DM20 and a great salad bar.

Entertainment

Jena's 'pub mile' is along Wagnergasse on the north-western edge of the city centre. Here you'll find hang-outs like **Café Bohème** (☎ 82 61 52) and **Café Stilbruch** (☎ 82 71 71), which serve coffee, beer and bistro fare to a student-age crowd. For live concerts and disco nights, head to **Rosenkeller** (☎ 93 11 90, Johannisstrasse 13), a historic student club with a network of cellars.

Getting There & Away

IC trains to Berlin-Zoo (DM81, three hours) and Hamburg-Altona (DM163, six hours) depart every two hours from Saalbahnhof. Hourly regional service to Saalfeld (DM12, 45 minutes) and Rudolstadt (DM9.80, 35 minutes) leave from here as well. To get to Weimar (DM9.80, 20 minutes) and Erfurt (DM12, 40 minutes), you must go to Westbahnhof station.

The regional bus station is slightly north of Paradiesbahnhof, though for buses bound for Weimar (DM7.20, 1¼ hours) you have to go to Westbahnhof.

Jena is on the A4 from Dresden to Frankfurt and just west of the A9 from Berlin to Munich. It's also crossed by the B7 (east-west) and B88 (north-south). The Mitfahrzentrale (☎ 194 40) is at Fürstengraben 30.

THURIN...

Getting Around

Day passes for buses and trams are DM5, and there are also 24 hour group passes for up to five people for DM8, but these are sold on weekends only. Rental bikes are at Fahrradhaus Kemter (☎ 44 15 33), Löbdergraben 24. For a taxi, call ☎ 45 88 88.

AROUND JENA
Dornburger Schlösser

This magnificent trio of palaces from different eras, romantically resting atop a steep hillside about 15km north of Jena, makes for a pleasant excursion.

The southernmost is the Renaissance palace where, after the death of his patron, Duke Carl August, Goethe sought solitude. The rooms he stayed in have been restored more or less to their 1828 state.

The central palace is a late rococo confection and beautifully blends with the garden. The uppermost structure is a mix of Romanesque, late Gothic, Renaissance and baroque elements, and may only be viewed from the outside.

The palace complex (☎ 036427-222 91) is open Wednesday to Sunday from 9 am to 6 pm, and 10 am to 4 pm in winter (DM6/4). The gardens are open daily year round from 8 am to dusk (free).

Trains go hourly from Saalbahnhof to Dornburg (DM4.60, 10 minutes), from where it's a steep 20 to 30 minute climb uphill. Bus No 407 leaves every two hours on weekdays (less frequently on weekends) from Jena's central bus station.

RUDOLSTADT
☎ 03672 • pop 30,000

The main residence of the princes of Schwarzburg-Rudolstadt until 1918, Rudolstadt experienced a heyday in the Age of Enlightenment in the late 18th century. It was here where the first meeting between Goethe and Schiller took place in 1788. Later, the musical virtuosi Franz Liszt, Richard Wagner and Paganini worked at the theatre, founded in 1793 and still in operation today. The manufacture of decorative porcelain 'kitsch but artfully painted figurines,

mostly) has been an important local industry since that period as well. The first factory, the **Volkstedter Porzellanmanufaktur** (1762) still has a showroom (☎ 35 20 12) at Breitscheidstrasse 7.

Rudolstadt's landmark is the local rulers' former digs, the baroque **Schloss Heidecksburg** (☎ 429 00), a hulking edifice on a lofty bluff. Besides lavishly decorated and furnished rooms, the complex also harbours regional history exhibits and collections of paintings, weapons and minerals (DM6/3). Perhaps the palace's best features, though, are free. These include a terrific view over the valley, the porcelain on view in the ticket office hall and, especially, the fantastic wooden sleighs by the entrance. Palace hours are from 10 am to 6 pm daily except Monday. It's a 10 minute uphill walk from the Markt in the town centre.

Sights around here include the **Stadtkirche St Andreas** on Kirchgasse, a Gothic hall-church rich in treasure; and the **Handwerkerhof**, a former convent for noble women. It recently metamorphosed into an assembly of galleries, shops and cafes wrapped around a flower-festooned inner courtyard. Enter from Mauergasse or Stiftsgasse.

Rudolstadt's tourist office (☎ 42 45 43, fax 43 12 86) is at Marktstrasse 57, and is open weekdays from 9 am to 6 pm and Saturday to noon.

There's hourly train service to Jena (DM9.80, 45 minutes). Long-distance train travel always requires a change in Saalfeld, which is served twice hourly (DM3, eight minutes). Rudolstadt is on the B88 between Ilmenau and Jena and the B85 to Weimar.

SAALFELD
☎ 03671 • pop 32,100

Saalfeld, about 15km south of Rudolfstadt, turned 1100 in 1999. It has an attractive centre brimming with historical buildings, and also one of Thuringia's most heavily visited natural attractions, the Feengrotten (Fairy Grottoes).

The train station lies east of the Saale river, about a 10 minute walk from Markt. The tourist office (☎/fax 339 50 or ☎ 194

33), at Markt 6, is open weekdays from 9 am to 6 pm, and weekends from 10 am to 2 pm.

Walking Tour

From the train station, head west on Bahnhofstrasse to the **Saaltor**, one of the four surviving town gates. It's worth climbing to the top for a peak at the town layout. Continue west via Saalstrasse to the Markt. On its south side looms the striking Renaissance **Rathaus**, a symphony of spiky turrets, ornate gables, frilly oriels and other design elements. Opposite is the partly Romanesque **Marktapotheke**, the former town hall and a pharmacy since 1681.

Behind the Markt, the twin towers of the Gothic **Johanniskirche** come into view. One of Thuringia's largest hall churches, it is richly decorated and features dramatic cross and net vaulting, plus a life-size carved figure of John the Baptist.

Brudergasse, west of Markt, leads uphill to the former Franciscan monastery at Münzplatz 5, since 1904 home of the **Thüringer Heimatmuseum** (☎ 59 84 71). Its major allure is the celestial building itself and the collection of local, late Gothic wood carvings. It's open from 10 am to 5 pm, but closed Monday (DM3.50/2).

Feengrotten

Saalfeld's main magnet are these underground grottoes (☎ 550 40), about 1.5km outside of town (free hourly bus service). The former alum slate mines were actively mined from 1530 to 1850 and opened for tours in 1914. In 1992 they made it into the *Guinness Book of Records* as the world's most colourful grottoes, but don't expect a kaleidoscopic spectacle. What counts as 'colour' here refers mostly to different shades of brown, ochre and sienna, with an occasional sprinkling of green and blue. Small stalactite and stalagmite formations further create a bizarre and subtly impressive series of grottoes with names like Butter Cellar and Blue-green Grotto. The highlight is the **Fairytale Cathedral**, with the 'Holy Grail Castle' – allegedly it inspired Richard Wagner's son Siegfried's *Tannhäuser* set design in the 1920s.

From March to October, tours of the grottoes are conducted daily from 9 am to 5 pm, and from 10 am to 3.30 pm the rest of the year. In November, it's only open on weekends (DM8/7).

Places to Stay & Eat

The nearest camping ground is the lakeside *Campingplatz Saalthal Alter* (☎ *036732-222 67*), which is about 15km east of Saalfeld in Gosswitz-Bucha. It's open from mid-April to mid-October. The town's newly restored *hostel* (☎ *51 73 20, Am Schieferhof 4*) is operated by the German Red Cross, and charges DM24 for B&B, plus DM7.50 for sheets.

Accommodation in general is comparatively inexpensive here. Pensions charging around DM40/80 for singles/doubles with private bath and breakfast include *Walter & Neranzakis* (☎ *67 25 25, Obere Strasse 14*) and *Fishermens Friend* (☎ *53 06 12, Sonneberger Strasse 44*).

Good eating options include the historical *Das Loch* (☎ *51 66 61, Blankenburger Strasse 8*) and the artistic *Zum Pappenheimer* (☎ *330 89, Fleischgasse 5*), which occasionally has jazz evenings.

Getting There & Away

Regional trains run twice hourly to Rudolstadt (DM3, eight minutes) and hourly to Jena (DM12, 55 minutes). There's also an IC connection to Berlin-Ostbahnhof every two hours (DM94, 3¾ hours). Saalfeld lies at the intersection of the B281 and the B85, which you'll use if coming from Weimar or Jena.

Saxony-Anhalt

The state of Saxony-Anhalt (Sachsen-Anhalt) comprises the former East German districts of Magdeburg and Halle. Originally part of the duchy of Saxony, medieval Anhalt was split into smaller units by the sons of various princes. In 1863, Leopold IV of Anhalt-Dessau united the three existing duchies in a single stroke, and eight years later his realm became a state of the German Reich.

The mighty Elbe River flows north-west through Saxony-Anhalt, past Lutherstadt-Wittenberg and Magdeburg on its way to the North Sea at Hamburg. Halle is on the Saale River south of Magdeburg.

The Harz Mountains, the most touristed part of the state, occupy its south-west corner and spread westward into Lower Saxony to Goslar. Quaint historical towns like Wernigerode and 1000-year-old Quedlinburg hug gentle, wooded slopes (see the Harz Mountains chapter for more information on these towns).

In the south-east, the Saale Valley's wine region makes for wonderful wine-tasting trips, using Naumburg – with its spectacular cathedral – as a base; alternatively, you could camp or stay in hostels along the way. The area is undertouristed, meaning that prices are correspondingly low.

Because renovation and investment into this area chugs on at a slower pace, it still provides travellers with the opportunity to see a bit of what's left of the GDR in eastern Germany. For the most part, this translates to small, untouristed and relatively unchanged villages that are only just beginning to acquire higher-end hotels and restaurants.

MAGDEBURG

☎ 0391 • pop 250,000

Magdeburg, on the Elbe River, lies at a strategic crossing of transport routes from Thuringia to the Baltic Sea and Western Europe to Berlin.

HIGHLIGHTS

Saxony-Anhalt Luminaries:
Otto von Bismarck, Georg Frederic Händel, Friedrich Gottlieb Klopstock, Martin Luther, Georg Philipp Telemann, Christa Wolf

- Renting a Trabant in Lutherstadt-Wittenberg, the famous 'Luther city'
- Rambling in the sprawling English-style park at Wörlitz
- Following the Vineyard Road in the Saale-Unstrut region
- Wine tasting in Naumburg (and seeing its Cathedral of Saints Peter and Paul)
- Taking in the timeless elegance of Dessau's Bauhaus
- Horse riding in the Altmark
- Visiting the Ferropolis, a fascinating technology museum

Magdeburg p335

Quedlinburg
(See Harz Mountains chapter)

Lutherstadt-
Wittenberg p341

On 16 January 1945 a 39 minute bombing raid left 90% of the city destroyed. Magdeburg was rebuilt under the GDR and they did a terrible job, using steel and concrete for everything.

These days, Magdeburg is a lively city struggling to come out from under its ham-fisted architecture. The centre of the city has generous boulevards (some of them lined with refurbished 19th century buildings), a Gothic cathedral and a few Romanesque churches.

Orientation

From Kölner Platz in front of the Hauptbahnhof, Ernst-Reuter-Allee leads east to the Neue Strombrücke that crosses the Elbe. Alter Markt, home to the tourist office, is on the left a block back from the river.

The broad, pedestrianised Breiter Weg runs north-south between Universitätsplatz and Ernst-Reuter-Allee. The chief sights are at the southern end of the Altstadt, between the Elbe and Otto-von-Guericke-Strasse.

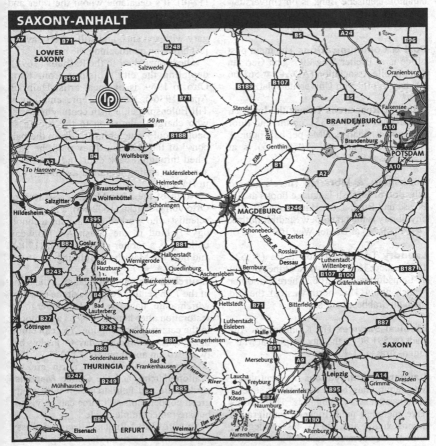

SAXONY-ANHALT

euro currency converter DM1 = €0.51

The Stadthalle and Stadtpark Rotehorn are on the east side of the Elbe; take tram No 6 from the centre.

Information

Tourist Office The tourist office (☎ 540 49 03, fax 540 49 10, email mi@magdeburg.de), open Monday to Friday from 10 am to 6 pm and Saturday to 1 pm, is at Alter Markt 12. German-language tours (DM5) leave from here daily at 11 am.

Money There's a Reisebank at the Hauptbahnhof. Deutsche Bank is on Universitätsplatz, and there's a NordLB ATM at Breiter Weg 193, 100m east of the youth hostel.

Post & Communications The main post office is at Breiter Weg 203. The German Automobile Association (ADAC; ☎ 561 66 44) has an office on Universitätsplatz.

Internet Resources To surf the Internet, Cyberb@r (☎ 620 98 35), on the 2nd floor of Karstadt, charges DM4 per half hour. A rival, Cyberspace (☎ 620 98 35) is at Heidestrasse 9.

Bookshops & Libraries There's a good selection of English-language books at HD Presse und Buch at the Hauptbahnhof. The city library is the brand-new Stadtbibliothek (☎ 540 48 21) at Breiter Weg 109.

Laundry Try Waschsalon Petra (☎ 622 1329), about 1km south-west of the Altstadt at Lemsdorfer Weg 106. There's another branch about 1km north-west of the old town at Grabbestrasse 8b.

Medical Services The Krankenhaus Altstadt (☎ 591 90) is the city hospital at Max-Otten-Strasse 11-15.

Dangers & Annoyances In recent years, Magdeburg has been the site of several vicious attacks by skinheads. The victims have included punk rockers, immigrants, homosexuals and, to a lesser degree, tourists. Use common sense in areas which tend to attract loiterers, especially around the Hauptbahnhof at night.

Alter Markt

The centre of the old town is called Alter Markt (old market), despite the fact that every building save one was built after the war. The square is home to a daily **market**, with an excellent range of fruits, vegetables, meats and clothes. It runs Monday to Friday from 9 am to 6 pm, Saturday till noon.

At the south-eastern end of the square is a copy of the bronze **Magdeburger Reiter** (1240). It's debatable whom the rider and maidens represent: some say King Otto and his two wives, others say the King of Hungary with servants, and still others say it's just any king approaching the city.

The bronze door to the **Rathaus** (1698), depicting the city's history from King Otto to 1969, is by local artist Heinrich Apel (1936-). Note the representation of Till Eulenspiegel, a 14th century trickster who charged admission to the square so people could watch him 'fly from the balcony' of the Rathaus. They paid, he vanished through a back door and was never seen here again (he pulled a similar stunt in Halle).

North of the Alter Markt is a **statue of Otto von Guericke** (1602-86), a mayor and scientist who worked on vacuum technology. Behind it, the lavish Art Nouveau building is a former police station (1906), and now the Magistrate Building.

Churches Behind the Rathaus are the ruins of the 15th century **Johanniskirche** (parts of which date back to 1131), undergoing restoration after long serving as a memorial to the catastrophic bombing. You can climb the southern tower Monday to Friday between 10 am and 6 pm (DM2/1).

Along the Elbe to the north are the **Wallonerkirche**, and the Gothic **Magdalenenkapelle** and **Petrikirche**, all with pretty green copper roofs. All three can be visited but are rather simple inside.

South of Ernst-Reuter-Allee, in a grassy expanse near the river, stands Magdeburg's

MAGDEBURG

To Uni-Hotel & Waschsalon Petra

To Herrenkrug Parkhotel, Die Saison, Bördelandhalle, & National Garden Showground

To Waschsalon Petra, University Clinic, Cyberspace & Airport

PLACES TO STAY
21 InterCity Hotel
22 Maritim Magdeburg
24 Jugendgästehaus Magdeburg
29 Roncalli Haus

PLACES TO EAT
2 Quartiere Latino
10 Flair
18 Otto-von-Guericke
19 McDonald's
25 Schlemmerland
33 Zum Alten Dessauer

OTHER
1 Deutsche Bank
3 Theater der Landeshauptstadt
4 City Library
5 Krankenhaus Altstadt
6 Magistrate Building
7 Otto von Guericke Statue
8 Tourist Office
9 Karstadt & Cyberb@r
11 Magdeburger Reiter Statue
12 Rathaus
13 Johanniskirche
14 Magdalenenkapelle; Petrikirche; Wallonerkirche
15 Weisse Flotte Dock
16 Fahnen Monument
17 Allee-Center
20 Main Train Station
23 Bus Station
26 Kloster Unser Lieben Frauen & Café
27 Kugelblitze Cabaret
28 Main Post Office
30 Kammerspiele Dramatic
31 Cultural History Museum
32 Dom
34 Boat Rental Stand
35 Stadthalle

oldest building, the 12th century Romanesque **Kloster Unser Lieben Frauen**, now a museum. The courtyard is lovely, and its cafe is a nice place to have coffee. Downstairs are religious exhibits, upstairs rotating exhibitions. Note the front door designed by Heinrich Apel – push down on the little hat to enter. Museum hours are Tuesday to Sunday from 10 am to 5 pm (DM4/2). Church and cloister are free.

Farther south is the soaring Gothic **Dom**, said to be the first built on German soil,

with the main construction taking place from 1209 to 1363. Inside you'll find the tomb of Otto I and art spanning eight centuries, including a pensive World War I memorial by Ernst Barlach. It's open daily from 10 am to 4 pm, with German-language tours at noon.

The quarter behind the Dom, which is located along Hegelstrasse and Hasselbach-platz, has nicely restored **villas** from the 19th century and a healthy number of restaurants and pubs.

Cultural History Museum

The Kulturhistorisches Museum (☎ 326 45), Otto-von-Guericke-Strasse 68-73, on the corner of Danzstrasse, houses the original *Magdeburg Rider* statue and a good collection of graphic arts and furniture. It's open Tuesday to Sunday from 10 am to 6 pm, and to 8 pm on Thursday (DM2/1).

Stadtpark Rotehorn

To the east of the Hubbrücke is the Stadtpark Rotehorn, with playgrounds, picnic areas and **Adolf-Mittag-See**, where you can rent rowboats. Tram No 6 stops about 300m north of the lake.

National Garden Showgrounds

On the east side of the Elbe lie the sprawling grounds of the *Bundesgartenschau* (National Garden Show), held here in the summer of 1999. When the flowers have been carted off, the lovely landscaped park, a former military compound, remains. Take tram No 6 to Grosse Cracauer Anger (direction: Herrenkrug).

Places to Stay

Campingplatz Barleber See (☎ 50 32 44), 8km north of town, is the last stop on tram No 10. It costs DM4/7 per person/car, and it's a nice, if simple, place right on a lake. There's a swimming beach as well.

The *Jugendgästehaus Magdeburg* (☎ 53 21 01, fax 53 21 02, Leiterstrasse 10), now expanded with a fitness centre and table tennis, is in a practical (if ugly) spot, only two minutes walk south-east of the Hauptbahnhof. It charges DM27/32 for juniors/seniors, plus DM6 for linen and DM6 for breakfast.

The tourist office has a free service booking *private rooms* from about DM30.

The *Roncalli Haus* (☎ 596 14 00, fax 596 14 40, Max-Josef-Metzger-Strasse 12) has clean, comfy singles/doubles with private facilities for DM80/130.

The *Uni-Hotel* (☎ 55 11 44, Walther-Rathenau-Strasse 6), near the university, has reasonable rooms with private shower and WC (toilet) for DM99/140.

InterCity Hotel (☎ 596 20, fax 596 24 99, Bahnhofstrasse 69), by the train station, offers its standard rooms from DM118/137.

Thanks to its strategic position, Magdeburg was invaded by Swedish forces during the Thirty Years' War.

Maritim Magdeburg (☎ 594 90, fax 594 99 90, email reservierung.mag@maritim.de, Otto-von-Guericke-Strasse 87) is perfectly located, with large rooms for DM222/288 and a pool.

The *Herrenkrug Parkhotel* (☎ 850 80, fax 850 85 01, email herrenkrug_hotel@ t-online.de, Herrenkrug 3) is the classiest of the lot, sited in an Elbe park mansion. Rates are DM189/238. The restaurants are superb, too (see Places to Eat).

Places to Eat
Restaurants & Cafes *Café im Kloster Unser Lieben Frauen* (☎ 656 02 33, Regierungsstrasse 6) is a lovely place for breakfast (DM5 to DM10) or lunch (light meals from DM8).

Flair (☎ 561 89 95), on the corner of Ernst-Reuter-Allee and Breiter Weg, has light dishes from DM7, pastas from DM11 to DM14, and salads from DM7.50 to DM14.

The *Quartiere Latino* (☎ 543 97 39, Universitätsplatz) has an enormous menu that includes pizzas and pasta (about 30 varieties) from DM8 to DM13, and mains averaging DM15.

The *Otto-von-Guericke* (☎ 543 91 81, Otto-von-Guericke-Strasse 104) is really cosy, with soups from DM7 and steaks/schnitzels for DM20 to DM30. Note the big spinning half-ball as you enter, honouring the physicist's famous vacuum experiment.

Zum Alten Dessauer (☎ 543 01 50, Breiter Weg 250) has nice lunch specials for DM7 to DM12 and steaks for DM19 to DM24.

Die Saison restaurant in the Herrenkrug Parkhotel (See Places to Stay) has seasonal menus, with mains ranging from DM24 to DM33, soups from DM8 and a few vegie items from DM17. There's also a *beer garden* that hosts regular jazz and classical concerts. The *Eiskeller*, the hotel's other restaurant, is in a genuine ice cellar. Prices are about DM10 higher than at Die Saison.

Fast Food There's a good *food shop* in the Hauptbahnhof, and downstairs *Ditsch* offers pizza and pretzels for DM3.50. There's also a *McDonald's* opposite the station.

The huge new *Allee-Center* shopping complex on Breiter Weg is a foodies' nirvana: there are places selling doner kebabs, pizzas and pastas, a *Nordsee* and several bakeries selling tasty filled rolls around the central fountain.

Schlemmerland, across the courtyard from the hostel on Leiterstrasse, has a great selection of breads and pastries, sausage from DM2, huge fruit and mixed salads for DM4, and soups for DM3 (closed Sunday).

Entertainment
StadtPASS is a free monthly calendar printed by the city. *Günter* and *DATEs*, two free private listings guides, are also excellent

Rock & Jazz Magdeburg hosts many big concerts. Top venues include the 2000 seat *Stadthalle* (☎ 593 45 29, Stadtpark Rotehorn) and the sparkling new *Bördelandhalle* (☎ 59 34 50, Berliner Chaussee 32) just east of town.

Theatre & Classical Music The *Kloster Unser Lieben Frauen* holds concerts featuring music by Georg Phillipp Telemann, the Magdeburger Kammerchor, and the energetic Gruppe M (chamber music from Debussy, Ravel, Ligeti and others).

The Magdeburg Philharmonic plays at the *Theater der Landeshauptstadt* (☎ 543 47 66, Universitätsplatz), which also hosts opera, ballet and theatrical performances.

The *Kammerspiele Dramatic* (☎ 598 82 26, Otto-von-Guericke-Strasse 64) stages dramas and free open-air theatre, the latter from late June to mid-July.

Die Kugelblitze (☎ 543 39 56, Breiter Weg 203) does satirical theatre and cabaret.

Getting There & Away
Flugplatz Magdeburg (☎ 622 78 77) is a regional airport with limited scheduled and charter services.

Trains to/from Berlin-Zoo take about 1½ hours (DM40). Magdeburg is on the main route from Rostock (DM76, 3¾ hours) and Schwerin (DM45, two hours) to Leipzig or Erfurt (DM34, 1½ hours).

The city is just south of the A2 Berlin-Hanover autobahn. From Wernigerode, take the B81 all the way.

Getting Around

Heading to the airport by public transport, take bus No 57 from the bus station and transfer to tram No 3 or 9. A taxi to/from the airport costs about DM30.

Single bus and tram tickets cost just DM2.40/1.80 for regular/short journeys, while four-trip tickets cost DM8.50. The day ticket (DM5) is valid from 9 am to midnight.

Free street parking is easier to find north and south of the city centre. Parking near the Hauptbahnhof and bus station is by permit only, but there's free parking in front of the Dom.

Taxis line up outside the Hauptbahnhof. Call Taxi Ruf (☎ 73 73 73) or Taxi Zentrale (☎ 56 88 88). Flag fall is DM3.50 and each extra kilometre costs DM1.90. The Bahntaxi is at the Kölner Platz exit.

Weisse Flotte (☎ 532 88 91) offers a 1½ hour scenic boat trip on the Elbe (DM12, children DM5). The mooring point is just north of the Neue Steinbrücke.

Northern Saxony-Anhalt

STENDAL

☎ 03931 • pop 41,000

About 60km north of Magdeburg lies Stendal, the largest town of the sparsely-populated Altmark region. This former Hanseatic trading centre flourished until the 17th century, when it was devastated by fires, the plague and finally, the Thirty Years' War. But many splendid medieval buildings survived and have been renovated since German unification, making it a pleasant stop for a day or two.

Orientation & Information

The Altstadt is a five minute walk northeast of the Hauptbahnhof along Bahnhof-strasse. The tiny tourist office (☎ 65 11 90, fax 65 11 95), Kornmarkt 8, is open weekdays from 8.30 am to 5 pm (in summer, also Saturday from 9.30 am to 3 pm). Breite Strasse is the pedestrian shopping street. The post office, with a Postbank inside, is on the corner of Poststrasse and Hallstrasse. Note that the churches are shut from noon to 3 pm.

Kornmarkt

The old market square is dominated by the fetching late-Renaissance **Rathaus** and to one side, an 8m-high statue of the legendary knight Roland (1525), clutching a 4m-long sword. The original was damaged by a storm in 1972 and replaced with a copy. (Roland statues are dotted about the country, the biggest being in Bremen, another Hanseatic League city.)

Behind the Rathaus is the **Marienkirche** (Church of St Mary), with two very different aspects: from the east, a pair of slim 14th and 15th century towers, from the west, a rather stolid congregational hall built later. Its main asset is the dazzling 16th century **astronomical clock** set under the organ gallery. The works of the timepiece resurfaced only in 1967 and were painstakingly reassembled. It's open Monday to Friday from 10 am to 5 pm, and weekends to 4 pm.

Other Churches

The exterior of **St Nicolauskirche**, commonly referred to as the Dom, is built in the economical Gothic brick style so typical of north German churches. Inside, the relative absence of decoration makes the colourful **stained-glass windows** a genuine relief. Of the 23 panes, only the crucifixion scenes are ones from the original 1430 church – the remaining ones were made in the 1800s in the same dark hues to enhance the mystical effect. The church, at the south-west of the centre on Am Dom, is open daily from 10 am to noon and 3 to 5 pm. In winter, opening hours are Monday to Friday from 1 to 2 pm only.

At the north end of Breite Strasse stands **Jakobikirche**, with some nice stained glass of its own, as well as a colourful **pulpit**, held up by a figure of St Jakob the Elder, patron saint of pilgrims. Just north-east of the church is a strikingly broad avenue with a village green called **Altes Dorf**, the oldest part of town.

Town Gates

At the extreme south and north-west of the Altstadt you'll find two handsome town gates, the **Tangemünder Torturm** and the **Uenglinger Tor**. Built more for prestige than defence, these fancy brick portals look a bit misplaced now that most of the town wall has gone. They both afford great views of the Altstadt, and are open daily from 10 am to noon and 3 to 5 pm (DM2/1). In front of the Tangermünder Tor is Nachtigalplatz, with a memorial to Africa explorer Gustav Nachtigal (1834-85).

Museums

South of Altes Dorf, in a half-timbered house at Winckelmannstrasse 36, is the **Winckelmann Museum** (☎ 65 17 54), dedicated to Johann Joachim Winckelmann (1717-68), regarded as the founder of modern archaeology. It's open Tuesday to Sunday, from 10 am to noon and 1 to 5 pm (DM3/1).

The **Altmärkisches Museum** is in the former Katharinenkloster near the Nicolauskirche and displays local artefacts, religious art and items from Stendal's heyday as a trading metropolis. Hours are Tuesday from 1 to 5 pm, Wednesday to Friday from 10 am to 5 pm, and weekends from 1 to 6 pm (DM3/2).

Places to Stay & Eat

The tourist office can book *private rooms* free of charge, from about DM35 per person. *Pension am Nordwall* (☎ 79 40 66, fax 79 40 67, Wendstrasse 9), three minutes walk from the centre, has a lovely terrace and fully equipped singles/doubles for DM65/96.

Pension Ramme (☎ 21 06 23, fax 71 58 09, Moltekestrasse 31c) on the edge of the Altstadt, has decent quarters from DM50/80, including breakfast and facilities.

The *Hotel am Uenglinger Tor* (☎ 684 80, fax 64 31 30, Moltkestrasse 17) charges DM80/110 for clean, modern rooms close to the old town gate, with all facilities.

Village Inn (☎ 79 38 20, Marienkirchestrasse 6) offers good soups for DM4.50 to DM6.50, pastas from DM8.50 and daily specials from just DM6.50.

Altstadt Bierstube (☎ 71 58 60, Mittelstrasse 6) is a cosy pub-restaurant with several schnitzel-and-dumpling dishes for under DM10. Most mains are under DM14.

The *Waldmannsheil* (☎ 21 33 42, Breite Strasse 31) specialises in game (eg wild boar for DM21.50). Main dishes average DM14.50 to DM25.50, and there are also good soups and salads.

Getting There & Around

Stendal is an important north-south/east-west rail junction, so there are trains to just about everywhere. There's an ICE service to Berlin-Zoo (DM45, 40 minutes) and regional trains to Magdeburg (DM14.80, 45 minutes) and Leipzig (DM50, two hours). The B188 and B189 intersect in the south of town.

The town is compact and easily seen on foot. You can rent bicycles from the tourist office on Kornmarkt 8 for DM10 per day, plus DM50 deposit.

AROUND STENDAL
Tangermünde

☎ 039322 • pop 10,000

Tangermünde, some 10km south-east of Stendal, was the second home of Charles IV, King of Bohemia, in the 14th century. A businessman at heart, Charles chose this market town because of its site at the confluence of the Elbe and Havel rivers. The place is straight out of a film set, and its ostentatious towers, gates and castle – some of them rather run-down – are worth at least a day of poking around.

The tourist office is at Marktplatz 13 (☎ 37 10, fax 437 70), and is open Monday to Friday from 10 am to 6 pm, and weekends from 11 am to 4 pm. Its friendly staff will book rooms for free. The Altstadt is a

Horse Riding

The Altmark is one of Germany's great horse-breeding areas, and there's no shortage of horse shows, parades or markets. With its abundance of unspoilt pastures and riverside paths, it's a charming spot to go riding, and you can hire a steed from DM15 per hour.

The Fremdenverkehrsverband Altmark (Altmark Tourist Association, ☎ 039322-432 32), Marktstrasse 13, 39590 Tangermünde, will send you a list of Reiterhöfe, which offer spartan lodgings for horse and rider (a B&B for the latter averages about DM40, though many are cheaper). All entries have stables charging DM10 to DM15 per horse per day (care including feed). Many Reiterhöfe offer riding lessons and have nice leisure facilities, making it a great way to spend a summer holiday.

five minute walk south of the train station, along Albrechtstrasse.

The **Stadtmauer** (1300) counts as one Germany's most complete municipal defences, crowned at the western end by the angular medieval **Neustädter Tor**, which looks very much like its cousins in Stendal. The soaring facade of the **Rathaus**, recalling the town's erstwhile wealth, resembles a huge, elaborate pipe organ. The local history museum is in its basement (DM2/1).

Moving east through the cobblestone lanes takes you past lovely half-timbered houses to the main house of worship, **St Stephanskirche**. The church houses a 17th century organ, the last working model by Hamburg craftsman Hans Schrer and reputedly one of the most valuable in Europe.

The **Schloss**, which overlooks a crook in the Elbe, was sacked in 1640 by the Swedes and quietly crumbled until the early 20th century, when it was made into a public park. Its only surviving building is the ruined **Kanzlei**, originally a dance hall. Bring a picnic – this is one of the most charming spots on the Elbe.

Getting There & Away

Trains run to Stendal hourly (DM3, 17 minutes). The *Reederei Kaiser* (☎ 0171-421 81 62) runs two-hour scenic trips up the Elbe (DM12), but also sails to Magdeburg and Havelberg (DM20/40 one-way/return).

Eastern Saxony-Anhalt

LUTHERSTADT-WITTENBERG
☎ 03491 • pop 53,000

Wittenberg is best known as the place where Martin Luther did most of his work, and nowhere else will you feel the great man's presence quite the same way. (The prefix 'Lutherstadt' was added in 1938 – the Nazis appreciated the reformer's marketing value.) As a leading university town it attracted its share of talent, including Renaissance painter Lucas Cranach the Elder, who lived here for 43 years. Wittenberg was also the seat of the elector of Saxony until 1547. It was here that Luther launched the Reformation in 1517, an act of the greatest importance to all of Europe.

Wittenberg can be seen in a day from Berlin, but it is well worth a longer look – especially to note the ceramic plaques around town that indicate past residents, both famous and infamous. You'll have plenty of company in summer, when thousands of Luther pilgrims come to see where it all began.

Orientation

There are two train stations: Hauptbahnhof Lutherstadt-Wittenberg is the stop for all the fast trains to/from Berlin, Leipzig, Magdeburg and Halle. Bahnhof Wittenberg-Elbtor is a minor stop for local trains. From the Hauptbahnhof, the city centre is a 15 minute stroll down Collegienstrasse.

All of the city's chief sights are within the Altstadt ring. The main street, Collegienstrasse, runs east-west through the Markt and becomes Schlossstrasse at its western end.

LUTHERSTADT-WITTENBERG

PLACES TO STAY
1 Art Hotel
2 DJH Hostel & Schloss Wittenberg
14 Pension am Schwanenteich
15 Park Inn Wittenberg
17 Gasthaus Central
25 Acron Hotel

PLACES TO EAT
4 Stadtkantine
5 Zur Schlossfreiheit
6 Zur Schwarzen Baer
8 Tante Emmas
19 Crêperie Lorette

OTHER
3 Tourist Office
7 Cranachhaus
9 Commerzbank
10 Rathaus
11 Luther & Melanchthon Statues
12 Independent
13 Stadtkirche
16 Klapsmühle
18 SSB-Com
20 Melanchthon Haus
21 Irish Harp Pub
22 Post Office
23 Lutherhaus
24 Luther's Oak

Information

Wittenberg-Information (☎ 49 86 10, fax 49 86 11, email wb_info@wittenberg.de) is at Schlossplatz 2 opposite the Schlosskirche. It's open weekdays from 9 am to 6 pm, Saturday from 10 am to 2 pm, and Sunday from 11 am to 3 pm. The regional tourist office (☎ 40 26 10) is located at Mittelstrasse 33. *The Historic Mile* (DM4.80) is a very good English-language guide to the city.

There's a Commerzbank at Markt 25 and a Hypovereinsbank at Collegienstrasse 24. The main post office, with a monument to the inventor of the telegraph, Wilhelm Weber, is at Friedrichstrasse 1. You can surf the Internet at SSB-Com, Collegienstrasse 73, for DM4 per half hour, and DM5 at weekends.

Buchhandlung Christoph Franzke (☎ 40 28 28), Collegienstrasse 82, has a small stock of English-language books. The city

library (☎ 40 21 60), Schlossstrasse 7, also has titles in English.

The biggest hospital is the Paul-Gerhardt Stiftung (☎ 500), Paul-Gerhardt-Strasse 42, 500m north-east of the centre. There's a walk-in clinic inside for everyday matters.

Lutherhaus

The Lutherhaus is a museum devoted to the Reformation, housed in a former Augustinian monastery at Collegienstrasse 54. Luther first stayed here in 1508, when he taught at Wittenberg University, and made the building his permanent home after returning in 1511. The house contains an original room furnished by Luther in 1535 and a copy of the papal bull threatening his excommunication (the original is in the state archives in Dresden). There's old graffiti, too: Russian Tsar Peter the Great signed his name above a door during a visit

Luther Lore

Martin Luther's '95 Theses' questioned Roman Catholic practices of the time, especially the selling of indulgences (or simony) to forgive sins and give the buyer reduced time in purgatory for past or even future sins. Luther's theses and questions created the Protestant church (the first one was in Wittenberg and the first service in 1522) and led to the Reformation, which changed the face of Europe.

Today hundreds of thousands make what amounts to a pilgrimage to the 'Luther town' of Wittenberg, where the great man lived and worked, and Eisleben, his place of birth and death.

Local lore and some guidebooks claim that in 1517 Luther hammered a copy of his 95 Theses to the door of Wittenberg's Schlosskirche for all to see. There's no proof either way, but he probably didn't.

Believers point to the fact that the door was used as a bulletin board of sorts by the university; that the alleged posting took place the day before the affluent congregation poured into the church on All Saints' Day (1 November), and the fact that at Luther's funeral, Philipp Melanchthon himself said he personally witnessed the deed.

But Melanchthon didn't arrive in town until 1518 – the year *after* the supposed event. It's also odd that Luther's writings never once mentioned what would have been a highly radical act.

While it's known that he sent his theses to the local archbishop to begin a discussion, some locals argue that it would have been entirely out of character for a devout monk, interested mainly in an honest debate of his points, to challenge the system so publicly and flagrantly without first exhausting all his options.

---

in 1702 (the scrawl is preserved under glass). The museum (☎ 40 26 71) is open from April to September, Tuesday to Sunday (closed Monday) from 9 am to 6 pm; the rest of the year, it's open from 10 am to 5 pm (DM7/4).

The **Luthereiche** (Luther's oak), the spot where he burned (yet another) copy of the document, is on the corner of Lutherstrasse and Am Bahnhof.

Melanchthon Haus

Philipp Melanchthon was born in 1497 at Bretten, near Heidelberg. A humanist and a master of ancient languages, he became a close friend of Martin Luther and his most eloquent advocate. He came to town in 1518 as a university lecturer and stayed until his death in 1560. Melanchthon's idea of reform went far beyond religious matters. His primary goal was to overhaul the German education system, which at that time taught entirely in Latin.

Melanchthon helped Luther translate the Bible into German from the Greek and Hebrew. Later he was heavily sought by other universities, and to keep him in town the last local elector gave him a house, at Collegienstrasse 60, in 1536.

Today the house functions as a museum (☎ 40 26 71). From April to October, it's open daily (except Monday) from 9 am to 6 pm, and the rest of the year from 10 am to 5 pm (DM5/3).

Stadtkirche St Marien

The large altarpiece in this church, designed jointly by Lucas Cranach the Elder and his son, was completed in 1547; it shows Luther, Melanchthon and other Reformation figures, as well as Cranach the Elder himself, in biblical contexts. In 1525 Luther married an ex-nun named Katherina von Bora in this church, where he also preached. Note the octagonal bronze baptismal font from the Fischer foundry. The church's altar is painted on two sides, and on the back is a representation of heaven and hell. Medieval students etched their initials into the divine section if they passed their final exams – and into purgatory if they failed.

There are also many fine paintings here; note especially *The Lord's Vineyard* by Cranach the Younger behind the altar in the south-east corner of the church.

Jewish Memorial

Outside the south-east corner of the Stadtkirche is a deplorable example of early German anti-Semitism. In 1305, to commemorate the first known expulsion of Jews from Wittenberg, the town's elders inscribed on the church facade a German translation of the most holy Hebrew words for God, partially covered by reliefs of pigs to mock the words.

On the ground below, placed here by the local church community in 1988, is a memorial to persecuted Jews and those murdered during the Holocaust. On the left and right, in Hebrew and German, is the opening line of Psalm 130: 'Out of the depths I cry unto you, O Lord'. The plaque shows water boiling through cross-shaped cracks, symbolic of guilt and reconciliation. Nearby stands a cedar tree, donated by the Jewish organisation, Children of Israel.

Corpus Christi Chapel

Just south of the Stadtkirche is the tiny Fronleichnamskapelle, which holds English-language services on Thursday at 12.30 pm and Saturday at 6.30 pm.

Cranachhaus

On one corner of the Markt, at No 4, is the house of Lucas Cranach the Elder, with a picturesque courtyard that visitors may enter. Inside is the superbly renovated **Gallerie im Cranachhaus** (π 420 19 15), which has rotating art exhibitions, and a groovy audio-visual presentation room (with shower heads for earphones).

Out the back, pick up some stern black-and-white sketches of Martin Luther in the **Historische Druckerstube**, which still sets type and prints by hand.

Schloss Wittenberg

At the western end of town is Wittenberg Castle (1499) with its huge, rebuilt **Schlosskirche** onto whose door Luther allegedly nailed his 95 Theses on 31 October 1517. The door itself was destroyed by fire in 1760 and has been replaced by a bronze memorial (1858) inscribed with the theses in Latin. Luther's tombstone lies below the pulpit, and Melanchthon's is opposite. Entry is free, but there's a German-language tour by church custodians for DM2.

Markt

On the northern side of the Markt is the **Rathaus** (1523-40), a banner example of an affluent central-German Renaissance town hall. In front of the Rathaus are two large statues. The one in the centre of the square is of Luther (1821), and on his right side is Melanchthon's (1865).

Hundertwasser Schule

North-east of the centre is the Martin-Luther-Gymnasium, the school which has been remodelled by Viennese architect Friedensreich Hundertwasser in his personal Art Deco style. It's quite a sight, with its mosque-like cupolas, bright kooky facade and roof-top vegetation. It's a 20 minute walk from the centre: go up Berliner Strasse, turn right into Schillerstrasse and it's the fourth corner on the left (at Strasse der Völkerfreundschaft.)

Organised Tours

From May to October, two-hour city tours in German start at 2 pm daily from in front of the Schlosskirche (DM10). One-hour tours in English cost DM75 for a group of up to 25 people.

Places to Stay

The nearest camping ground is *Bergwitz* (π 034921-282 28), some 11km south of town along the B100 on the Bergwitzsee, an artificial lake in a flooded mine pit. Trains leave from the Hauptbahnhof every hour (DM3, eight minutes). Go through the tunnel to Bahnhofstrasse, follow this to Walkstrasse and turn right. At the end of that street turn right, and you'll see the lake. From there it's 400m ahead on the right.

The 104 bed *DJH hostel* (☎ *40 32 55, fax 40 32 55)* is housed upstairs in Wittenberg Castle (DM20/25 for juniors/seniors, sheets DM6). It's a fun place, with table tennis and comfortable rooms.

Private rooms, for DM38 to DM76 per person, can be booked free of charge through Wittenberg-Information (☎ 41 48 48 for reservations).

Gasthaus Central (☎*/fax 41 15 72, Mittelstrasse 20)* has good bathless singles for DM61 and doubles with shower and WC for DM96.

Pension Am Schwanenteich (☎ *410 10 34, fax 40 28 07, Töpferstrasse 1)* is a very convenient, charming place with rooms for DM70 to DM80/125.

Acron Hotel (☎ *971 40, fax 971 41)* on Am Bahnhof is a shiny new budget option with rooms for DM79/99 and all amenities. It's right next to the Luther oak.

Art Hotel (☎ *46 73 10, fax 46 73 28, Puschkinstrasse 15b)*, just 300m north-west of the centre, is a semi-designer hotel with modern art exhibitions and nice rooms from DM85/110.

The lovely *Hotel Grüne Tanne* (☎ *62 90, fax 62 92 50, Am Teich 1)*, in Reinsdorf about 10 minutes drive north of town on Reinsdorfer Weg, is quiet and well organised, and has a decent restaurant. Singles range from DM78 to DM85, and doubles cost DM125.

Park Inn Wittenberg (☎ *46 10, fax 46 12 00, Neustrasse 7-10)* is a very modern business hotel with singles/doubles from DM135/165. It has big rooms, enormously friendly staff and a weird breakfast buffet.

Places to Eat

Much of the town's food scene is along Collegienstrasse. Try *Speckkuchen*, a pizza-like base topped with bacon and eggs scrambled with cream and onions. *Lutherbrot* is a scrumptious gingerbread-like concoction with chocolate and sugar icing.

The *Stadtkantine* (☎ *41 13 89, Coswigerstrasse 19)* is the best for a quick, cheap hot meal – try the stuffed pork roulade for DM6.50.

There's pub food like Irish stew and meat pies for under DM8 at the *Irish Harp Pub* (☎ *41 01 50, Collegienstrasse 71)*.

Tanta Emmas Bier-und Caféhaus (☎ *41 23 84, Markt 9)* is a cosy option for good, reasonably priced German cuisine.

Zum Schwarzen Baer (☎ *41 12 00, Schlossstrasse 2)* is a great place for snacks. Try *Bratkartoffeln* (fried potatoes with various ingredients) for DM4.50 to DM7, salads for DM7.50 to DM12, or pizzas. There's a cool pub in the back.

Creperie Lorette (☎ *40 40 45, Collegienstrasse 70)* is a charming little place with OK crepes, great salads and very friendly service – meat and fish-filled crepes are DM7.50 to DM14, vegetarian ones DM9 to DM11.

Zur Schlossfreiheit (☎ *40 29 80, Coswigerstrasse 24)* goes in for historical theme dishes, such as *Lutherschmaus* (duck in a peppery sultana sauce) for DM16.50.

Entertainment

The weekly *Wochenspiele* and the monthly *Wittenberg In* are the town's leading listing magazines.

Clubs & Bars The place to be is the *Irish Harp Pub* (see Places to Eat), with live music most weekends, great crowds and draught Guinness. *Klapsmühle* (☎ *40 00 10, Fleischerstrasse 4)* is a barn of a meat market with admission most nights under DM4 (drinks cost just 99 Pfennigs on Wednesday and Saturday). *Independent* (☎ *41 32 57, Collegienstrasse 44)* is a pub with live blues and an 'international table' (usually with English speakers) on Monday evenings.

Theatre & Classical Music The *Mitteldeutsches Landestheater* (☎ *40 20 85 for reservations, Collegienstrasse 74)* has operettas, classical music, Christmas concerts and the like. There's cabaret on offer in the **Brettl-Keller**, which has its entrance in the Schloss courtyard.

Wittenberger Kantorei is a church choir that performs at the Stadtkirche during services and at special concerts throughout the year. The Schlosskirche also has a choir and organ music every Tuesday in summer at 2.30 pm.

Getting There & Away
Lutherstadt-Wittenberg is on the main train line to Halle and Leipzig (DM16.20, one hour), and Berlin-Ostbahnhof (DM39, 1¼ hours). All the Berlin-bound trains stop at Schönefeld airport. For train tickets and times, go to the Hauptbahnhof or to Reise Welt travel agency at Markt 12.

Getting Around
The main bus station is along Mauerstrasse just west of Neustrasse; single tickets are DM1.50/0.90 for adults/children, blocks of 10 tickets are DM12/9.60.

Parking enforcement is quite stringent, so use the car parks on the fringes of the Altstadt, including the ones at Elbtor and Fleischerstrasse.

You can rent a Trabant through the private Tourismus Service Wittenberg (☎ 66 01 95), Dessauer Strasse 37. The cost is DM35/120/180 per hour/five hours/full day, or DM397 per person as part of a three day 'Trabi Safari' through the region, including accommodation and meals. You ain't lived till you've driven a plastic car.

AROUND LUTHERSTADT-WITTENBERG
Ferropolis
Some 24km south-west of the city is Ferropolis, one of eastern Germany's most fascinating destinations and one of the weirdest things you'll ever see.

Built on Golpa North, an unsightly openpit lignite coal mine, Ferropolis is now a technology museum and is being set up as an outdoor concert venue for up to 25,000 people – against the backdrop of some of the most hideous equipment ever devised.

Coal mining has played an enormous role in Saxony-Anhalt's history. The idea, conceived and executed by the Bauhaus school in Dessau, was to create a monument to the bravery of the miners, point out the ecological impact of the operations, and symbolise the changes wrought by industrial society. Today it's billed as an 'industrial garden realm' and Germany's largest openair technical museum.

By the time you read this, the pitted moonscape created by the strip mining will have been filled with water diverted from the Elbe – transforming one of the world's ugliest holes into one of its most interesting swimming holes. The blueprint is by Jonathan Park, the English designer who turned a rusting Ruhr-area plant into a work of art.

The equipment alone is worth the trip. The monstrously huge machines (with charming names like Mad Max, Big Wheel and Medusa) look like they were dispatched from some post-apocalyptic nightmare. If things go as planned, you'll be able to climb all over it. Admission is DM5/4.

Organised Tours For organised (two hour) tours of the site, call Ferropolis' office (☎ 034953-351 20) or the Bauhaus (☎ 0340-650 82 40). For concert information, check with the Dessau tourist office.

Getting There & Away If driving, take the B100 to its junction with the B107 in Gräfenhainichen and turn north; the entrance is on the right.

There's a bus link from Dessau train station (direction: Gräfenhainichen) to the Ferropolis gate (DM5 one-way, DM7.50 return, 30 minutes). From there, it's a dusty 2km walk into the grounds. Car park shuttles and direct train services from Dessau and Lutherstadt-Wittenberg are planned.

Wörlitz Schloss & Park
Some 15km west of Lutherstadt-Wittenberg is Schloss Wörlitz (1769-73) and its absolutely charming, 112-hectare Englishstyle park, a wonderful place to get away

from it all, with bike tracks, footpaths and hand-cranked ferries making quick jaunts (DM1/0.50) across the lake throughout the summer. Wörlitz-Information (☎ 034905-202 16, fax 217 04), Am Neuen Wall 103 just inside the town gate, will give you a free map of the grounds.

The park was constructed between 1764 and 1800 by Prince Leopold III, a duke of Saxony-Anhalt. Centred on the large Wörlizer See, the park has a wealth of formal gardens dotted with follies, including a **Venus Temple** and a **Pantheon**.

Admission is free, but several buildings around the grounds charge for entry. The classical **Schloss** was designed as a country house for Prince Leopold; considering the grand columns, the interior is surprisingly modest. You can take a guided tour from May to September daily from 10 am to 6 pm (DM6/4). Just east of the Schloss is the **Bibelturm** church; its tower offers a splendid view (DM3/2).

You can take a 45 minute **gondola tour** that departs as soon as eight people or more gather at the dock (DM8/5). Every summer there are weekend **concerts** on the lakeshore.

Getting There & Away Getting here using public transport from Lutherstadt-Wittenberg is a pain; by train you need to go to Dessau, change from the Dessau Hauptbahnhof to the Dessau Wörlitzer Bahnhof and then connect with another train. The journey takes two hours and costs DM20.

If you're under your own steam, take the B187 west to the B107 and turn south, which brings you right into town. *Don't* park at the huge car park by the lake, which charges DM6/2 for cars/motorbikes; there's another for DM1 per hour at the town gate.

DESSAU
☎ 0340 • pop 87,000

Dessau became a mecca for modern artists when the Bauhaus moved here in 1925 (see 'The Bauhaus' boxed text). One of Germany's first medieval settlements, it was a centre of the German Enlightenment in the 18th century under Prince Leopold III, who

framed the place in classical palaces, lakes and English-style parks. (His grandfather Leopold I was another creative spirit, having invented marching-in-step for Prussian troops and the steel ramrod).

The Renaissance-era town centre was devastated in WWII, and the city was rebuilt along uncompromising Stalinist lines. But key Bauhaus creations have been restored, and the green belt around town holds a wealth of undervisited castles, follies and unspoilt woodlands.

Orientation & Information

The town is just south of the confluence of the Elbe and Mulde rivers. Trams run southwest from the Hauptbahnhof to the Kavalierstrasse (B184), the main north-south artery, which borders on the old town centre to the east. The Bauhaus Building is a five minute walk west of the train station.

The tourist office (☎ 204 2242, fax 204 29 42, email touristinfo@net.stadt-dessau.de) is in the Rathaus, Zerbsterstrasse 4, a 10 minute walk down Antoinettestrasse and across Kavalierstrasse. The friendly staff sells the three day Dessau Card (DM15), which allows unlimited travel on buses and trams and free entry to several museums (but not the Bauhaus). Also pick up the useful *Bauhaus Architecture in Dessau*, a map pamphlet with all the major buildings.

There's a Dresdner Bank in the Rathaus-Center shopping mall at Ratsgasse 2. Here you'll also find the Karstadt department store with a Cyberb@r (☎ 252 90) on the top floor for Internet access (DM5 per half hour). The beautiful neo-Gothic post office is on the corner of Friedrichstrasse and Kavalierstrasse.

The Klinikum Dessau (☎ 50 10), Auenweg 38, is the town's main hospital.

To wash your smalls, try the SB-Waschsalon (☎ 220 1196), Stiftstrasse 18.

Bauhausgebäude

The Bauhaus Building is a touchstone of modern architecture on Gropiusallee, a five minute walk west of the Hauptbahnhof via Schwabestrasse and Bauhausstrasse. The

The Bauhaus

The most influential force in 20th century architecture was the Bauhaus. Founded in Weimar in 1919 by Berlin architect Walter Gropius, the Bauhaus School aimed to unite art with everyday function, from doorknobs and radiators to the layout of entire districts and apartment blocks. The movement attracted some of the era's most talented painters and architects, including Paul Klee, Wassily Kandinsky, Piet Mondrian, Lionel Feininger and Oskar Schlemmer.

Gropius' radical ideas raised too many eyebrows in Weimar and in 1925, the Bauhaus relocated to Dessau, where he built the Cubist headquarters of the Hochschule für Gestaltung (Institute for Design). Here the Bauhaus enjoyed its most fruitful phase, as disciples peppered Dessau with Bauhaus structures and mass-marketed their successes – simple but elegant lamps, chairs and wallpaper, to name a few items. Stuttgart even built the Weissenhof estate in this minimalist style; the suburb had clean lines, flat roofs and airy bay windows.

In 1932 the Bauhaus moved to Berlin to escape oppression by the Nazis, who claimed that it undermined traditional values (How could a flat roof be German? they asked). The school was dissolved by the Third Reich in 1933 and its leading lights fled the country. After WWII, the Bauhaus was hailed as the cutting edge of modern architecture but its chief followers remained in exile, creating cultural icons such as Wilhelm Wagenfeld's devastatingly chic desk lamp (a trinket in the Bauhaus Museum shop, at DM698).

three-sectioned ensemble of glass, steel and concrete was built in 1925-26 by Bauhaus director Walter Gropius as the new headquarters of the Hochschule für Gestaltung, the architectural school that put classrooms, workshops and residences under one roof. The interior was designed by Bauhaus disciples, and every detail adheres to the philosophy of 'form follows function' – even down to the doorknob recesses, which replaced conventional buffers. The work done here has inspired countless buildings around the world.

The Bauhaus was damaged during WWII and rather clumsily restored in 1975-76. Still, the design remains fascinating for its elegance, simplicity and timelessness. There are regular exhibitions in the workshop wing, including graphics, photos and furniture, including Ludwig Mies von der Rohe's celebrated cantilever chair. Hours are Tuesday to Sunday from 10 am to 6 pm (DM5/3). Call ☎ 650 82'51 for details of what's on.

Other Bauhaus structures around town include the **Meisterhäuser**, an estate five minutes walk to the north-west on Ebertallee. It originally consisted of three sets of semi-detached houses for senior Bauhaus staff and a detached one for director Gropius (which was destroyed in the war). Of them, the **Feiningerhaus** was restored in 1992-94 and today houses the **Kurt-Weill-Zentrum** (☎ 619 595), which is an exhibit on the work of Kurt Weill, the Dessau-born composer of the *Three-Penny Opera* and other collaborations with Bertolt Brecht. It's open Tuesday from 2 to 4 pm, Thursday from 10 am to noon and Saturday from 2 to 5 pm (DM5/3).

A further 15 minute walk north on Elballee, at a bend in the Elbe, stands the **Kornhaus**, a beer-and-dance hall designed by Carl Flieger, a Gropius assistant. Refurbished in 1996, the place is now a terraced restaurant with fine views of the river (see Places to Eat). Take tram No 1 north to Damaschkastrasse.

Georgium

For a pastoral counterpoint to Bauhaus, visit the Georgium, a sprawling 18th century park north-west of the Hauptbahnhof. At its heart stands the neoclassical **Schloss**; this houses the **Anhalt Art Gallery**, with a range of paintings by the old masters, including works by Rubens and Cranach the Elder. The museum (☎ 61 38 74) is open Tuesday to Sunday from 10 am to 5 pm (DM5/3). The leafy grounds, dotted as they are with ponds and fake ruins, make for a pleasant stroll. At the eastern side of the park is the **Lehrpark**, an educational garden and zoo with a huge domed **mausoleum**.

City Centre

Much of the Altstadt was pulverised by WWII bombs, leaving just a few old buildings worthy of inspection. The Markt offers the **Rathaus**, which was rebuilt in simplified form after the war; the carillon plays the Dessau March daily at noon.

Nearby is the **Marienkirche**, a late Gothic hall structure with Renaissance elements. Rebuilt in 1989-94, the church holds frequent concerts, and the tower can be ascended (DM1).

Places to Stay

Campingplatz Adria (*☎/fax 216 09 45, Mildensee*), 6km east of the centre on the B185, charges from DM4 for tents and DM6 per adult. There are laundry and sports facilities, including a lake swimming area and boat rentals. Take bus B or G from the Hauptbahnhof.

The **Jugendherberge Dessau** (*☎/fax 61 94 52, Waldkaterweg 11*), 3km west of the Hauptbahnhof in a wooded spot, charges DM21/26 for juniors/seniors, including breakfast.

The tourist office books *private rooms* free of charge, from DM30 per person (☎ 194 33).

The **Pension Damm** (*☎/fax 61 62 95, R Schirrmacher-Strasse 18*) is a nice place 1.5km from the centre, with a garden, sauna and solarium. Rates start at DM60/90 for singles/doubles.

Pension Bürgerhaus (*☎/fax 220 45 28, Mendelssohnstrasse 43*) asks DM69/99 for rooms, all equipped with private shower and WC.

The **Hotel-Pension An den Sieben Säulen** (*☎ 61 96 20, fax 61 96 22, Ebertallee 66*) is located in a villa opposite the Feinigerhaus, and charges from DM90/120 (all rooms with mod cons).

Hotel Astron (*☎ 251 40, fax 251 41 00, Zerbster Strasse 29*) is a comfortable, modern place close to the Rathaus, with rooms with all amenities from DM120/150.

Steigenberger Hotel (*☎ 251 50, fax 251 51 77, Friedensplatz*) is the top luxury option a minute's walk from the Hauptbahnhof, with great service and very stylish rooms from DM131/192.

Places to Eat

For snacks and fast food, you should try the Rathaus-Center. On the ground floor you'll find the popular **Stendaler Landbäckerei**, with scrumptious filled rolls for DM3.60. Nearby is the **Bey's Grill**, with half-chickens for DM2.95; and next door, *Pizza Pasta* sells its headline dishes from DM6.

The **Klub im Bauhaus** (*☎ 650 84 21, Gropiusallee*) is a hip student cafe in the basement, selling breakfast, pastas and other light dishes for under DM10.

Dessauer Bierstuben (*☎ 220 59 09, Hobuschgasse 2*) offers good German dishes such as pork loin in lemon-butter sauce (DM19.50). Most mains cost under DM20.

Jägerklause (*☎ 858 13 67, Alte Leipziger Strasse 76*) in the Törten district, specialises in game dishes, with mains averaging about DM22.

Kornhaus (*☎ 640 41 41, Kornhausstrasse 146*) is Bauhaus and culinary excellence rolled into one. (See also the earlier Bauhausgebäude section.) The steamed salmon and asparagus with hollandaise sauce we had was yummy (DM26).

Getting There & Around

Dessau is almost equidistant from Leipzig, Halle and Magdeburg (all DM14.80, one hour). The Berlin-Munich autobahn A9 runs just east of town.

Most of the sights are easily reached on foot, but bus/tram tickets cost DM2.50/1.50 for regular/short journeys. Fahrradverleih Dieter Becker (☎ 216 01 13), Coswiger Strasse 47, rents bicycles from DM10 per day.

HALLE
☎ 0345 • pop 270,000

Saxony-Anhalt's former state capital and its largest city, Halle, is about as romantic as a crime scene in a coal field. Grimy and crumbling buildings, dilapidated roads and smog-filled air are about what you'd expect of a city that was the centre of the GDR's chemical industry.

But there's a spark of life in Halle that belies its dreadful reputation. The city's keen preservation of historical landmarks – including those from the GDR days – reflects both restraint and a sense of humour.

First mentioned in 806, Halle was a powerful religious and financial centre – an important market town, a major salt producer and home to an archbishop. Its university merged with, and finally absorbed, the one in Lutherstadt-Wittenberg in 1817. The city was seat of the GDR's Halle district but its Communist links backfired after reunification, when Magdeburg became capital of Saxony-Anhalt.

Orientation
The main sights are all within spitting distance of the Ringstrasse, which marks the boundary of the former city walls. The Hauptbahnhof is to the south-east of the centre, west of Riebeck Platz. The Altstadt – the centre of town – is bordered by a rough ring road, collectively referred to as the Stadt Ring.

To walk to the city centre from the Hauptbahnhof, head through the underpass (Der Tunnel) and along pedestrianised Leipziger Strasse past the 15th century Leipziger Turm to the Markt, Halle's central square.

Information
Tourist Office The tourist office (☎ 202 33 40, fax 50 27 98, email Halle-Tourist@ t-online.de) is in the elevated gallery built around the Roter Turm in the middle of the Markt. It's open weekdays from 9 am to 7 pm (from 10 am on Wednesday), and on weekends from 10 am to 2 pm (closed Sunday in winter).

The office sells one/three-day HalleCard passes, covering public transport and most museums, for DM9/25. It also runs guided 1½ hour tram tours weekdays at 2 pm, Saturday at 11 am and 1.30 pm, and Sunday at 4 pm (DM10/7).

The German Automobile Association (ADAC; ☎ 202 64 93) has an office at Joliot-Curie-Platz 1a.

Money There's a Reisebank at the Hauptbahnhof, and Commerzbank branches at Leipziger Strasse 11 and on Markt.

Post & Communications The central post office is at Hansering 19, at the northeast corner of the Altstadt. There's a branch at the Hauptbahnhof. The Cyberb@r (☎ 862 80) in the Karstadt department store on Mansfelder Strasse charges DM5 per half hour on the Web (take tram No 9 to Mansfelder Strasse).

Internet Resources Events and hotel listings (in German and English) can be found at the town's Web site, www.halle.de.

Bookshops Haus des Buches (☎ 298 70), Marktplatz 2, has English-language novels.

Laundry Das Waschhaus (☎ 522 06 11) is a coin-operated laundrette on the corner of Richard-Wagner-Strasse and Böckstrasse.

Medical Services Ärztekammer Sachsen-Anhalt (☎ 388 09 36) is a clinic at Am Kirchtor 9. There are pharmacies at the Hauptbahnhof and the Markt.

Dangers & Annoyances Undesirables hang around the Hauptbahnhof at all hours. Use common sense in Der Tunnel, which runs between the station and the eastern end of Leipziger Strasse.

Protected Eyesores
The city is casting an interesting light on several GDR-era eyesores that it has decided to preserve. The legalisation of graffiti in **Der Tunnel** has attracted artists – some

excellent – from all over the country. At the eastern end of Der Tunnel in Riebeck Platz is **Die Faust** (The Fist), a goofy GDR-era monument to workers' pride that looks like a pulled tooth.

You can visit the **Stasi Archives** (☎ 64 40 63 or ☎ 66 10 74), Gemritzer Damm 4, on weekdays from 9 am to 4 pm, and Tuesday to 6 pm (free entry).

Markt

Halle's large Markt is punctuated by the 19th century **statue of Georg Friedrich Händel**, the celebrated composer born here in 1685, and the misleadingly named **Roter Turm** (Red Tower; 1506), which was once a courthouse, and now houses the tourist office and an art gallery. The tower is actually sooty in colour and the gallery below is surely one of the worst GDR offences ever perpetrated on a medieval structure.

Just south at Grosse Märker Strasse 10 is the **City Historical Museum** (☎ 202 62 43), with rotating exhibitions and a permanent display on the life of mathematician and physicist Christian Wolff. It's open daily from 10 am to 5 pm, and to 8 pm on Thursday (DM2/1).

Marktkirche

The four tall towers of the Marktkirche (1529) loom above the western end of the Markt. The late-Gothic hall church has a folding altar painted at the workshop of Lucas Cranach the Elder. There's a Romanesque bronze baptismal font, and two spectacular organs (Händel first doodled his *Messiah* on the smaller one). The chief treasure is the **death mask of Martin Luther**, cast when Luther's body was placed here for the night on its way back to Wittenberg for burial. It's locked in the chamber behind the altar (ask to see it during a city tour).

The church is open daily. There are organ concerts on Tuesday and Thursday at 4 pm, and services on Sunday at 10 am.

Händelhaus

Händelhaus (☎ 50 09 00), Grosse Nikolai Strasse 5-6, was the composer's birthplace

and now houses a collection of musical instruments. Händel left Halle in 1703 and, after stays in Hamburg, Hanover and Italy, resided in London from 1712 to his death in 1759. It was here he achieved his great fame. There's a Händel Festival during the first week of June. The house is open daily from 9.30 am to 5.30 pm (DM4/0.50). On Thursday, it's open to 7.30 pm (free).

Schloss Moritzburg

On Friedemann Bach Platz is the 15th century Moritzburg castle, a former residence of the archbishops of Magdeburg that contains a museum of 19th and 20th century art. It includes works by Edvard Munch and Johanna Schutz-Wolff, as well as a sculpture collection. It's open Tuesday from 11 am to 8.30 pm and Wednesday to Sunday from 10 am to 6 pm (closed Monday). Admission is DM5/3, but it's free on Tuesday. The **Maria Magdalenekapelle** across the courtyard is also worth a look, and if you're lucky you'll hear a choral recital.

Places to Stay

The municipal *Am Nordbad Campingplatz* (☎ 523 40 85, Am Nordbad 12) is near the Saale River on the northern edge of town. It's open from early May until late September. Sites are DM2, plus DM8 per person and DM8 per car. Take tram No 2 from the Hauptbahnhof and tram No 3 from the Markt to Am Nordbad.

The 72 bed *DJH hostel* (☎/fax 202 47 16, August-Bebel-Strasse 48a) in the town centre charges DM22/27 for juniors/seniors (including breakfast).

For *private rooms* (from DM30 per person), contact the tourist office's booking department (☎ 202 83 71). Otherwise, it's lean pickings for budget accommodation.

The *Pension Am Markt* (☎ 521 14 11, fax 523 29 56, Schmeerstrasse 3) is a well tended place with rates from DM85/110 for single/double rooms (including breakfast). Ask for a back room, away from the noisy trams.

The small *Kaffeehaus Sasse Hotel* (☎ 23 33 80, fax 283 63 55, Geiststrasse 22) near the Thalia Theater has rooms with shower and WC for DM95/135.

Akzent Hotel Am Wasserturm (☎ 298 20, fax 512 65 43, Lessingstrasse 8) is a bit away from the action but still a good deal, with rooms from DM99/140.

The sparkling *Steigenberger Esprix Hotel (☎ 693 16 00, fax 693 16 26, Neustädter Passage 5)* is the 'budget' version of the business-class hotel chain, with rooms costing from DM127/157.

The central *Dorint Hotel Charlottenhof (☎ 292 30, fax 292 31 00, Dorotheenstrasse 12)* has a fair amount of frills (including air-conditioning). Rooms start at DM189/224.

Places to Eat
Restaurants & Cafes The *Zum Schad (☎ 522 04 41, Reilstrasse 10)* is a brewery-restaurant with a nice ambience and a menu of hearty meat dishes. Smaller portions are available for around DM10.

The *Strieses Biertunnel (☎ 512 59 48, Grosse Ulrichstrasse 51)*, around the corner from the Neues Theater, serves bohemian food until midnight and has many beers on tap. *Gasthof zum Mohr (☎ 520 00 33, Burgstrasse 1)*, right on the Saale River across from Giebichstein castle, is quite popular with students.

Drei Kaiser (☎ 203 18 68, Berg 1), just off Kleine Ulrichstrasse, is our favourite place in town, with lots of bric-a-brac and fantastic service. One speciality is *ofenfrischer Brotlaib*, a cholesterol feast of smoked pork, white wine and *creme fraiche* baked in a hollow loaf (DM19).

The *Café Nöö (☎ 202 16 51, Grosse Klausstrasse 11)* is a cool haunt frequented by lots of locals, near the old cathedral.

In summer, other popular cafes that spill out onto the pavement include *Café Deix (☎ 522 71 61, Seebener 175)* and the pubby *Gosenschänke (☎ 523 35 94, Burg 71)*.

Fast Food Fast-food offerings are mostly along Leipziger Strasse, including a *Nordsee* at No 20 and the hugely popular *Eis Café Venezie*. Pizza and sausage vendors usually occupy the Markt, and the *Markthof*

(Grosse Ulrichstrasse 52) houses a bakery, an Asia Imbiss, pizza and Wurst stands and more, with lots of stuff under DM5.

Entertainment
Fritz is the most popular free monthly magazine. *Halle Blitz* is its competitor.

Pubs & Bars The *Miller's American Bar (☎ 202 53 33, Dorotheenstrasse 12)* is a Tex-Mex cocktail bar with occasional live music. There's copious beer-guzzling at the *Paulaner Keller (☎ 208 37 09, Waisenhausring 3)*, and also at *Strieses Biertunnel* (see Places to Eat).

The *Bulli (☎ 203 30 63, Sternstrasse 8)* has a cosy atmosphere and good, cheap drinks. *Don Camillo (☎ 304 17 41, Sternstrasse 3)*, almost opposite, is a quirky place that encourages you to confess your sins over big glasses of beer.

The *Potemkin (☎ 0177-666 66 78, Kleine Ulrichstrasse 25)* is another gem, with canned jazz music and furnished with comfy old padded chairs. Look out for the Cyrillic lettering in the front.

Theatre & Classical Music The best drama is staged at the *Neues Theater (☎ 205 02 22/23, Grosse Ulrichstrasse 50)*, and *Steintor Varieté Halle (☎ 208 02 05, Am Steintor)*, with variety and visiting shows.

Large concerts are held at the *Opernhaus Halle (☎ 51 00, Universitätsring 24)* and at the *Konzerthalle Ulrichskirche (☎ 202 89 36, Kleine Brauhausstrasse 26)*, home to the city's philharmonic orchestra. The brand-new, 1900-seat *Händel-Halle (☎ 292 90, Salzgrafenplatz 1)* hosts everything from music festivals to dance contests.

Rock & Jazz There's live rock music and jazz at *Easy Schorre (☎ 21 22 40, Philipp-Müller-Strasse 77-78)*, *Objekt 5 (☎ 522 00 16, Seebener Strasse 5)* and the *Turm (☎ 202 51 90, Kleine Ulrichstrasse 24a)*. Huge concerts fill the *Eissporthalle (☎ 690 22 74, Gimmritzer Damm 1)*, and other events take place at the *Wunder Tüte (☎ 550 04 63, Wörmlitzer Strasse 109)*.

Getting There & Away

Air Leipzig-Halle airport lies between both cities, which are about 25km apart. Because of Leipzig, the airport is a major link with Frankfurt and Munich, and also has services to other major German and European cities.

Train Leipzig and Halle are linked by hourly StadtExpress shuttle trains (DM9.80, 30 minutes). Halle is also on the fast train route from Magdeburg (DM19, 1¼ hours), Erfurt (DM29, 1½ hours) and Berlin-Zoo (DM48, two hours). Trains also come from Dresden (DM50, 1¾ hours), direct or via Leipzig. There are local trains to Eisleben (DM9.80, 35 minutes) and Lutherstadt-Wittenberg (DM16.20, one hour).

Car & Motorcycle From Leipzig, take the A14 west to the B100, and then west again to the B91. The B71 runs directly between Halle and Magdeburg. The B91 runs south from Halle and links to the A9 autobahn, which connects Munich and Berlin.

A ride-share agency, The Orange (☎ 294 22 83) is at Kleine Märker Strasse 7a.

Getting Around

To/From Airport Bus No 300 runs every 30 minutes during the day and less frequently at night between the airport and the Hauptbahnhof. The fare is DM10. Taxis cost about DM50.

Public Transport If you're not getting run over by Halle's trams they can be handy; bus and tram tickets cost DM1.50 for short rides of under 10 minutes and DM2.40 for others, and day tickets cost DM7.

Car & Motorcycle The one-way street system is fiendishly complex, and general traffic overload means you won't get anywhere quickly. The best bet is to look for parking near the Hauptbahnhof and walk.

LUTHERSTADT-EISLEBEN
☎ 03475 • pop 24,500

While Wittenberg was Luther's workplace, his heart and soul belonged in Eisleben.

This pleasant old mining town 30km west of Halle is where Luther was born and, after he'd shaken up the establishment, where he went to die. Eisleben (as it's still commonly known, despite the official prefix) is therefore a must on any Reformation-led itinerary. Any which way you turn it's Luther, Luther, Luther, from the churches and monuments down to the elongated Lutherbrot biscuits sold in local shops.

Orientation & Information

Most of Eisleben's sights are knotted together around the Markt, which lies just south-west of the Hallesche Strasse-Freistrasse (B80), the main thoroughfare. From the train station, it's a 10 minute walk north up Bahnhofsring and Bahnhofstrasse to the old market. The bus station is just north of the Altstadt on Klosterplatz.

The tourist office (☎ 60 21 24, fax 60 26 34) is at Bahnhofstrasse 36 on the corner of Hallesche Strasse; hours are weekdays from 10 am to 5 pm (Tuesday till 6 pm) and Saturday from 9 am to noon. There's a big Dresdner Bank at Am Markt 29, virtually on Freistrasse. The main post office is on the corner of Poststrasse and Schlossplatz.

Markt & Churches

The focal point of the Markt is the **Luther monument** (unveiled only in 1883), depicting the reformer as a sterner, less pudgy figure than in familiar paintings. At its base are four reliefs, one showing Luther strumming a lute among his family.

The Markt inclines uphill past the 16th century **Rathaus** to the **Andreaskirche**, a late Gothic hall church where Luther delivered his last sermons in 1546. Seen from the north side, it's an impressive sight, with the two large west towers paling in the shadow of an even bigger main spire. In the aisles are busts of Luther and Philip Melanchthon, both of whom were buried in Wittenberg, and to one side is Luther's **pulpit**, a relatively simple affair.

A stone's throw south of the tourist office is the **St Petri Pauli Kirche** (Church of Sts Peter and Paul), the church where Luther

Vista through to the Zwinger courtyard, Dresden

Fischmarkt with Gildehaus and street cafe, Erfurt

Goethe says to Schiller: 'I've had a great idea for an epic poem. Two guys walk into a bar ...', Weimar

Art Nouveau door, Nietzsche Archives, Weimar

Goslar building, with all the trimmings

The quaint fishing village of Warnemünde, where the Warnow River meets the Baltic Sea

was baptised. The chalky white columns and ribbed vault lend the place a light, airy feel. An oddity is the late Gothic **altar** dedicated to Saint Anne, Jesus' grandmother. She's also the patron saint of mining, and the altar panel depicts a group of shepherds as miners. Luther's baptismal font was destroyed, but remains of the original were built into the one we see today (1817).

Roughly 10 minutes west of Markt is the **St Annenkirche**, which was the miners' church. Luther stayed in the monk's quarters while he was district vicar. The church's most arresting feature is the *Steinbilder-Bibel* (stone-picture Bible; 1585), the only one of its kind in Europe, consisting of 29 sandstone reliefs and Old Testament scenes. Check out the pulpit here, too: rarely have Bible stories been illustrated with such obvious hilarity.

Note that all churches in town are locked from noon to 3 pm.

Luther Museums

A few steps north of the tourist office at Seminarstrasse 16 is **Luthers Geburtshaus** (Luther's birth house; ☎ 60 27 75), which goes through Luther's ancestry and upbringing in agonising detail. It claims to be Germany's oldest historical museum, having been a Luther memorial since 1693. In the forecourt is a bust of the reformer by Johann Gottfried Schadow, and just to the left on Seminarstrasse is an amusing bluish relief of – guess who – on the rear wall of the museum (DM4/2).

On Andreaskirchplatz is also **Luthers Sterbehaus** (Luther's death house; ☎ 60 22 85), where the reformer died on 18 February 1546. The Luther family owned a copperworks, and the patriarch had come to settle a contract dispute with local nobles. Already ill, Luther found the talks a strain but concluded them successfully on 17 February, only to expire a few hours later. The refurbished museum shows Luther's 16th century living quarters and death chamber, including copies of his plaster death mask and last testimony. Entry is DM4/2, but a combination ticket including Luthers Geburtshaus costs

DM6/3. Both museums are open from 9 am to noon and 2 to 5 pm.

Places to Stay & Eat

The *Seeburger See* camp site (☎ 034774-282 81), on the north side of the Süsser lake about 15km east of Eisleben, charges DM5 for sites and DM3 per adult. Take bus No 361 to Seeburg; it's a 10 minute walk west along the lakeshore.

The tourist office books accommodation for free. *Pension Morgenstern* (☎ 60 28 22, Hallesche Strasse 18), right by Luther's birth house, charges DM58/88 for nice singles/doubles with all the amenities. Ask for a room at the back, away from the noisy street.

The *Parkhotel* (☎ 540, fax 253 19, Bahnhofstrasse 12) has leafy views and modern singles/doubles from DM65/85, with private shower/WC.

For a snack, *Döner-Kebap (Hallesche Strasse 18)* offers big doners for DM4. There are also several *bakeries* and *butcher shops* on the Markt selling tasty filled rolls and pastries.

Mansfelder Hof (☎ 66 90, Hallesche Strasse 33) is lacking a bit in atmosphere but serves good local dishes averaging DM20.

Stadtgraben, in the so-named city park, is a great beer garden with schnitzels from DM12.

Getting There & Away

There are trains to Halle (DM9.80, 35 minutes), Leipzig (DM19.40, 70 minutes), Erfurt (DM24.40, 1½ hours) and Weimar (DM34, two hours). Bus No 361 goes regularly to/from Halle Hauptbahnhof (DM7.20, 40 minutes).

Eisleben is a half hour drive east of Halle on the B80.

Saale-Unstrut Region

The Saale and Unstrut (pronounced 'zah-leh' and 'oon-shtroot') rivers converge in a valley just north of Naumburg. The valley is

Wine & Apples

The Saale-Unstrut region has more than 750 vineyards, producing excellent, crisp white wines and let's just say, 'tangy' reds.

The Saale-Unstrut Weinbauverband (☎ 034462-202 12) has come up with the *Weinstrasse* (Vineyard Road). In any *Weingut* (vineyard) along it, you can sample the local product free. Or, for a fee of between DM5 and DM15, you can drink up to six large glasses accompanied by bread and cheese and a history of the vineyard. From tourist offices in the region pick up copies of *Weinstrasse – Land der Burgen* (DM6.80), a regional map that indicates the Vineyard Road as well as bicycle paths, and *Weinbau Saale-Unstrut* (DM1), a vineyard guide with tour and tasting prices.

There's something magical about riding a bike and stopping for wine tasting – you can rent bikes in Naumburg or Freyburg. If you plan to do some serious tasting, there's a ferry running from the Blütengrund camp site to Freyburg (see the Freyburg section).

The Saale-Unstrut region is also locally famous for its apples, and in the autumn they are everywhere.

The best apples and honey in the region are available from August to June, along with potatoes, other vegetables and fruit juices at the recently privatised Agrar-und Absatzgenossenschaft Naumburg (☎ 70 29 76), at the northern end of Naumburg on the road out to Henne.

Europe's northernmost wine-growing area, and in summer it's breathtakingly quaint. Its bicycle and hiking paths meander through rolling, castle-topped hills, there's horseback riding along the Saale, and the Vineyard Road that runs through here makes an irresistible one or two-day stopover for exploring and wine tasting.

The vineyards – many of them tiny family-owned operations – make some very good tipple, and if you're here between June and September you'll almost certainly run into a wine festival. Freyburg's do, which takes place on the second weekend in September, is the largest in eastern Germany.

You can find accommodation throughout the region, but Naumburg makes a good base; it has the most hotels, restaurants, camping sites and hostels, and it's within 8km of all the major sights and attractions, with frequent bus and train service to everything of interest.

This is the real eastern Germany, as yet relatively untouched by rampant westernisation. Things move slowly, prices stay lower and the people take the time to open up and welcome you. Although they're renovating and cleaning up the place, it's going to take at least another decade before you stop seeing crumbling buildings along cobblestone lanes in towns that are still heated by coal and wood stoves.

NAUMBURG
☎ 03445 • pop 31,500

Naumburg is one of those pretty little medieval towns for which Germany is so famous. Once a powerful market town and member of the Hanseatic League, it's best known for its exquisite cathedral. Naumburg's charms lie in its lovely buildings, friendly people and general accessibility. Its claims to fame are brief visits by Martin Luther (he stayed, preached, drank and taught here twice), and the fact that it was, for several years, the residence of Friedrich Nietzsche.

The town goes absolutely barking on the last weekend in June with the Kirsch Fest, held at the Vogelwiese at the south-east end of town. It celebrates the unlikely story, dating from the Middle Ages, of the lifting of a blockade by Czech soldiers when their leader, Prokop, gave in to requests by the town's children, dressed in their Sunday finest, to please leave and let the townfolk eat again.

Naumburg is a perfect base for exploring the region, but even if you can only make it a day trip from Halle or Leipzig, it's definitely worth putting on your itinerary.

Orientation & Information

The train station is 1.5km north-west of the old town. You can walk into town along Rossbacher Strasse, visiting Naumburg's famous cathedral along the way, or take bus Nos 1 and 2 from the train station to the Markt, Naumburg's central square. The Zentral Omnibus Busbahnhof (ZOB), or bus station, is at the north-eastern end of town on Hallesische Strasse.

Naumburg's helpful tourist office (☎ 20 16 14, fax 26 60 47, email stadt.naumburg@ t-online.de), Markt 6, is open from 9 am to 1 pm and 2 to 6 pm on weekdays, and from 10 am to 4 pm on Saturday (closed Sunday). It offers a room referral service, sells theatre tickets and also has a good range of information material.

There's a privately run service called Naumburg-Tourist (☎/fax 20 25 14) – more of a souvenir shop, really – in the shadow of the Dom at Steinweg 3 and at Steinweg 15 (same hours as above, but also open 10 am to noon and 1 to 4 pm on Sunday).

The main post office is just north of Marientor, and there's a Hypovereinsbank at Markt 9.

Dom

In the ancient western quarter of town stands the magnificent late-Romanesque/ early-Gothic Cathedral of Saints Peter and Paul. The cloister, crypt, sculptures and four tall towers of this great medieval complex are unique; the west rood screen and choir are adorned with a series of sculptures by the anonymous Master of Naumburg, and the choir includes the celebrated 13th-century **statues of Uta and Ekkehard**, along with the other founders of the cathedral. When looking at the statues, note Uta's crafty little smile.

The first, fourth and fifth stained-glass windows here date to 1250-60 and are considered some of the most valuable in the whole country.

Children and adults fall in love with the **banisters** – made by Magdeburg artist Heinrich Apel – of the staircases at the east and west sides of the crypt.

An informative, if droning, tour (in German) is included in the admission price (DM6/4, children DM3), but you can also walk around on your own.

Behind the Dom is a half-forgotten **park** with duck ponds and leafy paths – ideal for a picnic.

Marientor & Markt

The ruins of the city's medieval defence system are crowned by the newly renovated Marientor at **Marienplatz**, at the northern end of the city. The brick tower has a walled-in area that's used for concerts, puppet shows and film evenings in summer.

Walking south down Marienstrasse, passing the **Marien-Magdalen-Kirche**, on the right you'll see the 16th century **Samson-Portal**, a doorway with carvings of Samson and the Lion (above) and Sts Peter and Paul (below), at No 12a.

Marienstrasse twists to the right and leads into the Markt, which is dominated by the ornate **Rathaus** on the western side. The **Schlösschen**, home to the tourist office, is on the southern side, and the **Portal von 1680** is at the eastern end. All three are examples of a style known as Naumburg Renaissance. Closest to the southern side is a **statue of St Wenzel**.

The late 15th century **Hohe Lilie**, the white-gabled Gothic structure at the north-western end of the Markt along Herrenstrasse, houses the town museum.

Stadtkirche St Wenzel

This Gothic church, built between 1218 and 1523, has a 76m-high tower that rises above the southern end of the Markt. Inside, surprisingly enough, is a baroque interior complete with a Hildebrand baroque organ, a bronze Gothic baptismal font, and two paintings by Cranach the Elder: *The Adoration of the Three Magi* (1522) and *The Blessing of the Children* (1529). Visitors can climb the tower Wednesday to Sunday from 10 am to 1 pm and 2 to 5 pm (DM3/1.50).

Just outside is the entrance to **Jüdengasse**, a backwards L-shaped alley running into

SAXONY-ANHALT

Jakobstrasse, home to the town's Jewish community until they were expelled in 1494; a memorial on the southern side of the alley depicts the townsfolk chasing the (bearded) Jews out.

Nietzsche Haus
Fans of Friedrich Nietzsche will want to make a pilgrimage to Nietzsche Haus at Weingarten 18, which contains a permanent exhibition on his days in Naumburg. Nietzsche attended school here, and his mother and sister lived here. The museum (π 20 16 38) is open Tuesday to Friday from 2 to 5 pm and weekends from 10 am to 4 pm (DM3/1.50).

Special Events
The annual **Kirsch Fest**, five days around the last weekend of June, is huge. The main focus of the festival is at the Vogelwiese, a meadow at the north-eastern edge of town, with about 15 tents run by local organisations, each with live music every night, lots of regional food, wine and beer and, on Sunday, an enormous fireworks display. On Sunday a large parade at 2 pm goes from the Marientor to the Markt and on to the Vogelwiese.

The Peter Paul Messe – an emulation of a medieval market with goods half genuine handicraft, half tourist kitsch – sets up at Marienplatz.

Places to Stay
If you're after a *private room*, get in touch with Naumburg-Information; expect to pay from DM20 to DM50 per person (plus a 5% service fee) for somewhere central.

Camping Blütengrund (π 20 27 11, *Blütengrund Park*), 1.5km north-east of Naumburg at the confluence of the Saale and Unstrut rivers, charges DM2 for a tent site and DM5 per person; there are also bungalows with private facilities from DM30 per night. It's a family fun area, and your fellow campers most likely will be locals on holiday. There's a swimming area as well as a cinema.

Naumburg's large and well equipped *DJH hostel* (π 70 34 22, *Am Tennisplatz 9*),

1.5km south of the town centre, has multi-bed rooms for DM21/27 for juniors/seniors, and double rooms for DM26/30. There's another, better hostel 5km south-west of Naumburg in Bad Kösen (see that section later this chapter).

The *Gasthaus St Othmar* (π/fax 20 12 13, *Osthmarsplatz 7*) is a newly restored historic hotel with singles/doubles from DM40/80.

Gasthaus Zum Alten Krug (π/fax 20 04 06, *Lindenring 44*) halfway between the cathedral and the Markt, has lovely furniture, a great atmosphere and rooms for DM80/110.

Zur Alten Schmiede (π 243 60, fax 24 36 66, *Lindenring 36-37*) has really friendly staff, rooms from DM85/110, and a good restaurant.

Hotel Stadt Aachen (π 24 70, fax 24 71 30, *Markt 11*), tucked away behind the square, is more expensive at DM100/155. If you're going to spend that amount of money, try the excellent *Hotel Garni St Marien* (π 235 40, fax 23 54 22, *Marienstrasse 12*) for friendly staff, a free locked car park, spotless rooms and arguably the best morning coffee in Germany. Rates are DM80 to DM110 for singles, DM110 to DM130 for doubles, and a very large triple room for DM160.

Places to Eat
Restaurants *Gritti* (π 20 03 54, *Rosengarten 8-10*), just north of Lindenring, is a comfortable Italian place with friendly staff and pizzas, pastas, soups and salads for reasonable prices (pizzas DM7 to DM13).

Zur Alten Schmiede (see Places to Stay) has top-notch Argentinian steaks and sophisticated fish dishes for DM18 to DM24. *Carolus Magnus* (π 20 55 77 *Markt 11*) is a flashy, comfortable place with mains from DM22 to DM40 (closed Sunday).

Fast Food Doner kebabs (DM4.50) are great at *Anatolen* (π 201 74, *Herrenstrasse 1*), between the Markt and Lindenring; burgers are DM3.50 and pizzas cost DM4 to

DM6. Staff will make splendid vegie sandwiches for DM3, if you ask.

At Marienplatz there's an excellent *Bäckerei-Konditorei*. A *market* sets up on the Markt on Monday and Wednesday from 8 am to 5 pm, and Saturday to noon.

Entertainment

Kö Pi is a great little Irish pub just behind the Rathaus. With live music on weekends, draught Guinness and Kilkenny, it draws a young crowd.

Alt Naumburg at Marienplatz is a cosy place with wooden puppets, a good bar, local wines and occasional live music.

Down Marienstrasse through the alley opposite the (so-so) Greek restaurant is *Kaktus*, another comfortable neighbourhood hang-out with good local wine and beer.

In summer, the Markt is *the* place to be at night, as tables from the local bars and icecream places spill outside.

Kanzlei is a yuppie hang-out; downstairs, its Nachtschwärmer disco has a similar crowd on Friday and Saturday nights.

Nach Acht, in the Salzhof Passage, gets a good mixed crowd and plays Schlager and 1970s/80s hits.

Getting There & Around

There are fast trains to Naumburg from Halle (DM12, 40 minutes), Leipzig (DM14.80, one hour), Jena (DM9.80, 45 minutes) and Weimar (DM12, 30 minutes). A local line runs to Freyburg (DM3, eight minutes).

There are IC trains to/from Frankfurt-am-Main (DM89, 3½ hours), to/from Berlin (DM71, 2½ hours) and Munich (DM134, 4¾ hours).

By road from Halle or Leipzig, take the A9 to either the B87 or the B180 and head west; both lead right into town – the B87 is less direct and more scenic, though it's the first exit from the A9.

You can rent bicycles at the Radhaus (☎ 20 31 19), Rosengarten 6, for DM12/20 a day/weekend. Near the train station, Fahrrad Fiedelak (☎ 70 80), Bahnhofstrasse 4, charges DM10 per day for city/mountain bikes.

FREYBURG
☎ 034464 • pop 5000

Eight kilometres north-west of Naumburg, Freyburg lies in the heart of the lovely Unstrut Valley.

The tourist office (☎ 273 76) on the Markt is open weekdays from 7 am to noon and 2 to 5 pm, and Saturday to 1 pm (closed Sunday). It offers city tours in German on advance notice for DM50 for groups up to 20, but you can join a tour if one's running for DM3. Tours include a visit to the Rotkäppchen Sektkellerei and the castle. The tourist office also sells a huge range of locally produced wines, with bottles from DM6 to DM14.

The large medieval **Schloss Neuenburg** (☎ 280 28) stands on the wooded hill top directly above the town (DM5/3). The adjacent tower, the **Dicker Wilhelm**, offers splendid views (DM2). Both are open April to October, Tuesday to Sunday from 10 am to 6 pm, closing an hour earlier from November to March. Before you go in, illuminate the 103m-deep well near the castle gate for DM1. For a beautiful 20 minute walk, take the path running from the castle down to the *Herzoglichen Weinberg* (ducal vineyard).

Rotkäppchen Sekt Kellerei

Established in 1856, this *Sekt* (sparkling wine) producer (☎ 340), Sektkellereistrasse 5, is the most famous in the former GDR. The best thing about the place is its twostorey-high, 75,000L **Sekt barrel**, decorated with ornate carvings.

One-hour tours (including a tasting) run daily at 2 pm (DM6), and queues to get in can be enormous, particularly when the weekend coach tours pull in. You can buy a whole range of sekt from the shop out front – but frankly, many other brands taste a lot better.

Classical concerts called (get ready) *Sektivals* are held in the factory year round; tickets range from DM20 to DM40.

Getting There & Around

Trains run every two hours (DM3, eight minutes), and buses every hour (DM2,

15 minutes) between Naumburg's Hauptbahnhof/ZOB and Freyburg's Markt. The bicycle route *(Radwandern)* between the two cities is very well marked and makes for a wonderful ride. Rental bikes are available at Baldur Müller (☎ 273 02), Braugasse 1a.

Perhaps the most scenic way to get to Freyburg is by boat from Blütengrund, at the confluence of the Saale and Unstrut rivers just outside Naumburg. The *MS Fröliche Dörte* (☎ 03445-20 28 09) tootles its way up the Unstrut between March and September daily at 11 am, and 1.30 and 4 pm. It's more of a tour – it goes past Freyburg and then back to it. The journey takes 70 minutes and costs DM10/6 for adults/children one-way, and DM14/8 return. It runs back from Freyburg at 12.15, 2.45 and 5.15 pm.

SCHULPFORTE
Between Naumburg and Bad Köse is Schulpforte, a quiet little village worth a stop. The **Landesschule Pforta** (State school Pforta) was founded by Cistercian monks in 1137; in 1543 it was converted to a high school (grades 9 to 12, or pupils aged from about 14 to 18), which by the middle of the 19th century was one of Germany's finest.

Students here have included Friedrich Nietzsche (from 1858-64) and the philosopher JG Fichte (1774-80).

Today it's still one of the finest schools in eastern Germany, specialising in music, art and language. Students good enough to get in are blessed with subsidised tuition – including books, room and board – of around DM210 per month.

You can roam the romantic grounds, and the great park behind the main campus is perfect for a picnic.

On campus is the state-owned **Landesweingut Floster Pforta** (☎ 034463-30 00), a very pleasant little wine bar and shop open daily from 10 am to 6 pm. You can try all two dozen varieties of their wine for free, or order by the glass (DM2 to DM5). Bottles range from DM7 to DM10, though *Eiswein*, a late-season wine, runs in excess of DM110 per half-litre bottle. Across the

Saale is the main **vineyard** with its spectacular **Fasskeller**, a wine cellar where you can taste and buy.

Buses running between Naumburg and Bad Kösen stop in Schulpforte.

BAD KÖSEN
☎ 03446 • pop 5200
The spa town of Bad Kösen isn't exactly a bastion of young, energetic folk, but there's a great hostel and a couple of very interesting sights, including an intriguing saltworks.

The town straddles the Saale, 7km upstream from Naumburg, and its main sights are on the east side. At An der Brücke 3, near the main bridge, is the unhelpful tourist office (☎/fax 619 99). It's open Monday to Friday, 10 am to 6 pm and weekends from 10 am to 4 pm.

The **Romanisches Haus** was built in 1037 and is thus the oldest secular building in central Germany. It's open Tuesday to Friday from 10 am to noon and 1 to 5 pm, and weekends from 10 am to 5 pm (DM4/3). Today it's teamed up with the **Kunsthalle** behind it to form museums of local history and of dolls, the latter highlighting the Kösener stuffed toys.

Next door you'll see the **Wasserrad** (water wheel), which drove a long pair of drills leading to the **Soleschacht**, a brine well. The water was pumped up the hill to the **Gradierwerk** where the salt crystallised and helped purify the spa air. Nowadays, it's a technical monument, and beautifully lit at night.

West of the Saale, follow the signs towards the hostel, past the train station, up the hill, past the hostel and on to the lookout at **Himmelreich**. This peers down on a scene of such wondrous beauty – fairy-tale castle ruins at **Saaleck** and **Rugelsburg** towering over rolling hills, the Saale River and the little village of Saaleck – that you'll think you're looking at a children's pop-up book. There's a cafe at the lookout.

Places to Stay & Eat
The tourist office can book *private rooms* for between DM30 and DM50.

Camping An der Rugelsburg (☎ 287 05, fax 287 06), 1.5km south of town on the eastern bank of the Saale, is pretty and well equipped. It charges DM7.50 per adult, DM4 per tent and DM4.50 per car (plus DM1.40 in local *Kurtaxe*).

The *Jugendherberge Bad Kösen (☎ 275 97, no fax, Bergstrasse 3)*, 1.5km uphill from the train station, has beds for DM18/23 for juniors/seniors, plus DM6 for linen. The complex has three buildings and great food (barbecue in summer).

Hotel Loreley (☎/fax 287 88, Loreley-promenade 8) has nice doubles with private shower and WC for DM100. *Hotel Schöne Aussicht (☎ 273 67, fax 273 65, Ilskeweg 1)* has a commanding view of the valley, a fine restaurant and comfy singles/doubles for DM75/110.

The *Schoppe Café (☎ 285 85, Naumburger Strasse 1)*, across the road from the tourist office, offers dainty swirled cakes from just DM2.50, but be braced for hordes of customers and iffy service.

Shopping
Other than wine, there's a Spielzeug Bad Kösen factory outlet (☎ 331 05) selling furry toy animals – wonderful pigs, giraffes, squirrels, guinea pigs and elephants – at far below retail prices. It's located at Rudelsburgpromenade 22, which is on the way out to the hostel.

Getting There & Away
Bad Kösen is a six minute train ride from Naumburg (hourly, DM3). Bus service between the two towns (DM2) is also frequent.

Harz Mountains

The Harz Mountains rise picturesquely from the North German Plain and cover an area some 100km long and 30km wide. Until the Wende – the dramatic 'change' of 1989 – they were shared by West and East Germany. Although a far cry from the dramatic peaks and valleys of the Alps, the Harz region is a great year-round sports getaway, with plenty of opportunities for hiking, cycling and skiing.

The Brocken (1142m) is the focal point of the Harz. Goethe set 'Walpurgisnacht', an early chapter of his play *Faust*, on the Brocken, and Heinrich Heine spent a well oiled night here, described in his *Harzreise* (Harz Journey) in 1824. Narrow-gauge steam trains run to the peak and link major towns in the eastern Harz.

The eastern Harz is in the state of Saxony-Anhalt and borders Thuringia; the western Harz lies in Lower Saxony. Hochharz National Park was established in eastern Germany immediately after the Wende; Harz National Park in western Germany followed in 1994. These two parks form the region's heartland. Good entry points are Schierke, Drei Annen Hohne (Hochharz National Park), Bad Harzburg, Torfhaus and St Andreasberg (Harz National Park).

The Harz once had large deposits of silver, lead, copper and zinc. Mining began around the 10th century and continued up to 1988. All that remains of this industry today are several interesting mining museums and a system of dams and aqueducts that once supplied the mines with water. From 1945 to 1990 the Harz region was a frontline in the Cold War, and the Brocken was used by the Soviets as a military base.

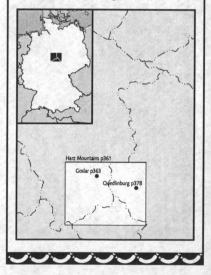

HIGHLIGHTS

- Trekking to the Brocken on Walpurgisnacht with the pagan masses
- Listening to the organist practise in the Gernrode Stiftskirche
- Hiking (or taking the cable car) up Hexentanzplatz, and through the Bode Valley from Thale to Treseburg
- Seeing Wernigerode Castle at dusk
- Exploring 1000-year-old Quedlinburg
- Enjoying the openness of the Harz people and listening to the bus drivers' bizarre stories
- Cross-country skiing in the Hochharz

Harz Mountains p361
Goslar p363
Quedlinburg p378

INFORMATION

The main information centre for the Harz Mountains is the Harzer Verkehrsverband (☎ 05321-340 40, fax 34 04 66, email harzer.verkehrsverband@t-online.de) in Goslar (see that section for details), but information on the eastern Harz is best picked up in towns there, particularly in Wernigerode. For details, see the Information sections under the individual towns.

Make sure you get the excellent *Grüner Faden* (Green Thread) booklet (DM6), available from most tourist offices in the

Harz region and at many hotels. It is especially useful for activities and equipment hire, but many telephone numbers and prices are outdated.

For information on camping, ask any tourist office for the free *Der Harz Camping* brochure (in German), which lists major camping grounds and facilities open all year.

The *Freizeit im Harz* map (DM12.80) provides the best general overview of sights and trails (cycling and hiking) for the entire Harz.

ACTIVITIES
Skiing
The main centres for downhill skiing are Braunlage, Hahnenklee and St Andreasberg, with many other smaller runs dotted throughout the mountains, though the quality of the slopes might disappoint real enthusiasts. Conditions for cross-country skiing can be excellent, with lots of well marked

trails and equipment-hire shops. For weather reports and snow conditions, ring the Harzer Verkehrsverband (☎ 05321-340 40) in Goslar. A German-language information service can be reached on ☎ 05321-200 24.

Hiking
The main attraction in summer is hiking. Every town has its own short trails, which often link up to long-distance ones, and there are usually traditional restaurants along the way. Trail symbols are colour-coded in red, green, blue and yellow on a square or triangular plate. Maps put out by the Harzclub hiking association also show trail numbers. The 1:50,000 Harzclub maps are the best for hikers. Harzclub offices in mountain towns are also good sources of information: hiking tips, itineraries, the availability of hiking partners and guides. Tourist offices usually stock the club's leaflets. Most trails are well

HARZ MOUNTAINS

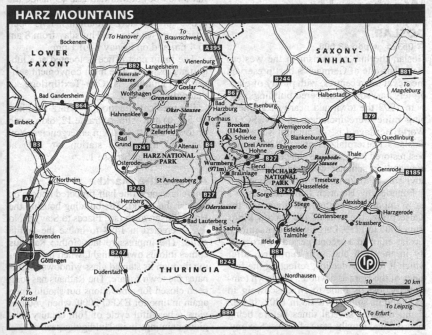

marked, but it doesn't hurt to ask occasionally to make sure you are heading in the right direction. Weather conditions can change quickly throughout the year; be prepared.

Cycling
Anyone seeking a challenge will enjoy cycling or mountain biking in the Harz, especially in quieter eastern areas. Buses will transport your bike when space allows. In some towns bikes can be rented.

Spas
Often dismissed by young Germans as a pensioners' paradise, the Harz region is sprinkled with thermal spas and baths where the weary and/or infirm can take the cure. The place to go for information in the various towns is the *Kurzentrum* (spa centre) or *Kurverwaltung* (spa administration), which often double as tourist offices.

Western Harz

GOSLAR
☎ 05321 • pop 48,000
Goslar, the hub of tourism in the western Harz, has one of Germany's best preserved medieval town centres, with plenty of elaborately carved half-timbered buildings.

In 1992 the town and nearby Rammelsberg mine were included on UNESCO's World Heritage List of cultural sites, and Goslar's Kaiserpfalz is one of Germany's best restored Romanesque palaces. It can get crowded on summer weekends, when it is advisable to make reservations in advance.

Founded by Heinrich I in 922, Goslar's early importance centred on silver and the Kaiserpfalz, the seat of the Saxon kings from 1005 to 1219. Largely due to its mines, Goslar enjoyed a second period of prosperity in the 14th and 15th centuries, after which it fell into decline, reflecting the fortunes of the Harz as a whole. The town temporarily lost its mine to Braunschweig in 1552 and its soul to Prussia in 1802. It then changed hands several times before being incorporated into the state of Lower Saxony.

Orientation
Goslar has a medieval circular layout, the heart of which is the Markt and a large pedestrian mall. Rosentorstrasse leads to the Markt, a 10 minute walk from the adjacent train and bus stations. The small Gose River flows through the centre south of the Markt. Streets in the old town are numbered up one side and down the other.

Information
The Goslar tourist office (☎ 780 60, fax 78 06 44, email goslarinfo@t-online.de), Markt 7, is open November to April weekdays from 9.15 am to 5 pm and on Saturday from 9.30 to 2 pm. From May to October it is open to 6 pm weekdays, to 4 pm Saturday and on Sunday from 9.30 am to 2 pm. German-language guided tours of the old town are conducted daily at 10 am (DM7/4.50 for adults/children).

The Harzer Verkehrsverband (☎ 340 40, fax 34 04 66) at Marktstrasse 45 inside the Bäckergildehaus is the central information office for the Harz Mountains. It is open year round Monday to Thursday from 8 am to 4 pm and on Friday until 1 pm.

The main post office is located at Klubgartenstrasse 10. The most convenient self-service laundry is City-Textilpflege at Petersilienstrasse 9.

For medical attention, try Harz Kliniken (☎ 55 50) at Kösliner Strasse 12, 6km north of town. Call ☎ 13 03 in emergencies. You can find the police station (☎ 791) at Heinrich-Pieper-Strasse 1.

Around the Markt
There are some fine half-timbered houses on or near the Markt. The building housing the **Hotel Kaiserworth** (see Places to Stay) at No 3 was erected in 1494 to house the textile guild. The impressive late-Gothic **Rathaus** comes into its own at night, when light coming through its stained glass windows illuminates the town square. The Rathaus has long been closed for renovations but should open again in time for EXPO 2000, when you can view a beautiful cycle of 16th century religious paintings in its Huldigungssaal.

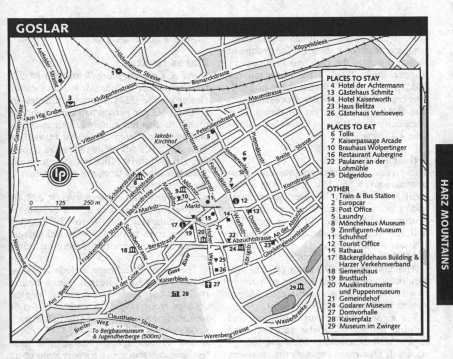

GOSLAR

PLACES TO STAY
4 Hotel der Achtermann
13 Gästehaus Schmitz
14 Hotel Kaiserworth
23 Haus Belitza
26 Gästehaus Verhoeven

PLACES TO EAT
6 Tollis
7 Kaiserpassage Arcade
10 Brauhaus Wolpertinger
16 Restaurant Aubergine
22 Paulaner an der Lohmühle
25 Didgeridoo

OTHER
1 Train & Bus Station
2 Europcar
3 Post Office
5 Laundry
8 Mönchehaus Museum
9 Zinnfiguren-Museum
11 Schuhhof
12 Tourist Office
15 Rathaus
17 Bäckergildehaus Building & Harzer Verkehrsverband
18 Siemenshaus
19 Brusttuch
20 Musikinstrumente und Puppenmuseum
21 Gemeindehof
24 Goslarer Museum
27 Domvorhalle
28 Kaiserpfalz
29 Museum im Zwinger

HARZ MOUNTAINS

In front of the Rathaus is a replica of the **Elle**, the local yardstick for cloth. A pillory for debtors who couldn't (or wouldn't) pay up once stood here; a local custom required the poor devils to drop their trousers before being led off for the next round of abuse.

The **market fountain**, crowned by an eagle symbolising Goslar's status as a free imperial city, dates from the 13th century, but the eagle itself is a copy of the original. Opposite the Rathaus is the **Glockenspiel**, a chiming clock depicting four scenes of mining in the area. It 'plays' at 9 am, noon and 3 and 6 pm.

The baroque **Siemenshaus** at Schreiberstrasse 12 is the ancestral home of the Siemens industrial family and can be visited on Tuesday and Thursday between 9 am and noon (free). **Brusttuch**, at Hoher Weg 1, and the **Bäckergildehaus**, on the corner of Marktstrasse and Bergstrasse, are two fine early 16th century houses.

Kaiserpfalz
This reconstructed 11th century Romanesque palace is Goslar's pride and joy. The interior frescoes of idealised historical scenes date from the 19th century. On the south side is **St Ulrich Chapel**, housing a sarcophagus containing the heart of Heinrich III. Below the Kaiserpfalz is the recently restored **Domvorhalle**, displaying the 11th century Kaiserstuhl, the throne used by Salian and Hohenstaufen emperors. In the pleasant gardens behind the palace is an excellent sculpture by Henry Moore, the **Goslarer Krieger** (Goslar Warrior). The Kaiserpfalz (☎ 75 78 10) is open in 2000 after renovation.

Rammelsberger Bergbaumuseum
About 1km south of the town centre along Rammelsberger Strasse, visitors can descend into the shafts of this 1000-year-old

mine (☎ 343 60), now a museum. Admission to the mine includes a German-language tour (or in English for groups of five or more) of the 18th and 19th century **Roeder Shafts** (DM9), the **mine railway** (DM13.50, or DM17 for the shafts and railway combined) and the **ore processing** section (DM9, or DM21 for all three). It is open daily from 9 am to 6 pm (last admission 4.45 pm).

Other Museums

The private **Musikinstrumente und Puppenmuseum** (☎ 269 45), Hoher Weg 5, will thrill kids or fans of musical instruments and/or dolls. The owner began collecting instruments more than 40 years ago. The doll collection is his daughter's addition. It's open daily from 11 am to 5 pm (DM5/2.50 for adults/children).

The **Zinnfiguren-Museum** (☎ 258 89) exhibits a colourful collection of painted pewter figures in a courtyard at Münzstrasse 11; it's open daily (DM4/2).

For a good overview of the natural and cultural history of Goslar and the Harz region, visit the **Goslarer Museum**, Königstrasse 1. One room contains the treasures from the former Goslar Dom, and there's also a cabinet with coins dating from the 10th century. It opens Tuesday to Sunday from 10 am to 5 pm; from November to March, it's open to 4 pm (DM3.50).

The **Mönchehaus Museum** (☎ 295 70), in a 16th century half-timbered house at Mönchestrasse 3, exhibits works of modern art, including some interesting sculptures and changing exhibitions. It's open Tuesday to Saturday from 10 am to 1 pm, and 3 to 5 pm (morning only on Sunday and public holidays). Admission is free.

For a real 'scream', take a look inside the **Museum im Zwinger** (☎ 431 40), set in gardens at Thomasstrasse 2. The 16th century Zwinger, a tower that was once part of the ramparts, has a collection of such late-medieval delights as torture implements, coats of armour and weapons used during the Peasant Wars. It's open from April to mid-November daily from 9 am to 5 pm, and

from 10 am to 4 pm in March (DM3.30). It's closed the rest of the year.

Places to Stay

Hotel & Campingplatz Sennhütte (☎ 225 02, Clausthaler Strasse 28) is 3km south of Goslar via the B241. Camping charges are DM5.50/4/3 per person/tent/car (open year round). It also has simple but clean single/double rooms from DM40/80 (closed on Thursday). It's advisable to reserve a room through the tourist office before setting out. Take bus No 434 from the train station to the Sennhütte stop.

The pretty *Jugendherberge* (☎ 222 40, Rammelsberger Strasse 25) is behind the Kaiserpfalz (take bus C to Theresienhof from the train station). The hostel charges DM21/26 for juniors/seniors, including breakfast.

The prices listed here include breakfast unless otherwise indicated. *Haus Belitza* (☎ 207 44, Abzuchtstrasse 11) has singles/doubles from DM35/55 with 1960s-style furnishings. Showers cost DM3.50 extra.

Gästehaus Schmitz (☎ 234 45, Kornstrasse 1), just east of the Markt, offers spotless, spacious rooms in a friendly atmosphere from DM55/70, and nice apartments for two for DM80 (without breakfast). Book ahead.

Gästehaus Verhoeven (☎ 238 12, fax 466 53, Hoher Weg 12) has basic but clean rooms for DM65/95 (DM75/115 with shower).

Hotel Kaiserworth (☎ 211 11, fax 211 14, Markt 3), in a magnificent 500-year-old building, has rooms from DM99/199 with bath and WC (toilet). Larger rooms are from DM149/219, and good-value weekend package deals are available.

The *Hotel der Achtermann* (☎ 210 01, fax 427 48, Rosentorstrasse 20) has rooms from DM169/259, including use of the pool and whirlpool (saunas half-price at DM8).

Places to Eat

Goslar has many good-value restaurants (some are closed on Monday).

The Kaiserpassage shopping arcade on Breite Strasse has a couple of good options. *Altdeutsches Kartoffelhaus* (☎ 454 25) serves generous portions of north German potato dishes for between DM6.50 and DM24.50. *Dolce Vita (☎ 218 71)* serves great pasta until 8 pm for around DM13.

Tollis (Sommerwohlenstrasse 5) is a friendly no-frills place, with budget cafeteria-style German food.

Brauhaus Wolpertinger (☎ 221 55, Marstallstrasse 1), in a brewery courtyard (a beer garden in summer), is a popular place to eat and drink, serving dishes from DM14 to DM28; but it also has jacket potatoes for under DM8. *Paulaner an der Lohmühle (☎ 260 70, Gemeindehof 3-5)* also has a beer garden in summer.

Didgeridoo (☎ 468 37, Hoher Weg 13) serves Australian 'cuisine' like kangaroo burgers for DM11 and kangaroo rump steak DM22.50. Other barbecue meals cost around DM16, and it has a good selection of Australian wines. It opens for lunch and dinner and kicks on till late.

Restaurant Aubergine (☎ 421 36, Marktstrasse 4) is much more upmarket and the quality of its Mediterranean cuisine is high – expect to pay from DM20 to DM40 for main courses. *Hotel Kaiserworth* has a restaurant that offers a lunch special for around DM20.

Shopping
Hoher Weg is packed with shops selling souvenirs. Local crafts such as ceramics, puppets and marionettes, many of them portraying witches, are available at a few shops. The better ones go for about DM200. Approach the local Harz fruit wines and herbal schnapps with caution – some of it will leave you the worse for wear. Try the Harzer Roller, a local, if somewhat bland, sour-milk cheese.

Getting There & Away
Train Frequent Bad Harzburg-Hanover trains (via Hildesheim) stop at Goslar, as do the Braunschweig-Göttingen trains. Though there's a direct train service to Wernigerode, there's also a more frequent service via Vienenburg (DM13, one hour), but you must change.

Bus The Regionalbus Braunschweig (RBB) office (☎ 343 10) at the train station, from where buses also depart, has free timetable leaflets for services in the Harz region. Bus Nos 408 and 61/432 run between Goslar and Altenau. Bus No 61/432 continues on to St Andreasberg (DM10.50, one hour). Bus Nos 408 and 434 (via Hahnenklee) run to Clausthal-Zellerfeld (DM8). For Bad Harzburg, where you can change buses for Torfhaus, take bus No 62/407 (DM3.70). The Berlinienbus BEX runs three times weekly to Berlin (DM61) via Magdeburg. For timetables and bookings, refer to DER-Reisebüro (☎ 757 90) at the train station.

Car & Motorcycle The B6 runs north to Hildesheim and east to Bad Harzburg, Wernigerode and Quedlinburg. The north-south A7 is reached via the B82. For Hahnenklee, take the B241. The car-rental chain Europcar (☎ 251 38) has a branch at Lindenplan 3.

Getting Around
Local bus tickets cost DM2.80 or can be bought in batches of four for DM9.50 from the Presseladen im Achtermann newsagent, next to Hotel der Achtermann on Rosentorstrasse. To book a taxi, ring ☎ 13 13. Mountain bikes can be hired for DM35 per day from Harz Bike (☎ 820 11) at Bornhardtstrasse 3-5, about 2km north of the station at the end of Hildesheimer Strasse.

AROUND GOSLAR
Oker Valley
The Oker Valley, which begins at Oker, a small industrial town now part of Goslar, is one of the prettiest in the western Harz. An 11km hike (marked with a red triangle) follows the course of the Oker River and leads to a 47 million cubic metre dam, constructed in the 1950s to regulate water levels and generate power. Along the way you'll pass the 60m-high **Römkerhalle** waterfall, created in 1863. The B498 leads to the dam. If travelling by bus, take No 407 from Goslar to Okertalsperre stop.

HARZ MOUNTAINS

HAHNENKLEE

☎ 05325 • pop 2200

This small thermal spa some 15km south-west of Goslar is one of the more tasteful ski resorts in the Harz Mountains and a good base for summer hikes in the western Harz.

The tourist office (☎ 510 40, fax 51 04 20) is in the Kurverwaltung building off Rathausstrasse at Kurhausweg 7. It's open from May to October weekdays from 9 am to 6 pm (closed for one hour at 1 pm), and Saturday till noon. Otherwise, it's closed Saturday and keeps slightly shorter weekday hours.

Things to See & Do

Hahnenklee is proud of its **Gustav-Adolf-Kirche** (1907), a Norwegian-style wooden stave church with an attractive interior of Byzantine and Scandinavian features.

In winter, however, most visitors are here to enjoy the downhill and cross-country **skiing**. Day tickets for the cable car and lifts cost DM30. The Skikeller in der Seilbahnstation (☎ 21 86), Rathausstrasse 6, hires out downhill ski equipment for DM20 a day, and cross-country gear for slightly less. Wehrsuhn (☎ 22 35) at Rathausstrasse 19 and Berghotel (☎ 25 05) at An der Buchwiese 1 are other options. Snow-Fun (☎ 21 72 or ☎ 30 45) at Hindenburgstrasse 4 has snowboards and skis for hire. Ice skates can also be rented at these places for when the Kranicher Teich (a large pond) freezes over. DSV-Ski-Schule Hahnenklee (☎ 21 86), Rathausstrasse 19, has weekend ski courses for DM60.

Hahnenklee is also popular for its **hiking**, with trails leading to the Bocksberg from the car park near the stave church and longer trails to Goslar (trail 2G, blue dot, 11km) via Windsattel and Glockenberg. Remember to take the Harzclub 1:50,000 walking map and be prepared for changing weather conditions.

Places to Stay & Eat

Hahnenklee levies a nightly resort tax of DM3.50 per person – keep your resort card for discounts. A reduced tax is charged on hostel and camping accommodation.

Campingplatz am Kreuzeck (☎ 25 70), on the B241 at the turn-off to Hahnenklee, has modern facilities and is open year round (bus stop: Kreuzeck). *Jugendherberge Bockswiese* (☎ 22 56, Steigerstieg 1) charges DM21/26 per night for juniors/seniors (bus stop: Bockswiese).

The tourist office has a free room reservation service and can book apartments for longer stays. *Steffens Café Restaurant* (☎ 22 35, Kurhausweg 6) has singles/doubles from DM42/84 and a traditional restaurant with well priced food, especially game/poultry.

Getting There & Around

Bus No 434 from Goslar to Bad Grund via Clausthal-Zellerfeld stops in Hahnenklee. The Berlinienbus BEX to Berlin stops here three times weekly. Hahnenklee is just west of the B241, between Goslar and Clausthal-Zellerfeld.

BAD HARZBURG

☎ 05322 • pop 25,000

Bad Harzburg is a pretty thermal spa town where fur coats and rheumatism are common among its visitors. Unless you fit into one of these categories, its main attraction is the nearby Harz National Park and trails. The town's proximity to Goslar (9km) makes it possible to stay in one town and commute to the other.

The tourist office (☎ 753 30) is in the Kurzentrum at Herzog-Wilhelm-Strasse 86, which also has information on thermal baths. It's open weekdays from 8 am to 8 pm and on Saturday from 9 am to 4 pm. Many shops are closed during the early afternoon *Ruhestunden*, a German siesta.

Things to See & Do

The **Haus der Natur**, a Harz National Park information centre at Berlinerplatz in the Kurpark, has audio-visual material, brochures on the park, and a collection of stuffed wild animals that does – despite any misgivings about taxidermy – allow you to view some of the rarer Harz Mountains creatures in the flesh (almost). It is open daily except Tuesday from 10 am to 5 pm.

It's worth hiking or riding up to **Grosser Burgberg**, a hill above Bad Harzburg with the ruins of an 11th century fortress built by Heinrich IV. The 481m-long cable car to the fortress costs DM4/6 one-way/return for adults. It operates May to September daily from 9 am to 6 pm and the rest of the year from 10 am to 5 pm. You can reach it by continuing up Bummelallee to the Kurpark. Not far from the fortress is a traditional cafe-restaurant.

Marked **hiking trails** lead into the national park from Berlinerplatz and Grosser Burgberg, the latter just over 3km from Berlinerplatz on foot. Among the many walks are those from Berlinerplatz to Sennhütte (1.3km), Molkenhaus (3km) and to scenic Rabenklippe (7km), overlooking the Ecker Valley. All destinations have restaurants; a blackboard inside the valley cable-car station indicates which ones are open.

From Grosser Burgberg you can take the Kaiserweg trail, which leads to Torfhaus and connects to the Brocken. A marked trail also leads to the 23m-high **Radau Waterfall**, some 7km from Grosser Burgberg. If snow conditions are good, it is possible to ski cross-country to/from Torfhaus, which has equipment-hire facilities (see Brocken & Torfhaus in the Eastern Harz section.)

Special Events
Bad Harzburg has plenty of concerts, though most are fairly staid affairs. Nevertheless, it pays to check out the tourist office's events calendar. An annual music festival is held in June. The Gallopp-Rennwoche horse race, a notable bright spot for punters, is held in July just outside town at the Pferde-Rennbahn racecourse (bus No 62/407 to the Silberbornbad stop).

Places to Stay & Eat
Campingplatz am Wolfstein (☎ 358 5), about 3km east of town at Ilsenburger Strasse 111, is reached by bus Nos 74 and 77 from the train station. *Campingplatz Stadtteil Göttingerode (☎ 812 15)*, about 4km west of town along the B6 (take bus No 62/407 from the train station) is another option.

Braunschweiger Haus hostel *(☎ 45 82, fax 18 67, Waldstrasse 5)* costs DM21.50/25 for juniors/seniors. Take bus No 73 from the station to the Lärchenweg stop.

A nightly resort tax of DM4 is charged on all hotel stays. You will find several good hotels west of the tourist office on Am Stadtpark; follow the small path below the tennis courts.

Hexenhaus, in the Kurpark near the cable car, serves up a full range of traditional German dishes, with mains in the DM18 to DM30 price range (closed Tuesday).

Getting There & Around
The train station and adjacent bus station are on the northern side of town, a 10 minute walk from the pedestrian mall. Bus No 62/407 leaves regularly for Goslar, and bus No 77 heads for Wernigerode (DM5.80, one hour). Bus No 63/422 shuttles almost hourly to Braunlage (DM7) via Radau Waterfall and Torfhaus. Frequent train services link Bad Harzburg with Goslar, Hanover, Braunschweig and Wernigerode. Bad Harzburg is on the A395 to Braunschweig. The B4 and B6 lead to Torfhaus and Wernigerode, respectively.

Distance buses double as city services in Bad Harzburg.

BRAUNLAGE
☎ 05520 • pop 6000
Braunlage is the largest centre for winter sports, and is popular with hikers in summer. The skiing here is usually the best in the Harz Mountains, although it can get a bit crowded on the slopes when the snow is good.

Orientation & Information
Braunlage's heart is the junction of Elbingeröder Strasse and Herzog-Wilhelm-Strasse, the latter a thoroughfare that changes names several times. The tourist office (☎ 194 33, fax 93 07 20) is in the Kurverwaltung building at Elbingeröder Strasse 7. It is open weekdays from 7.30 am to 12.30 pm and 2 to 5 pm, Saturday from 9.30 am to noon. The post office is off

euro currency converter DM1 = €0.51

Elbingeröder Strasse at Marktstrasse 3. The Volksbank at Herzog-Wilhelm-Strasse 19 has an ATM. The police station (☎ 553) is on Herzog-Johann-Albrecht-Strasse.

Skiing

A cable car will take you up the 971m Wurmberg, from where you can ski down or use the three lifts on the mountain itself. Day tickets cost DM32 (DM3 extra for closed cabins on the cable car). Downhill ski equipment can be rented at Café-Restaurant Zur Seilbahn (☎ 600) from DM20 a day, including boots and stocks, or from one of the many ski shops dotted around town. Braunlage has several smaller pistes, groomed cross-country trails, and a ski jump where high flyers can land on the former East German border.

Plenty of places in town offer cross-country skis for hire. Rosy's Souvenir Ecke (☎ 32 24), Elbingeröder Strasse 8a, has gear for DM12 per day.

Hiking

The tourist office has two good, free leaflets: *Wandervorschläge Rund Um Braunlage* (Hiking Suggestions around Braunlage), covering trails in the area and restaurant stops; and *Wanderwege Braunlage* (Hiking Trails Braunlage). If you are heading east, a trail follows the B27 to Elend (red triangle; 7km), where you can pick up the narrow-gauge railway to Wernigerode.

Places to Stay & Eat

A resort tax of DM3 is charged nightly on hotel stays in Braunlage, less for camping grounds and hostels.

Campingplatz Ferien vom Ich (☎ 413, fax 417) is 1.5km south of Braunlage, off the B27 to Bad Lauterberg.

The *Jugendherberge (☎ 22 38, fax 15 69, Von-Langen-Strasse 28)* is a 15 minute walk from the centre. Prices for juniors/seniors are DM21/26.

Hotel Berliner Hof (☎ 427, Elbingeröder Strasse 12) has singles/doubles from DM50/101 and a restaurant downstairs serving hearty fare from DM10 to DM25,

including a venison goulash for DM19. *Omas Kaffeestube und Weinstube (☎ 23 90, Elbingeröder Strasse 2)* serves coffee, cakes and light dishes during the day in an old-world atmosphere.

Getting There & Away

Bus No 65 runs to St Andreasberg (DM4.80) from the Von-Langen-Strasse stop. For Torfhaus and Bad Harzburg, take bus No 63/422 from the bus station, which is south of the town centre where Herzog-Wilhelm-Strasse becomes Bahnhofstrasse. The B4 runs north to Torfhaus and Bad Harzburg. The B27 leads south-west to the St Andreasberg turn-off and north-east to the eastern Harz.

ST ANDREASBERG
☎ 05582 • pop 2500

Known for its mining museums, clean air and hiking and skiing options, this hill-top resort sits on a broad ridge surrounded by mountains, 10km south-west of Braunlage. St Andreasberg is a pleasant town that offers a quiet base for trips into the national park. It's wonderful to visit during a warm snow-less spring or a 'golden October'.

The tourist office (☎ 803 36, fax 803 39) is in the Kurverwaltung building at Am Glockenberg 12. It is open weekdays from 9 am to 12.30 pm and 2 to 5 pm; from May to October it opens on Saturday from 10 am till noon.

Most shops close for several hours around noon.

Things to See & Do

German-language tours of the interesting **Grube Samson Mining Museum** (☎ 12 49) take you 20m down into the tunnels to view early forms of mine transportation. They leave daily at 11 am and 2.30 pm (DM6.50). Follow the signs from Dr-Willi-Bergmann-Strasse. The nearby Catharina Neufang tunnel includes a mining demonstration on weekdays at 1.45 pm (DM4).

Skiing in St Andreasberg can be excellent. The closest piste is on Mathias-Schmidt-Berg (☎ 265). Day passes are

DM28 or it's DM2 per ride. You'll also find pistes with lifts out of town on Sonnenberg (☎ 265 or ☎ 513) and Jordanshöhe (☎ 260), but they're difficult to reach by public transport. Skischule Pläschke (☎ 260), Dr-Willi-Bergmann-Strasse 10, rents downhill ski equipment from DM25 a day (DM20 for cross-country equipment) and has some good three-day deals. Hiring a snowboard costs DM15.

Cross-country skiers should pick up the *Wintersportkarte* map (DM4) from the tourist office, which shows groomed and ungroomed trails and some good ski hikes.

The **Rehberger Grabenweg** is a unique hiking trail that leads into the Harz National Park and to Rehberger Grabenhaus (☎ 789), a forest cafe 3km from St Andreasberg and only accessible on foot. In the evening from late December to early March you can sit in the darkened cafe and watch wild deer feeding outside (closed Monday). To avoid disturbing the animals, visitors have to arrive by 5 pm and aren't let out again until 7 pm.

There are exhibits on cultural history in the Harz, park information and a multimedia show in the new **Nationalparkhaus Samsoner Erzwäsche** (☎ 92 30 74) at the Grube Samson mine. Entry is DM3.

Places to Stay & Eat
A small resort tax is charged in St Andreasberg. *Campingplatz Erikabrücke* (☎ 14 31) is 8km south of St Andreasberg on the B27. The *Jugendherberge* (☎ 269, fax 89 00 19), at Am Gesehr 37, costs DM25 for both juniors and seniors.

Hotel Tannhäuser (☎ 918 80, fax 91 88 50, Am Gesehr 1a) has singles/doubles from DM60/120 and a good selection of traditional fare from DM19 and wholefood dishes from DM14.

Getting There & Away
Bus No 65 runs between St Andreasberg and Braunlage. Bus No 432 offers direct services several times daily to/from Goslar and Bad Lauterberg. The less frequent bus No 445 runs to/from Clausthal-Zellerfeld.

St Andreasberg can be reached by the B27, which winds along part of the scenic Oder Valley from Bad Lauterberg to Braunlage. The L519 (Sonnenberg) leads north to the B242 and Clausthal-Zellerfeld, to the B4 and Bad Harzburg, and to Goslar (B241 or the B498 along the Oker Valley).

CLAUSTHAL-ZELLERFELD
☎ 05323 • pop 17,000
Actually two settlements that were united in 1924, this small university town was once the region's most important mining centre. Its main attractions are mineral and spiritual: an excellent mining museum and a spectacular wooden church. But outdoors enthusiasts will feel at home here too, with 66 lakes and ponds, mostly created for the mines, in the immediate area.

Orientation & Information
As in many similar linear towns in the Harz, Clausthal-Zellerfeld's main street changes names several times, with Kronenplatz as the hub. Clausthal lies to the south, while Zellerfeld begins just beyond Bahnhofstrasse, roughly 1km to the north.

The tourist office (☎ 810 24), a 10 minute walk north of Kronenplatz, is in the former train station at Bahnhofstrasse 5a (turn left off Zellbach). It is open weekdays from 9 am to 6 pm, and on Saturday from 10.30 am to 12.30 pm. The building also houses the Kurverwaltung (same telephone number and hours) as well as the Harzclub (☎ 817 58). The latter is open on weekdays from 9 am to noon. The post office is at Kronenplatz 2. For medical services, go to the Robert-Koch-Krankenhaus (☎ 71 40) at Windmühlenstrasse 1. There's a police station (☎ 94 11 00) at Berliner Strasse 10.

Things to See
The **Oberharzer Bergwerksmuseum** (☎ 989 50), Bornhardtstrasse 16, has an interesting open-air exhibition of mine buildings and mining methods, including a model of a horse-driven carousel used to convey minerals. There are lots of mineral exhibits and artefacts in the museum building, and tours

in German (translators are available) take you down into the depths. The museum is open daily from 9 am to 5 pm (DM7). The last tour leaves at 4 pm.

Also of interest is the **Mineralogische Sammlung**, south of Kronenplatz at Adolph-Roemer-Strasse 2a, which has Germany's largest collection of mineral samples. It is open on Monday from 2 to 5 pm, and Tuesday to Friday from 9 am to noon (DM1).

The impressive baroque **Marktkirche Zum Heiligen Geist**, consecrated in 1642, seats more than 2000 people, making it Germany's largest wooden church. Its onion-shaped domes and lightness are a welcome change from the Harz's more stolid structures. The church is in Clausthal at Hindenburgplatz 1, off Adolph-Roemer-Strasse. Its decorative interior can be viewed Monday to Saturday from 9.30 am to 12.30 pm and from 2 to 5 pm, on Sunday and public holidays from 1 to 5 pm (times vary slightly according to the season).

The tourist office and Harzclub can help with information on cross-country ski hire and hiking.

Places to Stay & Eat

A nightly resort tax of DM1.50 is charged by hotels, less at camping grounds and hostels. *Campingplatz Waldweben (☎ 817 12, Spiegeltaler Strasse 31)* is about 1km west of Zellerfeld and open year round. Costs are DM6/8/4.50 per person/tent/car. Over-heated cyclists can cool off in the lakes nearby.

The *Jugendherberge (☎ 842 93, fax 838 27, Altenauer Strasse 55)* is set in forest about 2km from town. To get there, take bus No 408 (the Goslar-Altenau bus) from Kronenplatz and disembark at the Jugendherberge stop. The price for juniors/seniors is DM21/26. The hostel is often closed on the first weekend of the month from mid-September to mid-May.

Friese Hotel (☎ 938 10, Burgstätter Strasse 2), behind the Marktkirche, offers single/double rooms with facilities from DM85/130 and two restaurants.

Goldene Krone (☎ 93 00, fax 931 00, Am Kronenplatz 3) is centrally located and has tasteful rooms with shower and WC from DM105/160. Its restaurant is highly recommended, serving plenty of game (DM25 to DM30). Several cafes and cheaper eating options are also near Kronenplatz.

Getting There & Away

Regular bus services leave 'Bahnhof', the former train station, and Kronenplatz for Goslar and Bad Grund. Catch bus No 445 for St Andreasberg and bus No 408 for Altenau. The B241 leads north to Goslar and south to Osterode, the B242 goes east to Braunlage and St Andreasberg. To reach the A7, take the B242 west. Long-distance buses double as town buses in Clausthal-Zellerfeld. The number to ring for a taxi is ☎ 22 29.

Eastern Harz

WERNIGERODE
☎ 03943 • pop 35,000
Wernigerode is flanked by the foothills of the Harz Mountains. A romantic ducal castle rises above the old town, which counts some 1000 half-timbered houses spanning five centuries. In summer this busy tourist centre attracts throngs of German holidaymakers. It is also the northern terminus of the steam-powered narrow-gauge *Harzquerbahn*, which has chugged the breadth of the Harz for almost a century. The line to the summit of the Brocken, the highest mountain (1142m) in northern Germany, also starts here.

Orientation

The bus and train stations are adjacent on the northern side of town. From Bahnhofplatz, Rudolf-Breitscheid-Strasse leads south-east to Breite Strasse, which runs south-west to the Markt.

The roads Burgberg (where a path begins), Nussallee and Schlosschaussee all lead to the fairy-tale castle on a hill at Agnesberg to the south-east.

Information

The tourist office (☎ 194 33, fax 63 20 40, email wernigerod-tg@netco.de) is at Nicolaiplatz 1, just off Breite Strasse near the Markt. From October to April it is open weekdays from 9 am to 6 pm, Saturday from 10 am to 4 pm. From May to September it closes one hour later on weekdays and is open weekends from 10 am to 4 pm. Its excellent map, *Stadtplan Wernigerode* (DM4.90), includes hiking trails in and around Hochharz National Park.

You'll find several banks on Nicolaiplatz. There's a post office on the corner of Marktstrasse and Kanzleistrasse and a branch at the train station. A hospital, Harz-Klinikum Wernigerode (☎ 610), is at Ilsenburger Strasse 15. The police station (☎ 65 30) is at Nicolaiplatz 4.

Altstadt

On the Markt, the towered **Rathaus** began life as a theatre around 1277, but what you see today is mostly late Gothic from the 16th century. Legend tells us that the artisan who carved the town hall's 33 wooden figures fell out with authorities – and added a few mocking touches. The neo-Gothic **fountain** (1848) was dedicated to charitable nobles, whose names and coats of arms are immortalised on it.

The colourful 15th century **Gothisches Haus**, now a hotel, took its name from the 19th century habit of calling anything old 'Gothic'. Nearby, the quirky **Schiefes Haus** at Klintgasse 5 (reached via Marktstrasse) owes its appearance to a brook below what was once a mill. Downstairs you will find a good music venue (see Entertainment).

In Oberpfarrkirchhof, which surrounds the **Sylvestrikirche** nearby, you will find the **Gadenstedtsches Haus** (1582), with its Renaissance oriel. The **Harz Museum** (☎ 328 56), a short walk away at Klint 10, focuses on local and natural history. It is open Monday to Saturday from 10 am to 5 pm (DM3/2).

Cross the Markt to Breite Strasse. The pretty **Café Wien** building (1583) at No 4 is a worthwhile stopover both for architectural and gastronomical reasons. Elements of the carved facade of the **Krummelshes Haus**, Breite Strasse 72, depict Africa and America – the latter portrayed as a naked woman riding an armadillo. At No 95 you can visit the **Krell'sche Schmiede** (1678; ☎ 60 17 72), a blacksmith museum in a historic workshop built in the south German baroque style. It is open Tuesday to Saturday from 10 am to 4 pm (DM4/3).

Schloss

First built in the 12th century, Wernigerode Castle has been restored and enlarged over the centuries. It got its fairy-tale facade from Count Otto of Stolberg-Wernigerode in the last century. The museum includes portraits of Kaisers, beautiful panelled rooms with original furnishings and the opulent **Festsaal**. It's open from May to October daily from 10 am to 6 pm (last admission at 5.30 pm) and from November to April, Tuesday to Friday from 10 am to 4 pm, and weekends to 6 pm (DM8/7, children DM4).

The stunning **Schlosskirche** (1880) has an altar and pulpit made of French marble. For an extra DM2 you can climb the castle tower, but the views from the castle or restaurant terrace (best appreciated late in the day, when the grounds are empty of visitors) are free and just as spectacular. You can walk (1.5km) or take a Bimmelbahn or Schlossbahn wagon ride (DM3/2 each way) from stops at Marktstrasse (near Schiefes Haus) or Breite Strasse. In summer, horse-drawn carts make the trek from the Markt.

Activities

Highly recommended is the beautiful deciduous forest, crisscrossed by trails and *Forstwege* (forestry tracks), behind the castle. Wernigerode is also a good starting point for hikes and bike rides into Hochharz National Park (see Getting Around for bike-hire places).

Special Events

The **Harz-Gebirgslauf** is an annual fun run and hike program held on the second Saturday in October, which includes a

HARZ MOUNTAINS

Narrow-Gauge Railways

Fans of old-time steam trains or anyone who likes train travel will be in their element on any of the three narrow-gauge railways crossing the Harz. This 132km integrated network – the largest in Europe – is served by 25 steam and 10 diesel locomotives, which tackle gradients of up to 1:25 (40%) and curves as tight as 60m in radius. Most locomotives date from the 1950s, but eight historical models, some from as early as 1897, are proudly rolled out for special occasions. Timetables indicate which trains have steam locomotives.

The network, a legacy of the GDR, consists of three lines. The *Harzquerbahn* runs 60km on a north-south route between Wernigerode and Nordhausen. The serpentine 14km between Wernigerode and Drei Annen Hohne includes 72 bends; you'll get dropped off on the edge of Hochharz National Park.

From the junction at Drei Annen Hohne, the *Brockenbahn* begins the steep climb to Schierke and the Brocken. Direct services to the Brocken can also be picked up from the terminuses in Wernigerode and Nordhausen, or at stations en route.

The third service is the *Selketalbahn*, which begins in Gernrode and runs to Eisfelder Tal or Hasselfelde. At Eisfelder Tal, you can change trains for other lines. The picturesque Selketalbahn initially follows Wellbach, a creek with a couple of good swimming holes, through deciduous forest to Mädgesprung, before joining the Selke Valley and climbing past Alexisbad to high plains around Friedrichshöhe, Stiege and beyond.

Passes for three/five/seven days cost DM70/80/100 for adults and DM35/40/45 for children. Timetables, information and books on the network can be picked up from Harzer Schmalspurbahnen (☎ 03943-55 81 43, fax 55 81 48, www.hsb-wr.de) at Marktstrasse 3 in Wernigerode.

Brocken marathon (☎ 63 28 32 or email Harz.Gebirgslauf@t-online.de). An annual festival of music and theatre is held in the castle from early July to mid-August. Contact the tourist office for programs.

Places to Stay

Camping am Brocken (☎ 039454-425 89) is 10km south in Elbingerode. The city-run *Jugendgästehaus* (☎/fax 63 20 61, Friedrichstrasse 53) offers hostel-like accommodation for DM25 per person, breakfast included. Take bus No 1 or 4 from the train station to the Kirchstrasse stop; alternatively, take the narrow-gauge railway to the Wernigerode Kirchstrasse stop.

Hotel zur Tanne (☎ 63 25 54, fax 63 37 35, Breite Strasse 57) has singles/doubles from DM40/60, or with shower and WC from DM70/95. *Hotel am Anger* (☎ 923 20, fax 92 32 50, Breite Strasse 92) offers bright, pleasant rooms from DM70/120 with shower and WC. There's also parking. Small groups should consider its holiday flats, which cost from DM120. *Hotel Schlossblick* (☎ 63 20 04, fax 63 30 92, Burgstrasse 58) has basic rooms from DM55/75, or rooms with a bathroom from DM95/135. *Pension Schweizer Hof* (☎/fax 63 20 98, Salzbergstrasse 13) should be the first choice for those keen on hiking, with route information and rooms from DM65/100. This is also a branch of the Harzclub. *Hotel und Restaurant zur Post* (☎ 690 40, fax 69 04 30, Marktstrasse 17) has rooms for DM95/160.

The historic *Gothisches Haus* (☎ 67 50, fax 67 55 67, Am Markt 1) is an upmarket option with rooms from DM133/170 off season. Its package deals are good value, and the hotel has a sauna, gym and restaurant. The *Nonnenhof* adjoining it (same contact numbers) is no less historic (with rooms for the same price) and has a traditional restaurant with Harz specialities for around DM15.

Places to Eat

The Markt is a good hunting ground for restaurants. *Konditorei und Café am Markt*, near Breite Strasse, has a chic interior and tall windows. Lunch specials cost DM6.50 to DM14, larger main courses average DM17. It's also popular for ice cream (DM6 to DM11). *Firenze (☎ 63 26 46, Markt 9)* offers quite good Italian food averaging DM25 for main dishes, or DM12 for pizza and pasta, in a pleasant atmosphere. *Altwernigerode Kartoffelhaus (☎ 94 92 90, Marktstrasse 14)* serves well priced potato dishes (from DM6) and grills (closes at midnight). The *Krummelsches Haus (Breite Strasse 72)* has an Italian cafe that serves snacks from DM5 and light dishes for under DM20.

Self-caterers will find a *Spar* supermarket opposite the Café Wien on Breite Strasse.

Entertainment

The *d.a.g.-Guinnesskneipe (Kleine Bergstrasse 13)*, off Burgstrasse, is virtually unmarked except for a lantern. This small, friendly place (closed Monday) combines *Ost-Charme* ('eastern charm') with Irish conviviality. It serves snacks, occasionally has live music, and has been known to celebrate St Patrick's Day twice. The cellar of *Schiefes Haus*, south of the Markt, is a quality bar and music venue for night owls. *Karussell (Breite Strasse 44)*, in the passage, is a popular place to drink. It serves food and has a beer garden on warm summer evenings.

The *Filmkneipe Capitol (Burgstrasse 1)* is a glitzy bar and restaurant with movie-theme decor and standard dishes from DM12 to DM19.

Getting There & Away

Direct buses run to major towns in the region. Consider buying the WVB bus timetable (DM3) from the office (☎ 56 41 34) at the train station if you plan to explore the eastern Harz; it includes a train schedule as well. Bus No 253 runs to Blankenburg (DM4.50) and Thale (DM5.50), while bus No 257 serves Drei Annen Hohne and Schierke (DM4.50), both on the edge of Hochharz National Park.

There are frequent trains to Goslar (DM12, 30 minutes) and Halle (DM31, two hours). Change at Halberstadt for Quedlinburg (DM12, 50 minutes) and Thale (DM15, one hour), at Vienenburg for Goslar. Indirect services go to Braunschweig (DM17, one hour). Tickets on the narrow-gauge trains to the Brocken via Schierke cost DM26/42 one-way/return.

Getting Around

Bus Nos 1 and 2 run from the bus station, in front of the train station, to the Rendez-vous stop just north of the Markt, connecting with bus No 3. Tickets cost DM1.50. For car hire, go to Avis (☎ 498 14), Heinrich-Martin-Klapprothstrasse 30-32. For a taxi, call ☎ 411 44. Hallermann (☎ 63 25 08), at Breite Strasse 27, rents out mountain bikes for DM15 a day. Zweirad John (☎ 63 32 94), north-east of the train station at Zaunwiese 2, does the same for DM25.

RÜBELAND CAVES

Rübeland, a small, rather claustrophobic town just 13km south of Wernigerode, has two of Germany's more beautiful caves. **Baumannshöhle** was formed about 500,000 years ago, and the first tourists visited in 1646, just over a century after its 'rediscovery'. Human presence in the caves dates back 40,000 years. The Goethesaal, which has a pond, is sometimes used for concerts and plays.

Hermannshöhle was formed 350,000 years ago and was rediscovered in the 19th century. Its stalactites and stalagmites are spectacular, especially in the transparent Kristallkammer. Salamanders, introduced from southern Europe by researchers, inhabit one cave. Both caves are open from May to October daily from 9.30 am to 4.30 pm (last entry). During the rest of the year, only one cave is open (last entry at 3.30 pm), and it closes slightly later from February to October. Admission, which includes a guided tour in German, is DM7/3.50.

WVB bus No 258 leaves Wernigerode and Blankenburg for Rübeland hourly (DM3.50). Bus No 265 from Wernigerode to Hasselfelde (DM4.50) – on the Selketal-bahn (see the boxed text 'Narrow-Gauge Railways') – goes via the Wendefurth stop, where you can join the magnificent Bode-tal trail (blue triangle; 16km) to Thale. You can also start the trail from Rübeland itself and cross the Rappbodetalsperre, a 106m-high dam wall across the Harz's largest reservoir, on foot.

Frequent trains ply a small branch line connecting Rübeland with Blankenburg and Königshütte.

If driving from Wernigerode, take the B244 south to Elbingerode, then the B27 east towards Blankenburg.

SCHIERKE
☎ 039455 • pop 1000

Schierke, 16km south-west of Wernigerode, is the last stop for the Brockenbahn before it climbs to the summit. It's also a popular starting point for exploring the Hochharz National Park.

The tourist office (☎ 310, fax 403), Brock-enstrasse 10, is open weekdays from 9 am to noon and from 1 to 4 pm (till 5 pm from May to October). Nationalpark Info (downstairs from the tourist office, same telephone number) is open daily from 8.30 am to 4.30 pm. It has good material in English on the parks, and lots of hiking suggestions.

Activities
Schierke is a popular place for **climbing**, offering all levels of difficulty on nearby cliffs. The Aktiv-Center-Schierke (☎ 868 12), downstairs from the tourist office, hires climbing gear for DM25/20/15 a day for adults/students/children. The equipment is modern, and you can join a group. Courses are also offered. There's also a practice/learner's climbing wall (DM20/15/10, including equipment). It also rents out mountain bikes for DM20/15 for adults/children per half day and DM30/25 for 24 hours. Helmets and locks cost DM5, and child seats are extra. **Skiing** equipment can also be hired for the 70km of groomed trails.

You can **hike** to the Brocken via the bitumen Brockenstrasse (12km), closed to private cars and motorcycles. More interesting is the 7km hike via Eckerloch. Pick up the free *Wanderführer 2* hiking guide from Nationalpark Info. Marked hiking trails also lead to the rugged rock formations of Feuer-steinklippen (30 minutes from the tourist office) and Schnarcherklippen (1½ hours).

Horse-drawn wagons travel from Schierke to the Brocken and cost DM40/20 return for adults/children under 10. Reiter-hof Schierke (☎ 512 12) also operates horse-drawn sleigh services in winter.

On the night of 30 April, Walpurgisnacht, Schierke attracts about 25,000 visitors, many of whom set off on walking tracks to the Brocken.

Places to Stay & Eat
There is plenty of accommodation in town but you may need to book ahead. The tourist office can help. The *Jugendherberge (☎ 510 66, fax 510 67, Brockenstrasse 48)* charges DM27/32 for juniors/seniors.

Hotel König (☎ 383, fax 510 57, Kirch-berg 15) has a beautiful foyer, basic singles/doubles from DM60/80, and nice rooms with facilities from DM90/120. It also has a good restaurant, with hearty dishes from DM13 to DM25.

Getting There & Around
WVB bus No 76 runs six times daily between Braunlage and Schierke via Elend (DM3.50). The WVB bus No 257 is quite frequent and runs between Wernigerode and Schierke, connecting with bus No 76. Narrow-gauge railway services between Wernigerode and Schierke cost DM9/14 one-way/return. Tickets for the Brocken-bahn cost DM26/42 from all stations. If driving from the west, take the B27 from Braunlage and turn off at Elend. From Wernigerode, take Friedrichstrasse.

MITTELBAU DORA
From late 1943, thousands of slave labourers – mostly Russian, French and Polish prisoners of war – toiled under horrific conditions digging tunnels in the chalk hills north of Nordhausen. From a 20km

labyrinth of tunnels, they produced the V1 and V2 rockets that rained destruction on London, Antwerp and other cities during the final stages of WWII.

The camp, called Mittelbau Dora, was created as a satellite of the Buchenwald concentration camp after British bombers destroyed the missile plants in far northeastern Germany. During the last two years of the war, at least 20,000 prisoners died at Dora, many having survived Auschwitz only to be worked to death here.

The US army reached the gates in April 1945, cared for survivors and removed all missile equipment before turning the area over to the Russians two months later. Much of the technology was later employed in the US space program.

During the period of the GDR, Dora mouldered away, marked only by a couple of small memorials. The horrible truth of the place belies any need for extensive facilities, and a visit to the camp may be among the most unforgettable experiences you have in Germany.

Orientation & Information

Mittelbau Dora is 5km north of Nordhausen, an unfortunate town of interest only in regards to changing trains. The camp information office (☎ 03631-98 36 36) opens April to September daily from 10 am to 6 pm (till 4 pm the rest of the year).

The grounds, including the crematorium and a museum, are also open daily. The tunnels, which are the diameter of an aircraft hangar, are only accessible by guided tour. Within the dank walls you can see partially assembled rockets that have lain untouched for over 50 years.

Tours run from Tuesday to Friday at 11 am and 2 pm, and weekends at 11 am, 1 and 3 pm (also at 4 pm from April to September). No admission, of course, is charged.

Getting There & Away

The *Harzquerbahn* links Nordhausen with Wernigerode (three hours by narrow-gauge railway). The nearest stop to Dora is Nordhausen-Krimderode, served by almost hourly trains from the Nordhausen-Nord train station, immediately adjacent to the main Nordhausen station (11 minutes).

From the Krimderode stop, cross the tracks and walk south along Goetheweg, which curves and becomes Kohnsteinweg. Follow this for 1km towards the unassuming hill and you are at the camp.

Bus G goes directly to the memorial from Nordhausen's main bus station (ZOB) weekdays at 9.15 am and 1.45 pm, returning at 12.24 and 5.24 pm.

Trains run to Halle (DM24, 1½ hours) and Göttingen (DM25, 1½ hours) from Nordhausen.

BROCKEN & TORFHAUS
☎ 039455 (Brocken)
☎ 05320 (Torfhaus)

There are prettier landscapes and hikes in the Harz, but the Brocken is what draws the crowds – about 50,000 on a summer's day. When he wasn't exploring mines, Goethe also scaled the mountain – in stockings.

Goetheweg from Torfhaus

The 8km Goetheweg trail to the Brocken from the western Harz starts at Torfhaus. The Goetheweg, which is easier than other approaches, initially takes you through bog, follows a historic aqueduct once used to regulate water levels for the mines, then crosses the Kaiserweg. Anyone who has begun their sweaty Brocken ascent via the 11km Kaiserweg from Bad Harzburg to Torfhaus will probably feel a prickle of excitement here. Unfortunately, your next stop will be a dead forest, though the trail becomes steep and more interesting as you walk along the former border; you then hike along the train line on a ramp above soggy moorland. Enjoy the view, the pea soup and Bockwurst that's served at the top, and think of Goethe and Heine.

The **Nationalparkhaus** (☎ 263), at Torfhaus 21, has information on the parks and is open daily from 9 am to 5 pm. From November to March its reduced weekend hours are from 10 am to 4 pm. On top of the Brocken itself is the **Brockenmuseum**, an alpine garden and a 2.5km trail following what was once a wall around the summit.

Torfhaus is a good starting point for cross-country skiing or winter ski treks. Downhill skiing is limited to 1200m (two pistes); one recommended route is the 11km Kaiserweg trail to Bad Harzburg. Make sure you pack a good map and take all precautions.

The *Jugendherberge* (☎ 242, fax 254, *Torfhaus 3*) charges DM23.30/28.30 for juniors/seniors and runs nature programs, including hikes into the park. It also hires out cross-country ski gear for DM12.

Getting There & Away
Bus No 63/422 stops frequently at Torfhaus on the Bad Harzburg-Braunlage route.

QUEDLINBURG
☎ 03946 • pop 26,000
Unspoiled Quedlinburg is a popular year-round destination, especially since being added to UNESCO's World Heritage List 1992. Almost all the buildings in the historic town centre are half-timbered – street after cobbled street of them – and they are slowly being restored. The history of Quedlinburg is closely associated with the Frauenstift, a medieval collegiate foundation for widows and daughters of the nobility that enjoyed the direct protection of the Kaiser.

The Reich was briefly ruled in the 10th century from here by two women, Theophano and Adelheid, successive guardians of the child-king Otto III.

Orientation
The circular, medieval centre of the old town is a 10 minute walk from the train station along Bahnhofstrasse. To reach the Markt, turn left onto Heiligegeiststrasse after the post office. Hohe Strasse, off the Markt, leads south to the castle. The Bode River flows north-east through the town near the train station.

Information
The tourist office (☎ 77 30 12, fax 77 30 16) is at Markt 2. It is open from May to September weekdays from 9 am to 7 pm,

and weekends from 10 am to 4 pm. In October, December, March and April it is open weekdays from 9 am to 6 pm and weekends from 10 am to 3 pm. From November to February it is open weekdays only from 9 am to 5 pm. The accommodation service here is free. Book well in advance in summer.

There are several banks on the Markt, and the post office is on Bahnhofstrasse. The hospital, Dorothea Christiane Erxleben (☎ 90 90), is at Ditfurter Weg 24. The police station (☎ 97 70) is at Schillerstrasse 3.

Around the Markt
The Rathaus (1310) has been expanded over the years. It received its Renaissance facade in 1616. Quedel, the small hound above the entrance, is the city's symbol and is said to protect those who enter. Inside, the beautiful Festsaal is decorated with a cycle of frescoes focusing on Quedlinburg's colourful history. A German-language tour of the Rathaus (DM4/2) is conducted daily at 1.30 pm from April to October. The Roland statue (1426) in front of the Rathaus dates from the year Quedlinburg joined the Hanseatic League.

The late-Gothic Marktkirche St Benedikti is behind the Rathaus. On the tower you'll see a small house used by town watchmen until 1901. The mausoleum nearby survived the relocation of the church graveyard in the 19th century. There are some fine half-timbered buildings in Kirchhof, near the Marktkirche. At Breite Strasse 39 is the Gildehaus zur Rose (1612), arguably the city's most spectacular half-timbered house. The richly carved and panelled interior is the town's best night-time haunt (see Entertainment).

Return to the Markt and walk through Schuhhof, a shoemakers' courtyard on the east side, with shutters and stable-like 'gossip doors'. Alter Klopstock (1580) at Stieg 28 has scrolled beams typical of Quedlinburg's 16th century half-timbered houses. Also worth a peek is the Renaissance Hagensches Freihaus (1564), an impressive stone mansion at Klink 11.

Zwischen den Städten, an old bridge, connects the old town and **Neustadt**, which developed alongside the town wall around 1200, when peasants fled a feudal power struggle on the land. Many of the houses here have high archways, and courtyards are dotted with pigeon towers. Of special note are the **Hotel zur Goldenen Sonne** building (1671) at Steinweg 11 and **Zur Börse** (1683) at No 23.

Museums

Fachwerkmuseum Ständebau Located at Wordgasse 3, this museum (☎ 38 28) is in one of Germany's oldest half-timbered houses (1310), built with perpendicular struts supporting the roof. Inside, visitors can learn all about the history and construction of half-timbered buildings and view models of local styles. It is open daily except Thursday from 11 am to 5 pm (DM4/2.50).

Klopstockhaus The early classicist poet, Friedrich Gottlieb Klopstock (1724-1803), is one of Quedlinburg's celebrated sons. He was born inside this 16th century house at Schlossberg 12, which now houses a museum (☎ 26 10) containing some interesting exhibits on Klopstock himself and Dorothea Erxleben (1715-62), Germany's first woman doctor. Opening hours are Tuesday to Sunday from 10 am to 5 pm (DM5/3).

Lyonel-Feininger-Galerie This recently renovated gallery (☎ 22 38), at Finkenherd 5a, is devoted to the work of influential Bauhaus artist Lyonel Feininger (1871-1956), who was born in Germany and became an American citizen. The original graphics, drawings, watercolours and sketches on display are from the years 1906 to 1936 and were hidden from the Nazis by a Quedlinburg citizen. One highlight is Feininger's oil on canvas *Selbstbildnis mit Tonpfeife* (Self-Portrait with Clay Pipe). The gallery has the same hours as Klopstockhaus but closes from April to October at 6 pm (DM6/3).

Schlossberg

The castle district, perched above Quedlinburg on a 25m-high plateau, was established during the reign of Heinrich I, from 919 to 936. The present-day Renaissance **Schloss**, partly built upon earlier foundations, dates from the 16th century and offers good views over the town. The **Residenzbau** in the north wing houses the **Schloss Museum**, which has some mildly interesting exhibits on local natural and social history. The centrepiece, however, is its recently restored baroque **Blauer Saal** (Blue Hall). The museum is open from May to September daily (except Monday) from 10 am to 6 pm, and October to April from 9 am to 5 pm (DM5/3).

The 12th century Romanesque **Stiftskirche St Servatius** is one of Germany's most significant of the period. Its treasury contains valuable reliquaries and early Bibles. The crypt has some early religious frescoes and contains the graves of Heinrich and his widow, Mathilde, along with those of the abbesses. The church is open from May to October, Tuesday to Saturday from 10 am to 6 pm, and Sunday from noon to 6 pm. From November to April it closes daily at 4 pm (DM6/4).

Bimmelbahn rides through the Altstadt and Neustadt leave from the parking area on Carl-Ritter-Strasse, near Schlossberg, from April to October on the hour from 10 am (DM8, 45 minutes).

Münzenberg & Wipertikirche

Across Wipertistrasse, on the hill west of the castle, are the ruins of Münzenberg, a Romanesque convent. It was plundered during the Peasant Wars in 1525, and small houses were later built among the ruins. The settlement then became home to wandering minstrels, knife grinders and other itinerant tradespeople.

The Wipertikirche crypt dates from around 1000, and the church itself was used as a barn from 1812 until its restoration in the 1950s. The only way to see the church is by taking a tour (DM6/4 for adults/children), conducted by the tourist office daily from May to October (arrange the time in advance).

euro currency converter DM1 = €0.51

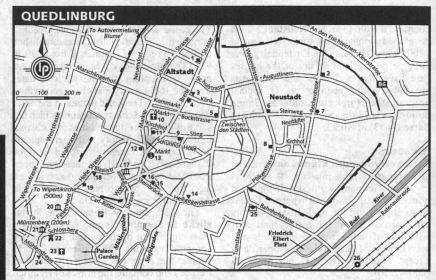

Special Events
A program of classical music is held in the Stiftskirche St Servatius each year from May to September. For tickets and information, contact the tourist office.

Places to Stay
The closest camping ground is *Am Bremer Dammteich* (☎ 039485-608 10, fax 500 55), along a forest lake approximately 7km south of Gernrode, near Haferfeld. Gernrode itself is about 8km south of Quedlinburg. The *hostel* there (same contact numbers) charges DM15 per person (no breakfast).

In Quedlinburg, *Familie Klindt* (☎ 70 29 11, Hohe Strasse 19) is basic but central and has reasonable singles/doubles with shower and WC for DM35/50. *Zum Augustinern* (☎ 701 60, fax 70 12 35, Reichenstrasse 35a) has nice rooms with full facilities from DM70/110; there's a traditional restaurant downstairs. *Hotel am Dippeplatz* (☎ 70 50 22, fax 91 59 92, Breite Strasse 16) has bright, clean rooms starting from DM80/110 with facilities. The historic *Hotel zur Goldenen Sonne* (☎ 962 50, fax 96 25 30, Steinweg 11) has a spacious and suitably wooden interior, with rooms from DM90/140. The hotel *Zum Alten Fritz* (☎ 70 48 80, fax 70 48 81, Pölkenstrasse 18), though less historic, offers pleasant rooms from DM95/125.

ROMANTIK Hotel Theophano (☎ 963 00 fax 96 30 36, Markt 13/14) is highly recommended for a night of baroque luxury. It offers rooms from DM120/160, four-poster beds, and a good restaurant (see Places to Eat) and vaulted wine bar in the cellar.

Places to Eat
The *Kartoffelhaus* (☎ 70 83 34, Breite Strasse 37) is difficult to beat for its filling potato dishes, priced from DM6 to DM23. Enter from Klink. *Fisch-Spezialitäten*, on Steinbrücke, serves good fish mains for under DM10 and cheap fish rolls. *Pasta Mia* (☎ 21 22, Steinbrücke 23) is a trendy Italian cafe and eatery with pizza for around DM12, but most main dishes are in the DM20 to DM25 price range.

Brauhaus Lüdde (☎ 32 51, Blasiistrasse 14), a lively microbrewery, serves up hearty

HARZ MOUNTAINS

QUEDLINBURG

PLACES TO STAY
1 Hotel am Dippeplatz
2 Zum Augustinern
6 Hotel zur Goldenen Sonne
8 Zum Alten Fritz
12 Hotel Theophano
19 Familie Klindt

PLACES TO EAT
3 Kartoffelhaus
14 Supermarket
15 Fisch-Spezialitäten
16 Pasta Mia
18 Brauhaus Lüdde
24 Café Romanik

OTHER
4 Gildehaus zur Rose
5 Hagensches Freihaus
7 Zur Börse
9 Alter Klopstock
10 Marktkirche St Benedikti
11 Rathaus
13 Tourist Office
17 Fachwerkmuseum Ständebau
20 Lyonel-Feininger-Galerie
21 Klopstockhaus
22 Schloss
23 Stiftskirche St Servatius
25 Post Office
26 Train & Bus Station

lunches and dinners for DM14 to DM22. We weren't all that thrilled by its Pilsener beer, but try the Lüdde-Alt or low-alcohol Pubarschknall. It stays open till midnight most nights.

Weinkeller Theophano, in the Hotel Theophano, serves light traditional dishes from DM10 to DM20 and a small range of seasonally varying main courses – lamb and beef fillet will probably feature. Expect to pay around DM35. It is closed on Sunday and Monday from November to March, and most of January.

Café Romanik (Mühlenstrasse 21), behind the castle, is highly recommended for tea and cakes, and has a comfortable old-world ambience.

The **supermarket** on Heiligegeiststrasse, just before the Markt, is convenient to the town centre.

Entertainment

After-dark options in Quedlinburg are extremely limited. **Gildehaus zur Rose** (Breite Strasse 39) is the most popular nightspot; the interior alone justifies a visit. It also serves light meals (closed Monday).

Getting There & Away

The QBus office (☎ 22 36) inside the train station has timetables and information on its frequent regional services, which leave from the train station for most towns in the eastern Harz. Quedlinburg's train station is one of the worst we experienced in the region. It has no toilets (beg inside the neighbouring Spielsalon if you're in dire straits), and too many clean-shaven heads kill time in the waiting hall for our taste – but the waiting hall is not always open. Check closing times before putting your luggage in the lockers, as there's no access once the main hall closes.

For trains to Wernigerode (DM12, one hour), change at Halberstadt. A branch line runs to Gernrode (DM3, 15 minutes); other frequent trains go to Thale (DM3, nine minutes). If the ticket office is closed, buy a ticket on the train.

The Romanesque Road (Strasse der Romanik) leads south to Gernrode. This theme road connects towns that have significant Romanesque architecture. The B6 runs west to Wernigerode, Goslar, the A395 (for Braunschweig) and the A7 between Kassel and Hanover. For Halle take the B6 east, and for Halberstadt the B79 north.

Getting Around

Infrequent city buses ply the ring road, but you probably won't need them. Cars can be hired from Autovermietung Blume (☎ 88 05), Schillerstrasse 10. For a taxi, call ☎ 70 70 70 or ☎ 88 88.

GERNRODE
☎ 039485 • pop 4000

Only 8km south of Quedlinburg, Gernrode makes an ideal day trip. Its Stiftskirche St Cyriakus is one of Germany's finest churches. Hikers, picnickers and steam-train enthusiasts will also enjoy this pretty town.

The tourist office (☎ 354) is a 10 minute walk from the train station on Suderode Strasse. It's open weekdays from 9 am to 4 pm (weekends by arrangement).

Stiftskirche St Cyriakus
This church is one of the purest examples of Romanesque architecture from the Ottonian period. Construction of the basilica, which is based on the form of a cross, was begun in 959. Especially noteworthy is the early use of alternating columns and pillars, later a common Romanesque feature. The octagonal **Taufstein** (Christening stone), whose religious motifs culminate in the Ascension, dates from 1150. In the south aisle you will find **Das Heilige Grab**, an 11th century replica of Christ's tomb in Jerusalem. The 19th century organ is both visually and aurally impressive. St Cyriakus is open from April to October weekdays from 9 am to 5 pm and on Saturday from 10 am. On Sunday it stays open after the 10 am service. Winter hours are from 10 am to 4 pm. Tours cost DM3 and are conducted at 3 pm daily, when the church is closed to general visitors for an hour. The tourist office has information on summer concerts here.

Activities
Especially picturesque is the 30 minute ride on the narrow-gauge railway from Gernrode to Mägdesprung (DM2). The trip can be broken at Sternhaus Ramberg, where a short trail leads through the forest to Bremer Teich, a pretty swimming hole with a camping ground and hostel (see Places to Stay in Quedlinburg). You can also walk to Mägdesprung and beyond from Gernrode along paths beside the train track.

From the corner of Bahnhofstrasse and Marktstrasse, marked trails lead east to Burg Falkenstein (11km), the historic castle in the Selke valley, and west to Thale (about 13km).

Getting There & Around
Regular QBus services stop at the train station and link Thale, Quedlinburg and Gernrode. Three night buses also stop here, including the Nacht3 to Thale. Small trains

chug almost hourly across the plain from Quedlinburg. Gernrode is the railhead for the Selketalbahn (see the boxed text 'Narrow-Gauge Railways' in the Eastern Harz section). Tickets and information can be picked up at the train station (☎ 94 00), where you can also hire bicycles (DM18 a day).

THALE
☎ 03947 • pop 15,000
Situated below the northern slopes of the Harz Mountains, Thale is blessed with a sensational landscape of rugged cliffs and a lush river valley that makes for ideal hiking. On the two cliffs at the head of the valley are Hexentanzplatz and Rosstrappe, both Bethlehems for postmodern pagans, who gather in grand style and numbers each year on 30 April to celebrate Walpurgisnacht.

Thale's mainstay was once its steelworks, the Eisen und Hüttenwerk Thale, which in GDR times employed some 8000 workers. That number has now dropped to 500, but Thale has kept its identity as a workers' town.

Orientation & Information
Thale's two main streets are Poststrasse, which runs diagonally off Bahnhofstrasse (go left on leaving the train station), and Karl-Marx-Strasse, which runs north-east to the Bode River.

The friendly tourist office (☎ 25 97, fax 22 77) is opposite the train station at Rathausstrasse 1. It is open from November to April weekdays from 9 am to 5 pm. From May to October it closes an hour later and is also open weekends from 9 am to 3 pm. Pick up the free English-language brochure *Thale Fabulous* here.

A Sparkasse bank is near the train station at the top of Karl-Marx-Strasse. The post office is at Karl-Marx-Strasse 16 in the Kaufhof department store. The police station (☎ 460) is at Rudolf-Breitscheid-Strasse 10.

Hexentanzplatz & Rosstrappe
These two rugged outcrops flanking the Bode Valley once had Celtic fortresses and were used by Germanic tribes for occult rituals and sacrifices (see the boxed text

'Witches & Warlocks'). The name of the Bode River is said to derive from a myth. Brunhilde, who symbolises the 'unnaturally' powerful woman, refuses to marry the uncouth Bohemian prince, Bodo. Unhappily crowned and dressed to the nines for the wedding, she flees on horseback, springing across the gorge, hotly pursued by Bodo. The impact of Brunhilde's (successful) landing leaves an imprint of the horse's hoof in the stone (which you can see, of course), on Rosstrappe; the crown, however, topples into the valley. Meanwhile, Bodo, who isn't much chop at hurdling gorges, plunges into

the valley, mysteriously turns into a black dog, and is destined to guard Brunhilde's crown there for evermore. It is worth a climb or ride up for the magnificent views alone.

A modern cable car runs to Hexentanz-platz (DM5/8 one-way/return), or you can take a chair lift to Rosstrappe for DM4/6 (discounts are available). Both run from May to September daily from 10 am to 6 pm. The cable car also runs from October to April daily from 10 am to 4.30 pm, and the chair lift also in October from 9.30 am to 6 pm. From November to April the chair lift sometimes runs on weekends and holidays.

HARZ MOUNTAINS

Witches & Warlocks

The area around the mouth of the Bodetal once contained Celtic fortresses built to fend off tribes descending from the north. The Celts had been driven out by 500 BC, when Germanic tribes took over the fortresses and turned them into sites for meetings and ritual sacrifices. These played an important role in the 8th century Saxon Wars, when Charlemagne embarked upon campaigns to subjugate and Christianise the local population. The mythology surrounding the sites blends these pagan and Christian elements.

One popular – but misleading – explanation for the Walpurgisnacht festival is that it was an invention of the tribes who, pursued by Christian missionaries, held secret gatherings to carry out their rituals. They are said to have darkened their faces one night and, armed with broomsticks and pitchforks, scared off Charlemagne's guards, who mistook them for witches and devils. A similar explanation appears in Goethe's *Faust*. The name 'Walpurgisnacht' itself probably derives from St Walpurga (or Walburga), who was born in England around 710 and became a Benedictine abbess at Hildesheim. Her name day is 1 May.

Originally considered benevolent, witches were only ascribed evil traits in the Middle Ages. A turning point came with the book *Hexenhammer*, published by two Dominican clerics in Strasbourg in 1486, which drew a connection between heresy and witchcraft. Natural disasters, disease, childlessness and impotence were blamed on heretics – mainly women. *Hexenhammer* described how witches met secretly in covens at night, renounced Christianity and paid homage to the devil. This was followed by a feast, often on the flesh of babies and children, and orgies between witches and warlocks. These orgies were said to represent copulation with the devil. The region's most notorious inquisitor was Duke Heinrich Julius of Braunschweig. In Quedlinburg, 133 people were convicted of sorcery in 1574, many ending up burnt at the stake.

According to local mythology, witches and warlocks gather on Walpurgisnacht at locations throughout the Harz Mountains before flying off to the Brocken on broomsticks or goats. There they recount the year's evil deeds and top off the stories with a bacchanalian frenzy. Frightened peasants used to hang crosses and herbs on stable doors to protect their livestock. Ringing church bells or cracking whips was another way to prevent stray witches from dropping by.

One of the best places to celebrate Walpurgisnacht is Thale. Schierke, also popular, is a starting point for Walpurgisnacht treks to the Brocken.

Go early or late in the day to avoid crowds. Signs direct you from the train station.

The wooden **Walpurgishalle** museum on Hexentanzplatz has exhibitions and paintings on matters heathen, including the **Opferstein**, a stone once used in Germanic sacrificial rituals. It is open from April to October daily from 9 am to 5 pm (DM2). Nearby is a 10 hectare **Tierpark** with lynx, wild cats and other animals. It's open year round (DM4/3, children DM2).

Hiking

The tourist-office brochures *Wanderführer* and *Führer durch das Bodetal* (DM3 each) are excellent if your German is up to it. Highly recommended is the Bode Valley walk between Thale and Treseburg (10km one-way; blue triangle). If you take the bus from Thale to Treseburg (QBus No 18; limited service), you can walk downstream and enjoy the most spectacular scenery at the end. Another 10km trail (red dot) goes from Hexentanzplatz to Treseburg; combine with the valley walk to make a round trip.

Special Events

The open-air Harzer Bergtheater on Hexentanzplatz has a summer program of music and plays, and a performance on Walpurgisnacht, when some 35,000 people flock to Thale. Tickets are sold at the venue or in advance from the tourist office (refunds/swaps are possible if performances are cancelled due to bad weather).

Places to Stay & Eat

Book extremely early for Walpurgisnacht. The number of cheap *private rooms* is limited, but the tourist office can help, especially in finding holiday flats, a good option if you plan to stay a few days.

The *Jugendherberge* (☎ 28 81, fax 916 53) is nestled in the lush Bode Valley, five minutes from the train station at Bodetal-Waldkater, and costs DM22/27 for juniors/

seniors. To reach it, go south along Hubertusstrasse from the top of Friedenspark. The Bode Valley trail begins at the door.

The friendly *Kleiner Ritter* (☎ 25 70, Markt 2), a small pension across the Bode River, has basic singles/doubles for DM35/70. It is best reached via Karl-Marx-Strasse (across the bridge and right onto Rosstrappenstrasse).

Pension Am Steinbach (☎ 93 50, fax 935 40, Poststrasse 9), near the train station, has cosy rooms for DM70/100. *Wilder Jäger* (☎ 95 00, fax 950 15, Poststrasse 18) has rooms with facilities from DM80/125. *Zur alten Backstube* (☎ 49 80, fax 498 31, Rudolf-Breitscheid-Strasse 15) has fine rooms for DM95/140 and free parking. Rudolf-Breitscheid-Strasse is a continuation of Poststrasse. Mains in the traditional restaurant downstairs cost around DM25. The rustic *Kleiner Waldkater* (☎/fax 28 26), in the valley alongside the hostel, is good value at DM60/100 for rooms with shower and WC. The location alone makes its restaurant a good place to drop in.

Restaurants and hotels can be found on Hexentanzplatz and Rosstrappe.

Getting There & Around

The bus station on Bahnhofstrasse is alongside the train station and tourist office. For Wernigerode, take WVB 253; for Treseburg, take QBus No 18 (both services have season restrictions). Night buses N3 and N4 go via Thale (and Hexentanzplatz) to Harzgerode and Quedlinburg respectively.

Frequent trains travel to Halberstadt (DM8, 30 minutes), Quedlinburg (DM3, nine minutes), Wernigerode (DM15, one hour) and Magdeburg (DM34, 1½ hours). Karl-Marx-Strasse leads to the main junction for roads to Quedlinburg and Wernigerode.

Call ☎ 24 35 or ☎ 55 35 for a taxi. Fahrradhaus Wagner (☎ 915 46), Bodestrasse 4, has bikes for hire from around DM25 per day.

Mecklenburg-Western Pomerania

Mecklenburg-Vorpommern (Mecklenburg-Western Pomerania) is a low-lying, post-glacial region of lakes, meadows, forests and the beaches of the Ostsee (Baltic Sea), stretching across northern Germany from Schleswig-Holstein to the Polish border. Most of the state is historic Mecklenburg; only the island of Rügen and the area between Stralsund and the Oder River belonged to the province of Pomerania, the bulk of which was handed over to Poland in 1945.

In 1160 the Duke of Saxony, Heinrich der Löwe (Henry the Lion), conquered the region (under the guise of introducing Christianity) and made the local Polish princes his vassals. Germanisation gradually reduced the Slavic element, and in 1348 the dukes of Mecklenburg became princes of the Holy Roman Empire. Sweden became involved in the area during the Thirty Years' War (1618-48). In 1867 the whole region joined the North German Confederation and, in 1871, the German Reich.

Some of the offshore islands, such as Poel and Hiddensee, are still undiscovered paradises, while others, including Rügen, are becoming increasingly popular with tourists. Just keep in mind the very short swimming season (July and August only). Spring and autumn can be cold.

In the centre of the state, the Mecklenburg Lake Plains (Mecklenburger Seenplatte) are wide open to hikers, cyclists and sailors, especially in the vast Müritz National Park. The medieval walled city of Neubrandenburg and its surrounding area is delightful. And the maritime cities of Rostock and Wismar are accessible and welcoming.

Accommodation

In addition to an excellent range of hostels and camping grounds, especially within the Mecklenburger Seenplatte area, dozens of the state's more than 2000 castles are open as castle hotels *(Schlösser und Her-*

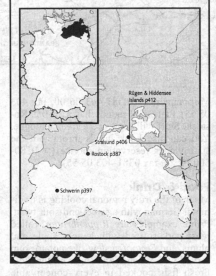

MECKLENBURG

renhäuser). Some are used as spas, others as resorts and executive retreats. Prices start at about DM75 per person per night.

For a comprehensive list of castle hotels, contact Tourismusverband Mecklenburg-

MECKLENBURG-WESTERN POMERANIA

Vorpommern (☎ 0381-403 06 00, fax 403 05 55), Platz der Freundschaft 1, 18059 Rostock. Staff will send you a free catalogue. You can also book hotels throughout the state via its reservation service (☎ 0180-500 02 23, fax 0381-403 05 55).

Food & Drink

Much of the truly regional cooking is traditional German with a sweet-and-sour twist. Prime examples are *Rippenbraten*, rolled roast pork stuffed with lemon, apple and plums, and *Eintopf*, a stew-like potato soup served with vinegar and sugar on the side. Fresh fish, cooked in every conceivable way, is very popular, as is *Heringe in Sahnestipp*, herring in cream sauce. In Wismar, try *Wismarer Spickaal*, young eel smoked in a way unique to the area.

Local firewaters include the powerful (45% alcohol) Rostocker Kümmel, an after-dinner drink made from caraway, and the wheat-based Rostocker Korn. The most popular beers are Rostocker Pils, slightly bitter, and Rostocker Dunkles, a dark beer.

ROSTOCK
☎ 0381 • pop 210,000

Rostock, the largest city in sparsely populated north-eastern Germany, is a major Baltic port and shipbuilding centre. First mentioned in 1161 as a Danish settlement, the city began taking shape as a German fishing village around 1200. In the 14th and 15th centuries, Rostock was an important Hanseatic city, trading with Riga, Bergen and Bruges. Parts of the city centre, especially along Kröpeliner Strasse, retain the flavour of this period.

As a major shipbuilding and shipping centre of the GDR, the city was pummelled by socialist architectural 'ideas', and the old city is surrounded by eyesores thrown up to house the longshoremen busy along the Warnow River. But much of the centre has been spruced up, and the mood among locals is relatively upbeat – even though its uncompetitive shipyards may not survive much longer.

Orientation

The city begins at the Südstadt (Southern City), south of the Hauptbahnhof, and extends north to Warnemünde on the Baltic Sea. Much of the city is on the western side of the Warnow River, which creates a long shipping channel from the Altstadt practically due north to the sea.

The Altstadt – the city centre – is a circular area about 1.5km north of the Hauptbahnhof. Blücher Strasse runs north from the station to Steintor, which unofficially marks the southern boundary of the Altstadt; the northern and eastern boundary is formed by the Warnow inlet; the western boundary is Kröpeliner Tor.

Information

Tourist Offices The tourist office (π 194 33 or 49 79 90, fax 497 99 23, email touristinfo@rostock.de) is at Schnickmann-strasse 13-14, 2km from the train station. Its helpful staff sell the Rostock Card (DM15), which gives you free bus/tram transport and discounts for many sights over a 48 hour period. Take tram No 11 or 12 outside the station and get off at the Lange Strasse stop.

Money There's a Reisebank in the Hauptbahnhof and a Citibank just north of Universitätsplatz on Kröpeliner Strasse.

Post & Communications Rostock's main post office is opposite the Rathaus, on the southern end of Neuer Markt, and has a Postbank inside. The Internetcafé Riz (π 496 11 61), Wismarsche Strasse 44, charges DM5 for half an hour's surfing.

Travel Agencies Atlas Reisewelt (π 38 00, Lange Strasse 38), in front of the Radisson

SAS Hotel, offers last-minute and discount tickets, as well as train tickets. Zimmerbörse Reisecenter Delphini (π 45 44 44), at Lange Strasse 19, books rooms and package tours.

Bookshops & Libraries The Pressezentrum (π 490 80 72) in the Gallerie Rostocker Hof shopping mall, Kröpeliner Strasse 26, and the Universitäts-Buchhandlung (University Bookshop; π 492 26 03) in Five-Gables Houses stock English-language books.

The Europa-Bibliothek (π 45 43 95), a multilingual offshoot of the university, is at Lagerstrasse 43. It's open Monday to Friday from 9 am to 4 pm (closed Wednesday). The main city library is at Kröpeliner Strasse 82.

University Established in 1419, Universität Rostock is the oldest in northern Germany. It has 10,000 students, mainly of medicine, law and theology. The main campus is in the city centre, at Universitätsplatz.

Laundry There's a laundrette (π 44 20 38) at Rudolf-Diesel-Strasse 1 in Südstadt. Walk under the Hauptbahnhof, turn right on the walkway in front of the Büro Hotel to Südring, go south one block, turn right, go one block to Rudolf-Diesel-Strasse and it's on the left.

Medical Services The Klinikum Süd (π 440 10) is at Südring. The Ärztehaus (π 456 16 22), Paulstrasse 48, will tackle less serious ailments during regular business hours.

Dangers & Annoyances Some tough-looking characters cruise around at night (more in the suburbs than in the Altstadt). Rostock became (in)famous for a 1992 arson attack on a home for asylum-seekers, and despite a police crackdown there are still occasional reports of right-wing violence.

Marienkirche

Rostock's pride and joy is the 13th century Marienkirche (St Mary's Church; 1290), which somehow survived WWII unscathed – the only one of Rostock's four main

euro currency converter DM1 = €0.51

MECKLENBURG

churches to do so. The long transept running north-south was added after the ceiling collapsed in 1398; this gives the building its unique shape.

The 12m-high **astrological clock** (1470-72), hand-wound every morning, is behind the main altar. At the very top are a series of doors; at noon and midnight the innermost right door opens and six of the 12 apostles march out to parade around Jesus (note that Judas is locked out). The lower section has a disc that tells the day, the date and the exact day on which Easter falls in any given year. The discs are replaceable and accurate for 130 years. The current one expires in 2017, and the university already has a new one ready.

Other highlights include the Gothic bronze baptismal **font** (1290), the **baroque organ** (1770) and, on the northern side of the main altar, some fascinating tombstones in the floor. Ascend the 207 steps of the 50m-high church tower for the view (free).

The church is open to visitors Monday to Saturday from 10 am to 5 pm, and Sunday from 11.30 am to noon (DM2).

Kröpeliner Strasse & Universitätsplatz

Kröpeliner Strasse, a broad, lively, cobblestone pedestrian mall lined with 15th and 16th century burghers' houses, runs from Neuer Markt west to Kröpeliner Tor.

At the centre of the mall is Universitätsplatz, positively swarming with people year round, and its centrepiece, the **Brunnen der Lebensfreude** (Fountain of Happiness). True to its name, the square is lined with university buildings and includes a handsome **baroque hall** with a fancy gable on the east side.

At the south side of the square stands an impressive bronze **statue of Field Marshal Blücher von Wahlstatt**, Rostock's most beloved military hero, who helped defeat Napoleon at Waterloo. On the statue's rear is a poem by Goethe, and on the other side a relief depicting the battle at Waterloo.

At the northern side of Universitätsplatz are the **Five Gables Houses**, modern interpretations of the residences that lined the square before WWII.

At the south-western end of Universitätsplatz is the **Kloster Zum Heiligen Kreuz**, a convent established in 1270 by Queen Margrethe II of Denmark. Today it houses the Cultural History Museum (☎ 45 59 13), with an excellent collection including sculptures by Ernst Barlach and Victorian furniture. The museum is open Tuesday to Sunday from 9 am to 5 pm (DM4/2).

City Walls & Gates

Today only two gates – at one time there were 32 – and a small brick section remain of the old city wall. The **Steintor**, at the southern end of the Altstadt, is surrounded by tram tracks. Its Latin inscription *Sit intra te concordia et publica felicitas* means 'Within these walls, let unity and general prosperity prevail'.

West of Steintor is **Wallstrasse**, which leads to the biggest surviving part of the Wallanlagen (Old City Wall). From here, you can stroll west through the pleasant park south of the wall to reach the 55m-high **Kröpeliner Tor**, containing the city's **Regional History Museum**. The top floor is dedicated to the GDR days, and includes a leather jacket given to GDR strongman Erich Honecker in 1980 by West German rocker Udo Lindenberg. It's open Wednesday to Sunday from 9 am to 5 pm (DM4/2).

Neuer Markt

The splendid and very pink 13th century **Rathaus** is at the eastern side of this square, just north of the Steintor. The baroque facade was added in 1727 after the original brick Gothic structure collapsed. Hensellmann, the architect of the northern addition to the Rathaus, was a GDR favourite; his works grace other eastern German cities with equal style and tact. Just behind the Rathaus is the intricate Gothic building housing the **State Archives**.

Opposite the Rathaus is a lovely series of restored **gabled houses**; the northern end of the square leads to the Marienkirche. Just behind the Marienkirche is the Renaissance

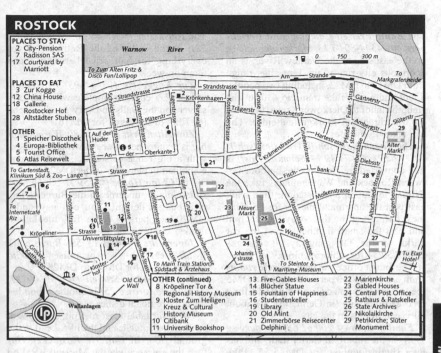

ROSTOCK

PLACES TO STAY
2 City-Pension
7 Radisson SAS
17 Courtyard by
   Marriott

PLACES TO EAT
3 Zur Kogge
12 China House
18 Gallerie
   Rostocker Hof
28 Altstädter Stuben

OTHER
1 Speicher Discothek
4 Europa-Bibliothek
5 Tourist Office
6 Atlas Reisewelt

OTHER (continued)
8 Kröpeliner Tor &
  Regional History Museum
9 Kloster Zum Heiligen
  Kreuz & Cultural
  History Museum
10 Citibank
11 University Bookshop

13 Five-Gables Houses
14 Blücher Statue
15 Fountain of Happiness
16 Studentenkeller
19 Library
20 Old Mint
21 Zimmerbörse Reisecenter
   Delphini

22 Marienkirche
23 Gabled Houses
24 Central Post Office
25 Rathaus & Ratskeller
26 State Archives
27 Nikolaikirche
29 Petrikirche; Slüter
   Monument

---

doorway on the former city **mint**, now a bank branch.

Maritime Museum

Rostock's good Maritime Museum (☎ 492 26 97), August-Bebel-Strasse 1, on the corner of Richard-Wagner-Strasse near the Steintor, has displays on the history of Baltic navigation, coins and medallions. It's open from Tuesday to Sunday year-round from 10 am to 5 pm (DM4).

Petrikirche & Around

The 117m-high steeple – a mariner's landmark for centuries – on the Gothic Petrikirche at Alter Markt was restored in 1994, having been missing since WWII. It's open from April to November on weekdays from 9 am to 5 pm, and the rest of the year from 10 am to 4 pm, with a one hour break at noon.

Next door, the **Slüter monument** honours Joachim Slüter, a reformer who preached in the *niederdeutschen* (Low German) dialect outside the church. Three blocks south is the **Nikolaikirche**, Rostock's oldest church.

Organised Tours

Guided tours lasting 1½ hours depart two to three days a week at 11 am and/or 2 pm, depending on the season, from the tourist office (DM7, children under 12 free). English-language tours can be arranged for DM85 for groups of up to 15 people.

Special Events

Every June to August the classical Festspiele Mecklenburg-Vorpommern is held at various venues in town and throughout the region. Tickets (DM16 to DM90) can be reserved by telephone (☎ 040-410 79 29) weekdays from 10 am to 5 pm.

euro currency converter DM1 = €0.51

MECKLENBURG

MECKLENBURG

Places to Stay

The *Baltic Freizeit Camping und Ferien-park* (☎ 04544-80 03 13, Markgrafenheide), on the east side of the Warnow River, is an enormous city-run affair. Tent sites range from DM17 to DM72, including two people, a tent and a car. Take tram No 4 from the Hauptbahnhof to Dierkower Kreuz, then bus No 18 (direction: Markgrafenheide). The trip takes 45 minutes.

The *Jugendgästeschiff Traditionsschiff* (☎ 71 62 24, fax 71 40 14, Schmarl-Dorf) is in a converted freighter on the harbour between Rostock and Warnemünde. Take the S-Bahn to Lütten Klein station, then walk east past the apartment blocks for 25 minutes, turn left at the three-way intersection and past the small lighthouse and the car parks to the far gangway. It charges DM27.50/34 for juniors/seniors.

The tourist office can book *private rooms* from around DM30 per person, plus a DM5 fee. After hours you can call ☎ 194 14 for a recorded message (in German only) about all vacant rooms in the city.

Familie Both (☎ 200 61 68, Fliederweg 17) is in the suburb of Gartenstadt, and has nice singles/doubles for DM35/55. Take bus No 25 towards Reutershagen and alight at Gartenstadt.

The *Etap Hotel* (☎/fax 122 22, Am Handelspark Süd), about 8km east of the Altstadt in the suburb of Broderstorf on the B110, is a great budget option if you have a car. Singles/doubles both start at DM49 (plus DM8.90 per person if you want breakfast). The *Inter-City Hotel* (☎ 495 00, fax 495 09 99, Herweghstrasse 51) at the Hauptbahnhof starts at DM78/156 for spotless rooms. They're a bit like 1st class sleeper compartments on a train.

City-Pension (☎/fax 459 07 04, Krönkenhagen 3) has rooms with private shower and WC (toilet) from DM85/134. *Courtyard by Marriott* (☎ 497 00, fax 497 07 00, Schwaansche Strasse 6), in the centre, has great service, lots of frills and rooms from DM175.

SAS Radisson (☎ 459 70, fax 459 78 00, Lange Strasse 40), of a similar standard, charges from DM152/162.

Places to Eat

The *Ratskeller* (☎ 45 48 50, Neuer Markt 22), in the cellar of the Rathaus, serves everything for half price between 3 and 5 pm on weekdays.

Zur Kogge (☎ 493 44 93, Wokrenterstrasse 27) comes complete with life preservers on the walls and very good seafood (eg fillet of sea perch for DM16).

Zum Alten Fritz (☎ 20 87 80, Warnowufer 65) is a shiny new place down on the docks with a big range of steaks, schnitzels and combination plates for under DM20.

The *China House* (☎ 459 10 03, Universitätsplatz 7), underneath the Burger King, is a budget delight. You can pay under DM20 per person for a full meal with drinks.

Jägerhütte (☎ 400 15 52, Barnstorfer Wald), near the zoo, specialises in *Wild* (game) dishes for DM16 to DM25.

The *Altstädter Stuben* (☎ 459 09 21, Altschmiedestrasse 25) is another good bet for tasty regional dishes.

For a veritable feast of fruit, fish, pizza, sandwiches, quiche and the like, head to the ground floor of *Gallerie Rostocker Hof* (use the entrance via the Marriott hotel on Schwaansche Strasse). The *Stadtbäckerei* there makes good sandwiches for under DM5, and just down the hall *Vino Veritas* lets you sample wines for DM4.50 to DM8.50 per glass.

Entertainment

The city puts out a free tri-monthly pamphlet *Die Stadt erleben*, listing everything from car repairs to concerts and events. It's available free at tourist attractions, bars and restaurants around the city.

Szene, a super-useful free monthly, is geared mainly to music but includes useful listings, articles, reviews and classified ads.

Discos & Clubs The *Studentenkeller* (☎ 45 59 28, Universitätsplatz) has been rocking on for years. Enter through the main university building at the eastern side of Universitätsplatz, go through the tunnel and it's on the left-hand side downstairs.

Disco Fun/Lollipop (☎ 768 37 82, Rigaer-strasse 5) has two dance floors, one haunted by the 20-to-40 crowd, the other dedicated to techno and other teeny stuff. Take bus No 39 or the S-Bahn to Lütten Klein.

Speicher-Discothek (☎ 492 30 31, Am Strande 3a), in a warehouse in the old port, has live music of just about every ilk (look for the big black eagle with the date '1935' about 30m up outside).

Getting There & Away
Air Flughafen Rostock-Laage (☎ 038454-313 39), about 30km south of town, is served by small private airlines, with frequent services to Hamburg, Dortmund, Hanover and Cologne/Bonn.

Train There are frequent direct trains to Rostock from Berlin-Lichtenberg (DM75, 2¾ hours), and several daily to Stralsund (DM19.40, one hour), Wismar (DM22.20, 1¼ hours) as well as Schwerin (DM22.20, 1¾ hours).

Car & Motorcycle From Berlin, head north or south out of the city to the A10; follow that north-west to the A24 (direction: Hamburg), which leads straight into the A19 running directly north to Rostock (2½ hours). From Neubrandenburg, take the B104 west to the A19 and turn north (1½ hours).

Ride Services For a lift, get in touch with the Mitfahrzentrale im DeTe 64 (☎ 493 44 38), Am Kabutzenhof 21. It's open Monday to Friday from 8 am to 6 pm.

Boat Several ferry companies, chiefly TT-Line ferries (☎ 67 07 90, fax 670 79 80) and Scandlines (☎ 673 40 40, fax 673 41 41) offer crossings to Trelleborg (Sweden, three to eight hours) and Gedser (Denmark, one to two hours) from Rostock Seaport on the east side of the Warnow. From the Hauptbahnhof, take tram No 4 to Dierkower Kreuz, then change for bus No 19 or 20 to the port.

To Gedser, Scandlines operates the only regular service (at least eight times daily), charging DM85/115 per car in winter/summer, DM40 for motorcycles and DM5/8 per adult.

To Trelleborg, TT-Line is more expensive but quicker, charging DM50 per adult year round, DM12 for bicycles and DM200/270 for cars (including driver) for the three hour trip in winter/summer. On Scandlines, adults cost DM20, cars DM140/195 in winter/summer and bicycles DM25 (including rider) for the six hour journey.

Getting Around
Public Transport The Rostock area, which includes Warnemünde, is zoned; for a single trip you pay DM2.20 for one zone, and DM3 for two or more zones. Day passes are DM5.50.

A *Familien-Tageskarte* (Family Day Pass), costing DM12 for two or more zones, covers up to three adults and two kids for travel until 3 am the following day. The weekend family card costs DM15.

Tram Nos 2, 11 and 12 travel from the Hauptbahnhof up Steinstrasse, around Marienkirche and down Lange Strasse. Take tram No 11 or 12 to get from the Hauptbahnhof to the university.

Car & Motorcycle With complicated one-way systems, confusing street layouts and dedicated parking-ticket police, Rostock is not a driver-friendly city. Use the *Parkschein* ticket machines or park in the lot next to the InterCity Hotel at the south end of the Hauptbahnhof for DM12 a day.

Taxi Flag fall is DM4, plus a varying per kilometre rate; prices actually go *down* at night. From Warnemünde to the Hauptbahnhof will cost about DM27.

Bicycle Cycling isn't much fun in the centre because of very heavy (and crazy) traffic, but just outside the city it quickly improves. You can rent bicycles from the Express-Guthalle (☎ 240 11 53), at the southern end of the Hauptbahnhof, from DM12 per day. In Warnemünde, try Wilhelm Meyer Touristen Service Mobil (☎ 519 19 55) at Am Leuchtturm 16.

MECKLENBURG

AROUND ROSTOCK
Warnemünde
☎ 0381 • pop 9500

Warnemünde, at the mouth of the Warnow River on the Baltic Sea just north of Rostock, is among eastern Germany's most popular beach resorts. It's a good choice if you want to enjoy the comforts of city life while staying in what is essentially a small fishing village on the beach.

Orientation & Information The train station is at the eastern end of town, east of the Alter Strom, the main canal on which all the fishing and tour boats moor. To the east of the train station is the Neuer Strom, across which is the Hohe Düne and the camping ground at Markgrafenheide.

The main action takes place along the promenade, which fronts the wide, surprisingly white beach. The town's main drags are Am Strom (the walkway along the Alter Strom) and Kirchenstrasse, which leads west from the bridge over the Strom to Kirchenplatz and finally on to Mühlenstrasse, lined with cafes, chic shops and cheap bistros.

The tourist office (☎ 511 42, fax 513 42), Am Strom 59, is open May to August from 10 am to 7 pm on weekdays and from 10 am to 4 pm on weekends.

There's a Reisebank at Am Bahnhof in the station area, open Monday to Friday from 8.30 am to 6 pm, and Saturday from 9 am to noon. There are ATMs in the station and throughout town.

Harbour Am Strom is a picturesque street lined with quaint fishers' cottages. The **Heimatmuseum** (Local Folklore Museum; ☎ 526 67), a converted fishers' cottage, is on Alexandrinenstrasse just south of Kirchenstrasse, the church and the main square. It's open Wednesday to Sunday from 11 am to 6 pm (DM3).

Restaurants (some quite kitschy) line the inlet on the west side, while boats moored at the quay below sell fish and rolls or offer cruises (DM9 to DM15 all year, weather permitting).

The crowded **promenade** to the north, on the sea, is where tourists congregate. Warnemünde's broad, sandy beach stretches to the west from the **lighthouse** (1898), and is chock-a-block with bathers on hot summer days.

Places to Stay The friendly *Jugendherberge Warnemünde* (☎ 548 17 00, fax 548 17 23, Parkstrasse 46) charges DM23.50/28.50 for juniors/seniors, with breakfast.

For *private rooms*, contact the tourist office or Warnemünde Zimmervermittlung und Reiseservice (☎ 591 76) at Am Bahnhof 1 outside the Hauptbahnhof. Expect to pay DM50 to DM75 in summer.

Pension Katy (☎ 54 39 40, fax 543 94 41, Kurhausstrasse 9), a pleasant family-run guesthouse, has doubles with private bath for DM55 to DM80.

The *Hotel am Alten Strom* (☎ 525 81, Am Strom 60) is a clean modern place with fully equipped single/double rooms from DM95/140.

The *Strand-Hotel Villa Hübner* (☎ 543 40, fax 543 44 44, Seestrasse 12) has very stylish, renovated quarters for DM198/238.

The *Arkona Hotel Neptun* (☎ 77 70, fax 540 23, Seestrasse 19), in a hulking GDR-era block, feels a bit like a big Moscow hotel but every room – yes, *every* one – has a great view of the beach. Rates start at DM200/300 in high season.

Places to Eat Lovers of smoked fish will be in heaven here, as many of the boats lining the Alter Strom smoke their catches on site and sell them cheaply.

Café Twee Linden (☎ 516 77, Am Strom 185) is a cosy harbourside place with light meals from about DM10.

Zur Gemütlichkeit (☎ 524 85, Mühlenstrasse 25) serves fish and other specials from around DM12. *Kettenkasten* (☎ 512 48, Am Strom 71) also has lots of affordable fish dishes.

Salsalitos Tex-Mex (☎ 519 35 65, Am Leuchtturm 9) has a nice atmosphere but isn't a bargain (eg two tacos for DM15.90, burritos for DM17).

Several Italian restaurants along Am Strom have pizzas from DM8 to DM10, pastas from DM7 to DM11 and bigger meals from DM12 to DM18.

Getting There & Away The sleek double-deck S-Bahn has frequent services from Rostock (DM3, 2nd class). Be careful which class you get into, as tickets are almost always checked.

Bad Doberan
☎ 038203 • pop 11,600
About 15km west of Rostock lies the former summer ducal residence of Bad Doberan, once the site of a powerful Cistercian monastery. It has an impressive Münster, regular horse races and is the starting point for the Molli Schmalspurbahn, a narrow-gauge steam train that runs to two fashionable resorts, Heiligendamm and Kühlingsborn.

The tourist office (☎ 915 30, fax 621 54) is at Goethestrasse 1. From May to September, weekday hours are from 9 am to 6 pm, and Saturday from 10 am to 4 pm; the rest of the year it's open only on weekdays to 5 pm (closed Thursday).

On the eastern side of town is the **Münster**, a stunning brick Gothic hall church typical of northern Germany. Its chief treasures include a lovely high altar and an ornate pulpit. It's open from April to October daily from 9 am to 4.30 pm (closed Monday, except in July and August). From November to March, it's open from 9 am to 3 pm (DM2, or DM3 with hourly guided tour in summer). Just north of the Münster is the **Beinhaus**, an octagonal-shaped crypt.

The train service, which everyone refers to simply as 'Molli', began huffing and puffing its way to Heiligendamm in 1886 for the likes of Duke Friedrich Franz I. Today it's operated by Mecklenburger Bäderbahn (☎ 038203-41 50) and also services Kühlingsborn, a Baltic resort full of lovely Art Deco buildings.

Trains depart year round from Bad Doberan's Hauptbahnhof 10 times a day from Monday to Friday, and slightly less frequently on weekends and holidays. There's a

bar car on some journeys and the scenery is lovely. The one-way/return fare is DM5/8.50 (children six to 14 years, DM2.50/4), while family tickets cost DM10.50/17.50.

Trains to Bad Doberan leave Rostock Hauptbahnhof at least hourly (DM8, 30 to 40 minutes). By car, you should take the B105 towards Wismar.

VORPOMMERSCHE BODDEN-LANDSCHAFT NATIONAL PARK
Covering an area of 805 sq km, the Western Pomeranian Boddenlandschaft National Park takes in Rostock, the Baltic coast to Stralsund, the islands of Weder, Bock and Hiddensee, the Darss/Zingst peninsula as well as Rügen's west coast. Created in 1990, its main features are mud flats, dunes, pine forests, meadows and heath; only one-eighth of its area consists of solid land. It's also the biggest resting ground in central Europe for migratory cranes – some 60,000 stop off here every spring and autumn.

In summer there are regular **guided tours** on Zingst, Hiddensee and other areas, both on foot and by bicycle. Contact the national parks authority, National-parkamt Vorpommersche Boddenland-schaft (☎ 038234-50 20, fax 502 24), Am Wald 13, 18375 Born, on Darss for further information. You can also hire horses from any number of places, including Reiterhof Gränert (☎ 0161-441 07 97), Grüne Strasse 66 in Prerow, from DM15 per hour. **Horse riding tours** through the park are also available from DM25 per hour.

WISMAR
☎ 03841 • pop 50,000
Wismar, about halfway between Rostock and Lübeck, joined the powerful Hanseatic trading league in the 13th century – the first town east of Lübeck to do so. For centuries the town belonged to Sweden, and traces of that rule can still be seen. Less hectic than Rostock or Stralsund, Wismar is definitely worth an overnight stay and is also the gateway to Poel Island, a lovely little piece of green to the north.

MECKLENBURG

Ossi v Wessi

The differences between *Ossis* (Easties) and *Wessis* (Westies) are manifold. One of the many subtle differences emerged when one of the authors was walking through Wismar with a *Wessi* and an *Ossi* guide. We saw a sign that read *Volkseigener Betrieb*, abbreviated VEB, which is a GDR-era term for 'people-owned company'.

The *Wessi* mentioned a local pun on the initials: locals call VEBs *'Vaters ehemaliger Betrieb'* – 'Father's former company'. We all laughed.

But after a moment it became clear that the *Ossi* and *Wessi* were laughing at two totally different interpretations. While the *Wessi* thought the joke meant that this company was owned by someone's father and then nationalised by the GDR government after WWII, the *Ossi* believed that it meant her father worked in this company until post-reunification budget cuts forced it out of business!

The misunderstandings, though, are usually that subtle. East and West Germans, though separated by the Cold War and so recently reunited, still both tell the same jokes about Austrians.

Orientation

The Altstadt is the city centre, built up around the Markt, which is said to be the largest medieval town square in Germany. The Hauptbahnhof is at the north-eastern corner of the Altstadt and the Alter Hafen port is at the north-western corner; a canal runs from Alter Hafen almost due east across the northern half of the Altstadt. The streets around the Markt are pedestrianised and the main night-time entertainment area is around Alter Hafen.

Information

The tourist office (☎ 25 18 15, fax 25 18 19, email touristinfo@wismar.de), Am Markt 11, is open daily from 9 am to 6 pm, and definitely has its act together.

You can change money at one of the three banks on the Markt (Sparkasse, Commerzbank and Deutsche Bank) and the main post office is south of the Markt on the east side of Mecklenburger Strasse. The town's Web site, with a good accommodation listing in English, is at www.wismar.de. There's a coin-operated washer-dryer in the little house in the harbour at Am Alten Hafen.

The town's medical clinic (☎ 330) is at Am Dahlberg, south of the centre.

Markt

The facades of Wismar's **gabled houses**, destroyed in WWII, have been lovingly restored; the interiors are near original. The **Rathaus** (1817-19) is at the square's northern end. Its basement houses the excellent new **Historical Exhibition**, with displays including an original 17th century *Wandmalerei* (mural) recently uncovered by archaeologists, maps and models of the city, and a glass-covered medieval well – stand over it if you dare. It's open daily from 10 am to 6 pm (DM2/1).

Alter Schwede, at the south-eastern side of the Markt, has an outlandish brick Gothic facade and is now home to one of the city's most popular restaurants. In front is the **Wasserkunst** (waterworks), an ornate, 12-sided well completed in 1602, which gave the town drinking water until 1897.

Busy **markets** are held on the Markt on Tuesday and Thursday from 8 am to 6 pm, and Saturday to 1 pm. Also on Saturday, a lively fish market takes place at Alter Hafen.

Churches

Wismar was a target for Anglo-American bombers just a few weeks before the end of WWII. Of the three great red-brick churches that once rose above the rooftops, only **St Nikolaikirche** (1381-1487), containing a font from its older sister church, St Marienkirche, is intact.

The massive red shell of **St Georgenkirche** is being restored for future use as a church, concert hall and exhibition space (partial opening is planned for 2005, and completion for 2010).

In 1945, a freezing populace was driven to burn what was left of a beautiful wooden statue of St George and the dragon. Cars now park where the 13th century **St Marienkirche** once stood, although its great brick steeple (1339), now partly restored, still towers above the city.

The 14th century Gothic **Heilige Geist Kirche**, in the courtyard west of the Markt (entered on Neustadt between Heide and Lübsche Strasse), contains the city **Music School**, and is a concert venue in summer.

Kittchen & Fürstenhof

Just west of the Marienkirche is the city's juvenile detention centre, also called the *Kittchen*, or 'clink'. Across the street from it is the prison restaurant and pool hall, decorated with huge caricatures of inmates laughing and pointing at the real ones across the street.

Around a little corner from the prison is the Italian Renaissance **Fürstenhof** (1512-13), now the city courthouse, which is undergoing a sweeping renovation. The facades are slathered in terracotta reliefs depicting town history and, under the arch in the courtyard, biblical scenes.

Historical Museum

The town's historical museum is in the Renaissance **Schabbellhaus** in a former brewery (1571) at Schweinsbrücke 8, just south of the Nikolaikirche across the canal. The museum's pride and joy is the large tapestry *Die Königin von Saba vor König Salomon* (The Queen of Sheba before King Solomon; 1560-75).

There are also displays on Wismar as a Hanseatic power and a Swedish garrison town. It's open Tuesday to Sunday from 10 am to 5 pm (DM3/1.50, free for children).

Regional artist Christian Wetzel's four charming **pig statuettes** grace the nearby **Schweinsbrücke**.

Scheuerstrasse

About 400m north-west of the Markt is Scheuerstrasse, a street lined with charming gabled houses, especially No 15, with its towering facade, and No 15a, with the cargo crane.

Activities

From May to September, Clermont Reederei operates hour-long **harbour cruises** five times daily from Alter Hafen (DM10). By arrangement, boats also go to Poel Island.

Hanse-Sektkellerei Wismar (☎ 63 62 82), a champagne factory at Turnerweg 4 south of the city centre, produces several varieties, from dry (Hanse Tradition) to extra dry (Hanse Selection). Tours are offered to groups of at least 15 (DM14 per person).

Organised Tours

In summer there are 1½ hour walking tours of the city, leaving the tourist office at 10.30 am (in German, DM7/3.50). English-language tours can be arranged for up to 20 people at a day's notice and cost DM80.

Special Events

In mid-June, the annual Harbour Festival (Hafenfest) features old and new sailing ships and steamers, music and food. Wismar holds a Schwedenfest every third August weekend from August 2000, celebrating the end of Swedish rule in 1903.

Places to Stay

Campingplatz (☎ 03841-64 23 77, Am Strand 19c) in Zierow, about 6km north-west of Wismar, can be reached via bus No 320.

A new youth hostel was about to open in Philipp-Müller-Strasse at the time of writing. Check with the tourist office for details. Otherwise, there's the *Beckerwitz Hostel* (☎/fax 038428-603 62, Haus Nr 21) in Gramkow, 15km north-west of Wismar, which charges DM24/29.50 for juniors/seniors. Take bus No 240 (direction: Boltenhagen) from the Hauptbahnhof.

Private rooms fill much of the city's accommodation needs. The tourist office can arrange private singles/doubles from DM30/75, plus a DM5 booking fee.

Hotel Gothia (☎ 73 41 56, fax 73 41 61, Sella-Hasse-Strasse 11) is a rustic but clean Scandinavian-style place, charging

MECKLENBURG

DM70 for singles and from DM45 per person for apartments.

Hotel Lippold (☎ *263 90, fax 26 39 79, Poeler Strasse 138)* is a simple place charging DM80/125, including breakfast. *Hotel Altes Brauhaus* (☎*/fax 28 32 23, Lübsche Strasse 37)* has rooms from DM80/120. The elegant *Hotel Alter Speicher* (☎ *21 17 46, fax 21 17 47 Bohrstrasse 12)* charges from DM110/165.

Hotel Stadt Hamburg (☎ *23 90, fax 23 92 39, Am Markt 24)* is a very flash place in a beautifully renovated building with rooms starting at DM145/185.

Places to Eat
Nur Hier Café and lots of *Stehcafés* are in and around the Markt. The *Grillmaster* budget grill is at Lübsche Strasse 49 and has fast and filling meals for DM8 or less.

Wismar's 'restaurant row' is along the pedestrianised Am Lohberg, near the fishing harbour. The *Brauhaus* (☎ *25 02 38, Kleine Hohe Strasse 15)* was the town's first brewery and has a good seafood menu (try the steamed pike-perch for DM16.50). *Kartoffelnhaus Nr 1* (☎ *20 00 30, Frische Grube 31)* offers good-value potato creations such as Budapester gratin, Hungarian potato soup, and *Himmel und Erde* (Heaven and Earth – potatoes and apples).

Zum Weinberg (☎ *28 35 50, Hinter dem Rathaus 3)* is a wine restaurant in a lovely Renaissance house. The *Alter Schwede* (☎ *28 35 52, Am Markt 18)* is pretty and has a prime location, but the food isn't all that hot – you're really paying for the atmosphere and service.

To'n Zägenkrog (pronounced 'tun tsaygencrokh'; ☎ *28 27 16, Ziegenmarkt 10)*, near the harbour, is a locals' hang-out surrounded by maritime mementos that serves excellent fish dishes. Main courses cost from DM9 to DM23.

Getting There & Away
Trains travel every hour to/from Rostock (DM22.20, 1¼ hours) and Schwerin (DM9.80, 30 minutes). Most trains to/from Berlin-Zoo (DM74, 2½ hours), Lübeck (DM19.60, 1¼ hours) and Hamburg (DM43, 1¾ hours) travel via Bad Kleinen.

Bicycles may be rented at the Hauptbahnhof and Beckerwitz youth hostel (from DM10 per day).

POEL ISLAND
☎ 038425 • pop 2000
The beaches on Poel Island, in Mecklenburg Bay inlet north of Wismar, are relatively undiscovered. It's a good spot for cycling, windsurfing and horse riding; in high summer its beaches accommodate everyone.

Orientation & Information
The island's main road access is just northwest of the village of Gross Strömkendorf. Most of the action takes place in Kirchdorf, in the centre of the island and home to Poel's main fishing port and marina.

The local tourist office (☎ 203 47, fax 40 43), Wismarsche Strasse 2 in Kirchdorf, hands out excellent street plans and cycling and hiking maps of the island. It's open weekdays from 8.30 am to noon and 2 to 5.30 pm (and in winter also on Saturday from 10 am to noon and 2 to 4 pm, and Sunday to noon).

There's a Sparkasse next to the tourist office at Wismarsche Strasse 1d and a Raiffeisenbank next door (both with ATMs). The post office is at the plaza at the junction of Möwenweg, Wismarsche Strasse and Ernst-Thälmann-Strasse.

Activities
The island is flat and perfect for cycling. Get maps at the tourist information office and rent bicycles for DM8 to DM12 per day at the tourist office. Horse riding is at Neuhof, west of Kirchdorf, and at Timmendorf. Horses cost DM20 per hour from Reiterhof Plath (☎ 207 60) in Timmendorf.

Places to Stay & Eat
You can camp in Timmendorf, near the beach and the lighthouse, from April to October at *Campingplatz Leuchtturm* (☎*/fax 202 24)*. Tent sites are from DM5, plus

DM5 per person (children DM2). Tempting as it may be, camping wild is prohibited.

The tourist office (☎ 203 47, fax 40 43) operates a free accommodation booking service, as does the privately run Ferienhausverwaltung und Zimmervermittlung Hanni Evers (☎ 209 94), Krabbenweg 5 in Kirchdorf. *Private rooms* range from DM20 to DM40 per person with breakfast.

There are restaurants at most of the hotels and pensions, serving mainly seafood and Mecklenburg specialities. In Niendorf, *Poeler Forellenhof* has sweeping views over Kirchdorf harbour.

Getting There & Away
From Wismar's Hauptbahnhof, take the hourly bus No 460 (DM4.50, 30 minutes) directly to the island.

By road from Wismar, take Poelerstrasse due north and follow the yellow signs to 'Insel Poel', through the village of Gross Strömkendorf and over a little bridge to the island. This lovely drive takes about 20 minutes.

Mecklenburger Seenplatte

The Mecklenburg Lake Plains is a band of wilderness spreading across the centre of the state. The area may well become one of the most popular outdoor and sport destinations for foreign visitors looking for peace, quiet and reasonably pristine wilderness.

The plains are crisscrossed by roads and highways that make getting around very easy. The roads (many of them canopied by trees planted by medieval fish merchants to shield wagons from the heat of the summer sun) meander through charming little villages and hamlets – many of them untouched by changes in government either after WWII or the Wende. In some places, like Penzlin, it's as if you've stepped back in time.

But in others, like Schwerin and Neubrandenburg, you'll have a chance to see eastern Germany in a state of flux that will be gone in just a few years' time. Get here fast; it's one of the country's most rewarding destinations.

SCHWERIN
☎ 0385   • pop 109,000
Schwerin, the state capital and oldest city (established 1160) in Mecklenburg-Western Pomerania, is one of the most picturesque towns in eastern Germany. It has so many lakes that locals and officials can't even agree on the number. Whatever the amount, the city's charm is certainly infectious.

The town gets its name from a Slavic castle known as Zaurin (Animal Pasture) on the site of the present Schloss. This former seat of the Grand Duchy of Mecklenburg is an interesting mix of 16th, 17th and 19th century architecture. The centre is small enough to travel on foot, but if you can spare the time, two to three days is best to really explore the city and its environs.

Orientation
The Altstadt is a 10 minute walk south from the Hauptbahnhof along Wismarsche Strasse. Just east of the Hauptbahnhof is the almost rectangular Pfaffenteich, an artificial pond marked (or marred, depending on your sense of humour) on its south-west corner by the wacky Arsenal building.

Farther south, there's the Old Garden (Alter Garten), which is a misnomer, as it's a field of mud in winter and dust in summer. Nearby, on the Schweriner See, you'll find the monumental Marstall (royal stables) and Burg Island, which is crowned with the lovely Schloss. Farther south, connected to Burg Island by a causeway, is the Palace Garden (Schlossgarten) and lesser-known Green Garden (Grüngarten).

Information
The Schwerin tourist office (☎ 592 52 13, fax 56 27 39, email stadtmarketing-schwerin@t-online.de) is at Am Markt 10. It's open weekdays from 10 am to 6 pm (to 5 pm in winter) and weekends from 10 am to 2 pm (closed Sunday in winter).

MECKLENBURG

There's a Reisebank in the train station and a Commerzbank on the corner of Mecklenburgstrasse and Helenenstrasse.

The main post office is on Mecklenburgstrasse, just south of Pfaffenteich. Schwerin's Web site, with a tourist section in English, is at www.schwerin.de.

Schweriner Buchhandel (☎ 56 59 76), Am Markt 13, is the best bet for English-language books.

SB Coin Laundry (☎ 56 86 27), Werderstrasse 6, is open from 6 am to 10 pm; take bus No 10 or 11 from the Hauptbahnhof and look for the Orient Snack doner kebab place on the corner.

In a medical emergency, call the city Klinikum (☎ 52 00) at 397 Wismarsche Strasse, the very end of tram No 1's route (direction: Nordstadt).

Dom

Above the Markt rises the tall, 14th century Gothic Dom (open daily), a superb example of north German red-brick architecture. Locals hotly point out that its 19th century church tower (118m high) is a whole *50cm taller* than Rostock's Petrikirche. You can climb to the tower's viewing platform for the view (DM1).

Another example of this type of architecture is the **Paulskirche**, south of the Hauptbahnhof, which is undergoing restoration.

Altstadt

The Markt is a bustling place, home to the **Rathaus** and the neoclassical **Neues Gebäude** (1780-83), which houses art exhibitions and is fronted by the better of the city's two lion monuments honouring the town's founder, Heinrich der Löwe (the other is on the south side of the Dom). Markets are held on Schlachtermarkt behind the Rathaus from Tuesday to Saturday.

There are several architectural styles in the old city, and a walk south-west of the Rathaus to the appropriately named **Enge Strasse** (Narrow Street) brings you past a lovely example of the city's earliest half-timbered houses at Buschstrasse 15 (now an antiques shop called Kunstdrechslerei

Zettler). To the east you'll pass **Hotel zur Guten Quelle** (see Places to Stay and Places to Eat).

But if you head west you'll emerge onto pedestrianised **Mecklenburgstrasse**, where you'll find the main **post office**, an early 20th century building. Many of the buildings along this street were built atop wooden pilings, a method devised by local architect GA Demmler, whose house is on the corner of Arsenalstrasse and Mecklenburgstrasse.

Staatliches Museum

In the Old Garden is the Staatliches Museum (☎ 59 24 00), which has a collection of works by old Dutch masters including Frans Hals, Rembrandt, Rubens and Brueghel, and works by Lucas Cranach the Elder. Enter the enormous neoclassical building from the steep stone staircase.

The museum is open on Tuesday from 10 am to 8 pm, and Wednesday to Sunday to 5 pm (DM7/4). Tours in German run on Wednesday and Saturday at 3 pm, and Sunday at 11 am and 3 pm.

Schelfstadt

Up Puschkinstrasse north of the Markt is Schelfstadt, a planned baroque village that was autonomous until the expansion of Schwerin in the mid-19th century. At No 12 is the restored **Schleswig-Holstein Haus** (1737), containing a gallery (☎ 55 55 27) with temporary exhibitions (DM5/3, or DM6/4 for special exhibits). Just north of here is the baroque **Schelfkirche** (also known as St-Nikolai-Kirche; 1708-1713), and **Schelfmarkt**, the former town market.

Schloss & Gardens

South-east of the Old Garden, over the causeway on Burg Island, is Schwerin's superb neo-Gothic **Schloss**, which is in turn connected to the **Palace Garden** by another causeway. The castle, built around the chapel of a 16th century ducal castle, is guarded by a **statue of Herzog Niklot**, a Frenchman defeated by Heinrich der Löwe. It's open Tuesday to Sunday from 10 am to

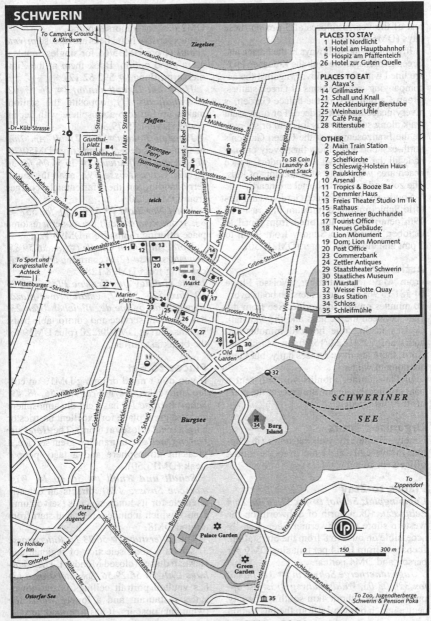

SCHWERIN

PLACES TO STAY
1 Hotel Nordlicht
4 Hotel am Hauptbahnhof
5 Hospiz am Pfaffenteich
26 Hotel zur Guten Quelle

PLACES TO EAT
3 Ataya's
14 Grillmaster
21 Schall und Knall
22 Mecklenburger Bierstube
25 Weinhaus Uhle
27 Café Prag
28 Ritterstube

OTHER
2 Main Train Station
6 Speicher
7 Schelfkirche
8 Schleswig-Holstein Haus
9 Paulskirche
10 Arsenal
11 Tropics & Booze Bar
12 Demmler Haus
13 Freies Theater Studio Im Tik
15 Rathaus
16 Schweriner Buchhandel
17 Tourist Office
18 Neues Gebäude;
   Lion Monument
19 Dom; Lion Monument
20 Post Office
23 Commerzbank
24 Zettler Antiques
29 Staatstheater Schwerin
30 Staatliches Museum
31 Marstall
32 Weisse Flotte Quay
33 Bus Station
34 Schloss
35 Schleifmühle

To Camping Ground & Klinikum

Ziegelsee

Knaudtstrasse

Landreiterstrasse

Dr.-Külz-Strasse

Grunthal-platz

Pfaffen-teich

Passenger Fern (summer only)

Zum Bahnhof

Mühlenstrasse

Gaussstrasse

Schelfmarkt

Körner-str.

Schliemannstrasse

Arsenalstrasse

Friedrichstrasse

Grüne Strasse

To Sport und Kongresshalle & Achteck

Wittenburger-Strasse

Marien-platz

Markt

Schlossstrasse

Grosser-Moor

Klosterstrasse

Old Garden

To Holiday Inn

Wallstrasse

Platz der Jugend

To Zippendorf

SCHWERINER SEE

Burgsee

Burg Island

Palace Garden

Green Garden

Ostorfer See

To Zoo, Jugendherberge Schwerin & Pension Poka

6 pm from mid-April to early October. The rest of the year, it closes at 5 pm on these days (DM6/4).

In summer, the walkways in the Palace and Green gardens, along with the **Kreuzsee** lake, are lined with flowers, lovely against the accompanying reproductions of Greek statues. **Green Garden**, east of the Palace Garden, is a very peaceful place indeed. For a pleasant walk along smooth paths for 5km or so, pick up the Franzosenweg at the Green Garden's north-east end and follow this lovely promenade all the way down to Zippendorf, a nice beach area with white sand and lots of kids. The zoo and the youth hostel are nearby.

South-east of the Palace Garden is the historic Schleifmühle, a museum in a restored 19th century mill. It's open from April to October, Tuesday to Sunday from 9 am to 5 pm, and closed in winter (DM3/1.50).

Activities
From May to September, Weisse Flotte (☎ 581 15 96) operates excursion boats every 30 minutes on the Schweriner See from the quay between the Schloss and the Marstall. Cruises lasting one hour/90 minutes/two hours cost DM12.50/15/20. In March and April, there are three cruises daily, but there are none in winter.

In the summer months you can rent a boat at Ruderboote am Burgsee, at the piers off the Old Garden.

Organised Tours
Ninety-minute city walking tours (in German) leave daily at 11 am from the tourist office year round (DM6/5).

Places to Stay
Campingplatz Seehof (☎/fax 51 25 40, Zum Zeltplatz), 10km north of Schwerin on the western shore of Schweriner See, is easily accessible on bus No 8 from the bus station. It charges from DM4 per tent site, DM9 per person and DM4 per car.

Jugendherberge Schwerin (☎ 326 00 06, fax 326 03 03, Waldschulweg 3) is just opposite the zoo, about 4km south of the city centre (catch bus No 15 from the bus station

or Platz der Jugend). Dorm beds cost DM23/28 for juniors/seniors.

Inexpensive hotel beds are rare, so *private rooms* (from DM35/65 for singles/doubles) are a good option. Book them at the Zimmervermittlung (☎ 592 52 12).

Hotel am Hauptbahnhof (☎ 56 57 02, Grunthalplatz 11), opposite the station, makes up for zero atmosphere with decent prices (DM44.75/79.50).

Pension Poka (☎ 550 71 60, Am Tannenhof 8) has decent rooms from DM50/70. *Hospiz am Pfaffenteich (☎ 56 56 06, fax 56 96 12, Gaussstrasse 19)*, near the small ferry landing on the Pfaffenteich, charges from DM70/120.

Hotel Nordlicht (☎ 55 81 50, fax 557 43 83, Apothekerstrasse 2) is a modern, restored place offering rooms from DM90/125.

Hotel zur Guten Quelle (☎/fax 56 59 85, Schusterstrasse 12) is charming and central, charging from DM98/128.

The *Holiday Inn Crowne Plaza (☎ 575 50, fax 575 57 77, email crown-plaza-schwerin@t-online.de, Bleicher Ufer 23)* has excellent service and comfortable beds. Rooms start at DM190/220 (plus DM19 for the breakfast buffet).

Places to Eat
If you don't mind dropping DM10 on coffee and cake, *Café Prag (☎ 56 48 49, Schlossstrasse 17)* has a chi-chi atmosphere and is a great place for excellent pastries or a light meal (closes at 6 pm). The *Hotel zur Guten Quelle* restaurant has great service, a pleasant atmosphere and a tasty pepper steak (DM13.50).

Schall und Knall (☎ 56 30 16, Wismarsche Strasse 128) attracts an eclectic clientele for its lunch specials (served until 5 pm), which include a beer and start from around DM8.

The *Ritterstube (☎ 56 23 15, Ritterstrasse 3)* serves a good selection of regional and German dishes (closed Monday). The *Weinhaus Uhle (☎ 56 29 56, Schusterstrasse 13)* has vaulted portrait ceilings in the downstairs restaurant and a lovely *Weinstube* (wine bar) upstairs. It has fine food, too.

Orient Snack (☎ 56 84 63, *Werderstrasse 6*) is a good Turkish place with cheap pizza, salads, doner and lots of other meaty stuff. It's open till midnight.

The *Grillmaster* snack bar, on the corner of Puschkinstrasse and Friedrichstrasse, has daily lunch specials such as cutlets and chips for under DM10. The *Mecklenburger Bierstube* (☎ 56 48 59, *Wismarsche Strasse 104*) serves barbecued half-chickens till midnight. *Ataya's* (☎ 557 47 81, *Zum Bahnhof 10*) has good and reasonably priced pizzas (DM6 to DM9).

Entertainment

Piste and *Schwerin Magazin* are free culture and listings publications, available at bars, restaurants and the tourist information office.

Large pop and rock concerts are held at the *Sport und Kongresshalle* (☎ 76 19 00, *Wittenburger Strasse*), 2km west of the centre; take bus No 5, 10 or 11 from the Hauptbahnhof.

The *Achteck* (☎ 76 08 60, *Wittenburger Strasse 120*) draws a very young crowd with house, techno and rave. *Speicher* (☎ 79 23 94, *Röntgenstrasse 22*) is another very popular place with live music.

Tropics (☎ 56 21 54, *Arsenalstrasse 16*) is a hot joint in the centre, packed with ever-so-fabulous types. Attached to it is the stylish *Booze Bar*, which we list here merely for its name.

The *Staatstheater Schwerin* (☎ 530 00, *Alter Garten*) hosts an impressive range of concerts and theatrical performances. There's also theatre, comedy, music and cabaret at the *Freies Theater Studio Im Tik* (☎ 56 24 01, *Mecklenburgstrasse 2*) on the corner of Arsenalstrasse.

Getting There & Away

Trains arrive regularly from Rostock (DM22.20, one hour), Magdeburg (DM52, 2½ hours) and Stralsund (DM44, two hours). Direct trains to/from Wismar (DM9.80, 30 minutes) leave frequently throughout the day. Trains from Hamburg, Lübeck and Berlin-Lichtenberg travel via Bad Kleinen.

Regional buses depart for Wismar and Lübeck from Grunthalplatz outside the Hauptbahnhof.

By road from Rostock, head south-west on the B105 (E22), then follow the signs in Wismar. There's perpetual construction on this road and it's busy as well, so count on a total travel time of about 1½ hours.

Getting Around

City buses and trams cost DM2. *Tageskarten* (24-hour day passes) cost DM6. In the summer months, a ferry plies the Pfaffenteich from east to west.

AROUND SCHWERIN
Lewitz

The Lewitz is a series of canals about halfway between Schwerin and Ludwigslust. Lewitzboot (☎ 03861-74 05), a kayak and canoe rental company, arranges independent or guided tours, including overnight stays throughout the region. It charges DM35/210 per day/week for kayaks and DM40/255 for canoes. The office is in the town of Banzkow; take bus No 119 (four a day, DM6.80, 30 minutes) from Schwerin's Hauptbahnhof to Banzkow.

GÜSTROW

☎ 03843 • pop 33,000

Some 50km south of Rostock and about 60km from Schwerin is the charming city of Güstrow. The city's Renaissance Schloss, a ducal residence of Herzog Ulrich III and once the home of sculptor Ernst Barlach (1870-1938), still towers above the city. It's definitely worth a day trip to view the impressive castle as well as the Barlach museums.

The city's Markt is at the centre of the Altstadt; the Schloss Museum is south-east, the Dom south-west, and the Barlach Museum north-west of the Altstadt.

The helpful tourist office (☎ 68 10 23, fax 68 20 79, email guestrow@twfg.de) is at Domstrasse 9. It's open Monday to Friday from 9 am to 6 pm, and Saturday from 9.30 am to 1 pm. From May to September it's open on Sunday as well.

MECKLENBURG

Things to See & Do

There has been a castle of some sort at Franz-Parr-Platz since 1556, but the **Schloss** (☎ 75 20) on the site today was completed in 1599. Today it's a museum with art exhibitions, a cultural centre and occasional concerts. It's open Tuesday to Sunday from 10 am to 6 pm in summer, and from 9 am to 5 pm in winter (DM5/2).

The Gothic **Dom** (☎ 68 20 77), begun as early as 1225, was completed in the 1860s. It contains Barlach's *Hovering Angel*. On the **Markt**, the Renaissance **Rathaus** competes with the **Pfarrkirche** for prominence.

Barlach Museums Ernst Barlach's expressionist work in bronze and wood carvings reflects the influence of his time spent in Russia. He was born and worked here and died just as Nazi bans of his work were reaching their peak. The **Atelierhaus** (☎ 822 99), his studio, is 4km south of the city at Inselsee (an hour's walk or 15 minutes on bus No 4). From March to October, hours are Tuesday to Sunday from 10 am to 5 pm, and in winter from 11 am to 4 pm (DM3/2). In town, the museum in the **Gertrudenkapelle** (☎ 68 30 01) displays many of his original works (same opening hours and admission).

Getting There & Around

Trains leave once or twice an hour from Rostock's Hauptbahnhof (DM9.80, 30 minutes) and hourly from Schwerin (DM19.40, one hour). Buses leave for Rostock's bus station at 5.15 am and 12.15 and 4.20 pm, returning at 6.40 am and 2 and 5.40 pm (DM14.50 return, 1¼ hours one-way).

You can rent bikes for DM12.50 a day from Zweiradhaus Dräger, at both Lange Strasse 49 and Plauer Strasse 71.

NEUBRANDENBURG

☎ 0395 • pop 75,000

At the eastern end of the Mecklenburger Seenplatte, on the Tollensesee some 95km south of Stralsund, lies the charming city of Neubrandenburg. While the old quarter dates back to the 13th century, it's surrounded by modern urban sprawl.

Writer and satirist Fritz Reuter (1810-74) lived for two years in a house (now a cafe) at Stargarder Strasse 35.

Orientation

The Hauptbahnhof is at the northern end of the Altstadt, and the bus station is 100m west of it. The Altstadt's wall effectively creates the largest roundabout outside Britain; it's circled by Friedrich-Engels-Ring. The best way to see the Altstadt is to walk around the interior wall and then cycle around the exterior pathways. The inside is more interesting visually; while the outside is also nice, the traffic on Friedrich-Engels-Ring is hellish and the dust atrocious in summer.

Inside the walls is a grid of north-south and east-west streets. The main shopping street is Turmstrasse, pedestrianised between Stargarder Strasse (the main north-south thoroughfare, which leads right to the Hauptbahnhof) and the eastern wall.

Information

Tourist Offices The Neubrandenburg tourist office (☎ 194 33, fax 582 22 67, email tourist@neubrandenburg.de) is at Treptower Strasse 1, tucked away in the little alley to the left as you walk east past the Radisson SAS Hotel on the Markt. It's open Monday to Friday from 9 am to 6 pm, and weekends from 10 am to 2 pm.

Money There's a Deutsche Bank on the corner of Treptowerstrasse and Stargarder Strasse, and a Sparkasse opposite the Haus der Kultur.

Post & Communications The main post office (☎ 558 40) is at Poststrasse 6, two blocks south of the Hauptbahnhof. The Mausklick bar in Hotel Horizont, Otto-von-Guericke-Strasse 107, charges DM10 per hour of Web surfing.

Library The Fremdsprachenbibliothek (foreign language library; ☎ 707 29 39) is at Einsteinstrasse 4, east of the centre in the Oststadt (closed Monday).

Laundry There's a laundrette on the south side of Ziolkowskistrasse between Leibnizstrasse and Keplerstrasse. Take bus No 8 from the Hauptbahnhof to the Lindetal Centre stop on Juri-Gagarin-Strasse, north of Ikarusstrasse, and walk east on Ziolkowskistrasse.

Medical Services There's an Ärztehaus (medical clinic; ☎ 544 26 34) behind (east of) the Marienkirche, with an electronic display of the Apotheken (pharmacies) on call.

City Gates
When the city was founded in 1248 by Herbord von Raven, a Mecklenburg knight granted the land by Brandenburg Margrave Johann I, it progressed in the usual manner: defence system, church, town hall, pub. The security system was the enormous stone wall, breached by four **city gates**.

The **Friedländer Tor**, begun in 1300 and completed in 1450, was first. **Treptower Tor**, at the western end of the Altstadt, is the largest, and contains what's billed as the **Regional History Museum** (☎ 582 65 57) but it's really more of an archaeological collection. It's open Tuesday to Friday from 9 am to 5.30 pm, and weekends from 1 to 5 pm (DM2/1).

At the southern end of the city is the gaudy **Stargarder Tor**, and the simple brick **Neues Tor** fronts the east side of the Altstadt.

Churches
Neubrandenburg's centrepiece was the once-enormous Gothic **Marienkirche** (1270), seriously damaged in WWII. Since then major portions have been rebuilt, notably the steeple, which crowns a 90m tower. For a long time, a heated debate raged about just how to restore the interior; it's finally being converted into a concert hall.

Inside is a photo exhibit of the church at different stages of construction and information on archaeological digs after the GDR took over. Get the key from the tourist office.

Also worth mentioning is the late-Gothic **Johanniskirche** (begun 1260), with its adjacent **cloister**.

Wiekhäuser
The city wall had 56 sentry posts built into its circumference. When firearms rendered such defences obsolete in the 16th century, the guardhouses were converted into *Wiekhäuser*, homes for the poor, handicapped and elderly. Some 26 of these remain today, some in the original form, and others (such as the pub at Wiekhaus No 45) rebuilt with white stucco and half-timber fronts.

Fangelturm
West of Johanniskirche is the Fangelturm, once the city dungeon. Ask for the key (free) at the tourist office, or at Wiekhaus No 11 or 21. Inside you can climb the 74 steps of the very steep and narrow staircase to the top, or just peer down through the grating to see the dungeon. At the top, kick the door to break the bird-crap seal and you will get a good view – invisible from the street – of a side of the Johanniskirche.

Grosse Wollweberstrasse
The only row of houses to survive WWII lines Grosse Wollweberstrasse, at the southwestern section of the city. The must-see house on the street is the very blue one at **No 25**, owned by graphic artist Gerd Frick. When he's home he'll give visitors a tour for the asking.

Haus der Kultur und Bildung
The saving grace of the city's **Haus der Kultur und Bildung** (House of Culture & Education), Marktplatz 1, with its obnoxious 56m tower and bunker-like foundation, is the viewing platform on the roof (DM1). It has great views of the region on clear days; there's also Bar No 14 and the Turm Café on the 13th floor.

Neubrandenburg's last **statue of Karl Marx** is in the beer garden adjacent to the building's north side; kids now put ice-cream cones (and sometimes condoms) in the statue's hand.

Activities
The tourist office publishes the very good *11 Radtouren rund um Neubrandenburg* (11

euro currency converter DM1 = €0.51

Bicycle Tours around Neubrandenburg). For rental outlets, see Getting Around.

Several moderate and clearly marked bicycle routes are near the town. There are cheap overnight accommodation options on routes south of the city.

Trail maps (DM2), and a detailed free pamphlet called *Auf Wanderschaft durch das Neubrandenburger Tollensebecken*, are available at the hostel or tourist office.

Organised Tours

The tourist office runs guided tours of the Altstadt (in German) from May to August daily at 10 am. The tours take 1½ hours (DM3.50/1.50).

Places to Stay

The nearest camping ground is at Gatsch-Eck at Tollensesee (see Around Neubrandenburg).

The *Jugendherberge Neubrandenburg* (☎/fax 422 58 01, Ihlenfelder Strasse 73) is 1.5km north-east of the Hauptbahnhof. From the station, take bus No 7 (four stops). Staff are cheerful and the buffet breakfasts are great. Dorm beds cost DM21/25.50 for juniors/seniors.

The tourist office books *private rooms*. Expect to pay DM50 to DM100 per night per couple (it's still cheaper than the hotels) without breakfast.

Hotel Weinert (☎ 58 12 30, fax 581 23 11, Ziegelbergstrasse 23), about three blocks west of the Altstadt, is a very modern, if uninspired, place with friendly service and clean rooms. Singles/doubles are DM98/130.

Hotel Horizont (☎ 569 84 28, fax 56 99 81 97, Otto-von-Guericke-Strasse 7) is in a quiet spot on the edge of town, and charges DM89/109 for well equipped rooms.

The *Radisson SAS Hotel* (☎ 558 60, fax 558 66 25, Treptower Strasse 1) has the typical pricey business-style rooms starting at DM175/205.

Places to Eat

Cheap meals (main courses from DM6 to DM12) in great surrounds can be had at *Boulevard Bistro* (☎ 582 64 69, Turmstrasse 8).

The very nice *Café im Reuterhaus* (☎ 582 32 45, Stargarder Strasse 35) serves light snacks and appetisers from DM5, soups from DM5 and main courses from about DM12. Next door, the *Bierstube im Reuterhaus* (☎ 582 22 05, Stargarder Strasse 35) has great brews from DM3, and snacks and light meals from DM4 to DM10.

Fürstenkeller (☎ 582 22 15, Stargarder Strasse 37) is a lovely old place with vaulted ceilings and good regional dishes from about DM15.

Tor Café (☎ 584 11 32, Friedländer Tor) has a very comfortable atmosphere and nice staff. Coffee and cake costs about DM6, and full meals are DM9 to DM15.

Wiekhaus 45 (☎ 566 77 62, 4-Ringstrasse 45) is a lovely example of a renovated guardhouse and a comfortable pub as well. It offers light meals under DM10, but mains range from DM13 to DM24.

For quick snacks, head for the pedestrian mall along Turmstrasse. Here you'll find stands selling Bratwurst, a *Grillstation* selling roasted chickens and *Die Brezelbäckerei*, which has a tasty pizza pretzel.

Entertainment

Blitz, a free monthly covering the entire Mecklenburg Lake Plains area, has a cultural calendar and club and pub listings. It's available at clubs, pubs and restaurants around the area.

Kelly's Irish Pub (☎ 582 60 05, Turmstrasse 28) and *Konsulat* (☎ 544 25 79, Jahnstrasse 12) are good for live music, mostly jazz, blues and rock.

Bar No 14 (☎ 582 36 20, 14th Floor, Haus der Kultur und Bildung) opens from 6 pm. It's pricey but the view is worth it.

Up To Date (☎ 422 62 60, Pasewalker Strasse 4) and *Café Destille* (☎ 582 54 85, Fritz-Reuter-Strasse 1a) are both more mellow drinking and talking spots, with lots of graphics and pictures on the walls.

Alter Schlachthof (☎ 582 23 91, Rostocker Strasse 33) is a disco in a former abattoir with several dance floors and a couple of restaurants. It gets a great mixed crowd – from 18 to 80.

Disco Colosseum (☎ *778 21 05, An der Hochstrasse 4*) attracts a teenage crowd, while the 30-somethings go for *Joy* (☎ *422 63 30, Demminer Strasse 49*).

Getting There & Away

From Berlin-Lichtenberg, trains leave every two hours (DM41, two to 2½ hours). There's an hourly service to/from Rostock (DM28, two hours) and Stralsund (DM22.20, 1¼ hours).

By road from Berlin take the A10 north-west (direction: Hamburg) to Neuruppin. At Neuruppin, head east towards Löwenberg, where you catch the B96 and head north; follow signs for Stralsund. From Stralsund or Greifswald, head south on the B96. From Rostock, take the A19 south to Güstrow and follow the B104 east all the way.

Getting Around

Single-trip tickets for city buses cost DM2.20 on board or DM1.50 at the bus station. Eight rides cost DM12.

Bike-rental outlets include Fahrradhaus Leffin (☎ 58 16 60) at Friedrich-Engels-Ring 23 and Kolping-Initiative Sozialwerkstatt (mobile ☎ 0171 217 47 16) at the Youth Centre, Lindenstrasse 12.

AROUND NEUBRANDENBURG

South and west of the city lies a wonderful region of wilderness (and oddities, including a witch museum) that's great for day trips, hikes or bike trips. Though most people stay in Neubrandenburg, there's camping in Müritz National Park and small guesthouses here and there.

Tollensesee

In the summer months, people flock to Tollensesee, a lake south-west of Neubrandenburg, for swimming, boating, camping and sunbathing.

The best swimming places are both free and fun: **Strandbad Broda** at the north-west tip of the lake and **Augustabad** on the north-eastern side. You can rent paddle, rowing, electric and motor boats from Thomas Behn (☎ 0395-566 51 22) at the northern end of the lake. Rentals range from DM7 to DM15 per hour.

Just south-east around the bend from Behn's place are the departure points for two touring ships: the *De Lütt* does one to two-hour tours for DM4 to DM15, and *Mudder Schulten* (☎ 368 21 95) tootles round the lake in summer from 10 am to noon, and 1 to 2.30 and 3 to 5 pm. Tickets for 1½/two-hour tours cost DM7/9.

Camping Gatsch-Eck am Tollensesee (☎ *0395-566 51 52*), on the western side of the lake, is a simple place with basic facilities, open from May to October. Camp sites cost DM15 per couple.

Penzlin

☎ 03962 • pop 5600

The main attractions at Penzlin, about 15km south-west of Neubrandenburg, are its witch museum and generally weird atmosphere. Penzlin is so drab it feels as if you've just walked into a black-and-white WWII movie.

The **Alte Burg Hexenkeller** (☎ 21 04 94), with displays on the Penzliner witches of the late 17th century, is worth a look. The museum is in the old **Burg**, a massive castle up a hill from the town's main **Markt**. It's open Tuesday to Sunday from 10 am to 5 pm (DM4.50/3.50). A nice beer garden opens in summer.

From the Markt, with its enormous **Marienkirche**, walk west to Alteburgstrasse and then north up the little hill to the Hexenkeller.

By car or motorcycle, take the B104 west out of Neubrandenburg and turn south on the B192, which leads into the Markt. Penzlin's sights can easily be seen in an hour.

Burg Stargard

☎ 039603 • pop 1200

About 12km south-east of Neubrandenburg is tiny Burg Stargard, in the middle of a lovely wilderness that's great for hiking and cycling. The town is a good base for trips into Müritz National Park.

Burg Stargard is half recovered from GDR rule: half is shiny and the other half dilapidated. Together they make an interesting

MECKLENBURG

contrast. The town is a common stop on hikes or bike trips, or it can be a short excursion from Neubrandenburg to check out the old Burg and the town's tiny zoo.

The Hauptbahnhof is at the western end of town. The post office is diagonally opposite. Bahnhofstrasse, the main drag, leads east to the Markt. The town's tiny tourist office (☎/fax 208 95), at Kurze Strasse 3, has lists of *private rooms* for rent in its window.

The **Klüschenberg Zoo** is a big drawcard for the town. It's across the pass along the eastern side of the pond and open May to September from 8 am to 6 pm, and October to April to 4 pm (DM4/2).

The chunky brick ducal **Burg** at the top of the hill, and visible throughout the town, is open Monday to Thursday from 10 am to 3 pm, Friday from 10 am to noon, and weekends from 1 to 3 pm. Inside, there's a **regional history museum**.

Marked hiking and cycling **trails** lead out of town throughout the region.

Getting There & Away Trains make the six minute journey from Neubrandenburg every two hours or so (DM3.50). There's also an infrequent bus service (No 8) from the bus station at Neubrandenburg. By road, take the B96 south from Neubrandenburg and turn left, following signs for Gross Nemerow and Burg Stargard; this brings you right into the centre of town, about 3km past the turning.

Neustrelitz
☎ 03981 • pop 20,000

Neustrelitz, 28km south of Neubrandenburg, is worth an afternoon's excursion. The city's tourist information office (☎ 25 31 19, fax 20 54 43, email stadtinformation@ neustrelitz.de) is at Markt 1. It's open from May to September on weekdays from 9 am to noon and 1 to 5 pm, and weekends from 10 am to 1.30 pm (shorter weekday hours and closed weekends in winter).

Private rooms are the best bet in Neustrelitz and can be arranged through the tourist office (DM2 fee). Rooms start at around DM25 per person without breakfast.

The first thing you'll notice in the enormous circular Markt is the clunky, square spire of the **Stadtkirche** (1768-78), dubbed the 'Butter Churn' by locals. You can climb the 174 steps to the viewing platform (DM1) atop this interesting piece of ecclesiastic architecture to get a panorama of the town.

The **Rondteil** at the centre of the Markt was once home to two memorials. The first (1866) was a bronze statue of Duke Georg, who was instrumental in the town's development. After WWII, the duke was removed in favour of a Soviet war memorial, which itself was carted off in 1995. The duke's statue was rediscovered in the 1980s and placed between the **Schlossgarten** and the **Schlosskirche**, just south-west of the centre. The Schloss was itself destroyed, but you can still walk through the gardens and into the mid-19th century church.

Getting There & Away There's an hourly train from Neubrandenburg (DM9.80, 30 minutes). By road, follow the B96 south from Neubrandenburg and you'll head straight into the Markt.

MÜRITZ NATIONAL PARK
☎ 03981

The two main sections of lovely Müritz National Park sprawl over 300 sq km to the east and (mainly) west of Neustrelitz. Declared a protected area in 1990, the park consists of bog and wetlands and is home to a wide range of waterfowl, mainly ospreys, white-tailed eagles and cranes. It has more than 100 lakes and countless other ponds, streams and rivers. Dedicated boaters can make their way from here clear to Hamburg. Working with a good set of maps from the park rangers, you can do a paddle-and-camp trip between Neustrelitz and Lake Müritz, at the park's western end.

Orientation & Information
The park's waterway begins on the Zierker See west of Neustrelitz. The main information centre is the Nationalparkamt (National Park Office; ☎ 458 90), An der Fasanerie 13, 17235 Neustrelitz.

Tourist offices, hostels and camping grounds in Neubrandenburg, Neustrelitz and Burg Stargard have trail and park maps, and also sell day passes giving you unlimited bus travel in the park, including bicycle transport (DM10), or a combination bus/boat pass (DM20).

Activities

The national park office arranges regular tours and excursions throughout the park. Contact the office for information about ranger-led tours. Hiking is permitted on marked trails.

Havel Tourist (☎ 247 90, fax 24 79 99) rents out one or two-person kayaks for DM10/45/200 per hour/day/week. It has offices at camping grounds throughout the park. Rowing boats (DM5/30/200), as well as sail and motorboats (from DM30/95/520), are available from Santana Yachting (☎ 20 60 42) at the eastern end of the Zierker See.

Places to Stay

You must use designated camping grounds, of which there are over a dozen within the park. The biggest operator is Havel Tourist (see Activities). Rates at all sites in high/low season are DM7/5.50 per tent, plus DM6/4 per person.

Western Pomerania

STRALSUND

☎ 03831 • pop 62,000

Stralsund, about 70km east of Rostock on the Baltic coast, is an attractive, historic town with imposing churches and elegant townhouses. In the Middle Ages, Stralsund was the second-most powerful member, after Lübeck, of the Hanseatic League of trading cities.

Stralsund was later absorbed into the Duchy of Pommern-Wolgast. In 1648, as a result of the Thirty Years' War, Stralsund (along with Rügen and Pomerania) came under the control of the Swedes, who had

helped in their defence. It remained Swedish until it was incorporated into Prussia in 1815.

The town's importance grew with the completion of the Rügendamm, the causeway to Rügen Island across the Strelasund channel, in 1936. After WWII, Stralsund became the third-largest port in the GDR, and today it's the biggest town in Western Pomerania. (The eastern part of the long-disputed province was ceded to Poland in 1945.)

Orientation & Information

The Altstadt's main hubs are Alter Markt in the north and Neuer Markt in the south. A few blocks south of the latter is the central bus station. The train station is across the Tribseer Damm causeway, west of the Neuer Markt. The harbour is on the Altstadt's eastern side.

The tourist office (☎ 246 90, fax 24 69 49, email info-hst@t-online.de) is at Alter Markt 9 near the Rathaus. Between May and mid-October, opening hours are weekdays from 9 am to 7 pm, and weekends to 2 pm. Winter hours are 10 am to 5 pm on weekdays, and 10 am to 1 pm on Saturday (closed Sunday). Here you can buy the amazing *Kultour-Ticket* for just DM1 for discounts to museums.

There's a Volksbank at Neuer Markt 7 and a Dresdner Bank at Tribseer Strasse 20. The post office is at Neuer Markt 4.

There's a Schnell und Sauber laundrette in the shopping mall in Knieper-West, about 3km north of the centre (catch bus No 4 to Hans-Fallada-Strasse). A police station is on the corner of Böttcherstrasse and Jacobiturmstrasse.

Northern Altstadt

The Alter Markt is dominated by the Nikolaikirche and the splendid **Rathaus**, with its late-Gothic decorative facade. The upper portion of the latter has slender copper turrets and gables with openings to prevent strong winds from knocking over the facade. This ornate design was Stralsund's answer to its rival city Lübeck, which has a similar town hall. The sky-lit atrium

WESTERN POMERANIA

STRALSUND

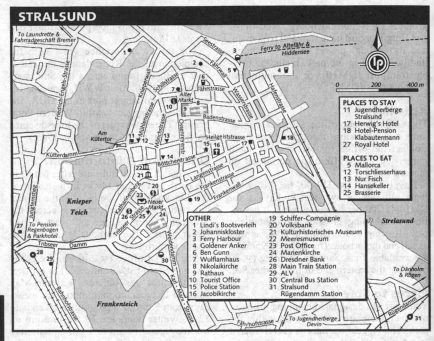

PLACES TO STAY
11 Jugendherberge Stralsund
17 Herwig's Hotel
18 Hotel-Pension Klabautermann
27 Royal Hotel

PLACES TO EAT
5 Mallorca
12 Torschliesserhaus
13 Nur Fisch
14 Hansekeller
25 Brasserie

OTHER
1 Lindi's Bootsverleih
2 Johanniskloster
3 Ferry Harbour
4 Goldener Anker
6 Ben Gunn
7 Wulflamhaus
8 Nikolaikirche
9 Rathaus
10 Tourist Office
15 Police Station
16 Jacobikirche
19 Schiffer-Compagnie
20 Volksbank
21 Kulturhistorisches Museum
22 Meeresmuseum
23 Post Office
24 Marienkirche
26 Dresdner Bank
28 Main Train Station
29 ALV
30 Central Bus Station
31 Stralsund Rügendamm Station

through the vaulted walkway has a gallery held aloft by shiny black pillars on carved and painted bases.

Exit through the eastern walkway to the main portal of the **Nikolaikirche** (1270), modelled after the Marienkirche in Lübeck. It's filled with art treasures, and is open weekdays and Saturday from 10 am to 5 pm (Sunday from 11 am to 2 pm). The main altar (1708), designed by the baroque master Andreas Schlüter, shows the eye of God flanked by cherubs, capped with a depiction of the Last Supper. Also worth a closer look is the high altar (1470), 6.7m wide and 4.2m tall, showing Jesus' entire life. Behind the altar is the astronomical clock (1394), allegedly the oldest in the world – but it has never worked very well.

Opposite the Rathaus, at Alter Markt 5, you'll find the **Wulflamhaus**, a beautiful 15th century townhouse named after a

mayor. Its turreted step gable somewhat mirrors the Rathaus facade.

On Schillstrasse, reached via Külpstrasse north off the Alter Markt, is the **Johanniskloster** (☎ 29 42 65), a former Franciscan monastery that's now a concert venue. It's famous for its 'smoking attic' (there was no chimney), chapter hall and cloister. Opening hours from mid-May to mid-October are daily from 10 am to 6 pm, except Monday (DM3/2).

Southern Altstadt

The Neuer Markt is dominated by the massive 14th century **Marienkirche**, another example of north German red-brick Gothic architecture. Its main draw is the huge **organ** (1659), built by F Stellwagen and festooned with music-making cherubs. The tower will be reopened after renovation in the summer of 2000, when you will be able to climb up (via steep wooden ladders at the end) for a sweeping view over to Rügen Island (DM2). The church is open daily from 10 am to 5 pm (in winter to 4 pm).

North of Neuer Markt is the **Meeres-museum** (☎ 29 51 35), an aquarium complex in a 13th century convent church at Mönchstrasse 25-27. There's a large natural history section and tanks with tropical fish, coral, and scary Baltic creatures. It's open daily from 10 am to 5 pm, and from 9 am to 6 pm in July and August (DM7/3.50).

The **Kulturhistorisches Museum** (Cultural History Museum; ☎ 29 21 80) is in the former St Catherine convent nearby at Katharinenberg 14-17. It has a large historical collection, paintings by Caspar David Friedrich and Philipp Otto Runge, faiences (tin-glazed earthenware), playing cards and Gothic altars. The museum is open daily (except Monday) from 10 am to 5 pm (DM6/3).

East of Neuer Markt, at Frankenstrasse 9, is the **Schiffer-Compagnie** (☎ 29 04 49) a small museum run by a sailors' association displaying model ships and paintings. It's open weekdays from 9 to 12.30 pm and 1 to 3.30 pm (DM3/1.50).

Activities

Ferries to the scenic fishing village of Alte-fähr on Rügen's southern coast operate every 30 minutes in high season and cost DM3 (bikes are DM2). One-hour harbour cruises depart daily at 11 am and 2.30 pm (DM8). Buy your tickets from the kiosk on the quay. The ferry harbour is on the north-eastern edge of the Altstadt.

You can rent boats at Lindi's Bootsver-leih (☎ 38 30 45) daily between 10 am and 6 pm (DM4.50 per person per hour).

Between May and September, the **Hanse-Bahn**, a miniature motorised train, travels to the town's sights at irregular intervals. The 40 minute tour starts after 11 am (on Saturday after 1.30 pm) and costs DM7/5. It doesn't run on Sunday. Stops often include the Neuer Markt, the Alter Markt and the ferry terminal, but the route changes; you can hop on almost anywhere it turns up.

Places to Stay

Campingplatz Altefähr (☎ 038306-754 83, fax 750 56, Klingenberg 15) is in the fishing village of Altefähr on the southern shore of Rügen. It's open from April to October. Take bus No 413 or the ferry.

Jugendherberge Stralsund (☎ 29 21 60, fax 29 76 76, Am Kütertor 1) is inside a 17th century town gate. Take bus No 4 or 5 to Kütertor or walk for 15 minutes from the train station. B&B costs DM23/28 for juniors/seniors.

Jugendherberge Devin (☎ 49 02 89, fax 49 02 91, Strandstrasse 21) is off the road to Greifswald in nearby Devin (20 minutes on bus No 3 from the train station). It charges DM20/24.

The tourist office books rooms from DM30 per person and may charge a DM5 fee (sometimes waived for foreigners). Prices listed are for summer, and some hotels charge around 10% less at other times.

Pension Regenbogen (☎ 49 76 74, fax 49 48 46, Richtenberger Chaussee 2a), about 2km from the centre, charges DM70/90 for decent singles/doubles.

Hotel-Pension Klabautermann (☎ 29 36 28, fax 28 06 12, Am Querkanal 2), near the port, has a view of the city and charges DM80/140.

Herwig's Hotel (☎ 29 39 54, fax 26 68 23, Heilgeiststrasse 50) is a small family-run outfit with rooms from DM75/120.

The *Parkhotel* (☎ 47 40, fax 47 48 6 0, Lindenallee 61), in a comfy complex 3km west of the Altstadt, has business-class rooms from DM99/119.

The *Royal Hotel* (☎ 29 52 68, fax 29 26 50, Tribseer Damm 4), near the train station, has rooms for DM125/155 in a stylish Art Nouveau building.

Places to Eat

Torschliesserhaus (☎ 184 39, Am Kütertor 1), next to the hostel, sells delicious steaks, fish and lots of snacks under DM10.

Hansekeller (☎ 70 38 40, Mönchstrasse 48) is in an old guardhouse and serves hearty regional dishes at moderate prices (DM15 to DM20) in its vaulted brick cellar.

euro currency converter DM1 = €0.51

Nur Fisch (☎ 28 85 95), at the corner of Mönchstrasse and Heilgeiststrasse, is a cafeteria-style restaurant with – as its name suggests – 'only fish' for DM10 or less. It's open weekdays to 6 pm, Saturday to 2 pm and is closed on Sunday.

The *Brasserie (☎ 70 35 14, Neuer Markt 2)* is a brass and wicker cafe-restaurant with a large bar. It has a moderately priced menu of salads, baguette sandwiches, steaks and fish.

The *Mallorca (☎ 29 84 01, Seestrasse 2)* uses Baltic fish for tasty, affordable Mediterranean cuisine. Spanish cook Domingo will come out for a chat (try not to smirk about the Greek interior).

Entertainment

Between May and September, organ recitals take place on Wednesday at 8 pm, either in the Marienkirche (DM8/5) or the Nikolaikirche (DM7/4).

For a throwback to GDR days, try the *Goldener Anker* at the northern end of Hafenstrasse in the harbour. It's got tattered furniture, a tile heating-stove and music out of a jukebox. Only the prices are post-Wende.

Another place popular with the young is the pub called *Ben Gunn (☎ 29 36 45, Fährstrasse 27)*.

Getting There & Away

Train Regional trains make the trip to/from Rostock (DM19.40, 1¼ hours), Berlin-Lichtenberg (DM68, 3¼ hours) and Hamburg (DM72.60, 3¼ hours) at least every two hours. There are less frequent services to Leipzig (DM123, 5½ to 7½ hours), but there are lots of trains to Sassnitz (DM14.80, one hour) and to Binz (DM14.80, 50 minutes), both on Rügen.

International trains between Berlin and Stockholm or Oslo use the car-ferry connecting Sassnitz Hafen on Rügen Island with Trelleborg and Malmö in Sweden.

Bus Buses travel to Bergen and Sassnitz on Rügen several times daily from the central bus station.

Car & Motorcycle If coming from the west – Lübeck, Wismar or Rostock – avoid travelling on the B105, a tortuously slow, jammed and speed-trapped country road. For an alternate route, leave Rostock on the B110 to Sanitz, then continue via Bad Sülze, Tribsees and Richtenberg to the B194 and head north. Coming from points east, you'll use the B96.

Boat Reederei Hiddensee ferries (☎ 0180-321 21 50) depart up to three times daily from the ferry terminal for Hiddensee Island. Singles/returns to Neuendorf cost DM11/21; to Vitte and Kloster it's DM14/ 24. Bikes are an extra DM10. You can buy tickets from the quay kiosk.

Getting Around

Your feet will do just fine in the Altstadt, but for the outlying areas there's a fairly comprehensive bus system. You can also rent a bicycle at Fahrradgeschäft Bremer (☎ 39 66 35), Lindenstrasse 26, or at ALV (☎ 28 01 55) at Bahnhofstrasse 10.

GREIFSWALD
☎ 03834 • pop 64,000

About 35km south-east of Stralsund lies the old university town of Greifswald, on the Ryck River. Greifswald went through a steep evolution from Cistercian monastery in 1199 to Hanseatic city only a century later. It's justly famous for its university, the second oldest in northern Germany (after Rostock's).

Like all of Pomerania, the town became Swedish in 1648 and Prussian in 1815. It escaped WWII largely unscathed thanks to a courageous German colonel who surrendered to Soviet troops in the final days of the war, a move usually punishable by execution. Today it's a bit off the beaten track, although its handsome Altstadt and student populace keep Griefswald from sinking into a backwater.

Orientation & Information

The Altstadt is in the north of town, northeast of the train station on the bank of the

Ryck. It's partly encircled by a road, partly by railway tracks. The mostly pedestrianised Lange Strasse bisects the Altstadt from east to west and is quickly reached via Karl-Marx-Platz, just north of the train station.

The tourist office (☎ 34 60, fax 37 88, email greifswald-information@t-online.de) is at Schuhhagen 22, a continuation of Lange Strasse. It's open weekdays from 9 am to 6 pm (in winter to 5 pm), and also on Saturday from 9 am to noon in the summer months. Guided walking tours (in German) are offered Monday, Wednesday and Friday (DM9).

There's a Commerzbank at Markt 7-8 and a Sparkasse next door. The post office is also here.

Marienkirche

Locals teasingly call this red-brick church on Brüggstrasse – a square tower trimmed with dainty turrets – 'Fat Mary' for its generous dimensions. The interior of this 12th century, three-nave hall church is modest except for one jewel: the awesome Renaissance **pulpit** (1587). Rostock carver Joachim Melekenborg used 60 types of wood for this masterpiece. The church is open weekdays from 10 am to noon and 2 to 4 pm, and on Sunday after services.

Markt & Around

The many historical buildings on the Markt hint at Greifswald's stature in the Middle Ages. The **Rathaus**, at the western end, had an earlier incarnation as a 15th century department store with characteristic arcaded walkways. The red-brick gabled houses on the eastern side are worthy of inspection. The one at No 11 is a good example of a combined living and storage house owned by Hanseatic merchants.

Walk one block east on Mühlenstrasse, which runs from the south-eastern corner of the Markt, to Thomas-Pyl-Strasse. At No 1-2 is the **Museum der Stadt Greifswald**, housed in a former Franciscan monastery. It's open Wednesday to Sunday from 10 am to 6 pm; in July and August it's also open on Monday and Tuesday (DM3/1.50). Displays

focus on the history of the town and the university; the prized exhibit is a small collection of paintings and drawings by local painter Caspar David Friedrich.

Dom St Nikolai & University Area

West of the Markt, the spires of Greifswald's **Dom** rise above a row of historic facades. Nicknamed 'Long Nicholas' for its 100m tower topped by an onion dome, it has an austere light-flooded, completely whitewashed interior with a large and solitary golden cross. The Greifswalder Bachwochen, a concert series, has been taking place in the Dom since 1946. The cathedral is open from May to October daily from 10 am to 4 pm (Sunday to 1 pm after the service). Its tower can be climbed (DM3/1.50) and, yes, there is a great view from the top.

Half-timbered, single-storey buildings in a sea of red brick make up the former **St Spiritus Hospital**, clustered around a small courtyard. It's an alternative cultural centre now, with a beer garden and a small stage for concerts in summer. For maximum visual effect, enter via the building at Rubenowplatz 12-14.

Rubenowplatz, to the west, is the heart of the university area. The **monument to Heinrich Rubenow** in the middle of the little park is dedicated to the university's founder. The university's main building flanks the square's south side. Only the former library, used as the assembly hall since 1881, is worth a closer look.

Places to Stay

The tourist office will book *private rooms* from DM30 per person (a free service). Wieck, a coastal village about 4km east of Greifswald, has the least expensive hotels.

The *Vario-Hotel* (☎ 51 60, fax 51 65 16, *Brandteich 5-8)* is a brand-new budget place just outside town, charging from DM48/64 for singles/doubles without breakfast (add 20% with). Take bus No 10 for three minutes from the train station – there's a stop right in front of the hotel.

WESTERN POMERANIA

Schipp In (☎ 34 60, fax 37 88, Am Hafen 2) has a nice view of the harbour and rooms for DM70/100, breakfast not included.

Zur Fähre (☎ 84 00 49, fax 84 18 24, Fährweg 2) is a friendly place charging from DM85/110 for rooms with private shower/WC.

If you're motorised, do try the *Hotel Alte Speicher (☎ 777 70, fax 77 70 77, Ross-mühlbachstrasse 25),* in a renovated warehouse 1.5km south-east of the centre off the B96. Lovely, spacious quarters cost from DM130/160 for singles/doubles, including breakfast.

Places to Eat

Braugasthof Zum Alten Fritz (☎ 578 30, Markt 13), in a step-gabled Gothic building, serves big, hearty portions. The service is friendly and the house brew smooth. The Sunday all-you-can-eat brunch costs just DM13.50.

The *Brasserie (☎ 79 01 00, Lange Strasse 22)* serves breakfast from 8 am and bistro fare for under DM12.

Hotel Alter Speicher is another excellent choice, with tasty regional dishes for DM16 to DM20.

The historical *Zur Falle (☎ 79 19 33, Schuhagen 1)* is mainly a pub and popular with students. There's a small menu with simple dishes.

A number of nice fish restaurants, such as *Zur Brücke* and *Fischerhütte*, are on the harbour at Wieck.

Getting There & Away

There's a regular train service from Rostock (DM28, 1½ hours), Stralsund (DM9.80, 20 minutes) and Berlin-Lichtenberg (DM60, 2½ to three hours).

Greifswald is well connected by bus to other communities in Mecklenburg-Western Pomerania, though service is either restricted or suspended on weekends.

To get to Stralsund or Rostock, take bus No 300. Bus Nos 508, 514 and 518 all go to Wolgast. Bus No 300 makes runs to Neubrandenburg. The express bus from Rügen to Berlin also stops here.

Greifswald is on the notorious B105 from Rostock. Another slow country road is the B96, which leads south to Berlin.

Getting Around

It's easy to get around Greifswald's centre on foot, but to reach the outlying sights, you may want to make use of the bus system. Single tickets cost DM2.20 and an eight-ticket block is DM14.

AROUND GREIFSWALD
Usedom Island

Usedom lies in the delta of the Oder River, about 30km east of Greifswald, and is separated from the Pomeranian mainland by the wide Peene River. The island's greatest asset is its 42km stretch of beautiful beach – sandy, festooned with dunes and facing the Baltic Sea. It earned the nickname Badewanne Berlins (Berlin's Bathtub) in the prewar period and was a much sought-after holiday spot in GDR days.

Since the Wende, Usedom has been somewhat overshadowed by neighbouring Rügen, but as the sprucing-up process continues, it is coming into its own. Elegant white villas with wrought-iron balconies from the 1920s grace many of the traditional resorts, including Zinnowitz and Koserow in the western half and Bansin, Heringsdorf and Ahlbeck further east.

Usedom's central tourist information office (☎ 038375-234 10, fax 234 29) is at Bäderstrasse 4 in Ückeritz, a resort between Koserow and Bansin.

The island's only *DJH hostel (☎ 038378-223 25, fax 323 01, Puschkinstrasse 7)* is in Heringsdorf, about 4km west of the Polish border town of Swinemünde (Świnoujście) at the island's eastern tip. It charges from DM25/30.50 for juniors/seniors.

Peenemünde Usedom's only attraction of historical importance is Peenemünde on the island's western tip. It was here that Werner von Braun developed the V2 rocket, first launched in October 1942. It flew 90km high and over a distance of 200km before plunging into the Baltic. This marked the

WESTERN POMERANIA

first time in history that a flying object had exited the earth's atmosphere. The research and testing complex was destroyed by the Allies in July 1944, but the Nazis continued their research in mine shafts in Nordhausen in the southern Harz region (see that section in the Harz chapter).

The **Historisch-Technisches Informations-Zentrum** (Historical and Technological-Information Centre), at Bahnhofstrasse 28, commemorates this era, immodestly billing Peenemünde as the 'birthplace of space travel'. The museum is open from April to October daily (except Monday) from 9 am to 6 pm, and in winter to 4 pm (DM6/4).

Getting There & Away Wolgast is the gateway to Usedom. It can be reached by train from Stralsund (DM16.20, one to 1½ hours) and Greifswald (DM19.80, one hour), and local trains continue the journey on to Peenemünde, Zinnowitz, Heringsdorf and the other resorts.

From Greifswald, take bus No 508, 514 or 518 here, then connect to island-bound buses which leave from the bus station at Wolgast-Hafen.

Rügen Island

Rügen's tourist tradition reflects Germany's recent past and the people who shaped it or played a role in it. In the 19th century, such luminaries as Einstein, Bismarck and Thomas Mann came to unwind here in the fashionable coastal resorts.

During the Third Reich, Hitler picked one of the island's most beautiful beaches to build a monstrous holiday resort intended to accommodate 20,000 of his loyal troops simultaneously. The GDR made Rügen the holiday choice for millions of comrades, not to mention the top apparatchik himself, Erich Honecker. Today, the island looks poised to become one of the most popular destinations in the Baltic.

Much of Rügen and its surrounding waters are national park or protected nature reserve. The Bodden inlet area is a bird refuge,

popular with bird-watchers. The main resort area is around the settlements of Binz, Sellin and Göhren on Rügen's east coast.

INFORMATION

Fremdenverkehrsverband Rügen (☎ 03838-807 70, fax 25 44 40), the head office for all the local tourist offices on the island, is at Am Markt 4 in Bergen. It provides information only. Room reservations are handled by the local tourist offices and a number of private agencies.

The latter include Rügen-Besucher-Service (☎ 038301-605 13, fax 613 95) at Bahnhofstrasse 2 in Putbus and Touristik Service Rügen (☎ 038306-61 60, fax 616 66) in Altefähr. In Binz, there's also Boy's Touristinformation (☎ 038393-325 15, fax 321 14) at Proraer Chaussee 2. Contact details of the local tourist offices are listed under the individual towns.

For emergency medical attention, ring ☎ 03838-802 30.

Dangers & Annoyances

Rügen is notorious for its gangs of skinheads who casually attack visitors, including tourists from western Germany. Use extreme caution in the areas around train stations, particularly in Sassnitz.

GETTING THERE & AWAY
Train

Local trains run almost hourly from Stralsund to Sassnitz and also to Binz (DM14.80, one hour). Both services pass Lietzow, 13km before Sassnitz, where you may have to change trains. To get to Putbus and Lauterbach, change in Bergen. To get to Sellin, Baabe and Göhren, you can catch the Rasender Roland historic train in Putbus or in Binz (see the Getting Around section).

Bus

BerlinLinienBus (toll-free ☎ 0130 71 91 07) runs a regular service between Berlin and the resort towns of Binz, Sellin, Baabe and Göhren. Trips cost DM55/99 one-way/return. If you're under the age of 26, you pay DM37/69. Reservations are essential.

euro currency converter DM1 = €0.51

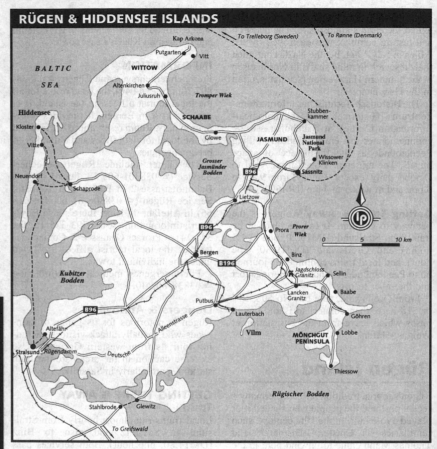

RÜGEN & HIDDENSEE ISLANDS

Car & Motorcycle

The most obvious way to get to Rügen is
via the Rügendamm, the causeway across
the Strelasund channel from Stralsund.
However, during rush hour or in the peak
season, it becomes a bottleneck with traffic
piled up for kilometres. And just to make
matters worse, in order to let major ships
pass through the channel, the causeway
opens five times daily for 20 minutes at
2.30 and 7.20 am and then again at 12.50,
6.20 and 9.30 pm.

Boat

Rügen is a stop for both domestic and international ferries.

The Mainland A good alternative to the
Rügendamm are the ferries. A small passenger ferry shuttles between Stralsund and
Altefähr on Rügen's south-western shore
every 30 minutes in high season (DM3 one-
way, bikes DM2).

If you want to take your car onto the island by ferry, you must drive to Stahlbrode,

about 15km south-east of Stralsund (direction: Greifswald). Between April and October, Weisse Flotte (☎ 038328-805 13) runs ferries to Glewitz on Rügen every 20 minutes between 6 am and 9.40 pm. From November to March, departures are every 30 minutes from 7 am to 6.45 pm. There's a DM7 charge per car up to 4m long, plus DM2 per person. Vehicles weighing up to three tonnes cost DM12 (including driver), and it's DM15 for those weighing up to five tonnes. Bikes cost DM2 extra

Hiddensee Reederei Hiddensee (☎ 038300-501 69) runs ferries between Schaprode on Rügen's western shore and Neuendorf, Kloster and Vitte several times daily between late March and mid-September. One-way/return fares to Neuendorf are DM11/21, and to Kloster and Vitte DM14/24. Children under 11 get a 30% discount. Bikes are DM10 return.

Sweden Scandlines HansaFerry runs five ferries daily from Sassnitz to Trelleborg and back. The crossing takes just under four hours and costs DM30 from June to mid-September and DM20 the rest of the year. Cars are DM155 to DM195 in summer (otherwise DM140). Motorcycles are DM35/25. Prices are return and include all passengers. For bookings, call ☎ 038392-644 20 or ☎ 0180-534 34 43, or visit a travel agent or the ticket kiosk on Trelleborger Strasse between Sassnitz train station and the harbour.

If you are taking the train to the Sweden-bound ferry, find out whether it terminates at Sassnitz's main train station or goes right to the quay at Sassnitz Hafen (in the case of a split train, you need to be in the appropriately labelled carriage). It's about a 10 minute walk downhill from the station to the harbour. Generally, local trains from Stralsund end at the main station, while services to/from Malmö connect with the ferry.

Denmark From June to mid-September, DFO HansaFerry runs three services daily between Sassnitz and Rønne on Bornholm Island. The trip takes almost four hours and costs DM30 each way. Same-day return tickets also cost DM30. During the rest of the year, the price is DM15 each way and there are only two daily crossings. For booking details, see Sweden.

GETTING AROUND
Train
The *Rasender Roland* steam train is not just a tourist attraction but an integral part of Rügen's public transport system. It shuttles between Putbus and Göhren daily between 6 am and 11 pm, stopping in Binz, Jagdschloss Granitz, Sellin and Baabe. The route is divided into four zones, each costing DM3 (eg Putbus to Binz, two zones; Putbus to Göhren, four zones). Bikes cost DM3.50.

Bus
Rügen has a fairly comprehensive bus system, with links to practically all communities. Services, however, are sporadic; sometimes there are just a few daily departures. The main hub is Bergen. The local tourist offices have bus schedules and maps, or you can call ☎ 03838-194 49. Most buses will let you transport your bicycle.

Car & Motorcycle
If you don't have much time, the car is the best mode of transport on Rügen Island. The main artery cutting through Rügen is the B96. Parking meters abound, so carry a lot of change.

Bicycle
Rügen's network of bicycle paths has not yet been completed, so sharing roads with cars cannot always be avoided. Ask for the *Fahrrad & Nahverkehrskarte Insel Rügen* at tourist offices. Besides being a map, it includes route recommendations and a list of bike rental and repair places.

DEUTSCHE ALLEENSTRASSE
After crossing the Rügendamm, if you turn east instead of continuing north on the B96, you will soon be driving beneath a lush canopy of chestnut, oak, elm and poplar trees that line the two-lane, sealed road for

the next 60km to the coastal resort of Sellin. This stretch is the first segment of the Deutsche Alleenstrasse, an ambitious project aiming to construct a route of leafy boulevards through Germany from here all the way south to Lake Constance. On Rügen, it leads through the island's largely agricultural, thinly populated south where, in spring, brilliant yellow fields of rape alternate with potato fields and meadows.

Putbus
☎ 038301 • pop 5000

Having passed through the modest farming villages that surround it, Putbus will seem like a mirage. Some 16 large white neoclassical buildings surround a gigantic **circular plaza** like candles on a birthday cake. Its 75 hectare **English park** – filled with ginkgoes, cypress, Japanese spruce and other exotic trees – lets you take a botanical journey around the world.

Putbus is an oddity, conceived and realised in the 19th century by an overly ambitious local prince, Wilhelm Malte I of Putbus (1783-1854). Putbus stands as the last European town to be purpose-built as a royal seat.

Today, Putbus prides itself on being Rügen's cultural centre, with the island's only theatre and the annual Rossini Festival held around May/June.

Putbus is the western terminus of the *Rasender Roland* (see Getting Around earlier in this section). The old-time steam train used to plough on for another 40km west to Altefähr near the Rügendamm, but this stretch is now covered with a wonderful bike trail including sections leading right through the forest.

The Putbus tourist office (☎ 870 60, fax 271) is at Markt 8, and is open weekdays from 8 am to 6 pm (in winter to 4 pm) and Saturday from 9 am to 2 pm.

MÖNCHGUT PENINSULA
The Mönchgut Peninsula in Rügen's southeast has a wildly irregular coastline, deep bays, sandy beaches, softly rising hillsides and stretches of forest. Much of the land is protected as a nature preservation area. The Mönchgut was first settled by monks in the 14th century. Because the monks prevented the people who settled with them from mixing with the other islanders – who were pagan Slavs – they developed their own traditions over the centuries. Some of these, such as costumes and dances, have survived to this day.

Göhren
☎ 038308 • pop 1200

Göhren is a pleasant and laid-back resort town, squatting on the Nordperd, a spit of land that juts into the sea like Pinocchio's nose. The beach is split into the quieter Südstrand and the livelier and more developed Nordstrand, with a pier, park and a promenade that leads to the neighbouring village of **Baabe**. Göhren is also the eastern terminus of the *Rasender Roland* steam train.

The tourist office (☎ 259 10, fax 259 11), Schulstrasse 8, is open weekdays from 7 am to 6 pm (closed Friday from 12.30 to 4 pm) and weekends from 4 to 6 pm. Hours are restricted between October and mid-May.

Places to Stay & Eat There are at least five sites to choose from: *Campingplatz Göhren* (☎ 21 22), open Easter to October; *Campingplatz Gager* (☎ 301 99, fax 82 10), open April to October; *Campingplatz Thiessow* (☎ 82 26, fax 82 97), open December to October; *Freizeitoase Rügen* (☎ 23 14, fax 251 27), open May to September; and *Campingplatz Baabe* (☎/fax 038306-142 99), partially open year round.

Private rooms in Göhren cost from DM20 per person. *Pension Franz* (☎ 23 40, Thiessower Strasse 23) is about 250m from the beach, and charges DM45 to DM55 for each person.

Travel Charme Hotel Nordperd (☎ 70, fax 71 60, Nordperdstrasse 11) charges DM65/85 per person in low/high season, with nice rooms in a modern complex close to the sands.

For food, try the huge *Ristorante Al Mare*, on the north beach promenade; or *Caprice* at Thiessower Strasse 32, with local fish dishes priced from DM15 to DM20.

BINZ
☎ 038393 • pop 6300

Binz is Rügen's largest and most celebrated seaside resort. It lies along one of the island's best beaches, fringed by dunes and forest with glorious views of Prorer Wiek bay. Thanks to heavy restoration, Binz has once again blossomed into a fully fledged beach town.

The tourist office (☎ 20 84, fax 20 83), may still be temporarily housed in a port-a-cabin outside Heinrich-Heine-Strasse 7 when you visit; it's open on weekdays from 9 am to 4 pm and Saturday from 9 am to noon (also on Sunday in July and August). There's a branch office with a free reservation service (☎ 27 82, fax 307 17) at Schillerstrasse 15, open weekdays from 9 am to 6 pm.

Things to See & Do

Binz is known for its **collection of houses** built in the late 19th century, Romantic style called Bäderarchitektur (spa architecture). Typical of this style are the large covered balconies, decorated with white filigree lattice work fashioned from wood and wrought-iron. Most of these elegant villas have recently been renovated, including the superb quartet at Schillerstrasse and Margaretenstrasse.

Binz has a 4km-long **beach promenade**; its focal points are the long pier and the palatial Kurhaus. At the northern end is the IFA holiday park with the state-of-the-art **Vitamar** pool, with slides, whirlpool, saunas and waterfalls. It's open daily to 9.30 pm (DM6 for one hour and DM14 for three hours).

Jagdschloss Granitz (1723), a hunting palace built on top of the Tempelberg (at 107m, the highest elevation in the Granitz Forest), was significantly enlarged and altered by Wilhelm Malte I, whose flights of fancy also gave Rügen the grandiose Putbus. Malte added the palace's main attraction, a 38m central tower.

The palace is open year-round from 9 am to 5.30 pm, except from October to March when it closes at 4 pm. It's also closed on Monday, except from July to September (DM4.50/3.50).

From Binz, you can walk an hour to the Schloss or catch the motorised mini-train that regularly shuttles between the pier and the palace (DM9 return, high season only). If you're driving, you must pay to leave your car or motorcycle in a parking lot and pay again for the shuttle up to the palace.

Places to Stay & Eat

Accommodation is quite plentiful here. The **Jugendherberge Binz** (☎ 325 97, fax 325 96, Strandpromenade 35) ain't cheap at DM34/40 for juniors/seniors, but it's popular, so book ahead.

Private rooms in Binz start at DM25 per person. Among the cheapest hotels is the **Pension am Schmachtersee** (☎ 322 37, Bahnhofstrasse 22), which has singles/doubles from DM60/120. **Pension Marion** (☎ 23 11, fax 328 19, Bahnhofstrasse 42) has clean, perfectly decent quarters from DM65/130. **Hotel Zur Promenade** (☎ 27 42, fax 38 60, Strandpromenade 46) will set you back DM90/180 in high season.

You'll find a number of nice restaurants along Strandpromenade, including the **Strandcafé** at No 29, where you can have coffee and cake or a pizza. You'll need deeper pockets for the **Brasserie** in the stylish Villa Salve at No 41, visited by Helmut Kohl while he was chancellor.

PRORA

Prora lies just north of Binz, along almost 5km of uninterrupted, fine white sand beach. Running parallel to this beautiful stretch of coast is a wall of hideous six-storey buildings, each 500m long. This eyesore, begun in 1936, was the Nazis' idea of a holiday resort for 20,000 people. The outbreak of WWII stopped its completion. After the war, Soviet troops tried to blow up the existing structures, but failed.

Today, one of its few occupants is **Museum zum Anfassen** (Hands-On Museum), a multimedia exhibit chronicling Prora's various stages, with 'period rooms' from the Nazi and GDR eras. The museum is at Objektstrasse, Block 1 (right at the back of the car park and down the road to the right).

euro currency converter DM1 = €0.51

ours are from 10 am to 7 pm daily,
om October to March when it closes
(DM8, children under 12 are DM4).

*Camping Meier (☎ 20 85, fax 326 24,
Proraer Chaussee 30)* is very well equipped
and open from late March to late October.
*Jugendherberge Prora (☎ 328 44, fax 328
55, Sandstrasse 12)* is housed in the Nazi-era
eyesore, charging DM20.50/25 for juniors/
seniors. It's a five minute walk from the train
station at Prora-Ost.

JASMUND NATIONAL PARK

The rugged beauty of Jasmund National Park
in Rügen's north-east has inspired a long line
of artists, led by the Romantic painter Caspar David Friedrich. His favourite spot was
the **Stubbenkammer**, an area at the northern
edge of the park, where jagged white-chalk
cliffs plunge into the jade-coloured sea.

The most famous attraction is the
Königstuhl (King's Chair) – at 117m it's
Rügen's highest elevation. Unfortunately,
most of the time, enjoyment of the scenery
is marred by the masses trying to do the
same thing. On busy summer weekends, up
to 10,000 people visit the Königstuhl, each
shelling out DM2 for the privilege. Fortunately, few make the trek a few hundred
metres east to the **Victoria-Sicht** (Victoria
View), which provides the best view of the
Königstuhl itself. And it's free.

Bus No 419a goes to the Stubbenkammer from Sassnitz. If you're driving, you
must pay to leave your vehicle in the parking lot in Hagen, then either pay again for
the ride on a shuttle bus or walk 2.5km past
the legendary Herthasee (Hertha Lake)
through the forest. After 6 pm you can
drive all the way to the Königstuhl. The
nicest way to approach the area, though, is
by making the 10km trek from Sassnitz
along the coast through the ancient forest
of Stubnitz. The trail also takes you past the
gorgeous **Wissower Klinken** chalk cliffs,
another famous vista painted by Friedrich.

Though it was once a popular resort
town, most people now only go to **Sassnitz**
to board one of the ferries headed for Denmark or Sweden.

The tourist office (☎ 51 60, fax 516 16),
Seestrasse 1, is open weekdays from 8 am
to 7 pm (in winter to 5 pm), and weekends
from 3 to 7 pm (closed in winter). It also has
information on the delights of the Jasmund
National Park.

WITTOW

Wittow, the northernmost area on Rügen,
began life as an island of its own. It was
later connected to the main island after
enough sand had washed up to form the
Schaabe. It's a thinly populated, windswept
stretch of land used mostly for agriculture.

Schaabe

This narrow strip of land, connecting the
Jasmund Peninsula with Wittow, has arguably the nicest beach on the island. It's a
10km-long crescent of fine white sand bordered by fragrant pine forest. The fact that
it's practically devoid of infrastructure (no
lifeguards, beach wicker chairs, snack bars
etc) only adds to its untamed charm. There
are parking lots with beach access on both
sides of the road that traverses it.

There's a *camping ground (☎ 038391-
237, Wittower Strasse 1-2)*, open from May
to mid-October, in Juliusruh at the northern
end of the Schaabe.

Kap Arkona

Rügen ends at the rugged cliffs of Cape
Arkona, with its famous pair of lighthouses.
The older of the two, designed by Karl
Friedrich Schinkel, was completed in 1827.
The so-called **Schinkel-Leuchtturm** (DM5/4)
is square and squat and 19.3m high. Inside
are exhibits by Rügen artists, and from the
viewing platform there's a wonderful view
over a colourful quilt of rape fields, meadows and white beaches, all set off against the
dark blue Baltic Sea. The views are better
still from the adjacent 36m-high **Neuer
Leuchtturm**, which has been in business
since 1902 (DM6/5).

A few metres east of the lighthouses is
the **Burgwall**, a complex that harbours the
remains of a *Tempelburg*, a Slavic temple
and fortress built for the four-headed god

Svantevit. The castle was taken over by the Danes in 1168, paving the way for the Christianisation of Rügen.

Vitt If you follow the coast for about 1.5km in a south-easterly direction, you will reach the charming fishing village of Vitt. The toy-sized village has 13 thatched cottages and a few restaurants and snack bars. The whitewashed octagonal chapel at the village entrance is open daily and contains a copy of an altar painting by Philipp Otto Runge (the original is in Hamburg).

Getting There & Away The gateway to Kap Arkona is the village of Putgarten, served infrequently by bus No 403 from Altenkirchen. If you're staying in the northern half of Rügen and you're not driving, it's probably best to travel by bicycle.

If you are in a car or motorbike, you have to leave the vehicle in a pay parking lot in Putgarten about 1.5km south of the lighthouses. The walk through the village to the cape is pleasant, though you can also cover the distance aboard a motorised mini-train (DM3 one-way, DM6 return). A second train services Vitt.

HIDDENSEE ISLAND
☎ 038300 • pop 1250

Hiddensee is a narrow island off Rügen's western coast, 17km long and 1.8km at its widest point. It's a quiet and peaceful place with no cars and little infrastructure. Locals refer to their island as *'Dat söte Länneken'*, which translates as 'The sweet little land'. In the 19th and early 20th centuries, Hiddensee bewitched artists like Thomas Mann, Asta Nielsen, Max Reinhardt, Bertolt Brecht and the writer Gerhart Hauptmann, who is buried here.

There's no mass tourism on Hiddensee, and its three villages – Kloster, Neuendorf and Vitte – have preserved an innocent charm rarely found these days. Hiddensee is best explored by bike, and there are rental places everywhere.

The tourist office (☎ 642 26/27/28, fax 642 25) is at Norderende 162 in Vitte. It's open on weekdays from 8 am to 5 pm. From July to mid-September it's also open on weekends from 10 am to noon.

There are no camping grounds or hostels on Hiddensee. A number of *private rooms* from DM20 per person in high season are available in all three villages, which is a good thing since there are basically no hotels either. One of the least expensive options is *Zur Boje* (☎/fax 65 20, *Königsbarg*) in Neuendorf, which charges DM45/90 for singles/doubles with private facilities.

Hiddensee is served by ferries from Schaprode on Rügen and from Stralsund. For details, see the earlier Getting There & Away sections under Stralsund and Rügen Island.

WESTERN POMERANIA

For many visitors to Germany, Bavaria (Bayern) is a microcosm of the whole country. Here you will find, in abundance, the 'olde-worlde' German stereotypes of *Lederhosen*, beer halls, oompah bands and romantic castles. But it also has a modern dimension: home to powerful companies such as BMW and Siemens, Bavaria is also Germany's most fertile breeding ground for new technologies. These contrasts heighten the Bavarians' sense of otherness – many feel like citizens of a separate country, only tenuously linked to the rest of Germany.

Bavaria was ruled for centuries as a duchy in the Holy Roman Empire, under a dynasty founded by Otto I of Wittelsbach. A transformation occurred in the early 19th century when Napoleon, in the course of empire-building, declared Bavaria a kingdom and doubled its size. The fledgling nation became the object of power struggles between Prussia and Austria and, in 1871, was brought into the German Reich by Bismarck (commonly known as the Iron Chancellor).

The last king of Bavaria was Ludwig II (1845-86), who earned the epithet the 'mad king', due to his kooky lifestyle and obsession with building fairy-tale castles at enormous expense, including the sugary Neuschwanstein at the foot of the Alps.

Bavaria was the only province that refused to ratify the Basic Law (Germany's near-constitution) following WWII, claiming that it ceded too much power to the central government. Instead, Bavaria's leaders opted to return to its prewar status as a 'free state', and drafted their own constitution. Ever since, the *Land* (state) has been ruled by the arch-conservative CSU, which refrains from running against its national partner, the CDU, in federal elections.

If you only have time for one part of Germany after Berlin, this is it. Munich, the 'Paris of Germany', is the heart and soul of the state. The Bavarian Alps, Nuremberg

HIGHLIGHTS

Bavaria Luminaries: Bertolt Brecht, Lucas Cranach the Elder, Ludwig Erhard, Rainer Werner Fassbinder, Henry Kissinger, Franz Marc, Franz Josef Strauss, Richard Strauss, Patrick Süskind

- Wandering around Bamberg's beautiful old town and canals
- Visiting Linderhof castle and its leafy grounds
- Exploring Munich's nightlife
- Sampling Regensburger sausages
- Hiring pedal boats on the Five Lakes
- Enjoying electric-boat rides on Königssee, near Berchtesgaden

The Romantic Road p464
Bamberg p508
Würzburg p467
Nuremberg p498
Rothenburg p472
CZECH REPUBLIC
Regensburg p521
Passau p531
Munich pp428-9
Greater Munich p423
AUSTRIA

and the medieval towns along the Romantic Road are other important attractions. Try getting off the beaten track in a place like the Bavarian Forest for a glimpse of Germany away from the tourist coaches.

BAVARIA

Orientation

Bavaria is Germany's largest state, embracing one-fifth of the country's land mass with 10 million inhabitants, or one-eighth of the national population. It's made up of several counties, but the boundaries of tourist offices and governmental organisations don't mesh. So, for example, you can't get information on Franconia from Munich tourist offices. For tourism purposes, Bavaria is broken up into five regions:

Munich (München) The capital of Bavaria, Munich is in the south-east of the state. A city of 1.3 million, Munich and its surrounding area is a separate region in itself.

Upper Bavaria (Oberbayern) This refers to the Bavarian Alps, at the southernmost point of the state.

East Bavaria (Ostbayern) This area includes Passau, the Bavarian Forest and Regensburg.

Franconia (Franken) The northernmost district of the state includes Nuremberg, Erlangen, Bayreuth, Bamberg, Würzburg and several Romantic Road cities, including Rothenburg ob der Tauber.

Allgäu-Bavarian Swabia (Allgäu-Bayerisch Schwaben) This includes Augsburg, eastern Lake Constance and the heart-stopper of the Romantic Road, Neuschwanstein Castle.

Accommodation

While Bavarian hostels (even the HI-member hostels) generally prohibit stays by anyone over the age of 26, some don't.

Unfortunately, we can't list all the hostels that welcome those over 26 (because the hostels would risk their membership). However, we will say that even if they *say* they don't, many hostels will take in people aged over 26, if there's room available, for a slightly higher price.

Bavaria's parks, as well as certain popular rafting routes, are in many cases open to free camping, and it's a wonderful thing to do. While cruising down a river in a canoe or rubber raft, you're permitted – generally speaking – to stop along the bank and pitch a tent.

Be sure to follow the local code of ethics and common decency and pack up everything you brought along – litter, bottles, cans – and bury human waste in cat holes at least 15cm deep before you leave.

Food & Drink

Prepare yourself: Bavarians enjoy beer, and one of the finer ways you can sample their brew is in beer gardens. In many places you can bring along a picnic lunch and just buy the beer; in some, though, outside food is forbidden.

You can be sure of one thing: travel in Bavaria involves a lot of stops in beer gardens, eating sausage and other meat, and drinking lots of glorious Bavarian beer – including some of the best brews in the world.

Munich

☎ 089   ● pop 1.3 million

Munich (München) is the Bavarian mother lode. It's the capital of the state of Bavaria, home to its finest museums, dotted with castles and one of Germany's most prosperous cities. Only since reunification has it become the nation's second most popular destination, after Berlin.

Munich has been the capital of Bavaria since 1503, but it really achieved prominence under the guiding hand of Ludwig I in the 19th century. It has seen many turbulent times, but this century has been particularly rough. WWI practically starved the city to death, and WWII (which in many ways began here with the infamous Munich Agreement) brought bombing and more than 200,000 deaths.

Whether you see the city during the tourist-packed summer, the madness of Oktoberfest or the cold stillness of a February afternoon, Munich offers the chance to see Bavarians and the values and attitudes that so dominate the exported image of 'Germany'.

History

There's evidence of settlements here as early as 525 AD, but it's generally agreed that the most important settlers were Benedictine monks around the 8th century; the

BAVARIA

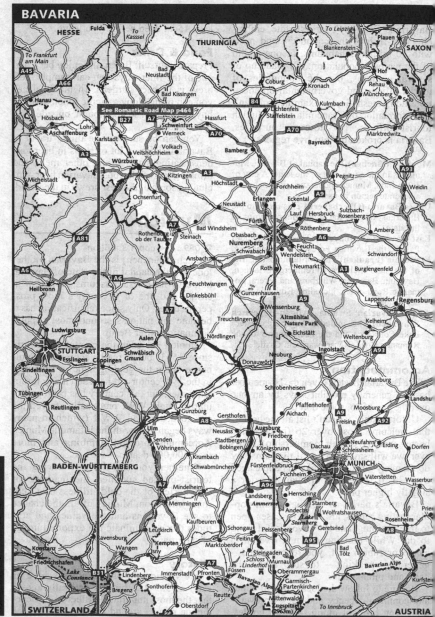

BAVARIA

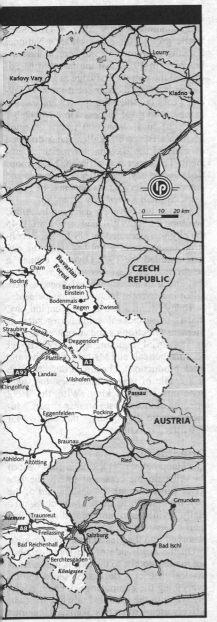

city's name derives from *Munichen*, or 'monk settlement'.

Heinrich der Löwe's rule was sanctioned by the Imperial Diet in Augsburg in 1158, which is the city's official birth date. Heinrich's control over the city, tenuous at the best of times, was repealed just 30 years later. In 1240, the city passed from the bishops of Freising to the House of Wittelsbach, which would run the city (as well as much of Bavaria) until the 20th century.

Munich became a ducal residence in 1255. In the next century, Ludwig the Bavarian expanded the city, rebuilt areas destroyed by the Great Fire of 1328, built many of the fortifications you can still see today and ensured Munich's regional power by granting it a salt-trade monopoly.

This established a wealthy trading city, and over the next 200 years Munich continued to prosper. By 1503 the city had 13,500 residents and had become the capital of the Duchy of Bavaria.

Dozens of outbreaks of the plague began in 1349 and continued for the next 150 years, despite frantic efforts to cordon off the city. Reinforcements were constructed and sewage and sanitation improved, but the city's population was ravaged. As the plague passed, the *Schäffler* (coopers) began a ritualistic dance in 1517, which they vowed to perform every seven years as long as the city was spared further outbreaks. Now the tradition can be witnessed more regularly: the *Schäfflertanz* is re-enacted daily by the little figures on the city's *Glockenspiel* on Marienplatz.

The Reformation hit Munich particularly hard. Under Duke Wilhelm IV, Protestants were persecuted and by the outbreak of the Thirty Years' War local residents were resolutely Catholic. During the war, the city was invaded with little fanfare – Imperial General Tilly (1559-1632), realising he was hopelessly outnumbered, wisely surrendered it to Swedish king Gustav Adolphus in 1632.

The city then fell under Habsburg rule from 1705 to 1714, and Munich was rejuvenated in the 18th century, with an explosion of spectacular baroque and Italianate architecture throughout the city.

In the 19th century, Napoleon's conquest of the territories and his rejigging of the German royal hierarchy elevated Bavaria to the rank of kingdom. The marriage in 1810 of Bavarian Crown Prince Ludwig I to the Saxon-Hildburghausen Princess Therese marked what would become the Oktoberfest.

In 1818 Bavaria became the first German state with a written constitution. The first half of the 19th century also saw runaway expansion under King Ludwig I, who was determined to transform his capital into a cultural and artistic centre. He hired architects including Leo von Klenze and Friedrich von Gärtner, and commissioned landmarks such as Königsplatz, the Alte Pinakothek and Ludwigstrasse, as well as the Königsbau and Festsaalbau sections of the Residenz. It was during this period that the university moved to Munich from Landshut and the Theresienwiese (site of the Oktoberfest), with its Ruhmeshalle (Hall of Fame), was constructed.

Ludwig II took the reins after his father's death and began spending the family fortune on projects that were seen by other members of the royal family as, to put it mildly, nutty. Ludwig's bizarre shyness, predilection towards ever more grandiose construction projects and lavish sponsorship (especially of Bismarck, the composer Richard Wagner and many of Ludwig's architects and planners) earned him the moniker 'Loony Ludwig'. Ironically, the very projects that bankrupted the government and royal house are today's biggest money-spinners for the Bavarian tourism industry.

Arrested after being declared mentally unfit, Ludwig was found drowned (with his doctor) in highly mysterious circumstances in Lake Starnberg (see the boxed text 'Ludwig II, the Fairy-Tale King' in the Around Füssen section). His brother Otto, a certified nutcase, was unable to take the throne, so his regent Prince Luitpold took charge and began another expansion of the city.

By the turn of the 20th century, Munich had over 500,000 residents. Political turmoil and infighting, along with runaway inflation and economic collapse after WWI, created fertile ground for Adolf Hitler's National Socialist movement. It was here, in the Hofbräuhaus in 1920, that the failed artist addressed the party's first large meeting.

The budding dictator spent the next several years consolidating power and raising money, with great success. On 8 November 1923, he and about 600 troops stormed Munich's Bürgerbräukeller and kidnapped officials of the Bavaria provincial government. The caper was a fiasco. Nazi troops fled the next day, and Hitler was arrested and jailed. While serving his sentence, he began work on *Mein Kampf* (My Struggle).

Munich was severely damaged by Allied bombing during WWII, and on 30 April 1945 the city was occupied by US forces. Reconstruction was largely finished when the city was awarded the 1972 Olympic Games, a celebration of West Germany's rebuilding that ended in tragedy when 10 people were killed in a terrorist hostage-taking incident.

Today Munich is a thriving capital city, thanks to unshakeable industries such as Siemens (electronics and computers as well as industrial equipment), BMW, Bayer pharmaceuticals and MAN (automotive and truck production). The area around Munich is a cradle of new technologies, too, with generous state backing. With the 1992 opening of Franz-Josef Strauss airport, Munich became the country's number two air hub after Frankfurt.

Orientation

The Hauptbahnhof is less than 1km west of the Altstadt, the centre of town. The Isar River flows through the eastern part of the city from south to north. Munich is officially divided into numerous districts; formerly separate villages, they have been absorbed into the greater metropolitan area.

On the north side of the Hauptbahnhof are mainly hotels; to the east is the 'gizmotronics' district – dozens of shops selling everything the computer geek could possibly want; to the south is Ludwigs-Vorstadt, a lively area – often mistaken as dangerous

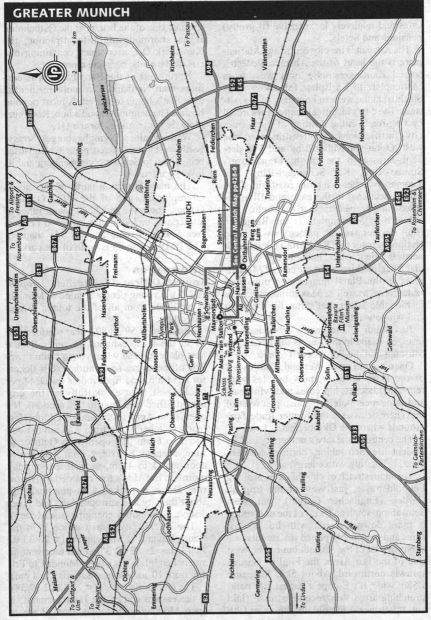

GREATER MUNICH

To Passau
Kirchheim
Vaterstetten
A94
E52
E45
B471
A99
B388
Haar
Hohenbrunn
Ismaning
Putzbrunn
Ottobrunn
To Airport & Freising
Garching
B11
River Isar
Unterföhring
Riem
Feldkirchen
Aschheim
Trudering
To Rosenheim & Chiemsee
A8
E52
E45
To Nuremberg
A9
E45
B471
E45
Taufkirchen
A95
E53
B13
Freimann
Unterschleissheim
MUNICH
Bogenhausen
Steinhausen
Berg am Laim
Ramersdorf
Unterhaching
E54
See Central Munich Map pp428-9
Ostbahnhof
Oberschleissheim
A92
E53
Hasenbergl
Haidhausen
Giesing
Bavaria Film Museum
Grosshesselohe
Geiselgasteig
Grünwald
Freimann
Milbertshofen
Olympic Park
Schwabing
Au
Harthof
Neuhausen
Maxvorstadt
Thalkirchen
Harlaching
River Isar
Feldmoching
Moosach
Gern
Main Train Station
Theresienwiese
Westend
Untersendling
Mittersendling
Obersendling
Pullach
B11
Karlsfeld
Schloss Nymphenburg
E54
Solln
Obermenzing
Nymphenburg
Laim
Pasing
Grosshadern
Maxhof
E33
A95
Allach
Gräfelfing
Kralling
Dachau
A8
E52
Aubing
B471
Neuaubing
Lochhausen
Starnberg
Gauting
To Garmisch-Partenkirchen
Olching
Puchheim
To Stuttgart & Ulm
To Augsburg
Maisach
Emmering
Germering
B2
To Lindau
A96
River Würm
River Amper

Speichersee
0   2   4 km

BAVARIA

– packed with Turkish shops, restaurants, cafes and relatively inexpensive (if grotty) pensions and hotels.

The Altstadt is the city centre and Marienplatz is the heart of the Altstadt. Pedestrianised Kaufingerstrasse runs west from Marienplatz to Karlsplatz (also known as Stachus) at the western boundary of the Altstadt. The city's historical centre is encircled by ring-roads in the position of the former city fortifications: Sonnenstrasse to the west; Oskar-von-Miller-Ring and Von-der-Tann-Strasse to the north; Franz-Josef-Strauss-Ring, Karl-Scharnagl-Ring and Thomas-Wimmer-Ring (one road with three named sections) to the east; and Blumenstrasse and Frauenstrasse to the south.

North of Marienplatz is the Residenz (the former royal palace), with the Nationaltheater and Residenz Theatre. Just north is Odeonsplatz, home to the spectacular Theatinerkirche. To the east of Marienplatz is the Platzl quarter for pubs and restaurants, as well as Maximilianstrasse, a fashionable street that's fun for strolling and window-shopping.

Just south of the centre on Museumsinsel, an island in the Isar, is the Deutsches Museum and the Forum der Technik.

Once a slum area, Westend, south-west of the Hauptbahnhof, now bristles with renovated houses, hip cafes and wine bars and some nicer hotels. It's also just west of the Theresienwiese, the former trade fairgrounds where the Oktoberfest is held.

The centre of the city's university and its student life, Schwabing, north of Marienplatz, is bursting with energy.

The main stretch of chi-chi cafes is along Leopoldstrasse, just west of the English Garden (Englischer Garten), but west Schwabing, south and west of the university, is more down-to-earth, with bookshops, cafes and reasonably priced restaurants.

North-east of the Altstadt but on the west side of the Isar River, the English Garden sprawls northward. About 5km long and 1.5km wide, it's Europe's largest city park, stretching from Prinzregentenstrasse (laid out by Prince Luitpold in the late 19th century) to the city's northern boundary. On the east side of the Isar, near the Ostbahnhof is an enormous nightlife attraction, the Kunstpark Ost, a complex containing discos, restaurants, bars and cinemas.

North-west of the Hauptbahnhof is cosmopolitan Neuhausen, a more residential area that's home to the city's most popular hostel. The neighbourhood's hub, Rotkreuzplatz, is the terminus for the U1.

Walking along Nymphenburger Strasse north-west from Rotkreuzplatz in Neuhausen brings you to Schloss Nymphenburg and its lovely gardens.

The main attraction north of the city is Olympiapark, site of the 1972 Olympic Games. Today the park hosts a wide range of attractions, including the Tollwood Festival (see Special Events later in this chapter). The BMW Museum is north of the park.

Information

Tourist Offices The excellent *Infopool* (DM1), a young people's guide to Munich, is available from all of the tourist offices listed here.

EurAide (☎ 59 38 89), near platform No 11 at the Hauptbahnhof, is generally the best place to head when you get into town. The office makes reservations, sells tickets for DB trains and finds rooms for DM7 per booking at least as skilfully as the city tourist office (see later in this section). It's open from April to the end of Oktoberfest (early October) daily from 7.45 am to noon and 1 to 6 pm. It's open from October to June, Monday to Friday from 9.30 am to noon and 1 to 4 pm, as well as Saturday morning. EurAide's free newsletter, *The Inside Track*, is packed with practical info about the city and surroundings, and gives discounts on money changing (see Money).

The central city tourist office is in the Neues Rathaus at Marienplatz (☎ 23 33 02 72/73, fax 23 33 02 33, email tourismus@muenchen.btl.de). It's open Monday to Friday from 10 am to 8 pm (Saturday to 4 pm).

The city tourist office (☎ 23 33 02 57/58), at the eastern end of the Hauptbahnhof, is open Monday to Saturday from 9 am to

8 pm, and Sunday from 10 am to 6 pm. Expect to queue during summer, and staff can be stunningly rude.

The room-finding service at the tourist office is free. You can book by calling with a credit card number (☎ 233 03 00), in person or by writing to Fremdenverkehrsamt München, 80313 Munich. The tourist office at the airport has been shut, but the airport information desk in the main hall will field simple inquiries (such as for a city map).

Jugendinformationszentrum (Youth Information Centre; ☎ 51 41 06 60), a couple of blocks south-west of the Hauptbahnhof on the corner of Paul-Heyse-Strasse and Landwehrstrasse, is open Monday to Friday from noon to 6 pm (to 8 pm on Thursday). It has a wide range of printed information for young visitors to Munich and Germany.

The German auto association (ADAC) has several offices in town. The biggest one (☎ 54 91 72 34) is at Sendlinger-Tor-Platz.

Money Reisebank has two branches at the Hauptbahnhof; note that presenting a copy of EurAide's newsletter *The Inside Track* will get you a 50% reduction on commissions at those branches. There are also branches of Deutsche Bank (with a currency-exchange machine outside), Hypovereinsbank and Sparkasse on Marienplatz; a Sparkasse is about 200m east at Sparkassenstrasse 2. Deutsche Bank and Citibank both have offices on Rotkreuzplatz, close to the DJH hostel. The Postbank, which offers very good exchange rates, is in the post office opposite the Hauptbahnhof at Bahnhofplatz 1. You'll find American Express (☎ 29 09 01 45) at Promenadeplatz 6 and Thomas Cook (☎ 383 88 30) at Kaiserstrasse 45.

Post & Communications Munich's main post office is at Bahnhofplatz 1, just opposite the Hauptbahnhof, with telephone and fax services. It's open weekdays from 7 am to 8 pm, Saturday 8 am to 4 pm and Sunday 9 am to 3 pm. The poste restante address is Postlagernd, Bahnhofplatz 1, 80074 Munich.

The Cyberb@r, on the 4th floor of the Hertie department store (☎ 551 20) at Bahn-hofplatz 7, charges DM3 for 30 minutes on the Net (you can surf for 15 minutes for DM1.50 if you ask). The Cyberb@r on the top storey of the Karstadt am Dom department store (☎ 260 02 30), Neuhauser Strasse 21, charges the same rates.

The Internet Café (☎ 260 78 15), Altheimer Eck 12 near Marienplatz, is also a passable Italian eatery with a dozen-odd cyber-terminals; send email and surf free with any food or drink purchase. There's a branch (☎ 129 11 20) at Nymphenburger Strasse 145, just east of Rotkreuzplatz near the hostel. On the south side of the Hauptbahnhof is the Times Square Online Bistro (☎ 550 88 00), open daily from 6 am till 1 am, where you can also phone and video-conference on the Web to your heart's content, but for a stiff DM4.50 per 15 minutes.

Internet Resources Munich has a voluminous and user-friendly Web site at www .muenchen-tourist.de, with good English-language sections.

Travel Agencies EurAide (see Tourist Offices) is the best place to go with complicated rail pass inquiries or to book train travel in Germany or elsewhere in Europe.

Munich is a great city for bucket shops and cheap airfares, with several helpful options. Council Travel (☎ 39 50 22), near the university at Adalbertstrasse 32, is one of the best around; take U3 or U6 to Universität. STA Travel (☎ 39 90 96), Königinstrasse 49, is also a good bet.

Travel Overland is a competent bucket shop with several locations, including a good one at Barer Strasse 73 (☎ 27 27 61 00); we've used it many times with great results. Studiosus Reisen (☎ 235 05 20) at Oberanger 6 organises educational trips. The ABR Reisebüro (☎ 120 40) in the Hauptbahnhof handles train tickets.

Atlas Reisen has outlets in the city's Kaufhof stores, including Kaufingerstrasse 1-5 (☎ 26 90 72).

Bookshops The best travel bookshop in town is Geobuch (☎ 26 50 30), opposite

Viktualienmarkt at Rosental 6. The best cultural book range is available at Hugendubel (☎ 238 90), opposite the Rathaus at Marienplatz, with an enormous selection of Lonely Planet guides and tons of English-language offerings. You can sit on sofas and read before you buy.

In Schwabing, the wacky but well stocked – if you can find anything – Anglia English Bookshop (☎ 28 36 42) is at Schellingstrasse 3. Down the street in the courtyard at Schellingstrasse 21a is Words' Worth Books (☎ 280 91 41).

The more expensive and limited but handy Sussmann international bookshop in the Hauptbahnhof has books in English and French, newspapers, magazines and Calvin & Hobbes collections (check the 'bargain' basket for books for DM10).

EurAide, also in the Hauptbahnhof, has a small selection of used English-language paperbacks for sale.

Max&Milian (☎ 260 33 20), Ickstattstrasse 2, south-east of Sendlinger Tor, is the best established gay and lesbian bookshop in Munich. You might also try Apacik & Schell (☎ 62 42 04 04), Ohlmühllerstrasse 18 (enter from Entenbachstrasse).

Libraries There are branches in Munich of *Stadtbüchereien* (city libraries), where you will usually find some books in English.

Branches include those at Rosenheimerstrasse 5 (☎ 48 09 83 13) in the Gasteig, at Schrenkstrasse 8 (☎ 50 71 09) in Westend, and at Hohenzollernstrasse 16 (☎ 33 60 13) in Schwabing. The Bavarian State Library (☎ 28 63 80), Ludwigstrasse 16, is one of Germany's largest.

The university libraries include the Universitätsbibliothek (☎ 21 80 24 28), Geschwister-Scholl-Platz 1, and the Technical University Library (☎ 28 92 86 21), opposite the Alte Pinakothek, at Arcisstrasse 21.

Libraries at the British Council (☎ 290 08 60), Rumfordstrasse 7; and at Amerika Haus (☎ 55 25 37 20), Karolinenplatz 3, both specialise in books about culture and business in those countries.

Universities Munich is home to some 100,000 students. Three-quarters of them attend the Ludwig-Maximilians-Universität München (☎ 218 00), at Geschwister-Scholl-Platz 1. The top three faculties are medicine, economics and law.

The Technische Universität München (☎ 289 01), Arcisstrasse 21, has about 22,000 students studying mainly mathematics, physics, chemistry, biology and earth sciences.

Cultural Centres Cultural organisations abound; the *München im ...* publication (see the Entertainment section) has the complete list. The city has active branches of Amerika Haus (☎ 55 25 37 20), Karolinenplatz 3; the British Council (☎ 290 08 60), Rumfordstrasse 7; the Institut Français (☎ 286 62 80), Kaulbachstrasse 13; and the Goethe Institut (☎ 551 90 30), Sonnenstrasse 25.

Laundry The best laundrette close to the centre is Der Wunderbare Waschsalon, Theresienstrasse 134, open daily from 6 am to midnight. It's spotless, has cafe-style tables, drinkable coffee and a pleasant atmosphere. A load of laundry costs DM6.

Close to the Hauptbahnhof but swarming with layabouts is Prinz Münz-Waschsalon at Paul-Heyse-Strasse 21, open daily from 6 am to 10 pm. Loads cost DM7, dryers are DM1 for 15 minutes and the last wash must be in by 8 pm.

Close by in Westend, there's the nicer SB Waschsalon at Schwanthalerstrasse that's the cheapest in town (just DM5 per load). The Waschcenter Schnell + Sauber, near the main theatre at Klenzestrasse 18, charges DM6 per load and DM1 per 15 minutes in the dryer.

In Neuhausen, there's a 24 hour *Waschsalon* on the west side of Landshuter Strasse at No 77, on the corner of Volkartstrasse, 10 minutes from the hostel. There's a tanning salon downstairs, lest you leave sallow.

Medical & Emergency Services The US and UK consulates can provide lists of English-speaking doctors on request.

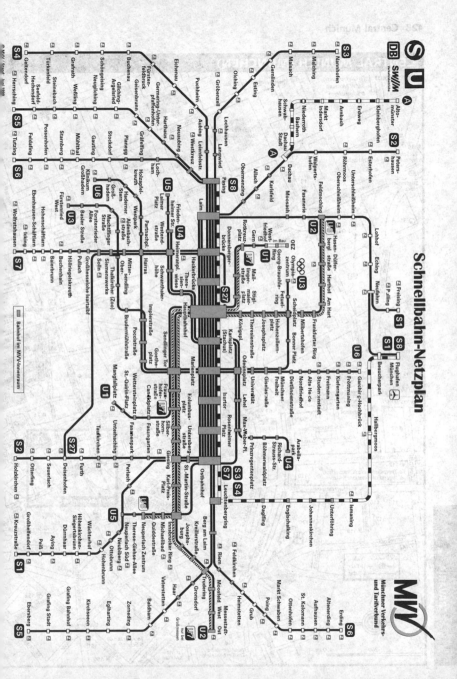

Schnellbahn-Netzplan

Münchner Verkehrs- und Tarifverbund

Bahnhof im MVV-Innenraum

CENTRAL MUNICH (MÜNCHEN)

MAXVORSTADT

To Olympiapark,
BMW Museum
& Schleissheim

To laundry

Theresienstrasse

Technische
Universität

To Schloss
Nymphenburg & DJH Hostel

Stiglmaier-
platz

Königsplatz

Karolinen-
platz

Hauptbahnhof

Bahnhof-
platz

Hauptbahnhof

Bayerstrasse

Schlosserstrasse

Adolf-Kolping-Strasse

Schwanthalerstrasse

To Theresienwiese (Oktoberfest)
& Jugendinformationszentrum

Landwehrstrasse

Pettenkoferstrasse

Sendlinger-
Tor-Platz

Lindwurmstrasse

To Frauentee-stube
& LeTra/Lesbentelefon

To Max
&Milian

To Apacik
& Schnell

Karlsplatz

Sendlinger Tor

Marienplatz
start

See Enlargement

St-Jakobs-
Platz

Frauenstrasse

Gärtnerplatz

Odeonsplatz

Hofgarte

Max-
Joseph-
Platz

Alter
Hof

Maximiliansplatz

Karlstrasse

Karlsplatz

Promenade-
platz

Löwengrube

Schäfflerstrasse

Neuhauser-strasse

Herzogspitalstrasse

Rottmannstrasse

Brienner Strasse

Brienner
Strasse

Elisenstrasse

Hirtenstrasse

Arnulfstrasse

Pfandhausstrasse

Prannerstrasse

Maxburgstrasse

Kaufingerstrasse

Rosental

Oberanger

Unterer Anger

Blumenstrasse

Schellingstrasse

Theresienstrasse

Gabelsbergerstrasse

Oskar - von - Miller - Ring

Walk
U-Bahn
S-Bahn

0   200   400 m

BAVARIA

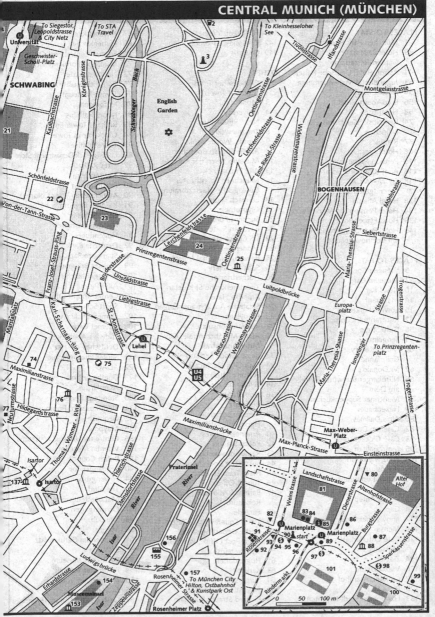

CENTRAL MUNICH (MÜNCHEN)

CENTRAL MUNICH

PLACES TO STAY
1 München Park Hotel
39 Hotel Bayerischer Hof;
   Garden-Restaurant
41 Astron Hotel Deutsche Kaiser
53 Jugendhotel Marienherberge
54 Hotel Cristal
56 Euro Youth Hotel
58 Hotel Eder
74 Kempinski Vier Jahreszeiten
   München
77 Rafael
106 Hotel Arosa
115 Pension Marie-Luise
116 Andi (Comfort) Hotel
118 CVJM-YMCA
   Jugendgästehaus
128 Hotel Atlanta
134 Hotel-Pension am Markt
139 Hotel Blauer Bock
143 Hotel Pension Mariandl; Café
   am Beethovenplatz

PLACES TO EAT
5 Crêperie Cocorico
7 Museum Café
10 News Bar
14 Maharani
15 Löwenbräukeller
52 Ristorante Ca'doro
55 Gute Stube
59 Tengelmann
60 Müller Bakery; Nordsee;
   Grillpfanne
62 McDonald's
68 Nürnberger Bratwurst Glöckl
   am Dom
70 Münchner Suppenküche
79 Haxenbauer
80 Alois Dallmayr
82 Café am Dom
93 Café Glockenspiel
95 Metropolitan
104 Prinz Myschkin
105 Hundskugel
110 Kandil Restaurant
112 Sultan
113 Kebab Antep
114 Gap
117 Jinny's Thai Food
119 Mensa
120 Café Osteria LaVecchia
   Masseria
124 Ziegler
126 Vinzenzmurr
127 Cipriani; Asamhof
129 Pizza Hut
133 Löwenbräu Stadt Kempten

141 Höflinger; Weiner's
142 Trattoria La Fiorentini
149 Shida

OTHER
2 Chinesischer Turm
   (Chinese Tower)
3 Monopteros
4 University
6 Neue Pinakothek
8 Treszniewski
9 Words' Worth Books
11 Anglia English Bookshop
12 Museum Reich der Kristalle
13 Alte Pinakothek
16 Münchner Volkstheater
17 Geologische Staatssammlung
18 Lenbach Haus
19 Glyptothek
20 Siemens Forum
21 Bavarian State Library
22 US Consulate
23 Modern Art Gallery
24 Bavarian National Museum
25 Schack Gallery
26 Hofgartnertor
27 Theatinerkirche St Kajetan
28 Amerika Haus
29 Staatliche Antikensammlungen
30 Propyläen
31 Russian Consulate
32 ADM-Mitfahrzentrale; City
   Mitwohnzentrale
33 Börse (Stock Exchange)
34 Soul City; Nachtcafé;
   Fortuna Musikbar
35 Feldherrnhalle
36 Lion Statues
37 Residenz
38 Kunsthalle der
   Hypo-Kulturstiftung
40 American Express
42 Police Station
43 Radius bicycle hire
44 Sussmann Bookshop
45 Main Train Station
46 Tourist Office
47 Bahnhof-Apotheke; ABR
   Reisebüro
48 EurAide
49 Times Square Online Bistro
50 Hertie Department Store
51 Main Post Office; Postbank
57 Hypovereinsbank
61 Hugendubel
63 Karlstor
64 Bürgersaal
65 Augustiner-Gaststätte
66 Richard Strauss Fountain

67 Michaelskirche
69 Frauenkirche
71 Former Central Post Office
72 Münzhof (Former Mint)
73 Nationaltheater
75 British Consulate
76 Jewish Museum
78 Hofbräuhaus
81 Neues Rathaus
83 Rathaus Tower Entry
84 Glockenspiel Tower
85 Tourist Office
86 Ludwig Beck Department Store
87 Altes Rathaus
88 Toy Museum
89 Fischbrunnen
90 Mariensäule (Mary Column)
91 Kaufhof Department Store
92 Sport Schuster
94 Hypovereinsbank
96 Hugendubel
97 Deutsche Bank
98 Sparkasse Bank
99 Weisses Bräuhaus
100 Heiliggeistkirche
101 Alter Peter
102 Central Tourist Office
103 Sport Scheck
107 Damenstiftskirche
108 Internet Café
109 Ludwigs-Apotheke
111 Deutsches Theater
121 Sauter Photographic
122 ADAC
123 Goethe Institut
125 Asamkirche
130 Studiosus Reisen
131 Stadtmuseum; Filmmuseum
132 Geobuch
135 Maypole
136 Centre for Unusual Museums
137 Valentin Museum
138 British Council
140 Sendlinger Tor
144 Löwengrube
145 The Stud
146 Marionettentheater
147 Ochsengarten
148 The Sub
150 Morizz
151 Theater am Gärtnerplatz
152 Bei Carla
153 Deutsches Museum
154 Forum der Technik
155 Müllerisches Volksbad
156 Muffathalle
157 Gasteig; City Library (Branch)

Medical help is available through the Kassenärztlicher Notfalldienst; call ☎ 55 14 71 and help will arrive. For an ambulance, ring ☎ 192 22. Most pharmacies will have some English-speaking staff on hand, but there are several designated 'international' ones with English-speaking staff: at the airport (☎ 975 92 95 0); Bahnhof-Apotheke (☎ 69 41 19), Bahnhofplatz 2; and Ludwigs-Apotheke (☎ 260 30 21) at Neuhauser Strasse 11. To find a pharmacy in an emergency, call ☎ 59 44 75. For an emergency dentist, call ☎ 516 00.

There's a police station at the Hauptbahnhof on the Arnulfstrasse side.

Dangers & Annoyances Crime and staggering drunks leaving the beer halls and tents are major problems during Oktoberfest, especially at the southern end of the Hauptbahnhof. (It's no joke: drunk people in a crowd trying to get home can get violent, and there are about 100 cases of assault every year.) Leave early or stay very cautious, if not sober, yourself.

The *Föhn* (pronounced 'foon') is a weather-related annoyance peculiar to southern Germany. Static-charged wind from the south brings exquisite views clear to the Alps – and an area of dense pressure that sits on the city. Asthmatics, rheumatics and hypochondriacs complain of headaches; other Münchners claim that it simply makes them cranky.

Marienplatz

Marienplatz is the heart and soul of the Altstadt, punctuated by the glowing **Mariensäule** (Mary Column), erected in 1638 to celebrate the removal of Swedish forces. At the top is the golden figure of the Virgin Mary, carved in 1590 and originally located in the Frauenkirche. Our tour of the square starts under the towering spires of the Neues Rathaus.

Neues Rathaus The late-Gothic new town hall (1867-1908) surrounds six courtyards, including the **Prunkhof**; there are festivals and events in them throughout the

---

Historic Centre Walking Tour

The attractions described in the sections from **Marienplatz** to the **Viktualienmarkt** are linked as a walking tour (see the Central Munich map), though you can also treat each entry as a separate sight, and pick and choose what you would like to visit.

This extensive circuit covers the main sights within the bounds of Munich's historic centre. Starting at Marienplatz, moving north to the Residenz and arching anticlockwise back to the starting point, the tour takes about 1¼ hours if walking at a leisurely pace. Include visits to all the museums and churches, however, and you've got (at least) a two day itinerary on your hands.

---

year. The building's blackened facade is festooned with gargoyles and statues, including, on the corner, a wonderful dragon climbing the turrets.

The highlight of the building is, of course, its incessantly photographed **Glockenspiel** (carillon), which has three levels. Two portray the **Schäfflertanz** (see the History section) and the **Ritterturnier**, a knights' tournament held in 1568 to celebrate a royal marriage. The apparatus springs into action to a wonderfully chimed tune at 11 am (November to April only), noon and 5 pm. The night scene, featuring the **Münchner Kindl** and **Nachtwächter**, runs at 9 pm. See Cafes & Bistros in the Places to Eat section for the two best cafes from which to watch the spectacle.

Visitors can take a lift to the top of the 80m-tall tower (DM3/1.50) Monday to Friday from 9 am to 7 pm, and from 10 am on Saturday, Sunday and holidays. The cashier is on the 4th floor; take the lift inside or use the staircase, taking a look at the stately corridors and views of the inner courtyard.

Fischbrunnen The Fish Fountain was used to keep river fish alive during the

BAVARIA

medieval markets; later it was used as the ceremonial dunking spot for butchers' apprentices and today it's a good meeting place. Local legend suggests that dipping an empty purse into the water here on Ash Wednesday guarantees that it will always be full.

Altes Rathaus The neo-Gothic old town hall building (1474) stands forlornly at the eastern end of the square; destroyed by lightning and bombs, it was rebuilt in a plainer style after WWII. In its south tower is the city's **Toy Museum** (Spielzeugmuseum; ☎ 29 40 01). The most amusing thing about it is right in front: the wind-powered sculpture that releases pent-up energy every few minutes by clanging and banging. That's a free exhibit. Inside (admission DM5/1) you'll stare at case after case of dolls.

St Peter & Heiliggeist Churches At the southern end of Marienplatz is the **Alter Peter** (also known as St Peterskirche), which was the city's first parish church in the 11th century. The Gothic building you see today was begun in the 14th century. You can climb its unique rectangular 92m-tall tower (297 steps, DM2.50/1.50) for spectacular views of the city. The flamboyant rococo interior was restored after WWII.

Behind the Altes Rathaus, the **Heiliggeistkirche** (Church of the Holy Spirit, 1392) first appears almost economical in design until you look up to see the Asam brothers' amazing rococo ceiling, completed during the interior revamp in 1724-30. This is also Germany's largest Gothic hall church.

Marienplatz to Max-Joseph-Platz

From the north-eastern end of Marienplatz, Sparkassenstrasse leads north past some exceptional buildings. Near the south end of the street is the **Alter Hof**, the Wittelsbach residence until they outgrew it and built the Residenz you'll see later on this tour.

Just opposite the Alter Hof, turn right onto Münzstrasse and walk one block to Orlandoplatz (teeming with tourist crap shops); look to the left-hand corner to see Munich's

celebrated **Hofbräuhaus**, crawling with tourists from opening time at 10 am. The ballroom upstairs was the site of the first large meeting of the National Socialist Party on 20 February 1920; you can visit if the rooms aren't being used for a function. Back downstairs, after guzzling a *Mass* (1L mug) or two of beer (DM11 to DM13 apiece), drivers can check their alcohol level in the coin-op breathalysers (DM3) by the toilets.

Return to Sparkassenstrasse, turn right and pass the former **Münzhof** (mint), which lies a block north of the Alter Hof. An inscription on the west side of the building reads *Moneta Regis* (Money Rules).

Max-Joseph-Platz

From the old mint you stroll north onto **Maximilianstrasse**, Munich's most glamorous shopping street, with splendiferously expensive shops and the grand Kempinski Vier Jahreszeiten Hotel. Turn left, and this avenue leads to the southern end of **Max-Joseph-Platz**, home to some of Munich's most beloved buildings. Among them is the five-tiered **Nationaltheater**, home to the Bavarian State Opera, and the grand-daddy of them all – the Residenz. The square's focal point is a **statue** of Bavarian king Max I Joseph, who promulgated Germany's first constitution in 1818.

At the southern end of the square is the **old central post office**, on the site of a former palace, with a frescoed Italianate arcade. The place still dispatches mail; enter at the west side.

Residenz On the north side of Max-Joseph-Platz looms the oldest section (1571) of the Residenz, the huge palace that housed Bavarian rulers from 1385 to 1918, and today contains more than 400 years of architectural history. Northern wings were added to create several interior courtyards, including the Emperor, Apothecary and Fountain courtyards and two smaller ones, Chapel and King's Tract. The enclosed Grotto Court, one of the first places you'll see when you enter, features the wonderful **Perseusbrunnen**. The west side of the building fronts Residenzstrasse and has the entrance to the Egyptian Art Museum and the Altes Residenztheater; the south side of the building, fronting Max-Joseph-Platz, holds the entrance to the Residenzmuseum and the Schatzkammer.

Residenzmuseum Within the palace, the Residenzmuseum (☎ 29 06 71) has an extraordinary array of more than 100 rooms displaying treasures of the Wittelsbach dynasty. The museum is so large that it's divided into two sections, which take about two hours each to see. You can do it on your own with a copy of the excellent English-language guide *Residence Munich* (DM6, at the cash desk), which has room-by-room tours with photographs and explanations.

A highlight is the **Ancestral Gallery**, remodelled in 1726-30 and including 121 portraits of the rulers of Bavaria (note the larger paintings of Charlemagne and Ludwig the Bavarian). There's also the **Schlachtensäle** (Battle Halls); **Porcelain Chambers**, containing 19th century porcelain services from factories in Berlin, Meissen and Nymphenburg; and the **Asian Collections**, with Chinese and Japanese lacquerware, tapestries, carpets, furniture and jewellery.

The museum is open Tuesday to Sunday from 10 am to 4.30 pm (DM7/5, free for children). Two-hour tours (DM8) in German are held on Sunday and Thursday at 11 am, and Thursday and Saturday at 2 pm; each tour starts at Maximiliansplatz and takes in half the collection.

Treasury The Residenzmuseum entrance is also the entrance to the Schatzkammer der Residenz (Residenz Treasury), which exhibits an enormous quantity of jewels, ornate goldwork and other precious objects. The mind-boggling treasures in this Aladdin's cave include portable altars, the ruby jewellery of Queen Therese, amazing pocket watches, and 'exotic handicrafts', including applied art from Turkey, Iran, Mexico and India. It's definitely worth the admission price (DM6/free). The English-language guide to the collection, *Treasury*

in the Munich Residence, is another DM6. The Schatzkammer is open Tuesday to Sunday from 10 am to 4.30 pm.

Altes Residenztheater The Old Residence Theatre, also known as the Cuvilliés Theatre, has a stunning, lavish interior, and is perhaps Europe's finest rococo theatre. While the building was destroyed during bombings in 1944, the interior furnishings had been removed, so what you see today is original. You can visit (except during state opera and theatre company rehearsals), Monday to Saturday from 2 to 5 pm and Sunday from 10 am to 5 pm (DM3/free). The entrance is at Residenzstrasse 1.

Egyptian Art Museum At the south side of the Hofgarten and the north side of the Residenz, the Staatliche Sammlung Ägyptischer Kunst (☎ 29 85 46) – at Hofgartenstrasse 1 but enter at the north side of the Residenz at the Obelisk – has an excellent display of Egyptian antiquities, artwork, monuments and statues from the Old, Middle and New Kingdoms (2670-1075 BC). It's open Tuesday to Friday from 9 am to 4 pm (also from 7 to 9 pm on Tuesday), and on Saturday, Sunday and holidays from 10 am to 5 pm (DM5/3).

Lion Statues At the entrance to the theatre and the Egyptian Art Museum on Residenzstrasse, note the two lions guarding the gates. Rubbing one of the lions' shields (look for the one that's been buffed to a gleaming shine) is said to bring you wealth.

Odeonsplatz

Residenzstrasse leads north from Max-Joseph-Platz to the **Feldherrnhalle** (Field Marshal's Hall) at the south end of Odeonsplatz. This square is the starting point of Ludwigstrasse, which is a broad Parisian-style boulevard shooting north past the university to the **Siegestor** (Triumphal Arch), which itself marks the starting point of chic Leopoldstrasse.

Odeonsplatz was the site of one of the earliest putsch attempts by Nazis in 1923, the

BAVARIA

so-called Beer Hall Putsch, which landed Hitler in jail. The Feldherrnhalle, dedicated to the field marshals under the Wittelsbachs, has several statues, including one of General Tilly, who surrendered Munich to the Swedes during the Thirty Years' War.

At the west side of the square is the landmark **Theatinerkirche St Kajetan** (1663-90), built to commemorate the conception (after a lengthy period of trying) by Henriette Adelaide) of Prince Max Emanuel. Designed by Agostino Barelli, the church's massive twin towers around a giant cupola are another landmark of Munich's skyline. Inside, the intensely stuccoed high dome stands above the *Fürstengruft* (royal crypt), containing the remains of Wittelsbach family members.

At the east side of Odeonsplatz, the neoclassical **Hofgartentor** (1816) leads the way to the former royal gardens (Hofgarten), with lovely paths around a **temple**. At the eastern end of the gardens is the modern **Bayerische Staatskanzlei** (Bavarian Chancellor's Office), with the city's **WWI memorial** in front.

South of the Theatinerkirche, on fashionable Theatinerstrasse at No 15, is the **Kunsthalle der Hypo-Kulturstiftung** (☎ 22 44 12), which has excellent rotating exhibitions (to get there, take the U-Bahn to Odeonsplatz or tram No 19 from the centre). Check with EurAide or the tourist offices to find out what's on when you're in town.

From the Kunsthalle, walk south down Theatinerstrasse (which turns into Weinstrasse), turn right into the alley opposite the grassy Marienhof and you'll face Munich's trademark, the oxidised copper onion domes atop the clunky late-Gothic **Frauenkirche** (Church of Our Lady, 1468-88). This twin-spired church, built of monotonous red brick and very Bavarian in its simplicity, belonged to the archbishopric of Munich-Freising. Its highlights are simple, but elegant: the magnificent St Nepomuk Altar by Cosmas Damian Asam and Johan Michael Ernst, and the tomb of Emperor Ludwig the Bavarian. You can climb the 98m-tall south tower (DM4/2) from April to October, Monday to Saturday from 10 am to 5 pm.

Frauenkirche to Karlsplatz

From the Frauenkirche, walk south through one of the several lanes to Kaufingerstrasse, a main shopping street. Turn right and continue 200m along what becomes Neuhauser Strasse to the **Michaelskirche** (St Michael's Church), widely acknowledged as Germany's grandest Renaissance church.

In front is the **Richard Strauss Fountain**, which shows scenes of the master's celebrated opera *Salomé*. Continue west to the corner of Kapellenstrasse (on your right) to regard the **Bürgersaal**, an 18th century church built for theology students. It also houses the crypt of Rupert Mayer, a Jesuit priest and noted opponent of the Nazis.

Just west of here is **Karlsplatz**, punctuated by the medieval **Karlstor**, the western gate and perimeter of the Altstadt, and an enormous modern **fountain**, a favourite meeting point. One of Germany's largest department stores, Karstadt, has a huge branch here; it's also a major tram, bus, U-Bahn and S-Bahn connection point. To the north is the city **Börse** (stock exchange).

Karlsplatz to Sendlinger Strasse

From Karlsplatz, double back and turn right onto Eisenmannstrasse, where you'll see the ornate **Damenstiftskirche** to your left, then continue south to **Sendlinger Tor**, the 14th century southern portal. From there, bear north-east onto Sendlinger Strasse; about 200m further on your left at No 32 is the St Johann Nepomuk church, better known as the **Asamkirche** (1733-46), designed and built by the Asam brothers. Above the entrance is a **statue** of St Nepomuk himself, a Bohemian monk who drowned in the Danube. The church shows a rare unity of style, with scarcely a single unembellished surface. The interior is particularly jaw-dropping (note, as you enter, the golden skeleton of Death trying to cut the string of Life to the right).

Carry on 300m along Sendlinger Strasse and take a right on Rosental, which runs into the **Stadtmuseum** on St-Jakobs-Platz. The outstanding exhibits cover brewing, fashion, musical instruments, photography

The White Rose

Public demonstrations against the Nazis were rare during the Third Reich: after 1933, intimidation and the instant 'justice' of the Gestapo and SS served as powerful disincentives. One of the few groups to rebel openly was the ill-fated Weisse Rose, led by Munich University students Hans and Sophie Scholl.

Robert Scholl had warned his children against the Nazis, but Hans joined the Hitler Youth, and his older sister, Inge, became a group leader of its female counterpart, the Bund Deutsche Mädels. Hans soon became disillusioned with the Nazis and attempted to build his own, liberal group within the Hitler Youth. This triggered a Gestapo raid on the Scholl home in Ulm in 1937, and from then on the family were marked as enemies of the state.

In 1942 Hans and Sophie met a group of like-minded medical students and formed the White Rose, which aimed to encourage Germans to resist Hitler. At first its members acted cautiously, creeping through the streets of Munich at night and smearing slogans such as 'Freedom!' or 'Down With Hitler!' on walls. Growing bolder, they printed and distributed anti-Nazi leaflets, leaving them in telephone boxes and sending them to other German cities. The leaflets reported on the mass extermination of the Jews and other Nazi atrocities. One read: 'We shall not be silent – we are your guilty conscience. The White Rose will not leave you in peace.'

In February 1943 Hans and Sophie took a suitcase of leaflets to university and placed stacks outside each lecture hall. Then, from a top landing, Sophie dumped the remaining brochures into an inner courtyard. A janitor saw her, and both were arrested and charged with treason along with their best friend, Christoph Probst. After a four hour trial, the three were condemned to death and beheaded the same afternoon. Sophie hoped that thousands would be stirred to action by their self-sacrifice, but there was to be no more resistance at Munich University – in fact, fellow students applauded the executions.

After WWII, Inge set up an adult education centre in Ulm to help ensure that the Nazi horrors should never happen again. In 1953, she and her husband Otl opened a design college in Ulm, hoping to continue the prewar Bauhaus tradition, but Inge devoted most of her time to preserving the memory of the White Rose.

and puppets (DM5, closed Monday). There are films shown nightly here as well; see Cinemas in the Entertainment section.

Viktualienmarkt

Carry on east down Rosental to emerge at the western edge of the bustling **Viktualienmarkt**, one of Europe's great food markets. It's crowded throughout the year. In summer the entire place is transformed into one of the finest and most expensive beer gardens around, while in winter people huddle for warmth and schnapps in the small *Kneipen* (pubs) around the square.

The merchandise and food are of the finest quality, but bargains don't exactly abound (see Self-Catering in Places to Eat for suggestions). On the south side you'll see a **statue** of famous comedian Karl Valentin holding out his hand – a perfect spot for a Chaplinesque flower (see also the Valentin Museum later in this chapter).

If thirsty, seek out the **Maypole** shooting up from the centre of the square, bearing craftsmen's symbols and the traditional blue-and-white Bavarian stripes. It will invariably point you towards the next beer garden. Marienplatz is just to the north-west.

BAVARIA

Königsplatz

North-west of the Altstadt is Königsplatz (take U2 or tram No 27), a Greek-revivalist pile created under Ludwig I to house several art museums. The square is flanked by the Glyptothek at the north and the Staatliche Antikensammlungen (Collection of State Antiquities) opposite, designed in the centre like a Corinthian temple. The centrepiece of the square is the Doric-columned **Propyläen** gateway.

The Glyptothek and the Antikensammlungen are worth a look. Either museum costs DM6/3.50, and to visit both costs DM10/6. Try to go on a Sunday when they're free; both are closed on Monday.

Glyptothek The Glyptothek (☎ 28 61 00), Königsplatz 3, contains a fascinating collection of Greek and Roman sculpture and portraits of Greek philosophers and leaders and Roman kings. It's open Tuesday to Sunday from 10 am to 5 pm (to 8 pm on Thursday).

Antikensammlungen The Staatliche Antikensammlungen (☎ 59 83 59), Königsplatz 1, features one of Germany's best antiquities collections, including vases, gold and silver jewellery and ornaments, bronzework, and Greek, Roman and other sculptures and statues. It's open Tuesday to Sunday from 10 am to 5 pm (to 8 pm on Wednesday).

Lenbach Haus Portraitist Franz von Lenbach (1836-1904), a leading *Gründerzeit* painter, used his considerable fortune to construct a residence in Munich between 1883 and 1889. It was sold to the city by his widow in 1924, and she threw in a bunch of his works as part of the deal. Today his fabulous residence is open as the Städtische Gallerie im Lenbachhaus (☎ 233 03 20), Luisenstrasse 33, featuring a staggering range of 19th century masterpieces by Munich and other German masters, and space for exhibitions of international modern art. A whole section upstairs is devoted to Der Blaue Reiter (Blue Rider) painters, members of a movement begun in 1911 by Franz Marc (1880-1916) and Wassily Kandinsky

(1866-1944), and considered the high point of German Expressionism (see Painting & Sculpture in the Facts about Germany chapter). Entry to the museum is DM8/4. Outside the museum is a beer garden and a lovely courtyard with fountains.

Mineral Museums Rock fans should head for the nearby **Geologische Staatssammlung** (☎ 520 31), Luisenstrasse 37, with exhibitions on the earth's crust and mineral wealth. Admission is free. Also popular is the **Museum Reich der Kristalle** (☎ 23 94 43 12), Theresienstrasse 41 (entrance at Barer Strasse, across the street from the Alte Pinakothek), with excellent exhibitions on the formation of minerals and crystals. It's open Tuesday to Friday from 1 to 5 pm, and Saturday and Sunday to 6 pm (DM2/1).

Alte Pinakothek The newly renovated Alte Pinakothek (☎ 23 80 52 16), at Barer Strasse 27 (north entrance), is a veritable treasure house of the works of European masters between the 14th and 18th centuries, including Albrecht Dürer's Christ-like *Self-Portrait* and his *Four Apostles*; Rogier van der Weyden's *Adoration of the Magi*; and Botticelli's *Pietà*. It's open Tuesday to Sunday from 10 am to 6 pm (DM7/4, free on Sunday).

Neue Pinakothek Just opposite the Alte Pinakothek at Barer Strasse 29 is the Neue Pinakothek (☎ 23 80 51 95); its entrance is on Theresienstrasse. It contains an extensive collection of 18th and 19th century paintings and sculpture, from rococo to Jugendstil. Don't miss Walter Crane's *The Seeds of Neptune* or Goya's chilling kitchen still-life, *Plucked Turkey*. It's open Tuesday to Sunday from 10 am to 5 pm, and Tuesday and Thursday to 8 pm (DM7/4, free on Sunday).

English Garden

The Englischer Garten is nestled between the Altstadt, Schwabing and the Isar River. The **Chinesischer Turm** (Chinese Tower), now in the centre of the city's best known beer garden, was constructed in 1789, which also marked the beginning of the park's construction. The largest city park in Europe, this is a great place for strolling, drinking, sunbaking and paddle-boating.

In balmy summer weather, nude sunbathing is the rule rather than the exception here. It's not unusual for hundreds of naked people to be in the park on a normal working day, with their coats, ties and frocks stacked primly on the grass. It's a lovely way to spend a sunny afternoon, but keep an eye firmly on your stuff.

Check out one of the three beer gardens here (see Entertainment), or head out for a little paddle on the lake. Just south of the Chinesischer Turm is the heavily photographed monument **Monopteros** (1838).

If you like the park so much you'd like to spend the night, remember that police patrol frequently, and muggers, junkies, proselytisers and other colourful characters are everywhere. In other words, forget it.

East of the Centre

Jewish Museum The Jüdisches Museum München (☎ 20 0 96 93) at Reichenbachstrasse 27 is an under-visited exhibition on the history of Jewish people in Munich and Bavaria. Admission is free, but the hours (Tuesday to Thursday from 2 to 6 pm) are limited due to budgetary constraints, so donations are encouraged.

Centre for Unusual Museums We could make lots of jokes about this place, but to paraphrase Groucho Marx, it doesn't need our help. The Zentrum für Aussergewöhnliche Museen (☎ 290 41 21), Westenriederstrasse 26 (take any S-Bahn to Isartor, or tram Nos 17 or 18), is a gathering of bizarre collections, including bottles, Easter bunnies, chamber pots, corkscrews and locks. There's also a collection of items associated with 'Sisi' (that's Empress Elisabeth of Austria to you). It's open daily from 10 am to 6 pm (DM8/5 – a bargain at twice the price).

Valentin Museum Dedicated to one of Bavaria's most beloved comic actors, this museum (☎ 22 32 66) celebrates the life and work of Karl Valentin and his partner, Liesl Karlstadt. It's in Isartor, the southernmost gate of the medieval fortifications and itself a work of 14th century art, bearing an impressive fresco of Ludwig the Bavarian's triumphant return to the city in 1322.

The museum is open Monday, Tuesday, Friday and Saturday from 11.01 am to 5.29 pm, Sunday from 10.01 am to 5.29 pm, and is closed Wednesday and Thursday (DM2.99/1.99). There's also a cafe at the top of the tower with a comical crowd. Take any S-Bahn to Isartor.

Deutsches Museum Said to be the world's largest science and technology museum, the Deutsches Museum (☎ 217 91), Museumsinsel 1 on the island (near Isartor, east of the city centre), takes up eight floors. The basement is devoted to mining and automobiles, and the ground floor to tunnel construction, railways and aeronautics. The 1st floor has a flimsy and dated section on physics and chemistry, but a wonderful section on musical instruments. The 2nd floor has the Altamira cave exhibit. The 3rd floor ranges from geodesy and weights and measures, to microelectronics and telecommunications. The 4th to 6th floors are dedicated to astronomy and amateur radio.

The museum is open daily from 9 am to 5 pm (DM10/4). It's free for children under six, and a family ticket costs DM22. A visit to the planetarium is DM3 extra. To reach it, take any S-Bahn to Isartor, U1 or 2 to Frauenhoferstrasse, or tram No 18 almost to the door.

Forum der Technik In the north-east corner of the museum complex on Museumsinsel, near Rosenheimer Strasse, is the Technical Forum (☎ 21 12 51 83), with a Zeiss planetarium show and an IMAX (bigscreen) cinema. Offerings generally look at nature and it's absolutely worth the admission price of DM12.50/9.50 (a combination ticket for the planetarium and IMAX is DM20.50/15.50). Several days a week, there are late-night performances of a Pink Floyd laser show (DM18.90/14.90). Programs for children run on weekdays (DM6.50) and

BAVARIA

prices are reduced on Monday, 'cinema day' (DM8.50).

Modern Art Gallery The Staatsgalerie Moderner Kunst (☎ 21 12 71 37), Prinz-regentenstrasse 1 in the Haus der Kunst east of the city centre (bus No 53 from the centre), displays some great German and international contributions to modern art, including wild paintings by Munch, Picasso and Magritte, as well as funky sculpture and some pop art. It's open Tuesday to Sunday from 10 am to 5 pm, and to 8 pm on Thursday (DM6/3.50).

Bavarian National Museum At the eastern end of Prinzregentenstrasse, at No 3 (take U4 or U5 to Lehel or tram No 17 or bus No 53 almost to the door), the formidable Bay-erisches Nationalmuseum (☎ 21 12 41) has the city's biggest collection of Bavarian and other German art, as well as artwork from around the world, modern and industrial art and prehistory. In the main building, there's folk art and history, including religious and folk costumes and artefacts.

The ground floor has early-medieval, Gothic, Renaissance, rococo, baroque and neoclassical works; and the 1st floor has applied arts, including clocks, ceramics, jewellery and stained glass. The Fine Art Collection has sculptures, carvings and paintings up to the 14th century. It's open Tuesday to Sunday from 9.30 am to 5 pm (DM3/2).

The **Neue Sammlung** (New Collection; ☎ 22 78 44) has rotating exhibitions from its huge collection of applied and industrial art.

At the northern section of the complex, the **Prähistorische Staatssammlung** (Prehistoric Collection; ☎ 29 39 11), Lerchen-feldstrasse 2, is packed with archaeological goodies, including artefacts from the city's first Roman and Celtic residents. It's open Tuesday to Sunday from 9 am to 4 pm, and to 8 pm on Thursday (DM5/3).

Southern Munich
Theresienwiese The Theresa Meadow, just south-west of the city centre (take U4 or U5 to Theresienwiese, or bus No 31 or 32),

is the site of the annual Oktoberfest (see Special Events). At the western end of the meadow, just near Theresienhöhe, is the **Ruhmeshalle** (Hall of Fame) containing statues of Bavarian leaders and the *Bavaria* statue, with a cunning design that makes it seem as if the thing is solid. It isn't – and you can climb to the head to get a so-so view of the city or a great view of the Okto-berfest for a mere DM4 (free for kids), Tuesday to Sunday from 10 am to noon and 2 to 5.30 pm.

Zoo The Hellabrunn Zoo (☎ 62 50 80), Tierparkstrasse 30 in Thalkirchen, was the first 'geo-zoo' (one with distinct sections dividing animals by continents). Today it has about 5000 animals representing 460 species, including rhinos, elephants, deer, bucks and gazelles. It's absolutely worth the DM10/5 admission if only to gain access to the petting zoo, crawling with sheep, deer and lambs that you can feed. Perhaps the best exhibit, though, is the tropical bird that shouts, loudly, *'Arschloch!'* (Asshole!) to giggling tourists. Take U3 to Thalkirchen or bus No 52 almost to the entrance.

Bavaria Film Museum Tour An often-missed treasure in Munich is the Bavaria Film Tour (☎ 64 99 23 04) of the **Bavaria Film Museum**, at Bavariafilmplatz 7 in the southern suburb of Geiselgasteig (take U1 or U2 to Silberhornstrasse, then tram No 25 to Bavariafilmplatz). You'll see sets of *Enemy Mine*, *Das Boot*, *Cabaret* and *The Never-Ending Story*, all of which were filmed here. German TV series and films are still shot here as well. The tour runs from March to October (DM17/12).

Western Munich
Schloss Nymphenburg If the Residenz hasn't satisfied your passion for palaces, visit the amazing Schloss Nymphenburg (☎ 179 80/00), north-west of the city centre (take tram No 17 or bus No 41). Begun in 1664 as a villa for Electress Adelaide of Savoy, the castle and gardens were continually expanded and built upon over the next century

to create the royal family's summer residence. Today the castle, porcelain factory and grounds (the surrounding park is worth a long stroll) are open to the public, and the grounds are also home to the Museum Mensch und Natur (Museum of Man and Nature), all definitely worth it if you're here with kids. A combined ticket to everything except the Museum Mensch und Natur costs DM8/7. Admission to the Schloss and the Schönheitengalerie is DM5/4; to Amalienburg or Badenburg, it's DM3.

Palace The main palace building (☎ 179 08) consists of two wings to the north and south of the main villa. You can visit Tuesday to Sunday from 9 am to 12.30 pm and 1.30 to 5 pm. The rooms are all sumptuous, but our favourite is Ludwig's **Schönheitengalerie** (Gallery of Beauties), in the southern wing, formerly the apartments of Queen Caroline. It's now the repository of 38 portraits of women whom Ludwig I considered beautiful; most famous of these is *Schöne Münchnerin*, the portrait of Helene Sedlmayr, daughter of a shoemaker.

Also in the south wing is the **Marstallmuseum** (☎ 179 08), with the coaches and riding gear of the royal families. It's open Tuesday to Sunday from 9 am to noon and 1 to 5 pm (DM3/2).

Tours of the palace are only offered to groups; pick up a copy of the unintentionally hilarious English-language translation of the guide *Nymphenburg* (DM5) at the cash desk.

The former factory of Nymphenburg Porcelain, on the 1st floor of the Marstallmuseum, is now a **Porcelain Museum** (Nymphenburger Porzellan Sammlung Bäuml; ☎ 17 90 80). Temporarily shut for renovation, the museum was expected to reopen sometime in 2000.

Gardens The royal gardens are a magnificently sculpted English park. In front (east) of the palace is a long canal, on which locals can be seen ice skating in winter. Behind (west of) the castle, the royal gardens ramble on around the continuation of the Nymphenburger Canal.

The whole park is enchanting and contains a number of intriguing buildings, four of which are open to the public.

Electress Amelia had the **Amalienburg**, a small hunting lodge with a large domed central room, built between 1734 and 1739. Don't miss the amazing Spiegelsaal (Mirror Hall). Amalienburg is open daily from 9 am to 12.30 pm and 1.30 to 5 pm. The two storey **Pagodenburg** (1717-19) was built as a Chinese teahouse by Prince Max Emanuel; by the time you read this, the building should have re-opened after a lengthy renovation. Opposite it, the **Badenburg**, by the lake of the same name, was also built by Max Emanuel, as a sauna and bathing house. You can visit it Tuesday to Sunday from 10 am to 12.30 pm and 1.30 to 5 pm.

Museum Mensch und Natur This natural history and science museum (☎ 17 64 94) is a fun place to bring the kids. Interactive, if aged, displays in German let kids take quizzes, but mostly they'll be racing to the upstairs exhibits on animals and the earth. There are rotating exhibitions in addition to the permanent collection, and a nice cafe downstairs. It's open Tuesday to Sunday from 9 am to 5 pm (DM3/1.50, children under six are free).

North of the Centre

Siemens Forum The Siemens Forum (☎ 63 63 26 60), on Oskar-von-Miller-Ring, has fascinating exhibits on electronics and microelectronics from the telegraph to the multimedia personal computer. It's a fun, hands-on kind of place, open Monday to Friday and Sunday from 10 am to 5 pm. Entry is free, so why not? Take the U4 or U5 to Odeonsplatz.

Olympiapark Quarter of a century after the Olympics for which it was built, Olympic Park (☎ 306 70) is still an integral part of life in the city. The centrepieces are the 290m **Olympiaturm** (Olympic Tower) and the 75,000 sq metre transparent 'tented' roof covering the west side of the Olympic Stadium, Olympic Hall and the swimming centre.

BAVARIA

Today the complex is open as a collection of public facilities, and the grounds are the site of celebrations, concerts, fireworks displays and professional sporting matches throughout the year. The swimming hall is open to the public, as is the ice arena.

There are two tours daily from April to October (meet at the information booth at the park's north-east): a soccer tour at 11 am, which visits the Olympic Stadium, VIP area and locker rooms (DM8, or DM6 for children under 15, one hour); and an adventure tour that covers the entire Olympiapark on foot and in a little train (DM13/8, 1½ hours).

If you like heights, go to the top of the Olympiaturm, open daily from 9 am to midnight, with the last trip up at 11.30 pm (DM5/2.50). When the weather's good you'll have stunning views of the city and, if you're feeling cashed up and hungry, you can have a meal at the revolving restaurant (☎ 308 10 39).

Olympic Spirit Welcome to the Virtual Games! Whether it's on a ski run, a tennis court, a kayak slalom or the 100m dash – at the press of a button, these simulations of Olympic events (housed in the former Olympic velodrome next to the main park) are stunningly realistic and your performance can even influence the outcome (it's unlikely, but you might win). Its **Action Cinema** has a 180° screen – a vicarious, bone-chilling way to experience the downhill. The less adventurous can turn sportscaster in a replica of an announcer's booth. Olympic Spirit (☎ 30 63 86 26) is open Monday to Friday from 10 am to 6 pm, and weekends and holidays to 7 pm (DM26/18, cinema included).

BMW Museum Opposite Olympic Park, at Petuel-Ring 130, is the popular BMW Museum (☎ 38 22 33 07). Behind the museum, the BMW (Bayerische Motoren Werke) headquarters building (1970-73), with its striking steel cylinders, is an architectural attraction in its own right.

The museum is as immaculate as you'd expect. Exhibits include many BMW cars, motorcycles, planes, concept cars and, near the top, simulators and interactive displays. It's open daily from 9 am to 5 pm, with last entry at 4 pm (DM5.50/4).

You can take the U3 from Marienplatz to Olympiazentrum. Look for the huge silver towers (and if you're flying overhead, the landing pad with BMW logo). The BMW factory (☎ 38 22 33 06), adjacent to the headquarters and museum, offers free tours of the factory line (in German and English).

Activities

Munich makes a perfect base for outdoor activities. For information about **hiking** and **climbing**, contact the Deutscher Alpenverein (German Alpine Club; ☎ 14 00 30), west of the centre at Von-Kahr-Strasse 2-4.

For hiking gear, the Sport Schuster, Rosenstrasse 1-5, and the better Sport Scheck (☎ 216 60), nearby at Sendlinger Strasse 6, both have multiple floors of everything imaginable for the adventurer, from simple camping equipment to expedition wear, plus excellent bookshops. There's also a discount Sport Scheck at the Ostbahnhof selling discontinued merchandise.

Swimming Bathing in the Isar River isn't advisable because of its high level of noxious bacteria. Germany's greatest water leisure complex is about an hour away at Alpamare (see Bad Tölz in the Around Munich section).

The two best swimming pools in town are at Olympiapark (☎ 23 61 34 34) and the spectacular Müllerisches Volksbad (☎ 23 61 34 29), Rosenheimer Strasse 1. The latter, a riot of Art Nouveau style, is worth visiting even if you don't swim. It has a large pool, sauna, steam baths and public baths; the cost is DM3.50/2.50 per hour, or with a private cabin (in which to take a hot bath) it's DM7.50. It's open to women only on Tuesday and Friday, and men only on Wednesday and Thursday.

The Olympic pool at Olympiapark is open to the public for varying sessions throughout the day. Admission is DM5/4; add a sauna and the price is DM15/11. Tanning beds (DM5) are available as well.

Boating There are several places in town to take a little tootle on a boat; the most popular spot is the English Garden's Kleinhesseloher See, where rowing/pedal boats cost DM10/12 per half hour for up to four people. Cheaper are the boats at Olympiapark, which you can rent for DM10/12 per hour for up to four people.

Skating The coolest thing in inline skating is Skate 'n' Fun (☎ 49 00 13 13), in Kunstpark Ost at Grafingerstrasse 6, behind the Ostbahnhof. It's a safe and clean indoor stunt park with ramps, shells and skating areas for people of all ages. Rented gear, including complete protection (pads, helmets and the like), costs from DM8, plus the DM5 entry fee. You can also rent standard skates (or with extra stunt protection) for DM30 a day or DM40 for the weekend. Courses are run daily.

Organised Tours
Among the best organised walking tours in Germany are those with Munich Walks (mobile ☎ 0177 227 59 01), which runs English-language tours daily from May to December. They last two to 2½ hours and cost DM15/12 for people over/under 26 (children under 14 free with an adult). The Discover Munich tour covers the heart of the city and gives good historical background and architectural information; from May to October it leaves at 10 am and 3 pm, and at 10 am only from November to 22 December. The Infamous Third Reich Sites tour covers exactly that, and runs on a more limited schedule. All tours leave from in front of the EurAide office, track 11 of the Hauptbahnhof. Bring transport tickets.

Mike's Bike Tours (☎ 651 42 75, mobile ☎ 0172 852 06 60) runs 3½-hour guided city cycling tours in English (DM31). They depart every day at 11.30 am and 4 pm from the archway in front of the Toy Museum on Marienplatz. You don't have to be in shape, because the guide stops about every 400m to explain a point of interest.

Panorama Tours (☎ 59 81 60) runs about six coach tours to various places within the city (from DM17/9 to DM100 per person, one to 4½ hours). They're all right but the commentary is given in two languages, so everything takes twice as long to explain. They leave from the front of the Hertie department store opposite the Hauptbahnhof.

You can hire English-speaking private guides from the city tourist offices for groups of up to 25 people from DM140.

Special Events
Oktoberfest Try to get to Munich for the Oktoberfest, one of Europe's biggest and best parties (see the boxed text). It runs from mid-September to the first Sunday in October. No entrance fee is charged but most of the fun costs something. Major Oktoberfest events are described in the following entries.

Grand Entry The parade through the city centre, from Sonnenstrasse to the fairgrounds via Schwanthalerstrasse, begins at 11 am on the first day of the festival. At noon, the lord mayor stands before the thirsty crowds at Theresienwiese. With due pomp, Hizzoner slams home a wooden tap with a mallet. When the tap breaks through the cask's surface and beer gushes forth, the mayor exclaims, *'Ozapft ist!'* (It's tapped!).

Münchner Kindl A young woman on horseback carrying a litre of beer in one hand and a huge pretzel in the other leads 7000 performers from all over Europe (wearing pretzel bras and other traditional drunkenwear) through the streets of the city centre during the ceremonial opening.

Oktoberfest Folklore International Music, dance and folklore events are held in the Circus Krone building at 8 pm on different nights.

In addition, there's a big gay meeting on the first Sunday of Oktoberfest at the Bräurosl tent, with legions of butch guys in leather pants. It is timed to coincide with a gay leather convention; it's huge fun and open to all.

euro currency converter DM1 = €0.51

BAVARIA

Oktoberfest

After the wedding on 12 October 1810 of Bavarian Crown Prince Ludwig I to the Saxon-Hildburghausen Princess Therese, an enormous party was held in front of the city gates. That was the beginning of what's now the largest beer festival in the world, Oktoberfest, a 16 day extravaganza that attracts over seven million people a year.

During the event, the Theresienwiese fairgrounds are practically a city of beer tents, amusements, rides – including a giant Ferris wheel and roller coasters (just what beer drinkers need after several frothy ones) – and kiosks selling snacks and sweets.

The Oktoberfest, which runs from late September to the 1st Sunday in October, is Munich's largest and most economically important tourist attraction. Visitors and locals leave behind almost DM1.5 billion, and a lot of that will be in chunks of DM8 and DM12 (the prices, respectively, of a pretzel and a 1L glass of Bavaria's finest).

There's not a whole lot you can do about the beer prices, but the food is where they really get you at the Oktoberfest tents. After a litre or two of amber liquid, the reluctance to part with DM20 for a beer and a chicken leg tends to fade, so make sure you eat before you arrive.

Self-catering is the cheapest way (see that section in Places to Eat). Avoid at all costs shops in the main train station, where prices for staple goods are 30 to 50% higher than in regular shops and markets.

Also, it's imperative that you reserve accommodation as early as you can (like a year in advance). Hotels are booked up very quickly and their prices skyrocket during the fair. If you show up during Oktoberfest, forget about finding a room in Munich.

Consider staying in the suburbs or nearby cities (eg Augsburg, Garmisch-Partenkirchen or Bad Tölz, all of which are under an hour away).

The festival is held at the Theresienwiese, a 15 minute walk from the Hauptbahnhof, and is served by its own U-Bahn station. If you're asking directions, say 'd'wies'n' (dee-**veezen**), the diminutive nickname for the grounds. Trams and buses heading that way, however, sport signs reading 'Zur Festwiese' (literally 'to the Festival Meadow').

The Oktoberfest runs daily from about 10.30 am to 11:30 pm. It's best to leave the fair early, about 9 or 10 pm, as crowds can get a bit touchy when the beer and schnapps supplies are turned off.

Thursday is Children's Day, when all children's rides and attractions are half price.

Tollwood Festival Another fine Munich tradition is the summer Tollwood Festival, held each June and July at the Olympiapark complex. It's a world culture festival, with music, food, clothes and merchandise from around the world, and nightly world-music concerts, weather permitting. Admission is free but the concerts cost something (anywhere from DM5 to DM35).

Opera Festival The Munich Opera Festival is held every July at the Bayerische Staatsoper (Bavarian State Opera) in the Nationaltheater. Consisting mainly of shows staged during the past year, it always concludes on 31 July with *Die Meistersinger von Nürnberg*.

Places to Stay

Prices in Munich tend to be expensive. Even if you book through EurAide or the city tourist offices (see Information), you're unlikely to find anything under DM60/90 for a single/double. The DJH and independent hostels are the cheapest options for a bed, bearing in mind that an age limit of 26

BAVARIA

generally applies. Otherwise, you'll find a slew of budget pensions and hotels – some a bit seedy and cramped, others quite OK – clustered around the Hauptbahnhof.

'Mid-range' in Munich can mean paying over DM200, but you may do far better by joining a package tour or booking through a travel agent. Also, many hotels will come down in price if you merely ask if there's anything cheaper. Hotels at the top of the heap are what you'd expect: clean, luxurious and very, very expensive.

As a rule, reserve if possible and tell them if you're arriving after 6 pm, when many places begin to cancel unconfirmed bookings. Note that rates in city hotels can rise about 10 to 15% during the summer; prices skyrocket during Oktoberfest.

Camping The most central camping ground is *Campingplatz Thalkirchen* (☎ 723 17 07, fax 724 31 77, Zentralländstrasse 49), south-west of the city centre and close to the hostel on Miesingstrasse. Open from mid-March to October, it can get incredibly crowded but there always seems to be room for one more tent. The price is DM8.40 per person, DM5.50 per tent, DM8.50 per car and DM4 per motorcycle. An extra charge of DM7 is levied during Oktoberfest. There are laundry facilities on the grounds. Take U3 to Thalkirchen station and bus No 57 to Thalkirchen, the last stop (about 20 minutes from the city centre).

A bit farther from the city centre are *Waldcamping Obermenzing* (☎ 811 22 35, fax 814 48 07) and *Langwieder See* (☎ 864 15 66, fax 863 23 42); the latter has a great location but can only be reached by car on the autobahn A8 towards Augsburg. It's open from early April to the end of October.

DJH Hostels Munich's summer budget favourite is the *Jugendlager am Kapuziner Hölzl* (☎ 141 43 00, fax 17 50 90, In den Kirschen), north of Schloss Nymphenburg. Take U1 to Rotkreuzplatz, then tram No 12 to the Botanical Garden (Botanischer Garten). Nicknamed 'The Tent', this mass camp is only open from mid-June to early

September. There's no night curfew but the usual 26-year age limit applies (with priority given to people under 23). The cheapest 'beds' (a thermal mattress and blanket in the big tent) cost DM13 with breakfast; showers are available. Bunk-style beds are DM17.

Most central is the sparkling *Jugendherberge München* (☎ 13 11 56, fax 167 87 45, Wendl-Dietrich-Strasse 20), north-west of the city centre (U1 to Rotkreuzplatz). One of the largest hostels in Germany, it is relatively loud and very busy, but also very popular and friendly. Beds cost from DM25.50 (DM23 if you're willing to sleep in a room with 36 others!). There's no curfew or daytime closing. The hostel has a restaurant, garden and bikes for rent (see Getting Around).

Still fairly accessible to the centre, and a better deal, is the more modern *Jugendgästehaus München* (☎ 723 65 50/60, fax 724 235 67, Miesingstrasse 4), south-west of the city centre in the suburb of Thalkirchen (take U3 to Thalkirchen, then follow the signs). Costs per person are DM26 in dorms, DM28 in triples and quads, and DM31.50/36.50 for singles/doubles. There is a 1 am curfew.

The *Jugendherberge Burg Schwaneck* (☎ 793 06 43, fax 793 79 22, Burgweg 4-6), via S7 to Pullach plus a 10 minute walk, is in a great old castle in the southern suburbs. Dorm beds cost from DM22.50 and rooms are DM31.50/63.

Independent Hostels Munich has quite a few non-DJH hostels or hotels that offer cheaper dormitory accommodation as well as simple rooms. A newcomer is the 24 hour *Euro Youth Hotel* (☎ 59 90 880, fax 59 90 88 77, email info@euro-youth-hotel.de, Senefelderstrasse 5), still wearing the decor of the grand Hotel Astoria it was until WWI. Beds in a 30 person dormitory cost just DM25 each, in a three and four-bed room DM36 and in a double room, DM42. Tapped half litres of Augustiner (the brewery owns the place) cost just DM3.60, and breakfast is DM7.90.

At the pernickety *CVJM-YMCA Jugendgästehaus* (☎ 552 14 10, fax 550 42 82,

BAVARIA

Landwehrstrasse 13), triples/doubles/singles are DM38/41/48 (or DM53 for a larger single), but prices are 16% higher for guests over 26. Smoking and alcohol are forbidden outside the house restaurant.

The **Kolpinghaus St Theresia** (*☎ 12 60 50, fax 12 60 52 12, Hanebergestrasse 8)*, a 10 minute walk north of Rotkreuzplatz (or via U1), has beds for DM34/36/49.

Women under 26 can try the Catholic **Jugendhotel Marienherberge** (*☎ 55 58 05, Goethestrasse 9)* behind the poorly marked black door (look for the tiny buzzer). Beds in common rooms start at DM30 and singles/doubles cost DM40/70. There's a midnight curfew.

Somewhat scruffy but clean and pleasant, the **Haus International** (*☎ 12 00 60, fax 12 00 62 51, Elisabethstrasse 87)*, via tram No 12 to Barbarastrasse, is a 'youth hotel', not a hostel, so travellers of any age can stay. It has more than 500 beds in all; prices range from DM40.50 in five-person dorms to DM55/104 for small and simple rooms, to DM85/144 for clean rooms with modern conveniences. There's also a pool, disco, beer garden and cafeteria.

Hotels – Budget The best option near the Hauptbahnhof is the cramped but reasonably clean **Pension Marie-Luise** (*☎ 55 25 56 60, fax 55 25 56 66, Landwehrstrasse 35)*, which offers singles/doubles from DM55/85. Reception is next door at the **Andi (Comfort) Hotel** *(same ☎ & fax, Landwehrstrasse 33)*, where the owner is charming and talkative, and well equipped rooms start at DM95/155.

The somewhat run-down but friendly **Hotel Atlanta** (*☎ 26 36 05, fax 260 90 27, Sendlinger Strasse 58)* is nicely located between Sendlinger Tor and the Asamkirche; go through the creepy door and up the creepy stairs to clean, simple, if brown, rooms from DM50/89, or DM79/98 with facilities.

Just north of the Hauptbahnhof sits the **Amba** (*☎ 54 51 40, fax 54 51 45 55, Arnulfstrasse 20)*, which offers simple rooms from DM80/120 and rooms with all facilities from DM140/180. The **Alfa** (*☎ 545 95 39, fax 545 95 32 99, Hirtenstrasse 20)* has cramped but

clean quarters from DM65/95, a bar and courtyard parking (DM15 per night).

An ideal compromise of location, price and cleanliness is **Pension Haydn** (*☎ 53 11 19, fax 54 40 48 27, Haydnstrasse 9)*, near the Goetheplatz U-Bahn station and within walking distance of the Hauptbahnhof. Rooms without bath start at DM60/90.

There's old-world charm, nice staff and clean, pleasant rooms at the **Hotel Pension Mariandl** (*☎ 53 41 08, fax 54 40 43 96, Goethestrasse 51)*; rooms cost DM70/95, or DM65/90 if you book through the city tourist office (not EurAide) at the Hauptbahnhof. Downstairs, the restaurant has live jazz or classical music every night at 8 pm (see Places to Eat and Entertainment).

Well south of the Hauptbahnhof off Kaiser-Ludwig-Platz, **Pension Schubert** (*☎ 53 50 87, Schubertstrasse 1)* has rooms without bath for DM50/85, while a fully equipped double isn't bad for DM95.

Located in Marienplatz, another value-for-money deal is the **Hotel-Pension am Markt** (*☎ 22 50 14, fax 22 40 17, Heiliggeiststrasse 6)*, just off the Viktualienmarkt. Simple singles/doubles start at DM60/110, while those with bath and toilet cost from DM116/160.

Clean, comfortable, central and reasonably spacious rooms can be found at **Hotel Blauer Bock** (*☎ 23 17 80, fax 23 17 82 00, Sebastiansplatz 9)*. Rooms with private shower and toilet start at DM100/150, or DM70/100 with communal facilities. A buffet breakfast is included and garage parking is available. Of a similar standard and price is **Hotel Arosa** (*☎ 26 70 87, fax 26 31 04, Hotterstrasse 2)*, with simple bathless rooms from DM77/102, including breakfast.

Comfortable but a bit out of the way in Neuhausen, the **CA Comfort Aparthotel** (*☎ 15 92 40, fax 15 92 48 00, Dachauer Strasse 195-99)* caters to the business crowd with modern, well appointed rooms and nice staff. Singles/doubles with facilities start at DM79/98 on weekends, jumping to DM140/170 during the week.

The **City Pension** (*☎ 54 07 38 64, fax 500 46 65, Gollierstrasse 36)*, located in

Westend, has simple, cheerful and bright rooms a whopping four flights up (and there's no lift) for DM60 to DM70 (singles) and DM100 to DM130 (doubles), plus DM10 for breakfast.

The best deal out here in Westend is the *Hotel Petri* (☎ 58 10 99, fax 580 86 30, Aindorferstrasse 82). Rooms have distinctive old wooden furniture and a TV, and there's also a garden and a small indoor swimming pool. Bathless singles cost DM95, while singles/doubles with shower and WC (toilet) start at DM115/175. Take U4 or U5 to Laimer Platz.

Hotels – Mid-Range In Westend, right near the Theresienwiese, two places can be bargained down outside the Oktoberfest season: the *Hotel Krone* (☎ 50 40 52, fax 50 67 06, Theresienhöhe 8), with posted rates of DM120/140 for singles/doubles; and *Siebel* (☎ 514 14 20, fax 54 01 42 99, Theresienhöhe 9), with prices from DM99/119.

North of the Hauptbahnhof is a veritable package-tourist heaven, with several hotels lining Arnulfstrasse. All seem to offer the same thing: moderately clean, moderately well appointed rooms and staff used to groups of up to 100. These can be an excellent bargain if you can get yourself booked into a group, so don't scoff at the idea. Rack rates for the hotels – the *Regent* (☎ 55 15 90, fax 55 15 91 54, Seidlstrasse 2), *REMA-Hotel Esplanade* (☎ 55 13 90, fax 59 34 03, Arnulfstrasse 12), and the *Astron Hotel Deutscher Kaiser* (☎ 545 30, fax 54 53 22 55, Arnulfstrasse 2) – all range between DM135 and DM230 for singles and DM185 and DM318 for doubles.

A bit south of the Hauptbahnhof are two options run by Best Western. We recommend only one of them: the *Hotel Cristal* (☎ 55 11 10, fax 55 11 19 92, Schwanthalerstrasse 36), with nice, clean rooms from DM215/250, and friendly staff.

Hotels – Top End The Hiltons are the 'bargain' of this segment. The *München Park Hilton* (☎ 384 50, fax 38 45 18 45, email fom_munich-park@hilton.com, Am Tucherpark 7) has rooms from DM195/215, while *München City Hilton* (☎ 480 40, fax 48 04 48 04, email fom_munich-city@hilton.com, Rosenheimerstrasse 15) is slightly more expensive at DM222/243.

The *Holiday Inn Crowne Plaza* (☎ 38 17 90, fax 38 17 98 88, Leopoldstrasse 194), in the heart of Schwabing, has nice rooms and great service from DM330/362.

One of the grand dames of the Munich hotel trade is the lovely *Bayerischer Hof* (☎ 212 00, fax 212 06 33, email hbh@compuserve.com, Promenadeplatz 2-6), with rooms for DM343.50/477 and suites from DM410/595. The hotel boasts a lovely location right behind Marienplatz, a pool and a great jazz club downstairs (see Entertainment).

The most famous hotel is the *Kempinski Vier Jahreszeiten München* (☎ 212 50, fax 21 25 20 00, email reservation.hvj@kempinski.com, Maximilianstrasse 17), with a grand facade featuring statues of the managers, the four seasons, and the four continents known at the time of construction in 1857. The rooms, with not as many amenities as you'd think, start at DM430/510 and suites range from DM495 to DM770.

If that's not dear enough for you, try the *Rafael* (☎ 20 09 80, fax 22 25 39, email info@hotelrafael.com, Neuturmstrasse 1), in a gorgeous renovated villa just round the corner from the Hofbräuhaus. Chambers here start at DM508/756, excluding the roll of notes you'll need for tipping swarms of well liveried servants.

Private Rooms & Long-Term Rentals The City Mitwohnzentrale (☎ 194 30, fax 194 20), Lämmerstrasse 4, on the north side of the Hauptbahnhof, lets furnished or unfurnished flats or rooms, from four days to indefinitely. Prepare to pay a fee for long-term rentals of up to 1½ months rent. Generally speaking, a room in a flat costs about DM500 per month, an apartment starts at DM800; some are cheaper, some more expensive. They'll send you a form in

BAVARIA

English; fill it out and fax it back with a photocopy of your ID/passport and credit card, or drop by with your documents.

Another agency is Antje Wolf Bed & Breakfast Munich (☎ 168 87 81, fax 168 87 91), which arranges apartments and guest rooms with or without breakfast from a day to a month.

Places to Eat

Munich has a fine selection of restaurants in all price ranges, including some excellent top-end places. Especially good value is Italian food, and the city has several excellent Vietnamese and Thai places and at least one fantastic Indian restaurant.

Eating cheaply in Munich is much like anywhere else in Germany: excellent Turkish fast food is the leader of the snack pack, especially in the area south of the Hauptbahnhof. Doner kebabs cost from DM5 to DM6 and are large enough to constitute a meal.

Vegetarian Restaurants For imaginative vegetarian cuisine at acceptable prices, nothing beats *Prinz Myschkin* (☎ 26 55 96, *Hackenstrasse 2)*, which gets rave reviews in the local press. It offers gourmet vegetarian cooking, blending East Asian, Indian and Italian influences. Daily menus and main courses cost DM18.50 to DM23.50; pizzas are expensive at DM16.50 to DM19.50. The sophisticated salads are a real treat, between DM7.50 and DM17.50. It's also a great place for a wine or coffee.

German Restaurants For German food, it's best to go local, like the less touristy beer halls and restaurants, or one of the many markets. However, since more people go to beer halls to drink than to eat – especially given the quality of the 'food' at places like the Hofbräuhaus – Beer Halls & Gardens have been listed under Entertainment.

The speciality of *Nürnberger Bratwurst Glöckl am Dom*, in the shadow of the Frauenkirche at Frauenplatz 9, is the small Nuremberg-style sausages, served with sauerkraut (DM12.50). *Haxenbauer (☎ 29 16 21 00, Sparkassenstrasse 8)*, with the

pig on a spit in the window, is a mid-range inner-Munich establishment offering hearty four-course menus from DM48 per person, and very cheap fast-food-like *Schweinshax'n* (pork thigh) for DM5.80 in the snack-room or for takeaway.

The *Hundskugel (☎ 26 42 72, Hotterstrasse 18)* right in the centre, is Munich's oldest restaurant, founded in 1440. It's a famous place to go, and the food's perfectly fine, if pricey for an evening meal. (Lunch specials often cost less than DM20.)

Another well known top-end place is the *Garden-Restaurant (☎ 212 09 93, Promenadeplatz 2-6)*, behind the Hotel Bayerischer Hof. It features fine decor, excellent service and exotic dishes that sound like endangered species (eg stuffed gurnard – a big-headed Mediterranean fish with armoured cheeks – for DM48).

Italian Restaurants Munich's proximity to Italy means that there are good and relatively inexpensive Italian options throughout the city. *Café Osteria LaVecchia Masseria (☎ 550 90 90, Mathildenstrasse 3)*, south of Landwehrstrasse, is one of the best-value places in Munich, and perfect for a romantic evening. The beautiful atmosphere comes with great service and nice touches like fresh aniseed bread on ceramic tiles. Pizzas cost DM9 to DM11, pastas are DM9 to DM14, and there are some fine three-course meals from DM40. The beer garden in the courtyard is lovely, too.

Also south of the Hauptbahnhof is the small *Trattoria La Fiorentini (☎ 53 41 85, Goethestrasse 41)*, a local hang-out that has good pizzas from DM7 to DM14. The menu, which changes daily, has main courses that average DM14 to DM18. Staff can get snooty if it's crowded, but the food's good.

Cipriani (☎ 260 43 97), in the Asamhof, occupying a small courtyard off Sendlinger Strasse behind the Asamkirche, has pastas from DM12 to DM14. The outside area is lovely in summer. Happy hour is daily from 5 to 9 pm, when cocktails are DM6.

The top restaurants in Munich usually serve (what else?) French food, but the

Hippocampus (☎ 47 58 55, Mühlbaur-strasse 5), a trendy, upmarket Italian place right near the Prinzregententheater east of the Isar River, can hold its own. Set menus range from DM60 to DM80, and many of its main courses (such as shark Genua style, DM35) have neat combinations.

French Restaurants There's *Le Bousquerey* (☎ 48 84 55, Rablstrasse 37) in Haidhausen, east of the Isar River, a splendid French restaurant that specialises in seafood. The place is small and intimate (reservations suggested). There's a good French and German wine list; set menus are about DM60 to DM70 per person, and main courses average DM20 to DM35.

Another very good but expensive French place is *Rue des Halles* (☎ 48 56 75, Steinstrasse 18), south of the centre in Mittersendling, with a very light, modern interior, comfortable atmosphere and slick but attentive service. Count on spending about DM150 per person without wine.

The restaurant upstairs at *Alois Dallmayr* (☎ 213 51 00, Dienerstrasse 14-15), near Marienplatz, is renowned for its excellent French and Continental food and great service; main courses range from DM30 to DM60.

Indian & East Asian Restaurants At Stiglmaierplatz, *Maharani* (☎ 52 71 92, Rottmannstrasse 24), diagonally opposite the Löwenbräukeller, is the best bet for dependable, authentic Indian food, and they'll make it spicy if you ask. Main courses average DM23 to DM31.

It's hard not to rave too much about *Vinh's* (☎ 123 89 25, Leonrodstrasse 29), near the corner of Landshuter Allee. Take the U1 to Rotkreuzplatz or bus No 33 or tram No 12 to Albrechtstrasse. This tiny place (reservations essential) offers spectacular Vietnamese food, with rice dishes from DM15 to DM18, and house specialities ranging from DM21 to DM35 (don't miss the roast duck for DM22.50). If he likes the crowd, the eccentric owner will dress up in silver duds and perform magic tricks.

Maitoi (☎ 260 52 68, Hans-Sachs-Strasse 10), near the gay area south of Sendlinger Tor, is a very slick, simple Japanese restaurant with takeaway sushi. Special evening prices apply after 7 or 9 pm, when everything is 25% less.

You could also try *Mangostin Asia* (☎ 723 20 31, Maria-Einsiefel-Strasse 2), in Thalkirchen near the zoo; it's a very chi-chi place with Thai, Japanese and Indonesian food. It's popular, but service can be reprehensible and the food varies from good to despicable depending on the night.

Shida (☎ 26 93 36, Klenzestrasse 32) is a very good and very intimate Thai place (it's small, so reservations are essential). Main courses range from DM20 to DM30.

Cafes & Bistros Centrally located cafes cater largely to tourists and therefore tend to be rather expensive. Cheap and central stand-up cafes that serve excellent homemade sweet and savoury pastries include *Höflinger*, on the corner of Sendlinger-Tor-Platz and Sonnenstrasse. The *Wiener's* buffet next door has great breakfasts (eg ham & eggs, rolls and coffee for DM8.50). Another excellent option is *Ziegler* (Brunnstrasse 11).

The *Stadtcafé* at the Stadtmuseum is a popular haunt of Munich's intellectual types, especially in summer when the lovely courtyard opens.

The *Gap* (☎ 54 40 40 94, Goethestrasse 34) is an arty, somewhat esoteric 'cantina culturale', with exhibits and occasional folk and classical music. A soup & sandwich combo costs DM7.50, and there are groovy daily specials (such as vegie platter with lentil mousse) for about the same price.

The *Interview* (☎ 20 23 94 21, Gärtnerplatz 1) has a pleasant street-side cafe with a nice view of the theatre and Italian set lunches for DM17 to DM19.

The *Kandil Restaurant* (☎ 54 82 82 52, Landwehrstrasse 8), south-east of the Hauptbahnhof, has a wide selection of full cafeteria-style but good meals from DM8.50 to DM13. It also offers breakfast (a simple one is DM5.50).

BAVARIA

In Marienplatz, the best places to watch the Glockenspiel are the bistro at the **Metropolitan** (☎ *230 97 70, Marienplatz 22)* on the 5th floor, and next door at *Café Glockenspiel*, a similar place but far more downmarket. Across the square on the west side is *Café am Dom*, where the view is so-so but the atmosphere is nicer outside in summer.

On Viktualienmarkt, seek out *Löwenbräu Stadt Kempten* at No 4 (closed Sunday). There, you'll get a half litre of Löwenbräu for DM5.20, and the daily set-menus start at around DM13.

Schwabing Among the many lively student hang-outs in Schwabing are the *Vorstadt Café* (☎ *272 06 99, Türkenstrasse 83)* and the *News Bar* (☎ *28 17 87, Amalienstrasse 55)*; both are open daily at least until 1 am, and the latter sells English magazines.

The cafes that line Leopoldstrasse are more for socialising, being seen and looking fabulous than eating, but food is available in spite of it all. Don't expect it to be good and do expect it to cost: they're all the same, but two notable entries are *Café Roxy* (☎ *34 92 92, Leopoldstrasse 48)*, with burgers for DM14.50 and sandwiches from DM8.50 to DM13.50; and the nearby *Eis Boulevard* (☎ *34 76 87, Leopoldstrasse 52)*, with lots of ice cream.

Farther west, *Egger* (☎ *39 85 26, Friedrichstrasse 27)* is a fine place with large plates and two-course lunch specials from DM11.50 to DM15. At dinner, vegetarian main courses average DM12 to DM15, and meat dishes from DM14 to DM21.

Neuhausen The *Löwenbräukeller* (☎ *52 60 21, Nymphenburger Strasse 2)*, via U1 to Stiglmaierplatz, is usually uncrowded, has great food and service, and the prices aren't bad either. Huge portions of Bavarian specialities (eg mushrooms in cream and anything with meat) are between DM12 and DM20. Do anything but lose your coat-check ticket – you may never retrieve your garment from the cloakroom.

Closer to Rotkreuzplatz, a really nice and totally untouristed place to sit and chat is *froh & munter* (☎ *18 79 97, Artilleriestrasse 5)*. This welcoming cafe serves excellent snacks, soups and great Spanish-style tapas, with offerings like rice balls with bacon and sweet-and-sour sauce, from DM4.50 to DM7.50. It also serves up organically prepared Unertl beer (DM5), some of the best Weissbier in town. The menu changes nightly. Food is served to 11 pm and the service is always friendly.

Westend The nicely renovated *Stoa* (☎ *50 70 50, Gollierstrasse 38)* is a fine place for lunch or dinner. It has a comfortable atmosphere, tapas from DM7.50 to DM15.50 and varied main courses like penne in a three-cream sauce from DM13.30, or chicken roulade with spinach in a mushroom cream sauce from DM10.50.

Student Cafeterias & Fast Food
Student-card holders can fill up for around DM4 in any of the university *Mensas*. The best one is on Schillerstrasse just north of Pettenkoferstrasse, and there are others at Leopoldstrasse 13, at Arcisstrasse 17 and Helene-Mayer-Ring 9.

For quick snacks, any Müller bakery *Stehcafe* offers coffee (around DM2) and pretzels or bread rolls covered with melted cheese (about DM3) or with bacon or ham (DM3 to DM4).

Throughout the city, branches of *Vinzenzmurr* have hot buffets and prepared meals; a very good lunch – like *Schweinebraten mit Knödel* (roast pork with dumplings) and gravy – can be as low as DM8, and pizza and hamburgers average about DM4.

The *Münchner Suppenküche* (☎ *52 38 94 42, Schäfflerstrasse 7)*, north of the Frauenkirche, has meat and vegetarian soups from DM3.50.

Hauptbahnhof Doner and pizza rule the fast-food scene in Munich. Opposite the Hauptbahnhof on Bayerstrasse are lots of tourist traps, but you can grab a quick cheap bite at the street window of *Ristorante Ca' doro*, where large slices are DM3.50 to DM4. *Don't* go inside – it's a tourist trap.

Just south of the Hauptbahnhof are about a dozen places selling doner kebab; two favourites are the *Gute Stube* on the corner of Schwanthalerstrasse and Schillerstrasse, with great kebabs for DM6; and the tiny *Kebab Antep* (☎ *53 22 36, Schwanthalerstrasse 45)*, with the entrance on Goethestrasse, where they cost DM5. There's also spinach pie and other vegetarian offerings.

Thai fans absolutely must head for *Jinny's Thai Food* (☎ *55 07 99 48, Schillerstrasse 32)*, just south of Landwehrstrasse, where exquisite soups (DM4.90) along with daily specials (DM9.90 to DM10.90) await. They're fantastic and the staff are really friendly, too.

Karlsplatz Cheap eating is also available in various department stores in the centre. Right opposite Karlsplatz, on the ground floor of Kaufhof, are three good options next to each other: a *Müller* bakery, *Nordsee* seafood and *Grillpfanne* doing sausages.

Schwabing North of the university, *Reiter Imbiss* (Hohenzollernstrasse 24) has heaps of meaty stuff for cheap prices, as well as changing daily specials.

Right next to the Haus International youth hotel is the *BP filling station*, with excellent and cheap sandwiches.

Neuhausen A spectacular deal for lunch is *Vinh's* (see Indian & East Asian Restaurants), with super set-lunch specials from DM7.50 (between 11.30 am and 2.30 pm).

Eis Ecke Sarcletti, at the southern end of Rotkreuzplatz, may well have the best Italian ice cream in the city, and the crowds know it. It's about DM1 per scoop, and there's a little outdoor cafe as well.

Breakfast Places When your train drops you at the Hauptbahnhof at 7 am, and everyone in the station is drinking large glasses of beer and eating Currywurst, get out of there before you join them.

If you must eat in the station, try the *bakery* on the ground level next to Sussmann's international bookshop, or the *kiosk*

at the head of Track 14, which has fine cappuccinos for DM3. The *cafeteria* is pleasant enough, with boiled eggs for DM1.30. And there's always *Burger King*, upstairs in the main hall, which serves breakfast.

Outside the Hauptbahnhof, go south, where breakfast is cheaper than in the expensive hotels to the north and east of the station. Two good spots here are *Sultan*, on the corner of Schwanthalerstrasse and Goethestrasse; and *Kandil Restaurant* (see Cafes & Bistros), which offers rolls with butter, marmalade and coffee for DM5.50. *Café am Beethovenplatz* (☎ *54 40 43 48, Goethestrasse 51)*, at the Hotel Pension Mariandl (see Places to Stay), offers breakfast from 9 am for DM8.50 to DM17, and on Sunday morning from 11 am (when prices are similar but there's live jazz as well).

In Neuhausen, the painfully trendy *Café am Platz der Freiheit* (☎ *13 46 86, Leonrodstrasse 20)* has very good *Milchcafé* (café au lait), served steaming hot in giant bowls, and three eggs with ham for DM8.50, but service is terrible.

Self-Catering In Neuhausen and close to the hostel is Munich's best bakery, the tiny *Schneider's Feinbäckerei* (☎ *26 47 44, Volkartstrasse 48)*, between Albrechtstrasse and Artilleriestrasse just east of Landshuter Allee. It bakes indescribably good bread rolls, other breads and cake.

Supermarkets large and small can be found throughout the city (the Turkish ones can be particularly cheap). *Norma* and *Aldi* supermarkets are the cheapest places to buy staples. For a last-minute stock-up before your train leaves, hit *Tengelmann* at Bayerstrasse 5, just opposite the Hauptbahnhof.

Aussies with Vegemite cravings should head for *Australia Service* (☎ *18 60 51, Dachauer Strasse 103)*, about 500m west of Stiglmaierplatz, with the famous spread plus Aussie everything from beer and wine to Akubra hats and Lonely Planet Australia guides. In a similar vein, the *English Shop* (☎ *48 84 00, Franziskanerstrasse 14)*, about 200m south of the Rosenheimer Strasse S-Bahn stop, has lots of British stuff.

BAVARIA

The **supermarket** in the basement of the Kaufhof department store opposite Karlsplatz has a far more upmarket selection, plus goodies like fresh mozzarella, superb sliced meats and cheeses, and a good bakery.

At Viktualienmarkt, just south of Marienplatz, you can put together a picnic feast of breads, cheeses and salad to take off to a beer garden for DM10 or less per person, but it's so good that chances are you'll get carried away and the price will soar. Make sure you figure out the price before buying, and don't be afraid to move on to another stall. **Nordsee** has simply awesome seafood from cheap to ridiculous. **Thoma** is a wonderful cheese and wine shop. Behind it you'll find the **Juice Bar**, with great fruity concoctions from DM3 to DM6. Right next to the maypole, look for the **Oliven & Essiggurken** stand, with olives and pickles plus pickled garlic and loads more.

More prosperous picnickers might prefer the legendary **Alois Dallmayr**, one of the world's greatest (and priciest) delicatessens, with an amazing range of exotic foods imported from every corner of the earth.

Entertainment

Munich's entertainment scene will keep you busy. Apart from discos, pubs and beer halls, try not to miss out on the city's excellent classical and opera scenes.

Not surprisingly, beer drinking is an integral part of Munich's entertainment scene. Germans drink an average of 127L of the amber liquid each per year, while residents of Bavaria average some 170L! If you're keen to keep up with the locals, a good investment is Larry Hawthorne's **Beer Drinker's Guide to Munich**, available locally, which lists and rates many of Munich's better beer gardens and brews.

Munich nightclub bouncers are notoriously rude and 'discerning', so dress to kill (or look, as locals say, **schiki-micki**) and keep your cool.

If you have even rudimentary German, the best sources of information are the free **in München**, available at bars, restaurants, ticket outlets and other venues; and the tall, thin, yellow, city-published monthly **München im ....** (DM3), which is an A-to-Z listing of almost everything the city has to offer except discos. It's the best source of information on new museum exhibitions, festivals, concerts and theatre.

Another great German guide (available at any newsstand) is the monthly **Münchner Stadtmagazin** (DM3), which is probably the most complete guide to bars, discos, clubs, concerts and nightlife in the city.

Bigger newsstands and shops sell **Munich Found** (DM4.50), an English-language city magazine with somewhat useful listings.

Tickets to different entertainment venues are available at official ticket outlets (Kartenvorverkauf) throughout the city, but these often specialise in certain genres. The exception is the Zentraler Kartenvorverkauf (☎ 26 46 20), which sells tickets to everything, including theatre, ballet, opera, rock concerts and all special events. Its office is conveniently located at Marienplatz, underground in the S-Bahn station.

Beer Halls & Gardens A few beer gardens have live music (from oompah to Dixieland) but the main thing is being outside with the beer. A recent Berlin offensive to have a closing law for beer gardens (10 pm, last orders at 9.30 pm) enforced in the rest of the country caused an uproar in Bavaria; locals promptly tagged it 'a Prussian' measure and predictably, a Bavarian court rejected it.

You sometimes have to pay a **Pfand** (deposit) for the glasses (usually DM5). Beer costs DM9 to DM12 per litre. For food options at beer halls, see the boxed text 'And There's Food, Too' later in this section.

Several breweries run their own beer halls; try at least one large, frothy litre of beer before heading off to another hall. Even in the touristy places, be careful not to sit at a **Stammtisch**, reserved for regulars (there will be a brass plaque).

Central Munich Most celebrated is the cavernous **Hofbräuhaus** (☎ 22 16 76, Am Platzl 9). A live band plays Bavarian folk music every night, but the place is generally packed with tipsy tourists.

The *Augustiner-Gaststätte* (☎ 55 19 92 57, Neuhauser Strasse 27) has a less raucous atmosphere than the Hofbräuhaus (not to mention decent food), yet it's a more authentic example of an old-style Munich beer hall.

The large and leafy beer garden at the *Augustiner Keller* (☎ 59 43 93, Arnulfstrasse 52), about 500m west of the Hauptbahnhof, has a laid-back atmosphere ideal for recreational drinking.

A Munich institution since 1807, the *Viktualienmarkt* (☎ 29 75 45, Viktualienmarkt 6) is a wonderful place right in the centre; see the earlier Viktualienmarkt section for details on the surrounding market.

English Garden Here you'll find the classic *Chinesischer Turm* (☎ 950 28, Englischer Garten 3), with a very weird crowd of businessfolk, tourists and junkies, all entertained by what has to be the world's drunkest oompah band (in the tower above the crowd, fenced in like *The Blues Brothers*). The *Hirschau* and *Seehaus* beer gardens (☎ 381 61 30), on the shore of the Kleinhesseloher See, are less crowded, though a more smug crowd abounds.

Western Munich We absolutely love the *Hirschgarten* (☎ 17 25 91, Hirschgartenallee 1), just south of Schloss Nymphenburg (take the S-Bahn to Laim). It's packed with locals and fewer tourists. The shady garden is enormous, and you can sit next to the deer that wander just on the other side of the chain-link fence.

The *Taxisgarten* (☎ 15 68 27, Taxisstrasse 12), north of Rotkreuzplatz, is another peaceful place with mainly local families. Take bus No 177 from Rotkreuzplatz to Klugstrasse.

Northern Munich The *Löwenbräukeller* (☎ 52 60 21, Nymphenburger Strasse 2) deserves another mention here (see Cafes & Bistros in Places to Eat) for its many earthy locals, a relative dearth of tourists and a grand main hall (which seats 2000) with

regular Bavarian music and heel-slapping dances on stage.

Waldwirtschaft Grosshesselohe (☎ 79 50 88, Georg-Kalb-Strasse 3), via the S7 to Grosshesselohe, is in one of the most expensive neighbourhoods in town. The wealthy residents decided that all the racket (Dixieland music, mainly) was too downmarket for their taste and tried to shut it down. The resulting city-wide brouhaha became headline news and the countermovement is written in Munich history as the 'Beer Garden Revolution'. It was, of course, successful.

Pubs & Bars Right in the centre, the *Nachtcafé* (☎ 59 59 00, Maximiliansplatz 5), stays open until 6 am, but they won't let you in unless you're *très chic*, female and dressed in a tight black dress, or throwing Deutschmarks around. Far more down-home Bavarian is *Jodlwirt* (☎ 467 35 24, Alten Hofstrasse 4), in an alley just north of Marienplatz. It's a nice, relatively untouristed place with good Ayinger beer and a pleasant atmosphere.

Julep's (☎ 448 00 44, Breisacherstrasse 18), in Haidhausen east of the centre, is a Mexican place with great drinks and a very rowdy crowd.

Schwabing The area along and around Leopoldstrasse between the university and Münchener Freiheit U-Bahn station is the bar district; the backstreets are teeming with places, big and small, and there's something to fit every taste. *Lardy* (☎ 34 49 49, Leopoldstrasse 49) is a quasi-exclusive bar, but the goons at the door don't really stop anyone from entering. There are DJs on Thursday and Friday nights and English-speaking staff.

Towards Königsplatz is *Treszniewski* (☎ 28 23 49, Theresienstrasse 72), a chic spot that attracts intellectual types and lots of people in black.

While *Munich's First Diner* (☎ 33 59 15, Leopoldstrasse 82) is truly a diner (complete with diner food and waiters on rollerblades), it's better known by the expat set as a great place for imported beer and

BAVARIA

And There's Food, Too

You'll find that Munich beer gardens allow you to pack food but no drinks, and everyone in town does just that: stock up (see Self-Catering under Places to Eat) and show up for the evening.

Food on offer includes roast chicken (about DM15 for a half), spare ribs (about DM20, and probably not worth it except in Taxisgarten), huge pretzels (about DM5) and Bavarian specialities such as *Schweinebraten* (pork roast) and schnitzel (for DM17 to DM22). There's both self-service and waiters. *Radi* is a huge, mild radish that's eaten with beer; it's cut with a *Radimesser*, which sticks down in the centre – you twist the handle round and round, creating a radish spiral. Buy a Radimesser at any department store and buy the radish at a market, or buy prepared radish for about DM7. If you do it yourself, smother the cut end of the radish with salt until it 'cries' to reduce bitterness (and increase your thirst!).

Obazda (**oh**-batsdah) is Bavarian for 'mixed up' – this cream-cheese-like beer garden speciality is made of butter, Camembert and paprika (about DM8 to DM12). Spread it on *Brez'n* (a pretzel) or bread. If you hate it while sober, you may like it after a few drinks.

cocktails. It's a fun flashback to the US of A, if that's what you're after.

Neuhausen This is a neighbourhood for little local, rather than tourist, pubs. *Kreitmayr's* (☎ 448 91 40, Kreitmayrstrasse), just east of Erzgiessereistrasse, is a real bar crawler's bar, with bar food, good drinks, a pool table, *Kugel* (a sort of bowling), darts and pinball, and live music on Thursday (from Irish folk to jazz). It also has a beer garden in summer. The *froh & munter* (see Cafes & Bistros in Places to Eat) is the best place for good Weissbier, with a great crowd of locals and good snacks as well.

Irish Pubs Munich has a huge Irish expat population; if you're out looking for friendly, English-speaking people, you're in luck. Most of the pubs have live music at least once a week.

In Schwabing, two very cool underground cellar bars are *Günther Murphy's Irish Tavern* (☎ 39 89 11, Nikolaistrasse 9a) and *Shamrock* (☎ 33 10 81, Trautenwolfstrasse 6). Both are fun, loud, boisterous and crowded every night. Get ready to be jostled, and come early if you want a table.

Also in Schwabing, *Shenanigans* (☎ 34 21 12, Ungererstrasse 19) has karaoke. It's bigger and less crowded than most of the others, and also sometimes has live music.

A divey atmosphere prevails at *Paddy's* (☎ 33 36 22, Feilitzschstrasse 17) in Schwabing, with locals and other interesting folks with interesting smokes.

Discos & Clubs Cover prices for discos change often, sometimes daily, but average between DM5 and DM15.

Despite occasional threats of closure, the *Kunstpark Ost* (☎ 49 00 27 30, Grafinger Strasse 6) remains a driving force in Munich's nightlife, with a multiple disco-restaurant-bar-cinema complex behind the Ostbahnhof in a former potato-processing factory. It's pure grungeville but swarmingly popular. Watch your valuables in the side alleys, where some very unsavoury characters hang out.

Discos at Kunstpark Ost often host live and sometimes very large concerts, and include *Bongo Bar* (☎ 49 00 12 60), with 1950s style weirdness, go-go dancers and kitsch extraordinaire; the *Milch + Bar Faltenbacher* (☎ 49 00 35 17), a cruising ground for a leathery twenty-something crowd; and the enormous *Babylon* (☎ 450 69 20), attracting big-name concerts and 'parties with thousands' on weekends. Friday nights are Fruit of the Room, with 1970s and 80s stuff and *Schlager*, popular updates of German folk songs.

Another large complex is the *Muffathalle* (☎ 45 88 75 00 00, Zellstrasse 4), which holds large concerts and, in summer, an open-air disco on Friday with drum/bass, acid jazz and hip hop (always crowded, so expect long queues). *P1 (☎ 29 42 52, Prinzregentenstrasse 1)* is still *the* seen-and-be-seen place for Munich wanna-bes, with extremely choosy and effective bouncers.

Opera (☎ 32 42 32 42, Helmholzstrasse 12), west of the Hauptbahnhof and off Arnulfstrasse, is a fun place with a strong contingent in its 30s, and lots of theme nights (eg metal, underground and oldies). On Saturday there's black beat and soul.

Backstage (☎ 33 66 59, Helmholzstrasse 18) is another concert place and disco – crossover, psychedelic, hip hop, trash and other freaky music is the rule.

Nachtwerk (☎ 578 38 00, Landsberger Strasse 186), next to the Nachtwerk Club about 2km west of the Hauptbahnhof, is another place with middle-of-the-road house and dance-chart music.

Party with soul and hip hop on the rooftop of the Hertie department store in Schwabing at *Skyline (☎ 33 31 31, Leopoldstrasse 82)*; it's right next to the Münchener Freiheit U-Bahn station.

Atomic (☎ 22 66 61, Am Kosttor 2), near the Hofbräuhaus, has mixed theme nights daily, attracting legions of twisting-and-gyrating under-30s.

Gay & Lesbian Much of Munich's gay and lesbian nightlife is centred in the area just south of Sendlinger Tor. Information for gay men and lesbians is available through Schwules Kommunikations und Kulturzentrum, dubbed 'the Sub' (☎ 260 30 56, Müllerstrasse 43), open Sunday to Thursday from 7 to 11 pm, and to 1 am on Friday and Saturday nights. It's a very cool gay community centre, with two floors (a bar downstairs and a library upstairs) that are home to extensive gay resources and support groups.

Lesbians can contact LeTra/Lesbentelefon (☎ 725 42 72, Dreimühlenstrasse 23), open Tuesday from 10.30 am to 1 pm, Wednesday from 2.30 to 5 pm and Thursday from 7 to 10 pm. A women-only teahouse, the *Frauentee-stube (☎ 77 40 91, Dreimühlenstrasse 1)* is on the corner of

Isartalstrasse south of the city centre (closed Wednesday and Saturday).

The *Rosa Seiten* (Pink Pages, DM5) is the best guide to everything gay and lesbian in the city; order it by mail from the 'Sub' or take the U2 to Theresienstrasse, where the Weissblauer Gay Shop (☎ 52 23 52) is just outside the station. An alternative is the shop Black Jump (☎ 448 10 73, Orleansstrasse 51) via the U-Bahn to Sendlinger Tor. These places also hand out free copies of *Our Munich*, a monthly guide to gay and lesbian life.

There's great service, good food and cocktails at *Morizz (☎ 201 67 76, Klenzestrasse 43)*, which looks a lot like a Paris bar: lots of mirrors, very quiet early in the night with lots of theatre types from Gärtnerplatz, but the later it gets, the rowdier it becomes. Another popular place is *Iwan (☎ 55 49 33, Josephspitalstrasse 15)*, a once ultra-chic place that's 'democratised' its crowd. Its two floors host a very mixed crowd, and in summer there's a nice outside area.

A fine exclusively lesbian bar is *Bei Carla (☎ 22 79 01, Buttermelcherstrasse 9)*, with a good mixed-age crowd and snack foods. There's a mainly lesbian crowd at *Karotte (☎ 201 06 69, Baaderstrasse 13)*, just south of the centre – it also serves food from a daily menu.

The *Ochsengarten (☎ 26 64 46, Müllerstrasse 47)* was Germany's first leather bar. It has a forbidding entrance, rustic interior, lots of boots hanging from the ceiling and a 30 to 40-year-old crowd. Leather lovers also head straight (or rather, 'gaily forward') to *Löwengrube (☎ 26 57 50, Reisingerstrasse 5)*, a small, exclusively gay place jammed with a tight-Levi's-and-rubber crowd.

The Stud (☎ 260 84 03, Thalkirchner Strasse 2) is a leather-Levi's place with a dark, coal-mine-like interior and lots of butch guys with no hair. The clientele is gay and lesbian (in fact, they're always looking for more lesbians, so if that fits, head on over). It's open Friday to Sunday from 11 pm to 4 am, and drinks start at DM5.

Fortuna Musikbar (☎ 55 40 70, Maximiliansplatz 5), in Reginahaus, changes its spots: Wednesday to Friday it's exclusively

euro currency converter DM1 = €0.51

gay and lesbian, Wednesday is also film night, Thursday it's house and live-music parties, and on Saturday it's lesbians only.

Together Again (☎ 26 34 69, *Müllerstrasse 1*) has live shows Sunday to Thursday from 10 pm, and disco on Friday and Saturday nights. *NY NY* (☎ 59 10 65, *Sonnenstrasse 25*) is a slick and very gay joint with a bar on the ground floor and a high-tech disco with a mixed crowd upstairs.

At the two level *Soul City* (☎ 59 52 72, *Maximiliansplatz 5*) there's a bar and cafe on the 1st level, while the 2nd level has a disco and dance floor with a young and extremely mixed crowd.

Rock Large rock concerts are staged at the Olympiapark. Most other rock venues are also listed in Discos & Clubs, including the *Muffathalle*, which also holds jazz, salsa, African and world music and other concerts as well; *Nachtwerk Club* and *Babylon* at Kunstpark Ost.

There are also concerts regularly at the *Schlachthof* (☎ 76 54 48, *Zenettistrasse 9*), via U-Bahns to Poccistrasse, which also hosts a regular TV show called 'Live aus dem Schlachthof' with Marc Owen, and comedy nights. It attracts a thirty-something crowd.

There's country and western music at the *Rattlesnake Saloon* (☎ 150 40 35, *Schneeglöckchenstrasse 91)*, via the S-Bahn to Fasanerie Nord; and at the *Oklahoma Country Saloon* (☎ 723 43 27, *Schäftlarnstrasse 156)*, reached by the U-Bahn to Thalkirchen. Both of them, as you might guess, are Wild West-style bars.

Jazz Munich is also a hot scene for jazz. *Jazzclub Unterfahrt* (☎ 448 27 94, *Einsteinstrasse 42)*, near the Ostbahnhof, is perhaps the best known place in town. It has live music from 9 pm (except Monday) and jam sessions open to everyone on Sunday night. There are also daily concerts in Munich's smallest jazz club, *Mr B's* (☎ 53 49 01, *Herzog-Heinrich-Strasse 38)*, not far from Goetheplatz.

You can go a bit more upmarket with jazz shows at the *Night Club* (☎ 212 09 94,

Promenadeplatz 2-6) in the Hotel Bayerischer Hof, which has regular jazz and other concerts including reggae, blues and funkabilly. An upmarket spot for open-air concerts is in the *Brunnenhof der Residenz* (☎ 29 68 36, *Residenzstrasse 1)*, which hosts a broad range of concerts, including rock, jazz, swing, classical and opera. There's a jazz brunch on Sunday at *Café am Beethovenplatz* (☎ 54 40 43 48, *Goethestrasse 51)*, at the Hotel Pension Mariandl.

Backstage Aluminium (☎ 18 33 30, *Helmholzstrasse 18)* right at the S-Bahn Donnersberger Brücke station, is a very popular jazz venue, with lots of live performances.

Munich's most infamous Dixieland venue (it also plays jazz) is the *Waldwirtschaft Grosshesselohe* (☎ 79 50 88, *Georg-Kalb-Strasse 3)*, which plays it nightly to the consternation of local residents.

Classical Music The Munich Philharmonic Orchestra performs at the *Philharmonic Hall* within the Gasteig (see Theatre), Munich's premier classical-music venue. It's also the home of the Bayerischer Rundfunk's orchestra, which performs on Sunday throughout the year.

There are occasional classical concerts at the *Theater am Gärtnerplatz* (☎ 201 67 67, *Gärtnerplatz 3)*, via the U-Bahns to Frauenhoferstrasse, but this is more an opera and operetta venue. There are always opera productions (some very good, some not) here.

Classical concerts are also often held in the lovely *Altes Residenztheater*, within the Residenz.

The Bayerische Staatsoper (Bavarian State Opera) performs at the *Nationaltheater*, Max-Joseph-Platz 2, which is also the site of many cultural events, particularly during the opera festival in July. You can buy tickets at regular outlets, at the theatre box office at Maximilianstrasse 11 (Monday to Friday from 10 am to 6 pm, Saturday to 1 pm) or by telephone (☎ 21 85 19 20).

Cinemas Call or check any listings publications for show information; cinema admission is between DM12 and DM15. Note that foreign films in mainstream cinemas are almost always dubbed (Westerns in German can be quite a hoot).

Two larger cinemas that show first-run (sort of) films in English daily are *Museum-Lichtspiele* (☎ 48 24 03, *Lilienstrasse 2*) and the excellent *Cinema* (☎ 55 52 55, *Nymphenburger Strasse 31*). Films are shown nightly in the *Filmmuseum* (☎ 233 55 86, *Stadtmuseum*), usually the originals with subtitles.

Other cinemas that show English-language movies include the *Atelier* (☎ 59 19 18, *Sonnenstrasse 12*), *Atlantis* (☎ 55 51 52, *Schwanthalerstrasse 2*) and *Cinerama* (☎ 49 91 88 19, *Grafinger Strasse 6*). *Amerika Haus* and the *British Council* (see Cultural Centres in the Information section) both show undubbed films as well.

Theatre Munich has a lively theatre scene. The two biggest companies are the Staatschauspiel and the Kammerspiele. The Staatschauspiel performs at the *Residenztheater*, at the intimate rococo *Cuvilliés Theater* (also within the Residenz) and at the *Marstall Theater*, behind the Nationaltheater (see Classical Music).

The *Kammerspiele* (☎ 23 33 70 00, *Maximilianstrasse 26*) stages large productions of serious drama from German playwrights or works translated into German. (These are the folks who said that Shakespeare sounded 'better' in German.)

The *Deutsches Theater* (☎ 55 23 44 44, *Schwanthalerstrasse 13*) is Munich's answer to the West End: touring road shows (usually light musicals) perform here.

The *Gasteig* (☎ 48 09 80, *Rosenheimer Strasse 5*), reached via the S-Bahn to Rosenheimerplatz or tram No 18, is a major cultural centre with theatre, classical music and other special events in its several halls. Theatre is performed in the Carl-Orff-Saal and on the far more intimate Black Box stage.

Other large venues include the *Prinzregententheater* (☎ 26 46 20, *Prinzregentenplatz 12*), via U4; and the *Neues Theater München* (☎ 65 00 00, *Entenbachstrasse 37*), via the U-Bahns to Kolumbusplatz.

There's regular comedy in the chic *Komödie im Bayerischen Hof* (☎ 29 28 10, *Passage Promenadeplatz*), via tram No 19, and at the *Kleine Komödie am Max II* (☎ 22 18 59, *Maximilianstrasse 47*) via the U-Bahn to Lehel.

Children's Theatre A big hit with children is the *Circus Krone* (☎ 545 80 00, *Marsstrasse 43*), with performances from Christmas to April.

For puppet theatre, there is *Marionettenstudio Kleines Festspiel* (*Neureutherstrasse 12*), with the entrance on Arcisstrasse. Admission is free; take the U-Bahn to Josephsplatz. Or, try *Das Münchner Marionettentheater* (☎ 26 57 12, *Blumenstrasse 29a*), via the U-Bahn to Sendlinger Tor. Performances (including puppet shows and children's theatre) are staged throughout the year at *Münchner Theater für Kinder* (☎ 59 38 58, *Dachauer Strasse 46*); take the U-Bahn to Stiglmaierplatz.

Shopping

Bavarian dress is the most distinctive of traditional German clothing. Loden-Frey, a specialist department store at Maffeistrasse 5-7 in the centre, stocks a wide range of Bavarian wear, but expect to pay at least DM400 for a good leather jacket, Lederhosen or a women's Dirndl dress.

Ludwig Beck, Munich's most venerable department store, on Marienplatz near the Toy Museum, has some chic but reasonably priced clothes, a large CD shop, a coffee bar and restaurant. It also has a branch of Heinemann's, which makes some of Germany's finest filled chocolates.

Also look out for optical goods (Leica cameras and binoculars), especially along Landwehrstrasse near Sonnenstrasse and at Sauter Photographic (☎ 551 50 40) at Sonnenstrasse 26, just off Sendlinger-Tor-Platz.

The Christkindlmarkt (Christmas market) on Marienplatz in December is large and well stocked but often expensive. The Auer Dult, a huge flea market on Mariahilfplatz in Au, has great buys and takes place during the last weeks of April, July and October.

BAVARIA

Beer steins and *Mass* glasses are available at all the department stores, as well as from the beer halls themselves.

Getting There & Away

Air Munich is second in importance only to Frankfurt for international and domestic flights. From here you can reach major destinations like London, Paris, Rome, Athens, New York and Sydney. Main German cities are served by at least half a dozen flights daily. The main carrier is Lufthansa Airlines (☎ 54 55 99), Lenbachplatz 1. For general flight information, call ☎ 97 52 13 13.

For some tickets, especially those to Asia or cheap flights to the USA, you need to reconfirm 24 to 48 hours before your flight.

Airlines serving Munich's Franz-Josef Strauss airport include:

British Airways/Deutsche BA
  (☎ 0180-334 03 40) Promenadeplatz 10
Delta Air Lines
  (☎ 0180-333 78 80) Maximiliansplatz 17
El Al
  (☎ 210 69 20) Maximiliansplatz 15
Finnair
  (☎ 01803-34 66 24) Franz-Josef Strauss airport, D section of passenger terminal
Japan Air Lines (JAL)
  (☎ 0180-222 87 00) Prielmayrstrasse 1
Scandinavian Airlines (SAS)
  (☎ 01803-23 40 23, nationwide reservation service)
Sabena
  (☎ 55 58 45) Schillerstrasse 5

Train Train services to/from Munich are excellent. There are rapid connections at least every two hours to all major cities in Germany, as well as frequent services to European cities such as Vienna (5½ hours), Prague (seven hours) and Zürich (six hours).

High-speed ICE services from Munich include Berlin-Zoo (DM175, 6¾ hours), Frankfurt (DM147, 3½ hours) and Hamburg (DM249, six hours).

Prague extension passes to your rail pass are sold at the rail-pass counters (Nos 19, 20 and 21) at the Hauptbahnhof, or through EurAide (see Tourist Offices under Information earlier in this chapter).

Bus Munich is a stop for Busabout, with links every two days from Austria and on to the Rhine Valley and France (see the Getting There & Away chapter). Munich is also linked to the Romantic Road by the Europabus Munich-Frankfurt service (see Getting Around in the Romantic Road section later in this chapter). Inquire at Deutsche Touring (☎ 545 87 00) near platform No 26 at the Hauptbahnhof.

BEX (BerlinLinienBus; ☎ 0130-83 11 44 from outside Berlin, ☎ 030-86 09 60 within Berlin) runs daily buses between Berlin and Munich (nine hours), via Leipzig, Bayreuth, Nuremberg and Ingolstadt. One-way/return SuperSpar tickets for passengers aged under 26 or over 60 cost DM76/139; full-fare tickets are DM129/149. See Getting There & Away under individual cities and towns for other fares and services.

Car & Motorcycle Munich has autobahns radiating on all sides. Take the A9 to Nuremberg, the A92/A3 to Passau, the A8 to Salzburg, the A95 to Garmisch-Partenkirchen and the A8 to Ulm or Stuttgart.

All major car-rental companies have offices at the airport. Sixt (Budget) and Hertz have counters on the 2nd level of the Hauptbahnhof; Europcar is outside, near the north entrance. Pick up and return the cars to the garage under the Maritim Hotel (enter from Senefelderstrasse).

If you're thinking about buying a car here (see Purchase under Car & Motorcycle in the Getting Around chapter) and you're not very technically minded, you should seriously consider having the vehicle vetted by ADAC's Prüfzentrum Gebrauchtwagenuntersuchung (ADAC Testing Centre for Used Cars; ☎ 519 51 88), Ridlerstrasse 35, which will run through the thing with a fine-toothed comb for DM85/110 for ADAC members/nonmembers.

Ride Services For arranged rides, contact the ADM-Mitfahrzentrale (☎ 194 40), near the Hauptbahnhof at Lämmerstrasse 4. It's open daily to 8 pm. Charges (including booking fees) are: Vienna DM42, Berlin

DM54, Amsterdam DM74, Paris DM79, Prague DM59 and Warsaw DM88.

The CityNetz Mitfahr-Service Kängaruh (☎ 194 44), at Adalbertstrasse 10-12, just 70m from the Universität U-Bahn stop, is slightly cheaper and also arranges lifts for women with female drivers. There's also a gay and lesbian Mitfahrzentrale at ☎ 0190-34 40 64 (DM1.20 per minute).

Getting Around
Even at the height of the summer tourist season, the central pedestrian zone leading from the Hauptbahnhof to Marienplatz makes for very pleasant walking.

To/From the Airport Munich's Flughafen Franz-Josef Strauss is connected by the S1 and S8 to the Hauptbahnhof – DM14 with a single ticket or eight strips of a *Streifenkarte* (a strip-card of 10 tickets). The service takes 40 minutes and runs every 20 minutes from 4 am until around 1 am.

The Lufthansa airport bus runs at 20-minute intervals from Arnulfstrasse near the Hauptbahnhof (DM16/26, 45 minutes one-way/return) between 6.50 am and 8.50 pm. A taxi will cost at least DM50 to the city limits, and about DM90 to the centre.

Public Transport Getting around is easy on Munich's excellent public-transport network (MVV). The system is zone-based, and most places of interest to visitors (except Dachau and the airport) are within the 'blue' inner-city zone *(Innenraum)*.

MVV tickets are valid for the S-Bahn, U-Bahn, trams and buses, but must be validated before use by time-stamping them in machines at entrances and on board buses and trams. Failure to validate puts you at the mercy of uniformed (sometimes plain-clothes) ticket inspectors who speak perfect English, have seen and heard all possible excuses and possess admirable Teutonic efficiency when it comes to handing out fines of DM60 for unauthorised travel.

The U-Bahn ceases at around 12.30 am on weekdays and 1.30 am on weekends, but there are some night buses. Rail passes are valid on S-Bahn trains. Bicycle transport costs DM3.60 per trip or DM4.50 for a day pass, but is forbidden on weekdays during the morning and evening rush hours (6 to 9 am and 4 to 6 pm).

Short rides (over four total stops with no more than two U-Bahn or S-Bahn stops) cost DM1.80, longer trips cost DM3.50. It's cheaper to buy a strip-card of 10 tickets called a *Streifenkarte* for DM15, and stamp one strip (DM1.50) per adult on rides of two or less tram or U-Bahn stops, two strips (DM3) for longer rides. Youths aged 15 to 20 can ride on the Streifenkarte for half-price.

The best value is in day passes for the inner zone, which cost DM9 for individuals and just DM13 for up to five people, and three-day inner-zone passes, which are DM22/33. You can also buy a weekly *Isarcard* pass covering four zones for just DM22.50, but the catch is that it's only valid beginning on a Monday (ie if you buy on Wednesday, the Isarpass is still only good through to Sunday).

A network of night buses *(Nachtbusse)* operates after standard hours – very convenient for disco and clubgoers; the routes, hours and schedules change often. Pick up the latest schedule from any tourist office.

Car & Motorcycle It's not worth driving in the city centre; many streets are pedestrian-only, ticket enforcement is Orwellian and parking is a nightmare. The tourist office map shows city car parks, which generally cost about DM3 per hour.

Taxi Taxis are expensive (more than DM5 at flag fall, plus DM2.20 per kilometre) and not much more convenient than public transport. For a radio-despatched taxi, ring ☎ 216 10/11 or ☎ 194 10. Taxi ranks are indicated on the city's tourist map.

The BahnTaxi stand (DM15; see the Getting Around chapter) is at the south-east end of the station near the Bayerstrasse exit.

Bicycle Guests of Jugendherberge München can rent bikes for DM22/40/54 for one/two/three days. Radius Fahrradverleih

(☎ 59 61 13), at the end of platform No 31 in the Hauptbahnhof, rents out city bikes for DM25/95 per day/week, and mountain and trekking bikes for DM30/90. Rail-pass holders get a 10% discount, and there's a 20% discount from Tuesday to Thursday.

Around Munich

DACHAU

'The way to freedom is to follow one's orders; exhibit honesty, orderliness, cleanliness, sobriety, truthfulness, the ability to sacrifice and love of the Fatherland'

Inscription from the roof of the
concentration camp at Dachau

Dachau was the very first Nazi concentration camp, built by Heinrich Himmler in March 1933. It 'processed' more than 200,000 prisoners, and 31,531 were reported killed here. In 1933 Munich had 10,000 Jews. Only 200 survived the war.

The camp is now one of the most popular day trips from Munich, though the experience can be so disturbing that we don't recommend it for children under age 12.

Outside the main exhibition hall is a monument, inscribed in English, French, Yiddish, German and Russian, that reads 'Never Again'. Nearby are large stakes onto which prisoners were hanged, sometimes for days, with their hands shackled behind their backs.

Inside the main hall, as you enter, is a large map showing camp locations throughout Germany and Central Europe. Indicators show which were the extermination camps. The exhibit inside shows photographs and models of the camp, its officers and prisoners, and of horrifying 'scientific experiments' carried out by Nazi doctors. There's also a whipping block, a chart showing the system for prisoner identification by category (Jews, homosexuals, Jehovah's Witnesses, Poles, Romas and other 'asocial' types), documents relating to the camp and the persecution of 'degenerate' authors banned by the party, and exhibits on the rise of the Nazi party and the establishment of the camp system.

Also on the grounds are reconstructed bunkers, and a (never used) crematorium and extermination gas chamber disguised as showers. Outside the gas chamber building is a statue to 'honour the dead and warn the living' and a Russian Orthodox chapel. Nearby are churches and a Jewish memorial.

Guided tours in English are essential if you don't understand German, and a good idea even if you do. Even if you take the tour, consider buying a copy of the catalogue, which has detailed descriptions of all the exhibits in the museum, as well as a written history. The DM25 goes directly to the Survivors Association of Dachau. An English-language documentary is shown at 11.30 am and 3.30 pm (and often at 2 pm). The camp is open daily except Monday from 9 am to 5 pm, and admission is free. Expect to spend two to three hours here.

Organised Tours

Dachauer Forum and Action Reconciliation runs free two-hour tours in English on Saturday and Sunday at 12.30 pm. They are excellent and informative; the bigger the group, the longer the tour.

Getting There & Away

The S2 to Dachau leaves Munich Hauptbahnhof three times an hour at 16, 36 and 56 minutes past. The trip takes 19 minutes and requires a two-zone ticket (DM7, or four strips of a Streifenkarte), including the bus connection.

In front of the Dachau Hauptbahnhof change for local buses; bus No 726 (from Monday to Saturday) and bus No 724 (on Sunday and holidays) are timed to leave the station about 10 minutes after the train arrives. Show your stamped ticket to the driver. The driver will announce the stop (KZ-Gedenkstätte); then follow the crowds – it's about a five minute walk from the bus stop to the entrance of the camp. Return buses leave from near the camp car park every 20 minutes. By car, follow Dachauer Strasse straight out to Dachau and follow the KZ-Gedenkstätte signs. Parking is free.

CHIEMSEE

Munich residents have a special place in their hearts for this lovely lake an hour east of Munich. So did Ludwig II, who liked it so much he built his homage to Versailles on an island in the centre.

Prien am Chiemsee

☎ 08051 • pop 8700

Blessed with a lovely setting and a stop on the Munich-Salzburg rail line, the harbour town of Prien is an ideal base for exploring the Chiemsee. Most tourists pass through en route to Schloss Herrenchiemsee, but the lake's wealth of natural beauty and the multitude of water sports justify a stay of a night or two.

Two tourist offices in town act as information centres for the entire lake district. There's a good branch at the Prien am Chiemsee Hauptbahnhof, open July to September only, Monday to Friday from 12.45 to 5.45 pm. The main office is at Alte Rathausstrasse 11 (☎ 690 50, fax 69 05 40, email info@prien.chiemsee.de), open Monday to Friday from 8.30 am to 6 pm, and Saturday from 9 am to noon. The town's Web site is www.prien.chiemsee.de.

There's a bicycle rental at Radsport Reischenböck (☎ 46 31), Bahnhofsplatz 6, a minute's walk east of the station behind the Sparkasse. It charges DM12/20 per day for city/mountain bikes.

Schloss Herrenchiemsee Begun in 1878 on the site of an Augustinian monastery on the island of Herreninsel, Schloss Herrenchiemsee provides insights into Ludwig's bizarre motivations. In a glorification of absolutist monarchy, the palace was meant to emulate the French 'Sun King' whom Maximilian II (Ludwig's father) had once admired. There's a portrait of Louis XIV in a more prominent position than any of the shy Ludwig himself, who is represented only by an unfinished statue.

The palace is both a knock-off and an attempted one-up of Versailles, with larger rooms, the immense **Ambassador Staircase** and the positively dazzling **Hall of Mirrors**,

which runs the length of the garden (98m). The 44 candelabra and 33 great glass chandeliers of the castle's main room took 25 servants half an hour to light; candle-lit concerts were held here until a few years ago, when the soot damage to the interior became alarmingly apparent. When cash ran out in 1885, only this central section had been completed.

Ludwig spent less than a month in the place. When he *was* in he was rarely seen, as the king normally read during the night and slept all day. If anything, the bedrooms are even more fantastic than at the other palaces; the **Paradeschlafzimmer** resembles a chapel, with the canopied bed standing altar-like on a ledge behind a golden balustrade. We especially enjoyed the **Kleines Blaues Schlafzimmer**, with a big blue glass bubble perched on top of a wildly extravagant golden pedestal, looking much like an eclipsed moon.

The palace also contains the **König-Ludwig II-Museum**, with a display including Ludwig's christening and coronation robes, blueprints for other projects and his death mask. The spacious garden is a lovely place for a walk, and there's a reasonable cafeteria.

The palace is open from April to October daily from 9 am to 5 pm, and in winter from 9.30 am to 4 pm. Admission is DM8/5, or DM10/6 for a combination ticket with the König-Ludwig II-Museum. Admission includes an obligatory guided palace tour that is a half hour rush of statistic superlatives – how much gold-leaf was used, etc.

In order to get to the palace, you must take the ferry from Prien (DM10/5 return). Note that the last ferry for the Schloss guided tour departs at 3 pm.

Fraueninsel This island is home to **Frauenwörth**, a 12th century Benedictine monastery. Benedictine monks returned to the area in the 1980s and founded another monastery, which functions today. The island also contains a memorial to (and the remains of) Irmengard of Fraueninsel, the great-granddaughter of Charlemagne, and

BAVARIA

the **Torhalle** (DM3), the gateway to the monastery (mid-9th century); inside is a chapel. Return ferry fare, including a stop at Herreninsel, is DM12.50/6.

Swimming & Boat Rental The most easily accessed swimming beaches are at Chieming and Gstadt (both free) on the lake's east and north shores, respectively. Fees for boat rental, available at many beaches, vary from roughly DM7 to DM40 per hour, depending on the type. In Prien, the Bootsverleih Stöffl (☎ 20 00), in front of the Westernacher am See restaurant, has two-seater paddleboats for DM8 per hour, and a huge array of electric-driven vessels for DM17 to DM36.

The new Prienavera, a weak pun on the Italian word for 'spring', will house an enormous pool complex (suitable for families), with sauna, steam baths and solaria. It was due to open near Prien harbour in the autumn of 1999.

Places to Stay The closest camp site is *Campingplatz Hofbauer* (☎ 41 36, fax 626 57, Bernauerstrasse 110), a 10 minute walk south of town on the main road to Bernau, a town just 2km south of Prien and largely overlooked by tourists. Charges are DM10.50 per adult, plus DM10 per tent and car. It's open from April to October.

The tourist office can set up *private quarters* in the centre from just DM20 a person. Beds at the *DJH hostel* (☎ 687 70, fax 68 77 15, Carl-Braun-Strasse 66), a 15 minute walk from the Hauptbahnhof, cost DM24 with breakfast.

With a nice view of the lakefront, the *Hotel Garni Möwe* (☎ 50 04, fax 648 81, Seestrasse 111) offers a reasonable deal at DM60/120 for singles/doubles.

For something really special but relatively cheap, head over to the *Bonn Schlössl* (☎ 890 11, fax 891 03, Kirchplatz 9), a mock Bavarian castle in Bernau. Take the hourly RVO bus 9505 from Prien am Chiemsee Hauptbahnhof, and alight at the Bernau mini-golf course near the hotel, which also has a nice restaurant (see

Places to Eat). Single/double rooms start at DM90/170.

Pride of place goes to the *Yachthotel Chiemsee* (☎ 69 60, fax 51 71, Harrasserstrasse 49), a ritzy place south of Prien harbour, with sauna and its own three-masted yacht, and rooms from DM187/DM249.

Places to Eat For a quick bite, the best bet is *Metzgerei Schmid* (☎ 15 62, Bahnhofstrasse 7), with sandwiches, pizza and fresh lasagne for DM3 to DM8. The *Scherer SB Restaurant* (☎ 45 91, Alte Rathausstrasse 1) is a self-service cafeteria with hearty dishes and salads for DM9 to DM19.

The best vistas in town are at *Westernacher am See* (☎ 47 22, fax 96 84 93, Seestrasse 115), with a great garden on the promenade for people-watching. The food's not bad, either (try the trout in garlic butter for DM18.90).

For truly great Bavarian cuisine with swift service, drop by the old-world *Der Alte Wirt* (see Bonn Schlössl under Places to Stay), a massive half-timbered inn in nearby Bernau. Main dishes average DM15 to DM25, with the misleadingly named *Leberkäse* (a smooth pork sausage without an ounce of liver) clearly the star of the menu. The waitresses dart round the dining halls as if on roller blades.

Getting There & Around Prien is served by hourly train from Munich (DM22.40, one hour). From the Prien am Chiemsee Hauptbahnhof, walk down the stairs and through the tunnel to Chiemsee Bahn station, where you catch the historic steam train from 1887 (DM3.50/1.50 one-way, DM5.50/2.50 return, 10 minutes) to the ferry terminal at Prien/Stock (Hafen). From there, Chiemsee Schiffahrt (☎ 60 90), Seestrasse 108, operates boats that ply the waters of the lake with stops every hour at Herreninsel, Gstadt, Fraueninsel, Seebruck and Chieming.

You can circumnavigate the entire lake and make all these stops (getting off and catching the next ferry that comes your way) for DM17.50.

STARNBERG
☎ 08150 • 22,000

Once a royal retreat and still a pretty afflu-ent neighbourhood, Lake Starnberg (Starn-berger See), just 30 minutes by S6 from Munich (two zones or four strips of a Streifenkarte), is a fast and easy way to get away from the urban bustle of Munich and out onto the water.

The city of Starnberg, at the northern end of the lake, is the heart of the Fünf Seen, the Five Lakes district. Lake Starnberg, about 22km long, 5km wide and between one 1m and 100m deep, is a favourite spot for Mu-nich windsurfers, who also skittle over nearby Ammersee, and the much smaller Wörthsee, Pilsensee and Osterseen.

The tourist office (☎ 08151-90 60 60, fax 90 60 90, email info@starnberger -fuenf-seen-land), Wittelsbacherstrasse 2c, is open Monday to Friday from 8 am to 6 pm, and from June to October also on Saturday from 9 am to 1 pm. The office gives out and sells maps and hiking maps of the entire area, and can help you plan pub-lic transport between here and other lake towns, as well as to the heavily touristed monastery at Andechs. It also books ac-commodation in the entire Five Lakes Dis-trict for free.

Starnberg is best known, though, as the place where King Ludwig II was found dead (see the 'Ludwig II, the Fairy-Tale King' boxed text in the Around Füssen sec-tion). The spot where Ludwig's body was found, near the **Votivkapelle** in Berg, is now marked with a cross erected in the water.

The Bayerische Seen Schiffahrt company runs electrically powered tour boats across the lake from their docks right behind the S-Bahn station (three hours cost DM23.50 in a two-seater). There are one-hour tours (DM12.50) to the five castles around the lake's edge, also passing the site of the Lud-wig II cross. These depart daily in summer at 8.50, 9.30 and 10.35 am, and 12.15, 1.15, 2.30 and 4.30 pm.

If that's too organised for your taste, head to one of the several boat-rental booths just west of the Hauptbahnhof, where you can rent rowing/pedal/electric-powered boats for DM12/15/20 per hour. The electric boats have about enough power to get you a third of the way down the lake and back.

ANDECHS
A short bus ride from Herrsching, on the east side of the Ammersee (from Munich take S5 to the last stop), is the Benedictine monastery of Andechs (☎ 08152-37 60), re-built in 1675 after the Thirty Years' War left it in ruins.

The lovely hill-top rococo structure (free entry) has always been a place of pilgrim-age – the hundreds of offertory candles and relics locked up in the Holy Chapel prove it. One-hour German-language tours (DM5) of the monastery run on Tuesday and Thurs-day at 4 pm.

But an overwhelming majority of today's visitors are after the beer that the monks here have been brewing for over 500 years. It's excellent beer, but the place is so over-run by tourists it's easy to forget that you're in a religious institution, pious as your love for the brew may be.

The **Klosterbrauerei** serves a litre of light (DM8), dark (DM9.40) and Weissbier (DM9) in the monastery restaurant, whose overpriced food, service counters and turn-stiles for queuing recall a Hauptbahnhof. Yet the terrace is lovely, with a sweeping view of the valley.

From Herrsching Hauptbahnhof, take the Rauner bus (DM3/2.50), which leaves at least once an hour between 7.55 am and 4.35 pm and returns from 9.55 am to 6.45 pm. Or, take a 3km walk on the well marked footpaths (be sure to stick to them, for it's a steep drop in spots).

SCHLEISSHEIM
☎ 089 • pop 11,500

Just north of Munich, the suburb of Schleiss-heim is home to two major castles that com-pete with anything in the heart of the city.

The **Neues Schloss Schleissheim** (☎ 315 87 20) in Oberschleissheim is another spec-tacular castle modelled after Versailles, this one ordered by Emperor Max Joseph in

BAVARIA

1701. The grounds are equally impressive (bring a picnic). Inside, you'll see the vaulted ceiling above the staircase, with frescoes by Cosmas Damian Asam. It's open Tuesday to Sunday from 10 am to 12.30 pm and 1.30 to 5 pm (DM2/1.50).

Nearby, the Renaissance **Altes Schloss Schleissheim** (☎ 315 52 72) is open as a museum of religion (DM5/3).

The other major castle here, on the grounds of Altes Schloss park, is **Schloss Lustheim** (☎ 315 87 20), with amazing frescoes and a stunning baroque interior, now home to the **Meissner Porzellan Sammlung**, said to be the largest collection of Meissen chinaware in Germany. It's open the same hours as Schloss Schleissheim (DM3/2). A combination ticket to both the Neues Schloss and Schloss Lustheim costs DM4/2.50.

Flugwerft Schleissheim

After Germany's defeat in WWI, the maximum power of German aircraft was heavily restricted. German engineers began a 'ground-up' approach to aerodynamics in an effort to increase performance and speed, and in doing so revolutionised the design of modern aircraft.

This museum (☎ 315 71 40), a 7800 sq metre display within three halls (including a renovated hangar built between 1912 and 1919), is the aviation branch of the Deutsches Museum and on the site of the birthplace of the Royal Bavarian Flying Corps in 1912. On exhibit are aircraft from around the world, including the USA, the former Soviet Union, Sweden, Poland and Germany; there's a great collection of glider 'alternative' flying kits.

The museum is open daily from 9 am to 5 pm (DM6/4, free for children under six).

Getting There & Away

Take S1 (direction: Freising) to Oberschleissheim. It's about a 15 minute walk from the station along Mittenheimer Strasse towards the palaces. By car, take Leopoldstrasse north until it becomes Ingolstadter Strasse. Then take the A99 to the Neuherberg exit, at the south end of the airfield.

BAD TÖLZ
☎ 08041 • pop 14,000

Bad Tölz is a pleasant spa town that's a favourite day trip for Munich residents because of the good swimming at Alpamare, the alpine slide at Blomberg Mountain and rafting down the Isar River. The resort's tourist office *(Kurverkehrsamt)* books accommodation, rents out bikes and organises tours.

Churches

Not to be missed is Bad Tölz's hill-top **Kalvarienbergkirche**, best viewed from the bridge crossing the Isar. The enormous baroque church, with its large central Holy Staircase is also the site of the tiny **Leonhardikapelle** (1718), which is the destination of the town's Leonhardifahrt, an equestrian pageant in early November. St Leonhardi, incidentally, is the patron saint of horses.

But the town's star attraction is the **Pfarrkirche Maria Himmelfahrt**, just south of Marktstrasse at the end of Kirchgasse. The enormous yellow Gothic building that stands today was built in 1466 (the neo-Gothic tower from 1875 to 1877) on the site of the 13th century original, which was destroyed in 1453.

East of the pedestrian zone of Salzstrasse is the **Mühlfeld Kirche** (1737), now in its third incarnation after fire and bomb damage. Its baroque interior boasts a painting of the Plague Procession by rococo master Matthäus Günter.

Alpamare

The *non plus ultra* of German water parks is south of Bad Tölz at Alpamare (☎ 50 93 34). This utterly fantastic complex for adults and kids has heated indoor and outdoor pools, a wave pool, a series of wicked waterslides including the longest one in Germany (the 330m-long Alpabob-Wildwasser), saunas, solariums and its own hotel.

Everything is included in one ticket price: four-hour passes for adults on weekdays/

weekends and holidays cost DM30/36, and DM23/25 for children aged five to 13. Day passes cost DM43/55 for grown-ups, and DM30/35 for children. Holders of a *Kurpass*, which overnight guests get when they pay their *Kurtaxe* (resort tax), get a DM5 discount on all tickets.

The park is open Monday to Thursday from 8 am to 9 pm, and Friday to Sunday to 10 pm; it is closed on 25-26 December and 1 January. From Bad Tölz take the B13 south in the direction of Lenggriess, then take the Stadt Krankenhaus exit and follow the 'Kurzonen/Alpamare' signs. Parking is free.

Blomberg
South-west of Bad Tölz towers the Blomberg (1248m), a family-friendly mountain with a natural toboggan track in winter and fairly easy hiking and a really fun alpine slide in summer.

The chair lift (☎ 37 26) runs from 9 am to 6 pm in summer and to 4.30 pm in winter, weather permitting. There's a station midway and at the top. A return ticket to the top/middle/alpine slide costs DM11/7/4 for adults, and DM5/7/4 for children.

The summer alpine slide is a 1226m-long fibreglass track that snakes down the mountain from the middle station. You ride down on little wheeled bobsleds that have a joystick to control braking (push forward to go, and pull back to brake). You can achieve speeds of about 40 to 50kmh, but chances are if you do that, you're going to either ram a rider ahead of you or, as one of us did, fly off the track and watch helplessly as the cart careens down the mountain (leaving our unfortunate author-rider with a massive friction burn and sore legs from walking back up the hill)! Take note of the warning – if you do try for speed, wear a long-sleeved shirt and jeans.

Getting There & Away
Bad Tölz has hourly train connections with Munich (DM16.80, one hour). Take the S7 to the end of the line at Wolfratshausen and connect from there.

The Romantic Road

The Romantic Road (Romantische Strasse) links a series of picturesque Bavarian towns and cities. It has so far been the most successful of Germany's marketing campaigns designed to get tourists away from the big cities and out into the countryside, and some two million people ply the route every year. That means, of course, lots of signs in English and Japanese, tourist coaches and kitsch galore.

Despite the tourists, it's worth falling for the sales pitch and taking time to explore this delightful route. You won't be alone, but you certainly won't be disappointed – the route travels through some of the most beautiful towns and cities in Germany.

Orientation & Information
The Romantic Road runs north-south through western Bavaria, from Würzburg in Franconia to Füssen near the Austrian border, passing through about a dozen cities and towns, including Rothenburg ob der Tauber, Dinkelsbühl and Augsburg.

The Romantic Road tourist office (☎ 09851-902 71, fax 902 79), Markt 1, 91550 Dinkelsbühl, can help you put together an itinerary and give you accommodation lists and prices. The office can also suggest excursions outside the Romantic Road towns. But the best places for information about the Romantic Road are the local tourist offices in Rothenburg (☎ 09861-404 92, fax 868 07) at Markt 1, and in Dinkelsbühl (☎ 09581-902 40, fax 902 79) at Markt 1 (in the same building as the Romantic Road tourist office).

Füssen's tourist office (☎ 08362-938 50, fax 93 85 20) is at Kaiser-Maximilian-Platz 1 (closed for lunch, Saturday afternoon and Sunday).

Places to Stay
Considering the number of tourists, accommodation along the Romantic Road can be surprisingly good value. Tourist offices in most towns are very efficient at

BAVARIA

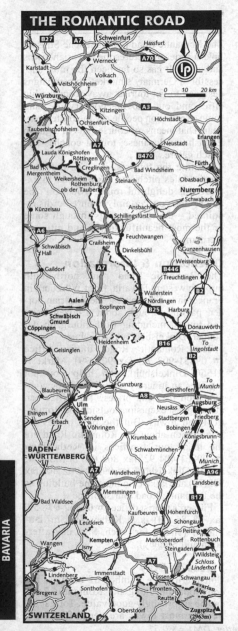

THE ROMANTIC ROAD

finding accommodation in almost any price range. Most of the DJH hostels listed here only accept people aged 26 and under, though some will in practice accept over 26s in 'emergencies', or when they have room.

Getting There & Away

Though Frankfurt is the most popular access point for the Romantic Road, Munich is a good choice as well, especially if you decide to take the bus (the stop is at the north side of the Hauptbahnhof).

Train To start at the southern end, take the hourly train link from Munich to Füssen (DM36, 2½ hours, some services change at Biessenhofen or Buchloe). Rothenburg is linked by train to Würzburg and Munich via Steinach, and Nördlingen to Augsburg via Donauwörth (DM27).

Bus Half a dozen daily buses connect Füssen and Garmisch-Partenkirchen (DM15.50, all via Neuschwanstein and most via Schloss Linderhof). There are also several connections between Füssen and Oberstdorf (via Pfronten or the Tirolean town of Reutte).

Heidelberg Deutsche Touring's Europabus runs a daily Castle Road coach service between Heidelberg and Rothenburg (DM47/94 one-way/return, 4¼ hours).

Nuremberg OVF has a daily morning bus (No 8805) from Nuremberg Hauptbahnhof to Rothenburg, which returns late in the afternoon.

Zürich & Berlin BerlinLinienBus (☎ 0130-83 11 44) runs buses between Zürich and Berlin, which pass through Rothenburg (DM96/105, seven hours).

Getting Around

Bus It is possible to do this route using train connections or local buses (see the individual town listings) or by car (just follow the brown 'Romantische Strasse' signs). But many foreign travellers prefer to take the

Europabus, which can get incredibly crowded in the summer. From April until October Europabus runs one coach daily in each direction between Frankfurt and Munich (12 hours), and another in either direction between Dinkelsbühl and Füssen (4½ hours). With either bus you're seeing about half the route. The only way to see all of it is by car.

The bus makes short stops in some towns, but it's silly to do the whole trip in one go (true for car travel, too), since there's no charge for breaking the journey and continuing the next day (you can reserve a seat for the next day before you disembark).

Reservations & Fares Tickets are available for short segments of the trip, and reservations are only necessary at peak-season weekends. For information and reservations, contact Deutsche Touring (☎ 069-790 32 81, fax 790 32 19), Am Römerhof 17, 60486 Frankfurt-am-Main.

The full fare from Frankfurt to Füssen is DM129/258 one-way/return (change buses in Dinkelsbühl, Nördlingen, Augsburg or Munich). Eurail and German Rail passes are valid. Inter-Rail pass-holders and people over 60 get a 50% discount, Europass holders get 30%, and students under 27 get 10% off. Here are the most heavily travelled circuits and the one-way/return fares from Munich:

Augsburg	DM30/60
Frankfurt-am-Main	DM116/232
Nördlingen	DM37/74
Rothenburg ob der Tauber	DM56/112
Würzburg	DM84/168

One-way/return fares from Frankfurt are:

Augsburg	DM98/196
Nördlingen	DM79/158
Rothenburg ob der Tauber	DM59/118
Würzburg	DM33/66

Bicycle With its gentle gradients and ever-changing scenery, the Romantic Road makes an ideal bike trip. Bikes can be rented from most large train stations. Tourist offices in all the towns keep lists of 'bicycle-friendly hotels' that permit storage, as well as providing information on public storage facilities. Radl-Tour (☎ 08191-471 77 or ☎ 09341-53 95) offers nine-day cycling packages along the entire route from Würzburg to Füssen for DM898 per person in double rooms (DM1048 in a single room for the duration), which covers bike rental, accommodation and daily luggage transport.

ASCHAFFENBURG
☎ 06021 • pop 65,000

Situated on the River Main at the foot of the rolling Spessart hills, and home to a magnificent Renaissance palace, Aschaffenburg would be a convenient gateway to the Romantic Road if city elders hadn't placed it on another German holiday route (the *Strasse der Residenzen*). A second domain of the Archbishops of Mainz in the 19th century, the city grew an ugly industrial shell after WWII but retains a charming old centre, with pretty churches and parks. Tucked into Bavaria's north-western corner, Aschaffenburg makes a nice day trip from either Würzburg or Frankfurt.

Orientation & Information

The Hauptbahnhof is on the northern edge of the Altstadt. The city's tourist office (☎ 39 58 00, fax 39 58 02, email info@aschaffenburg.de) is in the Stadthalle on Schlossplatz 1, about 10 minutes' walk from the Hauptbahnhof. It's open Monday to Friday from 9 am to 5 pm, and Saturday from 10 am to 1 pm. The city's Web site is at www.aschaffenburg.de.

Things to See & Do

Once a palace for the Mainz archbishops, the **Schloss Johannisburg** (☎ 224 17) is a model of 17th century German Renaissance (but looks distinctly French, with its bevelled turrets and decorative flair). Today it houses the **Schlossmuseum**, a collection of more than 400 paintings by German and Dutch masters. It's open from April to September, Tuesday to Sunday from 9 am to 5 pm, with a one hour break at noon; from November to March, hours are 11 am to 4 pm (DM5/4).

Behind the manicured hedges of its beautiful **Palace Garden** (Schlossgarten) is

BAVARIA

the **Pompejanum**, a replica of a Pompeii house built for Ludwig I. The Romanesque interior is worth a look, and the leafy gardens and vineyard trickling down the riverbank make for a pleasant walk. It's open from mid-March to mid-October, Tuesday to Sunday from 10 am to 12.30 pm and 1.30 to 5 pm (DM3/2).

From there, Schlossgasse takes you into the heart of the Altstadt, which is peppered with lovely cobbled lanes and half-timbered houses. On Stiftsplatz stands the city's other landmark building, the **Stiftkirche** (957 AD), which has an oddly skewed appearance with its mixture of Romanesque, Gothic and baroque. Its museum (☎ 33 04 63) is home to some intriguing relics and paintings, including Matthias Grünewald's *Lamentation of Christ* (1525). It's open daily except Tuesday from 10 am to 5 pm (DM5/2).

The eastern part of the Altstadt borders on **Park Schöntal**, another place for strolls, with a lake, ruins of a monastery and a **Fasanerie** (pheasantry). Three kilometres west of town lies **Park Schönbusch**, a shady 18th century expanse dotted with ornamental ponds and follies, including the charming **Schlösschen**, a country house of the bishops. There are guided tours in German from mid-March to mid-October daily from 10 am to 12.30 pm and 1.30 to 4.30 pm (DM4/3).

Places to Stay & Eat
Jugendherberge Aschaffenburg (☎ 93 07 63, fax 97 06 94, Beckerstrasse 47) on the southern edge of town charges just DM18 for juniors and seniors, with breakfast. Take bus No 5 to Kneippstrasse (10 minutes).

The *Hotel Pape Garni* (☎ 226 73, fax 226 22, Würzburger Strasse 16), not far from Schlossplatz, charges DM55/95 for singles/doubles.

Goldener Karpfen (☎ 239 46, fax 20 02 54, Löherstrasse 20) is a cosy place focused on the carp theme, with old-fashioned simple rooms from DM55/98 and a decent restaurant. The *Wilder Mann* (☎ 30 20, Löherstrasse 51) offers fine dining even if the interior is a bit dowdy. Regional specialities run from DM15 to DM35.

Getting There & Away
Aschaffenburg is on the regional and high-speed rail line between Frankfurt and Munich, with hourly service to Frankfurt (DM15, 35 minutes), Würzburg (DM19.60, 45 minutes) and Munich (DM95, 3¼ hours). The Frankfurt-Würzburg autobahn A3 runs right past town.

WÜRZBURG
☎ 0931   • pop 127,000
Surrounded by forests and vineyards, the charming city of Würzburg (**vurts**-boorg) straddles the River Main and is the official gateway to the Romantic Road. Although it's little known outside Germany, Würzburg is a centre of art, beautiful architecture and delicate wines.

Würzburg was a Franconian duchy when, in 686, three roving Irish missionaries – Kilian, Totnan and Kolonat – walked in one day and asked Duke Gosbert if he wouldn't mind converting to Christianity and – oh, yes – ditching his wife, the duke's brother's widow. Gosbert was said to be mulling it over when his wife, Gailana, had the three bumped off in 689. When the murders were discovered decades later, the three martyrs were canonised as saints and Würzburg became a pilgrimage city.

In 1720 the architect Balthasar Neumann was called in to design the new residence of the prince-bishops who had ruled the city from the hill-top fortress of Marienberg since the early 13th century; he was joined by Giovanni Battista Tiepolo, who painted the frescoes. Neumann's masterpiece is heralded as containing the finest baroque staircase ever to stand under a fresco (and the fresco itself is not bad either!).

About 90% of Würzburg's centre was destroyed by fire bombing in WWII, but the city has rebuilt with a vengeance. If Würzburg's highlights seem familiar to you, it's because you're rich: you've seen them (and Neumann) on the DM50 note.

Orientation
The train station is at the northern end of the Altstadt, which is shaped like a bishop's hat.

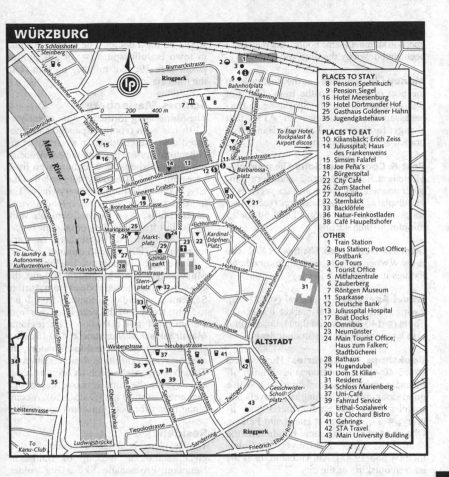

WÜRZBURG

PLACES TO STAY
8 Pension Spehnkuch
9 Pension Siegel
16 Hotel Meesenburg
19 Hotel Dortmunder Hof
25 Gasthaus Goldener Hahn
35 Jugendgästehaus

PLACES TO EAT
10 Kiliansbäck; Erich Zeiss
14 Juliusspital; Haus
   des Frankenweins
15 Simsim Falafel
18 Joe Peña's
21 Bürgerspital
22 City Café
26 Zum Stachel
27 Mosquito
32 Sternbäck
33 Backlöfele
36 Natur-Feinkostladen
38 Café Haupeltshofer

OTHER
1 Train Station
2 Bus Station; Post Office;
   Postbank
3 Go Tours
4 Tourist Office
5 Mitfahzentrale
6 Zauberberg
7 Röntgen Museum
11 Sparkasse
12 Deutsche Bank
13 Juliusspital Hospital
17 Boat Docks
20 Omnibus
23 Neumünster
24 Main Tourist Office;
   Haus zum Falken;
   Stadtbücherei
28 Rathaus
29 Hugendubel
30 Dom St Kilian
31 Residenz
34 Schloss Marienberg
37 Uni-Café
39 Fahrrad Service
   Erthal-Sozialwerk
40 Le Clochard Bistro
41 Gehrings
42 STA Travel
43 Main University Building

The River Main flows north through the western side of the Altstadt; the fortress, camp site, coin laundry and hostel are on the west bank; all the other sights are on the east. The boundaries of the Altstadt are roughly the river at the west and Friedrich-Ebert-Ring/Martin-Luther-Strasse, which runs in a rough circle around the east side and at the enormous roundabout at Berliner Platz, at the north-east corner of the Altstadt.

The stone footbridge, the Alte Mainbrücke, is the main route across the river;

it leads right into Domstrasse and the pedestrianised heart of the Altstadt. The Residenz and the Hofgarten are on the Altstadt's east side.

Information

Tourist Offices The main office is at the rococo masterpiece Haus zum Falken (☎ 37 23 98, fax 37 23 35, email tourismus @wuerzburg.de) on Oberer Markt and is open daily from 10 am to 6 pm (closed Sunday in winter). The branch in the pavilion

BAVARIA

outside the Hauptbahnhof (☎ 37 24 36) opens in summer (same hours), but may have been shut down by the time you read this.

Money Change money at the Postbank, in the post office next to the train station at Bahnhofplatz 2; or at the Sparkasse on Barbarossaplatz, which has an ATM that changes foreign notes. Deutsche Bank has a branch at Juliuspromenade 66.

Post & Communications The main post office is at Bahnhofsplatz 2, and there's another one with telephone and fax services at Paradeplatz. The Stadtbücherei (see Bookshops & Libraries) charges DM1.50 for 15 minutes of Web surfing.

Internet Resources The town's Web site is www.wuerzburg.de, with sights and hotel listings in English.

Travel Agencies STA Travel (☎ 521 76), Zwinger 6, is the local market leader. Go Tours (☎ 140 38) outside the Hauptbahnhof also has some attractive student deals.

Bookshops & Libraries Hugendubel (☎ 35 40 40) has an enormous branch off the main square at Schmalzmarkt 12, with a good stock of English-language novels and travel guides. The Stadtbücherei (city library; ☎ 37 34 38) is at Haus zum Falken, Oberer Markt, in the same building as the main tourist office. The Universitätsbibliothek (☎ 888 59 43), Am Hubland, is at the eastern outskirts of the city.

University You can study just about everything at Julius-Maximilian Universität (☎ 310), Sanderring 2, at the southern end of the Altstadt, but most of the 20,000 or so students are there for medicine or related fields. It was established in 1582.

Laundry The SB-run Waschsalon Waschhaus (☎ 41 67 73), Frankfurter Strasse 13a, is on the west side of the Main and relatively close to the hostel. A load costs DM7, and drying is DM1 for 10 minutes.

Medical & Emergency Services Call ☎ 192 22 for a doctor. The biggest hospital in town is Juliusspital (☎ 39 30), Juliuspromenade 19, five minutes on foot from the train station.

Schloss Marienberg

The Marienberg fortress, begun as early as 1201, has been rebuilt, expanded and renovated over the centuries in a variety of architectural styles. Built as the residence of the prince-bishops of Würzburg who lived here until 1718, it is today the symbol of the city, visible from almost everywhere. The huge castle sits atop the splendid vine-covered hills. It's a lovely 20 minute walk up the hill from the river, or take the twice-hourly bus marked 'Marienberg' from the train station (DM3.30, 15 minutes).

There are two museums. The **Fürstenbau Museum** (☎ 438 38), which features the episcopal apartments, is open from April to September, Tuesday to Sunday from 9 am to 5 pm; the rest of the year, hours are from 10 am to 4 pm (DM4/3). The regional **Mainfränkisches Museum** (☎ 430 16), covers Lower Franconia and local history, including wine exhibits and more statues by Tilman Riemenschneider. Its opening hours and days are the same as above, except that first entry is at 10 am (DM5/2.50). A combined ticket for both museums costs DM6.

Residenz

The Residenz, Neumann's baroque masterpiece, stands at the top of Balthasar-Neumann-Promenade like a big golden horseshoe. The admission (DM8/6) is well worth it. As you enter, the brilliant **Grand Staircase** (inspired by the one in the Versailles Palace) is to the left, a single central set of steps that splits and zigzags up to the 1st floor. Here you'll find Tiepolo's stunning fresco, *The Four Continents*, which depicts Europe as the cultural and financial capital of the world. (Neumann himself is at the bottom of the picture, perched smugly on a cannon.) The **Imperial Hall** and **Spiegelsaal**, in the **Imperial Apartments** upstairs, are just as impressive. Napoleon, who visited here in 1806, called the entire place 'the finest parsonage in Europe'.

Attached is the **Martin-von-Wagner Museum** (☎ 31 22 88), with graphics, 14th to 19th century paintings and Greek masterworks. Admission is free but it's closed on Monday. Behind this, the **Hofgarten** (open dawn to dusk) has spectacular French and English-style gardens and is the site of concerts and special events throughout the year.

Churches
In the Altstadt, the interiors of **Dom St Kilian** and the adjacent **Neumünster** (with crypts said to hold the bodies of Saints Kilian, Totnan and Kolonat), continue the baroque themes of the Residenz. The city Dom, heavily damaged, has been rebuilt around the remaining sections of choir and transept in several styles – Romanesque, Gothic and modern. You either like it or you don't.

Rathaus
At the end of the avenue leading to the Dom stands the Romanesque Rathaus, formerly an administrative seat of the bishops. The green tree still barely visible on its facade symbolises justice. On special occasions, wine was pumped from the ornate fountain in front.

Röntgen Museum
Würzburg's most famous modern scion is Wilhelm Conrad Röntgen, discoverer of the X-ray. The Röntgen Gedächtnisstätte (☎ 30 41 03), at Röntgenring 8, is a tribute to his life and work, and is open Monday to Friday from 9 am to 3 pm (free).

Wine Tasting
The fortified Alter Kranen (old crane), designed by Balthasar Neumann's son to service a dock on the river south of Friedensbrücke, is now the **Haus des Frankenweins** (☎ 120 93), where you can sample and buy some of Franconia's finest wines (for around DM2 per glass). From March to September, every Friday at 3 pm you can go on an hour-long tour (in German, English on request, DM7) of the splendid old wine cellars,

rooms and courtyards of the **Juliusspital** (☎ 393 14 00), Juliuspromenade 19. Tours at the **Bürgerspital** (☎ 35 28 80), Theaterstrasse 19, are just as good but in German only. They run on Saturday at 2 pm (DM7, including a glass of the local vintage).

Organised Tours
From late March to late October the tourist office runs guided city walks (two hours, DM15/12, including admission to the Residenz) from Tuesday to Sunday at 11 am. Meet in front of the Haus zum Falken.

For DM10, you can rent a cassette player and tape from the tourist office in the Haus zum Falken, with an English-language tape guiding you around the major sights.

Special Events
The largest European festival of black music, the **Africa-Festival**, is held in a Woodstock-like venue on the edge of town in late May, complete with tents, food stands and when it rains, lots of mud. Day and festival-long tickets cost DM30/78 at the tourist office.

Thousands flock to the **Mozart Festival** held in the Residenz courtyard from late May to early July (☎ 37 33 36 to reserve tickets). The mood is fantastic, with the golden facade of the palace serving as the ultimate backdrop.

Places to Stay
The nearest camping ground is *Kanu-Club* (☎ 725 36, Mergentheimer Strasse 13b), on the west bank of the Main (take tram No 3 or 5 to Jugendbühlweg). Two/four-person tents are DM3/6, plus DM4 per person.

Jugendgästehaus Würzburg (☎ 425 90, fax 41 68 62, Burkarder Strasse 44) below the fortress charges DM29 for beds (juniors only). Take tram No 3 or 5 from the Hauptbahnhof, alight at the Ludwigsbrücke stop and walk five minutes north along the river.

Two places with absolutely no frills but clean rooms are *Pension Siegel* (☎ 529 41, fax 529 67, Reisgrubenstrasse 7), with single/double rooms from DM48/92; and

BAVARIA

Pension Spehnkuch (☎ 547 52, 547 60, *Röntgenring 7)*, which charges DM50/92.

The *Gasthof Goldener Hahn* (☎ 519 41, *fax 519 61, Marktgasse 7)* offers perhaps the best value for a central location, with basic singles for DM50 and singles/doubles with bath and WC from DM80/140. There's an inviting beer garden, too. The *Hotel Dortmunder Hof* (☎ 561 63, fax 57 18 25, *Innerer Graben 22)* has comparable quarters from DM75/100. *Hotel Meesenburg* (☎ 533 04, fax 168 20, Pleichtorstrasse 8)* has various rooms, from simple singles (DM50) to fully equipped doubles (DM120).

If you have a car, the best option is about 5km east of the centre in the new *Etap Hotel* (☎ 270 82 20, fax 270 82 30, Nürnberger Strasse 129)*, with singles/doubles an outstanding deal for DM37/62. Up in the vineyards, the *Schlosshotel Steinburg* (☎ 970 20, fax 971 21, Auf dem Steinberg)* has well appointed rooms for DM130/190 and, so they claim anyway, a resident ghost.

Places to Eat

For a town its size, Würzburg has a bewildering array of enticing pubs, beer gardens, cafes and restaurants, with plenty of student hang-outs among them.

Restaurants & Cafes The *Café Haupelts-hofer* (☎ 134 17, Sanderstrasse 21)* has a very young, energetic crowd, and good salads and sandwiches. The *City Café* (☎ 145 55, Eichhornstrasse 21)* serves tasty snacks named after film stars for DM10 to DM14, including salads, soups, pastas, pancakes and toasted sandwiches. The *Sternbäck* (☎ 540 56, Sternplatz)*, a pub with 1920s decor and tables outside, has 32 baked-potato varieties from DM5.

One of Würzburg's most popular eating and drinking establishments is *Bürgerspital* (☎ 35 28 80, Theaterstrasse 19)*, a huge, labyrinthine place that was originally a medieval hospice. It offers a broad selection of Franconian wines and regional dishes (average DM16) served in some cosy dining nooks. Don't miss the *Mostsuppe* (DM4.50), a delicious soup made from freshly pressed

grapes. *Juliusspital* (☎ 540 80, Juliuspromenade 19)* is another lovely Weinstube with Franconian delicacies (closed Wednesday).

Mosquito (☎ 510 22, Karmelitenstrasse 31)* is a tiny Mexican place with fajitas, quesadillas and steak dishes for DM10 to DM25. *Joe Pena's* (☎ 57 12 38, Juliuspromenade 1)* is a popular rival with a big vegetarian menu and happy hour between 6 and 8 pm (book tables in advance).

The rustic *Backlöfele* (☎ 590 59, Ursulinergasse 2)* is perfect for a romantic evening under vaulted ceilings, with game, steak and fish dishes from DM20 to DM38 (much cheaper from 2 to 5.30 pm). The beautiful but over-touristed *Zum Stachel* (☎ 527 70, Gressengasse 1)*, behind Unterer Markt, has slightly dearer Franconian fare and a lovely courtyard (closed Sunday).

Snacks & Fast Food On the Kaiserstrasse near the Hauptbahnhof is a *Kiliansbäck*, at No 22, with cheap specials (eg three cheese rolls for DM3.33) and other tasty goodies. Next door, the butcher's *Erich Zeiss* offers chicken and roast pork sandwiches for around DM4.

Doner fans should head for *Simsim Felafel* (☎ 161 53, Pleichtorstrasse 2)*, right around the corner from the congress centre. Run by friendly Palestinians, it has outstanding doner and felafel (but no beer) from DM5. The *Natur-Feinkostladen* (☎ 189 81, Sanderstrasse 2a)* sells health-food snacks (such as grain burgers, DM4) and runs a specialist grocery next door.

Entertainment

Trend is the town's listing magazine. You could easily spend all night at the disco complex at Gattingerstrasse 17, which houses the *Airport* (☎ 237 71), a huge, techno-oriented joint; and *Rockpalast* (☎ 230 80)*, which plays metal for Easy Rider types with long manes. Both are open from Wednesday to Sunday. The *Zauberberg* (☎ 519 49, Veitshöchheimer Strasse 20)* has a healthy mix of soul, dance tunes and other styles. *Omnibus* (☎ 561 21, Theaterstrasse 10)* is the best place for live rock, jazz and folk music.

The Neubaustrasse has several popular student cafe-bars that stay open late and also serve good cheap food. They include *Gehrings* (☎ *129 07*) at No 26; *Le Clochard Bistro* at No 20, with good crepes and a daily *Schneller Teller* (fast dish) for DM9.90; and the hugely popular *Uni-Café* (☎ *156 72*) at No 2, with two floors, cheap snacks and a fun crowd.

Getting There & Away

Würzburg is 70 minutes by train from Frankfurt (DM45) and one hour from Nuremberg (DM42); both Frankfurt-Nuremberg and Hanover-Munich trains stop here several times daily. It is also handy if you want to join Europabus Romantic Road tours – from Rothenburg by bus is DM27 (2½ hours); by train via Steinach it costs DM15.40 (about one hour). The main bus station is next to the train station off Röntgenring. BerlinLinienBus (☎ 0130-83 11 44) runs daily from Berlin (DM89/97 one-way/return, six hours).

The Mitfahrzentrale (☎ 194 40/48 or 140 85) on Bahnhofplatz offers bargains to destinations in Germany and abroad.

Getting Around

The town is best seen on foot, but you can take a bus or tram for DM2.30/3.30 for short/regular journeys. The cheaper ticket will do for trips in town. Call a taxi at ☎ 194 10 (flag fall DM4).

There are several bicycle rental shops, including the Fahrradstation (☎ 574 45) at the Hauptbahnhof, with city/mountain bikes for DM12/17 per day (closed Sunday and Monday). Fahrrad Service Erthal-Sozialwerk (☎ 359 97 39), in the courtyard at Sanderstrasse 27, rents out two-wheelers for DM10 to DM15 (and you can try bargaining for a better deal).

ROTHENBURG OB DER TAUBER
☎ 09861 • pop 12,000

A well polished gem from the Middle Ages, Rothenburg is probably the main tourist attraction along the Romantic Road. Granted the status of a 'free imperial city' in 1274,

the place is full of cobbled lanes and picturesque old houses and enclosed by towered walls. Painfully crowded in summer and during the city's Christmas market, its museums are only open in the afternoon from November to March. Try to wander round in the evening, when the yellow lamplight casts its spell long after the last tour buses have left.

Orientation

The train station is about a five minute walk east of the Altstadt along Ansbacher Strasse. The main shopping drag is Schmiedgasse, and all signs along it are old-fashioned gold or brass ones. (Even McDonald's sports a pair of actual golden arches.) At the south end of the street is the *Plönlein* (little place), a scenic fork in the road with a half-timbered cottage and fountain. This spot has become Rothenburg's unofficial emblem, and is almost too cute for its own good.

Information

At Markt 2 you'll find the supremely helpful tourist office (☎ 404 92, fax 868 07, email info@rothenburg.de), which provides a great range of services, including room bookings. Hours are Monday to Friday, 9 am to 6 pm with a half hour break at 12.30 pm; it's also open Saturday and Sunday from 10 am to 1 pm.

There's a Volksbank with an ATM just to the right of the tourist office on the Markt. Dresdner Bank has a branch at Galgengasse 23.

The main post office is opposite the train station on Ansbacher Strasse, and there's also a small branch at Milchmarkt 5 in the Altstadt. The tourist office has a terminal for surfing on the Net and sending and receiving email, at a stiff DM1 for three minutes. Planet Internet (☎ 93 44 15), Paradiesgasse 8, offers a better deal at DM6 per half hour, and sells drinks (open daily from noon to midnight, Friday and Saturday to 1 am).

The town's excellent Web site (www .rothenburg.de) is also in English.

BAVARIA

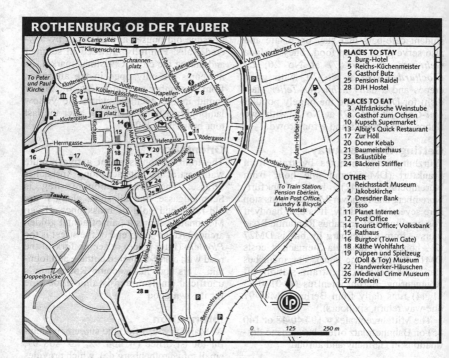

ROTHENBURG OB DER TAUBER

PLACES TO STAY
2 Burg-Hotel
5 Reichs-Küchenmeister
6 Gasthof Butz
25 Pension Raidel
28 DJH Hostel

PLACES TO EAT
3 Altfränkische Weinstube
8 Gasthof zum Ochsen
10 Kupsch Supermarket
13 Albig's Quick Restaurant
17 Zur Höll
20 Doner Kebab
21 Baumeisterhaus
23 Bräustüble
24 Bäckerei Striffler

OTHER
1 Reichsstadt Museum
4 Jakobskirche
7 Dresdner Bank
9 Esso
11 Planet Internet
12 Post Office
14 Tourist Office; Volksbank
15 Rathaus
16 Burgtor (Town Gate)
18 Käthe Wohlfahrt
19 Puppen und Spielzeug
    (Doll & Toy) Museum
22 Handwerker-Häuschen
26 Medieval Crime Museum
27 Plönlein

In the train station, Rothenburger Reisebüro (☎ 46 11) books Europabus and train transport.

The Wäscherei Then (☎ 27 75), at Johannitergasse 9 near the train station, charges DM6.50 per load, and dryers cost DM3 for 25 minutes.

Rathaus

The town hall on the Markt was begun in Gothic style in the 14th century but was completed during the Renaissance. The viewing platform (220 steps) of the **Rathausturm** offers a majestic view over the town and the Tauber Valley. It's open from April to October daily from 9.30 am to 5 pm, with a one hour break at 12.30 pm (DM1).

Jakobskirche

The Gothic Church of St James (1311-22, nave 1373-1436) has glorious stained-glass windows but the highlight is the carved *Heilige Blut* altar by Tilman Riemenschneider, made from 1499 to 1505. It depicts the Last Supper with Judas at the centre, taking bread from Christ. The other characters are set exactly as Tilman said they were in the Bible. There's an entry fee, except during services, of DM2.50/1. It's open daily from 10 am to noon and 2 to 4 pm; tours (in German) run at 11 am and 2 pm.

Medieval Crime Museum

The fascinating and extensive Mittelalterliches Kriminalmuseum (☎ 53 59), south of the Markt at Burggasse 3, displays brutal implements of torture (sorry, 'interrogation') and punishment used in centuries past (DM6/4, DM8 when combined with the Reichsstadt Museum). All exhibits are explained in English. The museum obtained its collections from various towns around the

Drink and Ye Shall Be Free

According to legend, Rothenburg was saved during the Thirty Years' War when the mayor won a challenge by the Imperial General Count Tilly and downed more than 3L of wine at a gulp. It's pretty much accepted that the wine legend is hooey, and that Tilly was placated with hard cash. Nevertheless, the *Meister Trunk* scene is re-enacted by the clock figures on the tourist office building (year round every hour from 11 am to 3 pm and 8 to 10 pm) and in costumed ceremonies in the Kaisersaal in the Rathaus during Whitsuntide (Pentecost) celebrations (mid to late May).

region; the building it is in today is a former hospital. It's open from April to October daily from 9.30 am to 6 pm, November to February from 2 to 4 pm, and during Christmas markets and March from 10 am to 4 pm.

Town Walls & Peter und Paul Kirche

The intact city walls are a 3.5km ring around the city (2.5km are walkable), on the west side of town they offer great views into the Tauber Valley. From this vantage point, you can see the double-deck **Doppelbrücke** bridge in the valley below, which is the best place to watch fireworks displays during the Reichsstadt Festtage (see Special Events). From here, too, you can see the head of a trail that leads down the valley and over to the lovely Peter und Paul Kirche in Detwang, which contains another stunning Riemenschneider altar. There's a beer garden about halfway along the trail.

Also at the west side of the city is the **Burgtor**, a town gate that now houses a **puppet theatre** (☎ 73 54), with shows from June to September, Monday to Saturday at 3 pm and 9 pm (closed Sunday). In April/May and October/November, shows are on the same days at 3 and 8.30 pm. Admission is DM10/7 for afternoon performances, and DM15/10 in the evening.

Reichsstadt Museum

The Reichsstadt Museum (Imperial Town Museum; ☎ 404 58), in a former convent on the Klosterhof, features the superb *Rothenburger Passion* (1494) in 12 panels by Martinus Schwarz, and the **Judaica room**, with a collection of gravestones with Hebrew inscriptions. Outside, the convent **gardens** are a quiet place to shake off the throngs (until a bus tour group walks through every now and then). Admission is DM5/3, or DM8 for a combination ticket to this and the Medieval Crime Museum.

Other Museums

The **Puppen und Spielzeugmuseum** of dolls and toys, at Hofbrunnengasse 13, is the largest private collection in Germany (DM6/4). **Handwerker-Häuschen** (☎ 942 80), Alter Stadtgraben 26, is a reconstruction of medieval life in the city (DM4/2).

Organised Tours

The tourist office holds English-language walking tours year round daily at 2 pm for DM6; meet in front of the Rathaus. Tours lasting 1½ hours (DM5) run at 11 am (in German only) and 2 pm daily (also in English) from Easter to Christmas. A very entertaining walking tour of the Altstadt is conducted every evening by the lantern-toting *Nachtwächter* (night watchman), dressed in his traditional costume. For the English-language tour (DM6), meet at the Markt at 7.55 pm; the German-language version (DM5) heads off at 9.30 pm.

Special Events

A play based on the Meister Trunk is combined with the **Meister Trunk Fest**, an enormous outdoor festival on Whitsunday weekend featuring parades, shows and a huge beer festival. From May to July and September to October, the play is performed on its own. Performances always take place in the Kaisersaal in the Rathaus; tickets range from DM20 to DM30 and are available from the ticket booth on the Markt in front of the tourist office, or at the Kaisersaal cashier.

BAVARIA

euro currency converter DM1 = €0.51

In September, the whole town history is re-enacted during the **Reichsstadt Festtage**, with different eras portrayed in different city streets. It runs from Friday to Sunday, and there's a huge fireworks display, best seen from the Tauber Valley, 10 minutes on foot from the city centre.

Schäfer (traditional shepherd's) dances are held around seven times a year in the Markt (four of which are in June). Tickets range from DM5 to DM8.

Places to Stay

The tourist office can find singles/doubles in hotels and pensions from around DM35/50 (plus a fee of DM2). The 24 hour room referral service number is ☎ 194 12.

The camping options are a kilometre or two north of the town walls at Detwang, west of the road on the river. Signs point the way to *Campingplatz Tauber-Idyll* (☎ 31 77) and the larger *Tauber-Romantik* (☎ 61 91). Both are open from Easter to late October.

Rothenburg's heavily booked *DJH hostel* (☎ 941 60, fax 94 16 20, Mühlacker 1), housed in two enormous renovated old buildings in the south of town, has beds from DM23, including breakfast. It's extremely well equipped (eg a film library in the TV room) and serves decent meals for DM7 to DM9. Reserve ahead or else.

The *Reichs-Küchenmeister* (☎ 97 00, fax 869 65, Kirchplatz 8), a lovely half-timbered house bang in the centre, offers basic singles from DM45 and singles/doubles with en-suite bath from DM90/120.

Pension Eberlein (☎ 46 72, fax 34 99, Winterbachstrasse 4), behind the train station, offers excellent value, with basic rooms from DM55/75. Inside the Altstadt are the *Pension Raidel* (☎ 31 15, Wenggasse 3), which is only slightly more expensive; and the *Gasthof Butz* (☎ 22 01, fax 861 55, Kapellenplatz 4), where rooms with bath cost from DM55/76.

The nicest views in town are from the expensive, family-run *Burg-Hotel* (☎ 948 90, fax 94 89 40, Klostergasse 1), built right into the town fortifications. If you're looking for a romantic getaway and price is no object, this is it – the views are phenomenal. Large double rooms with ugly carpets are DM210 to DM270 in summer and at Christmas, and DM160 to DM180 at other times.

Places to Eat

Bäckerei Striffler (☎ 67 88, Untere Schmiedgasse 1) is an excellent bakery with pastries, breads and a Rothenburg specialty called *Schneeballen* (sweet dough balls dipped in chocolate and nuts). Two cheap options on Hafengasse with sit-down and takeaway food are the imaginatively named *Doner Kebab* at No 2, where the prime dish costs DM6 and up, and *Albig's Quick Restaurant*, a no-pretensions trough at No 3, with German schnitzels with fries and salad from DM10 and burgers from DM2.30.

At *Gasthof zum Ochsen* (☎ 67 60, Galgengasse 26) you'll find light Franconian dishes from DM11 and schnitzels with all the trimmings from DM16.50 (closed Thursday). The *Bräustüble* (☎ 10 88, Alter Stadtgraben 2) has daily set menus for around DM14 and half litres of dark local brew for DM3.40.

The *Altfränkische Weinstube* (☎ 64 04, Klosterhof 7) is a cosy place with friendly, relaxed staff and an open hearth. Guests are treated to a riot of flowers and romantic lighting, and mains are incredibly good value for DM12 to DM18. The salads are particularly inventive.

Baumeisterhaus (☎ 947 00, Schmiedgasse 3) is in an elaborate Renaissance-era house with walls of antlers and a lovely inner courtyard. The daily specials are surprisingly cheap (such as breast of chicken with vegies for DM12.60).

Zur Höll (☎ 42 29, Burggasse 8), near the Medieval Crime Museum, is a Weinstube and a great tavern with a lovely atmosphere in the town's oldest original building. It has a few snacks and main dishes, but the wine list takes centre stage.

Shopping

A one-stop kitsch superstore that's built itself up from a local tourist stand to a powerful city industry, Käthe Wohlfahrt (☎ 40 90) has two main stores and four smaller outlets throughout the city, selling every Christmas trinket you could possibly imagine, and lots and lots of souvenirs. Prices are as you'd expect, but the tourists can't pass up those cuckoo clocks.

Getting There & Away

There's frequent train service from Würzburg (DM16.40, one hour) via Steinach, and Munich (DM77, three hours) via Augsburg. The Europabus stops in the main bus park at the train station. Rothenburg has its own turn-off on the A7 autobahn between Würzburg and Ulm.

Getting Around

The city has five parking lots at strategic points outside the walls (DM5 for up to five hours, or DM10 per day). Use them unless you're willing to shell out DM2 per hour within the Altstadt during the day. Note that the entire centre is closed to nonresident vehicles from 11 am to 4 pm (Sunday to 6 pm), although tourists with a hotel reservation are given access (there are occasional checks). The north-east gate at Würzburger Tor is the only exit that is always open.

Call ☎ 200 00 for taxis (flag fall DM4.50). Or you can rent bicycles at the Esso petrol station (☎ 67 06), Adam-Hörber-Strasse 38, for DM15 per day. Farther away and more expensive, but with a bigger selection, is Rad + Tat (☎ 879 84), Bensenstrasse 17, with bikes for DM25 per day. Horse-drawn carriage rides of 25 to 30 minutes through the city cost about DM10 per person, but you can haggle for a better price with some drivers. You'll find them right in the centre of town.

DINKELSBÜHL

☎ 09851 • pop 11,000

Another walled town of cobbled streets about 40km south of Rothenburg, Dinkelsbühl has a far less contrived feel than its more famous neighbour, as well as fewer tourists and buses. It's a pleasant walk of about an hour around the town's fortified walls, their 16 towers and four gates. Don't

miss the wonderful Museum of the 3rd Dimension, which is a real trip.

Orientation & Information

The Altstadt is five minutes walk south-east of the bus station, which occupies the defunct train station. The city tourist office (☎ 902 40, fax 902 79, email tourismus@ dinkelsbuehl.btl.de), in the centre at Markt 1, is open from April to November, weekdays from 9 am to noon and 2 to 6 pm, Saturday from 10 am to 1 pm and 2 to 4 pm, and Sunday from 10 am to 1 pm. In winter, it shuts at 5 pm on weekdays and is closed on the weekend. The office is also the main Romantic Road tourist information centre (☎ 902 71, fax 902 79).

The main post office is next to the police station, just south of Wörnitzer Tor at the east side of the city. The tourist office rents out bicycles for DM7/35 a day/week.

Weinmarkt

The city's main market square contains the Renaissance Gustav-Adolph and Deutsches Haus buildings. Its star turn, however, is the newly renovated **St Georg Münster**, one of southern Germany's purest late-Gothic churches. A look inside is well worthwhile, using the leaflet in English (DM1). Check out the bejewelled bones of the martyr St Aurelius, who was beheaded by Roman emperor Nero in 64 AD for his faith (the head was later returned to its rightful owner).

Museum of the 3rd Dimension

This museum (☎ 63 36) in Nördlinger Tor is probably the first museum dedicated entirely to simulating acid trips. It has three floors of entertainment, with holographic images, stereoscopic mind-blowers and lots of fun for the whole family. Watch a spiral and then see your hand turn concave; see lots of lovely 3D imagery (especially in the nude section on the 3rd floor) and much more. You can easily spend an hour here; borrow an English-language guide (which unfortunately isn't always available) and follow the numbers. It's open daily year

BAVARIA

round, but with reduced hours in winter. Admission is DM10/8 – it's expensive but worth it.

Organised Tours

There's a free night-watchman's tour in German, from April to November daily at 9 pm (Saturday and Sunday only in winter).

The city tourist office runs hour-long tours through the Altstadt (DM3.50) on Saturday and Sunday at 2.30 pm. They begin opposite the St-Georg-Münster on Weinmarkt. Horse-drawn carriage rides leaving from the same place cost DM7.

Special Events

In the third week of July, Dinkelsbühl celebrates the 10 day **Kinderzeche** (Children's Festival), commemorating a legend from the Thirty Years' War that the children of the town successfully begged the invading Swedish troops to leave Dinkelsbühl undamaged. The festivities include a pageant, re-enactments in the Stadt Festsaal, lots of music and other entertainment. You can order tickets in English at the dedicated Web site (www.kinderzeche.de).

The **Jazz Festival** 'Franken Schwingt' runs around the first weekend in July and involves local and international groups. It takes place throughout the Altstadt, and admission is DM10 per day, or DM25 for the three days.

Places to Stay

The tourist office books rooms (DM6 per person) in *private flats*, which run from about DM25 to DM30 per person, including breakfast.

The *DCC-Campingplatz Romantische Strasse* (☎ 78 17, fax 78 48) is about 300m north-east of Wörnitzer Tor (and well signposted). It costs DM11.50/7/5 per site/ person/car and is open all year.

Dinkelsbühl's *DJH hostel* (☎ 95 09, fax 48 74, Kopengasse 10), just west of the centre in an old granary storehouse, charges DM18 for beds (closed November to February).

The small *Pension Lutz* (☎ 94 54, Schäfergässlein 4) offers singles/doubles for

DM35/70; the owner, Rita, also runs a footcare shop downstairs. The *Fränkischer Hof* (☎ 579 00, fax 57 90 99, Nördlinger Strasse 10) has similar rooms from DM40/80.

The *Gasthof Sonne* (☎ 576 70, fax 74 58, Weinmarkt 11) offers one of the best deals in town: simple rooms, with a superb location on the main drag, for DM45/75. The *Goldene Rose* (☎ 577 50, fax 57 75 75, Marktplatz 4) is a lot better than the chalk tourist boards out front would have you believe, with nice rooms for DM49/98.

Its ornate medieval facade and fine coffered ceilings make *Deutsches Haus* (☎ 60 58, fax 79 11, Weinmarkt 3) one of the town's star attractions. Rooms are a bargain at just DM60/120.

Places to Eat

For fast food, try *Selvi Imbiss* (Nördlinger Strasse 8), with doner kebabs for DM5 and a bevy of Turkish package meals for DM9 to DM13. Stock up on picnic goodies at the supermarket **Tengelmann** (Nördlingerstrasse 13).

Gasthof Sonne (see Places to Stay) on Weinmarkt is a charming place that sets up a beer garden out front in summer, and is nice for people-watching. The *Eisenkrug* (☎ 577 00, Dr-Martin-Luther-Strasse 1) is a much fancier place with a wine cellar to boot. Food at the *Gasthof zum Goldenen Anker* (☎ 578 00, Untere Schmiedgasse 22) is really just as good, with fine Franconian mains averaging DM20.

Just outside Wörnitzer Tor, the *Zum Wilden Mann* (☎ 55 25 25, Wörnitzstrasse 1) is a comfortable brew-pub where a lot of locals go. Three-course specials, including salads and soups, cost between DM12 and DM25. The cosy *Deutsches Haus* (see Places to Stay) at Weinmarkt 3 has very friendly service, and most Franconian dishes cost under DM20.

Getting There & Away

The Europabus stops quite logically at the bus station, as do regional OVF buses to Rothenburg (DM10, one hour) and to Nördlingen (DM8, 40 minutes). By the time you read this, Deutsche Bahn may have resumed train service to Dinkelsbühl.

NÖRDLINGEN
☎ 09081 • pop 21,000
First mentioned 1100 years ago, the town of Nördlingen is still encircled by its original 14th century walls, measuring some 2.7km in diameter and dotted with five gates, 16 towers and two bastions – you can climb the tower of the St Georg Kirche for a bird's-eye view of the town. Nördlingen lies within the Ries Basin, a huge crater created by a megameteor more than 15 million years ago, which released energy nearly 250,000 times that of the bomb dropped on Hiroshima. The crater – some 25km in diameter – is one of the best preserved on earth, and was used by US astronauts to train for the first moon landing. Find out more at the Rieskrater Museum (and ask the watchman at the Daniel Tower, who met the Apollo crew).

Orientation & Information
The train station, which embraces the main post office, is south-east of the city and outside the city walls, about a 15 minute walk from the centre. The city is almost perfectly round, with concentric rings emanating from Markt, and access through the city gates.

The Eger River runs west to east across the very top of the Altstadt. North-east of the Altstadt is the Gerberviertel, the former tanners' quarter, which is packed with charming old buildings. There are free parking lots at all five city gates.

The tourist office (☎ 43 80, fax 841 13, email stadtnoerdlingen@t-online.de), behind the Rathaus at Markt 2, is open from Easter to November, Monday to Friday from 9 am to 6 pm, and Saturday from 9.30 am to 12.30 pm. In winter it's open weekdays from 9 am to 5 pm, and is closed on weekends. You'll find the town's Web site at www.noerdlingen.de.

Gates & Walls
You can circumnavigate the entire city by walking on top of its old walls (they're covered, so you can even do this in the rain).

Admission is free. Climb up at any of the town's five gates: **Baldinger Tor, Löpsinger Tor, Deininger Tor, Reimlinger Tor** and **Berger Tor**. They're all at the end of streets bearing their names.

St Georg Kirche
The late-Gothic Church of St George (1427-1519) is one of the largest in southern Germany. For a great view, climb to the top of the 90m-tall **Daniel Tower** (350 steps). It's open daily from 9 am to 8 pm, but to 5.30 pm in winter (DM3/2). The watchman who lives in the top of the tower – he's a real character, so stop for a chat – sounds out the watch every half-hour from 10 pm to midnight.

Rieskrater Museum
The Ries Crater Museum (☎ 841 43), Hinter der Gerbergasse 3, has examples of other craters, a genuine moon rock (on permanent loan from NASA) and a large display on the geology of the region. It's open Tuesday to Sunday from 10 am to noon and 1.30 to 4.30 pm (DM5/2.50).

Other Museums
The **Stadtmuseum** right in the centre of town has costumes and displays on local history, while the **Stadtmauermuseum**, in Löpsinger Tor, has an exhibition on the history of the town walls and fortification system, paintings of the city through history and a model of the medieval city. They're both closed on Monday.

Organised Tours
Hour-long German-language tours (DM4) leave daily at 2 pm from Easter through to early November in front of the tourist office. English-language tours can be arranged from DM60 for up to 30 people. The Rieskrater Museum offers 1½-hour geological tours of the area in several languages for groups of up to 30 people (DM50).

Special Events
The largest annual celebration is the 10 day **Nördlinger Pfingstmesse** at Whitsuntide/Pentecost (late May to early June). It's an

exhibition of regional traders, with a huge market featuring beer tents, food stalls and the usual entertainment. Tourists love it.

There's also the **Stadtmauerfest**, a three-day blowout every three years in September (the next is in 2001), featuring medieval costumes, huge parades, medieval-style food and grog etc.

The Christmas market is held in the pedestrian zone, along Schrannenstrasse and Bei den Kornschrannen.

Places to Stay

The nearest camping ground, *Erwin & Else Vierkorn* (☎ 07362-35 02), 5km away in Riesberg-Utzmemmingen, is nice and romantic (near an old mill and a pond) but because it's actually in Baden-Württemberg, bus service is difficult, with daytime departures only from the Rathaus in Nördlingen. By car, take the B466 (direction: Ulm), turn right in Holheim and follow the signs. It's DM5 per site plus DM7 per person.

The *DJH hostel* (☎ 27 18 16, Kaiserwiese 1) charges DM18 for juniors (and with cajoling, seniors for DM23.50). Reception is open from April to October daily from 8 to 10 am and 4 to 6 pm (don't arrive later). It's a 10 minute walk, well signposted, north of the centre.

You'll have views of the church at *Gasthof Walfisch* (☎ 31 07, Hallgasse 15), with singles/doubles for DM30/60 (with bath, it's DM50/100). The *Drei Mohren* (☎ 31 13, fax 287 59, Reimlinger Strasse 18) has rooms from DM35/70 (and a decent Swabian restaurant). The renovated *Altreuter Garni* (☎ 43 19, fax 97 97, Markt 11) has nice rooms for DM65/98.

Places to Eat

For a quick bite, the *Kochlöffel (Markt 9)* has half-chickens for DM4.25 and big drinks from DM2.60. The *Café Inle* (*Rübenmarkt 3*), with a street-side bakery behind the St Georg Kirche, has nice filled rolls for takeway (from DM4), and nonalcoholic drinks from DM1.50 (open Sunday, too).

The *Sixenbräu-Stüble* (☎ 31 01, Berger Strasse 17) has typical Swabian specialities

such as *Maultaschen* (big stuffed ravioli, DM9.80) and *Schäufele* (roast pork shoulder, DM15). It's closed on Monday.

Descend into the vaulted-ceiling wine cellar *Kaiserhof* (☎ 50 68, Markt 3), beneath the Hotel Sonne. The restaurant has daily lunch specials from DM13; in the evening, main courses cost around DM20.

La Fontana (☎ 21 10 21, Bei den Kornschrannen 2) is a freshly renovated Italian place in an old blood-red barnhouse, right in front of the kooky fountain. While it looks fancy, pizzas cost just DM7 to DM12 and salads DM4 to DM13, but meat dishes are expensive.

Getting There & Around

Hourly trains connect Nördlingen to Munich (DM36, 1½ hours) via Augsburg (DM19.60, one hour) and Stuttgart (DM32, two hours). The Europabus stops at the Rathaus. The regional VGN bus (No 868) to Dinkelsbühl also stops at the Rathaus (DM5.40, 30 minutes).

You can rent bicycles at Radsport Böckle (☎ 80 10 40), Reimlinger Strasse 19, from DM15 per day; or at Zweirad Müller (☎ 56 75), Gewerbestrasse 16. Call ☎ 16 60 or 877 78 for a taxi (flag fall is DM4).

AUGSBURG

☎ 0821 • pop 256,800

Established by the stepchildren of Roman Emperor Augustus more than 2000 years ago, Augsburg later became a centre of Martin Luther's Reformation: in 1530 the *Confessio Augustana* (Augsburg Confession) set forth the fundamentals of the Lutheran church.

A major trader in gold, silver and copper, Augsburg was an economic powerhouse in the Middle Ages. When Hans-Jakob Fugger arrived here around 1367 he was a weaver; within three generations the Fugger family was one of the wealthiest in Europe.

Today, Bavaria's third-largest city hides its treasures behind a carapace of shopping malls and office blocks, but the centre has a mellow feel that (in summer, anyway) is almost Mediterranean. The city is an easy day trip from Munich, only a half hour ICE-train ride away. But it's seldom used for accommodation during Oktoberfest, and also makes an ideal base for exploring the Romantic Road.

Orientation
The Hauptbahnhof is at the eastern end of Bahnhofsplatz, which runs into Fuggerstrasse at Königsplatz, the city's main bus transfer point. The heart of the Altstadt is Rathausplatz, reached on foot from Königsplatz up Annastrasse.

Information
Tourist Offices Augsburg's main tourist office is at Bahnhofstrasse 7 (☎ 50 20 70, fax 502 07 45, email stadtfuehrengen@regio-augsburg.de). The office is open weekdays from 9 am to 6 pm (to 5 pm in winter). There's a smaller branch at Rathausplatz (☎ 502 07 24) at Maximilianstrasse 4, open weekdays from 9 am to 5 pm, Saturday from 10 am to 4 pm in summer (10 am to 1 pm in winter) and Sunday in summer from 10 am to 1 pm.

Unless noted, all museums in Augsburg are closed on Monday and Tuesday.

Money The Postbank at the Hauptbahnhof has the best commissions on travellers cheques (open Monday to Saturday). Bahnhofstrasse has a slew of banks with ATMs: a Hypovereinsbank at No 11, a Citibank at No 2 and a Deutsche Bank next door.

Post & Communications The main post office is opposite the Hauptbahnhof. Surf the Internet at the Kolping education centre (☎ 344 30), Frauentorstrasse 29 near Mozarthaus, weekdays from 11.30 am to 8 pm (Friday till 5 pm). Half an hour costs DM5.

Internet Resources The town's Web site is www.regio-augsburg.de (with some sections in English).

Travel Agencies Fernweh (☎ 15 50 35), Dominikanergasse 10, is a representative office of STA Travel. Travel Overland (☎ 31 41 57) has an office at Zeuggasse 5.

Bookshops & Libraries Rieger und Kranzfelder Buchhandlung (☎ 349 08 10), in the Fugger Haus at Maximilianstrasse 36, is an enormous place with English-language books and everything else. The Stadtbibliothek (☎ 324 27 39) is at Schaezlerstrasse 25; the Stadtbücherei (☎ 324 27 56) is right in the centre at Gutenbergstrasse 2.

Laundry The Waschcenter HSB (☎ 41 94 51), Wolfgangstrasse 1 (take tram No 2), is open daily from 6 am to 11.30 pm; there's also Karkosch, at Vorderer Lech 27.

Medical Services The most central hospital is the Zweckverband (☎ 400 01), Stenglinstrasse 2. For a doctor or ambulance, call the Rotes Kreuz (Red Cross) on ☎ 192 22.

Rathausplatz
The twin onion-dome topped spires of the city's town hall (1615-20) dominate the pedestrianised Rathausplatz. Destroyed in 1944, the Rathaus was reconstructed from 1947 to 1962. Topping the building is a pine cone, Augsburg's emblem (also an ancient fertility symbol). Inside the lobby you can see the original **statue of Kaiser Augustus** that used to top the Renaissance **Augustus Brunnen** (fountain) in the square (which has a replica today).

Upstairs, the **Goldener Saal**, a dazzling restoration of the city's main meeting hall, is worth the DM2 entry. It's open daily from 10 am to 6 pm. Just 2.6kg of gold was used to cover the whole place with a thin layer of gold leaf, and the 14m-high, 32m-long room is spectacular.

Next to the Rathaus is the **Perlachturm**, a former guard tower. You can climb to the top (DM2/1) from April to September daily from 10 am to 6 pm (and in October to 4 pm) for a city panorama.

The square attracts throngs of people year round – at outdoor cafes in summer and for the Christmas market in December.

euro currency converter   DM1 = €0.51

BAVARIA

Dom

The Dom Mariae Heimsuchung (9th to 14th centuries), on Hoher Weg north of Rathausplatz, has amazing bronze doors at the south end, with 35 relief panels. The crypt, which dates to 1065, has a typical round Roman Madonna, and they say that passages leading from here went all the way to Ulrich Kirche at the other side of town. In the centre of the church is the *Weingartner Altar* by Hans Holbein the Elder. While modern 1960s glass mars some of the windows, others of medieval glass, dating to at least the 11th century, are spectacular.

St Anna Kirche

This former Carmelite monastery (1321) was expanded over the centuries and finally converted to a Protestant church; appropriate, since Luther himself slept here when in Augsburg. Inside the church are artworks by Lucas Cranach the Elder. It's closed Monday.

Fuggerei

One of the earliest welfare settlements, the charming little three-room houses and one-room widow's flats of the Fuggerei were established by Jakob Fugger in 1521 to provide homes for poor Catholics. The rent here is DM1.72 per *year*, plus utilities and a daily prayer. It's a nice place to walk through. To see how Fuggerei residents of the past lived, stop in at the **Fuggerei Museum**. It's open from March to October daily from 9 am to 6 pm (DM1/0.50), and is next door to the former home of Franz Mozart, Wolfgang Amadeus' great-grandfather, who lived here for 12 years. Gates close from 10 pm to 6 am (5 am in summer); residents returning after 10 pm are fined DM0.50, and after midnight a whole DM1! The chalk markings on the doors are placed there by priests blessing the houses on Epiphany (6 January).

Brecht Haus

The family home of the playwright and poet Bertolt Brecht, on the canal at Am Rain 7, is now the Bertolt-Brecht-Gedenkstätte, a museum dedicated to Brecht and the work of young artists. Brecht's work was banned by the Nazis for his communist leanings; he was later shunned by West Germans for the same reason, and it's only recently that the city has honoured one of its most heralded sons. It's open Wednesday to Sunday from 10 am to 6 pm (DM3). For more on Brecht, see the boxed text in the Berlin chapter.

Maximilianstrasse

This grand boulevard is more conventionally styled than the rest of the city, although one of Luther's more unconventional anti-papal documents was posted here after he was run out of town in 1518. Highlights of the street include the cafes; the **Mercur Brunnen** (a fountain with a statue of Mercury); and the restored **Fugger Haus** at No 36-38, the former residence of Jakob Fugger.

The **Schaezler Palais** (1765-70) is the rococo palace built for banker Liebert von Liebenhofen; today it's open as the German baroque art gallery and the Bavarian art gallery. Its inconceivably lavish ballroom makes the Goldener Saal in the Rathaus look shabby. It's open from October to April daily from 10 am to 4 pm, and to 5 pm in summer (DM4/2.50).

Synagogue

Synagogue Augsburg (☎ 51 36 58), Halderstrasse 8, right behind the tourist information office on Bahnhofstrasse, is an Art Nouveau temple (built 1914-17). Inside is the excellent **Jewish Cultural Museum**, with exhibitions on Jewish life in the region, Germany and Central Europe. It's open Tuesday to Friday from 9 am to 4 pm, Sunday from 10 am to 5 pm, and is closed Saturday and Monday (DM3/2). Tours are given most Wednesday evenings at 6 pm.

Marionette Theatre

The celebrated **Augsburger Puppenkiste** (☎ 43 44 49), next to the Heilig-Geist-Spital at Spitalgasse 15, holds performances of classic fairy tales such as *Puss in Boots* several times a week at 3 pm (tickets DM8 to DM14) and 7.30 pm (DM15 to DM22). The sets and costumes are fantastically elaborate, and half the fun is listening to the kids in the audience squeal in delight. Call ☎ 43 21 82 for advance bookings and program details.

Places to Stay

Campingplatz Augusta (☎ 70 75 75, fax 70 58 83) is 7km from the Augsburg Ost autobahn interchange north-east of the city. Apart from camp sites, it has a few family rooms. Bus Nos 301, 305 and 306 depart at least once an hour (DM4.80 each way) from the bus station.

The *DJH hostel* (☎ 339 09, fax 15 11 49, Beim Pfaffenkeller 3) is slightly down-at-heel but central. You can get a bed (if you're under 27) for DM20, plus DM5.50 for linen. From the station, take tram No 2 (direction: Kriegshaber) to Mozarthaus, then walk east on Mittleres Pfaffengässchen.

You can book pensions, which range from DM35 for singles and DM65 to DM80 for doubles, at the tourist offices. There's a charge of DM3 per room.

Behind the Hauptbahnhof is *Lenzhalde* (☎ 52 07 45, fax 52 87 61, Thelottstrasse 2), with simple single/double rooms from DM40/75.

Perhaps the best value in Augsburg is the *Jakoberhof* (☎ 51 00 30, fax 15 08 44, Jakobstrasse 39-41), a simple place with a decent Bavarian restaurant downstairs, and rooms from DM45/65. Also in this range is the *Hotel von den Rappen* (☎ 21 76 40, fax 217 64 60, Äussere Uferstrasse 3), where a modern bathless single goes for DM50, and doubles with WC and shower run to DM82. Another good one is the pleasant *Georgsrast* (☎ 50 26 10, fax 502 61 27, Georgenstrasse 31), run by a gaggle of older women, which offers rooms with WC and bath from DM65/85.

The *Privat Hotel Ost am Kö* (☎ 50 20 40, 502 04 44, Fuggerstrasse 4-6) is a whole lot better inside than the 1960s cube architecture would have you believe. As well as very friendly service, it has large, clean rooms without bath for DM89/130, and DM99/148 with bath and WC.

Right near the Hauptbahnhof are the *Ibis Beim Hauptbahnhof* (☎ 501 60, fax 501 61

50, Halderstrasse 25), with modern if sparse rooms from DM104.90/119.90; and the *InterCity Augsburg* (☎ 503 90, fax 503 99 99, Halderstrasse 29), with the usual InterCity rooms from DM140/160.

The *Steigenberger Drei Mohren Hotel* (☎ 503 60, 15 78 64, Maximilianstrasse 40) is a stunning place with rooms from DM239/350, right next to Fugger Haus.

Places to Eat

Cafes & Restaurants The *Café bei den Barfüssern* (☎ 15 93 08, Kanalstrasse 2), next to the Protestant Barfüsser Kirche, is a wonderful place to sit; it makes its own cakes and pastries, and you can sit outside next to the little canal. There are lots of cafes along Maximilianstrasse, including the *Max* and *Amadeus*, just in front of the Mercury fountain. *Café Stadler* (☎ 15 30 19, Bahnhofstrasse 30) has pastas for DM9 to DM11.

A local favourite – with enormous portions of good Bavarian food – is the *Bauerntanz* (☎ 15 36 44, Bauerntanzgässchen 1), which offers good deals at lunchtime (when main courses average about DM14). There's outdoor seating in nice weather.

The historic *Gasthaus zum Weissen Hasen* (☎ 51 85 08, Unter dem Bogen 4) has cheap lunch menus (eg veal ragout and asparagus, DM10) and lots of Bavarian-Swabian dishes for under DM20.

The decor at the *Fuggereistube* (☎ 308 70, Jakobstrasse 26), next to the north gate of the Fuggerei, is vintage 1970s hunting-lodge but the Bavarian food and service are very good. The leek soup (DM4.50) is delicious, and the tender pork loin with homemade noodles and salad (DM24) is a real treat.

Beer Gardens The three coolest are *Thing* (Vorderer Lech 45); *Lug Ins Land*, in the park at the northern tip of the Altstadt at Herwartstrasse; and *3 Königinnen (Meister-Veits-Gässchen 32)*, south of the Fuggerei. Right behind Maximilianstrasse, the outrageous *Zeughaus* (☎ 51 16 85, Zeughausplatz 4) was a 17th century armoury that is now a trade school, cinema and a superb place for a brew. It also offers tasty vegetarian dishes.

BAVARIA

Snacks & Fast Food *Farmers' markets* take place Monday to Friday from 7 am to 6 pm (to 1 pm on Saturday) between Fugger-strasse and Annastrasse. They have every-thing – from Thai to Bavarian and back.

The gleaming *Seval Imbiss* (☎ 395 18, *Karrengässchen 1)*, near the Fuggerei, has absolutely splendid doners for DM6. The bakery *Schuster* (☎ 56 08 50, *Provino-strasse 51)* has filled croissants and other goodies from DM3.

Getting There & Away
There are frequent RE and RB trains be-tween Augsburg and Munich (DM23.40, 30 minutes), Nuremberg (DM32, 1½ hours) and Würzburg (DM41.80, 2½ hours). The ICE trains are faster but more expensive. Connections to Regensburg take two hours via Munich (DM54). Augsburg is just off the A8 autobahn north-west of Munich. The Ro-mantic Road bus stops at the Hauptbahnhof.

The Mitfahrzentrale (☎ 15 70 19), Bart-hof 3, can arrange ride-shares for travellers for a modest fee.

Getting Around
Short rides on the bus and tram network cost DM1.70; two-zone rides are DM3.20. A day ticket costs DM8. The Lufthansa air-port bus (☎ 502 25 34) runs between Bahn-hofstrasse and Munich's airport eight times a day (last departure at 4.40 pm). The 50 minute ride costs DM32.

For bicycle rental, Bäuml (☎ 336 21), Jakobstrasse 70, has a good range of bikes from DM10/60 per day/week for a touring bike, DM15/65 for a trekking bike or DM30/120 for a tandem. If you have a rail pass or BahnCard, you get a 20% discount.

FÜSSEN
☎ 08362 • pop 17,000
After passing through the 1000-year-old Donauwörth, north of Augsburg at the con-fluence of the Danube and Wörnitz rivers, and Schongau, a lovely medieval town in the Alpine foothills, the road continues to Füssen, just short of the Austrian border. Füssen has a monastery, a castle and some

splendid baroque architecture, but the crowds flock here mainly for the famous cas-tles nearby: Neuschwanstein, Hohenschwan-gau and Linderhof, all legacies of mad King Ludwig II (see the Around Füssen section).

Orientation & Information
Füssen's Hauptbahnhof is at the western end of the city, about a three minute walk from the tourist office, the slick Kurverwaltung Füssen (☎ 938 50, fax 93 85 20, email kurverwaltung@fuessen.de) at Kaiser Max-imilian Platz 1, and behind the Sieben Stein Brunnen, a fountain with as many stone pil-lars. The town's Web site (www.fuessen.de) has a decent English-language section.

Neuschwanstein and Hohenschwangau are 4km to the east; Linderhof is an hour's drive towards Garmisch-Partenkirchen.

Museums
The **Museum of Füssen** in the Rathaus houses art, historical and cultural artefacts of the area, and its exquisite baroque inte-rior is just as good. It's open from April to October daily from 11 am to 4 pm, and the rest of the year from 2 to 4 pm (DM5/4). The **St Anna Kapelle**, the oldest wing of the monastery's church, is entered through the museum. On a hill above the town is the **Staatsgalerie im Hohen Schloss**, the former residence of the prince-bishops of Augs-burg, now a museum of religious artwork. It's open from April to October, Tuesday to Sunday from 11 am to 4 pm, and in winter from 2 to 4 pm (DM4/3).

Cable Car
Tickets for the Tegelbergbahn (☎ 983 60) are a bit, ahem, steep at DM25 but worth the dazzling views of the Alps and Forggensee. The mountain station is also a prime launch point for hang-gliders and parasailers; after an apple strudel in the restaurant, it's a wonderful hike down to the castles (follow the signs to Königsss-chlösser) in about two or three hours. The cable car runs in summer from 8.30 am to 5 pm, and in winter from 9 am to 4.30 pm (last ascent/decent is 30 minutes before

closing). To get there, take the RVA No 9713 bus from Füssen Hauptbahnhof to the Tegelbergbahn valley station.

Pleasure Flights & Hang-Gliding
A bird's eye view of this spectacular scenery isn't to be missed, and hired wings are the best way to do it. The Luftsportverein Füssen (☎ 08363-1639) at the Füssen airstrip offers glider trips around Neuschwanstein and Hohenschwangau (DM50, 30 minutes), and to the Zugspitze (DM100, one hour). Prices are similar for motor flights from Deutscher Alpenflug (☎ 0831-659 29) at Kempten-Durach airport.

If that sounds too tame, ride the air currents on a hang-glider or parasailer. The teachers at Aktiv Flugsport (☎ 98 34 54), Bullachbergweg 34a in Schwangau, charge DM150 for a day's instruction and equipment. Weekend courses cost DM250.

Places to Stay
There are several camping options near the castles; get the full list from the Schwangau tourist office (☎ 819 80), near the bus stop at the foot of the castles. From Schwangau, bus No 9715 takes you to *Campingplatz Bannwaldsee* (☎ 810 01, fax 82 30, Münchner Strasse 151), with camp sites from DM13 right on the Forggensee. With a car, the best bet is *Brunnen am Forggensee* (☎ 82 73, fax 817 38, Seestrasse 81) at the southern end of the Forggensee, which charges DM10.50 per person and DM10.50 per site.

Füssen's *DJH hostel* (☎ 77 54, fax 27 70, Mariahilferstrasse 5) is by the train tracks, 10 minutes west of the station. Dorm beds cost DM20 plus the Kurtaxe (DM1.20 to DM3), and curfew is a tourist-unfriendly 10 pm. The hostel is closed from mid-November to Christmas. Reserve early – showing up without a reservation is really pushing your luck.

The central *Hotel Alpenhof* (☎ 323 2, Theresienstrasse 8) has attractive singles/doubles from DM40/75. The *Hotel zum Hechten* (☎ 916 00, fax 91 60 99, at Ritterstrasse 6) has a fine spot near the main square and a quiet rear courtyard, with rooms from DM60/100.

The tourist office has lists of *private rooms* from DM30 per person. In Füssen there's a resort tax of DM3 per person per night (DM2.40 in the off-season).

Places to Eat
Schinagl (☎ 61 39, Brunnengasse 20) is a great bakery with wonderful pastries and breads. Weigh in at *Infooday* (Ritterstrasse 6), open weekdays to 6.30 pm and Saturday to 1 pm, where 100g of hot buffet food costs just DM2.53. Take away or eat in the glassed-in patio at the rear.

For restaurant dishes, check out the old *Franziskaner Stüberl* (☎ 371 24), on the corner of Ritterstrasse and Kemptener Strasse, which specialises in delicacies like roast trotters served with beer sauce and rye bread (DM11).

Next to the old fire station, *Weizenbierbrauerei* (☎ 63 12) has great beer and Bavarian specialities served by really nice staff (closed Friday). House specials range from DM13 to DM17, Schweinebraten from DM12.50 and daily lunch specials from DM12 to DM14.

Getting There & Away
From Munich (DM34, 2½ hours), the best train to catch to beat the crowds is the one that no one in their right mind would want: the No 4500 at 4.57 am, changing for the 6.31 am train at Biessenhofen and arriving at 7.23 am in Füssen. The most popular early train is the 6.50 am (No 5862), changing at Buchloe for the 7.46 am, arriving in Füssen at 8.57 am. Subsequent trains include ones at 7.52, 8.52 and 10.52 am; return trains run at five minutes past the hour until 11.05 pm. Always check schedules before you go.

If you're continuing into Austria by car, now's a good time to pick up a *Vignette* (fee sticker) required for Austrian motorways (not other roads). A one week permit costs DM10.50 for cars, DM7 for motorcycles.

Getting Around
The RVA buses go to the Neuschwanstein and Hohenschwangau castles (see Getting There & Away in the following section).

BAVARIA

With the Alps on one side and the lake-filled plains on the other, the area around Füssen is a cyclist's paradise. The cheapest rental is Hohenrainer Alwin (☎ 396 09), in the Altstadt at Hintere Gasse 13, with city, mountain and trekking bikes from DM10 per day (open daily). Two-wheelers at the Kurhotel Berger (☎ 913 30), Alatseestrasse 26, also cost just DM10. Radsport Zacherl (☎ 32 92), Rupprechtstrasse 8½, has a much bigger selection than the others, from DM12/14 per day in off-peak/peak season.

AROUND FÜSSEN
Schloss Neuschwanstein & Hohenschwangau

The castles provide a fascinating glimpse into Ludwig II's state of mind. Fortunately they're practically next to one another, so you can visit both on the same day. Hohenschwangau is where Ludwig lived as a child, but more interesting is the adjacent **Neuschwanstein**, which appears through the mountain-top mist like a kooky mirage.

Ludwig's own creation, it's perhaps the world's best known castle; the fantastic pastiche of architectural styles inspired Walt Disney's Sleeping Beauty Castle. Begun in 1869 and never finished, the grey-white granite castle was an anachronism from the start; by the time Ludwig died in 1886, the first New York skyscrapers were being built. For all the money spent on it, the king himself spent just 100-odd days there.

The initial blueprint was laid out by a theatre designer rather than an architect, which accounts for its dramatic packaging. Ludwig himself got the original idea of a high-standing castle from a visit to the Wartburg in Thuringia, where the bards used to hold singing competitions (see Eisenach in the Thuringia chapter). The muses lived 'here with us at stony heights, with heaven's zephyrs all around', as the king wrote to Richard Wagner.

Neuschwanstein was built at a lofty 200m above the valley floor, and its centrepiece became the lavish **Sängersaal** (Minstrels' Hall), so that Ludwig could feed his obsession with Wagner and medieval knights. (Wall frescoes in the hall depict scenes from the opera *Tannhäuser*). Though it wasn't used during Ludwig's time, concerts are now held there every September; contact the Hohenschwangau tourist office at ☎ 08362-819 80 for details.

Other completed sections include Ludwig's **bedroom**, a gaudy **artificial grotto** (another allusion to *Tannhäuser*) and the Byzantine **Thronsaal**. The sleeping chamber is dominated by a huge Gothic-style bed that bears a wood carving of a skyline. The throne room is in fact throneless, as Ludwig was removed before one could be constructed.

There are some wonderful walks you can do around the castle. For a great view of Neuschwanstein and the plains beyond, walk 10 minutes up to Marienbrücke (Mary's Bridge), which spans the spectacular Pöllat Gorge over a waterfall just above the castle. Down the other way lies the aquamarine Schwansee, a nature reserve.

Hohenschwangau was originally built by Schwangau knights during the 12th century, but its current visage stems from the 1830s. It's much less ostentatious outside, sporting a yellow neo-Gothic facade atop a modest hill just south of the grand Neuschwanstein, and the interior has a distinct lived-in feeling. Certain chambers are just as spooky as in Neuschwanstein, however. After his father Maximilian II died, Ludwig had stars painted on the ceiling of his royal bedroom; these were illuminated with hidden oil-lamps while his highness slumbered.

It was here that Ludwig first met Wagner, and the **Hohenstaufensaal** features a square piano where the bombastic composer would entertain Ludwig with excerpts from his latest effort. Some rooms have frescoes from German history and legends (including the Wagner subject Lohengrin, the Swan Knight).

Tickets & Tours The guided tours get awfully crowded after about 9.30 am, when train tourists from Munich arrive, so go

Ludwig II, the Fairy-Tale King

Few monarchs evoke an image as romantic (and ludicrous) as Ludwig II (1845-86), the last member of the Wittelsbach dynasty, which ruled Bavaria for nearly 800 years. As a patron of the arts, technology freak and recluse – and above all, builder of impossibly lavish castles – Ludwig was ready-made for the state's tourism industry, which opened his chambers to visitors just days after his death.

When the 18-year-old Prinz Otto Ludwig Friedrich Wilhelm ascended the Bavarian throne in 1864, a lonely and joyless childhood lay behind him. His parents, Maximilian II and Marie, took little interest in the romantic epics, architecture and music that fascinated the sensitive youth. In 1867, the king was engaged briefly to the sister of Elisabeth (Sisi), the Austrian empress, but as a rule he preferred the company of male hangers-on in the royal court. He also worshipped composer Richard Wagner, whose Bayreuth opera house was erected with Ludwig's funds.

Bavaria's days as a sovereign state were numbered, and Ludwig became a puppet king after the creation of the German Reich in 1871 (which had its advantages, as Bismarck gave Ludwig a hefty allowance). Never an enthusiastic leader, Ludwig now withdrew completely to drink, draw castle blueprints and view concerts and operas in private (he saw more than 200 on his own). His obsession with French culture and the 'Sun King', Louis XIV, inspired the fairy-tale fantasies of Neuschwanstein, Linderhof and Herrenchiemsee – incredibly expensive projects that spelt his undoing.

The castles ate up Ludwig's private fortune as well as substantial amounts of the state budget. As the bills mounted, several ministers and relatives arranged a hasty psychiatric test and in January 1886, Ludwig was diagnosed as mentally unfit to rule. That June he was removed to Schloss Berg, an asylum on Lake Starnberg. One evening the dejected bachelor – at 41, he was friendless, throneless and toothless – and his doctor took a lakeside walk and were found several hours later, drowned in just a few feet of water. The exact cause was never determined, although one leading theory implicates Prince-Regent Luitpold (who ruled after Ludwig's death).

That summer the authorities decided to open Neuschwanstein to the public to help pay off Ludwig's huge debts. Admission was stiff but the place was an instant hit, and today the three *Königsschlösser* are among Bavaria's biggest money-spinners – not to mention all those Ludwig T-shirts, beer mugs and ashtrays.

DAVID PEEVERS

Ludwig brought his fantasy to life with Neuschwanstein.

BAVARIA

early. Tickets to either palace cost DM12/9. When you reach the gate at Neuschwanstein, get in the line of the language of your choice; obligatory tours leave when there are enough people.

Neuschwanstein is open from April to September daily from 9 am to 5.30 pm, and October to March from 10 am to 4 pm. Hohenschwangau is open from mid-March to mid-October daily from 8.30 am to 5.30 pm, and mid-October to mid-March from 9.30 am to 4.30 pm.

The expense of an organised tour is worth it. EurAide's excellent three-castle tours visit Linderhof, Neuschwanstein and Hohenschwangau, along with Wieskirche. It's the best deal around – DM75 per person, including transportation – and leaves every Wednesday in summer from the EurAide office in Munich. Sign up as soon as you get to town, as it fills up fast.

If all that isn't enough Ludwig for you, from March 2000 the Musical Theater Neuschwanstein will stage an evening production in Füssen on the life and times of the Fairy-Tale King. To reserve tickets (costing a regal DM85 to DM230 for the three hour performance), call ☎ 01805-58 39 44.

Getting There & Away

Some fast and loose tourist information suggests easy train and bus links from Munich to Linderhof, Neuschwanstein and Hohenschwangau in one day, but if you miss one connection you've had it. Check with DB, EurAide in Munich or the Füssen tourist office before setting out. Munich train connections are listed in the Füssen Getting There & Away section.

By bus from Füssen, take the RVA bus No 9713 from the Hauptbahnhof (DM4.80 return, 10 minutes), share a taxi (around DM14) or walk the 5km. From the bus stop, it's a 20 to 30 minute walk up the hill to the castle entrance at Neuschwanstein, or a slightly longer trip by horse-drawn carriage (DM8 uphill, DM4 downhill). From Garmisch-Partenkirchen Hauptbahnhof, take the bus to Hohenschwangau (five daily, DM13, two hours).

Wieskirche

In the late spring of 1743, a farmer in Steingaden, a town on the Romantic Road northeast of Füssen, witnessed the miracle of his Christ statue crying. Over the next few years so many pilgrims poured into the town that the local abbot commissioned a new church to house the weepy work.

Enter master craftsman Dominikus Zimmermann, from nearby Landsberg, who supervised the construction of what became known as Wieskirche (1746-56). The church is an astounding festival of baroque. Admission is free.

At least three buses per day make the trip from Füssen. By car from Munich, head west on the A96 to Landsberg, then turn south on the B17 towards Füssen. From Füssen, take the B17 north-east and turn right (east) at Steingaden. The church is clearly signposted.

Bavarian Alps

Stretching west from Germany's remote south-eastern corner to the Allgäu region near Lake Constance, the Bavarian Alps (Bayerische Alpen) take in most of the mountainous country fringing the southern border with Austria.

The year-round resort of Garmisch-Partenkirchen is Munich's favourite getaway spot, though nearby Mittenwald is a less hectic alternative. Other suitable bases from which to explore the Bavarian Alps are Berchtesgaden, the Tegernsee area, Füssen (see the previous Romantic Road section) and Oberstdorf.

While not as high as their sister summits farther south in Austria, the Bavarian Alps rise so abruptly from the rolling hills of southern Bavaria that their appearance seems all the more dramatic.

For those with the time, energy and money, the Bavarian Alps are extraordinarily well organised for outdoor pursuits, though naturally skiing (or its increasingly popular variant, snowboarding) and hiking have the biggest following.

The ski season usually begins in late December and continues into April. Ski gear is available for hire in all the resorts; the lowest daily/weekly rates including skis, boots and stocks are around DM20/90 (downhill), DM12/60 (cross-country) and DM30/110 (snowboard). Five-day skiing courses (15 hours total) cost around DM190.

The hiking season goes from late May right through to November, but the higher trails may be icy or snowed over before mid-June or after October.

Large lakes are another feature of the landscape and are ideal for water sports. Rafting, canoeing, mountain biking and paragliding are popular summer activities.

Most of the resorts have plenty of reasonably priced guesthouses and private rooms, though it's still a good idea to ring ahead and book accommodation. Tourist offices can help you find a room; otherwise, look out for 'Zimmer frei' (vacancy) signs.

During the busy winter and summer seasons, some places levy a surcharge (usually at least DM5 per person) for stays of less than two or three days. In most resorts a Kurtaxe (usually an extra DM3 per night) is levied, but as a tax-paying guest you're usually entitled to certain perks, like free tours, city bus service and entry to special events.

Getting Around

While the public transport network is very good, the mountain geography means there are few direct routes between main centres; sometimes a short-cut via Austria works out to be quicker (such as between Garmisch and Füssen or Oberstdorf). Travelling by road rather than rail routes are often more practical.

For those with private transport, the German Alpine Road (Deutsche Alpenstrasse) is a more scenic way to go – though obviously much slower than the autobahns and highways that fan out across southern Bavaria.

Regional (RVO) passes giving free travel (with certain route restrictions) on the upper-Bavarian bus network between Füssen and Salzburg are excellent value; the day pass is DM13/6.50 for adults/children, and a pass giving five free days travel within one month costs DM40/20.

GARMISCH-PARTENKIRCHEN

☎ 08821 • pop 27,000

The combined resort towns of Garmisch-Partenkirchen were merged by Adolf Hitler to host the 1936 Winter Olympics. The reason they stayed merged is because their location is the best ski gateway in southern Germany. With access to four ski fields, including ones on Germany's highest mountain, the Zugspitze (2963m), the town is a favourite destination for skiers, hikers, snowboarders and mountaineers.

The huge ski stadium on the slopes right outside town has two ski jumps and a slalom course; it hosted more than 100,000 people for the 1936 Winter Olympics and is still used for professional competitions.

About 20km west of town is Ludwig II's charming Schloss Linderhof (see the Around Garmisch-Partenkirchen section). Garmisch can also serve as a base for excursions to Ludwig's extravagant castles, Hohenschwangau and Neuschwanstein, near Füssen (see the earlier Romantic Road section for more information); regular daily RVO buses from Garmisch to Füssen pass by Neuschwanstein en route (two hours each way).

Orientation & Information

The railway tracks that divide the two towns run right down the centre to the Hauptbahnhof. From it, turn east on St-Martin-Strasse to get to Garmisch and west on Bahnhofstrasse to get to Partenkirchen.

The tourist office (☎ 18 06, fax 18 07 55, email tourist-info@garmisch-partenkirchen .de), on Richard-Strauss-Platz, is open Monday to Saturday from 8 am to 6 pm, and Sunday and holidays from 10 am to noon.

Change money at the Commerzbank at Marienplatz 2a. The post office is across the street from the Hauptbahnhof. The town's Web site (www.garmisch-partenkirchen.de) has English sections.

BAVARIA

Skiing

The Zugspitze offers some of the most breathtaking views around. In winter, of course, it has some pretty amazing skiing. In summer, it offers spectacular hiking. Other than climbing the thing (see Hiking), there are two options for ascending – a cable car and a cog-wheel train *(Zahnradbahn)*, both a lot of fun.

On a standard day ticket, the cost for the two is the same; there are some discounts available for the train in conjunction with a train trip from Munich.

Both are spectacularly crowded at peak times in winter (around Christmas, New Year and festivals) and through much of the summer. Skiers may find it easier, if a little slower, to schlep their gear up on the train, which offers exterior ski-holders. Call ☎ 79 79 79 for a weather or snow report.

Ski Areas Garmisch is bound by four separate ski-fields: the Zugspitze plateau (the highest area), the Alpspitze/Hausberg (the largest area) and the Eckbauer and Wank areas (yes, Wank residents do jokingly say '*Ich bin ein Wanker*').

Day ski passes cost DM61 for Zugspitze (though this includes the cable car or Zahnradbahn ride up to the top), DM47 for Alpspitze/Hausberg, DM33 for Wank and DM28 for Eckbauer. The Happy Ski Card covers all four areas, but it's only available for a minimum of three days (DM143, or DM190 for four days).

Cross-country ski trails run along the main valleys, including a long section from Garmisch to Mittenwald.

Ski Hire Flori Wörndle (☎ 583 00) has the cheapest rates for ski hire (as well as convenient outlets at the Alpspitze and Zugspitze lifts). For skiing information and instruction (downhill), you can contact the Skischule Garmisch-Partenkirchen (☎ 49 31), Am Hausberg 8; or (cross-country) the Skilanglaufschule (☎ 151 6) at Olympia-Skistadion. Sport Total (☎ 14 25), Marienplatz 18, also runs skiing courses and organises numerous outdoor activities like paragliding, mountain biking, rafting and ballooning, as well as renting a wide range of gear.

If your skis are stolen (it hardly ever happens), call ☎ 88 39. You'll find that the Bayerische Grenzpolizei have a good chance of finding them!

Cable Car

What a high – the 10 minute journey aboard the Eibsee cable car is actually worth the admittedly high price (DM61 for adults, DM43 for teens aged 16 to 18, DM37 for kids), even if you're not skiing or hiking. The car, packed to the brim with people, sways and swings its way up from the base to the **Panorama Observation Terrace** – the ride is not for the fainthearted!

Zahnradbahn

Built from 1928 to 1930, this charming narrow-gauge railway makes its way from the mountain base up to Zugspitzplatt station, where you can switch for the Gletscherbahn cable car that takes you to the summit of the Zugspitze. Included in a day pass, this is the more scenic but slower way up the mountain. Without a day pass, it costs the same as for the Eibsee cable car.

Hiking

The best way to get to the top of the Zugspitze is to hike (it takes two days). A recommended hiking map is *Wettersteingebirge* (DM7.50), published at 1:50,000 by Kompass. For information on guided hiking or courses in mountaineering, call at the Bergsteigerschule Zugspitze (☎ 58 99 9), Dreitorspitz-Strasse 13, Garmisch.

A great short hike from Garmisch is to the Partnachklamm gorge via a winding path above a stream and underneath waterfalls. Take the cable car to the first stop on the Graseck route (DM5 per head) and follow the signs.

Places to Stay

The camping ground nearest to Garmisch is *Zugspitze (☎ 31 80)*, along highway B24. Take the blue-and-white bus outside the

Hauptbahnhof in the direction of the Eibsee. Sites cost DM8, plus DM9 per person and DM5 per vehicle.

The *hostel* (☎ *29 80, fax 585 36, Jochstrasse 10)* is in the suburb of Burgrain. Beds cost DM21 (including tourist tax) and there's an 11.30 pm curfew; note that it's closed from November until Christmas. From the Hauptbahnhof, take bus No 3, 4 or 5 to the Burgrain stop.

In the centre of Garmisch, *Haus Weiss* (☎ *46 82, Klammstrasse 6)*, *Gasthaus Pfeuffer* (☎ *22 38, Kreuzstrasse 9)* and the nearby *Haus Trenkler* (☎ *34 39, Kreuzstrasse 20)* all offer simple but pleasant singles/doubles for around DM35/70.

A five minute walk from the station is the quiet *Hotel Schell* (☎ *957 50, Partnachauen Strasse 3)*, with rooms from DM45/90 opposite a babbling brook.

Places to Eat

Do stop in at *Chapeau Claque* (☎ *713 00, Mohrenplatz 10)*, a very cosy and very French wine bar-bistro with soft lighting and great service. Good snacks include bagels with salmon and cream cheese (DM9.80), baked potato with bacon and onions (DM11.80) or wok dinners for DM14 to DM16. It also serves breakfast.

Despite – or perhaps because of – its weird pictures, Christmas lights and purple tablecloths, the *Café Max* (☎ *25 35, Griesstrasse 10a)* is quite charming, with snacks and mains such as French onion soup (DM5) and mixed grill with Swiss-style roast potatoes (DM19.20).

On the south side of the river near the Alte Kirche in Garmisch are two local favourites. The *Bräustüberl* (☎ *23 12, Fürstenstrasse 23)* is about as Bavarian as you can get, complete with enormous enamel coal-burning stove and Dirndl-clad (but sometimes curt) waitresses. The dining room is to the right, beer hall to the left; main courses (not a vegetable to be seen) are DM10.50 to DM26.50, though the average is about DM17.

Directly opposite the Cafeteria Sirch on Griesstrasse is the *Gasthaus zur Schranne*,

an old tavern with three-course evening menus from just DM12.80. The *Hofbräustüberl* (☎ *717 16)*, on the corner of Chamonixstrasse and Olympiastrasse, has home-made Hungarian specialities like *hajducki cevap* (skewered and grilled meat with paprika, DM18).

The local pizza and pasta guru is *Da Renzo* (☎ *41 77, Rathausplatz 6)*, with 100 varieties, mostly for DM10 to DM13.

A local favourite is *Isi's Goldener Engel* (☎ *566 77, Bankgasse 5)*, complete with frescoes, stags' heads and a golden vaulted main hall. The selection is huge, ranging from a simple pork thigh with potato dumplings (DM19.80) to game dishes such as roast boar or venison for around DM33 (closed Wednesday).

Bavaria Grill (☎ *33 08, Am Kurpark 16)* in Garmisch (entrance on the little alley) is a lot friendlier than it looks from the outside, and the food's good and cheap. Fill up on sausage dishes from DM6.90 to DM9.50, and add some excellent fries for DM4.50.

Also in Garmisch, *Konditorei Krönner* (☎ *30 07, Achenfeldstrasse 1)*, with an entrance on Am Kurpark, is a beautiful if pricey place for coffee and cakes, but the attached takeaway bakery is far more reasonable; try its speciality Mocca creme and almond Agnes Benaur torte for DM3.20.

Perhaps the best value in town is the excellent *Cafeteria Sirch* (☎ *21 09, Griesstrasse 1)*. It's not much to look at, but has excellent half-chickens for DM6.20, schnitzels for 7.20, and beef goulash and noodles for DM8.30.

Schnönegger Käsealm (☎ *17 33, Mohrenplatz 1)* has very friendly staff and cheese sandwiches from DM2 to DM5; it also sells a range of delicious all-natural yoghurt (DM6/4.50 with/without fruit), as well as fresh butter and honey.

There's an *Aldi* supermarket on the corner of Bahnhofstrasse and Enzianstrasse.

Getting There & Around

Garmisch is serviced from Munich by hourly trains (DM26, 1½ hours). A special return train fare from Munich or Augsburg

euro currency converter DM1 = €0.51

for DM68 (DM84 on weekends) includes the trip up the Zugspitze (or a day ski pass). The A95 from Munich is the direct road route. Trains between Garmisch and Innsbruck pass through Mittenwald.

Bus tickets cost DM2 for journeys in town. You can rent bicycles at Trek Pro Shop (☎ 795 28), Schnitzstrasse 1 near Rathausplatz, for DM18 (three gears), or DM25/32 for trekking/mountain bikes.

AROUND GARMISCH-PARTENKIRCHEN
Schloss Linderhof

About 20km north-west of Garmisch-Partenkirchen is Schloss Linderhof (1869-78), Ludwig II's hunting palace and the only one of his royal residences to be completed. Nestled at the crook of a steep hillside, it is fronted by formal French gardens with fountains, pools and follies as odd as you'd expect from the nutty monarch. Right in the front entrance is a statue of Louis XIV, the Sun King, with the inscription *Nec Pluribus Impar*, 'I'm the Greatest'.

Although the smallest of his residences, Linderhof boasts its fair share of unbelievable treasures, although the conflicting styles (eg quick switches from rococo to Gothic) could set your teeth on edge. Ludwig's **bedroom** is a shower of colourful ornaments set around an enormous 108-candle chandelier weighing 500kg. (It's checked regularly by the national safety board, so go ahead and stand beneath it.)

The dining room recalls the king's fetish for new invention: a **dumb-waiter** table that rises from the kitchen so that the shy Ludwig wouldn't actually have to see his servants.

On the grounds is more Francophilia, and the best part is that the sunnier the weather, the fewer the visitors. The fountains play in summer. Don't miss the oriental-style **Moorish Kiosk**, which Ludwig picked up at the 1876 World's Fair in Paris; or the **Venus Grotto**, an artificial stalactite cave used as a stage set for Wagner's *Tannhäuser*.

The palace is open from Easter to mid-October daily from 9 am to 5.30 pm, and from 9.30 am to noon and 1 to 4 pm the rest of the year. Admission is DM10/7 in summer and DM7/4 in winter (when only the main palace is open). A return bus fare from Garmisch-Partenkirchen costs DM11.

Getting There & Away From Munich, there's an hourly train service to Oberammergau with a change at Murnau (DM26, 1¾ hours), then take the hourly RVA bus No 9606 from the train station to Linderhof (DM9.20 return, 20 minutes). A bus from Füssen takes 90 minutes. From Garmisch-Partenkirchen, take the 'Oberammergau' bus from the Hauptbahnhof (DM4.80, 40 minutes), and change to the RVO No 9606 at Oberammergau train station.

Linderhof is about 20km north-west of Garmisch-Partenkirchen on the rural B23.

Mittenwald
☎ 08823 • pop 8500

Mittenwald, south-east of Garmisch Partenkirchen, was a famous violin-making centre long before the first tourists arrived. Nowadays it's a favourite Alpine getaway for weary urban types, with its clear air and snow-capped peaks. From almost any angle, the town looks like it comes straight out of a Bavarian travel leaflet.

The tourist office (☎ 339 81, fax 27 01, email kurverwaltung@mittenwald.de) is at Dammkarstrasse 3. It's open weekdays from 8 am to 5 pm, Saturday from 9 am to noon (and in summer, 10 am to noon on Sunday). You can get an overview of accommodation and events at its Web site, www.mittenwald.de.

Popular local hikes with cable-car access go to the Alpspitze (2628m), the Wank (1780m), Mt Karwendel (2384m) and the Wettersteinspitze (2297m). Return tickets to the Karwendel, which boasts Germany's second highest cable-car route, cost DM29/18 for adults/children. The tourist office sells a good map of hiking trails for DM4.

The Karwendel ski field has one of the longest runs (7km) in Germany. Combined day ski passes covering the Karwendel and nearby Kranzberg ski fields cost DM38. For equipment hire and ski/snowboard instruction, contact the Erste Skischule Mittenwald (☎ 35 82) at Bahnhofsplatz. A three hour ski lesson costs DM45, with rates lower from the second day.

Places to Stay & Eat The camping ground closest to Mittenwald is *Am Isarhorn (☎ 52 16, fax 80 91)*, 2km north of town off the B2 highway (bus No 9608 or 9610). Pitch sites start at DM8 (DM13.50 if you have a car).

The local *DJH hostel (☎ 17 01, fax 29 07)* is in Buckelwiesen, 4km outside Mittenwald. It charges DM18 per night and closes from early November until late December. It's impossible to reach by public transport, so take the road to Klais, bear left at the BMW dealer, go up the hill, round the lake and follow the signs – it's about 4km, and takes about an hour on foot.

Two good budget places in the middle of town are *Hotel Alpenrose (☎ 50 55, Obermarkt 1)*, with singles/doubles for DM45/85; and *Gasthaus Bergfrühling (☎ 80 89, Dammkarstrasse 12)*, which has basic but bright rooms from DM30/60.

The *Bäckerei Fleischmann (Hochstrasse 13)* has light bites, including pizza slices (DM3.50) and fresh pretzels (DM0.70). Across the street, *Salis Grillshop (☎ 82 26, Hochstrasse 14)* offers great roast chickens (DM5.60 for half).

Gasthof Alpenrose (☎ 927 00, Obermarkt 1), in an ornate 18th century building, offers affordable old-style eating – there's nothing on the menu over DM18 – and live Bavarian music almost every night. *Gasthof Stern (Fritz-Prössl-Platz 2)* has a spate of local dishes for DM15 to DM20, and a beer garden with fantastic views (closed Thursday).

Getting There & Away Mittenwald is served by regional trains from Munich (DM32, 1¾ hours), Garmisch-Partenkirchen (DM6, 20 minutes) and Innsbruck (DM18/AS126, one hour). There are also IC and ICE fast trains from Ulm (from DM72, three to 3½ hours).

Local buses depart from the Garmisch-Partenkirchen Hauptbahnhof every hour until late evening (DM3.30, 35 minutes).

Oberammergau
☎ 08822 • pop 5400

Approximately 20km north of Garmisch-Partenkirchen is the unbelievably touristy town of Oberammergau, celebrated for its Passion Play, performed every decade (see the boxed text).

The piece is *the* event for the locals. Unless you know someone, you wouldn't be likely to get tickets for performances in 2000, but you can visit the **Passionstheater**, which reopens in spring 2000 after refurbishment. Tours (in German and English, DM5) include a history of the play and a peek at the costumes and sets.

The city tourist office (☎ 10 21, fax 73 25, email info@oberammergau.de), Eugen-Papst-Strasse 9a, books accommodation as well as horse-drawn carriage rides to Schloss Linderhof (DM30). For more on the town and the Passion Play, check the Web site at www.oberammergau.de.

Throughout the town the highlights are the *Lüftmalerei*, trompe l'oeil paintings on the facades of buildings designed to impart an aura of wealth. Several houses have fairy-tale motifs, like *Hansel & Gretl* and *Little Red Riding Hood*. The crowning glory of the town's Lüftmalerei is on the front of Pilatus Haus, just off Dorfstrasse.

Oberammergau is also known for its intricate woodcarvings. You'll find that workshops throughout the village create everything imaginable, from figures of saints to corkscrews you wouldn't accept as a gift. There's also a carving school in the village.

Getting There & Away Regular buses run to/from Garmisch-Partenkirchen (DM4.80) on the B23.

OBERSTDORF
☎ 08322 • pop 11,000

Over in the western part of the Bavarian Alps is the car-free resort of Oberstdorf. The busy tourist office (☎ 70 00, fax 70 02 36, email info@oberstdorf.de) at Markt 7 is open weekdays from 8.30 am to noon and 2 to 6 pm, and Saturday from 9.30 am to

BAVARIA

The Passion Play

Name the world's longest-running play: is it *The Mousetrap*, the famous 'whodunnit' by Agatha Christie? Or one of Shakespeare's classics – *King Lear*, perhaps? The unlikely answer – the deeply religious *Passionsspiele* – performed in Oberammergau in 2000, draws more tourist buses than many an Andrew Lloyd-Webber evergreen.

In 1632, the chaos and famine of the Thirty Years' War helped to spread the Black Plague throughout Europe. Oberammergau was struck the following year, and survivors vowed to forever stage a play depicting the passion, death and resurrection of Christ – if they could be rid of the epidemic. The appeal seemed to work: after the premiere in 1634 there were no more plague deaths, even though many locals had shown early signs of the illness. To honour its pledge, the town continued to stage the play every 10 years (with a few exceptions), and although passion plays were commonplace in the 17th century, Oberammergau's has been the only one to endure.

It's a drama of Wagnerian proportions, lasting from 9 am to 5.30 pm with a three hour break for lunch. The cast consists of 2200 shaggy locals – haircuts are forbidden months ahead of time – with as many as 250 actors on stage at once. The play has changed with the times: in 1990 the part of the Virgin Mary was awarded to a mother of two, scandalising the traditionalists (the same actor plays Mary in 2000). A particularly anti-Semitic scene – depicting Jews as horned devils – has been rewritten, and the most gruesome bits have gone altogether.

The 100-odd performances between May and October 2000 were sold out well in advance – demand for the 470,000 tickets (costing DM65 and DM110 each, and coupled mostly with local hotel bookings) exceeded supply several times over. Lucky ticket-holders will enjoy the result of a DM17 million renovation of the open-air theatre, including wider seats and floor heating on chilly Alpine evenings. Move over, Jesus Christ Superstar.

noon. There's also a convenient room-finding service near the Hauptbahnhof.

Like Garmisch, Oberstdorf is surrounded by towering peaks and offers superb **hiking**. For an exhilarating day walk, ride the Nebelhorn cable car to the upper station, then hike down via the Gaisalpseen, two lovely alpine lakes.

In-the-know skiers value Oberstdorf for its friendliness, lower prices and generally uncrowded pistes. The village is surrounded by several major **ski fields**: the Nebelhorn, Fellhorn/Kanzelwand and Söllereck. Daily/weekly ski passes that include all three areas (plus the adjoining Kleinwalsertal lifts on the Austrian side) cost DM57/290.

For ski hire and tuition, try the Neue Skischule (☎ 27 37), which has convenient outlets at the valley stations of the Nebelhorn and Söllereck lifts.

The Oberstdorf Eislaufzentrum, behind the Nebelhorn cable-car station, is the biggest **ice-skating complex** in Germany, with three separate rinks.

Places to Stay

The local *Camping Oberstdorf* (☎ 65 25, fax 40 25, Rubinger Strasse 16) is 2km north of the station beside the train line. A tent site/car/adult costs DM5/5/9 per night, and there's a coin-op laundry.

The *youth hostel* (☎ 22 25, fax 804 66, Kornau 8), on the outskirts of town near the Söllereck chair lift, charges DM22 per night; take the Kleinwalsertal bus to the Reute stop.

Geiger Hans (☎ 36 74, fax 804 98, Frohmarkt 5) has small rooms from DM30 per person (DM40 with shower). The *Zum Paulanerbräu* (☎ 23 43, fax 96 76 13, Kirchstrasse 1), right in the heart of the Altstadt, charges DM45/90 for simple singles/doubles (DM57/114 with private shower). Also central is *Gasthaus Binz* (☎ 44 55, Bachstrasse 14), a quaint wooden inn with simple rooms for DM40 per person.

Places to Eat

The friendly bakery and butcher shop *Vinzenzmurr (Hauptstrasse 1)* is the best bet for a quick bite. The large *Zum Paulanerbräu* (see Places to Stay) has a wide range of belly-filling selections (such as *Grillhaxen*, or roast leg of pork) averaging DM16, with potent dark Salvator beer. The restaurant is closed on Tuesday.

Zum Wilde Männle (☎ 60 30, Oststrasse 15) is a bit splashier, with mains from DM19 to DM33, but lunch dishes can be extraordinarily cheap (eg calf goulash for DM12.80). The *Zum Kachelofen (☎ 56 91, Kirchstrasse 3)* is a good Tirolean restaurant with daily specials under DM20.

Getting There & Away
The direct 'Alpenland' InterRegio train runs daily to/from Hamburg and Oberstdorf (via Hanover, Würzburg, Augsburg and Buchloe). There are several daily bus connections to Füssen (via Reutte in Austria or Pfronten).

BERCHTESGADEN
☎ 08652 • pop 8200

Arguably the most romantically scenic place in the Bavarian Alps, the resort of Berchtesgaden enjoys a kind of splendid isolation created by centuries of monastic self-rule. Surrounded by Austria on three sides, the quirky droplet of terrain known as the Berchtesgadener Land (and site of the pristine Königssee, the country's highest lake) would now belong to Bavaria's southeastern neighbour but for the influence of the Holy Roman Empire. Nowadays visitors (including Americans in their tens of thousands) flock to nearby Obersalzberg to see the Eagle's Nest, a mountain-top teahouse built for Hitler to entertain foreign dignitaries. Ironically, the Nazi leader is said to have suffered from vertigo and rarely enjoyed the spectacular views himself.

Information
The Berchtesgaden tourist office (☎ 96 70, fax 633 00, email marketing@berchtesgaden.de), just across the river from the Hauptbahnhof at Königseer Strasse 2, is open in summer on weekdays from 8 am to 6 pm, Saturday to 5 pm, and Sunday and public holidays from 9 am to 3 pm. The rest of the year it opens on weekdays from 8 am to 5 pm, and Saturday from 9 am to noon.

Accommodation is surprisingly cheap (*private rooms* start at DM25) and the booking service is free. Outside office hours, you can use the self-service electronic reservation board out front. The town has a decent Web site (www.berchtesgadener-land.com), which includes an accommodation listing.

To change money, try the Hypovereinsbank on the main square at Weihnachtsschützenstrasse 2½.

The post office and bus station are at the Hauptbahnhof, perhaps the most grandiose surviving Nazi-era train station.

For bicycle rentals, turn to the Big Pack Country Store (☎ 94 84 50), Maximilianstrasse 16, for two-wheelers from DM10 per day. There's no laundrette in town.

Salt Mines
A tour of the **Salzbergwerk** (☎ 600 20) is a must. Visitors change into protective miners' gear before descending into the depths of the salt mine for a 1½ hour tour. It's open from 1 May to 17 October daily from 9 am to 5 pm; the rest of the year it's open Monday to Saturday from 12.30 to 3.30 pm. Admission is DM21 for adults, and DM11 for children.

Eagle's Nest
The area's most sinister draw is at Mt Kehlstein, a sheer-sided peak in Obersalzberg (east of Berchtesgaden) where Martin Bormann, a Hitler confidant, engaged 3000 workers to build a diplomatic meeting-house for the Führer's 50th birthday. Better known as the Eagle's Nest, the innocent-looking Kehlsteinhaus occupies one of Germany's most breathtakingly scenic spots. Visitors may be miffed by the absence of Nazi-related explanations – as a historical monument, the place is kept pretty much as it was. Nowadays there's a restaurant (☎ 29 69), open from late May to early October, that donates profits to charity. (The food can be hit-or-miss, depending on the cook's mood.)

BAVARIA

Hitler's Mountain Retreat

Hitler's holiday home, the so-called 'Berghof', was not far from the Eagle's Nest, with a labyrinthine bunker complex drilled into the alpine rock. (Neville Chamberlain, then British prime minister, came in 1938 for the first of several visits culminating in his infamous 'peace in our time' speech.) While the Eagle's Nest was spared – or simply overlooked – by Allied bombers, the Berghof was reduced to ruins and consigned to the undergrowth. US troops blew it up again in 1952 to discourage pilgrimages.

Kehlstein is reached from Berchtesgaden by RVO bus to Hintereck, then by special bus to the Kehlstein car park, where a lift (open mid-May to October) whooshes 120m to the summit through solid rock. Admission and car parking cost DM24 with a *Kurkarte* (the discount pass you get when you pay a Kurtaxe), but a ticket with return bus fare (No 9538) from the Berchtesgaden Hauptbahnhof runs just DM25.80. (When you alight, reserve a bus seat for the way down.) On foot, it's a 30 minute wheeze from the Kehlstein car park to the summit, and two to three hours from Berchtesgaden.

The creepy legacy of the place is best experienced on Berchtesgaden Mini Bus Tours (☎ 649 71 or 621 72), which is tremendous value at DM50 for the four hour guided tour in English (kids go half price). Buses depart at 1.30 pm from mid-May to October from the tourist office; reserve a ticket. It's the only historical tour of the area, as the local authorities prohibit German-language tours for fear of attracting Nazi sympathisers.

Königssee
Framed by steep mountain walls, the beautiful, emerald-green Königssee lies like a misplaced fjord 5km south of Berchtesgaden. There are frequent electric-boat tours (DM18, 1½ hours) in all seasons to

the quaint onion-domed chapel at **St Bartholomä**, which we all know from the glossy tourist leaflets.

In summer, boats continue to the far end of the lake. If you're lucky, the boat will stop and the guide will play a *Flügelhorn* towards the amazing **Echo Wall**. In the valley about one hour's hike from the dock at St Bartholomä is the **Eis Kapelle**. As snow gathers in the corner of the rocks here, a dome emerges that reaches heights of over 200m. In summer as the ice melts, the water digs tunnels and creates a huge opening in the solid ice.

Berchtesgaden National Park
The wilds of this national park unquestionably offer some of the best hiking in Germany. A good introduction to the area is a 2km path up from St Bartholomä beside the Königssee to the Watzmann-Ostwand – scores of mountaineers have died attempting to climb this massive 2000m-high rock face of Germany's second-highest mountain. Another popular hike goes from the southern end of the Königssee to the Obersee. The tourist office sells excellent topographical maps for DM10.80, and hiking maps from DM10 to DM15.

Skiing
The Jenner area (☎ 958 10) at Königssee is the main of Berchtesgaden's five ski fields. Daily/weekly ski-lift passes for its intermediate to advanced pistes cost DM37/155. The Gutshof and Hochschwarzeck are gentler and better suited to families – day passes cost DM22/16 and DM27/18.50 respectively for adults/children.

The Skischule Treff-Aktiv (☎ 667 10), Jennerbahnstrasse 19, rents skiing and snowboarding equipment at good rates. The Outdoor Club (☎ 50 01), Am Gmundberg 7, organises a vast range of activities and courses, from hiking and mountaineering to paragliding and rafting.

Places to Stay
Of the five camping grounds in the Berchtesgaden area, the nicest are at Königssee:

Grafenlehen (☎ 41 40) and *Mühleiten (☎ 45 84)*. Both charge DM10 per site, plus DM8 per person.

The *hostel (☎ 943 70, fax 94 37 37, Gebirgsjägerstrasse 52)* charges DM22 (including tourist tax and breakfast) for a bed. From the Hauptbahnhof, take bus No 3 to Strub, then continue a few minutes on foot. The hostel is closed from early November to late December.

The newly renovated *Hotel Watzmann (☎ 20 55, fax 51 74, Franziskanerplatz 2)* is just opposite the chiming church in the Altstadt. Simple singles/doubles cost just DM33/66 (DM39/78 in summer). The hotel closes in November and December.

Only 10 minutes walk from the station but with great views over the valley is the *Pension Haus am Berg (☎ 949 20, fax 94 92 30, Am Brandholz 9)*, where rooms start at DM38/76, including breakfast.

Rooms at the *Gästehaus Alpina (☎ 25 17, fax 21 10, Ramsauer Strasse 6)*, near the Hauptbahnhof, range from DM38 to DM45, and some have nice views to Kehlstein, Jenner, Göll and Brett.

Also near the station, the *Hotel Floriani (☎ 660 11, fax 634 53, Königsseer Strasse 37)* has rooms with bath, cable TV and minibar from DM40/80. Some rooms have balconies.

The *Hotel Rosenbichl (☎ 944 00, fax 94 40 40, Rosenhofweg 24)*, in the middle of the protected nature zone, is exceptional value, with singles from DM58 to DM85 and doubles from DM116 to DM170. Nonsmokers find solace here. There's also a sauna, whirlpool, solarium and a library (mainly German stuff).

The *Hotel Vier Jahreszeiten (☎ 95 92, fax 50 29, Maximilianstrasse 20)*, close to the centre, has panoramic views of the Alps, a good restaurant and rooms from DM75/130.

At Schönau am Königssee, the *Hotel-Pension Greti (☎ 946 50, fax 95 65 30, Waldhauserstrasse 20)*, a 15 minute walk from the lake, has well appointed rooms from DM58/116, all with bath and balcony.

Also in Schönau, the *Hotel Alpenhof (☎ 60 20, fax 643 99, Richard-Voss-Strasse 30)* is one of the area's swankier addresses at the foot of the Alps. Rooms start at DM112/224, including use of the tennis court and indoor swimming pool.

Places to Eat

There's a good weekly *market* at Weihnachtsschützenplatz from April to October, Friday from 8 am to 11 am, with an incredible array of fresh produce and meats. It's joined by a farmer's market on the last Friday of the month.

For a quick bite, the *Express Grill (☎ 23 21, Maximilianstrasse 8)* sells half-chickens for DM5.80 and burgers from DM3.50, while the butcher's *Fritz Kastner (☎ 23 39, Königseerstrasse 3)*, right opposite the tourist office, has unbeatable filled rolls from DM3.50.

Hotel Watzmann (see Places to Stay) deserves another mention for its well priced dishes, served to outside tables. The *Hubertus Stuben (☎ 95 20)*, part of Hotel Vier Jahreszeiten on Maximilianstrasse, offers vegetarian dishes alongside venison and sirloin steak specialities (from around DM18).

Gasthaus Bier-Adam (☎ 23 90, Markt 22) has a good range of traditional fare to suit all budgets, a nice dark beer and cheerful service. The nearby *Gasthaus Neuhaus (☎ 21 82, at Markt 1)* features old-style Bavarian cuisine with occasional folk music and a nifty terrace.

Grassl's Bistro-Cafe (☎ 25 24, Maximilianstrasse 11) is an ideal spot for lunch among all those cute porcelain jugs, with tasty soups, sandwiches and daily specials from DM10 to DM17. It's open 9 am to 6 pm (closed Sunday).

The *Bräustübl (☎ 14 23, Bräuhausstrasse 13)* is a huge beer hall that caters to carnivores, putting on a heel-whacking Bavarian stage show every Saturday night.

If you have a car, check out the *Holzkäfer (☎ 621 07, Buchenhöhe 40)* in a funky log cabin in the hills by Obersalzberg. Crammed with antlers, carvings and backwoods oddities, the place is great for an evening drink with the locals. Light meals and salads are priced from DM6.50 to DM15, but most

BAVARIA

nourishment is of the liquid variety. It's open from 5 pm to 1 am (closed Sunday).

Getting There & Away

For the quickest train connections to Berchtesgaden, it's usually best to take a Munich-Salzburg train and change at Freilassing. It's a 2¾ hour train trip from Munich (DM48), but just an hour from Salzburg (DM12.20), although from Salzburg it's more convenient to take a bus or even a tour. Berchtesgaden is south of the Munich-Salzburg A8 autobahn.

Franconia

Franconia occupies the northern part of the state of Bavaria, and its lovely rolling hills are home to a beautiful wine region, stunning parks and the unmissable cities of Nuremberg and Würzburg (for Würzburg, see the Romantic Road section earlier in this chapter).

The Franconian wine region, in the northwest of the state, produces some exceptional white and red wines, all served up in the distinctive Franconian bottle – the flattened teardrop-shape that is only used for these wines and for Mateus, the Portuguese table wine. The oldest variety of wine in Franconia is Bocksbeutel Silvaner. Labelling of wines in the region is simple: yellow labels mean dry, green half-dry and red somewhat sweet (locals say 'mild').

NUREMBERG

☎ 0911 • pop 500,000

Nuremberg (Nürnberg), capital of Franconia, is Bavaria's largest city after Munich. For centuries it was the unofficial capital of the (Germanic) Holy Roman Empire and preferred residence of German kings, who routinely convened their first Diet, or parliament, here. The city was also the empire's 'treasure chest' from 1424 to 1800, acting as guardian to the crown jewels and many of the priceless artworks we see today. Nuremberg played a pivotal role in several key peace treaties; in 1649-50, for instance, the town hosted a conference after the Thirty Years' War to agree on the demobilisation of the German, French and Swedish armies.

Today the city is more readily linked with, and heavily burdened by, the legacy of the National Socialists. Nazi party rallies were held here from 1927. This was also where the boycott of Jewish businesses was organised in 1933 and the infamous Nuremberg Laws revoking Jewish citizenship were enacted in 1935. Almost 8000 Jews lived in Nuremberg in 1933; by war's end, their ranks had thinned to 100.

Allied bombing raids killed about 6000 people, and by 2 January 1945 the city was reduced to rubble. After WWII, Nuremberg was the site of the War Crimes Tribunal, now known as the Nuremberg Trials.

Some prescient officials moved key artworks to a bomb shelter as early as 1940 – technically a form of resistance, since Hitler forbid such 'defeatist' thinking. The city's museums and churches – all of which converted to Protestantism in 1525, though the Frauenkirche converted back to Catholicism in 1810 – contain legions of valuable masterpieces. The Marshall Plan and local dedication spurred the reconstruction of almost all main buildings – including the castle and the three old churches in the Altstadt, which were painstakingly rebuilt using the original stone.

Nuremberg is one of Bavaria's biggest draws, and crowds get very thick in summer and during the spectacular Christmas Market. A compact city, it's easy to get around and makes a very enjoyable base for excursions into the Franconian wine country or the Romantic Road.

Orientation

Almost all main sights are within the Altstadt, surrounded by reconstructed city walls and a dry moat. The shallow Pegnitz River flows from east to west right through the centre of the city.

The Hauptbahnhof is just outside the city walls at the south-east corner of the Altstadt. The main artery, the mostly pedestrian

Königstrasse, takes you north from the Hauptbahnhof through Hauptmarkt and Rathausplatz and leads into Burgstrasse, which heads steeply uphill and brings you to the hostel and Kaiserburg.

The biggest attractions outside the Altstadt are the Reichsparteitagsgelände (also called Luitpoldhain), the Nazi rally ground southeast of the centre; and the Court of Justice (Justizgebäude), in which the Nuremberg Trials were held, just to the west.

Information

Tourist Offices There are tourist offices in the Hauptbahnhof's main hall (☎ 233 61 31/32, fax 23 36 16 11, email tourismus@ nuernberg.btl.de) and at Hauptmarkt 18 (☎ 233 61 35, fax 233 61 66). The former is open year round Monday to Saturday from 9 am to 7 pm; the latter opens the same days to 6 pm. From October to April and during Christkindlesmarkt, both offices also see visitors on Sunday from 10 am to 1 pm and 2 to 4 pm.

The ADAC service hotline is ☎ 01805-10 11 12. The city lost and found service (☎ 26 10 70) is at Rothenburger Strasse 10 at the east end of the Hauptbahnhof.

Money Change banknotes and travellers cheques at the Reisebank in the Hauptbahnhof. There's a Commerzbank at Königstrasse 21 and a Hypovereinsbank at Königstrasse 3. American Express (☎ 23 23 97) has an office at Adlerstrasse 2, just off Königstrasse.

Post & Communications The main post office is at Bahnhofplatz 1 by the station. Nuremberg has several Internet cafes, including Cyberthek (☎ 446 68 93) at Pillenreuther Strasse 34 and Maximum (☎ 23 23 84) at Färberstrasse 11.

Internet Resources Nuremberg has a comprehensive Web site in German and English at www.nuernberg.de.

Travel Agencies Atlas Reisen (☎ 20 67 50), Breite Gasse 72, offers the usual good discounts. Celtic Travel (☎ 45 09 74 20), Bulmannstrasse 26, specialises in travel to Ireland and Scotland. Plärrer Reisen (☎ 92 97 60), with an office at Gostenhofer Hauptstrasse 27, also has a last-minute ticket desk at the airport.

Bookshops & Libraries Hugendubel (☎ 236 20), Ludwigplatz 1, has a huge branch with lots of English-language books and a good selection of travel literature, including Lonely Planet titles. Buchhandlung Edelmann (☎ 99 20 60), Kornmarkt 8, has a German travel section upstairs and some English-language novels downstairs. The research library at the German National Museum (see that entry), has 50,000 volumes and 1500 periodicals.

Cultural Centres Amerika Haus (☎ 20 33 27), Gleissbühlstrasse 13 near the Hauptbahnhof, runs an impressive range of cultural and artistic programs each month. There's an English-language discussion group and a resource library.

Laundry Schnell & Sauber has three coin laundries, all outside the Altstadt, that open from 6 am to midnight: at Sulzbacher Strasse 86 in the north (tram No 8 to Deichslerstrasse), at Allersberger Strasse 89 in the south (tram Nos 4, 7 and 9 to Schweiggerstrasse), and at Schwabacher Strasse 86 in the west (U2 to St Leonhard). A load costs DM7, while drying is DM1 per 12 minutes.

Medical Services In a medical emergency, call the Bayerisches Rotes Kreuz (Bavarian Red Cross; ☎ 940 32 60). The city hospital, the Klinikum Nord (☎ 39 80), is at Professor-Ernst-Nathan-Strasse 1. Walk-in cases can also visit Dr Erler Unfallklinik (☎ 272 80) at Konthunazgarten 4-18.

Altstadt Walking Tour

This circuit, which goes north to the castle and loops anticlockwise back to the market square, covers the main sights of the historic city centre over a leisurely two hour walk. With stops, it can take the best part of two

BAVARIA

NUREMBERG (NÜRNBERG)

days; in this case, you may cleanly split the tour into north and south of the Pegnitz River.

The tour starts on the bustling **Hauptmarkt**, site of daily markets and also of the famous Christkindlesmarkt (see Special Events). At the square's eastern end is the ornate Gothic **Pfarrkirche Unsere Liebe Frau** (1350-58), or simply the Frauenkirche. The figures beneath the clock, seven electoral princes, march clockwise three times around Charles IV to chimed accompaniment every day at noon.

Near the tourist information office stands the 19m-tall **Schöner Brunnen** (Beautiful Fountain), a stunning golden vision of 40 electors, prophets, Jewish and Christian heroes and other allegorical figures rising from the square like a Gothic spire. It's a replica of the late 14th century original. On the market side hangs a seamless **golden ring**, polished bright by millions of hands; a local superstition has it that if you turn it three times, your wish will come true.

NUREMBERG (NÜRNBERG)

PLACES TO STAY		
1	Jugendgästehaus	
10	Agneshof	
34	Pension Altstadt	
35	Hotel Avenue	
47	Am Jakobsmarkt	
52	Pension Sonne	
55	Probst-Garni Hotel	
58	Gasthof zum Schwänlein	
60	Meridien Grand Hotel Nürnberg	
64	Maritim Hotel	
65	InterCity Hotel	

PLACES TO EAT	
5	Burgwächter Restaurant
14	Enchilada
17	Alte Küch'n
19	Bratwursthäusle
24	Kettensteg
25	Café am Trödelmarkt
27	Naturkostladen Lotus
29	Heilig Geist Spital
41	Wok Man
43	Stefansbäck

51	Kaufhof; Markthalle
54	Doneria
57	Historische Bratwurstküche

OTHER	
2	Kaiserburg
3	Tiergärtnertor
4	Pilatushaus
6	Historischer Kunstbunker
7	Der Hase (The Hare)
8	Altstadthof Brewery
9	Albrecht Dürer Haus
11	Dürer Statue; Felsengänge
12	Fembohaus; Stadtmuseum
13	Meisengeige
15	Altes Rathaus
16	St Sebalduskirche
18	Toy Museum
20	Neues Rathaus
21	Tourist Office
22	Pfarrkirche Unsere Liebe Frau
23	Schöner Brunnen
26	Weinstadel

28	Café Lucas
30	O'Shea's
31	Hypovereinsbank
32	Mach 1
33	American Express
36	Treibhaus
37	Naussauer Haus
38	Tugendbrunnen
39	Lorenzkirche
40	Commerzbank
42	Atlas Reisen
44	Peter-Henlein-Brunnen
45	Hugendubel
46	Ehekarussell Brunnen
48	Maximum Internet Café
49	Buchhandlung Edelmann
50	Police Station
53	Amerika Haus; Dai Cinema
56	German National Museum
59	Handwerkerhof
61	Main Post Office
62	Tourist Office
63	Main Train Station
66	Städtische Bühnen
67	Schauspielhaus/Kammerspiel

The site was the city's Jewish quarter until a pogrom in 1349, carried out under Charles IV, in which some 560 Jews were burnt outside the city after their homes, shops and synagogues were razed. In 1349, the community was restored at another location, only to be expelled again in 1499. Three and a half centuries elapsed before they were readmitted to Nuremberg in 1850.

Altes Rathaus & St Sebalduskirche Just north of Hauptmarkt is the Altes Rathaus (1616-22), a hulk of a building with lovely Renaissance-style interiors. It houses the **Lochgefängnisse** (medieval dungeons; ☎ 231 26 90), which might easily put you off lunch. You must join a tour (DM4/2); from April to mid-October and during Christkindlesmarkt, they run daily every 30 minutes from 10 am to 4.30 pm.

Opposite the Altes Rathaus is the 13th century St Sebalduskirche, Nuremberg's oldest church, whose exterior is replete with religious sculptures and symbols. Note the ornate carvings over the Bridal Doorway to the north, showing the Wise and Foolish Virgins. Inside, the highlight is unquestionably the bronze **shrine of St Sebald**, a Gothic and Renaissance masterpiece that took its maker, Peter Vischer the Elder, and his two sons more than 11 years to complete. (Vischer's in it too, sporting a skullcap.)

Felsengänge & Around Continue north along Rathausplatz, turn left onto Halbwachsengässchen and you'll encounter the **Albrecht Dürer statue** in the square that bears his name. Directly beneath it is the chilly Felsengänge (☎ 22 70 66), a four storey underground network burrowed into the sandstone in the 14th century to house a brewery and beer cellar. During WWII it served as an air-raid shelter. Take a jacket for the tours, daily at 11 am and 1, 3 and 5 pm (DM7/5). Groups must number at least three.

Just off the tour route to the north-east is **Fembohaus** (☎ 231 25 95), Burgstrasse 15 (*not* Bergstrasse), a 16th century merchant

BAVARIA

house with amazing stucco and wood panelling, home to the Stadtmuseum (DM4/2).
It was due to reopen in the spring of 2000
after renovation.

Kaiserburg At the northern end of Bergstrasse, with a capped tower looming like a
giant sentry, stands **Kaiserburg** castle, which
served for centuries as the 'treasure chest' of
the Holy Roman Empire. The complex affords stunning views of the city and consists
of three parts: the Kaiserburg and Stadtburg
(the emperor's palace and city fortress), as
well as the Burggrafenburg, which was
largely destroyed in 1420. Between its surviving towers the Kaiserstallung (Royal Stables) were built – today it is the DJH hostel.

The complex is roomier than the exterior
lets on, embracing the Kaiser's living quarters, a Romanesque chapel, the Imperial and
Knights' Halls and the **Sinwellturm** tower
(113 steps). There's also an amazingly deep
well (48m – they lower a platter of candles
so you can see the depth), which still yields
drinking water. View everything for DM9/8,
or just the well and tower for DM3/2.

The castle walls and dry moat spread
west to the **Tiergärtnertor** gate, through
which you can stroll behind the castle into
its lovely **garden**. The grassy knoll at the
south-east corner is Am Ölberg, a favourite
spot to sit and gaze out over the city's
rooftops. One fine place to do that is in the
Burgwächter restaurant (see Places to Eat).

Tiergärtnerplatz to Ludwigsplatz The
western side of the castle touches Tiergärtnerplatz, with **Albrecht Dürer Haus** (☎ 231
25 68). Here Dürer, Germany's Renaissance
draughtsman, lived from 1509 to 1528. The
house features a large number of Dürer artefacts (entry DM5/3) and was recently reopened with a new collection of the master's
graphic works.

Opposite, in front of **Pilatushaus** – marked
by an armoured St George atop the beast – is
Jürgen Goetz's 1984 bronze sculpture **Der
Hase – Hommage á Dürer** (The Hare – A
Tribute to Dürer). This nod to the *Junger
Feldhase* of 1502 shows the dire results of

tampering with nature (not that the tourists
clambering over it seem to notice).

Nearby is the **Historischer Kunstbunker**
(☎ 22 70 66), Obere Schmiedgasse 52, the
shelter that housed the city's art treasures
during the bombing raids of WWII. You can
visit on tours (DM5) from April to December on Thursday, Saturday and Sunday at
3 pm (the rest of the year, Saturday and
Sunday only).

A few blocks south of Dürer Haus, after
winding around the back of Sebalder Platz
you'll hit the **Toy Museum** (Spielzeugmuseum; ☎ 231 31 64) at Karlstrasse 13-15,
exhibiting playthings from many different
eras. It's open Tuesday to Sunday from 10
am to 5 pm, and Wednesday to 9 pm
(DM5/2.50).

From the Toy Museum carry on south,
take the first right on Weintraubengasse and
the first left into an alley that leads to the impressive half-timbered **Weinstadel**, an old
wine depot festooned with geraniums in
summer. This spot affords a wonderful view
of the Pegnitz River. Cross the covered
wooden **Henkersteg**, a two part bridge
spanning a tiny island that is the site of the
Trödelmarkt (flea market), and rest your
heels in the lovely cafe of the same name
(see Places to Eat).

Ludwigsplatz to Lorenzplatz South of
the Henkersteg, continue along Hutergasse
and turn south-west onto Ludwigsplatz,
named for Bavarian King Ludwig I and
lined today with unremarkable shops. At its
south end, before the fortified **Weisser
Turm** (White Tower), stands the amazing
Ehekarussell Brunnen, a large metallic
fountain with six interpretations of marriage
(some of them quite harrowing) based on a
verse by Hans Sachs, the medieval cobbler-
poet. To the north-east on Hefnerplatz,
you'll see another modern fountain, the
Peter-Henlein-Brunnen, dedicated to the
16th century tinkerer credited with making
the first pocket watch.

Continue on towards the east on Karolinenstrasse to reach the city's oldest house,
Nassauer Haus, at No 2.

Lorenzkirche Just east of Nassauer Haus is Lorenzplatz, which is dominated by the massive Lorenzkirche (Church of St Lawrence), of which only the towers survived the war. The highlight is its 15th century tabernacle, with delicate carved strands winding up to the vaulted ceiling. Remarkable also are the stained glass (including a rosetta window 9m in diameter) and artworks such as Veit Stoss' *Engelsgruss* (Annunciation), a massive wooden carving suspended above the high altar.

On the north side of the church stands the **Tugendbrunnen**, a fountain with seven Virtues proudly spouting water from their breasts, in the shadow of a figure of Justice. Continuing north up Königstrasse will return you to the Hauptmarkt, the start of the walking tour.

German National Museum

The Germanisches Nationalmuseum (☎ 133 10), Kartäusergasse 1, is the most important general museum of German culture, spanning the ancient to the early 20th century. It features works by German painters and sculptors, an archaeological collection, arms and armour, musical and scientific instruments and toys. Among its many highlights are Dürer's *Hercules Slaying the Stymphalian Birds*, confirming the artist's superb grasp of anatomical detail. It's open Tuesday to Sunday from 10 am to 5 pm, and to 9 pm on Wednesday (DM6/3, free on Wednesday from 6 to 9 pm). Free guided tours in English take place on the first and third Sunday of each month at 2 pm (but normal admission is still charged).

In Kartäusergasse at the museum's entrance is the **Way of Human Rights**, a symbolic row of 29 white concrete pillars (and one oak tree) bearing the 30 articles of the Universal Declaration of Human Rights. Each pillar is inscribed in German and, in succession, the language of a people whose rights have been violated. The oak, a sturdy specimen with generous foliage, represents the languages not explicitly mentioned. The intentions were noble, admittedly, but the result is a bit antiseptic.

Handwerkerhof

The Handwerkerhof, a recreation of a crafts quarter of old Nuremberg, is a walled tourist trap by the Königstor. Open from March to December, it's about as quaint as a hammer on your thumbnail, but if you're cashed up, you'll find some decent merchandise (eg quality leather goods). The Bratwurstglöcklein im Handwerkerhof (see Places to Eat) is also good, with friendly service and good sausages, but the other restaurants are a little cheesy, with accordion versions of *In the Mood* and violinists assaulting your table. The yard closes at 10 pm.

Nazi Rally Ground

Nuremberg's role during the Third Reich is emblazoned in minds around the world: the black-and-white images of ecstatic Nazi supporters thronging the city's flag-lined streets as goose-stepping troops salute their Führer.

The rallies at the Reichsparteitagsgelände were part of an orchestrated propaganda campaign that began as early as 1927 to garner support for the party. In 1933, Hitler decided that a purpose-built venue would be a better backdrop than the Altstadt, so the party planned a ridiculously outsized complex in the Dutzendteichpark to the southeast. Nazi leaders hoped to bridge a metaphorical link between Nuremberg's illustrious past as *Reichstagstadt* (the parliamentary seat of the Holy Roman Empire) and the Third Reich's new rally centre (the *Reichsparteitag*).

The premises were to have included the **Zeppelinwiese**, a military parade ground; the never-completed **Deutsches Stadion**, which was to seat 400,000; and the **Luitpoldarena**, designed for mass SS and SA parades. The half-built **Kongresshalle**, which was meant to outdo Rome's Colosseum in both scale and style, is a fitting monument to Nazi megalomania.

Commonly called the Luitpoldhain, the area was originally laid out for the Bavarian Jubilee Exhibition of 1906, long before the Nazis pressed it into party service. Discussion about a meaningful use of the grounds

BAVARIA

has been going on since 1945; nowadays the **Zeppelintribune** complex hosts sporting events (including the Noriscar races in June) and rock concerts, while the Kongresshalle acts as a warehouse for a large mail-order firm. The latest proposal is to install a permanent **documentation centre**, including an archive and museum, on the north side of the Kongresshalle by early 2001.

A chilling multimedia presentation, *Fascination and Terror*, can be seen in the current exhibit (☎ 231 56 66) in the rear of the Zeppelintribune. It's open from mid-May to October, Tuesday to Sunday from 10 am to 6 pm; the presentation costs DM2/1.

Take S2 to Frankenstadion (every 20 minutes), tram No 9 from the Hauptbahnhof to the Luitpoldhain-Volkspark, or tram No 4 or bus No 55 or 65 to Dutzendteich.

Court of Justice

The Justizgebäude (☎ 321 26 79), west of the Altstadt at Fürtherstrasse 110, is the state courthouse in which the war crimes trials were held after the conclusion of WWII. It's not normally open to visitors, though you can see the outside (take the U1 towards Fürth). The trials, held in Room 600, were set in Nuremberg by the Allies for symbolic and practical reasons. The very laws passed by the Nazis to justify the arrest and later extermination of Jews were called the *Nürnberger Gesetze* (Nuremberg Laws), passed in 1935. In addition, the building was easily accessible and one of few such complexes to survive the war intact.

The trials, which began shortly after the war and concluded on 1 October 1946, resulted in the conviction and sentencing of 22 Nazi leaders and 150 underlings, and the execution of dozens. Among those condemned early on were Joachim von Ribbentrop, Alfred Rosenberg, Wilhelm Frick and Julius Streicher, the notoriously sadistic Franconian party leader and publisher of the anti-Semitic weekly *Der Stürmer*. Hermann Göring, the Reich's portly field marshal, cheated the hangman by taking a cyanide capsule in his cell.

Organised Tours

The tourist office operates walking tours that meet at the tourist office on Hauptmarkt. There are daily two-hour tours in German (DM8) at 10 am and 2.30 pm (Wednesday only at 2.30 pm, no tours on major holidays). English-language walking tours (2½ hours, DM12) run daily from May to October at 2 pm (and as an added bonus, include a visit to the castle, which is not on the German tour). Tours are free for children under 14.

History For All (☎ 33 27 35) conducts two-hour tours of the Nazi rally area at Luitpoldhain from April to November on Saturday and Sunday at 2 pm (DM8/6). Meet at Luitpoldhain, the last stop of tram No 9.

Nürnberger Altstadtrundfahrten (☎ 421 91 9) is a tourist choo-choo that loops through the Altstadt for half-hour guided tours in German. The cost is DM7/6; they run daily from 10 am and start at Hauptmarkt.

Special Events

From the Friday before Advent to Christmas Eve, the Hauptmarkt is taken over by the most famous **Christkindlesmarkt** in Germany. During the duration of the market, scores of stalls line the Hauptmarkt, selling mulled wine, spirits, roast sausages and various trinkets. Not to be missed are *Lebkuchen*, the large, spicy soft cookies normally eaten at Yuletide (although you can buy them here year round).

Nuremberg celebrates its 950th birthday in the summer of 2000 – check with the tourist office for program details. The climax takes place in mid-July, when the city stages a three day anniversary blowout, although special events are scattered over the whole year.

Places to Stay

You can book rooms at the tourist information office for a booking fee of DM5 per room. Accommodation gets tight during the Christmas market and the toy fair (a closed event) in late January to early February. That said, cheap rooms can be found at other times, especially if you book ahead.

Campingplatz im Volkspark Dutzend-teich (☎ 81 11 22, Hans-Kalb-Strasse 56) is near the lakes in the Volkspark, south-east of the city centre (U1 from the Hauptbahnhof takes you to Messezentrum, which is fairly close). It costs DM8 per person, plus DM10 per site, and is open from early May to late September.

The excellent *Jugendgästehaus (☎ 230 93 60, fax 23 09 36 11, Burg 2)* is in the historic Kaiserstallung next to the castle. Dorm beds, including sheets and breakfast, cost DM29 (juniors only). The cheapest option for those aged over 26 is the *Jugend-Hotel Nürnberg (☎ 521 60 92, fax 521 69 54, Rathsbergstrasse 300)*, north of the city (take U2 to Herrnhütte, then bus No 21 north four stops). Dorm beds start at DM26, and there are singles/doubles from DM39/64; prices exclude breakfast (DM7.50).

The most reasonable pension in the city centre is the friendly *Probst-Garni Hotel (☎ 20 34 33, fax 205 93 36, Luitpoldstrasse 9)*, on the 3rd floor in a creaky building. The simple singles/doubles are minuscule but so are the prices – DM55/70, or DM70/110 with toilet and shower (including breakfast).

Another good deal is *Pension Altstadt (☎ 22 61 02, fax 22 18 06, Hintere Leder-gasse 4)*, with bathless rooms from DM50/90. Near the station is *Gasthof zum Schwänlein (☎ 22 51 62, fax 241 90 08, Hintere Sterngasse 11)*, which has basic rooms from DM35/70.

Pension Sonne (☎ 22 71 66, König-strasse 45) is one of the city's prize budget places near the theatre, with bathless rooms for DM56/92.

The simple and friendly *Pension Vater Jahn (☎/fax 44 45 07, Jahnstrasse 13)*, south-west of the Hauptbahnhof has rooms from DM43/75. *Haus Vosteen (☎ 53 33 25, Lindenaststrasse 12)*, just north-east of the Altstadt, charges from DM38/80.

South of the Pegnitz River, the *Hotel Avenue (☎ 24 40 00, fax 24 36 00, Joseph-splatz 10)* has modern, comfortable rooms with very good facilities for the price (from DM135/195). Entering the *Agneshof (☎ 21 44 40, fax 21 44 41 44, Agnessgasse 10)*,

near the castle, is a pleasure. The staff are polite and the rooms and facilities worth the DM155/188. Do ask about Agnes – the manager's an expert.

The *Am Jakobsmarkt (☎ 200 70, fax 200 72 00, Schottengasse 5)*, in a tiny courtyard near the Spittlertor in the south-west, has modern rooms with excellent amenities for DM148/194.

The *InterCity Hotel (☎ 247 80, fax 247 89 99, Eilgutstrasse 8)* at the Hauptbahnhof offers no surprises from the chain's usual standard, with rooms from DM190/245. Nicer is the *Holiday Inn Crowne Plaza (☎ 402 90, fax 40 40 67, Valznerweiher-strasse 200)* south-east of the centre, with rooms from DM185.

Probably the most luxurious top-end hotel is right in the centre – the *Le Meridien Grand Hotel Nürnberg (☎ 232 20, fax 232 24 44, Bahnhofstrasse 1-3)*, opposite the Hauptbahnhof. It features tonnes of amenities, great service, a good location and rooms from DM224/320.

Its competitor, *Maritim Hotel (☎ 236 30, fax 236 38 36, email reservierung.nur@ maritim.de, Frauentorgrabe 11)*, offers about the same level of luxury, plus an indoor swimming pool (rooms cost DM253/304).

Places to Eat

Restaurants & Bistros Probably the loveliest place to sit on a sunny day is the *Café am Trödelmarkt (☎ 20 88 77)*, on an island overlooking the covered Henkersteg bridge and the Weinstadel. It offers continental breakfasts from DM7, and filled baguettes and salads for DM11 to DM17.

The *Burgwächter Restaurant (☎ 22 21 26, Am Ölberg 10)*, in the shadow of the castle, is a great place to sit for drinks or a steak. Main courses average DM14, and it has a beer garden with wonderful views of the city.

A classic Nuremberg restaurant is the *Heilig Geist Spital (☎ 22 17 61, Spitalgasse 16)*, with a large dining hall spanning the river. There's an extensive wine list and Franconian specialities from DM17.

The best open-air option is the leafy *Kettensteg (☎ 22 10 81, Maxplatz 35)*, with

BAVARIA

a prime view of the Pegnitz away from the crowds. It has traditional Franconian fare averaging DM16 and a pretty interior, too.

Enchilada (☎ *244 84 98, Obstmarkt 5)* is a trendy Mexican place behind the market. Decent taco platters, combination burritos and nachos all cost between DM10 and DM17.

A tip for money-conscious diners is the *Sabberlodd* (☎ *33 55 52, Wiesentalstrasse 21)*, just north-west of the Altstadt in the backstreets of St Johannis (take tram No 6). It offers generous plates of ravioli and mixed salads for around DM10, along with inexpensive house wines and draught beers.

Snacks & Fast Food At the *Alte Küch'n* (☎ *20 38 26, Albrecht-Dürer-Strasse 3)* the house speciality is *Backers*, a kind of savoury cake of grated potato served with apple sauce or bacon accompanied by sauerkraut (from DM8.50). The *Markthalle* in the basement of the Kaufhof department store is a good deal, with Turkish meals for less than DM10. Here you'll also find a baker, a butcher and a wine bar.

Wok Man (☎ *20 43 11, Breite Gasse 48)* is a good Chinese fast-food place with beef fried noodles for DM4, mixed veg and beef with noodles for DM6.50 and big full meals for DM10 (closes at 8 pm). Nearby, *Stefansbäck (Breite Gasse 70)* has generous sandwiches from DM3.

The *Naturkostladen Lotus* (☎ *25 36 78 96, Untere Kreuzgasse)* is a health-food shop with vegie pizzas for DM3.50 and good hot meals for DM7.50 to DM8.50. The fresh bread and cheese counter is worth a look for picnic supplies.

Königstrasse is the ticket for conventional fast food, including *Doneria* at No 69 serving turkey doners for DM4.

Nuremberg Sausage There's heated competition between Regensburg and Nuremberg over whose sausages are the best; the latter's are certainly more famous. Judge for yourself: the *Bratwursthäusle* (☎ *276 95, Rathausplatz 2)* cooks 'em over a flaming grill for hordes of tourists willing to pay

DM9.50 for six or DM11.90 for eight (it's closed Sunday). Served typically with potato salad, sauerkraut or horseradish, the little links taste even better with a local Patrizier or Tucher brew. We found the *Bratwurstglöcklein im Handwerkerhof* (☎ *22 76 25)* to be just as good and as expensive – see the Handwerkerhof entry.

Locals seem to prefer the *Historische Bratwurstküche* (☎ *205 92 88, Zirkelschmiedegasse 26)* in the south-west part of the Altstadt in a renovated 15th century inn. It's cheaper and much more 'genuine'.

Entertainment

The excellent *Plärrer* (DM4) is available throughout the city and is heavy enough to kill someone with. It's also the best source of gay and lesbian places and events. The tourist office publishes *Das Aktuelle Monatsmagazin*, which also has cultural events listings.

Pubs & Bars A popular student bar is *Treibhaus* (☎ *22 30 41, Karl-Grillenberger-Strasse)*, with filling pastas and salads under DM6. *O'Sheas's* (☎ *23 28 95, Wespennest 6-8)* is a huge peach of a place on Schütt island in the middle of town, with cavernous vaulted rooms, Guinness and Kilkenny beers, and Irish dishes such as cottage pie and trimmings (DM13.60).

Café Lucas (☎ *22 78 45, Kaiserstrasse 22)* draws the designer set for cocktails; there's a nifty outside section with a platform overlooking the river. In the north-east Altstadt, *Meisengeige* (☎ *2082 83, Am Laufer Schlagturm 3)* is a comfortable hole-in-the-wall bar attached to a tiny cinema.

The *Altstadthof Brewery* (☎ *22 27 17, Bergstrasse 19)* near the castle is admittedly touristy but has a pleasant old-style pub.

Discos The *Mach 1* (☎ *20 30 30, Kaiserstrasse 1-9)*, right in the centre of town, is a cool basement club with house, hip hop, 1970s and 80s stuff, and soul music parties. *Planet Dance* (☎ *68 67 67, Kilianstrasse 108)*, north of the city centre near Freudenpark, is an enormous hall with neo-folk, romantic, pop, industrial-strength rock and a friendly crowd. *Hirsch (☎ 42 94 14, Vogelweiherstrasse 66)*, via U1 to Frankenstrasse in Gibitzen Hof Garden to the south, is a great live alternative music scene.

Forum (☎ 408 9744, Regensburger Strasse 334) hosts regular big-name concerts and has occasional gay parties (take the S2 to Frankenstadion).

Cinemas The *Roxy (☎ 488 40, Julius Lossmannstrasse 116)* shows English-language first-run films. The *DAI Cinema (☎ 23 06 90)* at Amerika Haus (see Cultural Centres) regularly screens first-run and classic Anglo-Saxon films.

Theatre & Classical Music The Schauspiel Nürnberg performs a huge range of theatre, including drama, comedy and young people's performances, at the *Schauspielhaus* and the *Kammerspiel*, while classical music and opera can be seen at the *Städtische Bühnen*. All venues are on Richard-Wagner-Platz; for tickets, call ☎ 231 35 14.

Getting There & Away
Nuremberg airport (☎ 350 60), 7km from the centre, is served by regional and international carriers including Lufthansa (☎ 26 61 15), Air Berlin (☎ 36 47 43), KLM-Royal Dutch Airlines (☎ 52 20 96) and Air France (☎ 529 85 22).

Trains run hourly to/from Frankfurt (DM69, 2¼ hours) and Stuttgart (DM54, 2¼ hours). There are connections several times daily to Berlin (DM144, 5¾ hours). Hourly trains run to/from Munich (DM61, two hours), and several daily trains travel to Vienna and to Prague (six hours each).

BEX BerlinLinien buses leave for Berlin daily at 12.10 pm and arrive from Berlin at 2.30 pm daily. The SuperSpar/standard cost for a one-way ticket is DM62/112; for a return ticket it's DM108/136.

Several autobahns converge on Nuremberg, but only the north-south A73 joins B4, the ring road.

There's an ADM Mitfahrbüro (☎ 194 40) at Strauchstrasse 1.

Getting Around
To/From the Airport Bus No 20 is an express shuttle (DM12) running every 20 minutes between the airport and the Hauptbahnhof from 5.30 am to nearly midnight. A taxi taking you to/from the airport will cost DM20 to DM25. By the time you read this, a U-Bahn connection to the airport may be open.

Public Transport Walking's the ticket in the city centre. Tickets on the VGN bus, tram and U-Bahn/S-Bahn networks cost DM2.50/3.30 per short/long ride in the centre. A day pass costs DM6.60 for one, and DM10.50 for two people.

Taxi Flag fall is DM4.80, and it's DM2.20 per kilometre. The BahnTaxi stand (DM12 per couple) is at the northern end of the Hauptbahnhof near the Mittelhalle exit.

Bicycle Allgemeiner Deutscher Fahrrad Club (ADFC, ☎ 39 61 32), with an office at Rohledererstrasse 13, organises group rides throughout the year. The Fahrradkiste (☎ 287 90 64), Knauerstrasse 9, has kids' bikes/trekking and mountain bikes/tandems for DM9/15/30 per day. Its rival, Ride on a Rainbow (☎ 39 73 37), at Adam-Kraft-Strasse 55, offers foldable bikes for DM10 per day, mountain bikes for DM14 and trekking bikes for DM18.

The city tourist office sells the ADFC's *Fahrrad Stadtplan* (DM8.50), a detailed map of the city and surrounding area. It also hands out a list of 'bicycle friendly' hotels in town that are willing to store bicycles for travellers.

ERLANGEN
☎ 09131 • pop 101,000
About 20km north of Nuremberg, the city of Erlangen (**air**-longen) is a charming little university and company town, with Siemens the major employer. Lined with quaint streets and ivy-covered buildings, and with a lovely little Schloss right in the centre, it's definitely worth a day of exploration, especially in summer.

BAVARIA

Orientation

The Regnitz River flows almost due north at the west side of the Hauptbahnhof. Just east of Bahnhofplatz is Hugenottenplatz, from where Universitätsstrasse and Obere Karlsstrasse run west to east. Friedrichstrasse is south of these two, running west-east as well. North of Hugenottenplatz is Schlossplatz and, of course, the Schloss; east of here is the Botanical Garden.

The campus of Universität Erlangen, Bavaria's second-largest, spreads east of Schlossplatz and serves 28,000 students.

Information

The city tourist office (☎ 895 10, fax 89 51 51, email citymanager@erlangen.de) is in the unsightly Rathaus, just off Nürnberger Strasse at Rathausplatz 1. It's open on Monday from 8 am to 6 pm, Tuesday to Thursday to 4.30 pm and Friday to 12.30 pm. Rooms are referred for free.

The ADAC has an office (☎ 356 52) at Henkestrasse 26. There's a Hypovereinsbank at Hugenottenplatz and a Dresdner Bank at Schlossplatz.

The main post office is two blocks southeast of the Hauptbahnhof on the corner of Henkestrasse and Nürnberger Strasse. Café Online (☎ 89 76 32) on Altstadtmarkt charges DM6 for 30 minutes of bobbing the cyber-waves, and DM10 for a full hour.

The city has a Web site with English sections at www.erlangen.de.

The Merkel Universitätsbuchhandlung, and next door, Merkel Jr, on Untere Karlsstrasse at Neustädter Kirchenplatz, have great maps and English books.

Just east is the Universitätsbibliothek, at Schuhstrasse 1a. Universität Erlangen's main office is at Schlossplatz 4.

Things to See & Do

The city's **Schloss** now houses university offices. Behind it, the **Botanical Garden** (open daily from 8 am to 6 pm) is a fabulous park; on any given day you can see concerts, theatre rehearsals, fencing or tai chi going on, and it's lovely in summer for a picnic. Speaking of lovely, the **Aromagarten**, near the Palmsanlage, is open from March to October daily from 8 am to 7 pm. The walk up to the **Burgberg** is definitely worthwhile. Simply follow the main drag north out of town. The site of a major folk and beer festival, its enormity (thousands of long wooden benches and well tended beer cellars) and leafy setting are impressive, even when empty.

Places to Stay

One of Germany's best-located camping grounds, *Naturfreunde Erlangen* (☎ 253 03) is about a five minute walk from the Hauptbahnhof right on the Regnitz. Enter the tunnel on Bahnhofplatz, carry on two blocks and follow the signs. It's DM4 per tent, DM9 per car, and DM7 per person.

The city's *DJH hostel* (☎ 86 25 55, fax 86 21 19, Südliche Stadtmauerstrasse 35) will admit people over 26 if there's room; beds are DM18/23 for juniors/seniors, plus DM5.50 for linen. It's in the Freizeitzentrum Frankenhof, a leisure centre with a swimming pool and inviting courtyard. The *Jugendgästehaus* (*same address and contact numbers*) has simple singles/doubles/triples from DM37/50/75 and singles/doubles with shower and toilet for DM47/74.

Despite its dull name, the *Bahnhof Hotel* (☎ 270 07, fax 20 50 78), adjacent to the Hauptbahnhof offers a good deal – DM57 for nice bathless singles and DM90/155 for singles/doubles with amenities. But it's hard to outdo the *Schwarzer Bär* (☎ 228 72, fax 20 64 94, Ludwigstrasse 16), with basic but pleasant rooms for DM45/70.

The *Luise* (☎ 12 20, fax 12 31 00, Sophienstrasse 10) is a four star hotel with a green conscience, sporting furnishings good for body and rainforest. Rooms start at DM129/175. The *Bayerischer Hof* (☎ 78 50, fax 258 00, Schuhstrasse 31) almost lives up to the elegance of its Munich counterpart, with rooms from DM160/210.

Places to Eat

There's a *bakery*, *butcher* and *Imbiss* (stand-up foodstall) right downstairs from the Bahnhof Hotel. The *Erlanger Teehaus*

Café (☎ 229 11, Friedrichstrasse 14) is a wonderful place with breakfast buffet specials, snacks for under DM7 and full meals for around DM15. There are two large rooms and a beer garden and the staff are a treat.

Nearby, *Umberto Pizzeria (☎ 20 95 29, Schuhstrasse 10)* has cheap pasta from DM9 to DM13, and pizzas from DM7.50 to DM10. *Daddy's Diner (☎ 20 50 80, Bahnhofplatz 6)* serves American diner food, including burgers (DM10 to DM15) and submarine sandwiches (DM8 to DM13); it's open to midnight.

Gastätte Römming Biergarten (☎ 229 70, Apfelstrasse 2), behind the Schloss, is a nice place to munch on vegie and Czech dishes. Meals average DM15, with lunch specials as low as DM10 (closed Saturday). With its reasonably priced fish and game dishes (many under DM20), the *Rotes Ross (☎ 956 50, Hauptstrasse 10)* pleases palates without straining budgets.

Entertainment

E-Werk (☎ 80 05 55, Fuchsenwiese 1) is a combination jazz club, disco, culture and communication centre, cinema and 'cultural meeting space' that always has something on. Theatre and cabaret is performed at *Fifty Fifty (☎ 248 55, Südliche Stadtmauerstrasse 1)* near the hostel.

Spruz (Weisse Herz Strasse 4), through the little courtyard, is a cool local bar with a nice garden and a wood interior. Hostellers spend lots of time at *De Old Inn (☎ 20 75 88, Holzgarten Strasse)* right around the corner. *Route 66 (Helmstrasse 9)*, next to the Hanf Centre (which sells hats, clothing, spirits and other products made from hemp) is an American-style cocktail bar.

Getting There & Away

There are four trains an hour from Erlangen to Nuremberg's Hauptbahnhof (DM6.30, 25 minutes). You can rent bicycles at Fahrradkiste (☎ 20 99 40), Henkestrasse 59, for DM9/15 for city/mountain bikes. Fahrrad Lang (☎ 241 44), Engelstrasse 14, is another good option. Erlangen is on the A73

autobahn, 24km north of Nuremberg and just north of the A3.

BAMBERG
☎ 0951   • pop 70,000

Tucked well off the main routes in northern Bavaria, the city of Bamberg is practically a byword for magnificence. This 1000-year-old monument dedicated to Heinrich II, the Holy Roman Emperor, and (for good measure) to the prince-bishops, clergy, patriciate and townsfolk, is acknowledged as one of Germany's most beautiful cities. In 1993 it made UNESCO's list of world heritage sites.

In the 17th century some of Europe's finest architects, including Küchel, the Dientzenhofers and Balthasar Neumann (see also the Würzburg section), went on a baroque frenzy and converted hundreds of buildings to this style. Many of them stand intact because Bamberg emerged from the WWII bombing raids, miraculously, with hardly a scratch.

The city's canals give Bamberg a relaxed feel, and its offerings to culture and the arts sustain the Bamberg Symphony Orchestra and the baroque ETA-Hoffmann-Theatre – the Calderon Festival here draws thousands every year.

The town's nine – and the region's 87 – breweries produce over 200 kinds of beer, including Keller Bier, a variety low on fizz, so you'll drink more of it faster, and *Rauchbier*, a dark-red ale with a smooth, smoky flavour. The hills surrounding the city are dotted with wonderful beer gardens, so in town or the environs, walk, behold and drink the unique brews.

Orientation

Two waterways flow through the city from north-west to south-east: the Main-Danube Canal, just south of the Hauptbahnhof, and the Regnitz River, which flows through the centre of town. From the station, take Luitpoldstrasse south, turn right onto Obere Königstrasse and left over the Kettenbrücke onto Hauptwachstrasse and onto Maximiliansplatz. The city's bus hub, the

euro currency converter   DM1 = €0.51

BAVARIA

Zentral-Omnibus Bahnhof (ZOB) is on Promenadestrasse, just off Schönleinplatz.

Information

The tourist office (☎ 87 11 61, fax 87 19 60, email touristinfo@bamberg.de) is at Geyerswörthstrasse 3 on the island in the Regnitz River, open year round Monday to Friday from 9 am to 6 pm, and Saturday from 8 am to 3 pm (Sunday 10 am to 2 pm from May to October and in December). Its friendly staff will sell you the Bamberg Card (DM13/24

for one/two people), which gives free or reduced admission to city attractions and use of city bus lines for 48 hours, plus a city tour. The tourist office also has tickets to performances by the splendid Bamberg Symphony Orchestra, which are sold only in July.

If you're planning an extended brewery tour, this is a good place to buy Stephan Mack's unique guide to Franconian brewpubs, *Die neue Fränkische Brauereikarte* (a bit dear at DM26.80, but well worth the 330 entries).

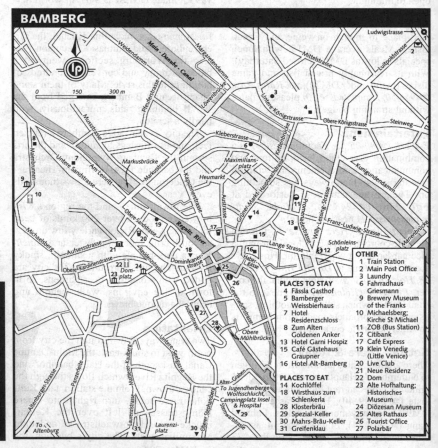

BAMBERG

PLACES TO STAY	OTHER
4 Fässla Gasthof	1 Train Station
5 Bamberger Weissbierhaus	2 Main Post Office
7 Hotel Residenzschloss	3 Laundry
8 Zum Alten Goldenen Anker	6 Fahrradhaus Griesmann
13 Hotel Garni Hospiz	9 Brewery Museum of the Franks
15 Café Gästehaus Graupner	10 Michaelsberg; Kirche St Michael
16 Hotel Alt-Bamberg	11 ZOB (Bus Station)
	12 Citibank
PLACES TO EAT	17 Café Express
14 Kochlöffel	19 Klein Venedig (Little Venice)
18 Wirtshaus zum Schlenkerla	20 Live Club
28 Klosterbräu	21 Neue Residenz
29 Spezial-Keller	22 Dom
30 Mahrs-Bräu-Keller	23 Alte Hofhaltung; Historisches Museum
31 Greifenklau	24 Diözesan Museum
	25 Altes Rathaus
	26 Tourist Office
	27 Polarbär

The Citibank on Schönleinsplatz is a good spot to change money.

The main post office is opposite the Hauptbahnhof at Ludwigstrasse 25.

The town has an excellent Web site (www.tourismus.bamberg.de) in English.

For laundry, try the Bamberger Waschsalon (☎ 215 17) at Untere Königsstrasse 32 right in the centre, or the SB Waschsalon (☎ 20 49 40) next to the Hauptbahnhof in the Atrium mall.

Altstadt

Bamberg's appeal lies in its sheer number of fine historic buildings, their jumble of styles and the paucity of modern eyesores. Most attractions are sprinkled along the Regnitz River, but the town's incredibly bombastic **Altes Rathaus** is actually on it, perched on twin bridges like a ship in dry dock. (Note the cherub's leg sticking out from the fresco on the east side, true to the 18th century fad for three dimensional artworks.) To the north-west are the charming half-timbered homes of **Klein Venedig** (Little Venice), complete with punts and river docks.

The princely and ecclesiastical roots of Bamberg can be sensed at Domplatz, a cross-section of German architectural history with the soaring Dom, housing the famous statue of the chivalric king-knight, the *Bamberger Reiter*.

Dom Today's cathedral is the outcome of a Romanesque-Gothic duel, fought by church architects after the original edifice burnt down (twice) in the 12th century. Politics, rather than passing styles, dictated the final floor plan of this dual chancel affair which conveniently recalls the Rhineland cathedrals of Henry II (who had been made a saint in the meantime).

The uniformity is remarkable, given the fact that the plans were altered each winter during 20 years of building. The pillars have the original light hues of Franconian sandstone thanks to Ludwig I, who ordered all post-medieval decoration be removed in the early 19th century. Traces of the bright 13th century reliefs, however, can be seen in the choir. Another highlight is the *Laughing Angel* in the north aisle, who smirkingly hands the martyr's crown to the headless St Denis. The star turn, however, is the *Bamberger Reiter* (see the boxed text).

Outside, an intriguing feature is the *Prince's Portal*, which shows Christ in an ornate sculpture of the Last Judgment, which broke plenty of conventions. King, pope and rich man are among the doomed shown screaming in desperation, while some key proportions are out of whack – the devil is larger than either Mary or John.

Diözesan Museum The highlight of the Diözesan Museum (☎ 502 32 5), in the cloister at Domplatz 5, is Heinrich II's Blue Coat of Stars. It's open Tuesday to Sunday from 10 am to 5 pm (DM4/2). The adjacent courtyard, the **Alte Hofhaltung** (partly Renaissance in style), contains the secular **Historisches Museum** (☎ 871 14 2), which focuses on the history of the region and of 19th century Bamberg. It's open from May to October, Tuesday to Sunday from 9 am to 5 pm (DM4/2).

Neue Residenz The episcopal Neue Residenz (☎ 563 51), though not as large as Würzburg's, is stately and superb, with its elaborate Kaisersaal and Chinese cabinet, and a collection of paintings from the Bavarian National Gallery. It's open from

---

Mystery Rider

The *Bamberger Reiter* is Bamberg's greatest and most enduring mystery. As with its counterpart in Magdeburg, nobody knows for sure who the fetching young king on the steed is. One leading theory points towards Konrad III, the Hohenstaufen king buried in the cathedral, another towards St Stephen, the king of Hungary and Henry II's brother-in-law. The Nazis seized on the image of the heroic medieval ideal, which became a symbol of Aryan perfection in classrooms during the Third Reich.

BAVARIA

April to September daily from 9 am to noon and 1.30 to 5 pm, and in winter to 4 pm (DM5/4). The **Rose Garden** (Rosengarten) behind offers one of the city's finest outlooks. For more, head to the tower of **Altenburg** castle, a few kilometres away (take bus No 10 from Promenadestrasse and finish with a walk to the hill top).

Michaelsberg Above Domplatz, at the top of Michaelsberg, is the former Benedictine **monastery** of St Michael (now an old people's home). The **Kirche St Michael** is a must-see for its baroque art and the carefully painted depictions of 600 herbal plants on the vaulted ceiling. The manicured garden terrace boasts a panorama of the city's splendour.

Also located up here is the **Fränkisches Brauereimuseum** (☎ 530 16), which shows plaster(ed) dummies of monks brewing their robust Benediktiner Dunkel beer, as well as exhibits from malt production to the final product. It's open from April to October, Tuesday to Sunday from 1 to 5 pm (DM3.50/2.50).

Places to Stay

The town is packed from May to September, so book ahead. The tourist office will book rooms for a DM5 fee (☎ 87 11 54).

Camping options are limited to *Campingplatz Insel* (☎ 563 20). Take bus No 18 (DM1.80) from the ZOB station to the suburb of Bug a few kilometres south of town (bus stop: Campingplatz). The grounds, in a calm spot right on the river, charge DM12 per site plus DM6.50 per adult.

The juniors-only *Jugendherberge Wolfsschlucht* (☎ 560 02, fax 552 11, Oberer Leinritt 70) is on the west bank of the Regnitz, closer to town than the camping ground. Take bus No 18 from the ZOB station (DM1.80) and alight at Rodelbahn. Walk north-east to the riverbank, turn left and there it is, past the mini-golf range. Beds cost DM20, plus DM5.50 for linen. The hostel is closed from mid-December to February.

Good deals on simple but central hotels include the *Hotel Garni Hospiz* (☎ 98 12 60,

fax 981 26 66, Promenadestrasse 3), just off Schönleinsplatz, with budget singles for DM50 and large doubles with a shower for DM80. Some rooms have balconies. *Hotel Alt-Bamberg* (☎ 98 61 50, fax 20 10 07, Habergasse 11), in a quiet location near the Rathaus, is also great value: DM58 for simple singles or DM68/115 for singles/doubles with all facilities.

Zum Alten Goldenen Anker (☎ 665 05, fax 665 95, Untere Sandstrasse 73) is an old-world inn north of Michaelsberg and has nice doubles with shower/WC for DM85 (singles aren't much cheaper, from DM75). *Café-Gästehaus Graupner* (☎ 98 04 00, fax 980 40 40, Lange Strasse 5) offers singles/doubles without shower for DM55/85 (with shower for DM65/95).

Pride of place goes to the ritzy *Hotel Residenzschloss* (☎ 609 10, fax 609 17 01, email hotel.residenzschloss@t-online.de, Untere Sandstrasse 32), in a magnificent baroque palace on the west bank of the Regnitz. With well trained staff, facilities include a Roman-style steam bath, whirlpool, two restaurants and a lovely house chapel. Rooms start at DM225/285, including the biggest breakfast buffet you're likely to see.

Brewery Hotels Two interesting options in town are brewery hotels – rooms upstairs, breweries downstairs (how practical) – and both come highly recommended. The *Bamberger Weissbierhaus* (☎/fax 255 03, Obere Königstrasse 38) has simple singles/doubles for DM39/70, or doubles with shower for DM80. The *Fässla Gasthof* (☎ 229 98 or ☎ 265 16, fax 20 19 89, Obere Königstrasse 19) has quiet rooms for DM63/98 and an earthy restaurant.

Places to Eat

Grüner Markt, Bamberg's main shopping drag, has a number of fast-food options, including a *Kochlöffel* at No 18.

The city's brewery-restaurants should be the first stop for local dishes, such as stuffed Bamberger onion with beef in smoked beer sauce, and (of course) for what's on tap. The 17th century *Wirtshaus zum Schlenkerla*

(☎ 560 60, Dominikanerstrasse 6) is a justly famous place, with tasty Franconian specialities (such as venison goulash, DM14) and its own superb Rauchbier (just DM3.40 per half litre mug). The *Greifenklau* (☎ 532 19, Laurenziplatz 20) serves Keller Bier in summer and, from October to November, awesome Bock beer.

Slurp great Pilsners in an Art Deco cellar at the *Mahrs-Bräu-Keller* (☎ 534 86, Oberer Stephensburg 36), as well as at the *Spezial-Keller* (☎ 548 87, Sternwartstrasse), with its own smoky ale and great views of the Dom from the beer garden. Another beautiful old half-timbered brewery is *Klosterbräu* (☎ 522 65, Obere Mühlbrücke 3), which has excellent beers for washing down its solid standard fare (between DM14 and DM20).

Entertainment
Consult the free listings mags *Franky*, *Treff* or *Fränkische Nacht*, usually laid out in pubs, for the latest 'in' spots and special events. *Café Express* (☎ 20 46 66, Austrasse 33) caters to students with stimulating cocktails (such as the Orgasmus for DM12) and Thai cuisine for afterwards. The *Polarbär* (☎ 536 01, Judenstrasse 7) has an intimate beer garden and an extra cosy interior, with salads and light meals from DM9. For eclectic disco, seek out the *Live Club* (mobile ☎ 0171 833 96 49, Obere Sandstrasse 7). There you'll find Marcel (the DJ You Can Trust).

Getting There & Around
There are hourly RE and RB trains from Nuremberg (DM16.40, 45 minutes) or from Würzburg (DM27, one hour), as well as daily trains from Munich (DM78, 2¾ hours) and Berlin (DM125, 5¼ hours). The A73 runs direct to Nuremberg.

Walking is the best option in town, but you can also rent bicycles from DM10 a day at either Fahrradhaus Griesmann (☎ 229 67), Kleberstrasse 25; or Rad im Hof Bredt (☎ 230 12), Untere Königstrasse 32. The tourist office has a huge selection of bicycle-path maps of the vicinity. Cars are a pain in town, so park on the outskirts and walk or

take a bus (DM1.80 for single journeys, DM7 for a five journey ticket). For a taxi, call ☎ 150 15 (flag fall is DM4).

BAYREUTH
☎ 0921　• pop 73,000
Every year over 600,000 people vie, by computer drawing, for fewer than 60,000 seats to the Bayreuth (buy-**royt**) Wagner Festival, started in 1876 by the cantankerous composer himself and now a pilgrimage for die-hard fans.

Bayreuth was first mentioned in 1194 as Baierrute, a name that is roughly translated from old German as 'Bavarians' forest clearing'. It was the seat of margraves from 1603, but gained prominence after Margravine Wilhelmine, sister of Frederick the Great, was forced into a marriage to Margrave Friedrich, dashing her dreams of moving to London. Wilhelmine – herself a composer, artist, actress and writer – managed to put Bayreuth on the cultural map by inviting the finest artists, poets, composers and architects in Europe to come to court here.

Money was somebody else's problem, and by the time she finished, the city was home to some of the most spectacular (and spectacularly gaudy) examples of rococo and baroque architecture in Europe.

Orientation & Information
The Hauptbahnhof is on the north-east corner of the historic centre, inside the Hohenzollernring. The Festspielhaus, the massive stage where the Wagner Festival is held, is on a hill to the north. The main drags are Richard-Wagner-Strasse and Maximilianstrasse, which is also the Markt.

The city tourist information office (☎ 885 88, fax 885 55, email tourismus@ bayreuth.btl.de) is at Luitpoldplatz 9 in the heart of town. The tourist office books rooms for a DM5 fee which rises to DM10 during the Wagner Festival. We'd recommend buying the three day Bayreuth Card here, which covers free bus transit around town, entrance to half a dozen museums and a two hour guided city walk (in German). The office also runs thematic English-language tours

euro currency converter DM1 = €0.51

BAVARIA

(eg 'In Wagner's Footsteps') for groups of at least 10 people starting at DM16 per head.

A Commerzbank is opposite the tourist office at Luitpoldplatz 8. The post office is close to the tourist office at Kanzleistrasse 3. To send emails, visit Café am Sternplatz (☎ 76 16 10) at Ludwigstrasse 1, where half an hour surfing the Net costs DM5. The town's primarily German-language Web site is at www.bayreuth.de.

In the same building as the tourist office are ticket agents for local concerts and opera (excluding the Wagner event), as well as Reisebüro Bayreuth (☎ 88 50), a leading travel agent with cheap flights and package deals.

Things to See

Except during the Wagner Festival in July-August (when the local population doubles), the streets can be very quiet as Bayreuth slips into a kind of provincial slumber. But this is really the best time to see the sights without queues, and the town's strong musical traditions ensure there are good dramatic and orchestral performances year round.

A favourite musical venue is the **Margräfliches Opernhaus** (☎ 759 69 22) on Opernstrasse. Designed by the Bibienas, a famous 18th century family of Bolognese architects, this stunning baroque masterpiece was Germany's largest opera house until 1871. Yet Richard Wagner deemed the place too quaint for his serious work, and conducted here just once. For more details, take the 'sound and light' multimedia tour in German, from April to September daily from 10 am to 5 pm, and in winter to 3 pm. The show, with projected images of the royals and lurid lighting, lasts 45 minutes and costs DM6 (free with student ID). In late May the house hosts a festival of opera and ballet, the Fränkische Festwoche.

Wilhelmine's **Neues Schloss** (☎ 759 69 21) and the **Hofgarten** are now open as museums of the margraves' residence, open April to September from 10 am to 5 pm, and in winter to 3 pm. This is the site of the annual opening celebrations of the Wagner Festival.

To discover the man behind the myth, visit the **Richard Wagner Museum** (☎ 757 28 16) in Haus Wahnfried, Richard-Wagner-Strasse 48. The great composer had this lovely home built with cash sent by Ludwig II, and it was worth every pfennig. Inside you'll find Wagner's death mask, details of his alternative lifestyle (his many mistresses, short temper etc) and marks showing his true and stated height. It's open daily from 9 am to 5 pm, and to 8 pm on Tuesday and Thursday (DM4/2). CDs of Wagner's music are played at 10 am, noon and 2 pm, while a video runs at 11 am and 3 pm.

The rather spartan **Festspielhaus** (1872), also constructed with Ludwig's backing, can be toured in September, October and December to early May at 10 and 10.45 am, and 2.15 and 3 pm (DM2.50/1.50). The acoustics of the place are truly amazing, as its builders took the body density of a packed house into account.

Outside the city are the **Eremitage** and **Altes Schloss**, two lovely palaces with an enormous formal garden and a 'pre-aged' grotto. The whole thing was a gift to Wilhelmine from her husband in 1735. The grounds had been built in 1714 by Margrave Georg Willhelm as a retreat, but Wilhelmine turned them into a pleasure palace. From the Markt, take bus No 2 (DM2.30, every 20 minutes).

For a fascinating look at how John Barleycorn is made, head to the enormous Maisel's **Brauerei-und-Büttnerei-Museum** (☎ 40 12 34) at Kulmbacherstrasse 40, next door to the eponymous brewery. A fascinating 90 minute guided tour (in German) takes you into the sweet-smelling bowels of a 19th century plant, covering all aspects of the business (including barrel-making). The *Guinness Book of World Records* lists it as the world's most comprehensive beer museum. Arguably, the best part is the foaming glass of Weissbier served at the end in the bottling room, which is now a private saloon with old-fashioned slot machines. Tours are from Monday to Friday at 10 am only (DM5). English-language tours can be arranged for groups of 12 or more.

A Munich street performer strikes a pose.

Lederhosen make a comeback? Maybe not.

Hedonists get high at Oktoberfest, Munich.

Medieval-style hotel sign, Rothenburg

DAVID PEEVERS

DAVID PEEVERS

DAVID PEEVERS

DAVID PEEVERS

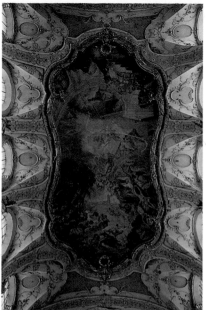

The ceiling of St Emmeram Basilika, Regensburg

Bamberg, home to many beautiful monuments

Before he drowned in a puddle of water, but after he went mad, King Ludwig built Neuschwanstein.

Special Events

The Wagner Festival has been held every summer for over 120 years. The event lasts 30 days, and a different opera is played every night for an audience of 1900. Demand is insane, and the board that runs the event has no mercy – the festival chairman, by the way, is Wolfgang Wagner, the composer's grandson. The enrolment process is quirky, and it takes an average of seven years to score tickets (although word has it that applicants from abroad needn't wait as long). To apply for tickets, send a letter (no phone, fax or email) to the Bayreuther Festspiele, Kartenbüro, Postfach 10 02 62, 95402 Bayreuth, before September of the year before you want to attend (but don't hold your breath). Although re-registration for the draw is allegedly automatic, it's advisable to write in every year until you 'win'. The lucky concert-goers face another endurance test – the seats are hard wood, ventilation is poor and there's no air-conditioning. But hang in there: on blister-ingly hot days, water is sprayed on the roof during the interval!

Places to Stay

The rooms at the **DJH hostel** (☎ 251 26 2, fax 51 28 05, Universitätsstrasse 28), south of the centre (take bus No 11, 18 or 19, DM2.30), are pleasant but the 10 pm curfew might cramp your style. Beds go for DM20, plus DM5.50 for linen. You can camp outside in summer.

Cheap but quite cheerful rooms are available at the **Gasthof Rotmainhalle** (☎ 661 77, Hindenburgstrasse 1), just outside the centre, from DM45/75 for singles/doubles.

The **Hotel-Gasthof Spiegelmühle** (☎ 410 91, fax 473 20, Kulmbacher Strasse 28), in an 18th century former mill five minutes walk from the ring, is great value from DM77/119 and has a lovely restaurant.

The perfectly located **Hotel Goldener Hirsch** (☎ 230 46, fax 224 83, Bahnhofstrasse 13), right in the centre, has nice rooms from DM90/130. The refined elegance of the

---

Richard Wagner

Richard Wagner (1813-83) was born in Leipzig but spent the last years of his life in Bayreuth. He arrived on 24 April 1872 from Switzerland with his wife, Cosima. With the financial backing of Ludwig II, his biggest patron and protector, Wagner built his spectacular house, Villa Wahnfried.

Wagner's operas, including *Götterdämmerung, Parsifal, Tannhäuser* and *Tristan and Isolde*, are powerful pieces supporting his grandiose belief that listening to opera should be work (his *The Ring of the Nibelungen* is literally four days long), not a social affair, and that music carries messages about life that are too important to ignore.

Wagner designed his own festival hall in Bayreuth. The acoustic architecture in the hall is as bizarre as his works are popular. The orchestra performs beneath the stage, and reflecting boards and surfaces send the sound up and onto the stage, where it bounces from the wall behind the singers and, mixed with the singers' voices, finally makes its way to the house. If you're scratching your head right now, visit the model of the stage and pit in the Wagner Museum.

Wagner is also well known for his reprehensible personal qualities: he was a notorious womaniser, an infamous anti-Semite and a hard-liner towards 'non-Europeans'. So extreme were these views that even fun-loving Friedrich Nietzsche called Wagner's works 'inherently reactionary, and inhumane'. Wagner's works – and by extension he himself – were embraced as a symbol of Aryan might by the Nazis, and even today there is great debate among music lovers about the 'correctness' of supporting Wagnerian music and the Wagner Festival in Bayreuth.

BAVARIA

Hotel Goldener Anker (☎ 650 51, fax 655 00, Opernstrasse 6), just a few metres from the opera house, is hard to beat at DM110/170.

Places to Eat

Bayreuthers are rightly proud of their tasty Bratwurst, just DM3 a link at the wooden stand in the pedestrian zone on Richard-Wagner-Strasse. *Hulinsky (☎ 640 89, Richard-Wagner-Strasse 25)* is a deli with enticing baked goods, filled rolls and wine for knock-down prices.

Wolffenzacher (☎ 645 52, Badstrasse 1) has Franconian dishes from DM15 to DM25, including *Krenfleisch* (finely sliced beef in horse-radish sauce). It's closed on Sunday evening. Or, toss back a dark Schinner beer at the aptly named *Braunbierhaus (☎ 696 77, Kanzleistrasse 15)*, a pub in the town's oldest surviving building, with decent local dishes from DM12. Another neat place is the *Hopfengwölb (☎ 95 95, Bindlacherstrasse 10)*, where you can watch production at the in-house brewery (closed Saturday and Sunday).

The *Schlosscafé Orangerie (☎ 98 01 14, Eremitage)*, about 1km south of the city centre, is a soothing place to sit and have pots of coffee (DM5.50, DM6.50 spiked with grappa). There's a beer garden, too, at the southern end of the park.

Getting There & Away

Bayreuth is well served by rail connections from Nuremberg (DM24.60, one hour), Munich (DM87, three hours) and Regensburg (DM53, 2½ hours).

AROUND BAYREUTH
Coburg
☎ 09561 • pop 44,000

If marriage is diplomacy by another means, Coburg's rulers were surely masters of the art. Over four centuries, the princes and princesses of the house of Saxe-Coburg intrigued, romanced and ultimately wed themselves into the dynasties of Belgium, Bulgaria, Denmark, Portugal, Russia, Sweden and (most prominently) Great Britain. The crowning achievement came in 1857,

when Albert of Saxe-Coburg-Gotha took vows with his first cousin, Queen Victoria, founding the present British royal family (which quietly adopted the name of Windsor during WWI).

A part of Saxony for many years, Coburg voted to join Bavaria after its last duke abdicated in 1918 – a wise choice, as it turned out. Saxony was absorbed by the GDR in 1947, and Coburg, just a few kilometres from the Iron Curtain, became a backwater for the next 40 years. Since reunification, the town has undergone a revival of sorts, rekindling visitors' interest in its proud Veste, one of Germany's finest medieval fortresses.

Orientation & Information The Hauptbahnhof is on the north side of town. The tourist office (☎ 741 80, fax 74 18 29, email info@coburg-tourist.de) is just off the town square at Herrngasse 4, and will find you a room (starting around DM30) for free. It's open from April to October, Monday to Friday from 9 am to 6.30 pm (November to March to 5 pm) and Saturday to 1 pm. Change money at the Postbank in the post office at Hindenburgstrasse 6.

Things to See & Do A masterful tribute to medieval defence, the **Veste Coburg** towers in a triple ring of fortified walls above town. This was the home of Duke Karl Eduard until he stepped down at the end of WWI. Up here you'll also find the **Kunstsammlungen** (☎ 87 90), an art collection that includes works by Rembrandt, Dürer and Cranach the Elder, as well as quarters occupied by Protestant reformer Martin Luther in 1530, the year he was tried for heresy. The museum is open from April to October, Tuesday to Sunday from 9 am to 5 pm, with a one hour lunch break at 1 pm; from November to March, it's open in the afternoon only (DM5/3).

Next door is the princely **Fürstenbau**, with its lovely half-timbered facade, which houses the apartments of the ducal family. It's open for half hour tours (in German) from April to October, Tuesday to Sunday from 9.30 am to 4 pm, with a one hour noon break, and November to March in the afternoon (DM4/3). Bus No 8 (DM2.50) takes you to the Veste from the Rathaus, or you can take on the steepish hill path (about half an hour).

In the heart of town, near the statue of Prince Albert on the handsome Markt, is the neo-Gothic **Schloss Ehrenberg** (☎ 808 80) in Herrngasse, a sumptuous tapestry-lined palace that was the royal residence in the 16th century. Albert spent his childhood here and Queen Victoria stayed in the room with Germany's first flushing toilet (1860). Guided tours (in German) are year round at 10 and 11 am, and 1.30, 2.30 and 3.30 pm; there's also a 4.30 pm tour in summer (DM4/3).

Also worth a look is Albert's childhood residence, the medieval **Schloss Rosenau**, and its English landscape gardens; it's 7km to the north-east in Rödenthal. Tours are Tuesday to Sunday from 11 am to 3.45 pm (DM3/2).

Places to Stay & Eat The spick-and-span youth hostel, *Schloss Ketschendorf* (☎ 153 30, fax 286 53, Parkstrasse 2) is in a mock castle 2km from town. Beds cost DM22, including breakfast, and linen is DM5.50. Take bus No 1 from the Markt (DM2.30).

The *Fink* (☎ 12 38, fax 240, Lützelbacher Strasse 24) is a smart modern guesthouse outside town with English-speaking staff. Well equipped singles/doubles with shower cost DM50/90 (take bus No 4, DM2.30, 10 minutes).

In town, *Gasthof Goldenes Kreuz* (☎ 904 73, fax 905 02, Herrngasse 1) on the Markt has agreeable rooms with shower for DM58.50/98.50. *Goldene Traube* (☎ 87 60, fax 87 62 22, Am Viktoriabrunnen 2) is the romantic blowout option for DM130/170, with a classy restaurant and sauna.

Loreley (☎ 924 70, Herrngasse 14) is a huge renovated 17th century inn just off the Markt with decent Franconian fare for DM13 to DM20. Try *Thüringer Klösse* (outsized dumplings) in a number of variations at the *Ratskeller* (☎ 942 00, Rathaus) on the

Markt, where mains average DM16. *Café Prinz Albert* (☎ 954 20, Albertsplatz) offers sweet goodies and ice cream for DM5 to DM7, and light meals for DM6 to DM10. The hills around Coburg are also chock-a-block with enchanting beer gardens (see the Vierzehnheiligen section).

Getting There and Away Trains go every hour from Bamberg (DM14.80, one hour), Bayreuth (DM22.40, 1¾ hours) and from Nuremberg (DM39, 1½ hours). There's also a BEX bus to Berlin (DM60, three hours) and to Nuremberg (DM45, 2¼ hours) from the Hauptbahnhof twice a day.

Vierzehnheiligen

Halfway between Coburg and Bamberg, with a commanding view of the River Main, stands the magnificent Vierzehnheiligen (Fourteen Saints), an 18th century pilgrimage church. Legend has it that on the same spot, a shepherd had recurring visions of the Christ child flanked by the 14 saints of Intercession. Their statues line the central altar, the focal point of Germany's most over-the-top rococo basilica (open daily from 8 am to 4 pm, and 7 am to 7 pm in summer). Designed by Balthasar Neumann, this and Würzburg's Residenz are acknowledged as the architect's greatest works.

On its perch across the valley is **Kloster Banz**, a former Benedictine monastery that is nowadays a conference centre for the Bavarian conservative party CSU. There's a lovely view from the Franz Josef Strauss memorial, which is dedicated to the former party leader.

Beer Gardens Round the back of Vierzehnheiligen, up the hill past the wooden stands peddling kitsch, is the wonderful *Alte Klosterbrauerei* (☎ 09571-34 88), a brewery tied to the adjacent convent. In the sprawling beer garden with a stunning outlook, quaff a half litre of the bracing 'Nothelfertrunk' (Auxiliary Saint's Drink) for DM3. Snacks such as hearty bread-and-sausage platters cost DM5 to DM9, but you can also bring your own. Stay long enough

BAVARIA

and you'll glimpse the nun in habit who brings in cases for refill. It's open daily from 10 am to 8 pm.

Getting There & Away Both churches are just off the B173 about 5km south of Lichtenfels, or about a 20 minute drive from Coburg or Bamberg. There are two buses from Lichtenfels Hauptbahnhof from Monday to Friday at 8.25 and 10.45 am (DM2.60, 10 minutes), except for Wednesday, when departure is at 1.45 and 5.45 pm.

ALTMÜHLTAL NATURE PARK

In the south of Franconia, the Altmühl River gently meanders through a region of little valleys and hills before joining the Rhine-Main Canal and emptying into the Danube at Kelheim. In 1969, a 3000 sq km area was set aside as Germany's largest nature park. Its main information centre is in the city of Eichstätt, a charming town at the southern end of the park that makes an excellent base for exploring.

Altmühltal covers some of Bavaria's loveliest lands, but it's relatively undiscovered by non-Germans. Some 90% of visitors are domestic, and another 5% are from German-speaking countries.

You can explore on your own via extremely well marked hiking and biking trails, or canoe for an hour or several days. There's free basic camping in several areas along the river, and camping grounds throughout the region, along with hotels, pensions, guesthouses and hostels.

Orientation

The park takes in the area just south-west of Regensburg, south of Nuremberg, east of Treuchtlingen and north of Eichstätt. The eastern boundaries of the park include the town of Kelheim and the Klosterschenke Weltenburg (see the Around Regensburg section later in this chapter).

Eichstätt, about a half-hour train ride north of Ingolstadt, sits about halfway between Kelheim and Gunzenhausen (at the north-west end of the park and the start of the Altmühl canoe trails). The river flows from west to east. There are bus and train connections between Eichstätt and all the major milestones along the river, including Gunzenhausen, Treuchtlingen and Pappenheim (from west to east).

North of the river, the activities focus around the towns of Kipfenberg, Beilngries and Riedenburg.

Planning a Trip

The Informationszentrum Naturpark Altmühltal (☎ 08421-987 60, fax 98 76 54), Notre Dame 1, 85072 Eichstätt, is a font of excellent information. Staff can put together an entire itinerary for free and send you (for face value) maps and charts of the area; information on bike, boat and car rental; and lists of hotels, camp sites and guesthouses throughout the park. However, they won't reserve rooms.

The information centre is also a good museum of the park's wildlife and habitats, complete with a re-creation of landscapes in its garden. It also sells the incorrectly titled *Altmühl Valley National Park*, an English guidebook to the area for DM9.80. Though it's dated in terms of contact information, it's good on basics. There's a German version as well.

Canoeing

The most beautiful section of the river is from Treuchtlingen or Pappenheim to Eichstätt or Kipfenberg, about a 60km stretch that you can do lazily in two to three days. There are lots of little dams along the way, as well as a few fun little pseudo-rapids about 10km north-west of Dollnstein. Signs warn of impending doom, but tourist officials say that if you heed the warning to stay to the right, these little canoe slides are pretty safe.

Tours San-Aktiv Tours (☎ 09831-49 36, fax 805 94), Nürnberger Strasse 48, 91710 Gunzenhausen, is the largest and best-organised canoe-rental company in the park, with a network of vehicles to shuttle canoes, bicycles and people around the area. It runs canoe packages through the park from April to October for three, five and seven days.

You can do it alone or join a group. Prices start at DM229 per person for three days, including boats, maps, instructions, two nights lodging in guesthouses (DM299 if you stay in hotels) and transport from the meeting point.

Natour (☎ 09142-961 10), Am Schulhof 1, 91757 Treuchtlingen, is another package canoe-trip operator that has similar trips and prices.

Rental Friendly, English-speaking Frank Warmuth runs Fahrradgarage (☎ 08421-67 67 69, mobile ☎ 0161 290 74 65), Herzoggasse 3 in Eichstätt, which rents four-person canoes for DM50 per day, including insurance, paddles, life-vests, and a waterproof box for your clothes. Staff will haul you and the boats for varying prices (eg DM37.80 from Eichstätt to Dollnstein, about 25km upstream), or just the canoe for a flat DM1 per kilometre between Eichstätt and the drop-off point. It's open every day.

There are canoe-rental stands in every town within the park, and prices are uniform; you can get a list of rental outlets from the Informationszentrum Naturpark Altmühltal.

Cycling & Hiking

Bicycle trails throughout the park are clearly labelled with long, rectangular brown signs bearing a bike symbol. Hiking-trail markers are yellow, and perhaps even better marked.

Fahrradgarage (see Canoeing, Rental) rents out bicycles for DM12 per day; and the Tretroller, a sort of high-tech push-scooter with handlebars and brakes, for DM5 per hour. Staff will bring the bikes to you or bring you with the bikes to anywhere in the park with the same conditions as for canoes.

There are bicycle-rental stands in every town within the park, and prices are uniform; you can get a list of rental outlets from the Informationszentrum Naturpark Altmühltal. Most bike-rental agencies will also store bicycles; Fahrradgarage charges DM1 per hour or DM3 per day.

Getting There & Away

Train Trains run between Eichstätt Bahnhof and Treuchtlingen hourly or better (DM7.60, 25 minutes), and between Treuchtlingen and Gunzenhausen hourly (DM7.50, 15 minutes). Trains from Munich that run through Eichstätt Bahnhof also stop in Dollnstein, Solnhofen and Pappenheim.

Bus On Saturday, Sunday and holidays from May to October, regional bus companies offer a bicycle transport service between Regensburg, Ingolstadt, Riedenburg, Kelheim, Beilngries, Eichstätt Stadtbahnhof, Kipfenberg and Wellheim. All-day tickets cost DM17 for passengers with bicycles, DM12 for passengers without, or DM38 per family with bikes, DM27 without. Routes and the companies that serve them are:

Ingolstadt-Riedenburg-Beilngries
 RBA (☎ 0841-97 37 40)
Regensburg-Kelheim-Riedenburg
 RBO (☎ 0941-99 90 80)
Wellheim-Eichstätt-Kipfenberg-Beilngries
 Jägle (☎ 08421-972 10)

Eichstätt

☎ 08421 • pop 13,000

Home to Bavaria's largest Catholic university, Eichstätt's buildings and streets haven't been damaged since Swedes razed the place during the Thirty Years' War. With several sights, in addition to a great hostel and several guesthouses, Eichstätt makes a perfect base for exploring Altmühltal Park. Note that businesses in Eichstätt close between noon and 2 pm.

Orientation There are two train stations. The Bahnhof, 5km from the centre, is the hub for trains between the Stadtbahnhof (south of the Altmühl River near the city centre) and everywhere on earth. From the Stadtbahnhof, Willibaldsburg is due south up Burgstrasse, uphill for about 10 minutes. For the hostel, take Burgstrasse to Reichenaustrasse and turn right; it's about four minutes ahead on the left side of the road.

The city centre is on the north side of the Altmühl. From the Stadtbahnhof, walk

BAVARIA

north across the Spitalbrücke and you'll end up in Domplatz.

For the tourist and nature park information offices, continue east at Domplatz to Ostenstrasse and then turn left on Kardinal-Preysing-Platz.

Information The city's fabulous tourist office (☎ 988 00), Kardinal-Preysing-Platz 14, in the Kloster of Notre Dame, is open in summer, Monday to Saturday from 9 am to 6 pm, and Sunday from 10 am to noon. In winter, hours are Monday to Thursday from 9 am to noon and 2 to 4 pm, and Friday from 9 am to noon (closed weekends). The Informationszentrum Naturpark Altmühltal right next door keeps the same hours.

Change money at Dresdner Bank, Westendstrasse 1 at the Markt. The post office is at Domplatz 7.

Universitäts Buchhandlung Sporer (☎ 15 38), Gabrielstrasse 4, has some books in English. The Universitätsbibliothek (☎ 93 14 14) is in the Ulmer Hof, Pater-Philipp-Jeningen-Platz 6.

In an emergency, you should call the regional Kreiskrankenhaus (☎ 60 10) hospital at Ostenstrasse 31.

Willibaldsburg The hill-top castle of Willibaldsburg (1355-1725) houses two museums: the **Jura-Museum Eichstätt** (DM6/4), with a fascinating collection of fossils from the region as well as other geological and natural history exhibits, and the **Museum of Pre-History & Early History**. Don't miss the 76.5m-deep well downstairs – toss in a coin and listen for about 10 seconds for the ting or the plop. There's also a lovely garden near the car park with fantastic views of Eichstätt.

On the other side, you'll see the **Kloster Rebdorf**, now also a boys' boarding school, which contains a splendid baroque church and some of Germany's most interesting arcades. On the hill above the school, you can visit the **limestone quarry**, a favourite spot for fossil-hunting locals. Drive up or take a JVB bus from Eichstätt (various lines, DM1.80, 10 minutes).

If you forget your tools, fear not: you can rent them at the **Museum Bergér** (☎ 46 83), at the base of the quarry, which displays a lot of geological samples. It's open Monday to Saturday from 1 to 5 pm, and Sunday from 10 am to noon and 1 to 5 pm. Chisel and hammer rental is DM2 per day.

Kloster St Walburga After the death of Walburga, sister of Eichstätt's first bishop, her body was buried in Heilige Kreuz Kirche, now the Kloster St Walburga. You can view the crypt in the church, at the north-west end of town, on Westenstrasse just south of the city's spectacular **fortifications**. At least once a year, a mysterious oily substance oozes from the crypt; nuns give it away as balm. It's free – just ask for a bottle of Walburgis Öl.

City Centre The city highlight, besides the churches and buildings designed by architects Gabriel de Gabrieli and Maurizio Pedetti, is the **Dom**, containing an enormous stained-glass window by Hans Holbein the Elder. Its prize, the Pappenheimer Altar (1489-97), was carved from sandstone and depicts a pilgrimage from Pappenheim to Jerusalem. The detail is worth an hour's gape.

Behind the Dom, in Residenzplatz, crowned by a golden statue of Mary atop a 19m-high column, is the **Residenz** (1725-36), a Gabrieli building with a stunning main staircase and the Spiegelsaal, with its mirrors and fresco of Greek mythology. There are free tours from Monday to Thursday at 11 am and 2 pm, and concerts 10 times a year.

Walk through the **Markt**, noting Café im Paradeis (see Places to Eat), a beautifully restored building with elements from 1313 and 1453 that's open to the public as a museum – just walk through. Continue up Westenstrasse, past the **Maria-Hilfe-Kapelle**, and you'll pass a moss-covered **water wheel**; turn right on Kapellbuck and you'll find the little **carp pond**.

Organised Tours The tourist office gives 1½ hour walking tours (DM5, kids under 12 free) from April to October at 1.30 pm on Saturday.

The tourist office in Treuchtlingen (☎ 09142-31 21) runs a bus tour to the eastern Altmühle Valley every Tuesday (DM30) that leaves at 9.20 am from the police station, opposite the Stadtbahnhof. The bus goes to Kelheim, where you get on a boat to the Weltenburg Monastery (see the Around Regensburg section later in this chapter).

Places to Stay & Eat *Bootsrastplatz Aumühle (no telephone)*, on the north side of the Altmühl River, is a free camping ground with toilets but no washing facilities. From the Stadtbahnhof, take a Green, Yellow or Red Line bus to Römerstrasse (Krankenhaus stop) and walk south along Universitätsallee.

The *hostel (☎ 980 40, Reichenaustrasse 15)* is a modern place overlooking the Altstadt, with dorm beds for DM22, but you can only book Monday to Friday from 8 am to noon and 5 to 7 pm – and they're frequently booked up with school groups. The hostel is closed in December and January.

Gasthof Sonne (☎ 67 91, Buchtal 17) is a perfectly pleasant place with clean rooms (though it's stingy with soap and shampoo), friendly service and singles/doubles from DM60/100. The best thing about the place is the *restaurant*, where a really good steak is DM21.

Gasthof Hotel Klosterstuben (☎ 35 00, Pedettistrasse 26), just east of the Kloster, has an extensive fish and game menu (eg fresh trout dishes for under DM15) and decent vegie dishes.

There's also fast food on the Markt at *Metzgerei Schneider*, which is open all day, and *markets* held here on Wednesday and Saturday mornings. Here, too, is *Café im Paradeis (☎ 33 13, Markt 9)*, with tasty tarts for DM4 to DM6, cappuccino for DM3.60 and sandwiches for DM8.

Getting There & Away There's train service hourly or better between Ingolstadt and Eichstätt (DM7.60, 25 minutes). For more connections, see the main Getting There & Away entry earlier in this Altmühltal Nature Park section.

Eastern Bavaria

A cluster of romantic ancient cities lies in the north-east of the state, stretching from Regensburg to the Czech border. Regensburg is one of Germany's loveliest and liveliest cities, and a bicycle ride from there along the Danube to Passau (about 120km away), where the Danube converges with the Inn and Ilz rivers, is a rewarding journey.

REGENSBURG
☎ 0941 • pop 142,000

A treasure trove of architecture, lovely Regensburg on the Danube has relics from all periods, yet integrates them into an unpretentious, very liveable whole. A former Roman settlement, Regensburg became the capital of Bavaria's first duchy in the 11th century, and was one of Germany's most prosperous trading hubs during the Middle Ages. The city has over 1400 listed landmarks in the centre alone. Here, as nowhere else in Germany, you enter the misty ages between the Roman and the Carolingian.

The patrician tower-houses in the centre of the city are as arresting as the populace is friendly and unspoiled – even by the relatively large hordes of tourists they see each year. Oskar Schindler lived in Regensburg for years, and now one of his houses bears a plaque to his recently celebrated achievements.

Regensburg is worth a couple of days on any Bavarian itinerary. If you do decide to visit, you must not miss sampling one of the best food products in Germany: Händlmaier's Süsser Hausmachersenf, a distinctive sweet mustard, made to go with another local speciality, Regensburger Bratwurstl. Wash it all down with a locally made Kneipinger Pils and you have the makings of a beautiful day.

Orientation
The city is divided by the east-flowing Danube, separating the Altstadt from the northern banks. Islands in the middle of the river, mainly Oberer and Unterer Wöhrd,

BAVARIA

are populated as well. The hostel is on Unterer Wöhrd, east of the Steinerne Brücke.

The Hauptbahnhof is at the southern end of the Altstadt. Maximilianstrasse leads straight north from there to Kornmarkt, at the centre of the historic district.

The twisting, pedestrianised streets of the Altstadt are closed to cars, but not buses.

Information

Tourist Offices The tourist office (☎ 507 44 10, fax 507 44 19, email touristmus@ info.regensburg.baynet.de), in the Altes Rathaus, is open Monday to Friday from 8.30 am to 6 pm, Saturday from 9 am to 4 pm, and Sunday and holidays from 9.30 am to 2.30 pm (from April to October to 4 pm). It's closed on New Year's Day. Ask about the *Verbundkarte* (DM10/5, DM20 per family), which gives free entry to four of the city's main museums.

ADAC has a service centre (☎ 556 73) on Ernst-Reuter-Platz.

Money Change money at the Postbank next to the Hauptbahnhof. There are also several banks along Maximilianstrasse, and a Hypovereinsbank at Neupfarrplatz.

Post & Communications The main post office is adjacent to the Hauptbahnhof, but the de facto main branch is the lovely Dom post office at Domplatz, in the former ducal court opposite the south side of the Dom.

C@fe Netzblick (☎ 599 97 00), Am Römling 9, is a fun Internet cafe in vaulted medieval chambers; surf or mail for DM5 per half hour. It's open from 10 am to 1 am in winter, and 7 pm to 1 am in summer.

Internet Resources Regensburg has a useful Web site at www.regensburg.de.

Bookshops & Libraries Get English books and magazines at the Hauptbahnhof's Internationale Presse stand. Hugendubel (☎ 58 53 20), Wahlenstrasse 17 (with another entrance on Tändlergasse), has the usual good collection of English and travel books (including Lonely Planet titles) and a

reading area. The Stadtbücherei (city library; ☎ 507 14 76) is at Haidplatz 8 in the Thon Dittmer Palais.

University Universität Regensburg (☎ 94 31) has its campus at the southern end of the city. Its 20,000 students are enrolled in major schools including theology, economics, medicine, philosophy and mathematics. Take bus Nos 6 and 11 to the Universität stop.

Cultural Centres Deutsch-Amerikanisches Institut (☎ 524 76), Haidplatz 8 in the Thon Dittmer Palais, has a good range of cultural programs and events.

Laundry There's a large and clean Schnell & Sauber coin laundry at Hermann-Geib-Strasse 5, on the corner of Landshuter Strasse. Other laundrettes are at Winklergasse 14 and at Hofgartenweg 4.

Medical Services & Emergency The largest hospital close to the centre is the Evangelical Hospital (Evangelisches Krankenhaus; ☎ 504 00) at Emmeramsplatz, near the Schloss Thurn und Taxis and the Hauptbahnhof. Call ☎ 192 22 for an ambulance. Police headquarters are on the south side of Bismarckplatz.

Dom St Peter

Dominating the skyline are the twin spires of Dom St Peter, considered one of Bavaria's most important Gothic cathedrals. Constructed on the site of four previous churches between 1275 and 1520, its distinctive jet-black grime layer was sandblasted in 1997 to reveal for the first time in centuries the green sandstone and limestone facade.

Inside the dark, cavernous church, you'll immediately see the cathedral's most prized possessions – its richly hued original 13th and 14th century **stained-glass windows**, above the choir on the east side. These, along with the 13th to 15th century windows on the south side, positively embarrass the 19th century glass at the west.

Just west of the altar are two more of the cathedral's prizes. They are the **statues**: *The*

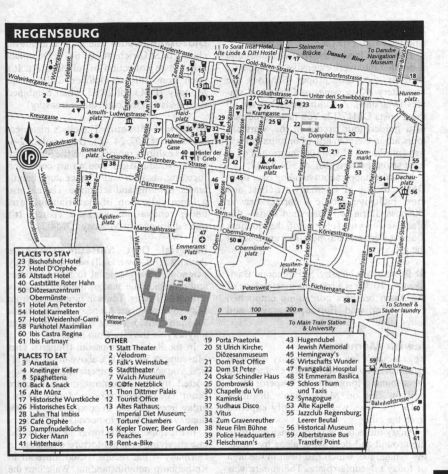

REGENSBURG

PLACES TO STAY
23 Bischofshof Hotel
27 Hotel D'Orphée
36 Altstadt Hotel
40 Gaststätte Roter Hahn
50 Diözesanzentrum Obermünste
51 Hotel Am Peterstor
54 Hotel Karmeliten
57 Hotel Weidenhof-Garni
58 Parkhotel Maximilian
60 Ibis Castra Regina
61 Ibis Furtmayr

PLACES TO EAT
3 Anastasia
4 Kneitinger Keller
8 Spaghettena
16 Back & Snack
16 Alte Münz
17 Historische Wurstküche
26 Historisches Eck
28 Lahn Thal Imbiss
29 Café Orphée
35 Dampfnudelküche
37 Dicker Mann
41 Hinterhaus

OTHER
1 Statt Theater
2 Velodrom
5 Falk's Weinstube
6 Stadttheater
7 Watch Museum
9 C@fe Netzblick
11 Thon Dittmer Palais
12 Tourist Office
13 Altes Rathaus; Imperial Diet Museum; Torture Chambers
14 Kepler Tower; Beer Garden
15 Peaches
18 Rent-a-Bike
19 Porta Praetoria
20 St Ulrich Kirche; Diözesanmuseum
21 Dom Post Office
22 Dom St Peter
24 Oskar Schindler Haus
25 Dombrowski
30 Chapelle du Vin
31 Kaminski
32 Sudhaus Disco
33 Vitus
34 Zum Gravenreuther
38 Neue Film Bühne
39 Police Headquarters
42 Fleischmann's
43 Hugendubel
44 Jewish Memorial
45 Hemingway's
46 Wirtschafts Wunder
47 Evangelical Hospital
48 St Emmeram Basilica
49 Schloss Thurn und Taxis
52 Synagogue
53 Alte Kapelle
55 Jazzclub Regensburg; Leerer Beutal
56 Historical Museum
59 Albertstrasse Bus Transfer Point

Smiling Angel of Regensburg, his charming mug beaming at *Mary* (on the north pillar) as he delivers the news that she's pregnant. At the west exit, note the **statuettes**: *Satan* and *Satan's Grandmother*, both reminders that outside these walls bad things await. Especially if you don't make a donation.

The church conducts tours in German from May to October, Monday to Saturday at 10 and 11 am, and 2 pm (Sunday and holidays at noon and 2 pm). Entry is free; the tour is DM4/2.

Around the corner from the Dom, the **Alte Kapelle** (8th to 15th centuries) has such an unbelievably lavish rococo interior that each person we saw walk in audibly gasped.

Schloss

The family castle, **Schloss Thurn und Taxis** (torn-und-**tak**-siss), has been handed down over the generations since Franz von Taxis (1459-1517) established the international postal system throughout Western Europe.

euro currency converter DM1 = €0.51

Taxis ran the post until 1867, when ownership passed to Prussia.

The castle is near the Hauptbahnhof and is divided into three extensive and separate sections: the castle proper (Schloss), the monastery *(Kreuzgang)* and the royal stables (Marstall). A combined ticket for all three costs DM17/12. You need to be part of a guided tour except in the Marstall; tours are in German only. For tours in English (minimum of DM100 for groups of at least seven persons) call ☎ 504 81 33.

If you're happy about handing over up to DM17 to one of Germany's richest and most reclusive people – former brewer Duchess Gloria von Thurn und Taxis – this place is for you (photos of the duchess looking stern and business-like are DM2 at the gift shop).

St Emmeram Nearby, St Emmeram Basilika (☎ 510 30) is a baroque masterpiece of the Asam brothers containing untouched Carolingian and Episcopal graves and relics (free).

Jewish Memorials

Regensburg's Jewish community was well established by the early 16th century, and Jews found a 'protector' in Emperor Maximilian. But on Maximilian's death in 1519, the Jews were summarily expelled from the city.

Angry mobs burned the Jewish ghetto to the ground and destroyed, piece by piece, the synagogue, which had been in the area of today's Neupfarrplatz. The square was named for the church that was erected on the site of the synagogue practically before the fires had gone out.

The city uncovered the foundations of the synagogue and several houses a few years ago. A memorial to the Jewish community stands near the entrance of Neupfarrplatz 7. Another synagogue (which had been partly wrecked by the Nazis) is about 200m southeast at Am Brixener Hof 2.

On the north side of the Steinerne Brücke you'll find a memorial to concentration-camp victims.

Museums

Diözesanmuseum The painted medieval church of St Ulrich (☎ 501 68) at Domplatz 2 houses a collection of religious art. It's open from April to October, daily except Monday (DM3, or DM5 when combined with a visit to the cathedral's **treasury**).

Historical Museum The city's historical museum (☎ 507 24 48), Dachauplatz 2-4, houses exhibits ranging from the Stone Age to the Middle Ages, and an art collection focusing on 14th and 15th century handicrafts, painting and sculpture. There's also a large collection of Bavarian folklore, under renovation when we visited. It's open daily except Monday (DM4/2).

Imperial Diet Museum The Altes Rathaus (Old Town Hall) was progressively extended from medieval to baroque times and remained the seat of the Reichstag for almost 150 years. Tours in English run from May to September, Monday to Saturday at 3.15 pm (DM5). Today, Regensburg's three mayors rule the city from here.

In the Reichstagsmuseum (Imperial Diet Museum; ☎ 507 44 11), above the tourist office, you can see the Imperial Chamber, supported by the enormous original centre beam. The museum is open Monday to Saturday from 9.30 am to noon and 2 to 4 pm, Sunday from 10 am to noon (DM5/2.50).

In the Imperial Diet tower are perhaps the last surviving original **torture chambers** in Germany – the reconstructed museum in Rothenburg notwithstanding. Walk into the old holding cell and look down to the dungeon before entering the interrogation room, which bristles with tools such as the rack, the Spanish Donkey (a tall wooden wedge on which naked men were made to sit), spiked chairs and other charming objects.

Watch Museum This breezy little privately owned museum (☎ 599 95 95), Ludwigstrasse 3, has a fabulous collection of valuable and notable watches, including the obvious stuff, from companies like Jaeger-LeCouitre, Patek Phillippe ... ahem ...

Swatch, and what is billed as the most 'complicated and expensive in the world', the Blancpain 1735. Also look out for the world's first digital watch, the 1972 Pulsar. Admission is DM8/4, worth it if you're a watch nut.

Danube Navigation Museum The Donau-Schiffahrts-Museum (☎ 525 10), Werftstrasse on Unterer Wöhrd not far from the hostel, is a historic paddle-wheel steam tugboat moored on the Danube, with exhibits on the history of navigation on the river. The museum is open from April to October daily from 10 am to 5 pm (DM4/3, or DM8 per family).

Kepler Tower
The astronomer and mathematician Johannes Kepler lived and died in the house at Keplerstrasse 5, which is now the Kepler-Gedächtnishaus (☎ 507 34 42). Guided tours are Tuesday to Saturday on the hour from 10 am to 3 pm, with a two hour break at noon, and Sunday at 10 am and 11 am (DM4/2). Of more immediate concern these days is the wonderful beer garden behind the house (see Entertainment).

Roman Wall
The Roman wall, with its seriously impressive **Porta Praetoria** arch, dates to 179 AD. It follows Unter den Schwibbögen onto Dr-Martin-Luther-Strasse and is the most tangible reminder of the ancient Castra Regina (Roman fortress), from which the name 'Regensburg' comes.

Stone Bridge
Steinerne Brücke (1135-46), the oldest in Germany, remains one of the most flabbergasting accomplishments of medieval architecture: until recently the 850-year-old bridge supported vehicular traffic. In a bid to conserve it, the city has banned all private vehicles, to the great consternation of car owners on the north bank of the Danube.

Canoeing & Kayaking
Christian Platzeck of Nautilus Canoes (☎ 09401-512 95, mobile ☎ 0172 851 69 13,

fax 65 52) can deck you out with kayaks or canoes along the Regen, Naab or Vils rivers. The cost per day is DM30 per kayak, or DM50/60 for three or four-person canoes. His address is Embacher Strasse 10, 93803 Niedertraubling, south-east of Regensburg on the B15 towards Landshut. Take one of the regular trains (DM3.50, six minutes) to Obertraubling and he'll meet you.

Kanu Tours (☎ 09964-10 93), Irschenbach 50, 94353 Haibach, rents out the same types of boats for DM30/60/70 per day.

Organised Tours
Walking tours of the Altstadt in German (DM8/4, 1½ hours) depart from the tourist office year round from Monday to Saturday at 2.45 pm (Saturday also at 10.15 am), and Sunday and holidays at 10.45 am and 2 pm. Meet at the tourist office. From May to September there's an extra tour from Monday to Friday at 10.15 am. English-language tours (DM8/4) start at the same spot on Wednesday and Saturday at 1.30 pm; call ☎ 507 34 13 to sign up.

Ferry cruises run by Regensburger Personenschiffahrt (☎ 56 56 68) depart from the landing near the Steinerne Brücke from late March to October hourly from 10 am to 4 pm (DM11/7, the trip lasts 50 minutes). There are also boat tours to Walhalla, a Ludwig I monument modelled on the Parthenon in Athens, from April to mid-October daily at 10.30 am and 2 pm (DM16/11 return, two hours including a one hour stop at Walhalla).

Places to Stay
The *Azur-Campingplatz* (☎ 27 00 25, fax 29 94 32, Am Weinweg 40) costs DM10 per adult, plus DM13 site fee if you have a car, DM7 if you don't, and DM4 per motorcycle. It's at the north-west end of the city just south of the Danube; from the Hauptbahnhof, take bus No 6 right to the entrance.

The *DJH hostel* (☎ 574 02, fax 524 11, Wöhrdstrasse 60), on Unterer Wöhrd east of the Steinerne Brücke, costs DM27 including breakfast (juniors only; closed in December). Its location is perfect, on the Danube about 10 minutes walk from the Altstadt.

BAVARIA

From the station, take bus No 3 from the Albertstrasse stop to the Eisstadion stop.

North of the river in a 13th century hospice, the **Hotel Spitalgarten** (☎ 847 74, St-Katherinen-Platz 1) has basic singles/doubles from DM40/80. **Diözesanzentrum Obermünster** (☎ 597 22 50, fax 597 22 30, Obermünsterplatz 7) has a prime location in the centre and similar rooms from DM50/90. Ring ahead if you're arriving after 5 pm.

Gaststätte Roter Hahn (☎ 59 50 90, fax 595 09 40, Rote-Hahnen-Gasse 10) and **Hotel Am Peterstor** (☎ 545 45, fax 545 42, Fröhliche-Türken-Strasse 12) both have simple rooms from around DM65/95 and DM75/95 respectively.

Hotel D'Orphée (☎ 59 60 20, fax 59 60 22 22, Wahlenstrasse 1), right around the corner from the tourist office, is a pleasure to recommend. Each room is unique and it's a lot cheaper than it should be: simple singles upstairs start at DM60, but the stunningly romantic room No 7 is DM125/140 and worth it. Downstairs rooms have baths (room No 5's bathroom entrance is hidden in a secret door) and prices range from DM125/140 to DM175/210. There's a nice common room downstairs with a large terrace, and breakfast is a block away at the Café Orphée – see Places to Eat.

Hotel Weidenhof-Garni (☎ 530 31, fax 56 51 66, Maximilianstrasse 23) is a nicely renovated place with pleasant staff and as good a location as the expensive Parkhotel at a fraction of the price. Clean, simple singles start from DM65, and singles/doubles with bathrooms begin at DM90/135.

Another good deal on simple rooms is at the **Hotel Karmeliten** (☎ 546 58, fax 56 17 51, Dachauplatz 1), east of the Dom, which charges DM80/120. Rooms with bath and toilet start at DM120/170.

The city's two Ibis hotels, the **Castra Regina** (☎ 569 30, fax 569 35 05, Bahnhofstrasse 22) and the **Furtmayr** (☎ 780 40, fax 780 45 09, Furtmayrstrasse 1), charge DM105/120 and DM115/130 respectively, including breakfast.

The **Bischofshof Hotel** (☎ 590 86, fax 535 08, Krautermarkt 3) is tucked away in a quiet courtyard right by the Steinerne Brücke, with room rates cheaper than you'd think, from DM110/195. Some rooms are within the Roman walls – nice touch, eh?

The **Altstadt Hotel** (☎ 586 60, fax 586 61 68, Haidplatz 4) is another city landmark that's been around forever. Its plush rooms, named after various royals who're slept in them, range from DM128/158 to DM219/280 for suites.

The modern and shining **Sorat Insel-Hotel** (☎ 810 40, fax 810 44 44, Müllerstrasse 7) on Oberer Wöhrd has a totally awesome location at the island's tip and great views of the town's skyline. Rooms start from DM200/240.

The **Parkhotel Maximilian** (☎ 568 50, fax 529 42, Maximilianstrasse 28) employs old-world European charm. It'll charm you right out of DM218/268, too.

The tourist office can find rooms from about DM30, and charges DM1.50 for every referral. The city Mitwohnzentrale (☎ 220 24) can arrange long-term stays.

Places to Eat
The **Historische Wurstküche** (☎ 190 98) may have a lock on the tourist trade in Bratwurst, but locals know that the best place to get the little links is **Kneitinger** (☎ 524 55, Arnulfsplatz 3). Walk around the corner onto Kreuzgasse for a peep into the brewery and then sit down to the best sausages around (DM8). It closes at 8 pm.

There's dependably good local food at the **Dicker Mann** (☎ 573 70, Krebsgasse 6), with Bavarian dishes for DM17 to DM24, good service and a little beer garden. Also great for solid Bavarian specialities (good steaks, too) is **Alte Münz** (☎ 548 86, Fischmarkt 7). It has a friendly atmosphere (lots of wood and booze bottles) and nice service.

The earthy **Hinterhaus** (☎ 546 61, Rote-Hahnen-Gasse 2), in a roofed-over lane, serves good vegetarian and meat dishes for about DM7 to DM15.

Sample fin-de-siècle elegance at **Anastasia** (☎ 584 15 79, Arnulfsplatz 4) in an old Russian consulate, with fine meat and vegetarian dishes for DM12.50 to DM18.

Specialties include the *Hussar's Spiess*, an enormous, tender pork and beef kebab with trimmings for DM25.80.

For heavenly pastas and a spirited crowd, step into the *Spaghetteria (☎ 589 25, Am Römling 12)* in a former 17th century chapel. You can pick fresh noodles, sauces and side dishes from the buffet and get out the door, with a glass of house wine, for under DM20.

Café Orphée (☎ 529 77, Untere Bachgasse 8) is as French as De Gaulle, serving nice breakfasts for two including fresh fruit, crepes, croissant and coffee. Sweet crepes are around DM8, meat and vegetable crepes are DM11, and main courses start from DM15.

The *Historisches Eck (☎ 589 20, Watmarkt 6)* offers amazing (and amazingly expensive) French food in a lovely setting with fine service. An eight course menu costs DM120 per person; don't miss one of its signature desserts, such as hazelnut pudding with quince jam and rum-raisin ice cream.

There's a daily fresh *produce market* at Neupfarrplatz (dubbed Viktualienmarkt, like its bigger namesake in Munich).

Back & Snack, Haidplatz 5, has good baked treats, as does the *bakery* in the Hauptbahnhof right next to the exit to the tracks – with a huge range of sandwiches from DM4.

The *Lahn Thai Imbiss (☎ 56 38 97, Untere Bachgasse 1)* offers good, cheap Thai meals such as red curry or sweet and sour chicken from DM8, and soups and spring rolls for DM3.50. More Asian fast food is available nearby at *Little Saigon (☎ 56 77 52, Domplatz 5)*, with egg rolls, salads and other vegie treats for under DM10.

The quirky *Dampfnudelküche (☎ 532 97, Am Watmarkt 4)* serves steamed doughnuts with custard (DM7.80), a local speciality of Regensburg. It's open Thursday to Friday from 10.01 am to 6.01 pm (to 3.01 pm on Saturday). It's closed Sunday and Monday.

Entertainment

The city publishes a seasonal *Kultur in Regensburg* guide, available at the tourist office (free). For gay information contact Rosa Hilfe (☎ 514 41), a gay switchboard service. Lesbians can contact the lesbian group Frauenzentrum (☎ 242 59). There's also the Regensburger Schwulen-und-Lesben-Initiative (☎ 514 41), a gay and lesbian contact group, at Blaue-Lilien-Gasse 1.

Beer Gardens The city's loveliest beer garden is probably the tiny *Kepler (☎ 56 06 35, Keplerstrasse 3)*, named after the famous astronomer. Walk through the tunnel into a sweet little yard beneath a tower. The *Alte Linde (☎ 880 80, Müllerstrasse 1)* runs a large and leafy beer garden just off the Steinerne Brücke – lovely on summer evenings (closed Wednesday). *Zum Gravenreuther (☎ 533 48, Hinter der Grieb 10)* is a worthy alternative, as is the *Bischofshof Hotel* (see Places to Stay), an excellent, if over-touristed, choice.

Pubs & Bars The *Dombrowski (☎ 573 88, Kramgasse 10-12)* is a chic place with intimate lighting and a nice street-side cafe right opposite the Dom. Two other fashionable haunts are *Hemingway's (☎ 56 15 06, Obere Bachgasse 6)*, and *Peaches (☎ 534 81, Baumhackergasse 2)* on Keplerstrasse.

Three places on Hinter der Grieb worth crawling into or out of are the *Chapelle du Vin*, a wine cellar in the 13th century Löblturm; *Kaminski*, sharp as a razor and peopled by a vain crowd; and the hugely popular *Vitus (☎ 526 46, Hinter der Grieb 8)*, with tasty salads, quiches and more.

A brand new, lively place with great cocktails and friendly staff is *Fleischmann's (☎ 580 82, Untere Bachgasse 15)*, on the edge of the main drinks quarter. Prepare to stand if you come after 8 pm.

Falk's Weinstube is in the lovely little white building across the street from the Stadttheater. About 100m south-east is a fashionable *Neue Film Bühne*, frequented by an eclectic theatre crowd.

Jazz The *Jazzclub Regensburg (☎ 56 33 75, Bertoldstrasse 9)* is open Tuesday to Sunday from 11 am to 1 am and features regular live music. The *Leerer Beutel (☎ 589 97, Bertoldstrasse 9)* is a popular rival.

euro currency converter DM1 = €0.51

BAVARIA

Classical Music Opera, operettas, ballet and classical-music performances are held at the *Stadttheater*. There are concerts of the Domspatzen boys' choir during Sunday services at the Dom, and classical concerts in lots of venues around town, including the baroque *Oswald-Kirche*, Weissgerbergraben 1 (just south of the pedestrian Eiserner Steg bridge), the *Rathaus*, and the *Theater am Haidplatz* (see Theatre).

Cinemas English-language films are screened regularly at *Film im Dai (☎ 524 76, Haidplatz 8)*, at the Deutsch-Amerikanisches Institut in the Thon Dittmer Palais.

Theatre Regensburg Städtische Bühnen runs (from September to July) the *Theater am Haidplatz* at Haidplatz 8, an open-air theatre venue in the courtyard of the Thon Dittmer Palais, as well as the *Velodrom (Kreuzgasse 12)*, a converted motorcycle rink through the passageway at Arnulfplatz. It stages performances of opera, theatre, musicals and ballet. Reserve tickets for the former at the tourist office (☎ 507 44 12); for the latter, ring ☎ 507 24 24.

The *Statt Theater (☎ 533 02, Winklergasse 16)* is a privately owned venue that stages alternative dramas, plays and cabaret.

Getting There & Away

Mainline trains run from Frankfurt through Regensburg on their way to Passau and Vienna (nine daily). Several Munich-Leipzig and Munich-Dresden services also pass through. Sample ticket prices are Munich (DM37, 1½ hours), Nuremberg (DM33, one hour) and Passau (DM34, one hour).

The A3 autobahn runs north-west to Nuremberg and south-east to Passau, while the A9 runs south to Munich.

For a lift, call the city Mitfahrzentrale (☎ 220 22).

Regensburg is a key player on the Danube Bike Trail (see the Central Black Forest section of the Baden-Württemberg chapter for details); all approaches to the city are well signposted along bike paths. There are bike lockers at the Hauptbahnhof on platform 1 (DM1 per day). See Getting Around for a bike rental station.

Getting Around

Bus The main point for city bus transfers is one block north of the Hauptbahnhof, on Albertstrasse. Other points include Arnulfsplatz, Domplatz and Neupfarrplatz. Bus tickets cost DM1.40/2.70 for short/long journeys in the centre; strip tickets cost DM10.50 for six rides (two strips per ride in town). An all-day ticket is a better deal, costing just DM6 for the centre. Bus Nos 6 and 11 course through the Altstadt for just DM1, but were in danger of being cancelled at the time of writing.

Car & Motorcycle The Steinerne Brücke is closed to private cars. To cross the river, you'll have to head east and work your way to Weissenburgstrasse, which becomes Nibelungenbrücke and leads to Nordgaustrasse. There's an exit from Nibelungenbrücke onto Unterer Wöhrd and the hostel.

The centre of the city is also closed to vehicles, but not buses and taxis. Car parks in the centre charge from DM2 per hour and are well signposted.

Taxi Taxis cost DM4.50 flag fall, plus DM2.50 per kilometre. For a taxi, call ☎ 194 10, ☎ 570 00 or ☎ 520 52.

Bicycle Rent-a-Bike (mobile ☎ 0177 831 12 34), on Donaumarkt, has daily rental from Monday to Saturday. Children's bicycles cost DM10, touring bikes DM15, cruisers DM16 and trekking bikes DM17. On Sunday and holidays there are cheap rates for hourly and three-hourly rentals. It also has bike storage, and staff can help plan bike trips along the Danube and in other regions.

AROUND REGENSBURG
Weltenburg
☎ 09441 • pop 400

When you're this close to the world's oldest monastic brewery, there's just no excuse to miss out. **Klosterschenke Weltenburg** has been brewing its delicious dark beer since

BAVARIA

1050. The hulking monastery (☎ 36 80), run by the Röhrl family since 1934, is set against the backdrop of the **Danube Gorge**, with dramatic hills and cliffs and rolling countryside. It also has a splendid baroque **church** built by the Asam brothers.

Only a half hour or so out of Regensburg, on summer weekends it's a favourite spot for Regensburgers (and now for hordes of tourists), who come by the boatload to sit in the beer garden and sample the beer (DM5 per half litre and worth every pfennig). There are several beer halls, including a *Bierstube* (the hard-to-get-into Asamstüberl), and one of the nicest beer gardens in the country.

The suds are served up from April to October daily from 8 am to 7 pm. From early November to late March, opening hours are more limited.

Getting There & Away From Regensburg's Hauptbahnhof, grab one of the hourly trains to Kelheim (DM7, 24 minutes), which actually bring you to Saal (Donau), from where there's connecting bus service to Kelheim. In Kelheim, climb aboard one of the boats run by Personenschiffahrt Altmühltal (☎ 218 01); these travel from Kelheim to Klosterschenke Weltenburg via Donaudurchbruch.

The schedule has four seasons within the March to November period, with more frequent service on weekends. Suffice to say that between 10 am and 4 pm, there are boats at least every 1½ hours. The return fare is DM9, plus DM6 per bicycle. Family tickets are DM25 return.

STRAUBING
☎ 09421 • pop 40,000

Straubing, some 30km south-east of Regensburg on the edge of the Bavarian forest, erupts into a beery roar for 10 days during **Gäubodenfest**, Bavaria's second-biggest collective drink-up. Begun in 1812 as a social gathering for grain farmers, the fair lubricates more than a million visitors in August, beating Munich's Oktoberfest by several weeks. The town centre becomes an enormous beer garden with 23,000 seats –

often it's standing room only – but the atmosphere is less contrived than at the more famous affair further south. Finding cheap lodging during the festival is a tall order.

Orientation & Information
The Altstadt, compact and easily walkable, is sandwiched between the Danube to the north and the Hauptbahnhof to the south. The tourist office (☎ 94 43 07, fax 94 41 03, email stadt@straubing.baynet.de), on the main square at Theresienplatz 20, will refer rooms for free. Ask ahead for exact dates of the Gäubodenfest.

The post office, housing a Postbank to change your money and travellers cheques, is opposite the Hauptbahnhof. Straubing has its very own Web site; you'll find it at www.straubing.baynet.de.

Things to See & Do
The Altstadt is chock-a-block with attractive historic buildings. Dividing the marketplace in two, the **Stadtturm** (city tower; 1316) is a proud, 68m-high Gothic watch tower that doubles as the town's symbol. Tours in German take place from April to October, Thursday at 2 pm, and Saturday and Sunday at 10.30 am (DM5/3). Meet at the tourist office except Sunday, when the tour starts at the tower entrance.

The **Rathaus** adjacent to the tower is almost as old, even if it doesn't show. Originally consisting of two 14th century merchants' homes, it was repackaged in neo-Gothic according to the 19th century vogue. Just east of the tower is the gleaming golden **Trinity Column** (Dreifaltigkeitssäule), erected in 1709 as a nod to Catholic upheavals during the Spanish War of Succession. Of the half-dozen historic churches in town, the most impressive is the **Karmelitenkirche**, of the begging monks' order north-east of the market on Hofstatt, with an illuminated nave typical of the late Gothic era (but which, like many edifices here, sports a baroque interior).

A minute's walk east of the town square at Frauenhoferstrasse 8 is the **Gäubodenmuseum** (☎ 818 11), with one of Germany's most important collections of Roman treasures, including some imposing armour and masks for soldiers and horses. It's open Tuesday to Sunday from 10 am to 4 pm (DM4/3).

Getting There & Away

Straubing is on a regional rail line from Regensburg (DM12.20, 30 minutes), Passau (DM19.60, one hour) and Munich (DM37, two hours), and is well placed at the junction of the B8 and B20 highways, just south of the Nuremberg-Passau autobahn A3.

INGOLSTADT

☎ 0841 • pop 115,000

Shunned by most as the industrial headquarters of the Audi car company, Ingolstadt is a fascinating medieval city with beautiful streets and buildings, and a church museum with the largest flat fresco ever made, the masterpiece of Cosmas Damian Asam inside the Maria de Victoria. Ingolstadt is also home to one of the best hostels in Bavaria and a fascinating military museum.

Local beer drinkers (read: the populace) are especially proud that Germany's Beer Purity Law of 1516 was issued in Ingolstadt. This demands an investigation, on the part of visitors, as to whether this claim to

---

Frankenstein's Baby

Ingolstadt contains the 'birthplace' of Frankenstein's monster, now the ghoulish Museum of the History of Medicine.

The museum was once the main medical faculty of the university (which was moved to Landshut in 1803), and its operating theatre was where professors and students performed experiments on dead bodies and tissues. Mary Shelley (1797-1851) chose the lovely baroque building (1732-37) as the setting for Frankenstein's laboratory in her classic novel. It was here that her title character famously combined harvested body parts and electrically animated a 'son'.

---

fame has affected the local brews, Herrnbräu, Nordbräu and Ingobräu.

Orientation

The Hauptbahnhof is 2.5km south-east of the city centre; bus Nos 10, 11, 15 and 16 make the trip every few minutes (DM2.70). The centre of the city is the Altstadt, roughly in the shape of a baseball diamond, with the Danube on the south side. The Altstadt's heart is formed at Am Stein, the convergence of its main north-south street, Harderstrasse, and its main east-west one, Theresienstrasse/Ludwigstrasse. Ludwigstrasse runs east from Harderstrasse to the Neue Schloss. Theresienstrasse runs west from Harderstrasse to the Kreuz Tor, west of which is the hostel. The Audi factory is at the northern end of the city.

Information

The city-run tourist office (☎ 305 10 98, fax 305 10 99, email touristinformation@ ingolstadt.de), Rathausplatz 4, has lots of pamphlets and overworked staff. They book hotels but not private rooms. It's open Monday to Friday from 8 am to 5 pm, and Saturday from 9 am to noon.

Change money at the post offices next to the Hauptbahnhof, at Am Stein, or at one of the several banks (including Sparkasse, Raiffeisenbank and Dresdner Bank) at Rathausplatz.

You can buy English books and copies of Frankenstein in any language (DM5 for English) at Schönhuber (☎ 934 50), Theresienstrasse 6. Menig Presse & Buch at the Hauptbahnhof also has a great selection. The city library is in the Alte Schloss, also known as Herzog's Kasten, on Theaterplatz.

Maria de Victoria

Built as a conference centre from 1732 to 1736, the Maria de Victoria isn't a church – though that didn't stop it from becoming one of the favourites of the Asam brothers, who designed and built it. The building was turned over to the Bavarian government in the early 19th century, which has since maintained it as a museum.

Cosmas Damian Asam's *trompe l'oeil* ceiling (painted in just six weeks in 1737) is the largest fresco on a flat surface in the world, and it does things so trippy you can spend hours staring at it.

To see the thing in proper perspective, walk in six paces from the door and stand on the little circle in the diamond tile and look ahead. The illusions begin when you walk around. From the circle looking east, look over your left shoulder at the archer with the flaming red turban. Wherever you walk in the room the arrow points right at you. Focus on anything – the Horn of Plenty, Moses' staff, the treasure chest – and it will appear to dramatically alter when you move around the room. Asam took the secret methods he used in the painting to his grave.

Ask the caretaker, Herr Schuler, to let you into the side chamber to see the *Lepanto Monstrance*, a gold and silver depiction of the Battle of Lepanto (1571).

Buzz for Herr Schuler (an absolute hoot if you can understand Bavarian) next door if the front door is locked during opening hours, which are Tuesday to Sunday from 9 am to noon and 1 to 5 pm (DM2.50/1.50).

Medicine Museum

The Museum of the History of Medicine (☎ 305 49 3), Anatomiestrasse 18/20, just screams 'body parts' – see the boxed text.

Downstairs isn't too bad, but upstairs isn't for the fainthearted: maternity gear, dental equipment, surgery tools (note the saw, ladies and gentlemen) and skeletons with preserved musculature. The grounds are lovely; bring a picnic if you still have an appetite. It's open Tuesday to Sunday from 10 am to noon and 2 to 5 pm; admission is DM4/2, and an extra DM2/1 during special exhibitions (we shudder to think!).

Neues Schloss

Unhappy with his local lot after returning from wealth-laden France, Ludwig the Bearded ordered this Gothic castle to be built in 1418. It's a little ostentatious, with its 3m-thick walls, Gothic net vaulting and individually carved doorways, but today it

makes a fine home for the **Bayerisches Armee Museum** (☎ 937 70), a fascinating collection of armaments from the 14th century through to WWII, including a collection of 17,000 tin soldiers in the tower.

Its extension is the **Reduit Tilly** across the river, named for the Thirty Years' War general, with exhibits on the history of WWI and post-WWI Germany. Admission is DM5.50/4 for either, and DM7.50/5.50 for both.

Münster

The city's Münster is less interesting for what it is – a reasonably impressive Gothic cathedral – than for what it isn't: finished. The city ran out of money several times during the construction, and a quick walk round reveals archways that were started and abandoned, bows that were left off and towers left devoid of ornamentation and at a fraction of their intended height. Regular concerts and recitals are held here.

Kreuz Tor

The Gothic Kreuz Tor (1385) was one of the four main gates into the city until the 19th century. This and the main gate within the Neues Schloss are all that remain of the main city gates, but the former **fortifications**, now flats, still encircle the city. There's a terrific beer garden next to the Kreuz Tor.

Audi Factory

You can take free one-hour tours of the Audi factory (☎ 890) from Monday to Friday at 9.40 am, noon and 1 pm; bus No 11 goes right there from the centre. Car nuts can't miss the **Audi Historical Car Museum** (☎ 89 12 41), Ettinger Strasse 40 just south of the factory, open Wednesday to Friday from 9 am to noon and 1 to 5 pm. Tours are held from Monday to Friday at 2.15 pm, and Saturday at 10.15 am (free).

Other Sights

The city's **Museum of Concrete Art** (☎ 30 57 28), Tränkorstrasse 6-8, has nothing to do with leftover building materials but does feature modern abstracts and some neat three-dimensional works. Opening times

euro currency converter DM1 = €0.51

are Tuesday to Sunday from 10 am to 6 pm, with a one hour lunch break (DM3/1.50).

The **Stadtmuseum** (☎ 30 51 30), in a squat fortification at Auf der Schanz 45, houses oodles of ancient artefacts as well as the **Toy Museum**, with playthings from the 18th to 20th centuries. It's open daily except Monday (DM4).

Places to Stay

The huge **Campingplatz Auwaldsee** (☎ 961 16 16), at the Auwaldsee lake about 3km south-east of the city centre, has five season changes during the year – in high/low season, sites are DM12/10 (DM6/5.50 without a car), plus DM9/7 per person. Bus service is screamingly inadequate; a taxi from the centre will cost about DM15.

The seriously nice **DJH hostel** (☎ 341 77, fax 91 01 78, Friedhofstrasse 4½) is in a renovated city fortification (1828). Rooms are a little crowded, with two to 12 beds, but staff are friendly and the place is very clean. Beds are DM20 with breakfast, DM7 with half-pension. There's a nice little pub on the corner, called Corner. Walk west through the Kreuz Tor, out of the Altstadt, and the hostel is 150m ahead on the right.

Gästehaus Bauer Pension (☎ 670 86, fax 661 94, Hölzstrasse 2) has simple singles/doubles from DM65/100, and nicer ones from DM85/120. Much nicer and more central is the **Bayerischer Hof** (☎ 93 40 60, fax 177 02, Münzbergstrasse 12), with spacious rooms from DM95/150.

Places to Eat

While the tourist office hypes the **Weissbräuhaus** (☎ 328 90, Dollstrasse 3), the oldest brewery restaurant in town, the food leaves much to be desired. Order an excellent Weissbier in the beer garden out back.

The best beer garden is **Glock'n am Kreutz Tor** (☎ 349 90, Oberer Graben 1), in the shadow of the Kreuz Tor. Open from 10 am, it has lots of great food starting from under DM10. The aromas coming from the kitchen at **Daniel** (☎ 352 72, Roseneckstrasse 1) were good enough to recommend it highly, and it's the oldest pub in town,

too. For decent Italian dishes, there's **Nudelstube Carrara** (☎ 340 43, Kanalstrasse 12), with pasta dishes from DM12 to DM15. It's closed Sunday and Monday.

The Wednesday and Saturday **markets** on Theaterplatz are wonderful.

The **Mensa** (Konviktstrasse 1) serves breakfast for DM2.50, and lunch and dinner for DM6 to DM8. It's one block from the Maria de Victoria. The chi-chi crowds at the **Mohrenkopf Café** (☎ 177 50, Donaustrasse 8) fill much of the pavement in summer, so maybe that's why the staff are so overworked and surly. The baked goodies are just as good at **Bar Centrale** right next door, and the staff are nicer, too.

Getting There & Away

Trains from Regensburg leave hourly and take one hour (DM19.60). From Munich, trains leave twice an hour (DM22.40, one hour). BEX BerlinLinien buses leave for Berlin daily at 10.55 am and arrive from Berlin at 3.45 pm daily. SuperSpar oneway/return tickets cost DM75/136.

PASSAU

☎ 0851 • pop 50,000

As it exits Germany for Austria, the Danube River flows through the baroque town of Passau, where it converges with the rivers Inn and Ilz. The town's Italian-baroque essence has not doused the medieval feel, which you will experience as you wander through the narrow lanes, tunnels and archways of the Altstadt and monastic district to Ortspitze, where the rivers meet.

Passau is not only at a meeting point of inland waterways, but is also the hub of long-distance cycling routes, eight of which converge here.

Orientation

The Altstadt is a narrow peninsula with the confluence of the three rivers at its tip. The little Ilz River approaches from the north, the Danube from the west and the Inn River from the south. The Hauptbahnhof is at the western end of the city, about a 10 minute walk from the heart of the Altstadt. The Veste

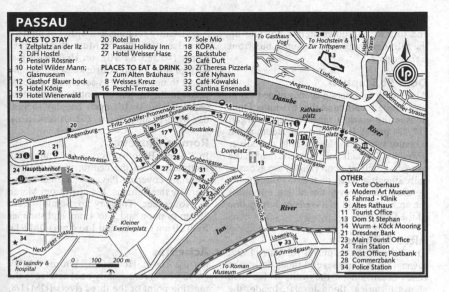

PASSAU

PLACES TO STAY
1 Zeltplatz an der Ilz
2 DJH Hostel
5 Pension Rössner
10 Hotel Wilder Mann; Glasmuseum
12 Gasthof Blauer bock
15 Hotel König
19 Hotel Wienerwald
20 Rotel Inn
22 Passau Holiday Inn
27 Hotel Weisser Hase

PLACES TO EAT & DRINK
7 Zum Alten Bräuhaus
8 Weisses Kreuz
16 Peschl-Terrasse
17 Sole Mio
18 KÖPA
26 Backstube
29 Café Duft
30 Zi'Theresa Pizzeria
31 Café Nyhavn
32 Café Kowalski
33 Cantina Ensenada

OTHER
3 Veste Oberhaus
4 Modern Art Museum
6 Fahrrad - Klinik
9 Altes Rathaus
11 Tourist Office
13 Dom St Stephan
14 Wurm + Köck Mooring
21 Dresdner Bank
23 Main Tourist Office
24 Train Station
25 Post Office; Postbank
28 Commerzbank
34 Police Station

Oberhaus and the hostel are on the north side of the Danube, reached by crossing the Luitpoldbrücke and walking up the hill.

Information

Tourist Offices There are two useful tourist offices: the main one opposite the Hauptbahnhof at Bahnhofstrasse 26 and another at Rathausplatz 3 (both serviced by ☎ 95 59 80, fax 572 98, email tourist-info@passau.de). For tours, ring ☎ 955 98 14. The latter is especially useful for bike and boat travel along the Danube. Staff provide maps, accommodation lists and help you plan your trip. *Pasta* is the town's free listings magazine.

The tourist offices sell a coupon booklet (DM2) worth DM9 in discounts to local attractions, one bus ticket plus a free drink at one of four hotels. ADAC has an office (☎ 01805-10 11 12) at Brunngasse 5.

Money There's a Postbank in the main post office adjacent to the Hauptbahnhof and a Dresdner Bank across the street at Bahnhofstrasse 23. There's also a Commerzbank at Ludwigstrasse 13.

Post & Communications The main post office, which also has a telephone centre, is immediately to the left as you emerge from the Hauptbahnhof.

Laundry Wash your smalls at Rent-Wash, Neuburger Strasse 19, for DM6 per load. Dryers cost DM3.

Fortress

Towering over the city is the 13th century **Veste Oberhaus** (DM6), containing the Cultural History Museum. It's closed in January and February.

The fortress, built by prince-bishops for defence (and taken over by Napoleonic troops in the early 19th century) commands superb views over the city, either from the castle tower (DM2) or from the **Battalion Linde**, a lookout that gives the only bird's-eye view of the confluence of all three rivers. The **Cultural History Museum** (DM2/1) includes a permanent exhibition of the work of local artist Hans Wimmer, whose 1970s social-realist bronze works recall a cold-war era long past. The hostel's up here as well.

BAVARIA

From the city, cross the Luitpoldbrücke and follow the Ludwigsteig path right up the hill, or simply take a shuttle bus from Exizierplatz.

Dom St Stephan

Along with fascinating scenes of heaven in the vaulted ceilings, the baroque Dom houses the **world's largest church organ** (17,774 pipes). It also has a **museum** and a **treasury** with a display of gold and silver jewellery. The half hour concerts held in the cathedral daily at noon (DM4) are acoustically stunning. Note, on the way out, the little cloth draped over the railing on top of the archway – said to have been left by one of the workmen.

Altes Rathaus

The bells in the colourful Rathaus (1399; tower 1891) chime several times daily (the times are listed on the wall, which also shows historical flood levels). Inside, the **Kleiner Rathaus Saal**, the **Registry** and the **Great Assembly Room** have wonderful paintings by local artist and crackpot Ferdinand Wagner.

Wagner, who used to live in the huge building on the north bank of the Danube, just to the right of where the Luitpoldbrücke suspension bridge is today, threatened to move out of town if the bridge was built. It was, he did, and after viewing the paintings, you wonder whether the city made the right choice. The fresco in the Small Assembly Room shows women representing the three rivers and the town.

Glasmuseum

The Passau Museum of Glass (☎ 350 71) has a splendid collection of over 30,000 examples of Bohemian glasswork and crystal from over 250 years. If you charge through the place, you'll need an hour to view all the 35 rooms containing Art Nouveau, baroque, classical and Art Deco pieces. The museum, in the Hotel Wilder Mann, is directly opposite the Rathaus. It's open in summer daily from 10 am to 4 pm, and in winter from 1 to 4 pm (DM5/3).

Modern Art Museum

A constantly rotating exhibition of modern art passes through the Museum Moderner Kunst (☎ 383 87 90), on Bräugasse just east of the Luitpoldbrücke. One of the nicest things about it is seeing the contrast between the building's Gothic architecture and the exhibits. It's open Tuesday to Sunday from 10 am to 6 pm (admission varies).

Roman Museum

In Kastell Boiotro, across the Innbrücke footbridge from the centre, is the Römermuseum, covering Passau's original settlement by the Romans. It's open from March to November, Tuesday to Sunday from 10 am to noon and 2 to 4 pm, and summer from 10 am to noon and 1 to 4 pm (DM2/1).

Activities

On the Ilz at Hochstein, Wurm + Köck (☎ 92 92 92) runs a daily **boat service** to the meeting point of the three rivers (DM11/8, 40 minutes). You can also take bus No 3 or 4 to Hochstein.

You can also take a pleasant, easy **hike** across the isthmus and through the tunnel to Zur Triftsperre (☎ 511 62), Triftparre Strasse 15, a very nice beer garden and restaurant along a peaceful section of the Ilz. Ask at the tourist office for hiking maps.

Places to Stay

There's camping at *Zeltplatz an der Ilz* (☎ 414 57, Halser Strasse 34), with a DM9 fee per adult and no tent price. It's over the Ilz River bridge on bus No 1, 2 or 3. No campervans are allowed.

It's a wheezy climb up to the fortress, which contains the *DJH hostel* (☎ 413 51, fax 437 09, Veste Oberhaus 125). The hostel only accepts juniors (DM22 including breakfast, plus DM5.50 for linen). There's a curfew from 11.30 pm to 7 am. Bus Nos 1, 2 and 4 go several times a day from Exerzierplatz (DM2.30) from April to October.

Travellers of all ages may prefer the more central *Rotel Inn* (☎ 951 60, fax 951 61 00), on the banks of the Danube just two minutes walk from the Hauptbahnhof. Built in the profile of a reclining man, the place has tiny yet clean singles/doubles for an amazing DM25/50, with a reasonably private hall shower/toilet. Breakfast costs an extra DM8. It's open from May to September.

The *Gasthof Blauer Bock* (☎ 346 37, fax 323 91, Höllgase 20) has quiet rooms (some with windows on the Danube) from DM49/98. The *Hotel Wienerwald* (☎ 330 69, fax 330 60, Grosse Klingergasse 17) has basic rooms from DM50/80, but the kitchen is noisy until late.

Better value is the *Pension Rössner* (☎ 93 13 50, fax 931 35 55, Bräugasse 19), with fortress panoramas from the eastern tip of the Altstadt peninsula and clean rooms from DM55/80.

Though it's often packed with busloads of tourists, the *Hotel König* (☎ 38 50, fax 38 54 60, Untere Donaulände 1) has well appointed and clean rooms right on the Danube from DM80/150.

Hotel Wilder Mann (☎ 350 71, fax 317 12, Am Rathausplatz), home to the Museum of Glass, has rooms from DM77/117. Just off the pedestrian zone, the *Hotel Weisser Hase* (☎ 921 10, fax 921 11 00, Ludwigstrasse 23) has friendly staff and very comfortable rooms from DM95/140.

Across the street from the Hauptbahnhof is the *Passau Holiday Inn* (☎ 590 05 25, fax 590 02 39, Bahnhofstrasse 24), with the usual standard rooms from DM70/140; there's a pool and sauna downstairs.

Places to Eat

There are *markets* every Friday morning at Domplatz. For cheap eats, Ludwigstrasse has a host of places. They include the *Kochlöffel* at No 26, the *Backstube* on the corner of Brunngasse (with big pizza slices for DM2.50) and the large *KÖPA* marketplace at No 16, complete with fruit stalls, meat and fish stand and a restaurant in the back with full meals from DM8.

Café Kowalski (☎ 24 87, Oberer Sand 1) is a cosy place with a young crowd, serving lunches for under DM10, as well as reasonably priced evening meals. *Café Nyhavn* (☎ 375 57, Theresienstrasse 31) has light Danish dishes for DM10 to DM15 and pleasant, airy decor.

Students flock to *Zi'Theresa Pizzeria* (☎ 21 38, Theresianstrasse 26), which has delicious pizzas and pastas for DM8 to DM13. At No 22, the *Café Duft* (☎ 34 6 66) has intimate lighting, vaulted ceilings, an individualistic crowd and mains for DM8 to DM15. Another great Italian place is *Sole Mio* (☎ 321 35, Rosstränke 12), which looks trendier than its prices suggest. Pizzas cost DM8 to DM13, and meat dishes DM20 to DM27.

Peschl-Terrasse (☎ 24 89, Rosstränke 4), an old-style pub-brewery with a spacious dining terrace overlooking the Danube, serves home-style German mains for DM13 to DM31. *Weisses Kreuz* (☎ 317 35, Milchgasse 15), in a back alley, is popular with local students, and serves big plates of cheesy wholemeal *Spätzle* (Swabian noodles) for DM14 and half litres glasses of local ale for DM3.80. It's open daily to 1 am. In a similar vein, *Zum Alten Bräuhaus* (☎ 21 25, Bräugasse 5) is an earthy beer hall serving pork roasts for DM13 or less and litres of beer for DM7.50 (and on Tuesday, all the ribs you can eat for DM10.80.)

Across the Inn bridge south of the Altstadt, the *Cantina Ensenada* (☎ 93 11 46, Löwengrube 4) is a great Spanish/Mexican evening restaurant with a cosy courtyard and mains from around DM15.

For good food and terrible service at great prices, jump on bus No 5 or 190, which will bring you right to the entrance of *Gasthaus Vogl* (☎ 537 53), a beer garden north of the fortress that offers typically Bavarian dishes for under DM15. It commands great views into the Ilz Valley.

Getting There & Away

Train Passau is on the main rail line linking Cologne, Frankfurt, Nuremberg, Regensburg and Vienna. Trains run direct to/from Munich (DM52), Regensburg (DM32) and Nuremberg (DM67). Change at Plattling for the Bavarian Forest.

There are 11 direct train connections daily to/from Linz (DM34, 1½ hours) and at least 11 to/from Vienna's Westbahnhof (DM67, 3¼ to four hours).

Bus Regional buses to and from Zwiesel (DM17.50), Grafenau and Bayerisch Eisenstein stop at the Hauptbahnhof concourse outside the main post office.

Car & Motorcycle The A3 runs from Passau to Linz (Austria) and Vienna, or back to Regensburg. The A92 from Munich connects with it.

Boat From May to October, Wurm + Köck (☎ 92 92 92), Höllgasse 26, has a daily boat service down the Danube to Linz in Austria, leaving Passau at 9 am and 2 pm (DM36 or AS256, five hours).

Getting Around
Passau is compact, so most sights are reachable on foot. A single ticket on the local SWP buses costs DM2, a four trip ticket DM5 and an eight trip ticket DM9. The Fahrrad-Klinik (☎ 334 11), Bräugasse 5 near the Luitpoldbrücke, rents out bikes from DM20 per day.

BAVARIAN FOREST
The largest continuous mountain forest in all of Europe, the Bavarian Forest (Bayerischer Wald) is a lovely landscape of rolling wooded hills interspersed with tiny, little-disturbed valleys. As is it is mostly visited by other Germans, the locals here speak little English. Go out of your way to do some hiking in this surprisingly wild and rugged region.

Orientation & Information
The ranges of the Bavarian Forest stretch north-west to south-east along the German-Czech border, and its wild frontier nature is still the region's chief attribute. At its heart is the town of Zwiesel, which makes an ideal base for exploring the Bavarian Forest. Zwiesel's helpful tourist office (☎ 09922-84 05 23, fax 56 55) is in the town hall at Stadtplatz 27, about 1km from the Hauptbahnhof. It has lots of free

brochures, maps and helpful hints for exploring the area.

The tourist office (☎ 08552-962 30) in Grafenau is at Rathausgasse 1. The best information about wildlife areas and trails is available from Dr-Hans-Eisenmann-Haus (☎ 08558-13 00) in Neuschönau.

Things to See & Do
Zwiesel's **Waldmuseum** (Forest Museum) deals with forestry and the wood industry (open daily), while the **Glasmuseum** covers local glass-making. Lindberg's **Bauernhausmuseum** features traditional Bavarian Forest houses, Regen has the **Landwirtschaftsmuseum** (Agricultural Museum), and there's the **Handwerksmuseum** (Handicrafts Museum) at Deggendorf.

The **Museumsdorf Bayerischer Wald** (☎ 08504-84 82) in Tittling, just north of Passau, is a museum of East Bavarian farm life from the 17th to 19th centuries, with over 140 houses on 20 hectares (DM5/3). It's really worth the trip. Take the RDO bus to Tittling from Passau Hauptbahnhof.

The **Dampfbier-Brauerei** (☎ 09922-14 09), at Regener Strasse 9-11 in Zwiesel, has a brewery tour at 10 am every Wednesday (DM13), which includes generous samplings of its peppery local ales.

The **Bayerwald-Bärwurzerei** (☎ 09922-15 15), 2km out of Zwiesel at Frauenauer Strasse 80-82, produces some 26 Bavarian liqueurs that you can sample and purchase.

The production of superior-quality glass is another important local industry. You can buy wares and watch glass being blown in many places, such as the Glasbläserei Schmid (☎ 09922-94 62), Am Daimingerstrasse 24 in Zwiesel.

Activities
Hiking & Skiing South of Zwiesel is the 130 sq km Bavarian Forest National Park, a paradise for the outdoors enthusiast. There are several superb long-distance hiking routes, with mountain huts along the way. The most famous is the 180km Nördliche Hauptwanderlinie (or E6) trail, a 10 day trek from Furth im Wald to Dreisessel.

Südliche Hauptwanderlinie (E8) is its shorter sibling at 105km, while the 50km trek from Kötzting to Bayerisch Eisenstein near the Czech border is the quickest way to experience the Bavarian Forest. A good walking map is the 1:50,000 *Mittlerer Bayerischer Wald* published by Fritsch (DM11.80).

Downhill skiing in the Bavarian Forest is relatively low-key, with the best resorts in the north around peaks such as Geisskopf (1097m), Grosser Arber (1456m), Pröller and Hoher Bogen (1079m). More exciting and popular here is cross-country skiing, with numerous routes through the ranges.

In Eukirchen bei Heiliger Blut, Freizeit-zentrum Hoher Bogen (☎ 09947-464) runs a summer alpine slope, from April to the end of October daily from 9 am to 5 pm.

Canoeing Waldschrat's Adventure Company (☎ 09926-731), at Flanitzmühle 9 in Fraueneau, rents three-person Canadian canoes for DM70/300 for one/five days, and kayaks for DM30/120. Staff transport the boats to a number of places within the forest for anywhere from DM50 to DM120. They have an agent at the booze-maker Bayerwald-Bärwurzerei (☎ 09922-15 15) in Zwiesel (see the earlier Things to See & Do section).

Places to Stay

Zwiesel's camping ground is called *Azur-Camping (☎ 09922-18 47)* and is located 1km from the Hauptbahnhof, near public pools and sports facilities.

The local *hostel (☎ 09922-10 61, fax 601 91, Hindenburgstrasse 26)* charges DM20 for beds. Other dormitory accommodation includes the Frauenau *hostel (☎/fax 09926-735, Hauptstrasse 29)*, with beds for DM16.50; and the *Waldhäuser (☎ 08553-60 00, fax 829, Herbergsweg 2)* in Neuschönau, where a dorm bed is DM24. All these hostels close for at least a month in early winter, and only accept guests under 27.

Zwiesel is crammed with budget pensions and apartments; prices include resort tax. Excellent value is the *Pension Haus Inge (☎ 09922-10 94, Buschweg 34)*, which stands at the edge of the forest and has

comfortable rooms with private shower and toilet from DM36/61 for singles/doubles. The *Naturkost Pension Waldeck (☎ 09922-32 72, Ahornweg 2)* is a nonsmokers' pension featuring organic vegetarian cooking. It costs from DM49 to DM58 per person for half board. Two quiet places in the hills at nearby Rabenstein are the *Pension Fernblick (☎ 09922-94 09, Brücklhöhe 48)* and the smaller *Berghaus Rabenstein (☎ 09922-12 45, Grosses Feld 8)*, which both charge around DM35 per person.

Grafenau's central *Gasthof Schraml (☎ 08552-619, Stadtplatz 14)* has basic rooms for DM26 per person (excluding breakfast). Nearby is *Gasthof Kellermann (☎ 08552-967 10, Stadtplatz 8)*, with better singles/doubles for DM35/65.

Places to Eat

In Zwiesel, *Bistro Flair (☎ 09922-13 49, Dr-Schott-Strasse 16)* has schnitzels from just DM7.80. Another good option in Zwiesel is the *Musikantenkeller (☎ 20 91, Stadtplatz 42)*, a live music pub where a pork cutlet served with chips and salad costs DM11.50. Wash it down with a half litre glass of local draught beer for DM3.80. *Zwieseler Hof Hotel-Restaurant (☎ 840 70, Regener Strasse 5)* has a comfortable ambience despite the plastic plants. The extensive menu (DM12 to DM25) includes fish, lamb and Bavarian dishes.

Two good restaurants in Grafenau are the *Gasthof Jägerwirt (☎ 08552-15 47, Hauptstrasse 18)* and *Zum Kellermann (☎ 967 10, Stadtplatz 8)*.

Getting There & Away

From Munich, Regensburg or Passau, Zwiesel is reached by rail via Plattling; most trains continue to Bayerisch Eisenstein on the Czech border, with connections to Prague. The direct buses between Zwiesel and Passau work out cheaper than a change of trains at Plattling, and run several times daily (DM10, one hour).

Two scenic narrow-gauge railways from Zwiesel go to Grafenau (DM10 one-way) and to Bodenmais (DM3.40).

Baden-Württemberg

Baden-Württemberg is one of Germany's main holiday regions. With recreational assets as varied as the Black Forest (Schwarzwald), Heidelberg and the ritzy spa town of Baden-Baden, the state is rivalled only by Bavaria in its breadth of sights and landscapes.

Lake Constance (Bodensee), which embraces sections of Germany, Switzerland and Austria, is justifiably one of Baden-Württemberg's biggest draws. But don't miss the less-travelled regions, including the gentle hills of the Schwäbische Alb and the medieval gem of Schwäbisch Hall. The student town of Tübingen, with its narrow lanes and hill-top fortress, positively oozes charm.

Stuttgart, home of Mercedes-Benz and Porsche, boasts some fascinating museums and attractive city parks. To the north and west are two big wine-growing regions (Baden and Württemberg), producing mainly whites and some very drinkable reds. Nestled in a snug valley near the Swiss border, Freiburg is a vibrant university town and an ideal base for exploring the Black Forest.

The prosperous state of Baden-Württemberg was created only in 1951 out of three smaller regions: Baden, Württemberg and Hohenzollern. Baden, the first to be unified, was made a grand duchy by Napoleon, who also promoted Württemberg to the rank of kingdom in 1806. Both areas, in conjunction with Bavaria and 16 other states, formed the Confederation of the Rhine under French protection, part of Napoleon's plan to undermine Prussia. Baden and Württemberg sided with Austria against Prussia in 1866, but were ultimately drafted into the German Empire in 1871.

STUTTGART

☎ 0711 • pop 630,500

Stuttgart is best known as the home of Mercedes-Benz (even the train station sports the familiar three-point star), and most travellers imagine it as an industrial

HIGHLIGHTS

Baden-Württemberg Luminaries: Boris Becker, Karl Benz, Gottlieb Wilhelm Daimler, Friedrich Hölderlin, Jürgen Klinsmann, Philipp Melanchthon, Erwin Rommel, Friedrich von Schiller, Ferdinand von Zeppelin

- Taking wine tasting trips in and around Stuttgart
- Checking out the Goethe plaque and everything else in Tübingen
- Taking in Ulm's magnificent Münster, with the highest spire in Europe
- Hiking through the Wutach Gorge
- Riding on the scenic Schwarzwaldbahn between Offenburg and Villingen
- Taking a trip to Mainau Island, especially the Butterfly House
- Indulging in Baden-Baden spas, like Friedrichsbad and Caracalla-Therme
- Visiting the Pilgrimage Church of Birnau

Heidelberg pp556-7

Black Forest (Schwarzwald) p574

Stuttgart p540

FRANCE

Baden-Baden p577

Ulm p568

Freiburg p591

Lake Constance (Bodensee) p604

city. Nothing could be further from the truth. Swathed in a belt of parks and thick hillside forests, Stuttgart could be the greenest city in Europe.

Over half its surrounding area is covered with orchards, vineyards, meadows and forest; you're never more than 15 minutes from dense woods. Over 500 vineyards turn out some excellent wines, many kept and consumed locally.

The city began as a stud farm (*Stuotgarten*, whence the name comes) on the Nesenbach Stream around 950. By 1160 it was a booming trade centre, and in the early 14th century Stuttgart became the royal seat of the Württemberg family.

The city is also the birthplace of two gadgets that have changed the world we live in: Gottlieb Daimler's petrol-powered, high-speed engine and Robert Bosch's spark plug. The Mercedes-Benz factory began automobile production here in 1926. (Daimler patented the motor coach, and Carl Benz the motor car, in 1886). Not to

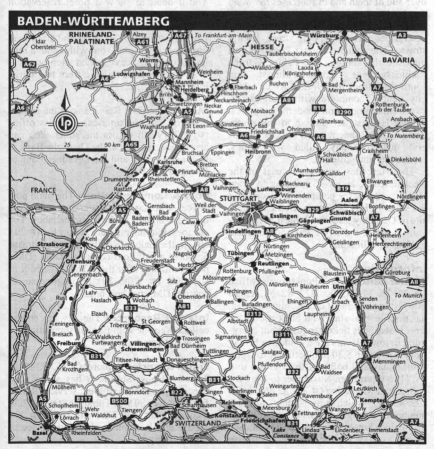

BADEN-WÜRTTEMBERG

be outdone, Ferdinand Porsche set up shop here as well.

After WWII, the city's architectural treasures were painstakingly reconstructed. Today, Stuttgart attracts almost a million visitors a year with its impressive museums and air of relaxed prosperity.

Orientation

The city lies in a valley just west of the Neckar River. The lovely Kriegsberg vineyards overlook town from the north-west. Steep grades are common on city streets – over 500 of them end in staircases *(Stäffele)* that lead to the top of the hills.

The Hauptbahnhof is just north of the central pedestrian shopping street, Königstrasse. The tourist office, i-Punkt, is just opposite the station. The Palace Garden (Schlossgarten) stretches almost 4km south-west from the Neckar River to the city centre, complete with swan ponds, street entertainers and modern sculptures. Across Hauptstätter Strasse to the southeast lies the Bohnenviertel, the old labourers' quarter today filled with pubs, restaurants and galleries.

The Mercedes museum is east of the Neckar River, about 15 minutes by tram from the centre; the company's factory is in the suburb of Sindelfingen. Bad Cannstatt, site of Germany's second-largest beer festival, is east of the city's zoo and botanical gardens at Wilhelma.

Information

Tourist Offices The i-Punkt tourist office (☎ 22 28 24 04, fax 223 82 53, email info@stuttgart-tourist.de), Königstrasse 1a, has multilingual staff who book rooms for free. It also sells tickets to just about everything in town. Hours are Monday to Friday from 9.30 am to 8.30 pm, Saturday to 6 pm, and Sunday and holidays from 11 am to 6 pm (1 to 6 pm from November to April).

Stuttgart-Marketing (☎ 222 82 46/48, fax 222 82 51), which runs i-Punkt, offers a number of very good deals during festivals that include hotel, train fares, passes etc. See Places to Stay for the excellent Surprise

deal, or write to Lautenschlagerstrasse 3, 70173 Stuttgart.

The ADAC motorists' association has a huge office (☎ 280 00) at Am Neckartor, north of the Hauptbahnhof.

Passes The new Stuttcard is a three day ticket providing free entry to all public museums, discounts for cultural events and leisure activities. It's a bargain at DM25.

The three day transport pass costs DM13 for the city centre and DM20 for the entire bus, tram and underground network. You'll need to show a hotel reservation when you buy it.

The three day Night-Pass (DM16) gives you admission to most clubs and discos and discounts on drinks – but with about a million exceptions, caveats and exemptions.

All passes are available from the tourist information office.

Money There's a Reisebank at the Hauptbahnhof and an American Express office (☎ 162 49 20) across the street. You can also change money at the Deutsche Bank at Königstrasse 1a, and the Dresdner Bank at Königstrasse 9.

Post & Communications The main post office is at Lautenschlagerstrasse 17, and there's a branch at the Hauptbahnhof. The cheapest Internet rates are at Surf Inn (☎ 203 60), in the Galeria Kaufhof at Königstrasse 6, where a half hour costs just DM3 (DM2 per 15 minutes after that). The Cyberb@r in Karstadt (☎ 208 20), Königstrasse 1, charges DM5 per half hour.

Internet Resources The city has an excellent Web site with English translations at www.stuttgart-tourist.de.

Travel Agencies Explorer (☎ 162 52 11) at Theodor-Heuss-Strasse 6 has some very cheap flight deals and great service. Reisefieber (☎ 649 80 94), Tübinger Strasse 72, is a good bucket shop. Discount Travel (☎ 794 20 55) is a last-minute ticketing service at Stuttgart airport.

Bookshops Wittwer (☎ 250 70), König-strasse 30, has great foreign-language and travel sections (with lots of Lonely Planet titles). It also runs the Internationale Presse newsagent at the Hauptbahnhof. Lindemann Books (☎ 24 53 23), Nadler-strasse 4-10, located south of the Rathaus, also has English-language books and a great travel section.

Libraries The Landesbibliothek (☎ 21 20), Konrad-Adenauer-Strasse 8, is a huge state collection. It's near the Stadtbücherei (☎ 21 65 70), on the same street at No 2, which is the city library. Next door at No 4 is the Staatsarchiv (☎ 212 43 35), which stores the original *Bannandrohungsbulle*, the papal bull that threatened Martin Luther with ex-communication for heresy.

Universities Universität Stuttgart has 130 institutes, 14 faculties and 21,000 students; its most important schools are of architec-ture, agriculture, economics and engineer-ing. The Universität Hohenheim, in the castle in the suburb of Hohenheim, has over 6000 students.

Cultural Centres Deutsch-Amerikanisches Zentrum (German-American Centre, ☎ 22 81 80), Charlottenplatz 17, in the Institute for Foreign Affairs, has lots of resource material in English.

Laundry The Waschsalon (☎ 236 19 05) on Hohenheimer Strasse is the closest to the town centre but charges a whopping DM19 per load (including drying). The SB Wasch-salon (☎ 52 30 08) at Kienbachstrasse 16 charges DM8 per load, and DM2 for 10 minutes drying (take S13 to Kienbach-strasse). There's also a washing machine at the Tramper Point Stuttgart hostel (see Places to Stay).

Medical Services For a doctor call ☎ 262 80 12 or ☎ 28 02 11. The largest hospitals are the Katharinen-Hospital (☎ 27 80), Kriegsbergstrasse 60; and the Marienhospi-tal (☎ 648 90), Böheimstrasse 37.

Dangers & Annoyances Stuttgart is gen-erally a safe city, but some rather sleazy characters gather after dark in the Klett Pas-sage below the Hauptbahnhof. Avoid the Palace Garden after sunset, too.

Schlossplatz

This square provides a crash course in ar-chitecture. Stand in the middle, beneath the **König Wilhelm Jubilee column**, flanked by fountains representing the eight rivers of Baden-Württemberg, then spin clockwise. The classical **Königsbau** is a focal point on warm evenings, when crowds gather to watch buskers perform amid its columns. Downstairs are shops, upstairs, the city's **Börse** (stock exchange).

To the right is a fine example of 1950s architecture in the **Olgabau**, home to the Dresdner Bank. Further right is the Art Nouveau **Kunstverein**, which contains the municipal art gallery and the Württemberg Art Society. The late-baroque/neoclassical front section of the **Neues Schloss**, once the residence of kings Friedrich I and Wilhelm I, now houses the state finance and culture ministries. At Karlsplatz, you'll find a statue of Wilhelm looking noble and serious on a bronze steed.

At the western end of Schlossplatz is Alexander Calder's **Mobile**, a modern sculpture the city bought in 1981 for almost DM1 million. Stuttgarters – known for what other Germans might call 'miserliness' but which they themselves call 'thrift' – ini-tially went ballistic over the cost (but are now happy since the work has tripled in value). There are concerts every Sunday in summer at the **Musik Pavillon** on the north-west corner of the square.

Schillerplatz

Opposite Schlossplatz is Schillerplatz – named after poet-dramatist Friedrich Schiller – whose statue stands in the centre. In its south-western corner, in the **Stifts-fruchtkasten**, a former wine depot topped by a Bacchus statue, is the **Instrumenten Museum** musical collection. Next to it stands the reconstructed **Stiftskirche**, with

euro currency converter   DM1 = €0.51

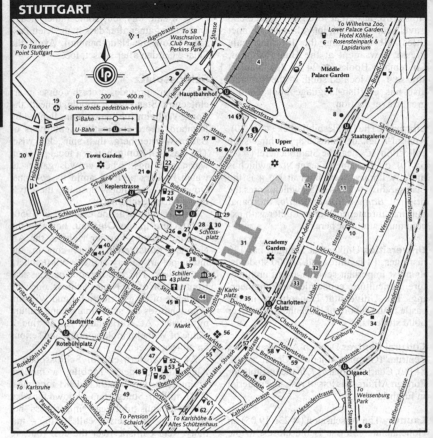

STUTTGART

its twin 61m-high late Gothic towers (by law, no Stuttgart building can be built taller). On the opposite side of the court-yard is the Renaissance **Alte Kanzlei** (Old Chancellory).

Through the tunnel to the east is **Altes Schloss**, with a large statue of Eberhard, Württemberg's first duke and the founder of Tübingen University. The old palace now holds the **Württemberg State Museum**, containing exhibitions on the Württemberg crown jewels. It's open Tuesday from 10 am

to 1 pm, and Wednesday to Sunday from 10 am to 5 pm. It costs DM5/3, which includes the Instrument Museum. Watch the elk above the clock on the tower – they ram their horns on the hour.

There are concerts and opera in the court-yard here in summer.

Museums

Staatsgalerie The State Gallery (☎ 212 40), Konrad-Adenauer-Strasse 30-32, contains Stuttgart's best art collection in two

STUTTGART

PLACES TO STAY
3 Steigenberger
  Graf Zeppelin
7 Inter-Continental
9 DJH Hostel
17 Hotel Unger
24 Pension Märklin
34 Wirt am Berg
40 Museumstube
41 Gasthof Alte Mira
45 Holl's Arche

PLACES TO EAT
10 Urbanstuben
20 University Mensa
44 Markthalle
46 Calwer-Eck-Bräu
49 Nirvan
55 Iden
57 Délice Vinothek
58 Weinhaus Stetter
59 Der Zauberlehrling
60 Pica Pao
61 Brunnenwirt

OTHER
1 Kriegsberg Vineyards
2 Lupe Cinema
4 Main Train Station
5 Bus Station
6 Beer Garden
8 Carl Zeiss Planetarium
11 Staatsgalerie
12 Staatstheater
13 Tourist Office
14 American Express
15 Karstadt; Cyberb@r
16 Galeria Kaufhof
18 Kommunales Kino
19 Katharinen Hospital
21 Varieté im Friedrichhaus
22 Palast der Republik
23 Climax Disco
25 Main Post Office
26 Wittwer Bookshop
27 Alexander Calder's *Mobile*
28 Börse (Stock Exchange)
29 Kunstverein
   (Municipal Art Gallery)

30 König Wilhelm Jubilee Column
31 Neues Schloss
32 Landesbibliothek (State
   Library) & Archives
33 Stadtbücherei (City Library)
35 Institute for Foreign Affairs;
   Amadeus Beer Garden
36 Altes Schloss;
   Württemberg State Museum
37 Freidrich Schiller Statue
38 Alte Kanzlei
39 Amex Travel
42 Instrumenten Museum
43 Stiftskirche
47 Lindemann Books
48 Hans im Glück
50 Deli
51 Max and Moritz
52 Paddock
53 Hans im Glück Statue
54 Club Zap
56 Breuninger Shopping Centre
62 Roger's Kiste
63 Waschsalon

buildings. The new section, housed in the spectacular postmodern Neue Staatsgalerie (1984), has a wealth of modern art, including the important **Steegmann Collection** which comprises works by Picasso, Giacometti and Klee. The old section features masterpieces from the Middle Ages to the 19th century.

The museum is open Tuesday to Sunday from 10 am to 5 pm, and to 8 pm on Tuesday and Thursday (DM9/5).

Motor Museums & Factory Tours The pioneers of the motor car were Gottlieb Daimler and Carl Benz, who, separately, began to make cars at the end of the 19th century.

The impressive **Mercedes-Benz Museum** (☎ 172 25 78), about 2km east of the Neckar, tells the story of their partnership via recorded commentary amid numerous gleaming vehicles. It's open Tuesday to Sunday from 9 am to 5 pm (free); take S1 to Gottlieb-Daimler-Stadion. Mercedes-Benz also runs free tours of its Sindelfingen plant at 8.50 am and 2.05 pm on weekdays

(children under 14 years are not allowed). You're well advised to call beforehand (☎ 07031-90 75 27).

The **Porsche Museum** (☎ 911 56 85), Porschestrasse 42, has its own share of very sexy cars. It's open Monday to Friday from 9 am to 4 pm, and weekends to 5 pm (free). Take S6 to Neuwirtshaus.

Beer Museum See how the suds are made at Schwäbisches Brauereimuseum (☎ 737 02 01), providing a complete history of brewing with entertaining displays on technology and methods from around the globe. It's open Thursday to Sunday from 11 am to 5.30 pm (free). Take S1, S2 or S3 to Vaihingen train station, walk west on Vollmoellerstrasse to Robert-Koch-Strasse – the museum's ahead on the left.

Linden Museum The state ethnological museum (☎ 202 24 56), Hegelplatz 1, has a large display focusing on South America, Asia and Africa. It's open Tuesday to Sunday from 10 am to 5 pm, but Wednesday to 8 pm and Friday to 1 pm (free).

euro currency converter DM1 = €0.51

Parks & Zoo

Royal Gardens All parts of the Palace Garden – Lower, Middle and Upper (Unterer, Mittlerer and Oberer) – are exceptional. They're filled with meandering walkways, fountains and sunbathing folk watching the world – and the inline skaters – go by. There's a very good beer garden in the Lower Palace Garden, about seven minutes walk north-east of the Hauptbahnhof.

At the north end of the Lower Palace Garden you probably won't even know that you've crossed into the **Rosensteinpark**, which jigs west through glorious copses to the corner of Nordbahnhofstrasse and Pragstrasse, through the **Löwentor**.

Within the park is the amazing **Schloss Rosenstein**, now the city's Natural History Museum, which is open Tuesday to Friday from 9 am to 5 pm, and weekends to 6 pm (DM4/2).

Wilhelma At the northern edge of Rosensteinpark is the Wilhelma zoo and botanical gardens, an enormously popular place that's open daily (DM14/7). It has animals from around the world in an amazing botanical garden on the grounds of Schloss Rosenstein.

Lapidarium Hardly known to tourists and many locals, the Lapidarium is an enchanting little park on a hillside near Marienplatz. Nestled amid its lush greenery are fragments of buildings destroyed in WWII: doorways, portals, facade ornamentation, statues, gargoyles and parts of fountains. There's also a collection of about 200 Roman artefacts.

You can enter (free) from April to mid-September on Wednesday and Saturday from 2 to 5 pm. At other times, peep through the fence; walk up the Willy-Reichert-Stäffel to Mörikestrasse 24/1 at the top of Karlshöhe Park.

Karlshöhe The hillcrest just north-east of the Lapidarium is Karlshöhe, another great park with sweeping views of the city and lovely hillside vineyards. You can reach it via the Willy-Reichert-Stäffel (steps) or through Humboldtstrasse.

That yeasty smell is coming from the nearby **Dinkel Acker Brewery** (☎ 648 10), Tübinger Strasse 46; call ahead and you may be able to take a free tour, though you'll have to join a group.

Weissenburg Park Another lovely hillside park offering great views of the city is Weissenburg (take the U5, U6 or U7 to Bopser then walk south). At the top of the hill is the spectacular **Teehaus**.

Planetarium

In the south-east of the Middle Palace Garden is the Carl Zeiss Planetarium (☎ 162 92 15), a pyramid-shaped building that houses one of the best planetariums in the country. General admission is DM9/5, but prices can be higher for special shows that run Tuesday to Friday at 10 am and 3 pm (extra 8 pm shows on Wednesday and Friday), and Saturday and Sunday at 2, 4 and 6 pm. You can catch most U-Bahn lines to Staatsgalerie.

Organised Tours

Bus The city runs 2½ hour bus tours every day from April to October, Monday to Saturday at 1 pm, and Sunday and holidays at 11 am. The DM32 charge includes admission to the TV Tower. They're fine if your German is good, otherwise overpriced. The i-Punkt office can arrange a great variety of walking tours as well.

Taxi If you're willing to invest DM200 for four people (DM250 on Saturday, Sunday and holidays), we highly recommend a 2½ hour taxi tour (in English, French or German) with official city guide, Anselm Vogt-Moykopf (☎ 0172-740 11 38). Herr Vogt-Moykopf is a knowledgeable and easy-going fellow who really loves the city, its architecture, his job and taking people to out-of-the-way, beautiful regions nearby.

Boat Between March and October, Neckar Personen Schiffahrt (☎ 54 10 73) operates one and two-hour Neckar River tours

(DM9.50/15) from its dock opposite Wilhelma in Bad Cannstatt. They depart Monday to Friday at 9 and 11 am, Saturday, Sunday and holidays at 11 am.

Special Events
The city organises a number of notable annual events, including the **Sommerfest** in August, an open-air festival with live music and food at Schlossplatz. Later in the same month, at Schlossplatz and the Upper Palace Garden, is the **Weindorf**, where hundreds of booths sell the year's vintages.

The **Cannstatter Volkfest** (locals call it the 'Wasen' after the river nearby) is Stuttgart's version of Oktoberfest. It's held in late September and early October, with better-behaved crowds and beer stands throughout town.

The **Christmas market** is held on Markt and Schillerplatz from late November.

Places to Stay – Budget
You can pitch your tent at *Campingplatz Stuttgart (☎ 55 66 96, fax 48 69 47, Mercedesstrasse 40)*, 500m from the Bad Cannstatt S-Bahn station on the Wasen river.

If you're between 16 and 27, the best deal in town is *Tramper Point Stuttgart (☎ 817 74 76, fax 237 28 10, Wiener Strasse 317)*, a spartan wooden hostel open late June to early September. B&B costs just DM13, and there are kitchen facilities and a washing machine. Check in between 5 and 11 pm for a maximum stay of three nights. Take U6 to Sportpark Feuerbach north-west of the centre.

The *DJH hostel (☎ 24 15 83, fax 236 10 41, Haussmannstrasse 27)* is a signposted 15 minute walk east of the Hauptbahnhof (or take U15 to Eugenplatz). Beds cost DM22/27 for juniors/seniors, and the curfew is midnight.

The non-DJH *Jugendgästehaus (☎ 24 11 32, fax 23 66 11 10, Richard-Wagner-Strasse 2)*, south-east of the centre, charges DM35/55 for singles/doubles (take U15 to Bubenbad).

For *private rooms* and long-term rentals, Stuttgart has two Mitwohnzentralen: AMB-Mitwohnbüro (☎ 194 22), at Hauptstätter Strasse 154; and the Home Company (☎ 22 13 92), at Frank-Korn-Lerchenstrasse 72.

If you're aged between 16 and 26, the Surprise deal from Stuttgart-Marketing (see Information earlier) costs DM88 and includes a hotel room with breakfast, a Stuttcard, Night-Pass and three day transport ticket. You can choose from a list of participating hotels.

You'll need to book ahead for the simple but central *Pension Märklin (☎ 29 13 15, Friedrichstrasse 39)*, which charges DM45/80 for single/double rooms (without breakfast).

Rooms at *Gasthof Alte Mira (☎ 29 51 32, fax 222 95 03 29, Büchsenstrasse 24)* start at DM60/100 or DM75/130 without/with private shower. Just around the corner is the *Museumstube (☎ 29 68 10, Hospitalstrasse 9)* with simple singles/doubles for DM60/90 and doubles with bath for DM110.

The *Pension Schaich (☎ 60 26 79, fax 60 83 25, Paulinenstrasse 16)* has large and sunny rooms (soundproofed against the noisy overpass outside) for DM65/100, or DM75/110 with shower cubicle in the room.

Places to Stay – Mid-Range
Hotel Unger (☎ 209 90, fax 209 91 00, Kronenstrasse 17) is very central, with a quiet location south-west of the i-Punkt office; it's also the outlet for bicycle rentals (see Getting Around). It has pleasant singles/doubles from DM159/219.

The best value in the city centre is offered by *Holl's Arche (☎ 24 57 59, fax 24 30 44, Bärenstrasse 2)*, an old tavern opposite the Markthalle. Rooms with private shower and WC (toilet) cost only DM80/130.

Service is excellent at the *Hotel Köhler (☎ 16 66 60, fax 166 66 33, Neckarstrasse 209)*, where simple rooms without bath range from DM68/110, and with shower and toilet from DM95/140. Take U1, U11 or U14 to Metzstrasse.

The *Wirt am Berg (☎ 24 18 65, fax 236 13 48, Gaisburgstrasse 12a)* is a quiet backstreet hotel with nicely furnished rooms for DM75/150.

euro currency converter DM1 = €0.51

BADEN-WÜRTTEMBERG

Places to Stay – Top End

Looming over the Hauptbahnhof is the newly renovated *Steigenberger Graf Zeppelin* (☎ 204 80, fax 204 85 42, Arnulf-Klett-Platz 7), with sumptuous rooms that start at DM215/235 and a fine restaurant.

A business travellers' favourite is the curvy *Inter-Continental* (☎ 202 00, fax 20 20 12, Willy-Brandt-Strasse 30), with the usual spotless rooms (all with bay windows overlooking the Lower Palace Garden) from DM345.

Places to Eat

Restaurants The *Iden* (☎ 23 59 89, Eberhardstrasse 1) is a cafeteria-type restaurant with an amazing spread of cheap wholefood eats – you can order a main course and drink for about DM10. It's open weekdays until 8 pm (or 9 pm on Thursday) and Saturday until 4 pm.

The *Weinhaus Stetter* (☎ 24 01 63, Rosenstrasse 32) has simple regional specialities like *Linsen und Saiten* (lentils with sausage) for under DM8 and a great wine selection.

Calwer-Eck-Bräu (☎ 226 11 04, Calwer Strasse 31) is a comfortable brewery/pub with excellent Swabian-Bavarian fare from

about DM15. More adventurous is *Pica Pao* (Pfarrstrasse 7) in the Bohnenviertel, open to 2 am, which features Latin American-inspired dishes such as maize pancakes (DM14.50).

Nirvan (☎ 24 05 61, Eberhardstrasse), just off the Eberhard-Passage, has great Persian dishes (eg lamb, fish and vegetarian) from just DM10.

The cosy *Urbanstuben* (☎ 24 51 08, Eugenstrasse 12), on the corner of Urbanstrasse, has Swabian and international dishes from around DM26 and some excellent local wines.

Délice Vinothek (☎ 640 32 22, Hauptstätter Strasse 61) is an upmarket place with 1st class Italian-international cuisine and a fine wine selection, with mains from around DM35.

Der Zauberlehrling (☎ 237 77 70, Rosenstrasse 38) is a fine restaurant in the Bohnenviertel featuring Swabian dishes infused with American, French and other influences. Mains start at DM25 to DM30.

Speisenmeisterei (☎ 456 00 37, Am Schloss Hohenheim) is a fitting spot to live out royal fantasies. It's housed in a castle south-east of town and has lavish dining

Besenwirtschaft

For one month in autumn and in spring, wine growers throughout the region attach brooms to the front of their homes to indicate that they're a *Besenwirtschaft*, a small restaurant that allows people to come in and taste the new vintage (around DM4 for .25L). They open from 11 am, and also serve lunch and dinner featuring typical Swabian dishes like *Kartoffelsuppe*, *Gaisberger March* (a stew of sliced potatoes, noodles and beef), and the evil-sounding *Schlachtplatte* (sauerkraut with pork belly, liver, lard sausage and smoked meat, with peas and other vegetables).

Some Besenwirtschaft open every year, but most don't. Check in *Lift Stuttgart* or *S-Trip*, published in the *Stuttgarter Zeitung* on the last Wednesday of the month during vintage times.

Besenwirtschaft that operate annually include the home of *Jürgen Krug* (☎ 85 90 81, Wildensteinstrasse 24), which is in the suburb of Feuerbach and holds free art shows and performances by artistes – singers, cabaret performers, variété types etc (take tram No 6 to Feuerbacher Krankenhaus). The *Family Ruoff* (☎ 32 12 24, Uhlbacher Strasse 31), Obertürkheim, is in a fabulous house built in 1550 (S1 to Obertürkheim). In Untertürkheim, *Helmut Zaiss* (☎ 33 11 49, Strümpfelbacher Strasse 40) has a romantic vaulted wine cellar. Bus Nos 60 and 61 (direction: Rotenberg/Fellbach) stop right in front.

Figures in Freiburg's magnificent Münster

Mainau Island's famous gardens, Lake Constance

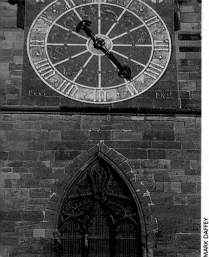

The Freiburg Münster dominates the town.

The Zeppelin Museum, Friedrichshafen

Germany's clock capital, Furtwangen

Boats on the Titi lake, Black Forest

The harvest crown, Black Forest

Smoking meat, Black Forest

Guild of Fools, Freiburg

A half-timbered house in picture-perfect Schiltach

The mostly ruined Heidelberg Castle

chambers that drip baroque. A three course meal with wine may set you back as much as DM150 to DM225.

Beer Gardens The best are in the Lower Palace Garden, Karlshöhe to the south-west of centre, and the Teehaus in Weissenburg to the south-east. The popular *Amadeus* (☎ 29 26 78, Charlottenplatz 17) is in the courtyard of the Institute for Foreign Affairs. You'll need to put down a DM3 deposit *(Pfand)* on your glass. They all sell Dinkel Acker beer and other brands, along with great food. Main courses cost from DM9 to DM18, and salads are under DM10.

The *Altes Schützenhaus* (☎ 649 81 57, Burgstallstrasse 99) at Südheimer Platz is typically packed with students who sit outside this old castle-like building. There's a disco on Saturday.

Snacks & Fast Food The *Marktstation* in the Hauptbahnhof is a cheap food court with the usual spread of burger, pizza and sausage places. Further into town, the *Markthalle*, a superb Art Nouveau-style market gallery on Dorotheenstrasse, is the ideal spot to buy delicatessen goodies for your picnic; it's open weekdays from 7 am to 6 pm and to 2 pm on Saturday.

The university *Mensa (Holzgartenstrasse 11)* has lunches for around DM7. The upstairs dining hall is reserved for students, but the ground-floor cafeteria and the small *Mensa Stüble* in the basement are open to all.

Brunnenwirt (☎ 56 94 75, Brunnenstrasse 15) is a quirky little sausage stand in the Bohnenviertel. Half grungy, half chic, this local institution draws everyone from passing vagrants to Mercedes coupé drivers.

Entertainment

Lift Stuttgart is a good publication with two versions: a free student-oriented guide and a twice-as-hefty *Stadtmagazin* (DM4.50). Both are easy-to-use (German-language) guides available throughout the city. *Prinz* (DM5) is another listings magazine that does about the same thing, but not as well.

Pubs & Bars The grandly named *Palast der Republik* (☎ 226 48 87, Friedrichstrasse 27) is a tiny kiosk bar with streetside tables that's become an institution. You won't find the name (there isn't room), but look for 'Schwaben Bräu' on the front.

Tiny Geissstrasse, just a block from Eberhardstrasse, has several little cafe-pubs that spill out onto what's unofficially called Hans-im-Glück Platz – a little square with a fountain depicting the caged German fairy-tale character 'Lucky Hans'.

The cafe-pubs here include the chi-chi *Ronny's* (☎ 23 66 46 11) at No 1; the very friendly *Max and Moritz* (☎ 239 92 39) at No 3, which also offers great pasta and pizzas; *Deli* (☎ 236 02 00) at No 7, a chic local favourite; and *Hans im Glück* (☎ 24 58 59) at No 8, which is probably the best-known pub in Stuttgart.

Discos & Clubs *Climax* (☎ 29 48 49, Friedrichstrasse 31) is a techno disco with an edgy twenty-something crowd, frenzied DJs and leather and rubber nights. The trendy *Club Prag* (☎ 817 56 02, Heilbronnerstrasse 261) launched the careers of those hip-hop superheroes, Die Fantastischen Vier (see the Contemporary Music section in the Facts about Germany chapter).

Perkins Park (☎ 256 00 62, Stresemannstrasse 39) is a massive place with two dance floors, a restaurant, a pool table and a very well mixed crowd aged from 16 to 60. There's techno, Brazilian, rock 'n' roll, soul ... you name it.

Club Zap (☎ 23 52 27, Hauptstätterstrasse 40), in the Schwabenzentrum, is an eclectic place where the crowd sways to jazz, soul and hip hop.

Gay & Lesbian The *King's Club* (☎ 226 45 58, Gymnasiumstrasse 21) is predominantly gay but some lesbians come as well. *Laura's Club* (☎ 29 01 60, Rothebühlplatz 4) is a lesbian disco that's also an information centre.

Rock & Jazz Live music is a regular fixture at *Longhorn/LKA* (☎ 409 82 90, Heiligenwiesen 6) and at *Ali's Litfass*

(☎ 24 30 31, Schwabenzentrum), near Club Zap (see Discos & Clubs). The latter is also a fine pub with drinks and great coffee served in bowls. *Roger's Kiste (☎ 23 31 48, Hauptstätter Strasse 35)* is a vintage hole in the wall that is the city's leading jazz venue. There's also regular jazz and rock at the *Theaterhaus* (see Theatre & Classical Music).

Cinema There's English-language cinema at the *Lupe (☎ 226 14 96, Kreigsbergstrasse 11)*, the *Atelier (☎ 29 49 95, Kronprinzstrasse 6)* and at the *Kommunales Kino (☎ 22 13 20, Friedrichstrasse 23a)* in the old Amerika Haus building. Check *Lift Stuttgart* and *Prinz* for details.

Theatre & Classical Music The Stuttgart area has 40 theatres and dozens of music venues. The *Staatstheater (☎ 22 17 95, Oberer Schlossgarten)* holds regular orchestral, ballet and opera performances. Tickets are heavily subsidised (eg opera tickets from DM16). The Stuttgart Ballet is renowned as one of the best in Europe.

The *Variété im Friedrichhaus (☎ 778 57 77, Friedrichstrasse 24)* is locally famous for its excellent variety shows and cabaret productions.

The *Theaterhaus (☎ 40 20 70, Ulmer Strasse 241)*, east of the centre in Wangen (take the U4 or U9 to Im Degen), stages anything from serious theatre to jazz concerts and cabaret.

Shopping

Of the many **weekly markets**, the biggest are the food markets on the Markt and the flower markets on Schillerplatz. They both take place on Tuesday, Thursday and Saturday from 7 am to 12.30 pm. There's a large flea market every Saturday at Karlsplatz.

Many varieties of **wine** are produced in the region; most are whites, but locals also go for Trollinger, a full-bodied red made from a variety of grape originally from South Tirol in Austria. Stuttgarters account for twice the national average consumption of wine, so while Trollinger is readily available here, they're not really exporting a lot. There's no shortage of wine shops in the city, and the tourist office has lists of vineyards open for tastings.

Stuttgart isn't renowned for bargain shopping but a neat place to browse is the Breuninger complex, a huge and expensive department store, south of the Markt.

Getting There & Away

Air Stuttgart international airport (☎ 94 80), south of the city, is served by domestic and international airlines. Connections are much more limited than at, say, Frankfurt airport.

Train There are frequent departures for all major German and many international cities, including IC and ICE trains to Frankfurt (DM62 to DM88, 1½ to two hours), Berlin (DM251, 5¼ to 6½ hours) and Munich (DM73, 2¼ hours).

There's frequent regional service to Tübingen (DM16.40, one hour), Schwäbisch Hall (DM22.40, 1½ hours), Ravensburg (DM49, two hours) and Ulm (DM24.60, one hour).

Bus Busabout coaches stop at the DJH hostel (see Places to Stay), with connections every two days to Heidelberg and Munich. Check the Getting There & Away chapter for details of Busabout passes.

Car & Motorcycle The A8 from Munich to Karlsruhe passes Stuttgart, as does the A81 from Würzburg south to Lake Constance.

Ride Services An ADM Mitfahrzentrale (☎ 636 80 36) is at Lerchenstrasse 65.

Getting Around

To/From the Airport S2 and S3 trains run frequently between the airport and the Hauptbahnhof and take about 30 minutes. A taxi to the town centre will cost between DM45 and DM50.

Public Transport On Stuttgart's public transport network, single fares will cost DM2/2.80 for short/longer trips within the central zone. A four-ride strip ticket costs

DM9.80. A three-day central-zone ticket is better value at DM12, and includes travel to/from the airport.

Car & Motorcycle The city is a pleasure to drive in – great roads and excellent street signs. There's underground parking throughout the centre costing about DM3.50 for the first hour and DM3 per hour after that.

There are Avis, Sixt and Europcar car-rental offices at the airport and in the Vermietungzentrum in the Hauptbahnhof.

Taxi Taxis cost DM4.70 at flag fall and DM2.60 per kilometre, plus DM2 for calling a taxi (☎ 194 10 or 56 60 61).

Bicycle You can rent bicycles (DM8/18/25/65/100 per hour/half-day/day/weekend/week) at Rent a Bike (☎ 209 90), which has a branch at the Hotel Unger, Kronenstrasse 17. The i-Punkt (☎ 222 82 27) rents fancy 24-gear jobs for DM20 a day, DM30 for a weekend and DM80 for a full week.

Bike transport on the commuter trains is restricted. The S-Bahn allows bikes Monday to Friday from 8.30 am to 4 pm and from 6.30 pm onwards, and all day on Saturday, Sunday and holidays. The U-Bahn allows bikes Monday to Friday, only after 7.30 in the evening, from 2 pm on Saturday and all day Sunday and holidays. Roving police will fine you at other times.

The ADFC has an office (☎ 636 86 37) at Breitscheidstrasse 82. Call for bike maps, information on organised rides etc.

AROUND STUTTGART

The region around Stuttgart is worth exploring and it's easy to get there on bus, tram, S-Bahn, U-Bahn or, better still, by bicycle. All the following places are within 20 minutes of the city centre by S-Bahn or U-Bahn.

Don't miss the spectacular vineyards and lovely paths along the Neckar, or the castles at Ludwigsburg.

Uhlbach

The best way to get into the spirit of the region is to head for the **Weinbaumuseum**

Pedal to the Metal

When Herman the German eases behind the wheel of his jet-black Mercedes, he's revving up for a pleasure as Teutonic as beer and bratwurst: fast driving. In a society famous for its adherence to rules and regulations, the autobahn is one of the few realms where Germans still taste freedom – or at least a lack of restraint. What other roads can you travel on at more than 200km (125 miles) per hour with no threat of a fine?

In fact, all but one-quarter of Germany's 11,000km of autobahns – the second-biggest network after the United States – have restrictions of 130km/h or less. But long stretches remain, where the only limits are warp drive and a motorist's own nerve. Here, too, unwitting foreigners are given a rough lesson in autobahn etiquette by a BMW, Porsche or Mercedes that appears out of nowhere in the rear-view mirror, angrily flashing its lights at the vehicle ahead to MOVE OVER.

But even this pastime may face regulation. Leading members of the ruling coalition – the Social Democrats and the Greens – have called for an autobahn limit of 100km/h (although 130km/h is a likelier outcome). Germany's carmakers, of course, hate the idea and related organisations do too. The magazine *Firmen Auto* wrote that 'the danger of being overtaken drops sharply at 200km/h, allowing the driver to concentrate fully on the traffic in front of the vehicle'. The AvD car club claims that 95% of all auto accidents in Germany involve drivers travelling less than 100km/h.

Remember that statistic the next time you hear of a massive autobahn pile-up – more often than not, it's the result of excessive speed and a blatant disregard for safe distance.

Uhlbach (☎ 32 57 18), Ulbacher Platz 4, in an old pressing house; look for the statue of the *very* happy-looking fellow outside. There are exhibits on the history of wine

euro currency converter DM1 = €0.51

making, but the tasting room is the big draw, with up to 16 wines available for tasting at any given time.

Tastes cost DM2. You can learn an awful lot about the region's wines here. Admission is free.

Opposite the museum is the late-Gothic/ Renaissance **Andreaskirche**, with its distinctive steeple and, next to it, a **WWII monument** to locals who died.

Take tram No 4 or S1 to Obertürkheim, then catch bus No 62 to the museum.

Württemberg

When Conrad von Württemberg established the Württemberg family dynasty, he sensibly built the family castle on this absolutely breathtaking hill south-east of Stuttgart. The hill is covered with vines and the castle has sweeping views down into a gorgeous valley.

Katherina Pavlovna, the daughter of a Russian tsar and the wife of Wilhelm I of Württemberg (1781-1864), reputedly told her husband that she'd never seen such a beautiful place and that she hoped to be buried here when she died. When she did, Wilhelm tore down the Württemberg family castle and in its place built a **Russian Orthodox chapel**. The crypt is amazingly ornate. The tombs of Wilhelm and Katherina lie to the east; their daughter, Marie, is to the south.

The chapel is open from March to October, Wednesday from 10 am to noon, and Friday to Sunday and holidays from 10 am to noon and 1 to 5 pm (free). The grounds outside afford lovely views of the countryside and are a perfect place for a picnic.

Bus No 61 runs here from the Obertürkheim S-Bahn station.

Max-Eyth-See & River Ride

Bring a bicycle on this little excursion along the most beautiful stretches of the Neckar, north-east of Stuttgart. On warm summer days, young Stuttgarters head for the lake recreation areas at the Max-Eyth-See (U14), a pleasant place for barbecues and picnics – though the water in the lake isn't too pristine. Ride or take the U-Bahn one

stop north to Seeblickweg, then bicycle down to the river bank.

There's a large, well maintained bike path along this spectacular stretch of river bank. The steep hills still have some of the older terraced-style vineyards, and many of the little **Wengerter Häuschen**, or tool sheds, which dot the hillside are over 200 years old and are protected landmarks. You can follow the river all the way back into town.

Ludwigsburg
☎ 07141 • pop 83,000

Ludwigsburg is named for Duke Eberhard Ludwig, who built the Residenzschloss in this lovely baroque city, the childhood home of dramatist Friedrich Schiller. It's a 20 minute train ride north of Stuttgart.

Orientation & Information The S-Bahn station is at the south-western end of town. Follow Myliusstrasse north-east to Arsenalstrasse and wend your way through the pedestrian centre to the Markt.

Ludwigsburg's tourist office (☎ 910 22 52, fax 910 27 74) is at Wilhelmstrasse 10, one block south of the Markt. It's open Monday and Thursday from 8.30 am to 5.30 pm, and on Tuesday, Wednesday and Friday from 9 am. On Saturday, it's open from 9 am to noon.

The main sights – the Residenzschloss and grounds, and Jagdschloss Favorit, a 'hunting palace' – are at the eastern end of town.

Things to See & Do The 18 buildings and 450-odd rooms comprising the baroque **Residenzschloss** (1704-33) can only be viewed on guided tours in German every 30 minutes; there's one tour in English daily at 1.30 pm (DM7/3.50). From April to September, the castle (☎ 18 64 40) is open daily from 9 am to noon and 1 to 5 pm. The rest of the year, German-language tours are Monday to Friday at 10.30 am and 3.30 pm, and every half hour on Saturday, Sunday and holidays from 10 am to noon and 1 to 4 pm.

Duke Karl Eugen, a businessman and bon vivant, established a porcelain factory in the castle in 1758. You can see samples from its heyday as well as the stuff it makes today in the **Porzellan-Manufaktur**.

The amazing **Blühendes Barock** (baroque in bloom) floral festival is held in the castle gardens from April to September. The grounds are yet another fabulous picnic area.

There are two more palaces of the former Württemberg rulers in the city. Just north of the Residenzschloss, in a cosy little nature reserve, is the **Jagdschloss Favorit**, the scene of Duke Eugen's glittering parties. From mid-March to November, it's open from 9 am to noon and 1.30 to 5 pm; the rest of the year, hours are 10 am to noon and 2 to 4pm. General admission is DM4/2, but a combined ticket including the Residenz-schloss costs DM11/5.50.

The other palace, east of the city, is the lakeside **Monrepos**, a former hunting lodge owned by the Württemberg family. There are concerts in summer (☎ 225 50 for program details), and you can rent boats on the lake.

The **Städtisches Museum** (☎ 910 22 90), Wilhelmstrasse 9/1, has exhibits on the town's history, industry and regional life. It's open Wednesday to Sunday from 10 am to noon and 1 to 5 pm (free). It's especially agreeable here during the Weihnachtsmarkt (Christmas fair).

Getting There & Away S4 and S5 go directly to Ludwigsburg train station. Alternatively, take a two hour ferry ride (DM21) from Bad Cannstatt to Ludwigsburg Hoheneck aboard a Neckar-Personen-Schiffahrt boat (☎ 0711-54 99 70 60).

SCHWÄBISCH HALL
☎ 0791 • pop 30,500

The site of ancient Celtic saltworks, the city of Reichstadt Hall became known as Schwäbisch Hall in 1806, when it was granted to the district of Swabia.

The city is celebrated for its open-air theatre and its ancient buildings along the Kocher River. It is also known for the Schwäbisch Hall banking and insurance company. But the best reason to come here is to see a German town that really does look like the ones portrayed on chocolate

boxes – a settlement of colourful half-timbered houses surrounded by rolling hills and covered bridges.

Because of its good hostel and camping grounds, it's also a cheap way to explore the area of the Schwäbisch Alb – a series of plateau-like hills crisscrossed by hiking and biking trails.

Orientation & Information
There are two main train stations: trains from Stuttgart arrive at the Hessental station; those from Heilbronn go to the one at Schwäbisch Hall. Trains and buses run regularly between the two stations. The Kocher River runs south through the city separating the Altstadt (on the east) from the Neustadt. The bus station (Zentraler Omnibus Bahnhof, or ZOB) is on the east side of the Kocher, north of Neue Strasse, the main shopping drag.

The Hauptbahnhof is south-west of the Altstadt; cross the bridge, walk down the stairs and follow the path, which will lead you across Roter Steg bridge and finally to the Markt.

The tourist information office (☎ 75 12 46, fax 75 13 75, email touristik@schwae-bischhall.de) at Am Markt 9 is open Monday to Friday from 9 am to 6 pm, and Saturday from 10 am to 3 pm. The Web site is www.schwaebischhall.de. The main post office is just west of the Markt.

From May to October, German-language guided tours of the Altstadt take place on Saturday at 2.30 pm; meet at the Fisch-brunnen (DM5/2.50).

Markt
The centrepiece of the Markt isn't the **Rathaus**, reconstructed in baroque style after a town fire in 1728 and again after WWII bombing, but rather the **Stadtkirche St Michael**, begun in 1156 but mainly constructed during the 15th and 16th century in late-Gothic style. Note the classical net vaulting on the ceiling of the choir.

Outside, the staircase has been used every summer since 1925 for **Freilichtspiele**, or open-air theatre (see Entertainment).

Next to the tourist office is the **Gotischer Fischbrunnen** (1509), a large tub used for storing river fish before sale. There are still markets here every Wednesday and Saturday morning.

Just south of the Markt, at the end of Pfarrgasse, is the massive **Neubausaal**, built as an arsenal and granary and now a theatre; walk up the stone staircase on its south side for a wonderful view of the city. Looking down to the river you can see the former **city fortifications** and, crossing the river, the covered **Roter Steg** bridge and the **Hangman's Bridge** connecting Neue Strasse to the west side of the Kocher.

Hällisch-Frankisches Museum

Housed in several buildings in the old city, the Hällisch-Frankisches Museum (☎ 75 12 89) covers the history of Swabia and Franconia. Exhibits include the houses themselves as well as artwork and crafts from the 17th century.

The museum's latest acquisition is an original **synagogue** (1738-39) from the town of Steinbach, near where the camping ground is today. It was torn down piece by piece by the Nazis and placed into storage; a local man rediscovered the bricks while renovating his house. The reconstructed synagogue will house an exhibit of Jewish life in the region.

The museum is open Tuesday to Sunday from 10 am to 5 pm, but on Wednesday it's open to 8 pm (free).

Activities

For a pleasant **day-hike** past the former monastery at Comburg (see the Around Schwäbisch Hall section) and up to the Einkorn tower, on a hilltop 25km outside the city, pick up maps from the tourist office. There are rest areas with barbecue grills and playgrounds along the way. Unfortunately, there's no public transport back to town; a taxi (☎ 25 26 or ☎ 61 17) will cost you between DM45 and DM65.

Rent **rowing boats** just north of Roter Steg bridge for DM5/8 per 30 minutes/hour. Horse riding from Reit- und Fahrverein Schwäbisch Hall (☎ 83 70) costs DM20 per hour (DM12 for kids), or DM100 for five hours.

Places to Stay

The idyllic *Campingplatz Steinbacher See* (☎/fax 29 84, Steinbacher See) charges DM9 per site plus DM7/5 per adult/child. There's a good restaurant, plus a washer/dryer and communal kitchen. Take bus No 4 to Steinbach Mitte.

The pristine *DJH hostel* (☎ 410 50, fax 479 98, Langenfelder Weg 5) charges juniors/seniors DM23/28 for dorm rooms or the same price in private two and three-bed rooms with showers and toilets (reserve early). Located in an attractive former retirement home, the hostel is antiseptically clean, but service is warm and friendly. It's just 10 minutes on foot from the Markt.

The *Gasthof Krone* (☎/fax 60 22, Klosterstrasse 1), next to the Stadtkirche St Michael, offers simple singles/doubles for just DM40/80, or for DM55/85 with shower and toilet. *Hotel Sölch* (☎ 518 07, fax 544-04, Hauffstrasse 14), on the edge of town, is a modern place with pleasant rustic interiors. Rooms with facilities cost DM65/105.

Hotel Garni Scholl (☎ 975 50, fax 97 55 80, Klosterstrasse 2-4), just behind St Michael, has very clean and nicely furnished rooms from DM95/150.

Hotel Hohenlohe (☎ 758 70, fax 75 87 84, Am Weilertor 14) is a smartly renovated, half-timbered inn and the town's chief blowout option. Rooms cost from DM159/218.

Places to Eat

Da Cesare (☎ 85 76 26), on the corner of Blockgasse and Hallstrasse, has enormous, scrumptious, New York-style pizza slices for around DM4. There's a takeaway window, a sit-down restaurant doing full Italian meals from DM9 to DM15, an ice-cream parlour and an outdoor cafe. *Hespelt (Am Spitalbach 17)* is a big butcher-deli that puts together great hot lunches for about DM10.

Weinstube Würth (☎ 66 36, Im Weiler 8), behind the Stadtkirche St Michael, offers delicious Swabian specialities for around

DM15 and has a lovely beer garden (closed Monday). *Schuhbäck (☎ 854 70, Untere Herrngasse 1-3)*, just down the steps from the Markt, has some really tasty lunch menus for DM14 or less (closed Tuesday).

Entertainment

The open-air theatre season is from June to September, typically with classics such as *The Hunchback of Notre Dame* or the comedy *Der Räuber Hotzenplotz*. Tickets ranging from DM10 (standing room) to DM50 are available at the tourist office (☎ 75 16 00 for reservations). And you can't peek: all the streets around the square are sealed off. Shows begin at sunset.

Plays and concerts take place year round in the *Alte Brauerei (☎ 85 58 72, Lange Strasse 35)*, a restored 19th century brewery just south of the river. It has a pleasant cafe, too.

Getting There & Around

There's train service at least hourly to Stuttgart (DM22.40, 1½ hours), and one that leaves every two hours for Heilbronn (DM14.80, 40 minutes). The best way to go to Ulm is via Crailsheim; trains run at least hourly (DM24.60, one hour). From Crailsheim, catch the regular service back to Schwäbisch Hall-Hessental and a connecting service to Schwäbisch Hall Hauptstadt.

Outfits renting bikes from DM10 a day include 2-Rad Zügel (☎ 97 14 00), Johanniterstrasse 55, and MHW-Radsport (☎ 484 10), Schmollerstrasse 43.

AROUND SCHWÄBISCH HALL
Comburg

This former Benedictine monastery just 5km south of Schwäbisch Hall was established in a baron's castle in 1078. Today it's a teacher's college, but its **Stiftskirche St Nikolaus** is a functioning Catholic church. The interior is impressive – note the huge Roman chandelier, lit only on special occasions. It's open from April to October, Tuesday to Friday, from 10 am to noon and 2 to 5 pm, and Saturday and Sunday from 2 to 5 pm only (DM4/2, free during church services on Sunday morning). The views

from the hilltop are terrific. Take bus No 4 to Comburg.

Hohenloher Freilandmuseum

If you've any romantic illusions about farm life, a visit to the open-air farming museum (☎ 97 10 10) in Wackershofen, 6km west of Schwäbisch Hall, will surely cure them. The ancient farmhouses reconstructed here show just how bucolic (read: back-breaking) agriculture was like before the 20th century. There are demonstrations of farming methods and equipment, and we nearly got blisters just watching.

Less strenuous is the **Weindorf**. Every weekend, the region's wine-makers give talks and tastings and sell snacks. It's good fun at good prices.

The farming museum and wine village are open from mid-March to October, Tuesday to Sunday from 10 am to 5 pm, and daily in July and August (DM9/5). Take bus No 7 to the front entrance.

Places to Stay & Eat The *Sonneck Hotel (☎ 97 06 70, fax 970 67 89, Fischweg 2)* in Gottwollshausen is a nice family-run place with clean singles/doubles from DM65/100 and good service. There's a restaurant downstairs and a games room with pool tables.

Gasthof zum Roten Ochsen (☎ 841 72, Freilandmuseum), right at the entrance to the farming museum, has good local specialities from DM14 and local beers from DM2.50 to DM5 (closed Monday).

TÜBINGEN

☎ 07071 • pop 8000

Just 40km south of Stuttgart, the graceful university town of Tübingen can rival the most picturesque of German medieval *burgs*. With its cobbled alleys, hill-top fortress and a stunning array of half-timbered houses, Tübingen is popular but lacks the summer crush of places like Heidelberg. The tourist office calls Tübingen University – founded in 1477 by Duke Eberhard – 'Germany's oldest university established by a member of the lower ranks of the aristocracy'.

With 25,000 students (triple the local population), an ivy-league atmosphere seems to permeate everything. The town was a favoured haunt of Goethe, who published his first works here, and today it's a lovely place to relax for a few days, hit some pubs and paddle your way down the Neckar River.

Orientation

The Neckar flows from east to west in a boomerang arc through town; the Altstadt and all key sights are to the north. The metre-wide Ammer River, a tributary, flows through the town north of the Neckar. The Hauptbahnhof is on the south side, a five minute walk from the Neckarbrücke, which links the north and the south banks with an exit onto the Platanenallee, a long, thin island in the middle of the Neckar extending to the west of the bridge.

Information

Tourist Office The tourist office (☎ 913 60, fax 350 70, email bvv.tuebingen@ t-online.de) is on An der Neckarbrücke beside the bridge. Its hours are Monday to Friday from 9 am to 7 pm, Saturday to 5 pm. From May to September, it's also open from 2 to 4 pm on Sunday and holidays. There's an electronic hotel board in front for booking at any time.

ADAC has an office (☎ 527 27) at Wilhelmstrasse 3.

Money There's a Postbank right opposite the Hauptbahnhof with an ATM, and a Sparkasse opposite the tourist office.

Post & Communications The main post office is in the Altstadt on the corner of Hafengasse and Neue Strasse. There's a very cool Internet cafe called H@ckers (☎ 219 19) at Neustadtgasse 11, which stays open to 1 am.

Bookshops & Libraries Buchhandlung Heckenhauer Antiquariat, Holzmarkt 5, is a national landmark: Hermann Hesse worked here from 1895 to 1899.

The Frauenbuchladen Thalestris (☎ 265 90), Bursagasse 2, has an enormous assortment of women's books (also in English). It's a women's information centre, too, and men aren't allowed inside. The British Corner (see Shopping) has cheap used books in English.

The city library (☎ 20 45 40) is at Nonnengasse 19. The university library is at Wilhelmstrasse 32.

Laundry There's the Steinlach-Waschsalon (☎ 720 67) at Albrechtstrasse 21, or you can try the Waschsalon im Studentenwerk at Rümelinstrasse 8, where washing and drying costs DM5.

Dangers & Annoyances The Platanenallee island in the Neckar attracts some particularly seedy characters and is often closed at night.

North River Bank

Walking west from the Neckarbrücke, beside the bank and the old city fortifications, you'll pass the one-room **Zimmer Theater**, the fraternity **punts** and the **Hölderlinturm**, where the poet Friedrich Hölderlin (1774-1843) was treated for mental illness until his death. Today it's a museum dedicated to his life and work.

Up the little hill is the **Burse**, the first university building (1477) and the centre of academic life in the city; today the university campus is spread throughout the city. West of the Burse is the **Stift**, the central Lutheran clerical training college from 1536. It's still a theology school today, and about half its students are women.

Schloss

From the heights of the Renaissance Schloss Hohentübingen (now part of the university) there are fine views over the steep, red-tiled rooftops of the Altstadt. The Schloss now houses an **Egyptology & Archaeology Museum**. It's open Wednesday to Sunday from 10 am to 6 pm, and to 5 pm in winter (DM4/2). Walk through the tunnel at the west side of the courtyard, past 'lovers' lane' and follow the path down through the narrow winding streets of the Altstadt and eventually onto Haaggasse.

Markt

On the Markt in the centre of town (which overflows with geraniums in summer) is the **Rathaus** (1433), with a riotous 19th century baroque facade. At the top is a glorious clock, astronomical clock and moon-phase indicator (1511). The four women of the **Neptune Fountain** represent the seasons, and the city council members who approved finance for the fountain modestly placed themselves in the decorative ironwork.

At the northern side of the Markt stands the **Lamm**, an erstwhile watering hole for many of Tübingen's leading figures; today it's owned by the Protestant church. Walk through the little passageway to see the beer garden.

Stiftskirche

The late-Gothic Stiftskirche (1470) nearby was the site of lectures before the main university buildings were erected. The church houses tombs of the Württemberg dukes and has excellent original medieval stained-glass windows (some dating to the early 15th century). It's open daily from 9 am to 5 pm, and to 4 pm from November to January.

Cotta Haus & Goethe Plaque

Opposite the western side of the Stiftskirche is the home of Johann Friedrich Cotta, who first published the work of both Schiller and Goethe. Herr Goethe, who was known to glean inspiration from the stock of the local pubs, stayed here for a week in September 1797. One night he apparently staggered back, missed the front door and wrote a technicolour poem on the wall next door. If you look up at the 1st floor window on that house, now a student dorm, you'll see a little sign: 'Hier Kotzte Goethe' (Goethe Puked Here).

Other Sights

The **Platanenallee**, the long sliver of an island in the middle of the Neckar, is especially pleasant in late June when the

fraternities hold their wildly popular punt races, which draw thousands of spectators.

Misbehaving students (as young as 14) were given the choice of losing their wine ration or being sent to the city's **Karzer**, the student jail on Münzgasse. If you've seen the one in Heidelberg, you can skip this one. If not, it'll be added to a city tour at no extra cost if you ask.

Shows at the **Kunsthalle** take place every couple of years, attracting droves of visitors; check with the tourist office for what's on.

Organised Tours

From April to October, the tourist office conducts a German-language walking tour of the city on Saturday at 2.30 pm, as well as Sunday and Wednesday at 10 am, starting at the Rathaus. The cost is DM5/2.50. It also arranges other tours, including one in Latin.

Places to Stay

The convenient *camping ground* (☎ 431 45, fax 250 70, Rappenberghalde 61) charges DM5.50 to DM7 per tent, plus DM9.50 per person (DM6 per child). Cars cost DM3.

The *DJH hostel* (☎ 230 02, fax 250 61, Gartenstrasse 22/2) has a very pretty location on the north bank of the Neckar, 1km east of the tourist office. Dorm beds cost DM23/28 for juniors/seniors, including breakfast.

Viktor-Renner-Haus (☎ 454 09, fax 44 00 03, Frondsbergstrasse 55), just north of the Altstadt, has an excellent deal at DM40/80 for clean, if pretty basic, singles/doubles. *Hotel-Restaurant Kürner* (☎ 227 35, fax 279 20, Weizsäckerstrasse 1) is a decent place right by the university, with a few bathless singles for DM58; with shower, singles/doubles cost DM68/108.

Gästehaus Marianne (☎ 937 40, fax 93 74 99, Johannesweg 14) is a pleasant family-run guesthouse just a 10 minute walk south-east of the Hauptbahnhof. Rooms with amenities start at DM60/85.

Hotel am Schloss (☎ 929 40, fax 92 94 10, Burgsteig 18), in the shadow of the castle, has a few simple rooms from DM45/95 (DM60/124 with shower) – very reasonable for the central location. Ask for room No 26, which has views in all four directions. There's also a great restaurant here – see Places to Eat.

Hotel Hospiz Tübingen (☎ 92 40, fax 92 42 00, Neckarhalde 2), very close to the Markt, has singles without baths from DM50; singles/doubles with amenities cost DM105/150. It's a solid choice.

Hotel Krone Tübingen (☎ 133 10, fax 13 31 32, Uhlandstrasse 1) is a very swish place near the Altstadt portals (and one of the few town hotels with air-con). Rooms start at DM155/190.

Places to Eat

The best chips/French fries (from DM2) in Baden-Württemberg are at *X* (☎ 249 02, Kornhausstrasse 6). It also has Bratwurst and burgers from DM3 to DM4.

For super coffee, *Hanseatica* (☎ 269 84, Hafengasse 2) can't be beaten; the coffee is only DM1.90 per cup, so follow your nose.

Naturgabe Backstube (☎ 56 03 35), at the corner of Froschgasse and Kornhausstrasse, has organic bread products and lovely outdoor tables; cross the little bridge over the Ammer River to the entrance.

The *Markthalle Kelter*, corner of Kelternstrasse and Schmiedtorstrasse, is a food hall with cheap takeaway and restaurants, many selling organic products. The university *Mensa (Hafengasse 6)* has full meals from DM4, but student IDs are often checked.

Inside the shopping mall at the Nonnenhaus, at the northern end of Neue Strasse, are *Pasta Fresca* (☎ 279 49) and *Eis Café San Marco* (☎ 352 39); the former has excellent home-made pasta from DM6 per portion and both have great outdoor cafes.

The *Collegium* (☎ 222 60), at the corner of Lange Gasse and Collegiumsgasse, has good-sized Swabian and vegetarian dishes from DM14.

The restaurant at the *Hotel am Schloss* (☎ 929 40, Burgsteig 18) literally wrote the book on the local speciality, a ravioli-like stuffed pasta called *Maultaschen*. The owner, Herbert Rösch, published the *Schwäbisches Maultaschen Buch*, which is available around town. The restaurant serves 28 types of Maultaschen costing from DM13 to DM18; salad plates and light meals range from DM8 to DM15. Sit on the back terrace for great views. Service is excellent.

Entertainment

Good bars include the *S'Urige* (☎ 92 75 21, Am Lustenauer Tor 8), a student cellar with a cryptic menu (main thing is, the beer's good and cheap). Quite convenient to the hostel is *Neckarmüller* (☎ 278 48, Gartenstrasse 4), a brewery/pub with a beer garden on the north side of the Neckarbrücke.

Patty (☎ 516 12, Schlachthofstrasse 9) is a theme disco with Turkish nights on Friday and Latin sounds on Saturday. *Tangente Jour* (☎ 245 72, Münzgasse 17) is the local *Szene* bar with lots of eats under DM15 – and not to be confused with *Tangente Night* (☎ 230 07, Pfleghofstrasse 10)*, a big disco and nightclub. *Club Voltaire* (☎ 512 14, Haaggasse 26b), at the end of the little alley, has gay and lesbian discos and cabaret.

JazzKeller (☎ 55 09 06, Haaggasse 15/2) has live jazz and 'funky soul' with a DM5 cover, while *Tapas* (☎ 550 89 5, Bursagasse 4) has flamenco music and tapas from DM5 to DM9.

English-language films run at the *Atelier* (☎ 212 25, Vor dem Haagtor 1) and at the *Museum* (☎ 133 55, Am Stadtgraben 2).

Check with the tourist office for what's on at the *Zimmer Theater* (☎ 927 30, Bursagasse 16) and at the *LTT Landestheater* (☎ 931 31 49, Eberhardstrasse 6).

Shopping

Vinum (☎ 520 52), Lange Gasse 6, has over 400 wines from around the region and the world, and samples are free. It also sells fine sherries and spirits and a wonderful selection of olive oil.

The British Corner (☎ 272 63), at Schmiedtorstrasse 13, is about as well stocked as the average (small) supermarket. It also buys and sells used English books priced from DM3 to DM5, and (Aussi Vegemite (DM8).

Getting There & Away
Tübingen can be easily visited on a day trip from Stuttgart. Direct trains link the two twice hourly (DM32.80 return, one hour). There's a Mitfahrzentrale (☎ 194 40) at Münzgasse 6 and a Mitfahrzentrale für Frauen (☎ 265 90) at the women's bookshop at Bursagasse 2.

Getting Around
You can book a taxi on ☎ 243 01. Rent bicycles (DM14 for the first day, less thereafter) from Radlager (☎ 55 16 51), Lazarettgasse 19-21. Rent rowing boats/pedal-boats/canoes at Bootsvermietung Märkle Tübingen (☎ 315 29) for DM10.50/16/9 per hour. It's just east of the bridge, behind the tourist office down the little stairs.

A more stylish way of cruising the river is aboard one of the university fraternities' *Stocherkähne*, or punts, for DM85 per hour for up to 16 people. They're on the north bank of the river, west of the bridge.

BURG HOHENZOLLERN
No other German dynasty ever wielded as much power as the Hohenzollerns. The family rose to prominence in the 15th century when it was put in charge of Germany's eastern border in the March of Brandenburg. By the early 18th century, the Hohenzollerns had taken control of Prussia from Poland, declared themselves royals and begun amassing an empire that would encompass much of modern Germany. They were also the first and last monarchical rulers of the short-lived first German Reich (1871-1918).

Their main stronghold was Burg Hohenzollern, about 25km south of Tübingen in the rolling Schwäbische Alb (Swabian Jura). The original 13th century castle was destroyed during the Peasants' War in 1423 but the Hohenzollerns quickly rebuilt. The neo-Gothic version you see today (1850-1867) cuts an impressive figure from a distance, rising dramatically from an exposed crag, its vast medieval battlements often veiled in mist. Up close it looks more contrived, in line with the 19th century fad of building roman- castles with little real defensive function.

The interior is definitely worth a look: its artworks, stained glass and fabulous **Schatzkammer** (treasury) justify the entry price (DM9/6, with German guided tour only). You can view the grounds at your leisure (DM4), and on clear days there's a view clear to the Swiss Alps. The castle (☎ 07471-24 28) lies a few kilometres south of the town of Hechingen, and is open daily from 9 am to 5.30 pm (to 4.30 pm in winter).

There's a single bus on Sunday from Hechingen train station at 11.20 am, return- ing at 2.20 pm (free if you've got a train ticket). Otherwise, taxis sell return journeys for DM17 per person. Frequent trains to Hechingen from Tübingen take 20 to 30 minutes (DM7.60).

HEIDELBERG
☎ 06221 • pop 140,000
Heidelberg, 130km from Stuttgart, is one of Germany's biggest tourist draws. It was dev- astated in 1622 during the Thirty Years' War and all but destroyed by invading French troops under Louis XIV in the late 17th cen- tury. The half-ruined castle looming over town is all the more romantic as a result.

American novelist and humorist Mark Twain began his European travels here in 1878 and recounted his comical observa- tions in *A Tramp Abroad*. Britain's William Turner also loved Heidelberg, inspiring him to paint some of his greatest landscapes.

With a student population of 32,000 (at- tending the oldest university in Germany), Heidelberg is a lively city. This is the place for a serious pub crawl: there are dozens of earthy, enjoyable bars and pubs with good beer, friendly locals and heaps of tradition. But be warned: more than three million vis- itors tramp through its narrow, twisting streets every year, and it'll seem like most of them are still there when you come.

Orientation
The modern and less interesting western side of the city starts near the train station. To find out what this place is really all about, head down Kurfürstenanlage to

euro currency converter DM1 = €0.51

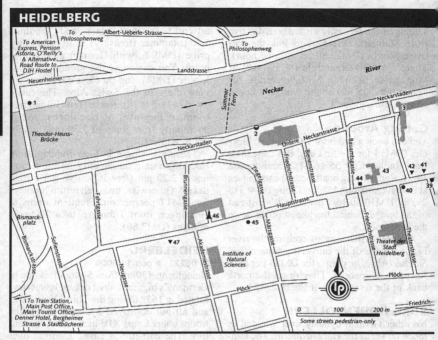

HEIDELBERG

PLACES TO STAY
6   Hotel Vier Jahreszeiten
9   Hotel Goldener Hecht
31 Hotel am Kornmarkt
33 Jeske Hotel
35 Hotel Zum Ritter
44 Hotel Futterkrippe
53 Hotel Zum Pfalzgrafen

PLACES TO EAT
12 Zur Herrenmühle
14 Sudpfanne
21 Vetter im Schöneck
22 Starfish
32 Vegethali; Raja Rani
38 Riegler
41 Güldenes Schaf
42 Viva Italia/
    Viva Mexico
47 Nordsee
48 University Mensa
54 Simplicissimus

OTHER
1   Boat Rental
2   Rhein-Neckar River Boats
3   Marstall; University Mensa
4   Karl-Theodor Statue
5   Monkey Statue
7   Napper Tandy's Irish Pub
8   Schnookeloch
10 Tourist Office
11 Transport Exhibition
13 Ethnology Museum
15 Zum Roten Ochsen
16 Zum Sepp'l
17 Palais Boissereé
18 Rathaus
19 Hercules Fountain
20 Cafe Max
23 Cafe Knösel
24 Goldener Reichsapfel
25 Gasthaus Zum Mohren
26 Destille
27 Palmbräu Gasse

28 i Punkt
29 Heiliggeistkirche
30 H+G Bank
34 Cave 54
36 Café Journal
37 Student Jail
39 Zimmertheater
40 Harmonie Cinema
43 Palatinate Museum
45 Koesters Bookshop
46 Bunsen Statue
49 Post Office
50 Jesuit Church
51 Drugstore Café
52 Waschsalon Wojtala
55 Zwinger3
56 Tangente – Disco
57 Scruffy Murphy's
58 Mata Hari
59 Funicular Railway
60 Schloss
61 Main Tourist Office

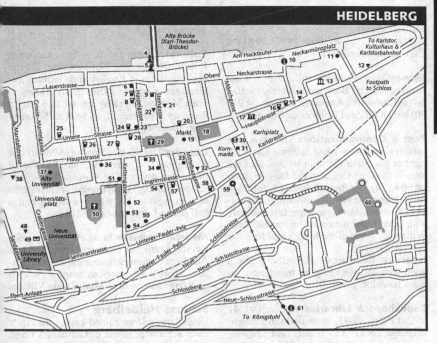

Bismarckplatz, where the romantic old Heidelberg begins to reveal itself. The Neckar River runs east-west just north of the Altstadt; streets that go from east to west are called 'Strasse', and north-south ones are called 'Gasse'. Hauptstrasse is the pedestrian thoroughfare, leading 1600m – the so-called Royal Mile – eastwards through the heart of the old city from Bismarckplatz via the Markt to Karlstor.

Two main bridges cross the Neckar from the Altstadt: at the western end, north of Bismarckplatz, is Theodor-Heuss-Brücke; north of the Markt is the Alte Brücke (also known as Karl-Theodor-Brücke). On the north side of the Neckar is Heiligenberg (Holy Hill); halfway up is Philosophenweg (Philosopher's Walk).

The Schloss is at the southern end of the ity up the hill. The DJH hostel is north of e Neckar, west of Theodor-Heuss-Brücke.

The US military communities of Mark Twain Village and Patrick Henry Village, with about 15,000 residents, are south-west of the Altstadt.

Information
Tourist Offices Heidelberg's main tourist office (☎ 194 33, fax 16 73 18, email cvb@heidelberg.de), outside the train station, has exceptionally friendly staff and mountains of good advice, though queues can get long. It's open Monday to Saturday, 9 am to 7 pm all year, plus Sunday from 10 am to 6 pm between mid-March and mid-November. There are tourist office branches open from May to October at the funicular station near the castle and on Neckarmünzplatz.

All the offices sell the Heidelberg Card (DM19.80), valid for 24 hours and including use of all public transport and discounts

euro currency converter DM1 = €0.51

to museums, theatres and even some hotels and restaurants.

The ADAC has an office (☎ 72 09 81) at Carl-Diem-Strasse 2-4.

Money There's a Reisebank at the train station and an H+G Bank conveniently located at Am Kornmarkt. American Express (☎ 912 70) has an office at Brückenkopfstrasse 1-2.

Post & Communications The main post office is in the huge white building just to the right as you leave the train station. Surf the Web in the Café Gekco at the Denner Hotel (☎ 60 45 10), Bergheimer Strasse 8, for DM4 per half hour. At the time of writing, the university was planning a huge Internet cafe with loads of terminals at Universitätsplatz, in the back foyer of the Mensa building.

Internet Resources Heidelberg has a good Web site, with English translations, at www.heidelberg.de/cvb.

Bookshops & Libraries Wetzlar (☎ 241 65), at Plöck 79-81, specialises in foreign-language books. You'll also find English-language books and Lonely Planet titles at Koesters Akademische Buchhandlung (☎ 298 69), Hauptstrasse 72. Antiquariat Schöbel (☎ 260 36), Plöck 56a, has some used novels in English.

The university library (☎ 54 23 80) at Plöck 107-109 and the Stadtbücherei (City Library; ☎ 58 36 13/14), Poststrasse 15, both have books in English.

University The Ruprecht-Karl-Universität (☎ 540), established in 1386 by Count Palatinate Ruprecht I, one of the seven imperial prince-electors at that time, is the oldest university in Germany.

The original university consisted of four faculties: philosophy, law, medicine and theology. Today it has over 30,000 students from 80 nations in 18 faculties. Women, first admitted in 1900, now make up about half of the student body.

Universitätsplatz is the historic centre of the university, but today the main campus is on the north side of the Neckar, which is west of the city.

Cultural Centre Deutsch-Amerikanisches Institut (☎ 607 30), Sofienstrasse 12, has concerts, films in English and German, lectures and frequent exhibits. Its library is open Monday to Friday from 1 to 6 pm (to 8 pm on Wednesday), as well as Saturday from 10 am to 2 pm.

Laundry The SB Waschsalon at Poststrasse 50 charges DM7 per load and DM1 for 20 minutes of drying. The Waschsalon Wojtala (closed Sunday) is an expensive alternative at Kettengasse 17, where washing and a half hour of drying cost DM15.

Medical Services In an emergency, contact the Ärztlicher Notdienst (☎ 192 92) on Alte Eppenheimerstrasse, near the train station. There's an American hospital (☎ 170) on Römerstrasse near Mark Twain Village.

Schloss Heidelberg

Heidelberg's large ruined castle, the city's chief attraction, is one of Germany's finest examples of a Gothic-Renaissance fortress. Begun in the 13th century, its oldest remaining structures date from 1400. The castle housed a branch of the Wittelsbachs, the Bavarian royal family. Over the years, family and court intrigues led to many changes in ownership; the place was first sacked in 1622 by forces of the Catholic Wittelsbachs against Protestants within the castle. At the end of the Thirty Years' War, the castle was rebuilt but destroyed again in 1693, along with most other buildings in the city.

The castle's dilapidation actually enhances its romantic appeal. Seen from anywhere in the Altstadt, this striking red sandstone pile dominates the hillside. The Renaissance **castle courtyard** is amazing. Outside, just east of the entry, is the **Pulver Turm** (gunpowder tower), destroyed by French forces in 1693. The wall remains and chimney behind it are worth a look. There are several places to eat up here, too (see Places to Eat).

As you enter the gates, look left at the tiny door with the iron ring, which is cracked. Legend has it that Ludwig V would give the castle to anyone who could bite through the ring; a witch supposedly gave it a shot.

The **terrace** provides huge views over the town and the Neckar. Look for the footprint in the stone, said to have been left by a knight leaping from the 3rd storey window when the prince returned early to his wife's bedroom. Don't miss seeing the **Grosses Fass** (great vat), an enormous 18th century keg, said to be capable of holding more than 220,000L. The contrast to the **Kleines Fass**, itself not exactly tiny, as you enter, earns a gasp from many visitors.

The **Deutsches Apothekenmuseum** (German Pharmaceutical Museum) recalls the chemistry and alchemy of earlier times. Downstairs on the left-hand side is a memorial to Robert Bunsen, inventor of that Bunsen burner we all used in science class, and of the colour-spectrum analyser. Other Bunsen-abilia in Heidelberg includes a plaque at the university and a statue on Hauptstrasse near Bismarckplatz.

The castle is open daily from 8 am to 5 pm. It costs nothing to walk around the grounds and garden terraces; entry to the castle courtyard, Grosses Fass and the German Pharmaceutical Museum is DM3/1.50, or sign up for the rather dull guided tour of the interior (DM4/2), which includes everything. For DM2 you can buy an English-language guide and map to the place.

To get to the castle either take the funicular railway from the lower Kornmarkt station (DM3/2 one-way, DM5.50/3.50 return), or make the 10 minute walk through steep cobbled lanes. On foot, it's nice to start from the less-touristed path at the east side of Karlplatz, which brings you past the Goethe statue near the fountain

Königstuhl & Fairy-Tale Park

The funicular continues up to the Königstuhl, where there's a TV tower; the return fare from Kornmarkt, with a stop at the castle, is DM8.50/6. Also at the top of the hill is the Fairy-Tale Park (☎ 234 16), a wonderful

playground with fairy-tale characters, hobby horses and other kiddie stuff. It's open from March to October daily from 10 am to 6 pm, and June to August from 10 am to 7 pm (DM5, children DM4).

Alte Brücke

To get the most out of a town walk, begin at the Alte Brücke. The **Karl-Theodor statue** refers to the local legend that the prince fathered almost 200 illegitimate children. At the base of the bridge is a statue of a **brass monkey** holding a mirror and surrounded by mice: touch the mirror for wealth; the outstretched fingers to ensure you return to Heidelberg; and the mice to ensure you have many children. The bridge foundation bears some pretty hairy high-water marks.

Opposite the bridge, note the plaque on the **Hotel Goldener Hecht**, which reads 'Goethe almost slept here'. Apparently, a clerk turned down the author who, to the enormous consternation of the owner, took rooms elsewhere.

Markt

At the Markt, the old town square, is the amazing **Heiliggeistkirche** (1398-1441), a Gothic cathedral with a baroque roof. There was, for a long time, a wall between one part used by Protestants and that used by Catholics, but it was torn down in 1936. Today, it's a Protestant place of worship.

You can climb the 204 steps to the top of the church spire (DM1) Monday to Saturday from 11 am to 5 pm, from 1.30 pm on Sunday.

The **market stalls** surrounding the church are a Heidelberg tradition. Across the street, on the south side of the square, the lavishly decorated former **royal pharmacy** has been reborn as a McDonald's.

In the centre of the Markt is a **Hercules fountain**; in medieval times petty criminals were chained to the fountain and left to face the townsfolk.

Palais Boisbereé

This former palace at Hauptstrasse 235, east of the Markt, is said to be the cradle of the

Romantic movement. It once housed a collection of medieval altars and artworks that attracted poets, writers and artists (including Goethe and the Brothers Grimm, among many others).

Jesuiten Viertel

East of Universitätsplatz is the Jesuit Quarter, a little square containing the city's former **Jesuit church** (1712-50), fronted by statues including St Ignatius Loyola, St Francis Xavier, Christ at the facade's top centre, and Faith on the rooftop. The church is still Catholic but not Jesuit.

University Buildings

Dominating Universitätsplatz are the 18th century **Alte Universität** and the **Neue Universität**, the old and new university buildings. Head south on Grabengasse to the **University Library** and then down Plöck to Akademiestrasse and the old **Institute of Natural Sciences**, where Robert Bunsen taught for more than 40 years. About 200m to the north of the square is the **Marstall**, the former stables and municipal armoury that now houses an ageing university cafeteria (Mensa).

Studentenkarzer

From 1778 to 1914, university students were tossed into the Studentenkarzer (student jail) if convicted of misdeeds such as singing, womanising, drinking or just plain goofing around. Sentences were generally a minimum of three days, during which they were fed only bread and water; during longer sentences, the recalcitrants could interrupt their stay for critical reasons (say, to take exams). A stint in the Karzer was considered *de rigueur* to prove one's manhood. Women, who were admitted to the university from 1900 onwards, were never imprisoned here. Detainees passed their time by carving inscriptions and drawing graffiti, which still cover the walls.

The jail (☎ 54 23 34), Augustinergasse 2, is open Tuesday to Saturday from 10 am to noon and 2 to 5 pm (DM1.50/1). In winter, the place closes on Saturday afternoon.

Palatinate Museum

The Palatinate Museum (Kurpfälzisches Museum; ☎ 58 34 02), tucked behind the courtyard at Hauptstrasse 97, contains regional artefacts and works of art, plus a copy of the jawbone of the 600,000-year-old Heidelberg Man. The original skeleton is kept across the river at the palaeontology centre, which is closed to the public.

The museum is open Tuesday to Sunday from 10 am to 5 pm (DM5/3).

Philosophenweg

A stroll along the Philosophenweg, north of the Neckar River, provides a welcome respite from the tourist hordes. Leading through steep vineyards and orchards, the path offers those great views of the Altstadt and the castle that were such an inspiration to the German philosopher Hegel. It's a well known lovers' haunt, and many young locals are said to have lost their hearts (and virginity) along the walkway. A little closer to the river bank is a meadow on which people gather to watch the tri-annual fireworks displays (see Special Events). There are also many other hiking possibilities in the surrounding hills.

You can rent rowing and pedal boats at the stand on the north side of Theodor-Heuss-Brücke. Charges are DM9/15 per half-hour/hour for up to three people.

Organised Tours

The tourist office arranges several tours of the city each week. There are daily guided tours (DM10/7) in English and German at 10 am from April to October, and in German only from January to March; they depart from the Lion Fountain in Universitätsplatz.

Rhein-Neckar Fahrgastschiffahrt (☎ 201 81), at the docks on the south bank of the Neckar, offers a huge range of tours and trips throughout the Neckar Valley. Three-hour cruises depart daily at 9.30 and 11 am, and 2 and 2.40 pm (extra trips are sometimes laid on). Return tickets are DM16.50/9.50.

Rowboats and paddleboats can be rented at Bootsverleih Simon (☎ 41 19 25), on the north shore of the Neckar by the Theodor-

Heuss-Brücke. A three-person boat costs DM9/15 per half-hour/hour; four-person boats cost DM12/18 (open daily from 10am to dusk).

Special Events

Heidelberg has many annual festivals. The most popular are **Heidelberger Herbst**, the huge autumn festival during which the entire pedestrian zone is closed off for a wild party on the last Saturday in September, and the **fireworks festivals**, held three times a year (on the first Saturday in June and September, and the second Saturday in July).

During these festivities the castle is specially lit and the whole town, plus members of the US military communities, show up to watch the magic. Best viewing sites are from the northern bank of the Neckar and from Philosophenweg.

The **Christmas market**, held at the centre square in December, is also a treat.

Places to Stay – Budget

Bargains are thin on the ground in Heidelberg, and in the high season finding *any* place to stay can be difficult. Arrive early in the day or book ahead – especially for the hostel.

Camping About 4.5km east of town by the river, *Camping Neckartal* (☎ 80 25 06, *Schlierbach)* costs DM8 per site and DM10 per person, plus DM2 per car. Take bus No 35 from Bismarckplatz and get off at the Orthopädische Klinik. It's open from Easter to October.

Camping Haide (☎ 21 11, fax 719 59, *Haide)*, across the river and back towards town about 1km, has sites for DM6, plus DM8 per adult, DM2 per car and DM1.50 per motorcycle. You can also rent a place in the dormitory lofts – like bunk barns – for DM9.50 per person, or in more private log huts for DM16.50/33/58 for one/two/four people. Take bus No 35 to the Schwäbische Brücke stop, cross the bridge and walk 10 minutes east along the river.

Hostels The huge *DJH hostel* (☎ 41 20 66, *fax 40 25 59, Tiergartenstrasse 5)* is a long

walk across the river from the train station. It's a lively, noisy place, with a cafeteria, pub and a small disco; downstairs there's also a token-operated laundry (DM5 per load). The rates are DM23/28 for juniors/seniors (including breakfast). From the station or Bismarckplatz, take bus No 33 towards the zoo, stopping at Jugendherberge.

Private Rooms The tourist office can book a limited number of *private flats* in town that cost from about DM65 to DM80 per double, but they book out very quickly and well in advance. However, the office can book rooms in the DJH hostel, hotels and pensions for free. You make a 7% deposit on the room when you book, and pay the balance when you check in.

The tourist information office (☎/fax 80 06 49) in Ziegelhausen, 4km east of the city, books *private rooms* from DM35/65 a single/double, including breakfast. Bus No 33 or 34 from Bismarckplatz goes there every 20 minutes.

Hotels & Pensions With a few exceptions, the cheap places are well outside the Altstadt. Many have rates that vary according to the season.

The veteran *Jeske Hotel* (☎ 237 33, *Mittelbadgasse 2)* is ideally situated just off the Markt. Frau Jeske can be a bit cranky and offers only doubles for a mere DM48, without breakfast.

The *Kohler* (☎ 97 00 97, fax 97 00 96, *Goethestrasse 2)*, within walking distance east of the station, has basic singles/doubles from DM72/92. The tiny *Astoria* (☎ 40 29 29, Rahmengasse 30)*, in a quiet residential street just north across Theodor-Heuss-Brücke, has bathless rooms from DM65/90. At the *Hotel Elite* (☎ 257 34, fax 16 39 49, *Bunsenstrasse 15)* all rooms come with private shower; it charges from DM75/95.

Places to Stay – Mid-Range

The *Hotel Vier Jahreszeiten* (☎ 241 64, fax 16 31 10, Haspelgasse 2)*, right near the Alte Brücke, has simple single/double rooms varying from DM85/125 in low season to

euro currency converter DM1 = €0.51

DM100/140 in high season. It's claimed that Goethe himself once creased the sheets here.

Hotel Goldener Hecht (☎ 536 80, fax 53 68 99, Steingasse 2) would also have kept the famous author had the clerk not been so uppity (see Alte Brücke earlier in this section). The hotel charges DM115/170 for rooms with amenities.

Hotel Am Kornmarkt (☎ 243 25, Kornmarkt 7) is an Altstadt favourite, charging DM120/165 for rooms with shower and toilet or DM75/130 without. Similar is the *Hotel Zum Pfalzgrafen* (☎ 204 89, fax 53 61 41, Kettengasse 21), where fully equipped rooms cost from DM100/150.

Denner Hotel (☎ 60 45 10, fax 60 45 30, Bergheimer Strasse 8) is a sleek new place with rooms decked out in south-east Asian furniture and modern decor by local artists. The smell of teak is heavenly, and there's a pleasant Internet cafe downstairs (see Post & Communications). Rooms with bath and toilet start at DM110/145.

Places to Stay – Top End

The *Heidelberg Marriott* (☎ 90 80, fax 90 86 98, Vangerowstrasse 16), north of the train station, has both singles and doubles from DM199. It's the stopping point for the Lufthansa Airport Express bus (see Getting There & Away).

The ornate, 16th century *Romantik Hotel Zum Ritter St Georg* (☎ 13 50, fax 13 52 30, Hauptstrasse 178), on the Markt, is one of the few town buildings to have survived the French attacks of 1693. Standard single/double rooms with amenities will set you back DM160/265.

Places to Eat

You might expect a student town to have plenty of cheap eating options, but free-spending tourists seem to outweigh frugal scholars in Heidelberg.

Restaurants The *Güldenes Schaf* (☎ 208 79, Hauptstrasse 115) is a huge old tavern with an extensive menu, vegetarian fare from DM13 and local specialities around DM20. *Sudpfanne* (☎ 204 86, Hauptstrasse

223) behind the barrel-shaped entrance has similar cuisine.

For fine French dining, head to *Simplicissimus* (☎ 18 33 36, Ingrimstrasse 16), where main courses start at DM36 (closed Tuesday). There's a pretty inner courtyard; book ahead.

Zur Herrenmühle (☎ 60 29 09, Hauptstrasse 237-39) is a slow but super-deluxe place serving small portions of outstanding nouvelle cuisine (don't blink or you'll miss it). You'll need loads of time and lots of dosh; main courses here cost from DM45 to DM60.

Starfish (☎ 125 87, Steingasse 16a) has quality 'natural food' like vegetable-and-nut tofu with chipped potatoes for DM16.50. The place is small, so it fills up quickly.

Cafes The *Bistro Backhaus* (☎ 979 70, Im Schlosshof), inside the Schloss, is a truly good deal with local specialities from DM10 to DM13 – don't miss the Maultaschen and, if it's going, the turkey Bratwurst with cabbage cooked in wine.

Café Knösel (☎ 223 45, Haspelgasse 20), on the corner of Untere Strasse, sells 'student kisses' (chocolate-covered wafers) and other tasty things, along with very good coffee and cocoa.

Café Max (☎ 295 69, Marktplatz 5) is a big favourite, and it's a bit more varied than some of the posey 'intellectual' cafes – of which one of the best is *Café Journal* (☎ 16 17 12, Hauptstrasse 162), where you can linger for hours over a cup of coffee and read the English-language papers.

Serious chess players (and other quiet guests) gather at the small *Drugstore Café* (☎ 227 49, Kettengasse 10) and at *Destille* (☎ 228 08, Untere Strasse 16).

Snacks & Fast Food The *Mensa* at Universitätsplatz charges students only about DM4 for a full meal. There's another, less comfortable *Mensa* in the Marstall, a two minute walk north of the university on Marstallstrasse. For takeaway food, there's *McDonald's* in the Markt and *Nordsee* (Hauptstrasse 40), or better still, there's the awesome pastry, pizza and bread offerings at *Riegler (Hauptstrasse 116)*.

Viva Italia/Viva Mexico (☎ 285 86, Hauptstrasse 113a) has excellent pizzas (DM2 for itty-bitty ones, larger ones from DM4) and some of the best Mexican food in Germany. They also offer doner kebab.

Raja Rani (☎ 244 84, Mittelbadgasse 5) serves some excellent Indian and Pakistani takeaways for around DM5; next door is the sit-down *Vegethali (☎ 16 86 78)*, with super-cheap lunches (eg vegie lasagne for DM5) and a spiritual-goods shop in the back.

Vetter im Schöneck (☎ 16 58 50, Steingasse 9) has good soups, salads and light dishes all under DM10, along with their own microbrewed beer (see also Pubs & Bars).

Entertainment

Meier (DM2) is a monthly publication with information on clubs, pubs, restaurants and gay and lesbian haunts. *Espresso* (DM9.80) is *the* guide to the region's nightlife, but it only comes out twice a year. The city prints *Heidelberg Aktuell*, available at the tourist information office.

Pubs & Bars A self-respecting university town, Heidelberg naturally has oodles of backstreet pubs and cafes. We went seriously overboard with the microbrewed beer at *Vetter im Schöneck* (see Places to Eat), which has a comfy atmosphere, lovely service and shiny beer vats.

Zum Roten Ochsen (☎ 209 77, Hauptstrasse 217) and *Zum Sepp'l (☎ 230 85, Hauptstrasse 213)* are the historical student pubs decorated with graffiti and street signs collected through the centuries. Nowadays students avoid these touristy joints.

Gasthaus Zum Mohren (Untere Strasse 5-7) is a more genuine place, as is *Schnookeloch (☎ 13 80 80, Haspelgasse 8)*, which first opened its doors in 1407. Some nights you'll catch fraternity members singing.

Goldener Reichsapfel (☎ 279 50, Untere Strasse 35) is one original student hang-out that hasn't quite gone the way of the others. There's noisy chat, even louder music and nowhere to sit just about every night. Just

opposite at No 30, *i Punkt (☎ 124 41, Untere Strasse 30)* is a modern place popular with 20-somethings.

Next door to i Punkt, in the passage between Untere Strasse and Hauptstrasse, is *Palmbräu Gasse (☎ 285 36, Hauptstrasse 185)*, an amazing place with a medieval feel and stonework, wooden benches, a great crowd and good service. *Mata Hari (☎ 18 18 08, Oberbadgasse 10)*, on the corner of Zwingerstrasse, is a popular gay bar.

Discos & Clubs The *Nachtschicht (☎ 16 44 04, Bergheimerstrasse 147)*, near the train station, has Top-40 canned music on weekends, live music on weekdays and, on Thursday, soul and hip hop. The *Schwimmbad Musik Club (☎ 47 02 01, Tiergartenstrasse 13)*, near the hostel, has lots of live music, and the program changes constantly – 1980s and 90s music, heavy metal and sometimes techno. Trendoids flock to *Tangente (☎ 277 63, Kettengasse 23)*, one of the town's most popular discos.

Rock, Jazz & Folk Music There's live music at the *Schwimmbad Musik Club* (see Discos & Clubs). *Cave54 (☎ 278 40, Krämergasse 2)* is said to be the oldest jazz club in Germany, opened in 1954 (Louis Armstrong played here). It's open daily, and famous for the Sunday jam sessions from 9 pm to 3 am.

The only folk music performed regularly is Irish, at *Napper Tandy's Irish Pub (☎ 259 79, Haspelgasse 4)* or at *Scruffy Murphy's (☎ 18 34 73, Ingrimstrasse 26a)*.

Cinemas *Gloria und Glorietta (☎ 253 19, Hauptstrasse 146)* shows English-language films regularly. *Harmonie*, on the corner of Hauptstrasse and Theaterstrasse, shows them less frequently.

Theatre & Classical Music The best-known stages are *Theater der Stadt Heidelberg (☎ 58 35 23, Theaterstrasse 4)* and the *Zimmertheater (☎ 210 69, Hauptstrasse 118)*, both running mainstream comedies, dramas and the odd avant-garde production. *Zwinger3* (☎ 58 35 46, *Zwingerstrasse 3)* has a series of plays for children and young adults.

Concerts are held in the castle and twice every summer at the *Thingstätte*, an amphitheatre on Heiligenberg, which is signposted along Philosophenweg (get both schedules from the tourist office). Organ concerts are held weekdays from 6 to 6.30 pm at the *Heiliggeistkirche* on the Markt (DM5).

The 19th century train station at Karlstor, east of the centre, has been converted to the *Kulturhaus Karlstorbahnhof* (☎ 97 89 11, *Am Karlstor 1)*, an 'alternative' cultural centre with theatre, cinema, music, art shows and other events.

Getting There & Away

Train There are frequent train connections to/from Frankfurt (DM22.40, one hour), Stuttgart (DM38, 40 minutes), Baden-Baden (DM22.40, one hour), Munich (DM104, three hours) and Nuremberg (via Frankfurt or Stuttgart; DM77 to DM93, three to 3½ hours).

Bus From mid-April to late October, Busabout coaches depart from Heidelberg every two days to Frankfurt and Stuttgart. The pick-up point is the youth hostel bus stop; the coach leaves at 10 am for Stuttgart (two hours) and at 3.30 pm for Frankfurt (1½ hours). You'll need a Busabout pass even for a single trip; see the Getting There & Away chapter for price details.

Lufthansa runs its Airport Express service to/from Frankfurt airport several times a day from the Heidelberg Marriott (see Places to Stay). Tickets cost DM38 one way, DM72 return; the journey takes one hour. (The timetable often shifts; ring ☎ 069-69 69 44 33 for details).

Car & Motorcycle The north-south A5 links Heidelberg with both Frankfurt and Karlsruhe.

Ride Services You can arrange a lift through Citynetz Mitfahr-Service (☎ 194 44) at Bergheimer Strasse 125.

Getting Around

Public Transport Bismarckplatz is the main transport hub. The bus and tram system in and around Heidelberg is extensive and efficient. Single tickets cost DM3 and a 24 hour pass costs DM10. Bus Nos 11, 21, 33, 34, 41 and 42, as well as tram No 1, run between Bismarckplatz and the train station.

Car & Motorcycle There are well marked underground parking garages throughout the city, charging DM2 to DM3 per hour. At weekends you can 'park and ride' for free, and take the frequent free shuttle buses to the Altstadt; look for the P&R signs.

Taxi Flag fall is DM4.20 plus DM2.20 per kilometre. Taxis line up outside the train station, or you can order one by ringing ☎ 30 20 30. It's about DM12.50 from the train station to the Alte Brücke.

Bicycle You can rent bicycles from Per Bike (☎ 16 11 48), south-west of Bismarckplatz at Bergheimer Strasse 125, for DM25/20/55/120 per day/subsequent-day/weekend/week.

AROUND HEIDELBERG

Excursions to the Neckar Valley offer a good introduction to the surrounding countryside. Check with Touristikverband Neckarland-Schwaben (☎ 07131-785 20), Lohtorstrasse 21, 74072 Heilbronn, for information on cycling opportunities in the region and for its guide to bike trails.

Rhein-Neckar Fahrgastschiffahrt (☎ 201 81), on the south bank of the Neckar in Heidelberg, offers the most scenic tours and some of the cheapest ways to get around the Neckar Valley, with boats to the main destinations (eg the castles at Neckarsteinach and Hirschhorn). See Other Sights for more information.

Schloss Schwetzingen

The fabulous **gardens** of Schwetzingen mark the apex of German rococo landscaping. When Prince-Elector Carl Theodor inherited the Palatinate region in the mid-18th century he made Schwetzingen his summer residence and commissioned a whimsical garden in keeping with the era's love of follies. Their secluded charm (and sheer lack of obvious use) make the gardens a great place to lose yourself for a few hours.

The grounds, which took three decades for French architect Nicolas de Pigage to lay out and complete, radiate from a formal French garden with delicate statues, floral beds and wide gravelled promenades. On the outer edges are theme-park-like sprinklings of architectural genres, from Rome to China, linked to one another by shady paths and a lacy waterway circuit.

The chief follies include **Tempel Apollos**, an auditorium built in the Greek columned style of a shrine to the gods, perched self-importantly on an artificial knoll. The silliness of the genre continues to come out in the **Römischer Wasserweg**, a fake fortress and aqueduct conceived as an ivy-covered ruin, and the **Moschee** (mosque), which sports an Oriental dome above a rather Germanic baroque entrance. One of the main routes back crosses the incongruous **Chinesische Brücke**, an arched Chinese bridge.

The main **Jagdschloss**, or hunting palace, is almost staid by comparison, its interiors a toned-down version of rococo stucco and curlicued wallpaper. The highlight within is the **Rokokotheater** (1752), another Pigage masterpiece with a deep-set stage that draws on light and a tunnel illusion to enhance the dimensions. Ask the gate-keeper about the **clock** on the facade, completed in 1700: the big and little hands were reversed so that horsemen could read time more easily from a distance.

The palace and grounds (☎ 06202-814 81) are open from April to October, Tuesday to Sunday from 10 am to 4 pm; the rest of the year, hours are Friday from 11 am to 2 pm, and weekends to 3 pm. Admission to both costs DM9/4.50 in summer or DM8/4 in winter.

Getting There & Away Schloss Schwetzingen is situated 10km west of Heidelberg, just off the A6 autobahn 8km south of Mannheim. From Heidelberg train station, you can take VRN bus No 717 (DM5.60, 40 minutes). From Mannheim, take the train to Schwetzingen Bahnhof (DM5.60, 25 minutes), where the VRN bus No 7000 (and others) depart for the Schloss (DM2.20, 12 minutes).

Heilbronn
☎ 07131 • pop 117,500

Pummelled to bits by Allied bombs, Heilbronn was able to preserve just a few old gems including the Gothic **Kiliankirche**, which has an amazing carved altar. These days the town, which lies about 60km southeast of Heidelberg, is much more of a gateway between Frankfurt and Heidelberg (DB's steam trains run through here) than an attraction in its own right.

The tourist office (☎ 56 22 70, fax 56 33 49) in the Markt is open year round Monday to Friday from 9 am to 6 pm, and from 9 am to 1 pm on Saturday. Among other sights, the **Städtisches Museum** is a free local history museum, and the **Rathaus** (opposite the tourist office) sports an astrological clock.

Frequent trains for Heilbronn depart from Heidelberg's main station (DM19.60, one hour). The Lufthansa bus leaves from the Hauptbahnhof to Frankfurt every one to two hours (DM38, 1¼ hours).

Other Sights

It's a nice day-trip upriver to **Neckarsteinach** and its four castles, built by four brothers between 1100 and 1250 as a result of a family feud. Two of the castles are still residences of family members. Take Bahnhofstrasse west and it will become Hauptstrasse; a path running north is marked 'Zu den Vier Burgen' (To the Four Castles). The tourist office (☎ 06229-920 00) is in the Altes Rathaus, Hauptstrasse 7.

From April to October, Rhein-Neckar Fahrgastschiffahrt boats (DM16.50/9.50 for adults/children, three hours return) leave from Heidelberg up to six times daily.

There are many castles in the Neckar Valley, such as the **Hirschhorn Castle** and, outside Neckarzimmern, **Burg Hornberg**. Deutsche Bahn runs scheduled services aboard steam-powered trains on several routes on weekends between Frankfurt and the Neckar Valley, through Heilbronn, Heidelberg and up to Neckarsteinach.

MANNHEIM
☎ 0621 • pop 322,000

You won't find Mannheim on any Top 10 (or likely even Top 100) listing of German tourist destinations. It's hard to imagine that this sprawling industrial centre 35km southwest of Frankfurt was once a tiny fishing village, rising to prominence only in the early 18th century when Elector Carl Philipp moved the Palatinate court here from Heidelberg.

Like Karlsruhe to the south, Mannheim's old town was flattened in 1945 and replaced, by and large, with unsightly steel and concrete blocks. However, it (sort of) compensates with its big-city sense of fun, lively cultural scene and some of the best shopping in Germany. Its streets also have a particularly quirky layout: a giant chessboard.

Orientation & Information

What's left of the old centre is north and north-west of the Hauptbahnhof, on a peninsula formed by the Rhine and Neckar rivers. The poorly equipped tourist office (☎ 10 10 11, fax 241 41, email info@ tourist-mannheim.de) is at Willy-Brandt-Platz 3 opposite the Hauptbahnhof. It's open weekdays from 9 am to 7 pm; and Saturday to noon.

The chessboard layout is a trip when you first arrive, with addresses such as 'Q3,16' or 'L14,5' sounding a bit like galactic sectors. But this grid system is practical once you get used to it. The centre is bisected by two largely pedestrianised shopping streets, the north-south Kurpfalzstrasse and the east-west Planken/Heidelberger Strasse.

The main post office is in O2 in the centre; there's a Reisebank in the Hauptbahnhof.

Wash your smalls at Waschsalon Stolz (☎ 33 32 99), on the corner of E3 and Mittelstrasse, from DM5 per load.

Things to See & Do

Coming by train from the north you'll pass the **Residenzschloss**, an imposing baroque palace. Soon after its completion, Elector Carl Theodor moved his court to Munich in 1777, rendering the Schloss a bit pointless. Today it's part of the university, and you can take a guided tour of the sumptuous interior for DM4/2.50. It's open Tuesday to Sunday from 10 am to 1 pm and 2 to 5 pm. The flowery **Schlosskirche** in the western wing holds the remains of Carl Philipp's third wife, Violante Thurn- und Taxis of the famous brewing dynasty.

Due north of the train station, on the loud and busy Kaiserring, is the elegant **Wasserturm** (Water Tower) in the middle of pretty Friedrichsplatz, flanked by a huge Art Deco fountain landscape. One of Mannheim's few oases of calm, the gardens are dotted with lazing students, ice-cream vendors and buskers in the warmer months.

On its south side is the highly acclaimed **Kunsthalle** (☎ 49 59 20), a museum of 19th and 20th century art, housing, among other great works, Cézanne's *Pipesmoker*, Manet's *Execution of Emperor Maximilian of Mexico* and sculptures by Ernst Barlach. It's open Tuesday to Sunday from 10 am to 5 pm, and Thursday from noon (DM4/2).

A few minutes north-east of centre is the lovely **Luisenpark**, a sprawling green belt with hothouses, gardens and an aquarium. It's open daily from 9 am to dusk (DM5).

Of its central churches, the grandiose **Jesuitenkirche** just west of the Schloss deserves a look, as does the **Untere Pfarrkirche**, which oddly enough shares a tower with the **Rathaus** on Marktplatz. The Jesuitenkirche was built extra big to celebrate the Palatinate's return to Catholicism.

Up on the Neckar is the **Museumsschiff Mannheim** (☎ 156 57 56), a paddle steamer converted to a display of navigation history. It's open Tuesday to Sunday from 10 am to 4 pm (DM2).

Places to Stay

The *Jugendherberge Mannheim* (☎ 82 27 18, fax 82 40 73, Rheinpromenade 21) is a

15 minute walk south of the Hauptbahnhof towards the Rhine. It charges DM21/26 for juniors/seniors, including breakfast.

Mannheim is primarily a business town and the hotel prices reflect this. The *Arabella Pension Garni (☎ 230 50, fax 156 45 27, M2/12)* is a rare exception in the centre of town. Just north of the Schloss, it has rates for basic single/double rooms from DM35/70.

Hotel Holländer Hof (☎ 160 95, fax 10 15 46, U1,11-12), close to the Congress Centrum, is pleasant enough and charges from DM75/110 with private facilities.

The newly renovated *Central Hotel (☎ 123 00, fax 123 01 00, Kaiserring 26)* is perfectly sited near the Hauptbahnhof for an early getaway. Comfy rooms (with sound-proofed windows) start at DM135/150.

Maritim Parkhotel (☎ 158 80, fax 158 88 00, Friedrichsplatz 2) next door offers the traditional 1st-class creature comforts and more for DM205/250.

Places to Eat
The area around the central Planken offers a number of fast-food places, including a *Pizza Hut (P3,12)* and a *Döner Iskender (Q1,19)* with kebabs from DM5. The *Mensa*, serving filling meals for DM6 or less, is in the south-west corner behind the Schloss.

The *Hoepfner Stuben (☎ 44 71 19)*, at the corner of S4/S5, is an earthy pub/restaurant with steaks, pizzas and fish dishes all under DM20. Students get a big discount with ID.

Café Moro (☎ 45 78 12, P7 passage ÖVA) has great Italian sandwiches and pastas for DM6 to DM10, and is a chic place to just hang out.

Broker's Inn (☎ 44 46 05, P7) on Planken has a nice street cafe and a stylish interior with a stock market display, serving reasonably priced pastas, salads and meat dishes.

The *Eichbaum Brauhaus (☎ 42 20 20, Käfertaler Strasse 168)*, Mannheim's largest brewery, sits north of the Neckar and serves hearty German dishes averaging DM18 with its signature beers.

Getting There & Away
To/From Airport The frequent Lufthansa bus takes about one hour to/from Frankfurt airport; the departure point is on the corner of L14 and Kaiserring (one-way/return for DM38/72).

Train Mannheim is a major junction on the Hamburg to Basel line, with ICEs from Frankfurt (DM40, 35 minutes), Basel (DM70, 2¼ hours) and Freiburg (DM73, 1½ hours). The fast IC trains are cheaper but a bit slower than the ICEs.

Car & Motorcycle Mannheim is extremely well connected at the junction of the A656 autobahn east to Heidelberg, the A650 west to Ludwighafen and the north-south A6/A67.

Ride Services To hitch a ride, try the City-Netz service in the tourist office.

Getting Around
Mannheim is huge, and the bus/tram network is well developed. Single short/regular journeys cost DM1.70/3.30; a triple-zone 24-Plus 24-hour transport pass costs DM10.

If driving, it's best to park just east of centre along the Augustaanlage and walk in (note that *Parkschein* machines are in use).

To rent bicycles, the cheapest option is Biotopia (☎ 122 30 77) in front of the Hauptbahnhof, near the small post office.

ULM
☎ 0731 • pop 165,000
On the Danube River at the border between the states of Baden-Württemberg and Bavaria, Ulm is famous for its Münster tower – the highest church spire in the world – and as the birthplace of Albert Einstein.

Ulm was a trading city as early as the 12th century and the *Ulmer Schachteln*, flat barges carrying local fabrics and goods, floated down the Danube as far as the Black Sea. The city's trade guilds, composed mainly of shipbuilders, fisherfolk and tanners, achieved political power through a new city charter in 1397.

euro currency converter DM1 = €0.51

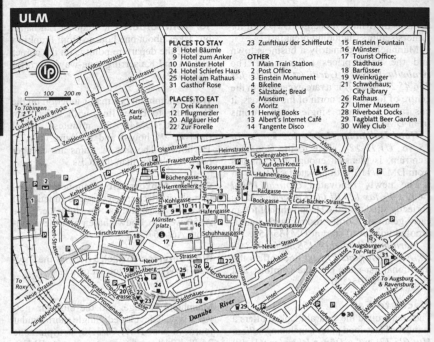

ULM

PLACES TO STAY
8 Hotel Bäumle
9 Hotel zum Anker
10 Münster Hotel
24 Hotel Schiefes Haus
25 Hotel am Rathaus
31 Gasthof Rose

PLACES TO EAT
7 Drei Kannen
12 Pflugmerzler
20 Allgäuer Hof
22 Zur Forelle

23 Zunfthaus der Schiffleute

OTHER
1 Main Train Station
2 Post Office
3 Einstein Monument
4 Bikeline
5 Salzstade; Bread Museum
6 Moritz
11 Herwig Books
13 Albert's Internet Café
14 Tangente Disco

15 Einstein Fountain
16 Münster
17 Tourist Office; Stadthaus
18 Barfüsser
19 Weinkrüger
21 Schwörhaus; City Library
26 Rathaus
27 Ulmer Museum
28 Riverboat Docks
29 Tagblatt Beer Garden
30 Wiley Club

0   100   200 m

To Tübingen
Ludwig Erhard Brücke

Ulm is also the place in which the hang-glider was invented in 1802 by Albrecht Berblinger, who made clothes for a living. A highly sceptical public watched as Berblinger attempted to fly across the river after leaping (some say he was kicked) from the city wall. The 'Tailor of Ulm', as the locals call him, made a splash landing but his design worked and became the prototype of the modern hang-glider.

Greater Ulm is actually split into two *Länder*, a curiosity that dates back to Napoleon, who decreed that the river would divide Baden-Württemberg and Bavaria. On the south side of the Danube, the Bavarian city of Neu Ulm, with a population of 50,000, is a rather bland, ugly and modern city that was formerly home to the US Army's Wiley Barracks, now used as low-income housing and a cultural and entertainment complex.

On the north side of the river is Ulm, which counts 115,000 people and contains all the main attractions. The two cities share transport systems and important municipal facilities.

Orientation

The Danube River splits the city: Ulm is to the north, Neu Ulm to the south. All the major sights are within the oval between Olgastrasse, a main thoroughfare, and the Danube to the south. The Hauptbahnhof is at the western end of the city, the university to the north-west and the hostel to the south-west.

Information

Tourist Offices The tourist information office (☎ 161 28 30, fax 161 16 41, email unt@tourismus.ulm), at Münsterplatz 50 in the Stadthaus building, is open Monday to

Friday from 9 am to 6 pm, Saturday to 1 pm. From May to October, it's also open Sunday from 11 am to 2 pm. The city publishes a monthly listings leaflet, the free *Wohin in Ulm/Neu Ulm*.

ADAC has an office (☎ 962 10 10) at Neue Strasse 40.

Money Change money at the Reisebank in the Hauptbahnhof or at the Hypovereinsbank across the street. There's a Deutsche Bank on Münsterplatz.

Post & Communications The main post office is at the Hauptbahnhof at Bahnhofplatz 2. Albert's (☎ 15 30 22) is an Internet cafe in the city high school at the Einsteinhaus, Kornhausplatz 5. Internet access is free with any purchase, such as coffee or tea (DM2).

Internet Resources Ulm has an English/German Web site at www.ulm.de.

Bookshops & Libraries Herwig (☎ 96 21 70), Münsterplatz 18, is a travel bookshop with Lonely Planet titles and lots of other travel literature and maps. There's a Wittwer Internationale Presse in the Hauptbahnhof. The main city library (☎ 161 41 40) is in the Schwörhaus at Weinhof 12.

University Universität Ulm is the smallest in Baden-Württemberg, with about 6000 students. It's a technical university north of the city, specialising in computer science, electronics and engineering.

Laundry The expensive central City-Wash (☎ 980 77 30) is at Schützenstrasse 46 (entrance around the corner). Loads cost DM10, plus DM3 for a half-hour's drying. Otherwise, there's the Waschsalon Kaiser, Memminger Strasse 72/235, at the former Wiley Barracks (bus No 42 to Memminger Strasse).

Medical Services For a doctor or an ambulance in an emergency, call the Deutsches Rotes Kreuz (☎ 622 22), Frauenstrasse 125.

Münster

The reason for coming to Ulm is to see the huge Münster (minster), celebrated for its 161.6m-high steeple – the tallest on the planet. Though the first stone was laid in 1377, it took over 500 years for the entire structure to be completed. Note the **hallmarks** on each stone, inscribed by cutters who were paid by the block.

Only by climbing to the viewing platform at 143m, via the 768 spiralling steps, do you fully appreciate the tower's dizzying height: there are unparalleled views of the Black Forest and the Swabian Jura mountains, and on clear days you can even see the Alps. The cathedral is open June to August from 8 am to 6.45 pm; the rest of the year, hours are 9 am to 5 pm (DM4/DM2.50). The last entry to the tower is an hour before closing. Allow 30 minutes for the ascent.

As you enter the church, note the **Israelfenster**, a stained-glass window above the west door which serves as a memorial to Jews killed during the Holocaust. The carved **pulpit canopy**, as detailed as lace, eliminates echoes during sermons; to one side is a tiny spiral staircase leading to a mini-pulpit for the Holy Spirit.

In the original 15th century oak **choir stalls**, the top row depicts figures from the Old Testament, the middle from the New Testament. The bottom and sides show historical characters such as Roman playwright Lucius Seneca, Nero's tutor (who committed suicide by slashing his wrists), and Pythagoras, who strums a lute.

The impressive **stained-glass windows** in the choir, dating from the 14th and 15th centuries, were removed for the duration of WWII. They are now back in place, including the oldest to the right of centre (1385) which shows the Münster as it was.

Services are held on Sunday at 8 and 9.30 am (10 am from January to Good Friday) and at 6 pm. There are also free daily organ concerts.

Stadthaus

The other highlight of Münsterplatz is the **Stadthaus** (1993), designed by American

Albert Einstein, Blundering Genius

Arguably the most influential scientist of the 20th century, Albert Einstein was born in Ulm in 1879 but spent his youth in Munich, where his family owned a small electrical machinery shop. He didn't talk until the age of three, but even as a child Albert showed a brilliant curiosity about nature and an ability to grasp tricky mathematical concepts – even if numbers weren't his forte.

When the family business failed, the 15-year-old Einstein withdrew from school and moved with his parents to Milan for a year. He finished secondary school in Arrau, Switzerland, and enrolled in the national polytechnic in Zurich. He often cut classes, preferring to study physics on his own or to play his beloved violin. When Einstein graduated in 1900 – by studying a classmate's notes – his professors wouldn't recommend him for a university posting, and the budding genius ended up a patent examiner in Bern.

In 1905, at age 26, Einstein emerged from obscurity to rock the scientific world. He published his Special Theory of Relativity, which shows that time and space vary systematically (disproving Isaac Newton's belief that both were constant). $E=mc^2$, Einstein's famous equation, still graces blackboards (and T-shirts) today.

MICK WELDON

It's a falsehood that Einstein failed mathematics (while it *is* true that he refused to wear socks). In any case, the great man – who became an unwilling cultural icon in his later years – was certainly prone to numerical blunders. His paper on the measurement of molecules, for instance, was riddled with mixed-up algebra, miscalculations and dodgy experimental data. If caught out in the classroom, the physicist usually countered with a classic quip. 'Do not worry about your difficulties in mathematics. I can assure you mine are greater still,' he told students at New Jersey's Princeton University, where the wild-haired physicist taught from 1933 until his death at age 76.

architect Richard Meier. He caused an uproar for erecting a postmodern building next to the city's Gothic gem, but the result is both gorgeous and functional. It stages exhibitions and special events and also houses the tourist office, the state's travel agency and an expensive cafe.

Rathaus

The town hall nearby was a commercial building until 1419. The eastern side has a Renaissance facade with ornamental figures and an amazing **astrological clock** (1520). There's a standard clock with Arabic numbers above it. Not accurate enough? Check the **sundial** above that or listen for the bells, which count off every quarter-hour. Inside the Rathaus you can see a replica of Berblinger's flying machine.

In the Markt to the south is the **Fischkasten Brunnen**, a tank where fishmongers kept their river fish alive on market days.

City Wall & Towers

On the north bank of the Danube you can walk along the **Stadtmauer**, the former city wall. Its height was reduced in the early 19th century after Napoleon decided that a heavily fortified Ulm was against his best interests. Note the **Metzger Turm**, leaning 2m off-centre to the north.

East of the Herdbrücke is a monument at the spot where Albrecht Berblinger attempted his flight.

Fischerviertel

Every first Monday in July, the mayor swears allegiance to the town's 1397 constitution at the **Schwörhaus** (Oath House). From here, stroll between the buildings whose roofs almost touch in **Kussgasse** (Kissing Alley) and cross **Lügner-Brücke** (Liar's Bridge) into the charming **Fischerviertel** (Fischer's Quarter), the old city's fishing and shipbuilding quarter, built along the tiny and sparklingly clear Blau River, which flows into the Danube.

Einstein Fountain & Monument

About 750m north-east of the Münster, stands a fiendishly funny fountain dedicated to Albert Einstein, who was born in Ulm but left when he was one year old. Before WWII he was granted 'honorary citizenship', but the Nazis revoked it. After the war, when Ulm asked the great man if he wanted this honour reinstated, he declined. The nearby health administration building, at Zeughaus 14, bears a single stone attached to the wall entitled *Ein Stein* (One Stone).

Over on Bahnhofstrasse is Max Bill's monument (1979) to the great physicist, a stack of staggered granite pillars on the spot where Einstein's home once stood.

Museums

The **Ulmer Museum** (☎ 161 43 00), Markt 6, houses a collection of ancient and modern art, including icons, religious paintings, and sculptures. A highlight is the 20th century **Kurt Fried Collection**, with works from artists including Klee, Kandinsky, Picasso, Lichtenstein and Macke. It's open Tuesday to Sunday from 11 am to 5 pm, and to 8 pm on Thursday (DM5/3, free on Friday).

The **Deutsches Brotmuseum** (☎ 699 55), Salztadelgasse 10, north of Münsterplatz, celebrates bread as the staff of life in the Western world. It also works with universities to develop new strains of wheat and other grain for use in developing countries. Hours are Tuesday to Sunday from 10 am to 5 pm (DM5/3.50).

Organised Tours

The tourist office conducts daily 1½ hour city walking tours in German from May to November at 10 am and 2.30 pm (11 am only on Sunday and holidays). The rest of the year there's only a morning tour. The fee is DM8/4.

You can take two to three-hour canoe tours from various points on the Danube and Iller rivers (DM31, or DM21 for children under 14). Book at the tourist office.

There are also cruises (DM10/7) up the Danube daily at 2, 3 and 4 pm, with extra ones at 1 and 5 pm on weekends. The docks are on the Ulm side, just south-west of the Gänstor Brücke.

Places to Stay

The *DJH hostel* (☎ 38 44 55, fax 38 45 11, Grimmelfinger Weg 45) charges juniors/seniors DM23/28, including breakfast. From the train station, take S1 to Ehinger Tor, then bus No 4 to Schulzentrum, from where it's a five minute walk.

Across the river in Neu Ulm, *Gasthof Rose* (☎ 778 03, Kasernstrasse 42a) has bathless but perfectly decent singles/doubles for DM40/80.

Hotel zum Anker/Spanische Weinstube (☎ 632 97, Rabengasse 2), right beside the Münster, has simple rooms from DM49/85.

euro currency converter DM1 = €0.51

There's a good restaurant, and it's a very popular stop for cyclists doing the Danube. *Münster Hotel (☎/fax 641 62, Münsterplatz 14)* has the same standard of accommodation, from DM45/90.

The family-run *Hotel am Rathaus (☎ 96 84 90, fax 968 49 49, Kronengasse 10)*, right behind the Rathaus, has very clean and comfortable rooms from DM70/100.

Hotel Bäumle (☎ 622 87, fax 602 26 04, Kohlgasse 6) is a snug little place with great views of the Münster – ask for a room in the back. It's a bargain too, at DM55/85 for basic rooms, or DM75/110 with amenities. The restaurant is very good (see Places to Eat).

One of Baden-Württemberg's nicest hotels is the *Hotel Schiefes Haus (☎ 96 79 30, fax 967 93 33, Schwörhausgasse 6)*. This romantic half-timbered house (1443) claims a *Guinness Book of Records* listing as the 'most crooked hotel in the world' (the building, that is). The beds have specially-made height adjusters and spirit levels, so you won't roll out during the night. Rooms start at DM195/255.

Places to Eat

Restaurants The *Zunfthaus der Schiffleute (☎ 644 11, Fischergasse 31)* is a typical Swabian place that has enormous portions of food from DM16 to DM20 and a good vegetarian menu. The *Allgäuer Hof (☎ 674 08, Fischergasse 12)* is a pancake house (42 varieties from about DM13).

Drei Kannen (☎ 677 17, Hafenbad 31), north of Münsterplatz, has an Italian loggia and courtyard next to a beautiful former patrician's home. The fare is typically Swabian and the prices reasonable.

Hotel Bäumle (☎ 622 87, Kohlgasse 6) is a rustic inn with loads of wood panelling, ceramic tiles, good wines and creative regional fare (ask for the tasty spinach-filled *Fröschle*) priced from about DM13. You can crawl upstairs after dinner (see Places to Stay).

Zur Forelle (☎ 639 24, Fischergasse 25) is widely held to be the best seafood restaurant in town, with daily specials for DM25 to DM30. (Note the cannonball lodged in

the wall outside.) The *Pflugmerzler (☎ 680 61, Pfluggasse 6)* reputedly has the best Swabian cuisine in town, and for corresponding prices.

Snacks & Fast Food The Hauptbahnhof's *Markt Im Bahnhof* has a Pizza Hut, a Kaffee Mit, a butcher, fruit market and La Mare, which has fish specialities. There's also a great bakery in the main entry hall.

Get good pizza slices for DM3.50 from the little *Pizza bar* on the south side of Markt. Right on Münsterplatz, the *Café Kassmeyer* bakery is open seven days a week, as is *Nudelmacher*, which has an all-you-can-eat pasta bar for DM9.90 from 3 pm Monday to Saturday and all day Sunday.

Entertainment

Roxy (☎ 968 620, Schillerstrasse 1) is a huge, multivenue centre with a concert hall, cinema, disco, bar and special-event forum. *Tangente (☎ 602 44 49, Frauenstrasse 20)*, 500m north-east of the Münster, is a disco that's been around for 25 years; it's open from 10 pm to 2 am.

Wiley Club (☎ 867 04, Memminger Strasse 72/234) hosts live jazz, rock and disco. Also on the former military base in *Arts & Crafts (☎ 980 76 64, Memminger Strasse 72/235)* in the former US Army gym, now a concert hall for everything from Brahms to head-banging.

One of the city's better beer gardens is *Zunfthaus der Schiffleute* (see Places to Eat). Other local favourites are the *Barfüsser (☎ 97 44 80, Paulstrasse 4)* and the seasonal *Tagblatt* on the tip of the Danube island west of the Herdbrücke.

Weinkrüger (☎ 649 76, Weinhofberg 7) is a quirky wine tavern in an old bathhouse on the Blau River, while *Moritz (☎ 666 99, Platzgasse 20)* is a sprawling pub with great atmosphere, decent food and indifferent service.

Getting There & Away

Ulm is on the main Stuttgart-Munich train line – trains cost DM24.60/40 respectively and take one to 1¼ hours. The B311 runs from Tuttlingen to Ulm, and the B16 from Ulm to Regensburg.

Getting Around

Buses leave from the Zentrale Omnibus Bushahnhof (ZOB) at the Hauptbahnhof, and the Rathaus is a major transfer point. Bus tickets cost DM2.80 for a single ride, DM7.50 for a day pass or DM9.50 for a four-ride strip ticket.

Rent bikes at Bikeline (☎ 602 13 58), Walfischgasse 18. Ulmer Fahrradverleih (☎ 38 24 07), west of the town centre at Klosterhof 17, rents out touring/mountain bikes for DM14.50/19.50 per day; it's open holidays.

Northern Black Forest

Resort Tax

If you're spending more than one night almost anywhere in the Black Forest, you will be subject to a *Kurtaxe*, a resort or visitors' tax of usually DM1.50 to DM4 per day. But unlike other places in Germany that also levy such a tax, here you'll be given a *Gästekarte* (guest card) that is valid in 178 towns and villages. Whenever you present this card, you will be entitled to discounts on museum admissions, boat trips, cultural events, public pools, bike rental and attractions such as the Europa Park Rust and the Black Forest Open-Air Museum. Details can be found in the *Schwarzwald Gästekarte* booklet available at most tourist offices.

KARLSRUHE

☎ 0721 • pop 287,000

Karlsruhe, which literally means 'Carl's Rest', was dreamed up in 1715 by Margrave Karl Wilhelm of Baden-Durlach as a residential retreat. The town is laid out like an Oriental fan: at its axis is the Schloss, nestled in the semi-circular Schlosspark. From this inner circle emanate 32 tines – straight streets, most of which feed into a ring road.

Imaginative as this is, were it not for the Schloss and some stellar museums, there would be little reason to visit Karlsruhe. Once a proud regional capital, the city lost that status in 1951 when Stuttgart became the seat of government for the newly merged Baden-Württemberg. Most of Karlsruhe's neoclassical buildings were pummelled in WWII and by and large, reconstruction hasn't flattered the place.

Modern Karlsruhe is known as an industrial centre and the site of the country's highest courts, the Bundesgerichtshof (Federal Supreme Court) and the Bundesverfassungsgericht (Federal Constitutional Court). Both were located here under Germany's postwar scattering of federal institutions, a decision that prevented Karlsruhe from sinking into obscurity.

Orientation & Information

The Hauptbahnhof is on the southern edge of the centre, with the Schloss 2km due north (tram No A, B or 3 to Markt). The Bundesverfassungsgericht, directly west of the Schloss, and the Bundesgerichtshof, on the south-west perimeter of the ring, are closed to the public.

The tourist office (☎ 355 30, fax 35 53 43 99, email vv@karlsruhe.de) is opposite the train station at Bahnhofplatz 6, and is open weekdays from 8 am to 7 pm, and Saturday to 1 pm. A branch office (☎ 35 53 43 76, fax 35 53 43 89) is at Karl-Friedrich-Strasse 22, with hours on weekdays from 9 am to 6 pm, and Saturday to 12.30 pm.

A Reisebank is in the train station, and the main post office is at Kaiserstrasse 217.

Schloss & Badisches Landesmuseum

The most compelling reason to visit Karlsruhe is to see the Schloss, which houses the superb collections of the Badisches Landesmuseum. The Schloss itself was destroyed in the war, but city custodians had enough sense – and money – to rebuild it in the original style, which reflects the transition from baroque to neoclassical. Be sure to climb the tower, really the only point from which to appreciate the town's eccentric layout.

euro currency converter DM1 = €0.51

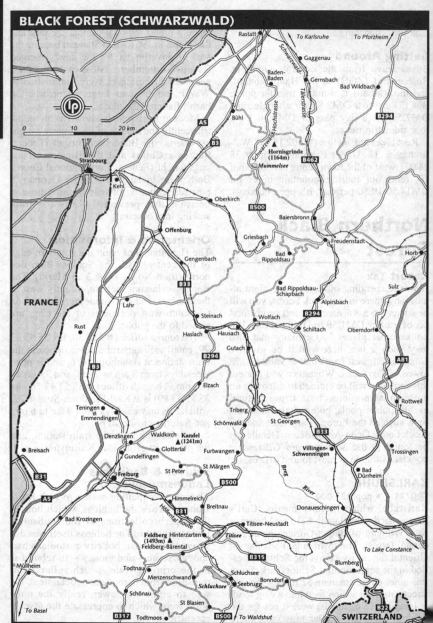

BLACK FOREST (SCHWARZWALD)

To Karlsruhe   To Pforzheim

Rastatt

Gaggenau

Baden-Baden

Gernsbach

Bad Wildbach

B294

A5

Bühl

B3

Schwarzwald-Hochstrasse

Hornisgrinde
(1164m)

B462

Mummelsee

Strasbourg

Kehl

Oberkirch

B500

Baiersbronn

Offenburg

Griesbach

Freudenstadt

Horb

Gengenbach

Bad Rippoldsau

B33

Bad Rippoldsau-
Schapbach

Sulz

FRANCE

Lahr

Steinach

Wolfach

B294

Schiltach

Alpirsbach

Oberndorf

B3

Rust

Haslach

Hausach

Gutach

A81

Elzach

B294

Rottweil

Teningen

Emmendingen

Triberg

Schönwald

St Georgen

B33

Denzlingen

Waldkirch

Kandel
(1241m)

Furtwangen

Villingen-
Schwenningen

Trossingen

Glottertal

Breisach

Gundelfingen

St Peter

B500

Bad
Dürrheim

Freiburg

St Märgen

Breg
River

A5

Himmelreich

Breitnau

Donaueschingen

Höllental Route

B31

Bad Krozingen

Titisee-Neustadt

Feldberg
(1493m)

Hinterzarten

Feldberg-Bärental

Titisee

B315

To Lake Constance

Blumberg

Müllheim

Todtnau

Menzenschwand

Schluchsee

Bonndorf

Schönau

Seebrugg

Schluchsee

St Blasien

B22

To Basel

Todtmoos

B317

B500   To Waldshut

SWITZERLAND

0   10   20 km

The palace's dual function as a residence and a retreat is apparent in the gardens. While the public side to the south adhered to a formal design, the huge park north of the palace is done in more relaxed English style. In fine weather, the latter is a popular gathering spot for university students.

The museum in this huge building deserves a couple of hours. At the entrance is the **antiquity collection**, with fascinating statues, jewellery, objects and even some mummies from Mesopotamia, Anatolia and Egypt. The opposite wing is filled with altars, statues and paintings which date from the Middle Ages. On the 1st floor you'll find some interesting booty, including guns, knives, saddles and clothing, brought back by Margrave Ludwig Wilhelm of Baden from his 17th century military campaigns against the Turks. Adjacent is the **Zähringer Saal**, which features the dazzling diadem, gem-encrusted crown and sceptre of that ruling family.

Museum hours are Tuesday to Sunday from 10 am to 5 pm (Wednesday to 8 pm), and closed Monday (DM5/3).

Kunsthalle

The private collections of the Baden margraves form the basis of this extensive art collection, which was first exhibited in 1846, making it one of the oldest public museums in Germany. On view is the full range of European masters from the 14th to the 20th centuries. A highlight is the **Gallery of Old German Masters** on the top floor, with works such as Matthias Grünewald's masterful *Crucifixion* and Lucas Cranach the Elder's *Frederick the Wise in Adoration of the Mother of God*. On the ground floor are 19th century paintings by French artists such as Manet, Degas and Delacroix and Germans Corinth, Liebermann and Slevogt. The impressive murals in the central stairwell show the consecration of the Freiburg Münster.

The Kunsthalle (☎ 926 3359), just west of the Schloss at Hans-Thoma-Strasse 2, is open Monday to Friday from 10 am to 5 pm, and weekends to 6 pm (DM5/3).

Places to Stay

Camping Turmbergblick (☎ 49 72 36, fax 49 72 37, Tiengerer Strasse 40) is in the eastern suburb of Durlach. It charges from DM8 for adults, DM6 for children and DM11 to DM13 per site.

The *DJH hostel (☎ 282 48, fax 276 47, Moltkestrasse 24)* near the Schloss charges DM22/27.50 for juniors/seniors. Take tram No 3 from the Hauptbahnhof to Europaplatz, then walk 10 minutes north on Karlstrasse to Moltkestrasse.

Hotels & Pensions The tourist office books rooms for free. The *Pension am Zoo (☎ 336 78, Ettlinger Strasse 33)*, has basic singles/doubles for DM55/100. Very central is *Pension Stadtmitte (☎ 38 96 37, Zähringer Strasse 72)*, which charges DM65 for bathless singles and from DM105 for doubles with amenities. The upmarket *Hotel Barbarossa (☎ 372 50, fax 37 25 80, Luisenstrasse 38)* has plushly furnished rooms with shower from DM98/128.

Places to Eat

Café Rih (☎ 220 74, Waldstrasse 3) is a bubbly bistro in the Baden art academy with simple fare from DM5. Several student haunts cluster around Ludwigsplatz, including the popular *Krokodil (☎ 273 31, Waldstrasse 63)*, a boisterous hall with tiled walls, wooden ceiling and an eclectic menu. Around the corner is *Trattoria Toscana (☎ 206 28, Blumenstrasse 19)*, a sophisticated Italian restaurant with mains from DM22. *Oberländer Weinstube (☎ 250 66, Akademiestrasse 7)* is the town's oldest wine locale, serving regional and French dishes from DM23. There's a huge wine list and lovely courtyard dining.

Getting There & Away

Karlsruhe is a major train hub with service in all directions. Trains leave regularly to Baden-Baden (DM10, 20 minutes), Freiburg (DM44, one hour) and Cologne (DM131, four hours).

Karlsruhe is on the A5 (Frankfurt-Basel) autobahn and the A8 to Munich, and is also

euro currency converter DM1 = €0.51

reached by the B3 and the B36. The Mit-fahrzentrale (☎ 194 40) is at Rankestrasse 14.

Getting Around

One/two-zone rides on Karlsruhe's KVV transport network (buses, S-Bahns and trams) cost DM1.50/3; four-block tickets are DM7/9.60. The best deal is the 24 hour Citykarte, which costs DM8 and covers two adults and two children over three zones (going as far as, say, Baden-Baden).

There's a Bahntaxi (DM15) in front of the main Hauptbahnhof entrance.

BADEN-BADEN

☎ 07221 • pop 50,000

When Roman legionnaires came to Baden-Baden some 2000 years ago, they must have felt right at home. Just like Rome, this idyllic enclave at the foot of the Black Forest is built on a group of hills, yielding curative mineral waters that, since the 19th century, have made the town the playground of the privileged classes. From Queen Victoria to the Vanderbilts, from Bismarck to Brahms and Berlioz, they all came – the royal, the rich and the renowned – to take the waters, or to lose their fortunes in the casinos.

Today, Baden-Baden is the grande dame among German spas, ageing but still elegant. It offers a townscape of palatial villas, stately hotels, tree-lined avenues and groomed parks. Spared from WWII bombing, Baden-Baden offers many salubrious activities in a sophisticated yet relaxed atmosphere that doesn't necessarily require deep pockets to enjoy.

Orientation

The train station is in the suburb of Oos, about 4km north-west of the town centre, with the central bus station immediately in front. To get to the centre, take bus No 201, 205 or 216, all of which make frequent runs to Leopoldsplatz, the heart of Baden-Baden. Most sights are within walking distance.

Information

Tourist Offices The main tourist information office (☎ 27 52 00, fax 27 52 02, email bbm.sales@baden-baden.de), Augustaplatz 8, is open daily from 9.30 am to 6 pm. If you're driving in from the autobahn, it's more convenient to stop at the office at Schwarzwaldstrasse 52 on your way into town. Hours here are 9 am to 8 pm between April and October and to 7 pm the rest of the year. If you're spending the night in Baden-Baden, you have to pay the Kurtaxe of DM4 (DM1.50 in the suburbs) which entitles you to the *Gästekarte* (see Resort Tax earlier in this section) good for discounts on concerts, tours, lectures and more.

Money There's a Sparkasse on Leopoldsplatz and a Commerzbank at Augustaplatz 4.

Post & Communications The post office is inside the Kaufhaus Wagener, a department store at Lange Strasse 44. Cafe Cont@ct (☎ 26 07 19), Eichstrasse 5, charges DM5 per half hour on the Web. It's open from 1 pm to 2 am (closed Tuesday).

Internet Resources The town's Web site is www.baden-baden.com, with sections in English.

Laundry The SB-Waschcenter Melcher (☎ 248 19), Scheibenstrasse 14, is open Monday to Saturday from 7.30 am to 9 pm.

Kurhaus & Casino

In the heart of Baden-Baden, just west of the river Oos, looms the palatial Kurhaus, the town's cultural centre, set in an impeccably designed and groomed garden. Two colonnades of shops, flanked by chestnut trees, separate the complex from the Kaiserallee. Corinthian columns and a frieze of mythical griffins grace the relatively modest exterior of this structure, designed by Friedrich Weinbrenner in 1824.

Modest, however, does not describe the Kurhaus interior. Besides a series of lavish festival halls – used for balls, conventions and concerts – it contains the casino, an undeniably opulent affair. Its decor, which seeks to emulate the splendour of French palaces, led Marlene Dietrich to call it 'the

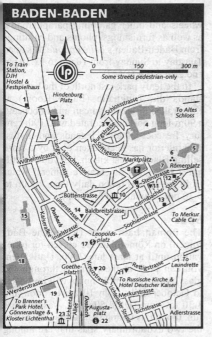

BADEN-BADEN

BADEN-BADEN

PLACES TO STAY
1   Steigenberger Badischer Hof
9   Hotel am Markt
12 Am Friedrichsbad
13 Hotel Römerhof

PLACES TO EAT
3   La Provence
11 Bratwurstglöckel
14 Leo's
20 Namaskaar
21 Piroschka-Stube

OTHER
2   Post Office
4   Neues Schloss
5   Caracalla-Therme
6   Römische Badruinen
7   Friedrichsbad
8   Stiftskirche; Markt
10 Stadtmuseum; Weinstube Baldreit
15 Trinkhalle
16 Police Station
17 Sparkasse
18 Kurhaus; Casino
19 Theater
22 Tourist Office
23 Staatliche Kunsthalle

most beautiful casino in the world'. After observing the action here, Dostoevsky was inspired to write *The Gambler*.

The rich and famous have passed through its doors since it opened in 1838 as Germany's first casino. The **Wintergarten**, decked out in a golden colour scheme, is crowned by a glass cupola interlaced with delicate wrought-iron ornamentation. Precious Chinese vases line the walls. Adjacent is the **Rote Saal** (red hall), draped in damask and modelled after a room in the Versailles palace. The **Florentiner Saal**, with its fleet of chandeliers, is also known as the 'hall of the thousand candles'.

The casino is open daily from 2 pm to 2 am, and to 3 am on Friday and Saturday; the baccarat tables are open to 6 am. You can also play French and American roulette, blackjack and poker. Admission is DM5, and you need your passport to enter. During the

week, minimum bets are DM5, on weekends DM10. You do not have to gamble, but men must wear jacket and tie (these may be rented at DM15 each), and women a suit or dress (trousers and blazer are acceptable).

A more casual alternative is to take a guided tour (English or German), offered daily every 30 minutes from 9.30 am to noon (DM6). Between October and March, the first tour is at 10 am.

Lichtentaler Allee
This elegant park promenade, comprising vegetation from around the world, follows the flow of the sprightly Oosbach from Goetheplatz, adjacent to the Kurhaus, to Kloster Lichtenthal about 3km south. Even today, it's not hard to imagine the movers and shakers of 19th century Europe – royals, aristocrats, diplomats and artists – taking leisurely strolls along this fragrant avenue.

The gateway to Lichtentaler Allee is formed by the Baden-Baden **Theater**, a white and red sandstone neobaroque confection whose frilly interior looks like a miniature version of the Opéra-Garnier in Paris.

Nearby stands the **Staatliche Kunsthalle** (State Art Gallery), featuring rotating international exhibits, mostly of contemporary art. It's open from 11 am to 6 pm, Wednesday to 8 pm, closed Monday (DM8).

A bit farther on is **Brenner's Park Hotel**, one of the world's poshest. It oozes the old-world charm, glamour and perfection that have largely become extinct. It's the type of place where the concierge would remember your poodle's favourite food.

About another kilometre south of here is the **Gönneranlage**, a rose garden ablaze with more than 300 varieties. For a quick detour, check out the **Russische Kirche** (Russian Church; 1882), just east of here on Maria-Victoria-Strasse. Built in the Byzantine style, it is topped with a shiny golden onion dome. It's open daily from 10 am to 6 pm (DM1).

Lichtentaler Allee concludes at the **Kloster Lichtenthal**, a Cistercian abbey founded in 1245. Generations of the margraves of Baden lie buried in its chapel, and there's also a **Museum of Religious Art**. It's closed mornings and all day Monday (DM3/1).

Altstadt

For wonderful views over Baden-Baden, climb to the terrace of the Renaissance **Neues Schloss** in Schlossstrasse. Until recently the palace was one of the residences of the margravial family of Baden-Baden, but acute cash flow problems forced them to auction off the furnishings and artworks. The palace itself still awaits a buyer.

On your way up you'll pass the **Stiftskirche** on the Markt, whose foundations incorporate the ruins of the former Roman baths. Otherwise, it's a hotchpotch of Romanesque, Gothic and baroque styles. Inside, look for the crucifix by Nicolaus Gerhaert, with a heart-wrenchingly realistic depiction of the suffering Christ.

Nearby in Küferstrasse 3 is the **Stadtmuseum** (City Museum, ☎ 93 22 72),

where highlights include historic roulette wheels and other gambling paraphernalia, as well as furnishings, photos and paintings from Baden-Baden's *belle époque*. It's open Tuesday to Sunday from 10 am to 12.30 pm and 2 to 5 pm (DM2).

In the leafy park just north of the Kurhaus stands the **Trinkhalle** (Pump Room) at Kaiserallee 3. Here you can amble beneath a 90m-long portico decorated with 19th century frescoes of local legends and myths. The interior has been taken over by a store selling Black Forest kitsch, but you can still get a free glass of curative mineral water from the springs (open daily from 10 am to 5.30 pm, in winter to 4.30 pm).

Spas

The **Roman bath ruins** (Römische Badruinen) on Römerplatz are closed for renovation until at least late 2000. Until then, you can peek at the remains through the glass. After reopening, hours will be Easter to October daily from 10 am to noon and 1.30 to 4 pm (DM2.50/0.50). Vastly more fun, though, is taking the waters yourself at the two extraordinary spas that are among Baden-Baden's main attractions. Built on either side of Römerplatz are the Friedrichsbad and the Caracalla-Therme.

The 19th century **Friedrichsbad** looks more like a neo-Renaissance palace than a bathhouse. Most stunning is the circular pool ringed by columned arcades that blend into a graceful cupola embellished with ornaments and sculptures. Two bathing options are offered: the Roman-Irish (DM36) and the Roman-Irish Plus (DM48) programs. Your three or more hours of humid bliss consist of a timed series of hot and cold showers, saunas, steam rooms and baths that leave you feeling scrubbed, lubed and loose as a goose.

No clothing is allowed inside, and several of the bathing sections are mixed on Wednesday and weekends, and from 4 pm on Tuesday and Friday – so leave your modesty at the reception desk. The Friedrichsbad (☎ 27 59 20) is open Monday to Saturday from 9 am to 10 pm, Sunday from 2 pm. Mixed bathing is all day.

The **Caracalla-Therme** (☎ 27 59 40), opened in 1985, has more than 900 sq metres of outdoor and indoor pools, hot and cold water grottoes, various whirlpools, therapeutic water massages, a surge channel and a range of saunas. Bathing suits must be worn everywhere except the upstairs sauna, but oddly enough, neither suits nor towels are available for hire. The baths are open daily from 8 am to 10 pm, but note that the last admission is two hours before closing time. Prices are DM19/25/33 for two/three/four hours.

Hiking

The low mountains around Baden-Baden make for good hiking excursions. The tourist office has put together a collection of pamphlets (DM9.80) with suggested hikes from the short and easy variety to some more serious climbs. Popular destinations are the Geroldsauer waterfalls, the Yburg castle ruin in the surrounding wine country, the Altes Schloss above the town and Mount Merkur. A cable car runs daily every 15 minutes from 10 am to 6 pm (DM7 return) up to the 660m-high summit of Mount Merkur. (Take bus No 205 from Leopoldsplatz to the cable car station).

Places to Stay

Campingplatz Adam (☎ 07223-231 94) is the closest camp site, about 12km southwest of town at Bühl-Oberbruch (no direct bus service).

The local **DJH hostel** (☎ 522 23, fax 600 12, Hardbergstrasse 34), 3km north-west of the centre, costs DM23/28 for juniors/seniors (from the train station, take bus No 201 to Grosse Dollenstrasse, then walk for 10 minutes).

As one might expect, hotels in Baden-Baden generally aren't cheap but a few bargains are available. The tourist office has a free room-reservation service and can help you find a *private room* from DM30 per person.

Altes Schloss (☎ 269 48, fax 39 17 75, Alter Schlossweg 10) has simple singles/doubles with shared shower and WC for

DM45/90. The Schloss, atop a hill, can only be reached by car or foot.

At the traditional *Hotel Deutscher Kaiser* (☎ 721 52, fax 721 54, Lichtentaler Hauptstrasse 35) you can get away with as little as DM60/90 for snug but quiet rooms; if you want your own shower and toilet, you'll have to fork out DM95/130.

Hotel am Markt (☎ 270 40, fax 27 04 44, Markt 17), up by the Stiftskirche, charges DM56/105 for simple rooms and DM90/140 for those with private facilities. Another nice place is *Am Friedrichsbad* (☎ 27 10 46, fax 383 10, Gernsbacher Strasse 31), with singles from DM67 to DM110 and doubles from DM99 to DM190.

The *Hotel Römerhof* (☎ 234 15, fax 39 17 07, Sophienstrasse 25) is classier, with bright clean rooms and private bath costing DM85/170; those without are DM10 less per person.

The *Steigenberger Badischer Hof* (☎ 93 40, fax 93 44 70, Lange Strasse 47) is a place for splashing out, with plush, spacious quarters from DM195/298. It has an elegant inner courtyard, attentive staff and droves of bathrobed guests shuffling to/from the house thermal baths.

Places to Eat

A good place to sample local Baden cuisine is at *Bratwurstglöckel* (☎ 906 10, Steinstrasse 7). It's rustic and small, and has dishes priced at DM13 to DM20 (closed Tuesday).

The *Piroschka-Stube* (☎ 220 39, Rettigstrasse 1) serves up regional and Hungarian specialities from DM13. *Leo's* (☎ 380 81, Luisenstrasse 10), near Leopoldsplatz, is a trendy movie-theme bistro that offers large salads and creative pasta dishes for DM15 to DM17.

At *Weinstube Baldreit* (☎ 231 36, Küferstrasse 3), in a cosy back courtyard beneath the Stadtmuseum, you can have filling snacks to go with crisp Baden wines or a full meal of regional fare. Main dishes average around DM22.

Vaulted ceilings, Art Nouveau mirrors and hanging baskets of dried flowers feature at *La Provence* (☎ 255 50, Schlossstrasse 20), where techno fiends to portly burghers dig into mouthwatering Franco-German dishes costing DM23 to DM28, and vegetarian dishes from DM16. Book ahead. It also has a much simpler and cheaper lunch menu (DM7 and under).

If you fancy something exotic, head to *Namaskaar (☎ 246 81, Kreuzstrasse 1)*, an Indian restaurant with imaginative meat, fish and vegetarian meals from DM24 per main course (closed Tuesday).

Entertainment
The town's new *Festspielhaus (Beim Alten Bahnhof 2)* at Robert-Schumann-Platz is in the historic old train station. Despite the top-notch orchestras, soloists and ensembles who perform here – including the New York Met Orchestra, Plácido Domingo, and the Vienna Philharmonic – the place has been plagued by poor attendance and financial troubles.

Baden-Baden's *Theater (Goetheplatz)* offers a repertory of classical and modern drama and musical theatre with most tickets priced from DM20 to DM40. Afternoon performances are slightly cheaper. The *Baden-Badener Philharmonie* performs in two concert halls in the Kurhaus and charges about the same prices (but students get a 50% discount).

Tickets for all three venues are available at the box office inside the Kurhaus (☎ 93 27 00) or from the ticket hot-line (☎ 27 52 33).

Getting There & Away
Air Baden-Baden's modern airport, about 15km west of town, is big enough to handle Boeing 747s, but is mostly used for hops within Germany and Europe and charter flights.

Train Baden-Baden is on the main north-south rail corridor. Trains leave every two hours for Basel (DM45, 1½ hours) and Frankfurt (DM65, 1½ hours). There are also services several times an hour to Karlsruhe (DM13, 20 minutes) and Offenburg (DM12.20, 30 minutes).

Bus Buses to many Black Forest towns depart from Baden-Baden. Bus No 212 makes hourly trips to Rastatt, while bus No 218 goes to Iffezheim, known for its prestigious annual horse race. Bus No 245 goes twice daily to Mummelsee (see the Schwarzwald-Hochstrasse section).

Car & Motorcycle Baden-Baden is close to the A5 Frankfurt-Basel autobahn and on the B3 and the B500, the scenic Schwarzwald-Hochstrasse.

Getting Around
Bus The Stadtwerke Baden-Baden (☎ 27 71) operates a decent bus system. Single tickets cost DM3 and four-block tickets are DM9. The best deal, though, is the 24 hour Day Pass (DM8), which entitles two adults and two children under 16 to unlimited travel in three zones (which includes Karlsruhe).

Car & Motorcycle To cut traffic in the centre, the main road goes underground near Verfassungsplatz in the north and emerges just south of the town centre. Note that much of the centre is either pedestrianised or blocked off from traffic. It's best to park and walk.

Bicycle Baden-Baden is *very* hilly. If you choose to cycle, you can rent from the Fahrradverleih at the train station or from the BBP bike shop at Geroldsauerstrasse 137a.

SCHWARZWALD-HOCHSTRASSE
The scenically beautiful Schwarzwald-Hochstrasse (Black Forest Highway), officially the mundanely named B500, wends its way from Baden-Baden to Freudenstadt, about 60km to the south. Large segments go right through the forest and along the ridge, with expansive views of the Upper Rhine Valley and, further west, the Vosges Mountains in Alsace, which form the border between Alsace and Lorraine in France.

The road also skirts a number of lakes, of which **Mummelsee** is the best known. It's at the foot of the Hornisgrinde, at 1164m the tallest mountain in the northern Black

Forest. According to legend, the lake is in-habited by water nymphs who emerge at night to party till 1 am, when the severe lake king orders them back. Mummelsee bustles with tourists during high season; if you want some quiet, rent a paddle boat (DM8 for 30 minutes).

The Schwarzwald-Hochstrasse is lined with hotels, and you'll find a *DJH hostel* (☎ 07804-611, fax 13 23) in Zuflucht, about 17km north of Freudenstadt, with its own bus stop. B&B costs DM23/28 for juniors/seniors. For truly rock bottom-priced lodging, you should check out the *Naturfreundehaus* (☎ 07226-238), about 2km from the B500 (bus stop Bühl-Sand), which charges only DM8 per bed, pro-vided you have your own sheets.

If you're not driving, you can get to the Mummelsee from Baden-Baden's central bus station by taking bus No 245. From Freudenstadt's Stadtbahnhof, take bus No 12 during the week and either bus No 2 or No 11 on weekends. Service is more fre-quent on Saturday and Sunday.

FREUDENSTADT
☎ 07441 • pop 23,500

This spa town on the eastern border of the Black Forest was the brainchild of Duke Friedrich I of Württemberg who, in 1599, decided to build one of the first planned residences north of the Alps. Together with his own architect, Heinrich Schickardt, he scoured Bologna and Rome for inspiration and came back with the idea for a town laid out like a spider web.

At Freudenstadt's centre is a gigantic market square – Germany's largest – with each side measuring 220m. Friedrich hoped to adorn the square with a palace, but this grandiose design was never realised; partly as a result, Freudenstadt fell into obscurity after the duke's death in 1610. It did not rise again until the mid-19th century, when a rail link brought in the first waves of tourists. The French wrecked the town in WWII, but thanks to restoration, Freuden-stadt retains some of its unique, quasi-urban charm.

Orientation & Information

Freudenstadt has two train stations, the Stadtbahnhof, centrally located about five minutes walk north of the Markt; and the Hauptbahnhof, about 2km south-east on Dietersweilerstrasse, on the corner of Bahnhofstrasse. Some trains link the two, as does the No B bus, but the latter only runs every two hours. The central bus station (ZOB) is right outside the Stadtbahnhof.

The tourist office (☎ 86 47 30, fax 851 76, email ktk.verwaltung@freudenstadt.de) is at Am Promenadeplatz 1 in the Kurhaus complex, and is open weekdays from 10 am to 6 pm (in winter to 5 pm) and Saturday to 1 pm. If the office is closed, see if someone inside the Kurhaus can help. If you're spending the night, you have to pay the DM3 daily Kurtaxe.

Several banks on Markt exchange money, including Kreissparkasse, Dresdner Bank and Deutsche Bank. The main post of-fice is also on the Markt and has a late counter open on weekdays until 7 pm.

Things to See & Do

From the Stadtbahnhof and bus station take a short walk south along Martin-Luther-Strasse to the **Markt**. It's too huge to truly feel like a square, especially since it's bi-sected by a major thoroughfare. It's entirely lined by Italianate arched arcades providing weatherproof access to dozens of shops.

On the south-western corner, the Markt is anchored by the **Stadtkirche** (1608), with its two naves built at a right angle, another un-usual design by the geometrically-minded duke. It's a bit of a mixture of styles, with Gothic windows, Renaissance portals and baroque towers. Of note inside are a **bap-tismal font** from the early 12th century with intricate animal ornamentations, a crucifix from around 1500 and a wooden lectern from 1140 carried on the shoulders of the four Evangelists.

In its early days, the church also pro-vided a safe place of worship for the many Protestants who settled in Freudenstadt after having been banished from their Aus-trian homeland.

BADEN-WÜRTTEMBERG

Located at elevations of 750 to 1000m, Freudenstadt is a place for moderately good winter sports, especially cross-country skiing, with eight groomed tracks between 4 and 12km long. There are also two ski lifts. For snow conditions, call ☎ 07442-69 22.

Places to Stay & Eat
If you want to camp in the area, head to *Camping Langenwald* (☎ 28 62), about 3km west of town along the B28 (take bus No 12, direction: Kniebis).

Freudenstadt's *DJH hostel* (☎ 77 20, fax 857 88, Eugen-Nägele-Strasse 69) is about 500m from the Stadtbahnhof and 2.5km from the Hauptbahnhof. B&B is DM23/28 for juniors/seniors, and you can rent bicycles and cross-country ski equipment.

Go to the tourist office if you need help finding a *private room* (no booking fee). These start at DM30 per person with private bath, but there's no shortage of central and reasonably priced hotels.

Gasthof Pension Traube (☎ 917 40, fax 853 28, Markt 41) charges DM50/100 for simple singles/doubles. Nearby is *Gasthof Ochsen* (☎ 26 67, fax 91 35 33, Markt 45), with identical room rates.

Between Stadtbahnhof and Markt is *Hotel Adler* (☎ 915 20, fax 91 52 52, Forststrasse 15-17), which charges DM66/110.

On the same street is *Hotel Schwanen* (☎ 915 50, fax 91 55 44 Forststrasse 6), a family-run operation where contemporary rooms cost DM63/126.

For a quick bite, try *Quick Snack* (☎ 91 49 38, Reichsstrasse 25), just off Lossburger Strasse south of Markt, with doner kebab for DM4.50 and pizzas from DM7.50.

Getting There & Away
The Kinzigtalbahn train leaves at two-hour intervals from the Stadtbahnhof. If you're northward-bound, there's the hourly Murgtalbahn to/from Rastatt (DM14.80, 1½ hours), which stops at both the Stadtbahnhof and the Hauptbahnhof.

Bus No 7628 makes a few trips on weekdays to/from Tübingen. Bus No 7161 travels daily along the Kinzig Valley with stops in Alpirsbach, Schiltach, Wolfach and Hausach.

Freudenstadt marks the southern terminus of the Schwarzwald-Hochstrasse (B500), which meanders northward for 60km to Baden-Baden. It also lies on the B462, the Schwarzwald-Tälerstrasse (Black Forest Valley Road) from Rastatt to Alpirsbach.

Getting Around
Freudenstadt's city bus network (☎ 89 50) has four routes; each one runs at two-hour intervals and each trip costs DM2.50. There's a bike-rental station in the Kurhaus (☎ 86 47 30) charging DM15 per day.

Central Black Forest

KINZIG VALLEY
The horseshoe-shaped Kinzig Valley begins south of Freudenstadt and follows the little Kinzig River south to Schiltach, then west to Haslach and north to Offenburg. Near Strasbourg, after 95km, the Kinzig is eventually swallowed up by the mighty Rhine. A 2000-year-old trade route through the valley links Strasbourg with Rottweil. The valley's inhabitants survived for centuries on mining and shipping goods by raft, and to this day you'll see plenty of felled trees awaiting shipping.

Getting There & Away
Train From Freudenstadt Stadtbahnhof, the *Kinzigtalbahn* train departs every two hours with stops in Alpirsbach, Schiltach, Wolfach and Hausach. At the latter, it hooks up with the Schwarzwaldbahn, with hourly links north to Haslach, Gengenbach and Offenburg, and south to Triberg, Villingen, Donaueschingen and Konstanz.

Bus The Kinzig Valley has direct connections with Freiburg by bus No 1066 with four daily departures (two on weekends). Bus No 7160 traverses the valley on its route between Offenburg and Triberg. Bus

No 7161 shuttles between Freudenstadt and Hausach.

Car & Motorcycle The B294 follows the Kinzig from Freudenstadt to Haslach, from where the B33 leads back north to Offenburg. If you're going south, you can pick up the B33 to Triberg and beyond in Hausach.

Alpirsbach
☎ 07444 • pop 7000
The main attraction of this village, 18km or so south of Freudenstadt, is the 11th century **Klosterkirche St Benedict**, formerly a part of a monastery and now a Protestant parish church. An almost unadulterated Romanesque basilica, its austere, red sandstone facade matches the streamlined interior with its flat ceiling and row of columned arcades. The entire building is based on symmetrical proportions: the central nave with its choir is twice as long as the transept, which is itself only half as wide as the aisles. Guided tours cost DM4 and run at 10 and 11 am, and at 2, 3 and 4 pm daily, except Sunday morning.

The tourist office (☎ 951 62 81, fax 951 62 83) is at Hauptstrasse 20 inside the Haus des Gastes. The *DJH hostel (☎ 24 77, fax 13 04, Reinerzauer Steige 80)* above town, about 2km from the train station, charges DM23/28 for juniors/seniors.

Schiltach
☎ 07836 • pop 4100
If you like half-timbered houses, then you should not miss this timeless jewel of a town about 18km south of Alpirsbach at the confluence of the Kinzig and Schiltach rivers. The wealth acquired by Schiltach in former times translated into a picture-perfect village that is at its most scenic around the triangular **Markt,** built against a steep hill. Take a closer look at the stepgabled **Rathaus**, whose murals provide a pictorial record of the town history.

At Hauptstrasse 5, you'll find Schiltach's tourist office (☎ 648, fax 58 58). *Campingplatz Schiltach (☎ 72 89, Bahnhofstrasse 6)* isn't far from the tourist office. There's no hostel here, but *private rooms* are available

from DM25 per person, though some require a three-day minimum stay. At the traditional *Gasthaus Adler (☎ 368, Hauptstrasse 20)*, singles/doubles go for DM65/95.

Wolfach
☎ 07834 • pop 6150
The main reason to stop at Wolfach, about 9km west of Schiltach, is to visit the **Dorotheenhütte**, a glass-blowing workshop at Glasshüttenstrasse 4. The finished items can be admired in the adjacent **museum**. The complex is open daily from 9 am to 4.30 pm (DM5/3).

To learn more about mining and logging in the area, you can visit the **Flösser- und Heimatmuseum** (Museum of Rafting & Local History), in the 17th century palace of the former Württemberg landgraves. It's open Tuesday, Thursday and weekends from 2 to 5 pm, and Sunday also from 10 am to noon; in winter it's only open on Thursday from 2 to 5 pm (DM3).

Wolfach's tourist office (☎ 83 53 51, fax 83 53 89) is at Hauptstrasse 41.

Gutach
☎ 07685 • pop 2200
Technically not in the Kinzig Valley, but only a 4km detour south along the B33, which parallels the Gutach river, is one of the Black Forest's biggest tourist draws, the **Schwarzwald Freilicht Museum** (Black Forest Open-Air Museum). It's worth braving the hordes of coach tourists for a first-hand look at the full range of historical farmhouses, brought here – and reassembled – from the entire region.

The museum centres around the **Vogtbauernhof**, a traditional farming village that has stood in the valley since 1570 and was saved from demolition in 1962 by Hermann Schilli, a former professor at the University of Freiburg and the museum's creator. The other farmhouses – along with a bakery, sawmill, chapel and granary – have been moved here from their original locations. It's not entirely kitsch-free, but the houses are authentically furnished and craftspeople at work inside seem to know

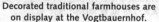

Decorated traditional farmhouses are
on display at the Vogtbauernhof.

what they're doing. The museum is open
from April to October daily from 8.30 am
to 6 pm, with the last admission at 5 pm
(DM7/5).

Haslach
☎ 07832 • pop 6600
Back in the Kinzig Valley, the next town
worth a brief stop is Haslach. During the
Middle Ages it prospered from the nearby
silver mines, but when these played out it
became a simple market town. Even today
it still is something of a shopping hub for
the immediate region, with 30 clothing
stores alone.

Haslach has a pretty Altstadt with some
half-timbered houses, but the most interesting building is the former Capuchin
monastery, which now contains the **Trach-
tenmuseum** (Museum of Folkloric Garments). This exhibit includes two types of
traditional women's headdresses. The *Bol-
lenhut* is a chalked straw bonnet festooned

with woollen pompoms – red for unmarried
women, black for married. Originally, it
hails from the village of Gutach, but is now
a symbol of the entire Black Forest. The
Schäppel is a fragile-looking crown made
from hundreds of beads that can weigh as
much as 5kg. These headdresses, along
with their appropriate costumes, are still
worn on important holidays, during processions and, occasionally, at wedding ceremonies. The outfits in this remote forest
region have stayed pretty much the same
over the centuries.

The museum is open Tuesday to Saturday
from 9 am to 5 pm and from 10 am on Sunday. From November to March, hours are
Tuesday to Friday from 1 to 5 pm (DM3.50).

Stop by the tourist office (☎ 706 71, fax 59
09), housed in the same building as the museum, for information on Haslach and its surrounds. Staff are friendly and speak English.
From April to October it's open Monday to
Saturday from 9 am to 5 pm and Sunday
from 10 am. The rest of the year, hours are
from 9 am to noon and 1 to 5 pm on weekdays only. They can help with finding *private
rooms* and hotel accommodation.

The nearest camping ground is *Campingplatz Kinzigtal (☎ 81 22)* in Steinach, about
3km north of Haslach. *Gasthaus Rebstock
(☎ 97 97 97, Kirchgasse 6)* charges from
DM40/50 for singles/doubles.

Gengenbach
☎ 07803 • pop 10,500
This romantic village, about 11km south of
Offenburg, is often compared to Rothenburg ob der Tauber but has remained relatively unspoiled by mass tourism. You can
stroll through its narrow lanes, past imposing patrician townhouses with crimson
geraniums spilling out of flower boxes, and
wander down to the Stadtkirche with its
lovely baroque tower.

On the market you'll find a fountain with
a statue of a knight, a symbol of the village's
medieval status as a 'free imperial city'.
Masks and costumes worn during Fasend
(a local version of Carnival) can be admired
on the seven floors of the **Narrenmuseum**.

It's open weekends from 2.30 to 5.30 pm, and Sunday also from 10 am to noon between April and October (DM2). The tourist office (☎ 93 01 43, fax 93 01 42) is at the Winzerhof building.

TRIBERG
☎ 07722 • pop 6000

Wedged into a narrow valley and framed by three mountains (hence the name) about 17km south of Hausach, Triberg is the undisputed capital of cuckoo-clock country. Countless shops, decorated with flags from around the world, simply crawl with coach tourists thinking they're buying 'typical' German trinkets when the label on that cute doll is more likely to say 'Made in Taiwan'. This is not to say that you can't find some authentic, locally made items including clocks, though usually at a high price.

Triberg also boasts not just one, but two of the 'world's largest cuckoo clocks' (see the boxed text later in this section). Fortunately, there are also some attractions unrelated to cuckoo clocks, including Germany's largest waterfall, some fine local museums and a historic Black Forest farmhouse where they still smoke their own hams.

Orientation & Information

Triberg's only thoroughfare is the B500, which bisects the valley and is called Hauptstrasse in town. The train station is at its northern end, where the B500 meets the B33. It's a little over a kilometre to walk from the station to the Markt, and there's also bus service. The Markt is the hub for regional buses.

Triberg's tourist office (☎ 95 32 30, fax 95 32 36) is at Luisenstrasse 10 inside the Kurhaus, just east of the waterfalls. It's open weekdays from 9 am to 5 pm, and in summer also on Saturday from 10 am to noon. The daily Kurtaxe is DM2. The Deutsche Bank at Markt 59 exchanges money and has an ATM that also accepts credit cards. The main post office is at the train station, but there's another at Markt 55 next to the Rathaus.

Things to See

Niagara they ain't, but Germany's tallest **waterfalls** do exude their own wild romanticism. Fed by the Gutach river, they plunge 163m in seven cascades bordered by mossy rocks. Energy has been generated from the falls since 1884, when it was first used to fuel the town's electric street lamps. You have to drop DM2.50/2 to even access the wooded gorge (open from April to October), but it's worth hiking the 20 to 30 minutes to the top of the falls.

For an imaginative overview of Triberg's history and social life in the region, head for the **Schwarzwaldmuseum** at Wallfahrtstrasse 4. It's open from November to April daily from 10 am to 5 pm, and from 9 am to 6 pm at other times (DM5/2). Note that it's closed from mid-November to mid-December. Continuing on Wallfahrtstrasse will get you to the baroque pilgrimage church **Maria in der Tanne** (Our Lady of the Pines), a single-nave structure with a flat wooden ceiling whose simplicity contrasts with the extravagant high altar adorned with biblical scenes.

One of Triberg's cuckoo clocks can be found a kilometre or so farther on at Untertalstrasse 28, inside a snug little house. It's open daily from 9 am to noon and 1 to 6 pm (DM1). Its rival is integrated into a large shop, open Monday to Saturday from 9 am to 6 pm, and from Easter to October also on Sunday from 10 am (DM2). It's on the B33 in Triberg-Schonachbach.

Hiking

Triberg is premier hiking territory, and the tourist office has lots of maps and suggestions. One enjoyable destination (reached after a one hour hike towards Schwarzenbach, south-west of Triberg) is the **Reinertonishof**, a Black Forest farmhouse from 1619. Inhabited until 1980, its chambers, stables and smokehouse can now be explored on a self-guided tour. The place is owned by Frau Duffner, who speaks excellent English, and who still smokes her own bacon while her husband makes schnapps strong enough to take the skin off your

euro currency converter DM1 = €0.51

BADEN-WÜRTTEMBERG

An Entirely Cuckoo Affair

Schwarzwälders know how to make capital with their cuckoo clocks, and like Texans and Alaskans, they have gone to absurd lengths in their claims of big, bigger, biggest.

The 'War of the Cuckoos' centres on Triberg and Schonach, which are pretty much the same village except perhaps to those who live there. As you enter Triberg on the B33 from the Gutach Valley, signs direct you to 'The World's Biggest Cuckoo Clock', a small house in which nests the Schwarzenegger of all cuckoos.

Problem is, as you exit Triberg in the direction of Schonach, you'll find the *other* 'World's Biggest Cuckoo Clock', also a legitimate contender.

The War of the Cuckoos hasn't yet come to an exchange of gunfire, but the acrimony over the issue is quite real. Civic pride is on the line.

Meanwhile, in elegant Wiesbaden, hundreds of kilometres away from the Black Forest, *another* 'World's Biggest Cuckoo' pops out of a storefront, chirping derisively at its deluded mountain cousins.

teeth. The farmhouse is open Tuesday to Sunday from 2 to 5 pm (DM2).

Most traditional Black Forest farmhouses are built into a hillside, with an entrance to the living quarters at the bottom of the slope and an opening to the threshing floor on the uphill side to provide easy entry for hay wagons. Animals, humans and fodder are all housed under the same low-hanging, shingled roof.

If you continue along the trail in the direction of Neustadt, after about another hour or so you'll get to the **Donauquelle**, source of the Danube. Technically, this modest little source springing from a stone is not yet the Danube but the Breg, the mighty Donau's main feeder, which merges with the Brigach in Donaueschingen (see that section) and then flows for another 2840km east to the Black Sea.

Places to Stay & Eat

Triberg's **DJH hostel** (☎ 41 10, fax 66 62, Rohrbacher Strasse 3) is on a scenic ridge on the southern edge of town. It's a 45 minute walk from the train station, but you take any bus to the Markt, from where it's 1200m uphill. It charges DM23/28 for juniors/seniors.

The tourist office can help you find a **private room** (no booking fee), starting at DM20 per person. The **Hotel Central** (☎/fax 43 60, Markt) charges DM51/88 for singles/doubles with all the facilities (it's DM5 more if you stay just one night).

Idyllically located on a little lake about 10 minutes on foot from the centre is **Pension Bergsee Stüble** (☎ 961 80, fax 96 18 20, Clemens-Maria-Hofbauer-Strasse 19), which charges DM80 to DM120 for doubles with private bath and balcony.

The **Romantik Parkhotel Wehrle** (☎ 860 20, fax 86 02 90, Gartenstrasse 7) is a haven of style in Triberg's sea of kitsch. Even the well travelled Ernest Hemingway, in Triberg to check out the local trout streams, enjoyed his stay here – you can too for DM109/200 for singles/doubles. In the kitchen, the chef works his magic with creativity and panache, but expect to pay DM25 and up for a main course.

All other hotels mentioned also have restaurants serving regional cuisine at average prices.

Bergcafé (Hermann-Schwer-Strasse 6) is a 15 minute trek uphill, but the views and reasonably priced good food are worth the effort.

Back in town at Markt 63 is the **Tresor** (☎ 215 60, Markt 61), a bit touristy to be sure, but the steaks and regional dishes are decent (from DM12.50).

Getting There & Away

Triberg is well connected to other Black Forest towns. The Schwarzwaldbahn line goes to Konstanz (DM34, 1¾ hours) and Offenburg (DM14.80, 45 minutes) with a service in either direction about once an hour. It's at the junction of the B500 and the B33.

The three main bus lines are No 7160, which travels north through the Gutach and Kinzig valleys to Offenburg; No 7265, which heads south to Villingen via St Georgen (one hour); and No 7270, which makes the trip to Furtwangen in 35 minutes.

Getting Around

There's local bus service between the train station and the Markt and on to the nearby town of Schonach. Trans-Alp (☎ 211 20) at Hauptstrasse 6 rents out mountain bikes, though you'll need to be in fairly good shape to bicycle around Triberg.

FURTWANGEN

☎ 07723 • pop 10,000

Furtwangen, about 15km south of Triberg, is considered one of the birthplaces of clock-making in Germany which, after 1700, became a cottage industry in large parts of the Black Forest. By 1870, more than 1.5 million clocks had been sold, and this manufacturing sector continues to play a role here to this day. The earliest models were rather primitive, often had only an hour-hand, relied on a field stone as a weight and were about as accurate as an Italian train schedule. You can learn more at the **Deutsches Uhrenmuseum** (German Clock Museum), with a comprehensive exhibit on timepieces from around the world. The museum is at Gerwigstrasse 11, and is open daily from 9 am to 5 pm, and from 10 am in winter (DM4/2).

Besides the museum, there's little to see in Furtwangen. The tourist office (☎ 93 91 11, fax 939 19 9) is at Markt 4. The town is easily reached by bus No 7270 from Triberg, bus No 70 from Villingen-Schwenningen, bus No 7272 from Freiburg and bus No 71 from Donaueschingen.

VILLINGEN-SCHWENNINGEN

☎ 07221 (Villingen)

☎ 07720 (Schwenningen)

• pop 80,000

When Villingen and Schwenningen were joined in 1972, the union couldn't have been more incompatible. Villingen is a spa town with a medieval layout; Schwenningen is a clock-making centre less than a century old. What's worse, Villingen used to belong to the Grand Duchy of Baden, while Schwenningen was part of the duchy of Württemberg, conflicting allegiances that apparently can't be reconciled. As one local was overheard to say, 'They decided to merge before they understood. Now they understand and can no longer decide.'

From the tourist's point of view, Villingen has more to offer, though Schwenningen has a couple of worthwhile museums.

Orientation & Information

Villingen's Altstadt is entirely contained within the ring road that follows the old fortifications. The train station is just east of the ring on Bahnhofstrasse; regional buses depart from here also. Most of the sights are in the northern half of the Altstadt. Bus No 20 connects Villingen with Schwenningen every 20 minutes in the daytime.

The Villingen tourist office (☎ 82 23 40, fax 82 12 07), Rietstrasse 8, is open weekdays from 8.30 am to 7 pm, Saturday to 4 pm and Sunday from 1 to 4 pm. There's also an information office inside the Schwenningen train station. The daily resort tax is DM1.

The Sparkasse on the Markt in Villingen exchanges money, and the main post office is at Bahnhofstrasse 6. Schwenningen's post office is at Friedrich-Ebert-Strasse 22.

Things to See

Unless noted otherwise, museums mentioned here are closed on Monday and cost DM3/1.50.

Villingen A few sights are clustered in the Altstadt, which wraps around two main streets laid out in the shape of a cross. Sections of the town wall and three towers still stand. The focal point is the vast **Münster**, with its striking pair of disparate spires, one completely overlaid with coloured tiles. This Romanesque church had its origins in the 12th century, though the choir, added after a major fire in 1271, is in the high Gothic style.

Head west of here to Schulgasse, then south for a couple of blocks until you get to Rietgasse 2 and the **Franziskaner Museum**, housed in a former Franciscan monastery, where there's a moderately interesting collection illuminating all aspects of the town's art and culture through the centuries; another department presents a wide range of folkloric and craft items. It's open weekdays from 10 am to noon; and also from 2 to 5 pm on Tuesday and Thursday to Saturday, from 2 to 8 pm on Wednesday, and from 1 to 5pm on Sunday and holidays.

At the eastern end of the Altstadt, just near the Bahnhof, is the 31m-high **Kaiserturm** (1372), once a town gate, whose five floors have exhibits on Villingen's medieval fortifications. It's open on Wednesday from 4.30 to 6.30 pm and Saturday from 2 to 4 pm.

Schwenningen Housed in the former factory of the oldest clock company in Württemberg at Bürkstrasse 39 is the **Uhrenindustriemuseum** (☎ 380 44), which looks at the industrial-production aspects of clock making (DM5/3). The **Uhrenmuseum**, at Kronenstrasse 16, on the other hand, showcases the actual finished products, with a special section dedicated to typical Black Forest clocks and another tracing the evolution of the timepieces. Both are open from 10 am to noon and 2 to 6 pm.

Places to Stay & Eat
The Villingen *DJH hostel (☎ 541 49, fax 526 16, St Georgener Strasse 36)* at the north-western town edge (bus No 3 or 4 to Triberger Strasse) charges DM21/26 for juniors/seniors.

The tourist office has a free booking service that includes *private rooms* from DM23 per person.

Perhaps the · cheapest option is the *Gasthof Schlachthof (☎ 982 90, 98 29 29, Schlachthausstrasse 11)*, which has a few shared-bath singles/doubles for DM50/85; rooms with private bath are DM72/120.

The central *Hotel Bären (☎ 555 41, fax 580 90, Bärengasse 2)* has modern and

spacious rooms for DM98/140 with private shower. Both hotels are in Villingen.

The *Ratskeller*, inside the Obere Tor at Obere Strasse 37, has a very cosy bar area and good vegie menu.

The bistro-cafe *Rietgarten (☎ 251 56, Rietgasse 1)* has lunch specials for DM9.50 and a 1970s bamboo interior.

Doner fans should head to the *Imbiss-Ecke (Färberstrasse 13)*, with stuffed doner pockets from DM3 and pizzas from DM4.

Getting There & Away
The town is on the Schwarzwaldbahn line from Konstanz to Offenburg, and there's also direct service to Donaueschingen and Rottweil. To get to Freiburg, you have to change in Donaueschingen.

From Villingen, bus No 7265 makes regular trips north to Triberg via St Georgen. Bus No 7281 goes to Rottweil and No 7282 to Donaueschingen. To get to Furtwangen, take bus No 70. IR trains between Kassel and Konstanz stop at Villingen-Schwenningen every two hours.

Villingen-Schwenningen is just west of the A81 (Stuttgart-Singen) and is also crossed by the B33 to Triberg and the B27 to Rottweil.

Getting Around
There's a bike-rental office at the station in Schwenningen. The tourist office sells a 1:30,000 bike map called *Rad und Wanderwege in Villingen-Schwenningen* (DM9.80).

DANUBE BIKE TRAIL
Donaueschingen, a small town about 50km east of Freiburg, marks the official beginning of one of Europe's greatest rivers, the Danube. The town itself isn't any great shakes, but offers a good launching point to the Donauradwanderweg (Danube Bike Trail), which ends 583km farther east in Passau on the Austrian border. The tourist office offers the *Donauradwanderführer*, with plenty of 1:50,000 maps and route descriptions (DM16.80), as well as a free brochure in English called *Tips, Info and Facts for Carefree Travels along the*

German Danube. The latter gives useful information about towns on the river and listings of camping grounds, hostels and bike-rental and repair shops.

Donaueschingen's tourist office (☎ 0771-85 72 21, fax 85 72 28) is at Karlstrasse 58. It's open weekdays from 8 am to noon and 2 to 5 pm (July and August also on Saturday from 9 am to noon). To rent bicycles, Josef Rothweiler (☎ 131 48) at Max-Egon-Strasse 11, charges from DM13 per day.

Southern Black Forest

Getting Around

SüdbadenBus (☎ 0761-361 72) offers special bus tickets that are good value and valid on all routes in the South Baden area. The region encompasses locales like Freiburg, St Peter, Titisee, Feldberg, Donaueschingen, Bonndorf, Villingen-Schwenningen and Schiltach, and reaches all the way east to Konstanz on Lake Constance.

The SBG-Freizeit-Ticket costs DM8 for one or DM12 for a family of two adults with children under 13, and is valid for unlimited travel on one weekend day or holiday. Those spending more time in the Black Forest can get the 7-Tage-SüdbadenBus-Pass, which costs DM38 for one person, DM55 for two people and DM68 for a family. Tickets are available from bus drivers.

FREIBURG
☎ 0761 • pop 200,000

As gateway to the southern Black Forest, Freiburg has the happy-go-lucky attitude of a thriving university community. Though badly disfigured by WWII, the city recovered with quick and tasteful restoration. It's framed by the velvety hills of the Black Forest and endowed with a wealth of historical attractions, led by the awe-inspiring Münster. Add to this a lively cultural scene and an excellent range of restaurants, bars and clubs, and it's easy to understand why Freiburg makes for a

terrific city to visit and to base yourself for exploring the Schwarzwald.

Founded in 1120 by Duke Bertold III and his brother Konrad of the Zähringer family, Freiburg came under the rule of the Urach counts in 1218. The Urachs proved to be immensely unpopular and so, just 150 years later, the people of Freiburg bought off the family with the proud sum of 15,000 silver marks, then placed themselves under the protection of the House of Habsburg. Freiburg prospered until 1677, when France's Louis XIV took such a shine to the place that he occupied it for two decades. The Habsburgs reclaimed the city and – after a brief second French interlude – governed here until 1805, when Freiburg became part of the Grand Duchy of Baden.

Orientation

The Hauptbahnhof and central bus station (ZOB) are on Bismarckallee, about 10 minutes west of the Altstadt. Follow either Eisenbahnstrasse or Bertoldstrasse east until you hit Kaiser-Joseph-Strasse, the centre's main artery. The Münster is on Münsterplatz, another block east. All sights are within walking distance from here.

Information

Tourist Office Freiburg's very friendly tourist office (☎ 388 18 80, fax 370 03, email freiburg@online.com.de) is at Rotteckring 14. From May to October it's open weekdays from 9.30 am to 8 pm, Saturday to 5 pm, and Sunday and holidays from 10 am to noon. The rest of the year, it closes on weekdays at 6 pm, Saturday at 2 pm and Sunday and holidays at noon.

The booklet *Freiburg – Official Guide* in English is a worthwhile investment (DM6). Also ask about the guided 'Kultour' walking tour in English (DM10, children DM8) daily between April and October for groups of at least six people (less frequent the rest of the year).

Money There's a Volksbank opposite the Hauptbahnhof and a Deutsche Bank opposite the tourist office.

Post & Communications The main post office is at Eisenbahnstrasse 58-62. Poste restante letters should be clearly marked *Postlagernd* and addressed to you at Haupt-post, 79001 Freiburg. There's a public fax-phone here and also one inside the Hauptbahnhof.

Surf the Web in the basement of the Herder bookshop, Kaiser-Joseph-Strasse 180, for DM5 per half hour. Its telecommunications link is super-quick.

Internet Resources Freiburg's best Web site is www.freiburg-online.com, with full English sections.

Bookshops The Herder bookshop (☎ 14 50 04 37), Kaiser-Joseph-Strasse 180, has a good assortment of foreign-language books, periodicals and maps. Rombach, Bertold-strasse 10, is another quality bookshop.

Laundry The Waschsalon in the central Café Fleck (268 29), Predigerstrasse 3, is open daily from 7 am to 1 am. A load with detergent costs DM7 and tumble-drying DM1 for 10 minutes.

Medical Services & Emergency For an ambulance, contact ☎ 192 22 and for 24 hour emergency medical care ☎ 809 98 00. There's a police station on Rotteckring near the corner of Bertoldstrasse, diagonally opposite the tourist office.

Münster

Freiburg's townscape is dominated by its magnificent Münster on the bustling market square. Begun as the burial church for the dukes of Zähringen, the cost of construction was shouldered by the local citizenry after the ruling family died out in 1218. A mere parish church until 1827, it was granted minster status when Freiburg became the seat of the Upper Rhenish bishopric, previously in Konstanz.

The minster has been called 'the most beautiful in Christendom'. Its **square tower** is adorned at ground level with rich sculptural ornamentation depicting scenes from the Old and New Testaments in a rather helter-skelter fashion. Look for allegorical figures such as Voluptuousness (the one with snakes on her back) and Satan himself on the west wall. The sturdy tower base gives way to an octagon, crowned by a filigreed 116m-high spire. An ascent of the tower (DM2, children DM1) provides an excellent view of the church's intricate interior, and up top you can see as far as the Kaiserstuhl and, in France, the Vosges Mountains on a clear day. The tower is open Monday to Saturday from 9.30 am to 5 pm, and Sunday from 1 to 5 pm. In winter, hours are Tuesday to Saturday from 10 am to 4 pm, and Sunday from 1 to 5 pm (closed Monday).

Inside the minster, the kaleidoscopic **stained-glass windows** are truly dazzling. The **high altar** features a masterpiece trip-tych of the coronation of the Virgin Mary by Hans Baldung, which is best viewed on a guided tour (DM1) of the ambulatory with its ring of richly outfitted side chapels.

South of Münsterplatz

Unless noted, museums mentioned here are open daily, except Monday, from 10 am to 5 pm and charge DM4/2.

Immediately south of the minster on Münsterplatz stands the arcaded, reddish-brown **Historisches Kaufhaus** (1530), a merchants' hall used as the central trade administration in the Middle Ages. The coats of arms in the oriels, as well as the four figures above the balcony, represent members of the House of Habsburg and indicate Freiburg's allegiance to these rulers.

The sculptor Christian Wentzinger built himself the **baroque townhouse** east of the Kaufhaus in 1761. Inside is a wonderful staircase whose wrought-iron railing guides the eye to the elaborate ceiling fresco. Nowadays, the building is occupied by the **Museum für Stadtgeschichte** (Town History Museum), where you can learn all about Freiburg's past up to the 18th century.

Admission to this museum also covers entrance to the **Augustinermuseum** (and vice versa) in a former monastery at Salz-

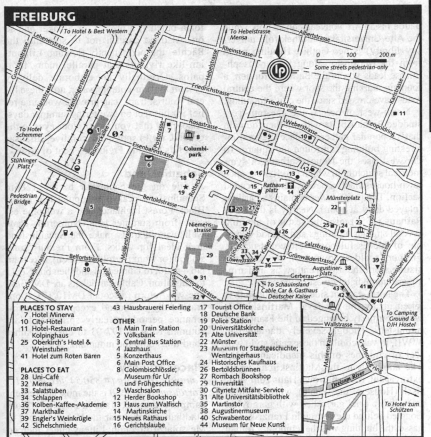

FREIBURG

PLACES TO STAY
7 Hotel Minerva
10 City-Hotel
11 Hotel-Restaurant Kolpinghaus
25 Oberkirch's Hotel & Weinstuben
41 Hotel zum Roten Bären

PLACES TO EAT
28 Uni-Café
32 Mensa
33 Salatstuben
34 Schlappen
36 Kolben-Kaffee-Akademie
39 Engler's Weinkrügle
42 Sichelschmiede
43 Hausbrauerei Feierling

OTHER
1 Main Train Station
2 Volksbank
3 Central Bus Station
4 Jazzhaus
5 Konzerthaus
6 Main Post Office
8 Colombischlössle; Museum für Ur und Frühgeschichte
9 Waschsalon
12 Herder Bookshop
13 Haus zum Walfisch
14 Martinskirche
15 Neues Rathaus
16 Gerichtslaube
17 Tourist Office
18 Deutsche Bank
19 Police Station
20 Universitätskirche
21 Alte Universität
22 Münster
23 Museum für Stadtgeschichte; Wentzingerhaus
24 Historisches Kaufhaus
26 Bertoldsbrunnen
27 Rombach Bookshop
29 Universität
30 Citynetz Mitfahr-Service
31 Alte Universitätsbibliothek
35 Martinstor
38 Augustinermuseum
40 Schwabentor
44 Museum für Neue Kunst

strasse 32, on Augustinerplatz. Its large collection of medieval art includes paintings by Baldung, Matthias Grünewald and Cranach, while its assembly of stained glass from the Middle Ages to the present ranks as one of the most important in Germany.

The **Museum für Neue Kunst**, about 200m farther south in a turn-of-the century former school building at Marienstrasse 10, makes an artistic leap into the 20th century with its collection of expressionist and abstract art (free entry).

Also in this neighbourhood, on Salzstrasse, is the muralled 13th century **Schwabentor** (Swabian Gate). Following the little canal west through the **Fischerau**, the former fishing quarter, will soon get you to the **Martinstor**, the only other surviving town gate. It's on Freiburg's main artery, Kaiser-Joseph-Strasse.

Western Altstadt
An eclectic mix of old and new buildings constitutes the **university quarter** extending

just west of the Martinstor. The **Kollegienge-bäude I** is an Art Nouveau concoction, while the **Alte Universitätsbibliothek** (old university library) is neo-Gothic. Heading north from the Martinstor along Kaiser-Joseph-Strasse leads you to the **Bertoldsbrunnen**, a fountain marking the spot where the central roads have crossed since the city's founding.

North-west of here is the chestnut-tree-studded **Rathausplatz** with another fountain that's a popular gathering place. Several interesting buildings surround the square. To the west rises the **Neues Rathaus**, a symmetrical structure in which two Renaissance town houses flank a newer, central arcaded section. The petite tower contains a carillon (played daily at noon). Nearby is the **Altes Rathaus** (1559), also the result of merging several smaller buildings and a good example of successful postwar reconstruction. Freiburg's oldest town hall, the **Gerichtslaube** from the 13th century, is in Turmstrasse immediately west of the square.

The north-eastern side of Rathausplatz is taken up by the medieval **Martinskirche**, which formerly belonged to the Franciscan monastery. Though severely damaged in WWII, it was rebuilt in the ascetic style typical of churches of this mendicant order. The antithesis to the Martinskirche is the extravagant, reddish-brown **Haus zum Walfisch** (House of the Whale), with its gilded late Gothic oriel garnished with gargoyles. Located behind the church in Franziskanergasse, the building was the temporary refuge of the philosopher Erasmus von Rotterdam after his expulsion from Basel in 1529.

Farther west, in a little park opposite the tourist office, is the neo-Gothic **Colombischlössle**, a villa housing the **Museum für Ur- und Frühgeschichte** (Museum of Pre- and Early History, free). Via the cast-iron staircase, you'll reach an eclectic bunch of archaeological exhibits spanning prehistory and the Middle Ages.

Freiburg Beneath Your Feet

As you stroll the town, be sure to look down at the pavement for the cheerful **mosaics** usually found in front of shopfronts. A diamond marks a jewellery shop, a cow is for a butcher, a pretzel for a baker and so on. Also be careful not to step into the **Bächle**, the permanently flowing, Lilliputian-like rivulets that parallel many footpaths. Originally an elaborate delivery system for non-potable water, now these literal 'tourist traps' can provide welcome relief for hot feet on sweltering summer days. Also, now that you've got your eyes to the ground, try to spot the decorative **canalisation lids** bearing Freiburg's coat of arms.

Schauinsland

A ride on the cable car to the 1286m Schauinsland peak is a popular trip to the Black Forest highlands and a welcome escape from summer heat. Numerous easy, well marked trails make the Schauinsland area ideal for walks. From Freiburg train station (or from Bertoldsbrunnen), take tram No 4 south to Günterstal and then bus No 21 to Talstation. Cable-car tickets are DM13/20 one-way/return (discount DM10/17). It operates daily year round, except during maintenance periods in early spring and late autumn. Ring ☎ 197 03 to check weather conditions atop the mountain.

Places to Stay

Camping Hirzberg (☎ *350 54, fax 28 92 12, Kartäuserstrasse 99)* is the most convenient camping ground. Take tram No 1 from Stadtbahnbrücke near the Hauptbahnhof to Messplatz (direction: Littenweiler), then go under the road and across the stream. Charges are DM6 to DM8 per site, DM8 per person and DM3.50 per car. It's open all year and gets very busy in summer.

Freiburg's huge *DJH hostel (*☎ *676 56, fax 603 67, Kartäuserstrasse 151)*, east of town, is often brimming with German students, so phone ahead. Take the same tram No 1 as for the camping ground to Römerhof and follow the signs down Fritz-Geiges-Strasse (about a 10 minute walk). B&B costs DM23/28 for juniors/seniors.

The tourist office has a room-reservation service (DM5 per booking). Finding an affordable room anywhere near the town centre can be difficult. The tourist office may be able to find a *private room* for you, but don't count on it. For long-term rentals, there's the *Mitwohnzentrale* (☎ 194 45, Konradstrasse 15a).

The least expensive hotel that's still fairly central is *Hotel Schemmer* (☎ 20 74 90, fax 207 49 50, Eschholzstrasse 63), behind the train station, where singles/doubles cost DM55/85 (DM90 for doubles with shower). Rooms with shared bath cost DM65/80 at the *Gasthaus Deutscher Kaiser* (☎ 749 10, fax 70 98 22, Günterstalstrasse 38), south of the Altstadt, but it also has rooms with private bath for DM95/125. *City-Hotel* (☎ 38 80 70, fax 388 07 65, Weberstrasse 3), in the northern Altstadt, starts at DM80/120 for basic rooms, but charges up to DM120/195 for those with shower and WC.

Best Western Hotel & Boardinghouse (☎ 896 80, fax 809 50 30, Breisacher Strasse 84) charges DM93/120 for modern rooms with full facilities. The historic *Hotel zum Schützen* (☎ 72 02 10, fax 720 21 33, Schützenallee 12), on the way to the hostel, is a reasonable compromise for location and good value, with rooms from DM75/110. Just north of the Altstadt is *Hotel-Restaurant Kolpinghaus* (☎ 319 30, fax 319 32 02, Karlstrasse 7), which has rooms for DM110/154.

The comfortable *Hotel Minerva* (☎ 202 06 16, fax 202 06 26, Poststrasse 8) is run by friendly young staff, has a great Art Deco lift and an OK deal with the Bahnhof parking garage (DM15 for 24 hours). Rooms cost from DM135/175.

If you're due a splurge, go for *Oberkirch's Hotel & Weinstuben* (☎ 310 11, fax 310 3, Münsterplatz 22), which asks for up to DM195/275. Or, try the classy but traditional *Hotel zum Roten Bären* (☎ 38 78 70, fax 387 87 17, Oberlinden 12), near Schwabentor, which claims to be the oldest guesthouse (since 1311) in Germany. It charges from DM185/250.

Places to Eat

As a university town, Freiburg virtually guarantees cheap eating. All in all, there are around 700 restaurants to choose from.

If you can produce student ID, the university-subsidised *Mensas* (Rempartstrasse 18 & Hebelstrasse 9a) have salad buffets and lots of filling fodder.

You'll find a good number of eating houses around the Martinstor, including the popular *Uni-Café* (☎ 38 33 55), on the corner of Universitätsstrasse and Niemenstrasse, which serves snacks and build-your-own breakfasts. *Schlappen* (☎ 334 94, Löwenstrasse 2) is an entrenched student pub with affordable food, a garden and a big selection of whiskies.

Next door is *Salatstuben* (☎ 359 11, Löwenstrasse 1), with a wide choice of wholesome salads for DM2.29 per 100g (after 5 pm the price goes down to DM1.89) and filling daily specials for around DM7.50. It's open to 8 pm on weekdays and to 4 pm on Saturday.

Upstairs in the *Markthalle* (Martinsgasse 235), you'll be hit with a wonderful confusion of smells from Mexican, Italian, Indian, French and other self-service counters offering fast, delicious and cheap lunches.

The *Kolben-Kaffee-Akademie* (☎ 387 00 13, Kaiser-Joseph-Strasse 233), around the corner, is an old-fashioned stand-up coffee house with large cups for DM2.50 (closed after 6.30 pm and on Sunday).

Pubs and restaurants also cluster along Konviktstrasse, where you'll find *Engler's Weinkrügle* (☎ 38 31 15, Konviktstrasse 12), which serves affordable Badener food and wine and has four-course meals for DM19 to DM21 (closed Monday). A haunt of the in-crowd is the *Hausbrauerei Feierling* (☎ 266 78, Gerberau 46) in a renovated old brewery, with a good vegetarian menu and absolutely enormous schnitzels with salad and *Brägele* (chipped potatoes) for DM16.50. Next door, the *Sichelschmiede* (☎ 350 37, Insel 1) is a snug wine bar decked out in wood and wrought iron (mains for DM19 to DM26).

Entertainment

The free cultural events listing *Freiburg Aktuell* is published monthly and available at hotels and at the tourist office. Also look for *Freizeit & Kultur*, a tad edgier and packed with up-to-date insider's tips.

The *Cräsh* (☎ *324 75, Schnewlinstrasse 7*) is a hard-core punk and heavy metal club open Friday and Saturday from 10 pm (free, except for concerts). Somewhat tamer is the hip hop, rock, pop and oldies played at *Sound* (☎ *259 59, Nussmannstrasse 9*), open Tuesday to Sunday from 9 pm. Cover charges start at DM5, but it's free to students on Wednesday.

A few doors on from Crash is *Jazzhaus* (☎ *349 73, Schnewlinstrasse 1*), one of Germany's hottest music venues, with live jazz nearly every night (admission generally costs no more than DM20), including appearances by internationally acclaimed artists.

Fine orchestras perform in the *Konzerthaus*, a hulking modern concert hall between the train station and the Altstadt, which doubles as a centre for other cultural events and conventions.

Getting There & Away

Train Freiburg lies on the north-south train corridor, and is therefore highly accessible. There are frequent departures for Basel (DM16.40, 40 minutes) and Baden-Baden (DM28, 45 minutes). Freiburg is the western terminus of the *Höllentalbahn* to Donaueschingen via Titisee-Neustadt. There's a local connection to Breisach (DM8, 30 minutes).

Bus Freiburg is a major hub for buses to rural Black Forest communities. Bus No 1066 travels to Hausach in the Kinzig Valley, with some departures continuing on to Wolfach and Schiltach. Bus No 7200 goes to the Europa Park Rust (see Around Freiburg), No 7205 and 7209 to St Peter, No 7211 to Breisach and No 7272 to Furtwangen.

Car & Motorcycle The A5, which links Frankfurt and Basel, also passes through Freiburg. The usually clogged but very scenic B31 leads east into the Höllental (Hell's Valley) and on to Lake Constance. The B294 leaves the town northward and travels into the central Black Forest. Car

rental agencies include Europcar (☎ 515 10 0) at Zähringer Strasse 42 and Avis (☎ 197 19) at St-Georgener-Strasse 7.

Ride Services The Citynetz Mitfahr-Service (☎ 194 44) is at Belfortstrasse 55.

Getting Around

Freiburg has an efficient public transport system that is part of a regional network called Regio, extending to all communities within a radius of approximately 30km. It's divided into three zones, with tickets costing DM3.30/5.70/8 for one/two/three zones. The 24-hour ticket is available either for one zone (DM8 one person, DM10 two people) or all zones (DM16/20); up to four children under the age of 15 travel for free on this ticket. Buy tickets from vending machines or the driver, and be sure to validate upon boarding.

AROUND FREIBURG
Breisach
☎ 07667 • pop 12,000

About 25km west of Freiburg, separated from France by the Rhine, is Breisach, an ancient town that has often been caught in the crossfire of conflict. The Romans first built a fortress atop the volcanic Breisachberg. After becoming an imperial city under Rudolf von Habsburg in 1275, Breisach became involved in a power struggle between Staufian and Habsburg rulers, the French and the Austrians. In 1793, the French demolished the town, and in 1815 it fell to the Grand Duchy of Baden.

Not to be missed on any visit to Breisach is the huge **Münster of St Stephan**. It is reached after a short walk from the train station: cross Bahnhofstrasse to Poststrasse, then keep going straight to the Gutgesellentor and up the Münsterberg. The Münster was built between the 12th and the 15th centuries and rebuilt after being badly damaged during WWII. Of note inside is the fairly faded fresco cycle (1491) of *The Last Judgment* by Martin Schongauer in the west end and the sweeping rood loft from around the same period. There's also a nice Renaissance pulpit (1597) and a silver shrine containing the relics of the town's patron saints. Top billing, though, goes to the magnificent **high altar triptych** (1526), with figures carved entirely of linden wood by an artist simply known as Master HL. From the Münster terrace, there's a great view across the Rhine into France and the Vosges Mountains.

The tourist office (☎ 94 01 55, fax 94 01 58) is on the Markt and can help with accommodation if you want to spend the night here. You'll find *Camping Münsterblick (☎ 939 30)* in the suburb of Hochstetten, about 2km south of town; it's open from April to October. The *DJH hostel (☎ 76 65, fax 18 47, Rheinuferstrasse 12)*, about a 15 minute walk south of the train station, charges DM23/28 for juniors/seniors.

Bus No 7211 shuttles between Freiburg and Breisach at least once an hour (40 minutes), and there's also direct train service (30 minutes) several times daily except Sunday.

Kaiserstuhl

North-west of Breisach is the Kaiserstuhl, a 560m-high mountain that's actually an extinct volcano. Its terraced slopes constitute one of Germany's finest wine-growing areas, noted especially for its late burgundies. The wines owe their quality to an ideal microclimate, the result of plenty of sunshine and the fertile loess (clay and silt) soil that retains the heat during the night.

Another popular grape variety here is the Grauburgunder (pinot gris). On weekends between April and October at least one wine estate opens for cellar tours and tastings on a rotating basis. For details, see the tourist office in Breisach.

The *Kaiserstuhlbahn* train from Breisach to Riegel is a good way to get to the area, though it's best explored by foot, for example by hiking the 15km Winzerweg (Wine Growers' Trail) from Riegel to Achkarren. By bicycle, you could pedal along the Kaiserstuhl Radwanderweg, a 64km loop trail starting in Breisach. Bikes may be rented at the train station in Breisach or at Zweirad-Sütterlin (☎ 63 99), Im Gelbstein 19.

St Peter
☎ 07660 • pop 2300
Little St Peter, on the southern slopes of Mt Kandel (1243m), is one of those supernaturally bucolic Black Forest villages that appears to be caught in a time warp. The fresh-faced people of St Peter are deeply committed to their ancient traditions and customs. One third of them still live in neat farmhouses often owned by the same family for centuries. At local events you can see the villagers – from young boys and girls to grey-haired matriarchs and patriarchs – proudly sporting their colourful *Trachten* (folkloric costumes), hand-fashioned locally by skilled craftspeople.

The most outstanding feature of St Peter is the former **Benedictine Abbey** (1727), a baroque-rococo jewel designed by the masterful Peter Thumb of Vorarlberg. Its predecessor was founded in 1093 by Duke Berthold II of Zähringen as a private monastery, as well as a burial place for his family. Secularised in 1806, it has been the seminary of the archdiocese of Freiburg since 1842.

The baroque church, which is always open, is a festive and light-flooded single-nave construction with six side chapels. Many of the period's top artists collaborated on the sumptuous interior decoration, including Joseph Anton Feuchtmayer, who carved the statues of the various Zähringer dukes affixed to the pillars. The high altar shows the coronation of the Virgin Mary and was painted by Johannes Cristoph Storer. The wall and ceiling frescoes, with scenes from the life of St Peter, are ascribed to Franz Joseph Spiegler.

You can take a guided tour (DM5) of the monastery complex but times vary, so check first with the tourist office (☎ 91 02 24, fax 91 02 44), next to the monastery at Klosterhof 11. It's open weekdays from 8 am to noon and 2 to 5 pm. From June to October, it's also open Saturday from 11 am to 1 pm. There's an electronic hotel reservation board out front.

From Freiburg's central bus station you can take bus No 7205 (one hour). Bus Nos

7209 and 7216 take only about 40 minutes but operate less frequently.

If you're driving, take the B3 north, then turn east in the direction of Glottertal. This will put you right onto the **Schwarzwald Panorama Strasse** (Black Forest Panorama Road), a scenic route across a plateau with dreamy views of the Feldberg and other mountains.

Europa Park Rust

So you don't have time to go to Paris, London, Amsterdam and Venice during your trip to Europe? Don't despair. The people of the Europa Park have brought the continent's best sights together right here at their theme park in Rust, about 30km north of Freiburg. Sure, it's not the real thing, but where else can you meander effortlessly from a Swiss mountain village to a Spanish *avenida* and be back in time for lunch at the Rock-Café – without even taking your passport? And if you need to brush up on German architectural styles, just take a walk down 'Main Street Germany', where you'll find it all – Gothic red brick and cute half-timber to curvy baroque. Add to that a bunch of rides, restaurants and glitzy shows and the fun is complete – provided you're into that sort of thing. They even have a big mouse walking around ... sound familiar?

The park (☎ 07822-77 66 77) is open daily from 9 am to 6 pm (longer in peak season, weather depending) from late March to early November. Admission is DM39 (DM35 for children four to 11 years).

From Freiburg's bus station, bus No 7200 makes daily trips directly to the park with several departures in the morning and return trips to Freiburg starting at 4 pm. By car, you should take the A5 north to the Herbolzheim exit.

Höllental

When in Freiburg, you shouldn't miss a ride through 'hell', the wildly romantic Höllental (Hell's Valley) to be precise, stretching east of the city en route to Titisee. It's easily seen by car along the B31 or by rail on the *Höllentalbahn* from Freiburg to Donaueschingen, although to truly experience its natural splendour, you should walk.

In a wonderful twist of names, the western gateway to 'hell' is the village of **Himmelsreich** (Kingdom of Heaven), after which you're plunged into the narrow, craggy stone canal that in parts is so steep that the sunlight doesn't reach the bottom until mid-morning. Near-vertical jagged rock faces, alternating with tree-covered hillsides, dwarf everything beneath them.

A famous landmark is the **Stag's Leap**, the narrowest point of the valley between Himmelsreich and Posthalde, and allegedly the spot where a male deer being pursued by hunters rescued itself by leaping across the crevice.

The valley was virtually impassable until the construction of its railway at the turn of the last century. This was another amazing feat of engineering accomplished by Robert Gerwig, who also built the Schwarzwaldbahn. On its way, the train passes through nine tunnels and travels along the 222m-long viaduct over the Ravenna Gorge before coming out of the valley at Hinterzarten.

Hiking Located at the northern foot of the Feldberg, the entire Höllental is terrific hiking territory. A convenient and particularly scenic base for your explorations is the Hofgut Sternen, an inn and restaurant at the mouth of the Ravenna Gorge in Höllsteig. The Hofgut Sternen is a Höllental institution and was already here in 1770 when the ill-fated Marie-Antoinette, daughter of Habsburg Empress Maria Theresa (1717-80), spent the night on her way from Vienna to Paris to marry Louis XVI. And only a few years later, Johann Wolfgang von Goethe also stopped by for a visit.

Today, the Sternen is a sprawling, largely kitsch-free Black Forest inn run with aplomb by energetic outdoor enthusiasts who know the area extremely well and are full of tips, information and suggestions. If you want to stay at the *Sternen* (☎ 07652-90 10, Höllsteig), expect to pay from DM108/156 for warmly furnished and very large singles/doubles with full facilities. Also ask here for the *Breitnau Wanderkarte* (1:25,000) hiking map.

Hike 1: Through the Höllental A particularly scenic, fairly steady and moderate hike (once you've worked your way out of the valley to an elevation of about 1000m) takes you above the Höllental towards Freiburg for a total of about 10km.

First you traverse the breathtaking, if claustrophobic, Ravenna Gorge that links up with the Querweg Freiburg-Bodensee. After about 5.5km on the Querweg you reach Nessellachen, with great views of Freiburg. From there it's on to Himmelsreich, where you can catch the Höllentalbahn back to Hinterzarten. It's about a 30 minute walk from here to the Sternen.

Hike 2: To the Feldberg Peak You need to be in reasonably good shape for this quite strenuous hike to the top of the Feldberg (1493m). It starts off with a challenging 6.5km uphill climb through the forest to Rinken at an elevation of 1200m. From here it's only another 300m gain to the top. Hike back down to Feldberg-Ort, where you can catch a bus to Feldberg-Bärental, then the Dreiseenbahn to Titisee and from there the *Höllentalbahn* to Hinterzarten, followed by the same 30 minute walk back to the Sternen.

FELDBERG
☎ 07655 • pop 1800
At 1493m the Feldberg is the highest mountain in the Black Forest and the region's premier downhill skiing area, with a dense network of runs and ski lifts. On clear days, the view of the chain of Alps in the south is stunning. The actual mountain top is treeless and not particularly attractive, looking very much like a monk's tonsured skull. This lack of trees is not because of an unusually low tree line, as some tourist brochures would have you believe, but the result of heavy logging by the area's early settlers.

Feldberg is also the name given to a cluster of five resort villages of which **Altglasshütten** is the administrative centre

and site of the tourist office (☎ 80 19, fax 801 43) at Kirchgasse 1. It's open weekdays from 8 am to 6 pm, in winter to 5.30 pm. During peak seasons (June to October and December to March) it's also open Saturday from 9 am to noon and Sunday from 10 am to noon. The daily Kurtaxe is DM2.10.

The post office is about 100m north of here on Bärentaler Strasse, with a bank immediately adjacent. Together with **Neuglasshütten**, Altglasshütten used to be a centre for glass-blowing, a tradition kept alive by just a single workshop today.

Just north of these twin communities is **Bärental** where traditional Black Forest farmhouses snuggle against the hillsides. Germany's highest train station (967m) is here. East of Bärental is **Falkau** in the Haslach Valley, a family-friendly resort with a cute waterfall for a nearby attraction. Also not far is the idyllic **Windgfällweiher**, a good lake for swimming or rowing.

About 7km west of these four villages, there's **Feldberg-Ort** (area code ☎ 07676) right in the heart of the 42 sq km nature preserve that covers much of the mountain. All the ski lifts are here, as is the popular chair lift to the Bismarck monument for wonderful panoramic views (DM10 return, DM8 up only, DM7 down only).

Skiing
The Liftverbund Feldberg comprises a network of 26 ski lifts, and you'll only need one ticket to use them all. There are 36 runs totalling 50km in length. Day lift-tickets are DM36, morning tickets (to 1 pm) are DM22 and afternoon tickets (after 1 pm) are DM25. Discounts on multi-day tickets are available. If you prefer cross-country skiing, you can choose from among four groomed trails ranging from 2.5 to 20km in length.

The snow season usually lasts from November to the end of February. For the latest snow conditions, ring the Schneetelefon (☎ 07676-12 14). Four different ski schools offer a variety of packages. If you want to rent downhill or cross-country skis, look for signs saying 'Skiverleih' or try Skiverleih Schubnell (☎ 07655-560).

BADEN-WÜRTTEMBERG

Schwarzwaldkaufhaus Faller (☎ 07676-223) rents snowboards. There's free shuttle service from all Feldberg communities to the ski lifts if you have a lift ticket or your Gästekarte.

Hiking

In summer, the Feldberg area is a great place for hiking with some rather challenging trails. Since much of the region is part of a nature preserve, you're quite likely to encounter rare wildflowers or animal species such as mountain hens and chamois. The trail to the top of the Feldberg is gravel-covered. Show up early to avoid the throngs of coach tourists headed up here in ant-like processions. The Westweg trail (Pforzheim to Basel) also crosses the Feldberg. The tourist information office has suggestions and an assortment of maps, including the *Wanderkarte Feldberg* (1:30,000), which costs DM5.80. (See the Höllental section for two recommended hikes in the region.)

Places to Stay

The *DJH Hebelhof* (☎ 07676-221, fax 12 32, Passhöhe 14) is perched at 1234m right in Feldberg-Ort (take bus No 7300 from the Bärental train station to Hebelhof). The hostel charges DM23/28 for juniors/seniors for B&B, plus DM2.50 for resort tax, and offers para-gliding courses year round and snowboard training in winter.

Altglasshütten's renovated *DJH Jugendgästehaus* (☎ 900 10, 90 01 99, Am Sommerberg 26) is about a 15 minute walk south of that village's train station. It charges DM23/28 for juniors/seniors but also has beds in modern two and four-bed rooms from DM38 per person, including breakfast buffet.

A more comfortable yet still affordable option is *Berggasthof Wasmer* (☎/fax 07676-230, An der Wiesenquelle 1), which charges DM65/120 for singles/doubles with full bath. It's right next to the ski-lift area.

If you need help finding a room that suits your budget, contact the tourist office (no service charge).

Getting There & Away

Bärental and Altglasshütten are stops on the Dreiseenbahn train from Titisee to Seebrugg on the Schluchsee. From the station in Bärental, bus No 7300 makes direct trips every 30 minutes to Feldberg-Ort.

If you're driving, take the B31 (Freiburg-Donaueschingen) to Titisee, then the B317 to Feldberg-Ort via Bärental. To get to Altglasshütten, get on the B500 in Bärental.

TITISEE-NEUSTADT

☎ 07651 • pop 12,000

Titisee, named for the glacial lake on which it is located, is an extraordinarily popular summer holiday resort with too much infrastructure for its own good. The village hugging the lake's north-eastern end is one giant beehive of activity filled with souvenir shops, kiosks, cafes and restaurants, and swarming mostly with families and elderly tourists taking advantage of the healthy air of the Black Forest's oldest spa.

The lake itself – 2km long and 750m wide – is reasonably scenic and best appreciated from the relative isolation of a rowing or pedal boat. **Windsurfing** and **sailing** are popular activities here, and equipment for both sports may be rented. The scenic trails around the lake provide more escape routes from tourists.

Neustadt is Titisee's less commercial twin town, about 3km east in the Gutach Valley at the foot of Mt Hochfirst (1190m). Titisee's train station is at Parkstrasse, only a short walk from the lake shore. The Bahnhof in Neustadt is also centrally located on Bahnhofstrasse. Post offices and banks are in the immediate vicinity of both stations. The tourist office (☎ 980 40, fax 98 04 40) is at Strandbadstrasse 4 in Titisee. The resort tax is DM2.80 (DM1 if staying at the hostels).

Places to Stay

Titisee has a good selection of camping grounds, including *Terrassencamping Sandbank* (☎ 82 43), open April to mid-October right on the lakeshore, and *Campingplatz Bühlhof* (☎ 16 06), open mid-December through October. Adults cost DM7.50 each and tent sites start at DM8.50.

The fabulous *DJH hostel (☎ 238, fax 756, Bruderhalde 27)* is on the northern lakeshore (bus No 7300 from the train station to Feuerwehrheim/Jugendherberge or 30 minutes on foot). There's a second *DJH hostel (☎ 73 60, fax 42 99, Rudenberg 6)* in Neustadt on the eastern town edge (20 minutes walk from Neustadt train station). Both hostels cost DM23/28 for juniors/seniors for B&B.

Private rooms start at DM18 per person, though there's often a small surcharge for stays of one or two nights. The tourist office has a free room-finding service. As for hotels and pensions, Titisee-Neustadt is flooded with options.

Getting There & Away

Train The *Höllentalbahn* from Freiburg to Donaueschingen stops at both Titisee and Neustadt train stations. The Dreiseenbahn to Feldberg and Schluchsee leaves from Titisee station. Neustadt is linked roughly every two hours with Donaueschingen and Ulm on the Donautalbahn.

Bus Titisee-Neustadt is a transport hub for the southern Black Forest. Bus No 7257 makes hourly trips to Schluchsee. From Titisee train station, bus No 7300 goes to Feldberg and continues to Basel in Switzerland. From Neustadt's train station, there are hourly links to Bonndorf with bus No 7258 and to St Märgen with bus No 7261.

Car & Motorcycle Titisee-Neustadt is at the junction of the B31 and the B500.

Getting Around

Bus No 7257 connects Titisee with Neustadt every hour. There's a free shuttle to the Feldberg ski area if you hold a lift ticket. Bikes may be rented from Ski-Hirt (☎ 74 94) on Wilhelm-Stahl-Strasse and Harry's Mountain Bike Verleih (☎ 40 93), Scheuerlenstrasse 15, both in Neustadt, as well as from Bootsvermietung Drubba (☎ 98 12 00) at Seestrasse 37 in Titisee.

SCHLUCHSEE
☎ 07656 • pop 2600

Schluchsee, the name of both a lake and town, is about 10km south of Titisee. Less commercial than its neighbour to the north, it's also a popular summer holiday-resort area and a centre for outdoor activities of all kinds, especially water sports. Originally, the Schluchsee was a 2km-long natural glacial lake (*Schluch* is a variation of *Schlauch*, meaning 'tube'). In the 1930s a 64m-high dam was built, which tripled the lake's length. An old farmhouse and other buildings fell victim to the raised water level and lie submerged. Because water from the Schluchsee is used to generate electricity, levels are not always constant. Water drained to power the turbines during the daytime is pumped back up from the Rhine – about 50km away and 600m lower in elevation – during the night.

Orientation & Information

The railway tracks and road are parallel to the Schluchsee's eastern shore. The community of Aha is at the north end of the lake, the town of Schluchsee is about two thirds down and Seebrugg forms the southern end. The western shore is accessible only by bike or on foot. The lake's circumference is 18.5km.

The tourist office (☎ 77 32 33, fax 77 59), inside the Haus des Gastes at Fischbacher Strasse 7, is open weekdays from 8 am to noon and 2 to 6 pm, in summer 8 am to 6 pm and also weekends 10 am to noon). The daily Kurtaxe is DM2.10. The post office is on Lindenstrasse, a short walk northwest from the tourist office.

Water Sports

The most popular activity at the Schluchsee is swimming, which is free and permitted everywhere. Keep in mind that even in summer water temperatures rarely climb above 20°C (the lake usually freezes over in winter). If that's too cold, you might prefer Aqua Fun, an outdoor pool complex with slides, playgrounds and a surge channel – though you better be fond of squealing children. It's open daily to 7 pm (DM6/4).

euro currency converter DM1 = €0.51

Those into windsurfing or sailing can rent equipment at the Segel+Surfschule Schluchsee (☎ 366), at the landing docks in Aha. Surfboards are DM15/60 per hour/day. Sailing boats cost DM20/100.

It's not the Caribbean but **scuba diving** is another activity practised in the Schluchsee. Visibility is relatively high, though below 12m a diver's torch is needed. Besides oodles of fish, the buildings and streets that were submerged by the damming are of particular interest. Tauchschule Lang (☎ 16 99) in Seebrugg rents equipment, but in order to dive on your own, you must present certification by a major international diving association (PADI, NAUI, BSAC etc). For the uninitiated, there are introductory courses (one hour of theory, one hour of practice, one dive) for DM100, including equipment.

Hiking
Thanks to its location at the foot of the Feldberg, the forests around Schluchsee offer some wonderful hiking on about 160km of trails. Even in winter, about 60km of paths are groomed for walking in the snow. To hike around the lake will take about four hours. Ask for the Schluchsee hiking map (1:25,000; DM3) at the tourist office.

Places to Stay & Eat
Campingplatz Wolfsgrund (☎ 573), open year round, is a modern facility on the eastern lakeshore, just north of the Schluchsee town centre.

The **DJH hostel** (☎ 329, fax 92 37, Im Wolfgrund 28) is nicely located on the peninsula jutting into the lake, about a 10 minute walk north of the Schluchsee train station. There's a second **DJH hostel** (☎ 494, fax 18 99, Haus Nr 9) in Seebrugg, about a five minute walk from the Seebrugg train station. B&B in either hostel is DM23/28 for juniors/seniors, plus Kurtaxe.

As you'd expect, the whole gamut of accommodation from top resorts to simple **private rooms** (from DM22 per person) is available along the Schluchsee. The tourist office can help you wade through the bewildering number of choices at no charge.

Among the less expensive places is **Pension am See** (☎ 513, Im Wolfsgrund 1), which charges DM32/64 for single/double rooms. **Haus Pfrommer** (☎ 867, Hinterer Giersbühlweg 4), where the rooms contain nicely painted furniture, charges the same. A bit more upmarket is **Pension Simone** (☎ 420, Dresselbacher Strasse 17), which charges DM57/114 for rooms with balcony. All prices are for rooms with full baths.

Good restaurants are at **Hotel Sternen** (Dresselbacher Strasse 1) and at **Hotel Haldenhof** on the same street at No 11, as well as at **Hotel Schiff** (Kirchplatz 7). If you're hiking or biking on the western lakeshore, stop in at the **Vesperstube**, a rustic – and solar-powered – restaurant with hearty and filling food.

Getting There & Away
Bus No 7257 makes regular trips to/from Titisee-Neustadt, though it's probably more convenient to take the Dreiseenbahn train, with hourly service between Titisee and Seebrugg. From the south, Seebrugg is also served by bus No 7319 to/from St Blasien. To get to the Wutach Gorge, take bus No 7343 to Bonndorf.

Schluchsee is on the B500, which hooks up with the B31 in Titisee.

Getting Around
Bicycles are available for rent at Haus Süsser Winkel (☎ 206) at Faulenfürster Strasse 4 in Schluchsee town. The tourist office has a map with bike trails available for DM3.

In season, G Isele (☎ 449) offers boat service around the Schluchsee, departing up to eight times daily with stops in Aha, at the dam (Staumauer), in Seebrugg and in Schluchsee town. You can get on and off as you please; the whole round trip takes one hour and costs DM9 (less for single stops).

ST BLASIEN
☎ 07672 • pop 4200
St Blasien is a health resort at the southern foot of the Feldberg, about 8km south of Schluchsee town. Despite its dwarfish size, St Blasien has been a political and cultural

giant in this region throughout its 1000-year history. This is reflected in its almost urban appearance and flair that's hardly typical of the Black Forest.

St Blasien's power was anchored in its Benedictine monastery, founded in the 9th century, whose influence reached its zenith in the 18th century under the prince-abbot Martin Gerbert. He was the one responsible for St Blasien's outstanding landmark, the magnificent Dom. After secularisation in 1806, the monastery did time as an ammunition then weaving factory before being turned into a boarding school by the Jesuits in 1933. Today, it ranks as one of Germany's top private schools.

Thanks to its healthy, fogless climate, St Blasien has also been a popular spa resort since the late 19th century. In winter, it offers a small range of cross-country skiing tracks and ski lifts. The community of Menzenschwand (area code ☎ 07675), about 8km to the north-west, is now a part of St Blasien.

Orientation & Information

The Dom and former monastery complex dominate St Blasien's small centre. Bus No 7321 shuttles between here and Menzenschwand. The tourist office (☎ 414 30, fax 414 38) is at Am Kurgarten 1-3. Opening hours are weekdays from 9 am to noon and 2 to 5 pm, and Saturday from 10 am to noon. The tourist office in Menzenschwand (☎ 07675-930 90, fax 17 09) is in the Rathaus at Hinterdorfstrasse 15 (same hours). The daily Kurtaxe is DM2.60.

There's a Sparkasse in St Blasien at Bernau-Menzenschwander Strasse 1, with the post office on the same road at No 5.

Dom St Blasien

The massive cathedral crowned by an enormous copper cupola seems oddly out of place in this remote town. It's an early masterpiece by French architect Pierre Michel d'Ixnard, who paved the way from the baroque period to neoclassicism. The former monastery complex surrounding the Dom is of equally generous proportions,

measuring 105m by 195m. The cupola has a diameter of 33.5m, making it the third largest in Europe after the Pantheon in Rome and the Église du Dôme, containing Napoleon's tomb, in Paris.

Having entered the Dom through a columned portico, you find yourself in a light-flooded rotunda of overwhelming symmetry and harmony. Twenty Corinthian columns support the cupola, whose massiveness is mitigated by 18 windows. The rectangular choir has the same length as the cupola's diameter. It's all bathed in white light.

Throughout the summer, the Dom is used as a venue for a series of free classical concerts. It's open to 6.30 pm between May and September and to 5.30 pm during the rest of the year.

Skiing

Positioned at the foot of the Feldberg, St Blasien and Menzenschwand provide access to seven ski lifts at elevations of 900 to 1400m. There are downhill runs rated for beginners to the more advanced, and about a dozen cross-country tracks. You can rent both types of ski at Sport Leber (☎ 504) in St Blasien, Skischule Gfrörer (☎ 733) at Albweg 11 and Wintersport Maier (☎ 498) at Vorderdorfstrasse 35, both in Menzenschwand. For up-to-date snow conditions, call ☎ 414 25.

Places to Stay & Eat

The *DJH hostel* (☎ 07675-326, fax 14 35, Vorderdorfstrasse 10) is in Menzenschwand in a gorgeous Black Forest farmhouse. It charges DM21/26 for juniors/seniors for B&B, plus Kurtaxe.

The tourist office can help find *private rooms* which cost from DM23 per person.

Pension Glatt (☎ 26 68, Klingnauer Strasse 2), in St Blasien, has rustic rooms for DM35 to DM55 per person. Roomy singles/doubles at *Hotel Klostermeisterhaus* (☎ 848, Im Süssen Winkel 2) in St Blasien, cost DM55/90.

A typical Black Forest guesthouse, not far from the ski lifts in Menzenschwand, is

Gasthof Birkenhof (☎ 10 79, Hinterdorfstrasse 25), which charges DM30/60. All prices in this section are for rooms with shower and WC.

Except for Pension Glatt, all hotels have a restaurant. In St Blasien you might also try the *Gasthaus Alter Hirschen (Hauptstrasse 39)*, closed Friday; and in Menzenschwand there's the *Hotel Sonnenhof (Vorderdorfstrasse 58)*. Both serve regional and standard German food, well priced daily specials and an inexpensive *Vesper* (supper) menu.

Getting There & Away

Train tracks into the Southern Black Forest terminate at Seebrugg, about 6km north of St Blasien. Seebrugg is reached on the *Dreiseenbahn* from Titisee (DM8.80, 25 minutes). The cross-country IR train from Norddeich in Friesland via Cologne, Mainz and Baden-Baden also terminates in Seebrugg.

From here, bus No 7319 provides an almost hourly connection to St Blasien (20 minutes). Bus No 7343 makes the trip from St Blasien to Bonndorf, the gateway to

---

More Things to Do in the Black Forest

If you have more time and you want to explore the Black Forest by car or on foot, there is a huge range of routes.

Scenic Roads Brochures on each of these drives are available from local tourist offices or from the Schwarzwald Tourismusverband (☎ 0761-313 17, fax 360 21), Bertoldstrasse 45, 79098 Freiburg im Breisgau.

- Schwarzwald-Täler-Strasse (Black Forest Valley Road) runs 100km through the Murg Valley from Rastatt to Alpirsbach in the Kinzig Valley
- Schwarzwald-Bäder-Strasse (Black Forest Spa Road) is a loop connecting all of the region's spa towns
- Badische Weinstrasse (Baden Wine Road) goes from Baden-Baden 160km south to Lörrach
- Deutsche Uhrenstrasse (German Clock Road) is a 320km loop starting in Villingen-Schwenningen
- Schwarzwald-Panoramastrasse (Black Forest Panorama Road) leads from Waldkirch to Hinterzarten over a stretch of 50km
- Grüne Strasse (Green Road) travels for 160km from the Vosges Mountains in France across the border as far as Titisee
- Schwarzwald-Hochstrasse (Black Forest Highway) connects Baden-Baden with Freudenstadt 60km to the south

Long-Distance Hikes Information on these and other hikes can be obtained from the Schwarzwaldverein (☎ 0761-38 05 30, fax 380 53 20), Bismarckallee 2a, 79098 Freiburg im Breisgau.

- Westweg: Pforzheim to Basel via Mummelsee, Hausach, Titisee, Feldberg; 280km, 12 days
- Mittelweg: Pforzheim to Waldshut via Freudenstadt, Schiltach, Schluchsee; 233km, nine days
- Ostweg: Pforzheim to Schaffhausen via Freudenstadt, Villingen; 239km, 10 days
- Querweg: Freiberg to Bodensee via Höllental, Wutachschlucht, Konstanz; 177km, eight days
- Querweg: Gengenbach to Alpirsbach; 50km, three days
- Querweg: Schwarzwald to Kaiserstuhl from Donaueschingen to Breisach; 110km, five days

the Wutach Gorge (see the following Wutachschlucht section).

St Blasien is on the B500, which crosses the B31 (Freiburg-Donaueschingen) in Titisee.

Getting Around

Use your own two feet to get about town; should you need a taxi, ring ☎ 90 70 90 in St Blasien. Mountain bikes can be rented for DM20 to DM25 a day from MTB Zentrum Kalle (☎ 10 74) at Grosse Bachwiesen 4 in Menzenschwand.

WUTACHSCHLUCHT

In a country as developed and densely populated as Germany, there are very few nature paradises left. The Wutach Gorge near Bonndorf, often billed as the 'Grand Canyon of the Black Forest' by tourist brochures, is one of them. It's a lovely ravine whose craggy rock faces make a near vertical rise skyward. Below lies a fertile habitat that harbours about 1200 types of wildflowers including orchids, rare birds like grey egrets, and countless species of butterflies, beetles and lizards.

Lined by ancient trees, the valley follows the flow of the 90km-long Wutach (loosely translated as 'angry river'), which originates as the placid Gutach (meaning 'good river') on the Feldberg at 1450m before flowing into the Rhine near Waldshut.

To appreciate the Wutach Gorge in all its splendour and complexity, you should take the 13km hike from the Schattenmühle in an easterly direction to the Wutachmühle (or vice versa). This can be accomplished in about 4½ hours. If you have the energy, add the 2.5km-long wildly romantic Lotenbach-Klamm (Lotenbach Glen) to your tour. The Bonndorf tourist office (☎ 07703-76 07, fax 75 07), Schlossstrasse 1, has maps and details about hiking in the Wutachschlucht.

To get to either trail head, take bus No 7344 from Bonndorf. The bus also stops in Boll, about 4km east of the Schattenmühle and 9km west of the Wutachmühle, which is a good place to end your hike if you don't want to walk the entire distance.

Bonndorf itself is served by buses from all directions. If you're coming from Neustadt, take bus No 7258 (40 minutes). From Donaueschingen, bus No 7260 travels to Bonndorf via the Wutachmühle (20 minutes). From St Blasien and the Schluchsee, bus No 7343 cuts west in about one hour.

If you're driving, take the B31 or B500 to Titisee, then the B315 in the direction of Bonndorf.

Lake Constance

Lake Constance (Bodensee) is a perfect cure for travellers stranded in landlocked southern Germany. Often jokingly called the 'Swabian Sea', this giant bulge in the sinewy course of the Rhine offers a choice of water sports, relaxation and cultural pursuits. It has a circumference of 273km, of which the southern 72km belong to Switzerland, the eastern 28km to Austria and the remaining northern and western 173km to Germany. It measures 14km at its widest point and 250m at its deepest level. The distance from Konstanz at its western end to Bregenz in the east is 46km. The snow-capped Swiss peaks provide a breathtaking backdrop when viewed from the German shore. During stormy weather, Lake Constance can get quite dangerous, with huge waves crashing onto the shores.

The Lake Constance region is popular with tourists and gets extremely crowded in July and August. It may be hard to find a room for the night, and drivers are bound to get very frustrated by the constantly choked roads. Be sure to call ahead to check on room availability, and be prepared to head into the hinterland to find a place to stay. The public transport system is well coordinated and a good alternative to the car.

April and May are among the best times to visit Lake Constance because that's when the fruit trees are flowering. Summers are humid, but at least the lake is warm enough for swimming (around 20° to 23°C), though the autumn wine harvest is also a pleasant

LAKE CONSTANCE (BODENSEE)

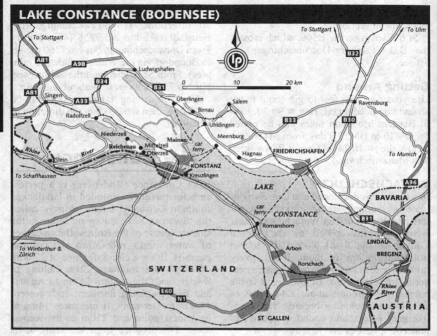

time to come. Winters are often foggy or misty at best.

Getting Around

Although most of the towns on Lake Constance have train stations (Meersburg is an exception), buses provide the easiest land connections. By car or motorbike, the B31 hugs the northern shore of Lake Constance, but it can get rather busy. By far the most enjoyable way to get around is on the ferries (☎ 07531-28 13 98) which, from March to early November, call several times a day at all the larger towns on the lake; there is a 50% discount for holders of most rail passes. The seven day Bodensee-Pass costs DM57 and gives two free days of travel plus five days at half price on all boats, buses, trains and mountain cableways on and around Lake Constance, including its Austrian and Swiss shores.

An international bike track circumnavigates Lake Constance, tracing the shoreline between vineyards and beaches. The route is well signposted, but Regio Cart's 1:50,000 *Rund um den Bodensee* cycling/hiking map (DM9.80) is useful and available at tourist offices.

KONSTANZ

☎ 07531 • pop 76,000

Konstanz (Constance) is the cultural and economic centre of the Bodensee. Bordering on Switzerland, it has an attractive location on a spit of land separating the Obersee (the main section of lake) from the Untersee. Its picturesque Altstadt never suffered through fire or war damage. Konstanz was first settled by the Romans and played a leading role in the Middle Ages when it was the centre of the Duchy of Swabia – whose territory included much of Central Europe – and was also the largest bishopric north of the Alps. The town reached its historical apex when the Council of Constance convened here from 1414 to 1418. The meeting chose a single pope (replacing three others), thereby healing the 'Great Schism' in the Catholic Church. This was the last great moment on the world stage for Konstanz, which then plunged into relative obscurity. The final blow came in 1821 when the bishopric – in existence for 1000 years – was dissolved and moved to Freiburg.

Today, Konstanz is a rather liberal town with little industry. About one in seven inhabitants – affectionately known as *Seehas* (sea hares) – is a student at the local university, which was founded only in 1966. Their presence is felt in a lively pub and restaurant scene that is unique in the otherwise rather staid region of Lake Constance.

Orientation & Information

Konstanz is bisected by the Rhine, which flows through a channel linking Obersee and Untersee, from where it continues its westward journey. On its left (south) bank is the Altstadt, where most sights are located, while the modern quarter is on the right (north) bank. Konstanz has a German and a Swiss train station adjacent to each other on Bahnhofplatz, on the eastern edge of the Altstadt next to the harbour. Most city buses and those bound for destinations in the countryside depart from here also.

Information

The tourist office (☎ 13 30 30, fax 13 30 60, email info@touristinformation.stadt .konstanz.de) is at Bahnhofplatz 13, about 150m to the right as you exit the train station. Between April and October, it's open weekdays from 9 am to 7 pm, and the rest of the year from 9 am to noon and 2 to 6 pm. From April to October, it's also open Saturday from 9 am to 4 pm and Sunday from 10 am to 1 pm.

If you're staying more than one night, your hotel or pension will give you the Gästekarte, which entitles you to unlimited bus rides and various discounts, for instance

at the island of Mainau. The daily resort tax is DM1.50 (April to October only).

In summer, the tourist office also sells the Konstanzer 2-Tages-Ticket (DM37) good for various boat rides, admission to Mainau, a guided city tour and an information package.

The Reisebank inside the train station is open weekdays from 8 am to 12.30 pm and 1.30 to 5.30 pm, Saturday from 8 am to 2.30 pm and Sunday to 12.30 pm. You can also change money at the ticket counter of the Swiss train station daily from 6 am to 8 pm.

The post office is opposite the German train station. The Internet cafe Schulze & Schulze, Pfauengasse 2, charges DM5 per 20 minutes of surfing.

The English Bookshop at Münzgasse 10 has a good selection. The Waschsalon is at Pfauengasse 2 and charges DM8 per load and DM6 for unlimited drying time.

For an ambulance, dial ☎ 192 22 or ☎ 07732-100 11 on weekends.

Harbour & Waterfront

To reach the harbour, take the passageway beneath the railway tracks just north of the tourist office. The imposing grey stone cube on your left is the Konzilgebäude (Council Building; 1388) that was a granary and warehouse before making its mark in history as the place where Pope Martin V was elected. It's a concert hall today.

On a perpetually turning pedestal over the lake, you'll see the newest Konstanz landmark, the Imperia, a sculpture of a scantily clad, voluptuous woman. Imperia was allegedly a prostitute who plied her trade in the days of the Council of Constance and was immortalised in a novel by Honoré de Balzac.

A few steps from here is the Zeppelin Monument, in honour of the airship inventor Count Ferdinand von Zeppelin. He was born in 1838 on the Insel, a tiny island a short stroll north through a small park. This handsome structure has housed a swanky hotel since 1875 but actually began life as a Dominican monastery in 1235. Just past the lobby is the former cloister with 19th century murals depicting the history of Konstanz.

Practically opposite the Insel is the **Theater**, whose facade sports a comical semi-relief showing the Fool's banishment from the theatre. The nearby **Rheinbrücke** links the Altstadt and Neustadt. Take a look across at Seestrasse on the opposite shore, with its row of handsome Art Nouveau villas. The one at No 21 houses the city **Casino**.

Münster
The Münster, where the Council of Constance held its sessions, sits on a slightly raised square marking the highest point in Konstanz's Altstadt. It's a showcase of architectural styles from nine centuries, starting with the original Carolingian church, built in 1000, which collapsed a mere 52 years later. Its reconstruction incorporated the original crypt beneath the choir that's decorated with large gilded copper medallions and – highly unusual for a crypt – bathed in muted daylight streaming in from a little window.

The new church in the Romanesque style still forms the core of today's structure. Between the 12th and 15th centuries, the Gothic vaulted side aisles, with their chains of chapels, were added, as were the masterfully carved oak main portal and choir stalls. The Renaissance brought the organ which perches on a stone balcony, while the high altar dates to the baroque era. The 19th century gave the church its neo-Gothic spires.

The Münster contains a number of treasures. A highlight is the **Schnegg** (literally 'snail'; 1438) in the northern transept, a vividly decorated spiral staircase. Exit left into the cloister to get to the **Mauritius Rotunda** with the 13th century **Heiliges Grab** (holy sepulchre), inspired by the one purportedly of Christ in Jerusalem. It's a crown-shaped, 12-sided stone structure festooned with highly emotional and artistic sculptures, including the apostles perched between each of the gables. Time and the elements have taken a toll on the Münster, which has not been without scaffolding since 1961.

Niederburg
Stretching north from the Münster to the Rhine, the Niederburg is the oldest quarter of Konstanz. The site of the original Roman settlement, it was later the quarter of the craftspeople and small merchants. An almost medieval atmosphere still permeates this maze of alleyways lined with centuries-old houses, some containing lovely antique stores, a snug wine bar or a lively restaurant.

At No 15 Brückengasse **Kloster Zoffingen**, founded in 1257 and still in the hands of Dominican nuns, is the only surviving convent in Konstanz. On the Rheinsteig, running parallel with the river, stands the 15th century **Rheintorturm**, a defensive tower whose upper section is covered by a mantle of wooden planks and topped by a steep tent roof. About 200m farther west is the **Pulverturm** (1321), with 2m-thick walls. Nearby in Rheingasse is the **Domprobstei** (1609), a red baroque structure that used to be the residence of the cathedral provosts.

Museums
At Rosgartenstrasse 5 stands the former guildhall of the butchers, now occupied by the **Rosgartenmuseum**, founded in 1871 and dedicated to regional art and history. The museum should have reopened after renovations by the time you read this; opening hours are Tuesday to Thursday from 10 am to 5 pm, and Friday to Sunday to 4 pm (DM3/1.50).

The **Archäologisches Landesmuseum** (Archaeological State Museum) is inside a former monastery at Benediktinerplatz 5, and has three floors filled with regional artefacts, models and reconstructions. It's open Tuesday to Sunday from 10 am to 6 pm (DM4/3).

Activities
Personenschiffahrt Wilfried Giess (☎ 811 01 75) offers one-hour cruises from the harbour landing docks daily in season between 10.30 am and 5.30 pm (DM9, kids DM4.50).

If you prefer to do your own pedalling, you can rent boats in the nearby Gondelhafen for DM8/14 per half-hour/hour.

Every Thursday at 7 pm between April and September wine tastings (DM13) take place at the Spitalkellerei (☎ 28 83 42) at Brückengasse 16. It's included in the guided city tour. A tour in English (DM10) takes place from May to September on Thursday at 10.30 am.

Places to Stay

Open from late March to September, *Campingplatz Klausenhorn* (☎ 63 72) is on the shore of the Überlinger See in the northern suburb of Dingelsdorf (take bus No 4 to Klausenhorn).

Other options are *Campingplatz Bruderhofer* (☎ 313 88, Fohrenbühlweg 50) and *Campingplatz Litzelstetten-Mainau* (☎ 94 30 30, Grossherzog-Friedrich-Strasse 43) in Konstanz-Litzelstetten, about a 20 minute walk to Mainau Island.

Konstanz's *DJH hostel* (☎ 322 60, fax 311 63, Zur Allmannshöhe 19) is pretty basic and located in a tower in the northern suburb of Allmannsdorf. From the train station, take bus No 4 to Jugendherberge or bus No 1 to Allmannsdorf-Post. The charge is DM22.50/26.50 for juniors/seniors.

The tourist office books accommodation for a DM5 fee (but the electronic booking board outside the front door is free).

Gasthaus Seeschau (☎ 51 90, fax 78 94, Zur Schifflände 11), in nearby Dingelsdorf, charges DM45/90 for no-frills singles/doubles.

Next up is *Gästehaus Holzer* (☎ 315 46, fax 321 24, Fischerstrasse 6), a pleasant little pension charging from DM70/110.

Sonnenhof (☎ 222 57, fax 203 58, Otto-Raggenbass-Strasse 3), right on the Swiss border, has a few shared-amenities rooms for DM75/85. Those with private bath will cost you from DM95/120.

The newly renovated *Hotel Gerda* (☎ 168 88, fax 226 03, Bodanstrasse 18), for nonsmokers only, has simple rooms for DM65/115 and some with full bath for DM125/195.

Decent value, if you can get one of the cheaper rooms, is the traditional *Hotel Barbarossa* (☎ 220 21, fax 276 30, Obermarkt 8-12), which asks DM70/160 for rooms with shower and WC.

Steigenberger Inselhotel (☎ 12 50, fax 264 02, Auf der Insel 1) is the town's major blow-out hotel, with cushy singles/doubles from DM190/300.

Places to Eat

The *Seekuh* (☎ 272 32, Konzilstrasse 1) is a relaxed student bar with black, white and red decor and a beer garden, serving up salads, pasta and pizza for around DM11. There's occasional live music.

Sedir (☎ 293 52, Hofhalde 11) is a lively Turkish restaurant with Turkish pizza, super salads and spiced noodle casseroles for under DM10.

The *Picco Palace* (☎ 202 90, Konradigasse 1) has good Indian cuisine, pizzas from DM3.50 and a range of vegie dishes. There's a takeaway window, too.

Pan (☎ 254 27), at the corner of Salmannsweiler and Hohenhausgasse, is a popular Greek restaurant that has preserved the beer hall look of its predecessor.

Brauhaus Johann Albrecht (☎ 250 45, Konradigasse 2) is a rambling beer hall with a rustic menu featuring daily specials and main courses under DM20.

Entertainment

The *Niederburg-Weinstube* (☎ 297 17, Niederburggasse 7) is a rustic hole in the wall with lots of regional wines. The locals start sipping at midday with a Bretzel. The *Wessenberg* (☎ 91 96 64, Wessenbergstrasse 41) is the hottest new chi-chi pub, with a really cool bar and good food.

Other neat watering holes include the *Rheinterrasse* (☎ 560 93, Hallenbad) in a quasi-medieval swimming complex to the north on the riverbank, and *Steg 4* (☎ 174 28, Hafenhalle) in a revamped warehouse down on the south side of the harbour.

A great place for a beer and a chat – and an occasional jazz concert – is the *Blue Note* (☎ 265 33, Hofhalde 11). The *Salzbüchsle* (Salmannsweiler 26), one of the first student pubs in Konstanz, has a James Dean/Marilyn Monroe gallery gracing the walls.

The *Konstanz Stadttheater* (☎ 13 00 50, Konzilstrasse 11) performs a repertoire of classical and contemporary drama and comedies. About 10% of the local casino's profits are earmarked for the theatre.

Getting There & Away

If you're going to Switzerland, the Thurgauer Tagesgarte day pass covers all bus, train, and boat links in the triangular zone Constance/St Gallen/Schaffhausen for DM27. It also includes the ferry from Romanshorn on the Swiss side over to Friedrichshafen in Germany.

Train Konstanz is connected to Frankfurt-am-Main (DM109, 4½ hours) by IR train every two hours. It is also the southern terminus of the scenic Schwarzwaldbahn, which travels hourly through the Black Forest to Offenburg.

To get to towns on the northern shore of Lake Constance – Salem, Friedrichshafen, Lindau – you must change in Singen, which is also where you catch the hourly Gäubahn to Stuttgart (DM56, 2½ hours).

Bus Bus No 7394 provides express service on weekdays to Meersburg (35 minutes) and Friedrichshafen (70 minutes). Bus No 7372 goes to the island of Reichenau (20 minutes) from outside the Swiss train station.

Car & Motorcycle Konstanz is reached via the B33, which connects with the A81 to/from Stuttgart in Singen. (See the following Boat section for the car ferry to Meersburg.)

Ride Services There's a Mitfahrzentrale (☎ 214 44) at Münzgasse 22.

Boat Between March and early November, Weisse Flotte (☎ 28 13 98) offers several departures daily between Konstanz and Bregenz (Austria) at the east end of Lake Constance (DM20.80). Boats stop at Meersburg (DM5.20, 30 minutes), Friedrichshafen (DM12, 1¾ hours), Lindau (DM18.80, 3¼ hours) and smaller towns in between. A second ferry headed for Überlingen (DM10.80, 1½ hours) travels also via Mainau and Meersburg.

The Schweizerische Schiffahrtsgesellschaft Untersee und Rhein (☎ 004152-625 42 82) offers service to Schaffhausen, Switzerland, and its Rhine Falls, Europe's largest waterfalls (DM36.50 return, 3½ hours) via Reichenau Island and Stein am Rhein. Boats leave from the harbour.

The frequent car ferry to Meersburg is the best bet to the north shore. Cars cost DM9.50 to DM14.50, plus DM2.20 per person. Bicycles are DM1.50 and motorcycles DM3. Boats leave from the landing docks in the north-eastern suburb of Staad.

Getting Around

Single tickets on SBG buses around town cost DM2.40. Day passes are DM7 (DM13 including the Swiss RAB network), covering two adults and up to four kids after 9 am. For a taxi, ring ☎ 222 22.

Touring and trekking bicycles may be rented from Kultur-Rädle (☎ 273 10), Blarerstrasse 19, for DM17 a day. There's also ProVelo (☎ 293 29), Konzilstrasse 3, right near the Waschsalon.

AROUND KONSTANZ
Mainau Island

Mainau is one of the finest attractions in the Lake Constance region and is something of a surprise. What was initially the island compound for the large Schloss of the Knights of the Teutonic Order has been transformed into a vast Mediterranean garden complex by the Bernadotte family, which is related to the royal house of Sweden. The current landowner, Count Lennart, has worked for more than 50 years to refurbish the island, which takes its name from the German *Maienaue* (May meadow).

More than two million visitors a year make their way over a narrow causeway to stroll around 45 hectares of splendid gardens and arboretums, visit the baroque church or attend special events and concerts. To avoid the crush, it's a good idea to arrive early in the day or in late afternoon.

The **Tropical Garden** is a lush hothouse brimming with banana trees, bamboo, orchids and other exotic flowers. The **Italian**

Cascade integrates bursting patterns of flowers with waterfalls and makes for a lovely photograph. The newly added **Butterfly House** is another highlight: you walk through a network of bridges and small canals while butterflies of the world flit and dart obliviously around your head.

Between mid-March and early November, Mainau (☎ 07531-30 30) is open daily from 7 am, with access until 8 pm (you can stay later if you want). Admission is DM18/9. In winter, opening hours are 9 am to 5 pm and admission is free (but you pay DM2 to DM9 for individual attractions).

Reichenau Island
☎ 07534 • pop 3300

In 724, a hard-working missionary named Pirmin founded a Benedictine monastery on Reichenau, the largest island (4.5km by 1.5km) in Lake Constance, located in the Untersee section about 12km west of Konstanz. Pirmin soon moved on to found other monasteries in the Upper Rhine area, but the abbots and monks he left behind ensured that, by the end of the 8th century, Reichenau had become a prominent cultural and artistic centre in south-west Germany. During its heyday from around 820 to 1050, it had more than 100 monks and one of the largest libraries anywhere. The so-called Reichenauer School of Painting produced stunning illuminated manuscripts and vivid frescoes.

Decline set in along with church reforms in the high Middle Ages, and the monastery's prime was essentially over by 1200, though it wasn't dissolved until 1757. Of its many buildings scattered across the island, three surviving churches provide silent testimony to the Golden Age of Reichenau. Today, about two-thirds of the island is taken up by vegetable cultivation, the prime source of income for the islanders. A 2km-long causeway connects the island with the mainland.

Getting There & Away The best way to get to and around Reichenau from Konstanz is by taking bus No 7372. Buses leave from the Swiss train station. Reichenau is a stop

on the Schwarzwaldbahn train, but the station is just off the island. The ferries from Konstanz to Schaffhausen and from Konstanz to Radolfzell also travel via Reichenau.

MEERSBURG
☎ 07532 • pop 5200

Meersburg is a picture-book romantic village, scenically perched on a rocky plateau overlooking Lake Constance and surrounded by vineyards and orchards. Its historic Oberstadt (upper town) has a labyrinth of narrow, car-free lanes that are lined by gorgeous red-tiled, half-timbered houses and stately baroque buildings. There are two castles, the Altes and the Neues Schloss (Old and New Palace), which lord over the bustling Unterstadt, the much more touristy section with a pretty promenade and plane trees.

Located 17km west of Friedrichshafen and reached by ferry from Konstanz, Meersburg makes for an extremely popular day excursion, and in July and August its tiny alleys are choked with visitors. If you're travelling in those months, try to show up early or late in the day to catch some of Meersburg's magic.

Orientation & Information

A steep vineyard separates the Oberstadt from the Unterstadt, and there's a scenic set of steps connecting the two (enter between the Altes and Neues Schloss). The northern boundary of the old part of the Oberstadt is the B33, here called Stettener Strasse.

Meersburg's tourist office (☎ 43 11 10, fax 43 11 20, email info@meersburg.de) is at Kirchstrasse 4 in the Oberstadt. Hours are weekdays from 9 am to noon and 2 to 6.30 pm. Between May and September, it's open Saturday from 10 am to 2 pm. Here you can pick up the useful *Rad-Urlaub* bike tour map for just DM2.50. The daily Kurtaxe is DM1.50.

The Volksbank on Marktplatz exchanges money and has an ATM that accepts credit cards. The post office is at Am Bleicheplatz, just north of Stettener Strasse. Unless noted otherwise, museums in Meersburg are closed between November and March.

Altes Schloss

Meersburg's landmark is the Altes Schloss, overlooking Lake Constance from its lofty Oberstadt perch. Its origin supposedly goes back to the 7th century Merovingian king Dagobert I, after whom the massive central keep is named. Between 1268 and 1803, the bishops of Konstanz used the castle as a summer residence before moving in permanently in 1526, after the Reformation.

The place was purchased in 1838 by Baron Joseph von Lassberg, who turned the castle into something of an artists' colony. His sister-in-law, the celebrated German poet Annette von Droste-Hülshoff (1797-1848), resided here for many years, and the Brothers Grimm and Ludwig Uhland were among those who also flocked to Meersburg.

The Altes Schloss is your quintessential medieval castle, complete with defensive walkways, knights' hall, moats, dungeons and subterranean tunnels. On a self-guided tour (English pamphlet available) you'll see the usual collection of furniture and arms and armoury but also a frightful 9m-deep prison hole for which the condemned only got a one-way ticket. You'll also pass through Droste-Hülshoff's living quarters, primly furnished in Biedermeier style.

The castle is open daily year round from 9 am to 6.30 pm (in winter 10 am to 6 pm), and admission is a rather steep DM9/8/5.50 for adults/students/children.

Neues Schloss

In 1710, the prince-bishop Johann Franz Schenk von Stauffenberg determined that the Altes Schloss was no longer suitable to meet the representational needs of his exalted office and began building the Neues Schloss on the terrace east of the old castle.

Construction continued under his successor, Damian Hugo von Schönborn, who added the impressive staircase designed by Balthasar Neumann (1741), the chapel with stucco by Joseph Anton Feuchtmayer, and frescoes by Gottfried Bernhard Göz (1743). The pink baroque palace was finally completed in the late 18th century, only a few years before the Grand Duchy of Baden gained its possession through secularisation.

Now state-owned, the palace houses the **Municipal Gallery** with changing exhibits. On the 1st floor is the very interesting **Dornier Museum** dedicated to Claude Dornier, the inventor of the seaplane.

The museums are open daily from 10 am to 1 pm and 2 to 6 pm (DM5/4).

Other Museums

Tiny Meersburg has an astonishing wealth of museums outside the two castles, including the **Deutsches Zeitungsmuseum** (☎ 71 58) at Schlossplatz 13, whose three floors trace the history of German newspapers. It's open daily from 11 am to 5 pm (DM3.50/3).

To learn more about Annette von Droste-Hülshoff, you should visit the exhibit in the **Fürstenhäusle** in Stettener Strasse 9. The poet bought this little garden house with the income from her first collection of poems. Though she never actually lived here, she frequently visited it for inspiration. It's open daily from 10 am to 12.30 pm and 2 to 5 pm, but is closed Sunday morning (DM5/3.50). By the way, you'll see Droste-Hülshoff's portrait, along with several Meersburg landmarks, on the DM20 note.

At Vorburgstrasse 11 is the diminutive but interesting **Weinmuseum**; it's open Tuesday, Friday and Sunday from 2 to 5 pm (DM1). Here you can see historical wine casks, including a giant one that holds more than 50,000L. There's also a wine press from 1607 that remained functional until the 1930s, plus lots of wine-making tools. Tastings take place here on Friday at 7 pm (DM15/13).

Places to Stay

The nearest camping grounds are in and around Hagnau, 4km east of Meersburg: *Camping Schloss Kirchberg* (☎ 07545-64 13), *Camping Seeblick* (☎ 07532-56 20) and *Camping Alpenblick* (☎ 72 10). The nearest *DJH hostels* are in Konstanz and Friedrichshafen (see Places to Stay in the relevant sections).

The tourist office can book *private rooms* from DM35 per person and up, free of charge.

The cheapest rooms are outside the Altstadt. Dive into the *Pension Santisblick (☎ 92 77, fax 15 35, Von-Lassberg-Strasse 1)*, which has simple singles/doubles for DM40/80 and also houses the Bodensee Scuba School.

The *Ferienhof Mohr (☎ 65 72, fax 41 42 05, Stettener Strasse 57)* charges DM60/90. At the *Gasthaus zum Letzten Heller (☎ 61 49, Daisendorfer Strasse 41)*, which also has a popular restaurant, rooms are DM48/95.

If you want to stay in a classic place, try the historical *Gasthof zum Bären (☎ 432 20, fax 43 22 44, Markt 11)* in the Oberstadt, whose traditionally furnished, comfortable rooms start at DM80/120.

All prices listed above include breakfast and are for rooms with private bath.

Places to Eat

Almost all restaurants and cafes have a daily special priced under DM20, often including locally caught *Felchen* (salmon trout). For coffee and cake or a snack, there's the *Burgcafé (☎ 800 00, Altes Schloss)*, which also has a little terrace with fantastic views (closed Monday).

In the Oberstadt, the *Winzerstube zum Becher (☎ 90 09, Höllgasse)* has a classy chef who infuses traditional Baden dishes with an international flavour.

The *Bistro 3 Stuben (☎ 800 20, Kirchstrasse)*, opposite the tourist office, serves light bistro fare in a yuppie-inspired contemporary decor (DM15 to DM35; closed Tuesday). The *Restaurant 3 Stuben* in the same building (enter on Winzergasse) has extremely good food at outrageous prices (mains start at DM49).

Getting There & Away

Bus Lacking a train station, Meersburg relies on buses for connections with the outside world. On weekdays, express bus No 7394 makes the trip to Konstanz (45 minutes) and Friedrichshafen (30 minutes). The latter is also served more frequently (and on

weekends) by bus No 7395. To get to Salem, take bus No 7397. Bus No 7373 connects Meersburg with Ravensburg and Konstanz four times daily from Monday to Saturday (no service on Sunday).

Car & Motorcycle Meersburg is just south of the B31 and reached via Daisendorfer Strasse. In the Oberstadt, it merges with the B33, which begins in Meersburg and continues north-eastward to Ravensburg.

Boat From March to November, Meersburg is a stop on the Weisse Flotte boat service between Konstanz and Bregenz and Konstanz and Überlingen. Some boats travel via the island of Mainau. The car ferry to Konstanz operates day and night and is the fastest way across the lake. All boats leave from the ferry harbour in the Unterstadt (see Getting There & Away under Konstanz for more details).

Getting Around

The best – actually the only – way to get around Meersburg is on foot. Those with motorised wheels must park in a pay parking lot, but even these can be full in high season. For excursions, you can rent bicycles from DM9/day at Hermann Dreher (☎ 51 76), Stadtgraben 5.

AROUND MEERSBURG
Birnau

The rococo pilgrimage church of Birnau is one of the artistic highlights of the Lake Constance region and is a sight worth braving the hordes for. Sitting majestically on a bluff overlooking the lake and surrounded by lush orchards, it looks more like a palace than a church. It was built by Peter Thumb of Vorarlberg, master architect of the rococo, who also gave the world the abbey in St Peter (see that section) and many other churches in the region. He was joined by two other household names of the period, the stucco master Joseph Anton Feuchtmayer and the fresco painter Gottfried Bernhard Götz.

The impression upon entering the church is awe-inspiring, the decor being so intricate and profuse you don't know where to look first. Your gaze is drawn to the ceiling, where Göz worked his usual magic, and there are whimsical details such as the tiny mirror in the cupola fresco.

Birnau is on the B31 about 10km north of Meersburg between Uhldingen and Überlingen. Bus No 7395 from Friedrichshafen and Meersburg stops right at the church. Entry to the church is free.

Schloss Salem

The 7km-long Prälatenweg (Prelates' Path) connects the church at Birnau with its mother church, the former Cistercian abbey of Salem. Founded in 1137, it was the largest and richest monastery in southern Germany. The huge complex, now named Schloss Salem, became the property of the Grand Duchy of Baden after secularisation and is still the main residence of the family's descendants. The west wing is occupied by an elite boarding school that was briefly attended by Prince Philip (Duke of Edinburgh and husband of Queen Elizabeth II).

The focal point is the **Münster** (1414), with a Gothic purity that has been diluted by a high altar and 26 alabaster altars fashioned in an early neoclassical style. Of particular note are the study of Abbot Anselm II, with superb stucco ornamentation, and the **Kaisersaal**, which contains a bewilderingly detailed amount of sculpture and stucco.

The complex has been turned into something of a low-key amusement park, integrating museums, artisans' workshops, a golf driving range, gardens and various restaurants. Schloss Salem is open late March to October from 9 am to 6 pm (Sunday from 11 am). Admission is a steep DM21/12 (children under 16 free), but that includes guided tours, entry to all museums, a welcome glass of wine and more.

Bus No 7397 travels to Salem from Meersburg via Oberuhldingen. From Friedrichshafen, travellers can catch bus No 7396 or the Bodensee-Gürtelbahn train, with departures roughly every 30 minutes.

FRIEDRICHSHAFEN

☎ 07541 • pop 56,400

Friedrichshafen is surely one of Germany's nicer industrial towns, stretched out for 11km along a placid bay of Lake Constance. Its name will forever be associated with the Zeppelin airships, first built here under the stewardship of Count Ferdinand von Zeppelin at the turn of last century.

It's a relatively young town, formed only in 1811 when King Friedrich of Württemberg merged the former imperial city of Buchhorn with the priory of Hofen. In WWII it was blown to smithereens and therefore has little in the way of historical sights. The extraordinary Zeppelin Museum, however, shouldn't be missed.

Orientation & Information

There are two train stations, the Hauptbahnhof and the better-connected Stadtbahnhof. The bus station is outside the Stadtbahnhof. The lakeside is a few metres south across Friedrichstrasse; its promenade is called Uferstrasse until the Gondelhafen, and then Seestrasse (where it culminates in the Zeppelin Museum).

The tourist office (☎ 300 10, fax 725 88, email tourist-infofriedrichshafen@t-online .de) is right outside the Stadtbahnhof and open weekdays from 9 am to noon and 2 to 5 pm (to noon on Friday in winter) and Saturday from 10 am to 2 pm (summer only). If it's closed, information may also be picked up at the Schulmuseum at Friedrichstrasse 14, about a five minute walk west of the station.

The Sparkasse on Seestrasse opposite the Zeppelin Museum exchanges currency and has an ATM that accepts credit cards. The post office is immediately to the right as you exit the Stadtbahnhof.

The self-service City Wash laundrette, Schwabstrasse 16, is open daily from 8 am to 11 pm.

Zeppelin Museum

At the eastern end of Friedrichshafen's pleasant, cafe-lined promenade you'll find the town's top tourist attraction. Inaugurated in

Legacy of the Zeppelin

Like many before him, Count Zeppelin (1838-1917) was obsessed with the idea of flying. With his vision and determination, he contributed significantly to the development of modern aircraft when the first Zeppelin made its inaugural flight over Lake Constance in 1900.

Unlike today's non-rigid airships (such as the Goodyear blimp), Zeppelins had an aluminium framework covered by a cotton-linen fairing. The cigar-shaped behemoths were soon used for passenger flights, outfitted as luxuriously and comfortably as ocean liners. The most famous of them all, the *Graf Zeppelin*, made 590 trips, including 114 across the Atlantic and, in 1929, travelled around the world in only 21 days.

The largest airship ever built was the 245m-long *Hindenburg*, which was destroyed in a terrible accident – or possible act of sabotage – while landing in Lakehurst, New Jersey, in 1937, killing 36 passengers and crew. Over 60 years later, several German firms are planning to revive the blimps as luxury liners and cargo carriers – held aloft this time by helium, rather than flammable hydrogen.

1996 in the reconstructed Hafenbahnhof, exactly 96 years after the first Zeppelin airship was launched, the museum is built around a full-scale (33m-long) recreated section of the *Hindenburg*, at 245m the largest airship ever. You can walk through its reconstructed passenger rooms and examine the filigree of the aluminium framework.

Exhibits, interactive information terminals (in German and English) and a series of short movies provide technical and historical insights. The top floor contains an eclectic collection of art. The museum is open from Tuesday to Sunday from 10 am to 6 pm, and to 5 pm in winter (DM12/6).

Schlosskirche

The western end of the promenade is anchored by the twin onion-domed, baroque Schlosskirche, built between 1695 and 1701 by Christian Thumb. It's the only accessible part of the Schloss, still inhabited by the ducal family of Württemberg. The lavish stucco ceiling was destroyed in WWII but recreated in 1950 by Joseph Schnitzer (*Schnitzer* means 'carver'). Also note the vividly carved choir stalls, whose end pieces represent, clockwise from the front left, Moses, St Benedict, an abbot and King David. The church is open from mid-April to the end of October daily from 9 am to 6 pm.

Activities

Friedrichshafen is an ideal base for cycling tours of Lake Constance. The tourist office has put together a well designed and useful folder (DM9.80), outlining 20 day trips with detailed map and sightseeing information (though in German only).

For excursions on the lake, you can rent motorboats (DM45 an hour for up to four people) as well as pedal and rowing boats (DM14 for up to two people) from the rental office at the Gondelhafen.

Places to Stay

Campingplatz Fischbach (☎ 420 59, *Meersburger Strasse)* operates on a first-come, first-served basis in the suburb of Fischbach. It charges DM7/8.50/3 per tent/person/car. The slightly cheaper private *Campingplatz Dimmler* (☎ 734 21, *Lindauer Strasse 20)* is east of the centre.

Immediately opposite, the *DJH hostel* (☎ 724 04, fax 749 86, *Lindauer Strasse 3)* charges DM24.90/29.50 for juniors/ seniors (bus No 7587 from the Stadtbahnhof). It's often full, especially in summer, so be sure to call ahead.

The tourist office has a room reservation service (DM5 fee for walk-ins). Also call ☎ 194 12 at any time of day. There's also a free automated booking terminal outside the office.

One of the cheapest places in town is *Gasthof Rebstock* (☎ 216 94, fax 215 73, *Werastrasse 35)*, which charges DM60/95 for singles/doubles with shared facilities and DM80/120 for rooms with private bath. *Hotel*

Schöllhorn (☎ 218 16, fax 330 60, Friedrich-strasse 65) asks DM50/90 or DM75/120 for similar quarters.

At **Hotel-Restaurant Knoblauch** (☎ 60 70, fax 60 72 22, Jettenhauser Strasse 30-32), rooms with full bath start at DM90/140. One of the top places in the centre is **Ringhotel Buchhorner Hof** (☎ 20 50, fax 326 63, email robert_baur@t-online.de, Friedrich-strasse 33), which will set you back up to DM200/300.

Places to Eat

Numerous cafes, snack bars and restaurants line the Seestrasse promenade.

Naturkost (Buchhornplatz 1), opposite the Zeppelin museum, offers a huge range of street snacks, including spinach pastry pockets for DM4.90 and grain burgers from just DM2. **Weber & Weiss** is an upmarket bakery with delectable pastries that go well with a cappuccino (DM2.50) from its stand-up cafe. It's at Wilhelmstrasse 23 and Char-lottenstrasse 11.

For Swabian specialities around DM15 and fish and meat dishes for DM20 and up, you could try **Old City** (☎ 70 50, Schanzstrasse 7) on the 1st floor of the Hotel City Krone.

The **Hotel Goldenes Rad** (☎ 28 50, Karl-strasse 43) has solid regional fare and a pleas-ant terrace for dining, with fish dishes from DM21 and meat and poultry from DM23.

Gourmet international cuisine with prices to match is served at the restaurant of the **Buchhorner Hof** (see Places to Stay).

Entertainment

The tourist office publishes a free monthly events schedule and also has copies of the biweekly Kultur-Blätter covering the entire Lake Constance area. For performance art, live music and cultural events of all sorts, there's the **Kulturhaus Caserne** (☎ 37 16 61, Fallenbrunnen 17) and the **Bahnhof Fischbach** (☎ 442 26, Eisenbahnstrasse 15) in an old train station.

Getting There & Away

Train Friedrichshafen is a stop on the Bodensee-Gürtelbahn between Singen and Lindau, and the Südbahn, which goes to Ulm (DM35, 1¾ hours) via Bad Schüssen-ried and Ravensburg (DM12.20, 45 min-utes) and to Lindau (DM7.60, 20 minutes).

Bus On weekdays, a fast way to get to Konstanz, via Meersburg, is on the express bus No 7394 (70 minutes). For local ser-vice to Meersburg and on to Birnau, take bus No 7395. Bus No 7395 makes the trip to Salem in 45 minutes.

Car & Motorcycle Friedrichshafen is on the B31 along the northern lake shore and is also the starting point of the B30 to Ravensburg.

Boat Friedrichshafen is a regular stop on the Konstanz-Bregenz route of the Weisse Flotte. See Getting There & Away under Konstanz for details.

Friedrichshafen is also the springboard for the car ferry (☎ 192 22) to Roman-shorn in Switzerland, the fastest way to get across the lake. Service is year round, with departures about every hour between 5.30 am and 9.30 pm. The trip takes 45 minutes and costs DM9.40 per person, DM4.70 for children under 16. Bicycles cost DM7, motorcycles DM21 (including driver) and cars DM36 to DM48 (includ-ing two people).

Getting Around

The town is compact and easy to get around on foot. Bikes can be rented at the Stadt-bahnhof (☎ 20 13 85) or from Sterzai Bikes (☎ 212 71), Paulinerstrasse 7. Expect to pay from DM10 to DM14 a day.

RAVENSBURG

☎ 0751 • pop 50,000

Half an hour's drive north of Lake Con-stance, Ravensburg was a Free Imperial City in medieval times and became exceedingly rich from the linen trade. It was also one of the first German cities to mass-produce paper, an industry that would later spawn the Ravensburg publishing house. Spared in the Thirty Years' War, Ravensburg still bears the hallmarks of past glories but bills itself nowadays as a regional shopping hub.

Orientation & Information
The train station and post office are at the western end of the city, a five minute walk down Eisenbahnstrasse to Marienplatz, the heart of the Altstadt. The hostel is at the south-eastern end of the Altstadt, perched on a hill top near the Mehlsack tower.

The tourist office (☎ 823 24, fax 824 66, email stadt.ravensburg@t-online.de) is in the Weingartner Hof building, Kirchstrasse 16, just east of Marienplatz. It's open Monday from 8 am to noon, Tuesday to Friday from 8 am to noon and 2 to 5.30 pm, and Saturday from 9 am to noon. Free walking tours in German run from 2 to 3.30 pm every Saturday, leaving from Holzmarkt.

W4 (☎ 342 59), Rossbachstrasse 8, is an Internet cafe that charges DM6 for a half hour's surfing. Buy English-language books and maps at Ravensbuch, Marienplatz 34.

Things to See & Do
The central **Marienplatz** is the site of a bustling market on Saturday mornings. At the western end of the square stands the **Lederhaus**, a 16th century domain of tanners and shoemakers that has an outrageous Renaissance facade. The teeny Flattbac River gurgles through a canal on the north side of the square, which is dominated by the stepped gable of the late-Gothic **Gewandhaus** and the impressive **Blaserturm**, part of the original city fortifications. The **Rathaus** doesn't look like much from the front, but the northern side is full of stained glass.

Ravensburger Publishing is one of Germany's largest manufacturers of board games. Its **Toy Museum** has an exquisite baroque door and shining brasswork; it's open Thursday from 2 to 6 pm (free).

The 41m-high Gothic **Obertor** in the south-east of the city is a sight, but it's overshadowed by the 51m-high **Mehlsack** (Flour Sack), the city's tallest tower, so named for its white, bulky form. You can climb the tower (free) from 10 am to noon every third Sunday between March and October (except in July).

To the north is the **Grünes Tor** (Green Tower), with its intricate tiled roof, and the weighty late-Gothic **Liebfrauenkirche**. The tower was constructed as a defence against soldiers who invaded from the hill-top **Veitsburg**, the 11th century castle believed to be the birthplace of Heinrich der Löwe. Nowadays it houses the hostel and a chic restaurant.

Places to Stay & Eat
DJH Jugendherberge (☎ 253 63, fax 137 69, Veitsburg Castle) is a rather severe place despite the stunning views. Check-in is from 5 pm, there's a 10 pm curfew and shower access is limited. Dorm beds cost DM22/23 for juniors/seniors.

The *Hotel Residenz (☎ 369 80, fax 36 98 50, Herrenstrasse 16)* has fine historic rooms, good service and great prices: simple singles/doubles cost from DM46/74. In its Weinstube you can sample Ravensburger tipple: the hotel owner runs the sole wine estate in the area.

Hotel Garni Bauer (☎ 256 16, fax 132 29, Marienplatz 1) is central and has very reasonable rooms from DM60/120. *Obertor Hotel (☎ 366 70, fax 366 72 00, Markstrasse 67)* right next to the tower, has well worn but comfy quarters from DM94/170.

For a quick bite, try the *Ravensburger Kebap Stube (☎ 35 31 28, Marktstrasse 14)*, with doner kebab and vegetarian sandwiches for DM5. *Tom's Elefant (☎ 269 63, Kirchstrasse 21)* has good Thai food, three-course lunches for DM12.50 and a popular streetside cafe.

Humpis-Stuben (☎ 256 98, Marktstrasse 47) is an earthy pub-eatery with organic food, schnitzels and Swabian dishes, all for DM15 or less. A trendier option is *Barbarossa (☎ 248 68, Rosenstrasse 4)*, a bistro that offers breakfast from DM7.50, tapas platters for DM9 and pastas from DM7.50.

Getting There & Away
Trains leave hourly for Stuttgart (DM49, two hours), via Ulm (DM22.40, one hour). From Markdorf, near Meersburg, trains run hourly (DM7.60, 40 minutes); from Friedrichshafen the ride takes 20 minutes and costs DM5.80.

LINDAU

☎ 08382 • pop 24,000

Lindau hugs a picturesque little island in the north-eastern corner of Lake Constance. It occupies the only snippet of Bavarian coastline on the entire lake, although you probably won't see any *Lederhosen*-clad visitors here. The town enjoyed a heady prosperity in the Middle Ages thanks primarily to its spot on a major north-south trading route. In the early 13th century is was made a free imperial city.

The place exudes old-world wealth and romance, and its superb views across to the Alps are worth a thousand postcards. Since 1951, annual Nobel-Prize winners and their colleagues have met in Lindau to promote scientific ideas, rub elbows and book the region's hotels solid at the end of June.

Orientation & Information

You'll find the train and bus stations, as well as a large pay car park, on the western side of the island; the harbour and its lovely promenade is to the south. Numerous suburbs line the mainland, and the Hauptbahnhof may have relocated there by the time you read this (supposedly to improve Lindau's rail links). The heart of the Altstadt is the east-west pedestrian **Maximilianstrasse**, lined by statuesque town houses.

The Lindau tourist office (☎ 26 00 30, fax 26 00 26, email tourist-information.lindau@ t-online.de) is at Ludwigstrasse 68 opposite the station. From May to September, it's open weekdays from 9 am to 1 pm and from 2 to 6 pm (to 7 pm in June and August), and Saturday from 9 am to 1 pm. The rest of the year it's open weekdays from 9 am to 5 pm, with a noon lunch break.

There's a Volksbank with an ATM and currency-exchange machine at the junction of Maximilianstrasse and Zeppelinstrasse. The post office, with a Postbank, is on the corner of Maximilianstrasse and Bahnhofplatz. You can surf the Web at B@boo's Internet Cafe (☎ 94 27 67), Dammsteggasse 4, for DM3 per 10 minutes or DM6.50 per half hour. It's open weekdays from 2 pm to 1 am, and weekends from noon to 1 am.

Altstadt

The Markt, in the north-east of the island, is dominated by the **Haus zum Cavazzen** (1730), a beautiful baroque construction with murals that appear three-dimensional. It contains the attractive **Stadtmuseum** with a fine collection of furniture and mechanical instruments, among other exhibits. Visits are by tour only, from Tuesday to Sunday at 3 and 4.15 pm (DM5/3).

Even more impressive are the frescoes of the Passion of Christ, painted by Hans Holbein the Elder, inside the former **Peterskirche** (St Peter's Church; circa 1000), now a war memorial.

Another visual highlight is the **Altes Rathaus** (1436), which has a stepped gable from the 16th century; the almost gaudy murals, however, were added only in 1975 and are based on 19th century designs. Alongside stands the **Diebstahlturm** (Brigand's Tower), a tiny jail once adjoining the town fortifications.

The **promenade** in summer offers an almost Mediterranean scene, with a sky bluer than blue, resort hotels and lots of well heeled tourists soaking up the sun. Out at the harbour gates you'll spot Lindau's signature **lighthouse** and on the other side – just in case you forget which state you're in – a pillar bearing the Bavarian lion. The squat **Mangturm**, the former lighthouse at the top of the sheltered port, offers a good view toward the Alps (DM2).

Places to Stay

Park-Camping Lindau am See (☎ 722 36, fax 97 61 06, Frauenhoferstrasse 20), on the water at the Austrian border, is a nice place with a coin-op laundry, supermarket and restaurant. Take bus Nos 1 or 2 to Anheggerstrasse, then bus No 3 to Leiblachstrasse.

The 240 bed *DJH hostel* (☎ 967 10, fax 96 71 50, Herbergsweg 11) is in a beautiful hotel-like complex charging DM28 for juniors/seniors. Take bus No 3 from Anheggerstrasse one stop east; remember to call to reserve first.

The *Gästehaus Lädine* (☎ 53 26, fax 15 80, In der Grub 25) is an understandably popular choice, at just DM45/80 for fully equipped singles/doubles.

The *Inselgraben* (☎ 234 37, fax 94 41 49, Hintere Metzgerstrasse 4-6) is a reasonable deal, charging DM65/100 for simple rooms and DM75/110 for ones with private facilities.

The family-run *Pension Noris* (☎ 960 85, fax 96 08 25, Brettermarkt 13) comes highly recommended, at DM60/120 for clean rooms with full bath.

Gasthof Engel (☎ 52 40, Schafgasse 4) offers quaint but well equipped rooms from DM85/140 and has a decent restaurant.

Hotel Bayerischer Hof (☎ 91 50, fax 91 55 91, email Bayerischer-Hof.Lindau@ t-online.de, Seepromenade) is the pride of the harbourfront and charges DM200/266.

All the listed hotels are on the island (rather than the mainland).

Places to Eat

The *Gasthaus zum Sünfzen* (☎ 58 65, Maximilianstrasse 1) is an island institution, with Swabian-Bavarian fare from DM15 under coffered ceilings and medieval vaults.

Alte Post (☎ 934 60, fax 93 46 46, Fischergasse 3) is the most atmospheric of local restaurants; every nook and cranny tells a story, and there's a huge regulars' table with the carved names of members. The food's excellent and affordable, too.

Café-Bistro Wintergarten (☎ 94 61 72, Salzgasse 5) has salads, pastas, vegie casseroles and more for DM8 to DM14 in an atrium-like chamber.

Landauer Hof (☎ 40 64, Seepromenade) has a great outside section (despite the canned kitsch music) at the east end of the harbour, with reasonably priced fish, steaks, pizzas, pastas and icecream.

For snacks try *Vinzenzmurr* (Maximilianstrasse 27), a butcher-deli with half-chickens for DM4 and other stand-up meals for under DM10. *Turkiyem* (Schafgasse 8) serves doners from DM4.50 and other takeaways.

Activities

There are 1½ hour organised tours in English on Monday at 10 am starting at the tourist office (DM6). Weisse Flotte offers a round-trip tour several times a day from Lindau harbour to Bregenz and the mouth of the Rhein (DM13, one hour).

Lindau is a paradise for sailing, windsurfing and water-skiing; the tourist office has a list of sports clubs and shops offering equipment rental and instruction. You can also rent row and paddleboats just west of the casino for DM10 to DM18 per hour.

Getting There & Away

Train Lindau has train connections to/from Friedrichshafen several times each hour (DM7.60, 20 to 30 minutes). It is the eastern terminus of the Bodensee-Gürtelbahn line to Singen and the southern terminus of the Südbahn to Ulm (DM35, 1¾ hours) via Ravensburg (DM12.20, 40 minutes). Bregenz is just 10 minutes away (DM3.80).

Car & Motorcycle Lindau is on the B31 and also connected to Munich by the A96. The scenic Deutsche Alpenstrasse (German Alpine Road), which winds eastward to Berchtesgaden, begins in Lindau.

Boat Weisse Flotte boats stop in Lindau several times daily between March and November on the route from Konstanz to Bregenz. For details, see Getting There & Away in the Konstanz section.

Getting Around

The island is tiny and perfect for walking. For buses to/from the mainland, singles cost DM2.50, a day pass is DM6 and a week pass is a great deal at just DM15.

There are a few metered car parks on the island, but the best bet is to park on the mainland and bus yourself over.

You can rent **bicycles** in the Hauptbahnhof (☎ 212 61) for DM13 to DM17 per day.

Lake Constance...

RHINELAND-PALATINATE

When French occupational forces patched together the state of Rhineland-Palatinate (Rheinland-Pfalz) after WWII from parts of Bavaria, Hesse and Prussia, they joined together territories and people that had never been under the same government. But they have one thing in common: the Rhine.

Europe's third largest river flows for 1320km from its source in the Swiss Alps to Rotterdam, but nowhere has it shaped the land and its people more than along the 290km stretch traversing the Rhineland-Palatinate. Here you'll find romanticism and industry intermingling to create the state's unique identity.

The headquarters of some of Europe's largest corporations, including the chemical giant BASF in Ludwigshafen, dominate the Rhine banks south of Mainz, the state capital. These firms have brought economic prosperity to the Rhineland-Palatinate, making it No 1 in the nation in exports. To find the state's great natural beauty – interspersed with legend and lore – that has drawn artists and tourists here since the 19th century, you have to travel north of Mainz to the Rhine Valley. Here, steep, vine-clad slopes guide the river's northward journey past turreted hill-top castles, snug wine villages and dense forests.

As the Rhine River flows through the Rhineland-Palatinate, so do Germany's rivers of wine. About two-thirds of all wine produced in Germany comes from one of the six growing regions here: the Ahr Valley; the Moselle-Saar-Ruwer; the Middle Rhine; the Nahe; the Rheinhessen; and the Rheinpfalz, with the German Wine Road (the latter being the only region not on a river). The local people's *joie de vivre* finds expression in the many wine festivals organised by the villages, however small they may be.

The Romans first brought grapevines with them when they established a number of settlements in this region in the early centuries AD. They left their legacy everywhere,

HIGHLIGHTS

Rhineland-Palatinate Luminaries: Hildegard von Bingen, Friedrich Engels, Johannes Gutenberg, Helmut Kohl, Karl Marx

- Travelling along the Romantic Rhine between Koblenz and Bingen
- Visiting Burg Eltz or the Marksburg, the ideal medieval castles
- Exploring Trier, with the best preserved Roman landmarks north of the Alps
- Drinking in the taverns of Bacharach, the quintessential wine town
- Admiring Kloster Eberbach, film set for *The Name of the Rose*, with its great architecture and wine
- Visiting the awe-inspiring Romanesque cathedrals at Mainz, Worms and Speyer

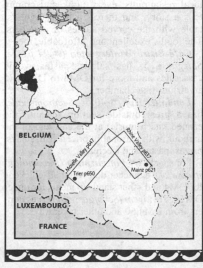

including in Bad Neuenahr-Ahrweiler on the Ahr River, Boppard and Bingen on the Rhine River and, above all, in Trier. Nowhere north of the Alps will you find more and better preserved Roman monuments than in this town on the Moselle.

The Middle Ages is represented by some of Germany's finest ecclesiastical architecture, most notably the magnificent trio of Romanesque cathedrals at Mainz, Worms and Speyer. This period also saw the construction of the popular Rhine castles.

Idealised today, their original purpose was anything but romantic. In fact, most of the castles were erected by a medieval Mafia of robber barons that extorted huge tolls from merchant ships by blocking their passage along the river with iron chains. Most of the castles were ruined by the passage of time and by French troops under Louis XIV during the War of the Palatine Succession in 1689. Some were restored in the 19th century.

Its gorgeous landscapes and innumerable attractions have been both a blessing and a

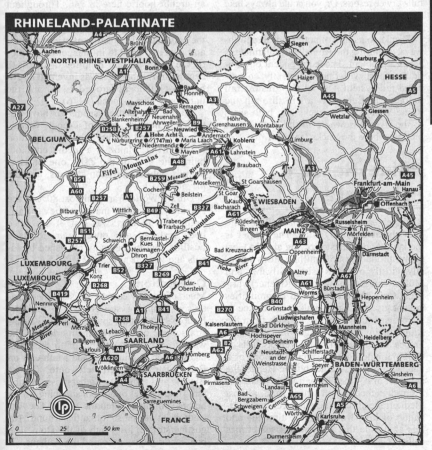

RHINELAND-PALATINATE

curse to the Rhineland-Palatinate. Mass tourism has tainted some of the towns. But getting away from the maddening crowds is easy. The low mountain areas of the Eifel, the Westerwald and the Hunsrück offer numerous escapes and plenty of outdoor recreation.

You'll find ample accommodation choices. Inexpensive private rooms abound, as do camping grounds, often right on the river banks. Most of the Rhineland-Palatinate's hostels have recently been overhauled and now offer upgraded accommodation. Hotels run the gamut from simple guesthouses to full-service resorts. Or, you could always take a room at one of the wine estates, with grapes ripening just outside your window.

Thanks to its mix of autobahns and highways, exploring the Rhineland-Palatinate is never a problem. Those dependent on public transport will find a perfectly coordinated rail system. One of the greatest rail journeys in Europe is a trip through the Rhine Valley, where tracks hug both sides of the river. Elsewhere in the state, buses pick up where the tracks leave off.

Rhine-Hesse & Palatinate

Rheinhessen and the Palatinate (Pfalz) are both characterised by wine. The former is the largest and oldest growing area in Germany, producing 250 million litres annually, mostly of the Riesling, Silvaner and Müller-Thurgau (now called Rivaner) varietals. Only three out of 136 communities are not given to bacchanalian commerce.

Farther south, the Pfalz extends from the Rhine plains to the Vosges mountains in France. It is bisected by the velvety hills of the Palatinate Forest, which functions as a temperature and weather buffer. Hence, the area east of it – the German Wine Road – is a sun-drenched region whose mild, almost Mediterranean, climate supports the cultivation of kiwi fruit, lemons, almonds and figs alongside the grapes. It is sometimes called 'Germany's Tuscany'.

MAINZ
☎ 06131 • pop 177,000

Mainz has a long pedigree as a state capital: its strategic location at the confluence of the Main and Rhine rivers spurred the Romans to found a military camp here in 39 BC. Called Mountiacum – possibly after the Celtic god Mogon – the settlement evolved into the capital of Germania Prima province by 300 AD.

After the Romans left in the 5th century, the town took a 250 year nap before being awoken by St Boniface, who established an archbishopric here in 746. Throughout the Middle Ages the archbishops of Mainz were immensely powerful, largely because they also held the position of prince-elector and thus managed to influence the politics of the Holy Roman Empire. In the 15th century moveable type was invented by Johannes Gutenberg (around 1446) and the university was founded (1476).

Mainz' population seems to have retained a healthy dose of French *savoir-vivre* from that country's brief occupation (1798-1814). Mainz is a media city too, being the seat of the ZDF, one of Germany's public television stations, and the private SAT1.

During World War II, almost 80% of the Altstadt, including many medieval half-timbered buildings, was lost. It has since been restored and once again forms a bustling centre of activity cherished by locals and visitors alike.

Orientation

Much of the city centre consists of pedestrianised shopping streets. You'll find the Hauptbahnhof at the southern end of Kaiserstrasse, one of the city's main arteries. The walk from the Hauptbahnhof to the Dom takes about 20 minutes. Head south-east on Bahnhofstrasse, then left onto Grosse Bleiche and right onto Lotharstrasse, which turns into a series of outdoor shopping streets before spilling out onto the Markt. The Altstadt is at its most romantic around Augustinerstrasse, just south of the Dom. The boat landing quay is behind the Rathaus.

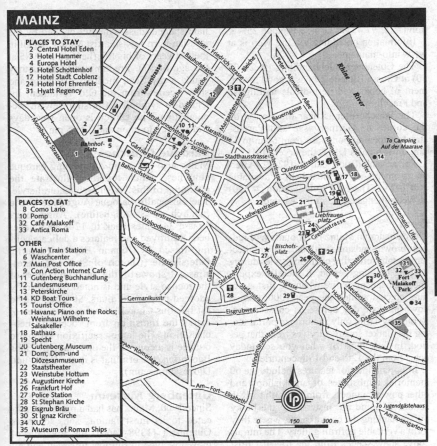

MAINZ

PLACES TO STAY
2 Central Hotel Eden
3 Hotel Hammer
4 Europa Hotel
5 Hotel Schottenhof
17 Hotel Stadt Coblenz
24 Hotel Hof Ehrenfels
31 Hyatt Regency

PLACES TO EAT
8 Como Lario
10 Pomp
32 Café Malakoff
33 Antica Roma

OTHER
1 Main Train Station
6 Waschcenter
7 Main Post Office
9 Con Action Internet Café
11 Gutenberg Buchhandlung
12 Landesmuseum
13 Peterskirche
14 KD Boat Tours
15 Tourist Office
16 Havana; Piano on the Rocks;
  Weinhaus Wilhelm;
  Salsakeller
18 Rathaus
19 Specht
20 Gutenberg Museum
21 Dom; Dom-und
  Diözesanmuseum
22 Staatstheater
23 Weinstube Hottum
25 Augustiner Kirche
26 Frankfurt Hof
27 Police Station
28 St Stephan Kirche
29 Eisgrub Bräu
30 St Ignaz Kirche
34 KUZ
35 Museum of Roman Ships

To Camping
Auf der Maaraue

RHINELAND-PALATINATE

Information

The tourist office (☎ 28 62 10, fax 286 21 55, email tourist@info-mainz.de) is at the Brückenturm am Rathaus, and is open Monday to Friday from 9 am to 6 pm and to 1 pm on Saturday. Staff sell the Mainz-Card (DM10), which entitles you to museum admissions (though most are free anyway), unlimited public transport, plus hotel, theatre and other discounts. It is valid for one week day or both weekend days. Two-hour guided city tours (in German)

operate every Saturday at 10 am from the tourist office (DM6).

Banks cluster in the centre, and there's a Reisebank in the Reisezentrum of the Hauptbahnhof. It's open to 7 pm, but only to 3 pm on Wednesday and Saturday; it's closed on Sunday. The post office also changes money.

The main post office is at Bahnhofstrasse 2; it is open weekdays from 8 am to 6 pm and to 12.30 pm on Saturday. There's a public fax-phone here and another in the

Reisezentrum. An Internet cafe is ConAction (☎ 27 97 45) at Grosse Bleiche 25.

Information on Mainz via the Web is at www.info-mainz.de.

The Gutenberg Buchhandlung (☎ 27 03 30) at Grosse Bleiche 29 has a good assortment of books and periodicals in English and French.

The Waschcenter is near the station on the corner of Gärtnergasse and Parcusstrasse. Opening hours are from 6 am to 11 pm; a wash costs DM7, the dryer DM1.

For an ambulance, call ☎ 192 22. After-hours emergency medical help is available at ☎ 192 92. There's a police station (☎ 650) at Weissliliengasse 12 in the Altstadt.

Dom

The cathedral in Mainz is a mountain of reddish-brown sandstone with fanciful architectural details reflecting changing styles during its long building period. It literally experienced a baptism by fire when the first structure, erected around the year 1000, burned down just one day before its consecration. Rebuilt by 1136, only the bronze portal facing the market square survives from that period. In fact, most of what you see today dates from the 12th and 13th centuries.

Important interior features include the 60 memorial tombstones of archbishops and other power-mongers from the 13th to 18th centuries. Some are fastened to the bulky pillars flanking the central nave, where they form a veritable portrait gallery. The murals above show scenes from the life of Christ but, despite their medieval appearance, they only date back to the 19th century.

The **Dom- und Diözesanmuseum** (☎ 25 33 44) is reached via the cloister. After renovation and enlargement, due for completion in 2000, it will once again present the cathedral treasury and important ecclesiastical artworks. Admission and hours were not available at the time of writing. A special exhibit on Gutenberg runs to October 2000.

St Stephan Kirche

On a hill at Kleine Weissgasse 12, St Stephan Kirche would be just another Gothic church were it not for the nine brilliant stained-glass windows created by the Russian-born Jewish artist Marc Chagall in the last years of his life (he died in 1985 at the age of 97). Predominantly blue, they exude a mystical, meditative quality and show scenes from the Old Testament intended to symbolise Christian-Jewish reconciliation. The church is open weekdays from 10 am to noon and 2 to 5 pm.

Baroque Churches

Mainz also has a trio of stunning baroque churches, which together illustrate the evolution of this lavish architectural style. The classically baroque **Augustinerkirche** (Church of St Augustine), Augustinerstrasse 34, dates back to 1768, has never been destroyed and features a delicate ceiling fresco by Johann Baptist Enderle. **Peterskirche** (Church of St Peter), Peterstrasse 3, shows off the sumptuous glory of the rococo style and is noted for its richly adorned pulpit and altars. **St Ignaz Kirche** (St Ignatius Church), Kapuzinerstrasse 36, marks the transition from rococo to neoclassicism. The large crucifixion sculpture outside is a copy of the one made by Hans Backoffen (the original is in the Dom- und Diözesanmuseum).

Gutenberg Museum

Since 1900, Mainz has had a museum dedicated to its most famous son, Johannes Gutenberg (1398-1468), the inventor of moveable type in Europe. Enlarged and altered through the decades, it has been expanded once again for the 600th anniversary in 2000 of the famous man's birth. Closed for renovation throughout 1999, it was set to reopen on 15 April 2000 as part of the city's jubilee celebrations.

On view once again, albeit in a modernised presentation, will be examples from Gutenberg's workshop, including a precious Bible, as well as illuminated manuscripts, wooden book-blocks, book-covers and historic presses. Also back will be a recreation of Gutenberg's workshop, where occasional demonstrations take place.

Johannes Gutenberg

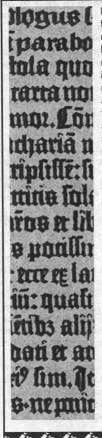

Few inventors have contributed more to the evolution of history and culture than Johannes Gutenberg, who developed moveable type in the middle of the 15th century. To be sure, the art of printing itself dates back many centuries earlier to the Chinese, and Koreans worked with moveable metal type from the mid-13th century, but it was Gutenberg's innovation that paved the way for mass publishing and thus the Information Age. Until then, knowledge had been the privilege of the clergy and the aristocracy. Book printing democratised the dissemination of information, setting in motion a revolution in science, literature, religion and almost every other field. Without Gutenberg, Martin Luther's reform movement would have been seriously hampered and Shakespeare's plays might have been lost to posterity.

Little is known about the man himself, who was born around 1400 in Mainz and spent about 20 years in Strassbourg, where he joined a goldsmith's guild. It was probably in this town where he made his first experiments with typography based on his knowledge of metalworking. Using techniques like casting, punch-cutting and stamping, he split text up into individual upper and lower case letters, punctuation marks and abbreviations. Each component was cast as type in reverse, then put together to form words, lines and pages.

Gutenberg returned to Mainz some time between 1444 and 1449 where, despite great advances, he was constantly plagued by money troubles. In 1450, he formed a partnership with a wealthy burgher named Johannes Fust to finance his most ambitious project: the 42 line Bible (so called because there are 42 lines in each column). While there's little doubt that Gutenberg made the type for this Bible and built the screw press used in its printing, it's possible that the printing was actually undertaken by Fust and another colleague. Legal records shows that Fust sued Gutenberg in 1455 to recover the money he advanced to Gutenberg. But Gutenberg, broke as usual, couldn't repay him in cash, and thus the court ordered that type and press be turned over to Fust. An appointment to the court of the Archbishop of Mainz eventually saved Gutenberg from the poorhouse and he died nearly penniless in 1468.

The museum is on Liebfrauenplatz 5. Call ☎ 12 23 82 for updated information. (Also see the boxed text 'Johannes Gutenberg'.)

Landesmuseum

The wonderfully eclectic collection of this state museum (☎ 285 70), housed in the former prince-elector's stables at Grosse Bleiche 49-51, provides a thorough history of the region from the Stone Age to today. A circuitous tour leads to a light-flooded hall filled with Roman monuments, including the **Jupitersäule**, a 1st century triumphal column with reliefs of 28 gods. In Room 6, you'll find the facade of the 14th century **Kaufhaus am Brand**, a trading house with reliefs depicting church and civil officials. Upstairs is a small who's who of 19th and 20th century art. Hours are from 10 am to 5 pm, Tuesday to 8 pm, closed Monday (DM5/3).

Museum of Roman Ships

Excavations for the Mainz Hilton Hotel in 1981 unearthed a spectacular collection of 4th century Roman shipwrecks, which are now housed in the Museum für Antike Schiffahrt (☎ 28 66 30). On view are the remains of five war ships and two full-size replicas, along with ship models, reliefs and monuments. It's at Holzhofstrasse, corner of Rheinstrasse, and open from 10 am to 6 pm, closed Monday (free).

Places to Stay

The camping ground *Auf der Maaraue* (☎ 06134-43 83) is nicely located at the confluence of the Rhine and Main rivers in Mainz-Kostheim, with a great view of the city. From the Hauptbahnhof, take bus No 17 or 19 to Castel Bahnhof, from where it's a five minute walk.

Mainz has a newly renovated and modernised *Jugendgästehaus* (☎ 853 32, fax 824 22, Otto-Brunfels-Schneise 4) near a city park. B&B in two-bed rooms is DM36.50, and in four-bed rooms it's DM27. Rooms have private bath, and prices include sheets and breakfast. From the Hauptbahnhof, take bus No 1 to the Jugendherberge or bus No 22 to the Viktorstift stop.

The tourist office can make room reservations for a DM5 fee. During the summer months, special weekend rates may be available at some hotels.

One of the cheapest options in town is *Hotel Stadt Coblenz* (☎ 22 76 02, fax 22 33 07, Rheinstrasse 47-49). It's on a busy street but near nice bars, the Rhine and the tourist office. Singles cost DM50 to DM80, and doubles DM80 to DM120. In the heart of the Altstadt in a quiet side alley is *Hotel Hof Ehrenfels* (☎ 22 43 34, fax 23 79 10, Grebenstrasse 5-7), with a wine tavern and modern singles/doubles for DM100/145.

Several decent hotels cluster around the Hauptbahnhof. *Hotel Hammer* (☎ 96 52 80, fax 965 28 88, Bahnhofplatz 6) has pleasantly furnished rooms from DM110/160. Amenities include a sauna. Next door at No 8, the *Central Hotel Eden* (☎ 27 60, fax 27 62 76) has rooms from DM140/180 and a

restaurant on the premises. Nearby is the friendly *Hotel Schottenhof* (☎ 23 29 68, fax 22 19 70, Schottstrasse 6), which charges from DM110/160 for singles/doubles.

One of the top hotels in town is the extravagant *Hyatt Regency* (☎ 73 12 34, fax 73 12 35, Malakoff-Terrasse 1), right on the Rhine in the southern Altstadt. Rooms and public areas are furnished with style and lack no comforts. Rates, though, start at a budget-straining DM190/280.

Places to Eat

In addition to the restaurants listed here, see Entertainment for tavern-style drinking/dining options.

For stomach-filling Italian food in a casual *ambiente*, jostle for a table at *Como Lario* (☎ 23 40 28, Neubrunnenstrasse 7). Fans of gourmet Italian and designer decor will feel more at home at *Antica Roma* (☎ 14 68 43) inside Fort Malakoff Park. It's easy to spend a fortune here, but if you choose carefully, you can get away with a tab of DM20 per person.

Also in the fort is the popular *Café Malakoff* (☎ 14 68 14), which goes through phases as a breakfast cafe, business lunch haunt, afternoon coffee and cake place, and night-time bar during its opening hours from 6 am to 5 am.

Thirty-somethings should feel comfortable at *Pomp* (☎ 23 55 19, Grosse Bleiche 29), a sparse but warmly lit bistro, where you can have breakfast till midnight, talk the day away over large cups of coffee or enjoy a small meal.

Entertainment

Look in the tourist office, in cafes and in pubs for a copy of the free magazines *Fritz* or *Der Mainzer* for event and other information for Mainz, Wiesbaden and Frankfurt.

Mainz is a wine town, and many atmospheric taverns are housed in the Altstadt's half-timbered gems. Locals flock to the low-key *Specht* (☎ 23 17 70, Rotekopfgasse) and to *Weinstube Hottum* (☎ 22 33 70, Grebenstrasse 3). Rustic and smoky, they have a cluttered living room atmosphere, delectable wines and a small menu with inexpensive, simple hot and cold dishes.

If beer is your thing, head for *Eisgrub Bräu (☎ 22 11 04, Weissliliengasse 1a)*. This brewery's network of vaulted chambers regularly buzzes with a mixed crowd that orders beer by the metre (12 glasses, DM30) and pub fare, including some vegetarian choices, for DM14 to DM25.

The small area immediately south of the tourist office has recently been injected with a dose of new life and now sports the trendy *Havana (☎ 23 46 08, Rheinstrasse 49)* for cocktails and Cuban-style fare, the intimate *Piano on the Rocks (☎ 22 72 61)* cocktail bar, the *Weinhaus Wilhelm* wine tavern and the Havana-affiliated *Salsakeller* for dancing.

The *Staatstheater (☎ 285 12 22, Gutenbergplatz 7)*, under partial restoration at the time of writing, has its own ensemble and stages plays, opera and ballet. Students get a 50% discount.

Mainz has two cultural centres worth checking out. The program at the *Frankfurter Hof (☎ 22 04 38, Augustinerstrasse 55)* runs the gamut from classical music to ethno jazz. *KUZ (☎ 28 68 60, Dagobertstrasse 20b)* is a bit more edgy and has lots of big party events, usually with live music.

Getting There & Away

Air Frankfurt airport is 30km north-east of Mainz and easily reached by S-Bahn No 8, which departs several times hourly from the Hauptbahnhof.

Train Mainz is a major hub for IC trains in all directions. There are regional connections to Wiesbaden and Frankfurt several times per hour. Services run to Koblenz (DM31.60, 50 minutes) and to Worms (DM12.20, 45 minutes) almost as frequently. There are also regional trains to Saarbrücken (DM46, 2¼ hours) and Idar-Oberstein (DM24.60, 1¼ hours).

Car & Motorcycle Mainz is easily accessible by autobahn. It's encircled by a ring road with connections to the A60, A63 and A66 in all directions. The nearest Mitfahrzentrale is in Wiesbaden (☎ 0611-33 35 55).

Getting Around

Mainz operates a joint bus and tram system with Wiesbaden, for which single tickets cost DM3.50 and day passes DM8. Tickets are available from vending machines and must be stamped before boarding.

A bike rental station (☎ 23 81 08) is on the ground level of CityPort-Parkhaus on Bingerstrasse near the Hauptbahnhof (open from 10 am to 3 pm). Maps and the booklet *Wandern und Radwandern in Mainz und Rheinhessen* are available at the tourist office and bookshops.

WORMS
☎ 06241 • pop 83,000

About 50km south of Mainz lies Worms, a small town that's continually managed to play a role in major moments in history. In 413 AD it became the capital of the short-lived but legendary Burgundian kingdom, whose rise and fall was later creatively embellished and immortalised in the 12th century Nibelungen epic (the basis of Richard Wagner's equally epic opera cycle *Der Ring des Nibelungen*).

After the Burgundians' downfall just about every other tribe had a go at ruling Worms, including the Huns, the Alemans and finally the Franks. Worms began to flourish under Charlemagne and rose to prominence under the succeeding Salian and Hohenstaufen emperors. From the early 11th century, a large Jewish community thrived in Worms.

In 1517 the town hosted the Imperial Diet, during which reformer Martin Luther refused to renounce his beliefs and was subsequently placed under imperial ban, effectively making him an outlaw. Not long afterwards, a succession of wars brought about Worms' demotion from imperial city to minor market town.

The most poignant reminder of Worms' heyday is its majestic late-Romanesque cathedral. Part of the Rheinhessen wine-growing region, Worms is also known as the birthplace of Liebfraumilch. Since that name

RHINELAND-PALATINATE

could not be trademarked, the original still produced here has nothing in common with the plonk served in pubs all over the world (to try the original, you must ask for the wine made by the Liebfrauenstift Kirchenstück).

Orientation & Information

Worms' train and bus stations are about 250m north-west of the ring road that encircles the Altstadt. It takes about 10 minutes to get from these to the Dom: head south-east on pedestrianised Wilhelm-Leuschner-Strasse (one of the main shopping streets) to Kämmererstrasse, turn right and continue on for another 200m or so.

The tourist office (☎ 250 45, fax 263 28, email worms-touristinfo@t-online) is just east of the Dom on Neumarkt 14, and is open weekdays from 9 am to 6 pm and to noon on Saturday. Guided city tours (in German) take place Saturday at 10.30 am (DM5/2.50). For a self-guided tour, pick up the excellent free walking tour map from the tourist office.

Banks offering exchange services include the Volksbank at Markt 19. The main post office is on the corner of Ludwigsplatz and Korngasse. Worms' Web page (German only) is at www.worms.de.

For after-hours medical help, call ☎ 192 92 or ☎ 59 45 04. The main police station (☎ 85 20) is at Hagenstrasse 5.

Kaiserdom

Worms' landmark Dom St Peter und St Paul, with its four towers and two domes, dominates the city skyline. Built in the 11th and 12th centuries in the late-Romanesque style, it ranks as one of the greatest accomplishments of medieval architecture.

The **Kaiserportal** on the north side was allegedly the scene of a fierce argument between the Burgundian queens Kriemhild and Brunhilde, which triggered the downfall of their nation. Today you enter through the Gothic **Südportal** (1300), richly decorated with biblical figures.

Inside, the cathedral's lofty dimensions impress as much as the lavish, canopied **high altar** (1742) in the east choir. Designed by the master of the baroque, Balthasar

Neumann, it shows sculptures of saints Peter and Paul flanking the Madonna. A stuffy **crypt** holds the stone sarcophagi of several ancestors of the later Holy Roman emperors from the Salian dynasty. To see a **scale model** of the huge original complex, which until 1689 also encompassed the imperial and bishop's palace north of the Dom, head to the south transept.

Jewish Quarter

From the early 11th century onward, a sizeable Jewish community lived in the northeast corner of the Altstadt along Judengasse and its side streets. The area was also known as Little Jerusalem and included a Talmudic school where Rabbi Salomon ben Isaak, also known as Raschi of Troyes (1040-1106), studied.

The first synagogue – from 1034 – was burned down by the Nazis. By 1961 the new **Alte Synagoge** off Judengasse – a serene whitewashed vaulted hall – had risen from its ashes. Also here is an exhibit on Jewish tombstones, as well as the oldest such stone (1036) from Worms' Jewish cemetery. Hours are daily to 4 pm, to 5 pm in winter; closed at lunchtime (free).

Behind the synagogue, on Hintere Judengasse, is the modern **Raschi Haus**, constructed on the 14th century foundations of a former dance hall that also saw incarnations as a hospital and school. Named after Raschi of Troyes, it now holds the **Jüdisches Museum** (☎ 85 33 46), with art from the 11th to the 20th century, ceremonial artefacts and documents. It's open from 10 am to noon and 2 to 4 pm, closed Monday (DM3/1.50). Just east of here is the impressive **Raschitor**, a surviving gate of the town wall that still partially encircles the Altstadt.

Worms' other major Jewish heritage site is across town, in the south-west corner of the Altstadt on Willy-Brandt-Ring: the **Heiliger Sand**, Europe's oldest Jewish cemetery, with more than 2000 graves. Buried here is Rabbi Meir of Rothenburg, who died in 1293 after being imprisoned by King Rudolf of Habsburg for leading a group of would-be emigrants to Palestine.

The grounds are open daily to sundown, in summer to 8 pm.

Museums

The **Museum der Stadt Worms** (☎ 946 39 12), the town's local history museum, is housed in the former Andreasstift church on Weckerlingplatz, behind the hostel. Exhibits chronicle Worms' turbulent history from prehistoric times onward. Hours are 10 am to 5 pm, closed Monday (DM4/2).

In a pretty park north of the Dom, on the grounds of the former imperial and bishop's palace, stands the **Kunsthaus Heylshof** (☎ 220 00). Its important private art collection includes Italian, Dutch, French and German paintings from the 15th to 19th centuries – including works by heavyweights Tintoretto, Rubens and Lenbach – as well as an assortment of Venetian, Bohemian and German glass. It's open from May to September daily from 10 am to 5 pm; otherwise, hours are 2 to 4 pm, Sunday also 10 am to noon, closed Monday (DM3/1).

Lutherdenkmal

On the south-western edge of the Altstadtring is the Lutherdenkmal (1868), which shows Luther surrounded by a who's who of the Reformation – from John Wyclif to Philipp Melanchton – as well as by allegorical figures and the coats of arms of the cities that endorsed the Reformation. It was in Worms where Luther uttered the defiant words 'Here I stand, I can do no other, so help me God' when being urged to renounce his reformist views before Emperor Karl V and the Imperial Diet in 1521.

Places to Stay

The location of Worms' *Jugendgästehaus* (☎ 257 80, fax 273 94, Dechaneistrasse 1) beats that of any five star hotel. It has an unimpeded view of the entire cathedral and has just been renovated; all rooms have private bath. A night in a four bed room costs DM27, in a two bed room DM36.50; sheets and breakfast are included.

The tourist office makes free hotel reservations, and when it's closed an automated

system indicates hotel vacancies and allows unlimited free calls to hotels of interest. The following prices are for rooms with private bath and breakfast.

One of the cheapest choices is the *Hotel Lortze-Eck* (☎ 263 49, Schlossergasse 10-14), which charges DM70/120 for single/ double rooms. A family atmosphere and friendly and modern rooms with basic amenities are offered by the *Hotel Kalisch* (☎ 276 66, fax 250 73, Neumarkt 9), between the Dom and tourist office. The cost here is DM80/120.

Hotel Kriemhilde (☎ 911 50, fax 911 53 10, Hofgasse 2-4) asks from DM80/120. Best of the bunch (and worth the extra DM10 or DM20) is the *Central Hotel* (☎ 645 70, fax 274 39, Kämmererstrasse 5), at the beginning of the pedestrianised shopping strip. Its charming owner runs the place with great panache and a personal touch. Rooms are largish and cost DM95/145.

Places to Eat

Worms offers plenty of good-value eateries. The cluttered *Weinkeller* (☎ 276 48, Wollstrasse 7-9) has a student-age clientele and serves mouthwatering *Flammekuche* and other affordable regional fare (open Friday to Sunday only). Yuppies congregate behind the panorama windows of the multifloor *Café Jux* (☎ 66 54, Judengasse 3), on the corner of Friedrichsstrasse. Its menu includes lots of snacks for around DM5. Across the street is *Zwiebel* (☎ 277 75, Kämmererstrasse 77), a hip joint with an Internet cafe upstairs.

By the Rhine is the excellent *Hagenbräu* (☎ 92 11 00, Am Rhein 3), which makes its own brew and also has an extensive menu of salads, schnitzel and snacks. A few steps south is the competition, *Kolb's Biergarten* (☎ 234 67). Both have outdoor seating in summer.

Getting There & Away

Worms has frequent train connections with Mannheim, a major hub for long-distance trains in all directions. The regional service to Frankfurt (DM16.40, 1¼ hours) and

RHINELAND-PALATINATE

Mainz (DM12.20, 45 minutes) leaves several times hourly.

Getting Around

All major sights are easily covered on foot, though Worms also has a bus system with single tickets that cost DM2.60 (one zone) and DM3.20 (two zones). Day passes cost DM10 and allow travel for up to five people after 9 am. For a taxi, call ☎ 31 41.

SPEYER
☎ 06232 • pop 50,000

On the left bank of the Rhine River about 50km south of Worms lies 2000-year-old Speyer, famed for its magnificent Romanesque cathedral.

First a Celtic settlement, then a Roman market town, Speyer catapulted to prominence in the early Middle Ages when a succession of emperors from the Salian dynasty made it one of the centres of the Holy Roman Empire. For more than seven centuries from 838, the town hosted 50 sessions of the imperial parliament.

In 1076 the king and later Holy Roman Emperor Heinrich IV – having been excommunicated by Pope Gregor VII – launched his penitence walk to Canossa in Italy from Speyer. He crossed the Alps in the middle of winter, an action that warmed even the heart of the pope, who granted him forgiveness and revoked his excommunication. He lies buried in the Kaiserdom.

Speyer's importance waned after being razed by the troops of France's King Louis XIV in 1689 during the War of the Palatine Succession. From 1792 to 1825, Speyer belonged to France, then became part of Bavaria until 1945 before being incorporated into Rhineland-Palatinate after WWII. Today, this provincial town possesses a lively spirit which, together with some interesting sights, makes it a worthwhile stopover.

Orientation & Information

The Hauptbahnhof is on Bahnhofstrasse, about 1km north-west of the city centre. Most city buses will drop you off at the Altpörtel city gate, from which Speyer's lifeline – the broad, pedestrianised Maximilianstrasse – leads you straight to the Dom in about 10 minutes.

The tourist office (☎ 14 23 92 or ☎ 194 33, fax 14 23 32) is at Maximilianstrasse 11, and is open weekdays from 9 am to 5 pm, Saturday from 10 am to noon.

Several banks along Maximilianstrasse exchange money, as does the post office on Postplatz 1 behind the Altpörtel gate. The town Web site is at www.speyer.de. If you need a doctor after hours, call ☎ 192 22.

Kaiserdom

In 1030 Emperor Konrad II of the Salian dynasty laid the cornerstone to the majestic Dom, whose towers float above Speyer's rooftops like the smokestacks of a giant ocean liner. It's the grandest of the trio of imperial cathedrals (the others are in Mainz and Worms) and has been a UNESCO World Heritage Site since 1981. Eight Salian emperors and kings, along with some of their queens, lie buried here.

Most startling about the interior are its awesome dimensions and dignified symmetry. The height of the central nave, the clear lines of construction and unadorned walls create a solemn atmosphere. Make sure you walk up the staircase to the transept to get a true sense of its vastness. Another set of steps leads down to the darkly festive crypt, whose candy-striped arches recall Moorish architecture. From here, a few more steps lead back up to the claustrophobic room beneath the altar area that holds the austere granite sarcophagi of the Salian rulers. Until 2006 the cathedral will be undergoing a DM50 million restoration, but it remains open for visitors weekdays from 9 am to 7 pm, weekends to 6 pm (in winter daily to 5 pm).

Historisches Museum der Pfalz

Though it may be hard to get excited about regional history museums, this museum (☎ 132 50) is a definite exception and should be a part of any visit to Speyer. Besides hosting world-class special exhibits, it has a permanent collection that values quality over quantity and presents each artwork in a unique, intimately lit fashion.

One of the highlights is the **Goldener Hut von Schifferstadt**, an incredibly ornate, perfectly preserved gilded hat in the shape of a giant thimble that dates back to the Bronze Age (14th century BC). Another section holds the **Wine Museum**, with ancient wine presses and a bottle containing a jellied substance from the 3rd century AD purported to be the world's oldest wine. Two more floors below is the **Cathedral Treasury**, where the prized exhibit is Emperor Konrad II's surprisingly simple bronze crown.

The museum is on Domplatz by the cathedral. It's open from 10 am to 6 pm, Wednesday to 8 pm, closed Monday (DM8/5, free on Tuesday after 4 pm).

Along Maximilianstrasse

Roman troops and medieval emperors once paraded down Maximilianstrasse, Speyer's 'Via Triumphalis' and still its main commercial drag. It is lined with baroque buildings, of which the **Rathaus** with its red facade and lavish rococo interior and the **Alte Münze** (Old Mint) deserve closer looks. The road finally culminates at the **Altpörtel**, the main city gate and only remaining part of the town wall. Standing 55m tall, it contains a viewing gallery and an exhibit about the city's fortification; it's open from April to October, weekdays from 10 am to noon and 2 to 4 pm, weekends from 10 am to 5 pm (DM1.50/0.50).

Technik Museum

A few minutes walk south of the Dom, at Geibstrasse 2, is the Museum of Technology (☎ 670 80). Displays in this former aircraft hangar include classic cars, aeroplanes, fire engines, trains and ships, including a 46m-long U-boat. The complex also incorporates two **IMAX** theatres (☎ 67 08 50). The museum is open daily from 9 am to 6 pm. Admission to either the museum or the IMAX is DM12/8; a combined ticket is DM22/15.

Places to Stay

Unofficial camping (both tents and campervans) is possible on land owned by several farmers around the Steinhäuserwühlsee, about 4km north of the city centre. The state-of-the-art *Jugendgästehaus* (☎ 615 97, fax 615 96, Geibstrasse 5), near the Rhine, offers lots of amenities and rooms with private bath. Bed, breakfast and sheets in four-bed rooms cost DM27, in two-bed rooms DM36.50.

The tourist office can help you find rooms in hotels and pensions. The closest to a budget option is the small and fairly central *Pension Grüne Au* (☎/fax 721 96, Grüner Winkel 28), whose singles/doubles with shared shower and WC (toilet) go for DM50/75; doubles with private bath cost DM90. Rooms at the *Hotel am Technik Museum* (☎ 671 00, fax 67 10 20, Geibstrasse 2) are small but modern and functional and a good deal at DM85/110, including private bath. Just one block south of Maximilianstrasse is *Hotel und Weinstube Trutzpfaff* (☎ 601 20, fax 60 12 30, Webergasse 5), which charges DM85/125.

Places to Eat

Most of Speyer's 200 restaurants are abuzz with locals and visitors alike. The *Domhof* (☎ 740 55, Grosse Himmelsgasse 6) is a bustling brewery-pub that specialises in traditional regional dishes. A good place to sample local wines is at *Zum Alten Engel* (☎ 709 14, Mühlturmstrasse 7), a lovely vaulted cellar where you can also get regional and Alsatian meals starting at DM13.

For a younger crowd and a chatty atmosphere, head for *Café Wunderbar* (☎ 759 85, Salzgasse 2). Almost next door is the yuppie hang-out *Zweierlei* (☎ 611 10, Johannesstrasse 1), a postmodern bistro serving pricey German *nouvelle cuisine*. A popular newcomer is the casual *Maximilian* (☎ 62 26 48, Korngasse 15), in the pedestrian zone near the Altpörtl. Waiters in long white aprons bring out French-influenced concoctions like snail ragout, Flammekuche and ratatouille alongside German favourites. It's recommended.

RHINELAND-PALATINATE

Getting There & Away

Buses depart from the Hauptbahnhof for Ludwigshafen (No 677) and Heidelberg (No 7007), but the train is more efficient (even though Speyer is on a minor rail line) and most trips require a change in Ludwigshafen or Schifferstadt. Regional trains to both destinations leave frequently. There is also an hourly direct service to Heidelberg via Mannheim (a major hub for IC and other long-distance trains).

Getting Around

Most sights are within walking distance, but for the weary there's the City-Shuttle minibus (bus No 565). Running at 10-minute intervals, it loops between the Hauptbahnhof and all major attractions from 6 am to 8.45 pm at the incredible price of DM1 for unlimited trips all day. Other local buses connect the suburbs with the town centre, but you're not likely to need them.

Speyer is a good base for exploring the surrounding wine country by bicycle. The booklet *Radspass im Süd-Westen* (DM7.50), available at the tourist office, has descriptions of 21 bike tours of various lengths. Rental bikes (DM20 a day) are available from Radsport Stiller (☎ 759 66), Gilgenstrasse 24, but you must book ahead.

GERMAN WINE ROAD

The German Wine Road (Deutsche Weinstrasse) begins about 15km west of Worms in Bockenheim and runs 80km south to the Deutsches Weintor (German Wine Gate) in Schweigen on the French border. The route is marked by yellow signs sporting a cluster of grapes.

Crowds flock to the more than 200 wine festivals, but otherwise the German Wine Road is not over-commercialised. Especially south of Neustadt, the towns take on a decidedly French flair. Streets are lined by an endless string of wine estates, their facades festooned with vines and ornate ironwork guild signs. This is a great place to taste the crisp white Pfälzer wines: just look for the sign saying 'Weinprobe'.

Information

The local tourist offices are the best sources of specific information on each town and can usually help with finding accommodation. Most will also have information about other towns on the German Wine Road. The central clearing house for the entire route is the Deutsche Weinstrasse office (☎ 06321-91 23 33, fax 91 23 30, email verein@ Deutsche-Weinstrasse.de) at Chemnitzer Strasse 3 in Neustadt.

Getting There & Away

Neustadt is a central hub from which to explore the German Wine Road and is served every half hour by trains from Kaiserslautern (DM9.80, 30 minutes) and Saarbrücken (DM27, one hour), and hourly from Karlsruhe (DM14.80, 45 minutes). There's also a bus service from Speyer.

Getting Around

Having your own vehicle is a great advantage when exploring the Weinstrasse, though it's possible to travel much of the route by public transport. Local trains connect Neustadt with Deidesheim and Bad Dürkheim to the north every 30 minutes.

For towns south of Neustadt, you have to connect with buses to Bad Bergzabern and down to Schweigen at the bus station in Landau.

Bad Dürkheim

☎ 06322 • pop 16,900

Bad Dürkheim is the third largest wine-growing community in Germany and one of four spa towns in the Rhineland-Palatinate. One of the main attractions here – and a tourist trap if we ever saw one – is the **Dürkheimer Riesenfass**, a gigantic wine cask built in 1935 for the Dürkheimer Wurstmarkt (Sausage Fair); it is actually a restaurant fit to seat up to 650 people.

The festival, which attracts half a million visitors, has been held on the second and third weekends in September for the past 500 years. The goings-on during this blowout are given expression in the **Wurstmarktbrunnen**, a comical fountain outside the train station.

The town's **Vitalis Spa** (☎ 96 40) is at Kurbrunnenstrasse 14, and is open from 9 am to 9 pm weekdays, and to 5 pm weekends (DM13 for 2½ hours, DM25 for unlimited day use including sauna). There's also a **hammam**, or Turkish bath, at the nearby Kurmittelhaus, where two-hour sessions cost DM55 (reservations are required).

Bad Dürkheim's tourist office (☎ 93 51 56, fax 93 51 59) is at Mannheimer Strasse 24; it's open weekdays from 8 am to 5 pm (Thursday to 6 pm). The post office is opposite the train station.

Bad Dürkheim's *camping ground (☎ 613 56, Am Badesee)* is open from February to October. The nearest hostel is in Neustadt, some 15km south (see that section). One of the cheapest places to stay is the familial and central *Pension Schillerstube (☎ 632 69, fax 98 10 39, Schillerstrasse 8)*, which charges DM35/60 for singles/doubles with shared bath. If you want to sleep at a wine estate, try *Gästehaus Karst (☎ 28 62, 659 65, In den Almen)*, where rooms with shower and WC cost DM80/95. It has wine tastings and also rents bicycles.

Deidesheim
☎ 06326 • pop 3650

Deidesheim is one of the Weinstrasse's most popular wine villages and is centred on the romantic, if diminutive, historical Markt.

The tourist office (☎ 967 70, fax 96 77 18), Bahnhofstrasse 5, is open weekdays from 9 am to noon and 2 to 5 pm (also on Saturday morning in summer). The post office is at Bahnhofstrasse 16.

The Markt is where the Gothic **Church of St Ulrich** and the **Rathaus**, with its double-sided, canopied exterior staircase, are located. Inside the Rathaus is a small **Museum für Weinkultur** (☎ 98 15 61), open from March to December, Wednesday to Sunday from 4 to 6 pm (DM2/1). On the north side of the Markt is **Deidesheimer Hof** (☎ 968 70), a stuffily stylish hotel-restaurant where former German chancellor Helmut Kohl used to feed visiting dignitaries the regional speciality *Saumagen*: a sheep's stomach stuffed with meat, potatoes

and spices, boiled, then cut in slices and briefly fried. (The dish sounds more intimidating than it is.)

On Bahnhofstrasse you'll find the cute **Geissbockbrunnen** (Goat Fountain) in honour of an unusual local custom, the **Goat Festival**. According to an ancient contract between Deidesheim and the nearby town of Lambrecht, the latter has to make an annual 'payment' of one goat for using pastureland belonging to Deidesheim. The presentation of this goat, and its subsequent auctioning, gives rise to this raucous festival held yearly in historical costumes on the Tuesday after Whit Sunday.

There's no camping ground here, and the nearest hostel is in Neustadt, 8km south (see the following section). The tourist office can help you find accommodation, including *private rooms* for DM25 per person. For DM40/90 for singles/doubles you can sleep at the wine estate *Winzerhaus Funk (☎ 52 52, Bennstrasse 49)*. Even more central is the comfortable *Gästehaus Ritter von Böhl (☎ 97 22 01, fax 97 22 00, Weinstrasse 35)*, integrated into a 15th century hospital complex. Its extremely spacious, modern rooms cost DM85/130.

A good dinner choice (in addition to the posh Deidesheimer Hof) is *Turmstübl (☎ 98 10 81, Turmstrasse 3)*, a contemporary, artsy wine cafe that also serves salads and uncomplicated hot dishes.

Neustadt an der Weinstrasse
☎ 06321 • pop 53,000

Neustadt, the heart of the German Wine Road, is the country's largest wine-growing community. It's a busy, modern town with a charming, largely pedestrianised **Altstadt** with row upon row of half-timbered houses. Especially picturesque lanes include Metzergasse, Kunigundengasse, Mittelgasse and Hintergasse. All are a few steps from the **Marktplatz**, an attractive square flanked by the surprisingly large baroque **Rathaus**, guarded by a bronze lion.

Also here is the town landmark, the Gothic **Stiftskirche** (1368), a red-sandstone concoction shared by a Protestant and a

RHINELAND-PALATINATE

Catholic congregation since 1708 (open only during services).

The tourist office (☎ 926 80, fax 92 68 10, email touristinfo@neustadt.pfalz.com) is in brand-spanking new digs at Hetzelplatz 1, across from the train station, and is open weekdays from 9.30 am to 6 pm, Saturday from 10 am to 1 pm (in September and October also Sunday from 10 am to 1 pm). The post office is just east of the train station.

Neustadt's *DJH hostel* (☎ 22 89, fax 829 47, Hans-Geiger-Strasse 27) is a modern, recently renovated facility. Charges are DM27 per person in four-bed rooms and DM36.50 in doubles, both with shower and WC and including sheets and breakfast. Another option is the *Naturfreundehaus* (☎ 881 69, Heidenbrunnerweg 100), which charges DM26 per person for a double room. Rooms at the *Gästehaus Villa Deco* (☎ 21 05, Haltweg 30), in an old park, have kitchenettes and cost DM75/110 for singles/doubles. It's a 15 minute walk from the centre.

Neustadt has a wonderful selection of restaurants, especially in the Altstadt. The *Novalis Cafe (Hintergasse 26)* serves such things as *ciabatta* sandwiches, salads and potato pancakes for under DM10. At No 6 on the same street, the traditional *Gerberhaus* (☎ 887 00) has home-style German food. At *Backblech* (☎ 812 50, Hintergasse 18-20), the speciality is Flammekuche. The *Wespennest* (☎ 72 45 or ☎ 350 07, Friedrichstrasse 36) is an alternative-culture pub with vegie lunch specials and other quick fare, plus live music at night.

Hambacher Schloss

On a bluff about 4km south of Neustadt is Hambacher Schloss (☎ 06321-308 81), known as the 'cradle of German Democracy'. It was here where students held massive demonstrations for a free, democratic and united Germany on 27 May 1832, during which the German tricolour of black, red and gold was raised for the first time. The event, which was called Hambacher Fest, is commemorated in an exhibit (DM5/3). There's a splendid view over the vineyards and the Rhine plains.

Daily hours are from 9 am to 6.30 pm (closed December to February). Admission to the grounds is free. From Neustadt, bus No 502 makes the trip up to 10 times daily.

Kaiserslautern

☎ 0631 • pop 109,000

To many American military personnel, Kaiserslautern will be a familiar name for, throughout the Cold War, 'K-Town' was home to up to 60,000 soldiers and their families at a time. To this day 40,000 remain, primarily playing supporting roles in regional wars like those that raged through the Balkans in the late 1990s.

Historically, the city's heyday was in the Middle Ages when Emperor Friedrich I (Barbarossa) chose the town as a governmental seat. It became a residence under Duke Johann Casimir in 1576, but was devastated by marauding French troops in 1635. In fact, they were so thorough that little of historical importance survived. Nonetheless, Kaiserslautern is still a livable place and a gateway to the Palatinate Forest, the largest contiguous forest area in Germany.

Orientation & Information Kaiserslautern's city centre, around the pedestrianised Marktstrasse, is about a 15 minute walk north of the train station. The tourist office (☎ 365 2317, fax 365 2723, email touristinformation@kaiserslautern.de) is at Willy-Brandt-Platz 1 inside the Rathaus. It's open weekdays from 8.30 am to 5 pm (Friday to 1 pm) and Saturday from 9 am to noon.

Things to See & Do Almost nothing remains of Barbarossa's palace, the **Kaiserpfalz** (1152), which once stood on a site next to the **Rathaus**, a modern skyscraper with a rooftop viewing platform. Incorporated into the town hall are the ruins of the **Casimirschloss** (1571), the former Renaissance palace of Johann Casimir.

Historical churches include the Gothic **Stiftskirche** off Marktstrasse and **St Martinskirche**, a curving two-nave structure whose incongruous decor blends a Gothic net vaulted apse with a baroque stucco ceiling.

For background on Kaiserslautern, visit the **Theodor-Zink-Museum** (☎ 738 88) at Steinstrasse 48 (closed Monday, free). It's adjacent to **Wadgasserhof**, an elaborate 17th century manor house. The **Pfalzgalerie** (☎ 364 72 01) on Museumsplatz harbours art from the 19th and 20th centuries, including works by Palatine artist Max Slevogt (DM2/1, closed Monday).

Hikers should stop by the tourist office for maps and suggestions. Easy favourites include trips to the wildly romantic **Karlstal Gorge** and to the **Humberg lookout tower**.

Places to Stay & Eat The nearest *hostel* (☎ 06305-336 51 52, Trippstädter Strasse 150) is about 8km west of town in Hochspeyer and charges DM26/32 per person in quads/doubles (with private shower and WC). The tourist office makes free hotel and private room reservations. Reasonable options include the *Pension Blum* (☎ 31 62 10, Rudolf-Breitscheid-Strasse 7) near the Hauptbahnhof, which asks DM70/110 for singles/doubles with private facilities, and the 1960s-style *City-Hotel* (☎ 130 25, fax 133 41, Rosenstrasse 28), where rates are DM110/150.

Restaurants and bars cluster on Steinstrasse and around St Martinsplatz. One recommended place is the historical *Spinnrädl* (☎ 605 11, Schillerstrasse 1), which has mouthwatering German favourites for DM15 to DM25. For a lively, youthful scene, head to *Café am Markt* (☎ 619 44, Stiftsplatz 3), where classy but affordable bistro fare is on the menu. Really cheap food in huge portions (DM8 to DM15) is available at *Leberecht* (☎ 225 48, Humboldtstrasse 31), owned by a former professional boxer.

Getting There & Away Regional trains leaving half-hourly connect Kaiserslautern with Saarbrücken (DM16.40, 45 minutes) and Neustadt/Weinstrasse (DM13, 20 minutes). Getting to Frankfurt requires a change in Mannheim (DM56, 1½ hours).

The A6 (Mannheim-Saarbrücken) passes just north of Kaiserslautern, which is also served by the B40 and the B270.

The Eifel

The Eifel, a rural area of gentle hills, tranquil villages and volcanic lakes, makes for a perfect respite from the mass tourism typical of the Moselle and Rhine valleys, which form its southern and eastern boundaries. In the west it merges with the Ardennes forest across the Belgian border. When formed about 400 million years ago, the Eifel mountains peaked at around 6000m but time has whittled them down to a maximum height of 747m at the Hohe Acht mountain.

The subtle charms of the Eifel landscape are best sampled during a bike ride or a hike, though major attractions include a world-class car racing track, a stunning Romanesque abbey and a lovely wine region.

AHR VALLEY

The Ahr River has carved its scenic 90km valley from Blankenheim – in the High Eifel – to the Rhine, which it joins near Remagen. It's one of Germany's few red-wine regions – growing Spätburgunder (pinot noir), in particular – with vineyards clinging to steeply terraced slopes along both banks. With a growing area of a mere 505 hectares, the Ahr is one of the smallest of German wine regions and very little is ever sold outside the valley. The quality is high but, because of the minuscule yield, bargains are rare.

The best time to visit is generally on weekdays or between November and May, when day-trippers and coach tourists are back home in Amsterdam or Blackpool. The valley is at its most idyllic between Ahrweiler and Altenahr, where it narrows dramatically and gentle hillsides give way to craggy cliffs.

Each town has its own tourist information office, but for details about the entire region, there's Touristik-Service Ahr, Rhein, Eifel (☎ 02641-977 30, fax 97 73 73, email tour-are@t-online.de) at Markt 11 in Ahrweiler, or on the Internet at www.ahr-rhein-eifel.de (German only).

Getting Around

The best way to travel through the Ahr Valley is by the Ahrtalbahn, which serves most villages between Remagen and Altenahr. Trains leave hourly, and the entire distance takes about 40 minutes, costing DM7.60. Bus No 841 also travels the route, but it's quite slow. If you're driving, make your way to the B266/267, which traverses the valley.

Rotweinwanderweg Hikers will enjoy trekking along the scenic Red Wine Hiking Trail, which leads right through grape country on its 35km route from Sinzig/Bad Bodendorf to Altenahr. The trail is marked by small signs with grape symbols, and you can walk as far as you like and then return on the Ahrtalbahn train. All Ahr Valley tourist offices have a detailed trail description and maps.

Remagen

☎ 02642 • pop 14,500

Remagen was founded by the Romans in 16 AD as Rigomagus, but the town would hardly figure in the history books were it not for one fateful day in 1945. As the Allies stampeded across France and Belgium to rid Germany of Nazism, the Wehrmacht tried frantically to stave off the attack by destroying all bridges across the Rhine. But the **Remagen Bridge** remained intact long enough for Allied troops to cross the river – and – bye-bye Hitler. The bridge itself is now gone, but one of its surviving towers houses the **Friedensmuseum** (Peace Museum; ☎ 201 46), with an exhibit commemorating the events leading to the dramatic finale of WWII. It's open from March to November daily from 10 am to 5 pm (DM2.50/1).

Bad Neuenahr-Ahrweiler

☎ 02641 • pop 25,000

The twin towns of Bad Neuenahr and Ahrweiler have very different characters. Bad Neuenahr is an elegant spa town whose healing waters have been sought out by Karl Marx, Johannes Brahms and other notables. It continues to be popular with the moneyed crowd crippled by the effects of rich and plentiful food and booze.

Ahrweiler, on the other hand, is a dreamy medieval village encircled by a town wall and crisscrossed by narrow, pedestrianised lanes lined by half-timbered houses. What the two have in common is wine, which can be enjoyed everywhere at taverns and estates.

Orientation & Information Bad Neuenahr forms the eastern half of the town, Ahrweiler the western half. The Bad Neuenahr train station is right in its city centre, from where it's a five minute walk west to the pedestrian-only Poststrasse, the main drag. Ahrweiler's centre is about 3km west. From the Ahrweiler train station, the medieval core is 200m west.

Bad Neuenahr has a tourist office (☎ 97 73 50, fax 297 58, email bad-neuenahr-ahrweiler@t-online.de) at Hauptstrasse 60, next to the train station. The Ahrweiler branch (☎ 97 73 62, fax 352 00) is at Markt 21. Both are open weekdays from 9 am to 6 pm, Saturday 10 am to 3 pm and Sunday 10.30 am to 4.30 pm. Hours are reduced from November to Easter.

To change money, options include the Sparkasse at Telegrafenstrasse 20 or the post office on the corner of Kölner Strasse and Hauptstrasse in Bad Neuenahr. The town Web site, with good English sections, is at www.bad-neuenahr-ahrweiler.de.

Things to See & Do The focal point of Bad Neuenahr is the stately **Kurhaus**, a turn-of-the-century Art Nouveau confection that also contains the posh **Casino** (☎ 757 50), the first to appear in post-WWII Germany. Here you can play roulette, slot machines and various card games (DM5 or DM10 minimum at most tables). It's a fairly elegant affair, and men must wear a jacket and tie. Opening hours are from 2 pm to 1 am (admission DM5); bring your passport.

Sore muscles are quickly soothed at the **Ahr-Therme** (☎ 80 12 00), Felix-Rüttenstrasse 3, Bad Neuenahr's state-of-the-art thermal mineral pools, open daily from 9 am to 11 pm. Unfortunately, prices are anything but relaxed: two hours cost DM18 and a day pass is DM26. A sauna is DM2.50 extra.

Many lovely houses line Ahrweiler's narrow lanes and all four of its **town gates** still exist. On pedestrianised Niederhutstrasse, at No 142, look out for **Haus Wolff**, with its octagonal oriel buttressed by generously sculpted and painted beams. This was one of only 10 houses to survive the fire storm triggered by marauding French troops in 1689.

Ahrweiler is anchored by the Gothic **Pfarrkirche St Laurentius** (St Laurentius Church) on the Markt, whose entire interior is covered with murals. Integrating floral and religious motifs, these date to the 14th century but had been whitewashed and were rediscovered only in 1903. Also note the hexagonal baptismal font (1570).

On the north-western edge of town are the extremely well preserved remains of a large 2nd century AD **Roman villa** (☎ 53 11), Am Silberberg 1, accidentally unearthed by construction workers in 1980. A functional floor heating system and a complete kitchen with stove, oven and smoking pantry are just a couple of highlights. Hours are Tuesday to Friday from 10 am to 6 pm, weekends to 5 pm, closed November to late March (DM7/3.50).

Places to Stay & Eat The *camping ground* (☎ 356 84) is in Ahrweiler and open from April to October. The snazzy *Jugendgästehaus* (☎ 349 24, fax 315 74, St-Pius-Strasse 7) is about halfway between Ahrweiler and Bad Neuenahr (a 15 minute walk east from the Ahrweiler train station). Rooms have private bath and cost DM27 in quads and DM36.50 in doubles with private facilities, breakfast and sheets included.

The tourist office staff offers a free room-finding service. Reasonable rates are offered by *Hotel Zum Ännchen* (☎ 977 70, fax 977 99, Niederhutstrasse 11-13) in Ahrweiler, where singles/doubles with private facilities are DM85/130. Good value too is *Hotel Eckschänke* (☎ 351 30, fax 373 94, Plätzerstrasse 52-58), also right in the old town. Charges are DM70/100 for rooms with private bath.

For a room with a view, try *Hotel Hohenzollern* (☎ 42 68, 59 97, Am Silberberg 50) in a location framed by vineyards. Rooms with all amenities start at DM100/150.

Both Bad Neuenahr and Ahrweiler teem with traditional German restaurants and dowdy cafes popular with spa visitors. For a younger ambience, head to *Apbell's* (☎ 90 02 43, Niederhutstrasse 27a) and its lovely chestnut-shaded beer garden. The menu features salads from DM15, small dishes from DM8 and bigger meals from around DM20. The most happening place is *Both's* (☎ 35 97 34, Wilhelmstrasse 58-60), which combines a jazzy bar, winter garden, beer garden, restaurant and disco. Most items on the American-style menu (bagels, nachos, salads) are under DM10.

Altenahr
☎ 02643 • pop 1900

Hemmed in on all sides by craggy peaks giving way to rolling hills and steep vineyards, Altenahr wins top honours for most romantic location on the Ahr. The landscape is best – and most easily – appreciated by taking a 10 minute walk to **Burg Are** (1100), whose weather-beaten tower stands guard over the valley. This is also the western terminus of the Rotweinwanderweg. A dozen more trails are accessed either from the village centre or picked up at the top of the **Ditschard**, whose 'peak' at 354m is easily reached by chair lift (DM3.50/2 uphill, DM6/3 return).

Altenahr is busiest from August to October, though finding accommodation is usually not a problem. There's an old-fashioned *DJH Hostel* (☎ 18 80, fax 81 36, Langfigtal 8), which charges DM20, plus DM5 for sheets. The tourist office (☎ 84 48, fax 35 16) inside the train station is open weekdays from 9 am to noon and Saturday from 2 to 5 pm (from 10 am in winter).

NÜRBURGRING

The Eifel is also home to the Nürburgring, a historic Formula 1 car racing track completed in 1927 and the site of spectacular races with legendary drivers. With 21km, its North Loop was the longest circuit ever built,

RHINELAND-PALATINATE

and it was also one of the most difficult, dubbed the 'Green Hell' by Jackie Stewart. After Niki Lauda's spectacular crash in 1976, the German Grand Prix moved to the Hockenheimring near Mannheim. Formula 1 returned to the shorter South Loop in 1996 with the Grand Prix of Europe.

If you have your own car or motorbike, you can take a spin on certain days between March and November (from DM20). Those who prefer someone else to do the driving can take the **'Renntaxi'**: up to three people pile into a 340hp BMW and are 'chauffeured' around the North Ring by a pro driving at speeds up to 320km an hour. Or you can hit the 1.3km-long **go-kart track** and see what 60km/h feels like with your tail scooting along 3cm above the asphalt. An automotive **theme park** opened on the grounds in May 1999. For details, contact ☎ 02691-30 26 30 or log on to www.nuerburgring.de (German only).

The Nürburgring is off the B258, reached via the B257 from Altenahr.

MARIA LAACH

About 25km north-west of Koblenz is the **Abbey of Maria Laach**, one of the most stunning examples of Romanesque architecture in Germany. Still a working Benedictine monastery, the abbey charms with its harmonious architecture and lovely setting beside a volcanic lake, the **Laacher Maar**.

Its striking outline is dominated by two central towers – one octagonal, the other square – each of which is flanked by two smaller ones. The interior is surprisingly modest, anchored in the west apse by the tomb of abbey founder Henry II of Palatine and the high altar in the east apse. Above the altar is a wooden canopy, which in turn is lorded over by an early 20th century Byzantine-style mosaic of Christ. The abbey is entered via a large **portico**, an architectural feature not usually found north of the Alps: note the quirky carvings in the capitals. The portico wraps around an inner courtyard with a **Löwenbrunnen** (Lion Fountain), oddly reminiscent of Moorish architecture.

A free 20 minute film (German only) takes visitors behind the monastery walls to reveal that the monks take the motto 'Ora et Labora' (Pray and Work) very seriously indeed. Five times each day, they take part in prayer services, which are well worth attending, if only to listen to the ethereal chanting.

The Abbey of Maria Laach is accessible by bus No 6031 from Andernach and bus No 6032 from Niedermendig, the town with the nearest train station. By car, take the Mendig exit off the A61 and follow the signs.

The Romantic Rhine

The Rhine's most evocative scenery lies between Koblenz and Mainz, as this legendary river carves deeply through the Rhenish slate mountains. This is where you'll encounter the most dramatic landscape, with fertile vineyards clinging to steep cliffs, dreamy wine villages of Roman origin and imposing castles framed by thick forests.

The Rhine Valley has been a favourite among travellers since the 19th century, and although visitor numbers have declined in recent years, the tiny towns are still regularly swamped by tourists.

Unfortunately, these hordes have turned some otherwise lovely towns into tourist traps with tacky shops and overpriced cafes and restaurants. The countryside surrounding these kitsch centres is, however, brilliant at any time. The busiest season is from May to September so, if you can, visit in early spring or late autumn when the crowds have disappeared. The area all but shuts down in winter.

Hiking & Cycling

The Rhine Valley is great hiking and biking territory, and each tourist office has specific suggestions and maps for long and short trips. One hiking option is the long-distance **Rheinhöhenweg**, which parallels the left river bank between Bonn and Oppenheim, south of Mainz, over a distance of 240km

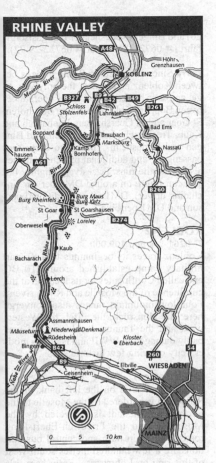

RHINE VALLEY

has nothing to do with the real thing, as you will soon discover when sampling some of Germany's finest at the local estates. Just look for the signs saying 'Weinprobe'. Some vintners only do wine tastings for groups but if you're really interested, just go to the winery and ask. Most will happily comply if they can tell you are serious. Don't drink too much without buying at least a bottle or two, though. In many places the tourist offices organise scheduled wine tastings for individual travellers.

Special Events

Every little river village holds at least one wine festival each year, with most of them crammed into the months of August and September, just before harvest time. The brochure *Veranstaltungskalender Rheinland-Pfalz*, with a complete listing of all festivals, is available from the local tourist offices.

Rhine in Flames This is the region's most famous series of festivals, held at five different settings each year. Water and fire combine in one spectacular show with castles, boats, monuments and the river banks all swathed in brilliant light and forming the backdrop to gargantuan fireworks displays. The following table shows where and when the festival is held.

Siebengebirge: villages between Linz to Bonn
    First Saturday in May
Bingen/Rüdesheim
    First Saturday in July
Koblenz to Braubach/Spay
    Second Saturday in August
Oberwesel
    Second Saturday in September
Loreley rock (St Goar/St Goarshausen)
    Third Saturday in September

Getting There & Away

Koblenz and Mainz are the best starting points for touring the region. For details on how to get to these towns, see their Getting There & Away sections. If you're pressed for time, you can also get a glimpse of the Romantic Rhine on a long day trip from Frankfurt.

through hills and vineyards. Another path travels along the right bank between the Bonn suburb of Bonn-Beuel and Wiesbaden, for a total of 272km. Trails are marked with an 'R'. A detailed brochure outlining these routes is available from local tourist offices, as are detailed maps. Bicycle paths also run along both banks.

Wine Tasting

Much of the cheap stuff sold in shops around the world as 'Rhine wine' actually

Getting Around

Train Train travel is an efficient and convenient way to go village-hopping along the Rhine. Local trains connect all villages on the left river bank between Koblenz and Mainz at least hourly. The entire trip takes 1¾ hours. Some trains stop only at the bigger towns, and IC trains make the direct trip between the two cities in 50 minutes. Both are also gateways for trains to Rhine villages on the right bank, though service is less frequent.

Car & Motorcycle The B9 highway travels along the left bank of the Rhine from Koblenz to Bingen, from where the A60 leads on to Mainz. On the right bank, the B42 hugs the river.

Boat Travelling by boat is certainly the most pleasant way to explore the Rhine Valley, because it allows you to absorb the scenic splendour slowly from the comfort of a deck chair. The most scenic stretch is the 70km between Koblenz and Bingen/Rüdesheim, with the Loreley rock being about halfway, near St Goarshausen.

Cruises Local boat operators offer excursions in most towns, and these are sometimes cheaper than the KD boat line. On the other hand, KD offers more options and flexibility. Besides a whole assortment of theme cruises (sunset, disco, dinner etc), it operates regular service between all Rhine villages on a set timetable, just like a bus or a train. You can travel to the next village or the entire distance. Once you've bought your ticket, you can get on and off as often as you like (eg if you're going from Boppard to Rüdesheim, you can also get off at St Goar, Bacharach and so on).

Many rail passes (Eurail, GermanRail etc) are valid for normal KD services. Children up to the age of four travel for free, while those up to age 13 are charged a flat DM5. Students get a 50% discount. Travel on your birthday is free. In general, return tickets cost only slightly more than one-way tickets.

Other operators include Rhein-und Moselschiffahrt Hölzenbein (☎ 377 44), the Boppard-based Hebel-Linie (☎ 06742-24 20) and Bingen-Rüdesheimer Fahrgastschiffahrt (☎ 06721-141 40 or ☎ 06722-29 72).

Ferry Since there are no Rhine bridges between Koblenz and Mainz, the only way to get across is by ferry. Car ferries operate between Boppard and Filsen/Kamp Bornhofen, St Goar and St Goarshausen, Bacharach and Kaub, Trechtinghausen and Lorch, and Bingen and Rüdesheim. These also carry foot passengers, and additional passenger ferries also make the runs. Prices vary slightly but you can figure on around DM5 per car (including driver), DM1.50 per additional person and DM1 per bike.

KOBLENZ
☎ 0261 • pop 109,000

Koblenz traces its beginnings to a Roman military camp established around 10 BC and called Confluentes for its location at the confluence of the Moselle and Rhine rivers. Four low mountain ranges also converge here: the Hunsrück, the Eifel, the Westerwald and the Taunus. Koblenz itself was badly damaged in WWII and is now a modern city offering few historic sites.

Orientation

Koblenz's core is on the left bank of the Rhine and is bordered by the Moselle to the north. The Altstadt is encircled by the Moselring and the Friedrich-Ebert-Ring roads. The main train and central bus stations are a few hundred metres south-west of this ring on Löhrstrasse. From here, it's about a 10 to 15 minute walk north on Löhrstrasse to the heart of the Altstadt. The landing stages of several boat operators are along the Konrad-Adenauer-Ufer on the Rhine just south of the Deutsches Eck.

Information

The tourist office (☎ 313 04, fax 100 43 88, email touristik@koblenz.de) is on Löhrstrasse 141 near the Hauptbahnhof. From May to September, hours are weekdays from 9 am to 8 pm, weekends from 10 am. In April and October, closing time is at

6 pm. From November to April it's open weekdays only from 9 am to 5 pm.

There's an ATM inside the Hauptbahnhof and a Sparkasse opposite at Emil-Schüller-Strasse 22. The post office is to the right (south) of the Hauptbahnhof.

For a great bookshop, try Bouvier (☎ 30 33 70), Löhrstrasse 30. The Waschcenter laundrette on the corner of Rizzastrasse and Löhrstrasse is open to midnight, and charges DM6 per load, plus DM1 for the dryer.

If you require emergency medical assistance or an ambulance, call ☎ 192 22. There's a police station (☎ 10 32) at Moselring 10.

Walking Tour

Löhrstrasse, which connects the Hauptbahnhof with the Altstadt, is Koblenz's main shopping drag, with run-of-the-mill chain boutiques and department stores. A block to the west is the **Löhr-Center**, a 130 store mall.

Of note on Löhrstrasse are the four carved and painted oriels clinging to the corner buildings of the intersection with Altergraben, which marks the gateway to the Altstadt. Turn right on Altergraben to get to **Am Plan**, a square that has seen incarnations as a butchers' market, a stage for religious plays, a place of execution and an arena for medieval tournaments.

The arched walkway at Am Plan's north-eastern end leads to the **Liebfrauenkirche**, built in a harmonious hotchpotch of styles: of Romanesque origin, it has a Gothic choir and baroque onion-domed turrets. Note the painted net vaulting above the central nave. Continue north through Mehlsgasse to Florinsmarkt, dominated by **Florinskirche** and flanked by the **Mittelrhein-Museum** (☎ 129 25 01), where highlights include paintings from the Romantic period. It's open Tuesday to Saturday from 10.30 am to 5 pm, Sunday from 11 am to 6 pm (DM5/4). The figure beneath the facade clock is that of the Augenroller (eye roller), a mistakenly executed medieval robber baron. You can watch it rolling its eyes and sticking its tongue out on the half and full hour.

The Moselle is just one block north. Strolling east along its banks will get you to the Deutsches Eck and also to the **Basilika St Kastor**, a gloomy, almost spooky, church from the late 12th century. The contemporary art collection of the **Ludwig Museum** (☎ 30 40 40) is in an adjacent building once owned by the Teutonic Knights (same hours and admission as Mittelrhein-Museum). Behind here, the **Rheinpromenade** leads along the Rhine to Pfaffendorfer Brücke and beyond.

Ehrenbreitstein

On the right bank, almost 120m above Koblenz, looms this monumental fortress in a strategic location above the confluence of the Rhine and Moselle. Over time, it was gradually enlarged into a bastion and proved unconquerable to all but the Napoleonic troops who levelled it in 1801. In 1817 it got a new lease on life from the Prussians, who turned it into Europe's strongest fortification. Indeed, walking beneath its massive bulwarks makes you feel Lilliputian. The fortress now houses a hostel, two restaurants and the **Landesmuseum** (☎ 970 31 50) with changing exhibits (DM3/2). The museum is open from mid-March to mid November daily from 9 am to 5 pm.

Bus Nos 7, 8 and 9 make the trip to Bahnhof Ehrenbreitstein from the central bus station, from where it's a 20 minute walk uphill. A Rhine ferry operates daily until around 7 pm between Easter and November (DM2/1 each way). From the landing dock, go through a tunnel, then take the chair lift to the castle (DM7/4, return DM10/6). Fortress admission is DM2/1.

Deutsches Eck

The Deutsches Eck is a promontory built on a sandbank right at the river confluence. It derives its name from the Deutscher Ritterorden (Order of Teutonic Knights), which had its headquarters in the 13th century building now occupied by the Landesmuseum. It's dominated by a statue of Kaiser Wilhelm II (1897), which was blasted in WWII. From 1953 to 1990, the stump served as a memorial to a united Germany. Soon after the *Wende* (the political

euro currency converter DM1 = €0.51

RHINELAND-PALATINATE

events of 1989), a wealthy local publisher donated DM3 million so that a replica could be mounted on the stone pedestal.

Schloss Stolzenfels

With its crenellated turrets, ornate gables and fortifications, Schloss Stolzenfels (☎ 516 56), 5km south of Koblenz, exudes the sentimental beauty for which the Romantic Rhine is famed. In 1823, the city donated the ruined castle to King Wilhelm IV of Prussia, who had it turned into a summer residence by famed Berlin architect Karl Friedrich Schinkel.

The guided tour takes you through the small and large Knights' Halls, and past displays of furniture, ceramics, weapons and other objects. Between Easter and September, Stolzenfels is open from 9 am to 5 pm; otherwise, from 10 am to 3.30 pm, closed December (DM5/3 with guided tour). Bus No 6050 from the central bus station goes to a parking lot from where it's a 15 minute walk.

Places to Stay

Of Koblenz's two camping grounds only *Campingplatz Rhein-Mosel* (☎/fax 80 24 89, Schartwiesenweg) accepts tents. It's on the Moselle north shore, opposite the Deutsches Eck, and is open from April to mid-October. It is served by ferry.

The *DJH hostel* (☎ 97 28 70, fax 972 87 30) is dramatically, if a bit inconveniently, located inside the Ehrenbreitstein fortress and is often full with school groups. Charges are DM24 to DM30 per bunk in four to eight-bed dorms, some of them with private facilities.

The tourist office has a free booking service for hotels, pensions and *private rooms*. *Hotel Jan van Werth* (☎ 365 00, fax 365 06, Von-Werth-Strasse 9) has imaginatively furnished singles/doubles for DM75/120. The family-run *Hotel Hamm* (☎ 30 32 10, fax 303 21 60, St-Josef-Strasse 32-34) near the Hauptbahnhof charges from DM98/130. *Hotel Am Schängel* (☎ 338 13, fax 386 48, Jesuitenplatz 1), in the Altstadt, charges DM65/125.

Places to Eat

Most of Koblenz's restaurants and pubs are in the Altstadt and along the Rhine. Of the traditional restaurants framing Am Plan, the cosy *Alt Coblenz* (☎ 16 06 56) has a good reputation and main courses from DM20 (dinner only). A tourist trap, though with decent food and drink, is the *Weindorf* (☎ 316 80, Julius-Wegeler-Strasse 2).

Young people gather at Görresplatz, where the happening *Café am Görresplatz* (☎ 100 22 30) draws a hip inter-generational crowd from breakfast to the wee hours. Salads, pizzas and sandwiches here are under DM10. In summer, seating spills out onto the square. It's recommended.

For a quiet chat, head to the *Pfefferminze* (☎ 144 57, Mehlgasse 12), which has snacks from DM4.50. *Havana* (☎ 100 46 84, Kornpfortstrasse 6) is a low-key cocktail bar that also serves food, including *rollos*, hot flatbreads stuffed with various ingredients. It's open for dinner only.

Getting There & Away

Train Koblenz is served by hourly IC train connections both north and south. Regional trains to Cologne (DM24.60, one hour) and Bonn (DM14.80, 40 minutes) depart at least hourly, as do trains heading south through the Rhine Valley and on to Frankfurt Hauptbahnhof (DM36, two hours) via Frankfurt airport. There's also regular service to Trier (DM30, 1½ to two hours).

Bus Koblenz is the hub for buses to nearby country towns. Bus No 6053 goes to Mayen in the Eifel, No 6050 to Boppard via Stolzenfels Castle. Other Rhine towns served include Braubach/Marksburg (bus No 6130) and St Goarshausen/Loreley (bus No 6129). To get to Höhr-Grenzhausen in the Westerwald, take bus No 6118.

Car & Motorcycle Several highways converge in Koblenz, including the B9 from Cologne/Bonn and the B49 from the Westerwald. The nearest autobahns are the A61 (Koblenz-Nord exit) and the A48/A1 to Trier.

Getting Around

There's a comprehensive bus system divided into zones, with most trips within the city costing DM2.20. Two zones (eg to the hostel) cost DM3.20 and day passes are DM11. To book a taxi, call ☎ 330 55.

AROUND KOBLENZ
Höhr-Grenzhausen
☎ 02624 • pop 8200

This little town lies in the heart of the Westerwald, a sparsely populated rural region of gentle hills and laid-back villages.

Thanks to its huge deposits of clay, the area has been renowned for its pottery since the Middle Ages. Today, it is the largest ceramic-producing region in Europe.

Höhr-Grenzhausen is one of the main towns on the **Kannenbäckerstrasse** (literally 'pot bakers' road'), a theme route that connects 10 communities. At many of the 40 potteries along the way you can watch the artists at work.

Everywhere you go along this route, you'll find the grey-blue glazed ceramics that are typical of the area. The region is also the main producer of beer steins, the kind that are so commonplace in Bavaria and other parts of Germany. They are also popular souvenir items.

A friendly and instructive pottery place to visit in Höhr-Grenzhausen is **Töpferhof Mühlendyck** at Lindenstrasse 39, just 200m up the street from the **Keramik Museum Westerwald** (☎ 94 60 10). This modern and spacious museum houses a comprehensive collection of both artistic and functional ceramics – from historical to contemporary – and also explains the production process. It's open from 10 am to 5 pm, closed Monday (DM4/1).

From the central bus station in Koblenz, bus No 6188 travels to Höhr-Grenzhausen.

BRAUBACH

Framed by vineyards and rose gardens, the snug 1300-year-old town of Braubach, about 8km south of Koblenz, unfolds against the dramatic backdrop of the **Marksburg** (☎ 02627-206). This hill-top castle's main claim to fame is that it has never been destroyed, thanks to several layers of fortification added by a succession of counts and landgraves. It has withstood all attacks, including those by the French in 1689, who laid to waste most other Rhine castles.

A tour takes in the citadel, the Gothic hall and the large functioning kitchen, plus the grisly torture chamber in the cellar with its hair-raising assortment of pain-inflicting instruments. The castle is open from 10 am to 5 pm; November to Easter hours are from 11 am to 4 pm (DM8/6). Take bus No 6130 from Koblenz's central bus station.

BOPPARD
☎ 06742 • pop 16,500

Boppard is about 20km south of Koblenz on a horseshoe-shaped river bend and has among the best tourist infrastructure of the Rhine villages. It began as a Roman military camp, remnants of which still exist today. Along with other attractions, they can be seen in the 200m-wide band between the Rhine and the train tracks. The main thoroughfare is the pedestrianised Oberstrasse.

Boppard's tourist office (☎ 38 88, fax 814 02, email tourist@boppard.de) is on the Markt and is open from May to September weekdays from 8 am to 5.30 pm (the rest of the year to 4 pm) and Saturday from 9 am to noon. English-language city tours run every Tuesday at 3 pm in season.

To change money, there's a Sparkasse at Oberstrasse 141. The post office is at Heerstrasse 177, just east of the train station. For information via the Internet, check www.boppard.de.

Things to See

A church has stood on the site of what once were Roman thermal baths at the Markt since the 5th century. Today's twin-towered **St Severus Kirche** dates to the 13th century and has a web vaulted ceiling. The triumphal cross above the main altar (1225) is considered the finest in the region.

A couple of blocks east of the church, in a 14th century palace on Burgstrasse, is the **Museum der Stadt Boppard** (☎ 103 10), with

RHINELAND-PALATINATE

an extensive exhibit of the furniture of Boppard's most famous son, Michael Thonet (1796-1871), creator of the 'Viennese coffeehouse style' of bent wood furniture. Museum hours are April to October from 10 am to noon and 2 to 5 pm, closed Monday (free).

Boppard's ancient origins come vividly alive in the **Archaeological Park**, often mistakenly called Römischer Park (Roman Park) on signs throughout town. While it does incorporate 55m of the original Roman camp wall, it also contains graves from the Frankish era (7th century) and a section of a medieval store/dance hall. The park's on Angertstrasse, one block inland from Oberstrasse (entry is free).

Activities

The 20 minute chair lift ride (DM7/4.50, return DM10/6.50) takes you from Mühltal station to the **Vierseenblick**, a hill-top spot where you have the illusion of looking at four lakes instead of a single river. It's also a good starting point for hikes.

A lovely excursion is a ride on the **Hunsrückbahn** (☎ 24 34), a train that travels through five tunnels and across two viaducts while ascending 330m on its scenic 8km trip from Boppard to Buchholz (DM3). Many people get off here and hike back to Boppard, though the train actually continues to Emmelshausen (DM4.60).

On Thursday in season, at 8 pm, the tourist office organises **wine tastings** with different vintners at different estates (DM8 for five wines).

Places to Stay & Eat

The nearest camping ground is *Camping-Park Sonneck* (☎ 21 21), beautifully located on the Rhine about 5km north of Boppard, and with modern facilities and a pool (bus No 6050, ask the driver to drop you off). The nearest *DJH hostel* is in St Goar (see the following St Goar section).

The tourist office has a free reservation service for hotel and private rooms. A good choice is the *Günther Garni* (☎ 23 35, fax 15 57, Rheinallee 40), which has an American co-owner, a riverside location and

modern rooms with TV, phone, hair dryer and private facilities for DM54 to DM69 for singles and DM96 to DM146 for doubles.

A bit old-fashioned, but with rooms sporting all amenities, is *Hotel Rebstock* (☎ 48 76, fax 48 77, Rheinallee 31) across from the car ferry landing. Prices are DM60 to DM90 for singles and DM90 to DM150 for doubles. Next to the Archaeological Park is *Weinhaus Sonnenhof* (☎ 32 23, fax 32 56, Kirchgasse 8), which charges from DM48/88.

Wine taverns serving traditional German food include the *Felsenkeller* (☎ 21 54, Mühltal 21) and *Weinhaus Heilig Grab* (☎ 23 71, Zelkesgasse 12). For a more upmarket meal, go to the snug *Zum Schnuggel-Elsje* (☎ 27 07, Untere Marktstrasse 24), in a historical half-timbered house. Boppard also has its share of inexpensive pizzerias.

ST GOAR/ST GOARSHAUSEN
☎ 06741/06771 • pop 3500

St Goar, 10km upstream from Boppard, is a routine stop on the tourist circuit, largely because of its proximity to the legendary Loreley rock. A much more impressive highlight, though, are the sprawling ruins of Burg Rheinfels above the town. St Goar's sister town, St Goarshausen, is across the river and served by ferry.

The train station is a couple of blocks inland on Oberstrasse, but train tickets must be bought at Reisebüro Müller at Heerstrasse 93, which also functions as the post office.

Heerstrasse, in fact, is the main drag and also the location of the tourist office (☎ 383, fax 72 09) at No 86. It's open weekdays from 8 am to 12.30 pm and 2 to 5 pm (plus Saturday morning in season). The Kreissparkasse across the street at No 81 is a convenient place to change money.

Things to See

Whatever you do, don't miss **Burg Rheinfels** (☎ 383), once the mightiest fortress on the Rhine. Built in 1245 by Count Dieter V of Katzenelnbogen as a base for his extortionate toll-collecting operation, its size and labyrinthine layout is astonishing, as is the network of subterranean tunnels and mine galleries. It's open from April to October daily from 9 am to 6 pm, and on fine weekends from November to March (DM5/3).

Kids might also like the **Doll and Bear Museum** (☎ 72 70), Sonnengasse 8, open daily from 10 am to 5 pm (DM5/4, children DM2.50).

From Rheinfels you have a good view of two castles on the Rhine's right bank. Downstream is **Burg Maus** (Mouse Castle), originally called Peterseck and built by the archbishop of Trier in an effort to counter Count Dieter's toll practices. In a show of medieval muscle-flexing, the latter responded by building yet another, and much bigger, castle above St Goarshausen. He called it **Burg Katz** (Cat Castle) and so, to highlight the obvious imbalance of power between count and archbishop, Peterseck soon came to be known as Burg Maus. These days, Burg Maus houses an eagle and falcon station (☎ 06771-76 69), reached by a 20 minute walk from St Goarshausen-Wellmich. Burg Katz is in Japanese hands and not open to the public.

One of the most anticipated sights of any trip down the Rhine Valley is the **Loreley rock**. Though nothing but a giant slab of slate, it owes its fame to a mythical maiden whose siren songs lured sailors to their death in the treacherous currents. You can make the one hour trek to the top from St Goarshausen, but once there you'll most likely be joined by throngs of day-trippers who came up by coach. A Loreley sculpture, depicting her as a buxom beauty, perches lasciviously at the tip of a strip of land jutting into the river.

Places to Stay & Eat

Camping Loreleyblick (☎ 20 66) is right on the Rhine opposite the Loreley; it's open all year but fills up quickly in season. *Camping Friedenau* (☎ 368, Gründelbachstrasse 103), a 20 minute walk west of the train station, is open from April to October. There's no public transport to either and both are rather old-fashioned. St Goar's basic *DJH hostel* (☎ 388, fax 28 69, Bismarckweg 17)

is right below Rheinfels Castle and charges DM20 plus DM5 for sheets.

Private rooms and true budget hotels are scarce. One of the cheaper digs is *Hotel Keutmann* (☎ 16 91, fax 72 20, An der Loreley 24), where rooms are DM50/95 for singles/doubles. *Hotel zur Loreley* (☎ 16 14, fax 25 50, Heerstrasse 87) has rooms topping out at DM75/130.

You'll find plenty of restaurants along Heerstrasse. Next to the train station is *Weinstube zur Krone* (☎ 76 80, Oberstrasse 38), which serves German mains for under DM20. Another option is the rustic *Vielharmonie* (☎ 78 79), the more casual of the two restaurants in Burg Rheinfels (closed Monday). Good Italian restaurants are *Bon Appétit* (☎ 73 78, Heerstrasse 99) and *Alla Fontana* (☎ 961 17, Pumpengasse 5).

BACHARACH
☎ 06743 • pop 2400

Bacharach hides its not inconsiderable charms behind a time-worn town wall and is therefore easily bypassed. Walk beneath one of its thick arched gateways, though, and you'll find yourself in a beautifully preserved medieval village with gorgeous half-timbered houses, including the **Altes Haus** on Oberstrasse, the town's main street. About a 15 minute walk above town looms **Burg Stahleck**, a 12th century castle occupied by the hostel. Halfway up the hill you'll pass the filigree frame of the **Wernerkapelle**, a medieval chapel destroyed, like so much else around here, by the French in 1689.

Back on Oberstrasse stands the late Romanesque **Peterskirche**, which has a particularly suggestive set of capstones. Look for the one of the naked woman with snakes sucking her breasts and another showing a man whose beard is being stroked by dragons (both are warnings about the consequences of adultery) at the end of the left aisle.

The diminutive tourist office (☎ 29 68, fax 31 55) is at Oberstrasse 1, and can help with finding accommodation. *Campingplatz Sonnenstrand* (☎ 17 52) is on the Rhine about 500m south of the town centre, and open from April to mid-November.

euro currency converter DM1 = €0.51

RHINELAND-PALATINATE

The *DJH hostel* (☎ *12 66, fax 26 84)* in Burg Stahleck has recently been renovated and charges DM24 for four-bed rooms, or DM30 for twin rooms with shared facilities but including breakfast and sheets. The cheapest accommodation in town is at *Haus Dettmar* (☎/fax *29 79, Oberstrasse 8)*, which charges just DM25 to DM35 per person for rooms with bath and breakfast.

Among the best of the many wine taverns is *Zum Grünen Baum (Oberstrasse 63)*, which has delicious, inexpensive wines and a friendly, English-speaking proprietor with an uncanny memory for faces. It's recommended.

BINGEN
☎ 06721 • pop 25,000

Strategically located at the confluence of the Nahe and Rhine, Bingen has seen its share of conflicts throughout the centuries, having been destroyed and rebuilt eight times since it was founded by the Romans in 11 BC. Far less touristy than Rüdesheim across the river, Bingen is a good alternative as a base from which to explore the southern section of the Rhine Valley and the Rheingau, the only section of the river that flows due west.

The Nahe River cuts right through Bingen, with the city centre spreading out on its eastern bank. Of Bingen's two train stations, the smaller train station is near the Rhine west of the Nahe. Most long-distance trains stop here. Local trains also stop here and at Bahnhof Bingen (Rhein) Stadt, only 2km farther east.

Bingen's tourist office (☎ 18 42 05, fax 162 75, email tourist-information@bingen .de) is at Rheinkai 21, and is open weekdays from 9 am to 6 pm, Saturday to 12.30 pm. On Mainzer Strasse are a Sparkasse branch at No 26 and the main post office at No 43. Bingen's Web site is at www.bingen.de.

Things to See & Do

One of Bingen's landmarks is **Burg Klopp**, resting on a hill top right in the town centre and occupied by the city hall and a **Heimatmuseum** (☎ 18 41 10) whose prized exhibit is a complete set of Roman surgical instruments. It's open Easter to October from 9 am to noon and 2 to 5 pm, closed Monday (DM1/0.50).

Housed in a former electricity works is Bingen's new **Historisches Museum am Strom** (☎ 99 06 54), Museumsstrasse 3, which addresses topics related to Bingen and the Rhine Valley. Its permanent exhibit may still be a work in progress, but topics like the life and works of Hildegard von Bingen (see the boxed text) and the Romantic Rhine as seen by artists are already part of the repertory. It's open daily except Monday from 10 am to 5 pm (DM8/4).

Up on Rochus Hill is the neo-Gothic **Rochuskapelle**, a pilgrimage church with a splendid canopied altar showing scenes from the life of Hildegard von Bingen. It's usually closed, but the interior is visible through a glass screen.

On an island in the Rhine is the **Mäuseturm** where, according to legend, the sadistic Bishop Hatto was devoured by mice when confined there. Previously, he had set fire to a barn in which he had locked a group of starving peasants who had asked him for grain after a bad harvest. In reality, though, the name is a mutation of *Mautturm*, or toll tower, which is what the building was during the Middle Ages.

Places to Stay & Eat

The *camping ground* (☎ *171 60, fax 169 98)* is on the Rhine in the eastern suburb of Bingen-Kempten (open from May to October; bus No 1). The *DJH hostel* (☎ *321 63, fax 340 12, Herterstrasse 51)* is downriver in the suburb of Bingerbrück and charges DM20, plus DM5 for sheets. It's a 10 minute walk from the train station.

The tourist office can help find accommodation and requires a 6% down-payment upon booking. If you don't mind the nearby railway line, the best hotel deal is offered by *Haus Clara* (☎/fax *92 18 80, Rheinkai 3)*, which has basic singles/doubles for DM50/100 and rooms with private bath from DM65/120. The top hotel is *Best Western Rheinhotel* (☎ *79 60, fax 79 65 00)*, where

Hildegard von Bingen

MICK WELDON

She's hip and holistic, a composer, dramatist and a courageous campaigner for the rights of women. She heals with crystals and herbs, her music frequently hits the New Age charts ... and she's been dead for more than 800 years.

Hildegard von Bingen was born in 1098 at Bermersheim (near Alzey), the 10th child of a well-off and influential family. At the age of three she experienced the first of the visions that would occur over the course of her extraordinarily long life. As a young girl she entered the convent at Disibodenberg on the Nahe River and eventually became an abbess who founded two abbeys of her own: Rupertsberg, above Bingen, in 1150; and Eibingen, across the river near Rüdesheim, in 1165. During her preaching tours – an unprecedented female activity in medieval times – she lectured both to the clergy and the common people, attacking social injustice and ungodliness.

Pope Eugen III publicly endorsed her, urging her to write down her theology and visionary experiences. This she did in a remarkable series of books that encompasses ideas as diverse as cosmology, natural history and female orgasm. Her overarching philosophy was that humankind is a distillation of all of God's greatness and should comport itself accordingly. Her accomplishments are even more remarkable considering her life-long struggle against feelings of worthlessness and the physical effects of her mysterious visions, which often left her near death.

Hildegard von Bingen was a force of nature who remains as much a cult figure today as she was during her life. She died in 1179.

you'll pay from DM165/235 for small but fully equipped rooms.

For eats, winners include **Brunnenstübchen** (☎ 106 63, *Vorstadtstrasse 58*), a wine bar near the tourist office whose creative young cook makes modern versions of regional favourites. Also popular with Bingen's in-crowd is **Life & Art House** (☎ 126 95, *Speisemarkt 3*), a bistro-cum-gallery in the heart of the pedestrian zone.

Getting Around

City-Linie minibuses shuttle between all major points of interest every 30 minutes

and are a good deal at DM1/0.50 per trip. The car/passenger ferry to/from Rüdesheim operates continuously to midnight.

RÜDESHEIM

☎ 06722 • pop 10,360

Rüdesheim is the capital of the Rheingau, famous for its superior Riesling. It is on the right bank, about 25km west of Wiesbaden. Rüdesheim is a quintessential wine town and a mecca for some three million yearly visitors – most of them middle-aged or older. Their 'shrines' are the wine bars and restaurants along the narrow Drosselgasse, the main drag. Every day between May and September, the ornate half-timbered houses here vibrate with music and the laughter of a rollicking crowd fond of a good time. If this is not your scene, simply wander beyond these 100m of drunken madness to discover that Rüdesheim is actually quite a classy place.

The tourist office (☎ 29 62 or ☎ 2194 33, fax 34 85) is at Rheinstrasse 16 and is open weekdays from 8.30 am to 6.30 pm, Saturday 10.30 am to 5.30 pm and Sunday 11.30 am to 3.30 pm. The post office is about 100m west on Rheinstrasse, with the train station and ferry landing dock just beyond here.

Things to See & Do
Rüdesheim is too small to avoid the Drosselgasse razzmatazz completely, though it's easy to escape. One island of calm is **Siegfrieds Mechanisches Musikkabinett** (☎ 492 17), Oberstrasse 29, a fun collection of mechanical musical instruments, such as pianolas, from the 18th and 19th centuries. Many are demonstrated during the guided tour offered from March to November daily from 10 am to 10 pm (DM9/5 – steep, but kinda worth it).

Also of interest is the **Weinmuseum** (☎ 23 48) in the 1000-year-old Brömserburg castle at Rheinstrasse 3, with a large collection of rare drinking vessels from Roman times onward. Hours are from March to November daily from 9 am to 6 pm (DM5/3).

A recent addition is the **Deutsches Motorroller Museum** (☎ 46 96), Rheinstrasse 5, which showcases more than 100 historical motor scooters (DM5/2.50).

For a bird's-eye view over the Rhine Valley and its vineyards, either walk or take the gondola up to the grandiose **Niederwald Denkmal** (1883). This giant monument glorifies the establishment of the German Reich in 1871 and is topped by a heroic figure of Germania. The gondola leaves from Oberstrasse and gains 200m in elevation during its 1500m journey (DM6.50/3.50, return DM10/5). There's also a chair lift from Assmannshausen (same prices), an island of red wine in a sea of white Riesling.

If you go up on the gondola and down on the chair lift, the cost is DM10/5.

The only wine estate that offers wine tastings to individuals is **Weingut Georg Breuer** at Grabenstrasse 8. Its wines are delicious, and the DM11 charge to try four or five wines is waived if you're buying.

Places to Stay & Eat
Campingplatz Auf der Lach (☎ 25 28), east of town on the Rhine, is open from May to October. The **DJH hostel** (☎ 27 11, fax 483 84) is in the vineyards above Rüdesheim at Am Kreuzberg and costs DM22/27 for juniors/seniors; sheets are DM6. It's about a 30 minute walk from the train station; there's no bus.

Hotel Zur Guten Quelle (☎ 27 57, fax 477 29, Katharinenstrasse 3) is one budget option, with singles/doubles from DM65/80. You'd never expect to find a modern, stylish and artsy hotel off the Drosselgasse, but that's just what the family-run **Rüdesheimer Schloss** (☎ 905 00, fax 479 60, Steingasse 10) is. Spacious rooms with one-of-a-kind designer furniture cost from DM150/180 and are well worth the splurge.

AROUND RÜDESHEIM
Kloster Eberbach
If you saw the 1986 film *The Name of the Rose*, starring Sean Connery, you've already 'visited' this one-time Cistercian monastery, where a number of scenes were shot. Dating back to the 12th century, the graceful structure went through periods as a lunatic asylum, jail and sheep pen after secularisation in the 19th century. In 1918, it was turned into a state-owned winery.

Visitors can walk through the monks' refectory and dormitory, as well as to the austere Romanesque basilica, the site of a classical concert series from May to October. Wine tastings are held on weekends and holidays (April to October) in the musty cellars (DM7.50 for three wines). Hours are daily from 10 am to 6 pm, and in winter to 4 pm (DM5/3).

Eberbach is about 20km from Rüdesheim but if you're not driving, the only way to get here is by taking the train or bus to Eltville, followed by a one hour signposted walk.

The Moselle Valley

Where other places in Germany demand that you hustle, the Moselle *suggests* that you mosey along at your own pace. The German section of the Moselle runs 195km north-east from Trier to Koblenz. The river follows a slow, winding course, revealing new scenery at every bend.

Exploring the vineyards and wineries of the Moselle Valley is an ideal way to get a taste for German culture, people and – of course – some wonderful wines. Slow down and do some sipping. There is, however, more to the Moselle than wine.

You'll encounter many historical sites and picturesque towns built along the river below steep, rocky, cliff-side vineyards. The entire route crawls with visitors from June to October, though getting off the beaten path is generally quite easy.

Wine Tasting

The main activities along the Moselle Valley are eating and drinking. Wine tasting and buying are why most people visit the area – just pick out a winery and head inside. It's considered impolite to drink too much without buying at least a couple of bottles. Organised tastings are also offered by local tourist offices and at central wine shops (such as the Vinothek in Bernkastel-Kues – see that section).

Hiking

The Moselle Valley is especially scenic walking country. Expect some steep climbs if you venture away from the river, but the views are worth all the sore muscles. The region is covered by a series of three 1:50,000-scale hiking maps; each sheet costs DM8.80.

A popular long-distance hike is the **Moselhöhenweg**, which runs on both sides of the Moselle for a total of 390km. A detailed booklet with route details is available, usually free, at local tourist offices.

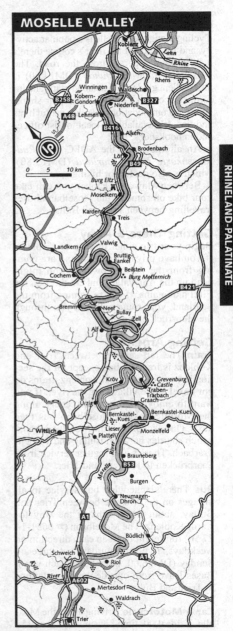

MOSELLE VALLEY

RHINELAND-PALATINATE

euro currency converter DM1 = €0.51

Cycling

Cycling along the Moselle is a popular activity, and for much of the river's course there's a bike track separate from the road. The *Moselland-Radwanderführer* (DM14.80) is an excellent guide, with detailed maps and information on bike rentals and repair shops, sights, accommodation and other useful hints and tips. It's available at local tourist offices and in bookshops.

An alternative is the ADFC map *Radtourenkarte Mosel-Saarland* (DM13.80), which is also useful for hiking.

Between May and October you can take your bike on some of the Moselbahn buses travelling between Trier and Bullay.

Getting There & Away

Begin your trip either in Trier or Koblenz. If you have private transport and are coming from the north, however, you might head up the Ahr Valley and cut through the Eifel mountains. If you're coming from the Saarland, your route will lead you through the Hunsrück mountains.

Getting Around

Train The rail service between Trier and Koblenz is frequent but, except for the section between Bullay and Koblenz, trains do not travel to the villages on the river. If you want to enjoy the beautiful scenery along the Moselle, take a Moselbahn bus (see next). One exception is the Moselweinbahn, which shuttles between Bullay and Traben-Trarbach. There's also regular service from Saarbrücken to Koblenz and Trier.

Bus There's scheduled bus service to all villages on the Moselle between Trier and Bullay, about three-fifths of the way towards Koblenz. The Moselbahn (☎ 0651-14 77 50) runs eight buses in each direction on weekdays, five on Saturday and three on Sunday (DM16.60, three hours each way). Buses leave from outside the train stations in Trier and Bullay.

Car & Motorcycle Driving along the Moselle is ideal, if time-consuming. The B53

from Trier, which continues as the B49 just north of Traben-Trarbach, follows the river course all the way to Koblenz, crossing it several times.

Boat The Moselle is at its most scenic between Trier and Bernkastel-Kues. The river's winding course, however, also makes water travel particularly slow. Add to that a fair number of locks – needed to compensate for the 70m difference in elevation between Koblenz and Trier – and it's easy to understand why boats take two days to cover the entire distance.

Between May and October, the KD line sails daily between Koblenz and Cochem, stopping several times along the way. Rail passes like Eurail and GermanRail are valid for scheduled KD services. Children up to age four travel for free, those up to age 13 are charged a flat DM5. Students get a 50% discount. Travel on your birthday is free. In general, return tickets cost only slightly more than one-way tickets.

Between Cochem and Trier, the Gebrüder Kolb Line (☎ 02673-15 15) is the dominant operation, with scheduled boat service from April to October. Its repertory also includes day excursions and one-hour panorama tours from various towns. In most villages, local boat operators offer additional options.

TRIER

☎ 0651 • pop 99,700

Trier shares the title of 'Germany's oldest town' with Worms and was founded by the Romans as Augusta Treverorum in 15 BC. In the 3rd century, it became the capital of the Western Roman Empire and the residence of emperors like Constantin the Great. More Roman ruins cluster here than anywhere else north of the Alps and, despite a host of architectural gems from later ages, they are still the main reason Trier garnered UNESCO World Heritage Site status in 1986.

Trier's second heyday began in the 13th century, when its archbishops acquired the rank and power of prince-electors. In the following centuries, the town see-sawed between periods of prosperity and poverty. Trier was briefly French in the early 19th century before being swallowed up by Prussia in 1815. It is the birthplace of Karl Marx (1818).

The town is beautifully located on the Moselle and hemmed in by the Eifel and Hunsrück mountains. Its proximity to Luxembourg and France can be tasted in the local cuisine, and about 18,000 students do their part to infuse a lively spirit.

Trier is an inspiring place that deserves at least a couple of days of exploration. It also makes an excellent base for trips down the Moselle River, to Luxembourg or into the nearby mountains.

Orientation
Sights cluster in the city centre, an area of approximately one sq km that is bordered by a ring road on three sides and by the Moselle to the west.

The Hauptbahnhof is in the north-eastern corner and connected to the Porta Nigra, the Roman gate that is Trier's main landmark, via Bahnhofstrasse, which turns into Theodor-Heuss-Allee. The pedestrianised centre begins south of the gate.

Boat tours leave from the docks at Zurlaubener Ufer.

Information
Tourist Office The tourist office (☎ 97 80 80, fax 447 59, email info@tit.de) is right at the Porta Nigra, and has maps and booklets in English and French and staff fluent in both. It's open April to November from 9 am to 6.30 pm, Sunday to 3.30 pm (slightly reduced hours the rest of the year).

Ask here about daily guided walking tours in English held between May and October (DM10/3), and rides aboard the Römerexpress, a trolley that ticks off the main sights in three languages and 30 minutes (DM10/5).

The TrierCard gives you free or reduced admission to main attractions and museums and is good for three consecutive days. It costs DM17 for one person, DM32 for families. TrierCardPlus includes public transport and costs DM25/44.

Money The banks include Sparkasse at Simeonstrasse 55 near the tourist office and Citibank on Grabenstrasse 12. Both also have ATMs that accept credit cards.

Post & Communications Trier's main post office is at the Hauptbahnhof and open to 8 pm on weekdays. It's also open to 2 pm on Saturday and from 11 am to noon on Sunday. A second branch is at Am Kornmarkt in the pedestrian zone.

Bookshops Trier's largest and most interesting bookshop is Akademische Buchhandlung Interbook (☎ 97 99 01), located at Fleischstrasse 62.

Laundry There's a convenient laundrette, the Waschcenter, at Brückenstrasse 19-21, which charges DM6 per wash and DM1 to use the dryer.

Medical Services & Emergency Call ☎ 11 50 for a doctor or pharmacist on night duty. There's a police station (☎ 977 00) at Christophstrasse 5 near the Hauptbahnhof.

Walking Tour
Trier's main Roman attractions – Porta Nigra, Kaiserthermen, Amphitheater and Barbarathermen – are open from Easter to October daily from 9 am to 6 pm, to 5 pm in winter (DM4/2 each or DM9/4.50 for all four sights).

Start your tour at Trier's chief landmark, the **Porta Nigra**, the imposing 2nd century city gate that was once part of the 6.4km-long Roman wall. Made from giant blocks of blackened sandstone held together by iron clamps, it has a central courtyard and two four-storey defensive towers jutting out from its northern facade. In the 11th century, it was turned into the church of St Simeon, whose surviving apse can be seen when touring the interior.

Right next to the Roman gate, in a converted monastery, is the **Städtisches Museum** (☎ 718 14 54), a regional history museum with an emphasis on art and artefacts from the Middle Ages onward. Hours

euro currency converter DM1 = €0.51

RHINELAND-PALATINATE

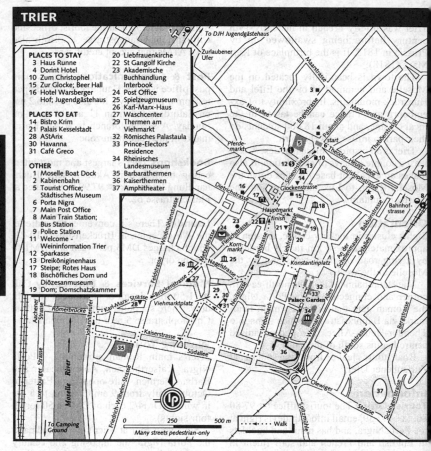

TRIER

PLACES TO STAY
3 Haus Runne
4 Dorint Hotel
10 Zum Christophel
15 Zur Glocke; Beer Hall
16 Hotel Warsberger
      Hof; Jugendgästehaus

PLACES TO EAT
14 Bistro Krim
21 Palais Kesselstadt
28 AStArix
30 Havanna
31 Café Greco

OTHER
1 Moselle Boat Dock
2 Kabinenbahn
5 Tourist Office;
    Städtisches Museum
6 Porta Nigra
7 Main Post Office
8 Main Train Station;
    Bus Station
9 Police Station
11 Welcome -
      Weininformation Trier
12 Sparkasse
13 Dreiköniginenhaus
17 Steipe; Rotes Haus
18 Bischöfliches Dom und
      Diözesanmuseum
19 Dom; Domschatzkammer

20 Liebfrauenkirche
22 St Gangolf Kirche
23 Akademische
      Buchhandlung
      Interbook
24 Post Office
25 Spielzeugmuseum
26 Karl-Marx-Haus
27 Waschcenter
29 Thermen am
      Viehmarkt
32 Römisches Palastaula
33 Prince-Electors'
      Residence
34 Rheinisches
      Landesmuseum
35 Barbarathermen
36 Kaisertermen
37 Amphitheater

are daily from 9 am to 5 pm, and in winter to 3 pm on weekends and closed Monday (DM3/1.50).

A short walk south on Simeonstrasse leads you past the ornate **Dreiköniginenhaus** (1230) at No 19 to the **Hauptmarkt** – the main square, anchored by a painted fountain whose sculptures represent St Peter and the four virtues. The market is framed by a harmonious ensemble of restored buildings, including the Gothic **Steipe**, a former banqueting house buttressed by an arched

arcade. Next door is the Renaissance **Rotes Haus**, with its early baroque gable.

The flowery portal on the square's south side leads to the 14th century **St Gangolf Kirche** with a muscular Gothic tower – once used to watch for fires – and nice floral frescoes inside.

Standing in the Hauptmarkt, the walls of the mighty **Dom** rise up to the east. The cathedral is mostly Romanesque, but incorporates an earlier Roman structure, as well as Gothic and baroque elements. Inside, it has a solemn simplicity, enlivened by a lavish stucco ceiling in the west apse, whose lower walls are clad in delicate inlaid panelling. A curiosity is the organ which, seemingly suspended from the ceiling, looks a bit like the fuel tanks of the NASA space shuttle. The **Domschatzkammer** (cathedral treasury) is open daily from 10 am to 5 pm, closed Sunday morning, restricted hours in winter (DM2/1).

More spectacular treasures are shown at **Bischöfliches Dom- und Diözesanmuseum** (☎ 710 52 55), north of the Dom at Windstrasse 6-8, where exhibits span from the early Christian era to the present. Highlights include a 4th century stucco ceiling, pieced together from countless fragments. The museum is open daily from 9 am to 5 pm, closed Sunday morning (DM4/2).

The Dom forms an ensemble with the **Liebfrauenkirche** (closed at lunchtime), one of Germany's earliest Gothic churches and built on the southern wing of an earlier Roman church. The cross-shaped structure is supported by a dozen round pillars symbolising the 12 apostles, and has a light, mystical quality, despite its strict symmetry.

Heading south on Liebfrauenstrasse will get you to another architectural masterpiece, the **Römische Palastaula**, a 4th century basilica that was once the throne room of Roman Emperor Constantin. Its dimensions (67m long and 36m high) are mindblowing, and no pillars or galleries support the immense coffered ceiling. It's open from April to October, Monday to Saturday from 9 am to 6 pm, and Sunday from 11 am to 6 pm. The rest of the year, it's open Tuesday to Saturday from 11 am to noon and 3 to 4 pm, and weekends from 11 am to noon.

In the 13th century, the prince-electors of Trier integrated the basilica into their residence, and it wasn't freed of its medieval alterations until King Friedrich Wilhelm IV of Prussia had it restored in the 19th century.

The **prince-electors' residence**, a pink rococo confection, still leans against the south side of the basilica. Here begins the stylised **Palace Garden** (Palastgarten), the green

axis ending at the Kaiserthermen ruins. On your way there, you'll pass the **Rheinisches Landesmuseum** (☎ 977 40) at Weimarer Allee 1, one of Germany's finest museums of prehistoric, Roman, early Christian and medieval art. It's open Tuesday to Friday from 9.30 am to 5 pm, weekends from 10.30 am, and is closed Monday (DM7/5).

The 4th century ruins of the **Kaiserthermen** (Imperial Thermal Baths) are a highlight of Trier. The arched remains of the eastern wall of these thermal baths rise 19m, and preside over a labyrinthine system of heating ducts, hot and cold-water pools and a sauna-like hot-air bath.

A few hundred metres east on Olewiger Strasse is the **Amphitheater**, once capable of holding 20,000 spectators during gladiator tournaments and animal fights. A visit includes the dank cellars once used to keep prisoners, caged animals and corpses. Both Kaiserthermen and Amphitheater are used as staging sites for the *Antikenfestspiele*, an annual open-air festival of tragedy, comedy and opera based on works by ancient Greek and Roman authors.

Head west on Kaiserstrasse, then turn right onto Neustrasse and left onto Viehmarktplatz, home of Trier's 'newest' Roman baths, the **Thermen am Viehmarkt**. Unearthed during excavations for a parking lot in the late 1980s, the ruins are sheltered by a dramatic glass cube designed by Cologne architect OM Ungers (free).

Head back to Kaiserstrasse via Hindenburgstrasse, then turn west past the synagogue to get to the final Roman structure, the **Barbarathermen**. Only the foundation, cellars and sections of the 1800-year-old floor heating system remain of these baths, whose stones were used to build a school in the 17th century.

From the baths, it's only a few steps west to the Moselle and the **Römerbrücke**, successor to a 2nd century bridge of which five of the seven pylons are still extant. Turn northeast onto Karl-Marx-Strasse, which becomes Brückenstrasse where, at No 10, stands **Karl-Marx-Haus** (☎ 430 11). The exhibit in this respectable town house, where the socialist

RHINELAND-PALATINATE

philosopher was born, encompasses photographs, first edition books, documents and manuscripts. Marx left Trier at age 17 to study law, philosophy and history at the universities of Bonn, Berlin and Jena. Hours are from 10 am to 6 pm, Monday from 1 pm, with curtailed hours in winter (DM3/2).

Kids especially will enjoy the whimsical collection of the **Spielzeugmuseum** (☎ 758 50), a block north-east at Nagelstrasse 4-5. Apart from the usual assortment of dolls and teddy bears, this toy museum contains some real rarities, including a miniature train environment on the 2nd floor. Hours are daily from 10 am to 5 pm, in winter from noon to 4 pm and closed Monday (DM7.50/4).

Continue right on Nagelstrasse, then turn left on Brotstrasse to get back to the Hauptmarkt.

Kabinenbahn

For a great view of Trier and the Moselle, as well as access to hundreds of kilometres of hiking trails, take this gondola (☎ 14 72 30) to the Weisshauswald. It departs from Easter to mid-November daily from 9 am to 6 pm (weekends to 7 pm) from the Zurlaubener Ufer. The restaurant Weisshaus (☎ 834 33) is a popular destination as well. Tickets are DM4.50/3, return DM8/4.

Places to Stay

The modern municipal camping ground **Trier-City** (☎ 869 21, fax 830 79, Luxemburger Strasse 81) is open all year and nicely positioned on the Moselle banks. The spick-and-span **DJH Jugendgästehaus** (☎ 14 66 20, fax 146 62 30, An der Jugendherberge 4), also by the river, charges DM27 per person in four-bed dorms or DM36.50 in doubles (all with shower and WC), sheets and breakfast included. Take bus No 3 or 40 from the Hauptbahnhof, change at Porta Nigra to bus No 7 or 8, get off at the bridge, then walk five minutes north along the river.

Trier's tourist office has a free room reservation service, and there's a surprisingly large number of good budget hotels. The central but simple **Hotel Warsberger Hof** (☎ 97 52 50, fax 975 25 40, Dietrich-strasse 42) charges DM39/78 for basic singles/doubles; it also operates the independent **Jugendgästehaus** (same ☎/fax), with beds for DM25 to DM27. Good value too is **Zur Glocke** (☎ 731 09, Glockenstrasse 12), which has functional singles/doubles for DM40/70 (DM80 with private bath).

It's worth paying a little extra to stay at **Haus Runne** (☎ 289 22, Engelstrasse 35), where clean, sunny rooms with private facilities cost DM45/90. Its restaurant is known for excellent Franco-German cooking. Right by the Porta Nigra is the spiffily renovated **Zum Christophel** (☎ 740 41, fax 747 32, An der Porta Nigra), which charges DM95 to DM120 for singles and DM160 to DM180 for doubles. The best view of the landmark gate, though, is from rooms at the **Dorint Hotel** (☎ 270 10, fax 270 11 70, Porta Nigra Platz 1), but expect to pay DM165/285 for the privilege.

Places to Eat

Trier has a wonderful repertory of restaurants catering for all budgets and tastes. For Franco-German cooking, head to **Bistro Krim** (☎ 739 43, Glockenstrasse 7), an innovative bar and eatery, which serves three-course set menus, including coffee, for around DM30 and interesting a la carte dishes, many under DM20. Across the street at No 12 (in the hotel of the same name) is **Zur Glocke** (☎ 731 09), a miniature beer hall that also has good wines and hearty food.

Facing the Dom and Liebfrauenkirche is the historic **Palais Kesselstadt**, a 650-year-old wine estate with a fancy restaurant, as well as a self-service wine bar with outdoor seating underneath a chestnut tree. Other traditional wine taverns cluster along the Moselle banks at the **Zurlaubener Ufer**, near the hostel and boat docks.

The area around Viehmarktplatz has evolved into a happening spot for younger people. Places to check out include **Havanna** (☎ 994 20 93, Viehmarktplatz 8), a stylish restaurant-bar with black club chairs, chrome bar stools and a reasonably priced Tex-Mex menu. Next door is **Café Greco** (☎ 490 98), a cosy cafe-bar with warm decor that blends antique and modern furniture. A favourite student hang-out is *AStArix* (☎ 722 39, *Karl-Marx-Strasse 11)*, where pasta, baked fetta and casseroles all cost well under DM10 (enter through the arcade).

Getting There & Away
The most convenient airport to Trier is in Luxembourg (☎ 00352-47 98 50 50), with flights throughout Europe and to New York. It's easily reached with the Trier-based Airport-Liner (☎ 71 72 73), a shuttle that must be ordered 24 hours in advance (DM20 per person each way).

Trier has several hourly train connections to Saarbrücken (DM22.10, one to 1½ hours) and Koblenz (DM30, 1½ to two hours). There are also frequent trains to Luxembourg and Metz (France). Regional buses into the Eifel or Hunsrück mountains leave from the central bus station in front of the Hauptbahnhof.

The city is connected to the A1 and A48 via the short A602 and is also crisscrossed by several *Bundesstrassen* (literally 'federal highways', but really secondary roads) from all directions.

Getting Around
Trier has a comprehensive public bus system, though the city centre must be explored on foot. Single tickets for the city area cost DM2.90, day passes are DM8.50 and six-ticket blocks are DM15. All are sold by bus drivers.

Rental bikes are available from the Radstation Bahnhof (☎ 14 88 56) in the Hauptbahnhof, at the DJH hostel and at the camping ground.

BERNKASTEL-KUES
☎ 06531 • pop 7500
About 70km downriver from Trier, at a dramatic river bend, is the 700-year-old double town of Bernkastel-Kues. It's the heart of the Middle Moselle region and a routine stop on many visitors' itineraries, making it pretty busy during the season. Bernkastel, on the right bank, is prettier and teems with wine taverns, while Kues has a younger

flair and most sights. The bus station is next to the boat docks in Bernkastel.

The tourist office (☎ 40 23/24, fax 79 53) is at Am Gestade 5, and is open weekdays from 8.30 am to 12.30 pm and 1 to 5 pm. In summer it's also open Saturday from 10 am to 4 pm. The Volksbank right next to the tourist office changes money, as does the Sparkasse a few metres downriver. The post office is in Bernkastel at Im Viertheil.

Things to See & Do
Bernkastel's main attraction is the **Markt**, a romantic ensemble of half-timbered houses with beautifully decorated gables. Note the medieval **pillory** to the left of the Rathaus. On Karlsstrasse, south-west of the Markt, you'll find the **Spitzhäuschen**, a tiny building looking a bit like a giant bird's house with its narrow base topped by a much larger, precariously leaning, upper floor. More such crooked gems line Römerstrasse and its side streets. Also take a look inside the 14th century **Pfarrkirche St Michael**, whose tower – ringed by a crown of eight smaller turrets – was originally part of the fortification wall.

Kues, across the bridge, is the birthplace of Nicolaus Cusanus (1401-64), a theologian (he died as general vicar of Rome) and one of the first German humanists to suggest that the earth was not at the centre of the universe. He built the town a hospice for exactly 33 men (one for every year of Christ's life) above the age of 50. Its inner courtyard, chapel and eastern cloister may be visited daily from 9 am to noon, and weekdays also from 2 to 6 pm (free). The hospice's famous library and its precious manuscripts can only be seen on a guided tour offered Tuesday at 10.30 am and Friday at 3 pm (DM5). To learn more about Cusanus himself, visit his birthplace at Nikolausufer 49 (☎ 28 31); it's closed Monday.

Also incorporated into the hospice complex is the Weinkulturelles Zentrum, with the **Mosel Weinmuseum** (☎ 41 55), open from mid-April to November daily from 10 am to 5 pm, afternoons only the rest of the year (DM3/1.50). An even greater draw is the adjacent **Vinothek** (☎ 41 41), housed

RHINELAND-PALATINATE

in the historic vaulted cellars where, for DM17, you can taste as much or as little of some 130 wines and sparkling wines from the Moselle-Saar-Ruwer as you wish. Bottles are available for purchase and priced from DM6. It's open daily from mid-April to November from 10 am to 5 pm, less in winter. Admission to the cellars is free.

Places to Stay & Eat

Campingplatz Kueser Werth (☎ 82 00) is 1km upriver from the bridge on a peninsula in Kues, while *Camping Schenk* (☎ 81 76) is in the Wehlen district and has its own wine estate.

The *DJH hostel* (☎ 23 95, fax 15 29, Jugendherbergsstrasse 1) charges DM26 in four-bed dorms and DM32 in double rooms, all with private bath and including breakfast and sheets.

The tourist office can help find accommodation for a fee of between DM3 to DM5, and plenty of *private rooms* from DM35 per person are available. Hotel options include the 32 bed *Hotel-Garni Arns* (☎ 68 25, fax 943 27, Jugendheimstrasse 1) in Kues, furnished in an old-fashioned way and charging only DM55/90 for singles/doubles with private facilities. In Bernkastel near the tourist office is *Hotel Bernkasteler Hof* (☎ 32 18, fax 77 94, Hebegasse 1), which asks DM65 for singles and DM110 to DM140 for doubles.

You'll find plenty of traditional eateries around the Markt in Bernkastel. For lighter versions of German food and good salads, try *Eulenspiegel* (☎ 65 70, Moselstrasse 7). Bars with a young flair are *Blue Heaven* (Gestade 3) and *Sammy's Keller* (☎ 943 44) in the old train station across the bridge in Kues.

TRABEN-TRARBACH
☎ 06541 • pop 5800

Those seeking relief from the 'romantic-half-timbered-town' circuit will welcome this smart double town. Art Nouveau (known as Jugendstil in Germany) is the architectural style that characterises Traben-Trarbach, and several grand old villas contribute to its provincial sophistication. It

was the trading – and not the production – of wine that brought wealth to this town which, at one time, was the second largest trading centre in Europe, after Bordeaux. Beneath the street surface lies a huge network of wine storage cellars.

Traben, on the left bank, is the commercial centre and was joined to Trarbach in 1904. The train station (with service to Bullay via the Moselweinbahn) is in Traben as well. It's a five minute walk south on Bahnstrasse to the centre and the tourist office (☎ 839 80, fax 83 98 39) at Bahnstrasse 22. It's open weekdays from 8 am to 5 pm (closed at lunchtime in winter). From May to October it's also open Saturday from 1 to 4 pm. Exchange facilities are at the Deutsche Bank, Bahnstrasse 38, and the Kreissparkasse at No 41 in Traben. The post office is on Poststrasse in Traben. For information via the Web, go to www.traben-trarbach.de (German only).

Things to See

Architecture fans will delight in Traben-Trarbach for its fanciful **Art Nouveau villas**, built after two fires (1857 and 1879) destroyed most of the older structures. Many were designed by the Berlin architect Bruno Möhring, already in town to build a bridge across the Moselle. The bridge itself was destroyed in WWII and replaced by the current steel monstrosity, but the **Brückentor**, on the Trarbach side, survived.

One of the best preserved and purest Art Nouveau villas is the **Hotel Bellevue** (1903) on the Moselpromenade, with its distinctive exterior incorporating an oriel with a slate-covered turret shaped like a champagne bottle. The dark oak lobby is bathed in muted light from stained-glass windows. The stylish restaurant has a slightly vaulted ceiling and walls decorated with stencilled friezes.

Unfortunately, the Hotel Bellevue is the only Art Nouveau house accessible to the public, since all the other villas are privately owned. But they are still worth admiring from the outside, especially **Haus Adolph Huesgen** at Am Bahnhof 20 and **Haus Breucker** at An der Mosel 7.

Of the surviving pre-19th century buildings, the baroque **Haus Böcking** on Enkircher Strasse in Trarbach houses the **Mittelmosel-Museum** (☎ 94 80), a local history museum; it's closed Monday (DM3/1).

High above the craggy hillside of Trarbach is the medieval **Grevenburg**, reached from the Markt via a steep footpath. Because of its strategic importance, the castle was destroyed 13 times between 1620 and 1734 by various enemy troops before being razed by the French in 1735.

Under King Louis XIV the French were also the architects of the giant **Mont Royal** fortress, built in 1697 on a high plateau on the left bank as a base from which to secure and expand France's power over the Rhineland. Little remains of the giant structure today, but it offers good views over the river valley.

Activities

Traben-Trarbach is also a spa town with hot mineral springs in its district of Bad Wildstein. You can experience these soothing waters at the **Moseltherme** (☎ 830 30), a state-of-the-art spa on Wildsteiner Weg, complete with sauna, indoor and outdoor pools, and jacuzzis. Day passes to both the pool and sauna are DM21, though you can spend as little as DM7 for one hour in the pool only.

You can rent a bike at Zweirad-Wagner (☎ 16 49), Brückenstrasse 42 in Trarbach; staff can also help with repairs.

Organised Tours

The tourist office organises **wine tastings** and cellar tours with different vintners every weekday evening (DM8). Pick up a schedule at the tourist office.

Places to Stay & Eat

Two camping grounds right on the Moselle and open from mid-April to October are *Campingplatz Rissbach* (☎ 31 11, Rissbacher Strasse 170) and *Campingplatz Wolf* (☎ 91 74, Wedenhofstrasse 25).

Beds at the newly modernised *DJH hostel* (☎ 92 78, fax 37 59, Hirtenpfad 6) in Traben cost DM26 in four-bed rooms and DM32 in

doubles, sheets and breakfast included (to get there, take bus No 6206 to Schulzentrum, or walk uphill for 20 minutes).

The tourist office makes free room reservations. If it's closed, you should find a list of vacancies posted on the door.

For those with tighter budgets, the *Altstadt Café* (☎ 81 06 25, fax 46 05, Mittelstrasse 12) in Trarbach charges DM45/88 for singles/doubles with private bath. If you can afford a splurge, spend the money at *Hotel Bellevue* (☎ 70 30, fax 70 34 00, Am Moselufer). Attention to detail and quiet and friendly service make a stay here a real treat; there's even a small sauna and pool. Dining in the classy gourmet restaurant is a culinary celebration. All this starts at a comparatively reasonable DM110/190 for large rooms with full facilities.

For a more rustic eatery, try the whimsically decorated *Alte Zunftscheune* (☎ 97 37, Neue Rathausstrasse) in Traben or the *Historische Kellerschänke Storcke Stütz* (☎ 68 18, Brückenstrasse 4) in Trarbach.

COCHEM

☎ 02671 • pop 5300

Cochem, 50km upriver from Koblenz, has all the trappings of a picture-postcard German village, complete with castle, narrow alleyways, half-timbered houses and town gates. But it's almost too cute for comfort and attracts more than its share of day-trippers.

Cochem's train station is at the northern end of town, from where it's only a short walk down Ravenéstrasse or Moselstrasse to the centre. The tourist office (☎ 600 40, fax 60 04 44, email verkehrsamt.cochem@lcoc.de), Endertplatz 1, is open weekdays from 10 am to 5 pm.

The Volksbank on the Markt changes money, as do other banks around town. On Ravenéstrasse, towards the train station, are both the post office and police station.

Things to See & Do

Cochem's *pièce de résistance* is the **Reichsburg** (☎ 255), poised atop a bluff south of the town. Although it matches everyone's imagined version of a medieval castle, it only dates from the last century, the 11th century original having fallen victim to frenzied Frenchmen in 1689. The walk up to the castle takes about 15 minutes. Guided tours (mid-March to January) last 45 minutes and cost DM8/4; English translation sheets are available.

For great views of town and river, head up to the **Pinnerkreuz** on the chair lift (☎ 98 90 63) leaving from Endertstrasse (Easter to mid-November from 10 am to 6 pm). The trip up costs DM6.90 (DM8.90 return), and it's a nice walk back down through the vineyards.

Places to Stay & Eat

Lovely riverside camping is offered at the *Campingplatz Am Freizeitszentrum* (☎ 44 09) on Stadionstrasse, about 1.5km downstream on the right bank. It's open from around Easter to late October; charges are DM6.50 per tent space and per person, plus DM3.50 per car. Cochem's *DJH hostel* (☎ 86 33, fax 85 68, Klottener Strasse 9) offers bed, breakfast and sheets for DM22.

A good budget place is *Pension Dapper* (☎ 74 71, fax 42 72, Moselstrasse 24) near the train station, which has basic doubles from DM54, or from DM64 with private shower and toilet. *Hotel Haus Erholung* (☎ 75 99, fax 43 62, Moselpromenade 64) counts a pool among its amenities and charges DM70/124 for singles/doubles.

A good sit-down fast-food choice is *Kochlöffel* (☎ 98 00 43, Markt 10), where a schnitzel with salad and chips (French fries) costs only DM7.80. A few paces uphill is *Zum Fröhlichen Weinberg* (☎ 41 93, Schlaufstrasse 11), which offers German home-style cooking for around DM15.

Getting There & Away

Trains to Cochem leave Koblenz several times per hour (DM12.20, 30 to 45 minutes). Boats to Beilstein and beyond also leave regularly.

AROUND COCHEM
Beilstein

On the right bank, about 12km upriver from Cochem, is Beilstein (population 160), a pint-sized village right out of the world of fairy tales. It's little more than a cluster of houses squeezed into whatever space has not been taken up by steep vineyards.

Its romantic townscape is further enhanced by the ruined **Burg Metternich**, a hill-top castle reached via a set of steps. There's little to do here but soak up the atmosphere during a stroll through the tiny lanes, taste some wine in one of the many cellars or walk up to the castle.

One of the finest buildings is the **Zehnthauskeller** where, in the Middle Ages, wine delivered as a tithing was stored. It now houses a romantically dark vaulted wine tavern.

From Cochem, catch bus No 8060 or alternatively, take the boat.

Burg Eltz

Victor Hugo thought this castle was 'tall, terrific, strange and dark', adding that he'd never seen anything like it. Indeed, Burg Eltz (☎ 02672-95 05 00), hidden away in the forest above the left bank of the Moselle, epitomises to many what medieval castles should look like.

The compact and impenetrable exterior is softened by scores of turrets crowning it like candles on a birthday cake. Eight residential towers stand gathered around an oval courtyard.

Burg Eltz has been owned by the same family for almost 1000 years and has never been destroyed. Highlights of the often crowded guided tour include the **Flag Room**, with its fan vaulted ceiling and the festive **Knights' Hall**. The **treasury**, which extends four floors beneath the rock, features a rich collection of jewellery, porcelain and priceless weapons.

The only direct access to Eltz, about 30km from either Koblenz or Cochem, is by private vehicle via the village of Münstermaifeld; it's a 10 minute downhill walk from the parking lot. Alternatively, take a train to the village of Moselkern (DM9.60, 30 minutes from Koblenz) and follow the signs for a scenic but strenuous one hour walk along the Elzbach stream up to the castle.

The castle is open from April to October daily from 9.30 am to 5.30 pm (DM9/6, entry to the treasury is an extra DM5/2).

Hunsrück Mountains

IDAR-OBERSTEIN
☎ 06781 • pop 34,300

The twin town of Idar-Oberstein is beautifully located in the Nahe River valley, about 80km east of Trier and about 90km north-east of Saarbrücken. Since the Middle Ages, its history and development have been inextricably linked to gemstone production and trade. Records of local agate mines go back to 1454, but the industry really took off after a bunch of local adventurers left for South America (especially Brazil) in the early 19th century. There they harvested raw stones as if they were potatoes, then sent them back home to be processed. To this day, Idar-Oberstein remains Germany's gem-cutting and jewellery manufacturing centre.

About one million day-trippers swamp the town annually, drawn by mines, museums and the minerals sold in countless shops. From about Easter to October, all attractions are open daily and, since all are indoors, they make ideal bad-weather destinations.

Orientation & Information

Idar-Oberstein consists of a string of communities lined up along the Nahe River for about 20km (you won't see much of the river, though, since it's been built over). The commercial centre is in Oberstein, also the site of the train station. The Markt is about 500m east of here. Bus Nos 1, 2, 3 and 4 regularly shuttle between Oberstein and Idar.

The tourist office (☎ 644 21, fax 644 25, email stadtverwaltung@idar-oberstein.de) is at Georg-Maus-Strasse 2, about 300m north of the train station, and is open weekdays from 9 am to 5 pm, plus Saturday from 9.30 am to 1 pm from May to October.

The Kreissparkasse on the Markt in Oberstein changes money and has a special counter open on weekends. The post office in Oberstein is at Hauptstrasse 34, about 200m north-west of the tourist office. The post office in Idar is inside the gemstone exchange building on Schleiferplatz. The town's Internet address is www.idar-oberstein.de (German only).

Things to See

Not surprisingly, most of Idar-Oberstein's attractions involve gemstones, and it's possible to learn about every stage of production from raw stone to brilliant bauble. Most sights are outside the city centre but easily reached by car or bus. Bus connections noted below leave from the train station in Oberstein.

In a natural park west of Idar are the **Edelsteinminen Steinkaulenberg** (☎ 474 00). Agates were still mined in this glittering underground world until 1870, but nowadays only hobby mineralogists dig for treasure in a designated 'miner's tunnel'. For DM25/10, you can keep whatever agates, amethysts, jasper, crystals or other gemstones you unearth during three hours of digging. Finds are guaranteed, but reservations are required and there's a minimum age of 16.

Non-diggers may visit the mines on a 30 minute guided tour from mid-March to mid-November daily from 9 am to 5 pm (DM7/4); take bus No 3 to Strassburgkaserne, then walk.

For a close-up look at how gemstones were traditionally processed, visit the **Historische Weiherschleife** (☎ 315 13), a 17th century cutting mill on Tiefensteiner Strasse. Lying belly-down atop tilting benches in front of water-driven wheels, the cutters demonstrate the stages of sawing, grinding, sanding and polishing. This is a tortuous process and in the old days, cutters rarely lived to be older than 30. It's open from mid-March to mid-December daily from 9 am to 5 pm (DM5/2.50); take bus No 1 to Weiherschleife.

The 9000 exhibits at the **Deutsches Edelsteinmuseum** (☎ 90 09 80), Hauptstrasse

RHINELAND-PALATINATE

118 in Idar, should dazzle even the most, well, jaded of visitors. Highlights include a 12.555 carat topaz from Brazil and copies of the famous Hope and Koh-i-Nor diamonds. Hours are daily from 9 am to 6 pm, in winter to 5 pm (DM8/6); take bus No 1, 2 or 3 to the Börse.

At the **Museum Idar-Oberstein** (☎ 246 19), near Markt in Oberstein, visitors are drawn by the fluorescent room, where special lamps produce interesting light effects, and the collection of crystals and quartz. Hours are daily from 9 am to 5.30 pm (DM6/3).

Wedged into the rockface above Markt, and reached via 230 steps, is the landmark 15th century **Felsenkirche** (☎ 228 40). Legend has it that this chapel was built by a knight inhabiting the castle above the church to atone for killing his brother over a woman. Inside there's a steadily trickling well and an unusual altarpiece. It's open from April to October daily from 10 am to 6 pm (DM3/1).

Above the church throne the twin castles **Burg Bosselstein** (1196) and **Schloss Oberstein** (☎ 1320) are reached by a 20 minute walk through a lovely beech forest. At the top, you'll be rewarded with great views over the town, the Hunsrück mountains and the Nahe Valley.

Places to Stay

The smallish *Campingplatz Im Staden* (☎ 318 21) is in the suburb of Tiefenstein, and charges DM5 per person, DM2 per car and DM2 per tent. It's open from April to October.

The following places are all in Oberstein. The town's modernised *DJH hostel* (☎ 243 66, fax 267 12, Alte Treibe 23) charges DM26/32 per person in quads/doubles (including private bath, breakfast and sheets). From the train station, take bus No 5 to the Café Weber stop or walk for 15 minutes.

Next door is the 37 bed *Naturfreundehaus* (☎ 224 50, fax 703 33) with B&B in doubles for DM26.30 or DM20.80 in dorm bunks. Facilities are shared.

The tourist office makes free hotel and private room reservations. A budget option is *Pension Trarbach* (☎ 256 77, fax 212 02, Wüstlautenbachstrasse 11), near the train station, where singles/doubles with shared facilities cost DM30/55 (DM35/75 with private bath). *Homericher Hof* (☎ 241 13, fax 211 82, Homerich 38-40) charges from a reasonable DM42/77 for rooms with shower and WC. More upmarket is the *Edelstein Hotel* (☎ 502 50, fax 50 25 50, Hauptstrasse 302), which has a pool and sauna and rooms for DM100/145.

Places to Eat

Unless you're a vegetarian, you shouldn't leave Idar-Oberstein without trying the local speciality, *Spiessbraten*. This is a large hunk of beef or pork, marinated in raw onion, salt and pepper, then grilled over a beechwood fire, which gives it its characteristic spicy and smoky taste. A good place to try this dish is *Badischer Hof* (☎ 240 71, Hauptstrasse 377), a respected restaurant right on Oberstein's pedestrianised main street. Another option is *Restaurant Kammerhof* (☎ 243 48, In der Kammer); closed Tuesday. For lighter or even meatless fare, go to *Café Extrablatt* (☎ 271 95, Kirchweg 1) above the Markt in Oberstein.

Getting There & Away

Idar-Oberstein has direct train links to Saarbrücken (DM19.60, one hour) and to Mainz (DM24.60, 1½ hours) at least once an hour. There are also direct trains to Frankfurt (DM36, 1¾ hours) every two hours.

Regional bus No 6440 leaves for Trier from the train station. The B41 and the B422 cross in Idar-Oberstein.

Saarland

Excluding the city-states of Berlin, Hamburg and Bremen, the Saarland is Germany's smallest state, covering a mere 2570 sq km. Yet this little piece of land has been hotly contested throughout its long history.

Already settled in Celtic and Roman times, the region was periodically governed by France throughout the Middle Ages. After Napoleon's defeat at Waterloo in 1815, it was divided by Prussia and Bavaria, both of whom coveted the area for its rich pockets of coal to fuel the burgeoning German economy. Under the Treaty of Versailles following WWI, Germany lost the Saarland, and it became an independent territory administered by the League of Nations under French guidance. In a referendum held in 1935, however, some 90% of all voters decided in favour of rejoining Germany. History repeated itself after WWII: the Saarland again became an autonomous region under French administration until another plebiscite in 1955 returned it to Germany. The Saarland has been a German *Land* since 1957.

With the steady decline of coal mining and steel production since the 1960s, the Saarland became one of the poorest and most depressed regions in western Germany. Restructuring began late – in the 1980s – and is still under way, with high-tech and service industries now making up for some of the jobs lost.

The state's scenery and its historical sights are assets that have been largely untapped, and the tourism industry is still in its infancy. This means that you won't find the same kind of infrastructure that you will along the Moselle, for instance, or in the alpine regions. On the other hand, you will find lots of natural beauty and a people unspoiled by the commercial trappings of mass tourism.

SAARBRÜCKEN
☎ 0681 • pop 191,000
Saarbrücken is the state capital of the Saarland and, though probably not tops on any-

HIGHLIGHTS

Saarland Luminaries:
Max Ophül,
Erich Honecker

- Visiting the monstrous Völklinger Hütte ironworks
- Cruising along the Saar river

LUXEMBOURG

Saarbrücken p662

FRANCE

SAARLAND

body's travel itinerary, it has a couple of museums and architectural sights worth exploring. It's also a good base from which to venture out to some of the other attractions in the Saarland. About 90% of the city was flattened in WWII and, in general, reconstruction has not been flattering. The proximity of smoking steel mills doesn't add much to its charm, either.

But Saarbrücken can hardly be called an industrial wasteland, as the entire city has

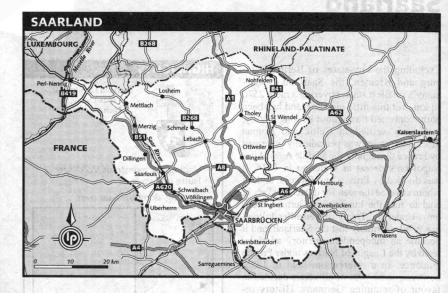

SAARLAND

been, and still is, undergoing a major face-lift. Vestiges of Saarbrücken's 18th century heyday under Prince Wilhelm Heinrich (1718-1768) survive in the baroque buildings designed by his court architect, Friedrich Joachim Stengel. Foodies will also find a trip to Saarbrücken rewarding – there are many atmospheric and well priced places in the historical centre around St Johanner Markt.

Orientation

Saarbrücken's centre is fairly compact. It's bisected by the Saar River, which runs north-west to south-east, parallel to the A620, the main artery through the Saarland. The Hauptbahnhof is at the north-western end of the centre on St Johanner Strasse. From here it's about a 15 minute walk south-east to St Johanner Markt.

Information

Tourist Offices The main tourist office (☎ 369 01, fax 390 35 3) is at Grossherzog-Friedrich-Strasse 1, and is open weekdays from 8 am to 5 pm. A second, more convenient, branch (☎ 365 15, fax 905 33 00) is

inside the Saar-Galerie on Reichsstrasse, the pedestrian street directly in front of the Hauptbahnhof. It is open weekdays from 9 am to 8 pm, and on Saturday to 3 pm (closed from 12.30 to 1 pm Saturday). Available here and in pubs and restaurants around town is *Kakadu*, the free monthly entertainment guide.

Money The Reisebank inside the Hauptbahnhof exchanges currency and travellers cheques, and is open weekdays from 7 am to 7.45 pm, Saturday from 8 am to 4 pm and Sunday from 9 am to 3 pm. In the foyer is an ATM that takes all major credit cards.

Post & Communications The main post office is at the Hauptbahnhof, and is open weekdays from 7.30 am to 6.30 pm and on Saturday to 1 pm. There's another one in the city centre on the corner of Dudweilerstrasse and Kaiserstrasse, open weekdays from 9 am to 6 pm and Saturday to noon.

Laundry There's a Waschcenter laundry at Beethovenplatz 7 and a slightly cheaper

Waschhaus laundry at Nauwieserstrasse 22. Both are open daily from 8 am to 10 pm.

Medical Services & Emergency The Caritasklinik St Theresia-Rastpfuhl (☎ 40 60) is a hospital at Rheinstrasse 2. There's a police station at Karcherstrasse 5.

Walking Tours

Northern Saar Bank Start your tour at the Hauptbahnhof. Just opposite is the **Saar-Galerie**, a huge, modern indoor shopping mall. Just east (left) of it begins Bahnhofstrasse, which is pedestrianised and lined by department and chain stores. Continue for about 600m to Betzenstrasse where, on the left, you can make out the cathedral-like **Rathaus** (1900). It's an imposing neo-Gothic red-brick pile by the architect Georg Hauberisser, who also built the town halls in Munich and Wiesbaden.

Continuing on Bahnhofstrasse you will soon reach **St Johanner Markt** which, along with its many alleyways and side lanes, forms Saarbrücken's historical core. In the centre of the square is the **Grosser Brunnen**, a fountain designed by Stengel with a filigreed wrought-iron balustrade; from its centre rises an ornamented obelisk crowned by a vase. The oldest houses are those at Nos 8 and 49, with windows from the late Gothic and early Renaissance periods.

The row of houses at Nos 18 to 28 dates to the baroque era. No 24 houses the **Stadtgalerie** (☎ 93 68 30), showcasing cutting-edge contemporary art, including video and performance art. It's open Tuesday and Thursday to Sunday from 10 am to 7 pm, Wednesday noon to 8 pm (free). Farther on you reach Türkenstrasse, from where you can make a short detour north for a look at **St Johannes Basilica**, another Stengel work.

Head back south on Türkenstrasse, then turn left (east) onto Bismarckstrasse; at No 11-19 you'll find the **Saarland Museum** (☎ 95 40 50). It's open from 10 am to 6 pm, Wednesday from noon to 8 pm, closed Monday (DM3/1.50). The main building houses the **Moderne Galerie**, which was being renovated at the time of research. Its permanent collection includes some nice works by German impressionists such as Slevogt, Corinth and Liebermann. There's also French 19th and 20th century art, and sculptures by artists like Richard Serra and Sigmar Polke.

In the building opposite at Karlstrasse 1 is the **Alte Sammlung** (same hours and prices as the Moderne Galerie) with almost a millennium's worth of paintings, porcelain, tapestries and sculptures from south-west Germany and the Alsace-Lorraine region of France. There are often special exhibits in either gallery (different prices apply).

Head west on Bismarckstrasse to the **Staatstheater** (☎ 322 04 for information and tickets), a grandiose yellow structure inspired by neoclassicism – a good example of the pompous architecture in vogue during the Third Reich. The theatre opened in 1938 with Richard Wagner's *The Flying Dutchman*.

Today's ensemble stages opera, ballet, musicals and drama (from classic to absurd). Just north of here is the **Alte Brücke**, a stone bridge that has connected the Saar's banks since 1546.

Southern Saar Bank Cross the Saar on Alte Brücke and head up to the **Saarbrücker Schloss**, which has risen from the ashes more times than a flock of phoenixes. The current incarnation dates back to 1810 and is a relatively plain, neoclassical U-shaped structure dominating the spacious Schlossplatz. The modern glass tower in the middle section was designed by Gottfried Böhm and put in place in 1989. Today, the palace houses administrative offices and sections of the **Historisches Saarmuseum** (☎ 50 65 49) in the basement of the right wing; there's more in the adjacent modern building. The museum documents the history of the Saarland with themed sections on WWI, the Third Reich and post-WWII reconstruction. It is open daily from 10 am to 6 pm, closed Monday (DM5/3).

Also on Schlossplatz, at No 16, is the **Museum für Vor- und Frühgeschichte** (Museum of Early History and Prehistory); it's open Tuesday as well as Thursday to

SAARLAND

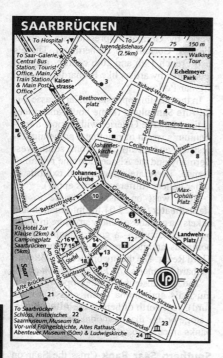

SAARBRÜCKEN

PLACES TO STAY
4 City-Hotel
5 Hotel Madeleine
6 Hotel Stadt Hamburg
14 Hotel Im Fuchs

PLACES TO EAT
1 La Carotte
13 Kerwan
15 Gasthaus Zum Stiefel
16 Hauck, Das Weinhaus
17 Stiefelbräu

OTHER
2 Police Station
3 Waschcenter
7 Post Office
8 Der Fahrradladen
9 Waschhaus
10 Rathaus
11 Main Tourist Office
12 St Johannes Basilica
18 Grosser Brunnen
19 Stadtgalerie; Kulturcafé
20 Mitfahrzentrale
21 Boat Landing
22 Staatstheater
23 Saarland Museum (Moderne Galerie)
24 Saarland Museum (Alte Sammlung)

Saturday from 9 am to 5 pm, Wednesday from noon to 8 pm and Sunday from 10 am to 6 pm (free).

Opposite the Schloss is the **Altes Rathaus**, originally built by Stengel in 1750 but simplified after WWII. Inside is the **Abenteuer Museum**, with a peculiar assortment of ethnic masks, sculptures and the like collected by Heinz Rox-Schulz on his solitary expeditions to Asia, Africa, South America and New Guinea. It's open Tuesday and Wednesday from 9 am to 1 pm, Thursday and Friday from 3 to 7 pm and some Saturdays from 10 am to 2 pm (DM3/2). There's a panoramic view of the river and town from atop the wall to the east of the palace.

From the Schloss, head west along Schlossstrasse to Eisenbahnstrasse and the impressive **Ludwigskirche** (1775), Stengel's crowning achievement. The festive sandstone structure dominates the generously sized Ludwigsplatz, lined with a collection of late-baroque town houses. Its main facade features a railing festooned with figures from the Old and New Testaments. As you enter, you may experience acute whiteout, for the entire interior is bathed in a pure, brilliant white – from the walls to the floor to the pews. A huge organ sits on a balcony above the main altar. The church has erratic opening hours but you can usually get at least a glimpse through the glass doorway.

This walk covers approximately 4km and takes about two hours excluding stops and museum visits.

Cruises

Saarbrücker Personenschiffahrt (☎ 340 84) runs three-hour boat trips from the landing near the Staatstheater, but don't expect too much in the way of scenery. It costs DM22 and includes a cup of coffee and a piece of cake. Every second Saturday, from May to early September, boats travel across the border to Sarreguemines in France (DM19, return DM26), sometimes also on market day (Tuesday).

Places to Stay
Camping The *Campingplatz Saarbrücken* (☎ 517 80, *Am Spicherer Berg*) is open from April to September and is near the German-French Garden (Deutsch-Französischer Garten) south of the city centre. Take bus No 42 from the Hauptbahnhof to the Spicherer Weg stop, from which it's a five minute walk. The cost is DM10 for a tent and DM8 per person.

Campingplatz Kanuwanderer (☎ 79 29 21, *Mettlacher Strasse 13*) is open year round and costs DM5 per tent and DM8 per person. Take bus No 10, 17 or 38 from the Hauptbahnhof to the Kirchen Burbach stop.

Hostels Saarbrücken's DJH *Jugendgästehaus* (☎ 330 40, *fax 37 49 11, Meerwiesertalweg 31*) is near the university in the north-east of town (take bus No 49 from the Hauptbahnhof or bus No 19 from Beethovenplatz near the Rathaus to Prinzenweiher). Single rooms cost DM51.60, a place in a two-bed room costs DM36.50, in a four-bed room DM27, including private shower and WC (toilet), breakfast and sheets.

Hotels The tourist office offers a free room-reservation service, but prices are relatively high because most hotels cater for business travellers.

Hotel Zur Klause (☎ 92 69 60, *fax 926 96 50, Deutschherrnstrasse 72*) is one of the cheapest. Rooms with shower and WC cost DM70/120 for singles/doubles. It's about 2km west of the centre. Take bus No 37 from the Hauptbahnhof. The central *Hotel Stadt Hamburg* (☎ 330 53, *fax 37 43 30, Bahnhofstrasse 71-73*) has basic singles for DM64 and singles/doubles with shower and WC for DM95/140. The *Hotel Madeleine* (☎ 322 28, *fax 37 47 04, Cecilienstrasse 5*) is also in the heart of the city. Rooms here cost DM95/120 with a shower and WC.

The small and rustic *Hotel Im Fuchs* (☎ 93 65 50, *fax 936 55 36, Kappenstrasse 12*) charges DM108/160 for rooms with private facilities.

The *City-Hotel* (☎ 340 88, *fax 320 35, Richard-Wagner-Strasse 67*) is funky and old-fashioned, with large rooms and friendly service. Rooms with full bath cost DM110/150.

Places to Eat
Saarbrücken has an active and attractive restaurant and bar scene that centres on St Johanner Markt. *Stiefelbräu* (☎ 936 36 17) is one lively place where you can enjoy the house brew and regional specialities at pub prices; enter from Fröschengasse. The affiliated *Gasthaus Zum Stiefel* (☎ 93 54 50), the oldest restaurant in town, serves more refined, and pricier, food (closed Sunday).

Hauck, Das Weinhaus (☎ 319 19, *St Johanner Markt 7*) is where you can relish just a glass of fine wine or choose from a smallish selection of wonderfully imaginative salads, soups and seasonal dishes. It's often filled with theatregoers after the curtain has come down.

La Carotte (☎ 31 41 11, *Karcherstrasse 15*) specialises in vegetarian food, with snacks and salads from DM5. Daily specials are around DM12.50 (closed Sunday).

The *Kulturcafé* (*St Johanner Markt 24*), in the Stadtgalerie building, is one good cafe. *Kerwan* (*Kappenstrasse 9*) serves tasty felafel and Turkish takeaway food.

Getting There & Away
Train Saarbrücken has at least once-hourly connections with Trier (DM23, one hour), Idar-Oberstein (DM20, one hour), Mainz (DM46, two hours) and Karlsruhe (DM48, three hours). Regional services to Völklingen (DM4.60, 10 minutes) and Homburg (DM10, 30 minutes) leave about every half hour. IC trains run to Frankfurt (DM60, 2½ hours), or take the IR/ICE via Mannheim (DM76, 2¼ hours).

Bus The central bus station for local and regional buses is on Bahnhofsplatz outside

SAARLAND

the Hauptbahnhof. Bus No 40 takes you right to the Völklinger Hütte (see the following section), though the train is faster and more frequent.

Car & Motorcycle Saarbrücken is bisected by the A620 leading north along the Saar to Merzig. It's also served by the A6 from Kaiserslautern and the A1 from the Moselle Valley. The B40 and B51 also cross the city.

Ride Services The Mitfahrzentrale (☎ 194 40) has an office at Grossherzog-Friedrich-Strasse 59.

Getting Around

For information on public transport in Saarbrücken, call ☎ 500 33 55. Bus and tram tickets valid for 4 stops cost DM2 and tickets for longer rides in the centre cost DM3. Both cost DM0.50 more if you purchase them from the driver instead of from machines at each stop. The 24 hour card costs DM7/10 for the city/region. Blocks of four cost DM6.50/10.50 short/city-trips and must be validated. A city version of the 24 hour card is also available for families with children, under the name *City-Familien Karte*. If you validate this pass after 5 pm on Friday, you can use it for the entire weekend.

You can book a taxi on ☎ 330 33.

Bicycles may be rented from Der Fahrradladen (☎ 370 98) at Nauwieserstrasse 19; prices start at DM15 a day for five-gear touring bikes and DM20 for 21-gear mountain bikes. There's a DM50 deposit.

VÖLKLINGER HÜTTE

About 10km down the Saar is the former Völklingen ironworks, one of Europe's great industrial monuments and a highlight of any visit to the Saarland. When it was founded in 1873, the Völklinger Hütte was among the last ironworks to be erected in Western Europe. Having survived the ravages of war, it fell into disuse as German manufacturing tapered off, was finally closed in 1986 and succumbed to rust and corrosion: an abandoned set from a version of *Metropolis* that was never filmed.

Today it exists as a testament to the Machine Age; its vast blast furnaces and the smelting houses that once spewed molten iron are now ice cold. Yet it has dignity, the sheer immensity of this industrial cathedral will have some people exclaiming, 'My God – *people* built this?'. So that future generations might understand the world of its time, the Völklinger Hütte was placed on UNESCO's World Heritage List in 1994.

The only way to see the plant is to take its two hour guided tour in German, offered daily except Monday from March to November at 10 am and 2 pm (DM6/4).

Völklingen is reached every 30 minutes by train from Saarbrücken. Völklinger Hütte is a short walk from the train station.

HOMBURG
☎ 06841 • pop 46,000

Homburg, about 35km north-east of Saarbrücken, in the gentle forested valleys of the Saarland-Palatinate, is a placid country town with a small student population from the Saarland University's School of Medicine.

Looking out over the town is the Schlossberg where you'll find one of Homburg's main attractions, the **Schlossberghöhlen caves**. The caves are open daily from 9 am to 6 pm, and to 4 pm from December to early February (DM5/3). The interior of the mountain has been hollowed out over six centuries, resulting in an amazing network of coloured sandstone caverns and tunnels that is purported to be the largest in Europe. Their original purpose was to provide an escape route and emergency supply channel for Hohenburg Castle, a fortress built atop the Schlossberg in the 12th century. Later they were used as ammunition magazines, as military barracks and, in WWII, as an air-raid shelter. Three of the 12 levels are accessible.

To get to the caves by foot, take the trail marked 'Zu den Höhlen' from the Markt in Homburg. By car, take the Schlossberghöhenstrasse to the top, from where it's a short walk back downhill to the entrance.

While you're in Homburg, it's also worth stopping by the **Römermuseum** (Roman Museum) in the suburb of Schwarzenacker. The Romans settled here between the 2nd and 3rd centuries AD. Some of their ruined houses and streets have been excavated and reconstructed, including a tavern and a house that supposedly belonged to an eye doctor. The house still has a functioning under-floor heating system; the skeleton of a Roman dog, who died trapped inside the ducts, lies here too. The museum is open from March to November daily except Monday from 9 am to 6 pm. The rest of the year it opens from 10 am to 4.30 pm (DM5/4).

Homburg's tourist office (☎ 20 66, fax 12 08 99) is in the Rathaus, Am Forum, and can help with finding accommodation. A pretty basic *DJH hostel (☎ 36 79, fax 12 02 20, Sickinger Strasse 12)* charges DM20 per bed, breakfast is included.

Homburg is easily reached by trains leaving from Saarbrücken every 30 minutes (DM10, 30 minutes). There are also frequent direct connections from Neustadt on the German Wine Road in Rhineland-Palatinate (DM17, one hour). If you're driving, take the Homburg exit off the A6 (Mannheim-Saarbrücken).

METTLACH
☎ 06864 • pop 11,500

Mettlach, about 30km downriver from Saarbrücken, was founded around 690 AD by the Merovingian Duke Luitwin, who served as bishop of Trier from 692 to 705. His bones lie buried in the octagonal **Alter Turm** (old tower), built around 990. Nearby is the former **Benediktiner Abtei** (Benedictine abbey), a baroque structure from the 18th century. The building was later sold to a paper manufacturer before being acquired by Johann Franz Boch-Buschmann, who turned it into a porcelain factory that is now known as Villeroy & Boch.

The abbey houses the company headquarters and a fairly commercial, if interesting, multimedia exhibit on their products. Called *Keravision*, it's open weekdays from 9 am to 6 pm, Saturday from 10 am to 1 pm

(free). A historical porcelain collection is housed in Schloss Ziegelberg. It is open April to October from 10 am to 5 pm, closed Monday, and the rest of the year also closed on Sunday (DM4/2).

The most scenic spot along the Saar River is the **Saarschleife**, where the river makes a spectacular hairpin loop. It's in the community of Orschholz, in a large nature park about 5km west of Mettlach (bus No 6300). The best viewing point is in Cloef, just a short walk through the forest from the village. Just look for signs saying Cloef or ask for directions.

If you want to experience the loop from a boat, you can take a 1½ hour tour (DM12) offered by Saar-Personenschiffahrt (☎ 06581-991 88) on Tuesday and Wednesday at 11 am, 2 and 4 pm, and on Thursday and Saturday at 11 am and 2 pm. Boats leave from the docks in Mettlach.

Mettlach's tourist office (☎ 83 34, fax 83 29) is at Freiherr-vom-Stein-Strasse 64. A *DJH hostel (☎ 06868-270, fax 06868-556)* in the community of Dreisbach charges DM20 per person for bed and breakfast.

Mettlach is on the Trier-Saarbrücken rail line, with services in either direction at least once an hour (DM13, 45 minutes in either direction).

By road, take the Merzig-Schwemlingen exit off the A8 (Saarbrücken-Luxembourg) and then follow the B51 north.

PERL-NENNIG
☎ 06866 • pop 6350

Right on the border with Luxembourg, about 15km west of Mettlach and 40km south of Trier, is Perl-Nennig. It is the Saarland's only wine-growing community and specialises in burgundies. On weekends between April and October, the wine growers open up their cellars for tastings on a rotating basis.

Perl-Nennig's real claim to fame, though, is the stunning, 160 sq metre **floor mosaic** in a 3rd century reconstructed **Roman villa**. Composed of three million tiny chips of coloured stone, it is the largest and best preserved such mosaic north of the Alps and shows scenes from a performance at an

euro currency converter   DM1 = €0.51

SAARLAND

amphitheatre. A farmer discovered it while digging in his garden in 1852.

Between April and September, the villa is open from 8.30 am to noon and from 1 to 6 pm, closed Monday. The rest of the year (except December, when it's closed) afternoon closing hours are at 3.30 or 4.30 pm. Admission is DM3/1.50.

Perl-Nennig's tourist office (☎ 14 39, fax 17 28), Bübinger Strasse 1a, has information on the villa, wine tastings and accommodation.

Moselcamping Dreiländereck (☎ *322, Sinzer Strasse 1*) is open from mid-March to mid-October, and costs DM8 for a tent and DM5 per person. It's about 500m from the bus and train stations in Nennig and on the bank of the Moselle River (cross the bridge behind the train station).

Perl-Nennig can be reached from Mettlach by bus No 6300. It also makes for an easy excursion from Trier, from where it is served by train at least every two hours (get off at Nennig; DM10, 50 minutes).

If you're travelling in from Saarbrücken, you must also change in Trier. Drivers can take the A8 from Saarbrücken or the B419 from Trier.

Hesse

The Hessians, a Frankish tribe, were among the first people to convert to Lutheranism in the early 16th century. Apart from a brief period of unity in that century under Philip the Magnanimous, Hesse (Hessen) remained a motley collection of principalities and, later, of Prussian administrative districts until it was made a state in 1945. Its main cities are Frankfurt-am-Main, the capital Wiesbaden and Kassel.

Frankfurt is Germany's most important transport hub but it can also be used as a base from which to explore some of the smaller towns in Hesse – those that remind you that you're still in Germany.

Wilhelm and Jakob Grimm were born in Hesse, and while they lived in Kassel they began compiling fairy tales. *Grimm's Fairy Tales* is now available in almost 200 languages and is read to children all over the world.

FRANKFURT-AM-MAIN
☎ 069   • pop 650,000

They call it 'Bankfurt' and 'Krankfurt' and 'Mainhattan' and more. Skyscraper-packed Frankfurt-on-the-Main (pronounced 'mine') is the financial and geographical centre of western Germany and plays host to some important trade fairs, including the world's largest book, consumer-goods and musical-instrument markets.

If you're not here for a trade fair, you're probably here because of air, train and road connections. Everybody, but *everybody*, changes planes in Frankfurt at some time or another.

Frankfurt produces a disproportionately large part of Germany's wealth. It is home to the most important stock exchange in the country, the Bundesbank (Germany's central bank), and the European Central Bank, the regulating bank for member countries of the European Monetary Union. The Rothschilds – the wealthy side of the family anyway – hail from here. Generous injections

HIGHLIGHTS

Hesse Luminaries: Georg Büchner, Anne Frank, Johann Wolfgang von Goethe, Wilhelm & Jakob Grimm, Paul Hindemith, Heinrich Hoffmann, Hans Holbein, the Rothschilds, August Weismann.

- Sampling Ebbelwei (apple wine) and Handkäse mit Musik (hand-cheese with music) and, oh yes, Frankfurt's Museums
- Visiting the Shoe and Leather museums in Offenbach
- Wandering around Wilhelmshöhe Park in Kassel
- Visiting Elisabethkirche, Germany's first Gothic cathedral, in Marburg
- Riding Wiesbaden's cable car up the Neroberg
- Stopping at Hessian towns on the Fairy-Tale Road

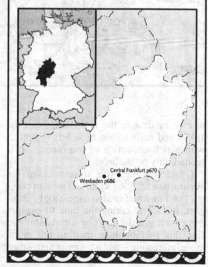

HESSE

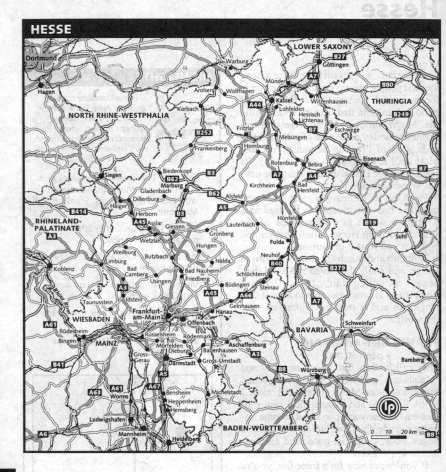

HESSE

of city funds into the arts throughout the 1980s and early 1990s have left Frankfurt with a rich collection of museums that is second only to Berlin's.

Glistening high-rise towers make the skyline an exception as far as German cities go, but Frankfurt is also surprisingly compact. It's worth taking the time to explore this city. If you do, don't be surprised if you find this cosmopolitan melting pot much more interesting – and a lot more fun – than you expected.

History

The first official mention of Frankfurt was in a document signed by Charlemagne in 794, which granted the town to the convent at St Emmeram – though by then it had been long established as a trading centre. Later, Frankfurt held a place of power in the Holy Roman Empire of Germany.

As its market flourished, so did its importance as a trade city; by the 12th century the 'Frankfurt Fair' attracted business from the Mediterranean to the Baltic.

With the election of Frederick I (Barbarossa) in 1152, Frankfurt became the site of the election and coronation of all German kings.

Throughout the history of the city and its market, Jews were invited to participate and then killed or driven out in pogroms. Frankfurt was among the first cities to convert to Protestantism.

The last German emperor was elected in 1792, and by the time the Holy Roman Empire collapsed in 1806 the region was under French control.

It was in Frankfurt in 1848 that Germany's first-ever parliamentary delegation met at the Paulskirche. Though that parliament was disbanded by the Prussians, Frankfurt was hailed, much later, by US President John F Kennedy as the 'cradle of democracy in Germany'.

By the early 20th century the walled city of Frankfurt had expanded to include a large Jewish quarter at its north-eastern end. The ghetto was abysmal, with poor sewerage and filthy conditions, but the city was again tolerant of Jews – until the rise of Nazism.

About 80% of the centre was destroyed by Allied bombing raids in March 1944. Plans to raze the remains of the Alte Oper were vigorously opposed by city residents and a reconstruction of it, along with much of the historical city centre, was undertaken. The Römerberg was completed in 1983.

The banking district is a shimmering symbol of Germany's postwar economic redevelopment, when high rise after high rise was erected.

Orientation

The Main River flows from east to west, dividing the northern section of the city, its traditional centre, from the southern section, whose focus is the lovely Sachsenhausen district.

Tour boats leave from the north bank of the Main, the Mainkai, between Alte Brücke and pedestrian-only Eisener Steg.

The south bank of the Main is Schaumainkai, called Museumsufer (pronounced 'moo-zay-umz-oofer'), or the Museum Embankment, for the high concentration of museums there.

Sachsenhausen's north-eastern corner, south of the DJH hostel, is known as Alt Sachsenhausen; it's full of quaint old houses and narrow alleys, and plenty of places to sample the local apple wine.

The Hauptbahnhof is on the western side of the city, about a 10 minute walk from the old city centre.

From the Hauptbahnhof, walk east along Kaiserstrasse and then on to a large square called An der Hauptwache. The Hauptwache itself is a lovely baroque building that was once the local police station; now it's a restaurant. The area between the An der Hauptwache and the Römerberg, the tiny vestige of Frankfurt's original old town, is the city centre.

The pedestrianised Zeil runs west to east between the Hauptwache S-Bahn/U-Bahn station and the Konstablerwache S-Bahn/U-Bahn station at Kurt-Schumacher-Strasse. East of there, Zeil is open to traffic and leads to the zoo.

Bockenheim, a student area north-west of the centre and due north of the Hauptbahnhof, and Bornheim, a cafe-laden, cosmopolitan district north-east of the zoo, are some of the neighbourhoods you'll see referred to in listings magazines (see Entertainment) and tourist brochures.

The airport is about 15 minutes by train south-west of the city centre.

Information

Tourist Offices Frankfurt's most convenient tourist office (☎ 21 23 88 49/51, fax 21 23 78 80) is in the main hall at the Hauptbahnhof. It's open weekdays from 8 am to 9 pm, weekends and holidays from 9 am to 6 pm. The staff are efficient at finding rooms (DM5 service fee). In the centre of the city, the Römer tourist office (☎ 21 23 87 08/09), Römerberg 27, is open weekdays from 9.30 am to 5.30 pm, weekends and holidays from 10 am to 4 pm. Call the Infoline (☎ 21 23 88 00) for event information in English.

People with particular needs or those staying longer in Frankfurt should contact

euro currency converter DM1 = €0.51

HESSE

CENTRAL FRANKFURT

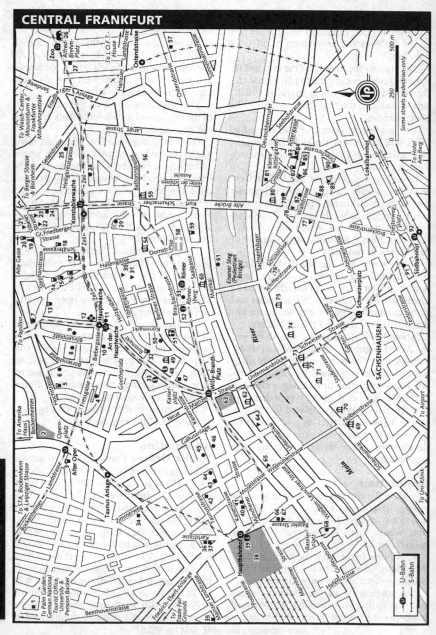

U-Bahn
S-Bahn

CENTRAL FRANKFURT

PLACES TO STAY
1   Hotel-Pension Gölz;
    Pension Sattler
24 Arabella Grand Hotel
27 Hotel am Zoo
34 Hotel Atlas
35 Glockshuber
36 Hotel Carlton
37 Concorde Hotel
40 Hotel Münchener Hof
41 Hotel Eden
42 Pension Schneider
47 Steigenberger Frankfurter Hof
57 Hotel-Garni Diplomat
66 Hotel Wiesbaden
81 Haus der Jugend hostel

PLACES TO EAT
21 Zu den Zwölf Aposteln
22 Iwase
23 Lahore Palace
30 Café Mozart
31 Kleinmarkthalle
64 Bistro im Gewerkschaftshaus
65 Ginger Brasserie
67 Gaylord
77 Café Satz
78 Tannenbaum
84 Mexir
86 Mr Lin
89 Café Noah

OTHER
2   Alte Oper
3   Fidelio

4   Jazzkeller
5   Blaubart Gewölbekeller
6   British Bookshop
7   Turm-Palast
8   Börse
9   ADAC
10 Hugendubel
11 Sussmann's Presse & Buch
12 Zeilgalerie &
    IMAX Cinema
13 Tangerine
14 The Blue Angel
15 The Cave
16 Sinkkasten
17 Main Post Office; Hertie
18 Zum Schwejk
19 Gay & Lesbian Memorial
20 The Dance Zone
25 Tiger Palast
26 Zoo
28 City Library
29 City Mitwohnzentrale
32 Cooky's
33 American Express
38 Main Train Station;
    Intercity Hotel
39 Tourist Office
43 Berlitz
44 English Theatre
45 ACC Telekom
46 Inlingua
48 Thomas Cook
49 Goethe Haus
50 Jazz-Kneipe
51 Paulskirche

52 Römer Tourist Office
53 Fountain
54 Museum für Moderne
    Kunst
55 Judengasse Museum
56 Jewish Cemetery
58 Frankfurter Dom
59 Metropol
60 Historisches Museum
61 Tour Boat Stand
62 Jüdisches Museum
63 Oper
68 ADM-Mitfahrzentrale
69 Liebighaus
70 Städel Art Institute
71 Postal Museum
72 Deutsches
    Architekturmuseum
73 Deutsches Filmmuseum &
    Kommunales Kino
74 Museum of Ethnology
75 Museum of Applied Arts
76 Krankenhaus
    Sachsenhausen
79 HL Markt
80 Icon Museum
82 Far Out
83 Frau Rauscher Brunnen
    Statue
85 O'Dwyers Pub
87 Wasch-Center Laundrette
88 Stereo Bar
90 Harmonie Cinema
91 Goethe Institut
92 Südbahnhof

Tourismus + Congress (☎ 21 23 03 96, fax 21 23 07 76, email info@tcf.frankfurt.de). This office makes free room reservations. Call ☎ 21 23 08 08 to reserve by telephone. The address for postal reservations is Kaiserstrasse 56.

The headquarters of the German National Tourist Office (☎ 97 46 40, fax 75 19 03, email gnto_fra@compuserve.com), Beethovenstrasse 69, north of the Hauptbahnhof, near the Palm Garden, has brochures on all areas of the country and very friendly staff.

Ask at any tourist office about the one/two-day FrankfurtCard, which costs DM12/19 and gives up to 50% reductions on admission to 15 museums and galleries,

the zoo and the airport visitors' terraces, as well as unlimited travel on public transport.

The German auto association (ADAC) has an office (☎ 25 09 29) on Börseplatz, opposite the stock exchange.

Money The Hauptbahnhof has a branch of the Reisebank (☎ 24 27 85 91) near the southern exit at the head of platform No 1; it is open daily from 6.30 am to 10 pm. There's an exchange machine accepting foreign currency at the head of platform No 15. There are several banks at the airport, most of them open till about 10 pm, and exchange offices and ATMs are dotted around the various arrival and departure halls.

euro currency converter DM1 = €0.51

HESSE

American Express (☎ 210 50) and Thomas Cook (☎ 13 47 33) offices are opposite each other on Kaiserstrasse at Nos 8 and 11 respectively.

Post & Communications The main post office is on the ground floor of the Hertie department store at Zeil 90. It's open weekdays from 9.30 am to 8 pm, and Saturday from 9 am to 4 pm. Another post office, on the 1st floor of the Hauptbahnhof above McDonald's, is open from 6.30 am to 9 pm weekdays, 8 am to 6 pm on Saturday and 11 am to 6 pm on Sunday and public holidays. The post office at the airport (in the waiting lounge of departure hall B) is open daily from 7 am to 9 pm.

ACC Telekom has a useful shop at Kaiserstrasse 40 where you can make cheap international calls using its pre-paid telephone cards (you can use their cards with any telephone). It also offers Internet and email access for DM5 per half hour. It's open daily from 10 am to 10 pm.

Cybercafé Cybers (☎ 29 49 64), stall 74 of the Zeilgalerie on An der Hauptwache, is another central Internet cafe for Web surfers.

Internet Resources Information on Frankfurt, with Web pages in English, is under www.frankfurt.de.

Travel Agencies Especially good deals on round-the-world tickets are available at outlets such as STA Travel (☎ 70 30 35, Bockenheimer Landstrasse 133); there are other branches in Bornheim at Berger Strasse 118 (☎ 43 01 91) and at No 109 (☎ 44 30 27). Last-minute tickets can be bought at the airport; the prices are usually lower than scheduled airfares.

There's a Lufthansa office (☎ 28 28 95 96) downstairs in level B of the Hauptwache U-Bahn station.

Bookshops The British Bookshop (☎ 28 04 92), Börsenstrasse 17, has the largest selection of English-language books in town. Hugendubel (☎ 28 98 21), Steinweg 12, also has English-language books, Lonely Planet titles and other travel resources, couches where you can sit and read before you buy, and a cafe downstairs.

Sussmann's Presse & Buch, on An der Hauptwache behind the Katharinenkirche, has a wonderful selection of English-language magazines. Schmitt & Hahn has two branches in the Hauptbahnhof with very good selections of fiction. Bauer Press International, with a dozen branches throughout the airport, has a good selection of best-selling English-language books.

Libraries The library at Amerika Haus (☎ 97 14 48 20) is an excellent reference source on economic and business matters (see Cultural Centres).

The city's central library (☎ 21 23 83 53), Zeil 17, and the Stadt- und Universitätsbibliothek (☎ 21 23 92 56), above the Bockenheimer Warte U-Bahn station, both have English-language books.

Universities Johann Wolfgang von Goethe Universität (☎ 798 21), with 28,000 students, has its main campus at Bockenheimer Warte, near the Palm Garden. University buildings are scattered throughout the city, housing schools of economics, law and social sciences.

Cultural Centres Amerika Haus (☎ 97 14 48 20), Staufenstrasse 1, is hugely popular with Germans who want to learn more about life and study in the USA. The Goethe Institut (☎ 961 22 70, fax 962 03 95), Diesterwegplatz 72, is *the* German cultural organisation, with concerts, openings, wine tastings and other events to introduce German culture to foreigners.

Laundry The Wasch-Center chain has coin-operated laundrettes at Wallstrasse 8 in Sachsenhausen (very near the hostel) and at Sandweg 41, just north-east of the city centre. They're open daily from 6 am to 11 pm and charge DM6 per wash, DM1 for the spinner extractor and DM1 for 15 minutes use of the dryer. SB-Waschcenter at Grosse Seestrasse 46 in Bockenheim is open daily from 6.30 am to 11 pm (DM8 per wash and DM1 for 10 minutes use of dryer).

Medical Services & Emergency Lists of English-speaking doctors are available at the UK consulate (☎ 170 00 20), Bockenheimer Landstrasse 42; and the US consulate (☎ 753 50), Siesmayerstrasse 21.

The Uni-Klinik (☎ 630 11), Theodor Stern Kai 7 in Sachsenhausen, is open 24 hours a day. Also in Sachsenhausen is the Krankenhaus Sachsenhausen (☎ 660 50), Schulstrasse 31. There's an emergency clinic (☎ 47 50) at Friedberger Landstrasse 430.

For routine medical queries, contact the 24 hour doctor service on ☎ 192 92. Pharmacies take turns staying open round the clock. To find out which one's open, check the list placed in all pharmacy windows or published in the *Frankfurter Rundschau* newspaper.

The emergency number for victims of rape is ☎ 70 94 94.

Dangers & Annoyances The area around the Hauptbahnhof is a base for Frankfurt's trade in sex and illegal drugs. To contain the problem of junkies publicly shooting up, *Druckräume* – shooting-up rooms – have been established in which drugs can be taken but not sold and where clean needles are distributed.

However, you *will* probably see junkies shooting up during your visit. Frequent police patrols of the station and the surrounding Bahnhofsviertel keep things under control. It is still advisable to use 'big city' common sense.

Zeilgalerie

A good place to start seeing the sights of Frankfurt is the Zeilgalerie, a shopping complex at An der Hauptwache. Here you can get an overview of the city. Ride the glass lift to the roof. From the roof you can see the **Römerberg**, the original city centre, to the south-west. Beyond it, across the river, is **Sachsenhausen**, an entertainment area with lots of pubs, bars and restaurants. To the west is the **banking district** with its everchanging jumble of high-rise towers,

including the reddish 256m-high peak of the elegant **Messeturm**, which locals call the *Bleistift* (Pencil). Its grace comes at the expense of space, for the service shaft takes up half of this slender building's interior. The upper echelons are occupied by the Bundesbank, whose employees can enjoy the view from their tea room on the 60th floor.

Römerberg

The Römerberg, west of the Dom, is Frankfurt's old central square, where restored 14th and 15th century buildings, including **Paulskirche**, provide a glimpse of the beautiful city this once was. It's especially lovely during December's *Weihnachtsmarkt* (see Special Events).

The old town hall, or **Römer**, in the northwestern corner of Römerberg, consists of three recreated step-gabled 15th century houses. The Römer was the site of celebrations of the election and coronation of emperors during the Holy Roman Empire. Today it's both the registry office and the office of Petra Roth, Frankfurt's mayor. Inside, you can view the Kaisersaal (Kaiser Hall), with portraits of 52 rulers. It's open daily from 10 am to 1 pm and 2 to 5 pm (DM3/1.50). Flags flying outside the building indicate the Kaisersaal is being used for official functions, in which case you won't be able to get inside.

Right in the centre of Römerberg is the **Gerechtigkeitsbrunnen**, the 'Font of Justice'. In 1612, at the coronation of Matthias, the fountain ran with wine, not water.

Frankfurter Dom

The restored Dom, east of Römerberg, is behind the **Historical Garden** (Historischer Garten), where you can wander through excavated Roman and Carolingian foundations. Dominated by the elegant, 15th century, 95m Gothic-style **tower** (completed in the 1860s), the Dom was one of the few structures left standing after the 1944 raids.

You can climb to one of the two viewing platforms (at 40m/180 steps or 75m/328 steps) daily from 9 am to 1 pm and 2.30 to 6 pm (DM3/1).

euro currency converter DM1 = €0.51

HESSE

The small **Wahlkapelle** (Voting Chapel) on the cathedral's southern side is where seven electors of the Holy Roman Empire chose the emperor from 1356 onwards. (A newly elected monarch usually kicked up his heels after that in the Kaisersaal.) The adjoining **choir** has beautiful wooden stalls.

Goethe Haus

Anyone with an interest in German literature should visit the Goethe Haus at Grosser Hirschgraben 23-25. Johann Wolfgang von Goethe was born in the house in 1749. This museum and library are open Monday to Saturday from 9 am to 6 pm, Sunday and public holidays from 10 am to 1 pm, with shorter hours in winter (DM4/3). Much of the furniture is reproduction, but some originals remain. There are guided tours in German daily at 10.30 am and 2 pm (morning only on Sunday). At other times, the staff might point out the highlights. Don't miss Goethe's original writing desk and the library on the top floor.

Alte Oper & Börse

Built in 1888, Frankfurt's lovely Renaissance Alte Oper (☎ 134 04 00), Opernplatz 8, bears a striking resemblance to Dresden's Semperoper. Destroyed in WWII, the Alte Oper – after a vote to save it from being razed to clear a path for 1960s-style cubes – underwent a DM220 million renovation. The outside is as original as possible but the inside is modern. There are statues of Goethe and Mozart on the building.

Between Opernplatz and Börsenstrasse is the pedestrianised **Fressgasse** (Munch Alley), a somewhat overrated mall scattered with snack bars and restaurants. If you're visiting in September, stop at the very nice Rheingau wine festival held here.

The city's **Börse** (stock exchange; 1874) on Börsenplatz is open to visitors who can watch the traders' frantic hand-gesturing from an observation section Monday to Friday from 11 am to noon. Admission is free. Enter from the small door under the glass awning on the east side of the front of the building.

Museums

Most museums are open Tuesday to Sunday from 10 am to 5 pm, Wednesday to 8 pm, and are closed Monday. Entry to almost all museums in Frankfurt is free on Wednesday.

Museumsufer A string of museums line the southern bank (Museum Embankment) of the Main River. The pick of the crop is the **Städelsches Kunstinstitut** (Städel Art Institute; ☎ 68 20 98), Schaumainkai 63, with a world-class collection of works by artists including Botticelli, Dürer, Van Eyck, Rembrandt, Renoir, Rubens, Vermeer and Cezanne, plus artists native to Frankfurt, including Hans Holbein. Entry costs DM8/4.

The **Deutsches Architekturmuseum** (German Architecture Museum; ☎ 21 23 88 44), Schaumainkai 43, is something of a disappointment – only rotating exhibitions and no permanent collection of the architecture of Frankfurt or even of Germany. Admission is DM8/4. Saturday opening hours are from 2 to 8 pm.

The **Deutsches Filmmuseum** (German Film Museum; ☎ 21 23 33 69) next door is, in contrast, a fascinating place. It has constantly changing exhibitions, extensive archives, plus premieres and special film events, all in their original languages, in the Kommunales Kino. Check with *MainCity* or the other listings magazines (see Entertainment). The museum is absolutely worth the admission price of DM5/2.50. Our favourite exhibit is the 'magic carpet' – watch yourself on a screen flying across the Frankfurt skyline.

The **Bundespostmuseum** (Postal Museum; ☎ 606 00), Schaumainkai 53, has restricted hours (open Wednesday to 5 pm and on weekends from 11 am to 7 pm) and displays on the history of communication, in addition to the collection of the former Reichspostmuseum in Berlin. Admission is free, so why not?

Other museums along this strip include the **Kunsthandwerkmuseum** (Museum of Applied Arts), Schaumainkai 17 (DM6/3); the **Museum für Völkerkunde** (Museum of

Ethnology), Schaumainkai 29 (DM6/3); and the **Liebighaus**, Schaumainkai 71, with classical, medieval, baroque and Renaissance sculptures and an exhibition of Egyptian art (DM5/2.50).

The **Icon Museum** (☎ 21 23 62 62), Brückenstrasse 3-7, houses a collection of Russian religious paintings (DM2/1).

Museum für Moderne Kunst The triangular Museum for Modern Art (☎ 21 23 04 47), Domstrasse 10, dubbed the 'slice of cake' by locals, has permanent and temporary exhibitions of modern art. The permanent collection contains works by Roy Lichtenstein, Andy Warhol, Claes Oldenburg and Joseph Beuys; temporary exhibits highlight local, national and international artists (DM7/3.50).

Historisches Museum This museum (☎ 21 23 55 99), just south of Römerberg at Saalgasse 19, is worth visiting, even if you have to skip the permanent exhibition (DM5/2.50) on Frankfurt in the Middle Ages in favour of the spectacular **model** (DM1) of the city from the 1930s in the foyer. Built by the Treuner brothers, the detail of the city centre is nothing short of wonderful. It's especially nice to go on Wednesday when pensioners, taking advantage of the free admission, stand around the model and point out shops and streets remembered from their youth. In the same foyer is a model of the ruins of the city after the war.

Jewish Museums The city has two notable museums on Jewish life in Frankfurt which call attention to the fact that the Jewish community here, with 35,000 people, was once one of the largest in Europe. The main **Jüdisches Museum** (☎ 21 23 50 00), in the former Rothschildpalais at Untermainkai 14-15, is an enormous place with an exhibit of Jewish life in the city from the Middle Ages to present day, with good detail on well known Frankfurt Jews persecuted, murdered or exiled by the Nazis. There are also religious items on display (DM5/2.50, free on Saturday).

The **Museum Judengasse** (☎ 297 74 19), along the north-eastern boundaries of the old city fortifications, is the annexe to the Jüdisches Museum. On display here are remains of ritual baths and houses from the Jewish ghetto, which was destroyed by the Nazis (DM3/1.50, or DM6/3 when combined with the Jüdisches Museum).

Behind the Museum Judengasse, on the western wall of the **Jewish Cemetery**, is a remarkable **memorial** with metal cubes bearing the names of all Frankfurt-born Jews murdered during the Holocaust, some with the date of death, others with merely a notation of the camp in which they died. The cubes allow visitors to place stones or pebbles, a Jewish tradition that shows that a grave is tended and the person not forgotten.

Palm Garden

The botanical **Palmengarten** (DM7, children DM3) is a nice place to relax. It has rose gardens and formal gardens, a playground for kids, a little pond with rowing boats (DM4/3 for adults/children plus DM1 per person per half hour) and a mini-gauge train that puffs round the place (DM2/1). It's near the German National Tourist Board office and the university, one block from Bockenheimer Warte (U-Bahn stop: Westend).

Monuments

On the corner of Alte Gasse, the city's main gay and lesbian drag, and Schaffergasse, north of Zeil, is a **memorial**, one of three in Europe, to homosexuals persecuted and killed by the Nazis during WWII. It is deliberate that the statue's head is nearly severed from the body.

In an altogether wacky departure from that sombre sight, the **Frau Rauscher Brunnen** on Klappergasse in Sachsenhausen is a treat. It's a bronze statue of a bulky, bitchy-looking *Hausfrau* who periodically spews a powerful stream of water about 10m onto the footpath. Stand around for a few moments east of the statue and you'll undoubtedly see pedestrians drenched. The idea is based on a popular Frankfurt song about drinking apple wine.

HESSE

euro currency converter DM1 = €0.51

Frankfurt Zoo & Airport

The zoo (take U6 to Zoo U-Bahn station), with its creative displays, signs and exhibits, is a relief from the cosmopolitan chaos (DM11/5).

Just as creative, and beloved by children, are the two visitors' terraces at Frankfurt airport (DM5, free with a FrankfurtCard) in Terminal 1, Level 3, and in Terminal 2, Level 4. It's only 11 minutes away from the Hauptbahnhof by S-Bahn (see the Getting Around section).

Language Courses

Due to the high percentage of foreign residents here, there are a number of language schools in the city. The most respected – and expensive – option is the Goethe Institut (☎ 961 22 70, fax 962 03 95), Diesterwegplatz 72.

Inlingua (☎ 23 10 21), Kaiserstrasse 37, offers a one month intensive course (DM990) and evening courses from DM230 per month. You might also try Berlitz (☎ 28 08 75) at Grosse Eschenheimerstrasse 1 or Kaiserstrasse 66.

Organised Tours

During weekends and holidays the city's Ebbelwei-Express (☎ 21 32 23 25) tram circles Frankfurt, stopping at the zoo, Hauptbahnhof, Südbahnhof, Frankensteiner Platz (near the Haus der Jugend hostel) and back several times a day. The fare is DM4/2.

Kulturothek Frankfurt (☎ 28 10 10) runs 2½ hour English-language walking tours on a variety of subjects on the first Sunday of the month (German tours every Sunday). Show up at 2 pm at the meeting point (it changes weekly). The cost is DM15/10.

The tourist offices offer excellent 2½ hour city tours, which include visits to the Historisches Museum and Goethe Haus, leaving daily at 2 pm (also at 10 am from April to October) from the Hauptbahnhof office. The cost is DM44/22. It also offers themed excursions, like Jewish Frankfurt, Frankfurt architecture and Goethe tours.

Elisabeth Lücke (☎ 06196-457 87) runs tours for individuals or groups (up to 25 people) in English, German and Spanish on the themes of architecture, the finance world and Jewish life in Frankfurt (about DM100 per hour).

Short cruises along the Main and longer Rhine trips to Rüdesheim and Loreley, which run from April to September/October, are available at varying prices from the docks on the northern embankment near the Eiserner Steg bridge.

Special Events

Frankfurt festivals include: **Dippemess**, in March and September, a fun fair with apple wine and food; **Kunsthandwerk Heute** in late May/early June, an arts and handicrafts festival held on Paulsplatz; and the **Sound of Frankfurt** in July, which takes place along the Zeil, with local and visiting groups playing techno mostly, but also soul, blues, jazz and rock. There's also the **Frankfurt Book Fair** in late September/early October; and **Weihnachtsmarkt** in December, a Christmas fair on Römerberg with mulled wine, choirs and traditional foods.

The Frankfurt Book Fair

If you're in publishing, there's no avoiding the world's largest book fair, held in Frankfurt in late September/early October. Over 250,000 publishers, agents, authors, wannabes, yahoos, drunks, Lonely Planet staffers and other nefarious characters descend on Mainhattan with a vengeance.

It's a scene and a half, and hotels are booked out a year in advance. If you plan to visit Frankfurt during the fair, you should reserve accommodation well in advance.

Admission for the general public to the Frankfurt Messe, where the fair is held, is only on the weekend. Take tram Nos 16 and 19, or S-Bahn No 3, 4 or 5 from the Hauptbahnhof. Expect to pay DM12 for one day.

HESSE

Places to Stay – Budget & Mid-Range

Camping *Heddernheim* (☎ 57 03 32, *An der Sandelmühle 35)* is the most recommended camping ground and is open year round. It's in the Heddernheim district north-west of the city centre, and charges DM5.50 for a site, DM9.50 per person and DM2 per car. It is a 15 minute ride on the U1, U2 or U3 from the Hauptwache U-Bahn station (one zone); get off at the Heddernheim stop.

Hostels The big, bustling and crowded *Haus der Jugend* (☎ 61 90 58, *fax 61 82 57, Deutschherrnufer 12)* on the south side of the Main River is within walking distance of the city centre and Sachsenhausen's nightspots. The postcode for bookings by mail is 60594 Frankfurt-am-Main. Rates (including breakfast) for beds in large dorms are DM26/33 for juniors/seniors or a fixed DM38.50 in four-person rooms. Evening meals of several courses cost DM8.70. From the Hauptbahnhof, take bus No 46 to Frankensteiner Platz; or from the Hauptbahnhof, take S-Bahn lines No 2, 3, 4, 5, or 6 to Lokalbahnhof. Check-in begins at 11 am, and there's a 2 to 6 am curfew.

Private Rooms The tourist information office books private rooms during trade fairs only. At all other times, contact one of the three Mitwohnzentrale offices in town: City Mitwohnzentrale (☎ 29 61 11), An der Staufenmauer 3, also has its own apartments; Mitwohnzentrale Mainhattan (☎ 597 55 61), Falkensteiner Strasse 68; and Frankfurter Mitwohnzentrale (☎ 44 77 06), Sandweg 106. All three can book rooms from about DM40 to DM100 per single.

Hotels In Frankfurt, 'cheap' can mean paying over DM100 for a spartan double room. During the many busy trade fairs, even that price may turn out to be unrealistic, since most hotels and pensions jack up their rates – in many cases close to double the standard rate. But don't give up hope – the tourist office has been known to perform miracles.

Most of Frankfurt's low-end accommodation is in Bahnhofsviertel, the rather sleazy area surrounding the Hauptbahnhof. The *Hotel Münchener Hof* (☎ 23 00 66, *fax 23 44 28, Münchener Strasse 46)* has reasonable basic singles/doubles for DM80/100, or DM100/140 with shower and WC (toilet). *Hotel Eden* (☎ 25 19 14, *fax 25 23 27, Münchener Strasse 42)* has immaculate rooms for DM85/100 with WC and shower. *Pension Schneider* (☎ 25 10 71, *fax 25 92 28, Taunusstrasse 43)*, a homely establishment in a sea of sleaze, has rooms from DM70/110. The *Hotel Carlton* (☎ 23 20 93, *fax 23 36 73, Karlstrasse 11)* has nice rooms for DM110/140 with shower and WC. The *Concorde Hotel* (☎ 23 32 30, *fax 24 24 22 88, Karlstrasse 9)* offers the same from DM140/180.

Glockshuber (☎ 74 26 28, *fax 74 26 29, Mainzer Landstrasse 120)* offers pleasant, clean and bright rooms without shower and WC from around DM75/110. *Hotel Wiesbaden* (☎ 23 23 47, *fax 25 28 45, Baseler Strasse 52)*, to the right of the Hauptbahnhof exit, is the pick of the mid-range crop. Its rooms, all with shower and WC, start from around DM105/140.

In the city centre, the modern *Hotel Atlas* (☎/fax 72 39 46, *Zimmerweg 1)* is away from the sleaze but still a convenient distance from the Hauptbahnhof. It has basic rooms from DM68/98.

Hotel-Garni Diplomat (☎ 430 40 40, *fax 430 40 22, Ostendstrasse 24-26)* offers quite good value on rooms for DM80/120. *Hotel am Zoo* (☎ 94 99 30, *fax 94 99 31 99, email Hotel_am_Zoo@t-online.de, Alfred-Brehm-Platz 6)* has reasonable rooms with shower and WC for DM128/195.

Hotel Am Berg (☎ 61 20 21, *fax 61 51 09, Grethenweg 23)*, in Sachsenhausen, is in a lovely sandstone building in the quiet back streets a few minutes walk from the Südbahnhof. Prices start at DM65/115 for simple rooms without breakfast; it's clean, pleasant and friendly.

Near the Palm Garden, in Frankfurt's quiet and pleasant Westend, are several attractive options. The *Pension Backer* (☎ 74 79 92,

euro currency converter DM1 = €0.51

HESSE

fax 74 79 92, Mendelssohnstrasse 92) has basic rooms for DM50/60. The *Hotel-Pension Gölz (☎ 74 67 35, fax 74 61 42, Beethovenstrasse 44)* offers comfortable rooms with shower and WC for DM80/135. The *Pension Sattler (☎ 74 60 91, Beethovenstrasse 46)* has rooms with shower and WC for DM99/160.

The *Hotel-Pension Uebe (☎ 59 12 09, Grüneburgweg 3)*, near the Grüneburg U-Bahn station in Westend-Nord, has singles with a shower for DM79, and doubles with shower and WC for DM129, excluding breakfast.

Falk Hotel (☎ 70 80 94, fax 70 80 17, Falkstrasse 38A) in Bockenheim has quiet and pleasant singles/doubles with shower and WC for DM120/160. Take the U-Bahn to Leipziger Strasse. *Hotel West (☎ 247 90 20, fax 707 53 09, Gräfstrasse 81)* offers small rooms with shower and WC for DM90/135. Take the U-Bahn to Bockenheimer Warte.

The *Pension Zur Rose (☎ 45 17 62, Berger Strasse 283)* in Bornheim charges DM60/100 for basic rooms and DM120/140 with shower and WC. The bowling alley below rumbles until 10 pm.

Places to Stay – Top End

If you're in Frankfurt on an expense account, there are several ways of staying here without having your hotel bill sent directly to the Raised Eyebrow Department. But remember, these prices usually double during important fairs.

The *InterCity Hotel (☎ 27 39 10, fax 27 39 19 99)*, attached to the Hauptbahnhof, is a very nice place; but so it should be, with singles/doubles from DM234/275 with breakfast.

There are two grand dames of the Frankfurt hotel scene. The *Steigenberger Frankfurter Hof (☎ 215 02, fax 21 59 00, email infoline@frankfurter-hof.steigenberger.de)* on Kaiserplatz has grandiose rooms and great service. It costs DM395/450 for rooms without breakfast, but it also offers good weekend deals, with breakfast, at almost half price.

Arabella Grand Hotel Frankfurt (☎ 298 10, fax 298 18 10, email reservation.grand-hotel-frankfurt@arabellaSheraton.de, Konrad-Adenauer-Strasse 7) offers friendly service but rather boxy rooms for DM435/505 without breakfast. There's a single and double weekend deal, which both cost DM268 with breakfast.

Places to Eat

Bahnhofsviertel The area around the Hauptbahnhof is filled with predominantly Southern European, Middle Eastern and Asian eating houses.

Gaylord (☎ 25 26 12, Baseler Strasse 54) has tasty Indian lunch specials for about DM15 and lunch or evening curry main courses for around DM22.

Ginger Brasserie (☎ 23 17 71, Windmühlenstrasse 14) has everything Asian on the menu – from good Sichuan to bad sushi, great salads, tandoori and Thai – with most main courses between DM19 and DM29. *Bistro im Gewerkschaftshaus (Wilhelm-Leuschner-Strasse 69-77)*, in contrast, is a plain union canteen that serves one set main dish weekdays from 12 to 2 pm for around DM9.

For snacks and fast food, the Hauptbahnhof has several options. *McDonald's* is at the head of track 22 and open for breakfast from 4 am. There's also a large *food hall* with lots of stalls at the opposite end of the station, and downstairs in the underpass running east from the Hauptbahnhof is a *Pizza Hut* and an overpriced *supermarket*, open daily.

Fressgasse & Northern Centre Known to locals as Fressgasse (Munch Alley), the Kalbächer Gasse and Grosse Bockenheimer Strasse area between Rathenauplatz and Opernplatz has many mid-priced restaurants and fast-food places with outdoor tables.

Moving east to Vilbeler Strasse, near Alte Gasse, are two excellent, if expensive, eateries. *Lahore Palace (☎ 28 08 54, Vilbeler Strasse 27)* is a pricey but mind-blowing Indian/Pakistani restaurant with excellent service and out-of-this-world food. The vindaloo is hot enough to make your nose run, and the starters (DM8 to DM15) are good.

Most main courses cost from DM25 to DM30. *Iwase* (☎ *28 39 92*), a few doors down, is an excellent Japanese restaurant that serves generous portions of sushi and miso soup for around DM25 at lunchtime, DM40 in the evening.

Zu den Zwölf Aposteln (☎ *28 86 68, Rosenberger Strasse 1)*, on the corner of Elefantengasse, serves fare with an emphasis on steaks and grilled food from about DM11 to DM30. It's open for lunch and dinner. Downstairs is an interesting beer cellar, open in the evening, where a house beer is still brewed.

Zeil & Römerberg If you're here and hungry, the best place for snacks or picnic supplies is the *Kleinmarkthalle*, off Hasengasse just south of Zeil. It's an active little city market (open weekdays from 7.30 am to 6 pm, Saturday to 3 pm) selling fruit, vegetables, meats, fish and hot food. Stalls have Italian, Turkish, Chinese and German food, and you can get salads and fresh fruit juices as well as wine and beer. At the western end of the hall there is a large mural of a bird's-eye view of Frankfurt. The nearby *Café Mozart (Töngesgasse 23)* is popular with tourists for its cakes and coffee.

Metropol (Weckmarkt 13-15), directly on the south side of the Dom, offers good dishes from its changing menu for about DM15 to DM20, and breakfast from DM3.50 to DM34. It's also a great place for coffee or a drink, and stays open until at least 1 am (closed Monday).

L.O.F.T.-House (Hanauer Landstrasse 181-185) is one of the trendiest discos in town for a mixed selection of dance music. It attracts a young crowd.

Sachsenhausen Sachsenhausen is everyone-friendly (gays, lesbians, heteros). There's an abundance of takeaway places at the top of Kleine Rittergasse *(Kleine Rittergasse 43)* is a large Thai eat-in/takeaway restaurant serving a good range of tasty curries, and more, for under DM10.

Ebbelwoi & Handkäse mit Musik

Frankfurt eating and drinking traditions are best experienced in the city's apple-wine taverns which serve *Ebbelwoi* (Frankfurt dialect for *Apfelwein*), an alcoholic apple cider, along with local specialities like *Handkäse mit Musik* (hand-cheese with music) and *Frankfurter Grüne Sosse* (Frankfurt green sauce).

The majority of Ebbelwoi taverns are in Alt Sachsenhausen – the area directly behind the DJH hostel – which is filled with eateries and pubs. In most of these you'll be served the stuff in *Bembel* jugs; it's something of a tradition to scrunch closer and closer to your neighbours and try to grab some from their pitcher too.

Classic Ebbelwoi joints in Sachsenhausen include the Lorsbacher Tal, Grosse Rittergasse 49; the Adolf Wagner, tucked away at Schweizer Strasse 71; and Zum Gemalten Haus, a lively place full of paintings of old Frankfurt, nearby at Schweizer Strasse 67. Fichte Kränzi, Wallstrasse 5, has an earthy atmosphere. In Bornheim, Zur Sonne, Bergerstrasse 312, is considered by Frankfurt locals to be the best in town.

Handkäse mit Musik is a name you could only hear in German. It describes a round cheese marinated in oil and vinegar with onions, served with bread and butter and with a knife only – no fork. As you might imagine, cheese marinated in oil and onions would tend to give one a healthy dose of wind – the release of which, ladies and gentlemen, is the 'music' part.

Frankfurter Grüne Sosse is made from parsley, sorrel, dill, burnet, borage, chervil and chives mixed with yoghurt, mayonnaise or sour cream; it's served with potatoes and meat or eggs – Goethe's favourite food.

HESSE

Café Noah (Affentorplatz 20) features inspired salads as well as daily specials that average DM15 per main course. *Café Satz (Schifferstrasse 36)* has a changing menu, but you'll always find chilli con carne on offer (DM8.50) and some traditional dishes.

The *Tannenbaum (Brückenstrasse 19)* is an upmarket designer pub/restaurant that will satisfy carnivores and herbivores alike with its main courses from DM15 to DM31. The unlikely *Mexir (☎ 96 20 11 58, Klappergasse 8)* is Sachsenhausen's Mexican-Iranian – that's right – speciality spot and restaurant. Staff are friendly, and the dishes are well priced, ranging from DM11 to DM30. It's next to the Frau Rauscher Brunnen (open in the evening).

Bornheim The *Café Gegenwart (☎ 497 05 44, Berger Strasse 6)*, is a large bar/restaurant serving traditional German dishes from DM13 and good breakfasts; if the weather cooperates you can sit outside. Heading north along Berger Strasse from here, you'll pass several cafes and bars. *Charivari (Berger Strasse 99)* is a comfortable and relaxed place to drink; the food, though, is less impressive. *Eckhaus (☎ 49 11 97, Bornheimer Landstrasse 45)* offers large servings of tasty salads and good main courses at reasonable prices. It opens in the evening and is also a nice place to enjoy coffee or a drink. Take the U4 to Merianplatz, walk north, then a few minutes west along Bornheimer Landstrasse.

Bockenheim Over to the west in bohemian Bockenheim, past the university, Leipziger Strasse branches off from Bockenheimer Landstrasse and becomes a very pleasant shopping and cheap eating area. (Take the U6 or U7 to Bockenheimer Warte, Leipziger Strasse or Kirchplatz.)

Prielok (☎ 77 64 68, Jordanstrasse 3), near the university, is a student favourite because of its hearty servings of fairly traditional main dishes from DM15 to DM22. *Ban Thai Imbiss (Leipziger Strasse 26)* is a small but very popular Thai stand-up and takeaway place with a good range of main dishes for under DM10. A few doors back towards the university is a courtyard with a *Bio-Laden* that sells organic produce and wines. The *Irish Shop (Leipziger Strasse 35)*, in a courtyard, has a limited lunch menu that includes good fish and chips for DM8. *Fisch Bader (Leipziger Strasse 55)* continues the 'stand-up fish for lunch' theme with a fish soup for DM5.50, a large variety of piscine rolls for under DM5 and baked fish with your choice of vegetables that should weigh in at under DM10.

Stattcafé (Grempstrasse 21), near the Kirchplatz U-Bahn station, offers vegetarian and meat dishes from around DM13 and serves good coffee and cakes. This is where students pass the time between (or during) lectures. *Casa Nostra (Konrad-Brosswitz-Strasse 42)*, off Grempstrasse, is open in the evening and serves well priced pasta and other Italian dishes. It's also a lively bar where you can tipple till late.

The *Andalucia (☎ 77 37 30, Konrad-Brosswitz-Strasse 41)* is a quality Spanish restaurant open in the evening (book ahead) with a menu strong on red-meat and seafood dishes for around DM25. But you might like to make a meal out of the excellent tapas. *Plazz am Kirchplatz (Kirchplatz 8)*, which is similar to Casa Nostra, opens for breakfast and closes late.

The Nordend area, east of Bockenheim, also attracts students and trendoids. *Grössenwahn (☎ 59 93 56, Lenaustrasse 97)* is a lively pub that serves fare with flare. You can eat here for under DM25. Take the U-5 to Glauburgstrasse.

Self-Catering Fresh produce *markets* are held on Thursday and Friday from 8 am to 6 pm at Bockenheimer Warte and Südbahnhof respectively. There are *supermarkets* in the basements of Kaufhof and Hertie on Zeil, and an HL Markt near the hostel in Sachsenhausen at Elisabethenstrasse 10-12. In Bockenheim there are HL, Penny Markt and Aldi supermarkets about 100m north of the Leipziger Strasse stop. (See the earlier Zeil & Römerberg section for the Kleinmarkthalle.)

Entertainment

Frankfurt is truly a *Weltstadt* – an 'international city' – with an exhaustive amount of evening entertainment.

The best source of information on what's happening in town is *Journal Frankfurt* (DM3.30), available at newsstands and kiosks. This German-language guide is published monthly and includes comprehensive listings for music, theatre, ballet, literary events, films and TV. It also has a section for gays and lesbians. Not all films showing in English are listed, though.

Fritz and *Strandgut* are free magazines with listings (in German) of concerts, clubs, restaurants etc, available throughout the city in clubs and bars.

Pubs & Bars The Irish influence on Frankfurt's drinking scene just can't be ignored. *MacGowan's (Berger Strasse 255)*, in Bornheim, is one of the best Irish pubs in town. The *Shamrock (Kleine Rittergasse 4)*, *Irish Pub (Rittergasse 11)* and the nearby *O'Dwyers Pub (Klappergasse 19)*, which has Irish folk music every Sunday night, are all in Sachsenhausen and are well worth a visit.

Blaubart Gewölbekeller (Kaiserhofstrasse 18) is a vaulted beer cellar with long tables, bright faces and a hearty atmosphere. It also serves a few standard dishes. *Zu den Zwölf Aposteln* (see Places to Eat) has a beer cellar and brews its own beer on the premises.

Fidelio (Bockenheimer Landstrasse 1) is an upmarket wine bar that attracts business-people during the day and a crowd from the nearby Alte Oper at night; it's closed on Sunday. *Bockenheimer Weinkontor (Schlossstrasse 92)* gets a mixed crowd of the young, the middle-aged and the business-suited. It stays open till late. The building, a 19th century workshop, has a courtyard out the back where you can drink in summer. Take tram No 16 from the Hauptbahnhof to Adalbert-Schlossstrasse. Enter through the arch next to the Vietnamese Restaurant.

Discos & Clubs
In Klappergasse just west of the Frau Rauscher Brunnen, *Far Out* is a disco and cafe open Wednesday to Sunday. It has a strong emphasis on soul music. *Stereo Bar (Abtgässchen 7)* has a 1970s interior and the music to match. *Cooky's (Am Salzhaus 4)* in the centre is another popular club – check the listings for what's on. *Dorian Gray* at the airport in Terminal 1, Hall C, is also worth checking out in the listings for what's on – techno, usually.

Gay & Lesbian *Fritz* has a gay listings page in every issue. Lesben Informations- und Beratungsstelle (☎ 28 28 83), Alte Gasse 38, provides information and assistance to lesbians; Rosa Telefon Mainz (☎ 06131-194 46) does the same for gay men.

The Oscar Wilde Bookshop on Alte Gasse sells gay and lesbian books and tapes, and is a great source of local information. Pick up a copy of *Frankfurt von Hinten* (Frankfurt from Behind), a good gay guide to the city.

Zum Schwejk (Schäffergasse 20) is a popular gay bar. *Harvey's (☎ 49 73 03)* is a restaurant on Friedberger Platz and a favoured meeting place for Frankfurt's guppies and luppies.

Frankfurt's premier gay street is Alte Gasse, north-west of Konstablerwache and east of Schäfergasse; here you'll find gay and lesbian discos, cafes and baths. *The Dance Zone (Alte Gasse 5)* gets a mixed crowd but is popular with gays. *The Blue Angel (Brönnerstrasse 17)* is strictly gay. Lesbian clubs include *Papillon (Bleichstrasse 34)* and *Tangerine (Stiftstrasse 39)*.

Rock & Jazz

The *Sinkkasten (☎ 28 03 85, Brönnerstrasse 5)* has leading rock and reggae live bands. *The Cave (Brönnerstrasse 11)*, a more recent addition to Frankfurt's music scene, is very similar.

Top jazz acts perform at the *Jazzkeller (☎ 28 85 37, Kleine Bockenheimer Strasse 18A)* and the *Jazz-Kneipe (☎ 28 71 73, Berliner Strasse 70)*. *Mampf (Sandweg 64)*, in Bornheim, also attracts a good crowd.

Cabaret Frankfurt has several good cabaret venues. *Tiger Palast (☎ 92 00 22 50, Heiligkreuzgasse 16-20)* has popular cabaret

HESSE

acts; but once you add the cost of a meal, it's an expensive night out. *Mousonturm (☎ 40 58 95 20, Waldschmidtstrasse 4)* is in a converted soap factory, and offers dance performances and politically oriented cabaret.

Cinemas Films screened in the original language are denoted in newspapers and programs by initials 'OF' or 'OmU'. Look for yellow *Kino* posters in U-Bahn stations; if the description's in English, so is the movie.

Turm-Palast (☎ 28 17 87, Am Eschenheimer Turm) is a multi-screen cinema that shows new films in original languages. The *IMAX* in the Zeilgalerie is where you can don the magic specs and watch films in 3D.

The *Kommunales Kino (☎ 21 23 88 30)* at the German Film Museum (see Museums) screens a range of old and new films, series and other special events.

Another venue is *Berger Kinos (☎ 945 03 30, Berger Strasse 177)* in Bornheim. *Harmonie (☎ 21 35 50, Driechstrasse 54)* in Sachsenhausen shows art films in their original languages.

Theatre & Classical Theatre, ballet and opera are strong points of Frankfurt's entertainment scene. The *English Theatre (☎ 24 23 16 20, Kaiserstrasse 52)* performs English-language plays and musicals with performances from Tuesday to Sunday. The *Chaincourt Theatre Company (☎ 79 82 31 63)*, administered by Frankfurt University's English Department, performs at Kettenhofweg 130. The *Freies Schauspiel (☎ 596 94 90, Hebelstrasse 15-19)* is a slightly offbeat venue with alternative theatre.

Die Städtischen Bühnen (☎ 21 23 79 99) runs, and takes bookings for, the *Kammerspiele* and *Schauspielhaus* (both theatres), as well as the *Oper* (all in the one complex at Willy-Brandt-Platz) and the *Alte Oper*, which is at Opernplatz 8. The Alte Oper has three venues: the Mozart Saal, Hindemith Saal and Grosser Saal, featuring an array of classical concerts, ballet and theatre. Die Städtischen Bühnen also runs *TAT*, Bockenheimer Warte, with experimental and alternative theatre, concerts and special events.

Tickets for classical and other performances can also be booked at the Hertie concert and theatre-booking service (☎ 29 48 48; commission charged), Zeil 90.

Shopping

The shopping in Frankfurt is excellent. It's an ideal place to satisfy any souvenir or last-minute requirements before boarding the plane or train home.

Frankfurt's main shopping street is Zeil, particularly the section between the Hauptwache and the Konstablerwache. It's reputed to attract more business than any other shopping district in Europe. Very serious splurging, however, takes place in the streets immediately south of Fressgasse, where you can browse through upmarket fashion boutiques and jewellery stores. Schweizer Strasse in Sachsenhausen and Berger Strasse in Bornheim are other streets with fairly good shopping.

There's a great flea market along Museumsufer (Schaumainkai) every Saturday between 8 am and 2 pm.

Getting There & Away

Air Flughafen Frankfurt-am-Main is Germany's largest airport, with the highest freight and passenger turnover in continental Europe (it's second to Heathrow in passenger turnover). This high-tech town has two terminals linked by an elevated railway called the Sky Line.

Departure and arrival halls A, B and C are in the old Terminal 1, the western half of which handles Lufthansa flights. Halls D and E are in the new Terminal 2.

Buses to Südbahnhof leave from Terminal 1, level 1. Regional train and S-Bahn connections are deep below Terminal 1 in Hall B. By the time you read this, IC/EC and ICE trains will depart from the new Fernbahnhof Flughafen Frankfurt, connected to the main terminal building by a walkway. ICE trains are scheduled to run between Hamburg and Stuttgart via Hanover and the airport every two hours, and to Berlin via Cologne and Dortmund, or south to Basel. Platforms 1 to 3 are in the regional station and platforms

4 to 7 are in the long-distance train station, where there's also a DB ticket office and service point. All trains leave from the regional station between 12.30 and 5 am.

The airport information number is ☎ 69 03 05 11. If you arrive well before your departure, be sure to bring a snack: cafes and bars are unforgivably expensive. And take a book, or you may end up in Dr Müller's – Germany's only airport sex shop/adult movie theatre.

If you're here in transit, you should know that for a mere DM8 you can enjoy a hot shower in Hall B; ask at the information counter for directions.

Train The Hauptbahnhof, west of the centre, handles more departures and arrivals than any other station in Germany, so finding a train to or from almost anywhere is not a problem. The information office for train connections and tickets is at the head of platform 9. For train information, call ☎ 018 05 99 66 33.

Bus Long-distance buses leave from the southern side of the Hauptbahnhof where there's a Europabus office (☎ 23 07 35/36). It caters for most European destinations, but the most interesting possibility is the Romantic Road bus (see Getting Around in the Romantic Road section of the Bavaria chapter). The Europabus head office is Deutsche Touring (☎ 790 30), Römerhof 17, 60486 Frankfurt.

Car & Motorcycle Frankfurt features the Frankfurter Kreuz, Germany's biggest autobahn intersection – modelled, it would seem, after the kind you might find in Los Angeles. All major (and some minor) car-rental companies have offices in the main hall of the Hauptbahnhof and at the airport.

Känguruh GmbH (☎ 596 20 35, fax 596 20 38), Eckenheimer Landstrasse 99, rents out older-model cars from DM59 per day or DM250 per week, including insurance and 200km allowance per day.

Ride Services The ADM-Mitfahrzentrale (194 40) is on Baselerplatz, three minutes

walk south of the Hauptbahnhof. It's open Monday to Friday from 8 am to 6.30 pm, and Saturday to 2 pm. Some samples of fares (including fees) are Berlin DM51, Hamburg DM47 and Munich DM39. The Citynetz Mitfahr-Service (☎ 194 44), Homburger Strasse 36, has slightly more expensive rates.

Getting Around

To/From the Airport S-Bahn line No 8 runs at least every 15 minutes between the airport and the Hauptbahnhof (DM5.90, 11 minutes), usually continuing via Hauptwache and Konstablerwache to Offenbach. At the Hauptbahnhof you can also jump on any train that stops at the airport if you have a valid S-Bahn ticket; see the list posted on every track that says (in English, German and French) 'Trains to Frankfurt Airport'.

Bus No 61 runs to/from the Südbahnhof in Sachsenhausen.

Taxis charge about DM45 for the trip into town but are slower than the train.

Public Transport Frankfurt's excellent – if expensive – transport network (RMV) integrates all bus, tram, S-Bahn and U-Bahn lines. Single or day tickets can be purchased from automatic machines (press the flag button for explanations in English) at almost any stop. Press *Einzelfahrt Frankfurt* for destinations in zone 50, which takes in most of Frankfurt (a plane symbol indicates the button for the airport). Short-trip tickets (*Kurzstrecken*; consult the list on machines) cost DM2.90, single tickets cost DM3.60 and a *Tageskarte* (24 hour ticket; also valid for the airport trip) DM8.20. Weekly passes – also valid for the airport – cost DM30.60.

Car & Motorcycle Traffic flows smoothly in central Frankfurt, but the one-way system makes it extremely frustrating to get to where you want to go. You're better off parking your vehicle in one of the many car parks (DM3 per hour, DM5 overnight) and proceeding on foot. Throughout the centre you'll see signs on lampposts for car parks, which give directions and the number of parking places left in each.

HESSE

Taxi Taxis are quite expensive at DM3.80 flag fall, plus a minimum of DM2.15 per kilometre. There are taxi ranks throughout the city, or you can ring for one on ☎ 230 00 33, ☎ 25 00 01 or ☎ 54 50 11.

Bicycle The city is good for cyclists, with designated bike lanes on most streets. Bikes are treated by the law as cars, so watch out for red lights. Bikes can be rented at the Hauptbahnhof's luggage counter for DM10 a day, or for slightly more at Per Pedale (☎ 707 23 63), Leipzig Strasse 4; Radschlag (☎ 45 20 64), Hallgartenstrasse 56; or Theo Intra (☎ 34 27 80), Westerbachstrasse 273.

AROUND FRANKFURT
Offenbach

Offenbach, though a city in its own right with 117,000 inhabitants, is all but in name a suburb of Frankfurt. It has a couple of interesting museums, a good Saturday market, and a pleasant waterfront. Until WWII, it was a centre for leather manufacturing, and the mansions once belonging to the tanners still line Main Strasse on the river and Frankfurter Strasse to the west.

After WWII, the leather industry vanished, never to return, but the city is home to the national **Leather Museum** (☎ 81 30 21), Frankfurter Strasse 86. Authentic down to the smell, anything and everything pertaining to tanned animal hides is celebrated in this large building. There is also a fascinating **Shoe Museum** here containing everything from a platform shoe autographed by the Spice Girls to Wild West and traditional German footwear (all in airtight cases). The museums are open Tuesday to Sunday from 10 am to 5 pm (DM5/2.50).

The pleasant **riverfront** on Main Strasse has several boat clubs with cafes, and the **market** on Saturday morning is a bustling, multicultural affair with a great range of fresh produce.

For an evening outing try *Weinstube* (*Taunusstrasse 19*), a relaxed pub, wine bar and restaurant better than many of its ilk in Frankfurt. Its serves good salads and vegie dishes, as well as steaks and the like (S-Bahn stop: Ledermuseum).

Getting There & Away The S-Bahn train S8 makes the 25 minute journey between Offenbach and Frankfurt's Hauptbahnhof four times an hour from 4 am to midnight. Day or weekly RMV passes are valid.

DARMSTADT
☎ 06151 • pop 138,000

Some 35km south of Frankfurt, Darmstadt is a city with a long history of artistic accomplishment – home to writers, composers and the Matildenhöhe, the art colony that truly brought the Art Nouveau (Jugendstil) style into vogue. It's a nice little side trip and if you decide to stay, there are a couple of very cool Irish pubs here, too.

Orientation & Information

The Hauptbahnhof is at the western end of the city, connected to the Altstadt by a long walk (or quick ride on bus D or F) down Rheinstrasse, which runs directly into Luisenplatz, in the pedestrianised heart of the city. The Hessisches Landesmuseum and Schloss are right in the centre. The Matildenhöhe is about 1km east of the centre.

The city tourist office (☎ 13 27 80, fax 13 27 83, email tourco@stadt.darmstadt.de) is right in front of the Hauptbahnhof, and is open weekdays from 9 am to 6 pm, and Saturday to noon. A second office is in the Luisencentre at Luisenplatz (☎ 13 27 81, fax 202 28). This office has the same weekday hours but is open on Saturday to 1 pm.

There's a post office at the Hauptbahnhof (open weekdays from 7 am to 7 pm, and Saturday from 8 am to 12.30 pm) and another in Luisenplatz (open weekdays from 9 am to 6 pm, and Saturday from 9 am to 2 pm).

There's also a Commerzbank at Rheinstrasse 34 with foreign exchange facilities and an ATM.

Books can be bought at the large international stand at the Hauptbahnhof; Lonely Planet titles and English-language books are available at Gutenberg Buchhandlung, Am Luisenplatz 4.

Things to See

Established in 1899 at the behest of Grand Duke Ernst-Ludwig, the artists' colony at **Mathildenhöhe** churned out some impressive works of Art Nouveau between 1901 and 1914. The **Museum Künstlerkolonie** (☎ 13 33 85) displays some of these works in its beautiful grounds. It's open Tuesday to Sunday from 10 am to 5 pm (DM5/3). Take bus F from the Hauptbahnhof. Also in the grounds is the **Braun Design Sammlung**, displaying 500 types of Braun products – from razors to radios. It's open Tuesday to Saturday from 10 am to 6 pm, and Sunday to 1 pm (free).

There's also a stunning **Russian Orthodox chapel**, built 1897-99 and designed by Louis Benois for the Russian Tsar Nicholas II after he married Princess Alexandra of Hesse in 1894. The chapel is open from April to September daily from 9 am to 6 pm, and the rest of the year to 5 pm (DM1.50).

One of the oldest art museums in Germany is the **Hessisches Landesmuseum** (☎ 12 54 34) at Friedensplatz 1. It houses Hessian artworks from 1550 to 1880 and exhibitions on the natural sciences and geology. It's closed Monday (DM5/1).

The **Schloss Museum** (☎ 240 35), in a former margrave's residence with an 18th century castle, is packed with ornate furnishings, carriages and paintings, including *The Madonna of Jakob Meyer, Mayor of Basle* by Hans Holbein the Younger. It's open Monday to Thursday from 10 am to 1 pm, and from 2 pm to 5 pm. On weekends it's open from 10 am to 1 pm. Admission is DM3.50/2.

Organised Tours

There are 1½ to two-hour guided city tours in German (DM15/8) on the first Saturday and Sunday of the month. You can buy tickets at the tourist offices (see Orientation & Information).

Places to Stay & Eat

The *Jugendherberge* (☎ 452 93, fax 42 25 35, Landgraf-Georg-Strasse 119) has beds for juniors/seniors for DM24/29, including breakfast. Take bus D to Am Woog from the Hauptbahnhof. *Hotel Zum Weingarten* (☎ 522 61, Weingartenstrasse 36) has the cheapest single/double rooms in town at DM45/70, or DM60/90 with shower and WC. Take tram No 6 or 7 to the suburb of Eberstadt. *Hotel Atlanta* (☎ 178 90, Kasinostrasse 129), north of the Herrngarten, has nice rooms from DM125/155 (ask for one away from the street).

The Luisencenter is a paradise for snackers and light eaters, with half a dozen good options. *Zum Goldenen Anker (Landgraf-Georg-Strasse 25)* has traditional fare at reasonable prices with a Bavarian focus.

Ann Sibin (Landgraf-Georg-Strasse 125) is a great Irish pub with good beer. *Goldene Krone (Schustergasse 18)* is the most popular night spot. It has a cinema, piano room, pool table, live music and positively ghastly toilets. *Café Kesselhaus (Rheinstrasse 97)* is a popular dance venue in this lively student town.

Getting There & Away

There's frequent S-Bahn service (DM10.50, 30 minutes) from Frankfurt's Hauptbahnhof. The A5 connects Frankfurt and Darmstadt.

WIESBADEN

☎ 0611 • pop 138,000

Wiesbaden, the capital of Hesse, is just an hour west of Frankfurt. It is a historic and attractive spa capital once favoured by ailing gentry. Goethe spent time here in 1814. More Russian writers than you can poke a stick at have swooned in over the centuries with dipped quills to partake of the cure. Fyodor Dostoevsky made a mess of his nerves here during the 1860s, when he amassed losses at the city's gambling tables. Rumour has it that in 1991 the Russian government offered to formally settle his debts, but Wiesbaden graciously wrote them off as a gesture of goodwill.

Wiesbaden still attracts the rich, the famous and the ailing. But it's a pleasant, bustling city, and well worth a visit for its charming atmosphere and fine parks.

HESSE

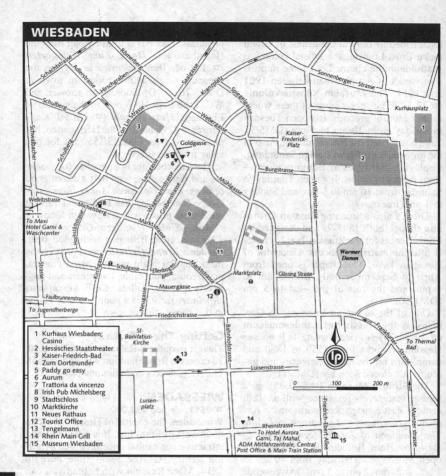

WIESBADEN

1 Kurhaus Wiesbaden;
   Casino
2 Hessisches Staatstheater
3 Kaiser-Friedrich-Bad
4 Zum Dortmunder
5 Paddy go easy
6 Aurum
7 Trattoria da vincenzo
8 Irish Pub Michelsberg
9 Stadtschloss
10 Marktkirche
11 Neues Rathaus
12 Tourist Office
13 Tengelmann
14 Rhein Main Grill
15 Museum Wiesbaden

Orientation & Information

The city centre is a 15 minute walk north from the Hauptbahnhof along Bahnhofstrasse or can be reached on bus No 1 or 8.

The cable car leading to the Russian Orthodox church at the top of Neroberg (Nero Hill) is at the northern end of the city. The Kurhaus is at the north-eastern end of the city. Bus No 1 goes to both of these.

The tourist information office (☎ 172 97 80, fax 172 97 98, email verkehrsbuero@ wiesbaden.de) is at Marktstrasse 6. It's open weekdays from 9 am to 6 pm, and Saturday to 3 pm. Staff book rooms in hotels and pensions (but not private rooms) for DM6 and sell tickets to the spas and attractions.

Change money at the Reisebank at the Hauptbahnhof. The central post office is at Kaiser-Friedrich-Ring 81, next to the Hauptbahnhof.

There's the Bauer Buchhandlung bookshop at the Hauptbahnhof, which has an English-language section, along with foreign newspapers and magazines. The

Waschcenter, Wellritzstrasse 41, is open daily from 6 am to 11.30 pm.

For a doctor, call ☎ 46 10 10 or ☎ 670 60.

Things to See & Do

The Schlossplatz is in the centre of the city and contains the stunning Gothic **Marktkirche** (1852-62) and the **Neues Rathaus** (1884-87) surrounding the **Marktbrunnen**, originally built in 1537. On the northern side is the neoclassical **Stadtschloss** (1840), built for Duke Wilhelm von Nassau and now the Hessian parliament.

Take bus No 1 to the **cable car** (DM2) for the trip up the Neroberg to the **Russian Orthodox Church**, often mistakenly called the 'Greek Chapel', built between 1847 and 1855 as the burial place of Elizabeth Mikhailovna, wife of Duke Adolf of Nassau and niece of a tsar of Russia. Elizabeth died here during childbirth in 1845 and Adolf built this five-domed church in her honour; it is modelled on the Church of the Ascension in Moscow.

Museum Wiesbaden (☎ 335 22 50, Friedrich-Ebert Allee 2) houses many paintings by Russian expressionist Alexei Jawlensky, who lived in Wiesbaden from 1921 until his death in 1941. It is open Wednesday to Friday from 10 am to 4 pm, Tuesday from 12 to 8 pm and weekends from 11 am to 5 pm (DM5, or DM6 for special exhibitions).

The **Kurhaus Wiesbaden** (☎ 172 92 90, Kurhausplatz 1) is a restored classical building (1907) that's been converted into the city's main theatre, convention centre and casino. If you want to do a Dostoevsky in the casino, men should pack a jacket and tie. You can view the obscenely lavish rooms with a guide (see Organised Tours) or just walk up to the desk staff and ask them to let you snoop around.

The grounds (free) are lovely to stroll in, and on Sunday there's a buffet brunch, accompanied by piano music, on the patio (DM45 per person; in the bistro in winter).

There are two main thermal baths in the city. The historic **Kaiser-Friedrich-Bad**, at the end of Langgasse, has been completely renovated and now resumes its place as Wiesbaden's premier bath. It's open Monday to Thursday from 10 am to 10 pm, and to midnight on Friday. Tuesday is for women only and Wednesday for men only. It costs a staggering DM31.50 (no discounts) for four hours of splashy fun. The more conservative **Thermal Bad**, with salt water, is at Leibnitzstrasse 7. Catch bus No 18 from Luisenstrasse or Schwalbacher Strasse. A day pass costs DM10.

Organised Tours

The tourist office runs bus tours on Wednesday at 2.30 pm and Saturday at 2 pm. Leaving from the Theatre Colonnade in front of the Hessisches Staatstheater, the tours usually take in the Kurhaus, Neroberg and the castle at Biebrich. On Saturday they sometimes include a glass of wine. The cost is DM20; DM10 for children up to age 14.

Places to Stay

Campingplatz Rettbergsau (☎ 31 22 77), on the island in the middle of the Rhine, has camp sites for DM8. Take bus No 3 from Schwalbacher Strasse, No 4 from Luisenstrasse, or No 38 from Europaplatz to Rheinufer Biebrich, then catch the ferry. The island is off-limits to cars. It's usually open from early May to September.

The *Jugendherberge* (☎ 486 57, Blücherstrasse 66) is a 10 minute walk west of the city centre. Despite the unattractive building, it's clean and the staff are helpful. A place in a six-bed dorm costs DM24/29 for juniors/seniors. There's a cafeteria downstairs that serves beer and apple wine. From the Hauptbahnhof, take bus No 14, in the direction of Klarenthal, to Gneisenaustrasse.

The thermal waters might heal the body, but Wiesbaden's hotel prices won't help anyone's budget. *Hotel Aurora Garni* (☎ 37 37 28, fax 33 36 50, Untere Albrechtstrasse 9) is friendly, convenient to the Hauptbahnhof and centre, and has nice singles/doubles from DM95/160 with shower and WC. *Maxi Hotel Garni* (☎ 945 20, fax 94 52 77, Wellritzstrasse 6) has tasteful rooms for DM130/170; these prices go down during seasonal lulls.

HESSE

Places to Eat

The unpretentious **Rhein Main Grill** *(Rheinstrasse 27)* has friendly service and good German food. Many of its main dishes come in at under DM20 (steaks are around DM25), and it has a cheap lunch special. **Zum Dortmunder** *(Langgasse 34)*, in the centre, offers traditional cuisine in a pub atmosphere from around DM15 to DM34 for main dishes.

Taj Mahal *(☎ 37 33 89, Bahnhofstrasse 52)* is more upmarket and serves good tandoori and curries in the DM20 to DM40 price range.

Goldgasse, in the centre, has several good eating and drinking options. **Trattoria da vincenzo** *(☎ 37 49 78)* at No 13 serves pasta and pizza, but its changing menu (around DM16) offers more interesting fare. **Aurum** at No 16 is a cafe and bar that offers light meals like baked whole potato with spinach and gorgonzola (DM13.50), and a great apple strudel and icecream (DM7.50). You can also drink here till late. **Paddy go easy**, an Irish pub on Goldgasse, next door to Aurum, opens in the evening and usually has live music. **Irish Pub Michelsberg** *(Michelsberg 15)* does the same.

Wellritzstrasse has lots of Turkish takeaway (and some eat-in) options available. The **Tengelmann** *(Luisenstrasse 23)* is a good supermarket with a salad section; there's another next door to the Zum Dortmunder restaurant.

Getting There & Around

S-Bahn trains leave every 20 minutes from Frankfurt's Hauptbahnhof (DM10.50, 45 minutes). The S8 runs via Frankfurt airport. There's an ADM Mitfahrzentrale office (☎ 194 40) just north of the Hauptbahnhof at Bahnhofstrasse 51-53.

Wiesbaden is connected to Frankfurt by the A66 Autobahn and is just off the A3, which leads to the Ruhr region.

City buses cost DM3.50 for a single ticket or DM8 for a 24 hour pass. The train station is a major hub for buses and you can buy tickets from the machines.

FULDA

☎ 0661 • pop 61,000

With a large baroque district and many fine and interesting churches, Fulda, 45 minutes from Frankfurt, is definitely worth a visit.

The Hauptbahnhof is at the north-eastern end of Bahnhofstrasse, five minutes from the baroque Altstadt, which begins just west of Universitätsplatz. Turn right at Universitätsplatz to get to the Stadtschloss, at the northern end of the Altstadt. The Dom and St-Michaels-Kirche are just west of the Stadtschloss. The bus station is at the southern end of the Hauptbahnhof.

The tourist office (☎ 10 23 46, fax 10 27 75, email tourismus@fulda.de), in the Stadtschloss, is open weekdays from 8.30 am to 6 pm, and Saturday from 9.30 am to 4 pm (from April to October, Sunday from 10 am to 2 pm).

There's a Commerzbank on Universitätsplatz, at the end of Bahnhofstrasse. The main post office is a block north-west of the station at Heinrich-von-Bibra-Platz. C@fé Online, Königstrasse 80-82, offers Internet access in a hip atmosphere for DM5 per half hour. It's open till midnight, and weekends till 1 am.

There are English-language books at the Buchexpress im Hauptbahnhof. The city library (☎ 974 90) is at Heinrich-von-Bibra-Platz. Wasch Insel, a laundrette, is at Petergasse 16. Ärztlicher Notdienst (☎ 192 92), Würtstrasse 1 on the corner of Leipziger Strasse, is an emergency medical service.

Things to See

The **Stadtschloss** (1707) was the former residence of the prince abbots and now houses the city administration and a museum. The Historical Rooms of the residence are a highlight of the museum and include the Fürstensaal, a grandiose banquet hall, the Spiegelkabinett (Chamber of Mirrors) and a good collection of porcelain dating from the 18th century. From the Green Room (which is, well, green) are views over the **gardens** to the **Orangerie**. It's open Tuesday to Sunday from 10 am to 6 pm, Friday from 2 to 6 pm (DM4/3). On the hill is the Frauenberg

Franciscan Friary. The church of this functioning convent is the only part open to the public (daily from 10 am to 5 pm; free).

West of the palace gardens (across Paulspromenade) is the remarkable **St-Michaels-Kirche** (820-22), the burial chapel belonging to a Benedictine monastic cemetery. The rotunda dates to the original construction and the pillars in the crypt of the chapel are from the Carolingian era.

The reconstructed **Dom** (1704-12) is across the street on the grounds of the Ratgar Basilica, which stood here from 819 to 1700. The cathedral has a richly decorated western portal.

Downstairs, inside the Dom, is the tomb of St Boniface, the English missionary who died a martyr in 754. Upstairs is an amazing painting of the *Assumption of Mary* and another of the *Holy Trinity* and a Gothic relief of Charlemagne (15th century). There are organ recitals (DM3/2) here every Saturday at noon during May, June, September and October.

The **Cathedral Museum**, in the former Stiftskirche, is the highlight of a visit to Fulda (DM4/3). The museum's collection includes Jewish gravestones (in the lovely front yard, packed with artefacts), the painting *Christus und die Ehebrecherin* by Lucas Cranach the Elder (1512), a fashion show of bishop's vestments and a spooky thing that is reported to be the skull of St Boniface. In the cloakroom, look through the glass floor at the foundations of the original basilica. The museum is open from April to October, Tuesday to Saturday from 10 am to 5.30 pm (Sunday from 12.30 pm). From November to March, it's open Tuesday to Saturday from 10 am to 12.30 pm and 1.30 pm to 4 pm (Sunday from 12.30 pm to 4 pm). It's closed in January.

Places to Stay & Eat

There's camping at *Ferienplatz Eichenzell-Rothemann* (☎ 066 59 22 85, *Mulkuppenstrasse 15)* in Rothemann, 12km south of Fulda. It's open from April to October and charges DM8 for a tent and car, DM7 per person. From Fulda's Hauptbahnhof take

bus No 5043; the last one leaves Fulda at 6.30 pm. If you're driving, take the B27 in the direction of Gersfeld.

The *Jugendherberge* (☎ 733 89, fax 748 11, Schirrmannstrasse 31), south-west of the centre, has dorm beds for DM23.50/28.50 for juniors/seniors. Take bus No 5052 from the Hauptbahnhof or 1B from the Schloss to Am Stadion.

Restaurant Mythos (☎ 739 55, Doll 2), in a square off Peterstor, serves well priced Greek fare in the DM15 to DM25 range. The *Zum Schwarzen Hahn* (☎ 24 03 12, Friedrichstrasse 18) offers Hessian specialities from DM15 to DM27.

The *Romantic Hotel Goldener Karpfen* (☎ 868 00, Simpliziusbrunnen 1-5) has an expensive restaurant where main courses are served for around DM30 to DM50, but the service is good and, in addition to its international and regional specialities, it always has a vegetarian dish for about DM25.

Getting There & Away

S-Bahn trains run to Fulda from Frankfurt (DM20), but the fastest method is by taking an IR train (DM29, one hour) or the ICE (DM47, 50 minutes). Fulda can be reached by the A7, which runs north towards Kassel and south to Würzburg.

MARBURG
☎ 06421 • pop 77,000

Some 90km north of Frankfurt, Marburg is a university city known for its charming Altstadt and the splendid Elisabethkirche – Germany's oldest pure Gothic cathedral. The Brothers Grimm studied here for a short time, and Philipps-Universität (1527) was Europe's first Protestant university.

It's also a great place to get fit: much of the city is built on a hillside, and staircases and ramps abound. But when the toil of the cobble-stoned Altstadt becomes too much, you'll also find some good bars and cafes in which to relax.

Orientation

The Lahn River flows south between the Altstadt and the Hauptbahnhof area. The

HESSE

Altstadt rises up the hill on the west bank of the river, divided into a fairly bland Unterstadt at the bottom and the charming Oberstadt on the hillside.

Bahnhofstrasse leads from the Hauptbahnhof to Elisabethstrasse, which takes you south past Elisabethkirche to a fork in the road; bear right for the Oberstadt and left for the Unterstadt. See the Altstadt section for information about the lifts and a delightful staircase that run between the two.

Philipps-Universität (☎ 20 21 62), Neue Kasseler Strasse 1, has 21 schools, including law, medicine, physics, languages and history. The campus is spread throughout the city, but the Old University building is in the centre of the Altstadt.

Information

The tourist office (☎ 99 12 23, fax 99 12 12, email mtm@scm.de) is in the Unterstadt at Pilgrimstein 26, opposite the Hotel Sorat and next to the lifts between the Unterstadt and Oberstadt. It's open Monday to Friday from 9 am to 6 pm, Saturday from 10 am to 2 pm.

There's an ATM in the Hauptbahnhof and a Sparkasse opposite the station. The main post office is at Bahnhofstrasse 6, where you'll also find another ATM. Internet TREFF, a cyberbar opposite the tourist office, charges DM4 per half hour and is open from 11 to 1 am (from 3 pm on Sunday).

Universitäts Buchhandlung (☎ 170 90, Reitgasse 7-9) has lots of English books and Lonely Planet guidebooks. There are always cheap English-language paperbacks (about DM5) in the bins outside Wohlfeile Bücher (☎ 669 19) at Neustadt 9.

Wash your clothes in style at the Bistro-Waschbrett (☎ 123 54, Gutenbergstrasse 16), a cafe-laundrette three minutes walk from the hostel. On Tuesday and Wednesday – the 'cheap' days – a wash costs DM5.

The main Uni-Klinikum (University Hospital; ☎ 28 36 97) is on the east side of the Lahn in Baldingerstrasse.

Elisabethkirche

The Elisabethkirche, Germany's oldest pure Gothic cathedral, was built between 1235 and 1283, though the twin spires weren't finished for another three decades. It's worthwhile going behind the screen to view the **Hohe Chor** (High Choir), the elegant **Elisabethschrein** (Elisabeth Shrine) and **gravestones**, but you'll have to pay DM3/2 for the pleasure, or join one of the German-language tours (DM4/3). The tours run from April to October daily except Saturday at 3 pm (there's an additional tour on Sunday at 11.15 am). At other times, an attendant might take you around (same price). Services are held on Saturday at 6 pm, and Sunday at 10 am and 6 pm.

Altstadt Walking Tour

From Elisabethkirche, walk south, take the left jig and get on to Steinweg, which leads up the hill. Steinweg becomes Neustadt and Wettergasse. Turn right onto the side street where Wettergasse becomes Reitgasse. This leads to the **Markt**.

In the centre of the Markt is the **Rathaus** (1512). Its beautiful clock strikes hourly with lots of pomp, and there's an odd half gable on the west side. A market is held here every Saturday morning.

From here, peer up through the narrow Nikolaistrasse to see part of the **Landgrafenschloss** (1248-1300), a massive stone structure that was the administrative seat of Hesse.

Follow the ramps up the amazingly steep **Landgraf-Philipp-Strasse** to the top, where there's a **Local History Museum** (DM3/2) and a great view. The Schloss and museum are open from April to October, Tuesday to Sunday from 10 am to 6 pm, and November to March from 11 am to 5 pm (DM3/2).

Concerts are held in the **Schlosspark** throughout the year. Ask at the tourist office for details.

Walk back to the Markt, turn down Reitgasse and you'll reach the **Universitätskirche** (1300), a former Dominican monastery; and the **Alte Universität** (1891), still part of the campus and still bustling.

Finally, walk round the church and across the Weidenhäuser Brücke; on the south side of the bridge and the east side of the Lahn is a stand with rowing boats (DM10 per hour).

If you want to see the Markt but don't want to climb Steinweg, begin this tour by walking south from Elisabethkirche, bear left at the fork and follow Pilgrimstein to **Rudolphsplatz**.

There's a monstrously steep **stone staircase** at Enge Gasse, just north of the tourist office, which was once a sewage sluice. Free **lifts** carry you from Rudolphsplatz up to Reitgasse from 7 am to 11.30 pm.

Other Sights

The **Universitätsmuseum für Bildende Kunst** (☎ 28 23 55), on the east bank of the river at Biegenstrasse 11, has artworks from the 19th and 20th centuries. It's open from Tuesday to Sunday from 11 am to 1 pm and from 2 to 5 pm (free).

The former city **botanical gardens**, just to the north-west of the museum, are now open as a city park (free).

Organised Tours

The tourist office runs two-hour walking tours of Elisabethkirche and Landgrafenschloss on Saturday from April to October (DM5); they leave from the Elisabethkirche at 3 pm. One-hour tours of the Markt and Altstadt leave Wednesday at 11 am from the Rathaus (DM3).

Places to Stay

Campingplatz Lahnaue (☎ 213 31, *Trojedamm 47*), just south of the Jugendherberge, is a fine option, right on the river, with tent sites for DM7, plus DM6 per person and DM3 per car (DM1 per bicycle). It's open from April to October.

The *Jugendherberge* (☎ 234 61, *Jahnstrasse 1*), about a 10 minute walk downstream along the Lahn from Rudolphsplatz in the Altstadt, is clean and well run. Rates for juniors/seniors are DM24/29. Staff can help plan outings, rent out three-person canoes (DM30 a day) and help to arrange bicycle rentals.

From the Hauptbahnhof, take bus No 1 to Rudolphsplatz. From there, walk south, cross the Weidenhäuser Brücke, take the stairs to the right at the east end of the bridge, turn

south (towards the waterfall) and it's five minutes ahead on the left.

The tourist information office books *private rooms* at no charge.

Hotels in town are expensive on the whole. *Gästehaus Einsle* (☎ 234 10, *Frankfurter Strasse 2A*), on the west side of the Lahn near the hostel, is pretty good value. Tacky but clean singles/doubles go for DM60/120 with shower and WC.

The boxy *Europäischer Hof* (☎ 69 60, *fax 664 04, Elisabethstrasse 12*), near Bahnhofstrasse, is a good deal for what it looks like: it's slightly seedy and in need of a charm-graft. Rooms start at DM78/135.

The *Hotel Sorat* (☎ 91 80, *fax 91 84 44, email marburg@SORAT-Hotels.com, Pilgrimstein 29*) is the most comfortable upmarket option and good for a splurge. During the week, rooms start at DM185/225 (weekends DM128/168). Prices include a champagne breakfast and use of the sauna and fitness room.

Places to Eat

Alter Ritter (☎ 628 38, *Steinweg 44*) is an upmarket traditional restaurant that has four and five-course set menus for DM65/78, but lunch specials for DM13.50. Otherwise, main courses average DM30. The *Brasserie* (☎ 219 92), opposite the Universitätsbuchhandlung on Reitgasse, is downmarket, traditional and inexpensive. *Bistro News Café* (☎ 212 05, *Reitgasse 5*) is a similar place but gets more students.

Café Barfuss (☎ 253 49, *Barfüsserstrasse 33*), a wacky student place with toy aeroplanes and ads hanging from the ceiling, serves breakfast till 3 pm; pasta costs around DM10 and vegetarian dishes average DM11.

Café 1900 (*Barfüsserstrasse 27*) has snacks, baked casseroles and light meals for under DM10, and a good bean soup for DM5.50. Both are open till 1 am.

Café Vetter (*Reitgasse 4*) is an old-fashioned cafe with great coffee, tea and cakes and a valley view to match. *Pizzeria da Pepe* (☎ 627 07, *Bahnhofstrasse 18A*), in the Bahnhof area, is a very popular but

HESSE

tiny place with smiling staff and good pizzas from DM6.

There's a *Plus* supermarket opposite the Europäischer Hof on Elisabethstrasse. *Naturkost Weidenhäuser*, on the south side of the Weidenhäuser Brücke, has organic wines and produce.

Entertainment

Pick up a free copy of *Marburger Magazin Express* for listings and music dates. The *Kino-Programm* leaflet lists film schedules and whether they're in the original language.

There are two cool places downstairs from the Bistro News Café at Reitgasse 5: *Hemingways*, an American bar; and *Dance Down Under* a bar and disco, both open until late.

Getting There & Around

Trains to Marburg run hourly from Frankfurt (DM25, 1¼ hours) and twice an hour from Kassel (DM27, 1½ hours). By car, the quickest way to reach Marburg from Frankfurt is via the A5 heading north towards Giessen. Marburg lies on the B3.

Velociped (☎ 245 11), Auf dem Wehr 3, hires bicycles for DM15 per day, and will also help in organising day trips to nearby towns, including accommodation on overnight trips. The youth hostel can help you plan an itinerary if you've got your own bike.

Bus Nos A1 and 7 run from the Hauptbahnhof to Rudolphsplatz. Tickets cost DM2.20.

KASSEL

☎ 0561 • pop 202,000

The term 'architectural crimes' could well have been coined to describe the reconstruction of Kassel, a once lovely city on the Fulda River, 1½ hours north of Frankfurt. The label does fit, but the sprawling town is doing its best to regain some of its former appeal.

There are a couple of must-sees here, including the city's unusual Museum of Death, and Wilhelmshöhe, a glorious nature park with waterfalls, a Roman aqueduct, two castles and the city's emblem – the massive Herkules monument.

Wilhelm and Jakob Grimm lived and worked in Kassel, and there's a museum here celebrating their work.

Every five years Kassel is host to one of Western Europe's most important contemporary art shows, the *documenta*. Lasting 100 days, it attracts up to 700,000 visitors. The next documenta will be held in 2002.

Orientation

There are two main train stations. ICE, IC and IR trains pull into the new Bahnhof Wilhelmshöhe (everyone calls it the ICE-Bahnhof), 3km west of the city centre. The Hauptbahnhof (in name only) is at the western end of the centre at Bahnhofsplatz and now serves as a train station for slower trains as well as a cultural centre.

Wilhelmshöhe and its attractions are all at the western end of Wilhelmshöher Allee, which runs straight as an arrow from the centre of the city to the castle.

The mostly pedestrianised centre of the city focuses on Königsplatz.

The Universität-Gesamthochschule is on the grounds of the former Henschl factory complex, south of the town centre, and at Holländischer Platz in the northeast of the city.

Information

The tourist office (☎ 340 54, fax 31 52 16, email ksg@kassel.de) is at the ICE-Bahnhof Wilhelmshöhe. It's open weekdays from 9 am to 1 pm and 2 to 6 pm (Saturday to 1 pm, closed Sunday) and sells the Kassel ServiceCard (DM12/19 for one/three days). The ServiceCard gives you unlimited access to public transport, guided coach or walking tours, and free or reduced admission to area attractions.

There is an ATM and a Sparkasse bank at the ICE-Bahnhof Wilhelmshöhe, and a Deutsche Bank and Commerzbank at Königsplatz. You'll find the main post office at the north-east corner of the centre on Königsstrasse, just south of Holländischer

Platz, but there's also a post office in the ICE-Bahnhof.

There's an Internet terminal inside the InterCity hotel near the ICE-Bahnhof. Information on Kassel can be called up at www.kassel.de.

Freyschmidts Buchhandlung (☎ 729 02 10), Königsstrasse 23, has English-language novels. You can wash your clothes at Schnell und Sauber Waschsalon, Friedrich-Ebert-Strasse 83, four blocks south of the hostel (see Places to Stay).

Wilhelmshöhe

Seven kilometres west of the centre, within the enchanting Habichtswald (Hawk Forest), stands the city's symbol – a massive statue of Herkules atop a huge stone pyramid atop an octagonal amphitheatre atop an impressive hill – which should be your first stop. You can spend an entire day here walking through the forest, down the hiking paths (all levels of difficulty) and, if you avoid the tour buses, it can be a very romantic spot to have a picnic.

The Herkules Herkules, at 600m above sea level, was built between 1707 and 1717 as a symbol of the area's power. The mythical hero himself (scantily clad as usual) looks down at the defeated Encelados, but the main attraction here, if you can climb the 449 steps to the top (DM3/2), is the unbelievable view you have in all directions.

Facing the town, you'll see Wilhelmshöhe Allee running due west towards the town. Until reunification, the hills east of the town formed the border with the GDR. To the south and north-west is the **Habichtswald**, with over 300km of hiking trails. At the bottom of the hill you'll see Schloss Wilhelmshöhe and, to its south, Löwenburg.

To get to Herkules from the ICE-Bahnhof, take tram No 3 to the terminus and change for bus No 43, which goes right up to the top once or twice an hour from 8 am to 8 pm.

Schloss Wilhelmshöhe Home to Elector Wilhelm and later Kaiser Wilhelm II, this palace (1786-1798) houses the **Old Masters Gallery**, featuring works by Rembrandt, Rubens, Jordaens, Lucas Cranach the Elder, Dürer and many others.

During renovation (until mid-2000) Dutch paintings are stored in the Neue Galerie (see Museums), while Italian and German works are at the **Hessisches Landesmuseum**, Brüder-Grimm-Platz 5 near the eastern end of Wilhelmshöher Allee. Its museum is open Tuesday to Sunday from 10 am to 5 pm (DM5/3).

To reach Schloss Wilhelmshöhe from the ICE-Bahnhof, take tram No 1 to the last stop. From there you can take bus No 23, which makes a loop around the lower regions of the park including the aqueduct and Schloss Löwenburg; or walk, following the well-marked hiking trails, straight to the top.

Schloss Löwenburg Modelled on a medieval Scottish castle, Löwenburg (1801) is only open to visitors on guided tours (DM6/4). They leave on the hour from 10 am to 3 pm (4 pm during daylight saving) and take in the castle's **Museum of Armaments** and **Museum of Chivalry**.

Fountains From April to October every Wednesday to Sunday the **Wasserspiel** takes place along the hillside. The fountain's water cascades from the Herkules down to about the halfway point, then follows underground passages until it emerges at the **Grosse Fontäne** in a 52m-high jet of water. The waterworks begin at 2 pm – follow the crowds.

Museums

Billed as 'a meditative space for funerary art', Kassel's excellent and undervisited Museum für Sepulkralkultur, or **Death Museum** (☎ 91 89 30), Weinbergstrasse 25-27, is certainly an interesting way to become familiar with German death rituals. Designed to end the taboo of discussing death, the museum's permanent collection consists of headstones, hearses, dancing skeleton bookends and sculptures depicting death. Upstairs are temporary exhibitions. It's open Tuesday to Sunday from 10 am to 5 pm (DM5/3).

HESSE

Fairy-Tale Road

The 650km Fairy-Tale Road (Märchenstrasse) is one of Germany's most popular tourist routes. It's made up of cities, towns and hamlets in four states (Hesse, Lower Saxony, North Rhine-Westphalia and Bremen), some of them associated with the works of Wilhelm and Jakob Grimm.

The Brothers Grimm, grammarians heralded in academic circles for their work on *German Grammar* and *History of the German Language*, travelled extensively through central Germany in the early 19th century documenting folklore. First published in 1812 as *Kinder und Hausmärchen*, their collection of tales (whose origins can be traced to Germany, Central Europe, Asia and India) gained international recognition after the release in 1823 of *Grimm's Fairy Tales*, most famously including *Hansel & Gretel*, *Cinderella*, *The Pied Piper*, *Rapunzel* and scores of others.

Every town, village and hamlet along the Fairy-Tale Road has an information office of sorts. For advance information, contact the central Fairy-Tale Road tourist information office (☎ 0561-787 80 01, fax 10 38 38), Postfach 102660, 34117 Kassel. Also most helpful is the tourist office in Hameln (see the Lower Saxony chapter).

For an organised tourist route, getting around the Fairy-Tale Road isn't very organised. There's no equivalent of the Romantic Road bus and, because the route covers several states, local bus and train services outside the major cities on the route aren't coordinated. The easiest way to follow the Fairy-Tale Road is by car. The ADAC map of the Weserbergland covers the area in detail.

There are over 60 stops on the Fairy-Tale Road. Major stops include:

Hanau This town east of Frankfurt on the Main River features a monument to its most famous sons: Jakob (1785-1863) and Wilhelm (1786-1859) Grimm, which is the obvious starting point of the Fairy-Tale Road. The puppet museum features some recognisable characters.

Steinau The Grimm brothers spent their youth here, and the Renaissance Schloss contains exhibits on their work. The Amtshaus, Renaissance palace of the counts of Hanau, was their grand home. The puppet theatre stages some of their best-known tales.

Marburg This university town on the Lahn River was where the Brothers Grimm were educated and began their research into German folk tales and stories.

The **Brothers Grimm Museum** (☎ 787 20 33), in the Bellevue Schlösschen at Schöne Aussicht 2, has displays on the brothers' lives, their work (before and after publishing the tales) and the tales themselves, with original manuscripts, portraits and sculptures. It's open daily from 10 am to 5 pm (DM5/3).

Across the street is the **Neue Galerie**, temporary home to the Dutch paintings from the Old Masters collection at Schloss Wilhelmshöhe. It is open Tuesday to Sunday from 10 am to 5 pm (free).

All city museums are closed on Monday.

Organised Tours

There are two-hour city bus tours, which include Wilhelmshöhe, on Saturday from April/May to mid-November at 2 pm (DM18/12); they leave from Königsplatz.

Walking tours leave twice-weekly from Königsplatz throughout the year (DM10, 1½ to two hours).

Two shipping companies offer cruises along the Fulda River from the docks on the east side of town. Rehbein Linie Kassel (☎ 185 05) and Söllner-Kasel (☎ 77 46 70) run one to six-hour cruises into the hinter-

Fairy-Tale Road

Kassel The Brothers Grimm collected a major part of their stories and legends in and around Kassel, where they lived from 1805 to 1830. The Brothers Grimm Museum has exhibits on their lives and works (see the Kassel section for details).

Göttingen The brothers were professors at the university (before being expelled in 1837 for their liberal views). In the summer months the Göttingen People's Theatre Company performs versions of the Grimms' fairy tales at the woodland stage in Bremke, south-east of Göttingen.

Bad Karlshafen This meticulously planned, baroque village is a major highlight of the Fairy-Tale Road (see the Bad Karlshafen section of the Lower Saxony chapter).

Bodenwerder The Rathaus is said to be the house in which the legendary Baron von Münch-hausen was born, famous for his telling of outrageous tales. The Rathaus contains an exhibition on the baron and his tales (see the Bodenwerder section of the Lower Saxony chapter).

Hamelin The biggest stop on the Fairy-Tale road is the quaint city of Hamelin (Hameln), associated forever with the legend of the Pied Piper. Hired by the city to rid the town of rats (he played his flute and the rats followed him out of town), the city later reneged on paying the Piper, and legend has it that he then played his flute to rid the town of its children! (See the Hamelin section of the Lower Saxony chapter).

Bremen Last stop on the route is the old Hanseatic city-state of Bremen, home to the Town Musicians of Bremen. The route that began with a statue of the Brothers Grimm ends at the statue of the famous foursome, at the western end of the Rathaus not far from the giant Roland statue (see the Bremen chapter for other town highlights). On Sunday in summer, a troupe performs a re-enactment of the charming tale.

MICK WELDON

land from where you can walk or take a train back. Prices start at DM10/6 one-way and DM16/8 return.

Places to Stay

The *Campingplatz* (☎ 224 33, Giessenallee 7), between Auestadion and the Messehallen on the Fulda River (open from March to October), is a very peaceful spot, with tent sites for DM10 per tent, DM5 per person and DM5 for parking. From the town centre, take tram No 7 to Auestadion.

Kassel's clean *Jugendherberge* (☎ 77 64 55, fax 77 68 32, Schenkendorfstrasse 18), is one of the best in the country. It is huge and airy, with friendly staff, good food and activities. Beds cost DM24.50/29.50 for juniors/seniors, sheets an extra DM6, and towels DM2. The cafeteria on the main floor is open all day. It's 10 minutes from the Hauptbahnhof on foot; follow Kölnische Strasse west, past the Martini Pils brewery to Schenkendorfstrasse, turn right and the hostel is at the end of the street on the right-hand side. Or, take tram No 4 or 6

HESSE

from the Hauptbahnhof to Annastrasse and walk north four blocks.

The *Jugendherberge* also has good deals on duplexes (covering two floors), which cost the standard junior/senior rate plus DM15/10 per person for a single/double. The bath is down the hall, but you have a WC and sink in the room.

Book *private rooms* at the tourist office (DM5 for the service). Rooms average DM40 to DM60 per person.

Hotel Lenz (☎ 433 73, Frankfurter Strasse 176) is the cheapest hotel in the central district. Basic singles/doubles here cost DM49/90, or DM90/130 with shower and WC. The friendly *Hotel Garni Kö 78 (☎ 716 14, fax 179 82, Kölnische Strasse 78)* has very fine rooms from DM69/98. It is a bit closer to town than the hostel and is bright and comfortable.

Above that you're pretty much looking at health spas and business hotels, of which there are several. The *Ramada Hotel (☎ 933 90, fax 933 91 00)*, near the ICE-Bahnhof, is a very nice place with good service and a sauna. Rooms start at DM160.

The *InterCity Hotel (☎ 938 80, fax 938 89 99, Wilhelmshöher Allee 241)*, attached to the east side of the station, has rooms from DM155/195, but weekend rates of DM117/136.

Places to Eat

The *Markt im Bahnhof* at the ICE-Bahnhof has a greasy assortment of cheap eats. There's also a *tegut* supermarket in the City Center complex at the ICE-Bahnhof.

The best place for a quick bite, however, is along Königsstrasse's pedestrian zone. Try *Udenhausener Brotstube*, a couple of doors down from the Kaufhof department store. It has quite good pastries, cookies, pizzas and breads.

The *Nordsee* restaurant at No 45 serves well priced fish dishes during the day. The *Café Paulus (☎ 97 88 90, Königsstrasse 28)*, at Opernplatz, is a very popular place for lunch and pastries, especially when it opens the footpath cafe. Its daily breakfast buffet costs DM18.50.

The *cafeteria* at the Jugendherberge is of good quality and value, with full lunches available from noon to 2 pm and dinners from 6 to 7 pm for DM8.70. No dinner is served on Sunday night.

Marmara (☎ 71 33 75, Friedrich-Ebert-Strasse 66), an eat-in and takeaway place on the corner of Annastrasse, near the hostel, serves huge portions of Turkish food and has friendly service. Felafel costs DM6, doner kebabs are from DM6 and there are great salads from DM5.50.

Wok (☎ 71 11 44, Kölnischestrasse 124) has good Thai food with a menu catering to herbivores as well as carnivores; expect to pay DM18 for noodle dishes and DM20 for meat dishes. Vegie main courses are from DM14.50 to DM17. There's a beer garden out the back.

Gleis 1, tucked away in the Hauptbahnhof, has absolutely no right to be as hip as it is. Looking much more like New York than Hesse, this very cool place has an American-style bar, a restaurant and live music and disco at nights. You can get ciabatta rolls from DM7.50, soups for DM6.50, pasta for around DM12.50 and full main courses from DM17 to DM25. It is open daily till late, and to 4 am on weekends.

Entertainment

The Hauptbahnhof is now called the Kultur Bahnhof (or KüBa) and has cafes and bars such as *Gleis 1* and *Caricatur*, art openings and sometimes original-language movies. Stop in or check out the magazine *KüBa*, available in the city at bars and pubs.

The stretch of Friedrich-Ebert-Strasse from the laundry running back towards the centre has lots of bars. *Joe's Garage (Friedrich-Ebert-Strasse 60)* looks like, well, Joe's Garage. It has live music most nights and occasional theme nights – everything from tattoos to transvestites.

Getting There & Away

Kassel is on the major north-south ICE route. ICE connections to/from Frankfurt-am-Main leave/arrive at the ICE-Bahnhof two to three times an hour (DM82, 1¾ hours). To/from Fulda, trains leave either twice hourly from the ICE-Bahnhof (DM47, 30 minutes) or hourly from the Hauptbahnhof (DM30, 1½ hours). To/from Marburg, trains leave from ICE-Bahnhof and the Hauptbahnhof (DM27, 1½ hours).

Direct RKH buses leave twice daily for Bad Karlshafen from the Hauptbahnhof (DM13.30, 1½ hours).

Getting Around
The KVG-Transport Centre (☎ 194 49), Königsplatz 36B, sells bus and tram tickets (DM3.60 for a single ticket, DM8.50 for 24 hours, DM25 for a week); you can also buy these tickets at kiosks and at the ICE-Bahnhof. Tram No 1 runs from the ICE-Bahnhof to the centre.

You can rent bicycles from Fahrrad Hof, which is located at the eastern end of the ICE-Bahnhof, for DM20 per day. For mountain bikes, head to Edelmann (☎ 177 69), Goethestrasse 37-39. Prices start at DM20 per day (you'll need to leave your passport as a deposit).

WARBURG
☎ 05641 • pop 3000
Some 40 minutes north-west of Kassel by train is the quaint village of Warburg. It makes a romantic day trip – an untouched German village filled with half-timbered houses, pleasant walking trails and nice churches.

If you have a bike, bring it along; trails through the woods are clearly marked. Don't get confused when you pull into the station and see the Südzucker sugar refinery!

The Altstadt is south of the Neustadt and the Hauptbahnhof.

From the Hauptbahnhof, you should follow Bahnhofstrasse south to the T-junction; to the right is Hauptstrasse, leading to Neustadt's main drag, to the left is the post office and Kasseler Strasse. Follow Kasseler Strasse to Bernhardi-Strasse, the Altstadt's main street, which brings you to Altstadt Platz.

Things to See & Do
Along Bernhardi-Strasse you'll come across numerous half-timbered houses, including the **Glockengiesserhaus** (1538), a Renaissance burgher's house; the **Eisenhoithaus** (1526), with its half-painted, half-carved doorway; and the absolutely massive **Arnoldi Haus**.

On the main Altstadt square is the huge **Altes Rathaus** (1336-7), now home to a pizzeria and beer garden.

For a bird's-eye view, walk through the narrow streets up the hill to the north of Bernhardi-Strasse. You'll first pass the **Altstadt Kirche** (1290-1297). From there, follow the ramps leading uphill, past the Gasthaus zur Alm, to the top of the hill, on which sits the late 12th century **Pfarrkirche**, with its choir stalls from the early 14th century.

A very interesting cultural series runs in Warburg throughout the year, with art openings, music nights (from organ concerts to swing), barbecues and dinners.

Look south from the stone terrace for a wonderful view over the town: to the south is **Der Biermannsturm** (1443), to the east and west is a view like a storybook illustration of medieval Germany.

Places to Stay & Eat
Most people don't make Warburg any more than an afternoon excursion, but you might like to stay overnight. If you do, you'll find accommodation available at the friendly *Warburger Hof (☎ 61 00, Bahnhofstrasse 19A)*, a clean, modern place with basic singles/doubles costing DM55, or DM75/100 with shower and WC. At the restaurant downstairs most main dishes are in the DM15 to DM25 price range. *Imbisstro* in Altstadt Platz has cheap fast food, plus vegetarian dishes.

Getting There & Away
Trains leave from Kassel's Hauptbahnhof every hour for the 40 minute journey (DM15). In Warburg, on weekdays only, you can take bus No 509 from the Hauptbahnhof to the Altstadt (DM2.60).

HESSE

North Rhine-Westphalia

Few German states have to contend with as many negative perceptions as North Rhine-Westphalia (Nordrhein-Westfalen). Billowing chimneys and heavy industry, crowded, faceless cities, a barren landscape devoid of trees and flowers – those are the images that first come to the minds of many. Few, however, realise that forests, fields and lakes cover about 75% of the state, that the cities are pulsating cultural centres and that high-tech and speciality industries – not coal and steel – form the backbone of North Rhine-Westphalia's economy today. There's a greater density of theatres, orchestras and museums here – many of international stature – than anywhere else in Germany. Churches, palaces and castles bulge with art treasures. And unique discoveries like the Neanderthal skeleton unearthed in a valley near Düsseldorf point to a historic richness that reaches back to prehistory.

Charlemagne's imperial headquarters were in Aachen, a city that belongs to any journey through North Rhine-Westphalia. Also a must is Cologne, with its breathtaking Gothic cathedral and first-rate art museums. A fascinating range of world-class museums also adds to the appeal of Bonn, which served as West Germany's 'temporary capital' for a little over four decades.

The state capital Düsseldorf is an elegant and cosmopolitan city that also possesses an earthy conviviality best experienced in the brewery pubs of its Altstadt. The cities of the Ruhrgebiet (Ruhr District) – Essen, Dortmund and Bochum – surprise with their wide spectrum of top-notch cultural events and vast green spaces.

To get completely off the main tourist path, head to the lush nature parks of the Sauerland and Siegerland, both popular getaways that Germans have kept largely to themselves. The skylines of the Westphalian towns of Soest and Paderborn are studded with the spires of medieval churches packed with a wealth of art treasures. And if there

HIGHLIGHTS

North Rhine-Westphalia Luminaries: Konrad Adenauer, Ludwig van Beethoven, Heinrich Böll, Herbert Grönemeyer, Heinrich Heine, Udo Lindenberg, Michael Schumacher, Wim Wenders

- Visiting the awe-inspiring cathedrals at Cologne and Aachen

- Indulging in a night of drink and merriment along the Rhine in Cologne or Düsseldorf

- Enjoying Essen's mindbending Meteorit, the quirky NRW Design Centre and Villa Hügel

- Spending time in Kalkar's St Nikolai Church with its intricate carved altars

- Admiring Schloss Augustusburg in Brühl

- Visiting the House of the History of the Federal Republic of Germany in Bonn

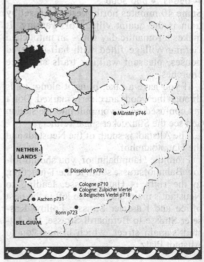

NETHERLANDS

● Münster p746

● Düsseldorf p702

Cologne p710
● Cologne: Zülpicher Viertel & Belgisches Viertel p718

● Aachen p731

Bonn p723

BELGIUM

were still an independent Westphalia, Münster, with its great Dom, university and historic centre would surely be its capital.

Travelling in North Rhine-Westphalia is easy, as the state is criss-crossed by a dense network of autobahns, country roads and major rail lines; even the smallest towns are served by trains and/or buses. Main cities, like Cologne and Düsseldorf, are comparatively expensive, and room rates can be astronomical during trade shows. When business slows, especially during summer,

these rates drop and good bargains abound. In addition, numerous youth hostels, many recently modernised, and camping grounds always provide low-budget alternatives.

HISTORY

Many towns in North Rhine-Westphalia, including Cologne and Xanten, were founded by the Romans, who settled here for about three centuries, having kicked out the Celts between 58 and 51 BC. Between the 3rd and the 5th centuries AD, Frankish tribes

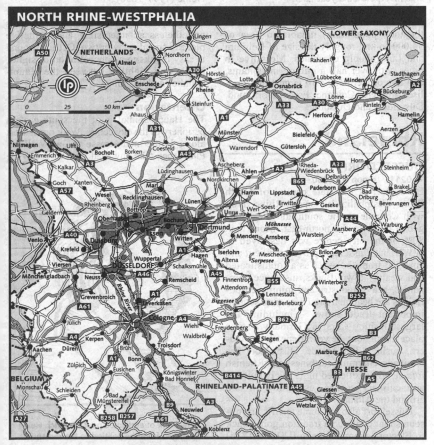

NORTH RHINE-WESTPHALIA

claimed the Lower Rhine area for themselves, while the Saxons took over today's Westphalia. This only lasted until the 8th century, when Frankish strongman Charlemagne subjugated Saxon Duke Widukind and incorporated the Saxon territory into the Holy Roman Empire.

As a modern political entity, North Rhine-Westphalia only came into existence in 1946. The British, who occupied the area after WWII, fused large portions of the former Prussian Rhine province with the province of Westphalia; the tiny state of Lippe-Detmold was incorporated a year later.

It is Germany's most densely populated state: 17 million people (about one fifth of the total population) inhabit an area of 34,000 sq km, roughly the size of Belgium and Luxembourg combined. Most live in cities with over half a million inhabitants, and five of Germany's 10 largest metropolises are here: Cologne, Essen, Dortmund, Düsseldorf and Duisburg.

Rhineland

DÜSSELDORF
☎ 0211   • pop 571,000

Düsseldorf is the state capital of North Rhine-Westphalia. It's on the Rhine river, with Cologne to the south and the Ruhrgebiet cities to the north-east. More than 80% of the city centre was destroyed in WWII, but Düsseldorf proved resilient and emerged from the ashes as a sophisticated and wealthy town. Banks, insurance companies, heavy industry and mining corporations are headquartered here, and several important trade shows – including the largest fashion fairs in Germany – take place throughout the year. Beneath its modern, business-like facade, Düsseldorf has retained a charming earthiness and Rhenish *joie de vivre*, reflected in its lively cultural and culinary scenes, especially in and around the Altstadt.

Düsseldorf also has some terrific art museums that continue a tradition going back to Elector Johann Wilhelm II (1679-1716)

– popularly known as Jan Wellem. His stunning collection of paintings was sent to Munich to protect it from Napoleon's troops, but it was never returned and in fact now forms the basis of that city's Pinakothek museum. But not all was lost for Düsseldorf. The late-baroque period saw the founding of the Düsseldorf School of Painting, which reached its zenith in the 19th century under Wilhelm von Schadow and still enjoys a fine reputation today as the Academy of Fine Arts. Düsseldorf is also the birthplace of the poet Heinrich Heine (1797-1856).

Although always in the shadow of Cologne, its fierce local rival, Düsseldorf is nonetheless an interesting and attractive place to spend a day or two. Getting around is easy thanks to a concentration of sights, hotels and nightlife between the Hauptbahnhof and the Rhine.

Orientation
The Hauptbahnhof is at the south-eastern periphery of the city centre. Walk north-west along Immermannstrasse to Jan-Wellem-Platz, then take any road west to get to the

MICK WELDON

The work of acclaimed poet, Heinrich Heine ranged from the political to the romantic.

Königsallee and the Altstadt with its high concentration of hotels, museums, restaurants and bars. The entire walk should take about 20 minutes. Alternatively, any U-Bahn from the Hauptbahnhof to the Heinrich-Heine-Allee stop will also put you right into the heart of things. The Rhine forms the Altstadt's western border. The main shopping areas are along both Königsallee and Schadowstrasse.

Information

Tourist Office The tourist office (☎ 17 20 20, fax 16 10 71) is opposite the main exit of the Hauptbahnhof towards the northern end of Konrad-Adenauer-Platz and is open daily from 8 am to 8 pm. A good deal for museum buffs is the Art Ticket, which buys two days of free admission and unlimited public transportation for DM20; the group ticket for up to four people costs DM60. It's sold at any museum or public transportation office.

Money The centre abounds with banks, and the Reisebank in the Hauptbahnhof's main hall is open daily to 9 pm. American Express (☎ 38 69 10) is at Königsallee 98a.

Post & Communications The main post office is at Immermannstrasse 1, just north of the tourist office. It's open weekdays until 8 pm and Saturday until 2 pm. The poste restante is here. Have letters clearly marked 'Postlagernd' and addressed to you at 40029 Düsseldorf. There's a public fax-phone in the Reisezentrum in the Hauptbahnhof.

Internet Resources For information via the Internet, check into www.duesseldorf.de (in English and German).

Medical Services & Emergency After hours, call ☎ 192 92 for medical assistance and ☎ 66 62 91 for dental help. Police headquarters are at Jürgensplatz 5. The municipal lost and found office is at ☎ 899 32 85.

Dangers & Annoyances As with most German cities, the area near the Hauptbahn-

hof – and especially around Worringer Platz just north of here – attracts a murky element and should be avoided after dark. The same is true of the city parks, the haunt of drug dealers and other unsavoury characters.

Königsallee & Hofgarten

Unless noted, museums are open from 11 am to 5 pm (from 1 pm on Saturday), closed on Monday.

For a glimpse of Düsseldorf's elegant lifestyle, head for the famed Königsallee – or 'Kö' – with its eastern side sporting stylish and expensive boutiques, often housed in futuristic glass and chrome arcades.

Stroll north on the Kö to the **Hofgarten** (Palace Garden), created in 1769 as Germany's first public city park, which features statues of Heine, Robert Schumann and others. The Hofgärtnerhaus at Jägerhofstrasse 1 houses the **Theatermuseum** (☎ 899 46 60), which traces 400 years of theatre in Düsseldorf. There are also noteworthy collections of marionettes and toy theatres made from paper. Admission is DM4/2; enter from the park side.

On the park's north-eastern edge is the pink **Schloss Jägerhof**, Jacobistrasse 2, the 18th century home of the eclectic **Goethe Museum** (☎ 899 62 62). The exhibit here is less about the great man of letters himself than about the historical context in which Goethe lived and worked, including political events, philosophical approaches and leading personalities. A 'trip' indeed is the epic oil triptych depicting the classical Walpurnisnacht scene from Faust II, painted in 1974 by Paul Struck. Admission is DM4/2.

Art Walk

Düsseldorf has several art museums that form the so-called 'Art Walk' running parallel to the Rhine. Farthest north, at Ehrenhof 5, the **Kunstmuseum Düsseldorf** (Fine Arts Museum; ☎ 899 24 60) is stocked with a collection of European art from the Middle Ages to the present. Highlights include Rubens' *Venus and Adonis* and 19th century landscape paintings by members of the Düsseldorf School. Also here is the **Glasmuseum**

DÜSSELDORF

PLACES TO STAY
18 Hotel AltDüsseldorf
19 Hotel Ludwig
28 Breidenbacher Hof
31 Carathotel
37 Appartementhaus am Schwanenmarkt
42 Hotel Komet
43 Hotel Max
45 Hotel Bristol
47 Haus Hillesheim

PLACES TO EAT
4 Zur Uel
5 Im Füchschen
20 Spitz
22 Zum Schlüssel
26 Herr Spoerl Deli
27 Zum Schiffchen
30 Marché; Kö Galerie
33 Bim's Marktwirtschaft
38 Citrus
46 Ram Thai

OTHER
1 Kunstmuseum; Glasmuseum Hentrich
2 Tonhalle
3 Ratinger Hof Nightclub
6 Theatermuseum
7 Goethe Museum; Schloss Jägerhof
8 Schauspielhaus
9 Kunstsammlung NRW
10 Deutsche Oper am Rhein
11 Kunsthalle
12 Kom(m)ödchen
13 Andreaskirche
14 Mahn- und Gedenkstätte
15 St Lambertus
16 Schiffahrt Museum; Schlossturm
17 Rathaus
21 Schnabelewopski
23 Zum Uerige
24 Kabüffke
25 Film Museum; Hetjens Museum; Black Box
29 Schadow Arcaden
32 Heinrich Heine Institut
34 Marionetten-Theater
35 Roncalli's Apollo Varieté
36 Rheinturm
39 Main Post Office
40 Tourist Office
41 Main Train Station
44 American Express
48 Police Station

Hentrich, with historic and contemporary glass exhibits. It's open Tuesday to Sunday from 10 am to 6 pm (DM8/4).

Top billing goes to the **Kunstsammlung Nordrhein-Westfalen** (Art Collection of North-Rhine Westphalia; ☎ 838 10), housed behind an undulating black syenite facade at Grabbeplatz 5. Its exquisite permanent collection includes paintings and sculpture by every leading light of the 20th century, presented in chronological fashion. Included are career-spanning selections of works by Picasso, Braque, Chagall and Modigliani; German Expressionists like Kirchner, Beckmann and Grosz; and a prestigious Paul Klee collection. Admirers of contemporary American artists, like Rauschenberg and Jasper Johns, as well as Düsseldorf's own Joseph Beuys, will also see their fill. The museum regularly hosts exhibitions of international calibre. Opening hours are daily from 10 am to 6 pm, and Friday to 8 pm (DM5/3, or DM12/8 during special exhibits). Immediately south, the **Kunsthalle**

(☎ 899 62 40) houses temporary art and photography exhibits (admission varies).

Altstadt

Just west of the Kunsthalle is **Andreaskirche** (1629), the former court church and burial place of Elector Jan Wellem. Stylistically a transition from Renaissance to baroque, it boasts complex stucco work, including 12 life-size figures of the apostles.

A few steps west on Mühlenstrasse at No 29 is the **Mahn-und Gedenkstätte** (Exhortation & Memorial Site; ☎ 899 62 05), with an interesting exhibit on persecution and resistance during the Nazi regime in Düsseldorf (free). Leaflets and tapes (DM50 deposit) in English are available at no charge. Continue on Mühlenstrasse, then turn right onto Schlössergasse to Stiftsplatz, lorded over by the 14th century **St Lambertus** parish church, with its peculiar twisted tower and rich interior.

Just beyond, on Burgplatz by the banks of the Rhine, is the **Schlossturm**, a forlorn reminder of the former glory of the electors. Today it houses the **Schiffahrt Museum** (Navigation Museum; ☎ 899 41 95), which deals with 200 years of Rhine shipping. Hours are Wednesday and Saturday from 2 to 6 pm, as well as Sunday from 11 am (DM5/2.50). In fine weather, the steps next to the tower are a happening gathering spot. From here you can stroll south along the river on the **Rheinuferpromenade**. It spills into the Rheinpark, which contains the 234m **Rheinturm**, with a viewing platform and restaurant at 180m (DM5).

Back in the heart of the Altstadt, the Renaissance **Rathaus** (1573) wraps around the Markt dominated by a striking **statue of Jan Wellem**. German-literature buffs may also want to visit the **Heinrich Heine Institut** (☎ 899 55 71), Bilker Strasse 12-14, where letters, portraits, first editions and manuscripts document this famed Düsseldorfer's career (DM4/3). His house at Bolkerstrasse 53 now contains a literary pub called Schnabelewopski (see Entertainment). The Palais Nesselrode at Schulstrasse 4 houses both the **Film Museum** (☎ 899 24 90) and the **Hetjens Museum** (☎ 899 42 00), with ceramics spanning a period of 8000 years. Both museums are open from 11 am to 5 pm, Wednesday to 9 pm and can be visited for a combined admission of DM6.

Schloss Benrath

This pleasure palace and park (☎ 899 72 71), some 12km south of the centre in the suburb of Benrath, was built by Frenchman Nicolas de Pigage in 1755 and makes for a lovely excursion. Its harmonious design – integrating architecture, garden landscaping, sculpture and decorative arts – is typical of the transition from late baroque to the neoclassical style. The rooms, which can be viewed on a one hour guided tour, are decorated with inlaid parquet floors, wood-panelled walls and stucco ornamentation in the style of Louis XVI. The west wing contains a natural history museum (☎ 899 72 19).

The palace is at Benrather Schlossallee 104 (take tram No 701 from Jan-Wellem-Platz or S-Bahn No 6 from the Hauptbahnhof). Both the palace and the park are open from 10 am to 5 pm (DM8/4).

Places to Stay

Room rates in Düsseldorf fluctuate enormously with demand and may triple in price during trade show activity, when hotels are booked far in advance. Check ahead on availability with the tourist office; there are usually no major fairs in summer. Prices quoted below are standard rates. Parking your car at the hotel or a public garage may add DM20 or more to your bill.

The tourist office charges DM5 per person per room reservation, which can be made in person or by calling ☎ 172 02 26. It also keeps a complete list of hotels with addresses and phone numbers posted in the window.

Places to Stay – Budget

Camping There are two camping grounds reasonably close to the city. *Campingplatz Nord Unterbacher See* (☎ 899 20 38) is at Kleiner Torfbruch in Düsseldorf-Unterbach (S-Bahn No 7 to Düsseldorf-Eller, then bus No 735 to Kleiner Torfbruch). It's open from

April to September. Camp sites on the southern lakeshore are reserved for long-term campers. *Camping Oberlörick* (☎ 59 14 01) is at Lütticher Strasse beside the Rhine in Düsseldorf-Lörick (U-Bahn No 70, 74, 76 or 77 to Belsenplatz, then bus No 828 or 838). It's open from mid-April to mid-September.

Hostels The 280 bed *Jugendgästehaus* (☎ 55 73 10, Düsseldorfer Strasse 1) is across the Rhine from the Altstadt. Bunks in three to six-person rooms cost DM37.50, including breakfast. Take U-Bahn No 70, 74, 76 or 77 from the Hauptbahnhof to Luegplatz, from where it's a 10 minute walk south via Kaiser-Wilhelm-Ring.

Hotels Düsseldorf and budget hotels are basically mutually exclusive, though a few older properties still offer singles/doubles under DM100. But even with these, rates skyrocket during trade shows. Don't expect luxuries, tasteful furnishings or a private bath. We're definitely talking no-frills. Places to try include *Hotel Komet* (☎ 17 87 90, fax 178 79 50, Bismarckstrasse 93) and *Hotel Bristol* (☎ 37 07 50, fax 37 37 54, Adersstrasse 8), both near the Hauptbahnhof. Best of the bunch is *Haus Hillesheim* (☎ 38 68 60, fax 386 86 33, Jahnstrasse 19), a historic hotel with matching old-fashioned flair but fairly progressive management. Ask for a room facing the garden.

Places to Stay – Mid-Range
For easy access to Düsseldorf's raucous nightlife, pick a hotel in the Altstadt. Reasonably priced options include *Hotel Alt-Düsseldorf* (☎ 13 36 04, fax 13 39 78, Hunsrückenstrasse 11) and the affiliated *Hotel Ludwig* (☎ 838 00, fax 32 34 61, Hunsrückenstrasse 50). Rooms are small, but all have private baths, phone and TV; if you want quiet, ask for one facing away from the street. Singles are DM110 to DM130, doubles go for DM160, slightly more at the Ludwig. *Carathotel* (☎ 130 50, fax 32 22 14, Benrather Strasse 7a) is a business-style property on the southern edge of the Altstadt charging DM160/210 for singles/doubles.

Style and a personal touch are the hallmarks of a couple of places outside the Altstadt. An absolute winner is the small *Hotel Max* (☎ 38 68 00, fax 386 80 22, Adersstrasse 65), between the Hauptbahnhof and Königsallee. Owned and managed by the young and energetic Christian Rosenstengel, this hotel has sparkling rooms with contemporary furnishings, private baths, telephone and cable TV. Year-round rates are DM115/130/165 for singles/doubles/triples. Call before you arrive.

Appartementhaus am Schwanenmarkt (☎ 13 40 96, fax 13 23 01, Hohe Strasse 41) is a sophisticated, quiet and friendly abode in a neighbourhood of galleries and antique stores just south of the Altstadt. Full baths, pantry kitchens, TV, direct phone lines and voice mail are standard amenities here, where year-round rates range from DM140 to DM160 for singles and DM220 to DM260 for doubles.

Places to Stay – Top End
The sky's the limit when it comes to Düsseldorf hotel rooms. If you like English country manor-style decor and happen to have DM323/351 for singles/doubles, then the all-suite *Villa Victoria* (☎ 46 90 00, fax 46 90 06 01, Blumenthalstrasse 12) may be your thing. A more traditional choice is the super-central *Breidenbacher Hof* (☎ 130 30, fax 130 38 30, Heinrich-Heine-Allee 36), which charges DM350/480. Some sections may be closed for renovation in 2000.

Long-Term Rentals
Düsseldorf has several room-sharing agencies, including Mitwohn-Centrale (☎ 194 30 or ☎ 36 30 25), the Home Company (☎ 194 45) and Mitwohn-Zentrale im Rheinland (☎ 938 50 56).

Places to Eat
Good eating places abound in the Altstadt. On its northern end is a strip along Ratinger Strasse that the locals have kept largely for themselves. This is where you'll find *Im Füchschen* (☎ 13 74 70, Ratinger Strasse 28), a smoky, crowded Rhenish beer hall

The grand Kaiserdom, Speyer

The chapel ceiling of the Marksburg castle

Powerful imagery at the Mainz Cathedral

Catching a cruise down the romantic Rhine River is a popular way to get around.

ANDREA SCHULTE-PEEVERS

Cologne Cathedral's twin spires

ANDREA SCHULTE-PEEVERS

Mona and friends on the plaza near the Cologne Cathedral

ANDREA SCHULTE-PEEVERS

A room of frozen shadows, just one of the visual effects at Essen's three-level Meteorit

DAVID PEEVERS

Bochum's German Museum of Mining

ANDREA SCHULTE-PEEVERS

A mix of styles, Cologne

that attracts all ages. Huge portions of hearty German food cost between DM10 and DM15 and wash down well with the delicious house brew. *Zur Uel (☎ 32 53 69)*, a few doors down at No 16, is a welcoming and popular hang-out for student types. The menu is a culinary journey across Germany with a median price of DM17, though a plate of spaghetti is just DM10.50.

More on the tourist track, but still happening, is Bolkerstrasse. At No 45, the traditional *Zum Schlüssel (☎ 32 61 55)* has a mid-priced menu heavy on regional favourites like *Sauerbraten* (marinated beef) and sauerkraut soup. *Zum Schiffchen (☎ 13 24 21/22, Hafenstrasse 5)* is similar but has the distinction of being Düsseldorf's oldest restaurant ('since 1628'). One wonders if the portions were as huge in 1811 when Napoleon dined here with his generals, or when Heinrich Heine hung out with his literary buddies.

The timelessly trendy *Spitz (☎ 32 27 70, Bolkerstrasse 63)* is a place to come for a cup of coffee, a beer or a small meal for all budgets. For tapas, sherry or paella, head to Schneider-Wibbel-Gasse, just off Bolkerstrasse, which is almost completely in the hands of Spanish restaurants, from cheap to frivolously pricey.

Herr Spoerl Deli (☎ 323 82 11, Benrather Strasse 6a) in the southern Altstadt is small but high-energy. Customer's taste buds are spoiled with freshly prepared gourmet sandwiches, many with a Mediterranean touch (manchego cheese, prosciutto ham). Prices start at DM4.50, though more substantial ones are DM10 or even more. It's closed Sunday.

Bim's Marktwirtschaft (☎ 32 71 85, Benrather Strasse 7), across from here, is an unpretentious place with cult status, inexpensive and delicious cross-cultural fare, and a clientele that ranges from street sweepers to ad execs and students.

The self-service *Marché (☎ 32 06 81, Königsallee 60)*, in the basement of the Kö-Galerie shopping mall, offers affordable dining on the Königsallee. In addition to salad and vegetable bars, various hot food stations offer plenty of choice at prices that let you fill up for under DM10. A pricier proposition is *Citrus (☎ 323 93 24, Grünstrasse 5)*, a chic hall-like restaurant with an endless bar and California-style world cuisine menu; main dishes start at DM20. A few steps south on Königsallee is the exquisite *Ram Thai*, an exotic food temple with tiled floors, mirrors and leafy plants and a comprehensive range of fragrant meat and vegetable dishes around DM20.

Entertainment

What's on in and around Düsseldorf is listed in great detail in the monthly magazines *Prinz* (DM5) and *Überblick* (DM4.50), on sale at newsagents. (Incidentally, the publisher of *Überblick* is also general manager of the legendary Düsseldorf punk band, Die Toten Hosen.)

Pubs & Beer Halls On evenings and weekends, especially in good weather, the atmosphere in the pedestrianised Altstadt is electric and, occasionally, a bit rowdy. The beverage of choice is Alt, a dark and semisweet beer typical of Düsseldorf. The best place to soak it all up is *Zum Uerige (☎ 86 69 90, Berger Strasse 1)*. Here the beer flows so quickly from giant copper vats that the waiters – called 'Köbes' – just carry huge trays of brew and plunk down a glass whenever they spy an empty.

Across from the Uerige at Flingerstrasse 1 is the *Kabüffke* where, besides Alt, you can also taste *Killepitsch*, a herb liqueur sold only here and in the shop next door. The former home of Heinrich Heine is now occupied by a charming literary pub called *Schnabelewopski (☎ 13 32 00, Bolkerstrasse 53)*, named after a Heine character.

Also refer to *Im Füchschen* and *Zum Schlüssel* in the Places to Eat section.

Discos & Clubs Düsseldorf's discos tend to be chic, trendy and expensive. A drink minimum, sometimes in addition to a cover charge (DM5 to DM25), is common. In some places, dim doormen decide on who fits in with the crowd and who doesn't.

Most clubs are open only Wednesday, Friday and Saturday after 11 pm and don't get going until midnight or 1 am.

An Altstadt institution that has always ridden the waves of the latest music trend is *Ratinger Hof* (☎ 32 87 77, Ratinger Strasse 10). Reliable stand-bys – with industrial flair, live music and huge crowd capacities – are *Stahlwerk* (☎ 730 86 81, Ronsdorfer Strasse 134) and *Tor 3* (☎ 733 64 97, Ronsdorfer Strasse 143), both in the district of Flingern, just east of the Hauptbahnhof. More intimate and alternative is *Zakk* (☎ 973 00 10, Fichtenstrasse 40), which has live jazz on Mondays, 1970s and 80s parties on weekends, plus an excellent Internet cafe and beer garden in summer.

Theatre, Classical Music & Cinema
Düsseldorf's main stage for theatre is the prestigious *Schauspielhaus* (☎ 36 99 11, Gustaf-Gründgens-Platz 1). For opera and musicals, head to the *Deutsche Oper am Rhein* (☎ 890 82 11, Heinrich-Heine-Allee 16a). Classical concerts are performed in the *Tonhalle* (☎ 899 61 23, Ehrenhof 2). A surprising gem is the *Marionetten-Theater* (☎ 32 84 32, Bilker Strasse 7), inside the baroque Palais Wittgenstein, with charming and beautifully orchestrated operas and fairy tales, many geared to an adult audience.

In the Palais Nesselrode (the same complex that houses the Film Museum and the Hetjens Museum) at Schulstrasse 4, the *Black Box* presents non-mainstream cinematic fare, often in the original language.

Varieté An evening of sparkle, glamour and visual surprises is the basic promise of the new *Roncalli's Apollo Varieté* (☎ 828 90 90, Haroldstrasse 1). It's housed in a customised 'performance palace' on the Rhine, and presents a lively menu of acrobats, jugglers, comedians and other variety acts, with tickets ranging from DM32 to DM86, drinks not included.

Shopping
For *haute couture* there are few places as exclusive as the boutiques along the Kö.

Department stores and mainstream shops are on Schadowstrasse and its sidestreets. Schadow Arcaden shopping centre has stunning contemporary architecture and a nice mix of shops. If funky club wear is your thing, head to the Altstadt. There's a large but mediocre flea market on Aachener Platz every Saturday from 9 am to 2 pm (tram No 712 from Jan-Wellem-Platz).

Getting There & Away
Air Düsseldorf International Airport (☎ 42 10) is Germany's third-largest and is currently being modernised and expanded to accommodate up to 20 million passengers a year by 2001. Major airlines with offices at the airport include British Airways (☎ 421 66 86/7), United Airlines, Air France (both ☎ 421 21 73) and Lufthansa (☎ 01803 80 38 03). Online air travel information is at www.duesseldorf-international.de.

Train Düsseldorf is part of a dense S-Bahn network in the Rhine-Ruhr region (the VRR; see Getting Around in the introduction to the Ruhrgebiet section), and regular services run to Cologne and Aachen as well; international rail passes are valid on these lines. ICE trains to Munich (DM181, six hours) and Berlin-Zoo (DM181, four hours), as well as IC service to Frankfurt (DM79, 2¾ hours), leave hourly. IC trains to Hamburg-Altona (DM123, 3½ hours) depart every other hour. Direct links also exist to Amsterdam (2¼ hours).

Bus Eurolines buses make daily trips to Paris (DM76/137 one-way/return) and Warsaw (DM105/180), to London twice weekly (DM101/182) and to Prague thrice weekly (DM80/140).

Car & Motorcycle Autobahns from all directions lead to Düsseldorf city centre; just follow the signs. Parking in the centre is pretty much limited to parking garages, which command DM2 to DM2.50 an hour.

Ride Services Mitfahr-Zentrale Citynetz (☎ 194 44) is at Kruppstrasse 102; ADM

(☎ 194 40) has a branch near the Hauptbahnhof at Konrad-Adenauer-Platz 13.

Getting Around
To/from the Airport S-Bahn Nos 7 and 21 shuttle between the airport and the Hauptbahnhof every 20 minutes. A new airport train station with direct ICE, IC and InterRegio service should be open by the time you read this and will significantly cut travel time to destinations in the Rhine-Ruhr region and beyond.

Public Transport Düsseldorf's network of U-Bahn trains, trams and buses is divided into zones, and prices vary according to how many zones you travel through. Single tickets are DM3.20/6/13 for one/two/three zones. Better value are the four-trip tickets that sell for DM9.60/18/39; day passes (which are valid for up to five people) cost DM10.80/16/30.50. Bicycles are DM3.10. Tickets are available from the orange vending machines at stops, though bus drivers also sell them. All tickets must be validated when boarding. For details, call ☎ 194 49.

Taxi For a taxi, call ☎ 333 33 or ☎ 194 10.

XANTEN
☎ 02801 • pop 16,500

In around 100 AD, Roman Emperor Trajan first put Xanten – about 60km north of Düsseldorf – on the map. He gave city status to a residential settlement adjacent to one of his military camps and named it Colonia Ulpia Traiana. Extending some 73 hectares and inhabited by up to 15,000 people (almost the same population as today), it lasted until the 4th century, when the Roman Empire – and its buildings along with it – began to crumble. The stones were later used in the construction of Xanten's Dom. The ancient city's foundations have been excavated and form the basis of the Archaeological Park, Xanten's main attraction.

In the Middle Ages Xanten thrived because of its location at the crossroads of major trade routes. Prosperity declined in the 16th century when the town lost its direct waterway access after the Rhine changed course. Xanten was badly damaged in WWII and, despite winning several conservation awards, today is a shadow of its medieval self. A few buildings, though, most notably the Dom and the Roman ruins, warrant a closer look. Xanten is also the mythical birthplace of Siegfried, one of the heroes of the medieval epic poem that inspired Richard Wagner's opera cycle *Der Ring des Nibelungen*.

Orientation & Information
The Dom and city centre are about a 10 minute walk north-east of the main train station via Hagenbuschstrasse or Bahnhofstrasse. The Archaeological Park is a farther 15 minutes north of here.

The tourist office (☎ 77 22 38/98, fax 77 22 09) is in the Rathaus on the eastern end of the Markt, and is open from April to September weekdays from 9 am to 4.30 pm. On weekends, there's an information booth on the square open from 10 am to at least 4 pm. In winter, opening hours are Monday to Thursday from 9 am to 4.30 pm and to 2 pm Friday to Sunday. Between May and September, free walking tours depart from here on Saturday at 11 am.

Xanten's post office is on the corner of Bahnhofstrasse and Poststrasse. There's a police station a few metres north of the tourist office on the corner of Rheinstrasse and Niederstrasse.

Walking Tour
Start with the crown jewel of Xanten's Altstadt, the **Dom St Viktor**, just west of the Markt. Framed by a walled close called an 'Immunity', it can only be entered through the fortress-like gate from the Markt.

Immediately in front are the flying buttresses and flamboyant facade characteristic of a Gothic structure (13th century). However, the sturdy twin towers at the Dom's western end were built first in the late-Romanesque style (late 12th century).

The sombreness of the five-nave interior is enlivened by a stunning collection of art treasures. Foremost among them is the **Marienaltar**, halfway down the right aisles, whose altar base (or predella) features an intricately carved version of the genealogical *Tree of Jesse* by Heinrich Douvermann (1535). Other masterpieces include the candelabrum in the central nave, with its **Doppelmadonna** (1500) and the 28 stone statues of the apostles and other saints affixed to the pillars.

Just outside the Dom is the **Regional Museum** (☎ 71 94 15), with Roman objects gleaned from the nearby excavation site on display, as well as presentations on the history of Xanten from the Ice Age to today. It's open Tuesday to Thursday from 9 am to 5 pm, 11 am to 6 pm weekends, closed Monday (DM4/2). A combination ticket that includes the Regional Museum, the Archaeological Park and the thermal baths (see below) is DM9/5.50.

Turning right as you exit the Immunity, follow the signs to Klever Strasse; at the end of that street you'll come upon the **Klever Tor** (1393), the only surviving double town gate on the Lower Rhine. The windmill visible from here is the **Kriemhildmühle**, also once part of the fortifications. It forms the terminus of Brückstrasse, where you can still admire some fine Gothic houses, including the **Arme Mägde Haus** with its step-gabled facade at No 9.

Archäologischer Park

Colonia Ulpia Traiana is the only Roman settlement north of the Alps that has never been built upon, allowing archaeologists to unearth the foundations of the fortification wall, streets and many buildings. In the mid-1970s, some of these were reconstructed and opened to visitors. Critics have ridiculed the results, and indeed the place does, on occasion, feel like a Roman theme park – especially in the restaurant, where toga-clad personnel serve 'Roman' fare. But overall, the reconstruction has been faithfully done and helps amateurs to visualise what a Roman colony looked like.

The self-guided tour begins at **Herberge**, the inn which, along with the restaurant, snack bar and furnished rooms, also contains an **Info-Center** with models and

explanatory panels. Next door, **Badehaus** points to the fairly high standard of hygiene enjoyed by the Romans 2000 years ago. Other highlights include the **Amphitheatre**, which seats about 12,000 people during Xanten's summer festival, and the partly rebuilt **Hafentempel**. Be sure to walk around the back for a glimpse of the original foundation. At the **Spielehaus** you can play a round of authentic antique board games, including backgammon (rules explained on the wall in German).

The Archäologischer Park (☎ 29 99) is open daily from 9 am to 6 pm, and from 10 am to 4 pm in winter (DM8/4.50).

Near the park are the newly excavated ruins of large-scale **Roman thermal baths** which are protected by an extravagant glass and steel construction. They're accessible Tuesday to Friday from 9 am to 5 pm, and weekends from 11 am to 6 pm (DM4/2).

Places to Stay & Eat

Xanten has two camping grounds but they are inconvenient unless you're motorised. *Campingplatz Bremer (☎ 47 30, Urseler Strasse 25)* is about 3km west of the centre and *Wald-Camping Speetenkath (☎ 17 69, Urseler Strasse 18)* is 5km away. The nearest *hostel (☎ 02832-82 67, Am Michaelsweg 11)* is 18km away in Kevelaer. It charges DM22 to DM24 for juniors and DM27 to DM29 for seniors.

The tourist office operates a free reservation service, with *private rooms* costing from DM25 to DM40 per person. As far as hotels go, your best bet is the central *Galerie an de Marspoort (☎ 10 57, fax 61 42, Marsstrasse 78)*, which has cosy singles for DM70 and doubles for DM110. Also in a central location is the family-run *Hotel Neumaier (☎ 715 70, fax 71 57 36, Orkstrasse 19-21)*, which offers a full range of amenities and services with singles/doubles costing DM110/160, though some are still available for DM75/120. Both hotels also operate decent restaurants.

Otherwise, Xanten has a huge number of ethnic eateries. On or around the Markt you will find Greek, Yugoslav, Japanese-Korean,

Chinese, Italian and Turkish restaurants. Young people gather for a beer and a chat at *Vips (Bahnhofstrasse 18)*, *Mäx (Klever Strasse 30)* and *Zentrale (Brückstrasse 2)*.

Getting There & Away

The only train stopping at Xanten's one-platform station is the hourly shuttle to and from Duisburg (DM12.20, 45 minutes). From here, bus No 44 leaves hourly to nearby Kalkar and Kleve, daily except Sunday. Xanten lies on route B57 (Kleve-Dinslaken). If travelling on the A57, take the Alpen exit, then route B58 east to B57 north.

AROUND XANTEN
Kalkar
☎ 02824 • pop 11,500

About 15km north of Xanten lies the little town of Kalkar, with a fairly intact medieval core anchored by the **Church of St Nikolai** and its astonishing carved altars. You'll find it on Jan-Joest-Strasse just west of the Markt. A rather bland Gothic brick building on the outside, St Nikolai's white-washed interior explodes with an extraordinary number of masterpieces. Many were created by artists from the Kalkar School of Wood-carving, founded in the late Middle Ages by Kalkar's wealthy burghers. Sadly, some of the treasures had to be sold off in the early 19th century to pay for the church's restoration, but enough are left to be admired.

Top billing goes to the **Passion Altar**, a depiction of the Passion of Christ in dizzying detail. The work was begun in 1490 by Master Arnt of Zwolle, who died before finishing it, a task then undertaken by Jan Halderen and Master Loedewig. Turn around and lift the first seat of the upper choir chair on the right – once reserved for the Duke of Cleves – to reveal the relief of a **monkey on a chamberpot**. Another eye-catcher is the **Altar of the Seven Sorrows** by Heinrich Douvermann in the south apse. It perches on a predella containing another version of the Tree of Jesse, reminiscent of the one in Xanten's Dom. If you look closely you can make out Jesse, the father of David, framed by two prophets, and Solomon with the sceptre.

Opening hours vary by season but between April and October you should be able to get inside in the mornings and afternoons (though not on Sunday during services); in winter, it's open in the afternoons only (DM2).

COLOGNE
☎ 0221 • pop 966,000

Cologne (Köln) is not only the largest city in North Rhine-Westphalia (and fourth largest in the country), it is also one of its most attractive and should be on everyone's must-see list. It spoils visitors with a cornucopia of sightseeing choices and activities: great architecture in its magnificent cathedrals, churches and public buildings; internationally renowned museums with world-class collections; funky boutiques and giant department stores; unique local cuisine and beer; cutting-edge dance clubs; first-rate theatre and concerts.

History

Cologne has been a major player in European history for two millennia, not least for its location on the Rhine and at a major trade crossroads. It's one of Germany's oldest cities, founded by the Romans around 50 BC under the reign of Emperor Julius Caesar. He made allies of the Germanic Ubier tribe and helped them settle along the river banks. About 100 years later, the settlement was given city status thanks to Agrippina, wife of Emperor Claudius, who was born here. Then called Colonia Claudia Ara Agrippinensium, the city prospered quickly. The Romans built a bridge, harbours and warehouses, and kept up a lively trade with ships carrying wheat from England and wine from Spain until they were gradually driven out by the Franks.

Cologne became a much-respected bishopric under Charlemagne in the 8th century. Throughout the Middle Ages, the city was a flourishing centre of commerce and culture, a development that culminated in it becoming a free imperial city in 1475.

In later centuries, Cologne remained one of northern Europe's most important cities

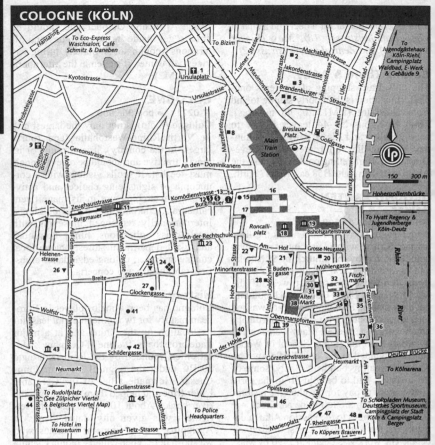

COLOGNE (KÖLN)

(it was the largest in Germany until the 19th century), and to this day it is one of the prime engines of the German economy. It's also the centre of the Roman Catholic church in Germany.

Though almost completely destroyed in WWII, the city was quickly rebuilt and boasts a stunning range of monuments and churches, many of them meticulously restored. Judging by the number of church steeples, one might suspect the Kölner not to be a particularly fun-loving bunch.

However, these people know how to party. All over Germany, they are appreciated for their wit and humour, which is best observed in the many bars or during the boisterous Carnival celebrations (see boxed text 'Fools, Floats & Revelry').

Orientation

Situated right on the Rhine River, the skyline of Cologne is dominated by its colossal cathedral (Dom). The pedestrianised Hohe Strasse – the main shopping street –

COLOGNE (KÖLN)

PLACES TO STAY		OTHER		24	WDR Arkaden &
2	Hotel DomBlick	1	St Ursula		Main Post Office
3	Hotel Thielen	6	Alter Wartesaal Disco	27	4711
4	Hotel Brandenburger Hof	7	Central Bus Station	30	Papa Joe's Klimperkasten
5	Hotel Berg	9	St Gereon	31	Flanagan's Pub
8	Station - Backpacker's	10	Roman Wall, Römerturm	32	Gross St Martin
	Hostel	11	Kölnisches Stadtmuseum &	34	Em Streckstump;
20	Hotel an der Philharmonie		Zeughaus		Biermuseum
28	Senats-Hotel	12	American Express	36	KD Landing Dock
33	Das Kleine Stapelhäuschen	13	Thomas Cook	37	Kölner Fahrradverleih
35	Rhein-Hotel St Martin	14	Tourist Office	38	Rathaus;
48	Hotel Allegro	15	Roman Arch		Praetorian Palace
		16	Dom	39	Wallraf-Richartz-Museum
PLACES TO EAT		17	Domforum	40	Mayersche Buchhandlung
21	Brauhaus Sion	18	Römisch-Germanisches	41	Schauspielhaus;
22	Früh am Dom		Museum; Diözesan		Opernhaus
25	Schmittchen		Museum	43	Käthe Kollwitz Museum;
26	Moderne Zeiten	19	Museum Ludwig;		Gonski Bookstore
29	Kaffeebud Alter Markt		Philharmonie;	44	Avis
42	Stausberg		Kölnticket	45	Schnütgen Museum
47	Brauerei zur Malzmühle	23	Museum of Applied Art	46	St Maria im Kapitol

begins just south of the Dom. The Hauptbahnhof is just north of the Dom, within walking distance of almost everything. The Busbahnhof is just behind the Hauptbahnhof, on Breslauer Platz.

The Altstadt, with its network of narrow lanes lined by pubs and restaurants, stretches out along the few blocks parallel to the western bank of the Rhine, between Hohenzollernbrücke and Deutzer Brücke. Other food and entertainment centres are the Zülpicher Viertel near Barbarossaplatz and the Belgisches Viertel around Friesenplatz (see map later in this chapter). Both are about 1.5km west of the Alstadt.

A series of ring roads encircles Cologne's core, each chronicling stages of the city's growth like the rings of a tree. While the Roman city was roughly confined to today's Altstadt area, the road called the Ring marks the line of the medieval fortifications. The next circle is the Gürtel (beltway), built with Prussian efficiency in the 19th century. And around it all wraps the ambitious six lane autobahn, the Kölner Ring, demanded by the 20th century's dramatic technological advances and population growth.

Information

Tourist Office The tourist office (☎ 22 12 33 45 or ☎ 194 33, fax 22 12 33 20, email koelntourismus@koeln.org) is at Unter Fettenhennen 19, opposite the Dom. The office is open from May to October, Monday to Saturday from 8 am to 10.30 pm, and Sunday from 9 am. Winter hours are Monday to Saturday from 8 am to 9 pm, and Sunday from 9.30 am to 7 pm.

Apart from the usual array of brochures, maps and books, the office also has a public fax-phone. For sale is the KölnTourismus Card, a voucher booklet (DM28) which buys admission to numerous museums, a guided city bus tour, unlimited public transportation, plus reduced prices for a river cruise, the zoo, Phantasialand amusement park and other activities.

Money The Reisebank (☎ 13 44 03) inside the Hauptbahnhof is open daily from 7 am to 10 pm. Other banks abound, and most have ATM machines that accept credit cards. Around the corner from the tourist office on Burgmauer are American Express (☎ 925 90 10) at No 14 and Thomas Cook (☎ 202 08 17) at No 4.

NORTH RHINE-WESTPHALIA

Fools, Floats & Revelry

Carnival in Cologne is one of the best parties in Europe and a thumb in the eye of the German work ethic. Every year at the onset of Lent (late February/early March), a year of painstaking preparation culminates in the 'three crazy days', which are actually more like six.

It all starts with *Weiberfastnacht*, the Thursday before Ash Wednesday, when women rule the day (and do things like chop off the ties of their male colleagues/bosses). The party continues through the weekend, with more than 50 parades of ingenious floats and wildly dressed lunatics dancing in the streets. By the time it all comes to a head with the big parade on *Rosenmontag* (Rose Monday), the entire city has come unglued. Those still capable of swaying and singing will live it up one last time on Shrove Tuesday before the curtain goes up on Ash Wednesday.

'If you were at the parade and saw the parade, you weren't at the parade,' say the people of Cologne in their inimitable way. Translated, this means that you should be far too busy singing, drinking, roaring the Carnival greeting *'Alaaf!'* and planting a quick *Bützchen* (kiss) on the cheek of whoever strikes your fancy, to notice anything happening around you. Swaying and drinking while sardined in a pub, or following other costumed fools behind a huge bass drum leading to God only knows where, you'll be swept up by one of the last completely innocent parties the world knows.

If you're not sure how to handle all these shenanigans, the Cologne tourist office has prepared a wonderful, and quite serious, little brochure chock-a-block with useful advice on pressing issues like how to deal with concerns of the bladder, sexual conduct and how to avoid getting crushed against a shop window. Further, it adds: 'The art is to drink as much as you need to attain a degree of merriment and to stop before your head starts spinning. And if you're dancing and jumping around – as you should be – then you'll be able to hold more drink than if you just stand around and stare.'

Words to live by.

Post & Communications The main post office (☎ 925 92 90) is inside the WDR Arkaden shopping mall on the corner of Breite Strasse and Tunisstrasse, and is open weekdays from 8 am to 8 pm and Saturday to 4 pm. The poste restante is here. Have mail clearly marked 'Postlagernd' and addressed to you at 50441 Köln, Breite Strasse 6-26. There's also a public fax-phone and a photocopy machine.

Internet Resources For more information, go to www.koeln.org/koelntourismus.

Bookshops Chain stores with large selections of foreign-language novels, as well as Lonely Planet titles, are the Mayersche Buchhandlung (☎ 920 10 90), Hohe Strasse 68-82; and Neumarkt 2 and Gonski (☎ 209 00), also at Neumarkt at No 18a.

Laundry The Eco-Express Waschsalon branches include Friedrichstrasse 12 near Barbararossaplatz; Richard-Wagner-Strasse 2, on the corner of Händelstrasse, near Rudolfplatz; Zülpicher Strasse 58, on the corner of Zülpicher Wall; and Hansaring 68, on the corner of Hamburger Strasse. All are open Monday to Saturday from 6 am to 11 pm and charge DM6 per load, with 10 minutes of drying costing DM1.

Medical Services & Emergency For an emergency doctor, call ☎ 192 92. Police headquarters (☎ 22 91) are on the corner of Nord-Süd-Fahrt and Blaubach.

Dom

The Kölner Dom – with its soaring twin spires – is the Mt Everest of cathedrals, Cologne's geographical and spiritual heart and its main tourist draw. It's easy to spend at least half a day exploring it. Building began in 1248 in the French Gothic style but was suspended in 1560 for lack of money. For nearly 300 years, the structure lay half-finished and was even demoted to a horse stable and prison by Napoleon's troops. In the 1820s the original architectural plans were found, and in 1880 the cathedral was finally completed, thanks to a generous cash infusion from Prussian King Friedrich Wilhelm IV. Luckily, it survived WWII's heavy night bombing almost intact. Since 1996, the Dom has been listed as a UNESCO World Cultural Heritage site.

To appreciate Dom's dimensions, encircle it before heading inside. Despite its overwhelming mass and height – it soars to 157m – its lacy spires and flying buttresses create a sensation of lightness and fragility.

The interior is equally overwhelming. A phalanx of pillars and arches supports the lofty central nave. An ethereal light shines through the radiant **stained-glass windows**, a highlight among the Dom's many art treasures. These also include the **Gero Crucifix** (970), a monumental work that shows a larger-than-life-size Christ figure with his eyes closed, and the largest **choir stalls** in Germany (1310). But the *pièce de résistance* is the **Shrine of the Three Magi** behind the altar, said to contain the bones of the kings who followed the star to the stable in Bethlehem where Jesus was born. The richly bejewelled and gilded sarcophagus was spirited out of Milan in 1164 as spoils of war by Emperor Barbarossa's chancellor, instantly turning Cologne into a major pilgrimage site. On the south side, in a chapel off the ambulatory, is the 15th century **Adoration of the Magi altarpiece**.

Core opening hours are daily from 10 am to 4 pm. Invest a mere DM1 in the informative, multi-language *Cologne Cathedral* booklet sold at the tourist office. Guided tours in English, including a slide show, are held at various times. Inquire at the **Domforum** information office in a building opposite the main portal. Tours in German are more frequent and cost DM5/3.

Tower For an exercise fix, pay DM3/1.50 to climb the 509 steps up the Dom's south tower to the base of the stupendous steeple, which dwarfed all buildings in Europe until the Eiffel Tower was erected. It is open daily from 9 am to 5 pm, in winter till dusk. En route, note the 24 tonne **Peter Bell** (1923), the largest working bell in the world. The view from the vantage point at 95m is absolutely breathtaking. With clear weather you can see all the way to the Siebengebirge (Seven Mountains) beyond Bonn.

Domschatzkammer Compared to the rest of the cathedral, the treasury, just inside the north entrance, is rather average. It is open Monday to Saturday from 9 am to 4 pm, and Sunday from 1 pm (DM3).

Romanesque Churches

Cologne's wealth during its medieval heyday is reflected in the abundance of Romanesque churches, built between 1150 and 1250. Many survived intact until WWII. A dozen have since been rebuilt; they are all scattered within the medieval city bordered by the Ring. The tourist office has a slim, multi-language guidebook with information on all of the churches for DM2.

Each church has unique architectural and artistic features and is well worth a visit. Winning top honours for most handsome exterior is **Gross St Martin**, whose ensemble of four slender turrets grouped around a central spire towers above Fischmarkt. It's open Monday to Saturday from 10 am to 6 pm, and Sunday from 2 to 4 pm only. Inside, the impressive clover-leaf choir is modelled on that in **St Maria im Kapitol** on Marienplatz; it's open daily from 9.30 am to 6 pm. Among this church's treasures is a carved door that predates its consecration date of 1065 by a few years.

The church with the most spectacular interior, though, has to be **St Gereon**,

Gereonsdriesch 2-4, whose four-storey decagonal dome was an astonishing architectural accomplishment in the early 13th century. It is open from 9 am to 12.30 pm and 1.30 to 6 pm, closed Saturday afternoon and Sunday morning.

If you look at Cologne's coat of arms, you'll see what looks like 11 apostrophes. These represent Christian martyrs St Ursula and the 10 virgins. The church of **St Ursula**, Ursulaplatz 24, was built atop the Roman cemetery where the virgins' remains were allegedly found. Opening hours are Monday, and Wednesday to Saturday from 9.30 am to noon. The highlight is the **Goldene Kammer** with 120 reliquary busts from the 14th to the 17th centuries. It's open from 1 to 5 pm, closed on Tuesday and Sunday.

Museums

Cologne's museum landscape is world-class and diversified enough to offer something for every interest, although the first three described here rank as absolute highlights. As usual, all museums are closed on Monday. A good deal is the Museumscard, valid for two days' admission to most museums and free public transportation. It costs DM20 per person (DM36 for families) and is available at the tourist office and museums. The Köln-Tourismus Card (see Information earlier in this section) is good value as well.

Römisch-Germanisches Museum Anyone even remotely interested in Roman history should *not* skip the extraordinary Roman Germanic Museum (☎ 22 12 45 90), right next to the Dom at Roncalliplatz 4. Numerous sculptures and parts from ruined buildings displayed outside and in the lobby give you a (free) taste of what is the most thorough collection of Roman artefacts found along the Rhine; inside it's all presented in an appealing fashion that is not overwhelming in any way. Highlights include the giant **Poblicius grave monument** (30 to 40 AD), the magnificent 3rd century **Dionysus mosaic** around which the museum was built, and astonishingly well preserved glass items.

Insight into daily Roman life is gained from such otherwise banal items as toys, tweezers, lamps and jewellery, the designs of which have changed little over the centuries. The museum is open weekdays from 10 am to 5 pm (Thursday to 8 pm), and weekends from 11 am to 4 pm (DM7/3.50).

Museum Ludwig The distinctive building facade and unorthodox roofline already signal that the Ludwig (☎ 22 12 23 79), just south of the Dom at Bischofsgartenstrasse 1, is no ordinary museum. Considered a European mecca of postmodern art, it offers a thorough overview of all genres – traditional to warped – generated in the 20th century. American Pop artists Andy Warhol, Robert Rauschenberg and Jasper Johns are especially well represented, as are German painters Georg Baselitz and AR Penck. But you'll also find plenty to look at by those who paved the way for these abstractionists: Paul Klee to Marc Chagall, Max Beckmann to Magritte and Dalí, to drop just a few names. It's all rounded off with a unique photography collection from the former Agfa Museum in Leverkusen. Opening hours are weekdays from 10 am to 6 pm, Tuesday to 8 pm and weekends from 11 am (DM10/5).

Wallraf-Richartz-Museum The collection of this museum ranks as one of the world's finest for art from the 13th to the 19th century. Previously sharing space with the Museum Ludwig, it recently moved to its customised postmodern cube. Designed by Cologne's own OM Ungers, it is just south of the Rathaus on Obenmarspforten.

Come here to admire medieval works by the Cologne Masters, known for their distinctive use of colour. Dutch and Flemish artists like Rembrandt and Rubens are as much part of the collection as Italians like Canaletto and Spaniards such as Murillo and Ribera. The exhibit continues with 19th century romanticists like Caspar David Friedrich and Lovis Corinth, and impressionists including Monet, Van Gogh and Renoir. Hours were not available at the time of writing. Call ☎ 22 12 43 43 for details.

Schnütgen Museum This museum (☎ 22 12 36 20), located in the former Church of St Cecilia at Cäcilienstrasse 29, houses an overwhelming display of medieval ecclesiastical treasures, including wooden sculptures, manuscripts, textiles and ivory carvings. It's open weekdays from 10 am to 5 pm, and weekends from 11 am (DM5/2.50). The **Diözesan Museum** (☎ 257 76 72) on Roncalliplatz also has 2000 years' worth of Christian art and treasures. Admission is free, but it's closed on Thursday.

Schokoladen Museum A *must*, and not just if you're in town with children, is a visit to the fabulous Chocolate Museum (☎ 931 88 80), Rheinauhafen 1a, a state-of-the-art temple to the art of chocolate making. A thorough section on the origin and growing process (with panelling in German *and* English) is followed by a live-production factory and an opportunity to sample the final product from a flowing chocolate fountain. Upstairs are departments on the cultural history of chocolate, advertising, and porcelain and other accessories. Stock up on your favourite flavours at the large shop downstairs. Museum hours are weekdays from 10 am to 6 pm, and weekends from 11 am to 7 pm (DM10/5).

Deutsches Sportmuseum A brand-new entry on Cologne's museum landscape, the German Sport Museum should have opened by the time you read this. Located in a former warehouse adjacent to the Chocolate Museum, its goal is to present exhibits on the subject of sport in all its infinite variety. Permanent departments focus on the evolution of the Olympic Games, exercising in ancient Greece and Rome, and sports as a universal pastime. Details about hours and admission were still unavailable at the time of writing. Call ☎ 22 12 43 43 for more information.

Other Museums In a bank branch at Neumarkt 18-24 is the **Käthe Kollwitz Museum** (☎ 227 23 63), with sculptures and stunning black-and-white graphics of the acclaimed socialist artist. Enter through the arcade, then take the glass-bubble lift to the 4th floor. It's open daily from 10 am to 5 pm, Thursday to 8 pm (DM5/2).

The **Kölnisches Stadtmuseum** (Cologne City Museum; ☎ 22 12 57 89), in the medieval former armory at Zeughausstrasse 1-3, is a journey into the history of Cologne. Besides an interesting scale model of the old city, there's also a fine weapons collection and exhibits on carnival traditions. It's open daily from 10 am to 5 pm, and Tuesday to 8 pm (DM7/3.50).

The **Museum für Angewandte Kunst** (Museum of Applied Art; ☎ 22 12 67 14), An der Rechtschule, traces the development of industrial design from the Middle Ages to today. Furniture to TV screens, tableware to bathroom fixtures, it's all here, including objects by big name designers like Mies van der Rohe and Charles Eames. It's open daily from 11 am to 5 pm, and Wednesday to 8 pm (DM7/3.50).

Fans of the Fab Four may enjoy visiting the **Beatles Museum** (☎ 923 13 13), at Heinsbergstrasse 13, which documents the rise of the cult band from Liverpool (Cologne's sister city). Hours are Wednesday to Friday from 10 am to 2 pm and 3 to 7 pm, Saturday to 3 pm; closed in August (DM5).

Roman Cologne

Lots of remnants from the former Roman settlement lie scattered around town. Outside the cathedral's main entrance is a **Roman arch** from the former town wall. Walk west along Komödienstrasse over Tunisstrasse to reach the **Zeughaus** (containing the Kölnisches Stadtmuseum), the Burgmauer side of which was built along the line of the **Roman wall**. On the pavement at the west end is a plaque tracing the wall's outline on a modern street plan (other plaques appear around the city near Roman sites). Continue west until you find a complete section of the north wall, which leads to the **Römerturm**, a corner tower standing among buildings on the street corner at St-Apern-Strasse. Walk south one block and you come to another tower ruin near Helenenstrasse.

On the southern wall of the Römisch-Germanisches Museum are the remains of the **Roman harbour street**, which led to the banks of the Rhine, and two **Roman wells**. The foundations of the **Praetorian Palace** (☎ 22 12 23 94), under Cologne's medieval town hall, are a highlight. The entrance is on Kleine Budengasse. It's open Tuesday to Friday from 10 am to 4 pm (closed Monday), weekends from 11 am (DM3/1.50). The **Rathaus** itself, with its Gothic tower and Renaissance loggia, is open from 7.30 am to 4.45 pm weekdays, and to 2 pm only on Friday (free).

Organised Tours

The daily guided city bus tour in English departs from the tourist office at 10 and 11 am and at 2 and 3 pm (from November to March at 11 am and 2 pm only). It lasts two hours and costs DM25. Three-hour German/English bicycle tours are operated by Kölner Fahrradverleih (☎ 72 36 27), Marksmanngasse in the Altstadt, daily from April through November at 9.30 am and 1.30 pm (DM29).

Cruises Between April and October, KD Line (☎ 208 83 18), Frankenwerft 15, runs hourly one-hour cruises (DM8.50/4) that let you enjoy the Cologne panorama from the Rhine. It also operates day excursions, eg to Königswinter in the Siebengebirge (DM30.60) and Linz (DM42.40). Rail passes (Eurail, German Rail, etc) are valid for scheduled KD services. Children up to four years of age travel free, and those up to 13 years for a flat DM5. Students get a 50% discount. Travel on your birthday is free. In general, return tickets cost only slightly more than one-way tickets.

Places to Stay

Cheap accommodation in Cologne is rare, and prices become outright ridiculous during trade shows, when some hoteliers are not shy about tripling their rates. Most trade shows are in spring and autumn. The good news is that if you arrive outside of such activity, it may well be possible to stay in an exclusive hotel at rock-bottom rates. Just contact the hotel directly and ask if there are any special rates. Prices quoted here should only be used as a guideline.

The tourist office runs a room-finding service for DM5 per person. If you're driving, keep in mind that parking your car in a hotel or public garage may add DM20 or more to your room rate.

Places to Stay – Budget

Camping The most convenient (though not very) camp sites are the municipal *Campingplatz der Stadt Köln* (☎ 83 19 66) on Weidenweg in Poll, 5km south-east of the city centre on the right bank of the Rhine (open from Easter to mid-October; take U16 to Marienburg, then walk across the bridge); *Campingplatz Waldbad* (☎ 60 33 15) on Peter-Baum-Weg in Dünnwald, about 10km north of the city centre (open all year; no public transport); and *Campingplatz Berger* (☎ 39 22 11, *Uferstrasse 53a)* in Rodenkirchen (open all year).

DJH Hostels Cologne has two DJH hostels. The big, 374 bed *Jugendherberge Köln-Deutz* (☎ 81 47 11, fax 88 44 25, email *jh-deutz@t-online.de, Siegesstrasse 5a)* in Deutz is a 10 minute walk east from the Hauptbahnhof over the Hohenzollernbrücke or three minutes from Bahnhof Köln-Deutz. Rates are DM32/37 for juniors/seniors, including sheets and buffet breakfast. *Jugendgästehaus Köln-Riehl* (☎ 76 70 81, fax 76 15 55, An der Schanz 14) is north of the city centre in the suburb of Riehl (U16 to Boltensternstrasse). The cost is a flat DM38.50, including breakfast and sheets.

Non-DJH Hostels A veritable godsend for Cologne visitors on a tight budget is the newish *Station - Backpacker's Hostel* (☎ 912 53 01, fax 912 53 03, email *station@t-online.de, Marzellenstrasse 44-48)*, a short walk north of the Hauptbahnhof. A large, welcoming lounge gives way to colourful dorms with one to six bunks.

Owner Ralf Kuhlmann and his team are fluent in English and very helpful. There's no curfew, and amenities include free safes, coin-op washer and dryer, Internet access, maps, mags and newspapers. Rates range from DM27 in a six-bed dorm to DM40 for singles, plus a one-time sheet fee of DM3.

Hotels Brandenburger Strasse, north of the train and bus stations, has a trio of low-budget, no-frills candidates that all list their lowest rates around DM50/75 for singles/doubles with shared facilities: *Hotel Berg* (☎ 12 11 24, fax 13 25 92) at No 6, *Hotel Brandenburger Hof* (☎ 12 28 89, fax 13 53 04) at No 2, and *Hotel Thielen* (☎ 12 33 33, fax 12 14 92) at No 1.

Another two reasonable options are near Fischmarkt, south of the Dom. They are the somewhat more upmarket *Rhein-Hotel St Martin* (☎ 257 79 55, fax 257 78 75, Frankenwerft 31-33), which has rooms with shower from DM55/105; and *Das Kleine Stapelhäuschen* (☎ 257 78 62, fax 257 42 32, Fischmarkt 1-3), which charges from DM55/122.

The *Pension Jansen* (☎/fax 25 18 75, Richard-Wagner-Strasse 18), in Zülpicher Viertel, is small but cheap and not far from restaurants and nightlife. Rooms here start at just DM45/90.

Places to Stay – Mid-Range & Top End
There are several mid-priced hotels centrally located in the Altstadt. The following rates for singles/doubles include private bath. *Hotel Allegro* (☎ 240 82 60, fax 240 70 40, Thurnmarkt 1-7) has rooms from DM130/160. *Senats-Hotel* (☎ 206 20, fax 206 22 00, Untere Goldschmied 9-17) is business-like yet pleasant and has good-sized rooms from DM110/135. Also nice is *DomBlick* (☎ 12 37 42, fax 12 57 36, Domstrasse 28), where room rates start at DM115/145. *Hotel an der Philharmonie* (☎ 258 06 79, fax 258 06 67, Grosse Neugasse 36) is super-central and charges DM100/160.

Being a major trade show centre, Cologne has the usual number of international chain hotels catering mainly for business travellers. *Hyatt Regency* (☎ 828 12 34, fax 828 13 70, Kennedy-Ufer 2a) clearly has the nicest view over the entire Cologne panorama, and rates from DM265/305. An extremely classy designer hotel is the historic *Hotel Im Wasserturm* (☎ 200 80, fax 200 88 88, Kaygasse 2). Rooms in this protected structure start at DM320/390.

Long-Term Rentals
Cologne's Mitwohnzentrale (☎ 21 05 11) is at Lindenstrasse 77.

Places to Eat
Restaurants Cologne's multiculturalism makes it possible to take a culinary journey around the world. True German food is best sampled in the beer halls (see later in this section). An eclectic mix of eateries clusters in the Zülpicher Viertel and the Belgisches Viertel.

Red velvet, nostalgic decor and romantic lighting add to the slightly mysterious atmosphere of *Hotellux* (☎ 24 11 36, Rathenauplatz 21), where Russian dishes from borscht to blinis (DM15 to DM30) and an extensive vodka menu attract an intellectual, trendy crowd (evenings only). *Alcazar* (☎ 51 57 33, Bismarckstrasse 39) has a boisterous atmosphere. It's famous for its creative and fresh – mostly Mediterranean – cuisine, topping out around DM20. Dishes like asparagus lasagne are typical here.

Lively Zülpicher Strasse is crowded with inexpensive eateries. *Magnus* (☎ 24 14 69) at No 48 has pizza from DM6.50 to DM12, snacks from DM6 and 250g steaks from DM20. Its big breakfast buffet is legendary, as are the cheap cocktails. At *Filmdose* (☎ 23 96 43), across the street at No 39, the speciality is Kölsche Pizza, where the dough is made of potato pancakes. It's all consumed in cheerful, cinematic surrounds with a long bar and red velvet curtains.

Two more candidates are on nearby Engelbertstrasse. For exotic fare, head to *Thali* (☎ 23 91 69) at No 9, which offers curries and tandoori dishes from DM15 to DM20. Next door, *Engelbät* is a friendly and

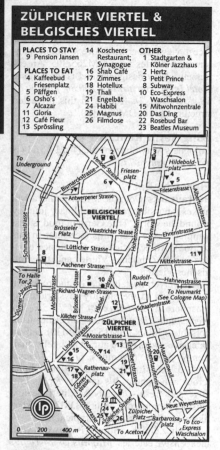

ZÜLPICHER VIERTEL & BELGISCHES VIERTEL

PLACES TO STAY	14	Koscheres	OTHER
9 Pension Jansen		Restaurant;	1 Stadtgarten &
		Synagogue	Kölner Jazzhaus
PLACES TO EAT	16	Shab Café	2 Hertz
4 Kaffeebud	17	Zimmes	3 Petit Prince
Friesenplatz	18	Hotellux	8 Subway
5 Päffgen	19	Thali	10 Eco-Express
6 Osho's	21	Engelbät	Waschsalon
7 Alcazar	24	Habibi	15 Mitwohnzentrale
11 Gloria	25	Magnus	20 Das Ding
12 Café Fleur	26	Filmdose	22 Rosebud Bar
13 Sprössling			23 Beatles Museum

usually packed pub/restaurant, popular for its habit-forming crepes – sweet, meat or vegetarian – for DM9.50 to DM13.

For sophisticated Turkish food, there's no place like *Bizim* (☎ 13 15 81, *Weidenstrasse 47*), north of the Hauptbahnhof, which offers professional preparation and service at price tabs of around DM50 per main course (closed Sunday and Monday).

Vegetarian Most restaurants now offer meatless dishes, but for dedicated vegie fare

head to *Sprössling* (☎ 23 21 24, *Mozart-strasse 9*), which uses only fresh ingredients in its daily changing menu with Thai, Oriental and Italian inflections (mains from DM15, closed Tuesday). A special touch is the flower-festooned courtyard. *Osho's* (☎ 574 07 45, *Venloer Strasse 5-7*) is affiliated with the Baghwan sect (there's a 'counselling centre' next door). Salad is sold by weight, and dishes cost DM10 and up. Both places are nonsmoking.

Kosher Cologne's two kosher restaurants are both around Rathenauplatz by the synagogue. *Koscheres Restaurant der Jüdischen Gemeinde* (☎ 240 44 40, *Roonstrasse 50*) is the only strictly kosher one (reservations mandatory, closed Saturday). At *Zimmes* (☎ 240 46 89, *Rathenauplatz 23*), you can get gefilte fish (DM22), sweet and sour pot roast (DM21), felafel (DM15) and other Jewish and Middle Eastern dishes.

Cafes Coffee-house culture is big in Cologne. Places that do more than traditional *Kaffee und Kuchen* (literally 'coffee and cake') include the bistro-style *Schmittchen* (☎ 257 84 36, *Breite Strasse 38*), where small meals – herring to steaks – range from DM15 to DM25. *Moderne Zeiten* (☎ 257 51 71), on the corner of Breite Strasse and Auf dem Berlich, is popular with media types from the WDR radio/TV studios across the street, and serves Italian and French morsels mostly costing DM15 or less. *Gloria* (☎ 258 36 56, *Apostelnstrasse 11*), nearby in a former cinema, is also a gay hang-out.

Cafe Schmitz (☎ 13 25 85, *Hansaring 98*) is a trendy and smoky corner cafe with 1950s decor where black-clad cool folk sip cappuccino behind panoramic windows. *Café Fleur* (☎ 24 48 97, *Lindenstrasse 10*) is a real Viennese-style coffee-house classic. It has great breakfasts, brunch and cakes, and is a good place to while away the time.

The *Shab* (☎ 23 22 64, *Lindenstrasse 93*) nearby is a low-key place with soft yellow walls and a relaxed crowd. It serves breakfast till 4 pm as well as coffee, salads and snacks.

Beer Halls Much like it is in Munich, beer reigns supreme in Cologne. There arc more than 20 local breweries, all producing a variety called Kölsch, which is relatively light and slightly bitter. The breweries in Cologne often run their own beer halls and serve their brew in skinny glasses called *Stangen* that hold a mere 0.2L. They also offer a selection of filling, hearty, regional dishes that usually cost DM20 or less.

Brauhaus Sion (☎ 257 85 40, Unter Taschenmacher 9) is packed most nights and for good reason: you'll eat your fill for well under DM20, including a couple of beers. *Brauerei zur Malzmühle (☎ 21 01 17, Heumarkt 6)*, in an ancient mill off Am Malzbüchel south of the Deutzer Brücke, has been pouring since 1858. *Päffgen (☎ 13 54 61, Friesenstrasse 64-66)*, considered one of the most original beer halls, is beloved by tourists and locals alike. *Früh am Dom (☎ 258 03 89, Am Hof 12-14)* is another good bet. It has a vaulted cellar and even serves pretty good breakfast.

Fast Food *Kaffeebud* stand-up coffee bars charge DM2.29 for all the coffee you can drink, and sell cakes, rolls and sandwiches for a song. There's one on the eastern end of Alter Markt and another on Friesenplatz. *Stausberg* at Schildergasse 92 is a bustling stand-up snack bar where you can get sausage and sandwiches for under DM10. Zülpicher Strasse is the place for doner kebab and other oriental fare like felafel and shwarma. For gourmet-quality shwarma, head to *Habibi (☎ 240 27 00)* at No 38.

Entertainment

Cologne is a happening place when it comes to nightlife with a scene that ranges from grungy and relaxed to upmarket chic. Centres of action include the Altstadt, with its rollicking pubs and beer halls; the 'Kwartier Lateng' (Cologne dialect for Quartier Latin, or student quarter), also known as Zülpicher Viertel, around Barbarossaplatz; and, a bit farther north near Friesenplatz, the Belgisches Viertel (Belgian Quarter), which has a more grown-up and trendy feel.

For an overview of cultural events, pick up a copy of the bilingual what's-on monthly *Monatsvorschau* (DM2), or the magazines *Kölner Illustrierte* (DM4) or *Prinz* (DM4.50), available at newsagents and bookshops.

Pubs & Bars Evenings and weekends in the Altstadt are like miniature carnivals, with bustling crowds and lots to do and see. The beverage of choice is, of course, beer and there are plenty of places to enjoy it. If you're feeling homesick, you're bound to find some company at *Flanagan's (☎ 257 06 74, Alter Markt 36-42)*, a happening Irish pub with live bands (no cover), nightly parties and English as the reigning language. If choice is what you want, head to the nearby *Biermuseum (☎ 257 78 02, Buttermarkt 39)*, which serves 39 varieties of beer.

Küppers Biergarten (☎ 93 47 81 18, Alteburger Strasse 157) is a great beer garden flooded with locals throughout the fine weather season. It's part of a historic brewery that also incorporates a beer museum. Opening hours vary, so call ☎ 962 99 49 for tour times. Take the U16 to Bayenthalgürtel.

For places to try the local brew, Kölsch, see Beer Halls earlier in this chapter.

Rosebud (☎ 240 14 55, Heinsbergstrasse 20) is one of Germany's best cocktail bars, according to that arbiter of taste, *Playboy* (German edition). All cocktails are DM10 during Happy Hour, which runs from 8.30 to 10 pm Monday to Thursday, and 10 pm to midnight on Friday and Saturday.

Daneben, on Lübecker Strasse, is a bizarre hang-out with a decor that seems to change with the owner's mood (though the nude barbie doll display above the bar is a permanent feature). The music is loud, but the audience is mixed in terms of age and walk of life. *Aceton (☎ 42 61 12, Luxemburger Strasse 46)* is a bar-cum-dance floor divided into three that's open from 9 pm.

Clubs & Live Music Most of Cologne's centrally located clubs – those lined up on Hohenzollernring between Friesenplatz and Gereonshof – are derisively regarded as 'meat markets' by Kölners in the know. Perhaps best of the bunch is *Petit Prince* (☎ *12 22 49, Hohenzollernring 90)*, where it's salsa one night, reggae the next and acid jazz on Tuesday. *Das Ding* (☎ *24 63 48, Hohenstaufenring 30-32)* nearby is mostly mainstream and usually packed with a student and teenie crowd, though more 'mature' folks show up on weekdays.

Alter Wartesaal (☎ *912 88 50, Johannisstrasse 11)* is a better alternative and has a super-central location. It's in a former train station waiting hall decked out with noble woods, stucco and marble in combination with bars and laser light shows. The Blue Monday parties – with go-go dancers – are legendary.

To get to the hippest venues – most of them in converted factories or industrial sites – you have to travel beyond the city centre. A main venue for rock concerts is *E-Werk* (☎ *962 79 10, Schanzenstrasse 37)*, in a former power station on the right bank of the Rhine in the suburb of Mülheim. It turns into a huge techno disco after 10 pm on Friday and Saturday. In the same neighbourhood, but with a distinctly industrial underground vibe, is *Gebäude 9* (☎ *240 30 39, Deutz-Mühlheimer Strasse 127)*. In the same vein is the appropriately named *Underground* (☎ *54 23 26, Vogelsanger Strasse 200)* which has a beer garden, two pubs and a live music stage. More mainstream again is *Halle Tor 2* (☎ *94 98 97 98, Girlitzweg 30)*, in a former oil drill factory in the western suburb of Müngersdorf.

Top acts appear at the *Kölnarena* (☎ *28 01, Willy-Brandt-Platz 2)* in Köln-Deutz.

Jazz The stand-bys for jazz are *Papa Joe's Klimperkasten* (☎ *258 21 32, Alter Markt 50)* and *Em Streckstrump* (☎ *257 79 31, Buttermarkt 37)*. While the first is large and lively, with a wonderful old pianola and progressive jazz, the latter hums with more traditional tunes. The intimate *Subway* (☎ *51 79 69, Aachener Strasse 82)* has mostly mainstream jazz, though if you're lucky, music quality can be very high. The same is true of *Stadtgarten* (☎ *95 29 94 10,*

Venloer Strasse 40) in the Kölner Jazzhaus. Check the listings magazines for details.

Theatre & Classical Music Lovers of classical music should not miss a concert at the *Kölner Philharmonie* (☎ *28 01 for box office, Bischofsgartenstrasse 1)*, below the Museum Ludwig. The box office is at Köln-Ticket on Roncalliplatz. Repertory theatre is based at the *Schauspielhaus*, on Offenbachplatz, the *Opernhaus* is also here. The box office for both is in the opera house foyer (☎ *22 12 84 00)*.

Shopping

Cologne is a fantastic place to shop, with lots of eccentric boutiques, designer stores and trendy second-hand shops, plus the usual selection of chain and department stores. The main shopping area is the pedestrianised Hohe Strasse, which meanders south from the Dom, then forks off into In der Höhle and Schildergasse, culminating in Neumarkt. Breite Strasse and adjoining side streets like Apostelnstrasse form another shopping haven with an eclectic mix of stores – some funky, some elegant.

If you want to bring something home to mother, consider a bottle of *eau de Cologne*, the not terribly sophisticated but refreshing perfume created – and still being produced – in its namesake city. The most famous brand is called 4711, after the number of the house where it was invented. There's still a perfumery and gift shop by that name on the corner of Glockengasse and Schwertnergasse. (Try to catch the Glockenspiel, with characters from Prussian lore parading above the store hourly from 9 am to 9 pm.)

Getting There & Away

Air Cologne/Bonn airport has many connections within Europe and to the rest of the world. For flight and general information, ring ☎ 02203-40 40 01/02.

Train Cologne is a major train hub. Regional and main-line trains service Bonn (DM9.40, 20 minutes), Düsseldorf (DM15.20, 20 minutes) and Aachen (DM19.60, one hour) several times an hour. Hourly IC trains include those to Hamburg (DM130, four hours), Frankfurt and Frankfurt airport (DM68, 2¼ hours), Hanover (ICE; DM104, 2¾ hours) and Munich (DM180, 5¾ hours). Trains to Leipzig (DM166, six hours) and Berlin-Zoo (ICE; DM190, 4½ hours) leave every two hours.

Bus Deutsche Touring's Eurolines buses go to Paris and back six times weekly (some trips overnight) for DM70/125, and Warsaw daily for DM105/180. Trips to Prague are scheduled three times a week for DM80/140. Copenhagen is served almost daily (DM130/209). The office is at the bus station outside the Breslauer Platz exit of the Hauptbahnhof.

Car & Motorcycle Cologne is also a major autobahn hub and is encircled by the immense Kölner Ring, with exits to the A1, A3, A4, A57, A555 and A559 leading in all directions. Note that the ring road is usually jammed with traffic.

Ride Services ADM Mitfahrzentrale (☎ 194 40) has two branches at Trierer Strasse 47 and at Maximinstrasse near the Hauptbahnhof. Citynetz Mitfahr-Service (☎ 194 44) is at Saarstrasse 22 near Barbarossaplatz.

Boat An enjoyable way to travel to/from Cologne is by boat. The KD Line has services all along the Rhine (see Organised Tours earlier in this section).

Getting Around
To/From the Airport Bus No 170 shuttles between Cologne/Bonn airport and the main bus station every 15 minutes from 5.30 am to 11 pm (DM8.50/4.30, 20 minutes). The taxi ride to/from the airport costs about DM45.

Public Transport Cologne's mix of buses, trams, U-Bahn and S-Bahn trains is operated by the Verkehrsverbund Rhein-Sieg (VRS; ☎ 20 80 80) in cooperation with Bonn's system. The fairly complicated

tariff structure is explained in the English-language brochure *Bus and Train Travel Made Easy*, available at VRS offices (there's one at the Hauptbahnhof).

Short trips within the city cost DM2.10, though for most trips you'll need the DM3.40 ticket; day passes are DM9.50. Groups of up to five people can travel with the Minigruppenkarte for DM13. Buy your tickets from the orange ticket machines and be sure to validate them when boarding.

Car & Motorcycle Driving in Cologne can be an absolute nightmare. Unless you're careful, you could easily end up in a tunnel or on a bridge going across the Rhine. Street parking in the city is usually reserved for residents, so head for one of the many car parks (DM2.50 an hour). Note that some close at night and charge an overnight fee.

Car-rental companies with branches in Cologne include Avis (☎ 23 43 33), Clemensstrasse 29-31; and Hertz (☎ 51 50 84) at Bismarckstrasse 19-21.

Taxi Taxis cost DM3.20 at flag fall, plus DM2.15 per kilometre (DM0.20 more at night); add another DM1 if you order by phone (☎ 28 82 or ☎ 194 10).

Bicycle Cycling is popular with Cologne's young people, but it requires major attention and skills to navigate safely through the heavy traffic. Kölner Fahrradverleih (☎ 72 36 27), at Marksmanngasse in the Altstadt next to the Deutzer Brücke, rents out bikes for DM4/10/20 per hour/three-hours/day and also does tours (see Organised Tours earlier in this section).

AROUND COLOGNE
Brühl
☎ 02232 • pop 40,000
About 15km south of Cologne, Brühl is the birthplace of former tennis star, Steffi Graf, and offers two major attractions that bring in the crowds. Aficionados of history, culture and architecture flock to **Schloss Augustusburg** (1745; ☎ 02232-440 00), a UNESCO World Cultural Heritage site that

is considered the most important baroque residential palace on the Rhine. Three well known architects of the period – Johann Conrad Schlaun, François Cuvilliés and Balthasar Neumann – worked on this elegant edifice, which is surrounded by a formal French garden. Also part of the complex is the much smaller **Schloss Falkenlust**, used as a private retreat by palace builder Clemens August (1723-1761), the flamboyant prince-elector and archbishop of Cologne.

The palace interior is a dizzying extravaganza that seems to incorporate every architectural and decorative element the baroque style had to offer. The most impressive feature is the ceremonial staircase by Neumann. A symphony in stucco, sculpture and faux marble, it is bathed in muted light and crowned by a multicoloured ceiling fresco by Carlo Carlone.

The palace opens daily from 9 am to noon and 1.30 to 4 pm, except Monday. Admission of DM6/4 to Augustusburg (DM4.50/3 to Falkenlust) includes a one hour guided tour.

Brühl's other attraction is **Phantasialand** (☎ 362 00), one of Europe's earliest Disneyland-style amusement parks (it turned 30 in 1997), which is naturally a winner with children. Settings include a Chinatown, Petit Paris, Viking ships, a fairy-tale park and a wild water ride. The park is located at Berggeiststrasse 31-41, and is open April to October from 9 am to 6 pm (to 9 pm in July). Day admission is DM36 (DM26 after 3 pm); children measuring below 1.2m get in for free. Brühl is regularly served by regional trains from Cologne. If you're driving, exit Brühl-Süd from the A553.

BONN
☎ 0228   • pop 290,000

When this friendly, relaxed city on the Rhine became West Germany's 'temporary' capital in 1949 it surprised almost everyone, including its own residents. Soon it was given the nickname 'Federal Village' for its supposed provincialism and lack of

sophistication. While Bonn was no world capital, these slights were not entirely deserved. Besides large international and student populations, it was also blessed with several first-rate museums, some packed with the biggest and the brightest names in art. Artists, in fact, also play a large role in the city's history. Bonn was the birthplace of Ludwig van Beethoven, the painter August Macke had his studio here, and Robert Schumann also lived here for a time.

Settled in Roman times, Bonn celebrated its 2000th anniversary in 1989. From the late 16th to the 18th century it was the permanent residence of the prince-electors and archbishops of Cologne, including the eccentric Clemens August. Some of the baroque architecture from this era survived the ravages of WWII and the postwar demand for modern government buildings. Since the move of the German federal government to Berlin was announced in 1991, Bonn has been in the process of reinventing itself (see the boxed text 'Bonn – The Future is Here').

Bonn is an easy day trip from Cologne and a good base for exploring some of the sights along this section of the Rhine.

Orientation

Bonn is about 30km south of Cologne and just north of the Siebengebirge (Seven Mountains) nature preserve. The Hauptbahnhof is on the southern edge of the largely pedestrianised Altstadt and city centre. The B9 from Cologne, which changes names several times within Bonn, connects the centre with the former government district before continuing south to Bad Godesberg and Koblenz. The landing docks for Rhine river cruises are at Brassertufer near the Opera House on the eastern edge of the Altstadt.

Information

Bonn's tourist office (☎ 77 50 00 or ☎ 194 33) is at Windeckstrasse 9. It's open from 9 am to 6.30 pm weekdays, to 4 pm Saturday, and from 10 am to 2 pm on Sunday. The office has good city maps and brochures

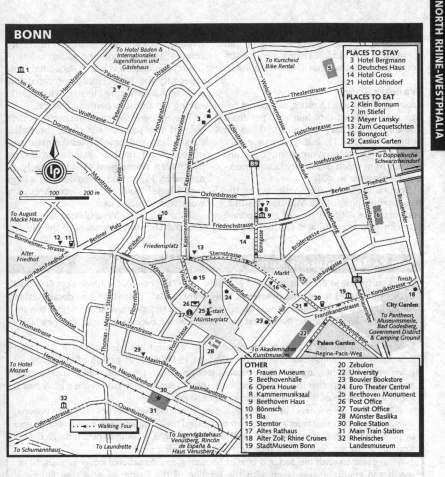

BONN

To Kurscheid
Bike Rental

PLACES TO STAY
3 Hotel Bergmann
4 Deutsches Haus
14 Hotel Gross
21 Hotel Löhndorf

PLACES TO EAT
2 Klein Bonnum
7 Im Stiefel
12 Meyer Lansky
13 Zum Gequetschten
16 Bonngout
29 Cassius Garten

Tu Doppelkirche
Schwarzrheindorf

To August
Macke Haus

To Hotel
Mozart

To Pantheon,
Museumsmeile,
Bad Godesberg,
Government District
& Camping Ground

To Akademisches
Kunstmuseum

To Jugendgästehaus
Venusberg, Rincón
de España &
Haus Venusberg

To Schumannhaus

To Laundrette

0   100   200 m

Walking Tour

OTHER
1 Frauen Museum
5 Beethovenhalle
6 Opera House
8 Kammermusiksaal
9 Beethoven Haus
10 Bönnsch
11 Bla
15 Sterntor
17 Altes Rathaus
18 Alter Zoll; Rhine Cruises
19 StadtMuseum Bonn
20 Zebulon
22 University
23 Bouvier Bookstore
24 Euro Theater Central
25 Beethoven Monument
26 Post Office
27 Tourist Office
28 Münster Basilika
30 Police Station
31 Main Train Station
32 Rheinisches
Landesmuseum

(some in English) and also sells the Regio BonnCard (DM24, families DM32), which grants unlimited public transportation in Bonn, Cologne and surrounds, admission to 20 museums in the region, plus discounts for tours, thermal baths and more. A three day version costs DM46 for either individuals or families.

The bank in the Hauptbahnhof is open weekdays from 9 am to 1 pm and 1.30 to 6 pm, and Saturday from 8 am to noon and 12.30 to 3 pm.

The main post office at Münsterplatz 17 is open from 8 am to 8 pm weekdays and to 4 pm on Saturday.

You'll find a superb bookstore with an excellent selection of English novels and other books in Bouvier (☎ 72 90 10), Am Hof 28, near the university.

There's a laundrette on the corner of Reuterstrasse and Argelanderstrasse, about a 15 minute walk south of the Hauptbahnhof. A basic wash costs DM6, plus DM1 for the dryer.

euro currency converter DM1 = €0.51

For medical emergencies, ring ☎ 192 92. A recorded message listing dentists on call is available at ☎ 115 00. There's a police station in the Hauptbahnhof U-Bahn station.

Walking Tour

From April through October, the tourist office runs a guided city tour at 2 pm from Tuesday to Saturday and at 10.30 am on Sunday (DM22/11), but you can easily cover the sights on your own. Cars are banned from much of the city centre, making it a pleasure to walk.

Start on Münsterplatz, dominated by the five soaring spires of the **Münster Basilika**, built in the transitional style of architecture between Romanesque and Gothic. On its site, two Roman officers, Cassius and Florentius, were allegedly martyred in the 3rd century; they are now the patron saints of Bonn. The church is richly decorated; note especially the 12th century baptismal font and the Romanesque cloister, which ranks among the finest in northern Europe.

The yellow building on the north-western side of the square was once the Palais Fürstenberg and now houses the main post office. Right in front stands the bronze **Beethoven Monument** (1845), largely financed by Franz Liszt, who donated a large sum himself and raised more through a worldwide concert tour.

Turn left onto Vivatsgasse, where you pass the **Sterntor**, a remnant of the old city

Bonn – The Future is Here

It was party time in Bonn on 10 May 1949, when the little city on the Rhine beat Frankfurt by just three votes to become Germany's 'temporary capital'. More than four decades later, on 20 June 1991, another vote was taken with no less historic implications: under the so-called Berlin-Bonn Decision, the federal government would relocate to Berlin, the 'new' German capital.

Bonn and its people, usually an optimistic and jovial bunch, plunged into an angst-ridden depression. Projections showed a net loss of about 15,000 jobs as a result of the exodus of government branches, along with embassies, lobbying groups and the media. Loss of pride and identity was another issue. Many Bonners, used to seeing their city on the nightly news, feared a regression of their town to provincial backwater.

Although things will never be the same, it now looks as if Bonn will not fade from national consciousness after all. Under a sweetheart deal called the Compensation Agreement, passed by parliament in 1994, the region will receive a total of DM3.4 billion to help through the restructuring process. Some of the money is already showing results.

A huge step towards the declared goal of becoming an international leader in scientific research and education was taken with the creation of the Centre of Advanced European Studies and Research (CAESAR). Other investments have gone – and continue to go – towards attracting international associations and large corporations to Bonn. Already here are the United Nations Volunteers and the head office of the UN Framework Convention on Climate Change (UNFCCC).

Politically, too, Bonn will retain a role as a *Bundesstadt* (federal city), a newly created term. The primary offices of seven ministries, including education and defence, will remain here. About two dozen federal institutions are scheduled to move to Bonn as well, including the Federal Cartel Office and the Federal Insurance Office. It is expected that this will add another 7500 jobs. These days, Bonners are worried no longer, aware that there's a future for their little city on the Rhine.

wall. Turn right onto Sternstrasse towards the Markt, a triangular square dominated by the pink, grey and gold rococo **Altes Rathaus**. Politicians from Charles de Gaulle to John F Kennedy have stood atop its stairway. Bonngasse, north of the Markt, leads to **Beethoven Haus** (see Museums later in this section), where the composer was born, but the tour continues via Stockenstrasse, which leads to the **Rheinische Friedrich-Wilhelm Universität** (1725), housed in the one-time residence of the prince-electors. The university (founded 1818) is bordered by the Hofgarten, a park and popular gathering place for students. On its south-western edge stands the **Akademisches Kunstmuseum** (Academic Art Museum; ☎ 73 77 38) in a structure by Berlin architect Karl Friedrich Schinkel. It holds one of the largest collections of copies of Greek and Roman sculpture. Hours vary (DM1, students free).

From the university, head back to Stockenstrasse, turn right (east) off Stockenstrasse onto Franzikanerstrasse, which leads past the new **StadtMuseum Bonn** (☎ 77 24 14) at No 9. Those interested in the history of Bonn and the region can visit it Friday to Monday from 11.30 am to 5 pm (DM5/3).

Cross Adenauerallee to get to **Alter Zoll**, a small section of the stone ramparts that once encircled Bonn, with great views of the river and the hilly surrounds. The embarkation point for river cruises is here as well.

Museums

If you plan to visit more than one or two of Bonn's fascinating variety of fine museums, it's worth getting the Regio BonnCard (see Information earlier in this section). Unless noted, museums are closed on Monday.

Beethoven Haus The modest appearance of the pink three-storey building at Bonngasse 20 belies its historic importance as the birthplace of Ludwig van Beethoven (1770-1827). Inside are letters, musical scores, paintings, the composer's last grand piano and public documents. Particularly memorable are the giant brass ear trumpets, used by Beethoven to combat his growing deaf-

ness, and a haunting death mask. The house (☎ 981 75 25) is open Monday to Saturday from 10 am to 5 pm (to 4 pm in winter), Sunday from 11 am to 4 pm (DM8/4).

Frauen Museum Housed in a former department store at Im Krausfeld 10, the Women's Museum (☎ 69 13 44) showcases contemporary paintings, installations, sculpture and other art forms by international women artists. It's all displayed in a friendly environment and complemented by readings, concerts, lectures and theatre performances. The museum is open Tuesday to Saturday from 2 to 6 pm, Sunday from 11 am (DM8/6).

Rheinisches Landesmuseum This regional history museum (☎ 988 10) at Colmantstrasse 14-16 is closed for expansion and modernisation until 2001.

Museumsmeile The Museum Mile consists of four museums all located along the B9 south of the Altstadt.

If you visit only one museum in Bonn, make it the **Haus der Geschichte der Bundesrepublik Deutschland** (House of the History of the Federal Republic of Germany; ☎ 916 50) at Adenauerallee 250. Five

MICK WELDON

Born in Bonn, Ludwig van Beethoven is one of the world's most acclaimed composers.

levels of rampways present an entertaining multimedia chronology of the entire post-WWII history of Germany – from bombed-out obliteration to the industrialised and unified powerhouse of today. This fascinating and engaging exhibit is a must for anyone interested in recent German history. Hours are from 9 am to 7 pm (free).

The **Kunstmuseum Bonn** (☎ 77 62 60), Friedrich-Ebert-Allee 2, is known for its 20th century collection, especially for its armload of works by August Macke and other Rhenish expressionists, as well as for German art after 1945 (Beuys, Baselitz, Kiefer, etc). It's all housed in a postmodern building with a generous and light-flooded interior. Unfortunately, the hostile glares from overzealous security personnel detract from the experience. Hours are from 10 am to 6 pm, Wednesday to 9 pm (DM5/3).

Immediately next door is the **Kunst und Ausstellungshalle der Bundesrepublik Deutschland** (Art and Exhibit Hall of the Federal Republic of Germany; ☎ 917 12 00), home of changing exhibits of German, European and world culture, science and the arts. The building, by Viennese architect Gustav Peichl, is easily recognised by its three distinctive cones jutting from its rooftop garden and a line of 16 columns representing the states of Germany. Opening hours are Tuesday and Wednesday from 10 am to 9 pm, and Thursday to Sunday to 7 pm (DM10/5).

A recent addition to the Museum Mile is the **Deutsches Museum Bonn** (☎ 30 22 55), Ahrstrasse 45, which highlights the accomplishments of German technology since WWII, including inventions like the airbag and the computer tomograph. It's open from 10 am to 6 pm (DM7/4).

Other Museums From 1910 until his death in 1914, August Macke had his first and only studio at Bornheimer Strasse 96, now **August Macke Haus** (☎ 65 55 31). The attic studio has been restored, and works by Macke and his contemporaries are displayed throughout. It's open weekdays from 2.30 to 6 pm, weekends 11 am to 5 pm (DM6/3).

Fans of Robert Schumann (1810-56) can study pictures, letters and documents in the two memorial rooms devoted to the composer in a former sanatorium at Sebastianstrasse 182, now called the **Schumannhaus** (☎ 77 36 56). Schumann suffered severe depressions and checked himself into the asylum in 1854 after a suicide attempt. He and his wife Clara are buried in **Alter Friedhof** on Bornheimer Strasse. The museum is open weekdays (except Tuesday) from 10 am to noon, plus Monday and Friday from 4 to 7 pm, and Wednesday and Thursday from 3 to 7 pm (free).

Former Government District

With the federal government move to Berlin in progress, it's no longer politics as usual for Bonn. Most buildings in the government district, which lies about 1.5km south-east of the Hauptbahnhof on Adenauerallee, will lose their original functions. While some are expected to become regular office buildings, others might be turned into concert halls, conference facilities and private function halls. No specific plans, however, had been made public at the time of writing.

Meanwhile, it's still possible to stroll through the area from which the nation of West Germany was governed for half a century. For a self-guided tour, simply ask for the free pamphlet *Bonner Spaziergänge: Bundesviertel* at the tourist office.

Highlights include **Villa Hammerschmidt**, once the official residence of the federal president, and **Palais Schaumburg**, which went through periods as Allied headquarters, home of Konrad Adenauer and chancellery. Nearby is the **Adenauer monument**, a gigantic bronze head with important events in the former chancellor's life engraved on the back. On Görresstrasse is the **Bundeshaus** complex with the former **Plenary Hall**, where the Bundestag, Germany's lower house, convened from 1992 to 1999.

Doppelkirche Schwarzrheindorf

On the right bank of the Rhine, in the suburb of Beuel, is this magnificent double church. It was donated by Arnold von Wied, a nobleman and imperial chancellor. Consecrated in 1152, it was used by the emperor himself during visits to this part of his Reich. The nobility sat in the *Oberkirche* (upper church) above an octagonal opening with a view of the altar below in the *Unterkirche* (lower church), where the congregation was assembled. The beautiful Romanesque architecture is impressive, but the church is especially famous for its extremely well preserved 12th century fresco cycles in the lower section which is open daily. The Oberkirche is open weekends only.

Places to Stay

The nearest *camping ground* (☎ 34 49 49, Im Frankenkeller 49) is on the Rhine about 5km south of Bad Godesberg and is open all year.

The state-of-the-art *Jugendgästehaus Venusberg* (☎ 28 99 70, fax 289 97 14, email jgh-bonn@t-online.de, Haager Weg 42) is about 4km south of the Hauptbahnhof (take bus No 621) and has a bistro and a garden terrace. Such relative luxury has its price: DM39 per bed in either quads or doubles, including sheets and breakfast.

The tourist information office operates a room-finding service (no phone reservations, a fee of DM3 for rooms costing up to DM100, otherwise DM5).

Beautifully located on a green hillside, *Haus Venusberg* (☎ 289 910, fax 289 91 59, Haager Weg 28-30) charges DM60/90 for singles/doubles with shared facilities and DM80/120 for rooms with private shower and WC (toilet). Bus No 620 runs here from the Hauptbahnhof.

Although calling itself *Internationales Jugendforum und Gästehaus* (☎ 989 60, fax 989 61 11, Graurheindorfer Strasse 149), amenities here are hotel-level with prices to match. Single rooms cost DM98 to DM128 and doubles range from DM140 to DM200, all with private bath and WC.

True budget hotels are rare, but you'll find two basic options on Kasernenstrasse. The better bet is the small *Hotel Bergmann* (☎ 63 38 91, fax 63 50 57) at No 13, where singles/doubles with shared shower go for DM60/95. At No 19 is *Deutsches Haus*

(☎ 63 37 77, fax 65 90 55), where rates start at DM65/100. Another kilometre or so north is *Hotel Baden* (☎ 96 96 80, fax 969 68 50, Graurheindorfer Strasse 1), which charges DM115/160 for rooms with all facilities. South of the Hauptbahnhof is *Hotel Mozart* (☎ 65 90 71, fax 65 90 75, Mozartstrasse 1), where rates range from DM70 to DM150 for singles and DM100 to DM185 for doubles, depending on amenities.

Hotel Gross (☎ 65 45 30, fax 604 53 60, Bonngasse 17), in the pedestrian zone near the Beethoven Haus, charges DM110/170. *Hotel Löhndorf* (☎ 65 54 39, fax 69 57 12, Stockenstrasse 6) has basic rooms for DM65/120, and several rooms with private bath for DM130/170.

Places to Eat

The city centre around the Markt is the place to find traditional Rhenish restaurant/ pubs. Choices include *Zum Gequetschten* (☎ 63 81 04, Sternstrasse 78) and the historic *Im Stiefel* (☎ 63 92 40, Bonngasse 30) next to Beethoven Haus. Both have generous main courses for around DM20.

More updated eateries include the excellent self-service *Cassius Garten* (☎ 65 24 29) inside the Cassius arcade opposite the Hauptbahnhof. There's a huge buffet with salad items and vegetarian dishes; prices are by weight, so be very careful how much you choose! *Bonngout* (☎ 65 89 88, Remigiusplatz 4) is a trendy cafe/bistro where those with an appetite can munch on a salad or have a hot meal, though it's also OK to simply linger over a big cup of coffee. *Meyer Lansky* (Bornheimer Strasse 24) is a chic bar and restaurant with courtyard seating and a menu of American-style dishes; the cocktails are reputedly very good (evenings only).

North-west of the pedestrian zone is *Klein Bonnum* (☎ 63 81 04, Paulstrasse 5), a student place with a remarkably creative menu, including several vegetarian dishes, all under DM20 (evenings only).

South of the centre is *Rincón de España* (☎ 23 96 09, Karthäuserplatz 21), where reasonably priced paella, tapas and other

Spanish dishes are so popular that the place bursts with people night after night.

In summer it's fun to put together a picnic from the *produce market* held daily (except Sunday) in front of the Rathaus and join the throngs of students in the nearby Hofgarten.

Entertainment

To find out what's on in Bonn, pick up a copy of the monthly *Bonner Illustrierte* (DM4) at any newsagent. The tourist office also has a smaller schedule of events called *Bonn-Info* (DM1.50). Central ticket reservations are at ☎ 910 41 61.

Pubs popular among students and younger people include *Zebulon* (☎ 65 76 90), on Stockenstrasse, near the university; the brew-pub *Bönnsch* (☎ 65 06 10, Sterntorbrücke 4); and the underground *Bla* (*Bornheimer Strasse 20*), which serves 60 different whiskies.

Congresses and concerts take place in the *Beethovenhalle* (☎ 722 20, Wachsbleiche 17) by the Rhine and also in the exquisite *Kammermusiksaal* (☎ 981 75 15, Bonngasse 24-26) next to Beethoven Haus. The Beethoven Festival is held every two or three years (the last one was in 1999).

Bonn's *Opera House* (☎ 72 81, Am Boselagerhof 1) is popular as well, as is the diminutive *Euro Theater Central* (☎ 65 29 51), on Mauspfad between the Markt and Münsterplatz. It stages plays in their original language, though most of them are in German. For biting satire, go to *Pantheon* (☎ 21 25 40, Bundeskanzlerplatz 2-10), where there's also a disco on weekends.

Getting There & Away

Air Bonn shares the Konrad-Adenauer airport (☎ 02203-404 00 12) with Cologne and offers connections within Germany, elsewhere in Europe and beyond.

Train Trains to Cologne (DM9.40, 20 minutes) leave several times an hour. IC trains to Hamburg (DM140, 4½ hours) and Frankfurt (DM59, two hours) depart hourly. There are also frequent trains to the Ruhrgebiet cities and Koblenz (DM21.80, 30 minutes).

Car & Motorcycle Bonn is at the crossroads of several autobahns, including the A565, A555 and A59. The B9 highway cuts north-south through the city.

Ride Services You'll find a Citynetz Mitfahrzentrale branch (☎ 69 30 30) at Herwarthstrasse 11, near the Hauptbahnhof.

Getting Around

Express bus No 670 shuttles between the Busbahnhof at the Hauptbahnhof and Cologne/Bonn airport every 20 or 30 minutes (DM8.50/4.30). A taxi to the airport from Bonn costs about DM60.

Buses, trams and the U-Bahn make up the public transportation system (☎ 711 48 13), which extends as far as Cologne and is divided into four zones. All you need within Bonn is an A-zone ticket, which costs DM3.40 each trip or DM9.50 for the 24 hour pass. Groups of up to five people travel for DM13, and a three-day ticket is DM23. The one-way trip to Cologne costs DM8.90. Tickets must be validated when boarding.

For a taxi, ring ☎ 55 55 55. Bikes may be rented at Kurscheid (☎ 63 14 33-35), Römerstrasse 4.

AROUND BONN
Siebengebirge

Across from Bonn, on the right bank of the Rhine, begins the Siebengebirge (Seven Mountains), a low mountain chain that is Germany's oldest nature preserve (1923). More than 200km of hiking trails lead through mostly deciduous forests, often allowing tremendous views of the Rhine, the Eifel and the Westerwald.

The Ölberg (461m) may be the highest of the seven mountains, but the **Drachenfels** (321m) is the most heavily visited. You can reach the summit on foot, by horse carriage, on the back of a mule or by riding the historic cogwheel train that has made the 1.4km climb since 1883 (the station is in Königswinter on Drachenfelsstrasse, just east of the B42). About halfway up the steep slopes, you will pass the neo-Gothic

Drachenburg and, farther uphill, the ruined **Drachenfels Castle** (1147).

The base for explorations of the Siebengebirge is **Königswinter**, reached from Bonn Hauptbahnhof via the U66 (DM5.30). The U-Bahn continues to **Bad Honnef**, the long-time home of West Germany's first chancellor, Konrad Adenauer. His house at No 8c in the street named after him has been turned into a museum (☎ 02224-92 10), with hours from 10 am to 4.30 pm (free).

AACHEN
☎ 0241   • pop 246,000
The Romans always knew a thing or two about soothing their war-weary bones in thermal waters, and so it's no surprise that they set up camp in the area of Aachen in the 1st century AD. A few centuries later, in 794 AD, Charlemagne too was so impressed with the revitalising qualities of the local waters that he made Aachen the capital of his kingdom. Today, the sulfurous springs still attract spa visitors with aching backs and bad circulation, but the city's main tourist draw is the magnificent cathedral, begun in Charlemagne's times, and now a UNESCO World Heritage Site. Aachen's proximity to the Netherlands and Belgium imbues it with a distinctly international feel, which is further enlivened by the students from the technical and general universities.

Orientation & Information
Aachen's compact city centre is contained within two ring roads and is best explored on foot. The inner ring road encloses the Altstadt proper and is called Grabenring because it's composed of segments all ending in 'graben' (meaning 'moat'). The Hauptbahnhof is south-east of the town centre just beyond Alleenring, the outer ring road. To get to the Dom and the Altstadt centre, head north from the train station for about 10 to 15 minutes. The Busbahnhof is at the north-eastern edge of the Grabenring on the corner of Kurhausstrasse and Peterstrasse.

Aachen's tourist information office (☎ 180 29 60/61 or ☎ 194 33, fax 180 29 30, email mail@aachen-tourist.de) is at Elisenbrunnen on Friedrich-Wilhelm-Platz, and is open weekdays from 9 am to 6 pm, and to 2 pm on Saturday.

Nearly all banks have exchange services, but the Sparkasse at Friedrich-Wilhelm-Platz 1-4, opposite the tourist office, is open weekdays till 6 pm and Saturday to 1 pm.

The main post office (☎ 41 20), Kapuzinergraben 19, is open to 6 pm, Saturday to 1 pm and has a fax-phone and photocopy machine.

Online information on Aachen is available at www.aachen-tourist.de.

For after-hours medical service, call ☎ 192 92; for dental problems, ring ☎ 70 96 16. The municipal Lost & Found (☎ 432 32 43) is on Bahnhofsplatz.

Dom
Aachen's drawing card is its cathedral, the coronation church of some 30 Holy Roman emperors, starting with Otto 1 in 936. The church was the brainchild of Charlemagne, who is buried here. It has been a major pilgrimage site since his death in 814, not least for its religious relics. Inspired by Byzantine architecture, the cathedral core was built as an octagon and was the largest vaulted structure north of the Alps when consecrated as Charlemagne's court chapel in 805. The Dom is open daily from 7 am to 7 pm.

A two storey gallery, supported by antique pillars, imported from Ravenna and Rome, rises towards a folded dome. The floral-patterned **mosaics** covering walls and vaults replaced the rococo decor about 100 years ago. A colossal brass **chandelier**, added to the octagon by Emperor Friedrich Barbarossa in 1165, hangs pendulously overhead.

Also of note are the altar, with its 11th century gold-plated **pala d'oro** (altar front) with scenes of the Passion; and the gilded copper **pulpit** donated by Henry II.

Unless you join a German-language tour (DM3, 45 minutes), you'll only catch a glimpse of Charlemagne's white marble **throne** in the first gallery of the octagon. Six

Charlemagne's court chapel in Aachen cathedral was the coronation site of 30 emperors.

steps lead up to it – the same number, supposedly, as those leading to the throne of King Solomon.

To accommodate the flood of pilgrims flocking to the cathedral, a **choir** in Gothic style was added in 1414. Most came to see the gilded **Karlschrein**, Charlemagne's final resting place, which stands at its eastern end. Commissioned by Barbarossa, it was completed under his grandson, Emperor Friedrich II, who allegedly insisted on personally placing Charlemagne's remains within this elaborate coffin on his coronation day in 1215.

The entrance to the **Domschatzkammer** (☎ 47 70 91 27), with one of the richest collections of religious art north of the Alps, is on nearby Klostergasse. It is open Monday from 10 am to 1 pm, Tuesday to Sunday to 6 pm, and Thursday to 9 pm (DM5/3).

Rathaus

North of the cathedral, the 14th century Rathaus overlooks the Markt and its fountain statue of Charlemagne. The eastern tower of the Rathaus, the Granusturm, was once part of Charlemagne's palace. Some 50 statues of German rulers, including 31 kings crowned in Aachen, adorn the building's facade. The 1st floor has fancy stuccowork and wall panelling, but the highlight is the grand **Empire Hall** on the 2nd floor, where Holy Roman emperors enjoyed their coronation feasts. The Rathaus is open daily from 10 am to 1 pm and 2 to 5 pm (DM3/1.50).

Museums

A combination ticket to all of Aachen's municipal museums is DM10 and is available at the tourist office. Museums are closed on Monday.

Suermondt Ludwig Museum This museum (☎ 47 98 00), Wilhelmstrasse 18, surveys art from the Middle Ages to modern times. Highlights include portraits by Lucas Cranach and Rubens, and sculptures from the late Middle Ages. Hours are weekdays from 11 am to 7 pm, Wednesday to 9 pm, and to 5 pm on weekends (DM6/3).

Ludwig Forum for International Art In a former umbrella factory at Jülicherstrasse 97-109, this museum (☎ 180 70) picks up where the Suermondt Ludwig leaves off, with a collection of Warhol, Lichtenstein, Baselitz and other postmodernists. Performance art events, including music, dance, poetry and film, complement the exhibits. It's open Tuesday and Thursday from 10 am to 5 pm, Wednesday and Friday to 8 pm, and weekends from 11 am to 5 pm (DM6/3).

Museum of Newspapers The Intenationales Zeitungsmuseum (☎ 432 45 08), Pontstrasse 13, is an often overlooked gem. Its collection of some 160,000 editions spans four centuries, with many first, last and special editions. A small portion of the material is presented according to milestones in

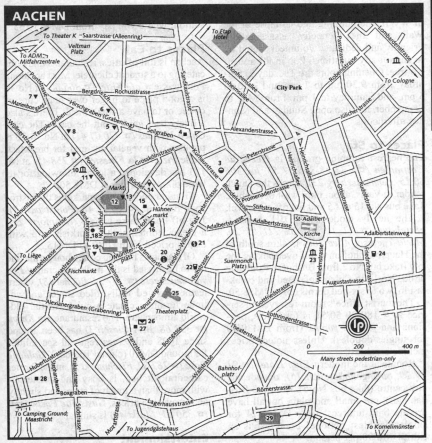

AACHEN

AACHEN

PLACES TO STAY
- 4 Hotel Reichshof
- 15 Hotel Brülls am Dom
- 27 Hotel Benelux
- 28 Hotel Marx

PLACES TO EAT
- 5 Efes
- 6 Am Knipp
- 7 Pizzeria la Finestra
- 8 Chico Mendes
- 9 Café Kittel

- 11 Egmont
- 13 Gaststätte Postwagen
- 14 Leo van den Daele
- 19 Goldene Rose

OTHER
- 1 Ludwig Forum for International Art
- 2 B9 Nightclub
- 3 Central Bus Station
- 10 Museum of Newspapers
- 12 Rathaus

- 16 Domkeller
- 17 Dom
- 18 Domschatzkammer
- 20 Tourist Office
- 21 Sparkasse
- 22 Aoxomoxoa
- 23 Suermondt Ludwig Museum
- 24 Club Voltaire
- 25 Theater Aachen
- 26 Main Post Office
- 29 Main Train Station

euro currency converter DM1 = €0.51

German and world history, such as the end of WWII, the building and collapse of the Wall and the Kennedy assassination. Friendly and dedicated volunteers stand by to answer any questions. Pop in for a visit: it's free. Opening hours are Tuesday to Saturday from 9.30 am to 1 pm and 2.30 to 5 pm, and Saturday to 1 pm. From May to September, it's also open Sunday and Monday afternoons.

Places to Stay

The nearest camping ground is *Hoeve de Gastmolen* (☎ +31-43-306 57 55, fax 306 60 15, Lemierserberg 23), across the Dutch border in Vaals, about 6km west of Aachen. Take bus No 15 or 65 and get off at Heuvel.

The newly modernised DJH *Jugendgästehaus* (☎ 71 10 10, fax 711 01 20, Maria-Theresia-Allee 260) is 4km south of the Hauptbahnhof on a hill overlooking the city (take bus No 2 from Bushof to Ronheide or bus No 12 to Colynshof). Bed and breakfast in two to six-bed dorms costs DM38.50.

The tourist office's room-reservation service at ☎ 180 29 50/51 is for hotels, pensions and *private rooms* (from DM30/40 for singles/doubles). Unless noted, prices include breakfast.

Rooms at the modern *Etap Hotel* (☎ 91 19 29, Strangenhäuschen 15), outside the city centre (take bus No 51 from the Busbahnhof), are small and plain but all have private bath and cost only DM62/74 for singles/doubles; optional breakfast is an extra DM8.90 per person.

Close to the Hauptbahnhof, but on a quiet street, *Hotel Marx* (☎ 375 41, fax 267 05, Hubertusstrasse No 33-35) has basic rooms from DM60/100 and those with facilities from DM85/140. Another central option is *Hotel Reichshof* (☎ 238 68, fax 238 69, Seilgraben 2), which tops out at DM112/160 for rooms with all facilities.

Small, comfortable and friendly is *Hotel Brülls am Dom* (☎ 317 04, fax 40 43 26), on Hühnermarkt, within a few steps of the cathedral. It charges from DM115/135 for rooms with private bath. *Hotel Benelux* (☎ 223 43, fax 223 45, Franzstrasse 21-23)

is a well run, elegant place not far from the station, where you pay from DM145/165.

Places to Eat

Aachen is full of cafes, restaurants and pubs catering to a student clientele. Most are along Pontstrasse. *Café Kittel* (☎ 365 60) at No 39 is a good place to linger over huge cups of coffee or to have a small meal. There's also a lively beer garden out the back. The cafe *Chico Mendes* (☎ 470 01 41) at No 74-76 is popular with vegetarians and for breakfast, while *Pizzeria la Finestra* (☎ 258 45) at No 123 has developed a loyal following for its large pizzas, starting at DM8.50.

Trendier and more upmarket is the bistro-style *Egmont* (☎ 40 77 46, Pontstrasse 1). Just off Pontstrasse is *Efes* (Neupforte 25), a clean, contemporary Turkish cafe with dishes priced from DM9 to DM15.

Of Aachen's historic coffee houses the one not to be missed is the nook-and-cranny *Leo van den Daele* (☎ 357 24, Büchel 18), where leather-covered walls, tiled stoves and antique furniture create a quintessential old-world atmosphere. The restaurant *Am Knipp* (☎ 333 68, Bergdriesch 3) has been around since 1698 and serves regional specialities for around DM20 (closed Tuesday). *Goldene Rose* (☎ 287 82, Fischmarkt 1), in the former cathedral kitchen, is busy and boisterous with more than a touch of style, and slightly above-average prices. *Gaststätte Postwagen* (☎ 350 01, Markt 40) is similar.

Entertainment

Aachen has a fairly lively club scene, and the unpronounceable *Aoxomoxoa* (☎ 226 22, Reihstrasse 15) is one of the cutting-edge venues. The *B9* (☎ 263 04, Blondelstrasse 9) offers music from hip hop to jazz and techno for a predominantly teenage clientele. The more mature crowd heads for *Club Voltaire* (☎ 54 34 27, Friedrichstrasse 9), which usually doesn't start swinging to funk and other black music until after midnight.

Domkeller (☎ 342 65, Am Hof 1), near the cathedral, has drawn students since the 1950s; there's live music on weekends.

Classic theatre, concerts and opera are staged most nights at the *Theater Aachen* (π *478 42 44*) on Theaterplatz. If you like your productions experimental and provocative, head for *Theater K* (π *15 11 55, Ludwigsallee 139*).

Shopping
Aachen is known for its Printen, a crunchy spiced cookie reminiscent of gingerbread. Traditionally shaped like a log, Aachen bakeries now churn it out in a variety of shapes, from the Easter Bunny to Santa Claus. One of the best places to buy them is Leo van den Daele (see Places to Eat).

Getting There & Away
Air Aachen is about 90km away from the airports at Düsseldorf and Cologne/Bonn. The Airport Express shuttles between Düsseldorf and Aachen 12 times daily, and between Cologne/Bonn four times. Call π 182 00 23 for details. Buses depart from the Busbahnhof.

Train Trains to Cologne (DM19.60, one hour) run several times hourly, with some proceeding to Dortmund and other Ruhrgebiet cities. Trips to most cities south of Aachen require a change in Cologne.

Car & Motorcycle If you're driving, Aachen is easily reached via the A4 (east-west) from Cologne and the A44 (north-south) from Düsseldorf. The B57, B258 and B264 also meet here.

Ride Services The ADM Mitfahrzentrale (π 194 40) is at Roermonder Strasse 4, on the corner of Ludwigsallee.

Getting Around
Bus tickets for travel within the area encircled by Alleenring cost a flat DM1.80. Otherwise, you can cover the entire city of Aachen, and the adjoining Dutch communities of Vaals and Kelmis, with a Zone 1 ticket for DM2.50. Day passes are DM8.80/16.50 and valid for up to five people travelling together. Buy tickets from the drivers.

Bicycles are for rent at the Hauptbahnhof. For a taxi, call π 51 11 11.

AROUND AACHEN
Kornelimünster
The romantic suburb of Kornelimünster is worth a short excursion. The main attraction here is the former Benedictine **Abbey Church of St Kornelius** (π 02408-64 92), Abteigarten 6. Upon its consecration in 817, Charlemagne's son, Ludwig the Pious, bestowed several important relics on the monastery. These are said to include Jesus' loin cloth and shroud, which are exhibited to the faithful every seven years. The abbey now functions as a gallery of contemporary art. It's open Tuesday and Wednesday from 10 am to 1 pm and 3 to 5 pm, and on Saturday and Sunday from 3 to 6 pm (free). Take bus No 68 or 166 from the Hauptbahnhof.

The Ruhrgebiet

Once Europe's largest industrial and mining region, the Ruhrgebiet is one of Germany's best-kept secrets. With the days of belching smokestacks and glowing furnaces largely a thing of the past, the area has evolved into a multifaceted and exciting cultural landscape with a charm and mythology all its own. A unique 'recycling program' embraces the industrial heritage in progressive and creative ways: a former gas processing tank is now a museum; concert crowds undulate where liquid steel once flowed; abandoned mining works are reincarnated as nightclubs.

Contrary to popular perception, the Ruhrgebiet is also surprisingly green, with 17.3% of the area given over to woodland and 43.2% to agricultural uses. The population of 5.5 million is concentrated in about 25 large cities in an area that stretches along the rivers Ruhr, Lippe and Emscher from the Dutch border to the eastern Westphalian flatlands. In medieval times the Hellweg, an important east-west trade route, cut right through here but the area remained completely rural until the 19th century.

The Age of Industrialisation gave birth to such corporate giants as Krupp, Thyssen and Hoesch, as well as to numerous regional mining companies. Workers were recruited from all over Europe, resulting in an ethnic and cultural stew not found elsewhere in Germany. While the Ruhrgebiet provided much of the fuel that turned Germany into a modern nation, its contributions to the German war machine also made it a prime target for Allied bombers in WWII. Thousands of raids caused widespread destruction, which is why most of the cities are built in a thoroughly modern and, shall we say, not always aesthetically pleasing style. Technology, administration, insurance and banking are major industries these days.

Unlike other German regions, the Ruhrgebiet does not have museum character. It's not evocative of a distant past but instead is constantly evolving and redefining itself. It's gritty, honest and unpretentious, just like its people.

Entertainment

For a thorough listing of current hot spots and events schedules throughout the Ruhrgebiet, pick up a copy of the free *Coolibri* (available in bars, restaurants and the tourist offices), or the magazines *Prinz* (DM5) or *Marabo* (DM5).

Getting Around

Each Ruhrgebiet city has an efficient and comprehensive public transportation system, usually composed of U-Bahns, buses and trams. Cities are also connected to each other by a network of S-Bahn and regional trains, managed by the Verkehrsverbund Rhein-Ruhr (VRR; ☎ 0209-194 49). The same tariffs apply within the entire region. There are three zones, depending on the distance you intend to travel. Look at the displays on the orange ticket vending machines to see which price applies in your case. Single tickets are DM3.20/6/13.80 for one/two/three zones. Better value are the four-trip tickets at DM9.60/18/39. Day passes are DM10.80/16/30.50 and valid for up to five people travelling together.

ESSEN

☎ 0201 • pop 615,000

Essen is the largest city in the Ruhrgebiet and the sixth largest in Germany. A settlement developed around a monastery founded in 852, and it obtained town rights in 1244. In the early 19th century, Essen plunged headlong into the Industrial Age, with the next 150 years dominated by steel and coal production. Essen is the home of the Krupp family of industrialists (see the boxed text 'The Krupp Dynasty – Men of Steel'). All of Essen's mines and steelworks have closed now, but several energy corporations still maintain their headquarters here.

To visitors, Essen has a surprising menu of attractions that includes some fine museums, generous green areas and a lively cultural scene. But most of all, Essen has a trio of unique sights: Villa Hügel, the Krupp family mansion; the Meteorit sensory exhibit and the NRW Design Centre. These offerings can make a stopover in this city a memorable experience.

Orientation & Information

Essen's sights are rather spread out, but all are easily reached by public transport. The Hauptbahnhof Nord (North) exit drops you right onto the centre's main artery, the pedestrianised Kettwiger Strasse. The museum complex and the recreational areas are both south of the station, while the Meteorit and Design Centre are to the north.

Essen's tourist office (☎ 194 33 or 887 20 46, fax 887 20 44) is on the ground floor of the Handelshof building opposite the Hauptbahnhof north exit and is open weekdays from 9 am to 5.30 pm, and Saturday 10 am to 1 pm.

The Reisebank inside the station is open daily but has irregular hours. If it's closed, the ATM machine outside the bank accepts all major credit cards.

The main post office is just on the left opposite the northern exit of the Hauptbahnhof, and is open from 8 am to 7 pm weekdays, 8.30 am to 2 pm Saturday and 10 am to noon on Sunday. For Web access,

The Krupp Dynasty – Men of Steel

Steel and Krupp are virtual synonyms. So are Krupp and Essen. For it's this bustling Ruhrgebiet city that is the ancestral seat of the Krupp family dynasty and the headquarters of one of the most powerful corporations in Europe. (To avoid confusion, Krupp has nothing to do with the company that produces coffee makers and other appliances – that's Krups.)

Through successive driven and obsessive generations, the Krupps amassed a huge private fortune, provided the German weaponry for four major wars and manipulated world economics and politics for their own gain. At the same time, however, they established a relationship between workers and management that's still the basis for today's social contract in industrialised Germany.

It all began rather modestly in 1811 when Friedrich Krupp and two partners founded a company to process 'English cast steel' but, despite minor successes, he left a company mired in debt upon his death in 1826. Enter his son Alfred, then a tender 14, who would go on to become one of the seminal figures of the Industrial Age.

It was through the production of the world's finest steel that the 'Cannon King' galvanized a company that – by 1887 – employed more than 20,000 workers. In an unbroken pattern of dazzling innovation, coupled with ruthless business practices, Krupp produced the wheels and rails for America's railroads and the stainless steel plating on New York's Chrysler building. It gave the world the first diesel engine and the first steam turbine locomotive. And – ultimately – it produced the fearsome weapons that allowed the Wehrmacht to launch the horror of the Blitzkrieg in WWII.

But in another pioneering move, Krupp also provided womb-to-tomb benefits to its workers at a time when the term 'social welfare' had not yet entered the world's vocabulary. Alfred realised that his company's progress and profit came at a price largely borne on the backs of his workers. He created a variety of measures, including company health insurance, a pension scheme, subsidised housing estates and company-owned retail stores.

But Krupp will forever be associated with the disastrous period in German history when a maniac from Austria nearly brought the world to its knees. It was their most glorious – and darkest – hour. Krupp plants were prime targets for Allied bombers. When the dust had settled, about two thirds of its factories had either been destroyed or damaged. An American military court sentenced Alfred Krupp von Bohlen and Halbach to prison, releasing him in 1951. He resumed the management of the firm in 1953.

In recent years, Krupp has merged with its main German competitors, the Dortmund-based Hoesch and its Essen rival, Thyssen.

An excellent source for an understanding of what the Krupp family has meant to Germany is William Manchester's brilliant chronicle *The Arms of Krupp* (1964).

---

there's a Cyberb@r inside the Karstadt at Friedrich-Ebert-Strasse 1.

The Baedeker bookshop (☎ 206 80) at Kettwiger Strasse 35 has a wide selection of maps and guidebooks and a fair number of English and French novels.

In medical emergencies, contact ☎ 192 92; for a dentist, dial ☎ 20 22 02.

City Centre

Essen's reputation as a shopper's haven reaches far beyond city limits. All along Kettwiger Strasse you'll find boutiques, speciality shops and department stores vying for your money. An island of quiet is the dignified **Münster** at Burgplatz 1 off Kettwiger Strasse, the seat of the Ruhr diocese since

1958. Of average architectural appeal, it is stocked with major Ottonian works of art from around 1000 AD, including a **seven-armed candelabrum** and the blue-eyed **Golden Madonna**. The **treasury** is one of Europe's richest, and boasts gemstone-studded processional crosses and a crown of Emperor Otto III (DM2).

East of the cathedral, at Steeler Strasse 29, the **Alte Synagogue** (☎ 884 52 25) is the largest synagogue north of the Alps. Completed in 1913, it survived WWII and now contains an exhibit on life in Essen during the Third Reich. It's open Tuesday to Sunday from 10 am to 6 pm (free).

Museum Complex
About 2km south of the Hauptbahnhof and flanked by Goethestrasse and Bismarckstrasse is Essen's museum complex (tram No 101, 107 or 127, or U11 to Rütten-scheider Stern). The moderately interesting **Ruhrlandmuseum** (Ruhr Area Museum; ☎ 884 52 00) focuses on the geology and industrial and social history of the Ruhrgebiet. The adjacent **Folkwang Museum** (☎ 884 53 14) enjoys an international reputation for its extensive collection of post-1800 painting. Romanticists like Caspar David Friedrich and Lovis Corinth are represented, as are all major impressionist, expressionist, cubist and Bauhaus artists. Both museums are open from 10 am to 6 pm, Thursday to 9 pm (DM5/3 each, free after 4 pm). All of Essen's museums are closed Monday.

Meteorit
A visit to the Meteorit (☎ 32 06 75 00) is a mesmerising journey into an underground fantasy world, a sensory immersion into sound, light, movement and mind-bending visual effects. André Heller, a multimedia artist from Vienna, has created a three-story subterranean stage, where you encounter such waystations as the **Light Cocoon**, a room clad in 90km of glass fibre and bathed in a meditative quality through multi-hued light patterns and sound poems. Bucky Fuller's vision is recalled with a building-sized **geodesic mirror dome**, inside which

videos create a dizzying kaleidoscope effect. In another room you'll encounter your own shadow, stroboscopically frozen against a naked wall for about 30 seconds. This is surrealism at its finest. Don't miss it.

The Meteorit is open daily from 10 am to 8 pm. Admission is DM15/10, and children under 1.35m get in free. Take tram No 106 to Katzenbruch.

Zeche Zollverein
One of the most accomplished conversions from industrial site to multi-use facility is the Zeche Zollverein (☎ 301 05 22), Gelsenkirchener Strasse 181. The red-brick complex, built in 1932 in Bauhaus style and once called the most beautiful mine in the world, was the last in Essen to close (in 1986). It is now a creative centre with artist studios, exhibit spaces and offices, as well as a performance venue.

The turbine building houses a superb restaurant (see Places to Eat), but the top draw is the **Design Centre Nordrhein-Westfalen** (☎ 30 10 40) in the ex-boiler-house, a showcase of the latest and best in international industrial design. It's a perfect marriage of space and function, conceived and realised by British architect Sir Norman Foster (who also redesigned the Reichstag in Berlin). Exhibit spaces are integrated into a four storey maze of original machinery: bathtubs and bike helmets balance on grated walkways, faucets dangle from snakelike heating ducts, and an entire bedroom perches atop a large oven. Walking around here feels like exploring the set of phantasmagoric sci-fi flick. It's bizarre, surprising and absolutely fascinating. The centre is open daily from 10 am to 6 pm, but is closed Monday (DM12/6, free if under 12 years of age).

A more traditional attraction is **Museum Zollverein**, an exploration of the mine itself. When active, about 12,000 tons of coal were unearthed here daily. Models explain the process and all the machinery is on view. Guided two-hour tours (German only) run Saturday at 2 pm, and Sunday at 11 am, and 2, 3 and 4 pm. Admission is DM8/5,

Hanover's Neues Rathaus enjoys commanding views over the Masch Pond.

One of Hanover's many parks and gardens

The original section of the Hamburg Kunsthalle

The prominent St Michaeliskirche, Hamburg

Hamburg's first archbishop, Ansgar

Harry's Hamburger Hafenbasar

Art imitates life: a fishwife and fishmonger get down to business at the Fischmarkt, Hamburg

and free if under 12. The best time to come is for the night tour at 7 pm on Fridays.

Zeche Zollverein is reached by tram No 107 from the Hauptbahnhof.

Villa Hügel

The Ruhr flows through Essen's southern suburbs, where it becomes the **Baldeney See**, a reservoir popular for windsurfing, sailing and rowing. A series of parks and forests fringes its northern shore. One of them contains **Villa Hügel** (1873; ☎ 42 25 59), the mansion inhabited by the Krupp dynasty until 1945. A two-part museum occupies the southern wing. The exhibit on the ground floor showcases the latest Krupp products and can easily be skipped. The upper floor, though, contains a fascinating family and company chronicle, starting with its beginning in 1811. The company's leading role in the manufacturing of guns, cannons and other military equipment, while not emphasised, is included as well. Panelling is in German only, though a free English-language brochure is usually available.

In the adjacent wing, you can stroll through the same generous salons, halls and galleries where the Krupps once received royalty and the Nazi party elite. Note the carved wooden ceilings and grand staircase that leads to a ballroom beneath a dramatic glass vault. Concerts are held here on occasion, and every two years, the entire estate hosts an internationally acclaimed exhibit. The lavish park is a pleasant place for a picnic or relaxing. The park and villa are open daily except Monday (DM1.50). Take S-Bahn No 6 to Essen-Hügel.

Werden

Now a suburb of Essen, Werden celebrated its 1200th anniversary in 1996 and still maintains a village atmosphere with a car-free centre of cobbled lanes flanked by half-timbered houses. Students of the Folkwang arts school (see Entertainment) fill the many pubs, cafes and restaurants, and the DJH hostel is here as well. Werden was built around the **Abbey of St Liudger** (1175), perched on a knoll at Brückstrasse 54 and

named after the Frisian missionary who is buried here. Architecturally a transition from Romanesque to Gothic, its interior is now largely baroque. The treasury (DM2) contains a hauntingly beautiful bronze crucifix from 1060.

Just north of here **St Lucius**, considered the oldest parish church north of the Alps, dates back to 1063 but was completely restored in 1965.

S-Bahn No 6 goes straight to Werden from the Hauptbahnhof.

Places to Stay

Essen has two camping grounds: the riverside **Stadtcamping Essen-Werden** (☎ 49 29 78, Im Löwental 67), near the Essen-Werden train station (S-Bahn No 6); and **Camping Manfred Erdhüter** (☎ 40 20 07, Hardenbergufer 369), on the southern lakeshore.

Also in Werden is the newly renovated **DJH Hostel** (☎ 49 11 63, Pastoratsberg 2) which charges DM22.50/27.50 for juniors/seniors. From Werden station, take bus No 190 in the direction of Ruhrlandklinik, or cross the Ruhr and walk uphill for 10 minutes. For private rooms, contact **B&B Martina Dietrich** (☎ 02323-133 53).

The tourist office operates a free hotel-booking service, though Essen is miserably devoid of budget options. **Ibis Hotel** (☎ 242 80, fax 2428600, Hollestrasse 50) by the station often has special rates, with singles/doubles under DM100. The **Hotel Zum Deutschen Haus** (☎ 23 29 89, fax 23 06 92, Kastanienallee 16) in the centre charges DM90/150 for simple digs with private bath. The plush **Behr's Parkhotel** (☎ 77 90 95, fax 78 98 16, Alfredstrasse 118) has a friendly owner and an integrated pub with occasional jazz jams. Rooms cost from DM110/140. Artistic types might be drawn to **Mintrops Burghotel** (☎ 57 17 10, fax 571 71 47, Schwarzensteinweg 81), where gorgeous rooms start at DM140/205.

Places to Eat

Skip Essen's city centre and head straight to the Rüttenscheid district ('Rü' for short), south of the station. Here pubs and bars rub shoulders with restaurants of all kinds, including **Bahnhof Süd** (☎ 23 65 75, *Rellinghauser Strasse 175)* in a former train station. There's a nonsmoking section, a beer garden and a menu with inexpensive pub fare. Vegetarians should try **Zodiac** (☎ 77 12 12, *Witteringstrasse 41)*, which offers 12 dishes from 12 countries in a jungle-like environment (evenings only, closed Thursday).

Click am See (☎ 48 08 49), on An der Kampmannsbrücke, serves French cuisine and excellent salads. In winter (closed Thursday) you can sit inside by the fireplace; in summer (open daily) there's a lakeside beer garden.

Essen's most spectacular, eccentric and stylish restaurant is the **Casino Zollverein** (☎ 83 02 40, *Gelsenkirchener Strasse 181)* in the converted turbine building of the former mine. The chef marries new German cuisine with typical local ingredients and charges DM18 to DM40 for mains. If that's too much, just enjoy the ambience over a drink. Make reservations (closed Monday).

Entertainment

Classic and contemporary theatre is presented at the **Grillo-Theater** (☎ 812 22 00), on Theaterplatz, off Kettwiger Strasse in the city centre, while the **Aalto Theater** (☎ 812 22 00, *Rolandstrasse 10)* is the main venue for opera, ballet and musicals.

Choreographer Pina Bausch and actor Jürgen Prochnow (*Das Boot*) are just two alumni of the prestigious **Folkwang Schule für Music, Theater und Tanz** (☎ 490 32 31, *Klemensborn 39)* in Werden. Current students can often be seen in performance at the school's home, the baroque former residence of the abbots of Werden (DM10/5).

Another crowd-pleaser is the **GOP Varieté** (☎ 247 93 93, *Rottstrasse 30)* where jugglers, acrobats, ventriloquists and other artists seize the stage (DM25 to DM65).

The **Zeche Carl** (☎ 834 44 10, *Wilhelm-Nieswandt-Allee 100)*, in the northern suburb of Altenessen (take tram No 101 or 106 to Karlsplatz), is an old mine reborn as a trendy cultural centre with live concerts, discos, cabaret, theatre and art exhibits.

Essen's premier techno temple is the labyrinthine **Mudia Art** (☎ 23 50 28, *Frohnhauser Strasse 75)* in an old factory (Saturday only). If you pass muster at the door – and are willing to drop DM20 – you'll plunge into a world of scantily clad go-go girls and a glass-encased naked woman holding court in one of the men's rooms.

Getting There & Away

Train IC trains leave in all directions hourly or every other hour for such cities as Frankfurt (DM91, 3¼ hours) and Hamburg (DM111, 3½ hours). The ICE to Berlin (DM168, 3¾ hours) comes through hourly. Essen is also efficiently linked to other cities in the Ruhrgebiet, as well as to Düsseldorf and Cologne, via the VRR network.

Bus Eurolines offers regular bus service primarily to Eastern European cities – eg to Warsaw (daily, DM100/170 one-way/return) and Prague (twice weekly, DM80/140). It also goes to Paris four times a week (DM85/153). For information and tickets, go to the Bahntouristik (☎ 182 41 88) office at the Hauptbahnhof's north exit. Buses leave from the stop outside the Hauptbahnhof's south exit.

Car & Motorcycle Essen is well connected in all directions via autobahns A40 and A52, but because of heavy commuter traffic these roads often slow to a crawl during rush hour.

Ride Services The ADM Mitfahrzentrale (☎ 194 40) is at Freiheit 4 outside the Hauptbahnhof's south exit.

BOCHUM
☎ 0234 • pop 394,000
Industrial cities are not exactly the stuff of heartfelt anthems, but that didn't stop singer-songwriter Herbert Grönemeyer from highlighting the assets and charms of his home town in the song *Bochum* (1984; also see 20th Century Music, under Arts, in the Facts about Germany chapter). The song not only boosted Grönemeyer's career

throughout Germany but also helped turn around people's perception about this Ruhrgebiet city, located halfway between Essen and Dortmund. With the opening of the musical *Starlight Express* in 1988, Bochum gained a cultural icon that has since brought thousands of people from throughout Europe to the modest city on the Ruhr. Add to that a vibrant nightlife, fine theatre, two superb technical museums and a lush recreational area (complete with medieval castles and a lake) and you have a city that makes for a surprisingly worthwhile stop.

Bochum is also the home of the Ruhr-Universität, which opened in 1965 as the Ruhrgebiet's first, and today has around 35,000 students. Along with a large Opel car factory, it is one of the region's major employers.

Orientation & Information

Bochum's almost completely pedestrianised city centre lies within an irregular loop made up of segments all ending in 'ring'. The Hauptbahnhof and Busbahnhof are on its south-eastern edge. The main shopping drag, Kortumstrasse, cuts through the entire centre. At its southern end it encompasses parts of the Bermudadreieck (Bermuda Triangle) pub district concentrated within the area between Südring and Konrad-Adenauer-Platz, about 200m west of the station. Bochum's sightseeing attractions are scattered across town but easily reached by public transport.

The tourist office (☎ 96 30 20, fax 963 02 55) is to the right of the Hauptbahnhof north exit and is open weekdays from 9 am to 5.30 pm and Saturday from 10 am to 1 pm. Banks in the city centre include a Sparkasse at Dr-Ruer-Platz and a Deutsche Bank at Husemannplatz 5a. The main post office is behind the Hauptbahnhof at Wittener Strasse 2. There's a Cyberb@r at the Know House at Kortumstrasse 73. Bochum's Web page is at www.bochum.de (in English and German).

Right on Kortumstrasse is Mayersche Buchhandlung, an excellent bookstore

stocked with English novels and Lonely Planet titles as well. There's a coin-operated laundrette at Südring 34 that is open daily from 6 am to 11 pm. For after-hours medical assistance, call ☎ 192 92; for dental emergencies, ring ☎ 77 00 55. Police headquarters (☎ 90 90) are at Uhlandstrasse 35.

Deutsches Bergbaumuseum

It may not seem a crowd-pleaser, but Bochum's German Museum of Mining (☎ 587 70), Am Bergbaumuseum 28, has one of the finest and most comprehensive exhibits on the subject around. The complex is easily spotted by its turquoise 68m mining tower, which can be ascended (DM2) for bird's-eye views of the city and surrounds. Far more unique and elucidating, though, is a trip *beneath* the earth's surface for a first-hand look at tunnels and mine shafts, as well as the machinery miners used and the working conditions they had to endure.

The museum exhibit itself is huge and imaginative and touches on every aspect of the industry. Of particular interest is the section on the role of women in mining. It's open Tuesday to Friday from 8.30 am to 5.30 pm, and weekends from 10 am to 4 pm (DM6/5). Take the U35 from the Hauptbahnhof.

Eisenbahnmuseum

In Bochum's southern suburb of Dahlhausen, this wonderfully nostalgic train museum (☎ 49 25 16) documents the evolution of trains. Based in a historic train station, its collection includes 160 vehicles, including 16 original steam locomotives. Between April and October, the museum organises rides through the Ruhr Valley aboard some of its oldest 'iron horses'.

The museum is located at Dr-C-Otto-Strasse 191 and is open Wednesday and Friday from 10 am to 5 pm, Sunday to 1 pm, and in summer to 3 pm (DM6.50/ 3.50). Rides are DM10/17 one-way/return (DM6/10 if under 12). Take tram No 318 or bus No 345 to Dahlhausen Bahnhof, then walk for 1300m or take the historic

Schweineschnäuzchen (little pig snout!) rail-bus shuttle to the museum grounds.

Other Sights

A couple of historic sights are located south of the centre, on the Ruhr, along the boundary with the town of Hattingen. **Burg Blankenstein**, resting on a hillside above the river, is the place where Bochum was given its town rights in 1321. It is open daily and entry is free. The view from its 30m tower gives you a good impression of how green the Ruhrgebiet can be. Right on the Ruhr banks along Kemnader Strasse, **Wasserburg Kemnade** (☎ 02324-302 68) is a moated Renaissance castle. Inside, there's a Gothic chapel, a Knights' Hall, and collections of Gobelins and musical instruments. It's open from November to April, Tuesday to Friday from 11 am to 5 pm, and weekends from 10 am. Opening hours from May to October are Tuesday from 9 am to 3 pm, Wednesday to Friday from 1 to 7 pm, and weekends from 11 am to 6 pm. Entry is free. Bus No C31 from the Hauptbahnhof stops at both Haus Kemnade and Burg Blankenstein.

Places to Stay

If you ever wanted to set up camp 'under a bridge', there's *Stolle* (☎ 800 38), on Ruhrbrücke, by the Ruhr river. The nearest hostel is the DJH Hostel in Essen-Werden (see Places to Stay in the Essen section).

If you don't mind monastic simplicity, check into the *Kolpinghaus* (☎ 601 90, Maximilian-Kolbe-Strasse 14), where singles with shared shower cost DM48 and doubles are DM76.

The business-style *Ibis Hotel* has two branches; one right inside the Hauptbahnhof (☎ 914 30, fax 68 07 78), the other immediately behind (☎ 333 11, fax 333 18 67). Singles/doubles at either cost DM123/138. If you can spend just a little more, stay at the *Art Hotel Tucholsky* (☎ 135 43, fax 687 84 21, Victoriastrasse 73), right in the Bermudadreieck pub quarter. Modern and stylish rooms with shower and WC range from DM80/140 to DM95/160.

Places to Eat

The restaurants in Bochum's centre seem to cater largely to a younger crowd. Nevertheless, traditional German restaurants are nicely represented with *Altes Brauhaus Rietkötter* (☎ 163 64, Grosse Beckstrasse 7). Otherwise, congenial cafes and bistros abound. One long-time favourite is *Café Ferdinand* (☎ 30 14 01, Ferdinandstrasse 44) behind the Hauptbahnhof. The decor is part Viennese coffee house, part modern and the food surprises with its French touches; it is especially popular for breakfast and at the close of the adjacent Saturday market.

The Bermudadreieck brims with fast-food places, but for a real Bochum experience, head to the *Dönninghaus* snack stand (☎ 68 42 70, Kortumstrasse 14) to indulge in a heartburn-inducing but delicious *currywurst* (sort of a bratwurst, served sliced in a spicy sauce and sprinkled with curry powder). Grönemeyer even made a song about it.

To find out that Turkish food is more than doner kebab, try the classy *Kokille* (☎ 666 11, Südring 24), which offers creative gourmet food, with mains costing DM20 and up. *Tucholsky* (see Art Hotel Tucholsky in Places to Stay) regularly draws a thirty-and-up crowd of artists and actors drawn by the Art Deco ambience, the reasonably priced menu and a good hot breakfast selection. The yuppy-ish *Zentral* (☎ 68 65 64, Luisenstrasse 15-17), with its large bar and wooden floors, is also a favourite among Italophiles.

Entertainment

Bochum's lively nightlife draws people from around the Ruhrgebiet and as far away as Cologne and the Sauerland.

Pubs & Bars Bochumers are serious pub and bar crawlers. As soon as the last winter storms have blown through, the Bermuda Triangle begins to look like an Italian piazza as life moves into the car-free streets. Anyone can find a favourite bar here. Popular candidates include *Mandragora*

(☎ 642 18, Adenauerplatz 1), a veritable scene 'dinosaur' that's far from extinct. It offers delicious crepes and the beer garden is an institution. For the hipper-than-thou, there's also the *Café Konkret* (☎ 670 70, *Kortumstrasse 19*).

Lately, a new scene has sprung up around the Schauspielhaus. The buzzing *Freibad* (☎ 31 21 35, *Clemensstrasse 8*) has a billiard room, a loud bar area and a comfy lounge with old theatre chairs. All this appeals to a mixed crowd, including a large gay and lesbian contingent.

About a 10 minute walk from here – and worth it – is *Stalowaja Majakowskij* (☎ 33 22 60, *Hattinger Strasse 103*), a stylish lounge/restaurant that serves borscht to blinis and other Russian fare for around DM20. The bar draws a hip, chatty and slightly older crowd who sip cocktails or coffee in a low-key living room atmosphere.

Discos & Clubs Live music, wild dance parties and a decent restaurant are part of the repertory of the *Zeche* (☎ 720 03, *Prinz Regent Strasse 50-60*), in a converted coal mining building. *Bahnhof Langendreer* (☎ 266 11 14, *Walbaumweg 108*), in a former train station in the eastern suburb of Langendreer, has a similarly eclectic program. *Tarm-Center* (☎ 45 90 70, *Rombacher Hütte 6-10*) and *Prater* (☎ 54 05 50, *Dorstener Strasse 425*) are hugely popular high-tech 'meat-market'-type discos.

Theatre The *Schauspielhaus* (☎ 333 31 11, *Königsallee 15*) was once one of the most innovative stages in Germany but has been in decline since the mid-1980s. Tickets cost from DM14 to DM39. The vastly superior Bochumer Symphoniker also play here, but performances are usually sold out.

Meanwhile, independent theatres have gained popularity. These include the *Prinz Regent Theater* (☎ 77 11 17) in the Zeche complex (see Discos & Clubs) and the *Theater Ecce Homo* (☎ 0231-953 61 85, *Hiltroper Strasse 13*).

The Andrew Lloyd Webber musical extravaganza *Starlight Express* has been playing (in German) in its custom-designed hall (☎ 01805-44 44, *Am Stadionring 24*) for more than a decade. Tickets range from DM70 to DM180.

Getting There & Away

There are frequent train links to other Ruhrgebiet cities from Bochum via the VRR network (see Getting Around at the start of the Ruhrgebiet section). Bochum is also an IC train stop with regular service in all directions. Regional trains to Cologne (DM27, one hour) and IC trains to Münster (DM26.60, 45 minutes) leave several times daily. Eurolines buses make daily trips to Warsaw (DM100/170) and twice weekly runs to London (DM101/182).

Bochum is served by a number of autobahns, including the A40 and A43, as well as the B51.

The Mitfahrzentrale (☎ 377 94) is at Ferdinandstrasse 20.

Getting Around

For prices on public transport, see Getting Around at the beginning of the Ruhrgebiet section. For a taxi, try calling ☎ 605 11 or ☎ 96 45 55. The Fahrradstation (☎ 68 43 40) inside the Hauptbahnhof rents out and repairs bicycles. Rental per day is DM4, with a DM50 deposit.

DORTMUND

☎ 0231 • pop 599,000

Dortmund is the second-largest city in the Ruhrgebiet and is celebrated for its six huge breweries – Ritter, Union, Kronen, Actien, Thier and Stifts – which collectively make 600 million litres of the amber brew every year. (Only the US city of Milwaukee and the Warsteiner brewery in the Sauerland produce more.) Historically, Dortmund goes back to 880, when a settlement sprang up around a Saxon castle (today's Hohensyburg) conquered by Charlemagne. In 1220, Dortmund became a free imperial city and a member of the Hanseatic League shortly thereafter.

The location on the Hellweg, an important trade route, brought the town prosperity.

The Thirty Years' War eventually plunged it into an economic slumber from which it awoke only with the onset of industrialisation in the early 19th century. Today it's an enjoyable down-to-earth place with a lively cultural and pub scene and several first-class sights and museums, as well as a university with 20,000 students.

Orientation & Information

Most attractions are located within an area bounded by a ring road and made up of segments ending in 'wall'. The Hauptbahnhof and the Busbahnhof are on Königswall on the north side of the ring. Cross Königswall from the southern exit of the Hauptbahnhof, then take any road to the pedestrianised Westenhellweg (which turns into Ostenhellweg), the main artery that bisects Dortmund's circular centre.

The tourist office (☎ 502 21 74, fax 16 35 93, email tourist-info@dortmund.de) is opposite the Hauptbahnhof Süd (South) exit at Königswall 18a, and is open weekdays from 9 am to 6 pm, and Saturday to 1 pm.

City centre banks include the Sparkasse at Freistuhl 2 and Commerzbank at Hansaplatz 2. The main post office is on Kurfürstenstrasse about 75m to the left of the Hauptbahnhof Nord (North) exit. It's open weekdays from 8 am to 6 pm, and Saturday from 9 am to 1 pm; it has a public fax-phone and credit card ATM. For Internet access, there's a Cyberb@r in the Karstadt Technikhaus at Kampstrasse 1. A Web site (in English) is at www.dortmund.de.

For a good selection of English books go to C L Krüger (☎ 540 10), Westenhellweg 9, or Universitätsbuchhandlung at Vogelpothsweg 85.

Walking Tour

Dortmund's main attractions are conveniently grouped within walking distance from the Hauptbahnhof. Museums are open 10 am to 5 pm, closed Monday.

The quasi-trapezoidal glass structure opposite the station's south exit contains the city library as well as the tourist office. Head up the staircase to the Gothic **Petrikirche**

(1353) on the pedestrianised shopping artery Westenhellweg. The show stopper here is the massive 7.4m x 5.6m altar carved in Antwerp in around 1520, with 633 gilded figurines and 54 pictures depicting the Passion of Christ and the Legend of the Cross.

You can then stroll east past the historic **Krügerpassage**, an arcade built in 1912 in neo-Renaissance style, to the sombre **Reinoldikirche** (1280), named after the city's patron St Reinoldus. According to legend, the church bells erupted in a wild peel after he had been martyred and the carriage containing his dead body rolled to Dortmund, stopping in the spot now occupied by the church. Inside is a life-size statue of the saint opposite another one of Charlemagne. Especially spectacular is the late Gothic **altar** (ask nicely in the sacristy for a close-up look). Also note the strangely outward-leaning walls and the landmark 100m steeple.

The last in this trio of churches is the **Marienkirche** (12th century) across Ostenhellweg, which is considered the oldest vaulted church in Westphalia. The star exhibit here is the **Marienaltar**, with a delicate triptych (1420) by Conrad von Soest who, despite his name, was actually born in Dortmund. In the northern nave is the equally impressive **Berswordt Altar** (1385). Also note the rather frivolous wood reliefs on the choir stalls and the ephemeral St Mary statue (1230).

From here head south along Kleppingstrasse, then east on Viktoriastrasse to Ostwall and the **Museum am Ostwall** (☎ 502 32 47), Ostwall 7. Renowned for its collection of German expressionists, it also has works by avant-garde artists like Christo and Beuys (DM4/1).

Follow Ostwall, then Schwanenwall north back towards the Hauptbahnhof. At the corner with Hansastrasse is the **Museum für Kunst und Kulturgeschichte** (Museum of Art & Cultural History; ☎ 502 55 22). It displays an eclectic mixture of pre-1900 paintings, arts and crafts, graphics, photography, archaeology and municipal history over the seven floors of a former bank in Art Deco style (DM4/2).

Go through the station to the north exit where, just beyond the cinema complex, is the entrance to the **Mahn- und Gedenkstätte Steinwache** (Exhortation and Memorial Site Steinwache; ☎ 502 50 02), Steinstrasse 50. This is a memorial exhibit about Third Reich atrocities housed in a notorious former Gestapo prison once known as the 'hellhole of Germany'. About 30,000 men and women were incarcerated, tortured and killed here. The cell block complex miraculously escaped WWII bombs and is completely intact. A free English-language pamphlet is available. Admission is free.

Industrial Museums

As a city of industry, it's only natural that Dortmund has its share of museums inspired by industrial themes. A visit to any of these makes a nice change from the usual 'church-castle-art museum' circuit and opens up different perspectives on German culture and history. Museums are closed on Monday and admission is free.

At the **Brauerei Museum** (☎ 502 48 50), Märkische Strasse 48, you can learn all about the history of brewing beer. Opening hours are from 10 am to 5 pm. Take U41, U45 or U47 to Markgrafenstrasse.

The coal mine Zeche Zollern II/IV at Grubenweg 5 in the suburb of Bövinghausen closed in 1966 and is now one of eight sites of the **Westfälisches Industriemuseum** (Westphalian Industrial Museum; ☎ 696 10). It's noted for its neo-Gothic features and an impressive Art Nouveau machine hall. An exhibit documents regional working and living conditions at the start of the 20th century. The grounds are accessible daily from 10 am to 6 pm, though the machine hall only opens weekends. Take S-Bahn to Dortmund-Marten Süd, then bus No 462.

Places to Stay

Dortmund has a *camping ground* (☎ 77 43 74, Syburger Dorfstrasse 62) in the suburb of Syburg (take bus No 444) but no youth hostel. The tourist office makes free room reservations and, in some cases, has negotiated special rates with hotels.

If you don't mind simple rooms with shared facilities, you might try the cute *Pension Cläre Fritz* (☎ 57 15 23, fax 57 96 23, Reinoldistrasse 6), which charges DM55/100 for single/double rooms. Nearby is the *Stadthotel Dortmund* (☎ 57 10 00, fax 57 71 94, Reinoldistrasse 14), where you pay DM100/130 for rooms with private bath. Recently renovated, the *Hotel City-Wall* (☎ 14 00 12/13, fax 14 56 09, Hoher Wall 2) offers good value with its 20 modern rooms with private bath, TV and telephone at DM89/135. Friendly and pleasant with smallish but new rooms is the *Stiftshof* (☎ 524701, fax 524702, Stiftsstrasse 5), where costs are DM89/119.

Places to Eat

Not-so-bitter Bitterbier and hearty meat-based fare from DM12 to DM30 are what draws an intergenerational crowd to *Hövel's Hausbrauerei* (☎ 14 10 44, Hoher Wall 5). In summer, the beer garden is a popular hang-out. For a fun ambience in an old-time interior, head to *Pfefferkorn* (☎ 14 36 44, Hoher Wall 38), in the shadow of the former Union brewery. Every budget and taste is catered for on a menu where big salads (around DM12.50) are as much at home as salmon steaks (DM30) and vegetable platters (DM15).

In the centre is the nostalgic *Am Alten Markt* (☎ 57 22 17, Markt 3), where you can indulge in Westphalian specialities like *Dicke Bohnen* (lima bean stew), *Wirsingroulade* (cabbage wrapped around spicy ground meat) and *Heringstipp* (marinated herring in cream sauce), all around DM14. Nearby, the self-service *Marché Mövenpick* (☎ 57 92 25, Kleppingstrasse 9-11) has several buffets and an inexpensive lunch menu.

In an unassuming setting about 10 minutes walk north of the Hauptbahnhof is the Portuguese *Ti Zé* (☎ 728 16 28, Altonaer Strasse 2), which has superb fresh fish and other dishes at a reasonable DM15 to DM20 for a main course.

The Kaufhof department store on Westenhellweg has a *food court* and an *Aldi* supermarket in the basement.

Entertainment

Discos & Clubs The *Stadtpalais* (☎ 165 54 30, Hansastrasse 5-7) is Dortmund's newest multi-sound dance temple with five different sections offering everything from techno to Top 40. It's open Friday and Saturday. The city's mainstay is *Live Station* (☎ 16 17 83), right inside the Hauptbahnhof, where you can hit the dance floor to soul, funk and hip hop. There are also about 100 live gigs a year. It's open Friday to Sunday.

Le Fou (☎ 81 00 24, Nordmarkt 26) in the Nordstadt quarter is a classy cocktail and dance bar for post-teenies that plays everything but techno (or so they say). It's closed Monday.

Nearby is *Jazzclub Domicil* (☎ 57 80 02, Leopoldstrasse 60), Dortmund's top jazz address for those older than 25. Concerts, which run the gamut from modern and new jazz to Afro and Latin rhythms, are usually on Friday or Saturday. Call ahead.

Theatre & Classical Music Dortmund's municipal theatre stages drama and musicals at the *Schauspielhaus (Hiltropwall 15)*, while operas and classical concerts are performed at the *Opernhaus* in Hansastrasse. One box office (☎ 502 72 22) takes care of both. Occupying a converted cinema from the 1950s is the popular *Luna Varieté & Theater (☎ 77 31 96, Harkortstrasse 57a)* where shows revolve around magic, cabaret, transvestites and music. Tickets range from DM19 to DM53, with about one-third off for students.

Getting There & Away

Dortmund's Hauptbahnhof is among Germany's biggest stations, with IC trains leaving every hour in all directions, for instance to Frankfurt (DM97, 3½ hours). There are also regional and local trains running even more frequently.

Eurolines has a daily bus service to Paris (DM90/162) and Warsaw (DM95/160) and twice weekly to London (DM101/182).

Dortmund is served by the A1, A2 and A45. The B1 runs right through the city and is the link between the A40 to Essen and the A44 to Kassel. It's very busy and often clogged. The Mitfahrzentrale office (☎ 194 44) is at Grüne Strasse 3.

Getting Around

For public transport, see Getting Around at the start of the Ruhrgebiet section. If you need to catch a taxi, try calling ☎ 14 44 44 or ☎ 194 10. ADFC (☎ 13 66 85), Hausmannstrasse 22, on the corner of Saarlandstrasse, rents out bikes.

CENTRO & GASOMETER

At the CentrO shopping mall (☎ 0208-828 20 55) in Oberhausen, in the northern Ruhrgebiet, a DM1.6 billion investment has resulted in an amusement park environment where 'shopping becomes an experience', to quote promoters. There are more than 200 shops and some 20 restaurants (including a Planet Hollywood branch).

While the grown-ups head to the shops, kids are entertained at the adjacent theme park, which features a pirate ship, a water playground, an English maze and other diversions. It's open March to October from noon to 6 pm, and weekends from 11 am (free). Also part of the complex are a nine-screen cinema and a 11,500-seat arena with top programming.

Right next to the mall looms the barrel-shaped **Gasometer** (gas tank, 1929; ☎ 0208-850 37 30), now one of Germany's most unique exhibit spaces. Shows, which usually run from spring to autumn, have included Christo and Jeanne-Claude's project 'The Wall', which bisected the vast interior with a stack of colourful oil drums. Accessible year round is a glass elevator that whisks you to a 117m platform, from where you have views over the entire western Ruhrgebiet.

Getting There & Away

CentrO is at Centroallee 267 in Oberhausen. Trains go from all Ruhrgebiet cities to Oberhausen's train station from which buses and trams make frequent departures to the complex. By car, you must get off at the Neue Mitte exit off the A42.

LANDSCHAFTSPARK DUISBURG-NORD

Another successful conversion of a 'cathedral of industry' is in Duisburg in the western Ruhrgebiet, where a blast furnace has been turned into an adventure playground. You can free-climb its walls or clamber around the giant steel tubes. After nightfall, a spectacular light show envelops the complex, making it look like a giant alien spacecraft. It's open from April to September, Friday to Sunday from dusk to 2 am. Concerts are occasionally held against this dramatic backdrop. The park is at Emscherstrasse 71. For information, call ☎ 0203-42 01 51.

The Deutsche Alpenverein (German Alpine Association; ☎ 0203-42 81 20) has a branch here.

WARNER BROS MOVIE WORLD

This sprawling amusement park – 'Hollywood in Germany', as the brochures call it – is the Ruhrgebiet's answer to EuroDisney. Opened by the movie giant Warner Brothers in 1996, it's a collection of thrill rides, restaurants, shops and shows providing 'nonstop entertainment'. Attractions include the Batman Show, the Lethal Weapon rollercoaster and the Bermudadreieck water ride. In 1999, a wooden roller coaster – the Riddler's Revenge – and the kiddie-ride – Looney Tunes Tea Party – were added.

Warner Bros Movie World (☎ 02045-89 98 99) is open daily from 10 am (in summer from 9 am) between late March and early November. Closing times range from 6 to 9 pm, depending on the time of year. Admission is DM38, or DM33 for children aged four to 11.

Getting There & Away

The park is located at Warner Allee 1 in Bottrop-Kirchhellen, about 15km north of Essen. If you arrive by train, you must get off at the Feldhausen stop. There are frequent direct connections from Essen and Oberhausen (both DM6, 30 minutes). If you're driving, take the Kirchhellen exit off the A31.

Westphalia

MÜNSTER
☎ 0251   • pop 264,000

Münster is an attractive university town and administrative centre in the flatlands of northern Westphalia, an hour's drive north of the Ruhrgebiet cities. Patrician townhouses and baroque city palaces characterise the Altstadt, but perhaps more than anything it's the bicycles – called *Leeze* in local dialect – that give the city its flair. On any given day, some 100,000 of them wheel through Münster's streets, making liberal use of special driving regulations and numerous designated bike paths and parking lots. Germany's fourth-largest university – and its 55,000 students – keep the cobwebs out of this otherwise conservative and Catholic town.

Münster got its start as a monastery founded in 794 by the Frisian missionary Liudger to help Charlemagne teach the obstreperous Saxons a thing or two about Christianity. In 805, Münster was made a bishopric and, in 1170, it got its town rights. In 1648, the Thirty Years' War concluded here (and in nearby Osnabrück, see Lower Saxony) with the signing of the Peace of Westphalia. During WWII, Münster received more than its share of bombs, but in rebuilding, the city centre's historic layout was faithfully recreated.

Orientation & Information

Most of the main sights are within the confines of the easy-to-walk Altstadt. The Schloss, now the university headquarters, is just west of the city centre, while the Hauptbahnhof is to the east. The Busbahnhof is right outside the west exit of the Hauptbahnhof. To get to the centre within minutes, head north-west on Windthorststrasse as you exit the station. The main recreational area is around the Aasee lake, southwest of the Altstadt.

The tourist office (☎ 492 27 10 or ☎ 194 33, fax 492 77 42), Klemensstrasse 9, is open weekdays from 9 am to 6 pm, Saturday to 1 pm and makes free room reservations. If

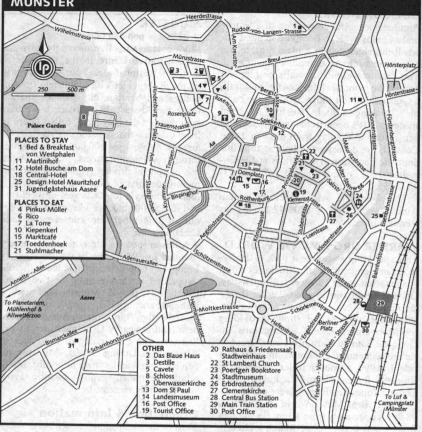

MÜNSTER

0   250   500 m

Palace Garden

PLACES TO STAY
1 Bed & Breakfast
   von Westphalen
11 Martinihof
12 Hotel Busche am Dom
18 Central-Hotel
25 Design Hotel Mauritzhof
31 Jugendgästehaus Aasee

PLACES TO EAT
4 Pinkus Müller
6 Rico
7 La Torre
10 Kiepenkerl
15 Marktcafé
17 Toeddenhoek
21 Stuhlmacher

To Planetarium,
Mühlenhof &
Allwetterzoo

Aasee

To Luf &
Campingplatz
Münster

OTHER
2 Das Blaue Haus
3 Destille
5 Cavete
8 Schloss
9 Überwasserkirche
13 Dom St Paul
14 Landesmuseum
16 Post Office
19 Tourist Office
20 Rathaus & Friedenssaal;
   Stadtweinhaus
22 St Lamberti Church
23 Poertgen Bookstore
24 Stadtmuseum
26 Erbdrostenhof
27 Clemenskirche
28 Central Bus Station
29 Main Train Station
30 Post Office

you read German, the brochure *Münster Aktuell* (DM1) is handy, with details on events,
hotels, sights and services. English-language
tours depart on Saturday at 11 am from the
Rathaus, from May to October (DM6).

Banks abound in the city centre, but the
Commerzbank in the Karstadt department
store on Salzstrasse is even open on Saturday to 4 pm.

Major post office branches are on Domplatz and just south of the Hauptbahnhof.
Both are open to 7 pm, Saturday to 2 pm.

The Poertgen Heinrich-Herdersche Buchhandlung at Salzstrasse 56 has an enormous
assortment of books over four floors, including a fair number of English and French
volumes.

Dom St Paul

The Dom's two massive towers match the
proportions of this 110m-long structure and
the enormous square it overlooks. The
three-nave construction was built in the
13th century on the cusp of the transition

from Romanesque to Gothic. Enter from the south through a portal, called the Paradies, festooned with magnificent sculptures of the 12 apostles. Once inside, you're greeted by a 5m **statue of St Christopher**, the patron saint of travellers (yes, that's a real tree branch in his left hand).

The cathedral's main attraction is the **astronomical clock** (1542) on the right side of the ambulatory. Look beneath the projecting pedestal in the gable of this 24 hour clock for a summary of its functions: it indicates the time, the position of the sun, the movement of the planets, and the calendar (with the Catholic holy days up to the year 2071). This was no mean feat in the year preceding the death of Copernicus.

The second chapel in the ambulatory contains the tomb of Clemens August Cardinal von Galen, who stood up to the Nazis in defending the right to display crucifixes in schools – a right outlawed in 1936. The cathedral treasury in the **Domkammer** can be reached via the cloister. It is closed Monday, Sunday morning and at lunchtime (DM1). The *pièce de résistance* is the 11th century gem-studded golden head reliquary of cathedral patron St Paul.

Around Domplatz

A few steps north-west of the Dom is the **Überwasserkirche** (also known as Liebfrauenkirche), a 14th century Gothic hall church with handsome stained-glass windows and an ornate square tower. Its name, which means 'Over the Water', was inspired by its location adjacent to Münster's tiny stream, the Aa, whose tree-lined promenade invites leisurely strolls.

In the 16th century, the iconoclastic Anabaptists (see St Lamberti Church later in this section) tore all sculptures out of this church, but fortunately many were saved and are now on view on the ground floor of the **Landesmuseum** (☎ 59 07 01), on the south-west corner of Domplatz. Head upstairs for an excellent display of the works of accomplished Westphalian painters, including Conrad von Soest and Hermann and Ludger tom Ring and other members of this

artistic family. Two rooms are dedicated to August Macke, a member of the Blue Rider group, an association of painters formed in Munich in the early 20th century that included Franz Marc, Paul Klee and Wassily Kandinsky. Opening hours are from 10 am to 6 pm, closed Monday (DM5/2); hours are longer during special exhibits.

Prinzipalmarkt

Münster's main artery is the Prinzipalmarkt, which is no longer a market but an upscale shopping street lined by stately townhouses with gabled facades that look down on the covered arcades of elegant boutiques and cafes.

The most majestic facade belongs to the **Rathaus**, begun in the late 12th century and enlarged and altered several times since. Inside is the Friedenssaal (☎ 492 27 24)

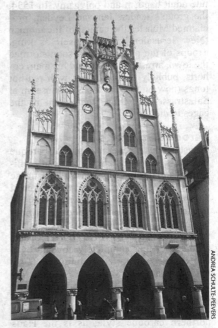

ANDREA SCHULTE-PEIVERS

The 12th century Rathaus has one of the most dramatic building facades in Münster.

where, in 1648, the Peace of Westphalia was signed, ending the calamitous Thirty Years' War. It's a spectacular hall with wood-panelled walls; note especially the elaborate carvings on the cabinet behind the mayor's table, with their clever mix of secular and religious themes. The open cabinet contains an incongruous display of the Goldener Hahn (golden rooster); a gilded silver container, as well as a slipper; and (gulp!) a mummified hand. The hall is open daily (DM1.50). As you exit, note the adjacent **Stadtweinhaus** (1615), once used for wine storage and now a part of the Rathaus.

Look north from here for a fine view of the late-Gothic **St Lamberti Church** (1450) and the three iron cages dangling from its slender openwork spire. These once held the dead bodies of the three leaders of the Anabaptists, a Protestant movement that sought to do away with money and to institute adult baptism and polygamy. In 1534, the group's leader, Jan van Leyden, proclaimed Münster the capital of the utopian 'New Jerusalem' with himself as king. Troops of the prince-bishop soon stormed the town, arrested Leyden and his main cohorts, publicly tortured them with red-hot tongs (now on view at the Stadtmuseum at Salzstrasse 28), then stuck them in the cages to die.

Baroque Buildings

Münster boasts several beautiful baroque buildings, most of them the work of architect Johann Conrad Schlaun. At Salzstrasse 38 in the Altstadt, you'll find the masterful **Erbdrostenhof** (1757), a town palace and former residence of the deputy prince-bishops. Nearby in Klemensstrasse is the small **Clemenskirche** (1753), which boasts a domed ceiling completely covered by a lavish fresco supported by turquoise faux-marble pillars. The **Schloss** (1773), the former residence of the prince-bishops and now the main university building, is another example of Schlaun's understated northern baroque style, as is the Haus Rüschhaus (see Münsterland Castles later in this chapter).

Aasee

South-west of the Altstadt, where the Aa flows into the Aasee, is a popular place for picnics and activities like sailing and windsurfing. On or near the lake shore are three more of Münster's attractions. On the northern lake end, the **Mühlenhof** (☎ 98 12 00), Theo-Breider-Weg 1, is an open-air museum of typical Westphalian buildings, including a mill and a bakery. It's open daily (DM5/3). The **Planetarium** (☎ 591 60 99) is at Sentruper Strasse 285 and has several shows daily except Monday (prices vary). On the western lake end is the **Allwetterzoo** (☎ 890 40), with more than 2000 animals, including dolphins and Asian elephants. It's open daily (DM18/9).

Places to Stay

Campingplatz Münster (☎ 31 19 82, fax 61 70 52, Laerer Werseufer 7) is open year round and is about 5km south-east of the city centre next to a public outdoor pool (bus No 320 or 330 to Kinnebrock). Tent space costs DM6 to DM10, plus DM7 per person.

Münster's modern hostel, the lakeside *Jugendgästehaus Aasee (☎ 53 24 70, fax 52 12 71, Bismarckallee 31)* charges DM39.50 in four-bed rooms and DM49.50 in two-bed rooms; sheets, towel and buffet breakfast are included. Take bus No 10 or 34 to Hoppendamm.

You pay even less if you can score one of the three doubles at *Bed & Breakfast von Westphalen (☎/fax 29 31 86, Rudolf-von-Langen-Strasse 8)* in the city centre, near the theatre. Showers and WC are shared, but charges are just DM60 per room. As for hotels, one of the cheapest is the traditional *Martinihof (☎ 41 86 20, fax 547 43, Hörsterstrasse 25)* with basic singles/doubles from DM75/120 and roomier ones with full bath for DM110/160. Super-central but quite old-fashioned is *Hotel Busche am Dom (☎ 464 44, Bogenstrasse 10)* with singles for DM70 to DM90 and doubles for DM130 to DM160. The pricier rooms have private baths.

Central-Hotel (☎ 51 01 50, fax 510 15 50, Aegidiistrasse 1) is owned by an avid art collector, which is reflected in the design.

Large rooms with modern furniture and private bath cost DM155 to DM185 for singles and DM195 to DM255 for doubles. Another property with an artsy touch is *Design Hotel Mauritzhof (☎ 417 20, fax 466 86, Eisenbahnstrasse 15-17)*, which charges DM185/235.

Places to Eat
The quarter to go for a bite, a beer or a full meal is the Kuhviertel, just north of the Dom. This is where you'll find the classic student pubs *Cavete (☎ 457 00, Kreuzstrase 38)*, *Das Blaue Haus (☎ 421 51, Kreuzstrasse 16)* and *Destille (☎ 437 26, Kuhstrasse 10)*, all of which have budget-priced dishes and a bustling ambience.

Those seeking local colour and traditional Westphalian food have plenty to choose from. Low-key and rustic are *Pinkus Müller (☎ 451 51, Kreuzstrasse 4)*, a brewery/restaurant with a network of wood-panelled rooms; and *Toeddenhoek (☎ 431 56, Rothenburg 41)*. A la carte items start at DM15, though daily dishes go for around DM10. Both are closed on Sunday.

More upscale food is served at the pretty but stultifying *Kiepenkerl (☎ 403 35, Spiekerhof 45)*. It's closed Tuesday. Equally historical but livelier is *Stuhlmacher (☎ 448 77, Prinzipalmarkt 6-7)*.

A considerably more contemporary atmosphere reigns at the *Marktcafé (☎ 575 85, Domplatz 7)*, a hall-like space with outdoor seating for the see-and-be-seen crowd. The food is excellent, and the all-you-can-eat lunch buffet (around DM13) is excellent value. Empty chairs are rare, especially on market days (Wednesday and Saturday). Another good-value lunch place (though their yummy pizza is good any time) is *La Torre (☎ 585 95, Rosenplatz 15-17)*, which serves main course, salad and beverage for DM8 to DM12 daily till 5 pm. Vegetarians should head to the casual *Rico (☎ 459 79, Rosenplatz 7)*.

Fairly new, but an instant winner with Münster's party crowd, is the canal-side *Luf (☎ 674 34 44, Hafenweg 46-48)*. There's something for everyone, including

a beer garden, an American-style restaurant (with mains around DM20) and a disco-bar sporting plush red sofas and artwork.

Getting There & Away
Train IC trains link Münster with Hamburg (DM86, 2¼ hours). There are also regular trains to the Ruhrgebiet cities, including Dortmund (DM14.80, 50 minutes) and Soest (DM16.40, one hour).

Bus Eurolines buses has a daily service to Paris (DM92/166) and to London twice weekly (DM101/182).

Car & Motorcycle Münster is on the A1 from Bremen to Cologne and is the starting point of the A43 in the direction of Wuppertal. It is also at the crossroads of the B51, B54 and B219. Parking in the centre is largely confined to parking lots and garages (DM2 per hour).

Ride Services Check the ride-share board at the university or call one of the Mitfahrzentralen, such as Citynetz (☎ 194 44), Aegidiistrasse 20a.

Getting Around
Bus Single tickets, available from the driver, cost DM2.90 (valid throughout the city); four-trip tickets are DM9.60. Group and family discounts are available. For information, call ☎ 694 16 80.

Bicycle When in Münster, do as the locals do and ride a bike. There's a rental station at the Hauptbahnhof, as well as at Terra Verde (☎ 566 53) at Überwasserstrasse 13 and Fahrzeughaus Gust (☎ 429 86), Handorfer Strasse 2. Daily rates range from DM11 to DM16. The tourist office stocks a palette of biking maps.

MÜNSTERLAND CASTLES
Münster is surrounded by the Münsterland, home to about 100 well preserved moated castles and palaces. In these rural flatlands, water was often the only way to protect the residences of bishops, counts,

dukes and landed gentry against the 'rabble' and rebels.

Some of these places are attractive destinations, either because of their unusual architecture, their idyllic country setting or both. Unfortunately, most are still in private hands and often can only be viewed from the outside; others require reservations. Also, unless you are driving, visiting these castles is not easy. Almost none are directly served by public transport and if they are, it's infrequent. As a rule, the bicycle is the most efficient method of travelling through this flat region. Bikes may be rented in Münster (see Getting Around) and at nearly all local train stations.

The Münster tourist office has maps, the free brochure *Schlösserträume* with details on all palaces, and other handouts with camping and hotel information. Another source of information is Münsterland Touristik (☎ 02551-93 92 91), located at Hohe Schule 13 in Steinfurt.

Following are profiles of a quartet of castles that offer the greatest tourist appeal and are comparatively accessible from Münster.

Burg Hülshoff

About 10km west of Münster, Burg Hülshoff (☎ 02534-10 52) is the birthplace of one of Germany's pre-eminent women of letters, Annette von Droste-Hülshoff (1797-1848). The large red-brick Renaissance chateau is embedded in a lovely – partly groomed, partly romantic – park, which is especially pleasant in spring. Inside is an unexciting restaurant and a small museum dedicated to the poet. It is open from March to December daily from 9.30 am to 6 pm (DM5/4). Bus Nos 563 and 564 make the trip out here from Münster's city centre, though service is sketchy on weekends.

Haus Rüschhaus

In 1826, Annette von Droste-Hülshoff moved to the smaller Haus Rüschhaus (☎ 02533-13 17) in the Münster suburb of Nienberge, just 3km north of Burg Hülshoff. The residence had formerly been the private home of master architect JC Schlaun (1749),

who infused baroque touches into what had been a Westphalian farmhouse. The strictly symmetrical garden makes for a lovely stroll. Guided tours run regularly (DM5); call for times. Bus No 5 from Münster's Hauptbahnhof stops right outside the grounds.

Burg Vischering

Burg Vischering (☎ 02591-797 90) is Westphalia's oldest (1271) and the quintessential medieval moated castle, the kind that conjures romantic images of knights and damsels. Surrounded by a system of ramparts and ditches, the complex consists of an outer castle and the main castle, connected by a bridge. Inside the main castle is the **Münsterland Museum**, open daily to 5.30 pm, in winter to 4.30 pm (DM2).

Burg Vischering is in the north of Lüdinghausen, about 30km south of Münster, and is served by train several times daily, albeit with a change in either Dülmen, Lünen or Coesfeld (DM12.20, 45 minutes). Connections tend to be quite good.

Schloss Nordkirchen

Very different in character from Burg Vischering, Schloss Nordkirchen (☎ 02596-93 34 02) is a grandiose baroque red-brick structure sitting on an island accessible via three bridges and surrounded by a lavish, manicured park. Nicknamed the 'Westphalian Versailles', this symmetrical palace was commissioned at the beginning of the 18th century by the prince-bishop of Münster, Christian Friedrich von Plettenberg. Gottfried Laurenz Pictorius began building it in 1703 and Johann Conrad Schlaun completed it in 1734. Now owned by the state government, it houses a college for economic studies.

The palace is well worth visiting just for the gardens and the exterior, though the interior – with its stuccoed ceilings, the festival hall, the dining room and other chambers – can only be viewed during guided tours (DM2). These are offered on Sunday from 2 to 6 pm and by reservation on other days.

Schloss Nordkirchen is 8km south-east of Lüdinghausen in the hamlet of Nordkirchen, which does not have a train station. Consult your bike map to find the route between the two castles.

SOEST

☎ 02921 • pop 43,000

Soest, a charming small town of neat, half-timbered houses and a web of idyllic lanes, has largely preserved its medieval appearance. It lies about 45km east of Dortmund and is the northern gateway to the Sauerland (see later in this chapter). Soest is also a 'green' town, not only because of parks and gardens but also for the unusual green sandstone used in constructing many of its buildings, most notably the churches. Brimming with outstanding works of art, these churches reflect the wealth Soest enjoyed in the Middle Ages, when its products – mostly textiles, salt and corn – were in great demand throughout Europe. They are also what makes Soest a popular destination for day-trippers from the nearby Ruhrgebiet cities and the Sauerland.

Orientation & Information

Soest is small enough to explore on foot. To get a sense of its dimensions, take a walk atop or along the almost completely intact 3.5km town wall. To get to the town centre from the train or bus stations, both just north of the Altstadt, weave your way through the medieval lanes to the area around St Patrokli. This should take around 15 minutes.

The tourist office (☎ 10 33 23, fax 330 39) is near St Patrokli in the town centre, at Am Seel 5. It's open weekdays from 8.30 am to 12.30 pm and 2 to 4.30 pm (Thursday to 5.30 pm), and on Saturday from 9.30 am to noon. You'll find a Deutsche Bank at Markt 14 and a Volksbank at Marktstrasse 6. The post office is at Hospitalsgasse 3. For emergency medical assistance or an ambulance, call ☎ 770 55.

Things to See

Soest's main attractions are its churches and their wealth of artworks. Closest to the Hauptbahnhof is the exquisite 14th century **St Maria zur Wiese**, known as Wiesenkirche

and easily recognised by its filigreed Gothic twin spires. It has a series of luminescent stained-glass windows, of which the **Westphalian Supper** is the most impressive (it's called 'Westphalian' because the dinner in this Last Supper consists of the local staples of ham, rye bread and beer). There are four altars, including one carved in 16th century Brabant. Its lower panels depict the Christmas cycle, while the upper shows the Passion of Christ. It is open daily from 10 am to 5 or 6 pm, in winter to 4 pm.

Just west of the Wiesenkirche is the smaller **St Maria zur Höhe**, better known as Hohnekirche, a squat and architecturally less accomplished hall church from the early 13th century. It features a beautiful ceiling with floral ornamentation and naive depictions of birds and other animals. The altar (1475) is ascribed to the Westphalian painter Master of Liesborn. Also note the Scheibenkreuz in the right aisle, a large wooden cross usually found in Scandinavian countries and the only one in Germany. To help you see better, there's a light switch on your left as you enter. It is open daily from 9.30 am to 5.30 pm, and in winter to 4 pm.

Near the Markt, Soest's main Catholic church is **St Patrokli**, referred to as the 'Dom' by locals. It's a three-nave Romanesque structure (965) and sports a stout square tower known as the Tower of Westphalia. There are delicate frescoes in the 12th century **Marienchor**. It's open daily from 10 am to 6 pm.

Of almost mystical simplicity is the tiny two-nave **Nikolaikapelle**, a few steps southeast in Thomästrasse. Also from the 12th century, it contains a masterful altar painting by the 15th century artist Conrad von Soest (born in Dortmund). It's open on Tuesday, Wednesday, Friday and Sunday from 11 am to noon. **St Petri**, west of the Dom, is considered the oldest church in Westphalia, with origins in the 8th century. It's open Tuesday to Sunday from 10 am to 6 pm.

Places to Stay & Eat

Soest's *DJH hostel (☎ 162 83, fax 146 23, Kaiser-Friedrich-Platz 2)* is just south of the Altstadt and charges DM21.60/26.60 for juniors/seniors. Take bus No 549 or 550 from the Hauptbahnhof. Hotels include **Stadt Soest** (☎ *362 20, fax 36 22 27, Brüderstrasse 50)* near the Hauptbahnhof, which charges DM95/150 for full-facility singles/doubles. **Hotel Im Wilden Mann** (☎ *150 71, fax 140 78, Markt 11)* is a local landmark where rooms cost DM100/160; there's a restaurant as well. The **Pilgrim Haus** (☎ *18 28, fax 121 31, Jakobistrasse 75)* is the oldest guesthouse in Westphalia (1304) and has rooms for DM120/175. Most restaurants, including the **Brauhaus Christ** at Walburger Strasse 36, serve artery-clogging Westphalian dishes.

Getting There & Away

Depending on where you're coming from, getting to Soest by train often requires a change in Hamm or Dortmund. There are several trains an hour to/from both cities, as well as to Paderborn. Through trains to Münster (DM16.40, one hour) leave hourly.

There's a regular bus service to the northern Sauerland, including Möhnesee lake (bus No 549), Warstein (bus No 551) and Arnsberg (bus No 550). If you're driving, take the Soest exit from the A44. Soest is also at the crossroads of the B1, B229 and B475.

PADERBORN

☎ 05251 • pop 134,000

Paderborn is a bustling, modern city about 90km northeast of Dortmund and the economic centre of east Westphalia. It derives its name from the Pader, Germany's shortest river; more than 5000L a second spurt from about 200 springs in the city centre to form the little stream that merges with the Lippe after only 4km.

Charlemagne used the royal seat and bishopric he had established here to control the Christianisation of the Saxon tribes. In 799, he received a momentous visit from Pope Leo III, which resulted in the foundation of the Holy Roman Empire and Charlemagne's coronation as its emperor in Rome. Religion – Catholicism, in this case – still characterises Paderborn to this day. Churches

abound, and religious sculpture and motifs adorn public facades, fountains and parks. Many of the city's 15,000 students are involved in theological studies (economics and technology are other major fields). Pope John Paul II visited Paderborn in 1996.

Orientation & Information

Paderborn's centre is small and easily explored on foot. The Hauptbahnhof lies about 1km south-west of the largely pedestrianised Altstadt. Exit right onto Bahnhofstrasse, then continue straight to Westernstrasse which leads to the Dom and other sights.

The tourist office (☎ 88 29 80, fax 88 29 90) is at Marienplatz 2a, and is open weekdays from 9.30 am to 6 pm, and Saturday to 2 pm; staff can make free room reservations. The post office is at Liliengasse 2, just off Westernstrasse. In an emergency, contact the police at ☎ 110; or BOSS (☎ 88 22 88), a cooperative between the city and the police, at Marienstrasse 6.

Walking Tour

Except where noted, Paderborn's museums are open Tuesday to Sunday from 10 am to 6 pm. A 50% discount applies to children and students.

Our tour starts at Paderborn's birthplace, the former site of Charlemagne's palace just north of the Dom. All that's left to see of the **Carolingian Kaiserpfalz**, where the fateful meeting with Pope Leo took place, are the foundations, discovered beneath WWII rubble and excavated in the 1960s.

Right behind looms the **Ottonian Kaiserpfalz**, a 44m-long and 16m-wide palace originally built in the 11th century and faithfully reconstructed in the 1970s. It exudes a dignified atmosphere because of its simple design and understated decor, and contains a museum (☎ 105 10) with unearthed items on display (DM2). Immediately adjacent is the tiny and beautiful **Bartholomäuskapelle** (1017), the oldest hall church north of the Alps, with otherworldly acoustics. It is open daily from 10 am to 6 pm.

As you enter the Gothic **Dom** (1270), a three-nave hall church, through the north portal, you'll immediately notice the unusual windows, some of which resemble a computer motherboard, an appropriate effect given Paderborn's close ties to computer technology.

One of the Dom's most charming features is the Hasenfenster in the cloister (follow the signs). It depicts three rabbits, arranged in such a way that each has two ears, even though there are only three ears in all, an illusion that gave rise to the following nursery rhyme: 'Count the ears. There are but three. But still each hare has two, you see?'. The window is supposed to represent the Holy Trinity and has become the city's symbol.

Beneath the cathedral choir is a hall-like crypt with the grave and relics of St Liborius, brought to Paderborn from Le Mans in France in 836. To see the Liborius shrine, though, exit through the sculpture-studded south portal – the Paradies – and head to the **Diözesanmuseum** (Diocese Museum; ☎ 12 54 00), housed in a 1970s architectural eyesore right outside the Dom on the Markt. Much more attractive on the inside, the museum boasts an impressive collection of ecclesiastical sculpture and paintings. The highlights from the Dom treasury – including Liborius' relics – are in the basement. Admission is DM4. As you exit the museum onto Domplatz, the octagonal tower (1180) of the **Gaukirche** leaps into view.

From here, walk west to Rathausplatz, dominated by the **Rathaus** (1616), a magnificent structure with ornate gables, oriels and other decorative touches typical of the Weser Renaissance architectural style. Just south of here is the **Jesuitenkirche**, whose curvilinear baroque exterior contrasts with the more subdued Gothic vaulted ceiling and rounded Romanesque arches inside. This mix of styles, however, is typical of Jesuit churches from the late 17th century.

Rathausplatz merges with Marienplatz, where the attractive **Heisingsche Haus**, a 17th century patrician abode with an elaborate facade, stands adjacent to the tourist office. A short walk north via Am Abdinghof leads to the **Paderquellgebiet**, a small park perfect for relaxing by the gurgling

springs of the Pader source. This is the starting point of a lovely walk along the little river to **Schloss Neuhaus**, a moated water palace, about 5km north-west.

Just east of the Paderquellgebiet, the twin Romanesque towers of the **Abdinghofkirche** (1015) come into view. Originally a Benedictine monastery but a Protestant church since 1867, it is almost overwhelmingly austere, with whitewashed walls, a flat wooden ceiling and a completely unadorned interior. A few steps east and you're back at the starting point of this tour.

Heinz Nixdorf MuseumsForum (HNF)

This innovative and interactive museum makes a stopover in Paderborn worthwhile even for those who could care less about churches. Established by the founder of one of Germany's big computer companies (now merged with Siemens), it opened in 1996 and offers visitors a fascinating journey through 5000 years of communication and information technology – from cuneiform to cyberspace.

There's so much to do, it's easy to spend an entire day here. Glass-encased treasures like a functional model of a calculating machine based on the binary system (developed by Leibniz, 1672) coexist with exhibits like the ENIAC, a room-sized forerunner of the modern computer. Built for the US Army in the 1940s, the ENIAC is neatly juxtaposed with a 6mm x 6mm chip providing the same functions today. You can learn all about the punch-card system, a form of automatic data processing (Hollerith, 1889); use machines like the comptometer, a mechanical calculator (Felt, 1887); play computer games or visit virtual reality in the Software Theatre.

English-language panels and a museum guide (DM8) are available. A comprehensive program of lectures, events and symposia (hence MuseumsForum) supplements the exhibits, though these are usually in German.

The HNF (☎ 30 66 00) is at Fürstenallee 7, and is open from 9 am to 6 pm on weekdays and from 10 am on weekends (DM6). Bus No 11 stops right outside.

Places to Stay

Paderborn has two camping grounds north of the city centre, of which only *Campingplatz Stauterrassen (☎ 45 04, fax 878 32, Auf der Thune 14)* is directly accessible by public transport (bus No 1, 8 or 11 to Schloss Neuhaus, then bus No 58 to Am Thunhof). The other, *Campingplatz Am Waldsee (☎ 73 72, Husarenstrasse 130)* is a 2km walk from the Husarenstrasse stop (bus No 11).

Paderborn's **DJH hostel** *(☎ 220 55, fax 28 00 17, Meinwerkstrasse 16)* is in the city centre but would benefit from an overhaul. B&B is DM22.60/27.60 for juniors/seniors. From the station, take bus No 2 to Detmolder Tor or No 5 to Maspernplatz.

The snug and central *Haus Irma (☎ 233 42, Bachstrasse 9)*, near the Paderquellgebiet, is an excellent deal, with simple singles for DM30 to DM65, while doubles clock in at DM80 to DM90. Pricier is the artsy *Galerie-Hotel Abdinghof (☎ 122 40, fax 12 24 19, Bachstrasse 1)*, which charges DM125/160 for singles/doubles with private facilities. Right in the Ükern pub quarter is the traditional *Hotel Zur Mühle (☎ 107 50, fax 10 75 45, Mühlenstrasse 2)*, where rooms with shower and WC cost DM120/175.

The most stylish digs in town are nearby at the new *Hotel StadtHaus (☎ 188 99 10, fax 188 99 15 55, Hathumarstrasse 22)*. Rooms and public areas are furnished in early 20th century style but sport all modern amenities. A restaurant and sauna (extra fee) are on the premises. Rates are DM158/188.

Places to Eat

The highest concentration of restaurants, student pubs and bars is in the Ükern quarter in the northern Altstadt along Kisau, Mühlenstrasse, Hathumarstrasse and Ükern. Candle-lit and casual *Café Klatsch (☎ 28 12 21, Kisau 11)* serves simple but interesting fare for slim wallets (it opens at 6 pm). On the same street is *Paderborner Brauhaus (☎ 28 25 54, Kisau 2)*, a local institution specialising in hearty Westphalian fare, which is best enjoyed in the Paderside beer garden. It's open daily after 5 pm, and Sunday after 11.30 am. Also here is

Adam's (☎ 224 14, Mühlenstrasse 2), a hugely popular pseudo US-style diner that caters to city trendoids.

In an arcade near the Rathaus, *Café Central (☎ 29 68 88, Rosenstrasse 13-15)* holds forth with theatrical decor, a library corner and velvet curtains. The place attracts couples, the grey-haired set and student groups alike. Come here for a cup of coffee or for a small meal costing DM8 to DM12. Alternatively, you could try *Alex (☎ 28 15 18, Libori-Galerie)*, a bustling bistro and hang-out for Paderborn's youth inside a new shopping mall. It's rightly famous for its lavish breakfast buffet.

Getting There & Away

Paderborn has direct a train link every two hours to Kassel-Wilhelmshöhe (DM29, 1¼ hours) and an hourly connection to the Ruhrgebiet cities, such as Dortmund (DM30, 1½ hours). Trains to Soest (DM14.80, 40 minutes) leave several times hourly. Paderborn is on the A33, which connects with the A2 in the north and the A44 in the south. The B1, B64, B68 and B480 also go through Paderborn. The Mitfahrzentrale (☎ 194 40) is at Bahnhofstrasse 10.

Sauerland

This gentle mountain range in the southeast of North Rhine-Westphalia is made up of five nature parks. The forest area is at its most scenic around the Kahler Asten, at 842m the Sauerland's highest mountain. Outdoor enthusiasts will find lots of hiking and biking trails, lakes for water sports and rivers for fishing. For culture buffs there are museums, tidy half-timbered towns and hill-top castles. The Sauerland is a fine destination for a brief respite.

The Sauerland tourist office (☎ 02961-943 22 9) is at Heinrich-Jansen-Weg 14 in Brilon. For specific information about a particular town, it's best to go to a local tourist office. If you're staying overnight, you'll be charged a visitor's tax from DM2.50 to DM5 in most resorts.

WINTER SPORTS
The Sauerland has around 170 groomed cross-country skiing tracks, 126 ski lifts and 44 ski schools. The season generally runs from December to March, but snow levels are not always reliable. The most dependable area is the High Sauerland, where elevations reach 700m. Most tourism is centred in the town of **Winterberg**, which also has a 1600m-long bobsled run, occasionally the site of German and European championships. Trips down the ice canal with an experienced driver last 60 seconds and cost DM50. For daily updates (in German) on snow conditions, call the Snowphone (☎ 0291-115 30). Expect big crowds after major snow falls, especially on weekends.

The brochure *Loipen und Pisten* (Cross-Country Trails & Downhill Runs) contains route descriptions and can be picked up at tourist offices. Equipment-rental shops abound; look for the sign saying 'Skiverleih' and figure on spending about DM20 for cross-country and DM25 for downhill skis and boots per day. Lift tickets cost around DM30 per day.

HIKING
More than 12,000km of hiking trails, mostly through dense beech and fir forests, crisscross the Sauerland. There's something for hikers of every level, from leisurely lakeside walks to long-distance treks. Maps and trail descriptions are available from the local tourist offices or in bookshops. A popular medium-level hike of 5km leads from Winterberg to the peak of the Kahler Asten; views from the tower here (DM1) are great. The new German Unity trail – cutting across the country from Aachen to Görlitz at the Polish border – also traverses the Sauerland.

WATER SPORTS
Sailing, windsurfing, diving, kayaking, swimming, fishing, rowing – the many lakes in the Sauerland offer plenty of choices.

For a list of equipment-rental places, contact the local tourist offices. The Biggesee in the southern Sauerland and the Möhnesee in the north are prime destinations.

The less active might enjoy a cruise on the Biggesee offered from April to October (DM12, children half price).

PLACES TO STAY
Camping grounds abound throughout the Sauerland. Scenic ones include *Waldenburger Bucht* (☎ 02722-955 00) on the Biggesee near Attendorn, *Campingplatz Hochsauerland* (☎ 02981-32 49, Remmeswiese 10) and *Campingplatz Winterberg* (☎ 02981-17 76, Kapperundweg 1) near Winterberg.

Hostels with charm include the one on Burg Altena (☎ 02352-235 22, fax 233 30), which charges DM21.60/26.60 for juniors/seniors. The hostel in Lennestadt-Bilstein, east of Attendorn, is in a medieval castle (☎ 02721-812 17, Von-Gevore-Weg 10) and costs DM23.70/28.70. The hostel in Winterberg (☎ 02981-22 89, Astenberg 1) charges DM21.50/26.50. All prices are for bed and breakfast; sheets are an extra DM6.50.

For *private rooms*, pensions or hotels, contact either the local tourist offices or the central reservation office at ☎ 02961-94 32 27.

GETTING THERE & AWAY
The A45 cuts through the Sauerland, connecting the Ruhrgebiet with Frankfurt. The area is also easily reached via the A4 from Cologne. For regional buses into the northern Sauerland, see Getting There & Away in the Soest section earlier in this chapter.

Regular train service – even to the smallest towns – exists, though you may have to make a number of changes. Travelling from the north, you'll most likely have to change in Hagen. Coming from points south usually requires a change in Siegen.

GETTING AROUND
It is most convenient to travel around the Sauerland under your own steam, though with some planning, it can also be explored by train and bus. Once you are based in a town, special buses head for the hiking areas and the surrounding towns. Each tourist office has information on the services available. If you're spending some time in the

region, consider investing in the Sauerland Urlauberkarte (DM15), which buys unlimited public transportation for three days (DM30 for 10 days) for up to two adults and four children. It's available from bus drivers and the tourist offices, which also have route maps and timetables.

ATTENDORN
☎ 02722 • pop 21,500

The tourist office (☎ 02722-642 29, fax 47 75) is in Rathauspassage in the new Rathaus, and is open weekdays from 9 am to 6 pm, Saturday in summer from 10 am to 1 pm.

The main attraction of this typical Sauerland town on the northern shore of the Biggesee lake is the **Attahöhle**, one of Germany's largest and most impressive stalactite caves. The daily 45 minute tour (DM9/4.50) covers a network of rooms with names like Candle Hall and Alhambra Grotto. Highlights include a 5m column and an underground lake.

In town, you'll find the **Church of St John the Baptist**, known locally as Sauerland Cathedral, whose main attraction is a 14th century Pieta. The lower section of the square tower reveals the Romanesque origins of this church, which is otherwise Gothic.

ALTENA
☎ 02352 • pop 24,000

Altena's tourist office (☎ 02352-20 92 12, fax 20 92 03) is at Lüdenscheider Strasse 22, and is open from 8 am to noon and 1.30 to 3.30 pm (Friday to noon).

The 12th century **Burg Altena**, perched romantically on a bluff, was originally the seat of the counts of Altena-Mark, but has spent time as an orphanage, a military command and a jail. In 1912 it became the world's first youth hostel, whose spartan furnishings are preserved as a museum. In the basement, you'll find the dormitory with 14 massive wooden bunks. Upstairs is the dank day room, which features a small open kitchen and long polished tables on a stone floor.

Two other museums are contained within the thick walls of the castle. The **Museum der Grafschaft Mark** is a regional history

museum with a splendid assortment of weapons and armour, furniture, ceramics, glassware and minerals.

The **Smithy Museum** traces this ancient craft through the ages and attests to the importance of the region's metal-working acumen. The museums are open Tuesday to Friday from 10 am to 5 pm and on weekends from 9.30 am (DM5/2.50).

Siegerland

The hills and mountains of the Sauerland continue southward into the Siegerland region, with the city of Siegen as its focal point. Frankfurt, the Ruhrgebiet and Cologne are all about 100km away.

SIEGEN
☎ 0271 • pop 110,000

Historically, Siegen has strong connections with the House of Nassau-Oranien (Nassau-Orange in English), which has held the Dutch throne since 1813. Around 1403, the counts of Nassau who ruled the area obtained large territories in the Netherlands; in 1530 they added the principality of Orange in southern France. When the Netherlands became a hereditary monarchy in 1813, the crown went to Wilhelm Friedrich of the House of Nassau-Oranien.

Two palaces and other buildings survive from those glory days. Though encircled by a lovely hilly landscape, modern Siegen has been scarred by steel production.

Siegen was the birthplace of Peter Paul Rubens (1577-1640), and there's a small collection of the Flemish painter's works in one of the town's museums.

Orientation & Information
Siegen's centre slopes up from the Hauptbahnhof in the north-west to the Oberes Schloss in the east, where the Altstadt is at its most scenic. It's traversed by the river Sieg.

The tourist office (☎ 404 13 16, fax 226 87) is in Room B219 of the Rathaus at Markt 2. Hours are erratic, so it's best to call ahead. There's also an Information

Pavilion outside the Hauptbahnhof, which is open to 6 pm weekdays and to noon on Saturday. Another information source is the regional tourist office (☎ 333 10 20) at Koblenzer Strasse 73, open weekdays till 5 pm. You can change money at the Commerzbank at Bahnhofstrasse 2 or the Dresdner Bank next door. The main post office is at Hindenburgstrasse 9.

Things to See

In 1623 the ruling family of Nassau-Oranien was split into two branches feuding over the Reformation. This required the construction of a second palace, the baroque **Unteres Schloss**, by the Protestant side, while the Catholic counts continued to live in the 13th century Oberes Schloss. The Unteres Schloss is a short walk south-east from the Hauptbahnhof. Today, it's primarily used as office space and only the family crypt has survived.

More interesting is the **Oberes Schloss**, reached via Burgstrasse. It houses the Siegerland Museum, a moderately interesting regional history museum. Its major drawing cards are eight original paintings by Rubens, including a self-portrait and *Roman Charity*. The Oraniersaal, with portraits of members of the dynasty, is another highlight. On a clear day, the view of the town and wooded surroundings from the tower can be superb. Hours are from 10 am to 5 pm, closed Monday (DM4/2).

Below the Oberes Schloss is the late Romanesque **Nikolaikirche**, whose galleried, hexagonal main room is unique in Germany. Also note the baptismal plate, made by Peruvian silversmiths in the 16th century and brought back by the counts of Nassau, who were involved in the colonisation of South America.

Places to Stay & Eat

Both the local and the regional tourist offices can help with room reservations. Of Siegen's few hotels *Hotel Bürger* (☎ 625 51, fax 89 69 60, Marienborner Strasse 134) has the lowest room rates with singles/doubles for DM55/90 without private facilities and DM85/125 with. The family run

Hotel Jakob (☎ 23 27 20, fax 232 72 11, Tiergartenstrasse 61), north of the Hauptbahnhof, charges DM75/125 for rooms with shower and WC. Also reasonable is the *Hotel Café Römer* (☎ 810 45/46, fax 87 01 49, Rijnsburger Strasse 4), which is in a quiet location with rooms with private bath for DM85/130.

The very central *Stadtschänke (Am Kornmarkt)* serves German food in a family atmosphere for reasonable prices. *Am Hasengarten (Burgstrasse 28)* is similar, and also has a beer garden. Somewhat more upmarket is *Efeu (Marienborner Strasse 7)*, where Italian food is on the menu. It's closed on Monday.

Getting There & Away

Direct trains depart for Cologne hourly (DM27, 1½ hours). Trips to Frankfurt require a change in Siegen-Weidenau or Giessen (DM38, 1¾ hours). To get to the Ruhrgebiet cities (eg Dortmund), you have to change in Hagen. Siegen is off the A45 connecting the Ruhrgebiet with Frankfurt and is also easily reached from Cologne via the A4.

AROUND SIEGEN
Freudenberg
☎ 02734 • pop 21,700

About 12km north of Siegen, the little town of Freudenberg would be unremarkable were it not for its stunning **Altstadt**, with its immaculate half-timbered houses set up in the 17th century equivalent of a planned community. Built in rows, the houses all face the same way, are roughly the same height and sport the same white facades, the same pattern of wooden beams and the same black-slate roofs. Conceptualised by Duke Johann Moritz of Nassau-Oranien, the area is called Alter Flecken (literally 'old borough') and was given preservation status in 1966. Also of interest to visitors is a **local history museum** at Mittelstrasse 4. Opening hours are Wednesday and weekends from 2 to 5 pm (DM1.50). To get to Freudenberg from Siegen, take bus No 45 from the Hauptbahnhof.

Bremen

Only 404 sq km, the state of Bremen comprises just two cities: Bremen, the capital, and the port of Bremerhaven, about 65km to the north. Along with Bavaria, Bremen is one of the oldest political entities in Germany and the second oldest city republic in the world after Italy's San Marino. Bremerhaven is Germany's most important port after Hamburg.

BREMEN
☎ 0421   • pop 550,000

This metropolis on the Weser River is celebrated for three things: beer (Beck's), liberal politics (the Green Party had its major breakthrough here) and a fairy tale *(The Town Musicians of Bremen)*. Of course, the charming quartet from the Brothers Grimm fable never actually made it through the town gates, but *you* should, for Bremen is an energetic city with much to offer. Besides a bevy of historical sights and museums, it has delightful parks, a vibrant nightlife and interesting restaurants. Bremen is also the end of the Fairy-Tale Road, which winds northward from Hanau, in Hesse, the Grimms' birthplace.

Like many German cities, Bremen has origins as an archbishopric. Founded in 787 by Charlemagne, it was the main base for Christianising Scandinavia, which earned the city its moniker as the 'Rome of the North'. Bremen grew by leaps and bounds, and by 1358 was ready to join the Hanseatic League. In 1646 it became a free imperial city, a status it still enjoys today as a 'Free Hanseatic City'. The Roland statue on the Markt is a symbol of Bremen's independent spirit and the focal point of a congenial Altstadt that is wonderful to explore on foot.

Orientation
Bremen's city centre is fairly compact and easy to get around on foot. To the north, the Altstadt is bounded by a lovely park called Wallanlagen that follows the old

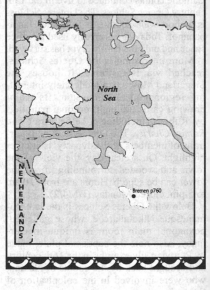

HIGHLIGHTS

- Admiring the Rathaus and other buildings around the Markt
- Wandering around Böttcherstrasse and the historic Schnoor quarter
- Exploring the pub and restaurant scene in Das Viertel and Auf den Höfen
- Meeting the Bremen folk – 'Hanseatic cool' meets warm-heartedness

North Sea

NETHERLANDS

Bremen p760

city walls and moat. The Hauptbahnhof and central bus station are just north of here. The centre's southern periphery is the Weser River.

To get to the Markt from the stations, walk along Bahnhofstrasse to Herdentorsteinweg, then continue along the pedestrianised Sögestrasse for another few minutes to Obernstrasse. The Rathaus and

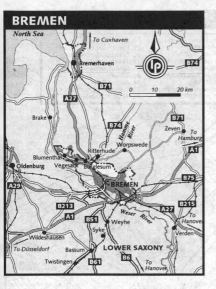

BREMEN

North Sea

To Cuxhaven

Bremerhaven

B74

B71

A27

Brake

B74

B71

Zeven

To Hamburg

Worpswede

Ritterhude

A1

Blumenthal

Oldenburg Vegesack Burglesum

A29

BREMEN

B75

B213

A27

Weser River

To Hanover

A1

B51

Weyhe

Syke

Verden

Wildeshausen

To Düsseldorf Bassum

LOWER SAXONY

Twistingen B61 B6 To Hanover

0   10   20 km

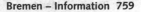

Markt are just east of here. The main entertainment quarter is east of the Altstadt along Ostertorsteinweg.

Information
Tourist Offices The main tourist office (☎ 30 80 00 or ☎ 194 33, fax 308 00 30, email btz@bremen-tourism.de) is at the Hauptbahnhof. Opening hours are Monday to Wednesday from 9.30 am to 6.30 pm, Thursday and Friday to 8 pm and weekends to 4 pm. There's also a smaller information kiosk at Liebfrauenkirchhof near the Rathaus that keeps the same hours.

Both offices hand out a free map of the city and an annual-events schedule. They sell the BremenCard, good for unlimited public transport, a 50% discount on museums and reductions of 10 to 20% on theatre tickets, sightseeing tours, guided walks etc. The two/three day card for one adult and one child costs DM19.50/26. A group card good for up to five people costs DM35/46.

Money Practically all banks in Bremen exchange money and travellers cheques,

but the Reisebank (☎ 132 19) in the Hauptbahnhof has the best hours: weekdays from 7.30 am to 7 pm, Saturday from 8 am to 12.15 pm and 1 to 4 pm. If it's closed, the ATM outside accepts all major credit cards.

Post & Communications The main post office is on Domsheide, but one with better opening hours (weekdays 9 am to 8 pm, Saturday to 2 pm) is outside the Hauptbahnhof. There's a public fax-phone inside.

Internet Resources Information on Bremen (in German only) is available at www.bremen-tourism.de.

Bookshops Georg Büchner Buchhandlung, Ostertorsteinweg 56, has a limited selection of novels in English and can order in Lonely Planet titles within 24 hours.

Laundry You'll find Schnell & Sauber laundrettes at Vor dem Steintor 105 and at Am Dobben 134. Expect to pay DM6 per wash, plus DM1 for the dryer. They're open from 6 am to 11 pm.

Emergency There's a police station (☎ 36 21) at Am Wall 201.

Markt
Most of Bremen's main sights are concentrated around Marktplatz, anchored on the northern side by the imposing **Rathaus** (1410) with its intensely ornate facade. Above the arched arcades is a row of tall windows separated by a cycle of sandstone figures representing Charlemagne and seven prince-electors. The balcony in the middle, added between 1595 and 1618 and crowned by three gables, is a good example of the flowery Weser Renaissance style. Tours of the Rathaus (in German) take place from Monday to Saturday at 11 am, noon and 3 and 4 pm; and Sunday at 11 am and noon (DM5/2.50). The highlight of the tour is the Upper Hall, with its wood-beamed ceiling and heavy brass chandeliers alternating with historic ship models.

BREMEN

BREMEN

PLACES TO STAY
- 6 Hotel Schaper-Siedenburg
- 7 Hotel Bremer Haus
- 10 Hotel Ibis
- 12 Jugendgästehaus Bremen
- 33 Hotel Weltevreden

PLACES TO EAT
- 15 Beck's Bistro
- 21 Gasthof zum Kaiser Friedrich
- 22 Scusi
- 23 Schnoor Teestübchen
- 28 Casablanca
- 29 Café Engel
- 30 Bio Biss
- 32 Savarin; Dos Mas; Zum Hofheurigen; Blue; Carnevale

OTHER
- 1 Main Train Station
- 2 Übersee Museum
- 3 Central Bus Station
- 4 Post Office
- 5 Tourist Office
- 8 Woody's
- 9 Stubu
- 11 Windmill

- 13 Kirche Unser Lieben Frauen
- 14 Tourist Office
- Liebfrauenkirchhof
- 16 Rathaus; Ratskelle
- 17 Martinianleger
- 18 Haus der Bürgerschaft
- 19 Dom St Petri; Dommuseum; Bleikeller
- 20 Main Post Office

- 24 Police Station
- 25 Kunsthalle; KuKuk Café
- 26 Gerhard Marcks Haus
- 27 Theater am Goetheplatz; Schauspielhaus
- 31 Türke
- 34 Airport Bar
- 35 Lagerhaus; Lagerhaus Kafé
- 36 ADM Mitfahrbüro

In front of the Rathaus, the 13m-tall **Roland statue**, which has been a symbol of justice and freedom in Germany since the Middle Ages, stands guard over the Markt. It's the original statue dating from 1404, though it has been restored several times. While Roland is often thought to be the symbol of Bremen, another statue (banished to the western side of the Rathaus) shows the friendly foursome that people associate more with the city. These are the **Town Musicians of Bremen** – the donkey,

dog, cat and rooster who star in the Brothers Grimm fairy tale. The bronze statue, by sculptor Gerhard Marcks, was erected in 1951. There's a charming re-enactment of the story by the Waldau Theater troupe from May to early October on Sunday at noon and 1.30 pm (free).

Immediately beside the statue of the Town Musicians loom the spires of the **Kirche Unser Lieben Frauen**, Bremen's oldest parish church. Its earliest section is the 11th century crypt from the Church of St

Vitus, which once stood on the site. A Romanesque structure followed from which only the south tower, with its round arches and arcades, survives. The church acquired its early-Gothic appearance in the middle of the 13th century and has been altered several times since. Today it's a three-nave hall church with bare red-brick walls that were originally plastered over and painted. Most of the interior decoration fell victim to iconoclastic zealots during the Reformation. Note the baroque memorial on the wall of the north tower and the carved pulpit.

The western side of the Markt is taken up by a row of stately townhouses containing several bars and restaurants. If not for the incongruously modern **Haus der Bürgerschaft** (State Assembly, 1966) opposite, it would be an almost perfectly preserved medieval square. This angled steel and concrete structure houses the parliamentary hall for both the city and state governments.

Dom St Petri

This magnificent cathedral, with its two landmark towers, stands to the east of the Rathaus. Its western portal is graced by two bronze doors with biblical scenes and flanked by sculptures of David and Moses (north door), and Peter and Paul, with a goofy-looking mustachioed Charlemagne in the middle. The vaulted central nave and aisles bear witness to the conversion of this Romanesque basilica into a Gothic hall church; but original Romanesque features remain in the form of crypts on the western and eastern sides. Look for the humorous figures riding lions on the **Taufbecken** in the western crypt. Other highlights are the 17th century pulpit, with its intricate carvings, and the sandstone rood loft, near the choir. The relief in its centre commemorates the founding of Bremen by Charlemagne and Bishop Willehad. You can climb the 265 steps to the top of the church tower between Easter and October, any day of the week (DM1).

Also part of the cathedral complex is the **Dommuseum** (☎ 36 50 40), Sandstrasse 10-12, with sculptures, murals, liturgical books and items such as rings and vestments dug

up recently from the graves of medieval archbishops. It's open weekdays from 10 am to 5 pm, November to April from 11 am to 4 pm; and Saturday to 1 pm and Sunday from 2 to 5 pm (DM3/2).

A trip to the cathedral's **Bleikeller** (Lead Cellar) is a unique, if somewhat macabre, experience. Here you can admire eight mummified corpses in black coffins, including that of a soldier with his mouth opened in silent scream and another of a student who died in a duel in 1705. It's still not known why corpses placed beneath the cathedral do not decompose. The cellar is open from Easter to October, the same hours as the Dommuseum (DM2/1).

Böttcherstrasse

Off the south side of the Markt towards the Weser winds this narrow 110m-long lane, the creation of Ludwig Roselius, a merchant who made his fortune from the invention of decaffeinated coffee at the beginning of the 20th century.

DAVID PEEVERS

The Town Musicians of Bremen pay homage to the Brothers Grimm and their fairy tales.

euro currency converter DM1 = €0.51

BREMEN

His dream became reality in 1931 in the form of a pleasing ensemble of red-brick gabled houses infused with expressionist, Art Nouveau and Art Deco architectural elements. Soon after the lane's completion, the Nazis declared it a prime example of 'degenerate art' and ordered it destroyed. It survived only because Roselius cleverly convinced the authorities to keep the street as a 'warning' to future generations of the depravity of 'cultural Bolshevism'.

A huge luminous golden relief greets you at the northern entrance to Böttcherstrasse. Called the **Lichtbringer** (Bringer of Light, 1936), it shows a scene from the Apocalypse with the Archangel Michael fighting a dragon. It was created by Bernhard Hoetger (1874-1959), one of the main designers of Böttcherstrasse. He also designed the **Haus Atlantis**, a stunning composition of steel, concrete and glass with a show-stopping spiral staircase. The building's interior is intended to evoke the mythical lost city of Atlantis. In 1965 it was given a new facade by Ewald Mataré.

Museums Hoetger also designed the **Paula Becker-Modersohn Haus**, another prime example of expressionist architecture, with its rounded edges and wall reliefs. Inside is a museum showcasing the art of the painter also known as Paula Modersohn-Becker (1876-1907), a member of the Worpswede artists colony, who paved the way for the development of German expressionism. Inspired by Cézanne and Gauguin, she created a series of portraits, still-lifes and landscapes in muted, earthy colours that evoke melancholy. The artist died suddenly at the age of 31, just after the birth of her first daughter. Note that Roselius put the artist's maiden name first in his museum to acknowledge her achievements *before* she married the landscape painter Otto Modersohn.

The upper floors of the same building contain the **Sammlung Bernhard Hoetger**, the sculptor of whom Auguste Rodin said: '(He) found the way I was searching for ... the way to monumental art, which is the only proper way.' You'll find Hoetger's own

portrayal of the Town Musicians of Bremen in the fountain of the **Handwerkerhof**, the courtyard once housing craftsmen's workshops, in the same building complex.

The museums are connected via a walkway to **Roselius Haus** (1588), the oldest house on Böttcherstrasse. Integrated into this furnished townhouse is Roselius' private collection of medieval art. Highlights are paintings from Lucas Cranach the Elder (1472-1553) and the Westphalian artist Conrad von Soest. There's also an emotional wooden sculpture by Tilmann Riemenschneider.

The museums (☎ 336 50 66) are open daily, except Monday, from 11 am to 6 pm. The admission price (DM8/4) allows entry to all three.

Der Schnoor

The south-eastern section of the Altstadt is occupied by the Schnoor quarter, whose name stems from the word *Schnur*, or 'string', and refers to the straight way in which its snug cottages line the quarter's alleyways. Once inhabited by fisherfolk, traders and craftspeople, these homes from the 15th and 16th centuries survived the bombings of WWII but almost succumbed to the destructive building boom of the 1950s. In the end they were spared, put under protection order and revived as a picturesque neighbourhood filled with cafes, restaurants and shops. You'll often find swarms of tourists squeezing through the tiny lanes, but otherwise it's idyllic and a peaceful place to stroll.

Museums

Kunsthalle The Kunsthalle (☎ 32 90 80), at Am Wall 207, ranks as Bremen's premier art museum and contains works spanning five centuries – from old masters like Rembrandt and Dürer to German expressionists, as well as paintings from the Worpswede artists' colony and sculptures by Rodin. *Quellnymphe* (Nymph of the Source) by Lucas Cranach the Elder is one early masterpiece you'll find here; and in room 4 is Jan Mertens' *Anbetung der Hirten* (Shepherds'

Adoration, 1527), a beautiful religious panel painting. The rooms are numbered, but not chronologically; if you pick up a copy of the free pamphlet that goes with the audioguide for the picture gallery, it's easy to find the highlights. The German-language audioguide itself (DM3, plus a DM20 deposit) provides interesting descriptions (or ambient noise if you don't speak German) of the 'best of' paintings and some background about the artists. The museum also has a large collection of copperplate etchings.

The Kunsthalle is open Wednesday to Sunday from 10 am to 5 pm, Tuesday till 9 pm (DM8/4).

Gerhard Marcks Haus (☎ 32 72 00) next door features the splendid works of this Bremen-born sculptor, and changing exhibitions; it's closed Monday (DM6/4, or DM10 for a combined ticket).

Übersee Museum The collection of the Overseas Museum (☎ 361 91 76), next to the Hauptbahnhof at Bahnhofsplatz 13, had its origins in a colonial trade exhibit from 1890, where merchants displayed goods imported from abroad. Items, which include a Japanese teahouse and an Alaskan totem pole, are arranged by continent and grouped in rooms around two skylit courtyards. Museum hours are from 10 am to 6 pm, closed Monday (DM6/3).

Beck's Brewery
Keen students of the amber brew can hone their knowledge with a look behind the scenes at **Beck's** (☎ 50 94 55 55), one of Germany's largest breweries, at Am Deich on the southern bank of the Weser, just west of Bürgermeister-Smidt-Brücke (tram Nos 1 and 8 to Am Brill). Tours of the facility cost DM5, last two hours and include a movie presentation and beer tasting. They run hourly Tuesday to Saturday from 10 am to 5 pm and Sunday till 3 pm. A tour in English runs daily at 1.30 pm.

Organised Tours
Basic, two-hour bus sightseeing tours of Bremen with English commentary depart

daily at 10.30 am from the central bus station (DM25, children DM15). Buy your tickets at the tourist offices. A city walking tour (a brief commentary in English can be provided on request) leaves from the tourist office outside the Hauptbahnhof daily at 2 pm (DM9, free for children up to age 14).

Schreiber Reederei (☎ 32 12 29, fax 32 61 36) operates a 75 minute Weser and harbour tour up to five times daily between March and October. The meeting point is the Martinianleger (Martini Landing) in the city centre (DM13, students DM9.50, children DM7).

Places to Stay
The tourist office runs a free hotel room reservation service (call ☎ 30 80 00 or ☎ 194 33).

Campingplatz Bremen (☎ 21 20 02, *Am Stadtwaldsee 1)* is north of the centre and fairly close to the university – take tram No 5 or 8 from the Hauptbahnhof to Kulenkampffallee, then bus No 28 to the Campingplatz stop. Tent sites cost from DM7.50, plus DM7.50 per person and DM2.50 per car.

Jugendgästehaus Bremen (☎ 17 13 69, *fax 17 11 02, Kalkstrasse 6)* is across the Weser from the Beck's brewery (closed between Christmas and New Year). The cost for juniors/seniors is DM29/34. From the Hauptbahnhof it's about a 15 minute walk, or a short ride on bus No 26 or tram No 1 or 8 to Am Brill.

For *private rooms*, contact Bed & Breakfast Bremen (☎ 536 07 71).

All hotel prices quoted include breakfast. *Hotel-Pension Weidmann* (☎/fax 498 44 55, *Am Schwarzen Meer 35)* has comfortable but basic singles/doubles for DM50/80. *Gästehaus Peterswerder* (☎ 44 71 01, fax 44 73 01, Celler Strasse 4)* charges DM60/100 for basic rooms, and DM80/130 for rooms with shower and WC (toilet). For either of these, take tram No 2 or 10 from the Hauptbahnhof to St-Jürgen-Strasse. The *Hotel Garni Gästehaus Walter* (☎ 55 80 27, fax 55 80 29, Buntentorsteinweg 86-88)* charges from DM43/75 for basic rooms and

euro currency converter DM1 = €0.51

BREMEN

DM65/98 for rooms with a shower and WC (tram No 4 or 5).

Hotel Bolts am Park (☎ *34 61 10, fax 34 12 27, Slevogtstrasse 23)*, behind the Hauptbahnhof, has very pleasant rooms from DM65/140 – it's well known, so book ahead.

The *Hotel Ibis* (☎ *369 70, fax 369 71 09, Rembertiring 51)* has fairly standard chain-hotel rooms for DM125 with breakfast, and better weekend or walk-in deals. The *Etap* (☎ *83 73 50, Borgwardstrasse 10)* is quite a bit south of the centre and difficult to reach without a car. Functional rooms cost DM58/70, or a fixed DM58 on weekends (breakfast DM9 extra per person). The family-run *Pension Galerie* (☎ *55 76 20, fax 557 98 12, Thedinghauser Strasse 46)* has basic rooms from DM55/85, and up to DM75/110 with shower and WC. It also offers free use of its bikes. Take tram No 6 to Gastfeldstrasse.

Hotel-Pension Domizil (☎ *347 81 47, fax 34 23 76, Graf-Moltke-Strasse 42)* has rooms from DM69/105. *Hotel Weltevreden* (☎ *780 15, fax 70 40 91, Am Dobben 62)* has basic rooms for DM60/100; those with facilities cost up to DM95/120. The *Hotel Haus Bremen* (☎ *43 27 20, fax 432 72 22, Verdener Strasse 47)* offers nice, quiet rooms for up to DM110/145 (though a few cheaper are available). Take tram No 3 to Verdener Strasse.

Hotel Schaper-Siedenburg (☎ *308 70, fax 30 87 88, Bahnhofstrasse 8)* is only a few minutes walk from the Hauptbahnhof. It serves a great breakfast and charges from DM135/160 for rooms with facilities. *Hotel Bremer Haus* (☎ *329 40, fax 329 44 11, Löningstrasse 16-20)*, only 300m from the Hauptbahnhof, charges from DM135/165. *Turmhotel Weserblick* (☎ *79 19 79, fax 791 97 88, Osterdeich 53)* offers rooms with a view in one of Bremen's poshest neighbourhoods. Rooms here cost from DM145/190, but there are also cheaper ones without the view (tram stop: Sielwall).

For long-term rentals, the Home Company Mitwohnzentrale (☎ 194 45) is at Humboldtstrasse 28.

Places to Eat

Markt In good weather, the western half of the Markt takes on the feel of an Italian piazza as parcel-laden shoppers, bohemians and grey-haired ladies jostle for a place in the sun at dozens of cafe tables. *Beck's Bistro (Markt 9)* has a regular menu complemented by inexpensive daily specials (around DM12). The *Ratskeller* is within sight from here, with its cosy network of vaulted cellar rooms decorated with large carved barrels. It serves regional and international cuisine, and an astonishing 650 varieties of German wine. This is stored in huge rooms that, at any given time, hold 50,000 bottles and countless casks containing half a million litres of wine.

Schnoor Quite a few interesting cafes and restaurants huddle together in this neat neighbourhood. The *Schnoor Teestübchen (Wüstestätte 1)* is actually a cafe, but it offers a couple of vegetarian soups and a vegetarian quiche for lunch, all from DM8 to DM12. *Scusi* (☎ *32 60 01)* is down the same lane at No 11; it's a popular Italian cellar restaurant open in the evening, with creative pizza and pasta concoctions in the mid-price range. The *Gasthof zum Kaiser Friedrich (Lange Wieren 13)* was a popular gathering place of sea captains some 200 years ago and now draws office workers and tourists alike (closed Sunday). Its many rooms sport hundreds of black-and-white photographs of famous and not-so-famous guests. The food is hearty, plentiful and mostly under DM16.

Das Viertel The place to go for food and drink, especially at night, is Das Viertel (The Quarter) – an area along Ostertorsteinweg, east of Goetheplatz. Here you'll find an eclectic mix of trendy restaurants, multicultural cafes, funky bars and bustling pubs, almost all of them offering good value. Many are open from breakfast till the wee hours.

Piano (☎ *785 46, Fehrfeld 64)* offers creative, Mediterranean-inspired cuisine in Art Deco rooms, including vegetarian dishes and tasty casseroles costing around DM12 to

BREMEN

DM16. *Casablanca (Ostertorsteinweg 59)* is a fashionable and noisy bistro. The menu includes salads (DM10 to DM16), plus soups, baguettes and baked potatoes. The breakfast buffet is good, though service is often slow. Housed in a former pharmacy, *Café Engel (Ostertorsteinweg 31)* is a popular student hang-out that matches black-and-white tiled floors with dark wood furniture and offers two-course daily specials for around DM11.

Bio Biss (☎ 70 30 44, Wulwesstrasse 18) serves fairly well priced organic vegetarian and vegan main dishes.

Auf den Höfen This narrow courtyard off Auf den Häfen offers a multicultural mix of restaurants, bars and cafes. On a balmy night, it's as jammed as a Rolling Stones concert, with an atmosphere almost as electric. *Savarin* offers creative casseroles for under DM15. *Dos Mas* has tapas, tortillas and nachos plus main courses for around DM15 to DM20. The Austrian *Zum Hofheurigen* seems incongruous with its southern German decor, but the schnitzel is quite good at around DM16.

Entertainment

For events information and tips on what's on and where in Bremen, buy a copy of *Prinz* or *Bremer* (both DM4.50) at any newsagent, or look for a free copy of *Mix* at the tourist office or in bars and restaurants. The monthly events guide *Bremer Umschau* is available for DM3. *Hinnerk*, the free gay guide for northern Germany, includes information on bars, pubs and services for gay men in Bremen.

Pubs & Bars Bremen's best nightspots convene in Das Viertel (see Places to Eat).

The *Lagerhaus Kafé (Schildstrasse 12-19)*, inside the cultural centre of the same name, is one of our favourites. *Türke (Beim Steinernen Kreuz 13)* is a mainstay of the quarter and still informally so-named because it once had a Turkish proprietor. *März (Sielwall 29)* is also a popular place. The dimly lit *Airport (Am Dobben 70)* is for true night owls – it doesn't even open until

11 pm and serves killer cocktails. *Blue*, in the courtyard of Auf den Höfen, is a trendy drinking place with minimalist blue and silver decor. *Carnevale*, which has an exotic Caribbean theme, is also here.

Discos & Clubs *Moments (☎ 780 07, Vor dem Steintor 65)* is one bar and music venue that has innovative bands. Check the listings, as it dishes up a very mixed bag of styles. Whatever it is, it's usually good. *Aladin/Tivoli (☎ 43 51 50, Hannoversche Strasse 1)*, in the suburb of Hemelingen, opens up on Wednesday, Friday and Saturday with lots of hard rock, but also German rock and occasional techno. *Stubu (☎ 32 63 98, Rembertiring 21)* specialises in oldies and 1980s music. *Woody's*, just down the road, changes its musical emphasis nightly from Tuesday to Sunday.

Cultural Centres *Schlachthof (☎ 37 16 61, Findorffstrasse 51)*, in a 19th century slaughterhouse north-west of the Hauptbahnhof, has ethnic and world-music concerts and also theatre, cabaret and variété, complemented by exhibits and a cafe. The *Lagerhaus (☎ 70 21 68, Schildstrasse 12-19)* has a varied schedule of theatre, dance parties, movies, live concerts and more (see also Pubs & Bars).

Cinema Bremen has plenty of movie theatres. *Kino 46 (☎ 587 67 31, Waller Heerstrasse 469)* shows lots of movies in the original language (look for the acronym OmU). Tickets cost DM9/8. Take tram No 2 or 10 to Gustavstrasse.

Theatre Bremen has a total of nine stages. *Theater am Goetheplatz (☎ 365 30, Goetheplatz)* stages opera, operettas and musicals (take tram No 2 or 3 from the Domsheide stop near the Rathaus). *Schauspielhaus (☎ 365 33 33, Ostertorsteinweg 57a)* behind Theater am Goetheplatz does the lot, from updated classic to avant-garde drama. The *Concordia (☎ 365 33 39, Schwachhauser Heerstrasse 17)* is dominated by dance theatre (take tram No 1 or 4 to Parkstrasse).

euro currency converter DM1 = €0.51

BREMEN

One of Bremen's private theatre troupes is the acclaimed Bremer Shakespeare Company. It performs at **Theater am Leibnizplatz** (☎ 50 03 33), about 500m south of the Weser off Friedrich-Ebert-Strasse (tram No 4, 5 or 6).

Besides contacting theatre box offices directly for tickets, you can also try the tourist office or the central Ticket Service Center (☎ 35 36 37, fax 333 80 55). All theatres offer discounts to students and children.

Shopping

Bremen's main shopping area is between the Hauptbahnhof and the Markt, and centres around Sögestrasse and Obernstrasse. Along Ostertorsteinweg in Das Viertel are eccentric boutiques, ethnic food stores and funky second-hand shops. There are also two flea markets: one along the north bank of the Weser, roughly between Bürgermeister-Smidt-Brücke and the bridge at Balgebrückstrasse (open Saturday from 8 am to 4 pm year round) and the other on the Bürgerweide, north of the Hauptbahnhof (open most Sundays from 7 am to 2 pm; check exact dates at the tourist office).

Getting There & Away

Air Bremen's small international airport (☎ 559 50) is about 4km south of the centre and has more than 300 weekly flights to destinations in Germany and Europe. Airlines with offices here include British Airways (☎ 55 91 92), Lufthansa Airlines (☎ 0180 380 38 03) and KLM/Eurowings (0180 53 64 30).

Train Bremen has hourly IC train connections to Dortmund (DM69, 1¾ hours, every hour) and Frankfurt (DM172, 3¾ hours). Trains to Hamburg (DM33, 1¼ hours) leave several times hourly. If going to Berlin (DM135, 3¼ hours), change in Hanover; or in Hamburg, which is cheaper but slower. Lockers (DM4/2) are plentiful in the north aisle of the station.

Bus Eurolines has a service to London every Monday, Thursday and Saturday. The journey takes 17 hours and costs DM126, return DM219. It also offers daily trips to Amsterdam (DM60/95, five hours). If you're under 26, you get a 10% discount.

Car & Motorcycle The A1 (from Hamburg to Osnabrück) and the A27/A7 (Bremerhaven to Hanover) intersect in Bremen. The city is also on the B6 and B75. All major car rental agencies have branches at the airport, including Avis (☎ 55 80 55), Hertz (☎ 55 53 50) and Alamo (☎ 55 20 26).

Ride Services The ADM Mitfahrbüro (☎ 194 40 or ☎ 720 11) is at Körnerwall 1.

Boat Schreiber Reederei (☎ 32 12 29, fax 32 61 36) offers regular scheduled service up and down the Weser River. The boats leave from the Martinianleger landing in the city centre between early May and mid-October. Boats travelling the entire distance from Bremen to Bremerhaven (DM22/36 one-way/return, 3½ hours), with numerous stops in between, depart at 8.30 am every Wednesday, Thursday and Saturday. Shorter tours ending at Brake (DM15/24, 2¼ hours) depart on Tuesday and Sunday at 2 pm. Additional boats on these days depart at 9.30 am for Vegesack (DM12/17, one hour). Students and children pay half price. Travel on your birthday is free (bring ID). Bikes cost DM2.50.

Getting Around

To/From the Airport Tram No 6 from the Hauptbahnhof gets you to/from the airport in under 20 minutes (DM3.40). A taxi ride costs about DM20.

Public Transport The Verkehrsverbund Bremen/Niedersachsen (☎ 536 32 88) operates a good system of buses and trams that extends to most corners of town. The main hubs are in front of the Hauptbahnhof and at Domsheide near the Rathaus. Short trips cost DM1.70, while a DM3.40 ticket covers most of the Bremen city area. Four-trip tickets are DM10.40 and the Day Pass (*Tageskarte*) DM8.50.

Taxi You can book a taxi on ☎ 140 14 or ☎ 144 33.

Bicycle Bremen is a bicycle-friendly town, with lots of specially designated bike paths. In fact, if you're walking, you'd better watch out for cyclists, since they also seem to claim the pedestrian areas (and just about any other ground) by proprietary right. It's safer just to join them. The Fahrradstation (☎ 30 21 14) just outside the Hauptbahnhof has bikes for DM15 for 24 hours and DM35 for three days, plus a DM50 deposit (bring your passport).

AROUND BREMEN
Bremen-Nord
Technically still a part of Bremen proper and only 20km north of the city centre, the communities of Bremen-Nord – Vegesack, Burglesum and Blumenthal – have retained their own identity. The maritime tradition is still alive in these villages on the Weser River, which built Germany's first artificial harbour (1619-22), constructed merchant ships and sent hardy whalers on their journeys to the Arctic. Bremen-Nord is also the birthplace of the German Sea Rescue Service.

Sightseeing attractions include the **White Swan of the Lower Weser** (☎ 658 73 73), a restored, fully rigged windjammer used as a training ship for sailors and as a museum. From May to September it's open Tuesday to Sunday, and Wednesday to Sunday the rest of the year (DM3). It lies at anchor in the mouth of the Lesum River at Friedrich-Klippert-Strasse 1 in Vegesack.

Besides old villas, warehouses and captains' houses, you'll also find the 300-year-old moated **Schloss Schönebeck** (☎ 64 34 32), a stately red-brick building that's now a local history museum. The exhibit concentrates on shipbuilding, seafaring, whaling and other activities important to the region's past. Opening hours are Tuesday, Wednesday and weekends from 3 to 5 pm, Sunday also from 10 am to 12.30 pm (DM3). To get to the Schloss, take bus No 78 or 79 from Bahnhof Vegesack to Herbartstrasse.

To get to Bremen-Nord, take the Stadt-Express train from Bremen's Hauptbahnhof to Bahnhof Vegesack.

Worpswede
☎ 04792 • pop 9000
Worpswede is a pretty village with an artistic tradition about 30km north-east of Bremen, which actually places it within the borders of Lower Saxony. The town surrounds the 55m-tall **Weyerberg**, a sand dune at the centre of a large peat bog called **Teufelsmoor** (Devil's Moor). This barren, melancholic landscape – where big clouds form dramatic skyscapes and the light creates deep shadows – drew painters here in 1889.

The original artists' colony included Fritz Mackensen, Otto Modersohn, Fritz Overbeck, Heinrich Vogeler and Hans am Ende. An exhibition of their works at the Glaspalast in Munich in 1895 catapulted the group to prominence overnight. Others, including writers, actors and composers, then began to flock to Worpswede as well. Paula Modersohn-Becker, who joined the group in 1898, is buried in the village cemetery. The future co-creator of Bremen's Böttcherstrasse, Bernhard Hoetger (see the earlier Bremen section), arrived here in 1914. As the density of studios and galleries shows, Worpswede continues to cast its creative spell on artists from all fields.

The **Grosse Kunstschau** (☎ 13 02), Lindenallee 3, displays works by the founding members. The **Ludwig Roselius Museum** next door has a large collection of items from European prehistory. Both museums are open daily from 10 am to 6 pm (DM5/3).

At Ostendorfer Strasse 10 stands the **Barkenhof**, a half-timbered structure remodelled in Art Nouveau style at the start of the 20th century by its then-owner Heinrich Vogeler. At one time, this house and studio formed the creative centre of the colony. Vogeler also designed the Art Nouveau **train station**. The rail line closed in 1978, and the structure is now a restaurant.

The moors and meadows surrounding Worpswede are an important **wetland** for wild geese, ducks, cranes and other birdlife.

euro currency converter DM1 = €0.51

BREMEN

The tourist office (☎ 95 01 21, fax 95 01 23, email info@worpswede.de), Bergstrasse 13, can suggest some walks and cycling routes, including the 20km signposted Teufelsmoor-Rundweg bike route. The tourist office is open weekdays from 9 am to 1 pm and 2 to 6 pm, weekends from 10 am to 3 pm, with restricted hours in winter.

Getting There & Around To get to Worpswede from Bremen, take bus No 140 from the central bus station, which makes the 50 minute trip about every 1½ hours. Personenschiffahrt Ruth Haferkamp (☎ 04404-35 14) offers boat trips from Bremen-Vegesack (2½ hours, DM18/25 one-way/return) via the Lesum and Hamme rivers from May to September every Wednesday and Sunday at 9.15 am. In August, there's an additional boat on Thursday. You can always take the bus back to Bremen.

Fahrradladen Eckhard Eyl (☎ 23 23), Finddorffstrasse 28, rents bikes for DM12 per day.

BREMERHAVEN
☎ 0471 • pop 130,000

Some 65km north of Bremen lies Bremerhaven, the state's only other city. It owes its existence to the silting up of the Weser in the early 19th century and the vision of the wily Bremen mayor at the time, Johann Smidt. For 73,000 thalers, he bought the land at the mouth of the river from King George of Hanover and laid the foundations for a brand-new harbour here in 1827. It was good timing, for the era of regular steamer traffic between Europe and North America was just picking up. Throughout the 19th and 20th centuries, Bremerhaven was the major exit ramp for about six million emigrants to the USA and other countries.

Bremerhaven *is* its port. The biggest city on Germany's North Sea coast boasts one of the largest and most modern container terminals in the world, handling 1.3 million of these giant steel crates each year. At the separate Banana Terminal, some 450,000 tonnes of cargo are discharged annually, while the Automobile Terminal loads and unloads about 750,000 cars.

Things to See & Do

Bremerhaven isn't pretty, but there's a certain excitement from all the activity surrounding the gigantic port. Between March and October you can stroll along the **waterfront promenade** or walk to the top of the **viewing platform** near the container terminal in the North Harbour to get an overview of its vastness (free).

Bremerhaven's main draw, though, is the **German Maritime Museum** (Deutsche Schiffahrtsmuseum; ☎ 48 20 70), Hans-Scharoun-Platz 1, near the radar tower in the city centre. It's the kind of place that can be enjoyed even by those who can't tell the bow from the stern. The museum's several floors are meant to resemble the decks of a passenger liner. The prized exhibit is the wooden hull of a merchant boat from 1388, the so-called **Hanse Kogge**. It was pieced together from thousands of fragments found during excavations in another harbour in 1962. This gem from the briny deep has sat out of view in a giant steel tank, submerged in a chemical bath, though it may be exhibited by the time you read this. A 1:10 scale model reveals what it looked like.

The museum has a thorough exhibition documenting the evolution of shipbuilding. The collection of about 500 ship models includes whalers, brigantines, three-masters and steamers. The entire range of ship and boat types is represented here, from an 11,000-year-old dugout to the engine control room of the nuclear-powered *Otto Hahn*. Outside, the **Museum Harbour** has a parade of eight historical ships open for viewing between April and September. They include the wooden sailing vessel *Seute Deern* (1919), the polar research ship *Grönland* (1868) and the fire ship *Elbe 3* (1909).

The Schiffahrtsmuseum is open from 10 am to 6 pm, closed Monday (DM6/3). To get there, take bus No 2, 3, 5, 6, 8 or 9 to Theodor-Heuss-Platz.

To get a glimpse of life on a U-boat, climb aboard the WWII-vintage **Wilhelm Bauer**, which is moored here as well. The only surviving boat of the XXI type, it was the first to go faster under water than above and was outfitted with a special snorkel that allowed it to stay submerged for extended periods. It's accessible from April to October daily from 10 am to 5.30 pm (DM3/1.50).

Another museum worth investigating is the **Morgenstern Museum** (☎ 201 38), in a modern complex at An der Geeste. It brings to life the early history of the port town with such exhibits as an old harbour pub, a fish shop, an American Jeep representing the occupation era after WWII, and older technology used to move cargo. It's open from 10 am to 6 pm, closed Monday (DM3/1.50). Take bus No 5 or 6 to the Borriesstrasse stop.

Bremerhaven's tourist office (☎ 946 46 10, fax 460 65, email TFG@bhv.ipnet.de),

Van-Ronzelen-Strasse 2, is open weekdays from 8 am to 6.30 pm, in winter to 4 pm on Thursday and to 3.30 pm on Friday. There's also an information pavilion (☎ 430 00, fax 430 80) at Obere Bürger 17 in the Columbus-Center mall, open Monday to Wednesday from 9.30 am to 6 pm, Thursday and Friday to 8 pm and Saturday to 4 pm.

Getting There & Away

Trains from Bremen to Bremerhaven are frequent and the trip takes about one hour (DM15.60). By car, Bremerhaven is quickly reached via the A27 from Bremen; get off at the Bremerhaven-Mitte exit. A slower alternative is a leisurely boat ride from Bremen (see Getting There & Away in the Bremen section).

Lower Saxony

Lower Saxony (Niedersachsen) is Germany's second largest state after Bavaria. Part of its attraction lies in its varied landscape, which spans the forested highlands of the western Harz Mountains, the northern German lowlands around Lüneburg, the low hills of the Weser region and the flat coastal area of Friesland with its offshore islands. Its natural resources are another major asset. Silver brought wealth to Goslar in the Middle Ages, and the salt mines in Lüneburg and the iron-ore deposits in Salzgitter contributed to those towns' riches. Fishing still provides a source of income to the coastal communities. And one of the largest car factories in Europe is the VW plant in Wolfsburg.

British occupational forces created the *Land* of Lower Saxony in 1946 when they amalgamated the states of Braunschweig (Brunswick), Schaumburg-Lippe and Oldenburg with the Prussian province of Hanover, formerly the Kingdom of Hanover. Between 1714 and 1837, Hanover and Britain were governed by the same series of rulers. Today, Hanover is the capital of the state and its largest city. Badly damaged in WWII, its charms lie in its wonderful museums and parks rather than in harmonious historic appearance. Every year, it hosts the world's largest industrial fair at the Hannover Messe.

North of Hanover is the Lüneburg Heath and the town of Lüneburg, with its splendid townscape dominated by redbrick Gothic buildings. Celle, once a residence of the Lüneburg dukes, boasts a picturesque half-timbered Altstadt. South of the state capital is Hannoversch-Münden, where the Weser River begins its 440km-long journey through a rural area of valleys, meadows, ruined castles and palaces before emptying into the North Sea near Bremerhaven. Göttingen is a pleasant university town whose hallowed halls have produced at least 40 Nobel Prize winners. The student life here is particularly lively, as is the nightlife.

HIGHLIGHTS

Lower Saxony Luminaries: Wilhelm Bausch, Leo von Klenze, Robert Koch, Wilhelm Raabe, Erich Maria Remarque, Georg Friedrich Bernhard Riemann, Werner von Siemens

- Visiting the Bergen-Belsen concentration camp
- Exploring the Herzog Anton Ulrich Museum in Braunschweig
- Visiting the half-timbered houses in Celle
- Wandering around Hanover's Markthalle
- Touring the Volkswagen factory in Wolfsburg

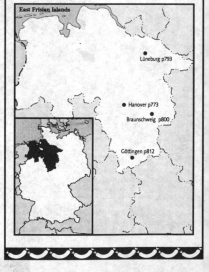

Braunschweig is Lower Saxony's second largest town and most closely associated with Heinrich der Löwe (Henry the Lion), who governed Bavaria and Saxony from

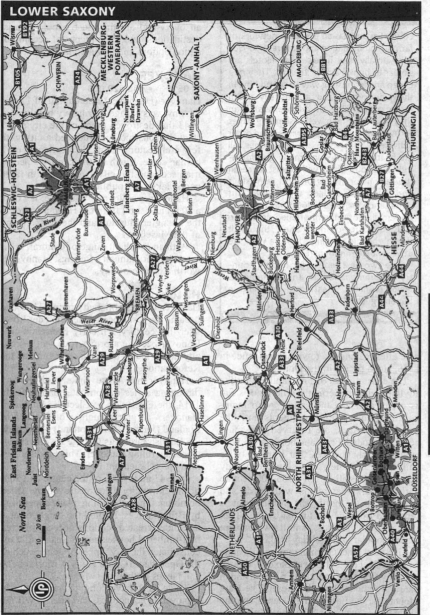

Hay Hotels

Lower Saxony has an excellent network of farm accommodation and several *Heu Hotels*, literally 'hay hotels'. Heu Hotels are similar to bunk barns in the UK. They're a cheap and interesting way to spend time in the countryside, and are usually much more comfortable (if odoriferous) than they sound. Some have horse riding, lakes for swimming, sledding in winter, and other activities. While some are bare-bones, all are heated in winter and many get downright luxurious. Check with tourist offices in the region for listings of local farm stays and hay hotels. Urlaub und Freizeit auf dem Lande (☎ 04231-966 50, fax 96 65 66, email info@bauernhofferien.de) is also a useful source of information, though it doesn't handle bookings. It has a Web site at www.bauernhofferien.de.

The two best centres for finding country accommodation in the Lüneburger Heide (Lüneburg Heath) are Celle and in Lüneburg itself.

here after making the town his residence in 1166. He is buried in the Dom.

The coastal areas of Friesland are unlike anything else in Germany. The land is flat as a pancake, and the people, who maintained republic-like governments until the late Middle Ages, are reserved and independent-minded. Friesland borders the Wattenmeer, a shallow sea that retreats twice daily with the tides, exposing the muddy ocean floor. It's all part of a 565,000 hectare national park that teems with birds and wildlife. To the north, the Wattenmeer is separated from the North Sea by the seven East Frisian Islands, small windswept places popular with holiday-makers.

Like most other German regions, it's quite easy to travel around Lower Saxony, though you may find a car useful in Friesland and in the rural regions along the Weser. The Harz Mountains, the East Frisian Islands and the picturesque towns along the Fairy-Tale Road

(see the boxed text in the Hesse chapter for an overview) are the most popular tourist destinations, and offer plenty of accommodation options and travel connections.

HANOVER
☎ 0511 • pop 520,000

Hanover (Hannover), the capital of Lower Saxony, was savaged by heavy bombing in 1943 that destroyed much of the city's Altstadt. Reconstruction produced a city with few architectural gems, but certainly on a human scale. Much of the centre is pedestrianised, and the city is dotted with large parks, lakes and public artworks.

Hanover is eminently walkable: it's only a 20 minute stroll from the Hauptbahnhof to the Spengler Museum and the northern end of the Maschsee.

With an excellent range of cultural, artistic and entertainment offerings, Hanover is worth a couple of days.

History

Hanover was established around 1100 and became the residence of Heinrich der Löwe later that century. An early Hanseatic city, Hanover became a prosperous seat of royalty and a major power by the time of the Reformation.

Hanover has close links with Britain through a series of intricate marriages. In 1714, the eldest son of Electress Sophie of Hanover – a granddaughter of James I of England (James VI of Scotland) – ascended the English throne as George I while simultaneously ruling Hanover. This English/German union lasted until 1837.

In 1943 up to 80% of the centre and 50% of the entire city were destroyed by Allied bombing. The rebuilding plan, supervised by British forces, limited the height of new buildings, created sections of reconstructed half-timbered houses and painstakingly reconstructed the city's prewar gems, such as the Opernhaus (Opera House), Marktkirche and Neues Rathaus.

Trade fairs have long played a role in Hanoverian economics, and after WWII the city was keen to get right back into them. It

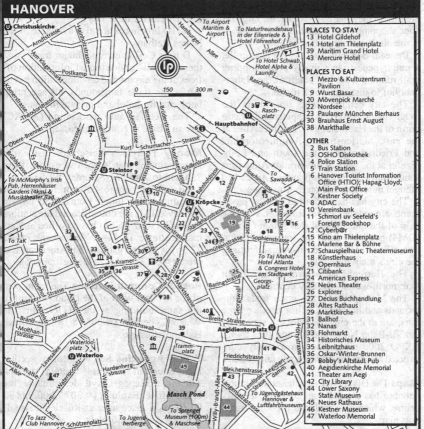

HANOVER

PLACES TO STAY
13 Hotel Gildehof
14 Hotel am Thielenplatz
39 Maritim Grand Hotel
43 Mercure Hotel

PLACES TO EAT
1 Mezzo & Kultuzentrum Pavilion
9 Wurst Basar
20 Mövenpick Marché
22 Nordsee
23 Paulaner München Bierhaus
30 Brauhaus Ernst August
38 Markthalle

OTHER
2 Bus Station
3 OSHO Diskothek
4 Police Station
5 Train Station
6 Hanover Tourist Information Office (HTIO); Hapag-Lloyd; Main Post Office
7 Kestner Society
8 ADAC
10 Vereinsbank
11 Schmorl uv Seefeld's Foreign Bookshop
12 Cyberb@r
15 Kino am Thielenplatz
16 Marlene Bar & Bühne
17 Schauspielhaus; Theatermuseum
18 Künstlerhaus
19 Opernhaus
21 Citibank
24 American Express
25 Neues Theater
26 Explorer
27 Decius Buchhandlung
28 Altes Rathaus
29 Marktkirche
31 Ballhof
32 Nanas
33 Flohmarkt
34 Historisches Museum
35 Leibnitzhaus
36 Oskar-Winter-Brunnen
37 Bobby's Altstadt Pub
40 Aegidienkirche Memorial
41 Theater am Aegi
42 City Library
44 Lower Saxony State Museum
45 Neues Rathaus
46 Kestner Museum
47 Waterloo Memorial

LOWER SAXONY

held its first postwar trade fair in August 1947 in the midst of all the rubble. As the majority of the city's hotels had been destroyed, the mayor made an appeal to the people of the city to provide beds for foreign guests. The people did, the money came and it's become a tradition: today there are about a third more beds for rent in private flats than in hotels.

The grand-daddy of all fairs is CeBit – the world's largest office information and telecommunications trade fair, attended by over 800,000 people annually. Look for CeBit's new home-electronics fair, which might eventually bring in even more than that. Some 25 million people are expected to visit during EXPO 2000, which runs from 1 June to 31 October 2000.

Orientation

The Hauptbahnhof is at the north-eastern end of the city centre. The centre contains the largest pedestrianised area in Germany, focusing on Georgstrasse and Bahnhofstrasse. Bahnhofstrasse runs south-west from the

Hauptbahnhof, Georgstrasse west-east from Steintor to the square at Kröpke; the large indoor shopping mall, called Galerie Luise, is at the north-eastern end of Kröpke.

Beneath Bahnhofstrasse is the Passarelle, a major pedestrian subway-cum-shopping mall running from just south of the Hauptbahnhof to just south of Kröpke.

The city centre's limits are within the rough ring formed by Raschplatzhochstrasse north of the Hauptbahnhof, Berliner Allee at the east, Marienstrasse, Aegidientorplatz and Friedrichswall at the south and Leibnizufer at the west. Willy-Brandt-Allee runs south from Friedrichswall to the Landes and Stengel museums and on to Maschsee.

The city has painted a red line on pavements around the centre; follow it, with the help of the multilingual *Red Thread Guide* (DM4) available from the tourist information office, for a quick do-it-yourself tour of the city's main highlights.

The Herrenhäuser Gardens are about 4km north-west of the city centre.

The Messegelände, the main trade fairgrounds and home to CeBit and other large fairs, are in the city's south-west, served by tram/U-Bahn No 8, and IC and ICE trains. EXPO 2000 takes place in a newly constructed area on the present trade fairgrounds.

Maps The DB service counter at the Hauptbahnhof has a good map covering the city centre, which also includes a public transport map.

Information

Tourist Offices The excellent Hanover Tourist Information Office (HTIO; ☎ 30 14 20), Ernst-August-Platz 2, next to the main post office and near the Hauptbahnhof, is open weekdays from 9.30 am to 7 pm and Saturday to 3 pm. It provides a wide range of services, including hotel and private room booking (the latter only during trade fairs and festivals), concert and theatre ticket sales, and tours and excursions. Consider buying the HannoverCard, which entitles you to unlimited public transport and discounted or free admission to museums

and other attractions. It costs DM14 for a day, DM23 for three days.

HTIO brochures are also available in the Neues Rathaus.

During CeBit and other major trade fairs, there are full-service tourist information offices at the airport and an information pavilion at the trade fairgrounds, all accepting bookings for hotel and private rooms.

The German auto association (ADAC) has an office at Nordmannpassage 4.

Money There's a Reisebank inside the Hauptbahnhof that is open weekdays from 7.30 am to 7.45 pm, Saturday till 5 pm and Sunday from 9 am to 4.30 pm. It closes for 45 minutes for lunch from 12.30 pm on Sunday. ATMs are dotted around the station. Citibank (☎ 32 76 81) has an office at Karmarschstrasse 12-14. A Vereinsbank (☎ 32 72 96) is at Georgstrasse 8a. American Express (☎ 36 34 28) is at Georgstrasse 54.

Post & Communications The main post office is north-west of the Hauptbahnhof in the same building as the HTIO. Surf the Web at Cyberb@r (☎ 305 18 18), upstairs at Bahnhofstrasse 6.

Travel Agencies See the Money section for American Express contact details. There's a Hapag-Lloyd desk inside the HTIO office. Explorer (☎ 307 72 00, fax 32 97 61) is a discounter at Röselerstrasse 1, towards Aegidientorplatz.

Bookshops & Libraries In the Passarelle on the corner of Georgstrasse is Schmorl uv Seefeld's Foreign Bookshop (☎ 367 50). Upstairs (separate entrance at Bahnhofstrasse 14) is a travel section with maps and Lonely Planet guides. A smaller selection is at Decius Buchhandlung (☎ 364 76 52), farther south on the corner of Marktstrasse and Karmarschstrasse.

The Stadt Bibliothek (city library) is on Georgstrasse just south of Aegidientorplatz.

Universities Hanover Universität has four campuses; the main one is west of the centre in and around the former Guelf Palace (take tram/U-Bahn No 4 or 5 to Universität). The university's 34,000 students are split into faculties of medicine, veterinary medicine, music and art.

Laundry The most central laundry is Schnell & Sauber, behind the Hauptbahnhof on the corner of Friesenstrasse and Eichstrasse. It's open daily from 6 am to 11 pm.

Medical Services & Emergency For medical emergency services call ☎ 31 40 44. There's a clinic (☎ 304 31) at Marienstrasse 37.

The police station is beneath the overpass on the north side of the Hauptbahnhof at Raschplatz.

Dangers & Annoyances The Passarelle and the area around the Hauptbahnhof feel a bit dodgy after dark; there's a huge police presence, but use common sense.

The red-light district hugs the western side of the pedestrian zone around Steintor. This area, along with legal brothels on and around Ludwigstrasse north of the railway tracks, attracts nefarious characters galore, including pimps and prostitutes of both genders. Use extreme caution at night in these areas, where robbery rates are the highest in the city.

Herrenhäuser Gardens
These gardens, especially the baroque **Great Garden** (Grosser Garten) and the **Mountain Garden** (Berggarten) are some of the last of their kind in Europe, and justifiably a favourite Hanoverian haunt. They were established on the estate of Duke Johann Friedrich in 1666, and up to 200 gardeners can be seen toiling on the grounds daily in summer.

The **Grosser Brunnen** (Great Fountain), at the southern end of the park, once blasted a stream of water (in perfectly still weather) some 82m high. It operates from Easter to early October from 11 am to noon and again from 2 to 4 pm (till 5 pm weekends and holidays).

The gardens open daily to 8 pm in summer (DM3, free with HannoverCard). In summer, international fireworks contests, concerts and theatrical performances are held regularly; many events are free or have small admission charges (see Entertainment). And if you've never walked through a real **maze**, now's your chance – just don't see *The Shining* before you do it. It's at the northwest end of the Great Garden. There you'll also find the **Fürstenhaus Herrenhausen-Museum** (DM6/3.50), with royal treasures and exhibits on the royal link between Britain and Hanover, and the **Wilhelm-Busch-Museum** (DM4/2) of caricature and satirical art, which contains the work of Busch and similar artists. Both are closed Monday and free with HannoverCard.

The Mountain Garden, north of the Great Garden, has a great range of flora, from a boisterous rhododendron grove to desert and heath plants and a marshland pond.

Tram/U-Bahn Nos 4 and 5 stop right at the northern end of the gardens.

Altstadt
What remained of the Altstadt after WWII was razed and rebuilt, with several liberties taken. The focal point of the Altstadt is the 14th century **Marktkirche** (1349-59). Apart from its truncated tower, it's characteristic

LOWER SAXONY

The **Wilhelm-Busch-Museum** sees the funny side of life, with its displays of satirical art.

euro currency converter DM1 = €0.51

of the northern German red-brick Gothic style. Its original stained-glass windows are particularly beautiful. The city has created an entire row of reconstructed **half-timbered houses** that line Kramerstrasse and Burgstrasse between the church and the Historical Museum.

The **Altes Rathaus** (begun 1455) across the marketplace was built in various stages over a century. Another highlight of the Altstadt is the **Ballhof** (1649-64), originally built for 17th century badminton-type games, but today staging plays.

Historisches Museum
The Historical Museum (☎ 168 30 52), Pferdstrasse 6, is especially popular with children. The exhibits include videos (with great postwar footage), and original gilded stagecoaches of the royal family. Downstairs is a section of the city's original fortification, around which the museum was built. Upstairs, don't miss the section on old German cars, with 1924 and 1928 Hanomags, early production automobiles, and the itty-bitty BMW Isetta 300. It's open Tuesday from 10 am to 8 pm, Wednesday to Friday to 4 pm, and weekends to 6 pm (DM5/3, free with HannoverCard).

Leibnizhaus & Fountain
Next to the Historical Museum, the home of mathematician and philosopher Gottfried Wilhelm Leibniz (1646-1716) is an impressive dwelling with a reconstructed Renaissance facade. Out front, walk up the little steps to the Oskar-Winter-Brunnen and, if you make a wish and turn the brass ring embedded in the ironwork three times, it'll come true – or so local lore tells us.

Neues Rathaus
In the domed Neues Rathaus (1901-13), off Friedrichswall west of Willy-Brandt-Allee (tram/U-Bahn No 10), the star of the show is the dome **lift** (elevator). It carries passengers in a shaft along the exterior of the dome (that's right, the lift slants as you go up) to a viewing platform at 98m. Not to be attempted with a hangover. It operates from

April to November daily from 10 am to 12.45 pm and 1.30 to 4.45 pm (DM3/2).

Inside the main lobby are four detailed city models that show what has been lost and gained in the march of time (free). From the display you'll gain a new appreciation of how extensive the WWII bomb damage was.

Kestner Museum
Opened in 1889, the original building (containing the core collection) of the Kestner Museum (☎ 16 84 21 20), Trammplatz 3, was rebuilt and restored after WWII and is now enclosed within the modern one. On the ground floor are rotating exhibitions and a small, permanent coin and medal collection.

The 1st floor is dedicated to **decorative art** from the Middle Ages to the present, including amazing oak chests. On the 2nd floor, turn left at the top of the stairs to view the museum's excellent **Egyptian collection**, including a bust of the Pharaoh Akhenaten. To the right at the top of the stairs is the **ancient art** section.

The museum is open Tuesday to Sunday from 11 am to 6 pm, Wednesday till 8 pm (DM5/3, free on Friday and with a HannoverCard).

Aegidienkirche Memorial
On Breite Strasse near the corner of Osterstrasse, at the ruin of the Aegidienkirche Memorial (1350), bashed by artillery in 1943, is an eloquent steel-cross memorial simply to *Unsere Toten* (Our Dead); the peace bell inside is a gift from one of Hanover's sister cities – Hiroshima. Every 6 August at 8.15 am, the date and time of the atomic detonation at Hiroshima, a delegation from both cities meets here to ring the bell.

Lower Saxony State Museum
By the time you read this, the Niedersächsisches Landesmuseum (☎ 980 75) should have reopened after renovation. It's home to an enormous display of natural history of the region. It also has paintings by Monet, Corinth and Cranach the Elder, along with 14th to 16th century Dutch and 17th and 18th century European works. It's at Willy-

Brandt-Allee 5 on the east side of the Masch-park, 10 minutes walk from the Neues Rathaus (tram/U-Bahn No 10 to Aegidientor-platz). It's usually open Tuesday to Sunday from 10 am to 5 pm, to 7 pm on Thursday.

Sprengel Museum

South of the Lower Saxony State Museum, the Sprengel Museum (☎ 16 84 38 75) at Kurt-Schwitters-Platz is a highly respected modern art museum with permanent and large rotating exhibitions and innovative programs for children.

The highlights of the impressive perma-nent collection include works by Picasso and Max Beckmann, Edvard Munch, Fran-cis Bacon, Marc Chagall and the Hanover-ian Kurt Schwitters. There's at least one Duane Hansen here as well. It's open Wednesday to Sunday from 10 am to 6 pm, Tuesday till 8 pm.

Other Museums

There are several noteworthy museums with rotating exhibits. The **Kestner Society** (☎ 70 12 00), Goseriede 11, has long been on the cutting edge of modern art shows (for which it was shut down by the Gestapo in 1936). Today it is housed in the city's beautiful former bathhouse.

The **Kunstverein** (☎ 32 45 94), Hanover's Art Association, has a great space in the **Künstlerhaus** (1853-56), Sophienstrasse 2, highlighting the work of many local artists.

The **Theatermuseum** at the Schauspiel-haus, Prinzenstrasse 9, has exhibitions re-lated to ongoing performances.

Out at Laatzen, south-west of the Messegelände, the **Luftfahrtmuseum** (☎ 879 17 91), Ulmer Strasse 2, is a museum of the history of aviation, with 30 aircraft includ-ing biplanes and triplanes, and British, Ger-man and Russian aircraft. It's open Tuesday to Sunday from 10 am to 5 pm (DM10/5).

Maschsee

The 2m-deep artificial Maschsee, a half hour walk (or five minute tram/U-Bahn ride) south of the Hauptbahnhof, was built by the unemployed in one of the earliest Nazi-led public works projects. Today, it's a favourite spot for swimming and boating.

Motorboats aren't permitted, as the lake is a prime breeding ground for carp; carp are harvested and served up on a platter for New Years' celebrations. A ferry plies the lake from Easter to October in good weather (DM5/2.50 to cross, DM10/5 for a tour). Stands here also rent sailing, pedal and rowing boats.

The Strandbad, a free swimming beach open from May to August, is at the south-east side of the lake; the DJH hostel is on the west side.

Waterloo Memorial

North-west of Maschsee is another city park (take tram/U-Bahn No 3, 7 or 9 to Waterloo), with a 42m-high column (1832) commemorating the German forces who fought here.

Special Events

The annual Maschsee festival, with drink-ing, performances and an enormous fire-works display, runs annually from 30 July to 17 August. Hanover hosts the ATP ten-nis world championship each year in late November. The women's Grand Prix tour-nament is held in mid-February. The inter-national fireworks festival at Herrenhäuser Garden is another big event, taking place throughout the summer months.

Places to Stay

Hanover's hotel scene becomes hectic dur-ing large trade shows: the city is positively awash with people, and even the hotel in-dustry approves of the HTIO booking pri-vate rooms as a pressure-release valve. Come CeBit time, hotel prices quadruple, quintuple and are generally outrageous: singles/doubles for DM450/550 are booked solid a *year* in advance. Many business-people stay in Hamburg and take the one hour ICE train ride to/from Hanover.

Hanover has dozens of hotels catering to expense-account holders. Check first – the more desirable mid to top-range places al-ways sell out before the cheapies.

LOWER SAXONY

EXPO 2000

The EXPO, Germany's first and held under the motto of 'Humankind-Nature-Technology', runs from 1 June to 31 October 2000 on the converted Messe site in Hanover. For five months, around 180 countries and international organisations will present some ideas on creating a better future.

About 2000 active projects – ranging from helping street children in Haiti to easing Britain's traffic problems – are being staged throughout the world as a practical aspect of the EXPO. The idea is for these to continue once the EXPO visitors have packed and gone home.

One of the highlights is the interactive Theme Park called 'Knowledge, Information and Communication', where the Protestant ethic meets cyberspace: the exhibit begins in the Garden of Eden, meditates Disney-like on the future of work and ends in a virtual reality airport/space station.

The German pavilion, an enormous transparent construction with timber and steel supports, has been designed to cope with about 60,000 visitors a day. A pre-show area contains an exhibition on the 50 year history of the Federal Republic of Germany. There's also a 'happening hall' with stage space, display screens and a media garden and large Tree of Knowledge with 16 branches, one for each state.

Between 20 and 30 million visitors are expected to attend EXPO 2000. A 30m-high gondola ferries visitors 2.5km across the site, with three stops.

The full/discount admission price for the EXPO 2000 is DM69/49 for a day ticket, DM49/39 for an afternoon ticket valid after 3 pm, and DM24/15 for an evening ticket valid after 7 pm. Discounts are for children or for students under 28. Tickets, which have been on sale since mid-1998, can be picked up from designated travel agents abroad and in Germany, from the Deutsche Bahn counter at any Hauptbahnhof, on the Internet at the official EXPO information Web site (www.expo2000.de), within Germany on ☎ 0-2000 or outside Germany on ☎ 49-2000. You can also buy them at the gate, but a surcharge of DM10 is levied on weekdays and DM20 on weekends. The exhibition site is open from 9 am to midnight and the national pavilions from 10 am to 11 pm.

A massive construction program to upgrade transportation facilities for the EXPO was under way at the time of research – evident by some sensational bottomless holes, construction barriers and 'container cities' of shops in and around Lower Saxony's train stations. A third terminal has been opened at Hanover's Langenhagen airport to cope with the extra flights scheduled for EXPO. Hanover Messe/Laatzen train station has also been upgraded and a new S-Bahn (the S5) between the airport and the EXPO/Messe site has opened. The frequent S-Bahn service runs via Hanover's Hauptbahnhof (12 minutes) to Messe/Laatzen (20 minutes from the airport).

Private Rooms Private rooms are only available during trade fairs and shows. You can book these or hotel rooms on arrival at the HTIO at Ernst-August-Platz or through Hannover Congress & Tourismus Center, Hotel- und Privatzimmer Service (☎ 811 35 00, fax 811 35 41), Theodor-Heuss-Platz 1-3, D-30175. Prices start at DM50 but average about DM80 and often go higher. The booking fee is DM10 to DM20 per stay.

Places to Stay – Budget
Camping There are three camping grounds in the area. *Campingplatz Blauer See* (☎ 05137-12 10 03), west of the city, has tent sites for DM3.90 plus DM9.50 per person. It also has dorm beds/singles/two-room

cabins, all with kitchens, for DM39/49/79, but you need your own blankets. Take tram/U-Bahn No 4 to Garbsen EKZ, then bus No 126 to Waldschänke Garbsen, from where it's 1km on foot. If you're driving, take the A2 to Garbsen and follow the signs.

Campingplatz Arnauer See (☎ *05101-35 34*), south of the city, has tent sites for DM7.50 plus DM6 per person. Take bus No 364 or 384 from the bus station to Arnum Mitte, from where it's a five minute walk. By car or motorcycle take the A7 south to Laatzen, or the B3 from Arnum and follow the signs.

Campingplatz Birkensee (☎ *52 99 62*), south-east of the city in Laatzen, is the most expensive and inconvenient. It costs DM8 for tent sites, plus DM10 per person. There's no public transport; take the A7 to Laatzen and the B443 to Birkensee.

Hostels The *Jugendherberge* (☎ *131 76 74, fax 185 55, Ferdinand-Wilhelm-Fricke-Weg 1*) is 3km from the centre and has recently been given a face-lift. The price for juniors/seniors is DM27/35 with breakfast. Take U-Bahn No 3 or 7 from the Hauptbahnhof to Fischerhof, then cross the river over the Lodemannbrücke and turn right.

The *Naturfreundehaus in der Eilenriede* (☎ *69 14 93, fax 69 06 52, Hermann-Bahlsen-Allee 8*), in the city park, has single rooms for DM43.80 and two or three-bed dorms for DM34.80 per person.

The *Jugendgästehaus Hannover* (☎ *86 44 40, fax 86 32 30, Wilkenburgerstrasse 40*) has rooms for DM36.50 per person with shared bath, DM50.50 with private bath.

Hotels The city centre has some affordable hotel options. The *Hotel Gildehof* (☎ *36 36 80, fax 30 66 44, Joachimstrasse 6*) offers basic singles/doubles for DM80/119, or with shower and WC for DM107/139. It also has a traditional restaurant serving food at reasonable prices. The *Hotel am Thielenplatz* (☎ *32 76 91, fax 32 51 88, email hotel.am.thielenplatz@t-online.de, Thielenplatz 2*) has one basic single for DM78, and rooms with shower and WC for DM99/180.

The friendly *Hotel Flora-Garni* (☎ *38 39 10, fax 383 91 91, Heinrichstrasse 36*) is a pleasant option, with basic rooms for DM65/110, and rooms with a shower and WC for DM85/130. It's a few minutes by foot north-east of the Hauptbahnhof.

Hotel Schwab (☎ *99 01 61, fax 336 00 44, Sedanstrasse 20*) is central but overpriced and the staff are unpleasant. But if you can't find anything else, a depressing basic room here will cost DM65, or DM85/120 with a shower. Take Friesenstrasse north-east.

Places to Stay – Mid-Range

The *Hotel Alpha* (☎ *34 15 35, Friesenstrasse 19*) has friendly staff and some weird and wonderful marionettes decorating the foyer. Nice single/double rooms cost DM118/178. Triples cost DM198, and all are with shower and WC. *Hotel Atlanta* (☎ *338 60, fax 34 59 28, Hinüberstrasse 1*), opposite the Taj Mahal restaurant, has comfortable and clean smoking and nonsmoking rooms. Prices start at DM135/185 for singles/doubles. It's a few minutes walk south-east of Raschplatz.

The Best Western-run *Hotel Föhrenhof* (☎ *615 40, fax 61 97 19, Kirschhorster Strasse 22*) offers comfortable small rooms from DM150/225. The *Mercure Hotel* (☎ *800 80, fax 809 37 04, Willy-Brandt-Allee 3*) is convenient to the centre. Prices start from DM135/155. The *Holiday Inn Crowne Plaza* (☎ *770 70, fax 73 77 81, Petzelstrasse 60*), out near the airport, has rooms of the usual Holiday Inn standard from DM235.

Places to Stay – Top End

Some of the top-end places away from the centre offer great amenities. The *Congress Hotel am Stadtpark* (☎ *280 50, fax 81 46 52, email CONGRHOTEL@aol.com, Clausewitzstrasse 6*) is next door to the Congress Centrum (take tram/U-Bahn No 6 towards Zoo). Singles/doubles start at DM190/298. It boasts Hanover's highest swimming pool. The *Fora Hotel* (☎ *670 60, fax 670 61 11, Grosser Kolonnenweg 19*) is towards the airport. It's a modern, comfortable place with a

LOWER SAXONY

great atmosphere, slick furnishings and a good breakfast buffet. Some rooms have kitchens, and the prices (from DM228/258 on weekdays, DM138/168 on weekends) include breakfast, a sauna, use of a city bike and a tram/U-Bahn ticket (tram/U-Bahn No 8 stops right outside).

The **Maritim Grand Hotel** (*☎ 367 70, fax 32 51 95, Friedrichswall 11*) has friendly staff and good service, but the rooms – even its DM1700 per night presidential suite – are a little like those at your grandparents' house: dated furniture, aged appliances and, when you really look closely, all kinds of coming-apart-at-the-seams. Still, its location is good, facing the Neues Rathaus. Rooms start at DM228/270. The **Airport Maritim** (*☎ 973 70, fax 973 75 70, Flughafenstrasse 5*) at the airport has the same prices.

Places to Eat

Hanover has some good, if unspectacular, nosh and an excellent market hall. The Altstadt area behind Marktkirche has a bundle of traditional-style places serving reasonably priced food.

Restaurants *Restaurant Gildehof* (see Places to Stay – Budget) has big servings of typical German food for under DM20. *Paulaner München Bierhaus*, opposite the Opernhaus and downstairs, is a chain restaurant-cum-pub that serves popular Bavarian fare in the DM12 to DM20 price range.

The Mövenpick **Marché**, next to the Kröpke passage, is about as stylish as a Mövenpick chain restaurant can be, with main courses from about DM18 to DM25. There's an attached snack-food stand and a good cafe as well.

Brauhaus Ernst August (*☎ 36 59 50, Schmiedestrasse 13A*) is a Hanover tradition. It serves somewhat basic traditional German main courses from DM11 to DM31 in a great atmosphere – with wooden tables and copper vats used to make its microbrew called Hannöversch.

Sawaddi (*☎ 34 43 67, Königstrasse 7*), on the corner of Hinüberstrasse, is a recommended Thai restaurant with a DM12.50 lunch menu and tasty main dishes for about DM23. The **Taj Mahal** (*Hinüberstrasse 21*), on the corner of Schiffgraben, has vegetarian curries for about DM16 to DM20 and meat dishes in the DM20 to DM30 range. Its lunch specials range from DM11 to DM16.

The vegetarian **Hiller** (*Blumenstrasse 3*) is a bit old-fashioned and staid, but it's been around for donkey's years and remains popular. Blumenstrasse is one block east of Schiffgraben, near the railway line.

Cafes *Mezzo* (*☎ 31 49 66, Leister Meile 4*) is a hip cafe, bar and restaurant that draws a mixed crowd from morning till late. It serves quite a good lentil curry for DM6.50, lots of other vegie dishes for under DM10, and pasta for under DM11. Meat dishes cost up to DM13. Or, you might want to go there just for a drink or to read the German newspapers.

Snacks & Fast Food The **Markthalle**, on the corner of Karmarschstrasse and Leinstrasse south of the Marktkirche, is a bargain paradise for hungry gourmands, including vegetarians. It has dozens of stalls selling a huge array of food, and on weekdays it's a major networking spot for local yuppies. Try Angelo Masala, which sells great hams, meats, cheeses and bottles of Italian wine. Vital Center has freshly squeezed fruit and vegetable juices from DM2.50 to DM4; Salad Erdal has a dozen different salads (100g from DM1 to DM2.50), and full meals for DM8.50. There are places here selling sausage and meats, doner kebab, pizza, spices, teas, cakes, bread … it's wonderful. The Markthalle is open Monday to Wednesday from 7 am to 6 pm, Thursday and Friday to 8 pm, and Saturday to 2 pm.

The **Nordsee** (*Karmarschstrasse 24*) serves what Nordsee does across the whole of Germany – tasty and well priced fish rolls and main dishes.

The **Wurst Basar** stand at the western end of Georgstrasse is perhaps more appropriately named the 'best basar', for it sells good roast chickens (half/whole for DM4.50/7.50), cheap sandwiches, and *Schweinehaxe* (pork joint) that will knuckle a hunger for a week. In the back there's a good fruit, cheese and meat market as well.

Entertainment

The best place to get tickets, rather than the box offices, is through the HTIO's booking service. *MagaScene* is an excellent and comprehensive free monthly publication packed with listings on music, concerts, gallery openings, museum exhibitions, theatre, film and football.

Pubs & Bars *Bobby's Altstadt Pub* (☎ 363 19 47, Am Markt 13) is a popular place to drink. *McMurphy's Irish Pub* (☎ 131 60 64, Königsworther Strasse 13) draws a lively crowd; *MacGowan's* (☎ 145 89, Brüderstrasse 4), a street parallel to, and north of, Kurt-Schuhmacher-Strasse, has live music and serves food. *Brauhaus Ernst August* (see Places to Eat) is a great German pub option – don't neglect to try its house brew.

Discos & Clubs *The Capitol* (☎ 44 40 66, Schwarzer Bär 2), a former movie theatre, has rock, pop, house, soul and more on weekends and frequently during the week. Take tram/U-Bahn No 3, 7 or 9 to Schwarzer Bär. *Musiktheater Bad (Am Grossen Garten 60)* has a regular mixed bag of live and dance offerings. *OSHO Diskothek*, behind the station on Raschplatz, is a dance venue where oldies get down and kick high.

Gay & Lesbian Venues Ask HTIO for its excellent bilingual pamphlet *Columbia Fun Map* with listings of clubs and bars for gays and lesbians. *The Hole* (☎ 352 38 95, Franckestrasse 5) is about what it sounds like – the leather and rubber crowd. Take tram/U-Bahn No 1, 2 or 8 to Vahrenwalder Platz. The *Schwule Sau* (☎ 700 05 25, Schaufelder Strasse 30a) has lesbian nights on Tuesday and another for gay men on Wednesday. The rest of the time it's mixed. Take tram/U-Bahn No 1 or 6 to Kopernikusstrasse.

Rock & Jazz *The Capitol* (see Discos & Clubs) and *Stadionsporthalle* (behind the

Niedersachsenstadion, south of the centre) are the venues for big rock concerts.

The *Kulturzentrum Pavilion* (☎ 34 45 58, Lister Meile 4) has jazz, world music and the like. The *Jazz Club Hannover* (☎ 45 44 55, Am Lindener Berge 38) is a premier venue of its ilk.

Cinema *Kino Am Thielenplatz* (☎ 32 18 79, Am Thielenplatz 2) shows films in their original language (usually English) daily. *Kino im Künstlerhaus* (☎ 168 47 32, Sophienstrasse 2) screens a good range of foreign films with German subtitles.

Theatre & Classical Music The *Schauspielhaus* (☎ 168 67 10, Prinzenstrasse 9) and the *Neues Theater* (☎ 36 30 01, Georgstrasse 54) are the big players in town for straight drama. *Theater am Aegi* (☎ 989 33 33, Aegidientorplatz) is home to comedies and musicals. *TaK* (☎ 44 55 62, Stephanusstrasse 29) is the city's cabaret theatre venue. *Marlene Bar & Bühne* (☎ 368 16 87), on the corner of Alexanderstrasse and Prinzenstrasse, also has regular cabaret.

The *Opernhaus* (☎ 268 62 40, Opernplatz 1) is the city's main classical music and opera venue, built in the mid-19th century (tram/U-Bahn stop: Aegidientorplatz). Curtain time is usually at 7.30 pm.

Shopping

On Saturday from 7 am to 1 pm year round, there's a weekly flea market at Hohen Ufer, behind the Historical Museum, along the Leine River Canal. It's a favourite with kids, and the whole affair is watched over by public art: the three playful Nanas, by Nicki de St Phalle.

Getting There & Away

Air Flights land at Hanover's sparkling airport (☎ 977 12 23), from which there's great transport to the city and the fairgrounds. City airline offices include:

Air France (☎ 977 27 75)
British Airways (☎ 77 87 55)
Czech Airlines (CSA; ☎ 0180-380 38 03)
KLM-Royal Dutch Airlines (☎ 0180-521 42 01)

LOWER SAXONY

Lufthansa Airlines (☎ 0180-380 38 03)
Sabena (☎ 728 18 14)
Scandinavian Airlines (SAS; ☎ 0180-323 40 23)
Swissair (☎ 0180-525 85 75)

Train Hanover is a major hub for train lines. ICE trains to/from Hamburg (DM67, 1¼ hours), Munich (DM215, 4½ hours), Frankfurt (DM140, 2¼ hours) and Berlin (DM101, 1½ hours) leave virtually every one or two hours from 5 or 6 am.

Bus Short-hop regional buses depart from the bus station north of the Hauptbahnhof.

Car & Motorcycle Hanover is well situated, with autobahns to Hamburg, Munich, Frankfurt and Berlin. There are also good autobahn connections to Bremen, Cologne, Amsterdam and Brussels. Major car rental firms have offices in the Hauptbahnhof, including Sixt (☎ 01805-25 25 25) and Avis (☎ 0180-555 77).

Getting Around

To/From the Airport
Bus No 60 shuttles between the Hauptbahnhof's city air terminal and the airport, 10km north-west of the city centre, from 5 am to 10.30 pm, and back from 5.25 am to 11.15 pm (weekends from 6.05 am). The one-way trip costs DM10.

During fairs, bus No 69 shuttles between the airport and the fairgrounds (DM15/20 one-way/return) every half hour from 8 am to 9 pm. A new S-Bahn line connecting the airport with the fairgrounds/EXPO site via the Hauptbahnhof in 25 minutes should be up and running by the time you read this.

The Fairgrounds
From the Hauptbahnhof, take tram/U-Bahn No 8 directly to the Messegelände. It's a two zone, 15 minute ride. See To/From the Airport for the S-Bahn connection. Is someone else paying? Grab the helicopter shuttle from the airport (☎ 977 22 87; arrivals level, gate Nos 1 to 6) to the helipad at the western end of the fairgrounds. They leave constantly during CeBit and some other fairs, and the eight minute flight costs DM130, with shuttle transfers.

Public Transport The excellent Hanover transit system of buses and a combination tram/U-Bahn line (the trams go underground in the centre of the city and pop up later) is run by Üstra (☎ 01803-194 49). The tourist brochure *Travel Tips for Visitors* is packed with information on how to get around town and to most attractions. Pick up a copy at the Üstra office in the Passarelle.

There are three zones: Hanover, Umland and Region. Single tickets/strips of six tickets for one zone cost DM3/17, two zones DM4/19.50, and single tickets/strips of four tickets for three zones DM5/19; 24-hour tickets for the zones respectively cost DM6/8/10. The HannoverCard (see Information earlier) includes free transport in all three zones.

Taxi Flag fall is DM4, and it's DM3.20 for the first kilometre, DM2.20 per kilometre after that. A taxi from the centre to the fairgrounds costs about DM35; from the airport it's about DM70.

FAIRY-TALE ROAD – SOUTH
The stretch of the Fairy-Tale Road (Märchenstrasse) between Hamelin and Bad Karlshafen is one of the prettiest along the route. It hugs the Weser River for much of the way, passing through several historic towns that ooze charm. South of Bodenwerder, the river is flanked on its eastern bank by the Solling-Vogler Naturpark, a relatively unpopulated and quiet corner of northern Germany favoured by hikers and cyclists. Two interesting stopovers on the Märchenstrasse that truly live up to the name of this route are Bodenwerder and the even more remarkable Bad Karlshafen.

Getting There & Away
It is difficult to travel along this section of the Fairy-Tale Road without your own transport. From Hamelin's Hauptbahnhof bus No 520 follows the Weser to/from Holzminden via Bodenwerder several times daily (DM16.10). In Holzminden (board at Hafendamm) bus No 221 runs to/from Höxter bus station (DM3.90), which connects with bus No 220 to/from Bad Karlshafen

(DM7.20). By car, take the B83 from/to Hamelin or Bad Karlshafen. See Hamelin's Getting There & Away section for bike hire.

Oberweser Dampfschiffahrt (see Hamelin for details) runs boats along the Weser between Hamelin and Bad Karlshafen (90km) from April to mid-October. The connection only works if you leave Hamelin or Bad Karlshafen on a Thursday, and involves stopovers along the way of one night going downriver or two nights if travelling upriver (DM73).

Bad Karlshafen is connected by frequent indirect trains to/from Göttingen (DM17, one hour).

HAMELIN
☎ 05151 • pop 59,000

Hamelin (Hameln), less than an hour's journey by train south-west of Hanover, is a major stopover on the Fairy-Tale Road. This pretty town is synonymous with *The Pied Piper of Hamelin (Der Rattenfänger)*, a folk tale that was written down by the Brothers Grimm in the 19th century and became popular with children throughout the world. Hamelin's tourist angle is based on just one thing – rats. If you've got a rat phobia or don't think rodents could ever be cute, maybe it's not the place for you. (See also the boxed text 'Fairy-Tale Road' in the Hesse chapter.)

Orientation & Information

Hamelin is on the east bank of the Weser River and retains a medieval circular Altstadt. The main streets are Osterstrasse, which runs east-west towards the Weser River, and Bäckerstrasse, the north-south axis. The Hauptbahnhof is about 800m east of the centre. To get to the centre from the Hauptbahnhof, follow Bahnhofstrasse to Diesterstrasse and turn left. Counters at the Hauptbahnhof stock the *Wohin heute* booklet, which has a good map of the town and useful addresses.

The helpful tourist office (☎ 20 26 19, fax 20 25 00) is just outside the Altstadt at Diesterallee 3. It has lots of good city and regional maps, and has a free room-finding service. From October to April it's open weekdays from 9 am to 5 pm (closed from

1 to 2 pm). From May to September it's also open Saturday from 9.30 am to 12.30 pm and 2 to 4 pm, and on Sunday till 12.30 pm. There is also a counter in the Hochzeitshaus from April to October. The Fremdenverkehrsverband Weserbergland-Mittelweser (☎ 930 00, fax 93 00 33), Inselstrasse 3, has useful information on the Mittel-Weser region.

The post office is at Am Posthof 1, off Osterstrasse.

Things to See & Do

Hamelin's **Altstadt** has many fine buildings in the ornamental Weser Renaissance style, which has a strong Italian influence. The **Rattenfängerhaus** (Rat Catcher's House; 1602-3), Osterstrasse 28, is the finest example of the style, with a typically steep and richly decorated gable. The **Leistehaus** (1585-89) at No 8-9 now houses a **museum** (☎ 20 22 15), with exhibits ranging from the town's history through to ceramics, childrens' toys and, of course, everything to do with the Pied Piper. It is open from Tuesday to Sunday from 10 am to 4.30 pm (DM3). Also not to be missed is the **Hochzeitshaus** (1610-17), at the Markt end of Osterstrasse, with a Rattenfänger **Glockenspiel** daily at 1.05, 3.35 and 5.35 pm.

For the other beauties of Hamelin – the restored 16th to 18th century half-timbered houses with inscribed dedications – stroll through the south-eastern quarter of the old town, around Alte Marktstrasse and Grosse Hofstrasse, or on Kupferschmiedestrasse, where at No 13 you'll find the **Bürgerhaus**.

A nice thing to do in fine weather is to take a one hour cruise on the Weser River. They run from early April to mid-October six times daily between 10 am and 4.15 pm. Drop by or contact the Oberweser Dampfschiffahrt (☎ 93 99 99, fax 230 40), Inselstrasse 3.

Places to Stay & Eat

The camping ground *Fährhaus an der Weser* (☎ 611 67, Uferstrasse) is across the river from the old town and 10 minutes walk north.

The *Jugendherberge* (☎ 34 25, fax 423 16, Fischbeckerstrasse 33) charges DM21/26 for juniors/seniors. Take bus No 2 from the Hauptbahnhof to Wehler Weg.

The central *Altstadt Wiege (☎ 278 54, Neue Marktstrasse 10)* has single rooms from DM55, and single/double rooms with shower and WC for DM65/120. The *Hotel zur Post (☎ 76 30, fax 76 41, Am Posthof 6)* has modern, bright rooms from DM95/149 with shower and WC. The *Hotel-Garni Christinenhof (☎ 950 80, fax 436 11, Alte Marktstrasse 18)* has stylish rooms from DM150/185, but the real hit is its swimming pool in a vaulted cellar.

Tandir (☎ 222 01, Diesterstrasse 38) offers eat-in and take-away Anatolian dishes from DM13 to DM20. The *Rattenfängerhaus (☎ 38 88)* has an excellent traditional restaurant. Main courses in the evening are from DM22 to DM38, but the servings are generous and it also has a cheaper lunch menu.

A *Plus* supermarket at the southern end of Bahnhofstrasse is a good place to stock up on food if you're driving along the Fairy-Tale Road. It has free parking at the rear.

Getting There & Around

Frequent trains rattle out to Hamelin from Hanover (DM15, 45 minutes). If travelling by car, take the B217 to/from Hanover. See the Fairy-Tale Road – South Getting There & Away section for information on bus and boat links.

The bus station is next to the Hauptbahnhof. Bus Nos 2, 3, 4, 12, 21, 33 and 34 will drop you opposite the tourist office.

Troches Fahrrad Shop (☎ 136 70), Kreuzstrasse 7, rents out bikes for DM15 per day or DM25 for the weekend.

BODENWERDER
☎ 05533 • pop 6500

Bodenwerder, straddling the Weser River, was originally a settlement of fisherfolk and river sailors and today is a pleasant town with a 114-strong bevy of historic half-timbered houses.

But the town is better known for its favourite son, the legendary Baron von

Münchhausen (the 'Liar Baron'), who was born here in 1720. The good baron's reputation was due to his telling of outrageous tales, the most famous of which was how he rode through the air on a cannonball. This very cannonball is in a room dedicated to the baron in the **Rathaus**. Also interesting is the **statue** of the baron, riding half a horse, in the garden outside the Rathaus, and the 12th century **Gertrudiskapelle** in Corvinusgang.

There is a pleasant **walking track** along the Weser River in both directions from Bodenwerder and a track leading through forest on the eastern side of the river to the **Königszinne** lookout, from where there are good views.

If you plan to stay overnight, drop by the tourist office (☎ 405 41, fax 61 52), Weserstrasse 3. It's open weekdays from 9 am to 12.30 pm and 2.30 to 6 pm. From April to October, it's also open Saturday from 9 am to 1 pm.

The *camping ground (☎ 49 38)* is on the east bank of the Weser River on Ziegeleiweg. The *Jugendherberge (☎ 26 85, fax 62 03, Richard-Schirrmann-Weg)* is on the edge of the forest and charges DM21/26 for juniors/seniors. The *Hotel Deutsches Haus (☎ 39 25, fax 41 13, Münchhausenplatz 4)* has singles/doubles from DM65/130.

BAD KARLSHAFEN
☎ 05672 • pop 4700

Bad Karlshafen, which belongs to Hesse, is that state's northernmost town, nestling just a stone's throw downriver from the border with Lower Saxony. It's a splendid anomaly among northern German towns: baroque, whitewashed and meticulously planned. Originally the city was planned with an impressive harbour and a canal connecting the Weser with the Rhine in the hope of diverting trade away from Hanover and Münden. These plans were laid by a local earl with help from Huguenot refugees from France. When the earl died, so too did his great ambition, but this incomplete masterpiece and the influence of the Huguenots is too beautiful to miss.

Orientation & Information

The tourist office (☎ 99 99 24, fax 99 99 25) is in the Kurverwaltung building on the Hafenbecken, in the town centre, across the river from the Hauptbahnhof. It is open from May to mid-October weekdays from 9 am to noon and 2 to 5.30 pm, Saturday from 9.30 am to noon and Sunday from 2.30 to 5 pm. The rest of the year it is open weekdays from 9 am to noon and 2 to 4 pm.

Things to See

Take a stroll around the **Hafenbecken** (Harbour Basin) with its surrounding baroque buildings such as the **Rathaus**. On the north-east side at Hafenplatz 9A is the **Deutsches Huguenotten Museum** (☎ 14 10) containing maps, copper-plate etchings and other exhibits explaining the history of the Huguenots in Germany. It is open Tuesday to Saturday from 9 am to 1 pm and 2 to 6 pm, and Sunday from 11 am to 6 pm (DM4/2.50).

Places to Stay & Eat

The camping ground *Am Rechten Weserufer* (☎ 710, fax 13 50) charges DM3 per tent, DM5 per person and DM2 for a car. It's on the north bank, just south of the Hauptbahnhof.

A few minutes walk north-east of the Hauptbahnhof is the *Hermann-Wenning-Jugendherberge* (☎ 338, fax 83 61, Winnefelder Strasse 7). It costs DM22/27 for juniors/seniors.

Hotel-Pension Haus Fuhrhop (☎ 404, fax 314, Friedrichstrasse 15) has singles/doubles from DM55/110 with shower and WC. *Hessischer Hof* (☎ 10 59, fax 25 15, Carlstrasse 13) has rooms for DM65/110, and a restaurant with regional Hessian specialities and international dishes ranging from DM8 to DM35.

Lüneburger Heide

North of Hanover along the sprawling Lüneburg Heath lies a land of beautiful villages and opportunities to get out into nature. The region is packed with history. Lower Saxony

was ruled from here before the court moved to Hamburg, and royal treasures and sagas, along with beautiful, exquisitely preserved buildings, await you in Celle. In Lüneburg, whose riches came from the salt trade in the Middle Ages, you can see fascinating museums and the largest Rathaus in Germany to have survived from the Middle Ages.

The area in between, along the Lüneburg Heath, can be covered on foot, by bike or in a boat, and there are plenty of hay hotels and camping grounds along the way. This is one of northern Germany's most rewarding areas; at the very least you should try to visit the two main cities, Celle and Lüneburg.

CELLE

☎ 05141 • pop 74,000

The hundreds of half-timbered buildings that line the tourist-thronged cobblestone streets are the main attraction in Celle. Many of the buildings, which date from the 16th century, were constructed by just the sort of pious, hardworking Germans who would take time to adorn the facades with inscriptions like 'Without the Lord's protection you need no guards' (that is, guards cannot save you) and 'Work harder'.

Celle has a lot to offer, with a very helpful and efficient tourist office, an excellent museum, one of the few surviving synagogues in northern Germany and a fascinating ducal Schloss. Carriage rides from here to the Lüneburger Heath are easy to arrange (see Organised Tours). It's a friendly town, and definitely worth an overnight stay – the spooky hostel notwithstanding.

Orientation

The mainly pedestrianised Altstadt is about 700m east of the Hauptbahnhof, reached by Bahnhofstrasse. The Markt is about 100m east of Schlossplatz. The Aller River flows around the northern section of the Altstadt with a tributary encircling it to the south. The Schloss is on the south-west corner. Just south of the Altstadt is the French Garden (Französischer Garten).

Note that the large, yellow castle-like building on the north side of Bahnhofstrasse,

LOWER SAXONY

behind the park, is not the city Schloss, but rather the city prison!

Information

The helpful Tourismus Region Celle (TRC; ☎ 12 12, fax 124 59, email touristinfo@ celle.de), Markt 6, offers walking and cycling tours for groups and books rooms. It's open from April to October, weekdays from 9 am to 7 pm, Saturday from 10 am to 4 pm and Sunday from 11 am to 2 pm. From November to March it's open weekdays from 9 am to 5 pm and Saturday from 10 am to 1 pm.

ADAC has an office (☎ 1060) at Nordwall 1a.

The most central place to change money is at the Sparkasse, Schlossplatz 10. You'll find several other banks dotted around town.

The main post office is at Runde Strasse 7, diagonally opposite the Schloss.

Schulzesche Buchhandlung (☎ 224 24), Bergstrasse 49, has English-language books and maps. Brandt Buchhandlung (☎ 228 04), Zöllnerstrasse 8, has a similarly sized collection.

The city hospital is Allgemeines Krankenhaus (☎ 720), Siemensplatz 4, just north-east of the centre. For routine matters, contact the Josefstift Krankenhaus (☎ 75 10), Canonenstrasse 8, south-west of the city centre.

Schloss

This magnificently restored ducal palace (☎ 123 73) is open to visitors on guided tours only.

Built in 1292 by Otto Der Strenge (Otto the Strict) as a town fortification, the building was expanded and turned into a residence in 1378. The last duke to live here was Georg Wilhelm (1624-1705), and the last royal was the exiled Queen Caroline-Mathilde of Denmark, who died here in 1775.

The highlight of the Schloss is the chapel. Its original Gothic form is evident in the high windows and vaulted ceiling, but the rest of the intricate interior is pure Renaissance. Many of the paintings are by the Flemish artist Marten de Voss (1532-1603). Inscriptions along the pews were created after the Reformation, and are therefore in German, not Latin. The duke's pew was above; the shutters were added later so his highness could snooze during the three-hour services.

In the left-hand corner closest to the glass is the chapel's prize – *Temptation*, represented by a woman (the New Church) surrounded by devils in various forms trying to lead her astray, but an angel descending from Heaven protects her. Reliefs on the left side depict the Apostles.

The painting on the south wall – de Voss' *Last Judgment* – is flanked by two others: on the left, *Faith*, and the right, *Love*. To the left of these is the splendid sandstone pulpit (1565).

Guided tours of the Schloss in German run daily except Monday hourly from 10 am to 4 pm; from November to March they run at 11 am and 3 pm (DM5/2.50). The TRC can arrange a tour in English – but at a much higher price.

Bomann Museum

Across from the palace, the Bomann Museum (☎ 125 44), Schlossplatz 7, is the town's history and modern art museum. It's housed in an enchanting series of buildings, parts of which span every architectural period in Celle's history, including aspects of half-timbered, Gothic, Renaissance, baroque and modern 20th century architecture. The historical museum is in the older building; the modern art collection and rotating exhibitions are in the new wing.

The museum is open Tuesday to Sunday from 10 am to 5 pm (DM4/2, including entry to the palace's east wing).

Altstadt

The heart of the Altstadt is the Renaissance **Rathaus** (1561-79) in the Markt, with its *trompe l'oeil* stone facade. At the northern end is a wonderful Weser Renaissance stepped gable, topped with a golden weather vane above the ducal coat of arms. On the south side are two whipping posts with shackles, used from 1786 to 1850. Prisoners guilty of minor offences were shackled by the neck to the posts for up to

The Sad Tale of Queen Caroline

Queen Caroline-Mathilde (1751-75) of Denmark was the last royal to live in Celle palace after she was exiled there by her brother, England's George III. The story of how an English-born queen of Denmark came to live in a German castle by order of an English king is a little convoluted, but bear with us – it's a good and gory one.

Caroline's husband, King Christian VII of Denmark (1749-1808), was a schizophrenic who needed constant looking after, so the German physician Dr Struensee (1737-72) was hired to come to Denmark and watch out for the king's welfare. Struensee did his job so well that he gradually managed to take over the day-to-day running of the country.

Struensee was something of a bleeding heart, freeing the serfs and the press, acts which didn't sit well with the Danish aristocracy, who wanted to flay the good man. But Struensee was smart enough not to push things too far – until he turned his attentions to the king's wife.

When Caroline gave birth to a daughter by Struensee, he was arrested. First they cut off his right hand and beheaded him, and then cut his body into four pieces, lengthwise and then crosswise at the waist. The body parts and his head were placed on stakes as a public warning.

Caroline was placed under house arrest at Kronborg, near Copenhagen, and was only released after appeals from George III, who then stuck her in the disused castle in Celle to keep her out of trouble.

For the next three years she wrote to her brother repeatedly, begging to return home to England. But she died of a fever in Celle in 1775, a few weeks shy of her 24th birthday.

12 hours; although prisoners weren't whipped, this was long enough to allow their neighbours to insult them, throw eggs and apples, and spit at them.

On the western end of the Rathaus is the Gothic **Marktkirche** (1292-1308), originally the Catholic Marienkirche, but Protestant since the Reformation. The church steeple dates from 1913. You can climb up the 234 steps to the top for a view of the city (DM2) or just watch as the city trumpeter climbs the 220 steps to the white tower below the steeple for a **trumpet fanfare** in all four directions. The ascent takes place at 8.15 am and 5.15 pm (9 am and 7.15 pm on Saturday).

Inside the church is a magnificent organ once played by Johann Sebastian Bach. It is covered with gold and other decoration and has carved faces on the pipes. The church is open from Tuesday to Saturday from 9 am to 12.30 pm and 3 to 6 pm (till 2 pm after the Sunday service). The tower is open from April to October, Tuesday to Saturday from 10 am to noon and 3 to 4 pm. Services are held year round on Sunday at 10 am.

In front of the church, jousting tournaments were held on the **Stechbahn**. The little horseshoe on the corner on the north side of the street marks the spot where a duke was slain during a tournament; step on it and make a wish, and local lore holds that it will come true.

Synagogue

Celle's synagogue (☎ 12 12), the oldest in Lower Saxony, was partially destroyed on Kristallnacht but is still open today as a museum (there aren't enough Jews in the area to form a *minyan* to hold services). From outside it looks like just another half-timbered house.

The synagogue is open to the public Tuesday to Thursday from 3 to 5 pm, Friday from 9 to 11 am and Sunday from 11 am to 1 pm. A guided tour can be organised through the tourist information office, or groups can arrange to pick up the key. The synagogue is at the south-eastern end of the Altstadt at Im Kreise 24, just off Wehlstrasse.

euro currency converter DM1 = €0.51

French Garden

This lovely bit of green at the southern end of the Altstadt is densely planted with flowers and grass and makes a great place to walk in summer. It's also home to the Lower Saxon Beekeeping Institute (☎ 60 54).

Other Sights

The **Hoppenerhaus** (1532), on the corner of Poststrasse and Runde Strasse, is one of the best of the Altstadt's Renaissance buildings, with a richly ornamented facade. This street contains buildings from the 16th to 20th centuries, culminating in the ugly Karstadt department store (1965).

Walk a block south to Bergstrasse, stand at the little blue **Trinkwasser** fountain and look south at the tiny alley between the pink and yellow Sparkasse buildings. One flight up you'll see a little box with a window – this was a **baroque toilet**. It's less glamorous than the name implies: waste would flush directly down into the alley.

Continuing east on Zöllnerstrasse you'll pass **No 37** (1570, now the Reformhaus), with its heart-warming inscription on the upper gable, 'Work! No chatting, talking or gossiping!'. Head one block north to Neue Strasse, whose highlights include the **green house** (1478) with the crooked beam at No 32 (now an interesting antique shop); and at No 11, the **Fairy-Tale House**, the facade decorated with characters such as a jackass crapping gold pieces.

Boating

Canoeing Hennings (☎ 287 91), near the Aller Brücke at the northern end of the Altstadt at Fritzenwiese 49, rents out kayaks from DM5 per hour. They can suggest several itineraries.

Organised Tours

The TRC runs city tours (DM4, free for children) in German on most days. From April to October, tours depart Monday to Saturday at 2.30 pm, Sunday at 11 am. From November to March tours operate on request. The departure point is the bridge in front of the Schloss.

From April to October there are half-hour, horse-drawn carriage rides through the Altstadt from DM5 per person. For longer carriage tours, check with the TRC; it has a list of about 20 companies offering two to three-hour tours onto the Lüneburg Heath (about DM20 per person).

Places to Stay

Camping Silbersee (☎ 312 23, fax 337 58) is the nicest and closest camping ground, about 4km from the centre; tent sites cost DM5 plus DM5 per person, DM3 for children. From Schlossplatz take city bus No 6 to the last stop.

The *Jugendherberge* (☎ 532 08, fax 530 05, Weghausestrasse 2) is clean and comfortable, but if Dracula himself popped out, you wouldn't be surprised at all. It charges DM21/26 for juniors/seniors, including breakfast. There's a charge of DM4.50 for laundry facilities. To get to the hostel from the Hauptbahnhof, walk under the tracks (west) to Kampstrasse and then north for about 15 minutes to Bremer Weg, turn left and walk the long block to Petersburg Strasse and the hostel's the apparition on the right. Or take bus No 3 to the Jugendherberge stop.

The TRC books *private rooms* free of charge. Rates average DM40 to DM45 per person in town, DM25 to DM30 in the countryside. The number for private room or hotel reservations is ☎ 12 12 or fax 124 59.

There are few budget hotels in Celle; the TRC can get you into a couple of small and central places if you give enough notice.

The central *Hotel Monopol* (☎ 240 35, fax 63 82, Bergstrasse 23-24) has fairly good singles/doubles/triples for DM80/120/150 with shower and WC. *Hotel Sattler Am Bahnhof* (☎ 10 75, Bahnhofstrasse 46) has surprisingly pleasant rooms near the Hauptbahnhof. Basic singles cost DM75, and singles/doubles DM92/140 with shower and WC.

Celler Residenz Hotels (☎ 20 11 41, fax 20 11 20) operates several nice places, including *Hotel Nordwall* (Nordwall 4), with rooms from DM98/150; and *Celler Hof (Stechbahn 11)* with rooms from DM115/170.

The *Hotel St Georg* (☎ *210 51, fax 217 25, St-Georg-Strasse 25-27)* is family-run and in a quiet neighbourhood. Comfortable and clean rooms with an ISDN modem system start at DM78/131 without breakfast, which is an extra DM17.

The *Steigenberger Esprix* (☎ *20 00, fax 20 02 00, Nordwall 22)* is a very pleasant place with rooms from DM125/140. The *Hotel Caroline Mathilde* (☎ *320 23, fax 320 28, Alter Bremer Weg 37)* is probably the best in town, with spotless rooms at DM120/160, and a good pool and sauna.

Places to Eat

Local specialities include *Roher Celle Roulade*, rolled, thinly sliced raw beef in a mustard marinade, and smoked or fried trout from local rivers. The local hooch is the *très* powerful Ratzeputz, 58% alcohol, brewed from ginger and said to cure all that ails you; and Heidegeist, a 50% alcohol brew made from 30 herbs that tastes predominantly of aniseed. You can buy these and other local spirits at Weinhandlung Richard Bornhöft, Zöllnerstrasse 29.

Schwejk, in the Marktpassage off Kanzleistrasse, is a popular restaurant serving fare from Bohemia in the DM20 to DM30 price range. The *König Stuben* (☎ *246 01, Neue Strasse 27)* has good German and Celle specialities. Lunch specials go for around DM12, several simple dishes cost around DM16 and others from DM20 to DM30.

Kartoffelhaus (☎ *78 15, Mauernstrasse 8)* has tasty potato dishes from DM12 to DM18 and good service (closed Monday). *Karstadt* has a restaurant on level two that serves plain but quite good food for under DM10; it also has a wok counter for pan-fried dishes at DM2.75 per 100g.

The town's *Ratskeller* (☎ *290 99)*, in the Rathaus, opened in 1378 and now claims to be the oldest restaurant in northern Germany. The food's fine, without being spectacular; main courses average DM35.

Waffel, opposite Kielhorn at the southeast corner of Brandplatz, has sweet and savoury crepes during the day from about DM5 to DM15. *Vis á Vis*, opposite the Schloss, serves breakfast from DM6.50 to DM20 and great hot drinks and cakes in a cheerful atmosphere (closes at 7 pm).

A *Nordsee* restaurant is on the corner of the Markt and Zöllnerstrasse. *H Kielhorn* (☎ *228 15, Brandplatz 2)* has good and filling food at budget prices. It's a stand-up place with a sumptuous selection of hearty soups (eg potato, split pea or lentil) for DM4.50 a huge bowl. Heaving plates of German fare – sausage, salad and potatoes and the like – cost DM8.50. It's popular with locals, and is open for breakfast as well.

Penny Markt (Schuhstrasse 20) is a convenient supermarket tucked away in a half-timbered house.

Entertainment

Celle Szene is a monthly listings guide to bars, banks, the tourist office etc. Another goodie is *Im Spiegel des Monats*, with the same type of information plus a good street map.

No Respect (Bahnhofstrasse 14), at the side entrance of Anja's Lolipop, has respectable soul and house music from Thursday to Saturday.

Concerts are held at the 360 seat *Schlosstheater* in the Schloss. Ticket prices and programs are erratic, so check with the tourist office when you're in town. The *Congress Union* (☎ *91 93, Thaerplatz 1)* also holds occasional concerts. In summer the *Stadtkirche* has free recitals every Wednesday at 6 pm.

Getting There & Away

Celle is within easy reach of Hanover, with trains making the 22 to 51 minute trip three times an hour (DM13). There's also regular service to/from Lüneburg (DM22, 45 minutes) and Braunschweig (DM28, 1½ hours).

If you're driving, take the B3 straight into the centre.

Getting Around

City bus Nos 2, 3 and 4 run between the Hauptbahnhof and Schlossplatz, the two main stations. Single tickets are DM2.10, six-ticket strips DM11. There are no family or day cards.

Regional buses serving Bergen-Belsen and Wienhausen operate from the bus station at the Hauptbahnhof and are run by KVC (☎ 88 11 80) and Lembke & Koschick (☎ 418 59), respectively.

Taxis (☎ 444 44 or ☎ 280 01) cost DM4 at flag fall, DM2.60 per kilometre.

Rent bikes from 2-Rad Meyer (☎ 413 69), Neustadt 42a, 1.5km west of the centre, for DM15 a day. You can cycle from here to nearby Wienhausen; ask at the shop about the shortcut through farms that saves you 5km each way.

BERGEN-BELSEN

It's difficult to overstate the impact of a visit to Bergen-Belsen, some 12km north of Celle. It's the most infamous Nazi death camp on German soil (the largest Nazi concentration camp, Auschwitz-Birkenau, is near Kraków in Poland). During WWII, 80,000 to 100,000 people were murdered here – 35,000 in 1945 alone.

Part of the emotional impact a visit to the camp has on people who were not directly affected by the Holocaust is that this is where Anne Frank died. The German-born Jewish girl was captured, along with her family, after two years of hiding in an Amsterdam attic. Anne and her sister, Margot, were brought to Bergen-Belsen from Auschwitz, and succumbed to typhoid only weeks before the camp was liberated.

The 13-year-old's diary was published by her father in 1947 as *The Diary of Anne Frank*. Her story brought people into the life of a bright, idealistic girl, on the cusp of adolescence, trying to come to terms with life in hiding, and it had the effect of humanising the statistics.

Established in 1940 as a POW camp, Bergen-Belsen officially became a concentration camp in December 1944, when SS captain Josef Kramer was put in command of the camp's 15,257 prisoners.

The prisoners – at first Russian and other Allied POWs, then later Jews, Poles, homosexuals and Romanian Gypsies – were subjected to some of the cruellest treatment ever perpetrated in human history. Beatings and torture were commonplace; many were starved to death or worked in the fields until they dropped. Prisoners, including children and the elderly, were used for 'medical experimentation'. As WWII progressed, prisoners were brought in from other camps, and as overcrowding became desperate, disease ran rampant. Death from dehydration was common.

British troops liberated the camp on 15 April 1945. The photographs and motion pictures taken by the liberating forces are so graphic and horrifying they literally defy description, and we won't attempt it here.

All told, approximately 50,000 concentration camp prisoners were murdered in Bergen-Belsen. Another 30,000 to 50,000 killed were POWs.

When the camp incinerators couldn't keep up with demand, mass graves were dug. These too were insufficient and thousands of corpses littered the compound. Days before liberation, the SS who hadn't fled the camp ordered a workforce of 2000 Jews to begin dragging bodies to mass graves, but on 15 April several thousand bodies remained unburied. In May 1945, British troops incinerated the camp's barracks to prevent the spread of typhus.

After WWII, the troop barracks were used by the Allied forces as a displaced-persons (DP) camp, the largest of a series of camps that housed refugees from the war, mainly Jews, waiting to emigrate to other countries. Those who didn't find their way to other countries ended up in Israel after its establishment in 1948. The DP camp at Bergen-Belsen closed in September 1950.

The Memorial

The camp is directly behind a large NATO training area, and you may hear artillery and small-arms fire during your visit.

Many photographs taken by liberating forces are on view in the main memorial, and a 25 minute documentary including the film shot on liberation day is shown daily, on the hour from 10 am to 5 pm. Free brochures sketch the layout and provide a historic outline; a fully illustrated guide to the exhibits is available in several languages, including English, Dutch, German, Hebrew and Polish (DM5); the one in Russian is free. Another free booklet, *Guide for Visitors to the Belsen Memorial*, has an excellent overview of the camp, suggested further readings, a chronology of the camp and the memorial.

The **Documentation Centre** is the main visitors' centre and has two theatres screening the documentary. Pick up booklets and buy guides here as well, before walking through the exhibition area, mainly photographs taken by the liberating forces but also containing uniforms, shoes (the children's shoes are particularly chilling) and other camp paraphernalia.

The **Belsen Memorial** is a large cemetery with group and individual graves. At the southern end are symbolic tombstones and a **Jewish monument**. Enter through the gate to the right of the Documentation Centre.

The **Hörsten Soviet Prisoner of War Cemetery** is at the north-western end of the camp and consists entirely of mass graves. There's a **Soviet memorial** here.

Getting There & Away

It's easy to reach Bergen-Belsen by car but unforgivably difficult by public transport.

There are only three direct buses per day to, and one from, the camp. From the Hauptbahnhof in Celle, take the KVC Belsen bus (DM8.20/16.40 one way/return, one hour) to the camp. These buses leave Celle at 11.55 am, and 1.40 and 3.45 pm. The only direct bus back leaves the camp at 4.54 pm. No buses run back to town from the memorial on the weekend. There are buses to the town of Belsen, 4km away, but you'll have to walk to the camp.

If you're driving, take Hehlentorstrasse north over the Aller River and follow Harburger Strasse north out of the city. This is the B3; continue north-west to the town of Bergen and follow the signs to Belsen.

Taxis from Celle's Schlossplatz cost about DM60.

LÜNEBURG

☎ 04131 ● pop 65,000

Lüneburg is a vibrant university town with a rich history based on its salt mines and lots of intact buildings.

Established in 956, many sources misinterpret the origin of the town's name to be from Luna, the Roman goddess of the moon. In fact, Lüneburg hails from the Saxon word *hliuni*, or 'refuge', granted at the duke's castle to those fleeing other territories. The Luna connection came later, in a deliberate attempt to anchor the city name to something grandiose. Nonetheless, there's a lovely fountain with a statue of the goddess in the town's market square, in front of the wonderfully quirky Rathaus.

In 1371, the townsfolk realised that they could run the local salt mines themselves, so they ran the feckless Duke Magnus out of town and destroyed his castle. But when salt production began winding down in the 17th century, the dukedom (apparently finding its feck) returned: the Ducal Palace from that period is on the north side of the Markt, and on the west side is the town's far more spectacular and wonderful Rathaus (1720).

The salt mines finally closed in 1980.

Orientation

The Hauptbahnhof is east, and the city centre west, of the Ilmenau River. The main sights are in the Altstadt. To reach the Markt by foot, turn left when leaving the station and go through the underpass on Altenbrückertorstrasse. This leads across the river to Am Sande, south of the Markt. Most of the centre is pedestrianised. Am Stintmarkt, dubbed 'the Stint' by students, is a veritable 'restaurant row' on the west bank of the Ilmenau, and also good for pubs and bars.

The Deutsches Salz (German Salt) Museum is in the south-west corner of the Altstadt, south-west of Lamberti Platz. Some 3km south of the centre is Universität Lüneburg.

Information

Tourist Offices Tourist-Information Lüneburg (☎ 30 95 93, fax 30 95 98), Am Markt,

LOWER SAXONY

in the south-western corner of the Rathaus facing the square, maintains a complicated regime of opening hours. Basic hours are Monday to Friday from 10 am to 5 pm, Saturday to 1 pm (closed from 1 to 2 pm). In May, August and September it's open uninterrupted till 7 pm, and Saturday and Sunday till 4 pm. In June, July, October and December it's open daily, closes weekdays at 6 pm and weekends at 4 pm (with lunch breaks again). In November it does the same but closes weekdays at 5 pm. It can also book private rooms (see Places to Stay).

ADAC has an office (☎ 77 93 11) at Bei der St Lamberti Kirche 9.

Money There's a Sparkasse at Am Sande 14-15 with ATMs, and another at An Der Münze 4 on the Markt.

Post & Communications The main post office (☎ 72 70) is at Sülztor 21, but the most convenient branch (☎ 84 09 27) is at the Hauptbahnhof, Bahnhofstrasse 14. Internet-Treff (☎ 73 30 01), Bei der St-Johanniskirche 5, has terminals for Web surfers.

Bookshops & Libraries Neue Buchhandlung, Grosse Bäckerstrasse 6, stocks Lonely Planet guides and has the best selection (though poor) of English-language books in town.

The city library is just across the street from the north-west corner of the Rathaus and has a fairly good collection of English literature. The university's library (☎ 78 12 60) is behind building No 9 on the campus at Scharnhorststrasse 1.

Universities Universität Lüneburg (☎ 78 12 60) was established in 1946 and has been expanding ever since. Today it includes colleges of education, business and cultural and environmental studies. From the Hauptbahnhof or Am Sande take bus No 11 or 12 to Blücherstrasse.

Laundry The most central laundry is two blocks south of Am Sande (the western end), on the corner of Rote Strasse and Wallstrasse.

Medical Services & Emergency In medical emergencies contact the Stadt Krankenhaus (☎ 770), Bögelstrasse 1. The police (☎ 290) are at Auf der Hude 1, just north of the Altstadt.

Rathaus & Markt

The focal point of the town is the **Markt**, packed with shoppers and farmers' stalls during markets held every Wednesday and Saturday morning. The **Rathaus** (begun in the 13th century, rebuilt in the 14th and 15th centuries) has a spectacular baroque facade (1720), and the steeple, topped with 41 Meissen china bells, was installed on the city's 1000th birthday in 1956. The top row of **statues** on the facade is the most important, representing (from left to right): Strength, Trade, Peace (the one with the big sword), Justice and Moderation.

On the north side of the Rathaus is the former **Court of Justice**, the little gated-in grotto-like area with paintings depicting scenes of justice being carried out throughout the centuries.

At the northern end of the Markt is the former **Ducal Palace**, now a courthouse, and west of that, on the corner of Burmeisterstrasse and Am Ochsenmarkt, is the home of the parents of poet Heinrich Heine – note the sandstone dolphins along the top of the building's facade. Heine, who hated Lüneburg, wrote the *Lorelei* here (for more on the Lorelei rock, see the St Goar/St Goarshausen section in the Rhineland-Palatinate chapter).

The Rathaus occupies the block running west from the Markt, 111m down to Reitende-Diener-Strasse. Heading west on Am Ochsenmarkt, you'll pass the entrance, which now houses city offices. Tours leave daily at 11 am, and 12.30 and 3 pm (DM6/4).

Diagonally opposite the mayor's offices, nine **16th century row houses** line tiny Reitende-Diener-Strasse.

Damaged Buildings

Many of the city's buildings are leaning, some more than 2m off true. Over the centuries, as salt was removed from the mines, ground shifts and settling occurred. From

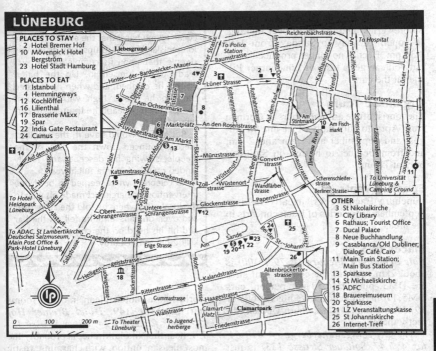

LÜNEBURG

PLACES TO STAY
2 Hotel Bremer Hof
10 Mövenpick Hotel
Bergström
23 Hotel Stadt Hamburg

PLACES TO EAT
1 Istanbul
4 Hemmingways
12 Kochlöffel
17 Lilienthal
17 Brasserie Mäxx
19 Spar
22 India Gate Restaurant
24 Camus

OTHER
3 St Nikolaikirche
5 City Library
6 Rathaus; Tourist Office
7 Ducal Palace
8 Neue Buchhandlung
9 Casablanca/Old Dubliner;
Dialog; Café Caro
11 Main Train Station;
Main Bus Station
13 Sparkasse
15 St Michaeliskirche
15 ADFC
18 Brauereimuseum
20 Sparkasse
21 LZ Veranstaltungskasse
25 St Johanniskirche
26 Internet-Treff

1994 to 1995, parts of the town sank an astounding 9cm into the ground.

The many buildings with bulging facades, though, are due to incompetence: artisans using gypsum plaster as mortar didn't maintain a uniform drying temperature, leaving the mortar susceptible to water absorption through rain or flooding, which caused the plaster to swell, resulting in the 'beer-bellied' buildings you see today.

Churches

At the eastern end of divided Am Sande is the clunky **St Johanniskirche** from the 14th century, whose 106m-high spire leans 2.2m off true.

Other churches include the partially reconstructed Gothic brick **St Nikolaikirche** (15th century), on the corner of Lüner Strasse and Koffmannstrasse (DM2). Behind it sits one of the best examples of the town's few half-timbered houses. At Johann-Sebastian-Bach-Platz is **St Michaeliskirche** (1376-1418).

Museums

The **Deutsches Salzmuseum** (☎ 450 65), Sülfmeisterstrasse 1, has taken the examination of salt to the extreme. With hands-on and interactive displays on the history of salt, salt production, salt tasting, salt boiling and even a salt tour of the city, salt fans will certainly feel they've had their money's worth – and it has a good section on the history of the city, too. It's open from May to September, Monday to Friday from 9 am to 5 pm, and weekends from 10 am; from October to April, it's open daily from 10 am to 5 pm (DM6/4/5 for adults/children/students). One-hour guided tours are available daily (an extra DM1.50).

The city's **Brauereimuseum** (☎ 410 21), Heiligengeiststrasse 39, shows the history of brewing in the city (once home to over 80 breweries) and the art of beer making. It's open Tuesday to Sunday from 1 to 4.30 pm. Beer is no longer produced here, but you can get a taste of Lüneburger Pilsner at the bar.

Organised Tours

The tourist office arranges tours in German from April to July daily at 11 am, in August and September at 11 am and 2 pm, and from October to March on Saturday only at 11 am.

Special Events

Lüneburg Bach weeks, usually held in September, are a series of Bach concerts in the area.

Places to Stay

Rote Schleuse Lüneburg (☎ 79 15 00) is about 2km south of the centre. Tent sites are DM3, plus DM6.50 per person, cars DM5. From Am Sande, take bus No 605 or 1977 (direction: Deutschebern/Uelzen) directly there.

The city's *Jugendherberge* (☎ 418 64, fax 457 47, Soltauer Strasse 133) is just west of the university, but the entrance is on Wichernstrasse. Juniors/seniors pay DM21/26, including breakfast. From the Hauptbahnhof, take bus No 11 (direction: Rettmer) or No 12 (direction: Bockelberg) to Scharnhorststrasse.

Book *private rooms* at the LTIO; expect to pay about DM45 per person, with breakfast.

During quiet periods, hotels band together and offer reduced packages; the best way to find out more is to contact one of the hotels directly, as LTIO doesn't always have a list of deals.

The *Hotel Stadt Hamburg* (☎ 444 38, fax 40 41 98, Am Sande 25), near St Johanniskirche, has comfortable singles/doubles from DM55/100 and young, friendly management. *Park-Hotel Lüneburg* (☎ 411 25, fax 40 71 41, Uelzener Strasse 27) has clean and comfortable rooms from DM 65/140.

Hotel Heidepark Lüneburg (☎ 650 91, Vor dem Neuen Tore 12) looks for all the

The Killer Drink

Local legend has it that the architect of the Johanniskirche was so upset by its leaning steeple that upon its completion he was ready to do himself in. Up the hated steeple he climbed, and when he reached the top he stood high with his arms spread. Then he leapt, he thought, to certain death.

But as fate would have it, the architect merely bounced down the side of the steeple, slowing his descent, and finally landed quite safely in a full haycart.

To celebrate what seemed to be divine intervention, the architect made his way to the local pub, where he told the story over and over, drinking until he fell off the bar and hit his head on the corner of a table, killing himself instantly.

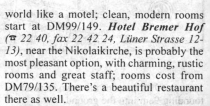

world like a motel; clean, modern rooms start at DM99/149. *Hotel Bremer Hof* (☎ 22 40, fax 22 42 24, Lüner Strasse 12-13), near the Nikolaikirche, is probably the most pleasant option, with charming, rustic rooms and great staff; rooms cost from DM79/135. There's a beautiful restaurant there as well.

The *Mövenpick Hotel Bergström* (☎ 30 80, fax 30 84 99, Bei der Lüner Mühle) has flashy and clean rooms for DM168, some with great views of the Ilmenau River. Its restaurant is in a wonderful location and offers good, if expensive, food.

Places to Eat

Restaurants & Cafes *Casablanca*, above the Old Dubliner bar on the corner of An den Rosen and Am Stintmarkt, has great service, a chic atmosphere, and is gay-friendly. It serves baked casseroles for about DM11 and well priced pizza and grills (open till 1 to 2 am).

Schröderstrasse, south of the Rathaus, has a couple of good options: *Lilienthal*, at No 5A, serves fare similar to Casablanca's, with almost all dishes costing under

DM15. *Brasserie Mäxx* (☎ 73 25 05) at No 6 serves 'new German' cuisine. That means much the same as above, but it offers a solid breakfast buffet during the week from 8 am to noon for DM8.50. It'll keep you going all day. If it doesn't, there's always the weekday lunch buffet from noon to 2 pm for DM11. Both stay open till late for tippling.

Hemmingways (☎ 23 22 55, *Bardowicker Strasse 27-28*) has Mexican and American specialities – appetisers from DM7 to DM9 and dinners from DM12 to DM25. It also offers a good Sunday breakfast buffet (DM16.90) from 10 am to 2 pm (open till late).

The *India Gate Restaurant*, next door to the Hotel Stadt Hamburg on Am Sande, has quite good lunch and dinner specials for about DM14. Main dishes are otherwise priced from DM17 to DM28. The curries are a bit on the tame side, but otherwise fine.

Mövenpick Brasserie (☎ 30 80, *Bei der Lüner Mühle*), where the dining room and the terrace both have good views of the Ilmenau, has main courses from DM27 to DM37. Its Sunday brunch, while admittedly bigger and more varied than the one at Hemmingways, is outrageously priced at DM40 per adult.

The restaurant at *Hotel Bremer Hof* is especially strong on local specialities. *Heidschnucke*, the cute-sounding local lamb, features heavily on the menu, but expect to pay around DM40 for Heidschnucke steaks, or DM29 for goulash. Many dishes range from DM17 to DM30 (lunch specials are about DM15), and the service is good.

Snacks & Fast Food *Istanbul* (☎ 359 29), on the corner of Lüner Strasse and Im Wendischen Dorfe, serves tasty Turkish food. *Camus* (☎ 428 20, *Am Sande 30*) is a popular student hang-out. *Kochlöffel*, on the corner of Glockenstrasse and Grosse Bäckerstrasse, has cheap German fast food.

Self-Catering The *Spar* (*Am Sande 8*) is one central supermarket with a good range of produce.

Entertainment
21Zwanzig magazine, the biggest 'what's on' guide, is available at the LTIO, pubs and bars.

The *Brauerei Museum* is a nice place to drink, but the most popular places are the bars along Am Stintmarkt, which heaves with activity in summer. You can also drink your beer on the river bank – pay a deposit for the glass. *Café Caro* is very hip; *Old Dubliner* has live music; *Dialog* is also worth trying and serves food.

Hemmingways (see Places to Eat) is a good place to start the evening.

Theater Lüneburg (☎ 75 20, *An den Reeperbahnen 3*) hosts drama, musicals, opera and classical music concerts. There are also classical concerts and recitals in St Johanniskirche, St Nikolaikirche and St Michaeliskirche.

The *Glockenhaus*, an arena seating 200-plus, holds art exhibits, classical and jazz concerts (and occasional craft fairs). *Heinrich Heine Haus* hosts literature forums, lectures and small concerts as well.

For concert ticket information, call or visit LZ Veranstaltungskasse (☎ 410 64) at Am Sande 16.

Getting There & Away
There's frequent train service to Hanover (DM35, one hour), Celle (DM22, 45 minutes), Schwerin (DM27, 1½ hours), Rostock (DM52, 3¼ hours) and Hamburg (DM12, 30 minutes).

The Lüneburg region is served by the bus companies: KVG (☎ 880 70), VOG (☎ 87 20 80, for Bleckede) and RBB (☎ 0581-97 62 80). Buses leave from the Busbahnhof beside the station and from Am Sande.

If you're driving from Hamburg, take the A7 south to the B250. From Schwerin take the B6 south to the A24 west and then exit No 7 (Talkau). From there, turn south on the B209, and you'll eventually get to town. From Hanover, take the A7 north to the B209.

Getting Around
Buses leave from the bus centre on Am Sande. Bus stops line both sides of the street. The ZOB (main bus station) is at the

Hauptbahnhof. Most buses stop running at around 7 pm. Tickets are DM2.30.

There are several taxi companies in town. Call ☎ 22 22, ☎ 520 25 or ☎ 370 37. For somewhat cheaper shared taxis, available after 8 pm, call AST (☎ 533 44).

Rent bicycles at the Hauptbahnhof (☎ 55 77) for DM10 per day, DM20 per weekend. There's a local branch of the ADFC (☎ 478 23, fax 475 12) at Katzenstrasse 2.

AROUND LÜNEBURG
Naturpark Elbufer-Drawehn

Some 20km east of Lüneburg, in an area of the Lüneburger Heide comprising wetland, are Bleckede and the Naturpark Elbufer-Drawehn. The nature reserve runs for 85km along the Elbe River and is a haven for birdlife such as white storks, wild geese and cranes. Cyclists and hikers will be well rewarded by this picturesque and interesting wetland, and if you don't have your own bike, you can hire one in Lüneburg or Bleckede. If you intend to come out here, drop by the tourist office in Lüneburg first, which is well stocked with brochures on accommodation and activities.

With its half-timbered houses, pretty **Bleckede** is a good starting point for trips in the Naturpark. The friendly tourist office (☎ 977 22, fax 977 99), Lüneburger Strasse 2A, has information on walks and other activities. It's open weekdays from 8 am to 4 pm. There's also a tourist information centre in the Elbtal-Haus Bleckede on weekends, near the Schloss.

A recommended **cycling** trip is along the Elbetour Radrundweg. For more information see the boxed text 'Elbetour Cycling Trail'.

Fahrgastschiffahrt A Haak (☎ 21 10, fax 21 26) runs two-hour **boat trips** daily except Monday from the harbour in Bleckede for DM14/7.

The tourist office can help with accommodation if you intend to stay overnight.

Getting There & Around There are no trains running to Bleckede. Buses leave at least hourly from Lüneburg at Am Sande or the Hauptbahnhof (DM8.20, 45 minutes; no

bikes permitted). If you're going by car, the B216 leads to the turn-off to Bleckede. A car ferry crosses the river here and in Neu Darchau to the south.

See the Lüneburg Getting Around section for bike hire there. Bikes can be hired in Bleckede at Fahrradverleih Weber (☎ 12 72), Breite Strasse 6, for DM10 per day. The tourist offices in Lüneburg and Bleckede can help with itineraries.

Elbetour Cycling Trail

One of the nicest cycling trails near Lüneburg and the Heide is the Elbetour Trail. It begins and ends at the Rathaus and tourist information office in Lüneburg and runs for some 80km through marshland, forest and meadows along and around the Elbe River. The advantage of this trail is that it takes in the most interesting parts of the Naturpark Elbufer-Drawehn, a nature reserve that briefly enjoyed national park status. (In this connection, also see the boxed text 'The Case of the Vanishing National Park' in the Facts about Germany chapter.)

From the baroque Rathaus in Lüneburg the trail runs north-east past Kloster Lüne (Lüne Convent, 1172) towards the Elbeseitenkanal (Elbe Side Canal) and Scharnebeck, where you'll find Europe's largest double-parallel hydraulic ship elevator. The next major stop is the pretty town of Lauenburg on the right bank of the Elbe, with its Altstadt of narrow lanes, the Maria-Magdalenen-Kirche and former Rathaus now housing the Elbe Shipping Museum (Elbeschiffahrtsmuseum). The trail then leads partially through forest to Boitzenburg, which has some nice buildings around the historic Marktplatz, including the Rathaus (1711), and the adjoining Kirchplatz. Near Gothmann the trail goes past some inland dunes, from where it eventually turns south to Bleckede (see Bleckede in this chapter) and on to the small town of Neetze, known for its tasty asparagus in spring.

South of Hanover

HILDESHEIM
☎ 05121 • pop 106,000

Established as a bishopric in the 9th century, Hildesheim grew as monasteries were established; by the 11th century it was a powerful market town. A new town (Neustadt) was formed, and the two merged in the 19th century.

The centre was completely destroyed by firebombs on 22 March 1945. Rebuilt in the 1950s in classic German Postwar Hideous, windowed concrete cubes took the place of the city's glorious half-timbered buildings. In the late 1970s a town movement was begun to rip them down and 'reconstruct' the town's historic heart. It was completed in 1989.

While the 'historic' core of Hildesheim is undeniably very pretty, it's just not, well, real. So while you're 'oohing' and 'aahing' at the buildings on the Markt, remember that they are, quite literally, five years younger than *Miami Vice*.

Hildesheim's true gems are the St Michaeliskirche and the bronze work inside the Dom, both of which are on the list of UNESCO World Heritage sites.

Orientation
The Hauptbahnhof is 750m north of the Markt, the centre of the old town. The pedestrianised Bernwardstrasse leads south towards the Markt, changing names to Almsstrasse and Hoher Weg, which meets Schuhstrasse, just south of the centre. The Markt is 100m east of Hoher Weg, reached via Marktstrasse.

The old Jewish quarter and Neustadt are south of Schuhstrasse. At Schuhstrasse's eastern end it becomes Goslarsche Strasse.

Information
The tourist office (☎ 179 80, fax 17 98 88) is on the south side of Markt at Rathausstrasse 18-20. Get a copy of *Hildesheimer Rosenroute* (DM3), a guide to the city's buildings and their history. The name comes from the tourist trail that is marked by roses painted on the streets of the town.

Change money at the Commerzbank, in the mall at Almsstrasse 29-30, which also has an ATM. Another ATM is at the post office, opposite the Hauptbahnhof. Online information on Hildesheim is at www.hildesheim.de.

There's a PANO laundrette (☎ 13 37 86) at Bahnhofsallee 10. The main city hospital is the Städtisches Krankenhaus (☎ 890, emergency room/casualty department ☎ 89 43 31) at Weinberg 1. There's a police station on the corner of Almsstrasse and Wallstrasse.

Churches
The first thing you should do in Hildesheim (if you're physically up to it) is climb the 364 steps to the top of **St Andreaskirche** (DM3/2). The viewing platforms at the top are on two levels. The bottom level has telescopes (DM0.50) and helpful directional indicators. The second offers the best view of the area.

The **Hildesheimer Dom** is an imposing reconstruction of the Gothic cathedral destroyed in 1945. The interior is quite severe, but many of the church's treasures remain, including the almost 5m-high **Bernwardstüren** (Bernward bronze doors), the wheel-shaped **chandelier**, 6m in diameter and the star of the show (commanding an extra DM0.50 admission), the **Christussäule** (Column of Christ), and the **Tausendjähriger Rosenstock**, a 1000-year-old rosebush. Alleged to be the very one on which Emperor Ludwig the Pious hung his gear in 815 AD, the rosebush climbs the walls of the chapel's apse.

The Dom is open Monday to Friday from 9.30 am to 5 pm, Saturday till 2 pm and Sunday from noon to 5 pm. It's at Domhof, south-west of the Markt. Next door, the cathedral treasury can be viewed in the **Dom-Museum**, open Tuesday to Saturday from 10 am to 5 pm, and Sunday from noon (DM6/4).

North-west of the Dom is the Romanesque **St Michaeliskirche** (1022), reconstructed after bombing raids badly damaged much of the original building.

Markt

The only thing that survived here was the **Marktbrunnen**, the fountain in front of the **Rathaus** on the east side of the square. The re-created highlights of the square are, on the west side, the **Knochenhauerhaus**, with entrance to the local history museum from the alley behind it and up a floor (DM3/2); and the **Bäckeramtshaus**. They are now both part of the Zum Knochenhauer restaurant. On the northern side of the plaza is the **Rokokohaus** (now the Meridien Hotel). At the east is the **Wollenweberhaus** and, at the south, the **Wedekindhaus**.

Lappenberg

Lappenberg, the former **Jewish Quarter**, is the oldest section of town. On Kristallnacht, as they let the synagogue burn, fire brigades saved the other houses around the square, including the former **Jewish school** (now owned by St Godehard's Church) on the corner.

In 1988, on the 50th anniversary of Kristallnacht, a memorial was installed on its site: an archaeological dig unearthed the synagogue's foundation, which was built up to indicate the dimensions. They were extended onto the pavement to be a constant reminder – you notice it because you have to walk around it. The memorial itself is topped by a model of Jerusalem.

Roemer- und Pelizaeusmuseum

The Roemer- und Pelizaeusmuseum (☎ 936 90), Am Steine 1-2, has one of Europe's best collections of Egyptian art and artefacts, and runs special temporary shows as well. The museum sends chunks of its core collection around the world, so check to see what's on and what's here during your visit. It's open Tuesday to Sunday from 9 am to 4.30 pm (DM3/1, usually DM12/7 during special exhibits).

Organised Tours

There are two-hour tours of the city (DM5) in German leaving from in front of the Rathaus from April to October daily at 2 pm, with an extra tour on Saturday at 10 am.

Places to Stay

Müggelsee, north of the city near the autobahn, is a beautiful private area with a small unofficial *camping ground* (☎ 531 51) on the corner of Kennedydamm and Bavenstedterstrasse, about 1km off the A7's Drispenstedt exit.

Campingplatz Derneburg (☎ 05062-565, fax 87 85), 13km south-east of the city on the B6, is open from April to mid-September. The cost is DM6 per person, DM6 per tent and DM3 per car. From Hildesheim's bus station, take bus No 2320 directly to the camping ground (the last bus is at 4.55 pm, though there's an indirect one at 6.15 pm to Derneburg Siedlung, a short walk from the place).

The modern *Jugendherberge* (☎ 427 17, fax 478 47), in the pretty house at the top of the hill, has friendly staff and spectacular views. From the centre, take bus No 1 or 4 to the Jugendherberge stop, then walk 750m up the hill; the entrance is on the right. Register from 8 to 9.30 am and 5 to 7 pm. There's a curfew at 10 pm. Beds cost DM20 for juniors, DM24.50 for seniors.

The *Hof-Café Wittenburg* (☎ 05068-37 65, fax 43 80), about 3km west of the city, is a hay hotel with places for DM19.19 per night with breakfast. To get there, take a train to Elze, then catch city bus No 2524 to Wittenburg. By car, take the B1 towards Hamelin (Hameln).

Hotel rooms are expensive in town. The *Hotel Weisser Schwan* (☎ 167 80, fax 16 78 90, Schuhstrasse 29) has nice singles/doubles for DM65/120 with a shower, or DM80/140 with shower and WC. Ask for one away from the street. *Hotel Bürgermeisterkapelle* (☎ 140 21, Rathausstrasse 8) has small but clean rooms available for DM100/150 with shower and WC.

The *Meridien Hotel* (☎ 30 00, fax 30 04 44, Markt 4) is in the splendid Rokokohaus. Expect to pay from DM265/295 for rooms. But its weekend deal of DM150 for a single or double is good value, especially as this price includes use of the fitness centre, sauna and pool. The hotel also has an upmarket restaurant.

Places to Eat

Paulaner im Kniep (☎ 382 82, *Kurzer Hagen 4*) serves up standard but well priced Bavarian fare for under DM20. The restaurant in the *Bürgermeisterkapelle Hotel* (see Places to Stay) is more expensive, with traditional main dishes in the DM20 to DM30 range.

Limerick (☎ 13 38 76, *Kläperhagen 6*) is a wonderful bar and cafe with a wood-fired oven and pizzas from DM6.70 to DM11.90. Great service, fun crowd. You can't miss the red phone booth just inside the front door. It closes at midnight on Sunday – the rest of the time it's open till late.

Friesenstrasse, parallel to and south of Schuhstrasse, has a high concentration of eateries, bars and nightspots. *Marmaris* (☎ 13 38 65, *Friesenstrasse 19*) offers doner kebab (DM5) and good pizzas (DM3 to DM8), and more substantial and well priced Turkish dishes. It is open to 2 am Sunday to Thursday, to 3 am Friday and Saturday. *Café-Brasserie Hindenburg* (*Hindenburgplatz 3*), at the eastern end of Friesenstrasse, offers a daily lunchtime buffet for DM11. If you've had your fill of heavy meals, try one of its fairly light dishes for under DM15. It's also good for a huge steaming bowl of cappuccino and stays open until at least 1 am.

Mexim's (*Friesenstrasse 15a*) has Mexican specials like jalapeno poppers – so called because you pop them into your mouth (DM8) – and nachos and chilli con carne for DM7. It's open in the evening and has American beer, drinks and service at German prices. *Two Pence Pub* (*Friesenstrasse 6*) is – surprise – an English pub.

Entertainment

Hildesheim Aktuell is a monthly entertainment guide put out by the city (free at the tourist information office) with excellent listings for cultural events. *Public* is another freebie that has information on discos, pop and rock concerts, parties and music reviews. Get tickets at the tourist office or at the venues themselves.

Vier Linden (☎ 272 44, *Alfelder Strasse 55b*) has a disco in the cellar and, on the ground floor, a concert hall that hosts many types of concerts. There's a restaurant and wine bar as well.

Die Kultur Fabrik (☎ 553 76, *Langer Garten 1*) is in an old paper mill behind the Hauptbahnhof and has alternative attractions, including performance art.

There's no concert hall in Hildesheim, but the large churches and the town's Stadttheater chip in to host classical concerts and ballet every weekend during winter.

Getting There & Around

There's frequent train service between Hildesheim and Hanover (DM10, 30 minutes), as well as to Braunschweig (DM13, 30 minutes) and ICE trains to Göttingen (DM40, 30 minutes to one hour).

Most sights in Hildesheim are within walking distance. If the legs are weary, bus No 1 (towards Himmelsthür) and No 2 (towards Ochtersum) will drop you at Schuhstrasse, near Friesenstrasse. Single tickets cost DM2.20, or DM10 for six.

From Hanover, the A7 runs right into town. MFZ Reisen (☎ 390 51), Annenstrasse 15 on the corner of Goschenstrasse, runs a Mitfahrzentrale.

Rent bikes for DM12 a day from Wico (☎ 380 58), Bahnhofsallee 12 (corner of Kaiserstrasse). You can book with them directly or through the tourist office.

The local ADFC (☎ 130 66 6) is at Wollenweberstrasse 30.

BRAUNSCHWEIG

☎ 0531 • pop 253,000

Busy, sprawling Braunschweig is Lower Saxony's second largest city. It lost 90% of its Altstadt in Allied bombing, was rebuilt and, until reunification, lived in the shadow of the Iron Curtain.

Its origins are as a trading centre, but when Heinrich der Löwe chose Braunschweig as his residence in the 12th century, it became the centre from which power was extended eastwards over the Slavic tribes.

The city developed out of five separate settlements. You can still today see where the old towns were – each had its own town

LOWER SAXONY

BRAUNSCHWEIG

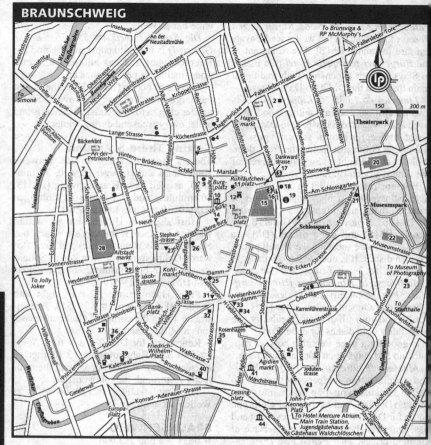

hall, church and market and was filled with solid granite buildings.

Despite its sprawling character, Braunschweig is a pleasant city with some fascinating architecture, fine museums and quiet parkland. Most of its sights are within its reconstructed centre, which can be easily covered by foot.

Orientation

The Hauptbahnhof is about 2km south-east of the town centre and is connected by Kurt-

Schumacher-Strasse, which leads to John-F-Kennedy-Platz and the south-eastern corner of the centre. The boundaries of the centre form a distorted rectangle, with Lange Strasse to the north, Bohlweg to the east, Konrad-Adenauer-Strasse to the south and Gülden-strasse to the west. A moat surrounds the centre, lending it the compact character of an island. A one-way system on the east side (see Getting Around) may cause problems if you're driving about. The heart of the pedestrianised shopping district is Kohlmarkt.

BRAUNSCHWEIG

PLACES TO STAY	OTHER	21	Staatstheater Kleines Haus
2 Hotel zum Stillen Winkel	1 Kinder und Jugendzentrum	22	Herzog Anton Ulrich
11 Deutsches Haus	Mühle; Fräuen Café		Museum
32 City-Hotel Mertens	3 Penny Markt	23	Brücke
34 Best Western Stadtpalais	4 Flugbörse	24	Glockmann & Sohn
37 Hotel Ritter St Georg	6 ADAC	25	Cats Statue
42 Courtyard by Marriott	7 Till Eulenspiegel Brunnen	26	Buchhandlung Karl
	8 LOT-Theater		Pfankuch
PLACES TO EAT	9 Konzertkasse	28	Altstadt Rathaus
5 Welfenhof/Packhof; Möven-	10 Landesmuseum	29	Gewandhaus; Stechinelli's
pick; Pasta Mania	12 Burg Dankwarderode		Kartoffel-Keller
14 Taj Mahal	13 The Dom	30	Post Office
27 Vegetarisches Vollwert	15 Neues Rathaus	35	Kottan
Restaurant Brodocz	16 Commerzbank	38	Merz
31 Delicato	17 Citibank	39	Liro Dando
33 Zum Löwen	18 Discount Travel	40	Brain Club
36 Tandir	19 Tourist-Büro Bohlweg-Pavillon	41	Jewish Museum
43 Java Indonesian	20 Staatstheater	44	Kunstverein

Information

Tourist Offices The tourist office (☎ 27 35 50, fax 273 55 19) in the Hauptbahnhof is open Monday to Friday from 8 am to 5 pm and Saturday from 9 am to noon. There's a second office, the Tourist-Büro Bohlweg-Pavillon (☎ 273 55 30/31) at Bohlweg 70, open Monday to Friday from 9 am to 6 pm, and Saturday from 9.30 am to 12.30 pm. Both have an excellent selection of brochures, and lots of city tours are available (see Organised Tours). They also sell the Museumsverbundtageskarte (DM10), which allows admission for one day to all city museums.

ADAC (☎ 440 14) has an office at Lange Strasse 63.

Money There's a Commerzbank with an ATM on the corner of Dankwardstrasse and Bohlweg, behind the Neues Rathaus, and a Citibank diagonally opposite.

Post & Communications The main post office is next to the Hauptbahnhof, but a more convenient branch is at Friedrich-Wilhelm-Strasse 3.

Travel Agencies Flugbörse (☎ 448 54, fax 126 93 8) is located at Hagenbrücke 15.

Discount Travel (☎ 24 27 20) has an office at Steinweg 44.

Bookshops & Libraries Buchhandlung Karl Pfankuch (☎ 453 03), in the Burgpassage mall between Damm and Kleine Burg, has an excellent collection of English-language books. The university's language library (☎ 391 35 06), Mülenpfordstrasse 22-23, is at the western end of the university campus.

Universities Technische Universität Braunschweig is the oldest technical university in Europe. There are 12,000 students. The main campus is at the northern end of town, with smaller institutes throughout the city.

Laundry There's an SB Waschsalon at Goslarsche Strasse 22, about 2km west of the centre, and another at Bültenweg 80, north-east of the centre.

Burgplatz

Landesmuseum The State Museum (☎ 484 26 02) covers Braunschweig and German history from the town's creation to the Trabant. There are great money exhibitions, with notes and coins from several periods, a coin press and the best notes you

LOWER SAXONY

could want: inflationary Weimar Republican *zweihundert Milliarden* (200 billion) and *zwanzig Millionen* (20 million) mark notes, emergency Braunschweig notes and Reichmarks. There is also some interesting Nazi propaganda and uniforms, and the 1950s and 1960s section is a hoot – the Trabi doesn't look out of place here at all.

The museum's other displays – uniforms, excellent furniture and weapons – are all worth the trip and admission price. It is open from Tuesday to Sunday from 10 am to 5 pm, Thursday till 8 pm, closed Monday (DM6/3).

The Dom In the crypt under St Blasius Cathedral (1173-95), the city's Romanesque and Gothic Dom, is the tomb of Heinrich der Löwe and Mathilde – an Englishwoman who was, depending on whom you believe, either his wife or (more probably) his 'consort'. Inside are some stunning murals from the 13th century, and large stone sculptures of Bishop Heinrich III of Hildesheim and Albert the Fat.

The Dom (☎ 130 26) is open daily from 10 am to 5 pm (closed January to Easter from 1 to 3 pm) and holds brief services Monday to Friday at 5 pm. There are Protestant services on Sunday at 10 am. Entry to the crypt costs DM2, students and children free, but it's pretty much the honour system. Turn right at the bottom of the stairs for the tomb.

Burg Dankwarderode The main attraction at this former residence of Heinrich himself is his original **lion statue**, copies of which stand in the square outside the museum and all over town. Upstairs is the enormous, spectacularly adorned **Knights' Hall**. Admission is DM5/2.50.

Herzog Anton Ulrich Museum

One highlight of a visit to Braunschweig is this wonderful museum. Its **Gemäldegalerie** on the 1st floor contains one of the best collections of Dutch, French and Italian paintings in Germany, with works by artists like Rubens, De Voss, Rembrandt and Vermeer. The collection is overwhelming in its sheer beauty, taking you through a fascinating array of portraits, biblical scenes, nudes and works with a playful theme, such as *Der Bacchuszug* (The Bacchus Procession) by Moses van Uetenbroeck (1590-1648). The gallery layout is straightforward, and the title of each painting and the artist's name are clearly marked, making things very easy for the visitor. The main painting galleries are in the large central halls, with separate halls in the wings to the right and left of the centre.

The 2nd floor houses sculpture, furniture, the most complete museum collection of Fürstenburg porcelain, as well as tapestries and other applied arts. The museum (☎ 484 24 00) is at Museumstrasse 1, and is open Tuesday to Sunday from 10 am to 5 pm, Wednesday from 1 to 8 pm (DM5/2.50).

Jewish Museum

In the former monastery of the **Aegidienkirche**, on Mönchstrasse at the south-eastern end of the centre, is Braunschweig's fascinating Jewish Museum (☎ 484 26 30). Inside are exhibits on Jewish life in northern Europe, the camp at Bergen-Belsen, remains from the synagogue in the village of Hornburg, including one of its Torah scrolls, and photos of the synagogue before its destruction by Nazis in 1940. You'll also find more Torah scrolls, ceremonial artefacts from throughout Germany and Poland, Shofar horns and other exhibits. Hours are the same as for the Landesmuseum (DM6/3).

Other Sights

The **Museum of Photography** (☎ 750 00), Helmstedter Strasse 1, has rotating exhibitions by local and international photographers. It's open Tuesday to Friday from 1 to 6 pm, weekends from 2 to 6 pm (DM5/3). The **Kunstverein** (☎ 495 56), Lessingplatz 12, is also worth visiting for its changing exhibitions.

The Gothic **Altstadt Rathaus** at the northern end of Altstadt Markt may be imposing and spooky, but its arches are adorned with some interesting statues. Inside is the Dronse meeting hall. The neo-Gothic **Neues Rathaus** (1894-1900), behind Burg Dankwarderode, has a pretty riotous facade of its own, but nothing in town is outdone by the step-gabled Renaissance **Gewandhaus** (1303, facade 1590) at the southern end of Altstadt Markt.

Kids will like the playful **cats statue** on the corner of Damm and Kattreppeln, in front of the Nordsee, and the lovely **Till Eulenspiegel Brunnen** at Bäckerklint, with Till sitting above owls and monkeys.

Boating

From Easter to the end of October, weather permitting, a boat-rental stand is set up at the foot of the bridge over a branch of the Oker River, near Kurt-Schumacher-Strasse. Rentals cost from DM8 to DM12 per hour.

Organised Tours

The tourist office organises several tours weekly, all in German. The two hour Mumme-Bummel tour is a favourite, with a walk around the town followed by a beer and a shot of Mumme, a local concoction dating from the Middle Ages that was used as an antidote to scurvy. It's sweet, malty and syrupy, but the beer cuts through all that quite nicely. The tours leave from in front of the Neues Rathaus at 6.30 pm on the second Friday of the month year round (DM11).

City tours lasting 1½ hours leave from the Tourist-Büro Bohlweg-Pavillon every Saturday at 2.30 pm and Sunday at 10.30 am year round (DM8).

Places to Stay

The non-DJH *Jugendgästehaus (☎ 26 43 20, fax 264 32 70, Salzdahlumer Strasse 170)*, near the hospital, has clean and comfortable six-bed dorms with bunks from DM19 to DM23. Breakfast costs DM7 extra. Take bus No 11 or 19 to Krankenhaus.

Hotel accommodation in Braunschweig is rather expensive; however, the tourist information offices, which book all types of accommodation free of charge, are very helpful.

Simoné (☎ 57 78 98, fax 57 43 13, Celler Strasse 111) is the cheapest pension in the city, with basic single/double rooms from DM43/79, rising to DM68/99 with shower and WC – but on the weekend you'll need to arrange check-in in advance, as the reception is not always staffed.

From here the scene gets depressing. *Hotel zum Stillen Winkel (☎ 448 82, fax 489 92 21, An der Katherinenkirche 12-15)* has fairly crummy singles with a shower cabinet in the corner for DM65, doubles with a shower for DM110 or with shower and WC for DM150. *Gästehaus Waldschlösschen (☎ 621 61, fax 639 59, Heidbleekanger 16)*, in the Südstadt (take bus No 11), charges DM60/90 for basic singles/doubles, and from DM70/120 for rooms with shower and WC.

The *City-Hotel Mertens (☎ 24 10 24, fax 24 24 18, Friedrich-Willhelm-Strasse 27-29)* has pretty standard rooms from DM115/130. The *Courtyard by Marriott (☎ 481 40, fax 481 41 00, Auguststrasse 6-8)* is clean and modern, with rooms from DM166 (breakfast DM23 extra).

Hotel Ritter St Georg (☎ 130 39, fax 130 38, Alte Knochenhauerstrasse 11-13) has large, very pleasant rooms for DM160/190, reduced to DM120/150 on the weekend. Many of the rooms have a balcony. The *Deutsches Haus (☎ 120 00, fax 120 04 44, Ruhfäutchenplatz 1)* is a very traditional place that has rooms from DM144/210, and suites from DM260 to DM369. *Hotel Mercure Atrium (☎ 700 80, fax 700 81 25, Berliner Platz 3)*, opposite the Hauptbahnhof, has rooms from DM150/192 and cheaper weekend deals.

The renovated *Best Western Stadtpalais (☎ 24 10 24, fax 24 10 25, Hinter Liebfrauen 1a)* is an excellent place with huge rooms, great service and lots of extras (staff will haul an exercise bike up to your room free for the asking). Drinks and snacks are available in your room 24 hours a day (no service charge), and they'll bring breakfast to your room at no extra charge (although there's a good breakfast buffet downstairs). If you're going to pay DM165 to DM185 for a single or DM225 for a double (DM250 for a suite), you should do it here. On weekend nights, it's a good deal at DM120/150.

euro currency converter DM1 = €0.51

Places to Eat

Restaurants The *Vegetarisches Vollwert Restaurant Brodocz* (☎ *422 36, Stephanstrasse 1)*, in the courtyard, has excellent vegie and vegan offerings. We found the service slow but the food was worth the wait. Vegetarian main dishes cost about DM10 to DM20, fish dishes DM17 to DM25 and salads DM10/15 for small/large. It also has cheaper lunch specials.

Java Indonesian (☎ *435 11, Auguststrasse 12-13)* gets quite pricey at night, but it also has good lunch specials from DM8 to DM14, including spring rolls or soup; at night main courses cost DM16 to DM19, or satay DM18 to DM21. *Taj Mahal* (☎ *433 44, Kleine Burg 14)* offers lunch specials from DM8 to DM12 and a la carte dishes from DM14 to DM30. Both of these are closed Monday.

Zum Löwen (☎ *12 45 11, Weisenhausdamm 13)* offers large servings of good German food. Main courses are in the DM20 to DM30 range, and there are some lunch specials. It brews its own tasty Pilsner and a top-fermented Weizen in the huge copper vats in the middle of the restaurant. When they're brewing, the whole place smells, well, interesting. All beers cost DM6.70/4.10 for 0.5L/0.3L glasses.

Stechinelli's Kartoffel-Keller (☎ *24 27 77, Altstadtmarkt 1)*, in the Gewandhaus, serves up satisfying potato and other dishes for under DM20. The upmarket *Gewandhaus* restaurant (☎ *24 27 77)* claims to be northern Germany's oldest restaurant (1352). The prices are fairly modern, though – around DM27 to DM45 for main courses (closed Sunday).

Another place where you can go the whole hog is the stylish restaurant in the *Hotel Ritter St Georg* (see Places to Stay). It has a set menu for DM87 with French-inspired fare; if you order a la carte, expect to pay DM15 to DM45 for main courses.

The Magni quarter near the Magnikirche has several traditional restaurants and places to drink. There are also a couple of good options in the Welfenhof/Packhof shopping complex near Hagenbrücke.

You'll find a *Mövenpick* restaurant here; or try *Pasta Mania* (☎ *408 43)*, where pasta dishes go for DM11 to DM17.50.

Snacks & Fast Food On the ground floor of the Landesmuseum there's a *bistro* with coffee and cake etc – try to get a seat on the glass floor over the foundation.

There are lots of Turkish food places in and around the pedestrian zones of the centre. *Tandir*, on the corner of Knochenhauerstrasse and Südstrasse, makes especially good salads, vegie and meat dishes.

Delicato (☎ *40 07 16, Münzstrasse 9)* has awesome speciality salads, roast potatoes, heaps of vegie offerings and budget hot dishes like lasagne (closed Sunday) – virtually everything comes in at under DM10.

Self-Catering There's a *Penny Markt* supermarket on Hagenbrücke. Fresh produce markets are held on Wednesday and Saturday mornings on the Altstadtmarkt.

Entertainment

The city prints the free monthly *Braunschweig Bietet* with listings of concerts and plays. Otherwise, there is no shortage of listings rags, which you can pick up at the tourist offices or in cafes and bars. Look for *Das Programm*, the more upmarket *Subway*, or *Da Capo*.

Pubs & Bars The beer is pretty good at *Zum Löwen* (see Restaurants under Places to Eat). *Merz* (☎ *181 28, Gieselerstrasse 3)* is a great place to eat, drink or dance. It serves well priced salads and pasta and has breakfast from DM8 to DM15. *Liro Dando* (☎ *157 09)* on Kalenwall also draws the crowds on a good night for drinks and eats (open from 5 pm).

Discos & Clubs The *Merz* (see Pubs & Bars) turns into a popular disco and bar at night that plays independent music. *Jolly Joker* (☎ *281 46 60, Broitzemerstrasse 220)* is a mainstream top-100 dance charts kind of place. *Brain Club* (☎ *408 62, Bruchtorwall 22)* has techno and a skeletal interior.

Kottan (Leopoldstrasse 7) is a heavy metal kind of place.

Folk & Traditional Music *Brücke (☎ 470 48 61, Steintorwall 3)* stages all kinds of cultural events, including cabaret, folk theatre and readings. *Brunsviga (☎ 23 80 40, Karlstrasse 35)* has small live performances of modern music, jazz, cabaret, classical and folk guitar, and even flamenco (but not rock). *RP McMurphy's (☎ 33 60 90, Bültenweg 10)* is an Irish pub that also has live Irish folk music on most weekends.

Theatre & Classical Music The main *Staatstheater (☎ 484 28 00, Am Theater)* hosts theatre, ballet and classical concerts. The smaller *Staatstheater Kleines Haus (same phone number, Magnitorwall 18)* hosts smaller events. The *LOT-Theater (☎ 173 03, Kaffeetwete 4A)* puts on more innovative theatre and sometimes has music. The *Dom (☎ 130 26 or ☎ 464 73)* holds regular choral and organ concerts.

The *Kinder und Jugendzentrum Mühle (☎ 470 25 71, An der Neustadtmühle 3)* is a children's theatre with educational and fantasy, role-playing games. There's a *Frauen Café* here as well.

The *Stadthalle (☎ 707 70, Leonhardplatz)* is an all-round venue, host to rock concerts as well to performances by the Philharmonisches Staatsorchestra. Buy tickets at the Konzertkasse (☎ 166 06), Schild 1A, or at the venues themselves.

Getting There & Away

There are hourly train connections to Hanover (DM16, 45 minutes), IC trains to Leipzig (DM 64, two hours), and ICE trains to Frankfurt (DM131, 2¾ hours) and Berlin (DM84, 1½ hours).

The A2 runs east-west between Hanover and Magdeburg across the northern end of the city. This connects with the A39 about 25km east of the city, which heads north to Wolfsburg. The A39 heads south from the city.

There's a Mitfahrzentrale (☎ 194 40) at Vollmarkt 3.

Getting Around

Bus & Tram Braunschweig is the heart of a new integrated transport network that extends throughout the region and as far south as the Harz Mountains. Ticket prices are determined by time, not distance: 90 minute-tickets cost DM2.80; and 24-hour tickets cost DM7, for groups of up to five people DM12. You can buy 90-minute tickets in blocks of four for DM9.50, and blocks of 10 for DM23.

Car & Motorcycle Roads aren't in pristine condition, and parking enforcement is stringent in the centre. Watch the one-way system that kicks in just north of the corner of Bohlweg and Ritterbrunnen.

Bicycle Rent bicycles at Glockmann & Sohn (☎ 469 23), Ölschlägern 29-30.

WOLFENBÜTTEL
☎ 05331 • pop 53,000

This charming little city, about 10 minutes by train south from Braunschweig's Hauptbahnhof, makes a nice day trip or, if you don't mind the lack of nightlife, can be used as an overnight alternative to Braunschweig. Wolfenbüttel was untouched by WWII, and it's almost a time capsule of half-timbered houses – there are over 600 of them, over 300 of which have been beautifully restored.

You can see all the town's sights on foot.

Orientation & Information

The Hauptbahnhof is a five minute walk south-west of Stadtmarkt, the town centre. To get to Stadtmarkt take Bahnhofstrasse north to Kommisstrasse. This joins Kornmarkt, the main bus transfer point. Stadtmarkt is just to the north. The Schloss and Herzog August Bibliothek are west of here.

At the time of writing, the tourist office (☎ 29 83 46, fax 29 83 47, email stadt@ wolfenbuettel.de) was at Rosenwall 1, but it will eventually move to the south-west corner of Stadtmarkt. Call the city administration on ☎ 860 if you can't reach it on the current telephone number. The tourist office is open Monday to Friday from 9 am to

LOWER SAXONY

12.30 pm and 2 to 4 pm; from April to October it's also open Saturday from 9 am to 1 pm. Ask for its free *Stadtrundgang* brochure in English, which takes you on an excellent city walk past the major sights, providing a lot of interesting detail.

The main post office is on Bahnhofstrasse, across the street from the Hauptbahnhof.

City Walk
The departure point for the city walk is Wolfenbüttel's pretty **Schloss**, once home to the dukes of Braunschweig-Lüneburg. Take a look inside the **Schloss Museum** (☎ 924 60), with its intricate inlaid wood and ivory walls in the main dining room and grand furniture. On the staircase at the entrance are trompe l'oeil pillars. The museum is open Tuesday to Saturday from 10 am to 5 pm, Sunday from 10 am to 1 pm (DM3, free for children and students).

Nearby is the **Herzog August Bibliothek** (DM6/4), one of the world's best reference libraries for 17th century books. Established by Duke August the Younger, the collection exceeds 800,000 volumes, including what's billed as the 'World's Most Expensive Book', an evangelistery (gospel book) owned by Heinrich der Löwe.

To the right as you enter is the research reading room. There's a huge collection of books in English. You can request books for no charge.

To the right of the main hall is the **vault** where, in September, you can see the original *Welfen Evangelia*, Heinrich der Löwe's evangelistery, valued at DM35 million. At other times facsimiles are on display.

Downstairs are fascinating maps and globes, and displays on book illustrations, with lots by Picasso.

Between the Schloss and the library is **Lessinghaus** (DM6/4), a museum dedicated to the writer Gotthold Lessing, who once lived here. The gabled pink building you can see nearby was once the **Zeughaus** (Armoury), but it is now used to store the library's catalogue.

From Schlossplatz, make your way east along Löwenstrasse to Krambuden and north up Kleiner Zimmerhof to **Klein Venedig** (Little Venice), which was built by Dutch canal builders in the late 16th century. Head southeast to **Stadtmarkt** (City Market) and the **Rathaus** (1602). Across the square at No 15 is the **wedding registry building** (1736) – outside the front door are two intertwined hearts in the stone pavement, and two more on the building's gable. Walk through to a lovely shared courtyard, where choral performances are held in summer. Continue south-east to **Marienkirche** (1608), a blend of Gothic, Renaissance and baroque styles, and east down Holzmarkt to the **Trinitatiskirche**. Behind the church is the **Bürgerfriedhof** (People's Cemetery), from where paths lead south along the **Wall** to the **Lessingtheater** (1909). This walk takes around one hour (2km), excluding visits, and is described in more detail in the *Stadtrundgang* brochure.

Places to Stay & Eat
The non-DJH *Jugendgästehaus* (☎ 271 89, fax 90 24 45, Jägerstrasse 17) has clean, comfortable dorm beds for DM19 for kids under 14, DM24 for people 14 to 25 years old, and DM30 for everyone else (prices include breakfast). From Kornmarkt, take bus No 95 to the Finanzamt stop; or bus No 91, 92 or 94 to Westring Adersheimer Strasse and walk back east, about 150m.

The *Akzent Hotel Waldhaus* (☎ 432 65, fax 420 21, Adersheimer Strasse 75) has clean singles/doubles from DM85/140. *Landhaus Dürkop* (☎ 70 53/4, fax 726 38, Alter Weg 47) is a nice option, with spotless rooms, a pleasant restaurant and a sauna/solarium. Rooms start at DM104/160. It's a 20 minute walk from Stadtmarkt. Take Breite-Herzog-Strasse north across the bridge. Alter Weg veers off to the left.

The *Ratskeller* in the cellar of the Rathaus offers the usual traditional fare for about DM18 to DM30. *Kartoffel Haus* (☎ 925 62, Kommisstrasse 10) has a great skewered lamb fillet (DM22) but also has cheap jacket potatoes and lots of extremely well priced and interesting vegetarian and meat dishes. The most expensive dish on the menu is DM26.

Wolfenbüttel folds up its footpaths at night, but there are a couple of drinking options on Grosser Zimmerhof. *Alter Fritz* at No 20 is your best bet.

Getting There & Around

Trains connect Wolfenbüttel with Braunschweig's Hauptbahnhof (DM5) twice an hour. There's a good bus service in town; the main transfer point is Kornmarkt. Single rides cost DM2.80, or DM9.50 for four tickets.

WOLFSBURG

☎ 05361 • pop 124,000

In Wolfsburg, 40km north-east of Braunschweig, you'll feel like a real bastard driving a Ford. Since its founding in 1938 under a Nazi plan to produce an economical car for the people, Wolfsburg has been home to a Volkswagen (VW) factory.

The city was built to make that car and to serve as a model factory town for propaganda purposes: *Mutter* and *Vater* with smiling *Kinder*, great salaries, perfect working and living conditions and the satisfaction of serving the people of the Reich.

During WWII, POWs and other forced labourers were put to work in the factory, which was producing jeeps, and plane and V2 parts.

When the British occupied Wolfsburg in 1945, they took over the Volkswagen factory and, employing German labour, made sure it kept churning out 'Beetles', as the first Volkswagen model is known.

The 1950s and 1960s saw the Volkswagen grow in popularity throughout Germany, as well as the UK and the USA. Pretty soon VW had become a household name worldwide.

Today it's a rather interesting place, although accommodation tends towards the expense-account trap. There's plenty of culture and a lot of parks, hiking and biking trails, swimming and leisure opportunities.

You can tour the VW factory, which may well be the largest under one roof in the world: the roofed factory area is the approximate size of Monaco.

Orientation

Wolfsburg's centre is just south of the Hauptbahnhof. Its main shopping street is the pedestrianised Porschestrasse, which runs north-south. Major suburbs include Alt Wolfsburg north-east of the centre, with the Schloss and artificial Allersee; Fallersleben to the west, with the Hoffmann Museum and Altes Brauhaus; and Rabenberg and Detmerode, south of the centre, with access to Hattorfer Holz, the huge forested area packed with cycling, hiking and horse-riding trails.

The factory entrance is on the north side of the Hauptbahnhof.

Information

Wolfburg's friendly and well stocked tourist office (☎ 28 28 28, fax 28 25 50, email infopavillon@wolfsburg.de) is at the pavilion in the centre of Porschestrasse, where Pestalozziallee meets Goethestrasse. It is open weekdays from 9 am to 6 pm, Saturday to 1 pm.

Along Porschestrasse there's a Citibank at No 19, a Sparkasse at No 70, and a Commerzbank on the corner of Kleiststrasse. The central post office is at Porschestrasse 22-24. Some suburbs have different telephone codes; unless otherwise indicated, the main code in use is ☎ 05361.

Volkswagen Factory Tour

Free two-hour tours of the Volkswagen factory (☎ 92 42 70) leave Tuesday to Friday at 1.30 pm. You'll see many aspects of car production – from the body press shop to the final product being loaded onto trains, and hear some of the mind-boggling facts about the enormous factory, its harbour, train station, 75km of track, huge car parks etc. For safety reasons, children under 10 aren't allowed in.

Show up at the factory, just north of the Hauptbahnhof, at around 1 pm to get your ticket.

Autostadt

A new Autostadt complex will open on the eastern portion of the Volkswagen site to coincide with the June opening of EXPO

2000. This permanent complex promises some interesting modern architecture and landscaping and will include a large piazza, a 3D cinema telling you all about the company, a five star hotel, and the relocated **AutoMuseum** (see Volkswagen AutoMuseum). Until the real thing opens, you can buzz through on a virtual trip of Autostadt in its **Kubis** information centre. At the time of writing, combined tickets for the (old) AutoMuseum and Kubis cost DM12. Discounts apply, and a shuttle bus runs every 30 minutes from the AutoMuseum, presently on Dieselstrasse, to the Kubis. Entrance to the information centre is via Tor Ost (the east gate).

Volkswagen AutoMuseum

Ferdinand Porsche (1875-1951) designed the air-cooled *Käfer mit dem Brezel Fenster* (Beetle with the pretzel rear window), a car that could run forever on tiny sips of fuel and practically no oil, could float, resist rust, and be fixed with spit and paper clips, and which became a symbol of 1960s hippie lifestyle in the USA.

The Volkswagen AutoMuseum (☎ 520 71), Dieselstrasse 35, is a great trip back in time, with hundreds of cars from the original Käfer to concept cars, including a Beetle balloon gondola, amphibious vehicle and catamaran; the original 1938 Cabriolet presented to Adolf Hitler on his 50th birthday, and the 1988 Passat embossed with the names of 134,535 VW workers at the factory on its 50th anniversary. In June 2000 the museum moves into its new home in Autostadt.

The museum is open daily from 10 am to 5 pm, closed 24 December to 1 January (DM9/5, DM25 per family).

Schloss Wolfsburg

The castle as it appears today was begun in 1600. From 1742 to 1942 the family of Graf von der Schulenburg lived here. Today it houses a museum of the city's history from 1938 to 1955, a small regional history museum and two art galleries that host rotating exhibitions. In summer, it puts on concerts. The museum is open Tuesday to Friday from 10 am to 5 pm, Saturday from 1 to 6 pm and Sunday from 10 am to 6 pm (DM2.50/1). A courtyard is the site of the Wolfsburg Summer Festival in June. Nearby, from May to September, there's also a **Museum of Agriculture** in the brewer's barn on the castle grounds.

Fallersleben

This lovely section of town is lined with original half-timbered houses from the mid-18th century. It was home to August Heinrich Hoffman (1798-1874), more commonly known as Hoffmann von Fallersleben, writer of the lyrics to Germany's national anthem in 1841, including the now infamous passage *Deutschland, Deutschland über Alles*.

Hoffmann was a liberal man, remembered far more for his charming children's songs. The 'über Alles' (above everything) words themselves were a call for an end to petty fiefdoms – a far cry from the nationalistic fervour they were later used to incite. The words are etched in the rear beam of the **Hoffmann Haus**, the place of his birth, now a hotel.

Nearby in the **Fallersleben Schloss** is a **Hoffmann Museum** (☎ 05362-526 23), with exhibits on his life and great exhibits for kids on his children's songs – the tree puzzle in the kids' room plays recordings of them when you plug in the pieces. Opening hours are the same as for the Städtisches Museum (DM2.50/1).

City Centre

In front of **Stadttheater** on the hill just southwest of the southern end of Porschestrasse is **Planetarium Wolfsburg** (☎ 219 39), built in 1982 after VW bartered Golfs for Zeiss projectors with the GDR. It's got laser and rock shows, star shows and spoken-word performances (like *The Little Prince*) set to the stars (DM8/5, or DM20 for families).

Both are in front of the city's historic landmark, the **Esso Station**, built in 1951 and restored in 1995 to its original splendour.

Also at the southern end is the excellent **Kunst Museum** (☎ 266 90), Porschestrasse 53. The building, designed by Hamburg architect Peter Schweger, is a delight in its own right, with an airy, modern but welcoming feel. It's home to temporary exhibitions of modern art. It's open Tuesday from 11 am to 8 pm, Wednesday to Sunday to 6 pm (DM7/4).

Places to Stay
Camping Allersee (☎ 633 95), right on the Allersee, is a somewhat rundown spot, but it's open year round and has great access to the water. It costs DM8 per caravan site (no tents), plus DM7 per person and there's a washer/dryer, but there's a 10 pm curfew.

The central **Jugendgästehaus** (☎ 133 37, fax 166 30, Lessingstrasse 60) has bare-bones dorm beds for DM23/28 for juniors/seniors.

Wolfsburg has few budget hotels, and even fewer we can recommend.

Hotel Am Hallenbad (☎ 266 60, fax 26 66 26, Kleiststrasse 35) is a bit long in the tooth but has clean singles/doubles for DM90/120 with shower and toilet. **Hotel Hoffmannhaus Fallersleben** (☎ 05362-30 02, fax 641 08, Westerstrasse 4), in Fallersleben, is a charming country inn sort of place with rooms from DM135/175, including breakfast. The **Parkhotel** (☎ 50 50, fax 50 52 50, Unter den Eichen 55) has clean rooms from DM120/195. The **Holiday Inn** (☎ 20 70, fax 20 79 81, Rathausstrasse 1) has dim and depressing rooms that start at DM155/185. However, the hotel's location, near the southern end of Porschestrasse, makes it a favourite with business travellers.

Places to Eat
Restaurants **Zum Tannenhof** (☎ 152 33, Kleiststrasse 49) is somewhat hidden and not well known, but it has good German specialities (main courses from DM9 to DM13) and has a terrific variety of German and imported beer. In summer it has a nice beer garden out the back. There's live music on some weekends.

M'Peyer (Porschestrasse 30) is a popular pub and restaurant with good grills. If you're up to a 500g T-bone it will cost DM38, but 180g rumps go for DM19, and its (non-grill) lunch specials are good value.

It's open for drinks till around midnight. The **Nordsee Restaurant** (Porschestrasse 64) serves up well priced fish dishes and rolls.

The **Hotel Hoffmannhaus Fallersleben** has a restaurant with some fairly average traditional mains from DM19 to DM32, and lunches from DM11 to DM15. The **Altes Brauhaus** (☎ 31 40), on Schlossplatz in Fallersleben, is a great place to eat and drink – long wooden tables, a beer hall atmosphere and boisterous crowds gathered round the copper brewing kettles. Typical is its hearty Bierhaus-Teller, a roast served with Nuremberg sausage, liver, potatoes and sauerkraut (DM18.50). Wash it down with half a litre of house beer for DM5.90.

Cafes & Wine Bars **Café Extreme** (☎ 322 44, Breslauerstrasse 198) is a student hangout with a big alternative scene; those who don't fit in elsewhere will be in their element here. It's gay and lesbian-friendly, with sort of an art gallery decor. **Frauen Café Rotezora** (☎ 220 88, Porschestrasse 90) is for women and girls only. It's a great source of information for women in the city.

Vini D'Italia (154 56, Schillerstrasse 25) is an interesting wine bar and shop that will give you a taste of Italy in Wolfsburg. It combines its wine promotions with one regional dish, which costs about DM10 to DM15. It also serves a cold entree for DM12, and a glass of wine costs from DM6.50. It's open till at least 10 pm, but closes on Sunday and at 4 pm on Saturday.

Self-Catering **Penny Markt** (Porschestrasse 74) is a cheap place to shop. A **fresh produce market** near the tourist office on Porschestrasse does a busy trade on Wednesday and Saturday mornings.

Entertainment
Wo und Was is a free monthly magazine with listings of bars, restaurants and what's happening in town. **Indigo** has more of the same. They're both available at bars, restaurants and clubs around the city. **Wolfsburg**, available from the tourist office, has information on events and concerts.

LOWER SAXONY

Pubs & Bars The Wolfburgers do much of their drinking in Kaufhof – not the department store, but a small strip of bars, pubs and a few eateries west of Porschestrasse. *Wunderbar* has cocktails and sometimes house music; *Alt Berlin* is open during the day and evenings and serves food.

The *Altes Brauhaus* in Fallersleben (see Places to Eat) is a great place to knock back a few. It brews and serves up Fallersleben Schlossbräu, an unfiltered Pilsner. There's live music on Friday and Saturday, though this gets a bit thigh-slappy sometimes.

Disco The *Esplanade* (☎ 129 40, Wieland-strasse 1) attracts a young crowd and gets down till very late.

Rock & Jazz The main car park of the *Volkswagen Werk* and *Allersee Park* are the sites of large outdoor concerts, especially by bands sponsored by VW – past performances included Pink Floyd, Genesis, Bon Jovi and the Rolling Stones. The *Congress Park* hosts smaller concerts.

Theatre & Classical Music The city's 777 seat *Stadttheater* hosts visiting performers from around the world: symphonies, theatrical performances and other events.

Getting There & Away

Wolfsburg's Hauptbahnhof sported an impressive hole out the front when we visited – a new Erlebniscenter was being built as one of the city's EXPO projects. There are frequent ICE train services from Wolfsburg to Braunschweig (DM19, 15 minutes), Hanover (DM33, 30 minutes) and Berlin-Zoo (DM74, one hour).

From Braunschweig, take the A2 east to the A39 north, which brings you right into town. Alternatively, take the B248 north to the A39.

Getting Around

Bus There's a comprehensive bus network in Wolfsburg. Tickets are sold in blocks of four for DM9.50, or 24-hour tickets are DM7. Single tickets cost DM2.80. The major bus transfer point is at the northern end of Porschestrasse. To get to the Schloss, Badeland, Eispalast and Camping Allersee, take bus No 1. For Fallersleben, it's bus No 3.

A free shuttle called City Mobil runs from the Hauptbahnhof down Porschestrasse with stops at the tourist office, Kaufhof, Südkopf Center (a shopping centre) and the Kunst Museum from Monday to Friday from 10 am to 7 pm, Saturday from 10 am to 4 pm.

Car & Motorcycle Once you leave the pedestrianised centre, distances become difficult to cover comfortably by foot. In every sense, Wolfsburg was built for cars. The car park behind the Planetarium and Stadttheater is free. An ADAC office (☎ 150 10) at Heinrich-Nordhoff-Strasse 125 has vehicle rental.

Taxi There are taxi ranks at the Hauptbahnhof and at the northern end of Porschestrasse. Taxis cost DM3.80 at flag fall, DM2.60 per kilometre. To order one, call City Taxi (☎ 23 02 36).

Bicycle Rent bicycles from Fritz Schael (☎ 140 64), Kleiststrasse 5, for DM10 per day or DM8 a day for more than three days.

GÖTTINGEN

☎ 0551   • pop 134,000

Göttingen, on the Leine River about 100km south of Hanover, is a historic university town with a pleasant atmosphere, a lively student scene and plenty of open space. Its compactness and the accessibility of the surrounding countryside make it a pleasant place to spend a few days between forays into Germany's larger cities. The university's 30,000 students set the tone of the place, making it a much more vibrant city than its size would suggest. This liveliness extends to a feral anarchist scene, which has attracted the attention of police. Nevertheless, the days are gone when plain-clothes police made up half the numbers in the more notorious student *Kneipen* (bars).

History
First mentioned in 953, Göttingen was the scene of some regional politicking until Heinrich der Löwe destroyed its castle in 1180. Soon afterwards, it developed into a small merchant centre, gaining town status in 1210. A network of walls and moats was constructed and improved upon up to the 18th century. From 1351 to 1572 Göttingen belonged to the Hanseatic League – the town owned half a ship – and enjoyed a period of relative prosperity.

The establishment of the Georg-August Universität in 1734 revived flagging fortunes. The Brothers Grimm, founders of modern German philology, once taught here, and Otto von Bismarck was one of its more famous students. More than 40 Nobel Prize laureates have either studied, taught or lived in Göttingen at some time or other, and plaques on buildings around town show who lived where and when.

Orientation
The circular city centre is surrounded by the ruins of an 18th century wall and is divided by the Leinekanal (Leine Canal), an arm of the Leine River. The centre has a large pedestrian mall, the hub of which is the Markt, a 10 minute walk east of the Hauptbahnhof.

Information
Tourist Offices The tourist information office (☎ 540 00, fax 400 29 98, email tourismus@goettingen.de) is in the Altes Rathaus at Markt 9. From April to October it's open weekdays from 9.30 am to 6 pm, weekends from 10 am to 4 pm. From November to March it has the same weekday hours but closes from 1 to 2 pm, on Saturday at 1 pm and isn't open Sunday. More convenient is the office (☎ 560 00, fax 531 29 28) in the white 'witches hat' tower outside the station. It's open year round weekdays from 9 am to 6 pm and Saturday from 10 am to 2 pm.

Reasonable hiking and cycling maps are sold at the tourist office for DM12.80 and DM5 respectively.

Money The main branch of the Sparkasse at Weender Strasse 13 changes money and travellers cheques, and has ATMs. There are several other banks in the centre.

Post & Communications The main post office is next to the Hauptbahnhof at Heinrich von Stephanstrasse 1-5, and there's a large branch at Friedrichstrasse 3 near Wilhelmsplatz.

Bookshops The Akademische Buchhandlung Calvör, in the mall at Weender Strasse 58, is excellent for ordering in English-language books quickly – many within 24 hours. Deuerlichsche Buchhandlung, across the street at No 33, also has good stocks. Peppmüller, Barfüsserstrasse 11, has a wide range of English-language books upstairs.

Laundry The central Waschcenter, Ritterplan 4, is open weekdays from 7 am to 10 pm. It costs around DM6 per load, but had a cheap deal at DM3 when we visited.

Medical Services & Emergency The main hospital is the Universitätsklinik (☎ 390) at Robert-Koch-Strasse 40. There's a police station (☎ 49 14 15) at Markt 3.

Around the Markt
The **Altes Rathaus**, at Markt 9, dates back to 1270. It once housed the merchants' guild and was enlarged between 1369 and 1463. The rich decorations of the Great Hall were added during 19th century restoration work. Frescoes depict the coats of arms of the Hanse cities, as well as local bigwigs, grafted onto historic scenes. In front of the Rathaus is the demure **Gänseliesel**, both the symbol of Göttingen and its 'most kissed woman'. Traditionally, those who have just passed their doctoral exams make a beeline to Gänseliesel and plant a kiss on her cheek. Nearby is the diminutive **statue** of Georg-Christoph Lichtenberg, aphorist and physicist, which was cast from old monuments to Lenin and Hoxha by an Albanian artist.

Half-Timbered Houses

The **Junkernschänke**, Barfüsserstrasse 5, is the prettiest of Göttingen's half-timbered buildings. Its colourful Renaissance facade dates from around 1548 when alterations were made, and the building now houses a good restaurant. Farther west at Barfüsserstrasse 12 is **Haus Börner**, built in 1536. Paulinerstrasse and Kurze Strasse are other historic streets worth a stroll for their fine buildings. **Schrödersches Haus**, Weender Strasse 62, was commissioned

by a clothmaker and now houses a men's fashion store.

Churches

Göttingen counts six Gothic churches. The 72m tower of **St Jacobikirche** (1361) on Weender Strasse rises elegantly above the pedestrian mall. One of the twin towers of **St Johanniskirche**, behind the Altes Rathaus, can be climbed Saturday from 2 to 4 pm (DM1). The tower was used by watchmen from the 15th century onwards

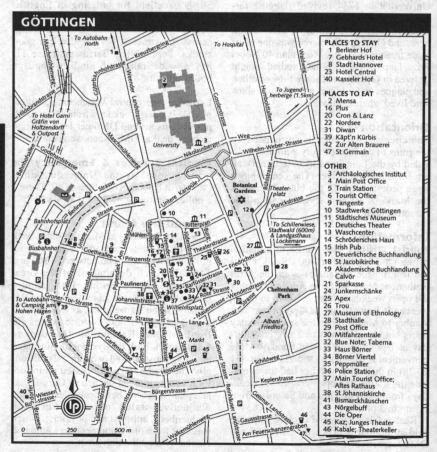

GÖTTINGEN

PLACES TO STAY
1 Berliner Hof
7 Gebhards Hotel
8 Stadt Hannover
23 Hotel Central
40 Kasseler Hof

PLACES TO EAT
2 Mensa
16 Plus
20 Cron & Lanz
22 Nordsee
31 Diwan
39 Käpt'n Kürbis
42 Zur Alten Brauerei
47 St Germain

OTHER
3 Archäologisches Institut
4 Main Post Office
5 Train Station
6 Tourist Office
9 Tangente
10 Stadtwerke Göttingen
11 Städtisches Museum
12 Deutsches Theater
13 Waschcenter
14 Schrödersches Haus
15 Irish Pub
17 Deuerlichsche Buchhandlung
18 St Jacobikirche
19 Akademische Buchhandlung Calvör
21 Sparkasse
24 Junkernschänke
25 Apex
26 Trou
27 Museum of Ethnology
28 Stadthalle
29 Post Office
30 Mitfahrzentrale
32 Blue Note; Taberna
33 Haus Börner
34 Börner Viertel
35 Peppmüller
36 Police Station
37 Main Tourist Office; Altes Rathaus
38 St Johanniskirche
41 Bismarckhäuschen
43 Nörgelbuff
44 Die Oper
45 Kaz; Junges Theater
46 Kabale; Theaterkeller

LOWER SAXONY

To Autobahn north
To Hospital
Kreuzbergring
Maschmühlenweg
Güterbahnhofstrasse
Weender Landstrasse
Gosslerstrasse
Humboldtallee
Waldweg
To Jugendherberge (1.5km)
Hildebrandstrasse
To Hotel Garni Gräfin von Holtzendorff & Outpost
Bahnhofsallee
Godehardstrasse
Maschmühlenweg
University
Nikolausberger
Weg
Wilhelm-Weber-Strasse
Bühlstrasse
Strasse
Berliner
Strasse
Botanical Gardens
Theaterplatz
Planckstrasse
Bahnhofsplatz
Untere Karspüle
Untere Masch Strasse
Mühlenstr
Am Leinekanal
Weender Strasse
Ritterplan
Burgstr
To Schillerwiese, Stadtwald (600m) & Landgasthaus Lockemann
Busbahnhof
Goethealle
Prinzenstr
Judenstrasse
Theaterstrasse
Friedrichstrasse
Cotmanstrasse
Paulinerstr
Barfüsserstrasse
Rote Strasse
Mauerstrasse
Wendenstrasse
Cheltenham Park
To Autobahn & Camping am Hohen Hagen
Groner-Tor-Strasse
Neustadt
Papendiek
Johannisstrasse
Wilhelmsplatz
Groner Strasse
Kurze Strasse
Geismar Strasse
Reinhäuser Landstrasse
Albani-Friedhof
Lange
Markt
Schildweg
Leinekanal
Angerstrasse
Gartenstrasse
Düstere Strasse
Nikolaistrasse
Hospitalstrasse
Keplerstrasse
Marienstrasse
Rosdorfer Weg
Wiesenstrasse
Bürgerstrasse
Lilienthalstrasse
Bunsenstrasse
Lotzestrasse
Walkemühlenweg
Geismar Landstrasse
Gaussstrasse
Am Feuerschanzengraben

0   250   500 m

– the last one died in 1921 – and it's now inhabited by students who admit visitors on open days.

Museums

The **Städtisches Museum**, Ritterplan 7-8, has displays on local history, a good collection of porcelain and interesting models of the city ramparts. It's open Tuesday to Friday from 10 am to 5 pm, weekends from 11 am (DM3/1).

In the **Archäologisches Institut** (☎ 39 75 02), Nikolausberger Weg 15, you can view reproductions of over 1500 classical sculptures. Entry is free, but visits must be arranged in advance (Monday to Friday from 9 am to 4 pm). When the university is in session, there are guided German-language tours on a particular theme on Sunday at 11.15 am.

The **Museum für Völkerkunde** (Museum of Ethnology; ☎ 39 78 92), Theaterplatz 15, has a collection of ethnographic art, including objects brought back from the Pacific by Captain Cook. It's open on Sunday only from 10 am to 1 pm, or by prior arrangement (DM3/1).

Parks & Gardens

Ideal for summer picnics, the small **Botanical Gardens** were Germany's first, and there's a pond and a section devoted to alpine plants. The gardens are open year round, weekdays from 8 am to 6 pm and weekends to 3 pm. The tropical greenhouses – highly recommended in winter – are open daily from 9 am to noon and 1.30 to 2.45 pm. The best entry point is from Untere Karspüle.

A 20 minute walk east of the Markt is the **Schillerwiese**, a large park that backs onto forest and has mini-golf. To reach it, follow Herzberger Landstrasse east, then turn right into Merkelstrasse.

Walks

City walking tours, in German, leave from the main tourist office from April to October daily at 2.30 pm (DM7); or pick up the excellent brochure *A Walk through the City* (DM2) and do it yourself.

Highly recommended is a walk along the 18th century city wall. It takes less than an hour, and the best starting point is the entrance near Cheltenham Park. This takes you past **Bismarckhäuschen** (Bismarck's Cottage) where, tradition holds, the town fathers banished 18-year-old Otto for rowdy behaviour in 1833. While this incident might be a case of rewriting history, the future Iron Chancellor was, however, later found guilty of the more serious offence of witnessing an illegal duel. The cottage is open Tuesday from 10 am to 1 pm, and Thursday and Saturday from 3 to 5 pm (free). Nearby are two old **water mills**, one of which operated until 1945. The walk ends near the **Deutsches Theater**.

Forest The Stadtwald is a 20 minute walk east from Wilhelmsplatz. One place to enter is from Borheckstrasse (near where Herzberger Landstrasse forms a hairpin bend). A bitumen track open to hikers and cyclists winds towards Hainholzhof-Kehr, a hotel and restaurant another 45 minutes away. Another option is to take bus A to Hainholzhof-Kehr from Jüdenstrasse and walk north-west back through the forest into town. From the terminus a path leads to **Bismarckturm**. This stone tower has spectacular views over the Leine Valley and is open April to late October on weekends and public holidays from 11 am to 6 pm (DM2/0.50).

Places to Stay

Camping *Camping am Hohen Hagen* (☎ 05502-21 47) is about 10km west of town in Dransfeld. It can be reached by bus No 120 from the Hauptbahnhof. Open year round, it charges DM10.50 per tent site (including car parking) and DM8.50/4.20 per adult/child. The per person charges are 20% less in winter.

Hostels The *Jugendherberge* (☎ 576 22, fax 438 87, Habichtweg 2) has beds in single, double and dormitory rooms for DM23/28 for juniors/seniors. It also has a laundry. To reach the hostel, cross Berliner

LOWER SAXONY

Strasse from the Hauptbahnhof, go south to Groner-Tor-Strasse and take bus No 6 or 9 from the stop across Groner-Tor-Strasse.

Hotels All prices quoted here, except for apartments, include breakfast. The friendly *Hotel Garni Gräfin von Holtzendorff* (*☎ 639 87, fax 63 29 85, Ernst-Ruhstrat-Strasse 4*) is a little outside the centre in the industrial area, but easy to reach by bus No 13 from the Hauptbahnhof or town centre (stop: Florenz-Sartorius-Strasse). Basic singles/doubles start at DM49/85, rising to DM75/120 with shower and WC.

Berliner Hof (*☎ 38 33 20, fax 383 32 32, Weender Landstrasse 43*) has clean rooms with shower from DM75/100 and basic singles for DM60. *Kasseler Hof* (*☎ 720 81, Rosdorfer Weg 26*) has well priced basic rooms from DM53/110, or DM95/130 with shower and WC. Apartments with cooking facilities are available for a minimum of four days at DM65/95. It's in a quiet area, some 10 minutes on foot south of the Hauptbahnhof. Check-in, after 2 pm on Sunday, should be arranged in advance.

The *Hotel Central* (*☎ 571 57, fax 571 05, Jüdenstrasse 12*) is more expensive but still good value, with basic singles from DM70, singles/doubles with a shower for DM90/130, rooms with all facilities for DM90/150, or double suites for DM250 with a bath and WC. Parking costs DM7 per night.

The *Landgasthaus Lockemann* (*☎ 20 90 20, Im Beeke 1*), 3km east of Göttingen in Herberhausen, has basic single/double rooms from DM45/70, doubles with shower and WC from DM70 as single occupancy and DM100 for two people. Bus No 10 from Jüdenstrasse stops nearby. There's an excellent restaurant here (see Places to Eat).

The *Stadt Hannover* (*☎ 459 57, fax 454 70, Goetheallee 21*) offers rooms from DM110/165. *Gebhards Hotel* (*☎ 496 80, fax 496 81 10, Goetheallee 22-23*) has quite good rooms from DM163/210 with shower and WC.

Places to Eat

The *Nordsee* chain of fish restaurants and snack bars offers good value at lunchtime, with herring rolls for around DM4.50, meals about DM12. You'll find one at Weender Strasse 50. *Cron & Lanz*, almost directly opposite at No 25, is a quality cafe with delicious confectionery and cakes. The *Mensa* university cafeteria offers the best value in town for students. There is one next to the Blue Note disco at Wilhelmsplatz 3, and a second on campus at Platz der Göttinger Sieben. In the early evening, the Wilhelmsplatz Mensa has a *Taberna*, which serves the daytime dish and a few extra basic dishes to nonstudents at rock-bottom prices.

Diwan (*Rote Strasse 11*) serves Turkish dishes (some vegetarian) for under DM20. The *Zur Alten Brauerei* is a very Bavarian option in a similar price range. You'll find it in a courtyard behind the half-timbered house at Düstere Strasse 20 (under the gallery walkover and to the right). The restaurant is at No 20a.

Käpt'n Kürbis (*Groner-Tor-Strasse 16*) is a lunchtime health-food restaurant serving one main dish on weekdays and Saturday for around DM12.

In the Börner Viertel, a yard behind Haus Börner at Barfüsserstrasse 12, you'll find *cocina mediterranea* (*☎ 531 30 01*), a quality southern European restaurant with main dishes in the DM25 to DM35 price range, as well as *Dr Wu* and *Champs*, two bars. The French *St Germain* (*☎ 464 64, Geismar Landstrasse 21a*) is one place where you're advised to book, especially on Friday and weekends. Open evenings only, it has fixed-price menus from DM23 to DM45. *Junkernschänke* (*☎ 573 20, Barfüsserstrasse 5*), in Göttingen's finest half-timbered house, is a very formal restaurant in the upper price category. The restaurant at the *Landgasthaus Lockemann* (see Places to Stay) specialises in game. Expect to pay around DM25 to DM35 for its hearty main courses.

A convenient *Plus* supermarket is on the corner of Prinzenstrasse and Stumpfebiel.

Entertainment

Pubs & Bars *Apex (☎ 468 86, Burgstrasse 46)* is open at 5.30 pm and offers good food, drink and company in a warm atmosphere. It is also an art gallery and has a performance area upstairs (mainly comedy, readings and music). *Trou*, 30m along Burgstrasse towards Wilhelmsplatz, is a small Gothic cellar where students meet to drink. *Kaz (☎ 471 45, Hospitalstrasse 6)* shares a 19th century building with the Junges Theater. On summer evenings the market square here, which is also a fruit and vegetable market (year round on Tuesday, Thursday and Saturday from 7 am to 1 pm), turns into a lively *beer garden*.

Kabale (Geismar Landstrasse 19) is another cosy place. Downstairs is the *Theaterkeller*, a nocturnal haunt for anarchists.

Discos & Clubs Göttingen has no shortage of clubs. Live-music venues don't get going until about 10 pm, discos much later. The *Blue Note (Wilhelmsplatz 3)* regularly has music and live bands. *Outpost (☎ 50 66 20, Königsallee 243)* is larger and less convenient, but it usually has excellent bands or dance music. Take bus No 1 or 7 to the Elliehäuser Weg stop. The *Irish Pub (☎ 456 64, Mühlenstrasse 4)* is an old favourite with cover bands and free admission. The *Nörgelbuff (☎ 438 85, Groner Strasse 23)* is a small live venue with an emphasis on blues.

Tangente (☎ 463 76, Goetheallee 8a) is the top disco in town for a slightly older student crowd. *Die Oper (☎ 48 79 98, Nikolaistrasse 1b)* is young, restless and hip. There are a couple of lively bars downstairs.

Theatre & Classical Music Göttingen's premier mainstream theatre is the *Deutsches Theater (☎ 496 90, Theaterplatz 11)*. The *Junges Theater (☎ 495 01 50, Hospitalstrasse 6)* is more innovative and draws a young crowd. Classical-music concerts are held regularly in the *Stadthalle* at Albaniplatz and in the *Aula*, a beautifully appointed hall upstairs on Wilhelmsplatz. The Händel Festival, held over several days in late May and early June, is a must for those keen on music. Inquire about tickets at the tourist office.

Getting There & Away

Train Frequent EC, ICE and IR train services link Göttingen with many towns. There are frequent direct ICE services to Kassel (DM30, 20 minutes), Frankfurt (DM94, 1¾ hours), Munich (DM180, four hours), Hanover (DM51, 30 minutes), Hamburg (DM103, 1¾ hours) and Berlin (DM122, 2¾ hours). Indirect regional services run to Weimar via Erfurt (DM46, 2¾ hours). Regional trains leave hourly for Goslar (DM23, one hour).

Bus Buses leave from the terminus alongside the Hauptbahnhof to surrounding towns and the Harz Mountains, but train services are more convenient.

Car & Motorcycle Göttingen is on the A7 running north-south. The closest entrance, often used by hitchhikers, is 3km south-west along Kasseler Landstrasse, an extension of Groner Landstrasse. The Fairy-Tale Road (B27) runs south-west to the Weser River and north-east to the Harz Mountains.

Ride Services The Mitfahrzentrale (☎ 194 44) is at Burgstrasse 7 (on Wilhelmsplatz). Sample prices include Berlin DM32, Hamburg DM26, and Frankfurt DM23.

Getting Around

Single bus tickets cost DM2.70, batches of four tickets go for DM8.40 (both valid for 60 minutes), and 24-hour tickets are DM6.50. Stadtwerke Göttingen (☎ 301 39), the city works office that runs the buses, is at Weender Strasse 80.

There's a taxi rank alongside the Altes Rathaus at Markt 9. To book a taxi by phone, ring ☎ 340 34. PUK Minicar (☎ 48 48 48) is good value, especially for women travelling either alone or with children after 8 pm (9 pm in summer): it gives a night discount of about DM3.80.

LOWER SAXONY

Göttingen has an excellent network of bike lanes throughout the city. At the Hauptbahnhof, Fahrrad Parkhaus am Bahnhof (☎ 599 94, open daily) rents out bikes for DM14 per 24 hours.

West of Hanover

OSNABRÜCK
☎ 0541 • pop 160,000

Osnabrück is a bustling modern university town that made its major mark on history in the 17th century. Together with Münster, about 60km to the south, it co-hosted the negotiations that brought about the Peace of Westphalia ending the devastating Thirty Years' War (1618-48).

Osnabrück has origins as a bishopric established by Charlemagne after he defeated the Saxon duke, Widukind, in 783. The battle, the last between Franks and Saxons, took place nearby. It wasn't just a military victory, but also a triumph of Christianity over paganism: two years after this encounter Widukind had himself baptised.

The Middle Ages brought relative wealth to Osnabrück as the town became an early and important member of the Hanseatic League. Most of the half-timbered and stone merchants' homes in the Altstadt date back to this era and are the few that survived the blazes that swept through Osnabrück during WWII. War and its devastation also played a major role in the works of native son, Erich Maria Remarque (1898-1970), who gained fame with his novel *All Quiet on the Western Front*.

Orientation
Osnabrück's egg-shaped city centre grew up within the boundaries of the old fortifications and is divided into the northern Altstadt and the southern Neustadt, with the Neumarkt at its centre. The Hauptbahnhof – an impressive two level construction from the last century – is on the eastern edge of the city centre. It's about a 20 minute walk from here to the Altstadt, where most sights are clustered. The little

Hase River traverses the centre in a north-south direction.

The DB Service desk at the station stocks free maps of the town centre.

Information
The tourist office (☎ 323 22 02, fax 323 27 09), Krahnstrasse 58 near the Markt, is open weekdays from 9 am to 6 pm and Saturday from 9.30 am to 1 pm.

There's an ATM in the Hauptbahnhof, and you can exchange money at the Sparkasse, Krahnstrasse 9-10, near the tourist office, or at the Volksbank, Nicolaiort 5A.

Look for the post office on your left as you exit the Hauptbahnhof.

Jonscher (☎ 33 16 80), Domhof 6, has a fair selection of novels in English and a few Lonely Planet titles.

You'll find information under the tourist office's homepage www.osnabrueck.de.

The most convenient laundry is the S-B Waschsalon, Hasestrasse 51A-52, just north of the Dom.

One city hospital is Kliniken Finkenhügel (☎ 40 50), Am Finkenhügel 1. Police headquarters (☎ 32 71) are at Kollegienwall 7.

Markt & Around
The two buildings dominating the small Markt are the Rathaus on its western side and the Marienkirche on its northern side. The facade of the **Rathaus** is festooned with neo-Gothic sandstone sculptures of Holy Roman emperors; the one above the portal is Charlemagne. It was from the town hall's double-sided open stairs that the Peace of Westphalia was proclaimed on 25 October 1648.

The peace negotiations took place in the **Friedenssaal** (peace hall), a stark rectangular room dominated by a flamboyant wrought-iron chandelier. Long wooden benches line the walls, which are decorated with portraits of the peace negotiators. The room is on the left as you enter. On the right is the small **Schatzkammer** (treasure chamber) with medieval manuscripts granting various town rights, and several goblets including the impressive late-13th century *Kaiserpokal*. The figurine inside the goblet was originally the knob of the goblet lid, but it migrated when replaced by a bigger figure of Charlemagne.

The four richly ornamented cross gables of the **Marienkirche** loom above the square. The church was first mentioned in 1177, but the current design dates back to the early 14th century. It was completely burned down in WWII and has been painstakingly rebuilt. Of note inside are a baptismal font from the workshop of Johann Brabender whose reliefs show scenes from the life of Christ, and a triumphal cross from 1320.

Opposite the Marienkirche, a small exhibit on **Erich Maria Remarque** chronicles the writer's life and work with photos, documents and a copy of his death mask. It's closed Monday, on each but the first Sunday of the month and at lunchtime (free).

The streets south of the Markt have various historic houses that provide glimpses of what the Altstadt must have looked like before WWII. At Bierstrasse 24 is the baroque **Walhalla** (today a hotel), with a portal flanked by cheeky cherubs. At Krahnstrasse 4 you'll find a beautiful **half-timbered house** (1533) with Café Läer taking up the ground floor (see Places to Eat). Best of the bunch, though, is the Renaissance **Haus Willmann** (1586), at No 7, with its carved relief of Adam and Eve.

The western boundary of the Altstadt is the **Heger Tor**, a former town gate turned triumphal arch. Nearby at Heger-Tor-Wall 28 is the **Cultural History Museum** (Kulturgeschichtliche Museum; ☎ 323 22 37). A recent addition to this four part museum complex is the **Felix-Nussbaum-Haus**, which houses the largest single collection of works by the Osnabrück-born painter Felix Nussbaum (1904-44), who was Jewish and died in Auschwitz. The building itself, a provocative angular structure of steel and concrete, was designed by the Polish-American architect Daniel Libeskind. All sections are open Tuesday to Friday from 9 am to 5 pm, Sunday from 10 am (DM8/4).

A short walk north along Natruper-Tor-Wall gets you to the **Bocksturm**, also formerly part of the fortification, which contains a hair-raising collection of torture implements – Osnabrück was a centre of witch persecution – and a unique wooden crate used to imprison an unpopular count in the 15th century.

Dom St Peter
The bulky cathedral on Domplatz in the eastern Altstadt is distinctive for its two towers; the slender Romanesque tower dwarfed by the much bigger Gothic one. This was a sturdy addition to house the new and bigger church bells. In the chapel on your left as you enter is the 13th century bronze **baptismal font** in the shape of a pail perched on feet so that a little fire could be built underneath to heat the water.

In the central nave is the **triumphal cross** (1230), at 6.8 x 4.2m the largest in Lower Saxony. On the wall in the north transept is a little stone **sculpture** of Mary holding the Infant Jesus carved by the Master of Osnabrück in 1520. She's depicted smiling angelically while stomping on a serpent. Also, take a look at the **wrought-iron gates**, with their unusual vanishing point perspective at the entrance to the square ambulatory, especially the one in the south transept. More treasures can be admired in the **Diözesan Museum** reached via the pretty cloister. It's open Tuesday to Friday from 10 am to 1 pm and 3 to 5 pm, weekends from 11 am to 2 pm (DM3/1.50).

Places to Stay
Camping *Campingplatz Niedersachsenhof* (☎ 772 26, Nordstrasse 109) is a modern, clean facility, about 5km north-east of the city centre (take bus No 71 to the Nordstrasse stop, then walk about 400m). It costs DM11 per site and DM6 per person.

Hostels The nice 147 bed *Jugendgästehaus* (☎ 542 84, fax 567 83, Iburger Strasse 183a) is about 2km south of the city centre alongside forest. B&B costs DM28/33 for juniors/seniors. From the Hauptbahnhof, take bus No 62 or Nos 463 to 468 (to stop Kinderhospital).

LOWER SAXONY

Hotels & Pensions The tourist office has a free room-reservation service. Prices quoted here are for rooms with shower and WC.

The *Intour Hotel* (☎ 466 43, Maschstrasse 10) charges DM75/95 for homely singles/doubles. The *Dom Hotel* (☎ 35 83 50, fax 358 35 35, Kleine Domsfreiheit 5) is central and has rooms from DM80/130. The *Hotel Westermann* (☎ 98 11 40, fax 981 14 11, Koksche Strasse 1), just south of the Altstadtring, charges DM85/140. It can be rather noisy and a reservation is advisable. The *Schlosspension* (☎ 33 83 30, fax 338 33 37, Schlossstrasse 15), in a lovely, tiny but cosy villa, costs from DM135/185. *Hotel Walhalla* (☎ 349 10, fax 349 11 44, Bierstrasse 24), near the tourist office, is – partly, at least – in a historic building. Clean and quite good rooms here cost DM150/195.

Places to Eat
Osnabrück has a wonderful range of pubs (most open in the evening only) that also serve inexpensive, simple food. The student-run *Unikeller* (☎ 216 98, Neuer Graben 29), in the west-wing cellars of the Schloss (now part of the university), has 27 different types of pizza from DM5 to DM8.50, as well as cheap salads.

Unicum (☎ 224 92), at No 40, is similar but slightly more alternative and sometimes has parties with music. Both stay open till late.

The Heger Tor quarter, just east of Heger Tor in the Altstadt, is a good area to bag a decent meal or just to tipple. *Grüne Gans* (Grosse Gildewart 15) is low-budget and traditional. *Weinkrüger* (☎ 233 53, Marienstrasse 18), a cosy upmarket restaurant and wine bar, serves German cuisine in the DM25 to DM35 price range – and some delicious wines.

If you can't hold out till evening, don't fret! *Hausbrauerei Rampendahl* (☎ 245 35, Hasestrasse 35) has a restaurant serving one set dish from noon till 6 pm for DM10. Otherwise, prices for traditional food, including game, range from DM15 to DM37;

there's jazz from 11 am on the last Sunday of the month and it produces two very tasty beers (an unfiltered top-fermented *helles* and the more potent Rampendahl Spezial), as well as its own brandy. *Kartoffelhaus* (☎ 211 72, Bierstrasse 38) offers well priced potato dishes, grills and baked casseroles from 11 am. The *Mensa* (university cafeteria) in the main university building is open to nonstudents.

Café Läer (Krahnstrasse 4), serves traditional *Kaffee und Kuchen* (coffee and cake) inside an ornate, historic building.

Entertainment
Irish Pub Remise (Heger-Tor-Wall 23) has occasional live music. *Stiefel*, on Heger Strasse, is good for a drink. For pubs that also serve food, see Places to Eat.

Hyde Park (☎ 12 81 23, Fürstenauer Weg 123) is a disco with indie, metal and punk canned music and occasional live concerts. It's open weekends after 8 pm and costs only DM1 admission (take bus No 81/82 to Sportpark).

Osnabrück's *municipal theatre* (☎ 323 33 14/40, Domhof 10/11) offers classical concerts, ballet and drama. The *Lagerhalle* (☎ 33 87 40, Rolandsmauer 26) is a large alternative cultural centre with a grab-bag of concerts, disco nights, movies, poetry readings and so on.

Getting There & Away
There are hourly IC/EC trains to Hamburg (DM73, 1¾ hours), Cologne (DM65, 2¼ hours) and Dortmund (DM36, 55 minutes). Regional/IR trains to Hanover also leave hourly (DM36, 1¾ hours).

Osnabrück is well connected by road via the A1 (Bremen to Dortmund) and the B51, B65 and B68.

There are two Mitfahrzentralen: one at Kleine Hamkenstrasse 4 (☎ 266 00 or ☎ 194 40) and another at Martinistrasse 9 (☎ 429 47 or ☎ 473 33).

Getting Around
The Stadtwerke Osnabrück (☎ 34 47 28) operates the city bus network. The best deal

is the 9-Uhr Tageskarte (one day ticket) for DM5. Single tickets cost DM2.70, or DM9.50 for batches of four tickets.

If you need a taxi, call ☎ 277 81, ☎ 320 11 or ☎ 830 83.

To rent a bicycle, try Pedals Fahrradstation (☎ 25 91 31) at the Hauptbahnhof, which charges from DM10 a day.

OLDENBURG

☎ 0441 • pop 154,000

Oldenburg, about 50km west of Bremen and 100km north of Osnabrück, is the economic and cultural centre of the Weser-Ems region. The town has a reputation for its high quality of life. Its university was founded in 1970 and has 12,000 students.

Oldenburg began life as Aldenburg in 1108. Around that time, it became the residence of the counts of Oldenburg, a family whose 'crowning' glory came in 1448 when Count Christian of Oldenburg became the king of Denmark. Though the Thirty Years' War bypassed the town, the 17th century nevertheless brought destruction in the form of a huge fire (1676) that spared only a few of the medieval buildings. After a century under Danish rule, Oldenburg wound up in Russian hands for a grand total of four days in 1773. In the same year it was then elevated to a duchy. The Schlosspark, the promenade and numerous neoclassical buildings date from that time.

Oldenburg escaped WWII almost unscathed, but swelled to a big city almost overnight when it had to absorb more than 40,000 German refugees from the east (Poland, the Sudetenland) after 1945. It's a pleasant town with a few sights worth exploring on a day trip from the Friesland coast or en route to Bremen or beyond.

Orientation

Oldenburg's centre is entirely pedestrianised and bounded by Heiligengeistwall to the north, Theaterwall to the west and Schlosswall to the south. The Hauptbahnhof is about a 10 minute walk north-east of the city centre.

Information

The tourist office (☎ 157 44, fax 248 92 02), Wallstrasse 14, is open weekdays from 9 am to 5 pm and Saturday from 10 am to 1 pm.

The Commerzbank, Heiligengeiststrasse 29, is open weekdays to 6 pm (Friday till 3 pm) and exchanges cash and travellers cheques. It also has an ATM that accepts all major credit cards.

The main post office, just west of the Hauptbahnhof at Bahnhofsplatz 10, has a special counter open weekdays to 7.30 pm and Saturday to 1 pm. Another is at Lange Strasse 51-52.

For a decent bookshop with volumes in English, go to Bültmann & Gerriets, Lange Strasse 57.

There's a self-service laundrette at Bloherfelder Strasse 200.

The Städtische Kliniken (☎ 40 30) is at Dr-Eden-Strasse 10. The number for medical emergencies after hours is ☎ 750 53. Police headquarters (☎ 79 01) are at Raiffeisenstrasse 25.

Around the Markt

Most of Oldenburg's main sights are a few steps from each other in the southern Altstadt. The **Lambertikirche** (open weekdays from 11 am to 12.30 pm and 2 to 5 pm, and Saturday from 11 am to 12.30 pm), with its five sky-piercing spires, dominates the Markt. It has a curious architectural history. When the original 13th century Gothic hall church partly collapsed in 1791, Duke Peter Friedrich Ludwig used the stones to build a new church in the neoclassical style. Based on the Pantheon in Rome, the interior of this square building features a large galleried rotunda with ionic columns that support a giant cupola. By the late 19th century, however, tastes had changed again and the entire edifice was encased in a neo-Gothic, red-brick shell with landmark towers.

Also on the Markt is the **Alte Rathaus** (open Monday to Thursday to 4 pm and to 1 pm on Friday), an unusual flat-iron building trimmed with little turrets. It dates only from the last century and is a good example of the style of historicism in vogue at the time. Inside, the assembly hall and the staircase warrant a quick look. Opposite the main portal of the town hall is the **Haus Degode** (1502), one of the few medieval buildings to survive the 1676 fire.

Schlossplatz

The **Schloss**, the former residence of the counts and dukes of Oldenburg, makes a rather unexpected appearance at the southern end of the Altstadt shopping district. It's a large yellow structure built in 1607 in transitional style from the Renaissance to the baroque. Its harmonious appearance conceals the many additions and alterations made in subsequent centuries. In the 18th century it was enlarged by a residential wing; a kitchen wing, library and carriage house followed. About 100 years ago, the neo-Renaissance wing was added.

Today, the Schloss contains the **Landesmuseum Oldenburg** (Oldenburg State Museum). The 1st floor features the representational rooms of the dukes of Oldenburg, preserved in their original neoclassical style. The Marble Room and the *Idyllenzimmer* with 44 paintings by court artist Heinrich Wilhelm Tischbein, a friend of Goethe, deserve special attention. Also noteworthy is the gallery of old masters focusing on Italian and Dutch art, including Rembrandt's *Angel in the House of Tobias*.

The 2nd floor provides insight into the lifestyle of the aristocracy between the 16th and 19th centuries, while the 3rd floor sheds light on the living conditions and customs of the working classes.

The museum's collection of 20th century art has been farmed out to the **Augusteum** on Elisabethstrasse 1. Showcased here are works by Heckel, Kirchner, Macke, the surrealist Franz Radziwill and others.

Both museums are open Tuesday to Friday from 9 am to 5 pm and Saturday from 10 am (DM4/2, admission to the Landesmuseum includes entrance to the Augusteum).

Opposite the Schloss, the four simple columns of the **Neue Wache** (1839), also in the neoclassical style, come into view. A

guardhouse until 1918, it is now part of the Sparkasse of Oldenburg, the oldest savings bank (1786) in the world. Unfortunately, the Bauhaus-style behemoth next to it, which houses most of the bank's administrative office, is not quite as classy a building.

Behind the Schloss is the sprawling English-style **Schlosspark**. Its pond, rose garden and masses of rhododendron bushes invite a leisurely stroll or a picnic.

Places to Stay

Camping-Park Flötenteich (☎ 328 28) is about 3km north of the city centre at Am Flötenteich. It's open from April to September. A tent site with car parking costs DM10.50, plus DM7.20 per person (take bus No 4 to Mühlenhofsweg).

The *Jugendherberge* (☎ 871 35, *Alexanderstrasse 65)*, about 20 minutes by foot north of the Hauptbahnhof, costs DM22.70/26.70 for juniors/seniors (take bus No 2 or 3 to Von-Finckh-Strasse).

The tourist office can help you find a room (DM4 per reservation), but budget options are basically nonexistent. *Private rooms* cost from DM45/75, and at that price they're a long way from the centre.

The *Hotel Sprenz* (☎ 870 33, fax 885 97 98, *Heiligengeiststrasse 15)* has singles/ doubles from DM50/100, or DM85/125 with a shower and WC. The *Hotel zum Lindenhof* (☎ 95 19 10, fax 951 91 44, *Bloherfelder Strasse 210)* is about 4km west of town (take bus No 9 to Schramperweg). Rooms with facilities cost DM80/120; three-person apartments are DM170.

The *Hotel Alexander* (☎ 980 20, fax 820 00, *Alexanderstrasse 107)* offers small rooms from DM100/140 with full facilities, and larger ones for DM140/190 (bus No 2 or 3). The *CCH City Club Hotel* (☎ 80 80, fax 80 81 00, *Europaplatz 4-6)*, next to the Weser-Ems congress hall, charges DM170/220 for its business-class rooms, and has a pool and whirlpool.

Places to Eat

One of the main eating drags at night is Wallstrasse, near the Lappan Tower, an

Oldenburg landmark. This car-free lane offers a strange but interesting hybrid of Parisian-style brasseries and American-style bars. In fine weather you can sit in wicker chairs under cheerful awnings. Otherwise, the decor in most places blends wood and brass into a fashionable ambience. Most serve a menu of tasty, filling snacks, such as baguettes, pizza, nachos and the like. *Alex Grand Café (Wallstrasse 1)*, one of the most popular haunts, serves a killer-bee double-meat hamburger for DM18. Most places are licensed to stay open until 5 am.

Chianti Classico (Achternstrasse 40), in a crooked half-timbered house tucked away in an alley, serves superb Italian food in a wonderfully romantic atmosphere. Pasta or pizza is under DM15, rising to steaks for up to DM30. *Die Stube*, upstairs at No 63, offers well priced vegetarian food during the day. *Kochlöffel* at No 8 on the same street has large portions of sit-down fast food.

Plus (Mottenstrasse 11) is one convenient supermarket. *Produce markets* are held near the Rathaus on Tuesday, Thursday and Saturday from 7 am to 2.30 pm.

Entertainment
Look for the free publications *Domino Kultur-Journal* and *Mox* in pubs or at the tourist office for up-to-date event information.

The *Rocktheater (Bloherfelder Strasse 2-4)* is a club that serves up nonmainstream rock and pop. *Jazzclub Alluvium (☎ 719 70, Zeughausstrasse 73)* is a popular jazz venue.

The *Oldenburgische Staatstheater (☎ 222 51 11, Theaterwall 28)* is the main venue for classical music and the performing arts. The alternative *Unikum (☎ 79 80, Ammerländer Heerstrasse 114)*, within the university building, has Kabarett, theatre and more. *Kulturetage (☎ 92 48 00, Bahnhofstrasse 11)* puts on theatre performances as well as rock and blues acts, and sometimes has dance parties.

Shopping
Oldenburg's pedestrian-only shopping area is one of the largest and earliest (1967) in Germany and covers practically the entire Altstadt. It stretches along Heiligengeiststrasse, Achternstrasse and Lange Strasse and has department stores, boutiques, chain stores and glass arcades. There's also a flea market every second Saturday of the month held in the Weser-Ems-Halle from December to March and on Schlossplatz from April to November.

Getting There & Away
Oldenburg is at the junction of rail lines to the north and to Bremen. There are trains at least once an hour to Bremen (DM16, 30 minutes) and Osnabrück (DM31, 1¾ hours), with further connections in all directions.

Oldenburg is at the crossroads of the A29 to/from Wilhelmshaven and the A28 (Bremen-Dutch border).

The Mitfahrzentrale (☎ 710 41) organises rides by telephone only.

Getting Around
Single bus tickets (valid for one hour) for the entire city area cost DM2.80; short trips are only DM1.90. Day passes are DM8.50. Buy your tickets from the driver. Bus Nos 7, 12 and 16 connect the Hauptbahnhof with Lappen, the central departure point for all buses.

If you need a taxi, call ☎ 22 55.

If you'd like to join the pedalling crowds, you can rent a bike at Fahrradstation (☎ 163 45), in a pavilion on Neue Strasse, opposite the tourist office (DM15/35 a day/three days).

EMDEN & AROUND
☎ 04921 • pop 50,000
The little town of Emden is in the northwesternmost corner of Lower Saxony – and of Germany – about 80km west of Oldenburg, where the Ems River meets the North Sea. With a past spanning some 12 centuries, Emden is an old town, but with a modern flair. The driving force behind the economy is the huge Volkswagen factory, employing 9000 people. After being essentially flattened in WWII, Emden was rebuilt successfully and aesthetically. Its largely pedestrianised city centre features red-brick walkways that match the architecture. The

euro currency converter DM1 = €0.51

harbour and little canals add some picturesque touches.

What makes a visit to Emden truly worthwhile, though, are its museums. Art aficionados especially will be rewarded by the Kunsthalle, whose collection of 20th century art can compete with similar houses in much larger cities.

Orientation

Emden's train and bus stations are about a 10 minute walk west of the city centre. As you exit, go east past the water tower to Neutorstrasse, passing the Kunsthalle, then head south to the small medieval harbour called Ratsdelft.

Information

The friendly, helpful tourist office (☎ 974 00, fax 974 09, email VerkehrsvereinEmden@ t-online.de) is in a pavilion next to the car park at the harbour. From May to September it's open weekdays from 9 am to 6 pm, Saturday from 10 am to 1 pm, and Sunday from 11 am to 1 pm. From October to April, the hours are weekdays from 9 am to 1 pm and 3 to 5.30 pm, Saturday from 10 am to 1 pm. The information terminal outside is useful when the office is closed.

A number of banks around town exchange money and travellers cheques, including the Commerzbank, adjacent to the tourist office, and the Citibank, on Neuer Markt, which also has an ATM that accepts all major credit cards. Most banks close at lunchtime.

The main post office is just north of the Hauptbahnhof.

There's a police station across the forecourt of the Hauptbahnhof.

Kunsthalle

Emden owes its place on the map of great art museums to local boy Henri Nannen, who left his home town to become the founder, publisher and editor-in-chief of the magazine *der Stern*, a glossy weekly read by millions of Germans. Upon retirement, he returned to Emden and donated the Kunsthalle to display his vast collection of paintings and sculpture. The red-brick building with blue wooden window frames blends harmoniously into its idyllic setting on a little canal.

Inside, its whitewashed, light-flooded rooms show off a stunning assembly of German expressionism and new realism. Emil Nolde alone is represented by about 30 paintings. There are works by the Russian Alex Jawlensky, Max Beckmann, Oskar Kokoschka, Erich Heckel, Max Pechstein and many more top names in 20th century art. Not all works are permanently displayed and part of the space is used for travelling exhibits. Three times a year, the museum closes its doors for one week while exhibits are changed.

The Kunsthalle (☎ 975 050) is at Hinter dem Rahmen 13, about a five minute walk east of the Hauptbahnhof. It's open Tuesday from 10 am to 8 pm, Wednesday to Friday to 5 pm and weekends from 11 am to 5 pm (DM9/5).

Ostfriesisches Landesmuseum

Inside the historic Rathaus is this regional history museum (☎ 87 20 57) with a vast collection spread over three floors. It's famous for its fine assortment of swords, halberds, pikes, muskets and other antique weapons from the 16th to 18th centuries.

Also on display are models, historic maps, costumes and other objects that document the history and lifestyle of East Friesland. There's also a gallery of old Dutch masters where you'll find such masterpieces as the evocative *Spaziergang nach Sandvoort* (Strolling to Sandvoort, 1642) by Isaack Luttichuijs and numerous works by the local 17th century painter Ludolf Backhuyzen. From the tower, you have a lovely view over the town.

From April to September the museum is open daily from 10 am to 5 pm. The rest of the year, hours are from 11 am to 4 pm, closed Monday (DM6/4).

Suurhusen

About 6km north of Emden, along the B70, stands the little church of Suurhusen (1262) which would be fairly unremarkable were it not for its unbelievably tilting tower.

Currently leaning 2.43m off true, it allegedly outdoes even the famous tower in Pisa by 4.7cm. The overhang is apparently the result of the decreasing groundwater levels in the peat-rich soil.

Activities
The flatlands in Emden and around are premier cycling territory, and the tourist office has at least half a dozen maps and even more suggestions on where to go (see Getting There & Around for bike rentals).

Another good way to travel is by water. The DJH hostel rents out canoes and kayaks from April to October for paddling around the placid canals (DM15/25 a half-day/day).

Organised Tours
You can take a harbour cruise (☎ 89 07 39), which leaves several times daily between March and October from the Delfttreppe steps in the harbour (DM9/4). There are also canal tours (DM6/3) leaving from the quay at the Kunsthalle between April and October on weekdays at 11 am and 3 pm, and on Sunday at noon and 3 pm. OLT (☎ 899 20) offers scenic flights over Emden.

Places to Stay
The *Campingplatz Knock* (☎ 567, fax 13 79, Am Mahlbusen) is about 10km west of town (DM7 per tent and DM4 per person). There are no direct bus connections.

Emden's *Jugendherberge* (☎ 237 97, fax 321 61, An der Kesselschleuse 5) is about a 15 minute walk east of the city centre. From the Hauptbahnhof, take bus No 3003 to Realschule/Am Herrentor. B&B costs around DM21/26 for juniors/seniors. It's closed in December and January, and on the first and third weekends in November and February.

The tourist office can help you find a room (no booking fee). *Private rooms* range from DM25 to DM50 per person. Several small guesthouses offer low-frills rooms at fairly low rates. *Gasthaus Rathausstübchen* (☎ 331 22, fax 221 50, Brückstrasse 5) charges DM70/100 for singles/doubles. *Gasthof zur Quelle* (☎/fax 319 91, Bollwerkstrasse 51-52) has singles/doubles for

DM70/90. The *Hotel Schmidt* (☎ 24 05 78, fax 327 02, Friedrich-Ebert-Strasse 79) is a step up. Singles/doubles with shower and WC cost DM98/155, but weekend rates are DM80/130. The owner speaks English well.

Places to Eat
Emden may not be the place to come for gourmet food, but you can always get a decent bite at the many cafes and bistros lining Neuer Markt. *Fischermann* (☎ 39 97 73) at No 19 offers lots of piscine dishes for under DM20. *Nordseewelle* nearby does cheap sit-down 'fast fish'. *Take it Easy* (a US-style bar) on Neuer Markt serves drinks only. *Sam's* next door (which serves good breakfasts) is similar – both are open till late.

The *Kunsthalle* has a nicely located cafe-restaurant (closed from 6 pm). *Pizzeria Peppino* (☎ 313 48, Grosse Strasse 24) has pizza and pasta dishes from DM10.

You'll find a *Neukauf* supermarket on Neuer Markt.

Getting There & Around
Emden is connected by rail to Oldenburg (DM23, 1¼ hours), Bremen (DM35, 1¾ hours) and Hamburg (DM74, three hours, change in Bremen). Despite its relative remoteness, Emden is also easily and quickly reached via the A31, which connects with the A28 from Oldenburg and Bremen. The B70/210 runs north from Emden to other towns in Friesland and to the coast.

Emden is small enough to be explored on foot but also has a bus system (DM1.50 per trip). The best transport method is the bicycle. Oltmanns (☎ 314 44), Grosse Strasse 53-57, rents out bikes at DM15 a day. Or, try MAC Zweiradverleih (☎ 275 00), Ringstrasse 17; it also rents out motorcycles.

JEVER
☎ 04461 • pop 13,000
Jever is at the heart of Friesland, a region just north of Oldenburg. Though a visitor would never notice a difference, the Frieslanders insist on not being confused with the people of East Friesland (for instance,

LOWER SAXONY

Emden, 50km to the west) and vice versa. In fact, both readily tell you about the so-called 'Golden Line', an imaginary border just a few kilometres west of Jever. That this rivalry has profound historic reasons goes without saying.

Jever has been settled for many centuries, as Roman coins from the 1st and 2nd centuries found would suggest. In the Middle Ages the town rose to prominence, largely because of its harbour. This is hard to imagine, given that it's landlocked today, with the sea about 12km away. In those days, Jever was ruled by elected judges called *Häuptlinge* (chieftains). The last of these rulers was the most famous and a woman to boot – the legendary Fräulein Maria (see the boxed text 'Fräulein Maria – the Last Chieftain' later in this section), who is revered by the people of Jever to this day. However, it wasn't Maria who made Jever a household name in Germany, but the dry Pilsner beer produced here since 1848.

Orientation & Information

Most of Jever's attractions are within a few hundred metres of each other in the eastern section of the Altstadt around the Schloss. The Hauptbahnhof is at Anton-Günther-Strasse, the south-western segment of the ring road that encircles the historic core. From there, it's only a short walk to the Schloss and Jever's tourist office.

The tourist office (☎ 710 10, fax 93 92 99), Alter Markt 18, is open from May to September, weekdays from 10 am to 6 pm and Saturday to 2 pm. The rest of the year, it's open Monday to Thursday from 9 am to 5 pm and Friday to noon. There's an information terminal outside the office.

The Landessparkasse, Alter Markt 4, exchanges money and has an ATM. The post office is at Mühlenstrasse 14, east of the Schloss.

Schloss

Jever's 14th century castle was first built by chieftain Edo Wiemken the Elder to keep out his overly assertive neighbours,

the counts of Oldenburg. The first structure proved too weak and was reconstructed and fortified by Edo Wiemken the Younger, the father of Fräulein Maria. Today the palace houses the **Kulturhistorische Museum des Jeverlandes**, a cultural history museum with 60 rooms packed with objects chronicling the daily life of the Frieslanders and their accomplishments in crafts and art. Precious Gobelin tapestries, faïences, period rooms and a portrait gallery round off the exhibits.

The *pièce de résistance*, however, is the magnificent audience hall, with a carved coffered oak ceiling of great intricacy. Fräulein Maria retained the Antwerp sculptor Cornelis Floris to create this 80 sq metre Renaissance masterpiece. Look for the grotesque figurines amid the garlands. Also note the 18th century leather wall coverings, gaudily decorated with gold leaf.

The Schloss is in the eastern section of the Altstadt and is open between March and mid-January from 10 am to 6 pm, closed Monday except in July and August (DM4/2). From May to September you can also climb the Schloss tower, which brings the entry fee up to DM5/3.

Friesisches Brauhaus zu Jever

This Frisian brewery (☎ 137 11), Elisabethufer 18, takes the mystique out of the beer-making process during tours of its production and bottling facilities. There's also a small **museum**. It's all capped off with a beer tasting. Tours take place weekdays from April to October hourly between 9.30 am and 3.30 pm. The rest of the year, they're given on weekdays at 10.30 am only. The cost is a fairly steep DM10, though that includes a pretzel and a commemorative glass mug. Reservations are necessary.

Other Sights

Most of Jever's sights are in some way connected to Fräulein Maria. She, her father and other historic figures are featured in the **Glockenspiel** on the facade of the Hof von

Fräulein Maria – the Last Chieftain

German history has a dearth of celebrated women, but the city of Jever has a champ: Fräulein Maria. The locals are so proud of this woman – the last in a long line of *Häuptlinge* (chieftains) – that they like to refer to their town as 'Marienstadt'.

Maria's legacy is everywhere: in a school that bears her name, in the statue near the Schloss where she lived and in the nearby Glockenspiel. The people so love their Maria, in fact, that they are loath to let her depart this world even centuries after her death. Legend has it that she hasn't gone to meet her Maker, but is merely lost in the labyrinth beneath the palace; those who have descended into the labyrinth to find her have suffocated, never to return. Every night at 10 pm (or 9 pm in winter), you'll hear the bells of the Stadtkirche pealing in an effort to guide Maria back to those who are waiting for her.

When Maria succeeded her chieftain father in 1517, she and her two sisters were immediately entrapped in a political power play. Her nemesis, Count Edzard of East Frisia, occupied Maria's palace and declared himself 'protector' of the young women. He should have left well enough alone: his promise that his three sons would marry the three daughters was soon broken. And Maria – proving that a woman scorned is not without options – promptly grabbed the reins of power for herself.

Her rule was tough but fair, the locals say. She gave Jever its town rights and, as a staunch Protestant, stamped out the local propensity for public drinking orgies. Having dealt with debauchery, she hurled her formidable energy into enlightening her people by founding a Latin school. When she died, the mantle of 'chieftain' was interred with her. But even in death she was to prove an agitator.

This century, feminists argued that the diminutive term 'Fräulein' – which originally referred to an unmarried, ie supposedly virginal, woman – was derogatory when applied to a mature woman such as Maria. But as she apparently died a virgin, this argument was soon dropped. 'Fräulein' Maria she will remain, and the bells of Jever will continue to ring in the hope that the last – and possibly greatest – chieftain will find her way home again.

Oldenburg opposite the Schloss (daily at 11 am, noon and 3, 4, 5 and 6 pm). Nearby, on Fräulein-Marien-Strasse, stands a **statue** of Fräulein Maria as a dignified matron wearing a large hat and accompanied by her dog. Head north, then turn left into Kleine Rosmarinstrasse to get to the **Stadtkirche** (open daily 8 am to 6 pm) containing the lavish **memorial tomb** of Edo von Wiemken (1468-1511), Maria's father. It miraculously survived eight fires (the last one in 1959), though the church itself succumbed to the flames and was rebuilt in a rather modern way.

The fantastical tomb – now glassed in – is another opus by Cornelis Floris whose imagination went into overdrive on this project. A huge octagonal two level wooden canopy shelters the sarcophagus topped with the life-sized figure of the chieftain dressed as a knight. This arrangement is propped up by a flock of caryatids representing Justice, Wisdom, Hope, Love, War and Peace.

One attraction *not* related to Maria is the little **shop** of Georg Stark, a former teacher who recently revived the long-lost art and tradition of *Blaudruckerei*, a printing and dying process similar to batik. Using original wooden embossing stamps he finds in old barns, at flea markets, antique shops and secret places, Stark makes everything from table cloths to jeans in his workshop on Kattrepel. The shop is open weekdays from 10 am to noon and 2 to 5 pm, Saturday to noon.

Places to Stay

The *Jugendherberge* (☎ 35 90, fax 35 65, *Mooshütter Weg 12)*, about a five minute walk from the Hauptbahnhof, charges DM19/24 for juniors/seniors for B&B. It's closed from November to the end of March.

Jever's tourist office doesn't make room reservations, though it can provide names and addresses. *Private rooms* start at DM22 per person.

There are only a few hotels in town, and they're quite inexpensive. *Hotel Weisses Haus* (☎ 68 39, fax 56 42, *Bahnhofstrasse 20)* charges DM60/90 for singles/doubles. *Pension Am Elisabethufer* (☎ 949 60, fax 94 96 10, *Elisabethufer 9a)* has quite nice rooms from DM66/100. *Hotel Pension Stöber* (☎ 55 80, *Hohnholzstrasse 10)* charges DM65/110. All rooms have private shower and WC.

Places to Eat

Bistro Neue 17 (☎ 60 89, *Neue Strasse 17)* offers basic but reasonable traditional dishes for under DM20 and a cheap lunch dish for around DM10. *Haus der Getreuen* (☎ 30 10, *Schlachtstrasse 1)* is one of the nicest restaurants in town. It's famous for regional specialities (DM16 to DM37), especially its tasty fish dishes. *Alte Apotheke* (☎ 40 88, *Apothekerstrasse 1)* is a stylish establishment for gourmets with deep pockets. One delicacy is the lamb with fetta crust (DM35).

A *Plus* supermarket is on Steintor, near the fountain.

On Alter Markt you'll find a couple of small-town drink 'n' dance type places where you can kick up your heels at night.

Getting There & Around

The train trip to Jever involves changing to a bus in Sand (DM15, 1½ hours). By road, Jever is easily reached by taking the exit to the B210 from the A29 (direction: Wilhelmshaven).

Jever is so small that all you need to explore it are your two feet. For explorations of the countryside, you can rent a bicycle at Rainer's Zweirad-Shop (☎ 735 98). The cost is DM10/50 per 24 hours/week.

East Frisian Islands

Trying to remember the sequence of the seven East Frisian Islands, Germans – with a wink of the eye – recite the following as a mnemonic device: '*Welcher Seemann liegt bei Nanni im Bett*?' (which translates rather saucily as 'Which seaman is lying in bed with Nanni?').

Lined up in an archipelago off the coast of Lower Saxony, the islands are (east to west): Wangerooge, Spiekeroog, Langeoog, Baltrum, Norderney, Juist and Borkum. Like their North Frisian cousins Sylt, Amrum and Föhr (see the Schleswig-Holstein chapter), the islands are part of the Wattenmeer National Park. And here too, nature is the islands' prime attraction. Those who make the trek are rewarded with long sandy beaches fringed by dunes and the shallow waters of the Wattenmeer.

Friesland itself covers an area stretching from the northern Netherlands, along the German coast, up into Denmark. Many inhabitants speak a language that is the closest relative of English but virtually incomprehensible to other Germans. The islands are popular with holiday-makers, though the Germans have kept them largely to themselves. Visits here aren't cheap, but those that have fallen under the spell of these islands swear that the pure sea breeze and wide open spaces are as invigorating and mind-clearing as hours of therapy. The main season runs from mid-May to September.

Resort Tax

Each of the East Frisian Islands charges a so-called *Kurtaxe*, a slap in the face to most visitors. Paying the tax gets you a *Kurkarte*, which entitles you to entry onto the beach and also gives you small discounts for museums, concerts and other events. The amount depends on the town and the season, though it rarely exceeds DM5 a day. If you're spending more than one night, your hotel will automatically obtain a pass for you for the length of your stay (the price will be added to the room rate).

Getting There & Away
Ferries to most of the islands don't operate on a fixed schedule because of the changing tides. It's best to call the ferry operator or Deutsche Bahn (DB), which also sells tickets, for details before you depart. Five of the seven islands don't allow cars, and you must leave your vehicle in a car park near the ferry pier, which can add up to an additional DM8.50 a day in expenses. If you're travelling by train, in most cases you'll have to change to a shuttle bus somewhere south of the harbour. For more details, see the Getting There & Away sections under each island.

WANGEROOGE
Wangerooge looks back on a rather turbulent past that saw it governed by Russia, the Netherlands, France, the duchy of Oldenburg and, finally, Germany. These days it's regularly invaded by visitors, most of them families coming for the wonderful sandy beaches and the car-free environment. The island lies along the shipping canal to Hamburg, Bremen and Wilhelmshaven, and the big ships can often be seen from the shoreline. Attractions here include the historic 39m-tall **lighthouse**, which can be climbed, a couple of **bird sanctuaries** and the **Wattenmeer Information Centre** in the Rosenhaus. There's also a sea-water adventure pool and a large list of sports activities.

For information, go to the Kurverwaltung (spa administration; ☎ 04469-990, fax 991 14) on the Strandpromenade, open Monday to Thursday from 8 am to 1 pm and 2.30 to 5 pm, and Friday to noon. There's also the Verkehrsverein (☎ 04469-948 80) in the pavilion at the Hauptbahnhof, which handles room reservations as well. A general warning: the tourist offices of the coastal spa towns change opening hours frequently and without notice. Call ahead if possible.

Getting There & Away
The ferry to Wangerooge leaves from Harlesiel two to four times daily (1¼ hours), depending on the tides. The one-way fare is DM28, same-day return tickets cost DM29. Large pieces of luggage are an extra DM5

each. If you want to take a bike along, it costs DM20 one-way. The price includes the tram shuttle to the village on the island (4km). The ferry is operated by DB (☎ 04464-94 94 11). If you're arriving by train, you must take the Bremen-Oldenburg-Wilhelmshaven line and get off in Sande, where you catch a shuttle bus to the ferry dock.

SPIEKEROOG
Rolling dunes dominate the landscape of minuscule Spiekeroog: about two-thirds of its 17.4 sq km is taken up by these sandy hills. It's the tranquillity of this rustic island that draws people, although it gets fairly busy in July and August, when most of the 50,000 annual visitors arrive. To prevent additional crowding, Spiekeroog is not only car-free but actually discourages bicycles too.

Spiekeroog's tourist office (☎ 04976-919 30, fax 91 93 47), Noorderpad 25, is open May to October on weekdays from 9 am to 5 pm year round, to noon on Saturday (closed November to February from 12.30 to 2 pm). For room reservations, ring ☎ 04976-91 93 25.

An attraction is the pint-sized **Alte Inselkirche** (1696), a church with a surprising interior: a flat wooden ceiling painted with red stars and model wooden ships dangling down into the hall. There's also a Spanish Pietà that washed ashore.

Getting There & Away
Neuharlingersiel to Spiekeroog takes 45 minutes and depends on the tides, which is why same-day returns aren't always possible. To get to the ferry by train, you must change to a shuttle bus in Esens or Norden. Prices are DM17.50 one-way and DM28 for same-day return tickets. Each piece of luggage is an extra DM4 return. Restrictions on cycling mean it's hardly worthwhile taking a bike. Call ☎ 04974-214 or any DB office for details and tickets.

LANGEOOG
Floods and pirates make up the story of Langeoog, whose population was reduced to a total of two following a horrendous

LOWER SAXONY

storm in 1721. But by 1830 it had recovered sufficiently to become a resort town.

Langeoog's tourist office (☎ 04972-69 30, fax 65 88), in the Rathaus at Hauptstrasse 28, is open Monday to Thursday from 7.30 am to noon and 1.30 to 5 pm, Friday from 7.30 am to noon. In July and August, it's also open on Friday from 3 to 5 pm and Saturday from 10 am to noon. For room reservations, ring ☎ 04972-69 32 01.

The island boasts the highest elevation in East Friesland – the 20m-high **Melkhörndüne** – and the **grave** of Lale Anderson, famous for her WWII song *Lili Marleen*. Nautical tradition is showcased in the **Schiffahrtsmuseum**, though the original **sea rescue ship** also on view is perhaps more interesting. In sunshine, the 14km-long beach is clearly the biggest attraction.

Getting There & Away

The ferry shuttles between Bensersiel and Langeoog up to nine times daily. The trip takes about one hour and costs DM18/30 one-way/return. Luggage is DM5 per piece return, and bikes are DM30 return. For details, call ☎ 04971-2501 or contact any DB office. To get to Bensersiel by train, you must change to a shuttle bus in Esens or Norden.

BALTRUM

Car-free Baltrum is tiny – only 1km wide and 5km long. It's so small that villagers don't even bother with street names. The houses, though, have numbers allocated on a chronological basis. Since houses 1 to 4 no longer exist, the oldest house is now No 5. Much of the available space is taken up by dunes and salty marshland. There's little to do except to go on walks or to the beach, or visit the exhibit on the Wattenmeer National Park environment in house No 177.

Baltrum's tourist office (☎ 04939-800, fax 80 27), in house No 130, is open Monday to Thursday from 7.30 am to 4.30 pm, Friday to noon. For room reservations, call ☎ 04939-91 40 03.

Getting There & Away

Ferries make the trip from Nessmersiel to Baltrum in 30 minutes. Departures depend on the tides, which means day trips aren't always possible. Tickets are DM20/36 one-way/return. Same-day return tickets cost DM24. Bikes are DM8 each way. Luggage is usually free. Details are available from ☎ 04939-913 00 or a DB office. To get to Nessmersiel by train, change to the shuttle bus in Norden.

NORDERNEY

Norderney is the 'Queen of the East Frisian Islands' and has been wooed by a long line of royal suitors, starting with Friedrich Wilhelm II of Prussia in 1797. He gave his blessing to the founding of Germany's first North Sea resort here. Georg V of Hanover liked Norderney so much that he made it his summer residence. Otto von Bismarck came here in 1844.

Norderney's tourist office (☎ 04932-918 50, fax 824 94), Bülowallee 5, is open from mid-May to September daily from 9 am to 6 pm. It is closed the rest of the year from 12.30 to 2 pm, and on Saturday afternoon and Sunday. It also handles room reservations (toll-free ☎ 0800-667 33 76 39).

The island's lavish **gardens**, **parks** and majestic architecture date back to this era of visits by the high and mighty. The red-brick post office and the **Kurhaus**, with its columns and arches, and the many neoclassical homes give Norderney a glamorous flair. One particular attraction is **Die Welle** (☎ 04932-89 11 41), an indoor ocean-water wave and fun pool at Kurplatz. There's also an outdoor pool at Weststrand. The **Nationalpark-Haus** is direct on the harbour. Because it is comparatively large, Norderney allows cars.

Getting There & Away

To get to Norderney you have to catch the ferry in Norddeich, with scheduled departures up to nine times daily (50 minutes). Prices are DM12/22.50 one-way/return; same-day returns are DM25 (including resort tax). Bikes are DM10. Details are available at ☎ 04931-98 70 or any DB office. There's a train service to Norddeich Mole, the ferry landing stage.

JUIST

Juist, shaped like a snake, is 17km long and only 500m wide. The only ways to travel are by bike, horse-drawn carriage or on your own two feet. What makes Juist special is what is *not* here: no high-rises, cars or shopping malls. Instead, you're often alone with the screeching seagulls, the wild sea and the howling winds. Forest, brambles and elderberry bushes blanket large sections of the island.

Juist's tourist office (☎ 04935-80 90, fax 80 92 23, email juist@t-online.de), Friesenstrasse 18, is open Monday to Thursday from 8.30 am to noon and 3 to 4 pm, and Friday to noon. Between Easter and September, it's also open on Friday from 3 to 5 pm and Saturday from 10 am to noon. Room reservations can be made on ☎ 04935-80 92 22.

One peculiarity of Juist is the idyllic **Hammersee** – the only freshwater lake on all the islands – which is also a bird sanctuary. There's also the Juister **Küstenmuseum** (Coastal Museum) on Loogster Pad.

Getting There & Away

Ferries to Juist also leave from Norddeich and take 1¼ hours. The cost is DM22/42 one-way/return; same-day returns are DM30 and include the resort tax. Luggage costs DM5.50 a piece, bikes DM17. More information is available from ☎ 04931-98 70 or any DB office. The train goes straight to the landing dock in Norddeich Mole.

BORKUM

The largest of the East Frisian Islands is also one of the most popular. Until ripped apart by a flood in the 12th century, Borkum was even larger than today. For many centuries, the men of Borkum made a living as seafarers and whalers. Reminders of those brutal days are the whale bones that you'll occasionally see, stacked up side by side, as garden fences. It wasn't until 1830 that the locals realised that tourism was a safer way to earn a living.

Borkum's Kurverwaltung (☎ 04922-30 33 10, fax 48 00), Goethestrasse 1, is open from April to September, weekdays from 9 am to 6 pm and Saturday from 10 am to noon. The rest of the year, hours are weekdays from 9 am to noon and 3 to 5.30 pm. There's another tourist office (☎ 04922-93 30, fax 93 31 04) at the Hauptbahnhof, which also handles room reservations.

To learn about the whaling era and other stages in the life of Borkum, visit the **Heimatmuseum** (Local History Museum) at the foot of the old lighthouse. Also of interest is the museum fireship *Borkumriff*, with its exhibit on the Wattenmeer National Park.

Getting There & Away

The embarkation point for ferries to Borkum is Emden. You can either take the car ferry, which takes two hours, or the catamaran, which makes the trip in half the time. Car-ferry tickets are DM25/47 one-way/return. Same-day return tickets also cost DM25. Weekend return tickets are DM37.50 (valid from Friday after 5 pm to Sunday). Tickets for the catamaran are DM15 more each way. Transporting a bike costs DM18 return. For information, call ☎ 04921-89 07 22.

Hamburg

☎ 040　● pop 1.7 million

Several years ago, a visit to Hamburg by Queen Elizabeth II of England presented city officials with a dilemma. Local tradition dictated that the mayor receive all visiting dignitaries on the 1st floor of the Rathaus. However, since the queen could hardly be expected to walk up the stairway unescorted, a compromise was struck: the mayor would descend the stairs – but only halfway – to meet Her Majesty.

It's an anecdote that could easily be a metaphor for why this northern German city-state (one of three besides Bremen and Berlin) is still called the 'Free and Hanseatic City' of Hamburg. Except during Napoleonic occupation in the early 19th century, Hamburg has never bowed to any foreign ruler. Instead, it has been governed by commerce and business.

In fact, in a letter from 1831, John Strang, then treasurer of Glasgow, called it 'the most mercantile city of the world' and, though in decline, Hamburg's bustling port is still the backbone of the city's wealth. And wealthy it is. Hamburg has more millionaires than any other German city, and the tree-lined avenues in neighbourhoods like Blankenese, Harvestehude and Winterhude are flanked by lavish mansions with matching cars parked outside.

But Hamburg is also a city of contrasts, where a free-wheeling liberalism thrives alongside clubby elitism. The former manifests itself as much in the revitalised red-light district along the Reeperbahn as in the eclectic mix of students, workers and immigrants that coexist quite harmoniously in such colourful quarters as the Schanzenviertel, Altona and St Pauli.

Rich or poor, Hamburgers are rightly proud of their city. Aesthetically it ranks high among major German metropolises. It boasts a lively cultural scene, vast urban green spaces and gorgeous architecture, despite the destruction wreaked upon it by a

Hamburg pp832-3
● St Georg p847
Altona p843

HIGHLIGHTS

Hamburg Luminaries:
Wolf Biermann, Johannes Brahms, Paul Dessau, Karl Lagerfeld, Felix Mendelssohn-Bartholdy, Helmut Schmidt, Michael Stich

- Sunday morning shopping and rock 'n' roll at the boisterous Fischmarkt

- Visiting the collections of the Kunsthalle including the dramatic new Galerie der Gegenwart

- Taking a boat trip through the Speicherstadt warehouse complex

- Having a night at the theatre: Schauspielhaus or Thalia, both top stages in Germany

- Barhopping through St Pauli with a stop at Angie's Nightclub

- Enjoying the hydraulic organ concerts in the Planten un Blomen park

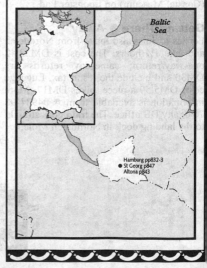

Baltic Sea

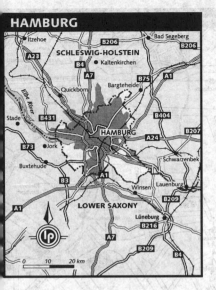

HAMBURG

(Map labels) Itzehoe, Bad Segeberg, B206, B206, SCHLESWIG-HOLSTEIN, A23, B4, Kaltenkirchen, A7, B75, A1, Quickborn, Bargteheide, Elbe River, B431, B404, Stade, HAMBURG, A24, B207, B73, Jork, Schwarzenbek, Buxtehude, B3, A1, Lauenburg, Winsen, LOWER SAXONY, B209, Lüneburg, B216, A1, A7, B209, B4

0   10   20 km

major fire in the 19th century and two world wars in the 20th. Exploring Hamburg properly takes time and good shoes, for the best way to see this city is by trekking through its neighbourhoods.

HISTORY
Hamburg's recorded history begins in the 9th century with the construction of a moated fortress called Hammaburg in today's city centre. The settlement that sprang up around it soon became a missionary stronghold, but it wasn't until the 12th century that the seeds for Hamburg's development into a wealthy trading city were laid.

This was accomplished largely by an ambitious nobleman, Count Adolf III, who in 1189, managed to wrangle a royal charter from Emperor Friedrich I (Barbarossa). It granted the fledgling city free trade rights and exemption from customs. A coup, to say the least, that turned Hamburg into an important port city and a leading member of the Hanseatic League.

The Great Fire of 1842, which burned one third of the city, was a major blow but the city soon recovered. By 1913, Hamburg's population exceeded one million and was again one of the premier ports in Europe. After WWI, most of Hamburg's merchant shipping fleet (almost 1500 ships) was forfeited to the Allies as reparations. WWII left more than half of all housing, 80% of the port and 40% of the industry in rubble. Fire bombs dropped by the Allies on 28 July 1943 created a conflagration so great that tens of thousands of civilians were killed and entire streets vaporised. Equal numbers of people perished at the hands of the Nazis in the concentration camps of Fuhlsbüttel and Neuengamme, including 8000 Jews.

In the postwar years, Hamburg showed its usual resilience and recovered quickly. Today it is Germany's second-largest city after Berlin, with about 15% of its population being immigrants. Some 68,000 students study at nine institutions, and the largest is the University of Hamburg, with 42,000 students.

Hamburg is also one of Germany's media capitals, represented by more than 6200 companies in the fields of publishing, advertising, film, radio, TV and music. The print media are especially prolific: 15 out of 20 of the largest German publications are produced here.

ORIENTATION
Like Venice and Amsterdam, Hamburg is a city shaped by water. Three rivers – the Elbe, the Alster and the Bille – traverse it, as does a scenic grid of narrow canals called *Fleete*. The beautiful Inner and Outer Alster lakes in the city centre contribute further to the maritime feel. Hamburg boasts 2600 bridges, considerably more than even Venice.

Most of Hamburg's main attractions cluster in the half-moon-shaped city centre, which arches north of the Elbe and is bordered by large roads whose names all end in *wall* (literally 'rampart') because they follow the former fortifications. The area is bisected diagonally by the Alsterfleet, the canal that roughly separates the Altstadt from the Neustadt, though the two merge seamlessly today.

HAMBURG

HAMBURG

To Camping Buchholz,
Hagenbecks Tierpark &
Camping Schnelsen
Nord

To Frauenbuchladen

To Abaton
Cinema, Bistro,
Balutschi, Hindukusch,
Arkadash, La Fattoria
& Logo

Sternschanzenpark

Schröderstiftstrasse

Langenfelder

Altonaer Strasse

To Neue Flora
& English Bookstore

Max. Brauer

Allee

Julius str

Lippmann strasse

Schulterblatt

Schanzenviertel

Susannenstrasse

B. Nissenstrasse

Schanzenstrasse

Kampstrasse

Sternstrasse

Sternschanze

Sternschanze

Lagerstrasse

Karolinenstrasse

Planten un
Blomen

Hamburg
Fairgrounds

Grabenstrasse

Glashüttenstrasse

Messehallen

Kleine
Wallanlagen

Gorch-Fock-Wall

Jungiusstrasse

Stremannstrasse

Allee

Wohlers

Otzenstrasse

Gilbertstrasse

Thadenstrasse

Neuer
Pferdemarkt

Neuer Kamp

Marktstrasse

Karolinenviertel

Feldstrasse

Feldstrasse

Messehallen

Johannes-
Brahms-
Platz.

Kaiser-Wilhelm-Strasse

Neustädter Strasse

Paul-Roosen-Strasse

Heiligengeistfeld

Grosse
Wallanlagen

Holstenwall

Pilatuspool

Neanderstrasse

Budapester Strasse

Glacischaussee

Kohlhöfen

Grossneumarkt

Wexstrasse

Alter Steinw

To Altona
Train Station

St
Pauli

Freiheit

Simon von Utrecht Strasse

Clemens-Schultz-Strasse

Hein-Hoyer-Strasse

Seilerstrasse

Talstrasse

Reeperbahn

St Pauli

Ludwig-Erhard-Strasse

Holstenstrasse

Grosse

start

Reeperbahn

finish

Spielbudenplatz

Hans-Albers-
Platz

Kastanienallee

Zirkusweg

Hopfenstrasse

Davidstrasse

Gerhardstrasse

Friedrichstrasse

Herbertstrasse

Bernhard-Nocht-Strasse

Hein-
Köllisch-
Platz

Elbpark

Helgoländer Allee

Seewartenstrasse

Böhmkenstrasse

Krayenkamp

Grossneumarkt

Venusberg

Neuer Neustädter Weg

Stubbenhuk

Herrengraben

Ditmar-Koel-Strasse

Rambachstrasse

Johannisbollwerk

Vorsetzen

Baumwall

Baumwall

St-Pauli-Hafenstrasse

St-Pauli-Fischmarkt

St Pauli
Landungsbrücken

To Fish Market,
Campingplatz Blankenese
& England Ferry Terminal

St-Pauli Elbtunnel

St Pauli Harbour

Elbe

River

H Blohm Strasse

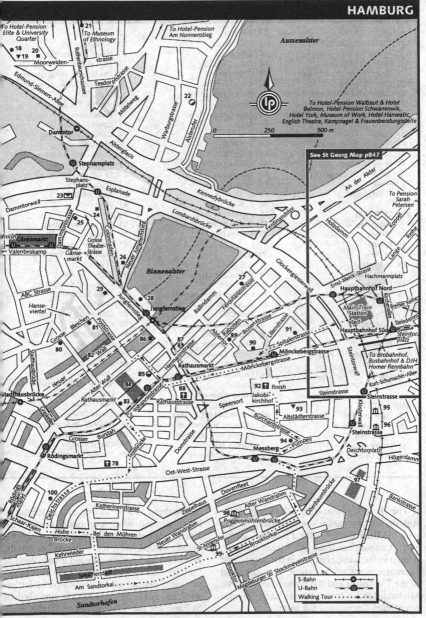

To Hotel-Pension
Elite & University
Quarter

21
To Museum
of Ethnology

18
19 20
Moorweidenstrasse

To Hotel-Pension
Am Nonnenstieg

Aussenalster

To Hotel-Pension Waltraut & Hotel
Belmon, Hotel-Pension Schwanenwik,
Hotel York, Museum of Work, Hotel Hanseatic,
English Theatre, Kampnagel & Frauenberatungsstelle

Edmund-Siemers-Allee

Rothenbaumchaussee

Tesdorpfstrasse

Mittelweg

Warburgstrasse

Alsterufer

22

0   250   500 m

Dammtor

Alsterglacis

See St Georg Map p847

Stephansplatz

Stephansplatz

Esplanade

Kennedybrücke

Ferdinandtor

An der Alster

To Pension
Sarah
Petersen

Dammtorwall

23

24
25

Colonnaden

Neuer Jungfernstieg

Lombardsbrücke

Holzdamm

Koppel

Lange Reihe

finish
Gänsemarkt

Valentinskamp

Grosse
Theaterstrasse

Gänsemarkt

26

Binnenalster

Glockengiesserwall

Ernst-Merck-Strasse

Hachmannplatz

Hauptbahnhof Nord

ABC Strasse

29

Jungfernstieg

27

Ferdinandstrasse

Main Train
Station
start

Hauptbahnhof Süd

Steindamm

Hanseviertel

28

Jungfernstieg

Ballindamm

Raboisen

Rosenstrasse

Lilienstrasse

91

Spitalerstrasse

Steintorplatz

Bleichen

81

Poststrasse

Hermannstrasse

87

Alstertor

89

90

Mönckebergstrasse

Steinstrasse

Grosser

80

82

86

Rathausmarkt

Mönckebergstrasse

To Brobahnhof,
Busbahnhof & DJH
Homer Rennbahn

Neuer

Alter Wall

85

84

Kurt-Schumacher-Allee

Stadthausbrücke

Rathausmarkt

83

88

Rathausstrasse

Speersort

92 finish

Jakobikirchhof

Steinstrasse

Grosser Burstah

St Johannisstrasse

Trostbrücke

Domstrasse

93
Altstädterstrasse

Burchardstrasse

95

96

Rödingsmarkt

78

94

Pumpen

Messberg

Steinstrasse

Deichtorplatz

Högerdamm

Ost-West-Strasse

Dovenfleet

97

Bankstrasse

Rödingsmarkt

100

Delichstrasse

Katherinenstrasse

Zippelhaus

Alter Wandrahm

Oberbaumbrücke

Schaar-Kajen

Hohe
Brücke

Bei den Mühren

Neuer Wandrahm

98
Poggenmühlenbrücke

St Annenufer

Brooktorkai

Kehrwieder

99

Brooktor

Magdeburger Str Stockmeyerstrasse

Speicherstadt

Am Sandtorkai

S-Bahn	
U-Bahn	U
Walking Tour	

Sandtorhafen

euro currency converter DM1 = €0.51

HAMBURG

PLACES TO STAY
1 InstantSleep Backpacker Hostel
2 Hotel Sternschanze
8 Schanzenstern Youth Hostel
20 Dammtorpalais
21 Gästehaus der Universität
24 Hotel-Pension Bei der Esplanade
26 Hotel Vier Jahreszeiten; Condi
31 Frauenhotel Hanseatin
42 Hotel Imperial
44 Hotel Monopol
103 Auf dem Stintfang DJH Hostel
104 Hotel Hafen

PLACES TO EAT
5 Café Unter den Linden
7 Shikara
11 Lokma
12 La Sepia
13 bok imbiss
14 bok restaurant
15 Frauenkniepe
16 Noodle's
19 Limerick
33 Café Klatsch
45 Café Absurd
48 Weite Welt
66 Phuket
75 Old Commercial Room
93 Saalbach
101 Sagres
102 O Pescador

BARS & CLUBS
3 Frank und Frei
6 Oma's Apotheke
10 Fritz Bauch
30 Madhouse
34 Café Oriental

35 Bob Bar
43 Café Keese
46 Spundloch
47 Toom Peerstall
49 Grünspan
50 Gretel & Alfons
51 Grosse Freiheit 36; Kaiserkeller
52 Funky Pussy Club
53 Safari
54 Tabu
55 Zur Ritze
58 Geyer Bar
59 Samba Do Brasil
60 Mary Lou's
61 Purgatory
62 La Paloma
63 EDK
69 Prinzenbar
71 Docks; Condomerie
79 Cotton Club

OTHER
4 Rote Flora
9 3001 Cinema
17 TV Tower
18 Heinrich Heine Bookshop
22 US Consulate
23 Post Office
25 Staatsoper
27 British Airways
28 Alster-Touristik Landing Stage
29 Streit's Cinema
32 Musikhalle
36 Laundrette – Neuer Pferdemarkt
37 Männerschwarm
38 Justizgebäude
39 Municipal Lost & Found
40 Museum of Hamburg History
41 Peterstrasse; Johannes Brahms Museum
56 Erotic Art Museum

57 Laundrette
64 privartmuseum
65 Harry's Hamburger Hafenbasar
67 Davidwache Police Station
68 Schmidt's Tivoli; Angie's Nightclub
70 Schmidt Theater
72 Panoptikum
73 Operettenhaus
74 Bismarck Monument
76 Michaeliskirche
77 Krameramtswohnungen
78 St Nikolai
80 Dr Götze Land und Karte
81 Thalia Bücher
82 Alsterarkaden
83 Börse
84 Rathaus
85 Rathaus Bus Station
86 Air France
87 American Express; International Pharmacy
88 St Petri
89 Thalia Theater
90 Cyberb@r; Karstadt
91 Thalia Buchhaus
92 St Jacobi
94 Chile Haus; Weinhexe
95 Kunsthaus
96 Kunstverein; Akademie der Kunste
97 Deichtorhallen
98 German Customs Museum
99 Speicherstadtmuseum; Hot Spice Gewürzmuseum
100 Deichstrasse
105 Tourist Office
106 HADAG Landing Stages
107 Rickmer Rickmers
108 Cap San Diego
109 Metropol Musical Theater

The Hauptbahnhof is on Glockengiesserwall on the city centre's north-eastern edge, with the Busbahnhof behind it to the southeast. Hamburg has three other train stations: Altona in the west, Harburg in the south, and Dammtor, north of the centre. The spiky top of the TV Tower and the bronze helmet-like Michaeliskirche spire provide handy visual orientation throughout the town.

Hamburg is a sprawling city made up of many distinct neighbourhoods. East of the Hauptbahnhof is St Georg, a schizophrenic quarter with lovely, leafy streets and seedy, prostitute and junkie-infested areas. West of the city centre lies the red-light and entertainment district of St Pauli which, farther west, merges with lively Altona. Just north of St Pauli are the Schanzenviertel and Karolinenviertel, both home to Hamburg's alternative scene. The city's most select neighbourhoods hug the 400 acre Outer Alster Lake north of the city centre, with Winterhude and Uhlenhorst on the eastern and Harvestehude and Rotherbaum on the western shores. The Universitätsviertel (University Quarter) takes up the western section of Rotherbaum.

The tourist offices hand out excellent free city maps.

INFORMATION
Tourist Offices
If you're not yet in Hamburg, information, room reservations and tickets are available through Hamburg Hotline (☎ 30 05 13 00), daily between 8 am and 8 pm (ask for an English-speaking operator).

The tourist office (☎ 30 05 12 00, fax 30 05 13 33, email info@hamburg-tourism.de) at the Kirchenallee exit in the Hauptbahnhof is open daily from 7 am to 11 pm. There's a larger office (same ☎ & fax) at St Pauli harbour, between piers 4 and 5 (S/U-Bahn: St Pauli Landungsbrücken), open daily from 10 am to 7 pm (in winter from 9.30 am to 5.30 pm). Both offices provide brochures, a room-finding service (DM6 fee) and tickets to city events.

The tourist offices also sell the Hamburg Card, which offers unlimited public transport and free or discounted admission to many museums, attractions and boat cruises. The Day Card is valid after 6 pm on the day of purchase and the entire next day, and costs DM12.80 (valid for one adult and up to three children under 12) or DM24.50 (for groups of up to five people). The Multiple Day Card is valid on the day of purchase and the following two days (DM26.50/43). If you don't want public transport included, you can get the Hamburg Light version, which is good for three days and costs DM10/21. These cards are also available from numerous hotels and hostels.

For those under 27, the best deal around is the Jugend Pass (DM12.50 the first day, DM5.50 for each additional day). Besides unlimited public transport, it offers even steeper discounts, plus a bunch of coupons good for savings on drinks, movie tickets and nightclubs.

Money
All major banks operate exchange stations during normal opening hours (weekdays to 4 pm, Thursday to 6 pm). Outside the city centre, branches may close at lunchtime.

The Reisebank, upstairs near tracks 3 and 4 at the northern end of the Hauptbahnhof, is open from 7.30 am to 10 pm daily. Other branches are at Altona station (closed Sunday) and at the airport in Terminal 4. There's also a Deutsche Bank counter at the airport, open from 6.30 am to 8.30 pm daily.

Also near the Hauptbahnhof, on Steindamm, is AGW Wechselstube, which charges no commission on cash; it's open weekdays from 8 am to 8 pm, and Saturday from 9 am to 3 pm. American Express is at Ballindamm 39, near Jungfernstieg, and is open weekdays from 9 am to 5.30 pm, and Saturday from 10 am to 1 pm. There's another branch in Terminal 4 at the airport that's open weekdays only from 6.30 am to 5 pm.

Post & Communications
The main post office (☎ 325 51 60), inside the Hauptbahnhof near the Kirchenallee exit, is open weekdays from 8 am to 8 pm, Saturday from 9 am to 6 pm, and Sunday from 10 am to 6 pm. The poste restante is here; letters should be clearly marked 'Postlagernd' and addressed as follows: Filiale Hamburg 101, Hachmannplatz 13, 20099 Hamburg, Germany. There's a photocopier on this floor and public fax-phones upstairs. Another post office is at Stephansplatz, on the corner of Dammtorstrasse. Hamburg has several Internet cafes, including a Cyberb@r in the Karstadt at Mönckebergstrasse 16.

Internet Resources
For comprehensive information on Hamburg via the Internet, you can try checking into www.hamburg.de.

Bookshops
For reasonably priced second-hand English novels, visit the English Bookstore at

euro currency converter DM1 = €0.51

Stresemannstrasse 169, just outside the Holstenstrasse S-Bahn exit. It is open from noon to 6.30 pm (closed Sunday). The Heinrich-Heine-Buchhandlung, Grindelallee 24-28 in the Universitätsviertel, also has a fair selection of foreign-language books, as do Thalia Bücher (☎ 302 07 01) at Grosse Bleichen 19 and Thalia Buchhaus at Spitalerstrasse 8, both in the city centre. Just about every map under the sun is available at Dr Götze Land und Karte (☎ 357 46 30), Bleichenbrücke 9, in the Bleichenhof arcade (S1/S3 to Stadthausbrücke). A smaller branch is at the Hauptbahnhof.

Laundry

There's a laundrette at Nobistor 34 in St Pauli (S1/S3 to Reeperbahn) and another at Am Neuen Pferdemarkt 27 (U3 to Feldstrasse). You might also try the one on Bahrenfelder Strasse in Altona.

Medical Services

In case of medical emergency, call ☎ 22 80 22 around the clock; 24 hour first-aid service is at ☎ 24 82 81 and dental emergency aid at ☎ 01 15 00. International pharmacies are at Ballindamm 39 (☎ 309 60 60) and in the Hauptbahnhof at the Kirchenallee exit.

Emergency

There are police stations all over the city, including one on the corner of Kirchenallee and Bremer Reihe in St Georg. In St Pauli is the Davidwache at Spielbudenplatz 31, corner of Davidstrasse.

Free counselling for women is offered by the Frauenberatungsstelle (☎ 652 77 11) at Kattunbleiche 31. A toll-free helpline for kids and teenagers is at ☎ 0800-111 03 33. A rape crisis centre can be reached at ☎ 25 55 66.

The municipal lost and found office (☎ 35 18 51) is at Bäckerbreitergang 73; it's open Monday to Thursday only.

Dangers & Annoyances

Overall, Hamburg is a safe city with a low crime rate. Junkies and pushers congregate at several places around town, most notably at the Kirchenallee exit of the Hauptbahn-

hof, at Hansaplatz in St Georg and in Sternschanzenpark in the Schanzenviertel. Since these areas cannot always be avoided, it pays to be extra careful around here.

There are prostitutes throughout St Pauli and on Steindamm and adjacent streets in St Georg. Locals claim that the area around the Reeperbahn is the safest place on earth because there are so many police around.

ALTSTADT WALKING TOUR

Starting at the Hauptbahnhof, head west down the pedestrianised Spitalerstrasse, a major shopping street, to the 12th century **St Petri**. The oldest of Hamburg's five main churches, it was rebuilt in the neo-Gothic style after the Great Fire of 1842. English-language services are held here at 5 pm on the first Sunday of the month; call ☎ 32 44 38 for information.

Farther on is the neo-Renaissance **Rathaus**, built in 1897. English tours (DM2) run hourly Monday to Thursday from 10.15 am to 3.15 pm, Friday to Sunday to 1 pm. The 40 minute tour passes through the Parliamentary Meeting Hall, which is about the only austere room out of a total of 647 (allegedly six more than Buckingham Palace). More typical are the opulent Emperor's Hall and the Great Hall, with its spectacular coffered ceiling.

Walk to the north side of the Rathaus for a look at the **Alsterarkaden**, an elegant row of Renaissance-style arcades sheltering shops and cafes. They parallel the Alsterfleet, which merges with the Binnenalster, the smaller of the two city lakes and departure point for lake cruises (see Cruises later in this chapter).

Backtrack to the south end of the Rathaus, then head south-west down Grosse Johannisstrasse. On the right is the **Börse** (☎ 361 30 20), Germany's oldest stock exchange. Free guided tours (with reservation) are offered Tuesday and Thursday at 11 am and noon.

From here turn left at Börsenbrücke, which takes you to the historic **Trostbrücke**, the oldest bridge linking the Altstadt and Neustadt. It features statues of Ansgar, Hamburg's first archbishop (801-65), and Neustadt founder Count Adolf III. Just beyond are the stark ruins of **St Nikolai**, now an antiwar memorial. The medieval original succumbed to the Great Fire, and the rebuilt St Nikolai was flattened by Allied bombers 100 years later.

The Great Fire broke out in **Deichstrasse**, which runs south off Ost-West-Strasse and features several restored 18th century homes. The best view of the street is from Hohe Brücke (turn left – east – at the southern end of Deichstrasse). Continue east, then cross the canal at Auf dem Sande for an exploration of the Speicherstadt.

Speicherstadt

Stretching from the Deichtorhallen in the east to Baumwall, where the Alsterfleet flows into the Elbe, the Speicherstadt (1885 to 1927) is the world's largest continuous warehouse complex. It's made up of rows of seven-storey high, statuesque red-brick buildings whose ornate gables and green copper rooftops are reflected in the calm waters of the narrow canals lacing this free port zone.

The building of a free port became necessary when Hamburg had to join the German Customs Federation after joining the German Reich in 1871. An older neighbourhood was demolished – and 24,000 people displaced – to make room for its construction. Today, goods such as coffee, tea, computers and oriental carpets are still hoisted into the storerooms via pulleys and remain there customs-free until the owner decides to sell.

All this and more is explained at the **Speicherstadtmuseum** (DM4/2) at St Annenufer 2. Other museums in the Speicherstadt are the **Deutsches Zollmuseum** (German Customs Museum; free) at Alter Wandrahm 15, and the **Hot Spice Gewürzmuseum** (DM3/1.50), Am Sandtorkai 32. They are open daily except Monday from 10 am to 5 pm.

The tourist office runs guided walking tours (in German) of the Speicherstadt on Tuesday at 2.30 pm between April and October (DM10/5), though it's also enjoyable just to wander around on your own. One of the loveliest views is from the Poggenmühlenbrücke. To leave the Speicherstadt, head

north from here, cross Ost-West-Strasse and turn right on Pumpen.

Merchant's District

Now you are in the Merchant's District, where much of Hamburg's money was, and is, being made. It's characterised by mighty edifices (looking very much like red-brick ocean liners) designed by expressionist architect Fritz Höger. His crowning achievement was the magnificent **Chile Haus** (1924), built for a merchant who derived his wealth from trading with Chile, and located between Burchardstrasse and Messberg. To fully appreciate its eccentric shape, stand on the corner of Burchardstrasse and Pumpen.

North of the Chile Haus, on Steinstrasse, is **St Jacobi**, another of Hamburg's main churches. The main attraction here is a 17th century organ built by Arp Schnitger. A few steps farther north takes you back to Mönckebergstrasse and the city's commercial centre.

NEUSTADT WALKING TOUR

This tour starts at the **Michaeliskirche** on Krayenkamp, the star attraction of the Neustadt and Hamburg's most prominent landmark. Popularly known as 'Michel', its distinctive tower presides over northern Germany's largest Protestant baroque church. The whitewashed, light-flooded interior exudes a cheerful elegance and sports a curved upstairs gallery. Concerts on one or all three of the organs often draw capacity crowds of up to 2500 people. Views from the tower, reached by a lift (DM4/2), help you grasp the city layout. A multivision show on the history of Hamburg (in German; DM5/2.50, 40 minutes) or a visit of the crypt (DM2.50/1) can easily be skipped. Combination tickets are DM9/4.50.

The church and tower are open from April to September, Monday to Saturday from 9 am to 6 pm (10 am to 4.30 pm in winter), and Sunday from 11.30 am to 5.30 pm (to 4.30 pm in winter).

Just below the church, in a tiny alley off Krayenkamp, are the **Krameramtswohnungen** (☎ 31 10 26 24), a row of tiny half-timbered houses from the 17th century that,

HAMBURG

for nearly 200 years, were almshouses for the widows of members of the Guild of Small Shopkeepers. Taken over by the city in 1863, they became seniors' homes until 1969 and are now just a tourist attraction. One home can be visited daily, except Monday, from 10 am to 5 pm (DM2/1, Friday half price).

Follow Krayenkamp north to Ludwig-Erhard-Strasse, head west, then north on Holstenwall to get to the cobbled **Peterstrasse**, with its restored baroque houses. The one at No 39 harbours the **Johannes Brahms Museum** (☎ 45 21 58), open Tuesday and Thursday from 10 am to 1 pm only (DM1). It's a tribute to the composer who was born in the city.

On the west side of Holstenwall at No 24 is the **Museum of Hamburg History** (Museum für Hamburgische Geschichte; ☎ 35 04 23 60), which chronicles the city's evolution from primal landscape to metropolis. Here you will learn that the Reeperbahn was once the quarter of the ropemakers (reep means rope) and how destructive the firebombs dropped in 1943 were. All exhibits have English commentary. Hours are Tuesday to Saturday from 10 am to 5 pm, Sunday to 6 pm (DM8/2, Friday half price).

Farther north on Holstenwall is the **Justizgebäude** (Halls of Justice) and the neobaroque **Musikhalle** (concert hall) fronting Johannes-Brahms-Platz. **Gänsemarkt**, to the east, is the western gateway to Hamburg's elegant shopping district.

KUNSTMEILE

A string of museums and galleries, known as the Art Mile, extends from Glockengiesserwall to Deichtorstrasse between the Alster Lakes and the Elbe. Unless noted, all museums are closed on Monday.

Hamburg Kunsthalle

Behind the green cupola and columns that dominate Glockengiesserwall, just north of the Hauptbahnhof, awaits the famed Kunsthalle (☎ 24 86 26 12), with its internationally important art collection from medieval portraiture to 20th century minimalism.

Top billing in the Gallery of Old Masters goes to the painted main altar of St Petri (1383), a work attributed to Master Bertram. An early work by Rembrandt called *Simeon in the Temple* heads the sampling of Dutch 17th century work.

The Kunsthalle's main strength is in its collection of 19th century German paintings. An entire room is dedicated to the haunting landscapes of romantic painter Caspar David Friedrich. Philipp Otto Runge, who signalled the trend towards subjectivity in painting, is strongly represented too, as is the impressionist Max Liebermann and the realist Wilhelm Leibl.

Among the early 20th century expressionist paintings that survived the sweep by the Nazis in 1937 are works by Kokoschka, Beckmann, Nolde, Marc and Klee.

It's easy to spend hours in the Kunsthalle, but if you're pressed for time, pick up a handy pamphlet (DM1) with highlights from the ticket office. Hours are from 10 am to 6 pm, Thursday to 9 pm (DM10/3, higher during special exhibits).

Galerie der Gegenwart The starkly white cube by Cologne architect Oswald Mathias Ungers, which houses the Kunsthalle's contemporary collection, opened adjacent to the museum's historic digs in 1997. Three floors wrap around a central light court, and between galleries large picture windows allow for great views of the Inner Alster and the city. Paintings by Georg Baselitz, Gerhard Richter, Sigmar Polke and other German artists dominate the 3rd floor, while the 2nd floor showcases installations, photographs, video, sculpture and other media by US artists of the 1980s and 1990s, with names like Jeff Koons and Cindy Sherman represented. More German works are on the 1st floor, while the basement features David Hockney, Claes Oldenburg, Joseph Beuys and other international heavyweights.

Museum für Kunst und Gewerbe The palatial, 19th century neo-Renaissance building at Steintorplatz 1 houses the Museum of Arts & Crafts (☎ 24 86 26 30).

Sculptures, furniture, jewellery, porcelain, musical instruments and even entire period rooms track the evolution of applied art and sculpture in Europe, from its roots in antiquity through to the 20th century. Highlights include an Art Nouveau room from the 1900 Paris World Fair and a Japanese teahouse, where tea ceremonies are held. The museum cafe *Destille* is integrated into the exhibition space. Museum hours are from 10 am to 6 pm, Thursday to 9 pm (DM8/2).

Other Kunstmeile Museums

A few metres south, at Klosterwall 15 and 23, respectively, are the **Kunsthaus** (Art House; ☎ 33 58 03) and the **Kunstverein** (Art Association; ☎ 33 83 44). While the former specialises in works by contemporary Hamburg artists, the latter presents the kind of conceptual and experimental art that makes most people say 'I can do *that*'. Behind the Kunstverein, accessed via a shiny aluminium drum, is the **Akademie der Künste** (Academy of Arts; ☎ 32 46 32), another venue for latter-day works.

Just south of here, at Deichtorstrasse 1-2, are the **Deichtorhallen** (☎ 32 10 30), former market halls that have been turned into dramatic exhibition spaces by Berlin architect Josef Paul Kleihues. Shown here are international touring exhibitions of contemporary art – Warhol, Lichtenstein, Haring, etc – as well as photography by Helmut Newton, Annie Leibowitz and other prominent shooters.

All museums are open from 11 am to 6 pm, and the Kunsthaus and Kunstverein are open to 9 pm on Thursday. Admission depends on the exhibit.

OTHER MUSEUMS
Museum der Arbeit

The Museum of Work (☎ 29 84 23 64) is on the grounds of the former New York-Hamburg Rubber Company at Maurienstrasse 19, in the north-eastern suburb of Barmbek (U2/U3/S1 to Barmbek). As its name suggests, the museum chronicles the development of the workplace in the Hamburg area, with a particular focus on the changing rights and roles of working men

and women. There's also an interesting section on the art of printing through the ages. Hours are Monday from 1 to 9 pm, Tuesday to Saturday from 10 am to 5 pm, and Sunday from 10 am to 6 pm (DM6/3, Friday half price).

Museum für Völkerkunde

The impressive Museum of Ethnology (☎ 428 48 25 24) at Rothenbaumchaussee 64 (U1 to Hallerstrasse) has exhibits from around the world, including ivory carvings from the kingdom of Benin and a complete, intricately carved Maori meeting hall. Hours are from 10 am to 6 pm, Thursday to 9 pm (DM6/2, Friday half price).

ST PAULI WALKING TOUR

The Reeperbahn is St Pauli's main artery, and getting off at the Reeperbahn S-Bahn station plunges you right into the heart of this legendary red-light district. A few steps from the station, on Reeperbahn itself, is the **Erotic Art Museum** (☎ 317 84 10), which showcases erotic art – soft porn to S&M – from the 16th century to the present, including Japanese wood prints, etchings, sculptures, and paintings from Henry Miller, Jean Cocteau, Eugene Delacroix and other artists. Hours are daily from 10 am to midnight, and Friday and Saturday to 1 am (DM15/10).

Just north of the station is the **Grosse Freiheit** (literally 'Great Freedom') street, with its bright lights, dark doorways and live sex nightclubs. Smarmy doormen try to lure the passing crowd into places like Tabu and Safari. If you're interested, be aware of the costs before entering. Admission tends to be fairly low (DM5 or DM10), but it's the mandatory drink minimum (usually around DM40) that drives up the cost.

The Star Club, forever associated with the Beatles (see the boxed text 'The Beatles in Hamburg – Forever' later in this chapter), once stood at Grosse Freiheit 39 but closed in 1969 and burned down later. The Fab Four also played in the basement of the Kaiserkeller, Grosse Freiheit 36, and this one still exists.

HAMBURG

The Renaissance of St Pauli

The character of St Pauli and its main artery, the Reeperbahn, is unique. Where else will you find live sex shows, a wax museum filled with stiff Germans and a mediocre musical by an English knight – all on the same street?

On a good night there may be as many as 30,000 people cruising the rip-roaring collection of bars, sex clubs, variety acts, restaurants, pubs and cafes known collectively by locals as the 'Kiez'. It is, of course, ironic that Paul, for whom Hamburg's 'sin centre' is named, was in fact a saint who did not take kindly to lust.

St Pauli's popularity reached its zenith in the liberated 1960s when the Beatles cut their musical teeth at the legendary – and sadly defunct – Star Club. Prostitution boomed along the lurid, spidery streets spilling off the Reeperbahn. But then a wave of hard crime and drugs sent St Pauli on a downward spiral, and rip-offs were commonplace (eg serving cheap wine from expensive bottles). Germany's Sündenmeile (Sin Mile) had to reinvent itself to survive – which it did.

These days another layer of attractions has usurped the tired red-light activity as the No 1 draw for tourists. The musical *Cats* has been playing to sold-out houses since 1986. Stylish nightclubs keep a hip, moneyed clientele entertained until dawn, and there are surprisingly good restaurants, bars and clubs.

The sex industry is still in full swing but it has lost some of its rougher edges: pimps no longer loiter and leer. Rather, they've been seen to lower – via pulleys – a bracing flagon of whisky to their hard-working girls in the street. The place has a feeling of calamity infused with a weird gentility.

Back on the Reeperbahn, head east past a jumble of sex shops, peep shows and questionable hotels, then cross the street where, on the corner with Davidstrasse, stands the **Davidwache** (1914). This dignified brick building, festooned with ornate ceramic tiles, is the home base for 150 police who ensure that St Pauli has a reputation for being the safest area in Hamburg.

Continue south on Davidstrasse where, after 50m, you'll see a metal wall on the right barring views into **Herbertstrasse**, a block-long bordello that's off-limits to men under 18 and women of all ages.

For tamer titillation turn right on Bernard-Nocht-Strasse for the **priv*art*museum** (☎ 317 47 57) at No 69. A branch of the Erotic Art Museum, it features changing exhibits with works of contemporary artists (same hours and admission as the Erotic Art Museum; combination ticket is DM20). A bit east at No 89-91 you'll find **Harry's Hamburger Hafenbasar**, the life work of Harry Rosenberg, a bearded character known to seamen

worldwide. For decades Harry has been buying trinkets and souvenirs from world travellers. The result is a shop crammed with oddities including Zulu drums, Indonesian masks and fertility sculptures. The admission price of DM4 is refunded with a minimum purchase of DM10, though it is hard to find anything costing less than DM50.

Turn left on Zirkusweg, then take Zum Trichter to Spielbudenplatz, the place to go for St Pauli's more 'respectable' entertainment. This is where *Cats* plays at the Operettenhaus and where a number of cafes and cabarets are (see Entertainment). At No 3 is the **Panoptikum** (☎ 31 03 17), a fancy name for wax museum, where models of prominent Germans from the arts, history and politics are on display. It's open weekdays from 11 am to 9 pm, Saturday to midnight and Sunday from 10 am to 9 pm. It's closed from mid-January to early February (DM7/4).

At Spielbudenplatz 18 is the **Condomerie**, with its extensive collection of amusing sex toys and protection devices. The shop owner offers DM100 to any gentleman who can properly wear the gargantuan condom shown in the window. They say the prize money has been awarded twice. Lucky devils.

PORT OF HAMBURG

St Pauli is fronted to the south by the port of Hamburg, one of the largest in Europe. Each year about 12,000 ships deliver and take on some 70 million tonnes of goods. The area is 75 sq km, accounting for 12% of Hamburg's entire surface area. An excellent way to experience this vast port is by taking a harbour cruise (see Boating & Cruises). For a panoramic view of the frenetic shipping activity, walk up the steps above the St Pauli

Landungsbrücken U/S-Bahn stop to the Stintfang stone balcony.

Below lies the **Rickmer Rickmers** (☎ 319 59 59), a three-masted steel windjammer from 1896 that is now a museum ship (DM6/4) and restaurant. Moored at the Überseebrücke (Overseas Pier) is the 160m-long behemoth, **Cap San Diego** (☎ 36 42 09), a 10,000 tonne freighter built in Hamburg and launched in 1962 (DM6/2).

Just west of the St Pauli landing stages stands a sturdy grey structure topped by a giant copper cupola. It marks the entrance to the **St Pauli Elbtunnel** (1911), a 426m-long passageway beneath the Elbe River. It is still in use, although most cars now use

Hamburg's Unique Fish Market

Every Sunday morning, in the wee hours, an unusual ritual unfolds along the banks of the Elbe, just a few hundred metres south of the Reeperbahn. A fleet of small trucks roars onto the cobbled pavement. Hardy types with hands the size of baseball gloves emerge from the driver's cabin and set out to turn their vehicles into stores on wheels. They artfully arrange their bananas, apples, cauliflower and whatever else the earth has yielded that week. Others pile up slippery eels, smoked fish fillets and fresh shrimp in tasteful displays. In another corner, cacti, flowers and leafy plants begin to wait for customers. It's not yet 5 am as the first of them begin to trundle in, their brains boozy, their eyes red, their moods hyper from a night of partying in St Pauli. May the trading begin.

The Fischmarkt in St Pauli has been a Hamburg institution since 1703 and still defines the city's life and spirit. Locals of every age and walk of life join curious tourists as the beer flows and you can buy everything from cheap sweatshirts and tulips to a hearty breakfast or a scorched Bratwurst.

The undisputed stars of the event – and great, free entertainment – are the boisterous *Marktschreier* (market criers) who hawk their wares at the top of their lungs. With lascivious winks and leering innuendo, characters like Aal-Dieter or Banana-Harry boast of the quality and size of their product. 'Don't be shy, little girl,' they might say to a rotund 60 year old, wagging a piece of eel in front of her face. But nobody minds the vulgar come-ons. Almost always, the 'girl' blushes before taking a hearty bite as the crowd cheers her on. It's all just part of the show.

More entertainment takes place in the adjoining Fischauktionshalle (Fish Auction Hall), where a live band cranks out cover versions of ancient German pop songs for which everyone seems to know the words. Down in the pit, the beer flows and sausage fumes waft through the air as if it were 8 pm and not just past dawn. For those who actually know what time it is, breakfast is served on the gallery, away from the crooners.

Hamburg life thrives here – at the edge of the river – in the good stink of mud and oil and fish. If Bruegel were to paint a picture of Hamburg life, this is where he'd set up his easel.

The Fischmarkt takes place Sunday mornings from 5 to 10 am (and from 7 am between October and March).

HAMBURG

the New Elbe Tunnel farther west. Cars and pedestrians descend some 20m in a lift, make their way through the tiled tube, then ride back up on the other end. The view back across the Elbe at the port and the city skyline is interesting (turn left as you exit).

SCHANZENVIERTEL & KAROLINENVIERTEL

North of St Pauli, the Schanzenviertel and Karolinenviertel are the home base of Hamburg's countercultural scene and the city's liveliest, youngest and most multiethnic quarters. Immigrants, students, workers and left-wing radicals inhabit rows of tall apartment buildings with ornate facades that have certainly seen better days. Turkish grocers display their produce streetside in artful pyramids, and there's no shortage of pubs, cafes and restaurants with character and decent prices.

The heart of the Karolinenviertel extends north of the Feldstrasse U-Bahn station along Marktstrasse, Ölmühle, Turmstrasse and Glasshüttenstrasse. An artistic vibe permeates this quarter, evident not only in the abundance of colourful wall-sized murals but also in the many small studios, often tucked away in building basements. Everything from jewellery to handmade wooden picture frames, from fetish clothing to funky clubwear is being made on the spot. Thrown into the mix are second-hand stores and happening bars.

A tad less edgy, the Schanzenviertel ensues north-west of here, just beyond Neuer Pferdemarkt. Its main artery is Schulterblatt where you can't miss the graffiti-covered building that looks one step away from demolition. This is the **Rote Flora**, now an alternative culture centre, but once the famous Flora Theatre. Plans to make this historic venue into a musical theatre were thwarted by a neighbourhood alliance that feared that an influx of theatregoers and tourists would lead to an undesired beautification of the quarter. Susannenstrasse is another lively street, but avoid Sternschanzenpark, a major stomping ground of drug dealers and junkies.

TV Tower

Properly known as Heinrich-Hertz-Turm, Hamburg's sleek TV Tower on Lagerstrasse looks down at the city from a height of 280m. The viewing platform, reached by a lift (DM6.50/4), and revolving restaurant, are at 132m. For a real scream (partly caused by having to part with DM250 to do so) you can leap from here in summer ... attached to a bungee rope, of course.

ALTONA

Just west of St Pauli, Altona is one of Hamburg's most delightful quarters and has become a fashionable place to live for young professionals and families. Lots of cool bars, restaurants, shops and markets have sprung up in this neighbourhood, which has a small-town feel quite distinct from the rest of Hamburg. And for good reason.

From 1640 to 1867, Altona was in fact separate city that belonged to Denmark, then to Prussia and only became part of Hamburg in 1937. A long-standing rivalry between the two peaked in 1800 when Altona's merchant fleet was actually larger than Hamburg's.

The **Stuhlmann fountain**, which you'll see when you turn south from the eastern exit of Altona train station, symbolises this age-old struggle for local supremacy. Just beyond lies the **Platz der Republik**, a rectangular park where locals congregate to play *boules* (bowls). Museumstrasse runs along its western side, and at No 23 is the **Altona Museum/North German State Museum** (☎ 380 75 14), with a focus on art and cultural history. Exhibits include exquisite ship models, harpoons, scrimshaw and other nautical memorabilia. An entire room is filled with an impressive display of bowsprits. The museum restaurant is inside an authentic 19th century farmhouse. Hours are from 10 am to 6 pm, closed Monday (DM8/2).

At the southern end of the park looms the stately **Altona Rathaus** (1898), a white neoclassical affair whose southern wing was once the foyer of the city's first train station. Immediately in front is the equestrian **Kaiser**

ALTONA

OTTENSEN

1 Fabrik
2 Zeisehallen, Eisenstein, Filmhauskneipe
3 Aurel
4 Chez Alfred
5 Blaues Haus
6 Mercado
7 Waschsalon
8 Stuhlmann Fountain
9 Altona Museum/North German State Museum
10 Altona Rathaus

Wilhelm I monument (1896). South of the Rathaus is the **Palmaille**, a beautiful boulevard lined with linden trees and elegant, neoclassical merchant houses built between 1790 and 1825; don't miss Nos 49 and 116. The name 'Palmaille', by the way, derives from the Italian *palla* for 'ball' and *maglio* for 'bat' and refers back to the street's intended (but never realised) use in the 17th century as a playing field. Farther west, Palmaille turns into Elbchaussee, one of Germany's grandest thoroughfares, lined by immense mansions with park-sized gardens.

The true character of Altona, though, is best sampled by heading west out of the train station along the pedestrianised Ottenser Hauptstrasse (this part of Altona is properly called Ottensen). Turn right onto Bahrenfelder Strasse, which runs into Friedensallee. This is where you'll find the **Zeisehallen**, a former propeller factory

that's been successfully converted into a shopping, entertainment and restaurant complex (see Places to Eat).

ÖVELGÖNNE & BLANKENESE
The people of Hamburg say that the better you're doing in life, the farther west in the city you live. Those who reside in Övelgönne are making it; those in Blankenese have arrived. Övelgönne was once home to captains who plied their trade on the Elbe River and North Sea. Its riverside walkway – past immaculate old homes and beneath a canopy of stately trees – is among the prettiest in Hamburg. At the **Museumshafen Övelgönne** (☎ 390 0079) on the Neumühlen ferry landing, some 20 working and fishing vessels dating from the 1890s to 1930s bob lazily in the water. All found as wrecks, they've been restored to shipshape condition (placards on the pier provide background on each).

Blankenese, a former fishing village and haven for cutthroats, now boasts some of the most expensive property in Germany. The labyrinthine, narrow streets with clusters of fine houses are best explored on foot via a network of 58 stairways with 4846 steps. For great views of the Elbe, (nearly 3km wide here) and the container ships putting out to sea, head to the top of the 75m-high Süllberg hill.

A clutch of restaurants and cafes is on Strandweg at Blankenese Landungsbrücke. The tiny bus No 48 – nicknamed the 'Mountain Goat' because of the steep, narrow alleys it has to navigate – shuttles between the hilltop town centre and the Elbe shores.

To get to Övelgönne by public transport, take bus No 112 from the Hauptbahnhof. To get to Blankenese, take the S1.

BOATING
Boating is a fine way to take in Hamburg's maritime charm. If you want to navigate under your own steam, you'll find sailing, rowing or pedal boats for hire all along the Alster Lakes. Prices start at DM13 per hour, plus DM2 per person. Also see Cruises under Organised Tours.

CYCLING

Hamburg is flat, so cycling is an excellent way to explore the city and the surrounding countryside. The paved path around the Outer Alster is a popular route (also good for walking or inline-skating), while another takes you along the Elbe Banks from St Pauli to Blankenese and Wedel past gorgeous homes and forests (20km each way).

The excellent *Fahrradtourenkarte für Hamburg*, available at Dr Götze Land und Karte (see Bookshops), contains more ideas and itineraries. If you want to rent a bike, try Fahrradladen St Georg, Schmilinskystrasse 6 in St Georg, or Fahrrad Richter at Barmbeker Strasse 16 in Winterhude. Both charge DM15 a day and require a DM100 deposit.

ORGANISED TOURS

If this is your first visit to Hamburg, you might consider taking a guided bus tour to gain an overview of the city layout as well as the major sights. Tours are operated by several companies, including those listed here. For more options, check with the tourist office.

Top Tour Hamburg is a standard 1¾ hour city sightseeing tour leaving daily every 15 minutes from 9.30 am to 4:45 pm (in winter from 11 am to 3 pm) from the Kirchenallee exit of the Hauptbahnhof or from St Pauli Landungsbrücken. It costs DM22, children under 14 pay DM13, and you can add a port cruise for an extra DM11.

For greater flexibility, board one of the red double-decker buses, which run tours eight times daily from April through September (less the rest of the year). Departing from Pier 1 at St Pauli Landungsbrücken, this tour allows you to get off and back on at or near the major sights (DM25, children under 12 are free).

An unashamedly touristy yet quite atmospheric way to travel is on the Hummelbahn trolley from the 1920s. Tours run hourly from 10 am to 5 pm between April and October, and three times daily throughout the rest of the year (DM25, children under 12 are free).

Cruises

Alster Cruises Alster-Touristik (☎ 357 42 40) runs several tours and ferries from its landing dock at Jungfernstieg between April and October. Kids under 16 pay half price.

Options include the 50 minute Alster Tour, which covers both the Inner and the Outer Alster lakes (DM16); the idyllic two hour Canal Tour, which floats past stately villas and gorgeous gardens (DM22); and the Waterway Tour of the Fleet canals, which takes you from the Alster to the Elbe and the historic Speicherstadt, via a couple of locks, in two hours (DM25). Free English-language pamphlets and tapes with a description of the sights are available for the Alster Tour and the Waterway Tour.

Hourly ferries call at nine stops on the Outer Alster and the river itself (DM1.60 per stop or DM13 for the entire trip).

Port Cruises Most Elbe cruises and ferries are operated by HADAG (☎ 311 70 70) between April and early October. Boats depart from St Pauli Landungsbrücken, usually from Pier 2. Kids up to age 16 pay half price.

The ferry service down the Elbe to Övelgönne takes 15 minutes (DM2.70 one way), to Blankenese it's 40 minutes (DM8). HADAG also offers a one hour steamer tour (DM15), including one with English commentary at 11.15 am.

Other cruise options include tours on funky wooden boats, called *Barkassen*, which are small enough to travel through the canals of the Speicherstadt (about DM20). For details, check with the various operators on the piers at St Pauli Landungsbrücken.

SPECIAL EVENTS

Hamburg has a busy year-round calendar of festivals, fairs, concerts and parties. Among the major ones is the **Hamburger Dom**, one of Europe's largest and oldest (1329) fun fairs, held on Heiligengeistfeld, a vast field between St Pauli and Schanzenviertel. Run in late March, late July and late November, it attracts up to 10 million visitors a year. Another big festival is the **Hafengeburtstag** (harbour birthday), a wild party ashore and in the water. It commemorates the day in 1189 when Emperor Barbarossa granted Hamburg customs exemption in the lower Elbe area, and runs for five days, beginning on 7 May.

PLACES TO STAY

Hamburg offers the entire range of accommodation, from 'fleabag' to frivolous, but true bargains are definitely rare. St Georg, the quarter east of the Hauptbahnhof, has many of the cheaper hotels, but these include several *Stundenhotels* that rent rooms 'by the hour' to prostitutes and their clients. Places listed below, or in the hotel brochure available at the tourist offices, are safe choices. You can also book a room through the tourist offices or by calling the Hamburg Hotline (☎ 30 05 13 00; DM6 per reservation). Except where noted, prices listed below include breakfast.

PLACES TO STAY – BUDGET

Camping and staying at a hostel are the only true budget choices in Hamburg. Stays in a somewhat central hotel or pension will cost at least DM60/100 for singles/doubles for a no-frills room with shared bath in a non-too-spiffy establishment.

Camping

Camping Buchholz (☎ 540 45 32, *Kieler Strasse 374*), in the suburb of Stellingen, is open year round and is a 10 minute walk from U-Bahn Hagenbecks Tierpark (U2). You can also take bus No 183 from Altona train station, which runs down Kieler Strasse. Tent sites cost from DM12.50 to DM18.50, plus DM7 per person. Warm showers are DM1.50. Sleeping in your car costs DM10.50, plus DM7 per person.

The newish *Camping Schnelsen Nord* (☎ 559 42 25, *Wunderbrunnen 2*) is open April to October and costs DM12.50 to DM13.50 per tent site, DM7 per person and DM4.50 per car. From the Hauptbahnhof take the U2 to Niendorf Markt, then bus No 291 (direction: Schnelsen Nord) to the Dornrösschenweg stop. From there it's 10 minutes on foot (follow the signs).

Campingplatz Blankenese (☎ 81 29 49, *Falkensteiner Ufer*), on the Elbe banks, is open from March to October and charges DM8 to DM20 per tent site, plus DM6 per person (children under 16 are DM3.50). Take the S1 to Blankenese, then bus No 189 (direction: Wedel) to Tindtsthaler Weg; then it's a 10 minute walk down to the shore.

DJH Hostels

Hamburg's two DJH hostels are large but often fill up with school groups. Reservations are always recommended, especially between June and September. *DJH Auf dem Stintfang* (☎ 31 34 88, *fax 31 54 07, email jh-stintfang@t-online.de, Alfred Wegener Weg 5*) has a great location above the St Pauli Landungsbrücken with superb views of the Elbe and the harbour. There's room for 336 in two to six-bed dorms, though staff will let you flop on a mattress in the common area or refer you to an inexpensive hotel if all beds are full. The place is closed for cleaning between 9.30 and 11.30 am. Rates depend on room size, and range from DM27 to DM35 for juniors and DM32 to DM40 for seniors, including breakfast and sheets. Hot and cold meals are available.

Somewhat less central is the *DJH Horner Rennbahn* (☎ 651 16 71, *fax 655 65 16, email jgh-hamburg@t-online.de, Rennbahn-strasse 100*). It's a modern 271 bed facility charging DM31.50/37 for juniors/seniors in six-bed dorms and DM5 more in twin rooms. There's a DM2.50 discount per day for stays of three nights and longer, but this only applies to advance bookings. Prices include buffet breakfast and sheets. Take the U3 to Horner Rennbahn, then walk 10 minutes north past the racecourse and leisure centre.

Independent Hostels

A couple of excellent hostels have opened in the happening Schanzenviertel. The *Schanzenstern* (☎ 439 84 41, *fax 439 34 13, Bartelsstrasse 12*), in a former Mont Blanc pen factory, has beds in sparse but clean dorms for DM33. Singles/doubles/triples/quads cost DM60/90/110/140. The

HAMBURG

breakfast buffet (DM11) is served in an adjoining cafe, where there is also a menu of healthy dishes at reasonable prices.

A recent addition to Hamburg's hostel scene is the *InstantSleep Backpacker Hostel* (☎ 43 18 23 10, fax 43 18 23 11, email backpackerhostel@instantsleep.de, Max-Brauer-Allee 277). Take U3/S3/S21 to Sternschanze, then a five minute walk. Amenities include cooking, washing and drying, and Internet, phone and fax. There's a communal area with TV and video, women-only bedrooms and no curfew. Bunks in eight or ten-bed dorms are DM29, DM33 in four or five-bed dorms, DM35 in triples, and DM38 in doubles. Singles are DM45. There's a one-time DM3 sheet fee.

Guesthouses

A good option for self-caterers is the *Gästehaus der Universität* (☎ 414 00 60, fax 41 40 06 22, Rothenbaumchaussee 34), which has 47 apartments for one and two persons with kitchenette, private bath, phone and TV. Rates are DM116/174 and drop to DM93/128 after five nights.

Pension Uhrlaub (☎ 280 26 34, Lange Reihe 63) in St Georg is above a bistro/pub and has apartments with kitchenette, bath and TV for just DM80/90 a single/double.

Private Rooms & Long-Term Rentals

For short-term stays, private rooms don't offer much of a saving over budget hotels. Most are in a flat shared by a group, often students. Expect to pay about DM60/120 for singles/doubles, inclusive of commission and tax. Long-term room rentals should run from DM500 to DM800 per month. Furnished apartments start at DM800, plus about 25% commission and 16% tax.

Agencies worth trying are: *Agentur am Fischmarkt* (☎ 317 27 13, fax 317 27 34, Bernstorffstrasse 14); *Bed & Breakfast* (☎ 491 56 66, fax 491 42 12, Methfesselstrasse 49); the *Hanseatische Zimmervermittlungs-Agentur* (☎/fax 655 56 00, Rhiemsweg 35); and *HomeCompany* (☎ 194 45, fax 43 13 57 50, Schulterblatt 112).

Hotels & Pensions

If you don't mind the seediness of St Georg, you'll find a few budget hotels here. Cheapest of the bunch is the *Hotel-Pension Annenhof* (☎ 24 34 26, fax 24 55 69, Lange Reihe 23), which charges DM56/98 for singles/doubles with shared bath and WC (toilet). *Hotel-Pension Kieler Hof* (☎ 24 30 24, fax 24 60 18, Bremer Reihe 15) has basic rooms for DM60/100 and some with shower for DM70/110. Triples are DM165.

Hotel St Georg (☎ 24 11 41, fax 280 33 70, Kirchenallee 23) has low-frills rooms from DM65/95 and some with showers (but no private toilet) for DM110/140. Phones, TV and in-room safe are available.

Hotel Sternschanze (☎ 43 33 89, fax 430 51 65, Schanzenstrasse 101) is in the Schanzenviertel, close to the S-Bahn station and has 20 rooms over several floors with TV but shared baths. Rates are decent at DM60/94.

In the Universitätsviertel, options include *Hotel-Pension Preuss* (☎ 44 57 16, fax 44 28 16, Moorweidenstrasse 34) in the Dammtorpalais, a huge brick building containing several hotels (also see Places to Stay – Mid-Range). Tasteful but rudimentary rooms start at DM80/120 and climb to DM110/150 for rooms with private facilities. Triples cost DM180. *Hotel-Pension Elite* (☎/fax 45 46 27, Binderstrasse 24) has reasonable prices with rooms costing DM90/110, including shower.

PLACES TO STAY – MID-RANGE

Hamburg has some medium-priced hotels and pensions that offer fairly good value. Many take up entire floors of a sprawling building or are upstairs from shops or restaurants. Often you must ring to enter. Expect to pay from DM85 to DM130 for doubles with shared facilities. Those with private bath cost around DM140/200.

St Georg

Located in a pleasant part of St Georg is the 11 room *Steen's Hotel* (☎ 24 46 42, fax 280 35 93, Holzdamm 43), which has

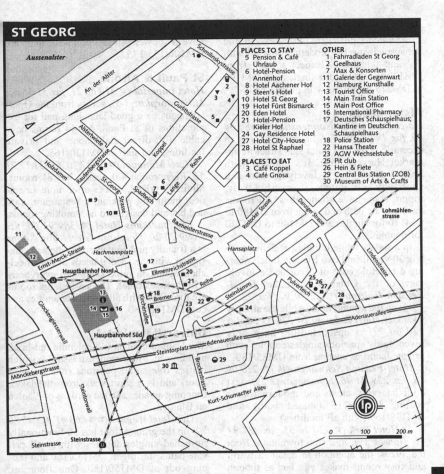

ST GEORG

Aussenalster

An der Alster

Schmilinskystrasse

Gurlittstrasse

Alsterwiete

Holzdamm

Rautenbergstrasse

St-Georg

Koppel

Spadteich

Lange

Reihe

Baumeisterstrasse

Rostocker Strasse

Danziger Strasse

Lohmühlen-strasse

Lindenstrasse

Hachmannplatz

Hansaplatz

Ernst-Merck-Strasse

Hauptbahnhof Nord

Ellmenreichstrasse

Reihe

Steindamm

Pulverteich

Adenauerallee

Glockengiesserwall

Kirchenallee

Bremer

Hauptbahnhof Süd

Steintorplatz

Adenauerallee

Mönckebergstrasse

Brockesstrasse

Kurt-Schumacher-Allee

Steintorwall

Steinstrasse

Steinstrasse

0   100   200 m

PLACES TO STAY	OTHER
5 Pension & Café Uhrlaub	1 Fahrradladen St Georg
6 Hotel-Pension Annenhof	2 Geelhaus
8 Hotel Aachener Hof	7 Max & Konsorten
9 Steen's Hotel	11 Galerie der Gegenwart
10 Hotel St Georg	12 Hamburg Kunsthalle
19 Hotel Fürst Bismarck	13 Tourist Office
20 Eden Hotel	14 Main Train Station
21 Hotel-Pension Kieler Hof	15 Main Post Office
24 Gay Residence Hotel	16 International Pharmacy
27 Hotel City-House	17 Deutsches Schauspielhaus; Kantine im Deutschen Schauspielhaus
28 Hotel St Raphael	18 Police Station
	22 Hansa Theater
PLACES TO EAT	23 AGW Wechselstube
3 Café Koppel	25 Pit club
4 Café Gnosa	26 Hein & Fiete
	29 Central Bus Station (ZOB)
	30 Museum of Arts & Crafts

singles/doubles/triples with showers from DM90/130/180. Amenities include minibar, cable TV and hair dryers, and non-smoking rooms are available, too.

Hotel Aachener Hof (☎ 24 14 51, fax 280 25 10, St-Georg-Strasse 10), in the same general area, has a few singles/doubles with shared facilities for DM68/110, though it charges twice that much for more pleasant and modern rooms. All have direct phones and TV, and there's a restaurant and bar on the premises.

The *Hotel City-House* (☎ 280 38 50, fax 280 18 38, Pulverteich 25) occupies a restored townhouse on a quiet side street. Single rooms with private bath go for DM138 to DM158, while doubles are DM178 to DM198.

Conveniently located at the Hauptbahnhof, *Hotel Fürst Bismarck* (☎ 280 10 91, fax 280 10 96, Kirchenallee 49) has 130 nicely appointed singles/doubles with private bath costing DM130/198. Rates drop DM20 in July and August.

euro currency converter DM1 = €0.51

HAMBURG

The *Eden Hotel (☎ 24 84 80, fax 24 15 21, Ellmenreichstrasse 20)*, next to the Schauspielhaus, has modern rooms, all with TV and telephone. Expect to pay from DM130 to DM170 for singles and DM190 to DM225 for rooms with private bath.

Alster Lakes

Hotel-Pension Am Nonnenstieg (☎ 480 64 90, fax 48 06 49 49, Nonnenstieg 11) is an eccentric place in a quiet side street in upmarket Harvestehude. It's jammed with knick-knacks, has a lovely garden and cheerfully decorated, if overly frilly, rooms; some have kitchenettes. All rooms have private bath and range from DM80 to DM150 for singles and DM140 to DM220 for doubles.

In a stately white building at Schwanenwik 30 you'll find two friendly hotels sharing a tasteful sense of decor and a lovely view of the Outer Alster Lake. *Hotel-Pension Waltraut (☎ 22 10 07, fax 22 28 73)* is on the ground floor, while the slightly swankier *Hotel Belmont (☎ 220 51 28, fax 220 80 77)* is upstairs. Both have only seven, fairly spacious singles/doubles with private facilities costing from DM85/130.

Hotel-Pension Schwanenwik (☎ 220 09 18, fax 229 04 46, Schwanenwik 29) next door has very clean and modern rooms costing DM85/115 (shared bath) and DM139/169 (with all facilities).

At *Hotel York (☎ 220 26 53, fax 227 31 19, Hofweg 19)*, in a slim townhouse from the 1920s, the attention to detail in warm and cosy rooms makes you feel as though you're a guest in a private home. Rates are DM135 to DM155 for singles and DM200 to DM250 doubles, all with private bath.

Frauenhotel Hanseatin (☎ 34 13 45, fax 34 58 25, Dragonerstall 11), which caters for women only, is a tranquil place on a busy street near the Musikhalle. Rates start at DM110/180 for singles/doubles and zoom as high as DM170/220, which buys amenities like direct phones, TV and room service.

Hotel-Pension Bei der Esplanade (☎ 34 29 61, fax 35 40 82, Colonnaden 45, 2nd floor) is near the opera and Jungfernstieg.

Rooms, some quite large, are modern and have a shower. Singles/doubles/triples are DM100/135/175.

St Pauli & Altona

Hotel Imperial (☎ 319 60 21, fax 31 56 85, Millerntorplatz 3-5), across from the Operettenhaus, is a good launching pad for explorations of St Pauli. All 44 rooms have cable TV, direct-dial phone and private facilities, and start at DM130/165.

Hotel Monopol (☎ 31 17 70, fax 31 17 71 51, Reeperbahn 48) nearby has 81 rooms. Similarly priced, it does offer more amenities, including parking, a restaurant, cafe and bar and designated nonsmoking rooms.

The *Stadthaus-Hotel (☎ 389 92 00, fax 38 99 20 20, Holstenstrasse 118)* in Altona is a friendly and contemporary hostelry designed with the special needs of the wheelchair-bound in mind (although everybody will feel welcome). The seven large rooms are furnished with all modern amenities and cost DM130/180.

Universitätsviertel

The Dammtorpalais is a splendid red-brick building at Moorweidenstrasse 34 which houses five small pensions (one on each floor) and is a short walk from the lakes, shopping arcades and the gardens of Planten un Blomen.

The *Hotel Wagner (☎ 44 63 41, fax 45 70 79)* on the ground floor has 50 functionally furnished singles/doubles with small private baths starting at DM135/160 and topping out at DM150/180. One floor up, *Hotel Amsterdam (☎ 441 11 10, fax 45 68 20)* has cheery public areas and 35 plain but clean and light-flooded rooms with shower and WC for DM149/194.

On the 3rd floor is the friendly, family-run *Hotel Fresena (☎ 410 48 92, fax 45 66 89)*, where rooms with private facilities cost DM150/190. Furnishings are tasteful if simple, and it has a welcoming feel to it. Up on the 4th floor, the *Hotel Bellmoor (☎ 413 31 10, fax 41 33 11 41)* has rooms with full bath and cable TV for DM150/185. Kids under eight years old stay free.

PLACES TO STAY – TOP END

In St Pauli, the urge to splurge is well directed towards the *Hotel Hafen (☎ 31 11 36 00, fax 31 11 37 51, Seewartenstrasse 9)*, a 19th century former home for retired seamen. It's often invaded by the coach crowds, but the public areas reflect an understated nautical theme and the 240 traditionally furnished singles/doubles (many with harbour views) cost from DM183/206.

The business-style *Hotel St Raphael (☎ 24 82 00, fax 24 82 03 33, Adenauerallee 41)*, a Best Western property, is in a relatively sedate part of St Georg. The staff are friendly and accommodating, and the modern rooms have all the creature comforts. Singles start at DM198 and doubles at DM248.

For the quintessential Hamburg hotel – stylish, discreet, quiet and often filled with celebrities – try to get a room at the *Hotel Hanseatic (☎ 48 57 72, fax 48 57 73, Sierichstrasse 150)* in the elegant Winterhude area. Each spacious room reflects the personal touch and attention to detail of the proprietors; they even make their own marmalade. A stay here is sure to be memorable, but so is the price tag of DM230/310.

Hotel Vier Jahreszeiten (☎ 349 40, fax 349 46 02, Neuer Jungfernstieg 9-14), a palatial edifice looming over the western shore of the Outer Alster Lake, is another haunt of the moneyed crowd. Rooms start at a gasping DM432/570 and spiral to DM562/700. At least they throw in breakfast for free.

PLACES TO EAT

As you would expect of a city that has, through its port, been a gateway to the world for centuries, the selection of restaurants is international indeed. Whether you fancy pizza or sushi, chateaubriand or tacos, you'll find it here – including, of course, these typical Hamburg dishes: *Aalsuppe* (eel soup), a sweet and sour soup made with dried fruit, ham, vegetables, lots of herbs and, yes, even some eel; *Labskaus*, consisting of boiled marinated beef put through the grinder with red beets and mashed potatoes and served with a fried egg, herring and pickles; and *Birnen mit Bohnen und Speck*, which is pears, beans and bacon, all cooked in one pot to allow the different flavours to mingle. (It all tastes better than it sounds.)

City Centre

Saalbach (☎ 33 55 26, Steinstrasse 19) is a trendy self-service eatery (lunch only) with a salad bar and main dishes priced around DM10. You pay about the same to eat in the company of actors at the basement *Kantine im Deutschen Schauspielhaus*, the theatre cafeteria at Kirchenallee 39 (weekday lunch only).

Weinhexe (☎ 33 75 61, Burchardstrasse 13c) in the 'bow' of the Chile Haus, is popular with business and media types. Stylish and cosy, it offers an opulent antipasto selection and daily specials starting at DM20 weekdays from 11 am to 8.30 pm only.

The *Old Commercial Room (☎ 36 63 19, Englische Planke 10)*, adjacent to the Michaeliskirche, is one of the city's best places for Hanseatic fare. Solid mahogany furniture and sparkling brass fixtures contribute to the maritime ambience that's been enjoyed by a roster of celebrities from Jon Bon Jovi to Lou Reed. Expensive.

St Pauli & Port Area

The small quarter just east of St Pauli Landungsbrücken U/S-Bahn station is where about a dozen earthy Portuguese restaurants have set up shop. One of the best is *Sagres (☎ 37 12 01, Vorsetzen 42)*, a snug spot brimming with maritime decor and always packed to the gills. The menu includes every type of fish caught that day, many under DM20. If it's full, try the more upmarket *O Pescador (☎ 319 30 00)*, on the corner of Reimarus and Dietmar-Koel-Strasse.

Phuket (☎ 31 58 54, Davidstrasse 31), practically across from the entrance to the Herbertstrasse bordello, is a popular traditional Thai restaurant with main dishes around DM25. It's open for dinner only.

The stylish *Weite Welt (☎ 319 12 14, Grosse Freiheit 70)* is in a quiet backyard with a small Japanese-style garden on the tame end of this raucous street. It serves

HAMBURG

world cuisine with a Californian touch (eg Caesar salad, nachos, pesto), with mains starting at DM16.50. Dinner only.

Schanzenviertel
This quarter is perfect for foodies on a budget. For delicious Mediterranean fishy fare, head to *La Sepia* (☎ *432 24 84, Schulterblatt 36)*. Dining takes place at long, communal wooden tables with candle light. *Noodle's* (☎ *439 28 40, Schanzenstrasse 2)* specialises in pasta, though the salads are good, too. Almost everything is DM10 or less.

Pan-Asian (Thai, Korean and Japanese) food is on the menu at *bok*, with several locations. For takeaway or stand-up eating, head to the *Imbiss* version (☎ *430 30 96, Bartelsstrasse 9)*, while sit-down dinners are served at the branch at Schanzenstrasse 27 (☎ *430 67 80)*. *Shikara* (☎ *430 23 53, Susannenstrasse 20)* is an Indian snack place; *Lokma*, on the corner of Bartelsstrasse and Susannenstrasse, makes Turkish food.

Universitätsviertel
Limerick (☎ *44 78 36, Grindelallee 18)* is a student hang-out with good pizzas, cooked in a beechwood-fired oven, from DM6.50. Ethnic eateries abound here. *Balutschi* (☎ *45 24 79, Grindelallee 33)* is a popular Pakistani haunt with great over-the-top Arabian Nights decor and a huge menu of fragrant dishes. Most are priced under DM20 and there are three dozen vegie choices.

Nearby, *Hindukusch* (☎ *41 81 64, Grindelhof 15)* touts its spicy and exotic Afghani food at very reasonable prices (around DM10). The weekday all-you-can-eat lunch costs just DM11.50. Seating is especially nice in the small garden. For Turkish food, try *Arkadash* (☎ *44 84 71, Grindelhof 17)*, where a main dish plus coffee/tea and desert cost just DM12 during 'Happy Hour' (3 to 6 pm and midnight to 2 am).

Abaton Bistro (☎ *45 77 71, Grindelhof 14a)*, across the street inside the Abaton Kino (see Entertainment), is where students boost their energy with biologically correct food and beverages. The vegetarian rice pan is a speciality.

La Fattoria (☎ *420 02 55, Isestrasse 16)*, a bit north of here, is a hole-in-the-wall gem of an Italian restaurant stuffed with antiques (all for sale). The antipasto bar alone is a feast for the eyes, and only choice ingredients make it into the creative dishes priced at DM20 and up. It's open till 6.30 pm Tuesday to Saturday only (U3 to Hoheluftbrücke). Lunch reservations are a must.

Altona
The hip *Eisenstein* (☎ *390 46 06, Friedensallee 9)*, inside the Zeisehallen, is a postmodern symphony of stone, steel and wood wrapped around the brick chimney of an old ship propeller factory. It's famous for wood-fired pizza, but the salads and fish dishes are good, too.

Slightly less expensive is the adjacent *Filmhauskneipe* (☎ *39 34 67, Friedensallee 9)*, where film executives and an intellectual crowd chow down on dishes with a south German/Italian touch while seated at unpretentious wooden tables.

Chez Alfred (☎ *390 85 69, Grosse Brunnenstrasse 61a)* is a French gourmet restaurant that's also housed in a former factory. Train tracks still run through the outdoor patio, while the interior charms with blue ceilings and surreal canvasses. Figure on DM25 and up for a la carte dishes; a four course meal is around DM60.

Cafes
Home-made breads and cakes are just part of the menu at *Café Koppel* (☎ *24 92 35, Koppel 66)* in St Georg. It's a quiet, non-smoking place with several choices for vegetarians and breakfast from morn' to night.

For a close-up look at Hamburg high society, treat yourself to an afternoon at the *Condi (Neuer Jungfernstieg 9)*, the Biedermeier cafe inside the Vier Jahreszeiten Hotel. Expect to part with DM7 for a cappuccino, and if you're on a tight budget, don't even think about selecting one of the mouthwatering cakes.

The clientele of *Café Absurd* (☎ *317 11 22, Clemens-Schultz-Strasse 86)* in St Pauli changes with the time of day and ranges from grunge types to young families with kids to hipsters. Come for coffee, breakfast or a snack.

In Karolinenviertel, *Café Klatsch* (☎ *439 04 43, Glashüttenstrasse 17*) is an island of calm and the place to come for a chat or to read a magazine.

For details on Café Gnosa and Café Unter den Linden, see Gay & Lesbian.

ENTERTAINMENT

For cultural event and lifestyle information, look for the monthly magazines *Szene* (DM5), *Prinz* (DM5) and *Oxmox* (DM4.30). The *Hamburger* is a free English-language booklet with general and event information, and is usually available at tourist offices and occasionally in bookshops, hotels and pubs. It's not the most reliable or up-to-date source, but it's useful if you don't read German. In the same places you might find the slightly more thorough *Hamburger Vorschau* (in German).

Pubs & Bars

It seems as though you're never more than a five minute walk from a bar or pub in Hamburg. In St Georg, these line up along Lange Reihe and the parallel Koppel. Two candidates are *Geelhaus* (☎ *280 36 60, Koppel 76*), popular with actors from the nearby Deutsches Schauspielhaus; and *Max & Konsorten* (☎ *24 56 17, Spadenteich 7*), sought out by an unpretentious and young neighbourhood crowd.

In the Schanzenviertel, you'll find the comfortable and neighbourly *Frank und Frei* (☎ *43 48 03, Schanzenstrasse 93*). Just opposite is *Oma's Apotheke* (☎ *43 66 20, Schanzenstrasse 87*), a converted pharmacy that uses the old counter as a bar. At *Fritz Bauch* (*Bartelsstrasse 60*) you can soak up the area's politically radical atmosphere. Punks, yuppies and environmentalists hunker over heavy wooden furniture in a room that never sees daylight.

Bars of a distinctly alternative vibe cluster in Karolinenviertel. *Bob Bar* (☎ *430 07 08, Marktstrasse 41*) is dungeon-like, with Gothic decor and chains for table bases.

Café Oriental (Glashüttenstrasse 21) is another popular hang-out which flaunts an Aladdin theme and has a multiethnic clientele.

A mainstay in Altona is *Aurel* (☎ *390 27 27, Bahrenfelder Strasse 15)*, a snug bar with an eccentric back room where stone-age meets baroque. Its Happy Hour goes till 9 pm. The cobalt blue facade of the *Blaues Haus* (☎ *39 90 58 42, Grosse Brunnenstrasse 55)* signals that this is no ordinary place. This is confirmed when you step through the door and behold an environment that seamlessly blends cowhide-covered bar stools with Madonna altars. It's open daily from 9 pm, in summer from 8 pm.

Back in St Pauli, *Geyer Bar* on Hein-Köllisch-Platz is the epicentre of the local bar scene; in summer, tables nearly fill the entire square. More typical (read: tawdry) St Pauli joints, with front-row views of the scene, include *La Paloma* (☎ *31 34 12, Friedrichstrasse 11)* and *Mary Lou's* (☎ *31 42 36, Hans-Albers-Platz 3)*. Always an eye-popper is the highly suggestive entrance of *Zur Ritze* (☎ *319 39 46, Reeperbahn 140)*. *Gretel & Alfons* (☎ *31 34 91, Grosse Freiheit 29)* is a low-key spot that purports to have been the Beatles' favourite watering hole. Popular with Hamburg locals are the bars at Schmidt Theater and Schmidt's Tivoli (see Theatre).

Discos & Clubs

Nightclubs cluster around the Reeperbahn and its sidestreets, but don't bother showing up before 10 pm.

One of Hamburg's top addresses is *Angie's Nightclub* (☎ *31 77 88 16, Spielbudenplatz 27)*, run by Angie Stardust, a big black transsexual who knows how to party. Spontaneous concerts by accomplished (and sometimes even famous) guests are common. It serves great cocktails, and is open Wednesday to Saturday (DM5 to DM15).

Some may think they've died and gone to hell when they find themselves surrounded by lava lamps, velvet Jesuses and plastic flowers, but it's only *Purgatory* (☎ *31 58 07, Friedrichstrasse 8)*. The music is loud and the crowd can get wild. Nearby at *Samba Do Brasil* (☎ *31 33 98, Silbersackstrasse 27)*,

HAMBURG

you can go Latin after 9 pm while sipping exotic cocktails (closed Monday and Tuesday).

Grünspan (☎ *31 36 16, Grosse Freiheit 58)*, Hamburg's oldest disco, is housed in a large kaleidoscopic building. It attracts all types and ages and is open Wednesday to Saturday. The *Funky Pussy Club* (☎ *31 42 36, Grosse Freiheit 34)*, a few doors down, plays progressive house and soul music Friday and Saturday only.

Outside St Pauli, *Madhouse* (☎ *34 41 93, Valentinskamp 46a)* near the Musikhalle has been a Hamburg mainstay for decades and these days usually vibrates with rock, pop and hip hop (open nightly after 10 pm).

If you enjoy dancing the tango, foxtrot and waltz – to a live band – head to 'Ball Paradox' at the hilariously old-fashioned *Café Keese* (☎ *31 08 05, Reeperbahn 19)*, where it's been 'ladies choice' since 1948. Couples may go together, of course, and the atmosphere is highly respectable. It's open Wednesday to Saturday and for Sunday tea. Dress smartly.

Live Music

Wedged between live sex theatres and peep shows is *Grosse Freiheit 36* (☎ *317 77 80)*, named after its St Pauli address. It's one of the hippest party places for live pop and rock concerts. The Beatles once played in the *Kaiserkeller* disco, in the basement. On weekends, one ticket gets you into both.

The acoustics at *Docks* (☎ *31 78 83 11, Spielbudenplatz 19)* may not be perfect, but that hasn't stopped people like Iggy Pop and Lou Reed playing here. The *Prinzenbar* (☎ *31 78 83 11, Kastanienallee 20)* around the corner opens from Friday to Sunday after 10 pm. It's a raucous joint and popular haunt of cast members of *Cats*.

In Altona, people flock to *Fabrik* (☎ *39 10 70, Barnerstrasse 36)*, an unusual venue in a former foundry, now painted pink and sporting a crane jutting from its roof. On most nights, the emphasis is on world music, but blues and jazz greats, including Miles Davis, have performed here at the annual jazz festival. The best place for jazz,

though, is the *Cotton Club* (☎ *34 38 78, Alter Steinweg 10)* in the city centre. Performances are almost nightly after 8 pm.

Logo (☎ *410 56 58, Grindelallee 5)*, in the Universitätsviertel, is one of Hamburg's best known venues for live rock.

Gay & Lesbian

Hamburg has a thriving and free-wheeling gay and lesbian scene but, as in every large city, what's hot and what's not is constantly in flux. An excellent source for up-to-date info is the gay centre Hein & Fiete (☎ 24 03 33), Pulverteich 21 in St Georg, open on weekdays from 4 to 9 pm, and Saturday to 7 pm. Also look for the free magazine *hinnerk*, which lists gay events around town. The bookshop Männerschwarm (☎ 43 60 93), Neuer Pferdemarkt 32 in the Schanzenviertel, caters for men; the Frauenbuchladen at Bismarckstrasse 98 in Eimsbüttel for women.

Gays won't have problems finding a hotel in liberal Hamburg but might prefer the *Gay Residence Hotel* (☎ *24 98 88, fax 280 32 25, Steindamm 24)* in St Georg. Rooms with private bath, cable TV and direct-dial phones are a veritable steal, starting at DM59/79/119/149 a single/double/triple/quad.

Hugely popular gathering and hang-out spots – for both heteros and gays – are *Café Gnosa* (☎ *24 30 34, Lange Reihe 93)* and *Café Unter den Linden* (☎ *43 81 40, Juliusstrasse 16)* in the Schanzenviertel. Both serve big bowls of coffee and delectable cakes and bistro fare. Lesbians meet at *Frauenkneipe* (☎ *43 63 77, Stresemannstrasse 60)*, while seriously male party places include *Pit* (☎ *280 30 56, Pulverteich 17)*, *EDK* (☎ *31 29 14, Gerhardstrasse 3)*, *Spundloch* (☎ *31 07 98, Paulinenstrasse 19)* and *Toom Peerstall* (☎ *319 35 23, Clemens-Schultz-Strasse 44)*.

Cinemas

Several nonmainstream cinemas screen movies in the original language with subtitles. Look for the acronym 'OmU' (Original mit Untertiteln). Venues include *Abaton Kino* (☎ *41 32 03 20)* on the corner of Grindelhof and Allende Platz in the

The Beatles in Hamburg – Forever

'I was born in Liverpool, but I grew up in Hamburg.' – John Lennon

It was the summer of 1960 and a fledgling band from Liverpool had been assured a paying gig in Hamburg, if only they could come up with a drummer in time. After a frantic search, Pete Best joined John, Paul and George in August 1960.

Within days, the band opened at the Indra Club on the notorious Grosse Freiheit to a seedy crowd of drunks and whores. After being egged on by the club's burly owner to 'Put on a show,' John went wild, screaming, leaping and shouting, even performing in his underwear and with a toilet seat around his neck.

After 48 consecutive nights of six-hour sessions, the Beatles' innate musical genius had been honed. The magnetism of the group that would rock the world began drawing huge crowds. When police shut down the Indra because of violence and noise, they moved a block south to the Kaiserkeller – and the crowds moved with them. But so did the police.

At the Kaiserkeller, they alternated with a band called Rory Storm & The Hurricanes, whose drummer was none other than Ringo Starr. But their reign at this top-ranked club abruptly ended in late November when an underage George Harrison was deported, and Paul and Pete were arrested for attempted arson. All escaped the German authorities and returned to England, taking their stage magnetism back with them.

Their Merseyside breakthrough came that year in December. Billed as 'The Beatles: Direct from Hamburg', they swept away the crowd with Little Richard's *Long Tall Sally* – Beatlemania was born.

In 1961, the Beatles returned to Hamburg, this time performing at the Top Ten Club on the Reeperbahn. It was during this trip that they made their first professional recording as back-up for rocker Tony Sheridan.

The Beatles' stint at the Top Ten would last 92 nights and – aided increasingly by drugs – their musicianship was becoming legendary. Enter manager extraordinaire Brian Epstein and the recording genius (now Sir) George Martin. The Beatles' recording contract with German producer Bert Kaempfert was bought out and they began their long recording career with EMI, with one proviso: exit Pete Best, enter one Ringo Starr, a far more professional drummer.

In the spring of 1962 the final constellation of the Beatles was to log 172 hours of performance at Hamburg's Star Club over the course of 48 nights. But by now the crowds in England held sway over the boys' ambition. They began to shuttle off more and more regularly for home and foreign shores. To usher in the New Year of 1963, the Beatles gave their final concert at the Star Club, immortalised in what would become known as the 'Star Club Tapes'.

The Beatles returned occasionally to Hamburg in later years. But it was the combined 800 hours of live performance on grimy German stages in the city's red-light district that burned away the rough protective covering of four Liverpool boys to reveal their lasting brilliance.

And how does Hamburg now feel about what she gave birth to? Perhaps, to the Beatles she would still utter, *'Sie Liebt Dich'*. Certainly, 'She Loves You'.

Universitätsviertel, *3001* (☎ *43 76 79, Schanzenstrasse 75)* in the Schanzenviertel, and **Streit's** (☎ *34 60 51)* on Jungfernstieg in the centre. Movies are usually expensive, with prices peaking at DM17 on Saturday night. Discounts are available on *Kinotag* (budget days, usually Wednesday) for some matinee shows and for students with ID.

euro currency converter DM1 = €0.51

Theatre

The *Deutsches Schauspielhaus* (☎ 24 87 13, Kirchenallee 39) is one of Germany's leading stages, and does solid productions of German classics, experimental interpretations and original stage designs. Also with a stellar reputation, the *Thalia Theater* (☎ 32 26 66, Alstertor 1) is an intimate, galleried venue with a central stage and cutting-edge adaptations of classics.

Hamburg also has a thriving private theatre scene. At the *English Theatre* (☎ 227 70 89, Lerchenfeld 14) in Winterhude, a cast of predominantly British actors perform light fare like mysteries and comedies. A former crane factory, also in Winterhude, houses *Kampnagel* (☎ 27 09 49 49, Jarrestrasse 20-24), a top venue for alternative and experimental theatre. For kids, there's *Theater für Kinder* at Max-Brauer-Allee 76 in Altona.

Not at all suitable for the underaged are *Schmidt Theater* (☎ 317 88 60, Spielbudenplatz 24) and *Schmidt's Tivoli* (☎ 317 78 80), a few doors down at No 27. Both venues are much loved for their shrill variety shows, wild cabaret and very casual atmosphere.

For a timewarp back to the early 20th century, catch a show at *Hansa Theater* (☎ 24 14 14, Steindamm 17) in St Georg, a wonderfully old-fashioned variété, in business since 1894. Seated in rows of chairs tucked behind slim tables with brass railings, you can nibble on nutcake while enjoying a parade of wacky acts. Performers include anything from Mongolian contortionists to a precision cross-bow shooter. Shows last 2½ hours, change monthly and start at DM28.

Opera & Classical Music

The citizen-founded *Staatsoper* (☎ 35 17 21, Grosse Theaterstrasse 34), in the city centre, is among the most respected opera houses in the world. Performances often sell out, but you can try the Hamburg Hotline (☎ 30 05 13 00) or go to the box office at Grosse Theaterstrasse 35, about 50m from the opera house. Tickets range from DM5 to a whopping DM260.

The premier address for classical concerts is *Musikhalle* (☎ 34 69 20, Dammtorwall 46), housed in a splendid neobaroque edifice. It's the home of the State Philharmonic Orchestra, the North German Broadcasting Network Symphony Orchestra and the Hamburg Symphonics.

Musicals

Cats, which celebrated its 10th anniversary here in 1997, still plays at the *Operettenhaus* (☎ 27 07 52 70, Spielbudenplatz 1) in St Pauli. Since 1990, the *Phantom of the Opera* has haunted the halls of the *Neue Flora* (☎ 0180-544 44, Stresemannstrasse 159a) in Altona. The yellow tent resembling a giant bee at Norderelbstrasse 6 in the free port area is the *Metropol Musical Theater* (☎ 0180-519 97) which hosts the *Buddy Holly Story*. A shuttle service takes you there from Pier 1 of the St Pauli Landungsbrücken.

SHOPPING

Central Hamburg has two main districts. East of the Hauptbahnhof, along Spitalerstrasse and Mönckebergstrasse (known as the 'Mö'), you'll find the large department stores and mainstream boutiques. The more elegant shops are located within the triangle created by Jungfernstieg, Fuhlentwiete and Neuer Wall. Most of them are in a network of 11 shopping arcades, which are sophisticated, covered avenues of brick, chrome, steel, marble and tile. Some, like the Hanseviertel, have domed glass roofs.

Shopping in Altona has a more relaxed feel. Along Ottenser Hauptstrasse west of the station you'll find the Mercado mall with clothing stores and a Safeway supermarket. The quarter is also infused with a Mediterranean feel from the many Turkish vendors who artfully display their fruit and vegies on the street. East of Altona station, department stores line the pedestrianised Grosse Bergstrasse. For second-hand shopping, try the Schanzenviertel or Karolinenviertel.

GETTING THERE & AWAY
Air

Hamburg's international airport (☎ 507 50) was among the first in Europe (opened 1911) and is in Fuhlsbüttel, north of the city centre. It serves 130 destinations, mostly cities within Germany and Europe, especially in Scandinavia. Lufthansa has an office here (☎ 35 92 55), but the main British Airways office (☎ 30 96 63 63 or ☎ 01803-340 340 for reservations) is at Ballindamm 7 in the city centre. Air France (☎ 0180-536 03 70) is nearby at Jungfernstieg 1.

Train

Hamburg has no fewer than four train stations: the Hauptbahnhof, Dammtor, Altona and Harburg. Many of the long-distance trains originate in Altona and stop at both Dammtor and the Hauptbahnhof before heading out of the city. Be aware of this as you read the timetables or you may end up at the wrong station.

There are several trains hourly to Lübeck (DM16.40, 45 minutes), Kiel (DM30, 1¼ hours), Hanover (DM50, 1½ hours) and Bremen (DM33, 1¼ hours). A direct service to Westerland on Sylt Island leaves every two hours (DM64, 2¾ hours).

There are direct IC connections to Berlin-Zoo (DM88, 2½ hours) and Cologne (DM130, four hours). Frankfurt is served hourly by the ICE train (DM191, 3½ hours), as is Munich (DM268, six hours). There's a direct service to Copenhagen several times a day, but the only direct train to Paris is the night train (otherwise, change in Cologne). Going to Warsaw requires a change at Berlin-Zoo.

Hamburg-Harburg handles some regional services (for instance, to Cuxhaven, the main port for Helgoland; DM28, 1½ hours). Plenty of lockers are available for DM4/2 at all stations.

Bus

The Busbahnhof (☎ 24 75 76) is south-east of the Hauptbahnhof between Adenauerallee and Kurt-Schumacher-Allee. Look for the cylindrical bunker with the letters 'ZOB' (Zentraler Omnibus Bahnhof). You could shop around for the best deal in the string of travel agencies next to the bus boarding gates. Autokraft goes to Berlin several times daily for DM42 one-way,

DM55 return. Eurolines has buses to Paris for DM108/184, London for DM136/229, Amsterdam for DM75/115, Copenhagen for DM63/109, Warsaw for DM70/115 and Prague for DM90/160. Students and anyone under 26 years of age or over 60 will get a 10% discount.

Several agencies specialise in trips to Eastern European countries such as Poland, the Czech Republic and Hungary. Prices for these change constantly, so it's best to check when you get there. The station has lockers (DM2 and DM3) in the entrance hall and closes from 9 pm to 5 am.

Car & Motorcycle

The autobahns of the A1 (Bremen-Lübeck) and A7 (Hanover-Kiel) cross south of the Elbe River. Three concentric ring roads manage traffic flow.

Ride Services There are Mitfahrzentralen on Lobuschstrasse 22 (☎ 391721) and Gotenstrasse 19 (☎ 194 44; U/S-Bahn to Berliner Tor, then a five minute walk).

Boat

Scandinavian Seaways (☎ 389 03 71) operates the car ferry from Hamburg to the English port of Harwich. The journey takes 20 hours, and services operate year round at least twice weekly in either direction (less frequently in January and February). The office is in the Edgar-Engelhard-Kai terminal (known as the England Ferry Terminal) at Van-der-Smissen-Strasse 4 off Grosse Elbstrasse, west of St Pauli harbour (S1 or S3 to Königstrasse). The one-way passenger fare to Harwich ranges from DM97 to DM495, depending on the season, the day of the week and cabin amenities, size and location. A car costs an extra DM80 to DM110, a motorbike DM45 to DM78, and transporting a bicycle will cost DM28 in the high season and DM5 the rest of the year.

From May to August, there's also a ferry to Newcastle every four days. The trip takes around 24 hours and costs from DM138 to DM515.

euro currency converter DM1 = €0.51

GETTING AROUND
To/From the Airport
Airport buses make the 30 minute trip to the airport from the Hauptbahnhof every 20 minutes between 5.40 am and 9.20 pm (DM8, return DM12). It's cheaper to take the U1 or S1 to Ohlsdorf, then change to the Airport Express (bus No 110), which leaves every 10 minutes (DM4.20). A taxi from the Hauptbahnhof takes about 35 minutes and costs around DM35.

Public Transport
The HVV (☎ 194 49) operates an extensive system of buses, ferries, U-Bahn and S-Bahn and has offices around town, including at the Hauptbahnhof and at Jungfernstieg station.

The service area is set up by zones. The central area (Nahbereich) covers the city centre, roughly between St Pauli and the Hauptbahnhof. The Greater Hamburg area (Grossbereich) covers the city centre plus outlying communities like Blankenese. Hamburg State (Gesamtbereich) covers the entire Hamburg area.

Tickets for the S/U-Bahn must be purchased from the orange machines at station entrances; bus tickets are available from the driver. Single journeys cost DM2.70 for the central area, DM4.20 for Greater Hamburg and DM6.80 for Hamburg State. Children cost a basic DM1.50. The express Schnellbus or 1st class S-Bahn supplement is DM2 per trip.

If you'll be using public transport a lot, day passes (Tageskarte) are a money-saving option (not available for Nahbereich). An individual day pass for unlimited travel after 9 am on weekdays and all day on weekends is DM8 for Greater Hamburg and DM12.90 for Hamburg State. Passes for groups of up to five people cost DM13.80/18.70. A three-day pass (available only for Grossbereich) is DM23.30. Weekly cards (valid from Monday through to Sunday) cost from DM24.50 to DM49.50.

At certain times, bikes may be taken onto U-Bahn and S-Bahn trains, buses and ferries for free. The fine for riding without a valid ticket is DM60. Checks are generally

sporadic but thorough: with up to five inspectors swooping into the U-Bahn or S-Bahn compartment, don't even think about trying to escape.

Service is suspended from 1 to 4 am when the night bus network takes over, converging on the main city bus station at Rathausmarkt. For transport options with the Hamburg Card, see the Information section at the beginning of this chapter.

Car & Motorcycle
Driving around Hamburg is surprisingly easy. Major thoroughfares cut across town in all directions, and road signs are ubiquitous. Parking is expensive, though, especially in the city centre. Expect to pay about DM2 an hour at meters or in parking garages. Parking your car at a hotel usually adds between DM15 and DM25 to your room rate.

All major car-rental agencies have branches in Hamburg. Represented both at the Hauptbahnhof and at the airport are Hertz, Budget and Europcar. Local agencies include Spar Car (☎ 468 83 00 or ☎ 654 41 10) or Profi Rent (☎ 656 95 95), both with cars available from around DM60/day or DM90/weekend.

Mot-In (☎ 550 03 33), Heidlohstrasse 1 in Hamburg-Schnelsen, rents out motorbikes from DM95 to DM205 a day (plus DM1200 deposit).

Taxi
You can book a taxi by ringing ☎ 21 12 11 or ☎ 66 66 66.

Around Hamburg

STADE
☎ 04141 • pop 45,000
Stade, about 60km west of Hamburg, is one of the oldest Hanseatic towns in the north and was first mentioned in a public record about 1000 years ago. Most of Stade's medieval buildings were destroyed in a major fire in 1659, so what you see today is nearly all post-17th century. Stade is an intensely neat little town with immaculately kept red-brick

houses, manicured gardens and litter-free streets. Its Altstadt is especially scenic around the harbour, which is lined by restored town houses and historic warehouses. Add to that a couple of churches and museums and Stade is well worth a day trip.

Information

The tourist office (☎ 40 91 70, fax 40 91 10) is in the Zeughaus at Pferdemarkt, and is open weekdays from 9 am to 7 pm (in winter to 6 pm), and Saturday to 2 pm. In summer, it also opens on Sunday from 11 am to 3 pm.

Walking Tour

Stade's train station is south-west of the Altstadt, which is encircled by a moat and a ring road. Cross the moat via Bahnhofstrasse, then continue north-east on the pedestrianised Holzstrasse to Pferdemarkt, where you'll find the tourist office. Head east from here via Sattelmacherstrasse to Flurstrasse and the **St Wilhadi Kirche**, a 14th century Gothic hall church with a badly leaning, squat tower. Of note here is the baroque organ, built around 1730 by E Bielfeldt of Bremen, and the ceiling frescoes, which had been painted over and were only rediscovered during recent restoration. Backtrack, then turn right onto Hökerstrasse, one of Stade's main shopping streets. On the right you'll see the **Rathaus**, with its columned portal flanked by the figures of Truth (with the mirror) and Justice (with the scales).

Stade's oldest church, just north of here in a courtyard off to the right, is the **Church of Sts Cosmas and Damiani**. It's easily recognised for its octagonal tower crowned by a baroque helmet. Inside, the marble baptismal font is festooned with alabaster likenesses of three of the Evangelists. The organ was the first work of local son (and later master organ builder) Arp Schnitger. Hökerstrasse ends at Fischmarkt, which marks one end of the **Alter Hafen**, the canal-like harbour and the prettiest part of the Altstadt. Beautiful historic houses are on both sides.

The houses on Wasser Ost were once owned by sea captains; the ones on the opposite side were merchants' homes. The **Kunsthaus** (☎ 448 24; DM2/1), Wasser West 7, contains an exquisite collection of works by painters from the Worpswede artist colony, including Paula Modersohn-Becker, Fritz Mackensen and Fritz Overbeck (also see Around Bremen in the Bremen chapter). It's open Tuesday to Friday from 10 am to 5 pm, and weekends from 10 am to 6 pm (closed Monday).

The **Bürgermeister-Hintze-Haus**, a lacy stucco confection with tall gables and a fancy portal, is at No 23. The large building at the harbour's northern end is the **Schwedenspeicher** (☎ 32 22), used as a food warehouse by the Swedish garrison during its occupation of Stade after the Thirty Years' War. It is now a regional history museum and has the same opening hours as the Kunsthaus (DM2/1).

Getting There & Away

There's a train service from Hamburg every 30 minutes (DM14.20, one hour). If you're coming from Bremen you require a change in Hamburg-Harburg (DM38, 1½ hours). If you're driving from Hamburg, take the B73; from Bremen, you can reach Stade via the B74.

From Hamburg, you can also hop on one of the super-fast Elbe-City-Jet (☎ 317 71 70) catamarans that leave St Pauli Landungsbrücken, Pier 4, up to 17 times daily (fewer on weekends and in winter) and speed down the Elbe to Stadersand in 50 minutes. From there, bus No 6 takes you to Pferdemarkt in the town centre. The trip costs DM16 each way, children and bikes are DM8.

BUXTEHUDE

☎ 04161 • pop 36,000

This bucolic town lies about 30km west of Hamburg on the Este River. The pedestrian-friendly Altstadt is at its dreamiest around the **Fleth**, a Dutch-style (ie canal-like) harbour in the western Altstadt. The Fleth dates back to the town's founding in 1285 and until 1962 was used by lighters transporting cargo weighing up to 100 tonnes. One of them, the **Ewer Margareta** (1897), is permanently moored here. Also here is the

HAMBURG

Flethmühle, a mill that was in operation until 1975 and has now been converted into apartments and shops.

Cafes and restaurants line both sides of the Fleth, and it's a nice place for a stroll. One block east, on the corner of Breite Strasse and the Markt, stands the ivy-clad **Rathaus**, a red-brick edifice with a monumental sandstone portal and copper roof. Built in 1911, it replaced its 15th century predecessor, which was destroyed by fire. North of here, the spires of **St Petri** come into view. The light-flooded, three-nave Gothic basilica contains small but vividly carved choir stalls, circa 1400, and a sumptuous baroque pulpit supported by a statue of Atlas. The star attraction is the late-Gothic **Halephagen Altar** below the organ, with scenes from the Passion of Christ. If the church is closed, pick up the key from the **Buxtehude Museum** (☎ 50 12 41) about 50m to the east at Am Stavenort 2. The museum focuses on regional history and also has special exhibits. It's open Tuesday to Friday from 1.30 to 5.30 pm, and weekends from 10.30 am (DM2/1).

The Buxtehude tourist office (☎ 50 12 97, fax 526 93) is in the same building as the museum, and is open Monday from 9 am to noon and 1.30 to 4 pm, from Tuesday to Friday to 5.30 pm and Saturday to 12.30 pm. If it's closed, general information and brochures are also available from the museum desk.

Getting There & Away

Buxtehude is easily reached by the same train connecting Hamburg Hauptbahnhof with Stade and Cuxhaven (DM9.60, 45 minutes). Drivers from Hamburg can catch the B73 west to Buxtehude. From Bremen, take the Rade exit off the A1, then travel via the B3 to the B73.

ALTES LAND

South of the Elbe, roughly bordered by Stade and Buxtehude is 'Hamburg's fruit basket', the Altes Land. All kinds of orchards blanket this fertile area that was reclaimed from marshy ground by Dutch experts in the Middle Ages. Thatched and panelled houses and farms, romantic windmills and sweeping dykes characterise this stretch of land that's at its most brilliant in May when the trees are blossoming. Its centre is the little town of **Jork**, which can be reached from Hamburg by taking the S3 to Neugraben and then bus No 257.

In fine weather, though, cycling is the most pleasant way to explore the region. The Obstmarschenweg is a particularly scenic bike path, following the Elbe. You can also travel here by boat. HADAG (☎ 311 70 70) cruises to Lühe from St Pauli Landungsbrücken, Pier 2, several times daily from April to October. The trip takes about 90 minutes and costs DM11 each way. The Elbe-City-Jet to Stadersand also stops at Lühe (DM12, 35 minutes).

Schleswig-Holstein

Schleswig-Holstein is a flat, windswept land of open skies, gentle hills and vast fields. Water has been the primary shaper in this northernmost of German states. From the beginning, Schleswig-Holstein's fate and prosperity have been inseparably linked to the savage North Sea in the west and the placid Baltic in the east. Its people have braved the seas as fisherfolk and whalers; its ports have been major launch sites for freighters, passenger ships and ferries. And, predictably enough, this predominantly agricultural land relies on its frequent rains.

Unlike some other states in Germany, Schleswig-Holstein doesn't owe its double-barrelled name to creative post-WWII mapping. The two territories were first united in 1460 under the Danish King Christian I. His oath that the two should 'remain forever undivided', however, was undermined only a generation later when his squabbling sons partitioned the land among themselves. For the next four centuries, both territories shuttled back and forth between independence and alliance with the Danish crown until, in 1864, a powerful Prussia ended the tug of war and both Schleswig and Holstein were incorporated into the German Reich. After WWI, the northern half of Schleswig was returned to Denmark following a referendum. The state – and national – border was moved southward to Flensburg, where it remains today.

With only 2.7 million people, Schleswig-Holstein is sparsely populated and almost devoid of cities. The largest is Kiel, the modern state capital, internationally famous for its Kieler Woche (Kiel Week) – the world's largest sailing regatta – and as a gateway to Scandinavia. An absolute highlight for visitors is the old Hanseatic city of Lübeck, the birthplace of Thomas and Heinrich Mann; the picturesque Altstadt here has been included on UNESCO's

HIGHLIGHTS

Schleswig-Holstein Luminaries: Willy Brandt, Dietrich Buxtehude, Thomas & Heinrich Mann, Emil Nolde, Max Planck, Jil Sander, Theodor Storm, Carl Maria von Weber

- Exploring the North Frisian Islands of Sylt, Amrum and Föhr
- Visiting the Landesmuseum in Schloss Gottorf in Schleswig
- Wandering around historic Lübeck
- Clambering through the WWII U-boat in Laboe

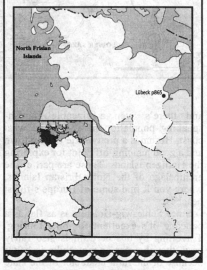

World Heritage List. Also well worth a visit is Schleswig, whose heydays under the Vikings and then the dukes of Gottorf have left their legacies around the town. Flensburg's location on the Danish border is reflected in its architecture and street names,

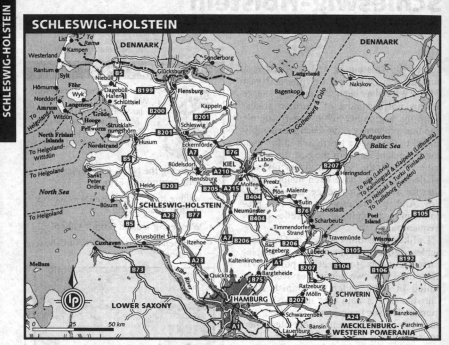

SCHLESWIG-HOLSTEIN

and there's even a sizeable Danish-speaking population here. On the west coast, Husum is a pretty little fishing town and a good jumping-off point for exploring the Halligen Islands. These are part of the archipelago of the North Frisian Islands, where you'll find some of Europe's finest beaches.

Since Schleswig-Holstein is as flat as a pancake, it's excellent for bike touring. Travelling by bus or train is also fairly easy, though a car or motorbike is better because of the rural character of the state and the relatively long distances between towns. Accommodation is plentiful and cuts across the entire budget spectrum. But the coastal areas are very popular with German holidaymakers and, even though finding a place to stay should not be a problem, it's probably best to phone ahead during the peak summer months.

KIEL
☎ 0431 • pop 243,000

Kiel, about 75km north-west of Lübeck and 80km north of Hamburg, is the state capital of Schleswig-Holstein. It came into being more than 750 years ago but, sadly, little of historical importance survived the ravages of war. Located at the end of the 18km-long Kiel Firth, it has long been one of Germany's most important harbours on the Baltic Sea.

Under the Prussians, who annexed Schleswig-Holstein in 1864, it became the headquarters of the Imperial Navy. During WWII it was the base for enormous German U-boat activity, making it a prime target for Allied bombers, which left more than 80% of the city in ruin.

After the war, economic survival – not architectural aesthetics – was the issue on city-planners' minds and, as a result, you wouldn't use 'Kiel' and 'picturesque' in the same sentence. Nevertheless, it's a vibrant city that's not without charm. Most of this comes from its rather scenic location on the water and the hubbub of its harbour. The city is the main gateway to Scandinavia, with about 2.3 million passengers annually boarding one of the colossal ferries headed for Oslo, Gothenburg, and even St Petersburg in Russia. Kiel also has a long tradition as a venue for sailing regattas; it hosted the Olympic sailing events in both 1936 and 1972. The international Kieler Woche sailing spectacle has been taking place here since 1882.

Orientation

Kiel's main thoroughfare is the pedestrianised Holstenstrasse, about 100m inland from the firth. It starts at the Kieler Schloss and runs south for about 1.5km before culminating in the Sophienhof, a huge indoor shopping mall on Sophienblatt, opposite the Hauptbahnhof. The central bus station (ZOB) is just north of the Hauptbahnhof.

The Deutsche Bahn (DB) service counter inside the Hauptbahnhof hands out good, free maps of central Kiel.

Information

Tourist Office The Kiel tourist office (☎ 67 91 00, fax 679 10 99, email info@Kiel-Tourist.de) is at Andreas-Gayk-Strasse 31, a northern extension of Sophienblatt and just five minutes by foot from the Hauptbahnhof. It opens December to February weekdays from 9 am to 6.30 pm, and Saturday from 9 am to 1 pm. On Saturday from May to September it opens to 4.30 pm. In June and July it stays open on Monday and Friday to 8 pm, and also opens Sunday from 9 am to 2 pm. The rest of the year it stays open to 6.30 pm, and 7.30 pm on Monday and Friday.

Money Banks closest to the Hauptbahnhof are the Sparkasse at Sophienblatt 21 and the Volksbank on the corner of Sophienblatt and Raiffeisenstrasse. An ATM outside the Reisezentrum (inside the station) accepts all major cards.

Post & Communications The main post office is at Stresemannplatz 5, about a five minute walk north of the Hauptbahnhof.

The Internet cafe Edit(ha's), Alter Markt 13, offers access from 11 am (Monday from 6 pm and Sunday from 4 pm) till midnight or later for DM14 per hour.

Bookshops The Fabulus bookshop, inside the Holstentörn Passage connecting the Holstenstrasse outdoor mall with the Sophienhof, stocks a number of English-language books.

Laundry The Schnell & Sauber laundry on the corner of Knooper Weg and Ziegelteich charges DM6 per wash and DM1 for the dryer (Bus stop: Exerzierplatz).

Medical Services & Emergency For medical attention, call the Universitäts-Kliniken on ☎ 59 70. Police headquarters (☎ 59 81) are at Gartenstrasse 7.

Walking Tour

You can easily see the sights in central Kiel on a walk. This one covers about 3.5km and takes about 1½ hours excluding museum and other visits. From the Hauptbahnhof, head through the nicely designed Sophienhof mall, then north onto Holstenstrasse. Turn left into Fleethörn to get to Rathausplatz and its impressive **Rathaus**, where baroque meets Art Nouveau. Completed in 1911, the Rathaus sports a 106m **tower** that is a city landmark. Unfortunately, the interior of the Rathaus can only be visited on a guided city tour. Tours run from May to October on Sunday and Wednesday at 9.40 and 10.40 am; details are at the tourist office.

Walk back to Holstenstrasse and continue north to Alter Markt and the **Nikolaikirche**, whose carved altar (1460), triumphal cross (1490) and bronze baptismal font (1344) deserve a closer look. Outside stands the statue **Der Geistkämpfer** (The Ghost Fighter) by Ernst Barlach, which was removed during the Third Reich because it was considered 'degenerate art'; it was later found buried in the Lüneburg Heath.

euro currency converter DM1 = €0.51

Dänische Strasse north of here is one of the more successfully restored sections of old Kiel. The lovely red-brick building with a rococo portal at No 19 is the Warleberger Hof, which contains the **Stadtmuseum** (☎ 901 34 25) with changing exhibitions. The museum is open daily from 10 am to 6 pm; it closes Monday and at 5 pm from April to October (DM2). The **Schloss** is only a short distance north. The west wing is the only part of the original Renaissance palace to survive. North of here, at the other end of the little park, stands the **Kunsthalle** (☎ 597 37 56) at Düsternbrooker Weg 1-3. It has a fine collection of paintings by Baltic artists and an entire section dedicated to Emil Nolde. It is open from 10.30 am to 6 pm, Wednesday to 8 pm, closed Monday (DM6/4, more for special exhibits).

Finally, walk south along the waterfront to the **Schiffahrtsmuseum** (Maritime Museum; ☎ 901 34 28), open daily from 10 am to 6 pm, April to October to 5 pm (DM2/1). Located in a former fish auction hall at Am Wall 65, it chronicles Kiel's maritime history with ship models, photographs and documents; one section focuses on nautical inventions and innovations coming out of Kiel. The **Museum Harbour** has a number of historical ships on display (April to October).

Kiel Canal & Locks

Kiel is the point at which this 99km-long shipping canal *(Nord-Ostsee-Kanal)* enters the Baltic from the North Sea. Inaugurated in 1895, the canal sees some 60,000 ships pass through it every year, and the *Schleusen* (locks) at Holtenau, 6km north of the city centre, are well worth a visit. Admission to the viewing platform on the southern side of the canal is DM2/1. Tours of the locks, offered daily at 9 and 11 am and 1 and 3 pm, depart from the northern side of the canal (DM3/2). To get to the locks, take bus No 11 to Wik, then walk north for about five minutes.

Special Events

Kiel's most famous attraction is the **Kieler Woche** (Kiel Week; ☎ 901 24 16) in the last full week of June. It's a giant festival revolving around a series of yachting regattas and attended by more than 4000 of the world's sailing elite and half a million spectators. Even if you're not into boats, the atmosphere is electric – just make sure you book a room in advance if you want to be in on the fun.

Places to Stay

Kiel's *Campingplatz Falckenstein* (☎ 39 20 78, Palisadenweg 171) is an inconvenient 15km north of the city centre (take bus No 501 to the Seekamp stop and walk about 1.5km). It is open from April to October. Tent sites cost DM8 to DM12, plus DM7 per person and DM3.50 per car.

Kiel's *Jugendherberge* (☎ 73 14 88, fax 73 57 23, Johannesstrasse 1) is in the suburb of Gaarden, across the firth from the Hauptbahnhof. To get there, walk over the new drawbridge. Alternatively, take bus No 11 or 12 from the Hauptbahnhof to Kieler Strasse. The hostel charges juniors/seniors DM27/32 (including breakfast and sheets) in two and four-bed rooms.

The tourist office charges DM3.50 for its accommodation booking service. It also stocks a helpful free accommodation guide. Be warned, though, even budget hotels are not exactly cheap and hotels are booked solid during Kieler Woche. *Private rooms* are a good alternative and cost from DM30 per person.

The *Hotel Runge* (☎ 73 19 92, fax 73 19 92, Elisabethstrasse 16) offers basic singles/doubles for DM60/100, or with shower and WC (toilet) for DM80/100. Take bus No 11 or 12 to the Augustern stop. The central *Hotel Schweriner Hof* (☎ 614 16, fax 67 41 34, Königsweg 13) offers good rooms from DM65/110, or doubles with shower and WC from DM110 to DM150. *Hotel Düvelsbek Garni* (☎ 810 21, fax 886 67 60, Feldstrasse 111) has well priced basic singles from DM59 and rooms with private showers (but not in the room itself) for DM70/110. Its best rooms go for DM85/130 with shower and WC. It's about 2km north of the city centre (take bus No 61 or 62 to Esmarch-Strasse).

Muhl's Hotel (☎ 997 90, fax 997 91 79, Lange Reihe 5) is centrally located and charges from DM110/150 for full-facility rooms. *Hotel Birke (☎ 533 10, fax 533 13 33, Martenshofweg 2-8)* is an excellent value, snug country inn, with standard category rooms from DM150/195 and comfort-class rooms from DM160/205 (ask about weekend deals). You'll find a sauna and fitness room on the premises. Take bus No 91 or 31 from the centre to the Waldesruh stop. *Steigenberger Hotel Conti-Hansa (☎ 511 50, fax 511 54 44, Schlossgarten 7)* is more central, but prices start from DM250/300.

Places to Eat
There are plenty of reasonably priced eateries. *Oblomov (☎ 80 14 67, Hansastrasse 82)* is a legendary student pub with dirt-cheap pizza, pasta, salads and baguette sandwiches. It also offers a choice of five dishes for lunch at DM9. *Viva (☎ 831 53, Knooper Weg 169)* is another favourite for cheap chow and a chat. *Frizz (☎ 80 56 60, Olshausenstrasse 8)*, a small bistro serving inexpensive, simple fare, is also near the university.

The *Friesenhof*, in the Rathaus, offers regional specialities and traditional daily lunch specials priced around DM10. Its tasty a la carte dishes range from DM16 to DM32; best of all, between 3 and 5 pm you can order all dishes at half price plus DM2. The *Klosterbrauerei (☎ 90 62 90, Alter Markt 9)* is a private brewery with a great atmosphere, good beer and lunch specials (including some vegetarian dishes) for under DM10. The *Forstbaumschule*, a big beer garden in a park about 3.5km north of the city centre, is a fun place to go on a warm day. *Kieler Ansichten (Hasselfelde 20)* offers great views of the firth in a historic building, where it serves surprisingly affordable international cuisine.

Ça Va (Holtenauer Strasse 107) is a popular gay and hetero bar that has a few snacks in the evening and stays open till late.

Getting There & Away
Train Numerous trains shuttle daily between Kiel, Hamburg-Altona and Hamburg

Hauptbahnhof (DM37, 1¼ hours). Trains to Lübeck leave hourly (DM23, 1¼ hours). There are regular local connections to Schleswig, Husum, Schwerin and Flensburg.

Bus Kiel's ZOB is a major hub for buses travelling to the nearby countryside and other towns in Schleswig-Holstein, although most are also served by trains that may be faster and more regular. Autokraft operates an express bus to Hamburg (2¼ hours) that runs up to a dozen times daily. There's also the direct No 4550 to Hamburg airport. Bus No 4320 goes to Lübeck (2¾ hours), and bus No 4810 to Schleswig (1¾ hours) and Flensburg (2½ hours). To get to Husum (2¾ hours), take bus No 4810 and change to bus No 1046 in Schleswig.

Car & Motorcycle Kiel is connected with the rest of Germany via the A210 and A215, which merge with the A7 to Hamburg and beyond. The B4, B76, B404, B502 and B503 also converge here.

Ride Services The ADM Mitfahrzentrale (☎ 67 50 01 or ☎ 1 94 40) is at Sophienblatt 54, near the Hauptbahnhof.

Boat At the time of writing, Langeland-Kiel (☎ 97 41 50) ran one or two ferries daily to Bagenkop (2½ hours) on the Danish island of Langeland. Trips cost around DM8/10 one-way/return. Cars cost DM25/45, including up to four passengers. No one knew how long this service would continue once duty-free allowances are abolished within the EU. Call the company for details.

Stena Line (☎ 0180-533 36 00) operates the daily overnight Kiel-Gothenburg ferry (14 hours) leaving from Schwedenkai. From early November to April, the fare for pedestrians is DM70/104 on all but a few days. It rises to DM200/256 on peak days in July and August. If you're under 26, you can buy the super-cheap Tramper-Ticket for DM48 in low season and DM158 in peak season (available only for return trips). Sleeping berths in air-conditioned four-bed cabins with shower and WC are an additional DM39.

Color Line ferries (☎ 730 03 00) has services to Oslo (19½ hours) throughout the year. One-way fares start at DM150/164 during the week/weekend in low season (around 30% extra in summer) per bed in very basic two-bed cabins. If you want a private shower and WC, expect to pay from DM256/270. Bikes are transported free; cars start at DM66. Return tickets are normally double the one-way fare. Ferries depart from the new Norwegenkai across the firth in Gaarden. A 50% student discount (with ID) is available.

Getting Around

The ZOB is right outside the Hauptbahnhof on Auguste-Viktoria-Strasse. Single trips cost DM3.30, six-ticket blocks are DM16.50. For a taxi, call ☎ 68 01 01.

A ferry service along Kiel Firth operates daily until around 6 pm (to 5 pm on weekends) from the Bahnhofbrücke pier behind the Hauptbahnhof. Prices depend on how many zones you travel through, and range from DM3.80 to DM5.40 (eg to Laboe). For information, ring ☎ 594 12 63.

AROUND KIEL
Laboe

At the mouth of the Kiel Firth and on its eastern bank lies the sleepy village of Laboe. It is home to the **U-boat** featured in Wolfgang Petersen's film *Das Boot* (1981). The sub, which served as a very real weapon of destruction during WWII, sits on struts in the sand and is now going through its third incarnation as a museum. The climb through its claustrophobic interior is well worth the DM3.50/2.50. You'll find it right below the **Marine Ehrenmal**, a naval memorial built in the shape of a ship's stern to commemorate sailors of all nations lost at sea. In fine weather, you can see all the way to Denmark from its 80m tower. Inside is a **navigation museum** (DM5/3). Both the U-boat and memorial/museum are open daily from 9.30 am to 6 pm, in winter to 4 pm. From Kiel, take bus No 100 or 101 or the ferry (see Getting Around in the Kiel section).

Schleswig-Holstein Open-Air Museum

South of Kiel, at Alte Hamburger Landstrasse in Molfsee, Schleswig-Holsteinisches Freilichtmuseum features some 70 traditional houses typical of the region, relocated from around the state. The houses, some of them furnished, provide a thorough introduction to the northern way of life. The museum is open from 9 am to 6 pm (closed Monday except in summer). In winter, it's only open on Sunday and holidays from 11 am to 4 pm. Admission is DM7/5. Take bus No 501 or 502 from the Kiel bus station.

LÜBECK

☎ 0451 • **pop 208,000**

Lübeck, about 65km north-east of Hamburg, was actually founded twice, once in 1143 by Count Adolf II of Holstein and again in 1159 – after a major fire had destroyed the modest settlement – by Saxon Duke Heinrich der Löwe (Henry the Lion). It was Heinrich who designed the orderly, grid-like street layout that still characterises the Altstadt today. He also laid the foundation stone for the grand Dom, having made Lübeck a bishopric in 1160.

Despite its many churches, Lübeckers proved to be incredibly adept at the rather secular art of trade and commerce. Within a century, Lübeck became the 'Queen of the Hanse', the flagship of the Hanseatic League, the powerful association of towns that ruled trade in much of Europe from the 13th to the 16th century (see the boxed text 'Hanseatic League' for details). The legal, political and societal structures developed in Lübeck became a model for many other cities around the Baltic. Its power was further reflected in its status as a free imperial city, which it was given in 1226 and retained until the Nazis revoked it in 1937.

The Altstadt's proud merchants' homes and seven church spires still attest to Lübeck's medieval halcyon days. In 1987, UNESCO placed the entire area (including more than 1000 historical buildings) on its World Heritage List. Yet the Altstadt is not just a giant museum but also an actual city

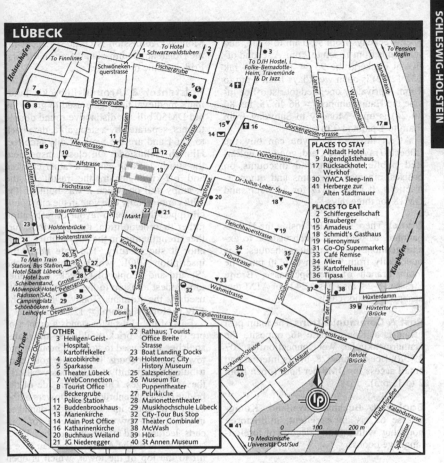

LÜBECK

PLACES TO STAY
1 Altstadt Hotel
9 Jugendgästehaus
17 Rucksackhotel;
Werkhof
30 YMCA Sleep-Inn
41 Herberge zur
Alten Stadtmauer

PLACES TO EAT
2 Schiffergesellschaft
10 Brauberger
15 Amadeus
18 Schmidt's Gasthaus
19 Hieronymus
31 Co-Op Supermarket
33 Café Remise
34 Miera
35 Kartoffelhaus
36 Tipasa

OTHER
3 Heiligen-Geist-
Hospital;
Kartoffelkeller
4 Jacobikirche
5 Sparkasse
6 Theater Lübeck
7 WebConnection
8 Tourist Office
Beckergrube
11 Police Station
12 Buddenbrookhaus
13 Marienkirche
14 Main Post Office
16 Katharinenkirche
20 Buchhaus Weiland
21 JG Niederegger
22 Rathaus; Tourist
Office Breite
Strasse
23 Boat Landing Docks
24 Holstentor; City
History Museum
25 Salzspeicher
26 Museum für
Puppentheater
27 Petrikirche
28 Marionettentheater
29 Musikhochschule Lübeck
32 City-Tour Bus Stop
37 Theater Combinale
38 McWash
39 Hüx
40 St Annen Museum

centre, with lively shopping streets and a host of cosy pubs, elegant restaurants and interesting cultural venues. Along with its seaside resort and port of Travemünde, Lübeck is a must-see destination in Schleswig-Holstein that needs at least a couple of days to appreciate fully.

Orientation

Lübeck's Altstadt is set on an island ringed by the canalised Trave River. Lübeck's landmark, the Holstentor, forms the western

gateway to the Altstadt, with the main train and bus stations a couple of hundred metres farther west of here. Königstrasse and several of its eastern side streets in the Altstadt are off limits to vehicles between 11.30 am and 6 pm (from 10 am on Saturday) unless you're going to a hotel there.

Information

Tourist Offices Lübeck's city-run tourist office has two branches. The office with the longest hours is at Breite Strasse 63, near the Rathaus (☎ 122 54 06, fax 122 54 19), open weekdays from 9.30 am to 6 pm, and weekends from 10 am to 2 pm. A second office at Beckergrube 95 (☎ 122 19 09, fax 122 12 02) is open weekdays from 8 am to 4 pm. A privately operated tourist office inside the Hauptbahnhof (☎ 86 46 75, fax 86 30 24) is open Monday to Saturday from 9 am to 1 pm and 3 to 6 pm.

At all three offices you can buy the Lübeck-Travemünde Card, good for unlimited public transport and discounts on cruises, cinemas, museums and other attractions. It costs DM9 for 24 hours and DM18 for three days.

Money There's an ATM inside the Hauptbahnhof, as well as a Wechselstube to exchange money and travellers cheques; it is open daily from 9.30 am to 6.30 pm. The main branch of the Sparkasse, Breite Strasse 18-28, also has a 24 hour ATM that accepts all major cards.

Post & Communications The main post office is at Königstrasse 46, opposite the Katharinenkirche. WebConnection (☎ 707 39 58), Beckergrube 78, offers Internet and email access for DM8 per hour (open from 2 to 11 pm).

Bookshop Buchhaus Weiland, Königstrasse 67, is an excellent, multistorey bookshop with a good selection of foreign-language books.

Laundry The large McWash laundrette is on the corner of Hüxterdamm and An der Mauer, and charges DM7 per wash and DM1.20 for the dryer. Opening hours are 6 am to 10 pm, closed Sunday and holidays.

Medical Services & Emergency Medizinische Universität Ost/Süd (☎ 5000) is at Ratzeburger Allee 160. There's a police station (☎ 13 11) at Mengstrasse 20.

Things to See

Unless noted otherwise, museums mentioned here are open from 10 am to 5 pm (to 4 pm from October to March) and closed Monday. Admission is DM5/3. Except for the Holstentor, admission is free on the first Friday of the month.

Holstentor & Around Lübeck's landmark medieval town gate used to grace the old DM50 bill. Its distinctive round double towers, separated by a step gable, date back to 1464 and are the work of city architect Hinrich Helmstede. On closer inspection, the sturdy-looking gate is a rather crooked and off-kilter affair, the result of the swampy soil on which it was built. In the 19th century, only one vote in the city council tipped the scale in favour of restoration rather than demolition, though it took further strengthening in the 20th century to anchor it successfully. The gate bears the inscription SPQL, which is Latin for the 'Senate and People of Lübeck' – a none-too-modest allusion to the signature SPQR used by the Romans. Today it houses the **City History Museum** (☎ 122 41 29).

East of the Holstentor stands a quintet of pretty gabled brick buildings, the **Salzspeicher**, once used to store salt brought into town from Lüneburg. This 'white gold' contributed significantly to Lübeck's wealth in the Middle Ages. On the other side of the bridge (the Holstenbrücke), the towers of the **Petrikirche** come into view. Badly damaged in WWII, it is now used as a venue for concerts, lectures and even techno parties. For a superb view of the Altstadt, you can take a lift to the top of the tower, which is open May to October from 9 am to shop closing time, which varies (DM3.50/2).

Head to the church via Grosse Petersgrube, which is lined by merchants' houses from various periods. In the parallel Kleine Petersgrube at No 4 is the **Museum für Puppentheater** (Puppet Theatre Museum; ☎ 786 26), a beautiful assembly of some 1200 puppets, props, posters and more, from Europe, Asia and Africa. It is open daily from 10 am to 6 pm (DM6/5, children DM3).

Markt & Around The majestic **Rathaus**, made of red and glazed-black bricks, flanks

Hanseatic League

The word 'Hanseatic' has its origin in the medieval German word *Hanse*, meaning 'guild' or 'association'. Northern Germany's rich merchants and ruling classes founded the league for reasons of enlightened self-interest in the late 12th century. It allowed them to take actions to ensure that neither petty wars nor predatory pirates would interrupt the prosperous flow of shipping and trade in the North Sea and Baltic regions.

The Hanseatic League was an accomplishment on a par with some of history's greatest empires. In a time of endless feudal squabbles and religious ruptures, it was a bastion of stability. Until the middle of the 17th century, Hanseatic merchants presided over a commercial confederation of member cities that stretched from Novgorod in Russia to London and as far south as the German Alps.

By the time Lübeck became the centre of Hanseatic activity in the middle of the 13th century, the league was much more than a guarantor of privileges and rights for the wealthy. By virtue of its collective power – and virtual monopoly on many strategic trade routes – it actually became one of the dominant political forces in Europe. The league dictated policy by threatening to withhold trading privileges. It even went to war. When challenged by Danish King Valdemar IV over control of the south-western Baltic, the league's members raised an army to thwart Danish goals and ensure their mastery over the Baltic region. But normally, well placed bribes to foreign officials were more than adequate to ensure unfettered trade.

For more than 500 years – and with little more in the way of central authority than its periodic meetings in Lübeck – the Hanseatic League brokered, bludgeoned or bribed Europe into the shape desired by its merchant member cities. It certainly lined the pockets of the rich, but even Thomas Mann was forced to admire its power in creating what he called 'a humane, cosmopolitan society'. It may have monitored, or often fixed, the prices of such commodities as grain, fur and ore, but it also established outposts in nations as vastly different as Russia and England which served, additionally, as forums for political exchange.

In essence, the Hanseatic League formulated many of the ideas of pragmatism, mutual protection and assured stability that guide today's commercially driven democracies. It was the distant forerunner of such powerful associations as NATO, the EU and the UN.

two sides of the Markt. Building began in 1230 and the complex grew over several centuries along with Lübeck's power and prosperity. The end result is a lavish, pan-shaped structure that's considered one of the most beautiful town halls in Germany. Most impressive is the southern facade of the north wing (1435), whose freestanding upper section sports three copper-clad spires and two large circular holes that lower the facade's resistance to wind, thus preventing it from being blown over. The cream-coloured Renaissance arcades are an embellishment from 1571. The comparatively plain, elongated middle section – part

of the 'panhandle' – is an expansion from the turn of the 14th century.

South of here is the so-called **Kriegs-stubenbau** (1444), which picks up the elements of the earlier sections – turrets, wind holes and arcades – with a row of coats of arms adding a splash of colour. The Breite Strasse side of this section boasts an elaborate Renaissance staircase. The inside of the Rathaus can only be seen on a guided tour, which runs weekdays at 11 am, noon and 3 pm (DM4/2). A highlight is the Audienzsaal (Audience Hall), a light-flooded hall decked out in festive rococo with 10 allegorical paintings showing the virtues of a

euro currency converter DM1 = €0.51

good town government – freedom, compassion, moderation, unity and so on.

Right behind the Rathaus rise the proud 125m spires of the **Marienkirche**, built between 1226 and 1350 by the town's secular leaders to demonstrate their power and independence from the church. The interior dimensions are overwhelming. The 80m-long centre nave rises 40m and is divided into two arcaded storeys. Floral ornamentation graces the vaulted ceilings and arches. Much of the interior decoration fell victim to WWII, whose destructiveness finds poignant expression in the chapel at the end of the south aisle: the shattered church bells – having crashed through the stone floor during a bombing raid – have been left where they fell as a memorial.

Another important chapel is the Marientidenkapelle (1518) behind the choir. Its stunning altar, a double tryptych with predella, contains elaborate gilded carvings portraying scenes from the life of Mary. Back towards the entrance on the south aisle stands the exquisite wooden statue of St John the Evangelist, clutching a goblet with a snake emerging from it. (In quite a reversed role for the biblical reptile, a serpent once warned the apostle that he was about to quaff poisoned wine – or so the legend goes). The Buxtehudeorgel (Buxtehude Organ) is one of the church's two and supposedly the largest mechanical one in the world.

On the north side of the Marienkirche at Mengstrasse 4 you'll find the **Buddenbrookhaus**, the house of the grandparents of literary giants Thomas and Heinrich Mann, which was immortalised in the former's 1929 novel *Die Buddenbrooks*. Today it houses an exhibit that documents, in chronological order, the literary accomplishments, family life, philosophical rivalry and years in exile of the brothers.

East of the Rathaus, at Breite Strasse 89, is **JG Niederegger**, a mecca for lovers of marzipan, a delicacy for which Lübeck is famous. The store has museum-quality displays that are worth checking out even if you don't have a sweet tooth.

Dom & St Annen Heinrich der Löwe laid the foundation for the Dom – Lübeck's oldest church – in 1173. Today's structure, in the southern Altstadt, is 130m long and harmoniously blends Romanesque and Gothic styles. If you approach the Dom from the north-east, you have to go through Hölle (hell) and Fegefeuer (purgatory) – the actual names of the streets – to get to the **Paradies**, the lavish vestibule through which you enter the Dom. Inside, the flamboyant 17m-high **Triumphal Cross** (1477) by Bernt Notke dominates. Immediately behind is the equally ornate, arcaded rood-loft, topped with another set of amazing carvings by Notke. Take a closer look at the integrated clock face: the eyes of the sun at its centre move from left to right (or should: apparently this mechanism doesn't always work).

Ecclesiastical art is the focus of the **St Annen Museum**, nearby at St-Annen-Strasse 15. Housed in a sprawling convent is a superb assortment of painted and gilded altars from the 15th and 16th centuries, of which the **Passion Altar** (1491) by Hans Memling stands out. Other exhibits illustrate the history of civilisation in Lübeck through to the end of the 18th century, with furniture, stoves, kitchen utensils, porcelain and even doll houses.

Northern & Eastern Altstadt In the Middle Ages, this charming section of central Lübeck was the quarter of craftspeople and artisans. When demand for housing outgrew the available space, tiny single-storey homes were built perpendicular to the streets and made accessible via little walkways from the main roads. More than 100 such passageways still exist today, but you have to look carefully to find their arched entrances. There's one, for instance, at Aegidienstrasse 47.

Also typical of Lübeck – and the age – are the charitable housing estates built for the poor by civic-minded citizens. They too are accessible via walkways, the so-called **Stiftsgänge**. Examples are Bruskows Gang at Wahmstrasse 47-51 and Glandorps Gang at Glockengiesserstrasse 41-51.

Glockengiesserstrasse meets König-strasse, where you'll see the towerless **Katharinenkirche**, built by the Franciscans. Part of the attractions here are the sculptures by Ernst Barlach and Gerhard Marcks set in niches in the facade, and *The Resurrection of Lazarus* by Tintoretto, poorly displayed on the right as you enter. Continuing north on Königstrasse you reach the pretty square Koberg. This is flanked by the **Heiligen-Geist-Hospital**, the oldest hospital in Germany (1246), which functioned as a home for elderly people until 1972 and is now the site of Lübeck's Christmas market. Four slender octagonal spires alternating with gables dominate its distinctive exterior. Inside is an early-Gothic hall church with a rood-loft decorated with scenes from the life of St Elisabeth. In the hospital hall you'll see the little chambers that were put in around 1820 to give the sick and old a certain degree of privacy. Admission to the complex is free.

Gothmund The charming settlement of Gothmund, nestled along one side of the Trave River on the northern outskirts of Lübeck, is a fishers' village with rows of historic (and a few modern) thatched cottages. What makes Gothmund unique is that it combines all the elements of a rural settlement in this region: quaint thatched cottages, pretty gardens planted with fruit trees, grassy ponds, small fishing boats moored in a harbour among reeds – it shimmers gloriously on a warm summer's day. The rural setting is marred somewhat by a quarry and transformer station across the river, but it's still worth the ride out here. Stroll along Fischerweg, a path running in front of the cottages, or take the same path west, which leads through a nature reserve beside the Trave.

To reach Gothmund, take bus No 12 to the last stop. The cottages are at the end (north) of the road. Buses leave three times an hour from Lübeck's main bus station.

Organised Tours

Guided two-hour city walking tours (DM8/6) depart daily from the tourist office at Breite Strasse 62, in May, June and October from Monday to Saturday at 2 pm, and Sunday at 11 am. In the summer months, they're available at 11 am and 2 pm (Sunday at 11 am only). From November to April they run at 2 pm on Saturday and 11 am on Sunday.

From May to September, the open double-deck City-Tour bus operates 50-minute tours at 10.30 and 11.30 am, and hourly from 1 pm to 5 pm. They leave from the corner of Kohlmarkt and Wahmstrasse (DM9/6).

A number of boat operators, like Quandt-Linie and Maak-Linie, run one-hour tours through the city canals encircling the Altstadt. Boats are scheduled to leave every half an hour, though many actually don't leave until they're at least half full. The landing docks are north of the Holstentorbrücke. Trips cost DM6/10/12 for children/students/adults.

Places to Stay

The city-run tourist offices can help with accommodation bookings; the tourist office at the Hauptbahnhof charges a DM5 booking fee. Unless noted, room rates listed below include breakfast.

Camping Open from April to October, *Campingplatz Schönböcken* (☎ 89 30 90, *Steinrader Damm 12)* is located in the western suburb of Schönböcken, with a direct bus connection (No 7) to the city centre. Charges are DM6 per tent, plus DM7 per person and DM2 per car.

Hostels Lübeck has two DJH hostels. The excellent *Jugendgästehaus* (☎ 702 03 99, *fax 770 12, Mengstrasse 33)* is well situated in the middle of the Altstadt, 15 minutes walk from the Hauptbahnhof (or bus No 3 or 12 to Beckergrube). The cost for juniors/seniors is DM30/38.50 in three or four-bed rooms and DM32/41 in single or two-bed rooms. Rates include breakfast and sheets, and discounts on subsequent nights are available. *Folke-Bernadotte-Heim* (☎ 334 33, fax 345 40, Am Gertrudenkirchhof 4) is a little outside the Altstadt. Take bus No 1, 3, 11, 12 or 31 from the Hauptbahnhof to

Gustav-Radbruch-Platz, from where it's a five minute walk. B&B costs DM27/32 for juniors/seniors.

The YMCA's *Sleep-Inn* (☎ *719 20, fax 789 97, Grosse Petersgrube 11)* charges DM15 per bed in dorms. A double room is DM40. It also has a two-bed apartment with private bath and kitchenette for DM30 per person, and another that sleeps three to four people for DM40 per person. Breakfast costs DM5 and sheets an extra DM6.50. It's closed from mid-December to mid-January.

The small *Rucksackhotel* (☎ *70 68 92, fax 707 34 29, Kanalstrasse 70)* has beds in four to eight-bed rooms with shared facilities for DM21 to DM26. It also has a few doubles with private bath for DM75 and a four-bed room, also with shower and WC, for DM128. Prices do not include breakfast but there are cooking facilities. It only has 28 beds, so you'd be wise to book ahead. A live concert venue, the Werkhof, is in the same building. Take bus No 8 to Falkenstrasse and walk back over the bridge.

Hotels The *Hotel zum Scheibenstand* (☎ *47 33 82, fax 325 74, Fackenburger Allee 76)* is a basic place south of the town centre. No-frills singles/doubles here cost DM40/60 with shared shower and WC. Breakfast is extra.

The family-friendly *Herberge zur Alten Stadtmauer* (☎ *737 02, fax 732 39, An der Mauer 57)* has basic rooms for DM50/110 and rooms with private shower and WC for DM75/130. Family rooms are available, too.

The *Pension Koglin* (☎ *62 24 32, fax 610 16 65, Kottwitzstrasse 39)* is a bit north of the centre and strictly nonsmoking. It charges from DM75/95 for rooms with private shower and toilet.

The *Hotel Stadt Lübeck* (☎ *838 83, fax 86 32 21, Am Bahnhof 21)* is just outside the Hauptbahnhof, opposite the bus station. It's quieter than its location suggests. Rooms with private bath start at DM75/129. Several mid-price hotels are on the other side of the bus station.

The central *Hotel Schwarzwaldstuben* (☎ *777 15, fax 70 54 14, Koberg 12-15)* has

rooms with full facilities ranging from DM75 to DM95 for singles, and DM135 to DM150 for doubles. The *Altstadt Hotel* (☎ *720 83, fax 737 78, Fischergrube 52)* is just as convenient, offering pleasant singles/doubles from DM135/185 and small suites for DM210/240.

The *Mövenpick Hotel* (☎ *150 40, fax 150 41 119)* is nicely situated opposite the Holstentor. Singles cost from DM175 to DM260, doubles from DM215 to DM300, and breakfast is an extra DM23. *Radisson SAS* (☎ *14 20, fax 142 22 22, Willy-Brandt-Allee 6)* is top of the line, with state-of-the-art singles/doubles during the week for DM200/250 without breakfast and weekend rates of DM205/240 with breakfast.

Places to Eat

Miera (☎ *772 12, Hüxstrasse 57)* is a gourmet food shop and bistro decked out in cheerful yellowish decor and serving Italian-style dishes from DM15 to DM30. Lübeck has at least two restaurants with a potato theme: *Kartoffelkeller* (☎ *762 34, Koberg 8)*, downstairs at the Heiligen-Geist-Hospital (closed Tuesday) and *Kartoffelhaus* (Schluhmacherstrasse 4). Dishes at both start at around DM10.

Tipasa (☎ *706 04 51, Schluhmacher-strasse 14)* is a popular student haunt that serves a variety of budget-priced meat, fish and vegetarian dishes as well as excellent pizzas. *Schmidt's Gasthaus* (☎ *761 82, Dr-Julius-Leber-Strasse 60-62)* is hard to beat for its steaks (from DM20), vegetarian dishes (from DM10), pizza (from DM7) and other dishes.

The *Brauberger* (Alfstrasse 36) serves a small selection of well priced pub fare and has a buffet with hot and cold dishes. It's closed Sunday. The rustic *Hierony-mus* (☎ *706 30 17, Fleischhauerstrasse 81)* is a cosy restaurant spread over three floors of a narrow 17th century building. Most dishes on the creative menu cost DM10 to DM20 and are quite filling. Lunch specials are served here until 5 pm weekdays for around DM10. It's open till at least 1 am.

Schiffergesellschaft (☎ *767 76, Breite Strasse 2*) is in the former sailors' guildhall. You sit beneath a painted and beamed wooden ceiling on long benches that resemble church pews. Above you are 17th century models of ships, while the walls are covered with large oil paintings. It's an atmosphere second to none, though you have to put up with crowds and a menu starting at DM30.

Amadeus (*Königstrasse 26*) is a good cafe to linger in over a cup of coffee and drinks till quite late. It also serves light meals, and is known for its generous breakfasts (open from 10 am). The trendy *Café Remise* (*Wahmstrasse 43-45*) has sparse decor and a bistro menu of salads, pasta and some creative dishes with an Italian flavour for under DM16.

JG Niederegger (see Markt & Around under Things to See) has a cafe at the rear. Self-caterers can head for the *Co-Op supermarket* near Kohlmarkt.

Entertainment

For up-to-date event information, pick up a copy of *Lübeck Heute*, free from the tourist offices. Geared towards a younger audience are the magazines *Szene* and *Piste*, free in pubs, restaurants and also the tourist offices. *Ultimo* is more subdued and *Nord* covers high-brow culture in northern Germany.

Rock & Jazz The *Werkhof* (☎ *757 18, Kanalstrasse 70*) is one of Lübeck's premier concert venues – from rock and blues to flamenco. *Hüx* (☎ *766 33, Hüxterdamm 14*) is a disco nearby. *Dr Jazz* (☎ *705 9 09, An der Untertrave 1*) is the place for cool jazz.

Classical Music The *Musikhochschule Lübeck* (☎ *150 50, Grosse Petersgrube 17-29*) is a music academy that puts on a number of high-calibre concerts throughout the summer and winter semesters. Most concerts are free. The Brahms Festival takes place here at the end of April.

Lübeck is famous for its organ concerts played on the two organs of the *Marienkirche* at least once a week throughout the year. Tickets are available on the night of the performance only and cost DM9/6. There are also organ concerts in the *Jacobikirche* on Königstrasse. Ask for the current schedule at the tourist offices or call ☎ 790 21 27.

Theatre The *Theater Lübeck* (☎ *745 52, Beckergrube 10-14*), housed in an Art Nouveau building, is the place to go for drama, musicals, dance, theatre and more. *Theater Combinale* (☎ *788 17, Hüxstrasse 115*) puts on avant-garde theatre by new playwrights.

The *Marionettentheater* (☎ *700 60*), on the corner of Am Kolk and Kleine Petersgrube, is a terrific puppet theatre. There is a children's show at 3 pm and one for adults on Friday (and sometimes Saturday) at 7.30 pm. Afternoon seats cost DM8; evening seats cost DM13 to DM16, depending on the play; discounts run from DM10 to DM13. The theatre is closed on Monday.

Getting There & Away

Train Lübeck has connections to Hamburg at least once an hour (DM17, 45 minutes) and also to Kiel (DM23, 1¼ hours). A direct train goes to Rostock every two hours (DM37, 1¾ hours).

Bus Regional buses stop opposite the local buses on Hansestrasse, around the corner from the Hauptbahnhof. Kraftomnibusse services to/from Wismar terminate here, as do the Autokraft buses to/from Hamburg, Schwerin, Kiel, Rostock and Berlin.

Car & Motorcycle If you're driving, Lübeck is easily reached via the A1 from Hamburg. The town also lies at the crossroads of the B75, the B104 to Schwerin, the B206 to Bad Segeberg and the B207 to Ratzeburg.

Boat Finnlines (☎ 150 74 43, fax 150 74 44), Grosse Alte Fähre 24-26, runs ships from Lübeck's Nordlandkai to Helsinki (36 hours) daily, year round. Prices depend on cabin class and range from DM360/460 to DM735/990 one-way in winter/summer. Return trips cost from DM650/830 to DM1320/1790 in winter/summer; there are cheap round trips on the same boat and discounts for kids.

Getting Around

Lübeck's city centre is easily walkable, but there's also an excellent bus system. Stadtwerke Lübeck (☎ 888 28 28) has a convenient office at the bus station. Short-trip tickets valid for three stops cost DM2.30, single tickets DM3.20 and blocks of six short-trip/single tickets are DM11.50/15.50. Weekly tickets cost DM21. All these, except short-trip tickets, are valid for Travemünde and Gothmund, as is the 24 hour Lübeck Karte (DM9, or DM17 for family tickets valid for two adults, three children). This is different from the Lübeck-Travemünde Card (see Information in the Lübeck section).

Leihcycle (☎ 426 60), Schwartauer Allee 39, rents out touring bikes for DM8 a day.

TRAVEMÜNDE
☎ 04502 • pop 12,000

In 1329 when the rich city of Lübeck bought Travemünde, 20km to its north, for what must have been the pocket change sum of 1060 marks, the motivation wasn't beach but business. The goal was to control the spot where the Trave River flows into the Baltic Sea and therefore to secure access for ships to the harbour at Lübeck.

It wasn't until 1802 that Travemünde also became a resort town, the third on the German seaside after Norderney and Heiligendamm.

In 1894, Emperor Wilhelm II brought a spot of glamour to the town when he participated in the Travemünde Week, a sailing regatta and the town's answer to Kieler Woche. Henceforth, until WWI, it became an event *de rigueur* for the aristocracy and industrial elite.

Today, Travemünde is a much more down-to-earth coastal playground, often bursting with visitors during the summer months. They come to stroll on its promenade or to catch the rays on its 4.5km of sandy beaches. Water sports (sailing, surfing, swimming, fishing) are popular here, and the casino offers glamorous entertainment at night. The Aqua Top outdoor pool, with slides, jacuzzis and other fun installations, is a recent addition to the list of activities.

Once a gateway to Scandinavia, Travemünde's importance has diminished somewhat in recent times. Services operate to Finland, Sweden and the Baltic region (see Getting There & Away later in this section).

The tourist office (☎ 804 30, fax 804 60) is near the Nordermole in the large Aqua Top swimming baths complex at Strandpromenade 1b.

Places to Stay

Strandcamping Priwall (☎ 717 92) is right on the beach. It is open from April to September. *Campingplatz Auf dem Priwall* (☎ 22 34, Mecklenburger Landstrasse 89a) is open from mid-March to September. Both are practically next to each other on the Priwall Peninsula on the southern side of the Untertrave River.

The *Jugendfreizeitstätte Priwall* (☎ 25 76, Mecklenburger Landstrasse 69) caters more for groups. It is open from June to mid-September. Beds in rustic cabins cost DM15/20 for juniors/seniors, plus a visitor's tax of DM5 in summer and DM2 in the off-season if you stay longer than one night.

Private rooms, hotel rooms or holiday flats can be booked through the free tourist office reservation service on ☎ 804 32.

Hotel Daheim (☎ 742 40, fax 742 47, Kaiserallee 35) has budget singles/doubles from DM45/65 during the high season.

Getting There & Away

Train There are regular connections from Lübeck to Travemünde, which has three stations: Skandinavienkai, Hafenbahnhof and Strandbahnhof. Most trains stop at all three.

Bus From Lübeck's central bus station, bus Nos 30 and 31 provide direct services to Travemünde.

Car & Motorcycle From Lübeck, the B75 leads north-east to Travemünde. If you're travelling on the A1, catch the A226 connecting road to the B75.

Boat TT-Line (☎ 801 81, fax 801 11, or in Hamburg on ☎ 040-360 14 42) operates boats from Travemünde to Trelleborg in Sweden daily (7½ hours). The cost per passenger is DM50/100 one-way/return, DM25/50 for students. The cost for a car plus up to five passengers is from DM180/310 to DM310/570, depending on the season (bikes DM10/20). The cost for a car plus a driver is from DM140/230 to DM270/490.

Finnlines Passagierdienst (☎ 0451-150 74 43, fax 0451-150 74 44), Grosse Alte Fähre 24-26 in Lübeck, runs ships year round between Helsinki and Travemünde four times a week. The trip takes 35 hours and costs from DM280/330 to DM630/825 one-way in the winter/summer period, or from DM500/590 to DM1140/1490 return in winter/summer, depending on the cabin class and ship. This includes all meals. The one-way cost for a car is from DM130/160 winter/summer, and return DM230/290 in winter/summer. There are discounts on short round trips on the same ship and for children.

Baltic Tours (☎ 52 01, fax 56 54) runs ships to Riga (Latvia) and Kaliningrad (Russia) twice weekly; Euroseabridge (☎ 862 40, fax 86 24 15) has a service to Klaipeda four times weekly, and LK-Linie (☎ 75 30 40, fax 753 04 20) runs boats to Kaliningrad once a week. All operators have offices at the Skandinavienkai (Scandinavia Quay).

Getting Around

Travemünde is small enough to be walked, but to get around quicker you can rent a bicycle from Beitsch (☎ 66 22) at Kurgartenstrasse 67 (DM10 a day) and Bruders (☎ 53 40) at Mecklenburger Landstrasse 14 (DM8 per day).

To get to Priwall, on the southern shore of the Trave River, there's a car ferry from Vorderreihe and also a passenger ferry from the quay near Nordermole (summer only).

SCHLESWIG

☎ 04621 • pop 26,500

First mentioned in public records in 804, Schleswig is the oldest town in northern Europe and its long history has bestowed on it a plethora of first-rate sights and attractions. About 34km east of Husum and the same distance south of Flensburg, Schleswig is a placid town scenically wrapped around the lake-sized terminus of the Schlei – at 40km, the longest and narrowest Baltic Sea fjord.

Schleswig muddled through the Middle Ages as a minor farming and artisans' town, not gaining much importance until 1544 when the dukes of Gottorf chose it as their residence. Thanks to their interest in art and science, Schleswig developed into a cultural centre in the late-Renaissance and baroque periods. The town's heyday lasted as long as the ducal power and, after 1721, Schleswig was once again relegated to a provincial backwater.

After the German-Danish War of 1864, Schleswig went to Prussia and it has been part of the state of Schleswig-Holstein since the end of WWII. Despite its relatively small size, you'll need at least one full day to explore it entirely.

Orientation

Schleswig's train station is about 1km south of Schloss Gottorf and 3km from the city centre (take bus No 1, 2, 4 or 5). The central bus station is on the corner of Königstrasse and Plessenstrasse, with the Altstadt and the Dom to the south-east.

Information

The tourist office (☎ 248 78, fax 207 03) is at Plessenstrasse 7. Between May and September, it's open weekdays from 9 am to 12.30 pm and 1.30 to 5 pm, and Saturday from 9 am to noon. In winter, it's closed on Friday afternoon and weekends. Here you can get the SchleswigCard, which offers unlimited access to public transport, admission to all museums and various reductions for three consecutive days (DM13, or families DM29). A touch screen and phone outside is useful for accommodation if the office is closed.

euro currency converter DM1 = €0.51

The Sparkasse at Stadtweg 49 exchanges money and also has an ATM machine that accepts all major credit cards. You'll find the post office practically next door at Stadtweg 53-55 (closed at lunchtime).

Bookshops with selections of English-language books are Liesegang at Stadtweg 8 and Die Eule at Mönchenbrückstrasse 10. There's a self-service Waschcenter next to Karstadt at Stadtweg 70, which is open from 6 am to 10 pm and costs DM6 per wash, plus DM1 for the dryer.

The local hospital, Martin-Luther-Krankenhaus (☎ 81 20) is at Lutherstrasse 22. The police station (☎ 841) is at Friedrich-Ebert-Strasse 8.

Dom St Petri

In the centre of the Altstadt is the imposing Cathedral of St Petri, a Schleswig landmark and the oldest surviving building in town (around 1134), which is filled with wonderful art treasures. Upon entering, the first thing you will see is a wooden **statue of St Christopher** (1515), the patron saint of travellers. It was carved by Hans Brüggemann, who was also responsible for the **Bordesholmer Altar** (1521) in the east choir – nothing will prepare you for this amazing display of complex, superb craftsmanship. The altar itself measures 12.6m x 7.14m, but it's the figurines, more than 400 of them – carved with amazing detail and perfectly composed – that impress most. In 24 scenes, they tell the story of the Passion of Christ. Bring binoculars, if you have some, to truly appreciate this roped-off masterpiece and the ceiling frescoes above.

To reach the altar, you pass through the rood-loft, in this case an arcade with pointed arches held up by Corinthian columns and carrying a **Triumphal Cross**. South of the main altar is the canopied **Dreikönigsaltar** (around 1300), which shows the three Magi with Mary and Jesus. In the niche north of the altar stands the monumental **tomb** of King Friedrich I of Denmark, formerly a Gottorf duke. Antwerp sculptor Cornelis Floris used black, green and red marble as well as alabaster for this work.

Opening hours for the Dom are from May to September, Monday to Thursday and Saturday from 9 am to 12.30 pm and 1.30 to 5 pm. On Friday it opens from 10 am and closes at 3 pm. On Sunday it opens from 1.30 to 5 pm. Shave an hour off all opening and closing times the rest of the year. Concerts take place in the cathedral at 8 pm on Wednesday in summer.

Holm

South-east of the Altstadt is this traditional fishing village, which was an island until 1935. Even today, about 20 active fishermen haul in eel, perch, salmon and herring from the Schlei waters. Right in the centre of Holm is an almost toy-sized **chapel** ringed by a starkly symmetrical cemetery whose graves are curiously framed by low hedges. Only residents of Holm may be buried here. Continue along Süderholmstrasse to get to the **Johanniskloster**, a former Benedictine convent and a collegiate foundation for noblewomen since the Reformation. Its Romanesque church was redecorated in the baroque style. It can be seen during a guided tour with the prioress (call ahead on ☎ 242 36) or on an official walking tour of Holm (ask at the tourist office about upcoming walks).

Schloss Gottorf

The rather plain exterior of this palace does not hint at the marvellous design and wealth of art treasures – from the Middle Ages to the 20th century – awaiting within. The building itself, which has its origins in 1161, was the former residence of the dukes of Gottorf and later used as a military barracks. After WWII it was chosen as the new home for the collections of the Schleswig-Holstein Landesmuseum (☎ 81 30), which lost its former domicile in Kiel to bombing raids.

Highlights include the **medieval section** on the ground floor (rooms 1-5) with altars, sculptures and paintings by such notables as Lucas Cranach the Elder. Upstairs you'll find an original wood-panelled 17th century wine tavern from Lübeck with carvings by Hinrich Sextra II. The adjoining rooms shed light on the lifestyle of the Gottorf family, with fancy furniture, paintings, tapestries and books from the baroque period. Don't miss the circular room 20, which boasts a fine collection of alabaster and marble sculpture. Also of note are rooms 48-56, filled with Art Nouveau furniture, paintings, objects and works by Henry van de Velde, Peter Behrens and Wenzel Hablik.

Architecturally, one of the most interesting rooms is the **Gotische Halle** (room 3) in the south wing, which is divided by a row of pillars supporting a cross-vaulted ceiling. Upstairs is the rococo **Plöner Saal**, with a collection of faïence originating from the Baltic region. In the north wing is the **Schlosskapelle** (room 26), a small church whose gallery is shouldered by a series of Ionic columns. Below is a small ebony altar with delicate silver decorations. The northern end of the gallery is taken up by the **Betstube**, a separate room reserved for the ducal family that is lavishly panelled with precious inlaid wood. It's the only room in the church that can be heated. Next door is the **Hirschsaal**, the former banquet hall, which derives its name from the deer frescoes on the walls. These contrast with the monochrome scenes from Roman history painted on the vaulted ceiling.

Turn left as you exit the main building to get to the **Kreuzstall**, whose three floors contain a striking collection of German 20th century art, including paintings by Brücke members Kirchner, Heckel, Pechstein, Nolde, Schmidt-Rottluff and Otto Müller.

The museum is open daily from 9 am to 5 pm. From November to February it opens from 9.30 am to 4 pm (DM7/3). If you read German, it pays to invest in the handy and thorough museum guide (DM8).

Viking Museum

The area of Haithabu, on the southern side of the Schlei Fjord, was the most important economic centre in northern Europe during the Viking era around the 9th century. The 24 hectare settlement is marked only by the remains of its semicircular wall. To make it all meaningful, visit the Wikinger Museum, about 3km from the train station (bus No 4810), east of the B76. A 30m-long Viking longboat has been artfully reconstructed inside, and objects displayed in glass cases provide insight into the everyday life of the Vikings. The museum (☎ 81 33 00) is open from April to October daily from 9 am to 5 pm, and the rest of the year from Tuesday to Sunday from 10 am to 4 pm (DM4/2). For ferry service across the Schlei to Haithabu, see Getting Around.

Places to Stay

Campingplatz Haithabu (☎ 324 50) is right on the southern shore of the Schlei in Haddeby, with a great view of the Schleswig skyline (take bus No 4810). It's open from March to October and costs DM6/11/4 per person/tent/car. The *Jugendherberge (☎ 238 93, fax 207 96, Spielkoppel 1)* charges DM21/26 juniors/seniors for B&B. From the train station, take bus No 1, 2 or 4 to the Stadttheater stop, then walk.

The tourist office has a room-booking service (DM8, or DM3 in advance). *Private rooms* start at DM25 per person.

Some hotels charge less in the low season. The *Hotel-Restaurant Schleiblick (☎/fax 234 68, Hafengang 4)* has singles/doubles from DM65/110 with shower and WC. The *Hotel Hohenzollern (☎ 90 60, fax 90 61 69, Moltkestrasse 41)* charges DM79/120 for rooms with shower and WC. The *Stadt Hamburg (☎ 90 40, fax 90 42 22, Lollfuss 108)* has rooms with shower and WC for DM85/135. *Hotel Olschewski's (☎ 255 77, fax 221 41, Hafenstrasse 40)* is also right on the harbour. Rooms with shower and WC cost from DM90/140; there's a good restaurant, too.

Places to Eat

Schleswig's main street for restaurants and bars is Lollfuss, one of the roads connecting the Altstadt with Schloss Gottorf to the west. *Patio (☎ 299 99)* at No 3, is a reasonably priced cafe-restaurant set in a lovely courtyard. The huge, rustic *Brauerei Schleswig (Königstrasse 27)* is the best all-round place for food and a drink. It sells decent house brews, a small range of well priced dishes and is open till at least midnight. *Panorama (Plessenstrasse 15)* offers wood-fired pizza, and has daily lunch specials for DM9.

The *Schleimöve (Süderholmstrasse 8)*, in Holm, is an excellent fish restaurant with dishes in the DM24 to DM35 price range. The *Stadt Flensburg (Lollfuss 102)* is small and cosy, serving a range of specialities from Schleswig-Holstein. The *Senatorkroog (Rathausmarkt 9-10)*, in a historic building, is one of the nicest (and priciest) places in town.

Getting There & Away

A direct train service to Hamburg (DM38, 1½ hours) runs every two hours, while trains to Flensburg (DM10, 30 minutes) leave several times hourly. There's also an hourly link to Husum (DM10, 30 minutes) and Kiel (DM14.80, 50 minutes). There are several daily buses, with restricted service on weekends, to Kiel (No 4810), Flensburg (No 4810) and Husum (No 1046). If you're driving, take the A7 (Hamburg-Flensburg) to the Schuby exit, then continue east on the B201.

Boat From mid-June to early September, the Schleischiffahrt A Bischoff (☎ 233 19) runs a scheduled boat service along the Schlei. Boats depart daily except Tuesday from the Schleihallenbrücke near Schloss Gottorf and travel as far as Ulsnis, about 15km to the north-east, which has a beautiful Romanesque church (about 1½ hours, DM8, return DM14). Trips from Schleswig all the way to the mouth of the Schlei into the Baltic Sea, just beyond Kappeln, are offered on Tuesday (DM13, return DM23, 3½ hours). Children up to age 12 pay half price. The company also runs three-hour excursions on the Schlei every Sunday, Wednesday, Thursday and holidays from May to mid-June and most of September (DM14).

Getting Around

Tickets for Schleswig's bus system cost DM1.90 per trip. Places that rent bicycles

are Splettstösser (☎ 241 02; DM9 per day) at Bismarckstrasse 13 and Peters (☎ 376 88) at Bahnhofstrasse 14. Ferries cross the Schlei channel to Haithabu daily between May and September from 12.30 to 5.30 pm and cost DM3.50/6 one-way/return; children pay DM2.50/4.

FLENSBURG
☎ 0461   • pop 90,000

Flensburg is the northernmost town on the German mainland, located about 150km north of Hamburg on the Danish border. It's an attractive town, hugging the shores of the Flensburg Firth and ringed by low hills – a strange sight on the plains of northern Germany. It's blessed with a handsome Altstadt, the work of visionary conservationists who, in the 1960s and 70s, silenced those in favour of razing and rebuilding. Flensburg is small enough to be explored in a day.

In 1284 Flensburg was awarded town rights but really only blossomed *after* the decline of the Hanseatic League in the 16th century. For centuries, squabbles between the dukes of Schleswig, the counts of Holstein and the Danish crown had kept Flensburg in the shadow of Lübeck and other Hanseatic cities. Only after King Christian I of Denmark was elected Duke of Schleswig and Count of Holstein in 1460 did Flensburg evolve into one of the region's most important merchant towns.

In the 18th century, its ships sailed as far as the Caribbean and returned loaded with rum, and to this day the town is also known as the 'Rumstadt'. From this prosperous era date the many *Kaufmannshöfe* (merchants' courtyards) that are unique to Flensburg. These complexes usually consisted of a section facing the main street that contained the merchant's living quarters, often with an office or store on the ground floor. Directly behind was a series of low buildings, wrapped around a central courtyard, where workshops were located. A tall warehouse stood on the other end – the harbour side – which made it easier to load and unload goods quickly and cheaply.

The Last 'Führer'

In 1945, with the Russians advancing quickly from the east and British and American armies closing in from the west, the small town of Mürwik, just outside Flensburg, became the final seat of government for the disintegrating Nazi regime.

In the final weeks of the war, Hitler, broken, paranoid and busily scribbling his final testament in a Berlin bunker, decided at the last minute against appointing one of his two henchman, Himmler and Goebbels, to take over the Nazi government and opted instead for Admiral Karl Dönitz. Dönitz had earned a reputation as the ruthless commander of the German naval fleet, having developed the nasty tactic of attacking Allied – and several neutral – merchant ships in submarine 'packs'. He was also a loyal officer who believed in traditional officer values and served the regime without ever questioning its brutality. He instilled in his submarine crews a sense of duty to the Third Reich that they could better have done without: three-quarters of his 40,000-strong submarine crew perished during the war.

Conveniently, Dönitz was based in Schleswig-Holstein, one of the few parts of Germany not occupied when Hitler committed suicide on 30 April 1945.

The government sat for some time in Plön, near Lübeck, then scrambled farther north to Flensburg for the final 20 days of the 'Thousand Year Reich'. From his headquarters in Mürwik/Flensburg, Dönitz, who neither wanted nor felt up to the job, declared Germany's total surrender.

But that was not the end of the matter for Dönitz. Hitler's loyal admiral was brought to trial in Nuremberg in 1946 for war crimes, accused of having issued an implicit order to kill rather than rescue the crews of enemy torpedoed ships. He was found guilty of committing war crimes and sentenced to 10 years in prison.

Today, these *Höfe* house restaurants, cafes, boutiques and galleries.

Flensburg escaped the bombing of WWII, and the local naval academy was in fact the seat of the last Third Reich government, under Admiral Karl Dönitz, who fled here to escape the Allied troops, finally surrendering on 7 May 1945 (see 'The Last Führer' boxed text).

Orientation & Information

It's easy to orientate yourself in Flensburg, for most of its sights are strung along the pedestrian zone anchored by Südermarkt and Nordermarkt and its sidestreets. The harbour is just north-east of here, while the train station is about a 10 minute walk south of Südermarkt. The central bus station (ZOB) is at the end of Rathausstrasse on Süderhofenden near the harbour area.

The tourist office (☎ 909 09 20, fax 909 09 36) is inside the Amalien-Lamp-Speicher, a former warehouse, opposite the car park at Speicherlinie 40, and is open weekdays from 9 am to 6 pm (also on Saturday from 10 am to 1 pm between June and September).

The Sparkasse bank on the corner of Holm and Rathausstrasse offers all services and has a currency exchange machine. The main post office is at Bahnhofstrasse 40, and there's a second branch on Nordermarkt. For a selection of English books, go to the Montanus bookshop at Holm 20. There are self-service laundrettes at Angelburger Strasse 45 and at Flurstrasse 27.

Walking Tour

From the train station, head north through the gardens, with sculptures carved out of tree stumps, to Platz der Gärtner. Cross here and veer left (west) to Rote Strasse, where you'll find some of Flensburg's typical **merchants' courtyards** – the Blumenhof at No 18-20 and the Krusehof at No 24.

Rote Strasse merges with Südermarkt, which is dominated by the **Nikolaikirche**, a Gothic red-brick hall church from 1390. The bronze baptismal font (1497) was the only piece of its medieval decoration to survive the Reformation. An artful work by Peter Hansen, it is supported by statues of the four Evangelists and shows scenes from the life of Christ. The church's *pièce de résistance* is the organ, with its flashy Renaissance encasement by Heinrich Ringerink.

Continue north on Holm and look for other courtyards, including the **Dethleffsen-Hof** at No 43-45, and the **Borgerforeningen Hof** at No 17 with a large chestnut tree. Turning left (west) onto Rathausstrasse and heading uphill will get you to the **Städtisches Museum** (Municipal Museum). The highlights are furnished farmhouse rooms from the 17th century and paintings by Emil Nolde. There's also a nice view from atop the Museumsberg. It's open Tuesday to Saturday from 10 am to 5 pm, and to 1 pm on Sunday (DM5/2.50). Keep your ticket, as it's valid for all city museums for up to one month.

Head back down Rathausstrasse and continue north on what is now Grosse Strasse where, after a short while, you'll pass the **Heiliggeistkirche** (1386), modestly integrated into a row of houses. It's the place of worship of the resident Danish minority, and is decorated with late-medieval frescoes and a baroque altar. Parallel to Grosse Strasse (east) is the Speicherlinie with the tourist office.

Grosse Strasse spills into Nordermarkt, above which rises the most magnificent of Flensburg's churches, the **Marienkirche**, begun in 1284. Of note are the frescoes, the only decoration predating the Reformation. Most impressive, though, is the sumptuous high altar (1598) by Ringerink. It's topped by a superstructure of gables and giant portraits of the merchant couple who donated the altar. In fact, the great number of epitaphs in this church confirms that modesty was apparently not a trait of Flensburg's rich merchants. Check out the Niels Hacke epitaph at the end of the northern aisle, which integrates a painting by Heinrich Jansen, a student of Rembrandt.

If you continue beyond the Marienkirche, on what is now Norderstrasse, you'll get to the **Nordertor** (1595), a Flensburg landmark and one of the few surviving town gates in Schleswig-Holstein. The town motto is inscribed on its north side: 'Friede ernährt, Unfriede verzehrt' (Peace nurtures, strife consumes).

To learn more about the history of shipping and the rum trade in Flensburg, visit the **Schiffahrtsmuseum** (Maritime Museum; same hours as the Städtisches Museum), Schiffbrücke 39, on the harbour.

Organised Tours

Boat trips leave from the firth at Schiffbrücke. Because most are connected in some way with duty-free shopping, there's likely to be a high attrition rate after 1999 once duty-free allowances are abolished within the EU. Consult timetables and operators on the dock to see what's currently on offer.

The tourist office can also help with information on short trips around the harbour and to Glücksburg. Most services operate from May to September. Nordlicht Reisen (☎ 980 02, fax 989 01) operates services to Glücksburg departing from Schiffbrücke up to five times a day in season (adults DM6, children DM4).

Places to Stay

Campingplatz Jarplund (☎ 932 34) is on the B76 south of Flensburg. It's open from April to October. Flensburg's *DJH hostel* (☎ 377 42, fax 31 29 52, Fichtestrasse 16) charges DM21/26 for juniors/seniors. From the train station, take bus No 1 to the ZOB, then No 3, 5 or 7 to the Stadion stop.

The tourist office reserves rooms for free. *Private rooms* start at DM15 per person without breakfast. The *Pension Ziesemer* (☎ 251 64 fax 215 41, Wilhelmstrasse 2) has basic singles/doubles for DM40/80 and rooms with shower and WC for DM60/110. The *Hotel Handwerkerhaus* (☎ 14 48 00, fax 144 80 44, Augustastrasse 2) offers nicely furnished rooms for DM70/110 with private bath. *Hotel am Rathaus* (☎ 173 33, fax 18 13 82, Rote Strasse 32) is nicer inside than its exterior and the staircase suggest. Rooms here cost from DM85/140 with shower and WC. The *Europa-Comfort-Hotel* (☎ 841 10, fax 841 12 99, *Norderhofenden 6-9*) has a great location on the harbour, and state-of-the-art rooms for DM135/160 with all facilities.

Places to Eat
The *Weinstube (Rote Strasse 24)* is a cosy place to go for a glass of wine. Food ranges from soup for DM5 to a succulent plate of shrimp for DM25 (dinner only). If beer is more to your liking, Flensburg has a very good microbrewery: *Hansens Brauerei (☎ 222 10, Grosse Strasse 83)*, near Nordermarkt. It makes an impressive pilsener beer that's 'hoppy' and full-flavoured. It also brews seasonal beers – ask at the bar. You can watch the wares being made, while sitting in a historic tram, downing big burgers, steaks and fish dishes at very reasonable prices.

Brasserie Napoleon (☎ 220 22, Grosse Strasse 42-44) is in a half-timbered building at the end of a courtyard. Here you can dine on regional fare from DM18 to DM28 for main courses in wood-panelled rooms surrounded by gold-leaf mirrors and oil paintings.

There are plenty of cheap places for snacks in the centre. *Kaiser's* supermarket is in the passage near the tourist office. The *Galerie (Holm 66)*, in the same passage, is an arty bar that opens in the evening and often has live music.

Getting There & Around
Flensburg has rail connections with Kiel (DM23, 1¼ hours), Hamburg (DM48, 1¾ hours) and Schleswig (DM10, 30 minutes). Trips to Husum (DM15, 1½ hours) require a change at Jübeck.

There's a regular Autokraft (☎ 90 33 90, bus No 4810) service to Schleswig (DM9.50, one hour) and on to Kiel (DM15, 2½ hours). Bus No 1044 goes daily to Husum (DM10, 1¼ hour).

Flensburg is at the beginning of the A7, which leads south to Hamburg, Hanover and

beyond. The town can also be reached via the B76, B199 and B200. The ADM Mitfahrzentrale (☎ 194 40) is at St-Jürgen-Platz 1.

You can easily cover all of Flensburg on foot. Fahrrad Petersen (☎ 254 55), at Hafermarkt 19, rents out bicycles for DM12 a day.

GLÜCKSBURG
☎ 04631 • pop 6400
The little spa town of Glücksburg is a mere 10km north-east of Flensburg. The main reason to visit is for the dreamy, horseshoe-shaped **Wasserschloss** (moated palace; ☎ 22 13), which virtually floats in the middle of a large lake. It's one of the state's most important Renaissance palaces and is partly furnished as a museum

Built between 1582 and 1622, it was the seat of the dukes of Glücksburg until 1779 and then temporarily fell under the rule of the Danes. It's a gleaming white structure, anchored by four octagonal corner towers, and can be explored either on a guided tour or by walking around independently.

Highlights of the Schloss include the lavish baroque palace **chapel** on the ground floor, and the two sweeping staircases that lead to the upper floors and the family's private quarters, with the **Kaiserin Salon** and **Kaiserin Schlafzimmer** (empress's salon and bedroom). Among the highlights on the 2nd floor are the series of **Gobelin tapestries** (1740) in the Weisser Saal (White Hall). Also note the precious goat-skin wall coverings, vividly painted with hunting scenes. In the **Schatzkammer** (treasure chamber) look for the Vogelservice porcelain from the royal manufacturer in Berlin.

If it's a nice day, you might want to check out the **Rose Garden** (Rosengarten) north of the palace, with more than 400 varieties of roses (DM4). Prime blooming season is usually around the end of June.

From May to September, the Schloss is open daily from 10 am to 5 pm; in April and October, hours are 10 am to 4 pm (closed Monday); and from November to March it's open only on weekends, but daily from 17 to 30 December (DM7.50/6).

euro currency converter DM1 = €0.51

Getting There & Away

Bus No 1574 makes regular trips between Flensburg and Glücksburg from the bus station. For information on boat services to Glücksburg, see Organised Tours in the Flensburg section earlier in this chapter.

HUSUM

☎ 04841 • pop 21,000

About 80km north-west of Kiel and 42km south-west of Flensburg lies this peaceful, pleasant coastal town, which has largely preserved its historical attributes. Husum was the birthplace of the famed 19th century German novelist Theodor Storm, who caustically referred to his hometown as 'the grey town by the sea,' a description rather undeserved, especially when the crocuses are in bloom in late March or early April.

Husum was first mentioned in 1252 in connection with the killing of King Abel of Denmark in Husumbro castle. Both disaster and serendipity struck in 1362 when a major storm rearranged the coast and carved out Husum's inland harbour. This direct access to the North Sea proved very profitable in the following centuries, as trade with the Netherlands picked up.

Despite this commercial success, Husum didn't get its town rights until 1603. A quarter of a century earlier, it had become a royal residence when the dukes of Gottorf built themselves a palace here. Husum continued to thrive as a merchant town and was largely spared from destruction during WWII. Today it's a relaxing place that is a good base for bike touring and exploring the Halligen Islands.

Orientation & Information

Husum's train station lies on the southern periphery of the city centre. To get to the central bus station, walk about 300m north from the train station along Herzog-Adolf-Strasse; it's just east of the Nordfriesisches Museum. The Markt is another 300m north. This merges with Grosstrasse, just south of which is the inner harbour. The outer harbour is about 500m west of the Markt, with the beach another 1.5km farther west.

The tourist office (☎ 898 70, fax 89 87 90), in the historical Rathaus at Grosstrasse 27, is open from mid-June to mid-September weekdays from 9 am to 6 pm, and Saturday from 9.30 am to noon. The rest of the year it's open weekdays from 9 am to noon and from 2 to 4 pm (Friday to 3 pm). If you're interested in seeing all of Husum's five main museums, consider buying the Museumsverbundkarte for DM12, available here or at each museum.

Banks around Grosstrasse/Markt that exchange cash and travellers cheques include the Commerzbank and a Sparkasse branch. The main post office is behind the train station, but a more central one is on Grosstrasse. The Kreiskrankenhaus Husum (☎ 66 00) is a hospital at Erichsenweg 16. There's a police station (☎ 66 80) at Poggenburgstrasse 9, near the train station.

Markt

The size of the Markt, and the merchants' houses that line it, attests to Husum's prosperity in the 16th and 17th centuries. The tower of the **Marienkirche**, which is supposed to symbolise a lighthouse, looms above the square. Built in the neoclassical style, the church replaced an earlier Gothic one, torn down in 1807. The interior is plain and streamlined with a flat ceiling and a phalanx of Doric columns holding up the gallery. The altar is framed by a construction that looks like the entrance to a Greek temple. The bronze baptismal font (1643) is one of the few pieces left over from the original church.

The **fountain** outside the church shows Tine, a young Frisian woman who figures in one of Storm's novellas. On the north side of the Markt is the old **Rathaus** (1601), where you'll find the tourist office. Adjacent is the **Herrenhaus**, whose gables sport a series of sandstone heads supposedly representing executed 15th century rebels. The house at No 11 is the birthplace of Theodor Storm. He lies buried in Klosterkirchhof, reached via Norderstrasse, which runs east from the northern side of the Markt.

Schloss vor Husum

The Schloss (☎ 897 31 30) is north of the Markt and easily reached via the narrow Schlossgang. The secondary residence of the dukes of Gottorf, it was built on a site formerly occupied by a Franciscan monastery. It was the Franciscans who, sometime in the Middle Ages, first planted oodles of crocuses in what is now the **Schlosspark**. If you happen to be here in late March or early April, you will witness the stunning spectacle of the entire park bathed in a sea of purple blossoms.

The palace was repeatedly altered through the centuries but finally got back its characteristic onion-shaped tower in 1980. Only the **Torhaus** (gateway), with its curvaceous gables, remained largely unchanged. Inside the Schloss is a moderately interesting collection of paintings and furniture, though the richly decorated fireplaces do warrant a closer look. The Schloss is open from April to October daily from 11 am to 5 pm, closed Monday (DM4/2).

Schiffbrücke & Around

Just south of Grosstrasse (follow Twiete, a narrow passage opposite Karstadt) is Schiffbrücke, the area around Husum's inland harbour. It is webbed by cobbled lanes, of which **Wasserreihe** is the most picturesque. At No 31 stands the **Theodor Storm Haus** (☎ 66 62 70). It is open from April to October daily from 2 to 5 pm, Tuesday to Friday also from 10 am to noon, and the rest of the year on Tuesday, Thursday and Saturday from 2 to 5 pm (DM4/2). The writer lived and worked in this townhouse from 1866 to 1880. On view are Biedermeier furniture, paintings and documents.

Across the street at No 52 is the curious **Tabak- und Kindermuseum** (Museum of Tobacco and Children; ☎ 612 76), which seems like an unusual fusion until you meet Herbert 'Floi' Schwermer, its eccentric owner. He has amassed a lifetime's worth of prams, teddy bears, toys, pipes and other smoking paraphernalia that are displayed in a charming, if somewhat chaotic, fashion. It's open daily from 10 am to 5 pm (DM3/2.50).

Wasserreihe parallels Hafenstrasse and the inland harbour on whose southern side stands the new modern Rathaus. A short way east of here at Am Zingel 15 is the **Schiffahrtsmuseum Nordfriesland** (Maritime Museum of North Friesland; ☎ 52 57), with a small but nicely displayed collection on Frisian shipping history. Exhibits include a historic ship's hull, scrimshaw and a good selection of ships in bottles. It is open from April to October daily from 10 am to 5 pm (DM4/2).

For an even wider look at local and regional history, go to the **Nordfriesisches Museum Nissenhaus** (☎ 25 45) at Herzog-Adolf-Strasse 25, near the train station. It is open daily except Saturday from 10 am to 5 pm, in winter to 4 pm (DM5/2).

Places to Stay

There are three camping grounds in the vicinity of Husum. *Campingplatz Doekkoog* (☎ 619 11, Doekkoog 17) is about 5km west of the town centre near the beach but inaccessible by public transport. It's open from late March to October and costs DM9/10 per person/tent.

Nordseecamping Zum Seehund (☎ 39 99) is in Simonsberg about 7km south-west of Husum (take bus No 1073 or 1077). It's open year round and costs DM6.50/10 per person/tent. It also rents out rooms from DM60 for two people.

Camping Seeblick (☎ 33 21, Nordseestrasse 32) is north of Husum in Schobüll (take bus No 1051). It's open from April to mid-October and costs DM6/9 per person/tent.

Husum's *DJH hostel* (☎ 27 1 4, fax 815 68, Schobüller Strasse 34), north-west of the city centre, charges DM22/27 for juniors/seniors. From the bus station, take bus No 1051 to Westerkampweg.

The tourist office offers a free room-reservation service. *Private rooms* start from around DM25 per person. Some hotels drop their rates in the low season.

The *Hotel-Restaurant Rödekrog* (☎ 37 71, Wilhelmstrasse 10) is about five minutes walk south from the train station. It charges DM45/90 for simple single/double rooms with private shower. The central *Hotel Wohlert (☎ 22 29, fax 21 25, Markt 30)* is good value, offering singles with a shower for DM65, and doubles with all facilities for DM130.

The *Hotel am Schlosspark (☎ 20 22 24, fax 620 62, Hinter der Neustadt 76-86)* is modern and quiet, has large rooms and serves a great breakfast. Rooms with shower and WC cost DM99/155. The newly renovated *Theodor-Storm-Hotel (☎ 896 60, fax 819 33, Neustadt 60-68)* has very nice rooms from DM140/190. The atmospheric *Hotel Altes Gymnasium (☎ 83 30, fax 833 12, Süderstrasse 6)* is Schleswig-Holstein's only five star hotel. Classy rooms in this former school start at DM215/255.

Places to Eat

Husums Brauhaus (☎ 896 60, Neustadt 66), in the Theodor-Storm-Hotel, brews its own Pilsener and a dark beer. You can sit among brewing vats or outside in the beer garden when the weather allows. Simple fare like spare ribs or a 'beer goulash' cost around DM14.

Friesenkrog (Kleikuhle 6), on the harbour, is best reached via Hafenstrasse. Expect to pay DM23 to DM30 at this rustic establishment, but daily specials are much cheaper. If you want something less expensive, grab a fish sandwich at one of several snack shops in the harbour area. Be sure to try the Husumer Krabben, the tiny brown shrimp for which Husum is famous. Sometimes, you can also buy the freshest catch right off the boat.

The *Fischereigenossenschaft (☎ 50 33, Am Aussenhafen 2)* is a fishers' cooperative that sells its wares. Trading hours depend on the tides, it's best to call ahead in the morning.

Café Central (☎ 87 15 48, Schiffbrücke 2) specialises in pancakes – it stays open till late and is something of a nightspot. *Speicher (☎ 650 00, Hafenstrasse 17)* is a cultural centre with regular live rock bands, jazz, blues and more.

Getting There & Away

There are direct hourly train connections to Kiel (DM24.60, 1½ hours), Hamburg-Altona (DM50, 2¼ hours) and Schleswig (DM10, 30 minutes), and several links daily to Westerland on Sylt (DM19.60, one hour).

Husum has many bus connections with other towns in North Friesland, but the service is irregular. If you're planning to return the same day, be sure to check schedules in advance so as not to be stranded. For detailed information, call ☎ 78 70. Bus No 1044 travels daily to Flensburg (1¼ hours). Bus No 1046 goes to Schleswig (one hour), though train service is more frequent and faster. Bus No 1071 goes to the resort town of St Peter-Ording (40 minutes). Some buses will transport your bicycle for an extra DM2. Husum is at the crossroads of the B5, the B200 and the B201.

See Sylt and Amrum in the North Frisian Islands section for boat services to these islands.

Getting Around

Husum is easily walkable, but it's nice to have a bike to get around. There are a few rental companies: Zweirad Clausen (☎ 729 75), Osterende 94, charges DM7.50 a day; the Fahrrad Center (☎ 44 65), Schulstrasse 4, costs DM10; and Eilrich (☎ 14 79), Ostenfelder Strasse 12, charges DM7.

AROUND HUSUM
Halligen

Husum is a good springboard for exploring the Halligen, a handful of tiny wafer-flat islands scattered across the Nationalpark Wattenmeer. In the Middle Ages, some 50 of these North Sea islets supposedly existed, but the sea has swallowed all but 10. Life here is rough and in constant conflict with the tides. Up to 60 times a year, floods drown the beaches and meadows, leaving the few reed-thatched farms stranded on the artificial knolls – or 'wharves' – they're built on. Electricity, water and even a few cars have reached these remote places, but essentially they're unique locales for walks in the sea breeze with your thoughts uninterrupted.

The largest island is **Hallig Langeness**, which is about 10km long, 1km wide and has 120 inhabitants. It can be reached by boat or by causeway via Oland. The prettiest islet is **Hallig Hooge**, which once sheltered a Danish king from a storm in the handsome **Königshaus** with its blue and white tiles and baroque ceiling fresco. Only 25 people on a single wharf eke out a living on **Hallig Oland** (2km x 500m), connected with the mainland by a 5km-long causeway. It's possible to rent rooms, though capacity is obviously limited and most people just experience the islands on day excursions.

From Husum, Wilhelm Schmid GmbH (☎ 04841-20 14) offers boat tours to the Halligen during high season. If you're prone to sea sickness, pick a day when the sea is fairly quiet. Boats leave from the Aussenhafen (outer harbour) in Husum, and trips cost between DM19 and DM27. Some boats pass sandbanks with seal colonies.

The main jumping-off point for Halligen explorations, though, is Schlüttsiel, about 35km north of Husum. The Husum tourist office has brochures on the various operators and tours. Prices range from DM20 to DM40. If you're driving to Schlüttsiel, take the B5; if not, bus No 1041 makes several runs daily from Husum right to the landing docks.

North Frisian Islands

SYLT

☎ 04651 • pop 21,000

Nature is the major draw of the North Frisian Islands, which lie west of the German mainland in the North Sea, and Sylt is no exception. On the west coast of the island, shaped not unlike an anchor attached to the mainland, the fierce surf of the North Sea gnaws mercilessly at the changing shoreline. The wind can be so strong that the world's best windsurfers meet here for one of their World Cup events each year. By contrast, the mood on Sylt's eastern Wattenmeer (Watt means 'mud-flats') shore is tranquil and serene. It's a rather unusual sight to witness the shallow ocean retreat twice daily with the tides, exposing the muddy sea bottom. In Sylt's north, you'll find wide expanses of shifting dunes with candy-striped lighthouses above fields of gleaming yellow rape flower. Everywhere you go there are typical Frisian homes, thatched with reeds and surrounded by heath the colour of burnt sienna.

Landscapes like these have long inspired writers such as Thomas Mann and Theodor Storm and painters like Emil Nolde and Lovis Corinth. For the past 40 years, Sylt has also been the preferred playground of the German jet-set and has provided much of the smut for Germany's gossip press. These days, the couplings – or triplings or what have you – have quietened down to the point where *Playboy* writer Benno Kroll remarked that Sylt was experiencing a 'sort of post-coital hangover'. But judging by the glut of fancy restaurants, designer boutiques, mega-Deutschmark homes and luxury cars, the moneyed set has not disappeared yet.

It's easy enough, though, to leave the glamour and crowds behind and get comfortably lost on the beach, in the dunes or on a bike trail.

Orientation

Sylt is 38.5km long and measures only 700m at its narrowest point. The largest town and commercial centre is Westerland in the centre of the island. At the northern end is List, Germany's northernmost town, while Hörnum is at the southern tip. Sylt is connected to the mainland by a trains-only causeway, though you can take your car on board (see Getting There & Away for details). The train station is in Westerland.

Information

For information on the entire island, the best place to go is the Bädergemeinschaft Sylt (☎ 820 20, fax 820 22 2), near the Westerland Rathaus at Stephanstrasse 6. It's open daily from 10 am to 5 pm (from November to March weekdays only). The office of Sylt

Tourismus Zentrale (☎ 60 26, fax 281 10) is at Keitumer Landstrasse 10b, just outside of town in Tinnum, and is open Monday to Saturday from 9 am to 6 pm. Local tourist offices are listed under each village.

If you need to exchange money, you can do so in Westerland at the Commerzbank at Strandstrasse 18 or the Volksbank at Friedrichstrasse 18. Other banks on the island also offer an exchange service, and there are various ATM machines accepting all major credit cards. There's a post office in Westerland at Kjeirstrasse 17 and a police station (☎ 70 47) at Kirchenweg 21.

Resort Tax All the communities on Sylt charge visitors a *Kurtaxe*. In the high season, this ranges from DM4 to DM5.50, less at other times. Paying the tax gets you a *Kurkarte*, which you need even to get onto the beach but which also entitles you to small discounts to museums or concerts and other events. If you're spending more than one night, your hotel will automatically obtain a pass for you for the length of your stay (the price will be added to the room rate). If you're just there for the day, you will need to obtain a *Tageskarte* (day pass) from a kiosk at the entrances to the beach. It's DM6 in all communities except Kampen, where it costs DM12.

Westerland

Westerland, the largest town on the island, is the Miami Beach of Sylt. In the centre, the view of the sea is sadly blocked by chunky high rises but there's a nice promenade along the beach. Another place to stroll is the pedestrianised **Friedrichstrasse**, the main drag, where swanky nightclubs rub shoulders with tourist shops and restaurants.

Westerland became Sylt's first resort back in the mid-19th century, its people having moved here much earlier from a little village to the east called Eidum. Don't look for it on the map, though; in 1436 it was swallowed up by the sea during a horrendous storm. Miraculously, the wily villagers managed to save their little church's altar, which can today be admired in the

Alte Dorfkirche on Kirchenweg to the east of the train station.

Westerland's tourist office (☎ 99 80, fax 99 82 34) is at Strandstrasse 33.

Kampen

If Westerland is the Miami Beach of Sylt, Kampen is its St Tropez. This is the island's ritziest village and the one that attracts all sorts of major and minor celebrities and aristocrats. The main artery is **Stroenwai**, better known as Whiskey Alley, which is lined with restaurants, cars and boutiques – all expensive, naturally. Grab a table at one of the outdoor cafes, plonk down DM8 or so for a cappuccino and watch the action.

Kampen has its landmarks too, among them the island's oldest **lighthouse** (1855), which rises 60m above sea level. Locals have baptised it 'Christian' in honour of all the Danish kings by that name who ruled the island until it became German territory in 1866. There's also the **Uwe Dune**, at 52.5m, Sylt's highest natural elevation and named after a local 19th century freedom fighter, Uwe Jens Lornsen. You can climb to the top via 115 wooden steps for a 360° view over Sylt and, on a good day, to the neighbouring islands of Amrum and Föhr.

Kampen's tourist office (☎ 469 80, fax 46 98 40) is at Hauptstrasse 12.

Keitum

About 3km east of Westerland is Keitum, the island's prettiest village. Here you'll find quiet streets flanked by old chestnut trees and lush gardens erupting in symphonies of colour. Historic reed-thatched houses (some of them the former homes of retired sea captains) abound.

In the old days, Keitum was Sylt's most important harbour, and there's plenty of evidence of this nautical tradition. **St Severin** is a late-Romanesque sailors' church known for its Gothic altar and pulpit, as well as for its romantic candlelight concerts. For excursions into the island's salty past, there's the Sylt **Heimatmuseum** (DM4) at Am Kliff 19 and the historic **Altfriesisches Haus** (DM3) at Am Kliff 13. Both are open daily from 10 am to 5 pm (check winter opening times at the tourist office or call ☎ 311 01).

Keitum's tourist office (☎ 33 70, fax 337 37) is at Am Tipkenhoog 5.

List

List's tourist brochures are filled with superlatives, for everything here is 'Germany's northernmost' – harbour, beach, restaurant etc … just fill in the blank. It's a windswept, tranquil land's end, but things usually liven up in the harbour when the ferry from Rømø dumps its load of day-tripping Danes in search of cheap drink. List has played important roles in both world wars. In WWI, Zeppelins headed towards England from its custom-built airport. In the 1930s List became an army post and its airport again a launchpad, this time for fighter planes. Remnants of List's wartime past can still be found around the village.

North of List is the privately owned Ellenbogen (literally 'elbow'). Two families own this banana-shaped peninsula which has 35m-high moving dunes and beaches that are unfortunately off-limits for swimming because of dangerous currents. It's under a nature-preservation order and you must pay a toll at the entrance (DM8 per ...

List's tourist off... ways to see the is...

Heikos Reiterwiese (☎ 56 00); in Keitum there's Reitstall Hoffmann (☎ 315 63).

Another activity unique to Sylt is a trip to the **beach-side sauna** (☎ 87 71 74). After you've heated up, the idea is to run naked into the chilly North Sea! To get to the sauna, take the road to Ellenbogen which branches off the main island road about 4km south-west of List. You will see a sign for the sauna on the left. The facilities are open from Easter to October from 11 am to 5 pm (DM23).

In Westerland, a fun thing to do is visit the **Sylter Welle** (☎ 99 80) indoor water park and health spa, especially when it's too cold for the beach. There are saunas, solariums, a wave pool and a slide. The complex is open daily from 10 am to 9 or 10 pm (DM17 without sauna, DM25 including sauna; no time limit).

Places to Stay

Private rooms tend to be the least expensive accommodation option on Sylt. They cost from DM30 per person, and the tourist offices can help you find one. If you're planning a longer stay, renting a holiday ... in high season a day in low season and Unless it's a particularly low season though, proprietors may ... time, rent or fewer than they fluctuate be... mir that prices ... gerason, and that the tw n low and his the earlier Sylt Information entry).

Camping Sylt has about half a dozen camping grounds. *Campingplatz Kampen* (☎ 42086) is about the nicest. It opens from Easter to mid-October and is located among dunes on Möwenweg at the southern entrance to Kampen. It's about a five minute walk to the beach, and costs DM7/9/3 per person/tent/car. *Campingplatz Westerland* (☎ 99 44 99) is the largest camping facility and is located in the dunes off Rantumer Strasse. It's open from April to October, and costs DM7/16/5 per person/tent/car.

1985. Because of the dang... tuming tides and treachei... should only venture o... tourist offices have li... **Horse riding** is a po... d is offered both ... enced. Usual... ember of group, and in high season uld boo. at least a few days ahead. at DM25 per hour, and the rides or two hours. In Westerland, try

...barefoot walk throu... Wattenmeer ... the ... park Wattenm... that's main... ... in ... founded in ... th a guide. The ... ar activity on ... ... tours on offer ... r beginners and ex... ou will need to go out

euro currency converter DM1 = €0.51

Hostels The *Jugendherberge (☎ 88 02 94, fax 88 13 92, Friesenplatz 2)* in Hörnum charges DM24/32.50 for juniors/seniors (with high-season Kurtaxe). From the bus station in Westerland, take the bus to the Hörnum-Nord stop, from where it's about a 1km walk. The other *Jugendherberge (☎ 87 03 97, fax 87 10 39)* is about 2km north-east of List, surrounded by dunes and just 800m from the North Sea. It costs DM24/29. Buses run from Westerland to List-Schule, and between April and September there's a shuttle to the hostel. Otherwise, it's a 2.5km trek.

Hotels Prices quoted here are for the high season; expect to pay 10 to 20% less in the low season.

Hotel Garni Diana (☎ 988 60, fax 98 86 86, Elisabethstrasse 19) is good value at DM65/130 for single/double rooms, or DM95/170 with shower and WC. *Haus Hellas (☎ 64 29, fax 265 69, Schützenstrasse 12)* is another budget option, with rooms from DM65/130, or DM105/180 with shower and WC. The lovely *Landhaus Nielsen (☎ 98 90, fax 98 69 60, Bastnstrasse 5)* hs r... shower and W... for DM83/1)5.

Th... *el Statt Hamburg (☎ 85 82 2..., ...dstrasse 2)* is top of t... offering tra... service and decor it th... modern price o... ...198/325. Low-se...son prices are DM172/2...

Places to Eat

Dining on Sylt can get pr...ty pricey, thoug... there are numerous shops a... stands selling fresh fish meals for DM10 a... under. Picnics on the beach are another fi... option.

Toni's Restaurant (☎ 258 10, ...orderstrasse 3) has good, inexpensive fare, with a variety of main courses from DM11 ... DM30, and a pleasant garden. *Blum's (☎ 294 20, Neue Strasse 4)* has a bit of a cafeteria feel to it, but serves some of the freshest fish for a sit-down meal or takeaway, at very reasonable prices. Westerland's *Alte Friesenstube (☎ 12 28, Gaadt 4)*, in a 17th century building, specialises in

northern German and Frisian cooking, with main courses ranging from DM25 to DM45 (closed Monday).

Kampen's *Kupferkanne (☎ 410 10)*, in Stapelhooger Wai, is one place where you can sit either inside a cosy Frisian house or outside in your private 'room', walled in by hedges, brambles and trees. A giant cup of coffee and equally large slice of pie will cost DM13.50, but the view of the Wattenmeer is complimentary. *Gogärtchen (☎ 412 42)* on Stroenwai in Kampen will offer you a closer look at the German jet-set. Here you can sit in the beer garden, on the terrace or inside the restaurant and munch on main courses from DM25.

List's harbour sports a number of colourful kiosks. *Gosch*, which prides itself on being 'Germany's northernmost fish kiosk', is an institution known far beyond Sylt. The food is delicious and, with prices from DM2.50 to DM6 for fish sandwiches, nobody has to leave hungry.

Fisch-Fiete (☎ 321 50, Weidemannweg 3) is a Keitum classic that serves red-meat and game dishes as well as fish (from DM28), and also has a nice garden. *Sansibar (☎ 96 46 46)* is on the beach between Rantum and Hörnum, south of Westerland. ...ooks like a shack, but having a drink or ... terrace at sunset, with a view ...

Get...

Getting ...ylt ... ...pricey o... to ...anks as a Sylt highdriving. ...h...to ... ...time. mainland ...ylan... causeway for t... only, than a basketball ...rt. Betw... ...assenger trains a... ...make the... ...our trek from Ham...g-Altona to ...lan... (DM64). If you b... a RegioTicket use ...ne of the frequer... ...regional tra... costs DM25.

If you are travelling by c..., yo... it onto a train in the town of N... are constant crossings (usua... an hour) in both directions...

reservations can be made. The cost per car is a shocking DM144 return, but at least that includes all passengers. A cheaper alternative is to drive across the Danish border to the seaport of Rømø, connected to the mainland by causeway, and catch the ferry to List on Sylt's northern tip (one hour). At least five daily ferries year round (up to 12 from May to mid-September) run in either direction. Return tickets are DM8 per person, DM16 if you're taking a bicycle. Cars cost DM94 return, which includes all passengers.

There are daily flights between Westerland airport and Hamburg, Munich and Berlin, and several weekly flights from other German cities.

If you want to visit the neighbouring islands of Amrum and Föhr, hop on one of the boats leaving from the harbour in Hörnum. Same-day return cruises through the shallow banks that attract seals and sea birds are offered by Adler-Schiffe (☎ 98 700 in Westerland) for DM34, and DM17 for children. Bicycles are an extra DM8.

Getting Around

Sylt is well covered by a bus system (☎ 70 27) with five lines serving every corner of the island. The main north-south buses ... DM2.20 to DM6.20).

... mode of transport on the island is a bike. Bicycle rental places ... 87 for the sign saying ... lace to find is ☎ 58 03, DM9 per pect to ... No 1 of the train station.

island. Amrum is different in character from Sylt; tranquil not glamorous, relaxing and far less touristy. Its landscape is a harmonious patchwork of dunes, woods, heath and marsh. Its villages have traditional Frisian architecture, with houses that are reed-thatched, gabled and with small doors. Besides the central village of Wittdün, there are Nebel, Norddorf, Steenodde and Süddorf.

Wittdün has northern Germany's tallest lighthouse (63m), which affords a spectacular view of the island and across to Sylt and Föhr. It's open from April to October on weekdays to 12.30 pm; for the rest of the year, it's only open on Wednesday (DM3). In Nebel, you can visit the **Öömrang-Hüs** at Waaswai 1, which is a historical sea captain's house with changing exhibits on North Frisian culture. It is open weekdays from 10 am to noon, and from 3 to 5 pm on Saturday and in summer.

Amrum has some fine walks, not least the 10km walk from the lighthouse to Norddorf through the ... ine forest, or the 8km return hike from Norddorf along the beach to the tranquil O...d Nature Reserve, an ideal place to observe birdlife. The tourist office can help with information on guided summer hikes across the ... att to Föhr. ... ist office (☎ 891, fa... 03 94) ... ...en at the ferry landing in W...dün.

Places to Stay & Eat

Cam...platz Schade (☎ 22 ... ute walk from the beach at the ... March to mid-Wittdün. It's open from ... re mandatory in October, and reserva...10 per person and summer. Prices ar...
DM8 for a tent. ...erge (☎ 20 10, fax 17 47, The Jugen... practically on the beach in Wittdün ...at 300m from the ferry landing. Mittelstrass... Mittelstrasat 300m from the ferry landing. B&B ... s DM23/28 for juniors/seniors. The tourist office has a free accommodation booking service. **Haus Südstrand** (☎ 2/ 08, fax 27 90, Mittelstrasse 30) is in Wittdün and has a few singles/doubles priced at around DM70/130 with shower and WC. **Hüttmann** (☎ 92 20, fax 92 21 13,

AMRUM
☎ 04682 • pop 2100
Amrum is the smallest of the North Frisian Islands – small enough in fact to walk round in a day. Yet it is also, arguably, the prettiest, blessed with the glorious Kniep-

– 12km of fine white sand, sometimes 1km wide – that takes up half the

euro currency converter DM1 = €0.51

Ual Saarepswai 2-6), in Norddorf, was the first hotel on the island – it opened more than 100 years ago – and is still owned by the same family. There's a sauna, steam room and other amenities. Rates are from DM115/DM225.

Amrum has only a few restaurants, and many close in winter. *Ual Öömrang (☎ 836, Bräätlun 4)*, in Norddorf, has a quaint nautical theme. This is Amrum's oldest restaurant, and serves main courses in the DM20 to DM40 range. *Burg Haus*, built on an old Viking hill fort above the eastern beach at Norddorf, has a relaxing teahouse atmosphere. Note that restaurants can be closed by 7 pm in the low season.

FÖHR
☎ 04681 • pop 10,000

Föhr is even more remote and tranquil than Amrum. Its main village is Wyk, which has been a resort since 1819. The island's best sandy beach is in the south. In the north you'll find 16 tiny Frisian hamlets tucked behind dykes that stand up to 7m tall. In the old days, Föhr's men went out to sea to hunt whales, an epoch you can learn more about at the Friesenmuseum at Rebelstieg 34 in Wyk. It's open Tuesday to Sunday from 10 to 5 pm, and from November to February from 2 to 5 pm (DM7.50). Some of these men are buried in the cemetery of St Lauren.

Also worth visiting is the church of Johannis in Nieblum. It dates from the 12th century and is known as the 'Frisian Cathedral' because it takes up to 1000 people (ask about guided tours up to 1000 people).

The information service the tourist office (☎ 30 40, fax 30 68) is at Wyk on Föhr. The spa administrations *(Kurverwaltungen)* in the various villages are also useful.

Places to Stay & Eat
Föhr does not have a camping ground. The *DJH hostel (☎ 23 55, fax 55 27, Fehrweg 41)* is in Wyk on Südstrand beach, about 3.5km from the ferry landing. B&B costs DM23.80/28.80 for juniors/seniors, and you should call ahead to check availability.

Private rooms on the island cost from DM25 per person.

The *Strandhotel (☎ 587 00, fax 58 70 77, Königstrasse 1)*, which is right on the beach in Wyk, charges from DM65/130 for singles/doubles. *Timpe Te (☎ 16 31, fax 83 69)* on Strandstrasse in Nieblum is a relaxing hotel with rooms that cost from DM55/110.

Wyk boasts a surprising number of restaurants. *Alt Wyk (☎ 32 12, Grosse Strasse 4)* is an upmarket traditional restaurant, with dishes from around DM32. The *Friesenstube (☎ 24 04, Süderstrasse 8)* is also popular. *Wyk End (Mittelstrasse 9)* is good for fishy fast food.

Getting There & Away
To get to Amrum and Föhr from the mainland, you must board a ferry operated by WDR (☎ 801 40) in Dagebüll Hafen. To get there, take the Sylt-bound train from Hamburg-Altona and change in Niebüll. In summer, there are also some through trains. Up to 10 boats make the trip in high season and, with prior reservation, it's possible to take your car aboard. The trip to Amrum takes 1½ hours, to Föhr about 45 minutes. The one-way trip to Wittdün costs DM15.80, same-day return DM23.50. Bikes are an extra DM7.50.

Getting Around
On Amrum, buses run at hourly intervals (hourly in winter) in winter in winter spine from the ferry terminal in Wittdün to Norddorf. On Föhr, there's an hourly service to all villages (less frequent in winter). There are bike-rental places in every village on both islands. They charge between DM5 and DM10 a day.

HELGOLAND
☎ 04725 • pop 1650

Technically not part of the North Frisian Islands, Helgoland is about 45km from the mainland and a popular day trip.

from 10 am to 5 pm (check winter opening times at the tourist office or call ☎ 311 01).

Keitum's tourist office (☎ 33 70, fax 337 37) is at Am Tipkenhoog 5.

List

List's tourist brochures are filled with superlatives, for everything here is 'Germany's northernmost' – harbour, beach, restaurant etc … just fill in the blank. It's a windswept, tranquil land's end, but things usually liven up in the harbour when the ferry from Rømø dumps its load of day-tripping Danes in search of cheap drink. List has played important roles in both world wars. In WWI, Zeppelins headed towards England from its custom-built airport. In the 1930s List became an army post and its airport again a launchpad, this time for fighter planes. Remnants of List's wartime past can still be found around the village.

North of List is the privately owned Ellenbogen (literally 'elbow'). Two families own this banana-shaped peninsula which has 35m-high moving dunes and beaches that are unfortunately off-limits for swimming because of dangerous currents. It's under a nature-preservation order and you must pay a toll at the entrance (DM8 per car).

List's tourist office (☎ 952 00, fax 87 13 98) is at Listlandstrasse 11.

Activities

One of the most unusual ways to see the island is by taking a barefoot walk through the sludge of the Wattenmeer, which stretches between Sylt's eastern shore and the mainland. It's a fragile environment that's part of the Nationalpark Wattenmeer, founded in 1985. Because of the danger from swiftly returning tides and treacherous channels, you should only venture out with a guide. The tourist offices have lists of tours on offer. **Horse riding** is a popular activity on Sylt, and is offered both for beginners and the experienced. Usually you will need to go out as a member of a group, and in high season you should book at least a few days ahead. Rates start at DM25 per hour, and the rides usually last for two hours. In Westerland, try

Heikos Reiterwiese (☎ 56 00); in Keitum there's Reitstall Hoffmann (☎ 315 63).

Another activity unique to Sylt is a trip to the **beach-side sauna** (☎ 87 71 74). After you've heated up, the idea is to run naked into the chilly North Sea! To get to the sauna, take the road to Ellenbogen which branches off the main island road about 4km south-west of List. You will see a sign for the sauna on the left. The facilities are open from Easter to October from 11 am to 5 pm (DM23).

In Westerland, a fun thing to do is visit the **Sylter Welle** (☎ 99 80) indoor water park and health spa, especially when it's too cold for the beach. There are saunas, solariums, a wave pool and a slide. The complex is open daily from 10 am to 9 or 10 pm (DM17 without sauna, DM25 including sauna; no time limit).

Places to Stay

Private rooms tend to be the least expensive accommodation option on Sylt. They cost from DM30 per person, and the tourist offices can help you find one. If you're planning a longer stay, renting a holiday flat is another possibility. This can cost as little as DM60 a day in low season and DM85 in high season (May to September). Unless it's a particularly slow time, though, proprietors may be reluctant to rent for fewer than three days. Keep in mind that prices generally fluctuate between low and high season, and that the Kurtaxe is extra (see the earlier Sylt Information entry).

Camping Sylt has about half a dozen camping grounds. *Campingplatz Kampen* (☎ 420 86) is about the nicest. It opens from Easter to mid-October and is located among dunes on Möwenweg at the southern entrance to Kampen. It's about a five minute walk to the beach, and costs DM7/9/3 per person/tent/car. *Campingplatz Westerland* (☎ 99 44 99) is the largest camping facility and is located in the dunes off Rantumer Strasse. It's open from April to October, and costs DM7/16/5 per person/tent/car.

Hostels The *Jugendherberge* (☎ *88 02 94, fax 88 13 92, Friesenplatz 2)* in Hörnum charges DM24/32.50 for juniors/seniors (with high-season Kurtaxe). From the bus station in Westerland, take the bus to the Hörnum-Nord stop, from where it's about a 1km walk. The other *Jugendherberge* (☎ *87 03 97, fax 87 10 39)* is about 2km north-east of List, surrounded by dunes and just 800m from the North Sea. It costs DM24/29. Buses run from Westerland to List-Schule, and between April and September there's a shuttle to the hostel. Otherwise, it's a 2.5km trek.

Hotels Prices quoted here are for the high season; expect to pay 10 to 20% less in the low season.

Hotel Garni Diana (☎ *988 60, fax 98 86 86, Elisabethstrasse 19)* is good value at DM65/130 for single/double rooms, or DM95/170 with shower and WC. *Haus Hellas* (☎ *64 29, fax 265 69, Schützenstrasse 12)* is another budget option, with rooms from DM65/130, or DM105/180 with shower and WC. The lovely *Landhaus Nielsen* (☎ *986 90, fax 98 69 60, Bastianstrasse 5)* has rooms with shower and WC for DM83/105.

The *Hotel Stadt Hamburg* (☎ *85 80, fax 85 82 20, Strandstrasse 2)* is top of the line, offering traditional service and decor at the modern price of DM198/325. Low-season prices are DM172/285.

Places to Eat

Dining on Sylt can get pretty pricey, though there are numerous shops and stands selling fresh fish meals for DM10 and under. Picnics on the beach are another fine option.

Toni's Restaurant (☎ *258 10, Norderstrasse 3)* has good, inexpensive fare, with a variety of main courses from DM11 to DM30, and a pleasant garden. *Blum's* (☎ *294 20, Neue Strasse 4)* has a bit of a cafeteria feel to it, but serves some of the freshest fish for a sit-down meal or takeaway, at very reasonable prices. Westerland's *Alte Friesenstube* (☎ *12 28, Gaadt 4)*, in a 17th century building, specialises in northern German and Frisian cooking, with main courses ranging from DM25 to DM45 (closed Monday).

Kampen's *Kupferkanne* (☎ *410 10)*, in Stapelhooger Wai, is one place where you can sit either inside a cosy Frisian house or outside in your private 'room', walled in by hedges, brambles and trees. A giant cup of coffee and equally large slice of pie will cost DM13.50, but the view of the Wattenmeer is complimentary. *Gogärtchen* (☎ *412 42)* on Stroenwai in Kampen will offer you a closer look at the German jet-set. Here you can sit in the beer garden, on the terrace or inside the restaurant and munch on main courses from DM25.

List's harbour sports a number of colourful kiosks. *Gosch*, which prides itself on being 'Germany's northernmost fish kiosk', is an institution known far beyond Sylt. The food is delicious and, with prices from DM2.50 to DM6 for fish sandwiches, nobody has to leave hungry.

Fisch-Fiete (☎ *321 50, Weidemannweg 3)* is a Keitum classic that serves red-meat and game dishes as well as fish (from DM28), and also has a nice garden. *Sansibar* (☎ *96 46 46)* is on the beach between Rantum and Hörnum, south of Westerland. It looks like a shack, but having a drink or dinner on its terrace at sunset, with a view of the crashing waves, ranks as a Sylt highlight. Prices are lower at lunchtime.

Getting There & Away

Getting to Sylt is a bit of an adventure and a pricey one to boot, especially if you're driving. The island is connected to the mainland by the Hindenburgdamm, a causeway for trains only, which is no wider than a basketball court. Between 13 and 18 passenger trains a day make the direct three hour trek from Hamburg-Altona to Westerland (DM64). If you buy a RegioTicket and use one of the frequent regional trains, it costs DM25.

If you are travelling by car, you must load it onto a train in the town of Niebüll. There are constant crossings (usually at least once an hour) in both directions every day, and no reservations can be made. The cost per car is a shocking DM144 return, but at least that includes all passengers. A cheaper alternative is to drive across the Danish border to the seaport of Rømø, connected to the mainland by causeway, and catch the ferry to List on Sylt's northern tip (one hour). At least five daily ferries year round (up to 12 from May to mid-September) run in either direction. Return tickets are DM8 per person, DM16 if you're taking a bicycle. Cars cost DM94 return, which includes all passengers.

There are daily flights between Westerland airport and Hamburg, Munich and Berlin, and several weekly flights from other German cities.

If you want to visit the neighbouring islands of Amrum and Föhr, hop on one of the boats leaving from the harbour in Hörnum. Same-day return cruises through the shallow banks that attract seals and sea birds are offered by Adler-Schiffe (☎ 98 700 in Westerland) for DM34, and DM17 for children. Bicycles are an extra DM8.

Getting Around

Sylt is well covered by a bus system (☎ 70 27) with five lines serving every corner of the island. The main north-south connections run at 20-minute intervals during the day. There are seven price zones, costing from DM2.20 to DM10.80. Some buses have bicycle hangers (DM2.20 to DM6.20).

The best mode of transport on the island is a bike. Bicycle rental places abound. Look for the sign saying *Fahrradverleih* and expect to pay about DM10 a day. Tieves (☎ 87 02 26), Listlandstrasse 15, rents out bikes. In Westerland, the easiest place to find is Fahrrad am Bahnhof (☎ 58 03, DM9 per day), at platform No 1 of the train station.

AMRUM
☎ 04682 • pop 2100

Amrum is the smallest of the North Frisian Islands – small enough in fact to walk around in a day. Yet it is also, arguably, the prettiest, blessed with the glorious Kniepsand – 12km of fine white sand, sometimes up to 1km wide – that takes up half the island. Amrum is different in character from Sylt; tranquil not glamorous, relaxing and far less touristy. Its landscape is a harmonious patchwork of dunes, woods, heath and marsh. Its villages have traditional Frisian architecture, with houses that are reed-thatched, gabled and with small doors. Besides the central village of Wittdün, there are Nebel, Norddorf, Steenodde and Süddorf.

Wittdün has northern Germany's tallest lighthouse (63m), which affords a spectacular view of the island and across to Sylt and Föhr. It's open from April to October on weekdays to 12.30 pm; for the rest of the year, it's only open on Wednesday (DM3). In Nebel, you can visit the **Öömrang-Hüs** at Waaswai 1, which is a historical sea captain's house with changing exhibits on North Frisian culture. It is open weekdays from 10 am to noon, and from 3 to 5 pm on Saturday and in summer.

Amrum has some fine walks, not least the 10km walk from the lighthouse to Norddorf through the pine forest, or the 8km return hike from Norddorf along the beach to the tranquil **Ood Nature Reserve**, an ideal place to observe birdlife. The tourist office can help with information on guided summer hikes across the Watt to Föhr.

The friendly tourist office (☎ 891, fax 94 03 94) is right at the ferry landing in Wittdün.

Places to Stay & Eat

Campingplatz Schade (☎ 22 54) has modern facilities and is about a 15 minute walk from the beach at the northern edge of Wittdün. It's open from mid-March to mid-October, and reservations are mandatory in summer. Prices are DM10 per person and DM8 for a tent.

The *Jugendherberge* (☎ 20 10, fax 17 47, Mittelstrasse 1) is practically on the beach in Wittdün, about 300m from the ferry landing. B&B costs DM23/28 for juniors/seniors.

The tourist office has a free accommodation booking service. *Haus Südstrand* (☎ 27 08, fax 27 90, Mittelstrasse 30) is in Wittdün and has a few singles/doubles priced at around DM70/130 with shower and WC. *Hüttmann* (☎ 92 20, fax 92 21 13,

Ual Saarepswai 2-6), in Norddorf, was the first hotel on the island – it opened more than 100 years ago – and is still owned by the same family. There's a sauna, steam room and other amenities. Rates are from DM115/DM225.

Amrum has only a few restaurants, and many close in winter. *Ual Öömrang* (☎ *836, Bräätlun 4)*, in Norddorf, has a quaint nautical theme. This is Amrum's oldest restaurant, and serves main courses in the DM20 to DM40 range. *Burg Haus*, built on an old Viking hill fort above the eastern beach at Norddorf, has a relaxing teahouse atmosphere. Note that restaurants can be closed by 7 pm in the low season.

FÖHR
☎ 04681 • pop 10,000

Föhr is even more remote and tranquil than Amrum. Its main village is Wyk, which has been a resort since 1819. The island's best sandy beach is in the south. In the north you'll find 16 tiny Frisian hamlets tucked behind dykes that stand up to 7m tall. In the old days, Föhr's men went out to sea to hunt whales, an epoch you can learn more about at the **Friesenmuseum** at Rebbelstieg 34 in Wyk. It's open Tuesday to Sunday from 10 am to 5 pm, and from November to February from 2 to 5 pm (DM7.50/3.50). Many of these men are buried in the **cemetery of St Laurenti** in Süderende.

Also worth visiting is the **church of St Johannis** in Nieblum. It dates from the 12th century and is sometimes called the 'Frisian Cathedral' that it seats up to 1000 people (ask about guided tours at the tourist office).

The information service on Föhr (☎ 30 40, fax 30 68) is at Wyk harbour. The spa administrations *(Kurverwaltungen)* in the various villages are also useful.

Places to Stay & Eat
Föhr does not have a camping ground. The *DJH hostel* (☎ *23 55, fax 55 27, Fehrstieg 41)* is in Wyk on Südstrand beach, about 3.5km from the ferry landing. B&B costs DM23.80/28.80 for juniors/seniors, and you should call ahead to check availability.

Private rooms on the island cost from DM25 per person.

The *Strandhotel* (☎ *587 00, fax 58 70 77, Königstrasse 1)*, which is right on the beach in Wyk, charges from DM65/130 for singles/doubles. *Timpe Te* (☎ *16 31, fax 83 69)* on Strandstrasse in Nieblum is a relaxing hotel with rooms that cost from DM55/110.

Wyk boasts a surprising number of restaurants. *Alt Wyk* (☎ *32 12, Grosse Strasse 4)* is an upmarket traditional restaurant, with dishes from around DM32. The *Friesenstube* (☎ *24 04, Süderstrasse 8)* is also popular. *Wyk End (Mittelstrasse 9)* is good for fishy fast food.

Getting There & Away
To get to Amrum and Föhr from the mainland, you must board a ferry operated by WDR (☎ 801 40) in Dagebüll Hafen. To get there, take the Sylt-bound train from Hamburg-Altona and change in Niebüll. In summer, there are also some through trains. Up to 10 boats make the trip in high season and, with prior reservation, it's possible to take your car aboard. The trip to Amrum takes 1½ hours, to Föhr about 45 minutes. The one-way trip to Wittdün costs DM15.80, same-day return DM23.50. Bikes are an extra DM7.50. One-way trips to Wyk cost DM9.80; same-day return tickets are DM15.

For information on getting to Amrum and Föhr from Sylt, see Getting There & Away in the Sylt section.

Getting Around
On Amrum, buses travel at 30-minute intervals (hourly in winter) along the island spine from the ferry terminal in Wittdün to Norddorf. On Föhr, there's an hourly bus service to all villages (less frequent in winter). There are bike-rental places in every village on both islands. They charge between DM5 and DM10 a day.

HELGOLAND
☎ 04725 • pop 1650

Technically not part of the North Frisian Islands, Helgoland is about 45km from the mainland and a popular day trip and duty-free port. Because of the North Sea's strong currents and unpredictable weather, however, the passage will be enjoyed only by those with iron stomachs. Helgoland was first ruled by the Danes, then by the British before it became German in 1891 in exchange for the African island of Zanzibar. It's a tiny place whose landmark is an 80m-tall red rock called 'Lange Anna' (Long Anna) sticking out from the sea in the south-west of the island.

In 1841, Heinrich Hoffmann von Fallersleben wrote the words to the German anthem in Helgoland. In WWII it was used as a submarine base and it's still possible to tour the remaining bunkers and underground tunnels. The island was heavily bombed and all of the houses are new.

Oddly, Helgoland's duty-free status continues to exist after the abolition of duty-free allowances within the EU in 1999 – this is because it's covered by an agreement made in 1840 and, economically at least, isn't part of the EU!

Take a walk along Lung Wai (literally 'long way'), filled with duty-free shops, and then up the stairway (180 steps) to Oberland for the view. There's also a scenic trail around the island.

There are no decent beaches on Helgoland, but to swim you can go to neighbouring **Düne**, a mere blip in the ocean that is popular with nudists. Little boats make regular trips to the pint-sized island from the landing stage in Helgoland.

The tourist office (☎ 81 37 11, fax 81 37 25), Lung Wai 28, is open from November to April and in October weekdays from 9 am to 4 pm (Wednesday to noon from November to February), and Saturday from 1 to 2 pm. It closes for an hour at 11.30 am. From May to September it opens weekdays from 9 am to 5 pm, and weekends from 11.30 am. The office can help with finding a room.

Places to Stay

There is a *camping ground (☎ 08 40)* and a bungalow village on Düne Island.

Helgoland's *Jugendherberge (☎ 341)* is about 15 minutes on foot north-east of the landing stages. B&B costs DM24/29 for juniors/seniors. It's only open from April to October and you must call ahead.

Getting There & Away

The WDR boat service (☎ 04681-801 40) makes the excursion from Hörnum on Sylt twice weekly (DM44). Ferries also travel to Helgoland from Dagebüll, Husum, Büsum, Cuxhaven, Bremerhaven, Wilhelmshaven and Borkum.

Language

German belongs to the Indo-European language group and is spoken by over 100 million people in countries throughout the world, including Austria and part of Switzerland. There are also ethnic-German communities in neighbouring Eastern European countries such as Poland and the Czech Republic, although expulsion after 1945 reduced their number dramatically.

High German used today comes from a regional Saxon dialect. It developed into an official bureaucratic language and was used by Luther in his translation of the Bible, gradually spreading throughout Germany. The impetus Luther gave to the written language through his translations was followed by the establishment of language societies in the 17th century, and later by the 19th-century work of Jacob Grimm, the founder of modern German philology. With his brother, Karl Wilhelm Grimm, he also began work on the first German dictionary.

Regional dialects still thrive throughout Germany, especially in Cologne, rural Bavaria, Swabia and parts of Saxony. The Sorb minority in eastern Germany has its own language. In northern Germany it is common to hear Plattdeutsch and Frisian spoken. Both are distant relatives of English, and the fact that many German words survive in the _____ vocabulary _____

_____ what's the good news. The ____ for ins ___ its tricky _____ English _____ ca-s, German does to hearing foreigners – and a few notable in-digenous spo_ts personalities – make a hash of their grammar, and any attempt to speak the language is always well received.

All German school children learn a foreign language – usually English – which means most can speak it to a certain degree. You might have problems finding English

speakers in eastern Germany, however, where Russian was the main foreign language taught in schools before the _Wende_ (change).

Pronunciation

English speakers sometimes hold onto their vowels too long when speaking German, which causes comprehension problems. Nevertheless, there are long vowels, like _pope_, and short ones, like _pop_. Another common mistake is a tendency to pronounce all vowels as if they have umlauts (ä, ö and ü). It's worth practising the difference, as they often change the tense and meaning of a word. In most other respects German pronunciation is fairly straightforward. There are no silent letters, and many foreign words (eg _Band_, for 'rock band') are pronounced roughly the same as in English.

Vowels

a	short, as the 'u' in 'cut', or long, as in 'father'
au	as the 'ow' in 'vow'
ä	short, as in 'hat', or long, as in 'hare'
äu	as the 'oy' in 'boy'
e	short, as in 'bet', or long, as in 'obey'
ei	as the 'i' in 'aisle'
eu	as the 'oy' in 'boy'
i	'marine', o long, as in _____ as in 'siege'
o	short, as in 'pot', or long, as in 'note'
ö	as the 'e' in 'fern'
u	as in 'pull'
ü	similar to the 'u' in 'pull' but with stretched lips

Consonants

Most consonants and their combinations are roughly similar to English ones, with a few exceptions. At the end of a word, consonants b, d and g sound a little more like 'p', 't' and 'k' respectively. There are no silent consonants.

ch	throaty, as in Scottish *loch*
j	as the 'y' in 'yet'
ng	always one sound, as in 'strong'
qu	as 'kv'
r	trilled or guttural
s	as in 'see' or as the 'z' in 'zoo'
sch	as the 'sh' in 'shore'
st	usually pronounced 'sht'
sp	usually pronounced 'shp'
v	more like an English 'f'
w	as an English 'v'
z	as the 'ts' in 'tsar'

Grammar

German grammar can be a nightmare for English speakers. Nouns come in three genders: masculine, feminine and neutral. The corresponding forms of the definite article ('the' in English) are *der*, *die* and *das*, with the basic plural form, *die*. Nouns and articles will alter according to the case (nominative, accusative, dative and genitive). Note that German nouns always begin with a capital.

Many German verbs have a prefix that is often detached from the stem and placed at the end of the sentence. For example, *fahren* means 'to go' (by mechanical means), *abfahren* means 'to depart'; a simple sentence with the prefixed verb *abfahren* becomes: *Um wieviel Uhr fährt der Zug ab?* (What time does the train leave?).

You should be aware that German uses polite and informal forms for 'you' (*Sie* and *Du* respectively). When addressing people you don't know well you should use the polite form (though younger people will be less inclined to expect it). In this language guide we use the polite form unless indicated by 'inf' (for 'informal') in brackets.

The following words and phrases should help you through the most common travel situations. Those with the desire to delve further into the language should get a copy of Lonely Planet's German *phrasebook*.

Greetings & Civilities

Hello.	*Hallo.* (*Grüss Gott* in Bavaria)
Good morning.	*Guten Morgen.*
Good day.	*Guten Tag.*
Good evening.	*Guten Abend.*
Goodbye.	*Auf Wiedersehen.*
Bye.	*Tschüss.*
Yes.	*Ja.*
No.	*Nein.*
Where?	*Wo?*
Why?	*Warum?*
How?	*Wie?*
Maybe.	*Vielleicht.*
Please.	*Bitte.*
Thank you (very much).	*Danke (schön).*
You're welcome.	*Bitte or Bitte sehr.*
Excuse me.	*Entschuldigung.*
I'm sorry/Forgive me.	*Entschuldigen Sie, bitte.*
I'm sorry. (to express sympathy)	*Das tut mir leid.*

Language Difficulties

I understand.	*Ich verstehe.*
I don't understand.	*Ich verstehe nicht.*
Do you speak English?	*Sprechen Sie Englisch?/Sprichst du Englisch?* (inf)
Does anyone here speak English?	*Spricht hier jemand Englisch?*
What does ... mean?	*Was bedeutet ...?*
Please write it down.	*Bitte schreiben Sie es auf.*

Paperwork

first name	*Vorname*
surname	*Familienname*
nationality	*Staatsangehörigkeit*
date of birth	*Geburtsort*
identification	*Geschlecht*
visa	*Reisepass*
	Viseis

Small Talk

What's your name?	*W... heisst du?*
	Ich heisse ...
My name is ...	*Wie geht es Ihnen?/Wie geht's dir?* (inf)
How are you?	*Es geht mir gut, danke.*
I'm fine, thanks.	*Woher kommen Sie/ kommst du?* (inf)
Where are you from?	*Ich komme aus ...*
I'm from ...	

Getting Around

I want to go to ...	Ich möchte nach ... fahren.
What time does the ... leave/arrive?	Um wieviel Uhr fährt ... ab/kommt ... an?
boat	das Boot
bus	der Bus
train	der Zug
tram	die Strassenbahn
Where is the ...?	Wo ist ...?
bus stop	die Bushaltestelle
metro station	die U-Bahnstation
train station	der Bahnhof
main train station	der Hauptbahnhof
airport	der Flughafen
tram stop	die Strassenbahn- haltestelle
the next	der/die/das nächste
the last	der/die/das letzte
ticket office	Fahrkartenschalter
one-way ticket	einfache Fahrkarte
return ticket	Rückfahrkarte
1st/2nd class	erste/zweite Klasse
timetable	Fahrplan
platform number	Gleisnummer
luggage locker	Gepäckschliessfach
I'd like to hire ...	... ein Auto
a bicycle	

Around Town

at the next corner	an der nächsten Ecke
north	Nord
south	Süd
east	Ost
west	West
I'm looking for ...	Ich suche ...
a bank	eine Bank/ Sparkasse
the church	die Kirche
the city centre	das Stadtzentrum
the ... embassy	die ... Botschaft
my hotel	mein Hotel
the market	den Markt
the museum	das Museum
the post office	das Postamt
a public toilet	eine öffentliche Toilette
a hospital	ein Krankenhaus
the police	die Polizei
the tourist office	das Fremden verkehrsbüro
I want to change some money/ travellers cheques.	Ich möchte Geld/ Reiseschecks wechseln.
What time does ... open/close?	Um wieviel Uhr macht ... auf/zu?
...phone call.	Ich möchte telefonieren.

Directions

Where is ...?	Wo ist ...?
How do I ...?	...er Vorort
	die Stadt
behind	hinter
in front	vor
opposite	gegenüber
straight ahead	geradeaus
(to the) left	(nach) links
(to the) right	(nach) rechts
traffic lights	an der Ampel

beach	der Strand
bridge	die Brücke
castle/palace	...g/das ...loss
cathedral	die Dom
coast	die Küste
...stan...	der Wa...
lak...	die See
mona...ry/convent	der... Kloster
...ntain	der Berg
river	der Fluss
sea	das Meer/die See
tower	der Turm

Accommodation

I'm looking for ...	Ich suche...
a hotel	ein Hotel
a guesthouse	eine Pension
a youth hostel	eine Jugendherberge
a campground	einen Campingplatz

Signs

Eingang/Einfahrt	Entrance
Ausgang/Ausfahrt	Exit
Auf/Offen/	Open
Geöffnet	
Zu/Geschlossen	Closed
Rauchen Verboten	No Smoking
Polizei	Police
WC/Toiletten	Toilets
Damen	Women
Herren	Men
Bahnhof	Train Station
Hauptbahnhof	Main Train Station
Notausgang	Emergency Exit

Where is a cheap hotel? — Wo findet man ein preiswertes Hotel?
Please write the address. — Könnten Sie bitte die Adresse aufschreiben?
Do you have a room available? — Haben Sie ein Zimmer frei?
How much is it per night/person? — Wieviel kostet es pro Nacht/Person?
May I see it? — Darf ich es sehen?
Where is the bathroom? — Bad?as.
It's very noisy/ ~~ty/expensive. — Es ist sehr lau~~ dreckig/teuer.

I'd like to b~~k~~ (a) ... — Ich möchte ... reservieren.
bed — ~~in Bett~~
cheap roo~~.~~ — ~~preiswerte~~
single room — ein E~~inze~~
double room — ein Doppe~~lzimmer~~
room with two beds — ein Zimmer mit ~~zwei~~ Betten
room with shower and toilet — ein Zimmer mit Dusche und WC
dormitory bed — ein Bett im Schlafsaal
for one night — für eine Nacht
for two nights — für zwei Nächte
I'm/We're leaving now. — Ich reise/Wir reisen jetzt ab.

Food & Drink

breakfast	Frühstuck
lunch	Mittagessen
dinner	Abendessen
menu	Speisekarte
restaurant	Gaststätte/Restaurant
pub	Kneipe
supermarket	Supermarkt
snack bar	Imbiss

I'm a vegetarian. — Ich bin Vegetarier(in).
I'd like something to drink, please. — Ich möchte etwas zu trinken, bitte.
It was very tasty. — Es hat mir sehr geschmeckt.

The bill, please? — Die Rechnung, bitte.
Please keep the change. — Das stimmt so. (lit: 'that's OK as is')

Shopping

I'd like to buy ... — Ich möchte ... kaufen
How much is that? — Wieviel kostet das?
Do you accept credit cards? — Nehmen Sie Kreditkarten?

bookshop — Buchladen
chemist/pharmacy — Apotheke (medicine)
— Drogerie (toiletries)
department store — Kaufhaus
bigg~~~~ — Wä~~sch~~

~~Hea~~
~~... hospital?~~
~~... I'm ill.~~
~~... hurts here.~~
~~I'm pregnant.~~

I'm ... — Ich bin ...
diabetic — Diabetiker
epileptic — Epileptiker
asthmatic — Asthmatike~~r~~

I'm allergic to antibiotics/ penicillin. — Ich bin allergi~~sch~~ Antibiotik~~a~~ Penizill~~in~~

Es tut ~~mir~~ schwan~~g~~
Ich bin schwan~~ger~~

Language

German belongs to the Indo-European language group and is spoken by over 100 million people in countries throughout the world, including Austria and part of Switzerland. There are also ethnic-German communities in neighbouring Eastern European countries such as Poland and the Czech Republic, although expulsion after 1945 reduced their number dramatically.

High German used today comes from a regional Saxon dialect. It developed into an official bureaucratic language and was used by Luther in his translation of the Bible, gradually spreading throughout Germany. The impetus Luther gave to the written language through his translations was followed by the establishment of language societies in the 17th century, and later by the 19th-century work of Jacob Grimm, the founder of modern German philology. With his brother, Karl Wilhelm Grimm, he also began work on the first German dictionary.

Regional dialects still thrive throughout Germany, especially in Cologne, rural Bavaria, Swabia and parts of Saxony. The Sorb minority in eastern Germany has its own language. In northern Germany it is common to hear Plattdeutsch and Frisian spoken. Both are distant relatives of English, and the fact that many German words survive in the English vocabulary today makes things a lot easier for native English speakers.

That's the good news. The bad news is that, unlike English, German has retained clear polite distinctions in gender and case. Though not as difficult as Russian, for instance, which has more cases, German does have its tricky moments. Germans are used to hearing foreigners – and a few notable indigenous sports personalities – make a hash of their grammar, and any attempt to speak the language is always well received.

All German school children learn a foreign language – usually English – which means most can speak it to a certain degree. You might have problems finding English speakers in eastern Germany, however, where Russian was the main foreign language taught in schools before the *Wende* (change).

Pronunciation

English speakers sometimes hold onto their vowels too long when speaking German, which causes comprehension problems. Nevertheless, there are long vowels, like *pope*, and short ones, like *pop*. Another common mistake is a tendency to pronounce all vowels as if they have umlauts (ä, ö and ü). It's worth practising the difference, as they often change the tense and meaning of a word. In most other respects German pronunciation is fairly straightforward. There are no silent letters, and many foreign words (eg *Band*, for 'rock band') are pronounced roughly the same as in English.

Vowels

a	short, as the 'u' in 'cut', or long, as in 'father'
au	as the 'ow' in 'vow'
ä	short, as in 'hat', or long, as in 'hare'
äu	as the 'oy' in 'boy'
e	short, as in 'bet', or long, as in 'obey'
ei	as the 'ai' in 'aisle'
eu	as the 'oy' in 'boy'
i	short, as in 'inn', or long, as in 'marine'
ie	as in 'siege'
o	short, as in 'pot', or long, as in 'note'
ö	as the 'er' in 'fern'
u	as in 'pull'
ü	similar to the 'u' in 'pull' but with stretched lips

Consonants

Most consonants and their combinations are roughly similar to English ones, with a few exceptions. At the end of a word, consonants b, d and g sound a little more like 'p', 't' and 'k' respectively. There are no silent consonants.

ch	throaty, as in Scottish *loch*
j	as the 'y' in 'yet'
ng	always one sound, as in 'strong'
qu	as 'kv'
r	trilled or guttural
s	as in 'see' or as the 'z' in 'zoo'
sch	as the 'sh' in 'shore'
st	usually pronounced 'sht'
sp	usually pronounced 'shp'
v	more like an English 'f'
w	as an English 'v'
z	as the 'ts' in 'tsar'

Grammar

German grammar can be a nightmare for English speakers. Nouns come in three genders: masculine, feminine and neutral. The corresponding forms of the definite article ('the' in English) are *der*, *die* and *das*, with the basic plural form, *die*. Nouns and articles will alter according to the case (nominative, accusative, dative and genitive). Note that German nouns always begin with a capital.

Many German verbs have a prefix that is often detached from the stem and placed at the end of the sentence. For example, *fahren* means 'to go' (by mechanical means), *abfahren* means 'to depart'; a simple sentence with the prefixed verb *abfahren* becomes: *Um wieviel Uhr fährt der Zug ab?* (What time does the train leave?).

You should be aware that German uses polite and informal forms for 'you' (*Sie* and *Du* respectively). When addressing people you don't know well you should always use the polite form (though younger people will be less inclined to expect it). In this language guide we use the polite form unless indicated by 'inf' (for 'informal') in brackets.

The following words and phrases should help you through the most common travel situations. Those with the desire to delve further into the language should get a copy of Lonely Planet's *German phrasebook*.

Greetings & Civilities

Hello.	*Hallo.* (*Grüss Gott* in Bavaria)
Good morning.	*Guten Morgen.*
Good day.	*Guten Tag.*
Good evening.	*Guten Abend.*
Goodbye.	*Auf Wiedersehen.*
Bye.	*Tschüss.*
Yes.	*Ja.*
No.	*Nein.*
Where?	*Wo?*
Why?	*Warum?*
How?	*Wie?*
Maybe.	*Vielleicht.*
Please.	*Bitte.*
Thank you (very much).	*Danke (schön).*
You're welcome.	*Bitte or Bitte sehr.*
Excuse me.	*Entschuldigung.*
I'm sorry/Forgive me.	*Entschuldigen Sie, bitte.*
I'm sorry. (to express sympathy)	*Das tut mir leid.*

Language Difficulties

I understand.	*Ich verstehe.*
I don't understand.	*Ich verstehe nicht.*
Do you speak English?	*Sprechen Sie Englisch?/Sprichst du Englisch?* (inf)
Does anyone here speak English?	*Spricht hier jemand Englisch?*
What does ... mean?	*Was bedeutet ...?*
Please write it down.	*Bitte schreiben Sie es auf.*

Paperwork

first name	*Vorname*
surname	*Familienname*
nationality	*Staatsangehörigkeit*
date of birth	*Geburtsdatum*
place of birth	*Geburtsort*
sex (gender)	*Geschlecht*
passport	*Reisepass*
identification	*Ausweis*
visa	*Visum*

Small Talk

What's your name?	*Wie heissen Sie?/Wie heisst du?* (inf)
My name is ...	*Ich heisse ...*
How are you?	*Wie geht es Ihnen?/Wie geht's dir?* (inf)
I'm fine, thanks.	*Es geht mir gut, danke.*
Where are you from?	*Woher kommen Sie/kommst du?* (inf)
I'm from ...	*Ich komme aus ...*

Getting Around

I want to go to ...	*Ich möchte nach ... fahren.*
What time does the ... leave/arrive?	*Um wieviel Uhr fährt ... ab/kommt ... an?*
boat	*das Boot*
bus	*der Bus*
train	*der Zug*
tram	*die Strassenbahn*
Where is the ...?	*Wo ist ...?*
bus stop	*die Bushaltestelle*
metro station	*die U-Bahnstation*
train station	*der Bahnhof*
main train station	*der Hauptbahnhof*
airport	*der Flughafen*
tram stop	*die Strassenbahn-haltestelle*
the next	*der/die/das nächste*
the last	*der/die/das letzte*
ticket office	*Fahrkartenschalter*
one-way ticket	*einfache Fahrkarte*
return ticket	*Rückfahrkarte*
1st/2nd class	*erste/zweite Klasse*
timetable	*Fahrplan*
platform number	*Gleisnummer*
luggage locker	*Gepäckschliessfach*
I'd like to hire ...	*Ich möchte ... mieten.*
a bicycle	*ein Fahrrad*
a motorcycle	*ein Motorrad*
a car	*ein Auto*

Directions

Where is ...?	*Wo ist ...?*
How do I get to ...?	*Wie erreicht man ...?*
Is it far from here?	*Ist es weit von hier?*
Can you show me (on the map)?	*Könnten Sie mir (auf der Karte) zeigen?*
street	*die Strasse*
suburb	*der Vorort*
town	*die Stadt*
behind	*hinter*
in front of	*vor*
opposite	*gegenüber*
straight ahead	*geradeaus*
(to the) left	*(nach) links*
(to the) right	*(nach) rechts*
at the traffic lights	*an der Ampel*

at the next corner	*an der nächsten Ecke*
north	*Nord*
south	*Süd*
east	*Ost*
west	*West*

Around Town

I'm looking for ...	*Ich suche ...*
a bank	*eine Bank/Sparkasse*
the church	*die Kirche*
the city centre	*das Stadtzentrum*
the ... embassy	*die ... Botschaft*
my hotel	*mein Hotel*
the market	*den Markt*
the museum	*das Museum*
the post office	*das Postamt*
a public toilet	*eine öffentliche Toilette*
a hospital	*ein Krankenhaus*
the police	*die Polizei*
the tourist office	*das Fremden verkehrsbüro*
I want to change some money/travellers cheques.	*Ich möchte Geld/Reiseschecks wechseln.*
What time does ... open/close?	*Um wieviel Uhr macht ... auf/zu?*
I'd like to make a phone call.	*Ich möchte telefonieren.*
beach	*der Strand*
bridge	*die Brücke*
castle/palace	*die Burg/das Schloss*
cathedral	*der Dom*
coast	*die Küste*
forest	*der Wald*
island	*die Insel*
lake	*der See*
monastery/convent	*das Kloster*
mountain	*der Berg*
river	*der Fluss*
sea	*das Meer/die See*
tower	*der Turm*

Accommodation

I'm looking for ...	*Ich suche...*
a hotel	*ein Hotel*
a guesthouse	*eine Pension*
a youth hostel	*eine Jugendherberge*
a campground	*einen Campingplatz*

Signs

Eingang/Einfahrt	Entrance
Ausgang/Ausfahrt	Exit
Auf/Offen/	Open
Geöffnet	
Zu/Geschlossen	Closed
Rauchen Verboten	No Smoking
Polizei	Police
WC/Toiletten	Toilets
Damen	Women
Herren	Men
Bahnhof	Train Station
Hauptbahnhof	Main Train Station
Notausgang	Emergency Exit

Where is a cheap hotel?	*Wo findet man ein preiswertes Hotel?*
Please write the address.	*Könnten Sie bitte die Adresse aufschreiben?*
Do you have a room available?	*Haben Sie ein Zimmer frei?*
How much is it per night/person?	*Wieviel kostet es pro Nacht/Person?*
May I see it?	*Darf ich es sehen?*
Where is the bathroom?	*Wo ist das Badezimmer?*
Ts very noisy/ ᵉrty/expensive.	*Es ist sehr laut/ dreckig/teuer.*

I'd likᵉ to book (a) ...	*Ich möchte ... reservieren.*
bed	*ein Bett*
cheap roo_k	*ein preiswertes Zimmer*
single room	*ein Einzelzimmer*
double room	*ein Doppelzimmer*
room with two beds	*ein Zimmer mit zwei Betten*
room with shower and toilet	*ein Zimmer mit Dusche und WC*
dormitory bed	*ein Bett im Schlafsaal*
for one night	*für eine Nacht*
for two nights	*für zwei Nächte*

I'm/We're leaving now.	*Ich reise/Wir reisen jetzt ab.*

Food & Drink

breakfast	*Frühstuck*
lunch	*Mittagessen*
dinner	*Abendessen*
menu	*Speisekarte*
restaurant	*Gaststätte/Restaurant*
pub	*Kneipe*
supermarket	*Supermarkt*
snack bar	*Imbiss*

I'm a vegetarian.	*Ich bin Vegetarier(in).*
I'd like something to drink, please.	*Ich möchte etwas zu trinken, bitte.*
It was very tasty.	*Es hat mir sehr geschmeckt.*
The bill, please?	*Die Rechnung, bitte.*
Please keep the change.	*Das stimmt so.* (lit: 'that's OK as is')

Shopping

I'd like to buy ...	*Ich möchte ... kaufen*
How much is that?	*Wieviel kostet das?*
Do you accept credit cards?	*Nehmen Sie Kreditkarten?*

bookshop	*Buchladen*
chemist/pharmacy	*Apotheke* (medicine) *Drogerie* (toiletries)
department store	*Kaufhaus*
laundry	*Wäscherei*

more/less	*mehr/weniger*
bigger/smaller	*grösser/kleiner*

Health

I need a doctor.	*Ich brauche einen Ärzt.*
Where is a hospital?	*Wo ist ein Krankenhaus?*
I'm ill.	*Ich bin krank.*
It hurts here.	*Es tut hier weh.*
I'm pregnant.	*Ich bin schwanger.*

I'm ...	*Ich bin ...*
diabetic	*Diabetiker*
epileptic	*Epileptiker*
asthmatic	*Asthmatike*

I'm allergic to antibiotics/ penicillin.	*Ich bin allergisch auf Antibiotika/ Penizillin.*

Emergencies

Help!	*Hilfe!*
Call a doctor!	*Rufen Sie einen Arzt!*
Call the police!	*Rufen Sie die Polizei!*
Leave me in peace.	*Lassen Sie mich in Ruhe.*
Get lost!	*Hau ab!* (inf)
I'm lost.	*Ich habe mich verirrt.*
Thief!	*Dieb!*
I've been raped/robbed!	*Ich bin vergewaltigt/bestohlen worden!*

antiseptic	*Antiseptikum*
aspirin	*Aspirin*
condoms	*Kondome*
contraceptive	*Verhütungsmittel*
diarrhoea	*Durchfall*
medicine	*Medikament*
the pill	*die Pille*
sunblock cream	*Sonnencreme*
tampons	*Tampons*

Times & Dates

What time is it?	*Wie spät ist es?*
It's (10) o'clock	*Es ist (zehn) Uhr.*
It's half past nine.	*Es ist halb zehn.*
in the morning	*morgens/vormittags*
in the afternoon	*nachmittags*
in the evening	*abends*
at night	*nachts*
When?	*wann?*
today	*heute*
tomorrow	*morgen*
yesterday	*gestern*

Monday	*Montag*
Tuesday	*Dienstag*
Wednesday	*Mittwoch*
Thursday	*Donnerstag*
Friday	*Freitag*
Saturday	*Samstag/Sonnabend*
Sunday	*Sonntag*

January	*Januar*
February	*Februar*
March	*März*
April	*April*
May	*Mai*
June	*Juni*
July	*Juli*
August	*August*
September	*September*
October	*Oktober*
November	*November*
December	*Dezember*

Numbers

1	*eins*
2	*zwei /zwo*
3	*drei*
4	*vier*
5	*fünf*
6	*sechs*
7	*sieben*
8	*acht*
9	*neun*
10	*zehn*
11	*elf*
12	*zwölf*
13	*dreizehn*
14	*vierzehn*
15	*fünfzehn*
16	*sechzehn*
17	*siebzehn*
18	*achtzehn*
19	*neunzehn*
20	*zwanzig*
21	*einundzwanzig*
22	*zweiundzwanzig*
30	*dreissig*
40	*vierzig*
50	*fünfzig*
60	*sechzig*
70	*siebzig*
80	*achtzig*
90	*neunzig*
100	*einhundert*
1000	*eintausend*
10,000	*zehntausend*
100,000	*hunderttausend*
one million	*eine Million*

Glossary

(pl) indicates plural

Abfahrt – departure (trains)
Abtei – abbey
ADAC – Allgemeiner Deutscher Automobil Club (German Automobile Association)
Allee – avenue
Altstadt – old town
Ankunft – arrival (trains)
Antiquariat – antiquarian bookshop
Apotheke – pharmacy
Arbeitsamt – employment office
Arbeitserlaubnis – work permit
Ärzte – doctor
Ärztehaus – medical clinic
Ärztlicher Notdienst – emergency medical service
Aufenthaltserlaubnis – residency permit
Auflauf, Aufläufe (pl) – casserole
Ausgang, Ausfahrt – exit
Aussiedler – German settlers who have returned from abroad (usually refers to post-WWII expulsions), sometimes called Spätaussiedler
Autobahn – motorway
Autonomen (pl) – left-wing anarchists
AvD – Automobilclub von Deutschland (Automobile Club of Germany)

Bad – spa, bath
Bahnhof – train station
Bahnsteig – train station platform
Bau – building
Bedienung – service; service charge
Behinderte – disabled
Berg – mountain
Bergbaumuseum – mining museum
Besenwirtschaft – seasonal wine restaurant indicated by a broom above the doorway
Bezirk – district
Bibliothek – library
Bierkeller – cellar pub
Bierstube – traditional beer pub
Bildungsroman – literally 'novel of education'; literary work in which the personal development of a single individual is central

BRD – Bundesrepublik Deutschland or, in English, FRG (Federal Republic of Germany): the name for Germany today; before reunification it applied to the former West Germany only
Brücke – bridge
Brunnen – fountain or well
Bundesland – federal state
Bundesrat – upper house of German Parliament
Bundestag – lower house of German Parliament
Bundesverfassungsgericht – Federal Constitutional Court
Burg – castle
Busbahnhof – bus station

CDU – Christian Democratic Union
Christkindlmarkt – Christmas market; see also Weihnachtsmarkt
CSU – Christian Social Union; Bavarian offshoot of CDU

DB – Deutsche Bahn (German national railway)
DDR – Deutsche Demokratische Republik or, in English, GDR (German Democratic Republic): the name for the former East Germany; see also BRD
Denkmal – memorial
Das Deutsche Reich – German Empire: refers to the period 1871-1918
Dirndl – traditional women's dress (Bavaria only)
DJH – Deutsches Jugendherbergswerk (German youth hostels association)
Dom – cathedral
Dorf – village
DZT – Deutsche Zentrale für Tourismus (German National Tourist Office)

Eingang – entrance
Eintritt – admission
Einwanderungsland – country of immigrants
Eiscafé – ice-cream parlour

Fahrplan – timetable
Fahrrad – bicycle
Fasching – pre-Lenten carnival (term used in Southern Germany)
FDP – Free Democratic Party
Ferienwohnung, Ferienwohnungen (pl) – holiday flat or apartment
Fest – festival
FKK – nude bathing area
Flammekuche – Franco-German dish consisting of a thin layer of pastry topped with cream, onion, bacon and, sometimes, cheese or mushrooms, and cooked in a wood-fired oven. Found on menus in the Palatinate and the Black Forest.
Fleets – canals in Hamburg
Flohmarkt – flea market
Flughafen – airport
Föhn – an intense autumn wind in the Agerman Alps and Alpine Foothills
Forstweg – forestry track
Franks – Germanic people influential in Europe between the 3rd and 8th centuries
Freikorps – WWI volunteers
Fremdenverkehrsamt – tourist office
Fremdenzimmer – tourist room
FRG – Federal Republic of Germany; see also BRD
Fussball – football, soccer

Garten – garden
Gasse – lane or alley
Gastarbeiter – literally 'guest worker'; labourer from primarily Mediterranean countries who came to Germany in the 1950s and 1960s to fill a labour shortage
Gästehaus – guesthouse
Gaststätte, Gasthaus – informal restaurant, inn
GDR – German Democratic Republic (the former East Germany); see also BRD, DDR
Gedenkstätte – memorial site
Gepäckaufbewahrung – left-luggage office
Gesamtkunstwerk – literally 'total artwork'; integrates painting, sculpture and architecture
Gestapo – Nazi secret police
Glockenspiel – literally 'bell play'; carillon, often on a cathedral or town hall,

sounded by mechanised figures depicting religious or historical characters
Gründerzeit – literally 'foundation time'; the period of industrial expansion in Germany following the founding of the German Empire in 1871

Hafen – harbour, port
Halbtrocken – semi-dry (wine)
Hauptbahnhof – main train station
Heide – heath
Das Heilige Römische Reich – the Holy Roman Empire, which lasted from the 8th century to 1806; the German lands comprised the bulk of the Empire's territory
Herzog – duke
Heu Hotels – literally 'hay hotels'; cheap forms of accommodation usually set in farmhouses and similar to bunk barns in the UK
Hitlerjugend – Hitler Youth organisation
Hochdeutsch – literally 'High German'; standard spoken and written German, developed from a regional Saxon dialect
Hochkultur – literally 'high culture'; meaning 'advanced civilisation'
Hof, Höfe (pl) – courtyard
Höhle – cave
Hotel Garni – a hotel without a restaurant where you are only served breakfast

Imbiss – stand-up food stall; also see Schnellimbiss
Insel – island

Jugendgästehaus – youth guesthouse of a higher standard than a youth hostel
Jugendherberge – youth hostel
Jugendstil – Art Nouveau
Junker – originally a young, noble landowner of the Middle Ages; later used to refer to reactionary Prussian landowners

Kabarett – cabaret
Kaffee und Kuchen – literally 'coffee and cake'; traditional afternoon coffee break in Germany
Kaiser – emperor; derived from 'Caesar'
Kanal – canal
Kantine – cafeteria, canteen
Kapelle – chapel

Karneval – pre-Lenten festivities (along the Rhine)

Karte – ticket

Kartenvorverkauf – ticket booking office

Kino – cinema

Kirche – church

Kloster – monastery, convent

Kneipe – pub

Kommunales Kino – alternative or studio cinema

Konditorei – cake shop

König – king

Konsulat – consulate

Konzentrationslager (KZ) – concentration camp

KPD – German Communist Party

Krankenhaus – hospital

Kreuzgang – monastery

Kristallnacht – literally 'night of broken glass'; attack on Jewish synagogues, cemeteries and businesses by Nazis and their supporters on the night of 9 November 1938 that marked the beginning of full-scale persecution of Jews in Germany (also known as *Reichspogromnacht*)

Kunst – art

Kunstlieder – early German 'artistic songs'

Kurfürst – prince elector

Kurhaus – literally 'spa house', but usually a spa town's central building, used for social gatherings and events and often housing the town's casino

Kurort – spa resort

Kurtaxe – resort tax

Kurverwaltung – spa resort administration

Kurzentrum – spa centre

Land, Länder (pl) – state

Landtag – state parliament

Lederhose – traditional leather trousers with attached braces (Bavaria only)

Lesbe, Lesben (pl) – lesbian (n)

lesbisch – lesbian (adj)

lieblich – sweet (wine)

Lied – song

Maare – crater lakes in the Eifel Upland area west of the Rhine

Markgraf – margrave; German nobleman ranking above a count

Markt – market

Marktplatz (often abbreviated to Markt) – marketplace or square

Mass – 1L tankard or stein of beer

Meer – sea

Mehrwertsteuer (MwST) – value-added tax

Meistersinger – literally 'master singer'; highest level in medieval troubadour guilds

Mensa – university cafeteria

Milchcafé – milk coffee, *café au lait*

Mitfahrzentrale – ride-sharing agency

Mitwohnzentrale – an accommodation-finding service (usually for long-term stays)

Münster – minster or large church, cathedral

Münzwäscherei – coin-operated laundrette

Nord – north

Notdienst – emergency service

NSDAP – National Socialist German Workers' Party

Ossis – nickname for East Germans

Ostalgie – a romanticised yearning back to the GDR era, derived from 'nostalgia'

Ost – east

Ostler – old term for an Ossi

Ostpolitik – former West German chancellor Willy Brandt's foreign policy of 'peaceful coexistence' with the GDR

Palast – palace, residential quarters of a castle

Pannenhilfe – roadside breakdown assistance

Paradies – architectural term for a church vestibule or ante-room; literally 'paradise'

Parkhaus – car park

Parkschein – parking voucher

Parkscheinautomat – vending machine selling parking vouchers

Passage – shopping arcade

Pfand – deposit for bottles and sometimes glasses (in beer gardens)

Pfarrkirche – parish church

Plattdeutsch – literally 'Low German'; German dialect spoken in parts of northwestern Germany (especially Lower Saxony)

Platz – square

Postamt – post office
Postlagernd – poste restante
Priele – tideways on the Wattenmeer on the North Sea coast
Putsch – revolt

Radwandern – bicycle touring
Rathaus – town hall
Ratskeller – town hall restaurant
Reich – empire
Reichspogromnacht – see Kristallnacht
Reisezentrum – travel centre in train or bus stations
Reiterhof – riding stable or centre
Rezept – medical prescription
R-Gespräch– reverse-charge call
Ruhetag – literally 'rest day'; closing day at a shop or restaurant
Rundgang – tour, route

Saal, Säle (pl) – hall, room
Sammlung – collection
Säule – column, pillar
S-Bahn – suburban-metropolitan shuttle lines; Schnellbahn
Schatzkammer – treasury
Schiff – ship
Schiffahrt – shipping, navigation
Schloss – palace, castle
Schnaps – schnapps
Schnellimbiss – stand-up food stall
Schwuler, Schwule (pl) – gay (n)
Schwul – gay (adj)
SED – Socialist Unity Party (Sozialistische Einheitspartei Deutschlands)
See – lake
Sekt – sparkling wine
Selbstbedienung (SB) – self-service (restaurants, laundrettes etc)
Soziale Marktwirtschaft – literally 'social market economy'; German form of market-driven economy with built-in social protection for employees
Spätaussiedler – see Aussiedler
SPD – Social Democratic Party (Sozialdemokratische Partei Deutschlands)
Speisekarte – menu
Sportverein – sports association
SS – Schutzstaffel; organisation within the Nazi party that supplied Hitler's bodyguards,

as well as concentration-camp guards and the Waffen-SS troops in WWII
Stadt – city or town
Stadtbad, Stadtbäder (pl) – public pool
Stadtwald – city or town forest
Stasi – GDR secret police (from Ministerium für Staatssicherheit, or Ministry of State Security)
Stau – traffic jam
Staudamm, Staumauer – dam
Stausee – reservoir
Stehcafé – stand-up cafe
Strand – beach
Strasse (often abbreviated to Str) – street
Strausswirtschaft – seasonal wine pub indicated by wreath above the doorway, also known as a Besenwirtschaft
Süd – south
Szene – scene (ie where the action is)

Tageskarte – daily menu or day ticket on public transport
Tal – valley
Teich – pond
Thirty Years' War – pivotal war in Central Europe (1618-48) that began as a German conflict between Catholics and Protestants
Tor – gate
Trampen – hitchhiking
Treuhandanstalt – trust established to sell off GDR assets after the Wende
Trocken – dry (wine)
Trödel – junk
Turm – tower

U-Bahn – underground train system
Übergang – transit or transfer point
Ufer – bank

Verboten – forbidden
Verkehr – traffic
Viertel – quarter, district
Volkslieder – folk song

Wald – forest
Waldfrüchte – wild berries
Wäscherei – laundry
Wattenmeer – tidal flats on the North Sea coast
Wechselstube – currency exchange office

Weg – way, path
Weihnachtsmarkt – Christmas market; see also Christkindlmarkt
Weingut – wine-growing estate
Weinkeller – wine cellar
Weinprobe – wine tasting
Weinstube – traditional wine bar or tavern
Wende – 'change' of 1989, ie the fall of communism that led to the collapse of the GDR and German reunification
Weser Renaissance – ornamental architectural style found around the Weser River
Wessis – nickname for West Germans
West – west
Westler – old term for a Wessi

White skins – skinheads wearing jackboots with white laces
Wiese – meadow
Wirtschaftswunder – Germany's post-WWII 'economic miracle'

Zahnradbahn – cog-wheel railway
Zeitung – newspaper
Zimmer Frei – room available (accommodation)
Zimmervermittlung – room-finding service, primarily for short-term stays; see also Mitwohnzentrale
ZOB – Zentraler Omnibusbahnhof (central bus station)

Acknowledgments

THANKS

Many thanks to the travellers who used the last edition, and wrote to us with helpful hints, useful advice and interesting anecdotes:

Christa Adams, Hugh Aitken, Alex & Oliver, Laura Balderree, Jan Bauer, Chad Bearden, Mark Bell, Dietmar Borgards, Eric Boudin, Keith Bowman, Marcia Breen, Nicole Brohan, Andy Broomfield, David Brown, Mark Buserill, Carolina & Susanne, Paolo Casoli, Kristin Certain, Patrick Chambers, Bridget Cleaver, Dr Peta Colebatch, Richard Colebourn, Tui Cordemans, Jolyne Daigle, Jay Davidson, Susan Davison, Hans Denruyter, Nick Detmold, Fionnuala Devine, Ronny Doering, Philip Edwards, Alan Eiger, Jon Eisenberg, Nick Evans, Ronit Fallek, Nathan Florence, Yossi Fogel, Alan Foster, Catherine Fox, David French, Eric Friedman, Eleanor & Alan Galt, Hollis Gardner, Sebastian Geddes, Rob Glas, Peter Goerig, Khrisslyn Goodman, M Goodwin, Gorrit Goslinga, Bianca Gravina, David Griffiths, Sebastien Hall, Lutz Hankewitz, Lea Harris, Amanda Harvey, Anthony Haywood, Regina Henry, Heide Hohenhaus, Matt Holland, Ingo Holzle, Thng Hui Hong, Martin Hula, Janet Ingall, Tom Jansing, Andre's Jaque, David Jeffrey, Rainer Kaduk, Keith Kaulfuss, Ann & Alan Keenan, Benedetta Kelly, William Kendrick, Shanna Kirkpatrick, Andre Ko, Stefanie Kohl, Julian Kolodko, Jochen Konrad, Carl Friedrich Kreiner, R James Krueger, Olaf Kuhmel, Gennady Kulikov, Bob Kunst, Tom Landenberger, David & Ortrud Lane, Alexandra Lehane, Lynette Leo, Marc Lobmann, Hermann-Josef Lohle, Mark Love, Nicholas Lowe, H E Mace, R & S Macgillicuddy, Brenda McIntyre, Mike McKenna, Erika Malitzky, Jerry Mann, Andrea Martin, Derek Mason, Charles Mays, Stan Menkyna, Stephanie Miles, Tony Milway, Jeremy Mittman, John-David Murray, Eric Nay, Dave Newham, Deirdre Ni Dhea, Kevin Nicholls, Stewart Nicolson, Paul Nithsdale, Tony Noble, Dick Ooms, H T Oosterheerd, Richard Owen, Warren Oxerford, Joona Palaste, Joseph Parsons, Brian Payne, Marta Porto, Oliver Posdziech, Leighton Prabhu, Vanessa Prowse, Scott Redding, Ralf Reinecke, William Rich, Jose Rojo, Al Rowley, Christine Rush, Karl Scharbert, Ingrid Selzer, Peter Slater, Sven Sommer, Jessie Stackhouse, Tim Stoecker, Pia Strubel, Mark Summers, Mayuko Tanigawa, Jonas Teubner, Huihong Thng, Dolores Tuttle, Chris & Ginie Udy, Cintha Verbraeken, Rick Vergets, Rasmus Villefrance, F Vrooland, Richard Wade, Bradley Waltermire, Sally Warthen, Florian Weber, Coryn Weigle, Piek Welge, Andrea White, Kate Wilford, Katherine Wilson, Rainer Winters, Tilmann Wittig, Charlotte Woschnagg, Jacqueline Zinder

LONELY PLANET
Guides by Region

Lonely Planet is known worldwide for publishing practical, reliable and no-nonsense travel information in our guides and on our Web site. The Lonely Planet list covers just about every accessible part of the world. Currently there are thirteen series: travel guides, shoestring guides, walking guides, city guides, phrasebooks, audio packs, city maps, travel atlases, diving & snorkeling guides, restaurant guides, first-time travel guides, healthy travel and travel literature.

AFRICA Africa on a shoestring • Africa – the South • Arabic (Egyptian) phrasebook • Arabic (Moroccan) phrasebook • Cairo • Cape Town • Cape Town city map• Central Africa • East Africa • Egypt • Egypt travel atlas • Ethiopian (Amharic) phrasebook • The Gambia & Senegal • Healthy Travel Africa • Kenya • Kenya travel atlas • Malawi, Mozambique & Zambia • Morocco • North Africa • South Africa, Lesotho & Swaziland • South Africa, Lesotho & Swaziland travel atlas • Swahili phrasebook • Tanzania, Zanzibar & Pemba • Trekking in East Africa • Tunisia • West Africa • Zimbabwe, Botswana & Namibia • Zimbabwe, Botswana & Namibia travel atlas
Travel Literature: The Rainbird: A Central African Journey • Songs to an African Sunset: A Zimbabwean Story • Mali Blues: Traveling to an African Beat

AUSTRALIA & THE PACIFIC Auckland • Australia • Australian phrasebook • Bushwalking in Australia • Bushwalking in Papua New Guinea • Fiji • Fijian phrasebook • Healthy Travel Australia, NZ and the Pacific • Islands of Australia's Great Barrier Reef • Melbourne • Melbourne city map • Micronesia • New Caledonia • New South Wales & the ACT • New Zealand • Northern Territory • Outback Australia • Out To Eat – Melbourne • Out to Eat – Sydney • Papua New Guinea • Pidgin phrasebook • Queensland • Rarotonga & the Cook Islands • Samoa • Solomon Islands • South Australia • South Pacific Languages phrasebook • Sydney • Sydney city map • Sydney Condensed • Tahiti & French Polynesia • Tasmania • Tonga • Tramping in New Zealand • Vanuatu • Victoria • Western Australia
Travel Literature: Islands in the Clouds • Kiwi Tracks: A New Zealand Journey • Sean & David's Long Drive

CENTRAL AMERICA & THE CARIBBEAN Bahamas, Turks & Caicos • Bermuda • Central America on a shoestring • Costa Rica • Cuba • Dominican Republic & Haiti • Eastern Caribbean • Guatemala, Belize & Yucatán: La Ruta Maya • Jamaica • Mexico • Mexico City • Panama • Puerto Rico
Travel Literature: Green Dreams: Travels in Central America

EUROPE Amsterdam • Amsterdam city map • Andalucía • Austria • Baltic States phrasebook • Barcelona • Berlin • Berlin city map • Britain • British phrasebook • Brussels, Bruges & Antwerp • Budapest city map • Canary Islands • Central Europe • Central Europe phrasebook • Corsica • Croatia • Czech & Slovak Republics • Denmark • Dublin • Eastern Europe • Eastern Europe phrasebook • Edinburgh • Estonia, Latvia & Lithuania • Europe on a shoestring • Finland • France • French phrasebook • Germany • German phrasebook • Greece • Greek Islands • Greek phrasebook • Hungary • Iceland, Greenland & the Faroe Islands • Ireland • Italian phrasebook • Italy • Krakow • Lisbon • London • London city map • London Condensed • Mediterranean Europe • Mediterranean Europe phrasebook • Norway • Paris • Paris city map • Poland • Portugal • Portugal travel atlas • Prague • Prague city map • Provence & the Côte d'Azur • Romania & Moldova • Rome • Russia, Ukraine & Belarus • Russian phrasebook • Scandinavian & Baltic Europe • Scandinavian Europe phrasebook • Scotland • Slovenia • Spain • Spanish phrasebook • St Petersburg • Switzerland • Trekking in Spain • Ukrainian phrasebook • Vienna • Walking in Britain • Walking in Ireland • Walking in Italy • Walking in Spain • Walking in Switzerland • Western Europe • Western Europe phrasebook
Travel Literature: The Olive Grove: Travels in Greece

INDIAN SUBCONTINENT Bangladesh • Bengali phrasebook • Bhutan • Delhi • Goa • Hindi & Urdu phrasebook • India • India & Bangladesh travel atlas • Indian Himalaya • Karakoram Highway • Kerala • Mumbai (Bombay) • Nepal • Nepali phrasebook • Pakistan • Rajasthan • Read This First: Asia & India • South India • Sri Lanka • Sri Lanka phrasebook • Trekking in the Indian Himalaya • Trekking in the Karakoram & Hindukush • Trekking in the Nepal Himalaya
Travel Literature: In Rajasthan • Shopping for Buddhas

LONELY PLANET

Mail Order

Lonely Planet products are distributed worldwide. They are also available by mail order from Lonely Planet, so if you have difficulty finding a title please write to us. North and South American residents should write to 150 Linden St, Oakland, CA 94607, USA; European and African residents should write to 10a Spring Place, London NW5 3BH, UK; and residents of other countries to PO Box 617, Hawthorn, Victoria 3122, Australia.

ISLANDS OF THE INDIAN OCEAN Madagascar & Comoros ● Maldives ● Mauritius, Réunion & Seychelles

MIDDLE EAST & CENTRAL ASIA Arab Gulf States ● Central Asia ● Central Asia phrasebook ● Hebrew phrasebook ● Iran ● Israel & the Palestinian Territories ● Israel & the Palestinian Territories travel atlas ● Istanbul ● Istanbul to Cairo ● Jerusalem ● Jordan & Syria ● Jordan, Syria & Lebanon travel atlas ● Lebanon ● Middle East on a shoestring ● Syria ● Turkey ● Turkey travel atlas ● Turkish phrasebook ● Yemen
Travel Literature: The Gates of Damascus ● Kingdom of the Film Stars: Journey into Jordan

NORTH AMERICA Alaska ● Backpacking in Alaska ● Baja California ● California & Nevada ● Canada ● Chicago ● Chicago city map ● Deep South ● Florida ● Hawaii ● Honolulu ● Las Vegas ● Los Angeles ● Miami ● New England ● New Orleans ● New York City ● New York city map ● New York, New Jersey & Pennsylvania ● Pacific Northwest USA ● Puerto Rico ● Rocky Mountain ● San Francisco ● San Francisco city map ● Seattle ● Southwest USA ● Texas ● USA ● USA phrasebook ● Vancouver ● Washington, DC & the Capital Region ● Washington DC city map
Travel Literature: Drive Thru America

NORTH-EAST ASIA Beijing ● Cantonese phrasebook ● China ● Hong Kong ● Hong Kong city map ● Hong Kong, Macau & Guangzhou ● Japan ● Japanese phrasebook ● Japanese audio pack ● Korea ● Korean phrasebook ● Kyoto ● Mandarin phrasebook ● Mongolia ● Mongolian phrasebook ● North-East Asia on a shoestring ● Seoul ● South-West China ● Taiwan ● Tibet ● Tibetan phrasebook ● Tokyo
Travel Literature: Lost Japan

SOUTH AMERICA Argentina, Uruguay & Paraguay ● Bolivia ● Brazil ● Brazilian phrasebook ● Buenos Aires ● Chile & Easter Island ● Chile & Easter Island travel atlas ● Colombia ● Ecuador & the Galapagos Islands ● Healthy Travel Central & South America ● Latin American Spanish phrasebook ● Peru ● Quechua phrasebook ● Rio de Janeiro ● Rio de Janeiro city map ● South America on a shoestring ● Trekking in the Patagonian Andes ● Venezuela
Travel Literature: Full Circle: A South American Journey

SOUTH-EAST ASIA Bali & Lombok ● Bangkok ● Bangkok city map ● Burmese phrasebook ● Cambodia ● Hanoi ● Healthy Travel Asia & India ● Hill Tribes phrasebook ● Ho Chi Minh City ● Indonesia ● Indonesia's Eastern Islands ● Indonesian phrasebook ● Indonesian audio pack ● Jakarta ● Java ● Laos ● Lao phrasebook ● Laos travel atlas ● Malay phrasebook ● Malaysia, Singapore & Brunei ● Myanmar (Burma) ● Philippines ● Pilipino (Tagalog) phrasebook ● Singapore ● South-East Asia on a shoestring ● South-East Asia phrasebook ● Thailand ● Thailand's Islands & Beaches ● Thailand travel atlas ● Thai phrasebook ● Thai audio pack ● Vietnam ● Vietnamese phrasebook ● Vietnam travel atlas

ALSO AVAILABLE: Antarctica ● The Arctic ● Brief Encounters: Stories of Love, Sex & Travel ● Chasing Rickshaws ● Lonely Planet Unpacked ● Not the Only Planet: Travel Stories from Science Fiction ● Sacred India ● Travel with Children ● Traveller's Tales

LONELY PLANET

FREE Lonely Planet Newsletters

We love hearing from you and think you'd like to hear from us.

Planet Talk

Our FREE quarterly printed newsletter is full of tips from travellers and anecdotes from Lonely Planet guidebook authors. Every issue is packed with up-to-date travel news and advice, and includes:

- a postcard from Lonely Planet co-founder Tony Wheeler
- a swag of mail from travellers
- a look at life on the road through the eyes of a Lonely Planet author
- topical health advice
- prizes for the best travel yarn
- news about forthcoming Lonely Planet events
- a complete list of Lonely Planet books and other titles

To join our mailing list, residents of the UK, Europe and Africa can email us at go@lonelyplanet.co.uk; residents of North and South America can email us at info@lonelyplanet.com; the rest of the world can email us at talk2us@lonelyplanet.com.au, or contact any Lonely Planet office.

Comet

Our FREE monthly email newsletter brings you all the latest travel news, features, interviews, competitions, destination ideas, travellers' tips & tales, Q&As, raging debates and related links. Find out what's new on the Lonely Planet Web site and which books are about to hit the shelves.

Subscribe from your desktop: www.lonelyplanet.com/comet

Index

Text

Bold indicates maps.

Boxed Text

MAP LEGEND

BOUNDARIES

............................International
....State
..................................Disputed

HYDROGRAPHY

....Coastline
................................River, Creek
....Lake
........................Intermittent Lake
....Salt Lake
....Canal
⊚ ⇀⇀..................Spring, Rapids
⌐.............................Waterfalls
....Swamp

ROUTES & TRANSPORT

....Freeway
....Highway
....Major Road
....Minor Road
=====..................Unsealed Road
....................................City Freeway
....................................City Highway
....City Road
............................City Street, Lane

....Pedestrian Mall
⇒〉====........................Tunnel
⊢⊢⊢⊢⊸⊢....Train Route & Station
⊸⊸⊙⊸....U-Bahn Route & Station
....Tramway
⊢⊩⊢⊩⊢⊩⊢....Cable Car or Chairlift
– – – – – – –..........Walking Track
· · · · · · · · · · ·..............Walking Tour
– – – – – –..................Ferry Route

AREA FEATURES

....Building
✿...............Park, Gardens
+ + × ×
⊥ ⊥ × ×.................Cemetery

.....................................Market
....Beach
....................................Urban Area

MAP SYMBOLS

✈..................................Airport
⌐..........Ancient or City Wall
∴.........Archaeological Site
⊖.....................................Bank
⊼..................................Beach
⍻..................Castle or Fort
⌒.......................................Cave
▢ ⬚...............................Church
⌐⌐⌐..........Cliff or Escarpment
◎...........................Embassy
⊕..........................Hospital
⚲.................Monument
▲.........Mountain or Hill
🏛.......................Museum

⊙ CAPITAL...........National Capital
◉ CAPITAL................State Capital
● CITY..............................City
● Town.................................Town
● Village.............................Village
○.............Point of Interest

■...............Place to Stay
⚑..........Camping Ground
⊞.............Caravan Park
⌂...........Hut or Chalet

▼.................Place to Eat
⊌.................Pub or Bar

☂.................National Park
←.............One Way Street
🅿.......................Parking
⊡..............................Petrol
★.................Police Station
✉...................Post Office
❖.........Shopping Centre
🏛.................Stately Home
▭.............Swimming Pool
▦.................Synagogue
⊙.........................Toilet
⊙.......Tourist Information
⊖.................Transport
🐃...............................Zoo

Note: not all symbols displayed above appear in this book

LONELY PLANET OFFICES

Australia
PO Box 617, Hawthorn, Victoria 3122
☎ 03 9819 1877 fax 03 9819 6459
email: talk2us@lonelyplanet.com.au

USA
150 Linden St, Oakland, CA 94607
☎ 510 893 8555 TOLL FREE: 800 275 8555
fax 510 893 8572
email: info@lonelyplanet.com

UK
10a Spring Place, London NW5 3BH
☎ 020 7428 4800 fax 020 7428 4828
email: go@lonelyplanet.co.uk

France
1 rue du Dahomey, 75011 Paris
☎ 01 55 25 33 00 fax 01 55 25 33 01
email: bip@lonelyplanet.fr
www.lonelyplanet.fr

World Wide Web: www.lonelyplanet.com *or* AOL keyword: lp
Lonely Planet Images: lpi@lonelyplanet.com.au